FOURTH EDITION

WORLDS TOGETHER, WORLDS APART

A History of the World from the Beginnings of Humankind to the Present

Robert **Tignor** • Jeremy **Adelman** • Stephen **Aron** • Peter **Brown**
Benjamin **Elman** • Stephen **Kotkin** • Xinru **Liu** • Suzanne **Marchand**
Holly **Pittman** • Gyan **Prakash** • Brent **Shaw** • Michael **Tsin**

W. W. Norton & Company
New York • London

W. W. Norton & Company has been independent since its founding in 1923, when William Warder Norton and Mary D. Herter Norton first published lectures delivered at the People's Institute, the adult education division of New York City's Cooper Union. The firm soon expanded its program beyond the Institute, publishing books by celebrated academics from America and abroad. By midcentury, the two major pillars of Norton's publishing program—trade books and college texts—were firmly established. In the 1950s, the Norton family transferred control of the company to its employees, and today—with a staff of four hundred and a comparable number of trade, college, and professional titles published each year—W. W. Norton & Company stands as the largest and oldest publishing house owned wholly by its employees.

Printed in the United States of America.

Editor: Jon Durbin
Director of High School Publishing: Jenna Barry
Associate Editor: Justin Cahill
Editorial Assistant: Penelope Lin
Project Editor: Diane Cipollone
Managing Editor, College: Marian Johnson
Copyeditor: Nancy Green
Editor, E-media: Tacy Quinn
Associate Editor, E-media: Lorraine Klimowich
Assistant Editor, E-media: Stefani Wallace
Photo Editor: Evan Luberger
Production Manager: Andy Ensor
Permissions Manager: Megan Jackson
Permissions Clearing: Bethany Salminen
Design Director: Rubina Yeh
Book Designer: Jillian Burr
Cartographer: Mapping Specialists
Composition: Cenveo® Publisher Services
Manufacturing: Courier, Kendallville

The Library of Congress has cataloged the one-volume edition as follows:

Tignor, Robert L.
Worlds together, worlds apart : a history of the world from the beginnings of humankind to the present / by Robert Tignor, Jeremy Adelman, Stephen Aron, Peter Brown, Benjamin Elman, Stephen Kotkin, Xinru Liu, Suzanne Marchand, Holly Pittman, Gyan Prakash, Brent Shaw, and Michael Tsin. — Fourth edition.
pages cm
Includes bibliographical references and index.
ISBN 978-0-393-92207-3 (hardcover : alk. paper) — ISBN 978-0-393-12376-0 (pbk. : alk. paper)
1. World history. I. Title.
D21.T53 2013
909—dc23

2013038525

This edition: ISBN 978-0-393-92333-9

W. W. Norton & Company, Inc., 500 Fifth Avenue, New York, NY 10110-0017
wwnorton.com

W. W. Norton & Company Ltd., Castle House, 75/76 Wells Street, London W1T 3QT
1 2 3 4 5 6 7 8 9 0 18 17 16 15 14 13

CONTENTS IN BRIEF

This registration code provides access to documents

and other sources available at the

Worlds Together, Worlds Apart 4e StudySpace site:

wwnorton.com/studyspace

WORL-DS4B

CONTENTS

Chapter 5
WORLDS TURNED INSIDE OUT, 1000–350 BCE 160

Chapter 11

CRISES AND RECOVERY IN AFRO-EURASIA, 1300–1500 404

Chapter 12
CONTACT, COMMERCE, AND COLONIZATION, 1450–1600 **440**

Chapter 13

WORLDS ENTANGLED, 1600–1750 476

Chapter 14

CULTURES OF SPLENDOR AND POWER, 1500–1780 518

Chapter 15

REORDERING THE WORLD, 1750–1850 **554**

Chapter 16

ALTERNATIVE VISIONS OF THE NINETEENTH CENTURY **594**

Chapter 21

Corporations are PEOPLE too ?!
JOBS NOT CUTS
99%

CURRENT TRENDS IN WORLD HISTORY

ANALYZING GLOBAL DEVELOPMENTS

PRIMARY SOURCES

Chapter 11

Chapter 12

Chapter 13

Chapter 14

Chapter 15

Chapter 16

Chapter 17

Chapter 18

Chapter 19

Chapter 20

Chapter 21

MAPS

PREFACE

Worlds Together, Worlds Apart has set the standard for three editions for those instructors who want to teach a globally integrated world history survey course. Just as the dynamic field of world history evolves, so too has *Worlds Together, Worlds Apart*. Building on the success of the first three editions, the Fourth Edition of *Worlds Together, Worlds Apart* continues to offer a highly coherent, cutting-edge survey of the field built around world history stories of significance that make it possible for students to readily make connections and comparisons across time and place and make the teaching of the course more manageable for instructors (e.g., the building of the Silk Road, the spread of the Black Death across Afro-Eurasia, the impact of New World silver on global trade, and alternative ways to organize societies during the rise of nineteenth-century capitalism). The new Fourth Edition has been further shortened and fully updated, and features a robust new suite of pedagogical and media tools designed to help students master core content, develop history skills, and make connections across time and place. In particular, more than any previous edition, *Worlds Together, Worlds Apart* provides an array of digital media that offers the materials faculty need to address their course goals—in the classroom and online—while providing students activities to develop core skills in reading comprehension, writing, and historical analysis.

HIGHLIGHTS OF THE NEW FEATURES OF THE FOURTH EDITION

- **Streamlined presentation with new pedagogical tools** make the text even more accessible.
  - Each chapter has been **shortened** to further highlight the global stories.
  - **The new robust suite of pedagogical features** is designed to make it easier for students to master core content and to readily make connections and comparisons.
    - The ***Before You Read This Chapter*** pedagogy includes new **Global Storylines** that highlight the chapter themes and new **Focus Questions** that focus on the core objectives students must understand to get a good grade on a quiz or exam.
    - The ***After You Read This Chapter*** pedagogy includes a new **Tracing the Global Storylines** feature, which serves as a chapter summary by showing the chapter themes in action in each region of the world. Bright new **Global Timelines** highlight by region the major developments in world history in the period. Refreshed **Key Terms** and **Study Questions** help students review core material.
- **Cutting-edge scholarship enables students to think like world historians.**
  - **New *Analyzing Global Developments*** features empower students to do historical analysis the way historians do: using historical data or comparative information. Each new *Analyzing Global Developments* feature highlights a major topic in world history, such as comparing the development of writing across cultures, quantifying the destruction caused by the Black Death, and measuring the impact of the Atlantic slave trade in human and economic costs.
  - **New *Current Trends in World History*** features showcase cutting-edge scholarship that is driving the field of world history. These brief essays with analysis questions focus on major research topics in the field, such as the environment, transnational developments, gender, and trade in global commodities, to let students

see the range of topics and ways that world historians think about and conduct their research. Examples include "Climate Change at the End of the Third Millennium BCE in Mesopotamia, Egypt, and the Indus Valley"; "Big Military Forces in Early Empires"; "Empires, Allies, and Frontiers in the Han and Roman Empires"; "Corn and the Rise of Slave-Supplying Kingdoms in West Africa"; "Stimulants, Sociability, and Coffee Houses"; and "Population Movements: Filling Up The Empty Spaces" and "Spread of Capitalism in the Early Twentieth Century."

   - **Completely rewritten coverage of South and East Asia in early world history** builds more social and cultural material into the narrative and makes each period of history in these regions more distinctive.

- **Robust map and primary source programs** build students' history skills.
   - **The updated, stellar map program** includes global and regional maps designed to highlight the main story in each chapter. Enhanced map captions ask students a series of questions to help them learn how to read maps and connect the content back to the narrative. Most maps have been simplified and made easier to read so that students can identify major developments more readily.
   - **A wealth of carefully selected primary sources empower students to carry out historical analysis.**
      - **More than 100 primary sources are integrated into the main text (five to six per chapter)**, each carefully chosen to highlight the chapter's main theme in a different region of the world.
      - ***Worlds Together, Worlds Apart: A Companion Reader,*** edited by Kenneth Pomeranz (University of Chicago), Laura Mitchell, and James Givens (both of University of California, Irvine) is an impressive collection of over 150 primary source documents carefully chosen to align with each chapter in *Worlds Together, Worlds Apart*. The reader also includes mini-casebooks on (1) women and power in the ancient world; (2) the Mongols and warfare; (3) the Atlantic world slave trade; and (4) rubber as a global commodity.
      - The **online world history reader on Norton StudySpace** includes 100 additional primary sources with headnotes and study questions.
- **Norton Coursepacks** allow you to bring strong assessment and lecture tools directly into your Learning Management System (LMS).
   - Available at no cost to professors or students in a variety of formats (including Blackboard, Moodle, and Angel), Norton Coursepacks include chapter-based assignments, test banks and quizzes, interactive learning tools, and selected content from StudySpace, the student Web site.
   - Content unique to the *Worlds Together, Worlds Apart* Coursepack includes new **Guided Reading Exercises**, new **Story Maps**, new **Map Exercises**, and new **Chrono-Quiz** (see below for more information).

Since work began on *Worlds Together, Worlds Apart*, world history has gained even more prominence in college classrooms and historical studies. Courses in the history of the world now abound, often replacing the standard surveys of European history and western civilization overviews. Graduate history students receive training in world history, and journals routinely publish studies in this field. A new generation of textbooks was needed to help students and instructors make sense of this vast, complex, and rapidly evolving field. We believe that *Worlds Together, Worlds Apart* remains the most cutting-edge, engaging, readable, and useful text available for all students of world history. We also believe that this text, one that has advanced the teaching of this field, could have only grown out of the highly collaborative effort of a team of scholars and teachers rather than the more typical single- or two-author efforts. Indeed, the idea to build each chapter around stories of world history significance and the execution of this model grew out of our monthly team meetings and our joint writing efforts during the development stage. As a team-driven text, *Worlds Together, Worlds Apart* also has the advantage of area experts to make sure the material is presented accurately, which is always a challenge for the single- or two-author texts, especially in world history. Finally, our book also reads with a single voice due to the extraordinary efforts of our general editor, and leader, Robert Tignor, who with every edition makes the final major sweep through the text to make sure that the voice, style, and level of detail are consistent throughout. Building on these distinctive strengths, we have worked hard and thoughtfully to make the Fourth Edition of *Worlds Together, Worlds Apart* the best one so far. While there are many exciting additions to the main text and support package, we have made every effort to remain true to our original vision.

OUR GUIDING PRINCIPLES

Five principles inform this book, guiding its framework and the organization of its individual chapters. The first is that

world history is global history. There are many fine histories of the individual regions of the world, which we have endeavored to make good use of. But unlike the authors of many other so-called world histories, we have chosen not to deal with the great regions and cultures of the world as separate units, reserving individual chapters to East Asia, South Asia, Southwest Asia, Europe, Africa, and the Americas. Our goal is to place each of these regions in its largest geographical context. Accordingly, we have written chapters that are truly global in that most major regions of the world are discussed in each one. We achieved these globally integrated chapters by building each around a significant world history story or theme. There are a number of wonderful examples throughout the book, including the peopling of the earth (Chapter 1), the building of the Silk Road (Chapter 6), the rise of universal religions (Chapters 8 and 9), the Black Death (Chapter 11), the effects of New World silver on the economies of the world (Chapter 13), alternative visions to nineteenth-century capitalism (Chapter 15), the rise of nation-states and empires (Chapter 16), and so on. It would be misleading, of course, to say that the context is the world, because none of these regions, even the most highly developed commercially, enjoyed commercial or cultural contact with peoples all over the globe before Columbus's voyage to the Americas and the sixteenth century. But the peoples living in the Afro-Eurasian landmass, probably the single most important building block for our study, were deeply influenced by one another, as were the more scattered peoples living in the Americas and in Africa below the Sahara. Products, ideas, and persons traveled widely across the large land units of Eurasia, Africa, and the Americas. Indeed, Afro-Eurasia was not divided or thought of as divided into separate landmasses until recent times. It is in this sense that our world history is global.

The second principle informing this work is **the importance of chronology in framing world history**. Rather than telling the story of world history by analyzing separate geographical areas, we have elected to frame the chapters around significant world history themes and periods that transcended regional and cultural boundaries—moments or periods of meaningful change in the way that human beings organized their lives. Some of these changes were dramatic and affected many people. Environments changed; the earth became drier and warmer; humans learned to domesticate plants and animals; technological innovations in warfare, political organization, and commercial activities occurred; and new religious and cultural beliefs spread far and wide. These changes swept across large landmasses, paying scant heed to preexisting cultural and geographical unity. They affected peoples living in widely dispersed societies. In other cases, changes occurred in only one locality while other places retained their traditions or took alternative routes. Chronology helps us understand the ways in which the world has, and has not, shared a common history.

The third principle is **historical and geographical balance**. Ours is not a history focused on the rise of the West. We seek to pay attention to the global histories of all peoples and not to privilege those developments that led directly into European history as if the rest of the history of the world was but a prelude to the rise of western civilization. We deal with peoples living outside Europe on their own terms and try to see world history from their perspective. Even more significantly, while we describe societies that obviously influenced Europe's historical development, we do so in a context very different from that which western historians have stressed. Rather than simply viewing these cultures in terms of their role in western development, we seek to understand them in their own terms and to illuminate the ways they influenced other parts of the world. From our perspective, it is historically inaccurate to annex Mesopotamia and Egypt to western civilization, because these territories lay well outside Europe and had a large influence on Africa, South Asia, and East Asia as well as on Europe. Indeed, our presentation of Europe in the period leading up to and including the founding of the Roman Empire is different from many of the standard treatments. The Europeans we describe are rather rough, wild-living, warring peoples living on the fringes of the settled parts of the world and looked down on by more politically stable communities. They hardly seem to be made of the stuff that will catapult Europeans to world leadership a millennium later—indeed, they were very different people from those who, as the result of myriad intervening and contingent events, founded the nineteenth- and twentieth-century empires whose ruins are still all around us.

Our fourth principle is **an emphasis on connections and what we call disconnections across societal and cultural boundaries**. World history is not the history of separate regions of the world at different periods of time. It is the history of the connections among peoples living often at great distances from one another, and it is also the history of the resistances of peoples living within and outside societies to connections that threatened to put them in subordinate positions or to rob them of their independence.

A stress on connections inevitably foregrounds those elements within societies that promoted long-distance ties. Merchants are important, as are military men and political potentates seeking to expand their polities. So are scholars and religious leaders, particularly those who believed that they had universalistic messages with which to convert others to their visions. Perhaps most important of all in pre-modern world history, certainly the most understudied, are the nomadic pastoral peoples, who were often the agents for the transmission of products, peoples, and ideas across long and harsh distances. They exploded onto the scene of settled societies at critical junctures, erasing old cultural and geographical barriers and producing new unities, as the Arabs did in the seventh century CE and the Mongols in the thirteenth century. *Worlds Together, Worlds Apart* is not intended to convey the message that the history of the world is a story of increasing integration. What for one ruling group brought benefits in the form of increased workforces, material prosperity, and political stability often meant enslavement, political subordination, and loss of territory for other groups. The historian's task, then, is not only to represent the different experiences of increased connectedness, describing worlds that came together, but also to be attentive to the opposite trends, describing peoples and communities that remained apart.

The fifth and final principle is that **world history is a narrative of big themes and high-level comparisons.** *Worlds Together, Worlds Apart* is not a book of record. Indeed, in a work that covers the whole of the historical record of humankind from the beginnings of history to the present, the notion that no event or individual worthy of attention would be excluded is the height of folly. We have sought to offer clear themes and interpretations in order to synthesize the vast body of data that often overwhelms histories of the world. Our aspiration is to identify the main historical forces that have moved history, to highlight those monumental innovations that have changed the way humans lived, and to describe the creation and evolution of those bedrock institutions, many of which, of course, endure. In this regard, self-conscious cross-cultural comparisons of developments, institutions, and even founding figures receive attention to make students aware that some common institutions, such as slavery, did not have the same features in every society. Or, in the opposite fashion, the seemingly diverse terms that were used, say, to describe learned and religious men in different parts of the world—monks in Europe, ulama in Islam, Brahmans in India, and scholar-gentries in China—often meant much the same thing in very different settings. We have constructed *Worlds Together, Worlds Apart* around big ideas, stories, and themes rather than filling the book with names and dates that encourage students only to memorize rather than understand world history concepts.

OUR MAJOR THEMES

The primary organizing framework of *Worlds Together, Worlds Apart*—one that runs through the chapters and connects the different parts of the volume—is the theme of **interconnection and divergence.** While describing movements that facilitated global connectedness, this book also shows how different regions developed their own ways of handling or resisting connections and change. Throughout history, different regions and different population groups often stood apart from the rest of the world until touched by traders or explorers or missionaries or soldiers. Some of these regions welcomed global connections. Others sought to change the nature of their connections with the outside world, and yet others resisted efforts to bring them into the larger world. All, however, were somehow affected by their experience of connection. Yet, the history of the world is not simply one of increasing globalization, in which all societies eventually join a common path to the present. Rather, it is a history of the ways in which, as people became linked, their experience of these global connections diverged.

Besides the central theme of interconnection and divergence, other themes also stand out in *Worlds Together, Worlds Apart.* First, the book discusses **how the recurring efforts of people to cross religious, political, and cultural borders brought the world together.** Merchants and educated men and women traded goods and ideas. Whole communities, in addition to select groups, moved to safer or more promising environments. **The transregional crossings of ideas, goods, and peoples produced transformations and conflicts**—a second important theme. Finally, the movement of ideas, peoples, products, and germs over long distances upset the balance of power across the world and within individual societies. Such movements changed the relationship of different population groups with other peoples and areas of the world and led over time to dramatic shifts in the ascendancy of regions. **Changes in power arrangements within and between regions explain which parts of the world and regional groups benefited from integration and which resisted it.** These three themes (exchange and migration, conflict and resistance, and alterations in the balance of power) weave themselves through every chapter of this work. While we highlight major themes throughout, we tell the stories of the people caught in these currents of exchange, conflict, and changing power relations, paying particular attention to the role that gender and the environment play in shaping the evolution of societies.

The history of the world is not a single, sweeping narrative. On the contrary, the last 5,000 years have produced multiple histories, moving along many paths and trajectories. Sometimes these histories merge, intertwining themselves in substantial ways. Sometimes they disentangle themselves and simply stand apart. Much of the time, however, they are simultaneously together and apart. In place of a single narrative, the usual one being the rise of the

West, this book maps the many forks in the road that confronted the world's societies at different times and the surprising turns and unintended consequences that marked the choices that peoples and societies made, including the unanticipated and dramatic rise of the West in the nineteenth century. Formulated in this way, world history is the unfolding of many possible histories, and readers of this book should come away with a reinforced sense of the unpredictability of the past, the instability of the present, and the uncertainty of the future.

OVERVIEW OF VOLUME ONE

Volume One of *Worlds Together, Worlds Apart* deals with the period from the beginnings of human history through the Mongol invasions of the thirteenth century and the spread of the Black Death across Afro-Eurasia. It is divided into eleven chapters, each of which marks a distinct historical period. Hence, each chapter has an overarching theme or small set of themes that hold otherwise highly diverse material together.

Chapter 1, "Becoming Human," presents biological and cultural perspectives on the way that early hominoids became truly human. We believe that this chapter is important in establishing the global context of world history. We believe too that our chapter is unique in its focus on how humans became humans, so we discuss how early humans became bipedal and how they developed complex cognitive processes such as language and artistic abilities. Recent research indicates that *Homo sapiens* originated in Africa, probably no more than 200,000 years ago. These early men and women walked out of the African landmass sometime between 120,000 and 50,000 years ago, gradually populating all regions of the world. What is significant in this story is that the different population groups around the world, the so-called races of humankind, have only recently broken off from one another. Also in this chapter, we describe the domestication of plants and animals and the founding of the first village settlements around the globe.

Chapter 2, "Rivers, Cities, and First States, 4000–2000 BCE," covers the period during which five of the great river basins experienced extraordinary breakthroughs in human activity. On the flood plains of the Tigris and Euphrates in Mesopotamia, the Nile in Egypt, the Indus valley in modern-day northern India and Pakistan, and the Yellow and Yangzi rivers in China, men and women mastered annual floods and became expert in seeding and cultivating foodstuffs. In these areas, populations became dense. Riverine cultures had much in common. They had highly developed hierarchical political, social, and cultural systems, priestly and bureaucratic classes, and organized religious and cultural systems. But they also differed greatly, and these differences were passed from generation to generation. The development of these major complex societies certainly is a turning point in world history.

Extensive climatic and technological changes serve as major turning points for **Chapter 3, "Nomads, Territorial States, and Microsocieties, 2000–1200 BCE."** Drought, environmental degradation, and political instability brought the first riverine societies to a crashing end around 2000 BCE. When aridity forced tribal and nomadic peoples living on the fringes of the settled populations to move closer to settled areas, they brought with them an insurmountable military advantage. They had become adept at yoking horses to war chariots, and hence they were in a position to subjugate or intermarry with the peoples in the settled polities in the river basins. Around 2000 BCE these peoples established new territorial kingdoms in Mesopotamia, Egypt, the Indus valley, and China, which gave way a millennium later (1000 BCE) to even larger, militarily and politically more powerful states. In the Americas, the Mediterranean, sub-Saharan Africa, and the Pacific worlds, microsocieties arose as an alternative form of polity in which peoples lived in much smaller-scale societies that showcased their own unique and compelling features.

Chapter 4, "First Empires and Common Cultures in Afro-Eurasia, 1200–350 BCE," describes the different ways in which larger-scale societies grew and became unified. In the case of the world's first empires, the neo-Assyrian and Persian, political power was the main unifying element. Both states established different models that future empires would emulate. The Assyrians used brutal force to intimidate and subjugate different groups within their societies and neighboring states. The Persians followed a pattern that relied less on coercion and more on tributary relationships, while reveling in cultural diversity. The Zhou state in China offered yet a third way of political unity, basing its rule on the doctrine of the mandate of heaven, which legitimated its rulers' succession as long as they were able to maintain stability and order. Vedic society in South Asia offers a dramatically different model in which religion and culture were the main unifying forces. Religion moves to the forefront of the narrative in other ways in this chapter. The birth of monotheism occurred in the Zoroastrian and Hebrew faiths and the beginnings of Buddhism. All three religions endure today.

The last millennium before the common era witnessed some of the most monumental developments in human history. In the six and half centuries discussed in **Chapter 5, "Worlds Turned Inside Out, 1000–350 BCE,"** teachers and thinkers, rather than kings, priests, and warriors, came to the fore. Men like Confucius, the Buddha, Plato, and Aristotle, to name only the best known of this brilliant group, offered new insights into the natural world and provided new guidelines for how to govern justly and live ethically. In this era, small-scale societies, benefiting from more intimate relationships, took the place of the first great empires, now in decline. These highly individualistic cultures developed new strategies for political organization, even including experimenting with a democratic polity. In Africa, the Bantu peoples spread across sub-Saharan Africa, and the Sudanic peoples of Meroe created a society that blended Egyptian and sub-Saharan influences. These were all dynamic hybrid societies building on existing knowledge. Equally dramatic transformations occurred in the Americas, where the Olmec and Chavín peoples were creating hierarchical societies of the like never before seen in their part of the world.

Chapter 6, "Shrinking the Afro-Eurasian World, 350 BCE–250 CE," describes three major forces that simultaneously integrated large segments of the Afro-Eurasian landmass culturally and economically. First, Alexander and his armies changed the political and cultural landscape of North Africa and Southwest and South Asia. Culturally, Alexander spread Hellenism through North Africa and Southwest and central Asia, making it the first cultural system to achieve a transregional scope. Second, it was in the post-Alexander world that these commercial roads were stabilized and intensified. For the first time, a trading network, known as the Silk Road, stretching from Palmyra in the West to central Asia in the East, came into being. Buddhism was the first religion to seize on the Silk Road's more formal existence as its followers moved quickly with the support of the Mauryan Empire to spread their ideas into central Asia. Finally, we witness the growth of a "silk road of the seas" as new technologies and bigger ships allowed for a dramatic expansion in maritime trade from South Asia all the way to Egypt and East Africa.

Chapter 7, "Han Dynasty China and Imperial Rome, 300 BCE–300 CE," compares Han China and the Roman Empire, the two political, economic, and cultural systems that dominated much of the Afro-Eurasian landmass from 200 BCE to 200 CE. Both the Han Dynasty and the Roman Empire ruled effectively in their own way, providing an instructive comparative case study. Both left their imprint on Afro-Eurasia, and rulers for centuries afterward tried to revive these glorious polities and use them as models of greatness. This chapter also discusses the effect of state sponsorship on religion, as Christianity came into existence in the context of the late Roman Empire and Buddhism was introduced to China during the decline of the Han.

Out of the crumbling Roman Empire new polities and a new religion emerged, the major topic of **Chapter 8, "The Rise of Universal Religions, 300–600 CE."** The Byzantine Empire, claiming to be the successor state to the Roman Empire, embraced Christianity as its state religion. The Tang rulers patronized Buddhism to such a degree that Confucian statesmen feared it had become the state religion. Both Buddhism and Christianity enjoyed spectacular success in the politically fragmented post-Han era in China and in the feudal world of western Europe. These dynamic religions represent a decisive transformation in world history. Christianity enjoyed its eventual successes through state sponsorship via the Roman and Byzantine empires and by providing spiritual comfort and hope during the chaotic years of Rome's decline. Buddhism grew through imperial sponsorship and significant changes to its fundamental beliefs, when adherents to the faith deified Buddha and created notions of an afterlife. In Africa a wide range of significant developments and a myriad of cultural practices existed; yet large common cultures also arose. The Bantu peoples spread throughout the southern half of the landmass, spoke closely related languages, and developed similar political institutions based on the prestige of individuals of high achievement. In the Americas the Olmecs established their own form of the city-state, while the Mayans owed their success to a decentralized common culture built around a strong religious belief system and a series of spiritual centers.

In **Chapter 9, "New Empires and Common Cultures, 600–1000 CE,"** in a relatively remote corner of the Arabian Peninsula another world religion, Islam, exploded with world-changing consequences. The rise of Islam provides a contrast to the way in which universalizing religions and political empires interacted. Islam and empire arose in a fashion quite different from Christianity and the Roman Empire. Christianity took over an already existing empire—the Roman—after suffering persecution at its hands for several centuries. In contrast, Islam created an empire almost at the moment of its emergence. By the time the Abbasid Empire came into being in the middle of the eighth century, Islamic armies, political leaders, and clerics exercised power over much of the Afro-Eurasian landmass from southern Spain, across North Africa, all the way to central Asia. The Tang Empire in China, however, served as a counterweight to Islam's power both politically and intellectually. Confucianism enjoyed a spectacular recovery in this period. With the Tang rulers, Confucianism slowed the spread of Buddhism and further reinforced China's development along different, more secular pathways. Japan and Korea also enter world history at this time, as tributary states to Tang China and as hybrid cultures that mixed Chinese customs and practices with their own. The Christian world split in this period between the western Latin church and the eastern Byzantine church. Both branches of Christianity played a role in unifying societies, especially in western Europe, which lacked strong political rule.

In the three centuries from 1000 to 1300 (**Chapter 10, "Becoming 'the World,' 1000–1300 CE"**) Afro-Eurasia experienced an unprecedented rise in prosperity and population that even spread into West and East Africa. Just as importantly, the world in this period divided into regional zones that are recognizable today. And trade grew rapidly.

A view of the major trading cities of this time demonstrates how commerce transformed cultures. Sub-Saharan Africa also underwent intense regional integration via the spread of the Mande-speaking peoples and the Mali Empire. The Americas witnessed their first empire in the form of the Chimu peoples in the Andes. This chapter ends with the Mongol conquests of the twelfth and thirteenth centuries, which brought massive destruction. The Mongol Empire, however, once in place, promoted long-distance commerce, scholarly exchange, and travel on an unprecedented scale. The Mongols brought Eurasia, North Africa, and many parts of sub-Saharan Africa into a new connectedness. The Mongol story also underscores the important role that nomads played throughout the history of the early world.

The Black Death brought Afro-Eurasia's prosperity and population growth to a catastrophic end as discussed in **Chapter 11, "Crises and Recovery in Afro-Eurasia, 1300s–1500s."** The dying and destruction of the fourteenth century saw traditional institutions give way and forced peoples to rebuild their cultures. The polities that came into being at this time and the intense religious experimentation that took place effected a sharp break with the past. The bubonic plague wiped out as much as two-thirds of the population in many of the densely settled locations of Afro-Eurasia. Societies were brought to their knees by the Mongols' depredations as well as by biological pathogens. In the face of one of humanity's grimmest periods, peoples and societies demonstrated tremendous resilience as they looked for new ways to rebuild their communities, some turning inward and others seeking inspiration, conquests, and riches elsewhere. Volume One concludes on the eve of the "Columbian Exchange," the moment when "old" worlds discovered "new" ones and a vast series of global interconnections and divergences commenced.

OVERVIEW OF VOLUME TWO

The organizational structure for Volume Two reaffirms the commitment to write a decentered, global history of the world. Christopher Columbus is not the starting point, as he is in so many modern world histories. Rather, we begin in the eleventh and twelfth centuries with two major developments in world history: the Mongols and the Black Death. The first, set forth in **Chapter 10, "Becoming 'the World,' 1000–1300 CE,"** describes a world that was divided for the first time into regions that are recognizable today. This world experienced rapid population growth, as is shown by a simple look at the major trading cities from Asia in the East to the Mediterranean in the West. Yet nomadic peoples remain a force as revealed in the Mongol invasions of Afro-Eurasia.

Chapter 11, "Crises and Recovery in Afro-Eurasia, 1300s–1500s," describes how the Mongol warriors, through their conquests and the integration of the Afro-Eurasian world, spread the bubonic plague, which brought death and depopulation to much of Afro-Eurasia. Both these stories set the stage for the modern world and are clear-cut turning points in world history. The primary agents of world connection described in this chapter were dynasts, soldiers, clerics, merchants, and adventurers who rebuilt the societies that disease and political collapse had destroyed.

The Mongols joined the two hemispheres, as we describe in **Chapter 12, "Contact, Commerce, and Colonization, 1450s–1600,"** bringing the peoples and products of the Western Hemisphere into contact and conflict with Eurasia and Africa. It is the collision between the Eastern and Western Hemispheres that sets in motion modern world history and marks a distinct divide or turning point between the pre-modern and the modern. Here, too, disease and increasing trade linkages were vital. Unprepared for the advanced military technology and the disease pool of European and African peoples, the Amerindian population experienced a population decline even more devastating than that caused by the Black Death.

Europeans sailed across the Atlantic Ocean to find a more direct, less encumbered route to Asia and came upon lands, peoples, and products that they had not expected. One item, however, that they had sought in every part of the world and that they found in abundance in the Americas was precious metal. In **Chapter 13, "Worlds Entangled, 1600–1750,"** we discuss how New World silver from Mexico and Peru became the major currency of global commerce, oiling the long-distance trading networks that had been revived after the Black Death. The effect of New World silver on the world economy was so great that it, even more than the Iberian explorations of the New World, brought the hemispheres together and marks the true genesis of modern world history. Sugar also linked the economies and polities of western Europe, Africa, and the Americas and was a powerful force in a triangular trade centered on the Atlantic Ocean. This trade involved the shipment of vast numbers of African captives to the Americas, where they toiled on sugar, tobacco, cotton, and rice slave plantations.

Chapter 14, "Cultures of Splendor and Power, 1500–1780," discusses the Ottoman scientists, Safavid and Mughal artists, and Chinese literati, as well as European thinkers, whose notable achievements were rooted in their own cultures but tempered by awareness of the intellectual activities of others. In this chapter, we look closely at how culture is created as a historical process and describe how the massive increase in wealth during this period, growing out of global trade, led to one of the great periods of cultural flourishing in world history.

Around 1800, transformations reverberated outward from the Atlantic world and altered economic and political relationships in the rest of the world. In **Chapter 15, "Reordering the World, 1750–1850,"** we discuss how political revolutions in the Americas and Europe, new ideas about how to trade and organize labor, and a powerful rhetoric of freedom and universal rights underlay the beginning of "a great divide" between peoples of European descent and those who were not. These forces of laissez-faire capitalism, industrialization, the nation-state, and republicanism not only attracted diverse groups around the world; they also threatened groups that put forth alternative visions. Ideas of freedom, as manifested in trading relations, labor, and political activities, clashed with a traditional world based on inherited rights and statuses and further challenged the way men and women had lived in earlier times. These political, intellectual, and economic reorderings changed the way people around the world saw themselves and thus represent something quite novel in world history.

These new ways of envisioning the world did not go unchallenged, as **Chapter 16, "Alternative Visions of the Nineteenth Century,"** makes clear. Here, intense resistance to evolving modernity reflected the diversity of peoples and their hopes for the future. Wahabbism in Islam, the strongman movement in Africa, Indian resistance in America and Mexico, socialism and communism in Europe, the Taiping Rebellion in China, and the Indian mutiny in South Asia catapulted to historical prominence prophets and leaders whose visions often drew on earlier traditions and led these individuals to resist rapid change.

Chapter 17, "Nations and Empires, 1850–1914," discusses the political, economic, military, and ideological power that thrust Europe and North America to the fore of global events and led to an era of nationalism and modern imperialism, new forces in world history. Yet this period of seeming European supremacy was to prove short-lived.

As **Chapter 18, "An Unsettled World, 1890–1914,"** demonstrates, even before World War I shattered Europe's moral certitude, many groups at home (feminists, Marxists, and unfulfilled nationalists) and abroad (anticolonial nationalists) had raised a chorus of complaints about European and North American dominance. As in Chapter 14, we look at the processes by which specific cultural movements rose and reflected the concerns of individual societies. Yet here, too, syncretistic movements emerged in many cultures and reflected the sway of global imperialism, which by then had become a dominant force.

Chapter 19, "Of Masses and Visions of the Modern, 1910–1939," briefly covers World War I and then discusses how, from the end of World War I until World War II, different visions of being modern competed around the world. It is the development of modernism and its effects on multiple cultures that integrate the diverse developments discussed in this chapter. In the decades between the world wars, proponents of liberal democracy struggled to defend their views and often to impose their will on authoritarian rulers and anticolonial nationalists.

Chapter 20, "The Three-World Order, 1940–1975," presents World War II and describes how new adversaries arose after the war. A three-world order came into being—the First World, led by the United States and extolling capitalism, the nation-state, and democratic government; the Second World, led by the Soviet Union and favoring authoritarian polities and economies; and the Third World, made up of former colonies seeking an independent status for themselves in world affairs. The rise of this three-world order dominates the second half of the twentieth century and constitutes another major theme of world history.

In **Chapter 21, "Globalization, 1970–2000,"** we explain that, at the end of the cold war, the modern world, while clearly more unified than before, still had profound cultural differences and political divisions. At the beginning of the twenty-first century, capital, commodities, peoples, and ideas move rapidly over long distances. But cultural tensions and political impasses continue to exist. It is the rise of this form of globalism that represents a vital new element as humankind heads into a new century and millennium.

We close with an **Epilogue**, which tracks developments since the turn of the millennium. These last few years have brought profound changes to the world order, yet we hope readers of *Worlds Together, Worlds Apart* will see more clearly how this most recent history is, in fact, entwined with trends of much longer duration that are the chief focus of this book.

MEDIA & PRINT ANCILLARIES

The Fourth Edition of *Worlds Together, Worlds Apart* is supported by an array of digital media with tools faculty need to meet course goals—in the classroom and online—and activities for students to develop core skills in reading comprehension, writing and historical analysis.

FOR STUDENTS

Free and open StudySpace Web site includes:

- **Chapter Quizzes.** Quiz feedback is aligned to student learning outcomes and chapter Focus Questions, accompanied by page references.
- **Flashcards** clarify key terms and events with brief descriptions and definitions.
- **iMaps** allow students to view layers of information on each map.
- **Map Worksheets** provide each map without labels for offline relabeling and quizzing.
- 100 **primary source documents and images** are included.
- **World History Tours,** powered by Google Earth, are dynamic, interactive primary source exercises that trace global developments over time.
- **Ebook links** tie the online text to all study and review materials.

FOR INSTRUCTORS

Classroom Presentation Tools

- **Chapter maps** and images are available as PowerPoint slides and JPG image files
- **Lecture slides** provide bullet points from the chapter outlines. Map and image files are inserted into the presentation.
- **New *Story Maps*** break complex maps into a sequence of five annotated screens that focus on the story behind the geography. Ten maps include such topics as "The Silk Road," "The Spread of the Black Death," and "Population Growth and the Economy."

Instructor's Manual (Grace Chee, West Los Angeles College, and Alice Roberti, Santa Rosa Junior College)

The Instructor's Manual for *Worlds Together, Worlds Apart*, Fourth Edition, is designed to help instructors prepare lectures and exams. The Instructor's Manual contains detailed chapter outlines, lecture outlines, lecture ideas, classroom activities, and lists of recommended books, films, and Web sites. It is available in print and downloadable formats.

Test Bank (Aaron Gulyas and Brian Harding, both of Mott Community College)

The Test Bank contains approximately 1,400 multiple-choice, true/false, and essay questions. All test questions are now aligned with Bloom's Taxonomy for greater ease of assessment (available in print, PDF, Word, and Examview formats).

Free Norton Coursepack (downloadable in Blackboard, D2L, and Moodle; additional formats can be provided upon request) includes:

- **NEW Guided Reading Exercises,** keyed to each chapter's *Focus Questions*, instill the three-step Note-Summarize-Assess pedagogy. Each chapter has three exercises, which are built around actual passages from the text. Feedback will provide model responses with direct page references. **(Coursepack Only)**
- **NEW *Story Maps*** break complex maps into a sequence of five annotated screens that focus on the *story* behind the *geography*. Ten maps include such topics as "The Silk Road," "The Spread of the Black Death," and "Population Growth and the Economy." **(Coursepack Only)**
- **NEW 35 Map Exercises** can be assigned for assessment. These activities ask students a series of questions about historical events that must be answered by clicking on the map to record the answer. **(Coursepack Only)**
- **NEW Chrono-Quiz.** Addressing reviewer feedback, the ever-popular *Chrono-Sequencer* is now available as an assessment activity that will report to the school's native LMS. **(Coursepack Only)**
- **Chapter Outlines and Quizzes.** Quiz feedback is aligned to student learning outcomes and chapter Focus Questions, accompanied by page references.
- **World History Tours,** powered by Google Earth, are dynamic, interactive primary source exercises that trace global developments over time.
- **iMaps** allow students to view layers of information on each map.
- **Map Worksheets** provide each map without labels for offline relabeling and quizzing.
- **Flashcards** align key terms and events with brief descriptions and definitions.
- **100 primary-source documents and images are included.**
- **Ebook links** tie the online text to all study and review materials.

ACKNOWLEDGMENTS

Worlds Together, Worlds Apart would never have happened without the full support of Princeton University. In a highly unusual move, and one for which we are truly grateful, the university helped underwrite this project with financial support from its 250th Anniversary Fund for undergraduate teaching and by allowing release time for the authors from campus commitments.

The history department's support of the effort over many years has been exceptional. Four chairs made funds and departmental support available, including the department's incomparable administrative talents. We would be remiss if we did not single out the department manager, Judith Hanson, who provided us with assistance whenever we needed it. We also thank Eileen Kane, who provided help in tracking down references and illustrations and in integrating changes into the manuscript. We also would like to thank Pamela Long, who made all of the complicated arrangements for ensuring that we were able to discuss matters in a leisurely and attractive setting. Sometimes that meant arranging for long-distance conference calls. She went even further and proofread the entire manuscript, finding many errors that we had all overlooked.

We drew shamelessly on the expertise of the departmental faculty, and although it might be wise simply to include a roster of the Princeton history department, that would do an injustice to those of whom we took most advantage. So here they are: Mariana Candido, Robert Darnton, Sheldon Garon, Anthony Grafton, Molly Greene, David Howell, Harold James, William Jordan, Emmanuel Kreike, Michael Mahoney, Arno Mayer, Kenneth Mills, John Murrin, Susan Naquin, Willard Peterson, Theodore Rabb, Bhavani Raman, Stanley Stein, and Richard Turits. When necessary, we went outside the history department, getting help from L. Carl Brown, Michael Cook, Norman Itzkowitz, Martin Kern, Thomas Leisten, Heath Lowry, and Peter Schaefer. Two departmental colleagues—Natalie Z. Davis and Elizabeth Lunbeck—were part of the original team but had to withdraw because of other commitments. Their contributions were vital, and we want to express our thanks to them. David Gordon, now at Bowdoin College, used portions of the text while teaching an undergraduate course at the University of Durban in South Africa and shared comments with us. Shamil Jeppie, like David Gordon a graduate of the Princeton history department, now teaching at the University of Cape Town in South Africa, read and commented on various chapters.

Beyond Princeton, we have also benefited from exceptionally gifted and giving colleagues who have assisted this book in many ways. Colleagues at Louisiana State University, the University of Florida, the University of North Carolina, the University of Pennsylvania, and the University of California at Los Angeles, where Suzanne Marchand, Michael Tsin, Holly Pittman, and Stephen Aron, respectively, are now teaching, pitched in whenever we turned to them. Especially helpful have been the contributions of James Gelvin, Naomi Lamoreaux, Gary Nash, and Joyce Appleby at UCLA; Michael Bernstein at Tulane University; and Maribel Dietz, John Henderson, Christine Kooi, David Lindenfeld, Reza Pirbhai, and Victor Stater at Louisiana State University. It goes without saying that none of these individuals bears any responsibility for factual or interpretive errors that the text may contain. Xinru Liu would like to thank her Indian mentor, Romila Thapar, who changed the way we think about Indian history.

The quality and range of reviews on this project were truly exceptional. The final version of the manuscript was greatly influenced by the thoughts and ideas of numerous instructors. We wish to particularly thank our consulting reviewers, who read multiple versions of the manuscript from start to finish.

First Edition Consultants

Hugh Clark, Ursinus College
Jonathan Lee, San Antonio College
Pamela McVay, Ursuline College
Tom Sanders, United States Naval Academy

Second Edition Consultants

Jonathan Lee, San Antonio College
Pamela McVay, Ursuline College
Steve Rapp, Georgia State University
Cliff Rosenberg, City University of New York

First Edition Reviewers

Lauren Benton, New Jersey Institute of Technology
Ida Blom, University of Bergen, Norway
Ricardo Duchesne, University of New Brunswick
Major Bradley T. Gericke, United States Military Academy
John Gillis, Rutgers University
David Kenley, Marshall University
John Kicza, Washington State University
Matthew Levinger, Lewis and Clark College
James Long, Colorado State University
Adam McKeown, Columbia University
Mark McLeod, University of Delaware
John Mears, Southern Methodist University
Michael Murdock, Brigham Young University
David Newberry, University of North Carolina, Chapel Hill
Tom Pearcy, Slippery Rock State University
Oliver B. Pollak, University of Nebraska, Omaha
Ken Pomeranz, University of California, Irvine
Major David L. Ruffley, United States Air Force Academy
William Schell, Murray State University
Major Deborah Schmitt, United States Air Force Academy
Sarah Shields, University of North Carolina, Chapel Hill
Mary Watrous-Schlesinger, Washington State University

Second Edition Reviewers

William Atwell, Hobart and William Smith Colleges
Susan Besse, City University of New York

Tithi Bhattacharya, Purdue University
Mauricio Borrerero, St. John's University
Charlie Briggs, Georgia Southern University
Antoinne Burton, University of Illinois, Urbana-Champaign
Jim Cameron, St. Francis Xavier University
Kathleen Comerford, Georgia Southern University
Duane Corpis, Georgia State University
Denise Davidson, Georgia State University
Ross Doughty, Ursinus College
Alison Fletcher, Kent State University
Phillip Gavitt, Saint Louis University
Brent Geary, Ohio University
Henda Gilli-Elewy, California State Polytechnic University, Pomona
Fritz Gumbach, John Jay College
William Hagen, University of California, Davis
Laura Hilton, Muskingum College
Jeff Johnson, Villanova University
David Kammerling-Smith, Eastern Illinois University
Jonathan Lee, San Antonio College
Dorothea Martin, Appalachian State University
Don McGuire, State University of New York, Buffalo
Pamela McVay, Ursuline College
Joel Migdal, University of Washington
Anthony Parent, Wake Forest University
Sandra Peacock, Georgia Southern University
David Pietz, Washington State University
Jared Poley, Georgia State University
John Quist, Shippensburg State University
Steve Rapp, Georgia State University
Paul Rodell, Georgia Southern University
Ariel Salzman, Queen's University
Bill Schell, Murray State University
Claire Schen, State University of New York, Buffalo
Jonathan Skaff, Shippensburg State University
David Smith, California State Polytechnic University, Pomona
Neva Specht, Appalachian State University
Ramya Sreeniva, State University of New York, Buffalo
Charles Stewart, University of Illinois, Urbana-Champaign
Rachel Stocking, Southern Illinois University, Carbondale
Heather Streets, Washington State University
Tim Teeter, Georgia Southern University
Charlie Wheeler, University of California, Irvine
Owen White, University of Delaware
James Wilson, Wake Forest University

Third Edition Reviewers

Henry Antkiewicz, Eastern Tennessee State University
Anthony Barbieri-Low, University of California, Santa Barbara
Andrea Becksvoort, University of Tennessee, Chattanooga
Hayden Bellonoit, United States Naval Academy
John Bloom, Shippensburg University
Kathryn Braund, Auburn University
Catherine Candy, University of New Orleans
Karen Carter, Brigham Young University
Stephen Chappell, James Madison University
Jessey Choo, University of Missouri, Kansas City
Timothy Coates, College of Charleston
Gregory Crider, Wingate University
Denise Davidson, Georgia State University
Jessica Davidson, James Madison University
Sal Diaz, Santa Rosa, Junior College
Todd Dozier, Baton Rouge Community College
Richard Eaton, University of Arizona
Lee Farrow, Auburn University, Montgomery
Bei Gao, College of Charleston
Behrooz Ghamari-Tabrizi, University of Illinois, Urbana-Champaign
Steven Gish, Auburn University, Montgomery
Jeffrey Hamilton, Baylor University
Barry Hankins, Baylor University
Brian Harding, Mott Community College
Tim Henderson, Auburn University, Montgomery
Marjorie Hilton, University of Redlands
Richard Hines, Washington State University
Lisa Holliday, Appalachian State University
Jonathan Lee, San Antonio College
David Kalivas, University of Massachusetts, Lowell
Christopher Kelley, Miami University, Ohio
Kenneth Koons, Virginia Military Institute
Michael Kulikowski, Pennsylvania State University
Benjamin Lawrence, University of California, Davis
Lu Liu, University of Tennessee, Knoxville
David Longfellow, Baylor University
Harold Marcuse, University of California, Santa Barbara
Dorothea Martin, Appalachian State University
David Mayes, Sam Houston State University
James Mokhiber, University of New Orleans
Mark Munzinger, Radford College
David Murphree, Virginia Tech University
Joshua Nadel, North Carolina Central University
Wing Chung Nq, University of Texas, San Antonio
Robert Norrell, University of Tennessee, Knoxville
Chandrika Paul, Shippensburg University
Beth Pollard, San Diego State University
Timothy Pytell, California State University, San Bernardino
Stephen Rapp, Professional Historian
Alice Roberti, Santa Rosa Junior College
Aviel Roshwald, Georgetown University

James Sanders, Utah State University
Lynn Sargeant, California State University, Fullerton
William Schell, Murray State University
Michael Seth, James Madison University
Barry Stentiford, Grambling State University
Gabrielle Sutherland, Baylor University
Lisa Tran, California State University, Fullerton
Michael Vann, California State University, Sacramento
Peter Von Sivers, University of Utah
Andrew Wackerfuss, Georgetown University
Ted Weeks, Southern Illinois University, Carbondale
Angela White, Indiana University of Pennsylvania
Jennifer Williams, Nichols State University
Andrew Wise, State University of New York, Buffalo
Eloy Zarate, Pasadena City College
William Zogby, Mohawk Valley Community College

Fourth Edition Reviewers

Andrea Becksvoort, University of Tennessee at Chattanooga
Hayden Bellenoit, United States Naval Academy
Volker Benkert, Arizona State University
Gayle Brunelle, California State University, Fullerton
Jessica Clark, California State University, Chico
Brian Harding, Mott Community College
Emily Hill, Queen's University at Kingston
Laura Hilton, Muskingum University
Dennis Laumann, University of Memphis
Elaine MacKinnon, University of West Georgia
Ronald Mellor, University of California, Los Angeles
Carol Miller, Tallahassee Community College
Greg O'Malley, University of California, Santa Cruz
David Ortiz, Jr., University of Arizona
Charles Parker, Saint Louis University
Juanjuan Peng, Georgia Southern University
Dana Rabin, University of Illinois, Urbana-Champaign
Matthew Rothwell, University of Southern Indiana
Teo Ruiz, University of California, Los Angeles
Jeffrey Shumway, Brigham Young University
Lisa Tran, California State University, Fullerton
Lela Urquhart, Georgia State University

We also want to thank Nancy Khalek (Ph.D. Princeton University), who now teaches at Brown University. Nancy was our jack-of-all-trades who helped in any way she could. She attended all the monthly meetings during the development of the early volume. She provided critiques of the manuscript, helped with primary research, worked on the photo program and pedagogical features, and contributed content to the student Web site. She was invaluable. For the Third Edition, Nancy authored a number of the new digital World History Tours powered by Google Maps. For the Fourth Edition, we want to thank Beth Pollard (San Diego State University) and Cliff Rosenberg (CUNY-City College) for their substantial help with creating the exciting new Analyzing Global Developments features. We also want to send a special thanks to Jon Lee (San Antonio College). Jon has worn many different hats on this project over the years. On this exciting new edition, Jon updated all the pedagogical features in the main text. He also read and critiqued all the new feature elements and the newly revised materials on South and East Asia in Volume 1. We would also like to thank Grace Chee (West Los Angeles College) and Alice Roberti (Santa Rosa Junior College) for authoring the Instructor's Manual. Finally, we'd like to thank Aaron Gulyas and Brian Harding (both of Mott Community College) for thoroughly revising the test bank.

For the Fourth Edition we have some familiar and new friends at Norton to thank. Chief among them is Jon Durbin, who once again played a major role in bringing this edition to publication. Sarah England has put together a creative marketing plan for the book. Jillian Burr is responsible for the book's beautiful and effective new design. Justin Cahill and Penelope Lin have been invaluable with their work on the maps, illustrations, and new feature boxes. Steve Hoge, Tacy Quinn, and Stefani Wallace have done a masterful job strengthening the media support materials to meet the ever more complex classroom and assessment needs of instructors. Lorraine Klimowich has strategically strengthened the Instructor's Manual and Test Bank. Diane Cipollone, our project editor, and Andrew Ensor, our production manager, have done a great job getting the book published on time with a very tight schedule. Nancy Green did a fine job with the copyediting, turning the chapters around quickly to meet our schedule. A special shout out goes to Debra Morton-Hoyt and her team of cover designers. *Worlds Together, Worlds Apart* has always been incredibly creative and distinctive looking, and the Fourth Edition covers are even more eye-catching and memorable than the first three editions. Bravo!

Finally, we must recognize that while this project often kept us apart from family members, their support held our personal worlds together.

ABOUT THE AUTHORS

ROBERT TIGNOR (Ph.D. Yale University) is Professor Emeritus and the Rosengarten Professor of Modern and Contemporary History at Princeton University and the three-time chair of the history department. With Gyan Prakash, he introduced Princeton's first course in world history nearly twenty years ago. Professor Tignor has taught graduate and undergraduate courses in African history and world history and written extensively on the history of twentieth-century Egypt, Nigeria, and Kenya. Besides his many research trips to Africa, Professor Tignor has taught at the University of Ibadan in Nigeria and the University of Nairobi in Kenya.

JEREMY ADELMAN (D.Phil. Oxford University) is currently the Director of the Council for International Teaching and Research at Princeton University and the Walter S. Carpenter III Professor of Spanish Civilization and Culture. He has written and edited five books, including *Republic of Capital: Buenos Aires and the Legal Transformation of the-Atlantic World,* which won the best book prize in Atlantic history from the American Historical Association, and most-recently *Sovereignty and Revolution in the Iberian Atlantic.* Professor Adelman is the recent recipient of a Guggenheim Memorial Foundation Fellowship and the Frederick Burkhardt Award from the American Council of Learned Societies.

STEPHEN ARON (Ph.D. University of California, Berkeley) is professor of history at the University of California, Los Angeles, and executive director of the Institute for the Study of the American West, Autry National Center. A specialist in frontier and Western American history, Aron is the author of *How the West Was Lost: the Transformation of Kentucky from Daniel Boone to Henry Clay* and *American Confluence: the Missouri Frontier from Borderland to Border State.* He is currently editing the multi-volume *Autry History of the American West* and writing a book with the tentative title *Can We All Just Get Along: An Alternative History of the American West.*

PETER BROWN (Ph.D. Oxford University) is the Rollins Professor of History at Princeton University. He previously taught at London University and the University of California, Berkeley. He has written on the rise of Christianity and the end of the Roman Empire. His works include *Augustine of Hippo, the World of Late Antiquity, the Cult of the Saints, Body and Society, the Rise of Western Christendom,* and *Poverty and Leadership in the Later Roman Empire.* He is presently working on issues of wealth and poverty in the late Roman and early medieval Christian worlds.

BENJAMIN ELMAN (Ph.D. University of Pennsylvania) is professor of East Asian studies and history at Princeton University. He is currently serving as the chair of the Princeton East Asian Studies Department. He taught at the University of California, Los Angeles, for over fifteen years. His teaching and research fields include Chinese intellectual and cultural history, 1000–1900; the history of science in China, 1600–1930; the history of education in late imperial China; and Sino-Japanese cultural history, 1600–1850. He is the author of five books: *From Philosophy to Philology: Intellectual and Social Aspects of Change in Late Imperial China; Classicism, Politics, and Kinship: the Ch'ang-chou School of New Text Confucianism in Late Imperial China; A Cultural History of Civil Examinations in Late Imperial China; On Their Own Terms: Science in China, 1550–1900;* and *A Cultural History of Modern Science in China.* He is the creator of Classical Historiography for Chinese History at www.princeton.edu/~classbib/, a bibliography and teaching website published since 1996.

STEPHEN KOTKIN (Ph.D. University of California, Berkeley) is professor of European and Asian history as well as international affairs at Princeton University. He formerly directed Princeton's program in Russian and Eurasian studies (1996–2009). He is the author of *Magnetic Mountain: Stalinism as a Civilization, Uncivil Society: 1989 and the Implosion of the Communist Establishment,* and *Armageddon Averted: the Soviet Collapse, 1970–2000.* He is a coeditor of *Mongolia in the Twentieth Century: Landlocked Cosmopolitan.* Professor Kotkin has twice been a visiting professor in Japan.

XINRU LIU (Ph.D. University of Pennsylvania) is associate professor of early Indian history and world history at the College of New Jersey. She is associated with the Institute of World History and the Chinese Academy of Social Sciences. She is the author of *Ancient India and Ancient China, Trade and Religious Exchanges, ad 1–600; Silk and Religion, an Exploration of Material Life and the Thought of People, ad 600–1200; Connections across Eurasia, Transportation, Communication, and Cultural Exchange on the Silk Roads,* co-authored with Lynda Norene Shaffer; and *A Social History of Ancient India* (in Chinese). Professor Liu promotes South Asian studies and world history studies in both the United States and the People's Republic of China.

SUZANNE MARCHAND (Ph.D. University of Chicago) is professor of European and intellectual history at Louisiana State University, Baton Rouge. Professor Marchand also spent a number of years teaching at Princeton University. She is the author of *Down from Olympus: Archaeology and Philhellenism in Germany, 1750–1970* and *German Orientalism in the Age of Empire: Religion, Race and Scholarship.*

HOLLY PITTMAN (Ph.D. Columbia University) is professor of art history at the University of Pennsylvania, where she teaches art and archaeology of Mesopotamia and the Iranian Plateau. She also serves as curator in the Near East Section of the University of Pennsylvania Museum of Archaeology and Anthropology. Previously she served as a curator in the Ancient Near Eastern Art Department of the Metropolitan Museum of Art. She has written extensively on the art and culture of the Bronze Age in the Middle East and has participated in excavations in Cyprus, Turkey, Syria, Iraq, and Iran, where she currently works. Her research investigates works of art as media through which patterns of thought, cultural development, and historical interactions of ancient cultures of the Near East are reconstructed.

GYAN PRAKASH (Ph.D. University of Pennsylvania) is professor of modern Indian history at Princeton University and a member of the Subaltern Studies Editorial Collective. He is the author of *Bonded Histories: Genealogies of Labor Servitude in Colonial India, Another Reason: Science and the Imagination of Modern India,* and *Mumbai Fables.* Professor Prakash edited *After Colonialism: Imperial Histories and Postcolonial Displacements* and *Noir Urbanisms,* coedited *the Space of the Modern City* and *Utopia/Dystopia,* and has written a number of articles on colonialism and history writing. He is currently working on a history of the city of Bombay. With Robert Tignor, he introduced the modern world history course at Princeton University.

BRENT SHAW (Ph.D. Cambridge University) is the Andrew Fleming West Professor of Classics at Princeton University, where he is director of the Program in the Ancient World. He was previously at the University of Pennsylvania, where he chaired the Graduate Group in Ancient History. His principal areas of specialization as a Roman historian are Roman family history and demography, sectarian violence and conflict in Late Antiquity, and the regional history of Africa as part of the Roman Empire. He has published *Spartacus and the Slaves Wars*; edited the papers of Sir Moses Finley, *Economy and Society in Ancient Greece;* and published in a variety of books and journals, including the *Journal of Roman Studies,* the *American Historical Review,* the *Journal of Early Christian Studies,* and *Past & Present.*

MICHAEL TSIN (Ph.D. Princeton) is associate professor of history and international studies at the University of North Carolina at Chapel Hill. He previously taught at the University of Illinois at Chicago, Princeton University, Columbia University, and the University of Florida. Professor Tsin's primary interests include the histories of modern China and colonialism. He is the author of *Nation, Governance, and Modernity in China: Canton, 1900–1927.* He is currently writing a social history of the reconfiguration of Chinese identity in the twentieth century.

THE GEOGRAPHY OF THE ANCIENT AND MODERN WORLDS

Today, we believe the world to be divided into continents, and most of us think that it was always so. Geographers usually identify six inhabited continents: Africa, North America, South America, Europe, Asia, and Australia. Inside these continents they locate a vast number of subcontinental units, such as East Asia, South Asia, Southeast Asia, the Middle East, North Africa, and sub-Saharan Africa. Yet this geographical understanding would have been completely alien to premodern men and women, who did not think that they inhabited continents bounded by large bodies of water. Lacking a firm command of the seas, they saw themselves living on contiguous landmasses, and they thought these territorial bodies were the main geographical units of their lives. Hence, in this volume we have chosen to use a set of geographical terms, the main one being Afro-Eurasia, that more accurately reflect the world that the premoderns believed that they inhabited.

The most interconnected and populous landmass of premodern times was Afro-Eurasia. The term Eurasia is widely used in general histories, but we think it is in its own ways inadequate. The preferred term from our perspective must be Afro-Eurasia, for the interconnected

landmass of premodern and indeed much of modern times included large parts of Europe and Asia and significant regions in Africa. The major African territories that were regularly joined to Europe and Asia were Egypt, North Africa, and even parts of sub-Saharan Africa.

Only gradually and fitfully did the divisions of the world that we take for granted today take shape. The peoples inhabiting the northwestern part of the Afro-Eurasian landmass did not see themselves as European Christians, and hence as a distinctive cultural entity, until the Middle Ages drew to a close in the twelfth and thirteenth centuries. Islam did not arise and extend its influence throughout the middle zone of the Afro-Eurasian landmass until the eighth and ninth centuries. And, finally, the peoples living in what we today term the Indian subcontinent did not feel a strong sense of their own cultural and political unity until the Delhi Sultanate of the thirteenth and fourteenth centuries and the Mughal Empire, which emerged at the beginning of the sixteenth century, brought political unity to that vast region. As a result, we use the terms South Asia, Vedic society, and India in place of Indian subcontinent for the premodern part of our narrative, and we use Southwest Asia and North Africa to refer to what today is designated as the Middle East. In fact, it is only in the period from 1000 to 1300 that some of the major cultural areas that are familiar to us today truly crystallized.

WORLDS TOGETHER,
WORLDS APART

FOURTH EDITION

BEFORE YOU READ THIS CHAPTER

wwnorton.com/
StudySpace

GLOBAL STORYLINES

- Hominids are ancestors to modern humans.
- All humans share a common heritage "out of Africa."
- Early humans populate the earth, adapting to changes in environment and diet, innovating, and accumulating knowledge.
- People domesticate plants and animals and settle in agrarian villages.

CHAPTER OUTLINE

1

Becoming Human

FOCUS QUESTIONS

- What traits made hominids different from other animal species?
- How did *Homo sapiens* become the only hominid species?
- How did art and language increase *Homo sapiens*'s chances of survival?
- What factors contributed to the domestication of plants and animals in some regions?
- How did agricultural revolutions change human relations?

In 2003, in a remote corner of the Ethiopian highlands of Africa, a team of evolutionary biologists came upon a remarkable cache of fossil remains lodged in volcanic rock. Identifying and reassembling these remains took six years, but the researchers eventually reconstructed one of the most revealing sets of human fossils ever found: a nearly complete skeleton of an adult male, and the partial remains of another adult and a juvenile. By dating the volcanic rock, the team determined that the bones were about 160,000 years old. Although the skeletal remains were not identical to those of modern men and women (who are technically *Homo sapiens sapiens*, the sole surviving subspecies of *Homo sapiens*), they were close enough to form part of the family of modern humans. In short, the bones represented the oldest record of *Homo sapiens*. The fossil finds confirmed what earlier studies had suggested: *Homo sapiens*, or modern humans, originated in a small region of Africa about 200,000 years ago and migrated out of Africa less than 100,000 years ago. As the team leader proclaimed, "We are all Africans."

Not everyone agrees with the "Out of Africa" thesis, which contends that modern human beings are all descendants of recent migrants out of Africa. Doubters claim that the world's "races" evolved separately in different regions for up to 1 million years after migrating out of Africa. These doubters argue that as the early descendants of modern men and women evolved in widely dispersed geographical settings, they took on diverse personality traits and distinctive physical appearances, with the result that they appear today as different "races." In this view, the story of humanity was about fundamental differences. Now the opposite is becoming clear: all humans share a common heritage, and our differences are not genetic or crudely physical, but mainly cultural. We are also much newer than scholars once imagined.

As a species we have been living apart for a comparatively short amount of time, and as a result the world's "races" have much in common. Most of the common traits of human beings—the abilities to make tools, engage in family life, use language, and refine cognitive abilities—evolved over many millennia and crystallized on the eve of the exodus from Africa. Only with the advent of settled agriculture did significant cultural divergences occur, as artifacts such as tools, cooking devices, and storage containers reveal. The differences in humankind's cultures are less than 15,000 or 20,000 years old.

This chapter lays out the origins of humanity from its common source. It shows how many different hominids (erect bipedal mammals, represented today only by humans, but in the past by many groups descended from Great Apes) preceded modern humans, and that humans came from only one—very recent—stock of migrants out of Africa. Fanning out across the world, our ancestors adapted to environmental constraints and opportunities. They created languages, families, and clan systems, often innovating to defend themselves against predators. One of the biggest breakthroughs was the domestication of animals and plants—the creation of agrarian settlements. With this development, humans could cease following food and begin producing it in their own backyards.

Before we begin our exploration, it will be useful to clarify two terms that occur frequently in this chapter's discussion: *evolution*, and *modern humans*. **Evolution** is the process by which the different species of the world—its plants and animals—adapted in response to their often changing environments in ways that enabled them to survive and increase in numbers. Biological evolution does not imply progress to higher and more exalted forms of life, only adaptation to environmental surroundings. The term *modern humans* refers to members of the *Homo sapiens* subspecies that evolved about 200,000 years ago. So when we say "modern" (and "recent") we are speaking in relative terms; compared to the life of the universe and even to the earliest hominids, the ancient creatures we call modern humans were indeed "modern." This chapter's discussion will show that as modern humans evolved, they passed through successive waves of migration, adaptation, and innovation.

PRECURSORS TO MODERN HUMANS

To understand the origins of modern humans (*Homo sapiens*), we must consider what is common to all humans and what distinguishes them from one another. We must also come to terms with time. Though the hominids that evolved into modern humans lived millions of years ago, our tools for analyzing them are relatively new. What we now know about the origins of human existence and the evolution into modern humans would have been unimaginable a century ago.

Creation Myths and Beliefs

Only 350 years ago, English clerics claimed on the basis of biblical calculations and Christian tradition that the first day of creation was Sunday, October 23, 4004 BCE. One scholar even specified that creation happened at 9:00 A.M. on the morning of that day. Now we see things differently. The origin of the universe dates back some 13.7 billion years, and the hominid separation from African pongids (members of the ape family) began some 6 or 7 million years ago. These discoveries have proved as mind-boggling to Hindus and Muslims as to Christians and Jews—all of whom believed, in different ways, in a creationist account of humanity's origins. (See Primary Source: A Hindu Creation Myth.) The Judaic-Christian belief in creation was based on the first book of the Old Testament, Genesis, which portrayed God creating the universe from nothingness, all of its plants and animals and the first set of human beings (Adam and Eve), over a period of seven days. This story became foundational for Western societies and also for the Islamic world, which accepted the Old and New Testaments—though not the divinity of Jesus—as the word of God.

Modern discoveries about humanity's origins have also challenged other major cultural traditions, because no tradition conceived that creatures evolved into new kinds of life, that humans were related to apes, and that all of humanity originated in a remote corner of Africa. The Yoruba peoples of West Africa, whose creation story is centuries old and is representative of many African creation accounts, believed that God descended from the heavens in human form. He became the godlike king Oduduwa, who established the Yoruba kingdom and the rules by which his subjects were to live. According to the Brahmanical Vedas and the Upanishads, which date to the seventh or sixth century BCE and remain fundamental to Hindu faith today, the world is millions, not billions, of years old. The Chinese, who do not appear to have their own creation story, and the Buddhists believed in a continuous reappearance of human and animal souls.

Even the million-year time frames and multiple planetary systems that ancient Asian thinkers endorsed did not prepare their

PRIMARY SOURCE

A Hindu Creation Myth

Around 1500 BCE a migrant people speaking an Indo-European language settled in South Asia. These Vedic people sang hymns while making sacrifices to their gods, and the hymns were later collected in the Rig-Veda—the earliest Hindu sacred text. This hymn describes the creation of the universe by the gods' sacrifice ("oblation") of a creature—Purusha, or "Man." From Purusha's body come four different kinds of people: the Brahman, the Rajanya, the Vaishya, and the Shudra. They represent the forefathers of the four castes, or hereditary social classes, of India.

Thousand-headed Purusha, thousand-eyed, thousand-footed—he, having pervaded the earth on all sides, extends ten fingers beyond it.

Purusha alone is all this—whatever has been and whatever is going to be. Further, he is the lord of immortality and also of what grows on account of food.

Such is his greatness; greater, indeed than this is Purusha. All creatures constitute but one-quarter of him, his three-quarters are the immortal in the heaven.

With his three-quarters did Purusha rise up; one-quarter of him again remains here. With it did he variously spread out on all sides over what eats and what eats not. . . . When the gods performed the sacrifice with Purusha as the oblation, then the spring was its clarified butter, the summer the sacrificial fuel, and the autumn the oblation.

The sacrificial victim, namely, Purusha born at the very beginning, they sprinkled with sacred water upon the sacrificial grass. With him as oblation, the gods performed the sacrifice, and also the Sādhyas [a class of semidivine beings] and the rishis [ancient seers].

From that wholly offered sacrificial oblation were born the verses and the sacred chants; from it were born the meters [*chandas*]; the sacrificial formula was born from it.

From it horses were born and also those animals who have double rows [i.e., upper and lower] of teeth; cows were born from it, from it were born goats and sheep.

When they divided Purusha, in how many different portions did they arrange him? What became of his mouth, what of his two arms? What were his two thighs and his two feet called?

His mouth became the brāhman; his two arms were made into the rājanya; his two thighs the vaishyas; from his two feet the shūdra was born.

The moon was born from the mind, from the eye the sun was born; from the mouth Indra and Agni, from the breath [*prāna*] the wind [*vāyu*] was born.

From the navel was the atmosphere created, from the head the heaven issued forth; from two feet was born the earth and the quarters (the cardinal directions) from the ear. Thus did they fashion the worlds.

QUESTIONS FOR ANALYSIS

- In early Vedic society the Brahman (priest) was the highest caste, and the Shudra (outsider/laborer) was the lowest. What parts of Purusha's body did these two castes come from, and what is the significance of each?
- According to this myth, what other beings came into existence fully formed?

Source: Sources of Indian Tradition, *vol. 1,* From the Beginning to 1800, *edited and revised by Ainslie T. Embree, 2nd ed. (1988), pp. 18–19.*

communities for the idea that humans are related to apes. In all traditional cosmologies, humans came into existence fully formed, at a single moment, as did the other beings that populated the world.

Evolutionary Findings and Research Methods

Revisions in the time frame of the universe and human existence have occurred over a long period of time. Geologists made early breakthroughs in the eighteenth century when their research into the layers of the earth's surface revealed a world much older than biblical time implied. Evolutionary biologists, most notably Charles Darwin (1809–1882), concluded that all life had evolved over long periods from simple forms of matter. In the twentieth century astronomers, evolutionary biologists, and archaeologists (scholars of ancient cultures whose information comes mainly from nonliterary sources such as fossils, monuments, and artifacts) have employed sophisticated dating techniques to pinpoint the chronology of the universe's creation and the evolution of all forms of life on earth. (See Current Trends in World History: Determining the Age of Fossils and Sediments.) Understanding the sweep of human history, calculated in millions of years, requires us to revise our sense of time.

A mere century ago, who would have accepted the fact that human beings are part of a long evolutionary chain stretching

CURRENT TRENDS IN WORLD HISTORY

Determining the Age of Fossils and Sediments

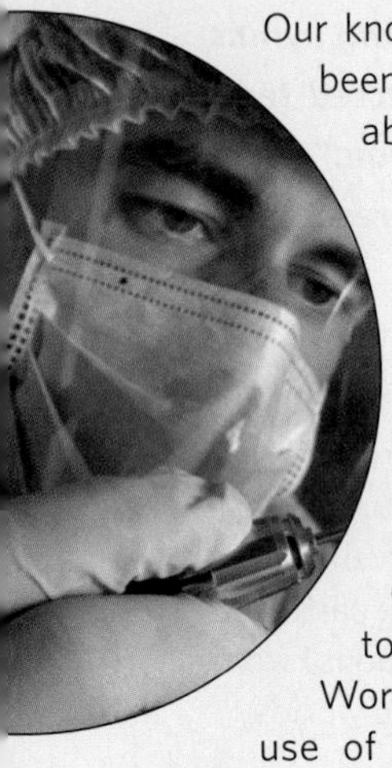

Our knowledge of human origins has been the result of several remarkable scientific breakthroughs. Only recently have scholars been able to date fossil remains and to use biological research to understand the relationships among the world's early peoples.

The first major advance in the study of prehistory (the time before written historical records) occurred after World War II, and it involved the use of *radiocarbon dating*. All living things contain the radiocarbon isotope C^{14}, which plants acquire directly from the atmosphere and animals acquire indirectly when they consume plants or other animals. When these living things die, the C^{14} isotope begins to decay into a stable nonradioactive element, C^{12}. Because the rate of decay is regular and measurable, it is possible to determine the age of fossils that leave organic remains for up to 40,000 years.

A second major dating technique, the *potassium-argon method*, also involves analysis of the changing chemical structure of objects over time. Scientists can calculate the age of nonliving objects by measuring the ratio of potassium to argon in them, since potassium decays into argon. This method allows scientists to calculate the age of objects up to a million years old. It also enables them to date the sediments in which researchers find fossils—as a gauge of the age of the fossils themselves.

DNA (deoxyribonucleic acid) analysis is a third crucial tool for unraveling the beginnings of modern humans. DNA, which determines biological inheritances, exists in two places within the cells of all living organisms—including the human body. *Nuclear DNA* occurs in the nucleus of every cell, where it controls most aspects of physical appearance and makeup. *Mitochondrial DNA* occurs outside the nucleus of cells and is located in mitochondria, structures used in converting the energy from food into a form that cells can use. Nuclear and mitochondrial DNA exists in males and females, but only mitochondrial DNA from females passes to their offspring, as the female's egg cells carry her mitochondria with their DNA to the offspring but sperm cells from males do not donate any DNA to the egg cell at fertilization. By examining mitochondrial DNA, researchers can measure the genetic relatedness and variation among living organisms—including human beings. Such analysis has enabled researchers to pinpoint human descent from an original African population to other, genetically related populations that lived approximately 100,000 years ago.

The genetic similarity of modern humans suggests that the population from which all *Homo sapiens* descended originated in Africa about 200,000 years ago. When these humans moved out of Africa around 100,000 years ago, they spread eastward into Southwest Asia and then throughout the rest of Afro-Eurasia. One group migrated to Australia about 50,000 years ago. Another group moved into the area of Europe about 40,000 years ago. When the scientific journal *Nature* published these findings in 1987, it inspired a groundswell of public interest—and a contentious scientific debate that continues today.

from microscopic bacteria to African apes that appeared about 23 million years ago? And no one would have accepted the findings that Africa's ape population separated into three distinct groups: one becoming present-day gorillas; the second becoming chimpanzees; and the third group, **hominids**, becoming modern-day humans only after following a long and complicated evolutionary process.

Early Hominids and Adaptation

What was it like to be a hominid in the millions of years before the emergence of modern humans? The first clue came from a discovery made in 1924 at Taung, not far from the present-day city of Johannesburg, South Africa. A scientist named Raymond Dart happened upon a skull and bones that appeared to be partly human and partly ape. Believing the creature to be "an extinct race of apes intermediate between living anthropoids (apes) and man," Dart labeled the creature the "Southern Ape of Africa," or *Australopithecus africanus*. This individual had a brain capacity of approximately one pint, or a little less than one-third that of a modern man and about the same as that of modern-day African apes. Yet these **australopithecines** were different from other animals, for they walked on two legs. Because Dart also found animal bones in the same vicinity, he mistakenly concluded that our early ancestors were bloodthirsty creatures who carried their prey to slaughtering grounds. It turns out that early hominids were only about five feet tall and weighed at most 110 pounds, so they were no match for big, muscular, and swift animal predators; the hominids were the hunted, not the hunters.

The fact that the hominids survived at all in such a hostile environment is a miracle. But they did, and over the first million years of their existence in Africa the australopithecines developed into more than six species. (A **species** is a group of animals or plants possessing one or more distinctive characteristics.) It is important

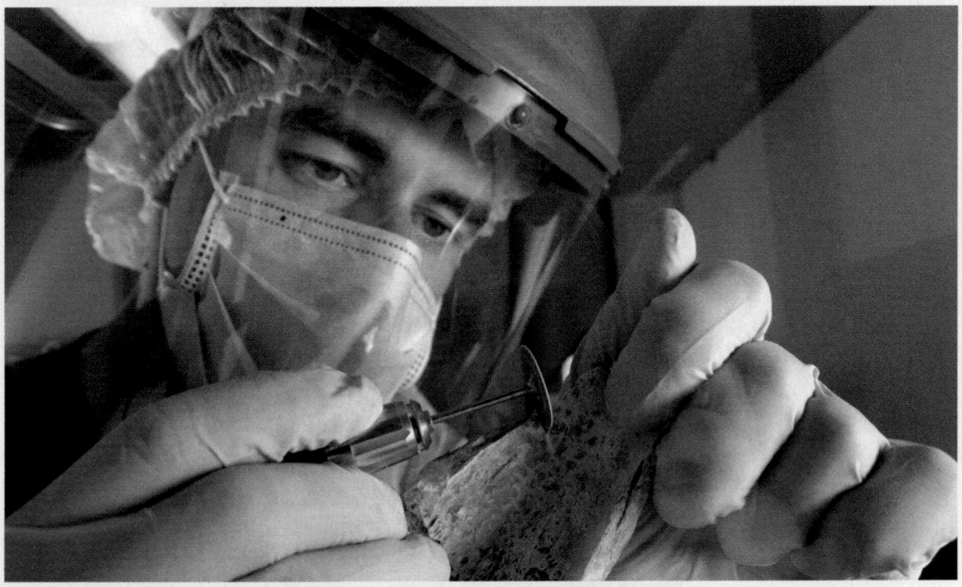

Neanderthal DNA Extraction. *This sample of fossilized Neanderthal bone will have its genetic material extracted and sequenced as part of the Neanderthal Genome Project.*

As this chapter demonstrates, the environment, especially climate, played a major role in the appearance of hominids and the eventual dominance of *Homo sapiens*. But how do we know so much about the world's climate going so far back in time? This brings us to the fourth of the scientific breakthroughs, known as marine isotope stages. By exploring the marine life, mainly pollen and plankton, deposited in deep sea beds and measuring the levels of oxygen-16 and oxygen-18 isotopes in these life forms, oceanographers and climatologists are able to determine the temperature of the world hundreds of thousands and even millions of years ago and thus to chart the cooling and warming cycles of the earth's climate.

QUESTIONS FOR ANALYSIS

- How has the study of prehistory changed since World War II? What are the consequences?
- How does the study of climate and environment relate to the origins of humans?

Explore Further

Lawrence Barham and Peter Mitchell, *The First Africans: African Archaeology from the Earliest Toolmakers to Most Recent Foragers* (2008).

Barker, Graeme, *Agricultural Revolution in Prehistory: Why Did Foragers Become Farmers* (2006).

to emphasize that these australopithecines were not humans but that they carried the genetic and biological material out of which modern humans would later emerge. These precursors to modern humans had a key trait for evolutionary survival: they were remarkably good adapters. They could make adaptations to deal with dynamic environmental shifts, and they were intelligent.

LUCY Australopithecines existed not only in southern Africa but in the north as well. In 1974, an archaeological team working at a site in present-day Ethiopia unearthed a relatively intact skeleton of a young adult female australopithecine in the valley of the Awash River. The researchers gave the skeleton a nickname, Lucy, based on the popular Beatles song "Lucy in the Sky with Diamonds."

Lucy was remarkable. She stood a little over three feet tall, she walked upright, her skull contained a brain within the ape size range, and her jaw and teeth were humanlike. Her arms were long, hanging halfway from her hips to her knees, and her legs were short—suggesting that she was a skilled tree climber, might not have been bipedal at all times, and sometimes resorted to arms for locomotion, in the fashion of a modern baboon. Above all, Lucy's skeleton was very, very old—half a million years older than any other complete hominid skeleton found up to that time. Lucy showed us that human precursors were walking around as early as 3 million years ago. (See Table 1.1.) But it also raised some significant questions: Was Lucy a precursor to modern-day humans? If so, what kind of a precursor?

ADAPTATION To survive, hominids had to adapt and evolve in order to keep pace with rapidly changing physical environments—for if they did not, they would die out. Many of the early hominid groups did just that. In fact, no straight-line descent tree exists from the first hominids to modern men and women. The places where researchers have found early hominid remains in southern and eastern Africa abounded in environmental changes, moving

TABLE 1.1 | Human Evolution

SPECIES	TIME
Orrorin tugenensis	6 MILLION YEARS AGO
Australopithecus anamensis	4.2 MILLION YEARS AGO
Australopithecus afarensis (INCLUDING LUCY)	3.4 MILLION YEARS AGO
Australopithecus africanus	3.0 MILLION YEARS AGO
Homo habilis (INCLUDING DEAR BOY)	2.5 MILLION YEARS AGO
Homo erectus and *Homo ergaster* (INCLUDING JAVA AND PEKING MAN)	1.8 MILLION YEARS AGO
Homo heidelbergensis (COMMON ANCESTOR OF *NEANDERTHALS* AND *HOMO SAPIENS*)	600,000 YEARS AGO
Neanderthals	200,000 YEARS AGO
Homo sapiens	200,000 YEARS AGO
Homo sapiens sapiens (MODERN HUMANS)	35,000 YEARS AGO

from being heavily forested and well watered to being arid and desert-like, and then back again. Survival required constant **adaptation** (the ability to alter behavior and to innovate, finding new ways of doing things), and some hominid groups were better at it than others. (See Map 1.1.)

In adapting, early hominids began to distinguish themselves from other mammals that were physically similar to themselves. It was not their hunting prowess that made the hominids stand out, because plenty of other species chased their prey with skill and dexterity. The single trait that gave early hominids a real advantage for survival was **bipedalism**: they became "two-footed" creatures that stood upright. At some point, the first hominids were able to remain upright and move about, leaving their arms and hands free for other useful tasks, like carrying food over long distances. Once they ventured into open savannas (grassy plains with a few scattered trees), about 1.7 million years ago, hominids had a tremendous advantage. They were the only primates (an order of mammals consisting of man, apes, and monkeys) to move consistently on two legs. Because they could move continuously and over great distances, they were able to migrate out of hostile environments and into more hospitable locations as needed.

Explaining why and how hominids began to walk on two legs is critical to understanding our human origins and how humans became differentiated from other animal groups. Along with the other primates, the first hominids enjoyed the advantages of being long-limbed, tree-loving animals with good vision and dexterous digits. Why did these primates, in contrast to their closest relatives (gorillas and chimpanzees), leave the shelter of trees and venture out into the open grasslands, where they were vulnerable to attack? The answer is not self-evident. Explaining how and why some apes took these first steps also sheds light on why humanity's origins lie in Africa. Fifteen million years ago there were apes all over the world, so why did a small number of them evolve new traits in Africa?

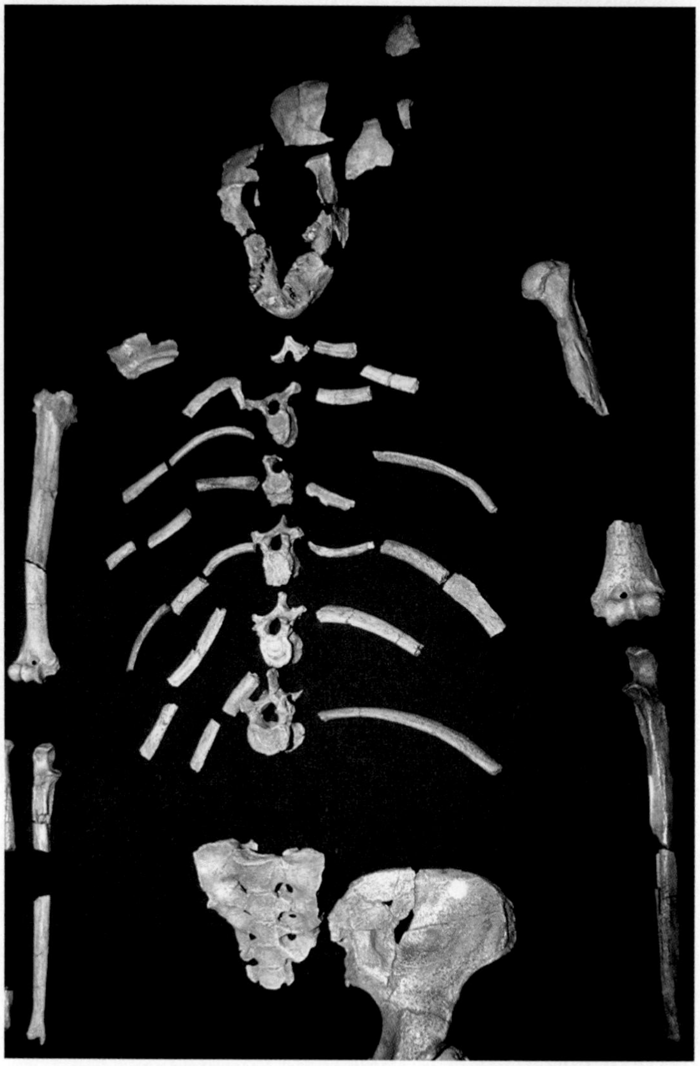

Fossil Bones of Lucy. *Archaeologist Donald Johanson discovered the fossilized bones of this young female in the Afar region of Ethiopia. They are believed to date from approximately 3.2 million years ago and provide evidence of some of the first hominids to appear in Africa. This find was of great importance because the bones were so fully and completely preserved.*

ENVIRONMENTAL CHANGES Approximately 40 million years ago the world entered its fourth great ice age, during which the earth's temperatures plunged and its continental ice sheets, polar ice sheets, and mountain glaciers increased. This ice age lasted until 10,000 years ago. Like all ice ages, it had alternating warming and cooling phases that lasted between 40,000 and 100,000 years each. Between 10 and 15 million years ago, the

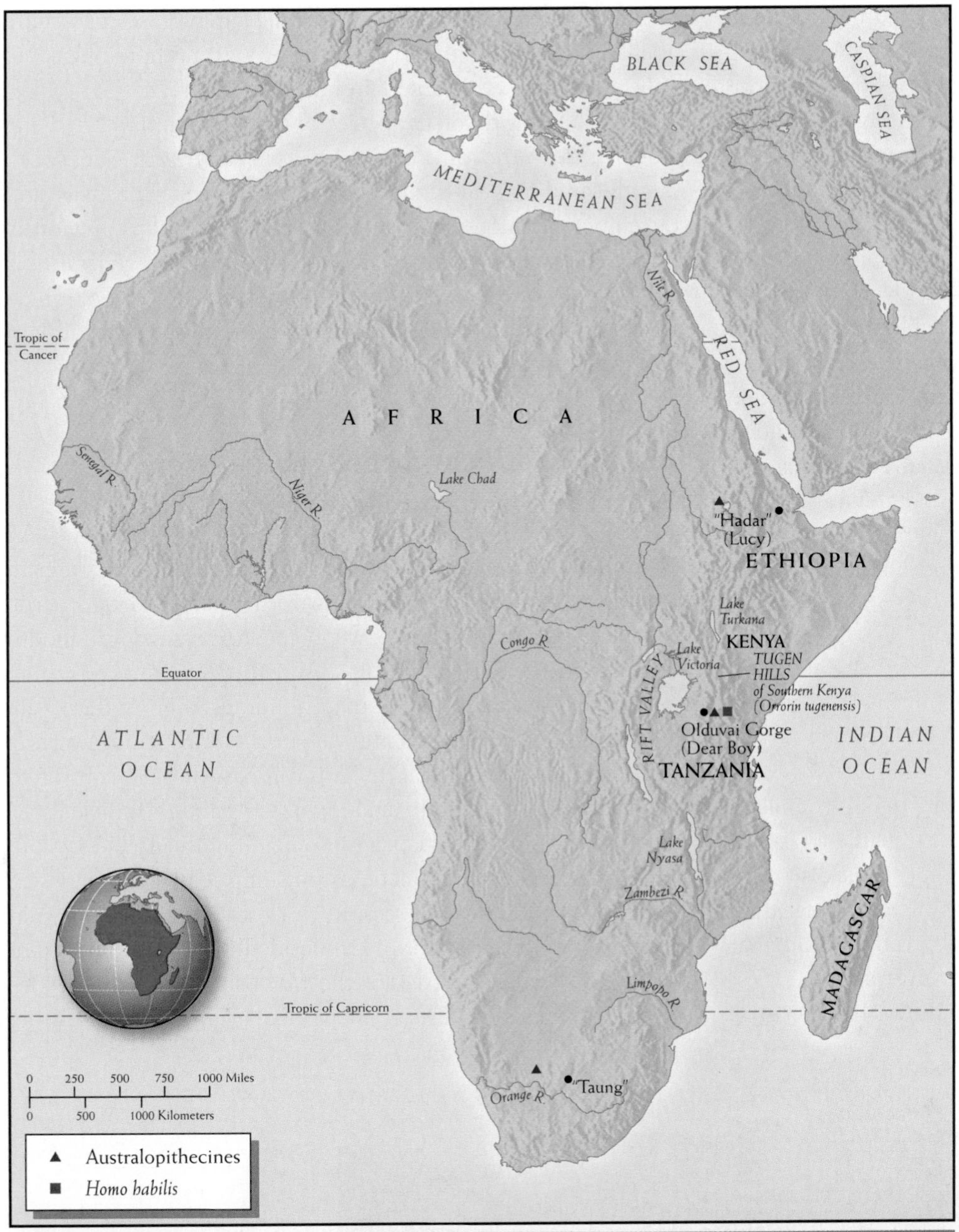

MAP 1.1 | Early Hominids

The earliest hominid species evolved in Africa millions of years ago.

- Judging from this map, what were the main geographic features of their environment?
- How did the changing environment of eastern and southern Africa shape the evolution of these modern human ancestors?
- What advantages did bipedalism give them?

climate in Africa went through one such cooling and drying phase. To the east of Africa's Rift Valley, stretching from South Africa north to the Ethiopian highlands, the cooling and drying forced forests to contract and savannas to spread. It was in this region that some apes came down from trees, stood up, and learned to walk, to run, and to live in savanna lands—thus becoming the precursors to humans, and distinctive as a new species. Using two feet for locomotion augmented the means for obtaining food and avoiding predators and improved the chances these creatures had to survive in constantly changing environments.

In addition to being bipedal, hominids had another trait that helped them to survive and create and use tools—opposable thumbs. This trait, shared with other primates, gave hominids great physical dexterity, enhancing their ability to explore and to alter materials found in nature. Manual dexterity and standing upright also enabled them to carry young family members if they needed to relocate, or to throw missiles (such as rocks and sticks) with deadly accuracy to protect themselves or to obtain food. They also used increased powers of observation and memory, what we call **cognitive skills**, such as problem solving and—much later—language, to gather wild berries and grains at this stage and to scavenge the meat and marrow of animals that had died of natural causes or as the prey of predators. All primates are good at these activities, but hominids excelled at them. Cognition was destined to become the basis for further developments and yet another characteristic that separate hominids from their closest species.

The early hominids were highly social. They lived in bands of about twenty-five individuals, trying to survive by hunting small game and gathering wild plants. Not yet a match for large predators, they had to find safe hiding places. They also sought ecological niches where a diverse supply of wild grains and fruits and abundant wildlife ensured a secure, comfortable existence. In such locations, small hunting bands of twenty-five could swell through alliances with others to as many as 500 individuals. Like other primates, hominids communicated through gestures, but they also may have developed an early form of spoken language that led (among other things) to the establishment of cultural codes such as common rules, customs, and identities.

The early hominids lived in this manner for up to 3 million years, changing their way of life very little except for moving around the African landmass in their never-ending search for more favorable environments. Even so, their survival is surprising. There were not many of them, and they struggled in hostile environments surrounded by a diversity of large mammals, including predators such as lions.

As the environment changed over the millennia, these early hominids gradually altered in appearance. Over a period of 3 million years their brains more than doubled in size; their foreheads became more elongated; their jaws became less massive; and they took on a much more modern look. Adaptation to environmental changes also created new skills and aptitudes, which expanded the ability to store and analyze information. With larger brains, hominids could form mental maps of their worlds—they could learn, remember what they learned, and convey these lessons to their neighbors and offspring. In this fashion, larger groups of hominids created communities with shared understandings of their environments.

DIVERSITY We know that hominids were much older than we thought, but it turns out that they were also much more diverse. Consider some startling finds from Ethiopia and Kenya. In southern Kenya, researchers discovered bone remains, at least 6 million years old, of a chimpanzee-sized hominid (named *Orrorin tugenensis*) that walked upright on two feet. This discovery indicates that bipedalism must be millions of years older than we used to think. Moreover, these hominids' teeth indicate that they were closer to modern humans than to australopithecines. In their arms and hands, though, which show characteristics needed for tree climbing, the *Orrorin* hominids seemed more apelike than the australopithecines. So *Orrorin* hominids were still somewhat tied to an environment in the trees.

The fact that different species of early hominids were living side by side in the same environment in eastern Africa between 3 and 4 million years ago indicates much greater diversity and development among their populations than scholars previously imagined. The environment in eastern Africa was generating a fair number of different hominid populations, a few of which would provide our genetic base, but most of which would not survive in the long run.

Homo Habilis and the Debate over Who the First Humans Were

One million years after Lucy, the first examples of creatures,to whom the scholarly community gave the name *homo*, or "true human," appeared. They, too, were bipedal, possessing a smooth walk based on upright posture. And they had an even more important advantage over other hominids: brains that were growing larger. Big brains are the site of **innovation**: learning and storing lessons so that humans can pass those lessons on to offspring, especially in the making of tools and the efficient use of resources (and, we suspect, in defending themselves). Mary and Louis Leakey, who made astonishing fossil discoveries in the 1950s at Olduvai Gorge (part of the Great Rift Valley) in present-day northeastern Tanzania, identified these important traits. The Leakeys' finds are the most significant discoveries of early humans in Africa—in particular, an intact skull that

Searching for Hominid Fossils. *Olorgasalie in Kenya has proved to be one of the most important archaeological sites for uncovering evidence of early hominid development. Rick Potts, a leader in the field, is shown here on-site. Among his discoveries were hand axes and indications that hominids in this area had learned to use fire.*

was 1.8 million years old. The Leakeys nicknamed the creature whose skull they had unearthed Dear Boy.

Other objects discovered with Dear Boy demonstrated that by this time early humans had begun to make tools for butchering animals and, possibly, for hunting and killing smaller animals. The tools were flaked stones with sharpened edges for cutting apart animal flesh and scooping out the marrow from bones. To mimic the slicing teeth of lions, leopards, and other carnivores, the Oldowans had devised these tools through careful chipping. Dear Boy and his companions had carried usable rocks to distant places where they made their implements with special hammer stones—tools to make tools. Unlike other tool-using animals (for example, chimpanzees), early humans were now intentionally fashioning implements, not simply finding them when needed. More important, they were passing on knowledge of these tools to their offspring and, in the process, gradually improving the tools. Because the Leakeys believed that making and using tools represented a new stage in the evolution of human beings, they gave these creatures a new name: ***Homo habilis***, or "Skillful Man." By using the term *Homo* for them, the Leakeys implied that they were the first truly human creatures in the evolutionary scheme. Their toolmaking ability made them the forerunners, though very distant, of modern men and women.

Although the term *Homo habilis* continues to be employed for these creatures, in many ways, especially in their brain size, they were not distinctly different from their australopithecan predecessors. In fact, just which of the many creatures warrant being seen as the world's first truly human beings turns on what traits are identified as most decisive in distinguishing bipedal apes

The Leakeys. *Louis Leakey and his wife, Mary, were dedicated archaeologists whose work in East Africa established the area as one of the starting points of human development. Mary Leakey was among the most successful archaeologists studying hominids in Africa. Her finds, including the one in this photograph from Laetoli, Tanzania, highlight the activities of early men and women in Africa. The footprints, believed to be those of an* Australopithecus afarensis, *date from 3.7 to 3 million years ago.*

Olduvai Gorge, Tanzania. *Olduvai Gorge is arguably the most famous archaeological site containing hominid finds. Mary and Louis Leakey, convinced that early human beings originated in Africa, discovered the fossil remains of* Homo habilis *("Skillful Man") in this area between 1960 and 1963. They argued that these findings represent a direct link to* Homo erectus.

from modern humans. If that trait is toolmaking, then *Homo habilis* is the first. If being entirely bipedal, then *Homo erectus* is the one; if having a truly large brain, then it might only be *Homo sapiens* or their immediate predecessors.

Early Humans on the Move: Migrations of *Homo Erectus*

All the different species of hominids flourished together in Africa between 1 and 2.5 million years ago. By 1 million years ago, however, many had died out. One surviving species, which emerged about 1.8 million years ago, had a large brain capacity and walked truly upright; in fact, its gait was remarkably similar to that of modern humans. It therefore gained the name ***Homo erectus***, or "Standing Man." Even though this species was more able to cope with environmental changes than other hominids had been, its story was not a predictable triumph. Only with the hindsight of millions of years can we understand the decisive advantage of intelligence over brawn—larger brains over larger teeth. Indeed, there were many more failures than successes in the gradual changes that led *Homo erectus* to be one of the few hominid species that would survive until the arrival of *Homo sapiens*.

One of the traits that contributed to the survival of *Homo erectus* was the development of extended periods of caring for their young. Although their enlarged brain gave these hominids advantages over the rest of the animal world, it also brought one significant problem: their heads were too large to pass through the females' pelvises at birth. Their pelvises were only big enough to deliver an infant with a cranial capacity that was about a third an adult's size. As a result, offspring required a long period of protection by adults as they matured and their brain size tripled.

This difference from other species also affected family dynamics. For example, the long maturing process gave adult members of hunting and gathering bands time to train their children in those activities. In addition, maturation and brain growth required mothers to spend years attending to their infants, via lactation as well as food preparation for children after weaning. This investment of time and energy was so critical to survival that mothers devised means to share the burden of childrearing. They figured out how to reduce the risks of accidents or attacks, sometimes even fending off assaults by predatory fathers and other males. Mothers relied on other women (their own mothers, sisters, and friends) and girls (often their own daughters) to help in the nurturing and protecting, a process known as allomothering (literally, "other mothering").

Two main features of *Homo erectus* distinguished them from their competitors: bipedalism and their attempts to control the environment. Being bipedal, they could move with a smooth and rapid gait, so they could cover large distances quickly. They were the world's first long-distance travelers, forming the first mobile human communities. In addition, they began to make rudimentary attempts to master their environments. Not only did these early human ancestors make stone tools for hunting and food preparation, but they also began to control fire—another significant marker in the development of human culture. It is hard to tell from fossils when humans learned to use fire. The most reliable evidence comes from cave sites, less than 250,000 years old, where early humans apparently cooked some of their food. Less conservative estimates suggest that human mastery of fire occurred nearly 800,000 years ago. Fire provided heat, protection from wild animals, a gathering point for small communities, and perhaps most importantly a way to cook food. It was also symbolically powerful, for here was a source of energy that humans could extinguish and revive at will. The uses of fire

Skulls of Ancestors of *Homo sapiens*. *Shown here are seven skulls of ancestors of modern-day men and women, arranged to highlight brain growth over time. The skulls represent (left to right):* Adapis, *a lemur-like animal that lived 50 million years ago;* Proconsul, *a primate that lived about 23 million years ago;* Australopithecus africanus; Homo habilis; Homo erectus; Homo sapiens *from the Qafzeh site in Israel, about 90,000 years old; and Cro-Magnon* Homo sapiens sapiens *from France, about 22,000 years old.*

ANALYZING GLOBAL DEVELOPMENTS

The Age of the Universe and Human Evolution

Our universe is nearly 14 billion years old. Our sun, earth and solar system appeared nearly 4.5 billion years ago, and the earliest life forms on earth appeared 3.8 billion years ago. Hominids, however, only appeared on the scene about seven million years ago, which represents not even 1% of the total time that the earth has existed. They were for a long time confined to the African land mass, learning to walk on two legs there, devising simple tools at first and perfecting their use over time. Africa remained the homeland for many different hominid groups for nearly five million years before *Homo erectus* ventured out of the continent, moving into Central Asia, East Asia, Southeast Asia, and Europe though not into the Americas. There were probably other waves of hominid migrations out of Africa, but the most important of the migrations out of Africa occurred about 50,000 years ago when modern humans, *Homo sapiens* left the continent and, with amazing rapidity, filled up all of the globe's land masses. (See Map 1.2 to trace the migrations of *Homo erectus* and *Homo sapiens*.)

The Big Bang Moment in the Creation of the Universe	13.8 BILLION YEARS AGO (BYA)	
The Formation of the Sun, Earth, and Solar System	4.5 BYA	
Earliest Life Forms appear	3.8 BYA	
Multi-Cellular Organisms appear	1.5 BYA	
First Hominids appear	7 MILLION YEARS AGO (MYA)	>1% of Earth's Existence
Australopithecus afarensis appears (including Lucy)	3.4 MYA	
Homo habilis appears (including Dear Boy)	2.5 MYA	
Homo erectus appears (including Java and Peking Man)	1.8 MYA	
Homo erectus leave Africa	1.5 MYA	
Neanderthals appear	200,000 YEARS AGO	
Homo sapiens appear	200,000 YEARS AGO	
Homo sapiens leave Africa	100,000 YEARS AGO	
Homo sapiens migrate into Asia	60,000 YEARS AGO	
Homo sapiens migrate into Europe	40-50,000 YEARS AGO	
Homo sapiens migrate into Australia	40,000 YEARS AGO	
Homo sapiens migrate into the Americas	16,000 YEARS AGO	
Homo sapiens sapiens appear (modern humans)	35,000 YEARS AGO	

QUESTIONS FOR ANALYSIS

- How do we know the age of the universe and when and how hominids first appeared and their evolutionary patterns?
- Why are hominids and *Homo sapiens* so late in the evolutionary cycle and why did they prevail over other hominids?
- In your opinion which of the different families of hominids deserves the designation of the first humans and why?
- Why are scientists disinclined to see a straight line evolution from the earliest hominids to modern humans?

Sources: Chris Scarre (ed.), The Human Past: World Prehistory and the Development of Human Societies *(2005); Ian Tattersall,* Masters of the Planet: The Search for Our Human Origins *(2012).*

had enormous long-term effects on human evolution. Because they were able to boil, steam, and fry wild plants, as well as otherwise undigestible foods (especially raw muscle fiber), early humans could expand their diets. Because cooked foods yield more energy than raw foods and because the brain, while only 2 percent of human body weight, uses between 20 and 25 percent of all the energy that humans take in, cooking was decisive in the evolution of brain size and functioning.

The populating of the world by hominids proceeded in waves. Around 1 or 2 million years ago, *Homo erectus* individuals migrated first into the lands of Southwest Asia. From there, according to some scholars, they traveled along the Indian Ocean shoreline, moving into South Asia and Southeast Asia and later northward into what is now China. Their **migration** was a response in part to the environmental changes that were transforming the world. The Northern Hemisphere experienced thirty major cold phases during this period, marked by glaciers (huge sheets of ice) spreading over vast expanses of the northern parts of Eurasia and the Americas. The glaciers formed as a result of intense cold that froze much of the world's oceans, lowering them some 325 feet below present-day levels. So it was possible for the migrants to travel across land bridges into

Southeast Asia and from East Asia to Japan, as well as from New Guinea to Australia. The last parts of the Afro-Eurasian landmass to be occupied were in Europe. The geological record indicates that ice mantles blanketed the areas of present-day Scotland, Ireland, Wales, Scandinavia, and the whole of northern Europe (including the areas of present-day Berlin, Warsaw, Moscow, and Kiev). Here, too, a lowered ocean level enabled human predecessors to cross by foot from areas in Europe into what is now England.

It is astonishing how far *Homo erectus* traveled. Discoveries of the bone remains of "Java Man" and "Peking Man" (named according to the places where archaeologists first unearthed their remains) confirmed early settlements of *Homo erectus* in Southeast and East Asia. The remains of Java Man, found in 1891 in central Java, turned out to be those of an early *Homo erectus* that had dispersed into Asia nearly 2 million years ago. In 1969, at Sangiran (also on the island of Java), archaeologists uncovered remains with a fuller cranium that was very thick, indicating that the individual's brain was about half the size of a modern human's. Because this discovery dates from about 800,000 years ago, scientists realized that hominids were moving northward and eastward into Asia at least a million years ago and had reached Java, which was then connected by land to the rest of the Afro-Eurasian landmass.

Similar twentieth-century finds in China give a clearer picture of the daily lives of these pioneering hominids. Peking Man was a cave dweller, toolmaker, and hunter and gatherer who settled in the warmer climate in northern China perhaps 400,000 years ago. Peking Man's brain was larger than that of his Javan cousins, and there is evidence that he controlled fire and cooked meat in addition to hunting large animals. He made tools of vein quartz, quartz crystals, flint, and sandstone. These *Homo erectus* hominids were more adept at toolmaking than their predecessors. Their major innovation was the double-faced axe, a stone instrument whittled down to sharp edges on both sides to serve as a hand axe, a cleaver, a pick, and probably a weapon to hurl against foes or animals. Even so, and in spite of their enlarged brains, these early predecessors still had a long way to go before becoming modern humans.

Rather than seeing human evolution as a single, gradual development, increasingly scientists view our origins as shaped by a series of progressions and regressions as hominids adapted or failed to adapt and went extinct (died out). Several species existed simultaneously, but some were more suited to changing environmental conditions—and thus more likely to survive—than others. Although those in the *Homo habilis* and *Homo erectus* species were among some of the world's first humanlike inhabitants, they probably were not direct ancestors of modern man and woman. The early settlers of Afro-Eurasia from the *Homo erectus* group went extinct. Later waves of hominids followed them, walking out of the African landmass just as their predecessors had done. By 500,000 years ago, caves and rock shelters in many areas of Afro-Eurasia housed residents who made fire, flaked stones into implements, and formed settlements. Yet we are not their immediate descendants. Although the existence of *Homo erectus* may have been necessary for the evolution into *Homo sapiens*, it was not, in itself, sufficient.

THE FIRST MODERN HUMANS

The first traces that we have of *Homo sapiens* come from two sites in modern-day Ethiopia and suggest that the first modern humans emerged sometime between 200,000 and 150,000 years ago. *Homo sapiens*, unlike other hominids, did not take long to become highly mobile, moving out of Africa about 60,000 years ago. If we consider the 5 million years of hominid life as a single hour of our time today, then our own history (that of *Homo sapiens*) is slightly less than two minutes.

The early hominids could not form large communities, as they had limited communication skills. They could utter simple commands and communicate with hand signals, but complex linguistic expression eluded them. This achievement was one of the last in the evolutionary process of becoming human; it did not occur until between 100,000 and 50,000 years ago. Many scholars view it as the critical ingredient in distinguishing human beings from other animals. It is this skill that made *Homo sapiens* "sapiens," which is to say "wise" or "intelligent"—humans who could create culture. Creating language enabled humans to become modern humans.

Homo Sapiens's Precarious Beginnings and Their Migration

About 200,000 years ago, massive shifts in Africa's climate and environment put huge pressures on all types of plants and animals, including hominids. Temperatures dropped, plummeting 40 degrees Fahrenheit below present-day averages. A sheet of ice 2.5 miles thick blanketed Northern Europe and North America. With much of the earth's water frozen in glaciers, the climate went dry. The Sahara and Kalahari deserts expanded; Africa's large tropical rain forests became isolated pockets. Many plant and animal species died out all across Afro-Eurasia. To make matters worse, about 73,000 years ago Mount Toba, in present-day Sumatra, erupted, spewing into the atmosphere an enormous quantity of volcanic ash which created a global volcanic winter that lasted for six full years. The hominid populations declined precipitously, and its new species, *Homo sapiens*,

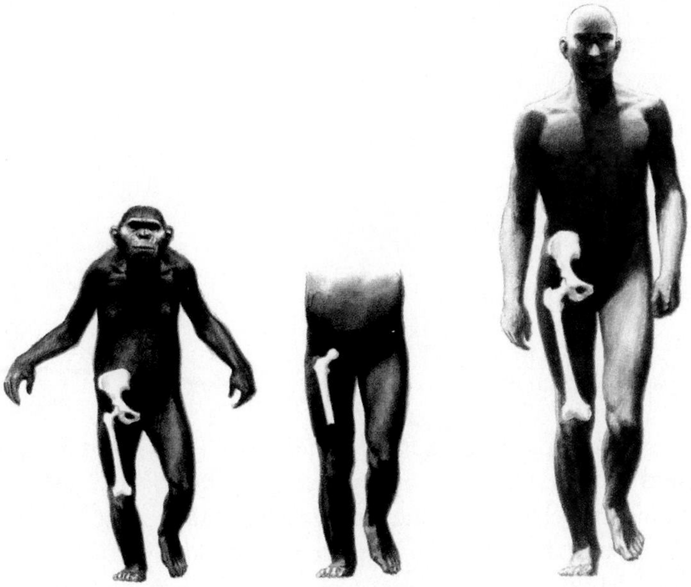

The Physical Evolution of Hominids. *These three figures show the femur bones of Lucy,* Orrorin tugenensis *(one of the earliest of the hominids, who may have existed as many as 6 million years ago), and* Homo sapiens. Homo sapiens *has a larger femur bone and was bigger than Lucy—a representative of the hominid species* Australopithecus afarensis*—but has the same bone structure.*

threatened to go extinct before it could get started. Only a few thousand survivors huddled together in what remained of the once rich tropical rain forests of equatorial Africa—a fact that means that all 7 billion of us today descend from an incredibly small African core population. In these extremely cold and dry environments, what counted for survival was superior intelligence and extraordinary mobility, precisely the traits that *Homo sapiens* possessed in abundance. What *Homo sapiens* lacked in large size and brute strength, it made up for in cognitive abilities and a capacity to search out and move with great speed into habitable locations.

The highlands of eastern Africa was one of the regions least affected by climate change, and it was there that this new bigger-brained, more dexterous, and more agile species of humans congregated. ***Homo sapiens*** differed notably from their precursors. Yet the eclipse of *Homo erectus* by *Homo sapiens* was hardly inevitable. After all, *Homo erectus* was already scattered around Africa and Eurasia. But the *Homo sapiens* population did rebound from its environmental crisis, and when members of the species began to move out of Africa and the two species encountered each other in the same places across the globe, *Homo sapiens* prevailed—in part because of their greater cognitive and language skills.

The *Homo sapiens* newcomers followed the trails blazed by earlier migrants from Africa. (See Map 1.2.) In many places, they moved into the same areas as their genetic cousins, migrating by way of the Levant (the area encompassing modern-day Lebanon, Israel, Palestine, Jordan, and Syria), into other parts of Southwest Asia and from there into central Asia—but not at this stage into Europe. They flourished and reproduced. By 30,000 years ago, the population of *Homo sapiens* had grown to about 300,000. Between 60,000 and 12,000 years ago, these modern humans were surging into areas tens of thousands of miles from the Rift Valley and the Ethiopian highlands of Africa. In the area of present-day China, they were thriving and creating distinct regional cultures. Consider Shandingdong Man, a *Homo sapiens* whose fossil remains and relics date to about 18,000 years ago. His physical characteristics were closer to those of modern humans, and he had a similar brain size. His stone tools, which included choppers and scrapers for preparing food, were similar to those of the *Homo erectus* Peking Man. His bone needles, however, were the first stitching tools of their kind found in China, and they indicated the making of garments. Some of the needles measured a little over an inch in length and had small holes drilled in them. Shandingdong Man also buried his dead. In fact, a tomb of grave goods includes ornaments suggesting the development of aesthetic tastes and religious beliefs. The social unit of these hominids may have been some sort of clan descended from a common ancestor and thus linked by genealogy.

Homo sapiens were also migrating into the northeastern fringe of East Asia. In the frigid climate there, they learned to follow herds of large Siberian grazing animals. The bones and dung of mastodons, large-tusked mammals, for instance, made decent fuel and good building material. Pursuing their prey eastward as the herds sought pastures in the steppes (treeless grasslands) and marshes, these groups migrated across the ice to Japan. Archaeologists have discovered a mammoth fossil in the colder north of Japan, for example, and an elephant fossil in the warmer south. Elephants in particular roamed the warmer parts of inner Eurasia. The hunters and gatherers who moved into Japan gathered wild plants for sustenance, and they dried, smoked, or broiled meat by using fire. They refined these practices once the seas separated the islands from Asia and limited the supplies of game and plants.

About 18,000 years ago, *Homo sapiens* began edging into the weedy landmass that linked Siberia and North America (which hominids had not populated). This thousand-mile-long land bridge, later called Beringia, must have seemed like an extension of familiar steppe-land terrain. For thousands of years, modern humans poured eastward and southward into the uninhabited terrain of North America. The oldest known location of human settlement in the Americas is Broken Mammoth, a 14,000-year-old site in central Alaska. A final migration occurred about 8,000 years ago by boat, since by then the land bridge had disappeared under the sea. (See Table 1.2.)

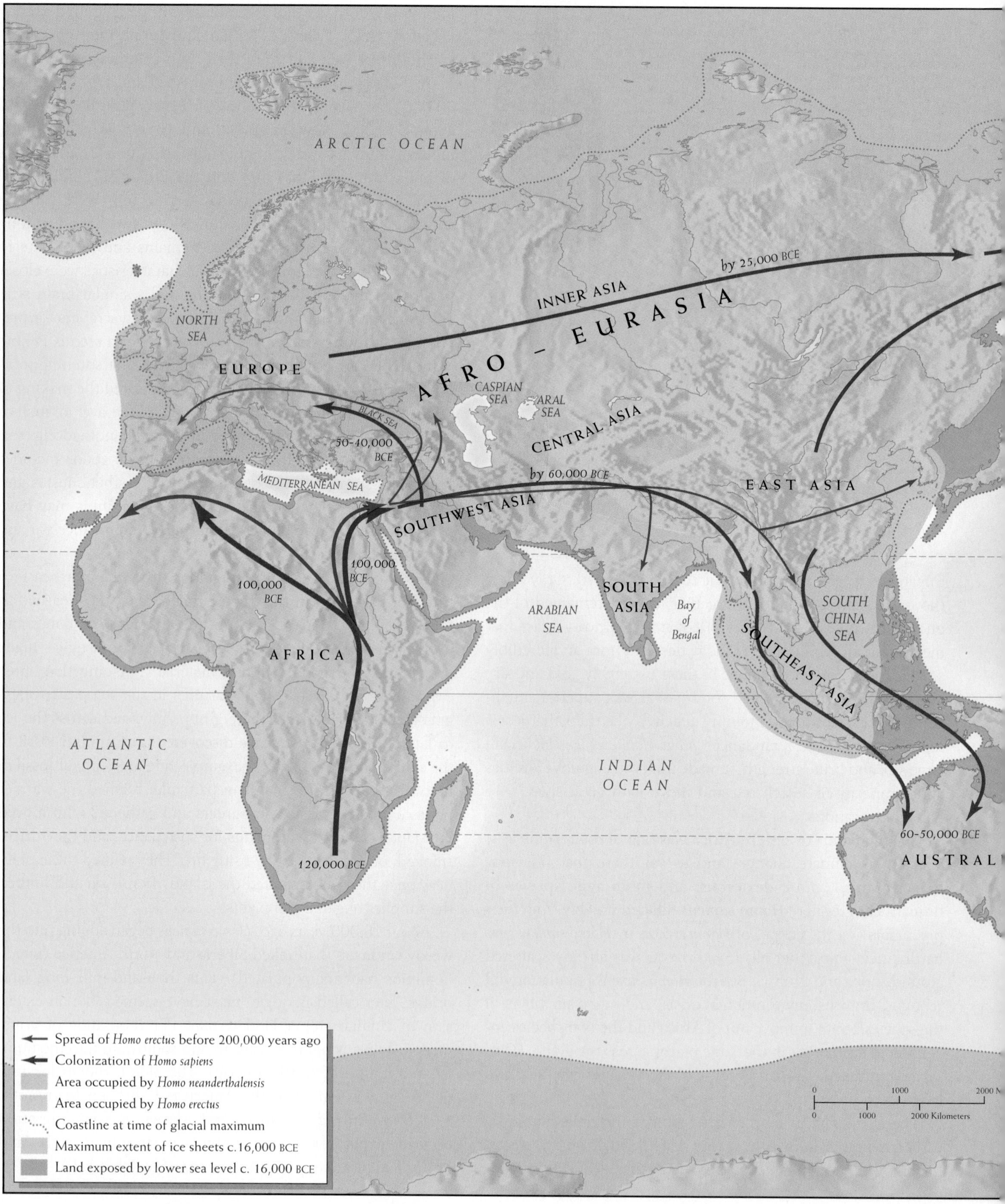

ARCTIC OCEAN
NORTH SEA
EUROPE
AFRO – EURASIA
INNER ASIA
by 25,000 BCE
CASPIAN SEA
ARAL SEA
BLACK SEA
CENTRAL ASIA
50-40,000 BCE
MEDITERRANEAN SEA
by 60,000 BCE
SOUTHWEST ASIA
EAST ASIA
100,000 BCE
100,000 BCE
ARABIAN SEA
SOUTH ASIA
Bay of Bengal
SOUTH CHINA SEA
SOUTHEAST ASIA
AFRICA
ATLANTIC OCEAN
INDIAN OCEAN
120,000 BCE
60-50,000 BCE
AUSTRAL
Spread of Homo erectus before 200,000 years ago
Colonization of Homo sapiens
Area occupied by Homo neanderthalensis
Area occupied by Homo erectus
Coastline at time of glacial maximum
Maximum extent of ice sheets c.16,000 BCE
Land exposed by lower sea level c. 16,000 BCE
0 1000 2000 Kilometers

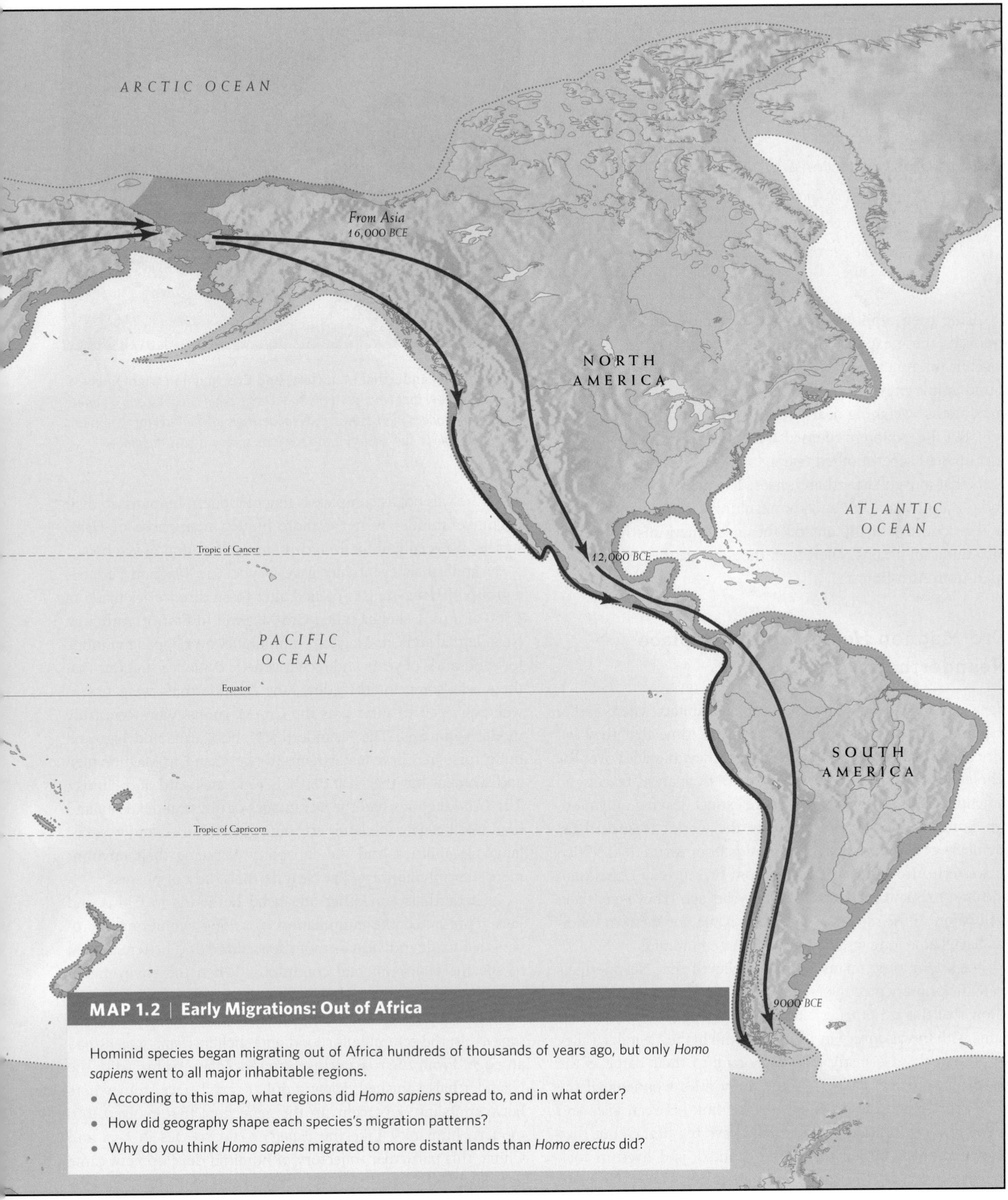

MAP 1.2 | Early Migrations: Out of Africa

Hominid species began migrating out of Africa hundreds of thousands of years ago, but only *Homo sapiens* went to all major inhabitable regions.

- According to this map, what regions did *Homo sapiens* spread to, and in what order?
- How did geography shape each species's migration patterns?
- Why do you think *Homo sapiens* migrated to more distant lands than *Homo erectus* did?

TABLE 1.2 | Migrations of *Homo sapiens*

SPECIES	TIME
Homo erectus *leave Africa*	c. 1.5 MILLION YEARS AGO
Homo sapiens *leave Africa*	c. 100,000 YEARS AGO
Homo sapiens *migrate into Asia*	c. 60,000 YEARS AGO
migrate into Europe	c. 40–50,000 YEARS AGO
migrate into Australia	c. 40,000 YEARS AGO
migrate into the Americas	c. 11–16,000 YEARS AGO

Skulls of a Neanderthal Man (left) and Cro-Magnon (right). *These two skulls show that Neanderthals had a large brain capacity and a larger head than modern man. However, Neanderthals lost out to* Homo sapiens *in the struggle to survive as* Homo sapiens *spread across the globe.*

Using their ability to adapt to new environments and to innovate, these expansionist migrants, who were the first discoverers of America, began to fill up the landmasses. They found ample prey in the herds of woolly mammoths, caribou, giant sloths (weighing nearly three tons), and 200-pound beavers. But the explorers could also themselves be prey—for they encountered saber-toothed tigers, long-legged eagles, and giant bears that moved faster than horses. The melting of the glaciers about 8,000 years ago and the resulting disappearance of the land bridge eventually cut off the first Americans from their Afro-Eurasian origins. Thereafter, the Americas became a world apart from Afro-Eurasia.

Cro-Magnon *Homo Sapiens* Replace Neanderthals

Homo sapiens spread out and occupied habitats where earlier hominid migrants had dwelled. From the time that they left Africa, approximately 60,000 years ago, they migrated over the whole globe. By 25,000 years ago, as DNA analysis reveals, all genetic cousins to *Homo sapiens* were extinct, leaving only modern humans' ancestors to populate the world. Neanderthals, members of an early wave of hominids from Africa, had settled in western Afro-Eurasia (ranging from present-day Uzbekistan and Iraq to Spain) perhaps 150,000 years ago. They were there well before *Homo sapiens*. Therein lies a tale, for Western scholars have had a long fascination with these hominids.

For a long time, many scholars believed that Neanderthals were the primary precursors of modern-day Europeans. We now know that this is not true. The first knowledge of Neanderthals came with the discovery in 1856 of a skull in the Neander Valley of present-day Germany (the *thal* or *tal* in their name is the German word for "valley"). Some authorities wondered if the skull represented the so-called missing link between apes and humans. Not only did Neanderthals have big brains, but they also used tools, buried their dead, hunted, and lived in rock shelters and caves. To judge from their behavior, their brain structure was not as complex as that of modern humans, so their cognitive abilities were far more limited than those of *Homo sapiens,* especially in their perception and creation of symbols.

Neanderthals eventually gave way to Cro-Magnon peoples, a group of *Homo sapiens* named after fossil discoveries made in 1868 at a rock shelter called Cro-Magnon in France. Although Neanderthal and Cro-Magnon communities overlapped in Europe for thousands of years and recent genetic evidence suggests that there was some interbreeding, the Neanderthals were not as well equipped to survive as the Cro-Magnons, who were truly modern humans. The Neanderthals' short arms and legs and bulky torso may have made them stronger than Cro-Magnon men and women, but the Neanderthals were awkward and clumsy. The Cro-Magnons had the advantages of physical dexterity and high intelligence; the latter attribute gave them cognitive skills, language abilities, and the capability of seeing their environment in symbolic ways that Neanderthals did not possess.

Neanderthals and other advanced hominids in China and Java represented the culmination of a long evolutionary process that made individuals more specialized and better adapted to specific environmental conditions. When the environment began to change, these descendants from Africa had difficulty coping. They lacked the range and adaptive fluidity of *Homo sapiens*. In the scramble for food and shelter, *Homo sapiens* had an edge. From their last refuge around Zafarraya in Spain, the Neanderthals vanished, leaving only a small trace, somewhere between 1 and 4 percent, in the gene pool that evolved into modern humanity. Like the *Homo erectus* species in Java and China, this particular trajectory of hominid development came to a dead end.

PRIMARY SOURCE

Problems in the Study of Hunters and Gatherers

One of the challenges in studying the origins of humanity is that the evidence is incomplete. Archaeologists and anthropologists have to theorize on the basis of what they can lay their hands on. In the case of archaeologists, these include fossil records. In the case of anthropologists, their subjects are tribal peoples—such as the San of southern Africa—whose lifeways today may resemble those of their ancestors tens of thousands of years ago.

To date, the hunting way of life has been the most successful and persistent adaptation man has ever achieved.

. . . It is appropriate that anthropologists take stock of the much older way of life of the hunters. This is not simply a study of biological evolution, since zoologists have come to regard behavior as central to the adaptation and evolution of all species. The emergence of economic, social, and ideological forms are as much a part of human evolution as are the developments in human anatomy and physiology . . . .

. . . Ever since the origin of agriculture, Neolithic (new stone age) peoples have been steadily expanding at the expense of the hunters. Today the latter are often found in unattractive environments, in lands which are of no use to their neighbors and which pose difficult and dramatic problems of survival. The more favorable habitats have long ago been appropriated by peoples with stronger, more aggressive social systems.

. . . Taking hunters as they are found, anthropologists have naturally been led to the conclusion that their life (and by implication the life of our ancestors) was a constant struggle for survival.

At the dawn of agriculture 12,000 years ago, hunters covered most of the habitable globe, and appeared to be generally most successful in those areas which later supported the densest populations of agricultural peoples. By 1500 CE the area left to hunters had shrunk drastically and their distribution fell largely at the peripheries of the continents and in the inaccessible interiors. However, even at this late date, hunting peoples occupied all of Australia, most of western and northern North America, and large portions of South America and Africa. This situation rapidly changed with the era of colonial expansion, and by 1900, when serious ethnographic research got under way, much of this way of life had been destroyed. As a result, our notion of unacculturated hunter-gatherer life has been largely drawn from peoples no longer living in the optimum portion of their traditional range.

To mention a few examples, the Netsilik Eskimos, the Arunta, and the Kung Bushmen are now classic cases in ethnography. However, the majority of the precontact Eskimos, Australian aborigines, and Bushmen lived in much better environments. Two-thirds of the Eskimos, according to Laughlin, lived *south* of the Arctic circle, and the populations in the Australian and Kalahari deserts were but a fraction of the populations living in the well-watered regions of southeast Australia and the Cape Province of Africa. Thus, within a given region the "classic cases" may, in fact, be precisely the opposite: namely, the most isolated peoples who managed to avoid contact until the arrival of the ethnographers. In order to understand hunters better it may be more profitable to consider the few hunters in rich environments, since it is likely that these peoples will be more representative of the ecological conditions under which man evolved than are the dramatic and unusual cases that illustrate extreme environmental pressure. Such a perspective may better help us to understand the extraordinary persistence and success of the human adaptation.

QUESTIONS FOR ANALYSIS

- Why is it important to study hunting and gathering communities?
- Why are the "classic cases" not necessarily the most representative of this early lifeway?

Source: Richard B. Lee and Irven De Vore, "Problems in the Study of Hunters and Gatherers" from Man the Hunter, pp. 3 and 5. Copyright © 1968 by Aldine Publishers. Reprinted by permission of Aldine Transaction, a division of Transaction Publishers.

Early *Homo Sapiens* as Hunters and Gatherers

Like their hominid predecessors, modern humans were hunters and gatherers, and they subsisted in this way until around 12,000 years ago. They hunted animals, fished, and foraged for wild berries, nuts, fruit, and grains, rather than planting crops, vines, or trees. Even today **hunting and gathering** societies endure, although only in the most marginal locations, mainly driven there by peoples living in settled societies. For example, researchers consider the present-day San peoples of southern Africa as an isolated remnant continuing their traditional hunting and gathering modes of life. On the basis of analogy, modern scholars use the San to reveal how men and women must have lived hundreds of thousands of years ago. (See Primary Source: Problems in the Study of Hunters and Gatherers.) As late as 1500, hunters and gatherers occupied a third of the globe, including all of Australia, most of North America, and large tracts of South America, Africa, and North and Northeast Asia, and constituted as much as 15 percent of the world's population.

The fact that hominid men and women survived as hunters and gatherers for millions of years, that early *Homo sapiens* also lived this way, and that a few contemporary communities still forage for food suggests the powerful attractions of this way of life. Hunters and gatherers could find enough food in about three hours of foraging each day, thus affording time for other pursuits such as relaxation, interaction, and friendly competitions with other members of their bands. Scholars believe that these small bands were relatively egalitarian, and one scholar described foragers as "the original affluent society," producing much and wanting little. Men specialized in hunting and women in gathering and child rearing but men and women contributed equally to the bands' welfare. Scholars also believe that women made a larger contribution than men and enjoyed high status because the dietary staples were cereals and fruits, whose harvesting and preparation were likely women's responsibility.

The San Hunters and Gatherers of Southern Africa. *The San, who live in the Kalahari Desert in present-day Botswana, continue to follow a hunting and gathering existence that has died out in many parts of the world. Hunting and gathering was the way that most humans lived for millennia.*

ART AND LANGUAGE

Despite the remorselessly nature-bound quality of life for early humans, the first *Homo sapiens* made an evolutionary breakthrough. They developed cultural forms that reflected a consciousness of self, a drive to survive, an appreciation of beauty, and an ability to manipulate information symbolically.

Art

Few of the cultural achievements of early *Homo sapiens* communities have engaged modern-day observers more than their artistic endeavors. Accomplished drawings have come to light in areas in Europe. The ability to draw allowed *Homo sapiens* to understand their environment, to bond among their kin groups (groups related by blood ties), and to articulate important mythologies. In times of stress, such behaviors gave individuals an adaptive advantage in surviving in extremely challenging circumstances.

"Look, Daddy, oxen!" That is what the daughter of Marcelino Sanz de Sauruola cried to her father as she looked at the ceiling of a deep cave on his property at Altamira, Spain, that he was exploring one summer afternoon. As he looked up, Sauruola could not believe what he saw. Arranged across the ceiling of the huge chamber were more than two dozen life-size figures of bison, horses, and wild bulls, all painted in vivid red, black, yellow, and brown. He did not think that anyone would believe these fabulous images were tens of thousands of years old, but he knew in his heart that they were. That was in 1879. Only in 1906 did the world accept that the Altamira paintings were the work of early humans and are at least 35,600 years old. Even today, with researchers having found more than 50,000 works of art by early humans in Europe, these paintings compel wonder and awe at the innate artistic abilities unique to humans. (See Primary Source: The Art of Chauvet Cave.)

The images were rendered on cave walls over a period of 25,000 years, and they changed very little during that long

PRIMARY SOURCE

The Art of Chauvet Cave

A spectacular discovery at Chauvet Cave in southwestern France in 1994 overturned all previous ideas about the development of prehistoric art. Dating to about 35,000 years ago (much older than the 20,000-year-old paintings from Lascaux in southeastern France, or the 17,000-year-old paintings from Altamira in northwestern Spain), they are the oldest prehistoric cave paintings known in Europe. The hundreds of representations found at Chauvet Cave are more detailed and more brilliant than the ones at Altamira and Lascaux. There are drawings of mammoths, musk oxen, horses, lions, bears, and even rhinoceroses, as well as human palm prints (and footprints on the cave's floor) and "Venus" figures with exaggerated female genitalia—the latter apparently signifying a preoccupation with human fertility. These amazing engravings and paintings shocked scholars because they were produced only a few thousand years after the first modern humans appeared in Europe.

QUESTIONS FOR ANALYSIS

- These drawings show horses, a musk ox, and a rhinoceros. What characteristics of these animals might have inspired the early *Homo sapiens* artists, and why?
- What does their decision to portray certain animals but not others tell us?

Almost as soon as their first appearance in western Europe, modern humans seemed to have rapidly developed a sense, ability, and desire to portray other living beings in their environment. This brilliant drawing shows the detail in a depiction of horses' heads.

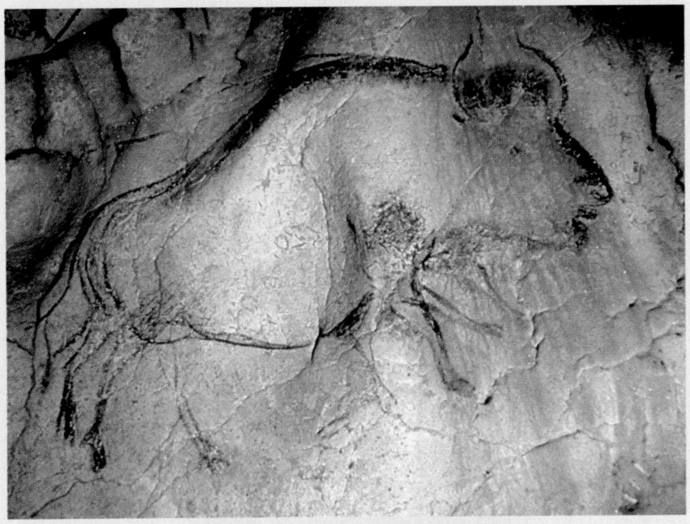

This image uses a doubling effect—drawing additional hindquarters and legs—to give the bison the appearance of motion and speed. The ability to portray dynamic movement was once thought to be a skill that humans developed much later.

time. The earliest wall decorations are at least 41,000 years old. The subjects are most often large game—animals that early humans would have considered powerful symbols. The artists rendered these animals with a striking economy of line, frequently painted in such a way that the natural contours of the cave wall defined a bulging belly or an eye socket. Many appear more than once, suggesting that they are the works from several occasions or by several artists. The remarkably few human images show naked females or dancing males. There are also many handprints made by blowing paint around a hand placed on the cave wall, or by dipping hands in paint and then pressing them to the wall. There are even abstract symbols such as circles, wavy lines, and checkerboards; often these appear at places of transition in the caves. But they are accomplished with such consummate skill that one of the twentieth century's most celebrated painters, Pablo Picasso, is alleged to have exclaimed that the Ice Age artists left him little to do.

We can only speculate what the images meant to ancient humans. Scholars have rejected an initial explanation that they were decorative, for the deep caves were not the ancients' homes and had no natural light to render the images visible. Perhaps the images had a social function, helping the early humans to define themselves as separate from other parts of nature. Among other interpretations is a theory that they were the work of powerful shamans, individuals believed to hold special powers to understand and control the mystifying forces of the cosmos.

Paintings were not the only form of artistic expression for early humans. Archaeologists also have unearthed small sculptures of animals shaped out of bone and stone that are even older than the paintings. Most famous are figurines of enormously fat and pregnant females. Statuettes like the so-called Venus of Willendorf, found in Austria, demonstrate that successful reproduction was a very important theme. Among the most exquisite sculptures are those of animals carved in postures of movement or at rest.

The caves of early men and women also resounded to the strains of music. In 2008 archaeologists working in southwestern Germany discovered a hollowed-out bone flute with five openings that they dated to approximately 35,000 years ago, roughly the same time that humans began to occupy this region. When researchers put the flute to musical tests, they also concluded that this seemingly primitive instrument was capable of making harmonic sounds comparable to those of modern-day flutes, no small achievement for these early humans whose artistic prowess must have provided much enjoyment to listeners and viewers.

Only *Homo sapiens* had the cognitive abilities to produce the abundant sculptures and drawings of this era, thus leaving a permanent mark on the symbolic landscape of human development. Such visual expressions marked the dawn of human culture and a consciousness of men's and women's place in the world. Symbolic activity of this sort enabled humans to make sense of themselves, nature, and the relationship between humanity and nature.

Willendorf Venus. *This squat limestone statuette—only about six inches in height—was discovered in 1908 near the village of Willendorf, Austria, and dates back about 25,000 years. As one of the earliest representations of a female figure found in Europe, it is a famous icon of prehistoric art. The emphasis on the woman's breasts and reproductive organs—to the exclusion, for example, of her facial features—and the presence of a red ochre dye on her genitalia suggest the maker's concern with the woman's fertility and procreative functions.*

Language

Few things set humans off from the rest of the animal world more starkly than their use of language, whose genesis and evolution spark heated controversies. Scholars do agree, however, that the cognitive abilities involved in language development marked an evolutionary milestone.

It is important to distinguish between meaningful vocal-utterance speech, possessed by many precursor hominids, and natural **language** (the use of sounds to make words that when strung together convey complex meaning to others), which is unique to modern humans. The development of language necessitated a large brain and complex cognitive organization to create word groups that would convey symbolic meaning. Verbal communication thus required an ability to think abstractly and to communicate abstractions. Language was a huge breakthrough, because individuals could teach words to offspring and neighbors and could use them to integrate communities for survival. Language also enhanced the ability to accumulate knowledge that could be transmitted across both space and time.

Biological research has demonstrated that humans can make and process many more primary and distinctive sounds, called phonemes, than other animals can. Whereas a human being can utter many more than fifty phonemes, an ape can form only twelve. Also, humans can process sounds more quickly than other primates can. With fifty phonemes it is possible to create more than 100,000 words; by arranging those words in different sequences and developing syntax in language, individuals can express endless subtle and complex meanings. Recent research suggests that use of complex languages occurred about 80,000 years ago and that the nearest approximation to humanity's proto-language (earliest language) existing today belongs to two African peoples, the !Kung of southern Africa and the Hadza

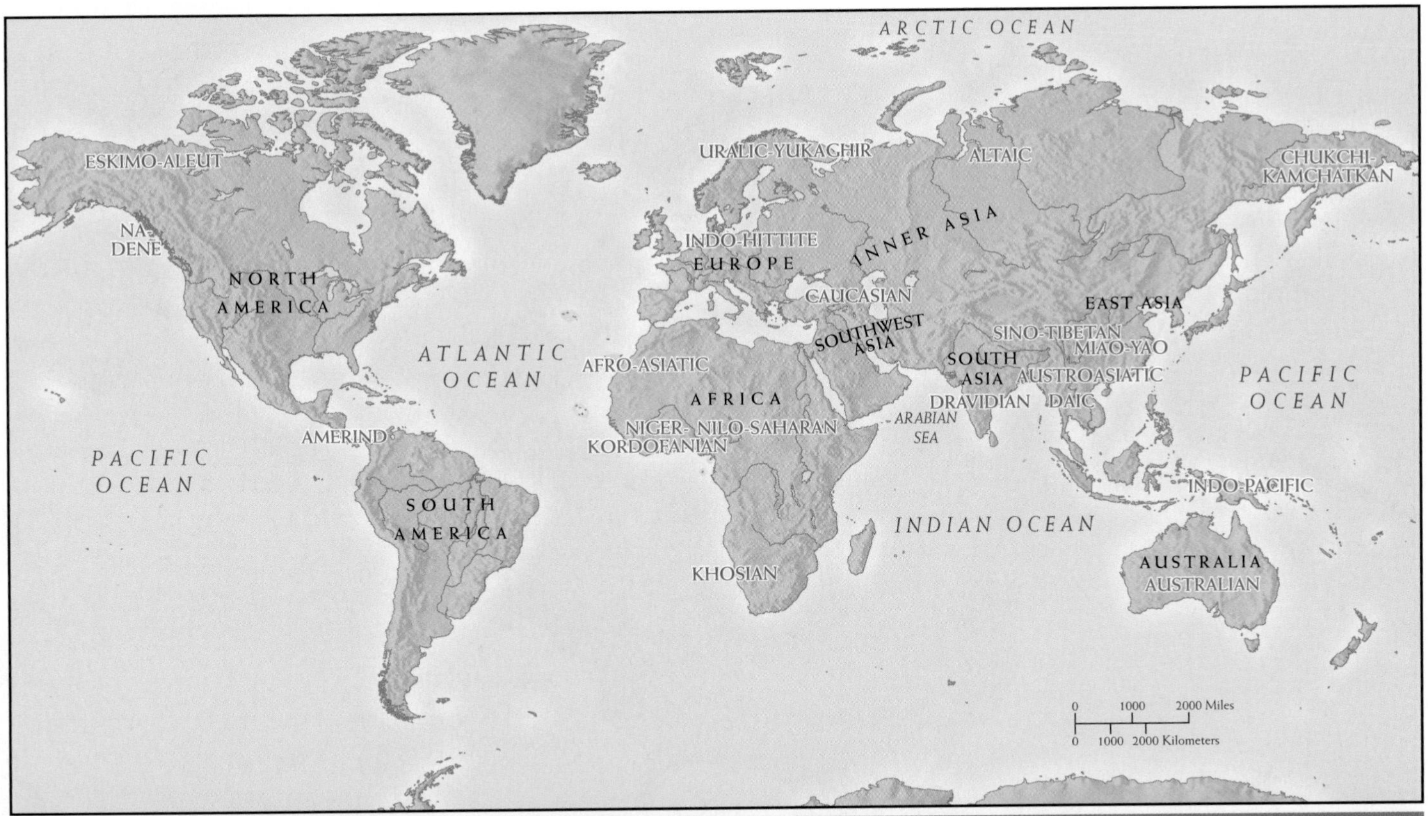

MAP 1.3 | Original Language Family Groups

The use of complex language developed 100,000 years ago among *Homo sapiens* in Africa. As humans dispersed throughout the globe, nineteen language families evolved from which all modern languages originate.

- How many different landmasses did language evolve on?
- On the basis of this map, what geographic features kept emerging language families distinct from one another?
- Why do you think separate languages emerged over time?

of Tanzania. As humans moved out of Africa and dispersed around the globe, they expanded their original language into nineteen language families, from which all of the world's languages then evolved. (See Map 1.3.) It was the development of cultural forms and language that allowed *Homo sapiens* to engage dynamically with their environments.

THE BEGINNINGS OF FOOD PRODUCTION

About 12,000 years ago, a fundamental change occurred in human behavior. It involved a shift in the way humans controlled and produced food for themselves—what some scholars have called a revolution in agriculture and ecology. In this era of major change, some communities gradually stopped going out in search of wild grains and wild animals and learned instead how to propagate edible plants and **domesticate** (bring under human control) wild animals. In doing so, they also settled down in villages, expanding their numbers, and gaining control over nature. Eight locations that scholars acknowledge to be independent centers of this agricultural revolution were Southwest Asia, East Asia, Southeast Asia, the New Guinea highlands, sub-Saharan Africa, Andean South America, central Mexico, and the eastern United States. (See Map 1.4.)

Precisely what factors triggered the move to settled agriculture remains hotly contested. Undoubtedly, the significantly warmer temperatures and wetter climates made the move to settled agriculture easier. Population pressure was also a decisive precipitant, as hunting and gathering alone could not sustain growing foraging populations. The agricultural revolution shattered the population ceiling of natural food supplies—and led to a vast population expansion because men and women could now produce more calories per unit of land than in the past. But the changeover from foraging to settled agriculture did

NORTH AMERICA
Eastern Woodlands
3000 BCE
(Squash)
ATLANTIC OCEAN
Gulf of Mexico
Tehuacan Valley
Mesoamerica
8000–4000 BCE
(Maize, Squash)
SAHA
Sahel
2000 BCE
(Millet, Sorghum)
Equator
PACIFIC OCEAN
ANDES MOUNTAINS
SOUTH AMERICA
Mesotropics
8000–5000 BCE
(Manioc, Squash, Palms, Yams)
Central Andes
8000–5000 BCE
(Llamas, Potatoes, Guinea Pigs)
Origin of food domestication
Present-day agricultural land
0 1000 2000 Miles
0 1000 2000 Kilometers

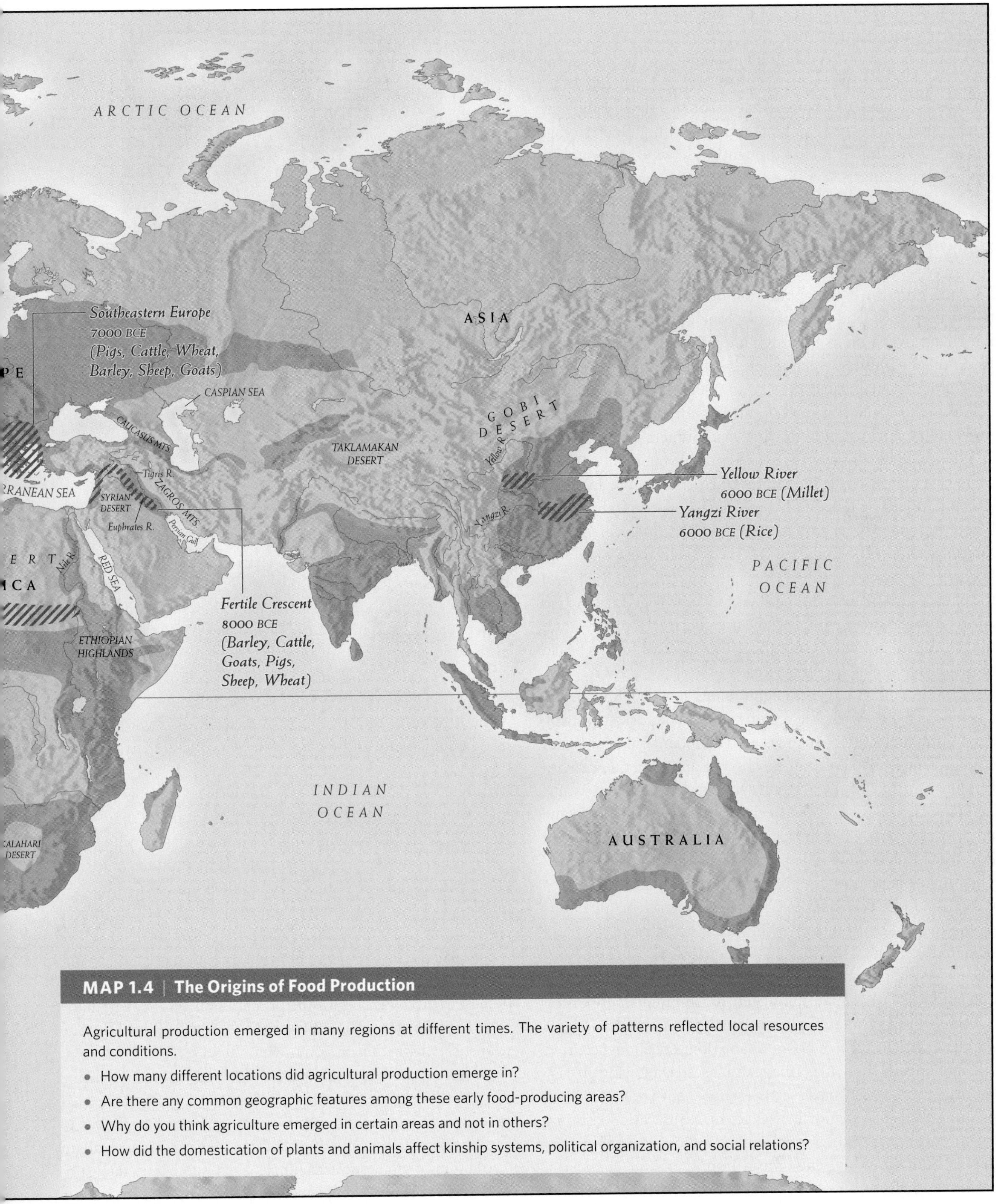

MAP 1.4 | The Origins of Food Production

Agricultural production emerged in many regions at different times. The variety of patterns reflected local resources and conditions.

- How many different locations did agricultural production emerge in?
- Are there any common geographic features among these early food-producing areas?
- Why do you think agriculture emerged in certain areas and not in others?
- How did the domestication of plants and animals affect kinship systems, political organization, and social relations?

not occur quickly. It took many thousands of years for foragers to add farming and herding to their traditions of hunting and gathering and then eventually to rely entirely on farming and herding for their subsistence. To be sure, learning to control environments and domesticate resources did not liberate humans from the risks of natural disasters. Without food storage systems, for example, a sharp drought could wipe out or uproot entire communities.

Early Domestication of Plants and Animals

Settled agriculture, the application of human labor and tools to a fixed plot of land for more than one growing cycle, entails the changeover from a hunting and gathering lifestyle to one based on agriculture, which requires staying in one place until the soil has been exhausted. Around 9000 BCE, abundant rainfall and mild winters created optimal conditions in Southwest Asia for humans to settle down. Once hunters and gatherers could meet their subsistence needs in a single but highly diverse ecological niche, they could afford to settle in a single location. They did so throughout Southwest Asia in greater numbers than before, learning to exploit mountainous areas covered with forest vegetation and home to wild sheep, wild goats, and long-horned wild oxen. In attractive locations such as the valleys of the Taurus Mountains in Upper Mesopotamia (present-day Iraq and Syria), the Anatolian plateau (in modern-day Turkey), and the hillsides of present-day northern Israel, early humans began to establish permanent settlements.

The formation of these communities enabled humans to take advantage of favorable regions and to take risks, spurring agricultural innovation. In areas with abundant wild game and edible plants, people began to observe and experiment with the most adaptable plants. For ages, people gathered grains by collecting seeds that fell freely from their stalks. At some point, observant collectors perceived that they could obtain larger harvests if they pulled grain seeds directly from plants. The process of plant domestication probably began when people noticed that certain edible plants retained their nutritious grains longer than others, so they collected these seeds and scattered them across fertile soils. When ripe, these plants produced bigger and more concentrated crops. It took time to understand this process, but ultimately a community supporting this kind of innovation realized that it could sustain a larger population than its neighbors. Plant domestication occurred when the plant retained its ripe, mature seeds, allowing an easy harvest. People used most seeds for food but saved some for planting in the next growing cycle, to ensure a food supply for the next year. The gradual domestication of plants began in the southern Levant and spread from there into the rest of Southwest Asia.

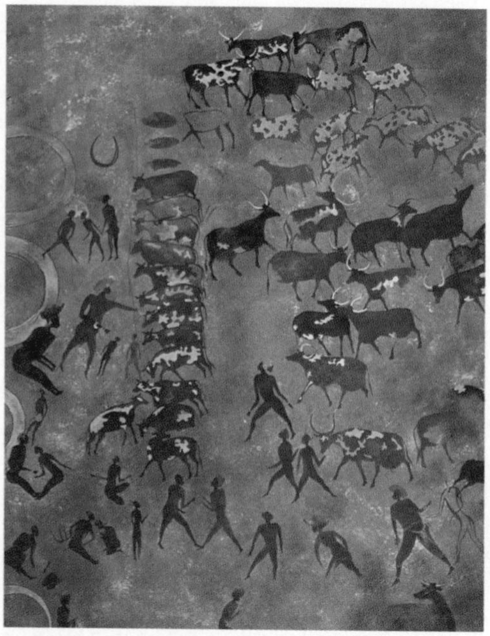

Domestication. *This detail from a wall painting in the Tassili n'Ajjer mountain range in modern Algeria depicts early domestication of cattle and other animals.*

DOMESTICATION OF ANIMALS If dogs are a man's best friend, we are now beginning to learn how long and important that friendship has been. Dogs were the first animals to be domesticated (although in fact they may have adopted humans, rather than the other way around). At least 14,000 years ago, in the area of present-day Iraq, dogs became an essential part of human society. They did more than comfort humans, however, for they provided a vital example of how to achieve the domestication of other animals. Moreover, dogs with herding instincts aided humans in controlling sheep once they had been domesticated.

Wild sheep and wild goats were the next animals to come under human control. This process took place in the central Zagros Mountains region, where wild sheep and wild goats were abundant. A favored explanation is that hunters returned home with young wild sheep, which then grew up within the human community. They reproduced, and their offspring never returned to the wild. The animals accepted their dependence because the humans fed them. As it became clear that controlling animal reproduction was more reliable than hunting, domesticated herds became the primary source of protein in the early humans' diet. This shift probably happened first with the wild sheep living in herds on the mountain slopes.

When the number of animals under human control and living close to the settlement outstripped the supply of food needed to feed them, community members could move the animals to grassy steppes for grazing. Later this lifestyle, called **pastoralism** (the herding of domesticated animals), became an important subsistence strategy that complemented settled farming. Pastoralists herded domesticated animals, moving them to new pastures on a seasonal basis. Goats, the other main domesticated animal of Southwest Asia, are smarter than sheep but more difficult to control. The pastoralists may have introduced goats into herds of sheep to better control herd movement. Pigs and cattle also came under human control at this time.

Pastoralists and Agriculturalists

The domestication of plants and animals offered new and powerful subsistence strategies that at first augmented and then replaced hunting, gathering, and foraging. Both of these new sources of food and raw materials required radically different ways to use the land which in turn led to different modes of social, political, and economic organization.

Pastoralism, which involved the herding of sheep and goats but also cattle, appeared as a way of life around 5500 BCE, essentially at the same time that full-time farmers appeared. The first pastoralists were closely affiliated with agricultural villages whose inhabitants grew grains, especially wheat and barley, which required large parcels of land. Pastoralists produced both meat and dairy products, as well as wool for textiles, and exchanged these products with the agriculturalists for grain, pottery, and other staples. In the fertile crescent surrounding the Mesopotamian alluvium, many extended families farmed and herded at the same time, growing crops in fertile flat lands and grazing their herds in the foothills and mountains nearby. These herders moved their livestock seasonally, usually pasturing their flocks in higher lands during summer and in valleys in winter. This movement over short distances is called transhumance and did not require herders to vacate their primary locations, which were generally in the mountain valleys.

A quite different form of pastoralism, often called nomadic pastoralism, also based on the herding of cattle and other livestock, came to flourish much later in other settings, notably in the steppe lands north of the agricultural zone of southern Eurasia. This way of life was characterized by horse-riding herders of livestock. These herders often had no fixed home, unlike the transhumant herders of Southwestern Asia, though they often returned to their traditional locations, but moved in response to the size and needs of their herds. The northern areas of the Eurasian landmass stretching from present-day Ukraine across Siberia and Mongolia to the Pacific Ocean became the preserve of these horse-riding pastoral peoples beginning in the second millennium BCE in a region unable to support the extensive agriculture necessary for large settled populations.

Historians know much less about these horse-riding pastoral peoples than about the agriculturalists and their transhumant cousins, as their numbers were small and they left fewer archaeological traces or historical records. Their role in world history,

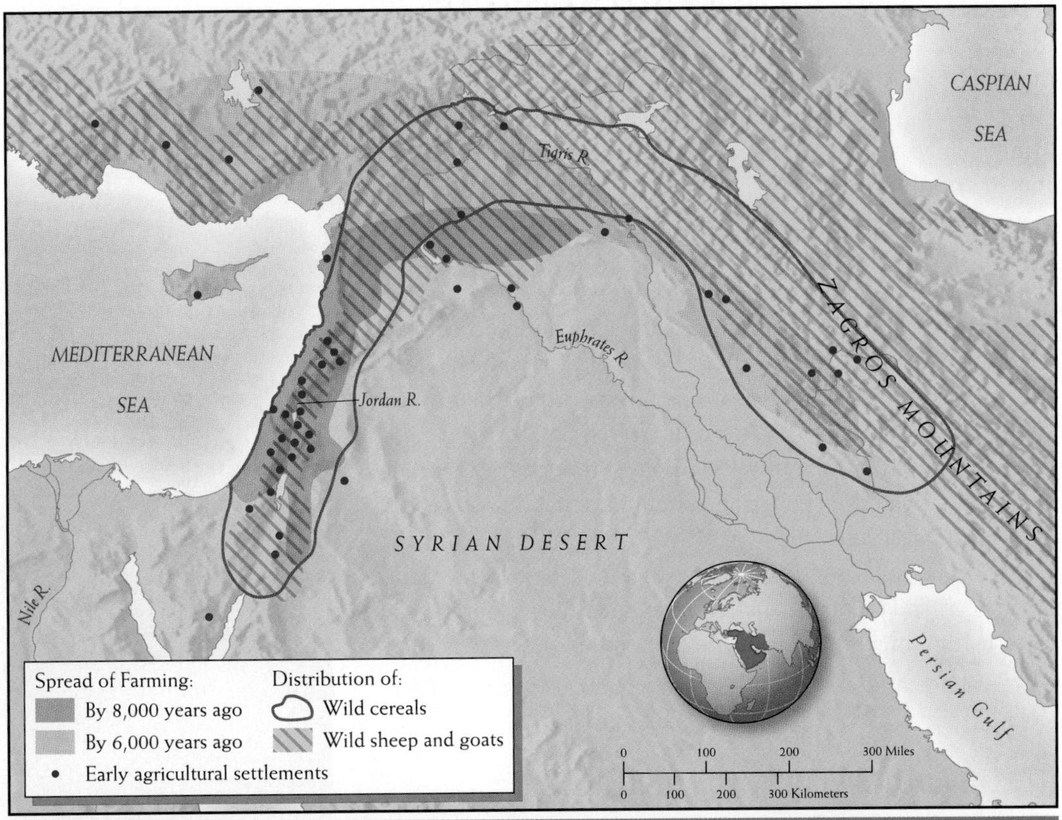

MAP 1.5 | The Birth of Farming in the Fertile Crescent

Agricultural production occurred in the Fertile Crescent starting roughly at 9000 BCE. Though the process was slow, farmers and herders domesticated a variety of plants and animals, which led to the rise of large-scale, permanent settlements.

- What does the map reveal about the environment and natural resources in the Fertile Crescent?
- Why was agriculture absent in the region of the southern Tigris and Euphrates rivers during this period?
- What relationship existed between cereal cultivators and herders of goats and sheep?

however, is as important as that of the settled societies. In Afro-Eurasia, they domesticated horses and developed weapons and techniques that at certain points in history enabled them to conquer sedentary societies. They also transmitted ideas, products, and people across long distances, maintaining the linkages that connected east and west.

The archaeological record indicates that full-fledged pastoralism crystallized on the steppe lands of northern Eurasia by 2000 BCE. By this time, the peoples living there had learned to yoke and ride animals, to milk them, and to use their hair for clothing, as well as to slaughter them for food. Of all the domesticated animals in the steppe lands, the horse became the most important. Because horses provided decisive advantages in transportation and warfare, they gained more value than other domesticated animals. Thus, horses soon became the measure of household wealth and prestige.

EMERGENCE OF AGRICULTURE

Agricultural revolutions occurred worldwide between 9000 and 2000 BCE. They had much in common: the same factors of climatic change; increased knowledge about plants and animals; and the need for more efficient ways to feed, house, and promote the survival of larger numbers. These concerns led peoples in Afro-Eurasia and the Americas to see the advantages of cultivating plants and domesticating wildlife.

The following sections examine early agriculture in five key regions: (1) Southwest Asia, where control of rivers was decisive; (2) the southern part of China in East Asia, where water and rice were critical; (3) western Europe, where the new cultivators borrowed from Southwest Asia; (4) the Americas, which had the disadvantage of offering few animals that humans could usefully domesticate; and (5) Africa, where Sahelian farmers carried their skills south to West Africa and east to the Ethiopian highlands. Our discussion highlights the broad array of patterns that humans tried out as they settled down as farmers and herders.

Southwest Asia: The Agricultural Revolution Begins

The first agricultural revolution occurred in Southwest Asia in an area bounded by the Mediterranean Sea and the Zagros Mountains. Known today as the Fertile Crescent because of its rich soils and regular rainfall, the area played a leading role in the domestication of wild grasses and the taming of animals important to humans. Six large mammals—goats, sheep, pigs, cattle, camels, and horses—have been vital for meat, milk, skins (including hair), and transportation. Humans domesticated all of these except horses in Southwest Asia.

Around 9000 BCE, in the southern corridor of the Jordan River valley, humans began to domesticate the wild ancestors of barley and wheat. (See Map 1.5.) Various wild grasses were abundant in this region, and barley and wheat were the easiest to adapt to settled agriculture and the easiest to transport. Although the changeover from gathering wild cereals to regular cultivation took several centuries and saw failures as well as successes, by the end of the ninth millennium BCE, cultivators were selecting and storing seeds and then sowing them in prepared seedbeds. Moreover, in the valleys of the Zagros Mountains on the eastern side of the Fertile Crescent, similar experimentation was occurring with animals around the same time.

East Asia: Rice and Water

A revolution in food production also occurred among the coastal dwellers in East Asia although under different circumstances. (See Map 1.6.) As the rising sea level created the Japanese islands, hunters in that area tracked a diminishing supply of large animals, such as giant deer. After all big game became

Large Two-handled Yangshao Pot. *This pot comes from the village of Yangshao in Henan Province, along the Yellow River in Northwest China, where remains were first found in 1921 of a people who lived more than 6,000 years ago. The Yangshao lived in small, rammed-earth fortresses and, without the use of pottery wheels, created fine white, red, and black painted pottery with human faces and animal and geometric designs. This jar dates back to the third or second millennium BCE.*

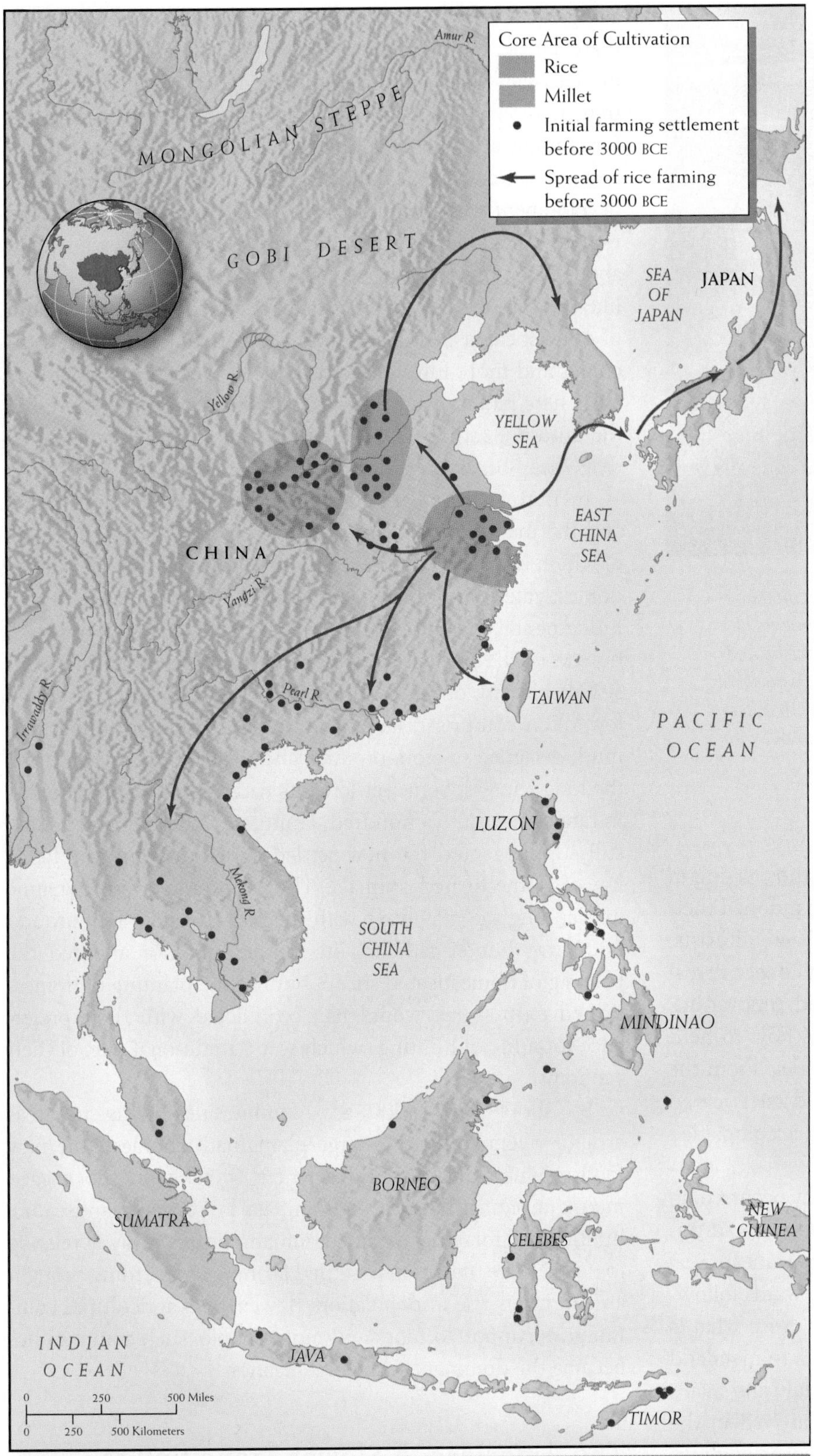

MAP 1.6 | The Spread of Farming in East Asia

Agricultural settlements appeared in East Asia later than they did in the Fertile Crescent.

- According to this map, where did early agricultural settlements appear in East Asia?
- What types of crops and animals were domesticated in East Asia?
- How did the physical features of these regions lend themselves to agricultural production?

extinct, men and women sought other ways to feed themselves, and before long they settled down and became cultivators of the soil. In this postglacial period, divergent human cultures flourished in northern and southern Japan. Hunters in the south created primitive pebble and flake tools, whereas those on the northernmost island, Hokkaido, used sharper blades about a third of an inch wide. Earthenware pottery production also may have begun in this period in the south. Converting mud into pottery—a hard, lightweight substance—was a breakthrough that enabled people to store food more easily.

Throughout the rest of East Asia, the spread of lakes, marshes, and rivers created habitats for population concentrations and agricultural cultivation. Two newly formed river basins became densely populated areas that were focal points for intensive agricultural development. These were the Yellow River, which deposited the fertile soil that created the North China plain, and the Yangzi River, which fed a land of streams and lakes in central China.

Rice in the south and millet in the north were for East Asia what barley and wheat were for western Asia—staples adapted to local environments that humans could domesticate to support a large, sedentary population. Archaeologists have found evidence of rice cultivation in the Yangzi River valley in 6500 BCE, and of millet cultivation in the Yellow River valley in 5500 BCE. Innovations in grain production spread through internal migration and wider contacts. When farmers migrated east and south, they carried domesticated millet and rice. In the south, they encountered strains of faster-ripening rice (originally from Southeast Asia), which they adopted. Rice was a staple in wetter South China, but millet and wheat (which spread to drier North China from Southwest Asia) were also fundamental to the food-producing revolution in East Asia.

Europe: Borrowing along Two Pathways

Peoples living at the western fringe of Afro-Eurasia, in Europe, borrowed the technology of settled agriculture from their neighbors. By 6000–5000 BCE, people in regions of Europe

Pottery in Banpo Village (c. 4800–4200 BCE). *This remarkable, intact village, one of the best-known ditch-enclosed settlements of Yangshao culture, provides us with clear evidence of a sophisticated agriculture based on millet and Chinese cabbage. One of China's first farming cultures, the people of Banpo interacted directly with other villages on the North China Plain and were indirectly in contact with peoples from as far away as Southeast Asia.*

close to the societies of Southwest Asia, such as those living in what are modern-day Greece and the Balkans, abandoned their hunting and gathering lifeways to become settled agriculturists. (See Map 1.7.) Places like the Franchthi Cave in Greece reveal that around 6000 BCE the inhabitants borrowed innovations from their neighbors in Southwest Asia, such as how to herd domesticated animals and to plant wheat and barley. From the Aegean and Greece, settled agriculture and domesticated animals expanded westward throughout Europe, accompanied by the development of settled communities.

The emergence of agriculture and village life occurred in Europe along two separate paths. The first and most rapid trajectory followed the northern rim of the Mediterranean Sea. Domestication of crops and animals moved westward, following the prevailing currents of the Mediterranean, from what is now Turkey through the islands of the Aegean Sea to mainland Greece, and from there to southern and central Italy and Sicily. Once the basic elements of domestication had arrived in the Mediterranean region, the speed and ease of seaborne communications aided astonishingly rapid changes. Almost overnight, hunting and gathering gave way to domesticated agriculture and herding.

The second trajectory took an overland route: from Anatolia, across northern Greece into the Balkans, then northwestward along the Danube River into the Hungarian plain, and from there farther north and west into the Rhine River valley in modern-day Germany. Change here likely resulted from the transmission of ideas rather than from population migrations, for community after community adopted domesticated plants and animals and the new mode of life. This route of agricultural development was slower than the Mediterranean route for two reasons. First, domesticated crops, or individuals who knew about them, had to travel by land, as there were few large rivers like the Danube. Second, it was necessary to find new groups of domesticated plants and animals that could flourish in the colder and more forested lands of central Europe. Agriculturalists here had to plant their crops in the spring and harvest in the autumn, rather than the other way around. Cattle rather than sheep became the dominant herd animals.

In Europe, the main cereal crops were wheat and barley, and the main herd animals were sheep, goats, and cattle—all of which had been domesticated in Southwest Asia. (Residents domesticated additional plants, such as olives, later.) These fundamental changes did not bring dramatic material progress, however. The normal settlement in Europe at this time consisted of a few dozen mud huts. These settlements, although few, often comprised large "long houses" built of timber and mud, designed to store produce and to shelter animals during the long winters. Some settlements had sixty to seventy huts—in rare cases, up to a hundred. Hunting, gathering, and fishing still supplemented the new settled agriculture and the herding of domesticated animals. The innovators were dynamic in blending the new ways with the old. Consider that around 6000 BCE, hunter-gatherers in southern France adopted the herding of domesticated sheep, but not the planting of domesticated crops—*that* would have conflicted with their preference for a life of hunting, which was a traditional part of their economy.

By about 5000–4000 BCE, communities living in areas around rivers and in the large plains had embraced the new food-producing economy. Elsewhere (notably in the rugged mountain lands that still predominate in Europe's landscape), hunting and foraging remained humans' primary way of relating to nature. The transition to settled farming and herding brought an enormous rise in population, however. As agricultural communities supported more and more people, such communities became the dominant social organization.

The Americas: A Slower Transition to Agriculture

When people crossed Beringia and trekked southward through the Americas, they set off an ecological transformation but also adapted to unfamiliar habitats. The flora and fauna of the

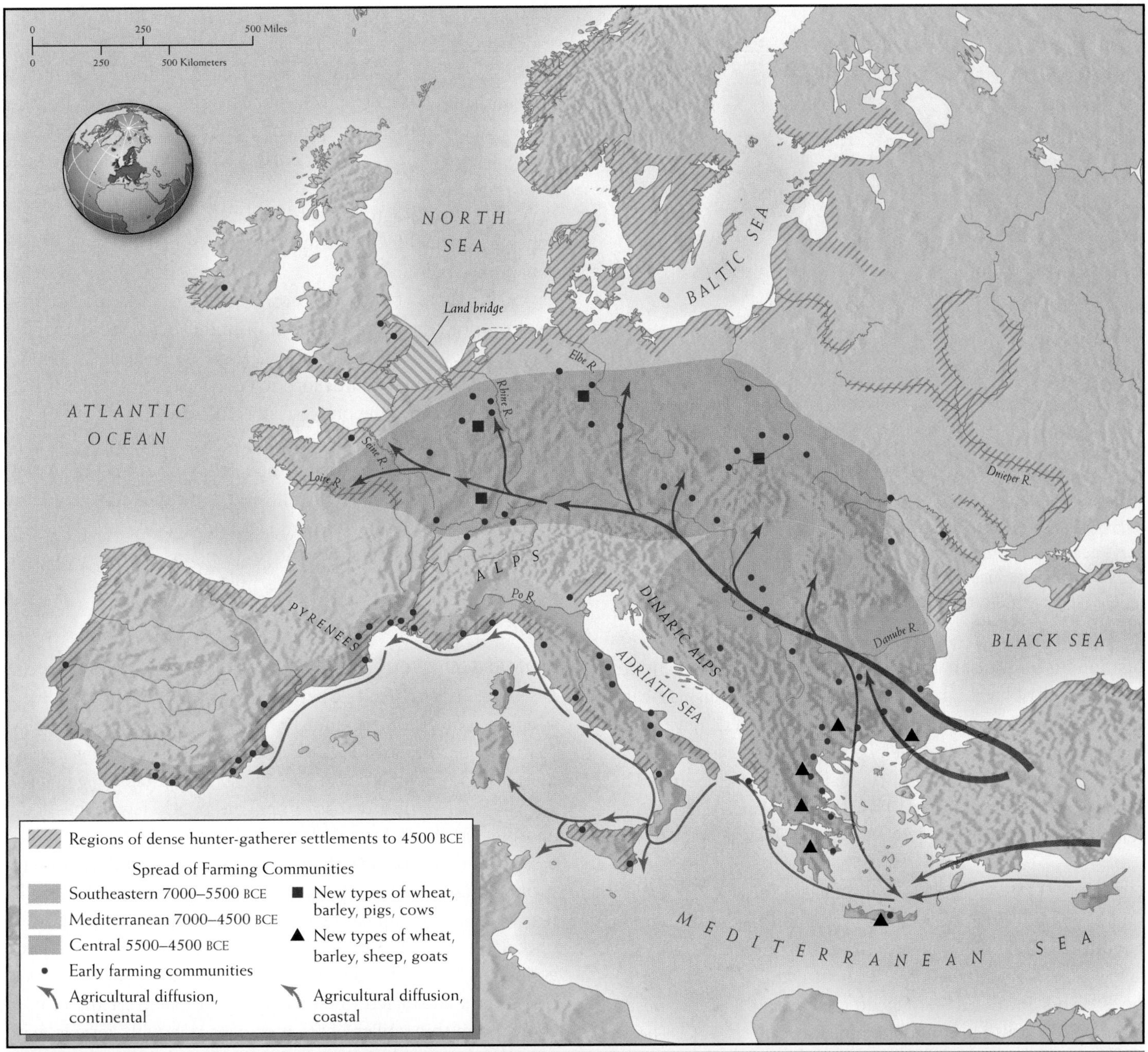

MAP 1.7 | The Spread of Agriculture in Europe

The spread of agricultural production into Europe after 7000 BCE represents geographic diffusion. Europeans borrowed agricultural techniques and technology from other groups, adapting those innovations to their own situations.

- Where did the ideas and techniques originate?
- Through what two pathways did agriculture spread across Europe?
- Did Europe's settled agricultural communities have different features from those that appeared in Southwest Asia, East Asia, and Africa?

Americas were different enough to induce the early settlers to devise ways of living that distinguished them from their ancestors in Afro-Eurasia. Then, when the glaciers began to melt around 12,500 BCE and water began to cover the land bridge between East Asia and America, the Americas and their peoples lost their connections with Afro-Eurasia.

Early humans in America used chipped blades and pointed spears to pursue their prey, which included mastodons, woolly

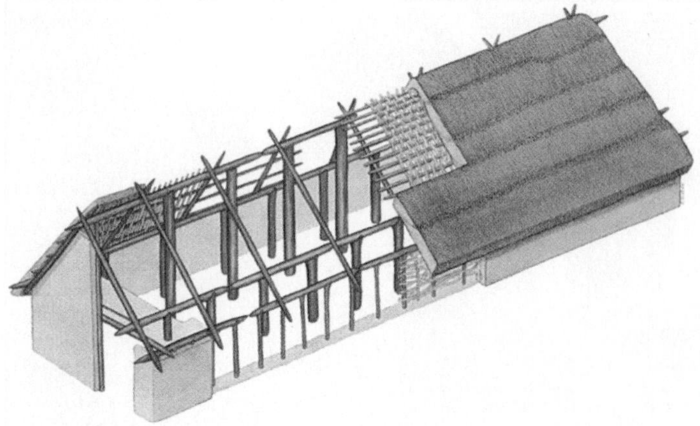

"Long House." *The people who opened up the whole of central Europe to agriculture typically lived in communities of six to twelve "long houses." Although large in size (varying between 60 and 120 feet in length), long houses were built on simple principles: a framework of wooden beams and posts with walls made of mud and woven branches beneath a thatched roof. These dwellings probably sheltered large extended family or kinship units that cooperated to provide the hard work needed to carve out pioneer farming settlements along river valleys. This cutaway reconstruction of a long house shows the placement of wall timbers and internal support posts.*

mammoths, and bison. In doing so, they extended the hunting traditions they had learned in Afro-Eurasia, establishing campsites and moving with their herds. Researchers have named these hunters "Clovis people" because a site near Clovis, New Mexico, first yielded their typical arrowhead point. Their archaeological sites located all over North America contain the remains of their weaponry.

CLIMATIC CHANGE AND ADAPTATION For many years, scientists thought that the Clovis communities had wiped out the large ice-age mammals they found in America. Recent research suggests, though, that climatic change destroyed the indigenous plants and trees—the feeding grounds of large prehistoric mammals—and that abundant forage became scarce. The vast spruce forests that had fed the great mastodons, for instance, shrank into isolated pockets, leaving undernourished mastodons vulnerable to human and animal predators until they vanished. The tall grassland prairies gave way to areas with short grass; where short grass once flourished, cacti took over. As in Afro-Eurasia, the arrival of a long warming cycle compelled those living in the Americas to adapt to different ecological niches and to create new subsistence strategies. Thus, in the woodland area of the present-day northeastern United States, hunters learned to trap smaller wild animals for food and furs. To supplement the protein from meat and fish, these people also dug for roots and gathered berries. What is important is that even as most communities adapted to the settled agricultural economy, they did not abandon basic survival strategies of hunting and gathering.

Food-producing changes in the Americas were different from those in Afro-Eurasia because this area did not undergo the sudden cluster of innovations that revolutionized agriculture in Southwest Asia and elsewhere. Tools ground from stone, rather than chipped implements, appeared in the Tehuacán Valley by 6700 BCE, and evidence of plant domestication there dates back to 5000 BCE. But villages, pottery making, and sustained population growth came later. For many early American inhabitants, the life of hunting, trapping, and fishing went on as it had for millennia.

On the coast of what is now Peru, people found food by fishing and gathering shellfish from the Pacific. Archaeological remains include the remnants of fishnets, bags, baskets, and textile implements; gourds for carrying water; and stone knives, choppers, scrapers, bone awls, and thorn needles. Oddly enough, there is no evidence of watercraft even though thousands of villages likely dotted the seashores and riverbanks of the Americas. Some made breakthroughs in the management of fire that enabled them to manufacture pottery; others devised irrigation and water sluices in floodplains. And some even began to send their fish catches inland in return for agricultural produce.

DOMESTICATION OF PLANTS AND ANIMALS The earliest evidence of plant experimentation in Mesoamerica dates from around 7000 BCE, and it went on for a long time. Maize (corn), squash, and beans (first found in what is now central Mexico) became dietary staples. The early settlers foraged small seeds of maize, peeled them from ears only a few inches long, and planted them. Maize offered real advantages because it was easy to store, relatively imperishable, nutritious, and easy to cultivate alongside other plants. Nonetheless, it took 5,000 years for farmers to complete its domestication—that is, to settle in one place, live there year-round, plant maize, and stay beyond a single growing and harvesting cycle. Over the years, farmers had to mix and breed different strains of maize for the crop to evolve from thin spikes of seeds to cobs rich with kernels, with a single plant yielding big, thick ears to feed a growing permanent population. (See Primary Source: A Mesoamerican Creation Myth.) Thus the agricultural changes afoot in Mesoamerica were slow and late in maturing. The pace was even more gradual in South America, where early settlers clung to their hunting and gathering traditions.

Across the Americas, the settled, agrarian communities found that legumes (beans), grains (maize), and tubers (potatoes) complemented one another in keeping the soil fertile and offering a balanced diet. Unlike the Afro-Eurasians, however, the settlers did not use domesticated animals as an alternative source of protein. In only a few pockets of the Andean highlands is there evidence of the domestication of tiny guinea pigs, which may have been tasty but unfulfilling meals. Nor did people in the

Head of Mayan Corn God. *Corn, or maize, was a revered crop in Mesoamerica, where people ritually prayed to their deities for good harvests. Notice the crown made not of precious metals and stones but of corn husks as an example of the cultural emphasis on maize.*

Americas tame animals that could protect villages (as dogs did in Afro-Eurasia) or carry heavy loads over long distances (as camels did in Afro-Eurasia). Although llamas could haul heavy loads, their patience and cooperation were limited. Considered at best semi-domesticates, llamas were mainly useful for clothing.

Nonetheless, the domestication of plants and animals in the Americas, as well as the presence of villages and clans, suggests significant diversification and refinement of technique. At the same time, the centers of such activity were many, scattered, and more isolated than those in Afro-Eurasia—and thus more narrowly adapted to local geographical climatic conditions, with little exchange among them. This fragmentation in migration and communication was a distinguishing force in the gradual pace of change in the Americas, and it contributed to their taking a path of development separate from Afro-Eurasia's.

Africa: The Race with the Sahara

Some societies, like those in Southwest Asia and East Asia, were innovators, while others, like those in Europe, were borrowers. What about Africa, where the story began? The evidence for settled agriculture in different regions there is uncertain. Most scholars think that the Sahel area (spanning the African landmass just south of the Sahara Desert) was most likely where hunters and gatherers became settled farmers and herders without any borrowing. In this area, an apparent move to settled agriculture, including the domestication of large herd animals, occurred two millennia before it did along the Mediterranean coast in North Africa. In fact, the Sahel agricultural revolution was so early that it cannot serve as an example of diffusion from Southwest Asia via the Nile River valley. From this innovative heartland, Africans carried their agricultural breakthroughs across the landmass.

It was in the wetter and more temperate locations of the vast Sahel, particularly in mountainous areas and their foothills, that villages and towns developed. These regions were lush with grassland vegetation and teeming with animals. Before long, the inhabitants had made sorghum, a cereal grass, their principal food crop. Residents constructed stone dwellings, underground wells, and grain storage areas. In one such population center, fourteen circular houses faced each other to form a main thoroughfare, or a street. Recent archaeological investigations have unearthed remarkable rock engravings and paintings, one often composed on top of another, filling the cave dwellings' walls. Many images portray in fascinating detail the changeover from hunting and gathering to pastoralism. Caves abound with pictures of cattle, which were a mainstay of these early men and women. The cave illustrations also depict daily activities of men and women living in conical huts, doing household chores, crushing grain on stone, and riding bareback on oxen (with women always sitting behind the men).

The Sahel was colder and moister 10,000 years ago than it is today. As the world became warmer and the Sahara Desert expanded, around 4,000 years ago this region's inhabitants had to disperse and take their agricultural and herding skills into other parts of Africa. (See Map 1.8.) Some went south to the tropical rain forests of West Africa, while others trekked eastward into the Ethiopian highlands. In their new environments, farmers searched for new crops to domesticate. The rain forests of West Africa yielded root crops, particularly the yam and cocoyam, both of which became the principal life-sustaining foodstuffs. The enset plant, similar to the banana, played the same role in the Ethiopian highlands.

REVOLUTIONS IN SOCIAL ORGANIZATION

With the domestication of plants and animals came settlement in permanent villages. These villages were near fields accessible for sowing and cultivating, and near pastures for herding

PRIMARY SOURCE

A Mesoamerican Creation Myth

There are very few extant texts from indigenous peoples of the Americas before the time of European conquest and colonization. The* Popol Vuh *is an extraordinary exception. Representing a whole body of mythological and historical narratives, it explained the elements of Mayan cosmology and established the Mayan right to rule by virtue of their descent from gods—although some scholars dispute this interpretation.

Here, then, is the beginning of when it was decided to make man, and when what must enter into the flesh of man was sought.

And the Forefathers, the Creators and Makers, who were called Tepeu and Gucumatz said: "The time of dawn has come, let the work be finished, and let those who are to nourish and sustain us appear, the noble sons, the civilized vassals: let man appear, humanity, on the face of the earth." Thus they spoke.

They assembled, came together and held council in the darkness and in the night; then they sought and discussed, and here they reflected and thought. In this way their decisions came clearly to light and they found and discovered what must enter into the flesh of man.

It was just before the sun, the moon, and the stars appeared over the Creators and Makers.

From Paxil, from Cayalá, as they were called, came the yellow ears of corn and the white ears of corn.

These are the names of the animals which brought the food: *yac* [the mountain cat], *utiú* [the coyote], *quel* [a small parrot], and *hob* [the crow]. These four animals gave tidings of the yellow ears of corn and the white ears of corn, they told them that they should go to Paxil and they showed them the road to Paxil.

And thus they found the food, and this was what went into the flesh of created man, the made man; this was his blood; of this the blood of man was made. So the corn entered [into the formation of man] by the work of the Forefathers.

■ ■ ■

The animals showed them the road. And then grinding the yellow corn and the white corn, Xmucané made nine drinks, and from this food came the strength and the flesh, and with it they created the muscles and the strength of man. This the Forefathers did, Tepeu and Gucumatz, as they were called.

After that they began to talk about the creation and the making of our first mother and father; of yellow corn and of white corn they made their flesh; of corn meal dough they made the arms and the legs of man. Only dough of corn meal went into the flesh of our first fathers, the four men, who were created.

■ ■ ■

It is said that they only were made and formed, they had no mother, they had no father. They were only called men. They were not born of woman, nor were they begotten by the Creator nor by the Maker, nor by the Forefathers. Only by a miracle, by means of incantation were they created and made by the Creator, the Maker, the Forefathers, Tepeu and Gucumatz. And as they had the appearance of men, they were men; they talked, conversed, saw and heard, walked, grasped things; they were good and handsome men, and their figure was the figure of a man.

They were endowed with intelligence; they saw and instantly they could see far, they succeeded in seeing, they succeeded in knowing all that there is in the world. When they looked, instantly they saw all around them, and they contemplated in turn the arch of heaven and the round face of the earth.

The things hidden [in the distance] they saw all, without first having to move; at once they saw the world, and so, too, from where they were, they saw it.

Great was their wisdom; their sight reached to the forests, the rocks, the lakes, the seas, the mountains, and the valleys. In truth, they were admirable men, Balam-Quitzé, Balam-Acab, Mahucutah, and Iqui-Balam.

Then the Creator and the Maker asked them: "What do you think of your condition? Do you not see? Do you not hear? Are not your speech and manner of walking good? Look, then! Contemplate the world, look [and see] if the mountains and the valleys appear! Try, then, to see!" they said to [the four first men].

And immediately they [the four first men] began to see all that was in the world. Then they gave thanks to the Creator and the Maker: "We really give you thanks, two and three times!"

QUESTIONS FOR ANALYSIS

- From what material did the creators make living creatures?
- Why do you think they chose this material?
- What commands did the Creator and the Maker convey to the first men? Why do you think this is significant?

Source: Adrian Recinos, from Popol Vuh: The Sacred Book of the Ancient Quiché Maya, *trans. Delia Goetz and Sylvanus G. Morley, pp. 165–68.*

livestock. Villagers collaborated to clear fields, plant crops, and celebrate rituals in which they sang, danced, and sacrificed to nature and the spirit world for fertility, rain, and successful harvests. They also produced stone tools to work the fields, and clay and stone pots or woven baskets and later on potter-vessels to collect and store the crops. As populations grew and lands yielded surplus food, some villagers became craftworkers, devoting some of their time to producing pottery, baskets, textiles, or tools, which they could trade to farmers and pastoralists for food. Craft specialization and the buildup of surpluses contributed to early social stratification, as some people accumulated more land and wealth while others led the rituals and sacrifices.

Settling in villages also made possible the rise of the extended family as a new and ultimately humankind's principal social unit, eroding the influence of clans and free-floating communities that had been the predominant social units among hunters and gatherers. Because successful families strove to accumulate wealth and power and to pass their successes on to offspring, the family also promoted social inequality and stratification.

Settlement in Villages

The earliest dwelling places of the first settled communities were simple structures: circular pits with stones piled on top to form walls, with a cover stretched above that rested on poles. Social structures were equally simple, being clanlike and based on kinship networks. With time, however, population growth enabled clans to expand. As the use of natural resources intensified, specialized tasks evolved and divisions of labor arose. Some community members procured and prepared food; others built terraces and defended the settlement. Later, residents built walls with stones or mud bricks and clamped them together with wooden fittings. Yet all were involved in securing food.

As construction techniques changed, houses changed from the traditional circular plan to a rectangular one. Because the rectangular shape does not exist in nature, it is a truly human mark on the landscape. This new shape reflected new attitudes and social behaviors: in rectangular houses, walls did more than support and protect—they also divided and separated. The introduction of interior walls meant that family members gained separate spaces and that privacy improved. Human relations would never be the same as they had been in the relatively egalitarian arrangements of the mobile hunters and gatherers.

Although the food-producing changes were gradual and dispersed, a few communities stand out as pioneers in the long transition from hunting and gathering to agrarian and pastoral life. Around Wadi en-Natuf, located about ten miles from present-day Jerusalem, a group of people known historically as Natufians began to dig sunken pit shelters and to chip stone tools around 12,500 BCE. Over the next two millennia these bands stayed in one place, improving their toolmaking techniques, building circular shelters, and developing various ways to preserve and prepare food. They dwelled in solid structures, buried their dead, and harvested grains. Although they did not plant seeds and did not give up hunting, their increasing knowledge of wild plants paved the way for later breakthroughs.

It was only a matter of time before the full transition to settled agriculture and full-scale pastoralism took place. One of the best examples of this development occurred in central Anatolia (the area encompassing modern-day Turkey), The village of Çatal Höyük, a dense thirty-two-acre honeycomb settlement that may have contained several thousand residents, featured rooms covered with wall paintings and sculptures of wild bulls, hunters, and pregnant women. Here, men and women made their own structures where they worshipped the forces of nature and the spirit world, interacting with one another according to rituals that defined their place in society. This settlement, called by one scholar a precocious city, flourished from 7300 BCE to 6200 BCE. Its houses were constructed as rectangular boxes, the walls of one house attached to four others. The village lacked lanes, and thus residents had to climb up on the roofs to enter their homes through trap doors.

Another example of village settlement occurred after 5500 BCE, when people moved into the river valley in Mesopotamia (in present-day Iraq) along the Tigris and Euphrates rivers, and small villages began to appear. The inhabitants collaborated to build simple irrigation systems to water their fields. Perhaps because of the increased demands for community work to maintain the irrigation systems, the communities in southern Mesopotamia became stratified, with some people having more power than others. We can see from the burial sites and myriad public buildings uncovered by archaeologists that for the first time, some people had higher status derived from birth rather than through the merits of their work. A class of people who had access to more luxury goods, and who lived in bigger and better houses, now became part of the social organization.

It is important to emphasize that changes arising from agriculture enabled larger numbers of people to live in denser concentrations, and the household with its dominant male replaced the small, relatively egalitarian band as the primary social unit.

Men, Women, and Evolving Gender Relations

One of the fundamental divisions evident in the fossil remains of early hominids and humans is the division between males and females. This observation raises questions about the relationships between the sexes in prehistoric times.

For millions of years, biological differences—the fact that females give birth to offspring and that males do not—determined

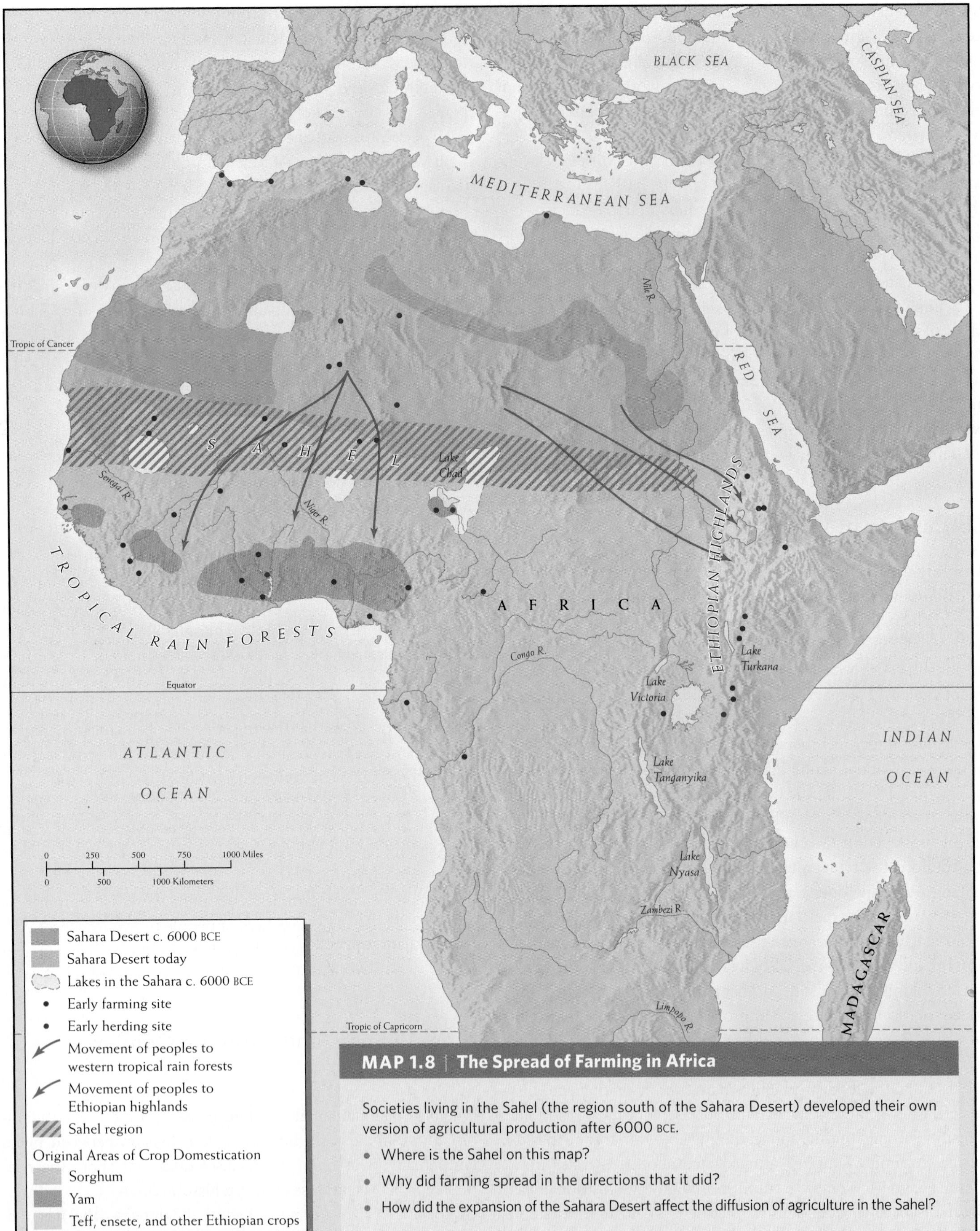

MAP 1.8 | The Spread of Farming in Africa

Societies living in the Sahel (the region south of the Sahara Desert) developed their own version of agricultural production after 6000 BCE.

- Where is the Sahel on this map?
- Why did farming spread in the directions that it did?
- How did the expansion of the Sahara Desert affect the diffusion of agriculture in the Sahel?

Hunting. *This wall painting from Catal Huyuk (in present-day Turkey) depicts humans hunting a bull.*

female and male behaviors and attitudes toward each other. Thus it is incorrect to think of these biologically based sexual relations as "gender" (social and cultural) relations. One can speak of the emergence of "gender" relations and roles only with the appearance of modern humans (*Homo sapiens*) and, perhaps, Neanderthals. Only when humans began to think in complex symbolic ways and give voice to these perceptions in a spoken language did true gender categories as *man* and *woman* crystallize. As these cultural aspects of human life took shape, the distinction between "men" and "women," rather than between "males" and "females," arose. At that point, around 150,000 years ago, culture joined biology in governing human interactions. (See Primary Source: Mothering and Lactation.)

Gender roles became more pronounced during the gradual transition to an agriculturally based way of life. As human communities became larger, more hierarchical, and more powerful, the rough gender egalitarianism of hunting and gathering societies eroded. However, an enhanced human power over the environment did not bring equal power to everyone, and it is possible to say that women were the net losers of the agricultural revolution. Although their knowledge of wild plants had contributed to early settled agriculture, they did not necessarily benefit from that transition.

Advances in agrarian tools introduced a harsh working life that undermined women's traditional status as farmers. Men, no longer so involved in hunting and gathering, now took on the heavy work of yoking animals to plows. This left to women the backbreaking and repetitive tasks of planting, weeding, harvesting, and grinding the grain into flour. Thus, although agricultural innovations increased productivity, they also increased the drudgery of work, especially for women. Consider the evidence from fossils found in Abu Hureyra, Syria: damage to the vertebrae, osteoarthritis in the toes, and curved and arched femurs suggest that the work of bending over and kneeling in the fields took its toll on female agriculturalists. These maladies do not usually appear among the bone remains of (male) hunters and gatherers.

The increasing differentiation of the roles of men and women also affected power relations within households and communities. The senior male figure became dominant in these households, and males became dominant over females in leadership positions. The agricultural revolution marked a greater division among men, and particularly between men and women. Where the agricultural transformation was most widespread, and where population densities began to grow, the social and political differences created inequalities. As these inequalities affected gender relations, patriarchy (the rule of senior males within households) began to spread around the globe.

CONCLUSION

Over thousands of generations, African hominids evolved from other primates into *Homo erectus* hominids, who migrated far from their native habitats to fill other landmasses. They did so in waves, responding to worldwide cycles of glaciation and

PRIMARY SOURCE

Mothering and Lactation

One of the dividing lines among all animals, humans included, involves child rearing and the division of labor between mothers and fathers. This text argues that lactation (milk production) became a major factor shaping the social roles of primate mothers.

"Is sex destiny?" When this question is posed, it's a safe bet that the underlying agenda has to do with what women *should* be doing. Should they be home caring for their children or off pursuing other interests? A comparative look at other creatures that (like humans) breed cooperatively and share responsibilities for rearing young with other group members reveals that sex *per se* is not the issue. Lactation is.

Caretakers of both sexes, wet-nurses, even "daycare"—none of these are uniquely human, nor particularly new. They are standard features of many cooperatively breeding species. As we saw, cooperative breeding is exquisitely well developed in insects such as honeybees and wasps. Shared provisioning is also common among birds such as acorn woodpeckers, bee-eaters, dunnocks, and scrub jays. Although cooperative breeding is uncommon among mammals generally, it is richly developed in species such as wolves, wild dogs, dwarf mongooses, elephants, tamarins, marmosets, and humans. In all these animals, individuals other than the mother ("allomothers") help her provision or otherwise care for her young. Typically, allomothers will include the mother's mate (often but not necessarily the genetic progenitor). Individuals other than either parent ("alloparents") also help. These helpers are most often recruited from kin who are not yet ready to reproduce themselves, or from subordinates who do not currently—or may never have—better options. In the human case, the most important alloparents are often older, post-reproductive relatives who have already reproduced.

Among mammals, the trend toward having young who require costly long-term care began modestly enough. It probably began with an egg-laying brooding reptile that started to secrete something milklike. Such egg-layers gradually developed glands especially equipped for milk production. Only among mammals did one sex come to specialize in manufacturing custom-made baby formula, to provide something critical for infant survival that the other sex could not. This peculiarity has had many ramifications, especially as infants became dependent for longer periods in the primate line.

The ante was upped substantially when primate mothers, instead of bearing litters, began focusing care on one baby at a time. These singletons were born mature enough to cling to their mother's fur, to be carried by her right from birth and for months thereafter. Whether or not this intimate and prolonged association is the mother's destiny, *sex* is not the issue. Lactation is.

QUESTIONS FOR ANALYSIS

- How does lactation affect mothers' child-rearing roles differently from fathers'?
- Why is the difference more marked among humans than among other species?

melting. These human predecessors had some features in common with modern humans (*Homo sapiens*): they stood erect on two feet, made stone tools, lived in extended families, and, to a certain extent, communicated with one another (by means other than language).

What separated humans from other animal species was their ability to adapt to environmental change, to innovate, and to accumulate their breakthroughs in knowledge. *Homo sapiens*, who had greater cognitive skills than other hominids had, also emerged in Africa and migrated out of Africa about 60,000 years ago. Since *Homo sapiens* had greater adaptive and cognitive skills, they were better prepared to face the elements when a cooling cycle returned and better able to understand the world around them and even to represent it symbolically through art and language. Eventually they eclipsed their genetic cousins. Critical to their success was their use of language, which allowed them to engage in abstract, representational thought, and to convey the lessons of experience to neighbors and descendants. As modern humans stored and shared knowledge, their adaptive abilities increased. Another remarkable development was the use of art to portray the world around them and to locate themselves within it.

Although modern men and women shared an African heritage, these individuals adapted over many millennia to the environments they encountered as they began to fill the earth's corners. Some settled near lakes and took to fishing, while others roamed the northern steppes hunting large mammals. No matter where they went, their dependence on nature yielded broadly similar social and cultural structures. It took a powerful warming cycle for people ranging from Africa to the Americas to begin putting down their hunting weapons and start domesticating animals and plants.

The changeover to settled agriculture was not uniform worldwide, although there were some common features. These included reliance on wood, stone, and natural fibers to make tools, shelter, and cultural items; and increasing social hierarchies—especially an unequal status between men and women. As communities became more settled, though, the world's regions began to vary as humans learned to modify nature to fit their needs. The varieties of animals that they could domesticate, the wild plants that they learned to cultivate, and the differing climatic conditions and topography that they encountered shaped the ways in which people drifted apart in spite of their common origins.

One important commonality remained: there was a limit to the scale and complexity of settlements and communities. As a result, most people continued a life of moving in search of more reliable and plentiful amounts of food. Villages grew—but they did not become cities. Peoples moved across mountains or deserts to find fresh pastures for their animals, richer lands for their crops, or new waters where fish were spawning. The remains of rudimentary pottery, tools, and dwellings reflect worlds that were rural, socially egalitarian, and dependent on the natural flow of fresh water and the natural fertility of soils. As we will see in Chapter 2, another round of technical advances was necessary before humans could further change their relationship to nature and create the foundations for complex societies.

AFTER YOU READ THIS CHAPTER

Review and research materials are available on **StudySpace:** wwnorton.com/studyspace

TRACING THE GLOBAL STORYLINES

FOCUS ON: *What Makes Us Human*

- *Bipedalism:* Hominids come down from the trees in Africa, become upright, and walk on two legs.
- *Big brains:* Ancestors to modern humans make tools and fire and acquire larger brains.
- *Language: Homo sapiens* learn to communicate with one another, develop a sense of self, and produce art.
- *Writing:* In a few places on the globe, humans invent systems of writing.
- *Village life:* People domesticate plants and animals and settle in villages.

CHRONOLOGY

Southwest Asia and Egypt
- Earliest Sumerian cities appear in Mesopotamia **3500 BCE**

South Asia

East Asia
- Yangshao culture thrives along Yellow River **5000 BCE**

Europe and the Mediterranean

The Americas
- Chicama Valley culture thrives on Pacific Coast of South America **3500 BCE**
- Tehuacán Valley in Mexico thrives **3500 BCE**

Sub-Saharan Africa
- Dense village life along many lakes and rivers **3500 BCE**

Inner and Central Asia
- Spread of nomadic pastoralism begins **3500 BCE**

5000 BCE — **4000 BCE**

KEY TERMS

adaptation p. 8

australopithecines p. 6

bipedalism p. 8

cognitive skills p. 9

domesticate p. 23

evolution p. 4

hominids p. 6

Homo erectus p. 12

Homo habilis p. 11

Homo sapiens p. 15

hunting and gathering p. 19

innovation p. 10

language p. 22

migration p. 13

pastoralism p. 26

settled agriculture p. 26

species p. 6

STUDY QUESTIONS

1. **Explain** how evolutionary biologists and archaeologists working in recent decades have transformed our understanding of human origins. What tools and discoveries led them to their conclusions?
2. **Describe** the evolutionary process through which *Homo sapiens* emerged. Was it a linear progression?
3. **Identify** the advantages that language and symbolic art gave *Homo sapiens* over other species. What can modern observers learn about early humans by studying their artistic expressions?
4. **List** the eight regions where agricultural production first emerged. What common factors in all these places facilitated the domestication of plants and animals?
5. **Analyze** the advantages and disadvantages of agricultural production versus nomadic foraging. How were agricultural or pastoral communities different from those of hunters and gatherers?

First Dynasty emerges in Egypt **3100 BCE**

Sargon's Akkadian territorial state in Mesopotamia **2334–2103 BCE**

Old Kingdom Egypt **2649–2152 BCE**

Cities appear in Indus Valley **2500 BCE**

Longshao Culture emerges in Yellow River Valley **5000–2000 BCE**

Fortified villages in the Aegean **2500 BCE**

Stonehenge constructed **2000 BCE**

3000 BCE **2000 BCE**

BEFORE YOU READ THIS CHAPTER

wwnorton.com/
StudySpace

GLOBAL STORYLINES

- Complex societies form around several river basins.
- The world's first cities arise from the river-basin societies, transforming human life.
- Most people around the globe still live in interdependent villages or as hunters and gatherers.
- Pastoral nomadic peoples appear, herding animals and trading animal products for grains, pottery, and tools.

CHAPTER OUTLINE

2

Rivers, Cities, and First States, 3500–2000 BCE

FOCUS QUESTIONS

- Why did complex urban societies first appear in a few river basins during this time period?
- What key features separated complex urban societies from smaller agricultural settlements and communities of hunters and gatherers?
- How similar and different were the complex societies in Mesopotamia, Egypt, and the Indus Valley?
- How did social and cultural developments in East Asia differ from those in Egypt, Mesopotamia, and the Indus Valley?
- How did the growth of complex urban societies in river basins affect people living in the Aegean region, Anatolia, and Europe?

One of the first urban centers in the world was the ancient city of Uruk. Located in southern Mesopotamia on a branch of the Euphrates River, it was home to more than 10,000 people by the late fourth millennium BCE and boasted many large public structures and temples. One temple had stood there since before 3000 BCE; with a lime-plastered surface of niched mud-brick walls that formed stepped indentations, it perched high above the plain. In another sacred precinct, administrative buildings and temples adorned with elaborate facades stood in courtyards defined by tall columns. Colored stone cones arranged in elaborate geometric patterns covered parts of these buildings, making Uruk the "shining city" of King Gilgamesh.

Over the years Uruk became an immense commercial and administrative center. A huge wall with seven massive gates surrounded the metropolis, and down the middle ran a canal carrying water from the Euphrates. On one side of the city were gardens, kilns, and textile workshops. On the other was the temple quarter where priests lived, scribes kept records, and lu-gal ("the big man") conferred with the elders. As Uruk grew, many small industries became centralized in response to the

Uruk. *A contemporary depiction of the sacred precinct of Uruk, the "shining city" of King Gilgamesh.*

increasing sophistication of construction and manufacturing. Potters, metalsmiths, stone bowl makers, and brickmakers all worked under the city administration.

Uruk was the first city of its kind in world history, marking a new phase in human development. Earlier humans had settled in small communities scattered over the landscape; gradually, however, some communities became focal points for trade. Then a few hubs grew into cities—concentrations with large populations and institutions of economic, religious, and political power. Most inhabitants no longer produced their own food, working instead in specialized professions.

Between 3500 and 2000 BCE, a handful of remarkable societies clustered in a few river basins on the Afro-Eurasian landmass. These regions, located along the banks or in the deltas of five rivers with regular annual floods (in Mesopotamia, northwest India, Egypt, northern China, and central China), became the heartlands for densely populated settlements with complex cultures. Here the world saw the birth of the first large cities and territorial states. One of these settings (Mesopotamia) brought forth humankind's first writing system, and all laid the foundations for kingdoms radiating out of opulent cities. This chapter describes how each society evolved, and it explores their similarities and differences. It is important to note how exceptional these places were—and thus we cannot ignore the many smaller societies that prevailed elsewhere, far from urbanizing locales. The Aegean, Anatolia, and Western Europe serve as reminders that most of the world's people continued to dwell in small communities, far removed culturally from the monumental architecture and well-developed bureaucracies of the big new states.

SETTLEMENT, PASTORALISM, AND TRADE

Over many millennia, people had developed strategies to make the best of their environments. As populations expanded and sought out locations capable of supporting larger numbers, often it was reliable water sources that determined where and how people settled. Village dwellers gravitated toward predictable water supplies that allowed them to sow crops adequate to feed large populations. Abundant rainfall was involved in the emergence of the world's first villages, but the breakthroughs into big cities occurred in drier zones where large rivers formed beds of rich alluvial soils (created by deposits from rivers when in flood). With irrigation innovations, soils became arable. Equally important, a worldwide warming cycle caused growing seasons to expand. These environmental and technical shifts profoundly affected who lived where and how.

As rivers sliced through mountains, steppe lands (vast treeless grasslands), and deserts before reaching the sea, their waters carried topsoils and deposited them around the deltas. The combination of fertile soils, water for irrigation, and availability of domesticated plants and animals made **river basins** (areas drained by a river, including all its tributaries) attractive for human habitation. Here, cultivators began to produce agricultural surpluses to feed the city dwellers.

With cities came greater divisions of labor, as dense settlement enabled people to specialize in making goods for the consumption of others: weavers made textiles, potters made ceramics, and jewelers made precious ornaments. Soon these goods found additional uses in trade with outlying areas. And as trade expanded over longer distances, raw materials such as wool, metal, timber, and precious stones arrived in the cities. These materials served in the construction and decoration of city walls, temples, and palaces, as well as in the fashioning of tools and weapons. One of the most coveted metals was copper: easily smelted and shaped (not to mention shiny and alluring), it became the metal of choice for charms, sculptures, and valued commodities. When combined with arsenic or tin, copper hardens and becomes **bronze**, which is useful for tools and weapons. For this reason the new age is often called a Bronze Age, though the term simplifies the breadth of the breakthroughs.

Early Cities along River Basins

The material and social advances of the early cities occurred in a remarkably short period—from 3500 to 2000 BCE—in three locations: the basin of the Tigris and Euphrates rivers in central Southwest Asia; the Indus River basin in northwestern South Asia; and the northern parts of the Nile River flowing toward the Mediterranean Sea. (See Map 2.1.) In these regions humans farmed and fed themselves by relying on intensive irrigation agriculture. Gathering in cities inhabited by rulers, administrators, priests, and craftworkers, they changed their methods of organizing communities by obeying divinely inspired monarchs and elaborate bureaucracies. They also transformed what and how they worshipped, by praying to zoomorphic and anthropomorphic gods (taking the form and personality of animals and humans) who communicated through kings and priests living in palace complexes and temples. About a millennium later a similar process began along the Yellow River in North China, laying the foundations for a culture that has flourished unbroken until this day.

As people congregated in cities, new technologies appeared. The wheel, for example, served both as a tool for mass-producing pottery and as a key component of vehicles used for transportation. At first vehicles were heavy, using four solid wooden wheels drawn by oxen or onagers (Asian wild asses). Two other technologies, metallurgy and stoneworking, both developed in the surrounding highlands near the raw materials and provided luxury objects and utilitarian tools.

The emergence of cities as population centers created one of history's most durable worldwide distinctions: the **urban-rural divide**. Where cities appeared, people adopted lifestyles based on specialized labor and the mass production of goods. In contrast, residents of the countryside remained on their lands, cultivating the land or tending livestock; but they exchanged their grains and animal products for goods from the urban centers. Therefore the new distinction never implied isolation, because the two lifeways were interdependent. Despite the urban-rural divide, both worlds remained linked through family ties, trade, politics, and religion.

As the dynamic urban enclaves evolved, they made intellectual advances. One significant advance was the invention of writing systems, which enabled people to record and transmit sounds and words through visual signs. An unprecedented cultural breakthrough, the technology of writing used the symbolic storage of words and meanings to extend human communication and memory: scribes figured out ways to record oral compositions as written texts and, eventually, epics recounting life in these river settlements.

Smaller Settlements around 3500 BCE

It is essential to remember that in 3500 BCE, the vast majority of people worldwide lived either as hunters and gatherers or in small villages close to the animals and plants they used for food. As we have seen, they hunted, gathered, fished, and cultivated plants, forming small, egalitarian communities organized on the basis of clan and family allegiances. They used tools made of wood and stone, and carried gourds to transport food and water. In some locations, artisans formed and fired clay to make vessels for storing and preparing food. In other locations, craftworkers pounded native copper into small items of personal adornment. As the population in certain areas increased, divisions between artisans and manual laborers emerged, community life became more hierarchical, and villages grew into towns. The Americas and sub-Saharan Africa provide good examples of this way of life.

THE AMERICAS In certain places, environmental factors limited the size of human settlements. Here the techniques of food production and storage, transportation, and communication restricted the surpluses for feeding those who did not work the land. Thus these communities did not grow in size and complexity. For example, in the Chicama Valley of Peru, which opens onto the Pacific Ocean, people still nestled in small coastal villages to fish, gather shellfish, hunt, and grow beans, chili peppers, and cotton (to make twined textiles, which they dyed with wild indigo). Around 3500 BCE, these fishermen abandoned their cane and adobe homes for sturdier houses, half underground, on streets lined with cobblestones.

Thousands of such villages dotted the seashores and riverbanks of the Americas. Some made the technological breakthroughs required to produce pottery; others devised irrigation systems and water sluices in floodplains (areas where rivers overflowed and deposited fertile soil). Some even began to send their fish catches inland in return for agricultural produce. In the remains of these villages, archaeologists have recovered sacred spaces, fire-pit chambers, and tombs that reveal an elaborate religious life. These ceremonial structures highlighted communal devotion and homage to deities, and rituals to celebrate birth, death, and the memory of ancestors.

NORTH AMERICA
ATLANTIC OCEAN
TEHUACAN VALLEY
SAHA
SAHE
ANDES MOUNTAINS
PACIFIC OCEAN
CHICAMA VALLEY
SOUTH AMERICA
Desert
Pastoral belt – steppe lands
Tropical rain forest
Agricultural society 3000 BCE
Riverine societies (early cities)
Widespread village culture
0 1000 2000 Miles
0 1000 2000 Kilometers

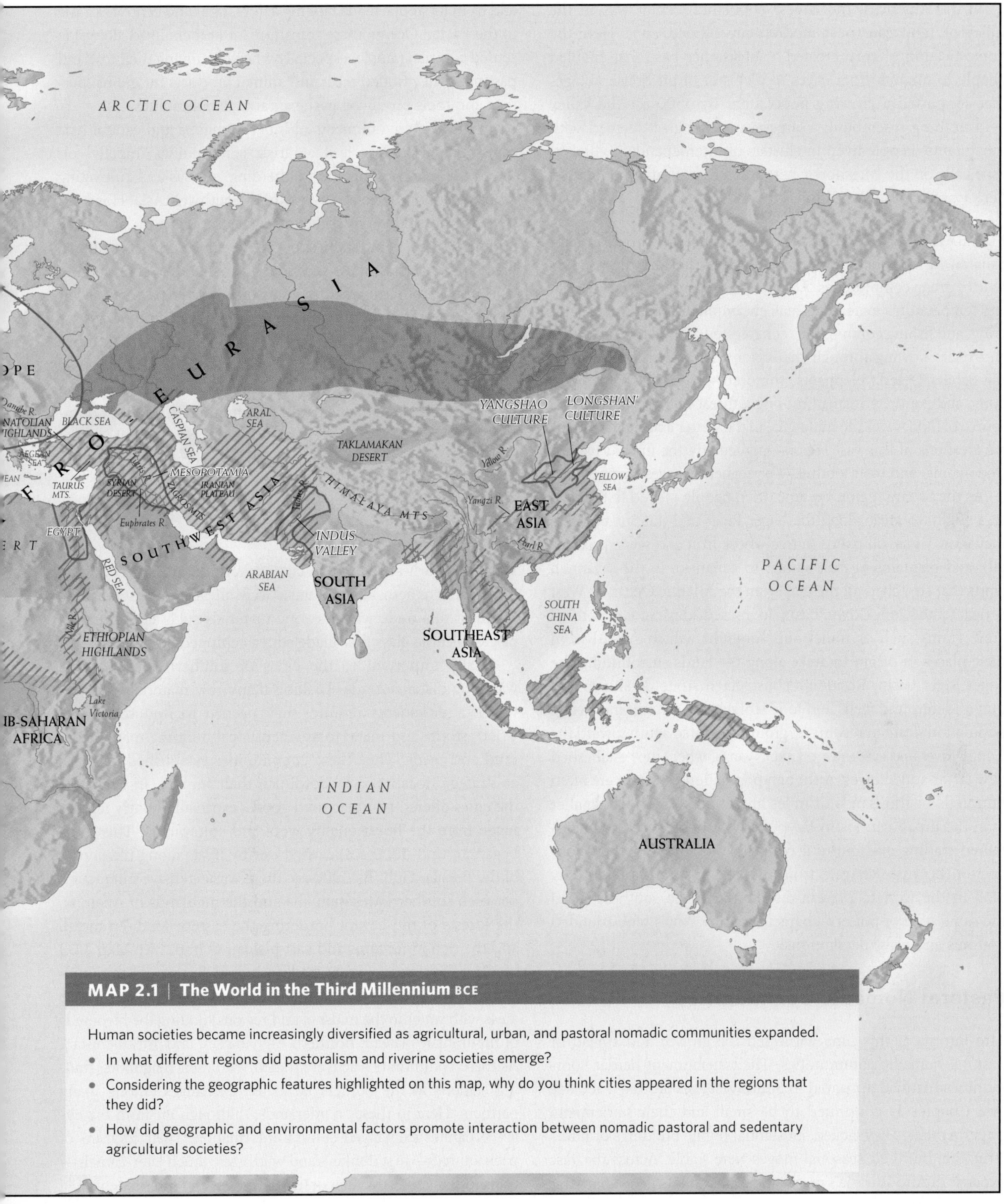

MAP 2.1 | The World in the Third Millennium BCE

Human societies became increasingly diversified as agricultural, urban, and pastoral nomadic communities expanded.

- In what different regions did pastoralism and riverine societies emerge?
- Considering the geographic features highlighted on this map, why do you think cities appeared in the regions that they did?
- How did geographic and environmental factors promote interaction between nomadic pastoral and sedentary agricultural societies?

In the Americas, the largest population center was in the valley of Tehuacán (near modern-day Mexico City). Here the domestication of corn created a subsistence base that enabled people to migrate from caves to a cluster of pit-house villages that supported a growing population. By 3500 BCE the valley held nothing resembling a large city, although it teemed with inhabitants. People lived in clusters of interdependent villages, especially on the lakeshores: here was a case of high population density, but not urbanization.

SUB-SAHARAN AFRICA The same pattern occurred in sub-Saharan Africa, where the population grew but did not concentrate in urban communities. About 12,000 years ago, when rainfall and temperatures increased, small encampments of hunting, gathering, and fishing communities congregated around the large lakes and rivers flowing through the region that would later become the Sahara Desert. Elephants, rhinoceroses, gazelles, antelopes, lions, and panthers roamed, posing a threat but also providing a source of food. Over the millennia, in the wetter and more temperate locations of this vast region—particularly the upland massifs (mountains) and their foothills—permanent villages emerged.

As the Sahara region became drier, people moved to the desert's edges, to areas along the Niger River and the Sudan. Here they grew yams, oil palms (a tree whose fruit and seeds produce oil), and plantains (a fruit similar to bananas). In the savannah lands that stretched all the way from the Atlantic Ocean in West Africa to the Nile River basin in present-day Sudan, settlers grew grains such as millet and sorghum, which spread from their places of origin to areas along the lands surrounding the Niger River basin. Residents constructed stone dwellings and dug underground wells and food storage areas. As an increasing population strained resources, groups migrated south toward the Congo River and east toward Lake Nyanza, where they established new farms and villages. Although population centers were often hundreds or thousands of miles apart and were much smaller than the urban centers in Egypt and Mesopotamia, they maintained trading and cultural contacts. We know of their connection because villagers from the area spanning present-day Mali in the west to present-day Kenya in the southeast used the same style of pottery, characterized by bowls with rounded bottoms and wavy decorations.

Pastoral Nomadic Communities

Afro-Eurasia at this time witnessed the growth and spread of pastoral nomadic communities. The transhumant herder communities that had appeared in Southwest Asia around 5500 BCE (see Chapter 1) continued to be small and their settlements impermanent. They lacked substantial public buildings or infrastructure, but their seasonal moves were stable. Across the vast expanse of Afro-Eurasia's great mountains and its desert barriers, and from its steppe lands ranging across inner and central Eurasia to the Pacific Ocean, these transhumant herders lived alongside settled agrarian people, especially when occupying their lowland pastures. They traded meat and animal products for grains, pottery, and tools produced in the agrarian communities.

In the arid environments of Inner Mongolia and central Asia transhumant herding and agrarian communities initially followed the same combination of herding animals and cultivating crops that had proved so successful in Southwest Asia. However, because the steppe environment could not support large-scale farming, these communities began to concentrate on animal breeding and herding. As secondary pursuits they continued to fish, hunt, and farm small plots in their winter pastures. Their economy centered on domesticated cattle, sheep, and horses. As their herds increased, these horse-riding nomads had to move often to new pastures, driving their herds across vast expanses of land. By the middle of the second millennium BCE, some had become full-scale nomadic pastoral communities, and they dominated the steppes. In these pastoral nomadic economies of the arid zones of central Eurasia, horses became crucial to survival.

The Rise of Trade

When the earliest farming villages developed around 7000 BCE, trade patterns across Afro-Eurasia were already well established. Much of this trade was in exotic materials such as obsidian, a black volcanic glass that made superb chipped-stone tools.

Vitally important to the cities of southern Mesopotamia was long-distance trade. Lacking many raw materials that developed settlements require, they needed to find sources of wood, stone, and metal to augment local building materials of mud and reeds. Thus these communities established outposts at strategic locations to coordinate their import. In exchange the cities offered manufactured goods, especially luxury textiles made from the finest quality wool and embroidery. This trade began around 5000 BCE, carried out by boats along the shores of the Persian Gulf. By 3000 BCE there was extensive interaction between southern Mesopotamia and the highlands of Anatolia, the forests of the Levant bordering the eastern Mediterranean, and the rich mountains and vast plateau of Iran. (See Map 2.2.)

Over thousands of years, trade increased. By the mid-third millennium BCE, flourishing communities populated the oases (fertile areas with water in the midst of arid regions) dotting the highlands of the Iranian plateau, northern Afghanistan, and Turkmenistan. As these communities actively traded with their neighbors, trading stations at the borders facilitated exchanges among many partners. Here in these "borderlands," although far from big cities, urbanites exchanged cultural information. Their caravans of pack animals—first donkeys and wild asses; much later, camels—transported goods through deserts, steppes, and forests. Stopping

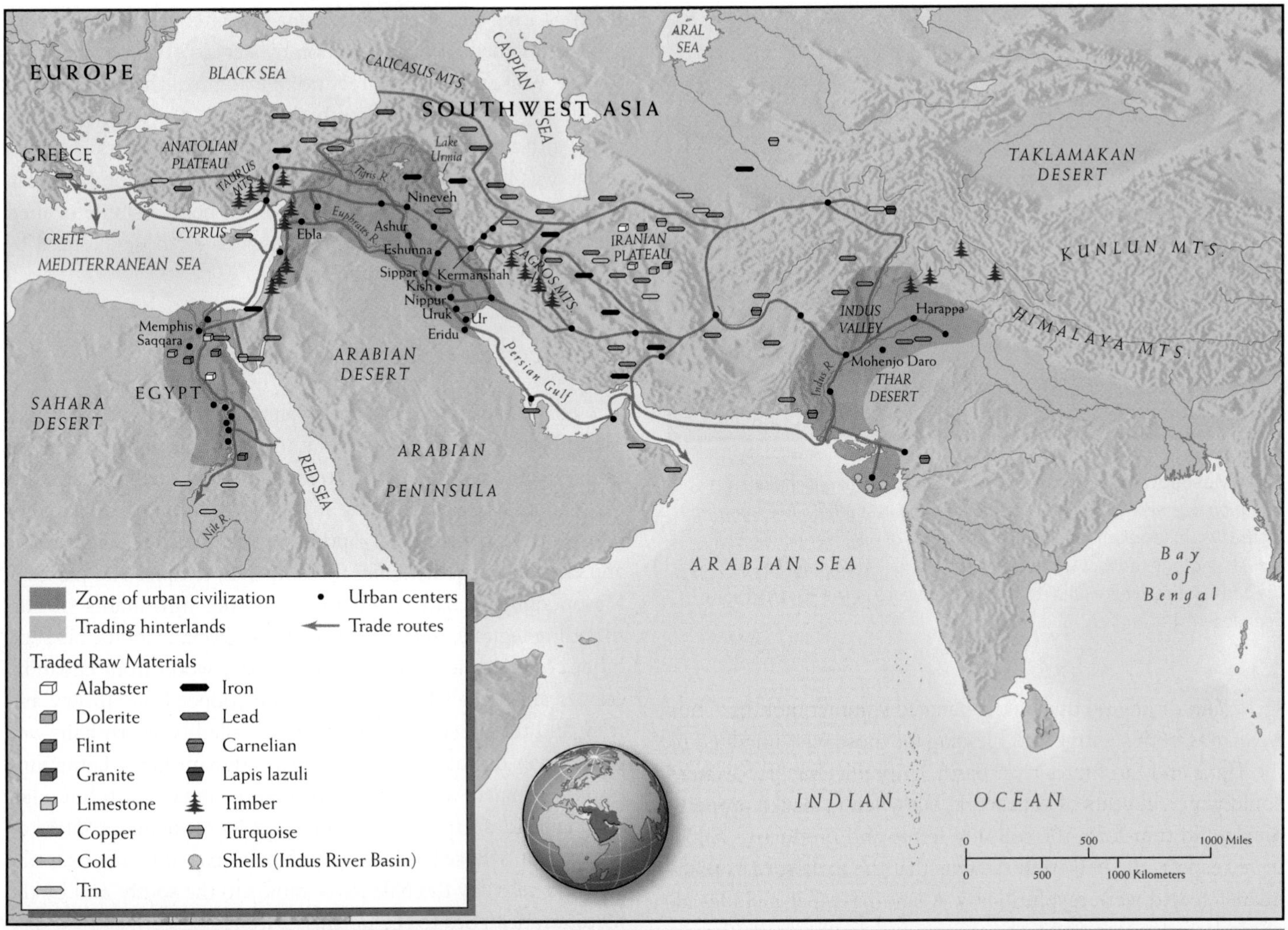

MAP 2.2 | Trade and Exchange in Southwest Asia and the Eastern Mediterranean—Third Millennium BCE

Extensive commercial networks linked the urban cores of Southwest Asia.

- Of the traded raw materials shown on the map, which ones were used for building materials, and which ones for luxury items?
- Why were there more extensive trade connections between Mesopotamians and people to their northwest and east than with Egypt to the west?
- According to the map, in what ways did Mesopotamia become the crossroads of Afro-Eurasia?

at oasis communities to exchange their wares for water and supplies, these caravans carried ideas across Afro-Eurasia. In this way, borderlands and borderlanders—along with the cities they connected—have played a vital role in world history.

BETWEEN THE TIGRIS AND EUPHRATES RIVERS: MESOPOTAMIA

In 3500 BCE, in a world where people had been living close to the land in small clans and settlements, a radical breakthrough occurred in one place: the Mesopotamian river basin. Here the world's first complex society arose. Here the city and the river changed how people lived.

Tapping the Waters

Mesopotamia, whose name is a Greek word meaning "[place] between two rivers," is not at first glance a likely landscape for a dramatic social transformation to occur. From their headwaters in the mountains to the north and east to their destination in the Persian Gulf, the Tigris and Euphrates rivers are wild and unpredictable, flooding in periods of heavy rainfall and

Early Mesopotamian Waterworks. *From the sixth millennium* BCE, *irrigation was necessary for successful farming in southern Mesopotamia. By the first millennium* BCE, *sophisticated feats of engineering allowed the Assyrians to redirect water through constructed aqueducts, like the one illustrated here on a relief from the palace of the Assyrian king Sennacherib at Nineveh.*

snow, and drying up during the parched summer months. Thus water was both scourge and blessing for those who migrated to the Tigris and Euphrates river basin. Unpredictable floodwaters could wipe out years of hard work, but when managed properly they could transform the soil into fertile and productive fields. In retrospect, the irrigation systems that the earliest Mesopotamians created were revolutionary. A landmass that includes all of modern-day Iraq and parts of Syria and southeastern Turkey, Mesopotamia embraces a rich variety of topography and cultures—all unified by natural drainage basins. Both rivers provided water for irrigation and, although hardly navigable, were important routes for transportation and communication by pack animal and by foot.

Converting the floodplain of the Tigris and Euphrates rivers into a breadbasket required mastering unpredictable waters. Unless controlled by waterworks, both were profoundly unfavorable to cultivators because the annual floods and low-water seasons came at the wrong times in the farming sequence. Floods occurred at the height of the growing season, when crops were most vulnerable. Low water levels occurred when crops required abundant irrigation. To prevent the river from overflowing during its flood stage, farmers built levees (barriers to the waters) along the banks and dug ditches and canals to drain away the floodwaters. Their solution was ingenious. Since the bed of the Euphrates is higher than that of the Tigris, and the Euphrates floods sometimes drained toward the Tigris, engineers devised extensive irrigation systems contoured to follow the downward sloping grade between the two rivers. Under this scheme the Euphrates served as the supply and the Tigris as the drain of the southern river basin. Storing and channeling water year after year required constant maintenance and innovation by a corps of engineers.

The Mesopotamians' technological breakthrough was in irrigation, not in agrarian methods. Because the soils were fine, rich, and constantly replenished by the floodwaters' silt, soil tillage was light work. Farmers sowed a combination of wheat, millet, sesame, and barley (the basis for beer, a staple of their diet). Their yields may have been as high as those afforded by modern-day wheat fields in Canada.

Crossroads of Southwest Asia

Though its soil was rich and water was abundant, southern Mesopotamia had few other natural resources apart from the mud, marsh reeds, spindly trees, and low-quality limestone that served as basic building materials. To obtain high-quality, dense wood, stone, metal, and other materials for constructing and embellishing their cities (notably their temples and palaces), Mesopotamians had to interact with the inhabitants of surrounding regions. In return for textiles, specialty foods, oils, and other commodities, they imported cedar wood from Lebanon, copper and stones from Oman, more copper from Turkey and Iran, and the precious blue gemstone called lapis lazuli, as well as the ever-useful tin, from faraway Afghanistan. Maintaining trading contacts was easy, given Mesopotamia's open boundaries on all sides. (In this crucial respect Mesopotamia contrasted with Egypt, whose land was cut off by impassable deserts to the east and west, by the Nile River rapids to the south, and by the Mediterranean Sea to the north.)

Mesopotamia's natural advantages—its rich agricultural land and water, combined with easy access to neighboring regions—favored the growth of cities. The area became a magnet for waves of newcomers from the deserts and the mountains (an early version of migration from the countryside to cities), and thus a crossroads for the peoples of Southwest Asia, the meeting grounds for distinct cultural and linguistic groups. Among the dominant groups were Sumerians, who concentrated in the south; Hurrians, who lived in the north; and Akkadians, who populated western and central Mesopotamia.

The World's First Cities

During the first half of the fourth millennium BCE, a demographic transformation occurred in the Tigris-Euphrates river basin. The population expanded as a result of the region's agricultural bounty, and swelling ranks of Mesopotamians migrated from country villages to centers that eventually became cities. (A **city** is a large, well-defined urban area with a dense population.) The earliest cities—Eridu, Nippur, and Uruk—developed over about 1,000 years, dominating the southern part of the

ANALYZING GLOBAL DEVELOPMENTS

The Development of Writing

Agricultural surplus, and the urbanization and labor specialization that accompanied it, prompted the earliest development of writing and the profession of the scribes whose job it was to write. Early forms of writing were employed for a variety of purposes such as keeping economic and administration records, recording the reigns of rulers; and preserving religious events and practices (calendars, rituals, and divinatory purposes). By the third millennium BCE, some early societies (Mesopotamia and Egypt, in particular) used writing to produce literature, religious texts, and historical documents. Different types of writing developed in early societies, in part because each society developed writing for different purposes (see table below):

- **Ideographic/Logographic/Pictographic Systems:** symbols represent words (complex and cumbersome).
- **Logophonetic and Logosyllabic Systems:** symbols represent sounds, usually syllables (alphabetic, fewer symbols).
- **Syllabic Systems:** symbols represent syllables.
- **Inalphabetic Systems:** symbols are letters that are assembled to create words.

Scholars know more about early cultures whose writing has since been deciphered. Undeciphered scripts, such as the Indus Valley Script and Rongorongo, offer intrigue and promise to those who would attempt their decipherment.

QUESTIONS FOR ANALYSIS

- What is the relationship between writing and the development of earliest riverine societies? (See also Map 2.1).
- To what extent does the type of society (riverine, sea-faring, etc.) seem to impact the development of writing in that region (date, type, purpose, etc.)?
- How has the decipherment, or lack thereof, of these scripts impacted scholars' understandings of the societies that produced them?

Name/Type of Society	Writing Form and Date of Emergence	Type of Writing and Purpose	Date and Means of Decipherment
Mesopotamia (Sumer)/ Riverine (Tigris-Euphrates)	Cuneiform, 3200 BCE	Transitions from ca. 1000 pictographs to about 400 syllables (record-keeping)	Deciphered in 19th century via Behistun/Beisitun inscription
Egypt (Old Kingdom)/ Riverine (Nile)	Hieroglyphs, 3100 BCE	Mixture of thousands of logograms and phonograms (religious)	Deciphered in early 19th century via tri-lingual Rosetta Stone
Harappan/Riverine (Indus)	Indus Valley Script, 2500 BCE	375–400 logographic signs (nomenclature and titleature)	Undeciphered
Minoan/Mycenaean Greece/Seafaring micro-society	Phaistos Disk and Linear A (Minoan Crete); Linear B (Mycenaean, Crete and Greece); 1900 BCE–1300 BCE	Phaistos Disk (45 pictographic symbols in a spiral); Linear A (90 logographic-syllabic symbols); Linear B (roughly 75 syllabic symbols with some logographs) (record-keeping)	Phaistos (undeciphered); Linear A (undeciphered); Linear B (deciphered in mid-20th century)
Shang Dynasty/Riverine (Yellow River)	Oracle bone script, 14th–11th century BCE	Thousands of characters (divinatory purposes)	Deciphered in early 20th century
Maya/Central American rainforest	Mayan glyphs, 250 BCE	Mixture of logograms (numeric glyphs), phonograms (around 85 phonetic glyphs), and hundreds of "emblem glyphs" (record of rulers and calendrical purposes)	Decipherment begun in 20th century
Vikings/Seafaring (Scandinavia)	Futhark (runic alphabet), 200 CE	24 alphabetic runes (ritual use; or to identify owner or craftsperson)	Deciphered by Elder Futhark in 19th century
Inca/Andean highlands	Quipu, 3000? BCE	Knotted cords, essentially a tally system (record-keeping)	Deciphered
Easter Island/Sea-faring micro-society	Rongorongo, 1500 CE	120 glyphs (calendrical or genealogical)	Undeciphered

Sources: Chris Scarre (ed.), The Human Past: World Prehistory and the Development of Human Societies *(2005); Luigi Luca Cavalli-Sforza,* Genes, Peoples, and Languages, *translated by Mark Selestad from the original 1996 French publication (2000).*

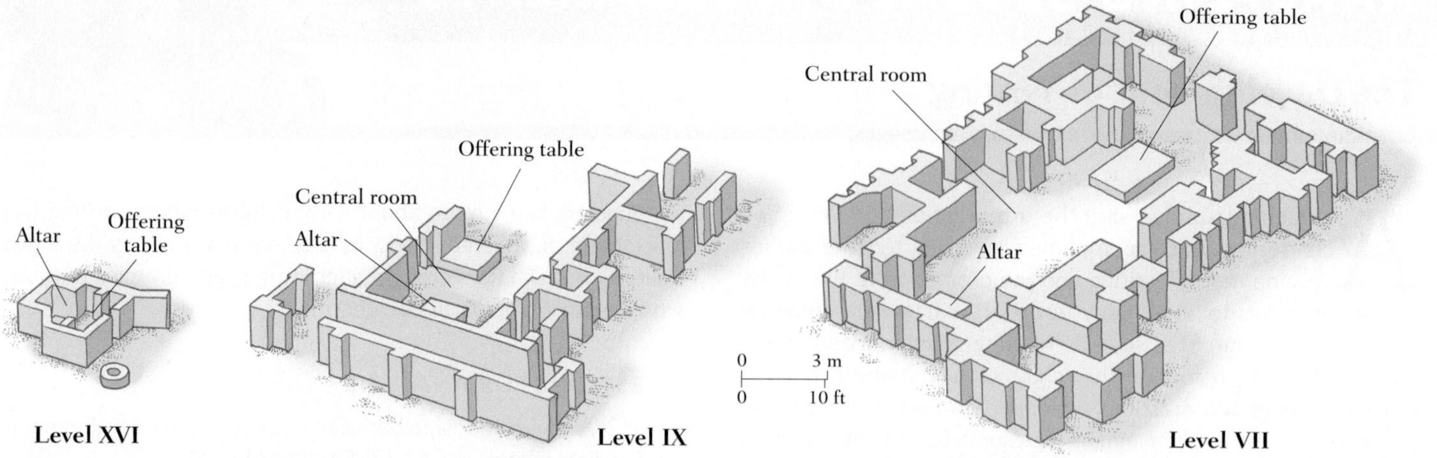

Layout of Eridu. *Over several millennia, temples of increasing size and complexity were built atop each other at Eridu in southern Iraq. The culmination came with the elaborate structure of level VII.*

floodplain by 3500 BCE. Here archaeologists have found buildings of mud brick marking successive layers of urban development. Consider Eridu, a village dating back to 6000 BCE. Home to the Sumerian water god, Ea, Eridu was a sacred site where temples piled up on top of one another for over 4,000 years. Throughout more than twenty reconstructions the temples became increasingly elaborate, standing on an ever-higher base. The final temple rose from a platform like a mountain, visible for miles in all directions.

As the temple grew skyward, the village expanded outward and became a city. Gods oversaw the sprawl. From their homes in temples located at the center of cities, they broadcast their powers. In return, urbanites provided finery, clothes, and enhanced lodgings for the gods and their priestly envoys. In Sumerian cosmology, man was created solely to serve the gods, so the urban landscape reflected this fact: with a temple at the core, with goods and services flowing to the center, and with divine protection and justice flowing outward.

Some thirty-five cities with divine sanctuaries dotted the southern plain of Mesopotamia. Sumer glorified a way of life and a territory composed of politically equal city-states, each with a guardian deity and sanctuary supported by its inhabitants. (A **city-state** is a political organization based on the authority of a single, large city that controls the surrounding countryside.) Local communities in these urban hubs expressed homage to individual city gods and took pride in the temple, the god's home.

Because early Mesopotamian cities served as meeting places for peoples and their deities, they gained status as religious and economic centers. Whether enormous (like Uruk and Nippur) or modest (like Ur and Abu Salabikh), all cities were spiritual, economic, and cultural homes for Mesopotamian subjects.

Simply making a city was therefore not enough: it had to be made great. Urban design reflected the city's role as a wondrous place to pay homage to the gods and their human intermediary, the king. The early cities contained enormous spaces within their walls, with large houses separated by date palm plantations. The city limits also encompassed extensive sheepfolds (which became a frequent metaphor for the city). As populations grew, the Mesopotamian cities became denser and the houses smaller. Some urbanites established new suburbs, spilling out beyond old walls and creating neighborhoods in what used to be the countryside.

The typical layout of Mesopotamian cities reflected a common pattern: a central canal surrounded by neighborhoods of specialized occupational groups. The temple marked the city center, while the palace and other official buildings graced the periphery. In separate quarters for craft production, families passed down their trades across generations. In this sense, the landscape of the city mirrored the growing **social hierarchies** (distinctions between the privileged and the less privileged).

Gods and Temples

The worldview of the Sumerians and, later, the Akkadians included a belief in a group of gods that shaped their political institutions and controlled everything—including the weather, fertility, harvests, and the underworld. As depicted in the *Epic of Gilgamesh* (a second-millennium BCE composition based on oral tales about Gilgamesh, a historical but mythologized king of Uruk), the gods could give but could also take away—with searing droughts, unmerciful floods, and violent death. Gods, and the natural forces they controlled, had to be revered and feared.

Ziggurat. *The first ziggurat of Mesopotamia, dedicated to the moon god Nanna, was built by the founder of the Neo-Sumerian dynasty, Ur-Nammu (2112–2095 BCE). Although temples had been raised on platforms since early times, the distinctive stepped form of the ziggurat was initially borrowed from the Iranian plateau. It became the most important sacred structure in Mesopotamia.*

Faithful subjects imagined their gods as immortal beings whose habits were capricious, contentious, and gloriously work-free. Each major god of the Sumerian pantheon (an officially recognized group of gods) dwelled in a particular city that he or she had created, giving rise to each city's character, institutions, and relationships with its urban neighbors.

Temples served as the gods' home and as the symbol of urban identity. (A **temple** is a building where believers worshipped their gods and goddesses and where some peoples believed the deities had earthly residence.) Rulers lavished resources on temple construction and adornment to demonstrate their cities' power. Inside the temple was an altar displaying the cult image. (A **cult** is a religious movement, often based on the worship of a particular god or goddess.) Benches lined the walls, with statues of humans standing in perpetual worship of the deity's images. By the end of the third millennium BCE, the temple's platform base had changed to a stepped platform called a *ziggurat*. On top of the temple tower stood the main temple. Surrounding the ziggurat were buildings that housed priests, officials, laborers, and servants—all bustling about to serve the city's god.

While the temple was the god's home, it was also the god's estate. As such, temples functioned like large households engaging in all sorts of productive and commercial activities. Their dependents cultivated cereals, fruits, and vegetables by using extensive irrigation. The temples owned vast flocks of sheep, goats, cows, and donkeys. Those located close to the river employed workers to collect reeds, to fish, and to hunt. Enormous labor forces were involved in maintaining this high level of production. Other temples operated huge workshops for manufacturing textiles and leather goods, employing craftworkers, metalworkers, masons, and stoneworkers.

The Palace and Royal Power

The palace, as both an institution and a set of buildings, appeared around 2500 BCE—about two millennia later than the Mesopotamian temple. It joined the temple as a landmark of city life, upholding order and a sense of shared membership in city affairs. Over time, the palace became a source of power rivaling that of the temple. (A **palace** is the official residence of a ruler, his family, and his entourage.) While palaces were off limits to most citizens unless they were connected to the royal court, elite members of the Sumerian community did enjoy access to the cult chamber. As time went on, the god, like the king, became inaccessible to all but the most elite.

Although located at the edge of cities, palaces soon became the symbols of permanent secular, military, and administrative authority distinct from the temples' spiritual and economic power. As the population grew, competition among the city-states increased over scarce arable land and access to water for irrigation. Gradually the more powerful city-states came to dominate their weaker neighbors, thereby upsetting the balance of power within and among Mesopotamian cities.

The Royal Tombs of Ur. *The Royal Tombs of Ur, excavated in the 1930s, contained thousands of objects in gold, silver, lapis lazuli, and shell that were buried along with elites of the First Dynasty of Ur. In one grave, along with the skeletons of more than sixty members of a royal household, were musical instruments, including this large harp with a golden bull's head. Such instruments would have been played at the ritual meal associated with these fabulously rich burials. Pu-Abi, identified as a queen by the cylinder near her body, was buried in a separate chamber. She was interred in full regalia, including the elaborate headdress shown here.*

Rulers tied their status to their gods through elaborate burial arrangements. The Royal Cemetery at Ur offers spectacular archaeological evidence of how Sumerian rulers dealt with death. Housed in a mud-brick structure, the royal burials held not only the primary remains but also the bodies of people who had been sacrificed—in one case, more than eighty men and women. Artifacts including huge vats for cooked food, bones of animals, drinking vessels, and musical instruments enable scholars to reconstruct the lifestyle of those who joined their masters in the graves. Honoring the royal dead by including their followers and possessions in their tombs reinforced the social hierarchies—including the vertical ties between humans and gods—that were the cornerstone of these early city-states.

Social Hierarchy and Families

Social hierarchies were an important part of the fabric of Sumerian city-states. Mesopotamia's city-states at first had assemblies of elders and young men who made collective decisions for the community. At times, certain effective individuals took charge of emergencies, and over time these people surrounding the leaders acquired more durable political power. The social hierarchy set off the rulers from the ruled. Ruling groups secured their privileged access to economic and political resources by erecting systems of bureaucracies, priesthoods, and laws. Priests and bureaucrats served their rulers well, championing rules and norms that legitimized the political leadership.

Occupations within the cities were highly specialized, and a list of professions circulated across the land so that everyone could know his or her place in the social order. The king and priest in Sumer were at the top of the list, followed by bureaucrats (scribes and household accountants), supervisors, and craftworkers. The latter included cooks, jewelers, gardeners, potters, metalsmiths, and traders. The biggest group, which was at the bottom of the hierarchy, comprised workers who were not slaves but who were dependent on their employers' households. Movement among economic classes was not impossible but, as in many traditional societies, it was rare. There were also independent merchants who risked long-distance trading ventures, hoping for a generous return on their investment.

The family and the household provided the bedrock for Sumerian society, and its organization reflected the balance between women and men, children and parents. The Sumerian family was hierarchical, so the senior male dominated as the patriarch. Most households were composed of a single extended family, all of whose members lived under the same roof. The family consisted of the husband and wife bound by a contract: she would provide children, preferably male, while he provided support and protection. Monogamy was the norm unless there was no son, in which case a second wife or a slave girl would bear male children to serve as the married couple's offspring. Adoption was another way to gain a male heir. Sons would inherit the family's property in equal shares, while daughters would receive dowries necessary for successful marriage into other families. Most women lived inside the contract of marriage, but a special class of women joined the temple staff as priestesses. By the second millennium BCE, they gained economic autonomy that included ownership of estates and productive enterprises. Even in this case, though, their fathers and brothers remained responsible for their well-being.

First Writing and Early Texts

Mesopotamia was the birthplace of the first recorded words of history, inscribed to promote the power of the temples and kings in the expanding city-states. Small-scale hunter-gatherer societies and village-farming communities had developed rituals of oral celebrations based on collective memories transmitted by families across generations. But as societies grew larger and more complex, and their members more anonymous, oral traditions provided inadequate "glue" to hold the centers together.

Those who wielded new writing tools were **scribes**; from the very beginning they were at the top of the social ladder, under the major power brokers—the big man and the priests. As the writing of texts became more important to the social fabric of cities, and facilitated information sharing across wider spans of distance and time, scribes consolidated their grip on the upper rungs of the social ladder.

Mesopotamians became the world's first record keepers and readers. The precursors to writing appeared in Mesopotamian societies when farming peoples and officials who had been using clay tokens and images carved on stones to seal off storage areas began to use them to convey messages. These images, when combined with numbers drawn on clay tablets, could record the distribution of goods and services.

In a flash of human genius, someone, probably in Uruk, understood that the marks (most were pictures of objects) could also represent words or sounds. A representation that transfers meaning from the name of a thing to the sound of that name is a *rebus*. Before long, scribes connected visual symbols with sounds, and sounds with meanings. As people combined rebus symbols with other visual marks, they discovered they could record messages by using symbols or signs to denote concepts. Such signs later came to represent syllables, the building blocks of words. (See Primary Source: The Origins of Writing According to the Sumerians.)

By impressing signs into wet clay with the cut end of a reed, scribes pioneered a form of wedge-shaped writing that we call *cuneiform;* it filled tablets with information that was intelligible to anyone who could decipher the signs, even in faraway locations or in future generations. This Sumerian innovation enhanced the urban elites' ability to produce and trade goods, to control property, and to transmit ideas through literature, historical records, and sacred texts. The result was a profound change in human experience, because representing symbols of spoken language facilitated an extension of communication and memory. Although these gradual steps toward literacy were fundamental to the innovative process occurring in cities, only a tiny but influential scribal elite mastered writing at first.

Much of what we know about Mesopotamia rests on our ability to decipher cuneiform script. Rebus writing appeared around 3200 BCE, but not until 700 years later could the script record spoken utterances completely. By around 2400 BCE, texts began to describe the political makeup of southern Mesopotamia, giving details of its history and economy. Northern cities borrowed cuneiform to record economic transactions and political events, but in their own Semitic tongue. In fact, cuneiform's adaptability to different languages was a main reason its use spread widely.

As city life and literacy expanded, they gave rise not only to documents but also to written narratives, the stories of a "people" and their origins. One famous set of texts written around 2100 BCE, "The Temple Hymns," describes thirty-five divine sanctuaries. The magnificent Sumerian King List, known from

Cylinder Seal of Adad Carved from Green Stone. *Many people in Mesopotamia involved with administration and public life had one or more cylinder seals. Cylinder seals were carved with imagery and inscriptions and were impressed into clay tablets and other documents while they were still malleable in order to guarantee the authenticity of a transaction. The cylinder seal shown here carries the inscription of the scribe Adda. The imagery includes representations of important gods of the Akkadian pantheon. The sun god Shamash rises from between the mountains in the center. Ishtar as a warrior goddess stands to the left. To the right is Ea, the god of wisdom, who is associated with flowing water and fish. Behind him is the servant Usmu, whose double face allows him to see everything. At the far left is a god of hunting.*

PRIMARY SOURCE

The Origins of Writing According to the Sumerians

One Sumerian myth records the invention of writing by the Lord of Kulaba, Enmerkar. He wanted to transmit complex messages across vast distances to the Land of Aratta, where his rival for the love of the goddess Inanna lived. Normally messengers would memorize messages and responses and deliver them orally after making an arduous journey across the mountains. Enmerkar felt he could not trust his messenger's memory to deliver one particularly complicated message, so he invented writing in the form of cuneiform script.

His speech was substantial, and its contents extensive. The messenger, whose mouth was heavy, was not able to repeat it. Because the messenger, whose mouth was tired, was not able to repeat it, the lord of Kulaba patted some clay and wrote the message as if on a tablet. Formerly, the writing of messages on clay was not established. Now, under that sun and on that day, it was indeed so. The lord of Kulaba inscribed the message like a tablet. It was just like that. The messenger was like a bird, flapping its wings; he raged forth like a wolf following a kid. He traversed five mountains, six mountains, seven mountains. He lifted his eyes as he approached Aratta. He stepped joyfully into the courtyard of Aratta, he made known the authority of his king. Openly he spoke out the words in his heart. The messenger transmitted the message to the lord of Aratta:

Cuneiform version of the myth "Enmerkar and the Lord of Aratta."

"Your father, my master, has sent me to you; the lord of Unug, the lord of Kulaba, has sent me to you." "What is it to me what your master has spoken? What is it to me what he has said?"

"This is what my master has spoken, this is what he has said. My king is like a huge *meš* tree, . . . son of Enlil; this tree has grown high, uniting heaven and earth; its crown reaches heaven, its trunk is set upon the earth. He who is made to shine forth in lordship and kingship, Enmerkar, the son of Utu, has given me a clay tablet. O lord of Aratta, after you have examined the clay tablet, after you have learned the content of the message, say whatever you will say to me, and I shall announce that message in the shrine E-ana as glad tidings to the scion of him with the glistening beard, whom his stalwart cow gave birth to in the mountains of the shining *me,* who was reared on the soil of Aratta, who was given suck at the udder of the good cow, who is suited for office in Kulaba, the mountain of great *me,* to Enmerkar, the son of Utu; I shall repeat it in his *ĝipar,* fruitful as a flourishing *meš* tree, to my king, the lord of Kulaba."

After he had spoken thus to him, the lord of Aratta received his kiln-fired tablet from the messenger. The lord of Aratta looked at the tablet. The transmitted message was just nails, and his brow expressed anger. The lord of Aratta looked at his kiln-fired tablet. At that moment, the lord worthy of the crown of lordship, the son of Enlil, the god Iškur, thundering in heaven and earth, caused a raging storm, a great lion, in . . . He was making the mountains quake . . . , he was convulsing the mountain range . . . ; the awesome radiance . . . of his breast; he caused the mountain range to raise its voice in joy. (lines 500–551)

QUESTIONS FOR ANALYSIS

- What passages in this reading reveal the Sumerians' familiarity with pastoralism?
- What aspects of Sumerian history and geography does this mythic story preserve and transmit?

Source: J. A. Black, G. Cunningham, E. Fluckiger-Hawker, E. Robson, and G. Zólyomi, The Electronic Text Corpus of Sumerian Literature *(Oxford, 1998–2006), www-etcsl.orient.ox.ac.uk/.*

texts written around 2000 BCE, recounts the reigns of kings by dynasty, one city at a time. It narrates the fabulously long reigns of legendary kings before the so-called Great Flood, which, in turn, is one of many traditional stories that people transmitted orally for generations (and it later evolved into the book of Genesis as part of the Bible's creation story). The Great Flood, a crucial event in Sumerian identity, explained Uruk's demise as the gods' doing. Flooding was the most riveting of natural forces

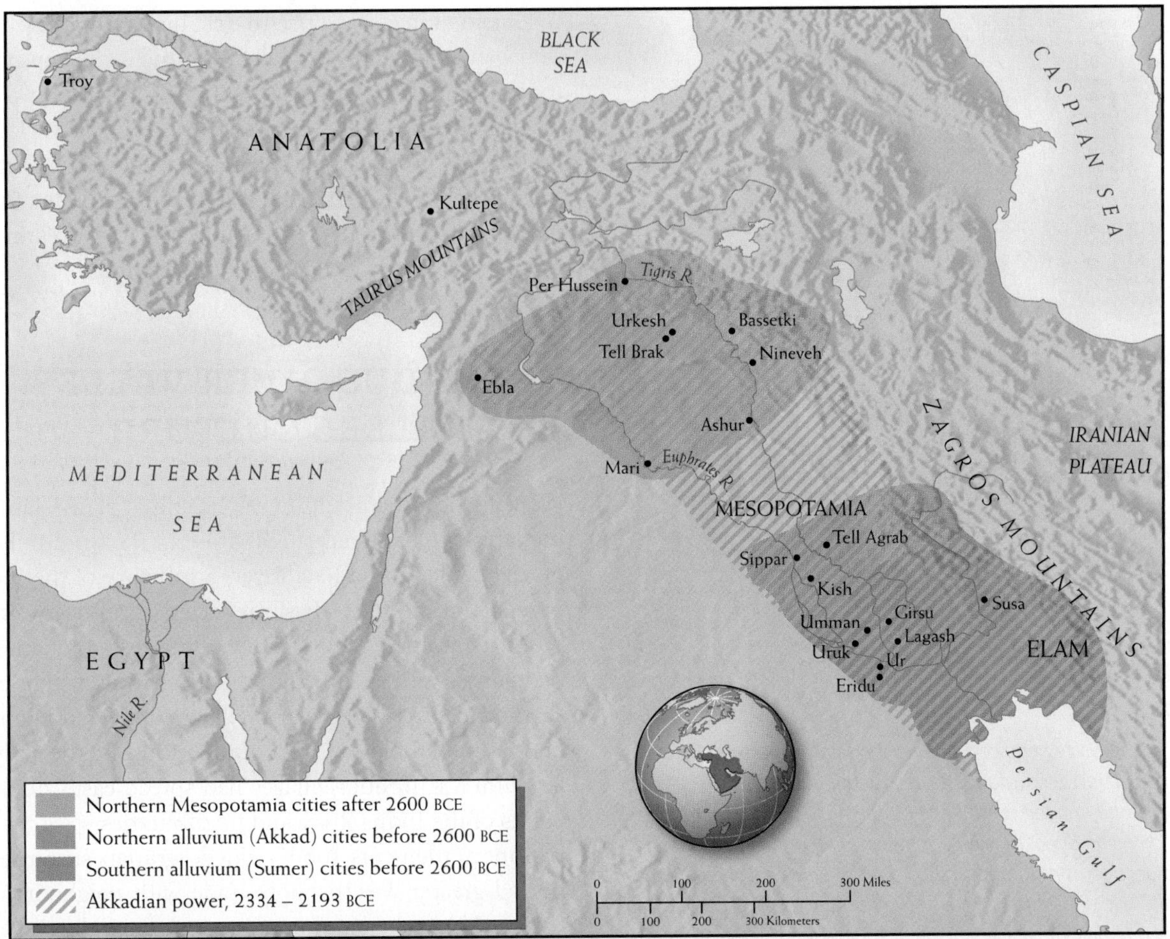

MAP 2.3 | The Spread of Cities in Mesopotamia and the Akkadian State, 2600–2200 BCE

Urbanization began in the southern alluvium of Mesopotamia and spread northward. Eventually, the region achieved unification under Akkadian power.

- According to this map, what were the natural boundaries of the Mesopotamian cities?
- How did proximity to the Zagros Mountains affect the new urban centers?
- How did the expansion northward reflect the continued influence of geographic and environmental factors on urbanization?

in the lives of a riverine folk, and it helped shape the material and symbolic foundations of Mesopotamian societies.

Spreading Cities and First Territorial States

Although no single state dominated the history of fourth- and third-millennia BCE Mesopotamia, a few stand out. The most powerful and influential were the Sumerian city-states of the Early Dynastic Age (2850–2334 BCE) and their successor, the Akkadian territorial state (2334–2193 BCE).

While the city-states of southern Mesopotamia flourished and competed, giving rise to the land of Sumer, the rich agricultural zones to the north inhabited by the Hurrians also became urbanized. (See Map 2.3.) Beginning around 2600 BCE, northern cities were comparable in size to those in the south. Though their inhabitants were culturally related to the Sumerians and Akkadians, the northern cities had economic, political, and social organizations that were distinct and independent.

As Mesopotamia swelled with cities, it became unstable. The Sumerian city-states with expanding populations soon found themselves competing for agrarian lands, scarce water, and lucrative trade routes. And as pastoralists far and wide learned of the region's bounty, they journeyed in greater numbers to the cities, fueling urbanization and competition.

Cities also spawned rivalry and struggles for supremacy. In fact, the world's first great conqueror emerged from one of these cities, and by the end of his long reign he had united (by force)

Naram Sin. *This life-size head of a ruler cast of almost pure copper was found at Nineveh in northern Iraq in the destruction levels of the Assyrian Empire. The style and imagery of this sculptural masterpiece identify it as a ruler of Old Akkadian dynasty. While sometimes identified as Sargon, it is most likely a portrait of his grandson, Naram Sin, who consolidated and transformed the Akkadian state. It must have stood for over 1,500 years in the courtyard of a temple at Nineveh before it was defaced by the Medes and Elamites, whose savage attack on Nineveh cause the Assyrian Empire to fall.*

the independent Mesopotamian cities south of modern-day Baghdad. The legendary Sargon the Great (r. 2334–2279 BCE), king of Akkad, brought the era of competitive independent city-states to an end. His most remarkable achievement was unification of the southern cities through an alliance. Although this unity lasted only three generations, it represented the first multi-ethnic unification of urban centers—the **territorial state**. (A territorial state is a form of political organization that holds authority over a large population and landmass; its power extends over a wider area than that of city-states.)

The most obvious legacy of Sargon's dynasty was sponsorship of monumental architecture, artworks, and literary works. These cultural achievements stood for centuries, inspiring generations of builders, architects, artists, and scribes. And by encouraging contact with distant neighbors, many of whom adopted aspects of Mesopotamian culture, the Akkadian kings increased the geographic reach of Mesopotamian influence.

The riches and competition among cities also lured invaders, with the result that Sargon's "empire" was short-lived. Foreign tribesmen from the Zagros Mountains infiltrated the heartland of Akkad, conquering the capital city around 2190 BCE. This cycle of urban magnificence punctuated by disintegration triggered by outside forces gave rise to epic history writing, and its myth of urban civility and rural backwardness still captivates readers today. The fall of Sargon's "empire" underscores a fundamental but often neglected reality of the ancient world: living side by side with the city-state dwellers were peoples who followed a simpler way of life. They often did not enter the historical record except when they intruded on the lives of their more powerful, prosperous, and literate neighbors.

THE INDUS RIVER VALLEY: A PARALLEL CULTURE

We call the urban culture of the Indus area "Harappan" after the large site of Harappa that arose in the third millennium BCE on the banks of the Ravi River, a tributary of the Indus. Developments in the Indus basin reflected an indigenous (local) tradition combined with strong influences from Iranian plateau peoples, as well as indirect influences from distant cities on the Tigris and Euphrates rivers. Villages appeared before 5000 BCE on the Iranian plateau west of the Indus. By the early third millennium BCE, frontier villages had spread eastward to the fertile banks of the Indus River and its tributaries. (See Map 2.4.) The riverine settlements soon yielded agrarian surpluses that supported greater wealth, more trade with neighbors, and public works. In due course, urbanites of the Indus region and the Harappan peoples began to fortify their cities and to undertake public works similar in scale to those in Mesopotamia, but strikingly different in function.

The Indus Valley environment boasted many advantages—especially compared to the area near the Ganges River, the other great waterway of the South Asian landmass. The semitropical Indus Valley had plentiful water from melting snows in the Himalayas that ensured flourishing vegetation, and the region did not suffer the yearly monsoon downpours that flooded the Ganges plain. The expansion of agriculture in the Indus basin depended on the river's annual floods to replenish the soil and avert droughts (as in Mesopotamia, Egypt, and China). From June to September, the rivers inundated the plain. Once the waters receded, farmers planted wheat and barley. They harvested crops the next spring as temperatures rose. At the same time, the villagers improved their tools of cultivation. Researchers have found evidence of furrows, probably made by plowing, that date to around 2600 BCE. Farmers were soon achieving harvests like those of Mesopotamia, yielding a surplus that freed many inhabitants from producing food and allowed them to specialize in other activities.

In time, rural wealth produced urban splendor. More abundant harvests, now stored in large granaries, brought migrants into the area and supported expanding populations. By 2500 BCE

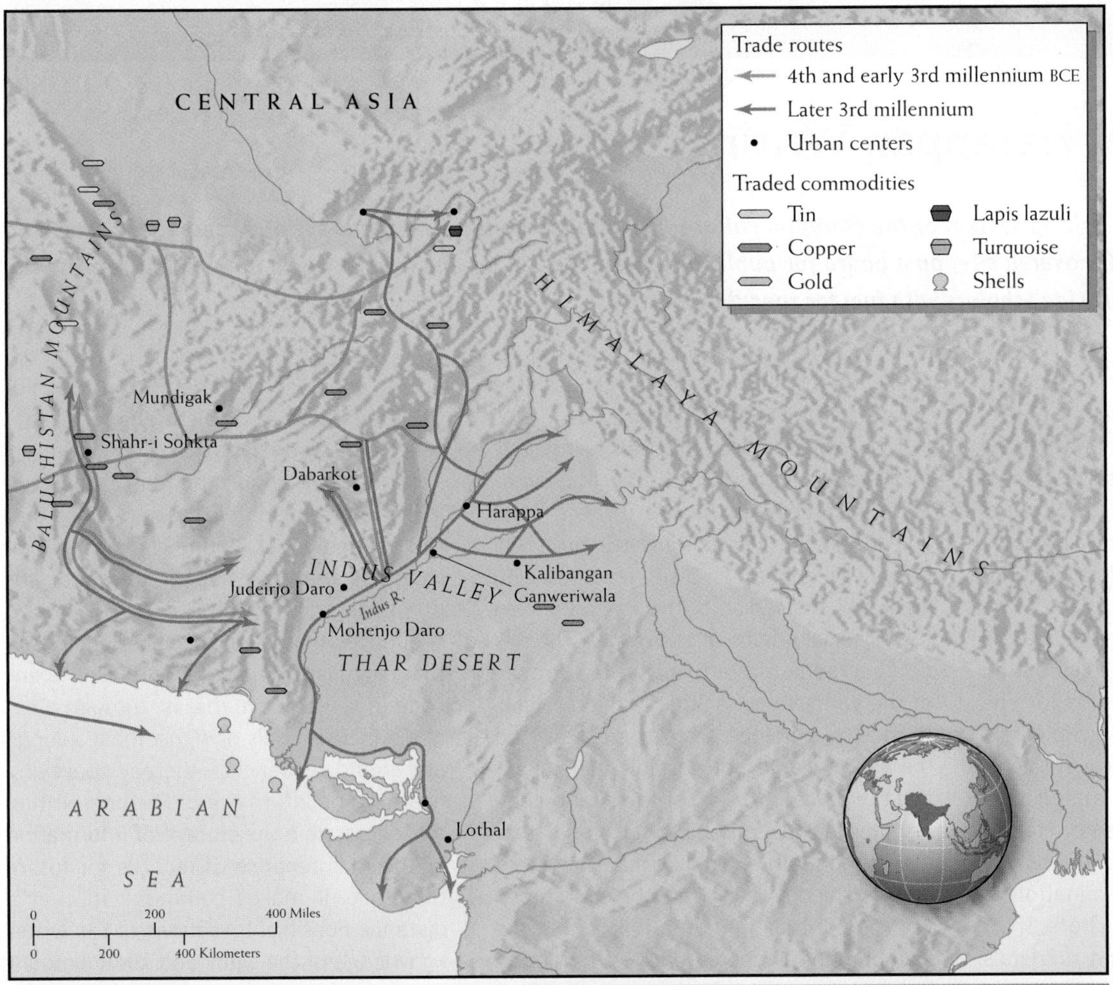

MAP 2.4 | The Indus River Valley in the Third Millennium BCE

Historians know less about the urban society of the Indus Valley in the third millennium BCE than they do about its contemporaries in Mesopotamia and Egypt. Still, archaeological evidence gives insight into this urban complex.

- Where were cities concentrated in the Indus Valley?
- How did the region's environment shape urban development?
- What functions do you think outposts such as Lothal played in Harappan society?

cities began to replace villages throughout the Indus River valley, and within a few generations towering granaries marked the urban skyline. Harappa and Mohenjo Daro, the two largest cities, each covered a little less than half a square mile and may have housed 35,000 residents. As in Mesopotamia, such population densities were unprecedented departures from the more common agrarian villages or nomadic communities, which remained self-sufficient.

Harappan cities sprawled across a vast floodplain covering 500,000 square miles—two or three times the Mesopotamian cultural zone. At the height of their development, the Harappan peoples reached the edge of the Indus ecological system and encountered the cultures of northern Afghanistan, the inhabitants of the desert frontier, the nomadic hunter-gatherers to the east, and the traders to the west.

Harappan City Life and Culture

We know less about Harappan culture than about other contemporary cultures of Afro-Eurasia, because many of its remains lie buried under deep silt deposits accumulated over thousands of years of heavy flooding. Further, scholars have been unable to identify the Indus peoples' language or decipher the script of about 400 symbols. The script might not represent a spoken language; instead, it might be a nonlinguistic symbol system. (See Primary Source: The Mystery of Harappan Writing.) Most of what remains is visible on a thousand or more stamp seals and small plaques excavated from the region, which may represent the names and titles of individuals rather than complete sentences. Moreover, because the Harappans did not produce King Lists (as the Mesopotamians and Egyptians did)—and may not even have had kings—scholars cannot chart a Harappan political history by tracing the rise and fall of dynasties and kingdoms.

We base our knowledge about Harappa on archaeological reconstructions, and these are sketchy. The sketchiness reminds us that "history" is not what happened but only *what we know about what happened*. Relying only on fragmentary archaeological evidence, scholars have been unable to draw the rich portraits of Harappan life that they have supplied for the Mesopotamians and the Egyptians.

What we know is impressive nonetheless. The layout of Harappan cities and towns followed a well-planned pattern: a fortified citadel housing public facilities, alongside a large

PRIMARY SOURCE

The Mystery of Harappan Writing

No one has deciphered the writing system of the Harappa culture in the Indus Valley. The Indus script appeared on seals and tablets—and in a recently discovered site, on a board for public display. Although no one is sure which language it represents, some of its characteristics provide scholars with fuel for speculation.

As for verbal communication through writing, it needs to be understood that no one has as yet succeeded in deciphering the Harappan script and that this will remain an unlikely eventuality unless a bilingual inscription—in Harappan and a known form of writing—is found, that incorporates the names of people or places. The Harappan script is logographic: there are 375 to 400 signs, which rules out an alphabet (where one sign stands for one vowel or consonant) because alphabets usually have no more than thirty-six signs. Often Harappan bangles or metal tools are inscribed with just one sign. Harappan writing goes from right to left, as can be made out from close examination of overlapping signs scratched on pots. Short strokes indicate numbers, and numerals precede other signs, which could mean that in the Harappan language adjectives preceded the nouns they qualified. Certain signs, computer concordances reveal, tend to occur frequently at the end of inscriptions, which points to a language using a set of phonetic suffixes.

The Harappan language was probably agglutinative, or a language which added suffixes to an unchanging root. This feature is characteristic of the Dravidian language family rather than the Indo-Aryan languages. This, and the fact that the earliest Indo-Aryan text, the *Rigveda*, shows Dravidian influence (indicating that the early Indo-Aryans in the northwest had some contact with Dravidian speakers), make it likely that the language of the Harappans was a Dravidian one. (Note, also, that Brahui, spoken in the hills of southern Baluchistan today, is a Dravidian language.)

The inscriptions on the seals being brief, on average five to six signs long, they probably gave little more than the owner's name and designation. Perhaps it was the pictorial (often solo animal) emblem, rendered with great skill, that indicated the lineage, ancestry, or social origins of the owner. There is no geographic pattern to the occurrence of the various seal animals (unicorn, bull, rhinoceros, antelope, tiger, or elephant), so the animal could not possibly have signified the place of origin of the seal owner. Perhaps it was this pictorial image that lent authority to any spoken message that accompanied a seal or an object stamped with one. It may be noted that so far it is Harappa and Mohenjo-daro—and mound E rather than the 'citadel mound' AB at Harappa—that have yielded the evidence for the most intensive writing activity. These were probably centres of administration.

Harappan writing occurs on pots, seals, terracotta (stoneware) and shell bangles, copper tablets and tools, and ivory rods. Large numbers of scored goblets with pointed bases that occur at Harappa and Mohenjo-daro are important as they are one of the very few pottery forms that can occasionally carry seal impressions (as distinct from scratched signs)—their use remains a mystery. We get the impression that writing was for humdrum purposes. A striking exception to this is the occurrence of a huge "public" inscription that seems to have been set up on a street at Dholavira in Kutch, with letters about 37 centimetres high cut out of stones and, R. S. Bisht suggests, fastened on a wooden board.

The most important point, however, is the enormous intellectual advance that the emergence of writing signifies. When we speak we utter sounds in one or another language using a series of sound sequences that carry specific meanings in that language. What writing does is to encode in visual form, that is, through a set of distinct symbols or signs, those sounds and sound sequences—thereby conveying meaning or information. Further, writing makes possible the storage of information or the maintenance of records for future reference. It makes communication at a distance possible. It requires of the writer knowledge of the signs and some amount of manual dexterity, and of the reader, knowledge of how the visual signs are vocalized and of course familiarity with the relevant language. Writing has been termed the most momentous invention human beings have ever made.

QUESTIONS FOR ANALYSIS

- Even though we cannot read Harappan script, why is the knowledge that the Harappans wrote in script important?
- Judging from the information above about Harappan writing, what language do you think the script most likely represents?

Source: Shereen Ratnagar, "The Mystery of Harappan Writing" from Understanding Harappa Civilization in the Greater Indus Valley *(New Delhi: Tulika Publishers, 2001), pp. 60–62.*

Mohenjo Daro. *Mohenjo Daro, the "mound of dead," is a large urban site of the Harappan culture. The view of the city demonstrates a neat layout of houses and civic facilities such as sewer draining.*

residential area. The main street running through the city had covered drainage on both sides, with house gates and doors opening onto back alleys. Citadels were likely centers of political and ritual activities. At the center of the citadel of Mohenjo Daro was the famous great bath, a brick structure 39.3 feet by 23 feet and 9.8 feet deep. Flights of steps led to the bottom of the bath, while other stairs went up to a level of rooms surrounding it. The bath was sealed with mortar and bitumen (a sticky, tarlike form of petroleum), and its water came from a large well nearby. The water drained out through a channel leading to lower land. The location, size, and quality of the structures all suggest that the bath was for public bathing rituals.

The Harappans used brick extensively—in houses for notables, city walls, and underground water drainage systems. Workers used large ovens to manufacture the durable construction materials, which the Harappans laid so skillfully that basic structures remain intact to this day. While common construction materials were used throughout Harappan communities, the differences in the size of dwellings, particularly in urban settings, suggests that social distinctions did exist within the society. A well-built house of a more wealthy family could be two to three stories high. It contained at least one interior courtyard, and had private bathrooms, showers, and toilets that drained into municipal sewers. More typical dwellings in the cities were one-room apartments with shared bathrooms. Houses in small towns and villages were made of less durable and less costly sun-baked bricks, which are used throughout southern Eurasia even today.

Harappan beliefs and religion are equally difficult to discern due to our inability to understand their writings. Scholars, however, have been able to draw some insights from the hundreds of seals and the symbols and images on those seals. Like many early agriculture-based societies, the Harappans were strongly concerned about fertility and other natural forces. The images on the seals quite often portrayed deities who displayed "mothering" qualities or blended human and animal characteristics, all of which suggested the importance of procreation. Trees and animals were also considered sacred. Scholars have long debated whether the similarities in Harappan and Hindu deities suggest that some Harappan deities survived the collapse of their society and live on today within Hinduism.

Trade

The Harappans engaged in trade along the Indus River, through the mountain passes to the Iranian plateau, and along the coast of the Arabian Sea as far as the Persian Gulf and Mesopotamia. They traded copper, flint, shells, and ivory, as well as pottery, flint blades, and jewelry created by their craftworkers, in exchange for gold, silver, gemstones, and textiles.

Some of the Harappan trading towns nestled in remote but strategically important places. Consider Lothal, a well-fortified port at the head of the Gulf of Khambhat (Cambay). Although distant from the center of Harappan society, it provided vital access to the sea and to valuable raw materials. Its many workshops

Harappan Seal Stamps. *The stamp seals of the Indus Valley culture are distinctive. Cut from the soft stone steatite and fired to a white color to make them hard, they have a rounded boss pierced for suspension on the back. The images carved on their surface are usually animals: elephants, tigers, bulls. Occasionally human figures, perhaps deities, perhaps rulers, are depicted seated on a platform, or dancing, or surrounded by animals. Many of the stamp seals have inscriptions across the top edge. The script of the Harappan people has not been deciphered, nor has its underlying language been identified.*

Harappan Gemstone Necklace. *Beadmakers perforated lapis lazuli and other semiprecious stones using a bow drill to make tiny holes for suspension.*

processed precious stones, both local and foreign. Because the demand for gemstones was high in Mesopotamia, the Harappans knew that controlling their extraction and trade was essential to maintaining economic power. Carnelian, a precious red stone, was a local resource, but lapis lazuli had to come from what is now northern Afghanistan. So the Harappans built fortifications and settlements near its sources. Extending their frontier did not stop at gemstones, however. Because metals such as copper and silver also had strategic commercial importance, the Harappans established settlements near their copper mines as well.

Through a complex and vibrant trading system, the Harappans maintained access to mineral and agrarian resources. To facilitate trade, rulers relied not just on Harappan script but also on a system of weights and measures that they devised and standardized. Archaeologists have found Harappan seals, used to stamp commodities with the names of their owners or the nature of the goods, at sites as far away as the Persian Gulf, Mesopotamia, and the Iranian plateau.

The general uniformity in Harappan sites suggests a centralized and structured state. Unlike the Mesopotamians and the Egyptians, however, the Harappans apparently built neither palaces, nor grand royal tombs, nor impressive monumental structures. The elites expressed their elaborate urban culture in ways that did not proclaim their high standing, with the exception, in some cases, of more substantial private homes. As a result, the Harappans were as unassuming as the Egyptians and Mesopotamians were boastful. This quality has puzzled scholars, but it underscores the profound differences in ancient societies: they did not all value the same things. The advent of writing, urban culture, long-distance trade, and large cities did not always produce the same social hierarchies and the same ethos (a set of principles governing social and political relations). What the Indus River people show us is how much the urbanized parts of the world were diverging from one another, even as they borrowed from and imitated their neighbors.

"THE GIFT OF THE NILE": EGYPT

The earliest inhabitants along the banks of the Nile River were a mixed people. Some had migrated from the eastern and western deserts in Sinai and Libya as these areas grew barren from climate change. Others came from the Mediterranean. Equally important were peoples who trekked northward from Nubia and central Africa. Ancient Egypt was a melting pot where immigrants blended cultural practices and technologies.

Egypt had much in common with Mesopotamia and the Indus Valley. Like them, it had densely populated areas whose inhabitants depended on irrigation, gave their rulers immense authority, and created a complex social order. Like the Mesopotamians, they built monumental architecture. Tapping the Nile waters gave rise to agrarian wealth, commercial and devotional centers, early states, and new techniques of communication.

Yet the ancient Egyptian culture was profoundly distinct from its contemporaries in Mesopotamia and the Indus Valley. To understand its unique qualities, we must begin with its geography. The environment and the natural boundaries of deserts, river rapids, and sea dominated the country and its inhabitants. The core area of ancient Egypt covered 386,560 square miles, of which only 11,720 square miles (7.5 million acres) were cultivable. Of this total, roughly 6 million acres were in the Nile delta—the rich alluvial land lying between the river's two main branches as it flows north of modern-day Cairo into the Mediterranean Sea.

The Nile River and Its Floodwaters

Knowing Egypt requires appreciating the pulses of the Nile. The world's longest river, it stretches 4,238 miles from its sources in the highlands of central Africa to its destination in the Mediterranean Sea. In this way (and many others), Egypt was deeply attached to sub-Saharan Africa. Not only did its life-giving irrigation waters and rich silt deposits come from the African highlands, but much of its original population had migrated into the Nile valley from the west and the south millennia earlier.

The Upper Nile is a sluggish river that cuts through the Sahara Desert. Rising out of central Africa and Ethiopia, its two main branches—the White and Blue Niles—meet at present-day Khartoum and then scour out a single riverbed 1,500 miles long to the Mediterranean. The annual floods gave the basin regular moisture and alluvial richness. Although the Nile's floodwaters did not fertilize or irrigate fields as broad as those in Mesopotamia or the Indus Valley, they created green belts flanking the broad waterway. These gave rise to a society whose culture stretched along the navigable river and its carefully preserved banks. Away from the riverbanks, on both sides, lay a desert rich in raw materials but largely uninhabited. Egypt had no fertile hinterland like the sprawling plains of Mesopotamia and the Indus Valley. In a sense, Egypt was the most "riverine" of the riverine cultures.

The Nile's predictability as the source of life and abundance shaped the character of the people and their culture. In contrast to the wild and uncertain Euphrates and Tigris rivers, the Nile was gentle and bountiful, leading Egyptians to view the world as beneficent. During the summer as the Nile swelled, local villagers built earthen walls that divided the floodplain into basins. By trapping the floodwaters, these basins captured the rich silt washing down from the Ethiopian highlands. Annual flooding meant that the land received a new layer of topsoil every year.

Nile Agriculture. *The Nile is fed by the Blue Nile, which has its source in the Ethiopian highlands, and the White Nile in southern Sudan. It rises and falls according to a regular pattern that was the basis for the ancient Egyptian agricultural cycle. Flooding the valley in August and September, the Nile recedes, depositing a rich layer of silt in which the crops were planted in the fall and harvested in April and May.*

The light, fertile soils made planting simple. Peasants cast seeds into the alluvial soil and then had their livestock trample them to the proper depth. The never-failing sun, which the Egyptians worshipped, ensured an abundant harvest. In the early spring, when the Nile's waters were at their lowest and no crops were under cultivation, the sun dried out the soil.

Egypt's Unique Riverine Culture

The peculiarities of the Nile region distinguished it from Mesopotamia and the Indus Valley. Some 2,500 years ago, the Greek historian and geographer Herodotus noted that Egypt was the gift of the Nile and that the entire length of its basin was one of the world's most self-contained geographical entities. Bounded on the north by the Mediterranean Sea, on the east and west by deserts, and on the south by cataracts (large waterfalls), Egypt was destined to achieve a common culture. The region was far less open to outsiders than were Mesopotamia and the Indus River basin.

Like the other pioneering societies, Egypt created a common culture by balancing regional tensions and reconciling regional rivalries. Ancient Egyptian history is a struggle of opposing forces: the north or Lower Egypt versus the south or Upper Egypt; the sand, the so-called red part of the earth, versus the rich soil, described as black; life versus death; heaven versus earth; order versus disorder. For Egypt's ruling groups—notably the kings—the primary task was to bring stability or order, known as *ma'at*, out of these antagonistic impulses. The Egyptians believed that keeping chaos, personified by the desert and its marauders, at bay through attention to *ma'at* would allow all that was good and right to occur.

The Rise of the Egyptian State and Dynasties

Once the early Egyptians harnessed the Nile to agriculture, the area changed from being scarcely inhabited to socially complex. Whereas Mesopotamia and Harappa developed gradually, Egypt seemed to grow overnight. It quickly became a powerhouse state, projecting its splendor along the full length of the river valley.

A king, called pharaoh, was at the center of Egyptian life. His primary responsibility was to ensure that the forces of nature, in particular the regular flooding of the Nile, continued without interruption. This task had more to do with appeasing the gods than with running a complex hydraulic system—hence, Egypt's large clerical class. The king also had to protect his people from invaders from the eastern and western deserts, as well as from Nubians on the southern borders. These groups threatened Egypt with social chaos. As guarantors of the social and political order, the early kings depicted themselves as shepherds. In wall carvings, artists portrayed them carrying the crook and the flail, indicating their responsibility for the welfare of their flocks (the people) and of the land. Moreover, under the king an elaborate bureaucracy organized labor and produced public works, sustaining both his vast holdings and general order throughout the realm.

The narrative of ancient Egyptian history follows its dynasties—a structure that gives a sense of deep continuity. According to a third-century BCE Egyptian cleric named Manetho, Egypt saw no fewer than thirty-one dynasties, spanning three millennia from 3100 BCE down to its conquest by Alexander the Great in 332 BCE. (See Table 2.1.) Since the nineteenth century, however, scholars have recast the story around three periods of dynastic achievement: the Old Kingdom, the Middle Kingdom, and the New Kingdom. At the end of each era, cultural flourishing suffered a breakdown in central authority, known respectively as the First, Second, and Third Intermediate Periods.

Rituals, Pyramids, and Cosmic Order

The Third Dynasty (2686–2613 BCE) launched the foundational period known as the Old Kingdom, the golden age of ancient Egypt. (See Map 2.5.) By the time it began, the basic

TABLE 2.1 | Dynasties of Ancient Egypt

SPECIES	TIME
Pre-dynastic Period dynasties I and II	3100–2686 BCE
Old Kingdom dynasties III–VI	2686–2181 BCE
First Intermediate Period dynasties VII–X	2181–2055 BCE
Middle Kingdom dynasties XI–XIII	2055–1650 BCE
Second Intermediate Period dynasties XIV–XVII	1650–1550 BCE
New Kingdom dynasties XVIII–XX	1550–1069 BCE
Third Intermediate Period dynasties XXI–XXV	1069–747 BCE
Late Period dynasties XXVI–XXXI	747–332 BCE

Source: Compiled from Ian Shaw and Paul Nicholson, eds., The Dictionary of Ancient Egypt *(1995), pp. 310–11.*

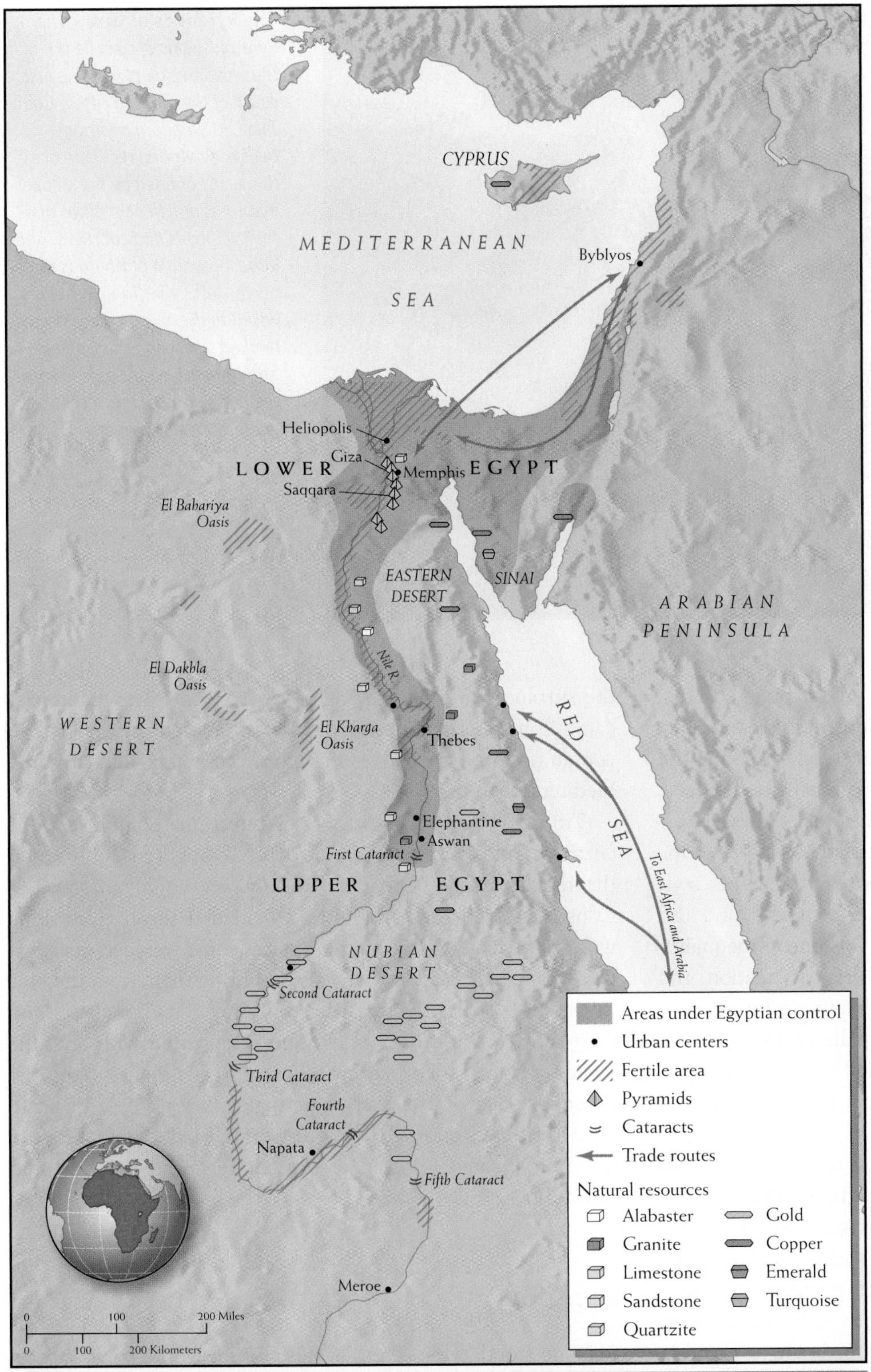

MAP 2.5 | Old Kingdom Egypt, 2686–2181 BCE

Old Kingdom Egyptian society reflected a strong influence from its unique geographical location.

- What geographical features contributed to Egypt's isolation from the outside world and the people's sense of their unity?
- What natural resource enabled the Egyptians to build the Great Pyramids?
- Based on the map, why do you think it was important for upper and lower Egypt to be united?

institutions of the Egyptian state were in place, as were the ideology and ritual life that legitimized the dynastic rulers.

The king as god presented himself to the population by means of impressive architectural spaces, and the priestly class performed rituals reinforcing his supreme status within the universe's natural order. The most important ceremony was the Sed festival, which renewed the king's vitality after he had ruled for thirty years. Although it focused on the king's well-being, its origins lay in ensuring the perpetual presence of water.

King Djoser, the second king of the Third Dynasty, celebrated the Sed festival in his tomb complex at Saqqara. This magnificent complex, the world's oldest stone structure (rather than the mud-brick temples and palaces of Mesopotamia), took shape during his reign. It began as a huge flat structure identical to earlier royal tombs. However, the architect, Imhotep, was not satisfied with the modest shape of earlier burial chambers. Throughout six renovations he transformed the structure into a step pyramid that ultimately rose some 200 feet above the plain, dominating the landscape like the later Mesopotamian ziggurats did (see p. 53). This mountainlike structure stood at the center of an enormous walled precinct housing five courts where the king performed rituals emphasizing the divinity of kingship and the unity of Upper and Lower Egypt. Because most of the structures were facades, the whole complex became a stage for state rituals. The symbolism of the unity of Upper and Lower Egypt was pervasive, embodied in the entwined lotus and papyrus—symbols of each region. The step pyramid complex incorporated artistic and architectural forms that would characterize Egyptian culture for millennia.

The Egyptian pharaoh—the king as god—used the royal tomb to embody

The Pyramids of Giza. *The Pyramid Fields of Giza lie on the western side of the Nile just south of the modern city of Cairo. The Old Kingdom pharaohs built their eternal resting places there, surrounded by the smaller pyramids and bench tombs of their relatives and courtiers. The largest pyramid of Khufu is to the north (left). Khafra's (right) is linked to the Nile by a causeway flanked by the famous Sphinx. The smallest is that of Menkaure, the penultimate king of the glorious Fourth Dynasty.*

the state's ideology and the principles of the Egyptian cosmos. The ritual of death, leading to everlasting life, became part of the cultural myth. So did a common ideology stressing the unity of the long river valley's distinct regions. The pharaoh also employed symbols (for example, the dual crown representing Upper and Lower Egypt), throne names, and descriptive titles for himself and his advisers to represent his own power and that of his administrators, the priests, and the landed elite. The Egyptian cosmic order was one of inequality and stark hierarchy. Established at the time of creation, the universe was the king's responsibility to maintain for eternity. The belief that the king was a god compelled him to behave like one: serene, orderly, merciful, and perfect. He always had to wear an expression of divine peace, not the angry snarl of mere human power.

Pyramid building evolved rapidly from the step version of Djoser to the grand pyramids of the Fourth Dynasty (2613–2494 BCE). These kings erected their magnificent structures at Giza, just outside modern-day Cairo and not far from the early royal cemetery site of Saqqara. The pyramid of Khufu, rising 481 feet above ground, is the largest stone structure in the world, and its corners are almost perfectly aligned to due north, west, south, and east. Khafra's pyramid, though smaller, is even more alluring because it retains some of its original limestone casing and because it enjoys the protective presence of the sphinx. Surrounding these royal tombs were those of high officials, almost all members of the royal family. The enormous amount of labor involved in constructing these monuments provides another measure of the degree of centralization and the surpluses in Egyptian society at this time. The manpower came from peasants and workers who labored for the state at certain times of year, slaves brought from Nubia, and captured Mediterranean peoples.

Through their majesty and architectural complexity, the Giza pyramids reflect the peak of Old Kingdom culture and the remarkable feats that its bureaucracy could accomplish. Construction of these monuments entailed the backbreaking work of quarrying the massive stones (some weighed over two tons), digging a canal so barges could bring them from the Nile to the base of the Giza plateau, building a harbor there, and then constructing sturdy brick ramps that could withstand the stones' weight as workers hauled them ever higher along the pyramids' faces. Most likely a permanent work force of up to 21,000 laborers endured 10-hour workdays, 300 days per year, for approximately 14 years just to complete the great pyramid of Khufu.

Religion

Religion stood at the center of this ancient world, so all aspects of the culture reflected spiritual expression. Egyptians understood their world as inhabited by three groups: gods, kings, and the rest of humanity. Official records only showed representations of gods and kings. Yet the people did not confuse their kings with gods—at least during the kings' lifetimes. Mortality was the bar between rulers and deities; after death, kings joined the gods whom they had represented while alive.

Egyptian Gods. *Osiris (left) is the dying god who rules over the netherworld. Most frequently he is depicted as a mummy wearing a white crown with plumes and holding the scepter across his chest. The god Horus (right), who was also rendered as Ra-Horakhty, is the falcon-headed Egyptian sky god. Horus is the earliest state god of Egypt and is always closely associated with the king. Horus is a member of the nine deities of Heliopolis and is the son of Osiris and Isis.*

CULTS OF THE GODS As in Mesopotamia, every region in Egypt had its resident god. The fate of each deity found expression in the history of its region. Some gods, such as Amun (believed to be physically present in Thebes, the political center of Upper Egypt), came to transcend regional status because of the importance of their hometown. Over the centuries the Egyptian gods evolved, combining often-contradictory aspects into single deities represented by symbols: animals and human figures that often had animal as well as divine attributes. They included Horus, the hawk god; Osiris, the god of regeneration and the underworld; Hathor, the goddess of childbirth and love; Ra, the sun god; and Amun, a creator considered to be the hidden god.

Official religious practices took place in the main temples, the heart of ceremonial events. The king and his agents cared for the gods in their temples, giving them respect, adoration, and thanks. In return the gods, embodied in sculptured images, maintained order and nurtured the king and—through him—all humanity. In this contractual relationship, the gods were passive and serene while the kings were active, a difference that reflected their unequal relationship. The practice of religious rituals and communication with the gods formed the cult, whose constant and correct performance was the foundation of Egyptian religion. Its goal was to preserve cosmic order fundamental to creation and prosperity.

One of the most enduring cults was that of the goddess Isis, who represented ideals of sisterhood and motherhood. According to Egyptian mythology, Isis, the wife of the murdered and dismembered Osiris, commanded her son, Horus, to reassemble all of the parts of Osiris so that he might reclaim his rightful place as king of Egypt, taken from him by his assassin, his evil brother Seth. Osiris was seen as the god of rebirth, while Isis was renowned for her medicinal skills and knowledge of magic. For millennia her principal place of worship was a magnificent temple on the island of Philae. Well after the Greeks and Romans had conquered Egypt, the people continued to pay homage to Isis at her Philae temple.

THE PRIESTHOOD The responsibility for upholding cults fell to the king. However, the task of upholding the cult, regulating rituals according to a cosmic calendar, and mediating among gods, kings, and society fell to one specialist class: the priesthood. Creating this class required elaborate rules for selecting and training the priests to project the organized power of spiritual authority. The fact that only the priests could enter the temple's inner sanctum demonstrated their exalted status. The god, embodied in the cult statue, left the temple only at great festivals. Even then the divine image remained hidden in a portable shrine. This arrangement ensured that priests monopolized communication between spiritual powers and their subjects—and that Egyptians understood their own subservience to the priesthood.

Although the priesthood helped unify the Egyptians and focused their attention on the central role of temple life, unofficial religion was equally important. Ordinary ancient Egyptians matched their elite rulers in faithfulness to the gods, but their distance from temple life caused them to find different ways to fulfill their religious needs and duties. Thus they visited local shrines, just as those of higher status visited the temples. There they prayed, made requests, and left offerings to the gods.

MAGICAL POWERS Magic had a special importance for commoners, who believed that amulets (ornaments worn to bring good fortune and to protect against evil forces) held extraordinary powers—for example, preventing illness and guaranteeing safe childbirth. To deal with profound questions, commoners looked to omens and divination (a practice that residents of Mesopotamia and ancient China also used to predict and control future events). Like the elites, commoners attributed supernatural powers to animals. Chosen animals received special treatment in life and after death: for example, the Egyptians adored cats, whom they kept as pets and whose image they used to represent certain deities. Apis bulls, sacred to the god Ptah, merited special cemeteries and mourning rituals. Ibises, dogs, jackals, baboons, lizards, fish, snakes, crocodiles, and other beasts associated with deities enjoyed similar privileges.

Writing and Scribes

Egypt, like Mesopotamia, was a scribal culture. Egyptians often said that peasants toiled so that scribes could live in comfort; in other words, literacy sharpened the divisions between rural and urban worlds. By the middle of the third millennium BCE, literacy was well established among small circles of experts in Egypt and Mesopotamia. The fact that few individuals were literate heightened the scribes' social status. Although in both cultures writing emerged in response to economic needs, people soon grasped its utility for commemorative and religious purposes. As soon as literacy took hold, Mesopotamians and Egyptians were drafting historical records and literary compositions.

Both the early Mesopotamian and Egyptian scripts were complex. In fact, one feature of all writing systems is that over time they became simpler and more efficient at representing the

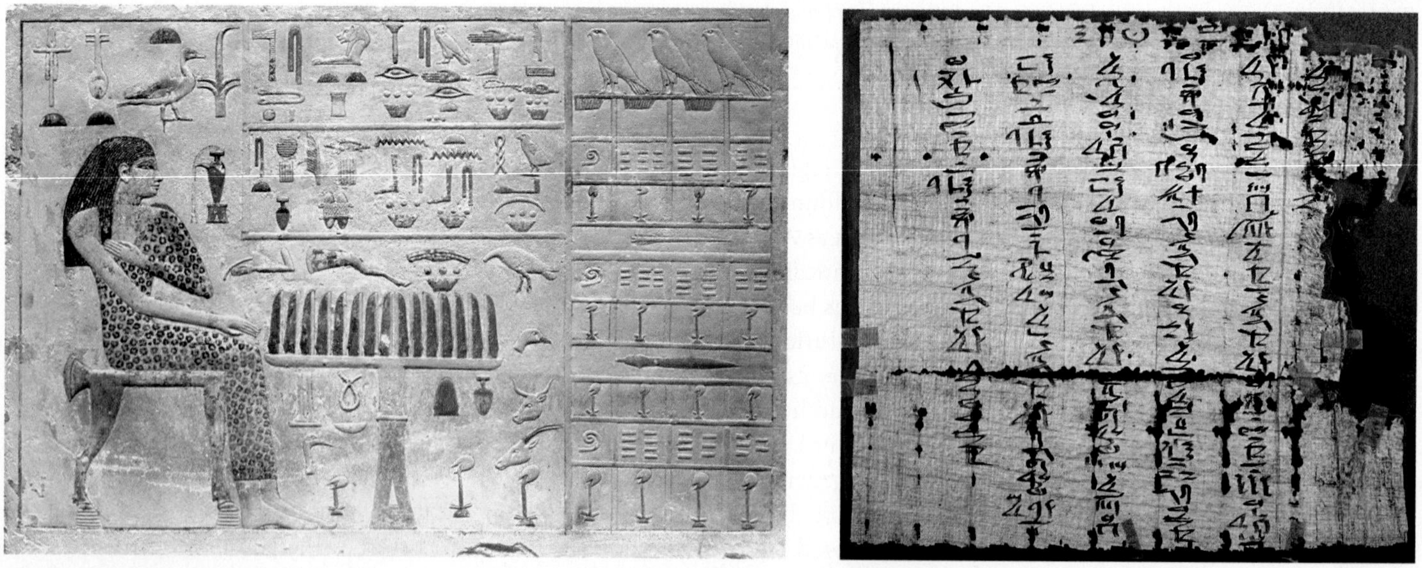

Egyptian Hieroglyphs and "Cursive Script." *The Egyptians wrote in two distinctive types of script (left). The more formal is hieroglyphs, which is based on pictorial images that carry values of either ideas (idiograms) or sounds (phonemes). All royal and funerary inscriptions, such as this funerary relief from the Old Kingdom, are rendered in hieroglyphic script. Daily documents, accountings, literary texts, and the like were most often written in a cursive script called demotic, which was written with ink on papyrus (right). The form of the cursive signs is based on the hieroglyphs but is more abstract and can be formed more quickly.*

full range of spoken utterances. Only when the first alphabet appeared (in Southwest Asia, to record Aramaic around 1500 BCE) did the potential for wider literacy surface. To judge from remaining records, it seems that more Egyptians than Mesopotamians were literate. Most high-ranking Egyptians were also trained as scribes working in the king's court, the army, or the priesthood. Some kings and members of the royal family learned to write as well.

Egyptians used two basic forms of writing throughout antiquity. *Hieroglyphs* (from the Greek "sacred carving") served in temple, royal, or divine contexts. First Dynasty tombs yield records in a cursive script written with ink on papyrus, pottery, or other absorbent media. This *demotic writing* (from the Greek *demotika*, meaning "popular" or "in common use") was more common. Used for record keeping, it also found uses in letters and works of literature—including narrative fiction, manuals of instruction and philosophy, cult and religious hymns, love poems, medical and mathematical texts, collections of rituals, and mortuary books.

Becoming literate involved taking lessons from scribes, and these skills clustered in extended families. Most students started training when they were young, before entering the bureaucracy. After mastering the copying of standard texts in demotic cursive or hieroglyphs, students moved on to literary works. The upper classes prized the ability to read and write, regarding it as proof of high intellectual achievement. When they died, they had their student textbooks placed alongside their corpses as evidence of their talents. The literati produced texts mainly in temples, where these works were also preserved. Writing in hieroglyphs and transmitting texts continued without break in ancient Egypt for almost 3,000 years.

The Prosperity of Egypt

The agrarian surpluses, urbanization, elaborate belief systems, population growth, and splendor that characterized Mesopotamian, Harappan, and Egyptian societies led to heightened standards of living and rising populations. Under pharaonic rule, Egypt enjoyed spectacular prosperity. Its population grew at an unprecedented rate, swelling from 350,000 in 4000 BCE to 1 million in 2500 BCE and nearly 5 million by 1500 BCE.

The state's success depended on administering resources skillfully, especially agricultural production and labor. Everyone, from the most powerful elite to the workers in the field, was part of the system. In principle, no one possessed private property; in practice, Egyptians treated land and tools as their own—but submitted to the intrusions of the state. No one challenged the state's control, especially over taxation, prices, and the distribution of goods. Such control required a large bureaucracy that maintained records, taxed the population, appeased the gods, organized a strong military, and aided local officials in regulating the Nile's floodwaters.

Later Dynasties and Their Demise

As the Old Kingdom expanded without a uniting or dominating city like those of Mesopotamia or Harappa, the Egyptian state became more dispersed and the dynasties began to look increasingly outward. Expansion and decentralization eventually exposed the dynasties' weaknesses. The shakeup resulted not from external invasion (as in the Indus Valley) or bickering between rival city-states (as in Mesopotamia), but from feuding among elite political factions. In addition, an extended drought strained Egypt's extensive irrigation system, which could no longer water the lands that fed the region's million inhabitants. Imagery of great suffering filled the royal tombs' walls. The long reign of Pepy II (2278–2184 BCE) marked the end of the Old Kingdom. Upon his death, royal power collapsed. (See Primary Source: The Admonitions of Ipuwer.) For the next hundred years, rivals jostled for the throne. Local magnates assumed hereditary control of the government in the provinces and treated lands previously controlled by the royal family as their personal property. And local leaders plunged into bloody regional struggles to keep the irrigation works functioning for their own communities. This so-called First Intermediate Period lasted roughly from 2181 to 2055 BCE, until the century-long drought ended.

THE YELLOW AND YANGZI RIVER BASINS: EAST ASIA

Like the Mesopotamians and Egyptians, East Asian peoples clustered in river basins. Their settlements along the Yellow River in the north and the Yangzi River in the south became the foundation of the future Chinese state. By 5000 BCE, both millet in the north and rice in the south were under widespread cultivation.

Yet in the following three millennia (when Mesopotamia, Egypt, and the Indus Valley were developing complex, city-based cultures) the Chinese moved slowly. China's great riverine cultures did not arise until the second millennium BCE. (See Map 2.6.) Like the other regions' waterways, the Yellow and Yangzi rivers had annual floods and extensive floodplains suitable for producing high agricultural yields and supporting dense populations. In China, however, the evolution of hydraulic works, big cities, priestly and bureaucratic classes, and a new writing system took longer.

PRIMARY SOURCE

The Admonitions of Ipuwer

In order to maintain power during a period of increasing drought, Pepy II (r. 2278–2184 BCE) gave many advantages and tax exemptions to provincial nobles. At the end of his long reign, no successors were capable of maintaining centralized power. The collapse of the central state was traumatic, and Egyptian society fell into chaos. A number of poignant texts written by prophets and wise men captured this situation. One of the most moving was the text known as the Ipuwer Papyrus, written by an Egyptian sage.

Behold, the fire has gone up on high, and its burning goes forth against the enemies of the land.

Behold, things have been done which have not happened for a long time past; the king has been deposed by the rabble.

Behold, he who was buried as a falcon [is devoid] of biers, and what the pyramid concealed has become empty.

Behold, it has befallen that the land has been deprived of the kingship by a few lawless men.

Behold, men have fallen into rebellion against the Uraeus, the [. . .] of Re, even she who makes the Two Lands content.

Behold, the secret of the land whose limits were unknown is divulged, and the Residence is thrown down in a moment.

Behold, Egypt is fallen to pouring of water, and he who poured water on the ground has carried off the strong man in misery.

Behold, the Serpent is taken from its hole, and the secrets of the Kings of Upper and Lower Egypt are divulged.

Behold, the Residence is afraid because of want, and [men go about] unopposed to stir up strife.

Behold, the land has knotted itself up with confederacies, and the coward takes the brave man's property.

Behold, the Serpent [. . .] the dead: he who could not make a sarcophagus for himself is now the possessor of a tomb.

Behold, the possessors of tombs are ejected on to the high ground, while he who could not make a coffin for himself is now [the possessor] of a treasury.

Behold, this has happened [to] men; he who could not build a room for himself is now a possessor of walls.

Behold, the magistrates of the land are driven out throughout the land: [. . .] are driven out from the palaces.

Behold, noble ladies are now on rafts, and magnates are in the labor establishment, while he who could not sleep even on walls is now the possessor of a bed.

Behold, the possessor of wealth now spends the night thirsty, while he who once begged his dregs for himself is now the possessor of overflowing bowls.

Behold, the possessors of robes are now in rags, while he who could not weave for himself is now a possessor of fine linen.

Behold, he who could not build a boat for himself is now the possessor of a fleet; their erstwhile owner looks at them, but they are not his.

Behold, he who had no shade is now the possessor of shade, while the erstwhile possessors of shade are now in the full blast of the storm.

Behold, he who was ignorant of the lyre is now the possessor of a harp, while he who never sang for himself now vaunts the Songstress-goddess.

QUESTIONS FOR ANALYSIS

- In this reading, the "Residence" is the palace and the "Two Lands" are Upper and Lower Egypt. Who do you think "he who was buried as a falcon" is?
- What were the effects of the collapse of Egypt's Old Kingdom?
- How can we use such a document as "The Admonitions of Ipuwer" to understand conditions in Egypt at this time?

Source: James B. Pritchard, ed., "The Admonitions of Ipuwer" from Ancient Near Eastern Texts Relating to the Old Testament, *Third Edition with Supplement.*

Living conditions and the environment played a key role in ancient Chinese society, just as they did in the riverine cultures of Mesopotamia, Harappa, and Egypt. In the river basins of China, abundant food and the fact that communities were widely dispersed encouraged the development of localized agrarian cultures. Complex cities would come later. Also contributing to their different development were a lack of easily domesticated animals and plants and an abundance of geographic barriers. Geography isolated China, for the Himalayan Mountains and the Taklamakan and Gobi deserts prevented large-scale migrations between East Asia and central Asia and hindered the diffusion of cultural breakthroughs occurring elsewhere in Afro-Eurasia.

From Yangshao to Longshan Culture

China's classical histories have claimed that China's cultural traditions originated in the Central Plains of the Yellow River basin and spread outward to less developed regions inside and even beyond mainland China. This location, seen by many as the birthplace of China's imperial traditions, was thought to have exercised a civilizing influence on these other communities. These histories place the beginnings of Chinese culture at the Xia dynasty, dating from 2200 BCE. Archaeological studies of riverine environments in East Asia tell a different story, however. Whether or not the Xia existed as a historical dynasty, archaeological evidence suggests our study of the Yellow River basin and Yangzi delta should begin earlier—in the two millennia from 4000 to 2000 BCE.

China in 4000 BCE was very different geographically and culturally from what it is today. A warmer and moister climate divided its vast landmass into quite distinctive and separate regions. The Shandong Peninsula was an island separated from mainland China. Lakes abounded in southern Manchuria and southern Mongolia, and the Central Plains was a smaller area than it is today. Only after a long cycle of cooler and drier weather did these bodies of water dry up and the landmass become a single geographical unit. Recent archaeological research records that at least eight distinct regional cultures appeared between 4000 and 2000 BCE, and only as these communities interacted did their institutions and ways of life come together to create a unified Chinese culture that in time produced the Han Empire (see Chapter 7).

In addition to being geographically and culturally divided, China was never devoid of outside influences. Unlike the Americas, East Asia was not separated from the rest of Afro-Eurasia by great oceans. Some travelers did arrive via the ocean, but more came via the Mongolian steppe, through which nomads introduced important technologies such as metal works. Nomads were drawn to the agricultural settlements (as they were in Mesopotamia), and they brought innovations, bronze, and other goods from the west. Through trade and migration, nomadic cultures and technologies filtered from the steppes to settled communities on the rivers.

Yangshao Bowl with Dancing Figures, c. 5000–1700 BCE. *The Yangshao, also referred to as the "painted pottery" culture, produced gray or red pottery painted with black geometric designs and occasionally with pictures of fish or human faces and figures. Because the potter's wheel was unknown at the time, the vessels were probably fashioned with strips of clay.*

The major divide in China was between the Yellow and Yangzi river basins. Not only did these two regions rely on different crops—millet in the north and rice in the south—but they built their houses differently, buried their dead in different ways, and produced distinctive pottery styles. The best known of these early cultures developed along the Yellow River and in the Central Plains area and is known as the Yongshao culture. Although it began on a small scale, in time it extended its influence northward to the present-day provinces of Qinghan and Gansu. Yangshao villages covered ten to fourteen acres and were composed of houses erected around a central square. Villagers had to move frequently because they practiced slash-and-burn agriculture. Once having exhausted the soil, residents picked up their belongings, moved to new lands, and constructed new villages. Their lives were hard ones. Excavated cemeteries reveal that nearly twenty percent of the burials were of children fifteen years and younger; only a little more than half of those buried lived past the age of forty. Markings found on red pottery near the village of Yangshao along the Yellow River also indicate that some residents were proficient in manipulating signs and symbols from as early as 5000 BCE. Yet writing, such as that developed by the Sumerians, did not appear until much later. Nevertheless, shamans in the emerging villages of the fourth and third millennia BCE may have used signs in performing rituals, music, and healing, as well as in divination.

Around 3000 BCE the Yangshao culture gave way to the Longshan culture, which had an even larger geographical scope and would provide some of the cultural foundations for the first strong states that emerged in the Central Plains. Longshan flourished from 3000 BCE to 2000 BCE, having its center in Shandong Province. Although the Longshan way of life first took form in coastal and southern China, outside the Central Plains, it moved quickly into this hub of economic and political activity. Proof of its widespread cultural influence can be seen from the appearance of a unique style of black pottery, stretching all the way from Manchuria in the north through the Central Plains to the coast and beyond to the island of Taiwan. (See Primary Source: Archaeological Evidence for the Longshan Culture.) Near the village of Longshan itself in Shandong province on the North China plain, for example, archaeologists discovered polished black pottery and a complete town enclosure

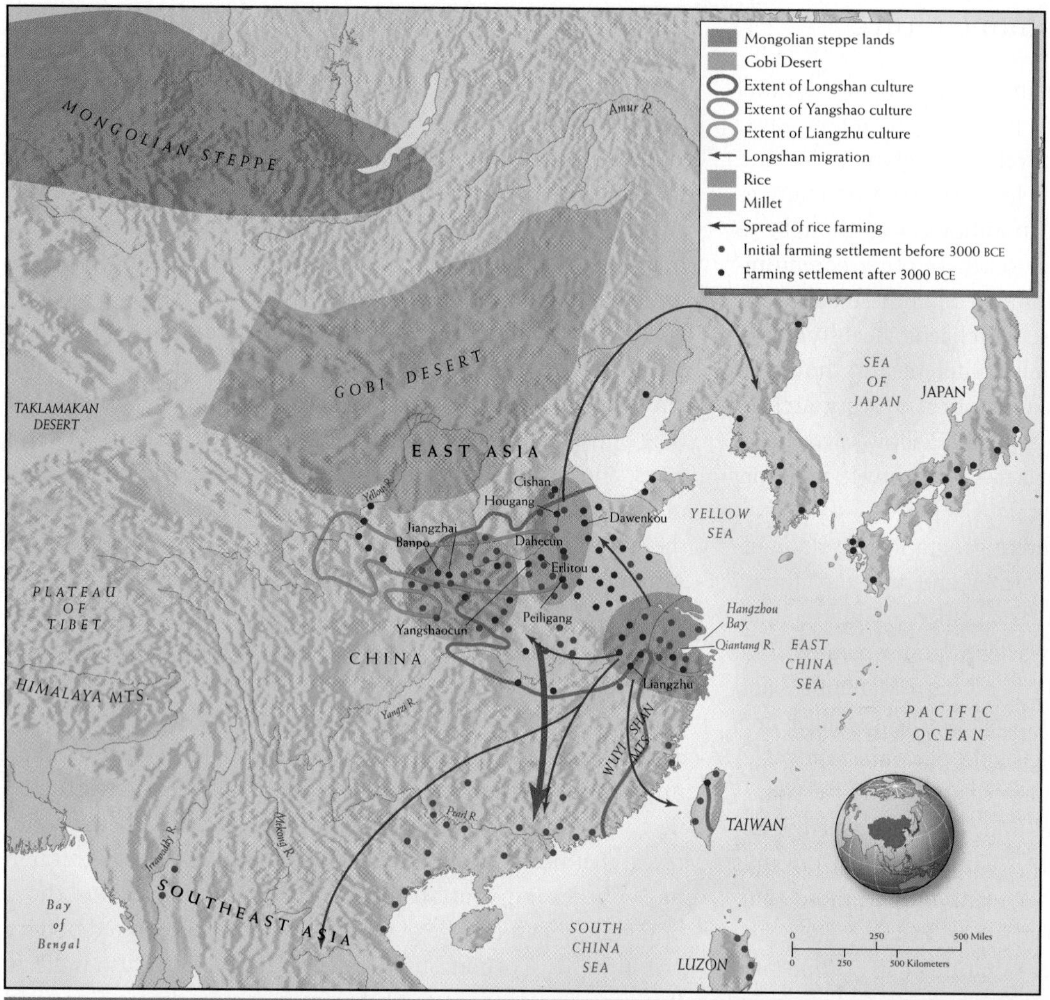

MAP 2.6 | Riverine Peoples in East Asia, 5000–2000 BCE

Complex agricultural societies emerged in East Asia during the third millennium BCE.

- What were the regional cultures that flourished here during this time?
- What are the major geographic differences between the northern and southern regions of China in this period?
- Based on geographic differences among the areas, how were these cultures different, and how were they similar?

of compacted earth. Such finds contrast with the simpler artifacts of the Yangshao sites. Furthermore, Longshan residents burned deer scapulas (shoulder blades) so that diviners could interpret the cracks that formed. This ritual probably gave rise to the inscribed oracle bones introduced later during the Shang dynasty (1600–1045 BCE), which diviners consulted for advice from ancestors when making important decisions.

The Longshan people likely migrated in waves from the peripheries of East Asia to the eastern China seashore. Their achievements, compared to those of the Yangshao, suggest marked development between 5000 and 2000 BCE. Several independent regional cultures in northern and southern China began to produce similar pottery and tools and to plant the same crops, probably reflecting contact. They did not yet produce city-states, but agriculture and small settlements flourished in the increasingly populated Yellow River valley.

Some of the hallmarks of early urban life are evident. For example, the Longshan buried their dead in cemeteries outside their villages. Of several thousand graves uncovered in southern Shanxi province, the largest ones contain ritual pottery vessels, wooden musical instruments, copper bells, and painted murals. Shamans performed rituals using jade axes. Jade quarrying in particular indicated technical sophistication, as skilled craftworkers incised jade tablets with powerful expressions of ritual and military authority. The recent discovery of a Longshan household whose members were scalped demonstrates the danger of organized violence. Attackers filled the water wells with five layers of human skeletons, some decapitated. Clearly, the villages' defensive walls were essential.

As communities became more centralized, contact between regions increased. Links between northern and southern China arose when Longshan peoples began to migrate along the East Asian coast to Taiwan and the Pearl River delta in the far south. Similarities in artifacts found along the coast and at Longshan sites in northern China, such as the form and decoration of pottery and jade items, also point to a shared sphere of culture and trade. (See Primary Source: Archaeological Evidence for Longshan Culture.)

Archaeologists also have found evidence of short-lived political organizations. Although they were nothing like the dynastic systems in Egypt, Mesopotamia, and the Indus Valley, they were wealthy—if localized—polities. They constituted what scholars call the era of Ten Thousand States (*Wan'guo*). One of them, the Liangzhu, has drawn particular interest for its remarkable jade objects and its sophisticated farmers, who grew rice and fruits. The Liangzhu domesticated water buffalo, pigs, dogs, and

PRIMARY SOURCE

Archaeological Evidence for Longshan Culture

Over the course of a millennium, multiple cultures with strong similarities emerged in north and northwest China. Some scholars argue that a single Longshan culture grew out of these close-knit groups. While these were not fully integrated spheres interacting with one another, the changes that Longshan represented were remarkable.

Let us take a quick look at the kind of innovations that sprouted everywhere and that, because of the similarities of style, must be interrelated:

1. Archaeologically acceptable evidence of copper objects, mostly trinkets and small tools of no agricultural value, has been unearthed in Shantung, western Honan, southern Shansi, and Ch'i-chia from archaeological horizons comparable in age. The finds do not suffice to point to a major metal industry as yet, but in light of what happened later on one must regard the Lung-shan metallurgy as worthy of note. . . .

2. Industrially much more important is the extremely widespread use of potter's wheels for the manufacture of ceramics. There was tremendous variation in the pottery wares of the various Lung-shan cultures, but the overwhelming change from red to gray and the general decline of painted decoration must have been the result of a conscious choice on the part of the potters, who, armed with improved kilns and the wheel, must have represented a specialized profession in the Lung-shan society.

3. The stamped-earth construction technology and the construction of town walls using that technology are separate issues, but the town walls in Shantung, east Honan, north Honan, and west Honan indicate both the transmission of a technology and the rise of the necessity for defensive public works.

4. Related to the rise of defensive ramparts is the archaeological evidence of institutionalized violence. This takes two forms—evidence of raids or wars, such as the Chien-kou-ts'un finds of skulls and bodies in the water well; and burials of possible ritual victims relating to the construction of chiefly or royal monuments.

5. There are several manifestations of rituals, especially ones closely tied to persons of high political status. The first is the role of some animals and birds in ritual art, such as those found or identified recently in Liang-ch'eng, Shantung; the Liang-chu sites, in Kiangsu and Chekiang; and T'ao-ssu, Shansi.

6. The *ts'ung* tube, especially if associated with animals and birds, is a very distinctive ritual object manifesting a unique cosmology. Its discovery in Liang-chu on the coast and T'ao-ssu in the interior cannot be accidental; it indicates without question an interregional transmission of cosmology or even a spherewide substratum featuring that cosmology. If we include jade rings (*pi*) in this cosmological bag, the Ch'i-chia Culture also becomes involved.

7. The virtually universal occurrence of scapulimancy among the Lung-shan cultures is another manifestation of the spherewide communication or substratum of cosmology.

8. The archaeological evidence for violence and for ritual on an institutional basis almost inevitably means a society featuring sharp political and economic divisions, and that is exactly what we find in the mortuary remains of many of the Lung-shan cultures. We have already seen archaeological indications of social ranking in the mortuary remains of the Neolithic sites of the fifth and fourth centuries B.C. . . . These trends accelerated and further intensified in the Lung-shan cemeteries. Furthermore, as the Ch'eng-tzu (Shantung) and T'ao-ssu (Shansi) cemeteries show, the economic and political polarization appears to have taken place within the framework of the unilinear clans and lineages.

All of the above happenings are plainly indicated by archaeological evidence, but they do not point to a single Lung-shan culture. Instead, they indicate a series of interrelated changes in culture and society that took place within each of the regional cultures in the Chinese interaction sphere. From the point of view of each of the regional sequences, both the external interaction network and internal changes during a period of two thousand years were essential for its readiness, toward the end of the third millennium B.C., to step over the next threshold into the state society, urbanism, and civilization.

QUESTIONS FOR ANALYSIS

- What were the key features of Longshan culture?
- What does *scapulimancy* mean, and how widespread was its use?
- What does the evidence of violence reveal about Longshan society?

Source: Kwang-chih Chang, The Archaeology of Ancient China, *4th ed. (New Haven: Yale University Press, 1986), pp. 287–88.*

Longshan Beaker, c. 2500 BCE. *Longshan has been called the "black pottery" culture, and its exquisite black pottery was not painted but rather decorated with rings, either raised or grooved. Longshan culture was more advanced than the Yangshao culture, and its distinctive pottery was likely formed on a potter's wheel.*

Oracle Bone Artifact. *The Shang dynasty use of oracle bones (such as the one above) may have grown out of the Longshan people's ritual of interpreting the cracks in burned deer scapulas.*

sheep. Archaeologists have discovered the remains of net sinkers, wooden floats, and wooden paddles, which demonstrate a familiarity with watercraft and fishing. Artisans produced a black pottery from soft paste thrown on a wheel, and like the Longshan they created ritual objects from several varieties of jade. Animal masks and bird designs adorned many pieces revealing a shared cosmology that informed the rituals of the Liangshu elite.

In the late third millennium BCE, a long drought hit China (as it did Egypt, Mesopotamia, and India). Although the climate change limited progress and forced migrations to more dependable habitats, the Chinese recovered early in the second millennium BCE. They created elaborate agrarian systems along the Yellow and Yangzi rivers that were similar to earlier irrigation systems along the Euphrates, Indus, and Nile. Extensive trading networks and a stratified social hierarchy emerged; like the other river-basin complexes of Asia and North Africa, China became a centralized polity. Here, too, a powerful monarchy eventually united the independent communities. But what developed in China was a social and political system that emphasized an idealized past and a tradition represented by sage-kings, which later ages emulated. In this and other ways, China diverged from the rest of Afro-Eurasia.

LIFE ON THE MARGINS OF AFRO-EURASIA

Those dwelling in river basins and established cities with hierarchies, bureaucracies, and strong militaries were inclined to see outsiders—particularly nomads—as "barbarians." Actually, the city people's imagery and narratives that depict nomads as uncivilized are not objective, because they were more concerned with promoting themselves than with portraying the nomads accurately. The nomads surely would not have recognized themselves as savages lacking culture, faith, and organized life. In fact, they had frequent contact with the urbanites and became skilled users of their technologies. (See Map 2.7.) Despite being less urbanized and stratified than city dwellers, they fashioned institutions and belief systems that were as durable as those of the metropolitan centers.

The people living outside the river basins had a distinctive warrior-based ethos, such that the top tiers of the social ladder held chiefs and military men instead of priests and scribes. This feature was especially evident in Europe and Anatolia, where weaponry rather than writing, palisades (defensive walls and turrets) rather than palaces, and conquest rather than commerce dominated everyday life. Here, too, the inhabitants moved beyond stone implements and hunting and gathering, but they remained more egalitarian than riverine folk and did not evolve much beyond small societies led by chiefs.

Aegean Worlds

Contact with Egypt and Mesopotamia affected the Aegean worlds, but it did not transform them. Geography stood in the way of significant urban development on the mountainous islands, on the Anatolian plateau, and in Europe. Even though people from Anatolia, Greece, and the Levant had populated the Aegean islands in the sixth millennium BCE, their small villages endured for 2,000 years before becoming more complex.

On mainland Greece and on the Cycladic islands in the Aegean, fortified settlements housed local rulers who controlled a small area of agriculturally productive countryside. Metallurgy developed in both Crete and the Cyclades, a group of small islands in the Aegean Sea, southeast of mainland Greece. There is evidence of more formal administration and organizations in some communities by 2500 BCE, but the norm was scattered settlements separated by natural obstacles. Consider rocky and mountainous Crete, the largest island in the Aegean, where seafaring peoples occupied settlements sprinkled throughout its rugged interior. By the early third millennium BCE, Crete had made occasional contact with Egypt and the coastal towns of the Levant, encountering new ideas, technologies, and materials as foreigners arrived on its shores. People coming by ship from the coasts of Anatolia and the Levant, as well as from Egypt, traded stone vessels and other luxury objects for the island's abundant copper.

Lacking a rich agrarian base, most communities remained small at fewer than 100 inhabitants, and only a few grew over time. By the middle of the third millennium BCE, a more complex society was emerging in eastern Crete. During the second millennium BCE, Knossos, located in a rich agricultural plain, became the primary palace-town in an extended network of palaces. Evidence from burial sites suggests that some households belonged to an elite class, for they took gold jewelry and other exotic objects with them to their graves. Aegean elites did not reject the niceties of cultured life, but they knew that their power rested as much on their rugged landscape's resources as on self-defense and trade with others.

Anatolia

The highland plateau of Anatolia shows clear evidence of regional cultures focused on the control of trade routes and mining outposts. This area had been populated almost from the time that humans walked out of Africa, and the pace of change was slow because people clung to their village ways and stone tools. True cities did not develop here until the third millennium BCE, and even then they were not the sprawling population centers typical of the Mesopotamian plain. Instead, small communities emerged around fortified citadels housing local rulers who competed with one another. Two impressively fortified centers were Horoz Tepe and Alaça Hüyük, which have yielded more than a dozen graves—apparently royal—full of gold jewelry, ceremonial standards, and elaborate weapons.

Another important site in Anatolia was Troy to the far west. It is legendary as the place of the famous war launched by the Greeks (the Achaeans) and recounted by Homer in the *Iliad*. Troy developed around 3000 BCE on the Mediterranean coast in a fertile plain. In the 1870s the German archaeologist Heinrich Schliemann identified Troy level I as a third-millennium BCE fortified settlement with monumental stone gateways and stone-paved ramps. The extremely rich Troy level II had five large buildings called *megarons,* forerunners of the classic Greek temple. Here, Schliemann found gold and silver objects, vessels, jewelry, and other artifacts. Many are similar to the ones found in graves at Alaça Hüyük. Moreover, since they parallel finds on Crete and on the Greek mainland and even as far away as the royal tombs of Ur, they indicate that Troy participated in the trading system linking the Aegean and Southwest Asian worlds. At the same time, Troy faced predatory neighbors and pirates who attacked from the sea—an observation that explains its impressive fortifications.

Europe: The Western Frontier

At the western reaches of the Eurasian landmass was a region featuring more temperate and also more frigid climates with smaller population densities. Its peoples—forerunners of present-day Europeans—began to make objects out of metal, formed permanent settlements, and started to create complex societies. Here, too, hierarchies replaced egalitarian ways. Yet, as in the Aegean worlds, population density and social complexity had limits.

More than in the Mediterranean or Anatolia, warfare dominated social development in Europe. Two contributing factors were the persistent fragmentation of the region's peoples and the type of agrarian development they pursued. The introduction of the plow and the clearing of woodlands expanded agriculture. Agrarian development here was not the result of city-states or dynasties organizing irrigation and settlement (as in Mesopotamia and Egypt), but rather the result of households and communities wielding axes for defense and for cutting down trees. Compared to the riverine societies, Europe was a wild frontier where violent conflicts over resources were common.

CURRENT TRENDS IN WORLD HISTORY

Climate Change at the End of the Third Millennium BCE in Egypt, Mesopotamia, and the Indus Valley

During the long third millennium BCE, the first urban centers in Egypt, Mesopotamia, Iran, central Asia, and South Asia flourished and grew in complexity and wealth in a wet and cool climate. This smooth development was sharply if not universally interrupted beginning around 2200 BCE. Both archaeological and written records agree that across Afro-Eurasia, most of the urban, rural, and pastoral societies underwent radical change. Those watered by major rivers were selectively destabilized, while the settled communities on the highland plateaus virtually disappeared. After a brief hiatus, some recovered, completely reorganized and using new technologies to manage agriculture and water. The causes of this radical change have been the focus of much interest.

After four decades of research by climate specialists working together with archaeologists, a consensus has emerged that climate change toward a warmer and dryer environment contributed to this disruption. Whether this was caused solely by human activity, in particular agriculture on a large scale, or was also related to cosmic causes such as the rotation of the earth's axis away from the sun is still a hotly debated topic. It was likely a combination of factors.

The urban centers dependent on the three major river systems in Egypt, Mesopotamia, and the Indus Valley all experienced disruption. In Egypt, the hieroglyphic inscriptions tell us that the Nile no longer flooded over its banks to replenish the fields with fresh soil and with water for crops. Social and political chaos followed for more than a century. In southern Mesopotamia, the deeply down-cut rivers changed course, disrupting settlement patterns and taking fields out of cultivation. Other fields were poisoned by salts brought on through overcultivation and irrigation without periods of fallow. Fierce competition for water and land put pressure on the central authority. To the east and west, transhumant pastoralists, faced with shrinking pasture for their flocks, pressed in on the river valleys, disrupting the already challenged social and political structure of the densely urban centers.

In northern Mesopotamia, the responses to the challenges of aridity were more varied. Some centers were able to weather the crisis by changing strategies of food production and distribution. Some fell victim to intraregional warfare, while others, on the rainfall margin, were abandoned. When the region was settled again, society was differently organized. Population did not drastically decrease, but rather it distributed across the landscape more evenly in smaller settlements that required less water and food. It appears that a similar solution was found by communities to the east on the Iranian plateau where the inhabitants of the huge urban center of Shahr i Sokhta abruptly left the city and settled in small communities across the oasis landscape.

The solutions found by people living in the cities of the Indus Valley also varied. Some cities, like Harappa, saw their population decrease rapidly. It seems that the bed of the river shifted, threatening the settlement and its hinterland. Mohenjo Daro, on the other hand, continued to be occupied for another several centuries, although the large civic structures fell out of use, replaced by more modest structures. And to the south, on

The gradual expansion of agricultural communities eventually reached a critical point. The growth of flint mining to an industrial level (as evident in the thousand shafts sunk at Krzemionki in Poland and the flint-mining complex of Grimes Graves in England) indicates a social and economic transformation. Most important, mining output slashed the cost and increased the availability of raw materials needed to make tools for clearing forested lands and tilling them into arable fields. As agricultural communities proliferated, some became villages that dominated their regions. But nowhere did these folk create large cities and corresponding states.

By 3500 BCE the more developed agrarian peoples had coalesced into large communities, constructing impressive monuments that remain visible today. In western Europe, large ceremonial centers shared the same model: enormous shaped stones, some weighing several tons each, set in common patterns—in alleyways, troughs, or circles—known as *megalithic* ("great stone") constructions. These daunting projects required cooperative planning and work. In the British Isles, where such developments occurred later, the famous megalithic complexes at Avebury and Stonehenge probably reached their highest stages of development just before 2000 BCE. No matter how forbidding the ecology of Europe was in this period, in the centuries after 3000 BCE, culminating in new developments around 2000 BCE, the whole of the northern European plain came to share a common material culture the Gujarat Peninsula, population and the number of settlements increased. They abandoned wheat as a crop, instead cultivating a kind of drought-enduring millet that originated in west Africa. Apparently conditions there became even more hospitable, allowing farming and fishing communities to flourish well into the second millennium BCE.

The evidence for this widespread phenomenon of climate change at the end of the third millennium BCE is complex and contradictory. This is not surprising, because every culture and each community naturally had an individual response to environmental and other challenges. Those with perennial sources of fresh water were less threatened than those in marginal zones where only a slight decrease in rainfall can mean failed crops and herds. As important, certain types of social and political institutions were resilient and introduced innovations that allowed them to adapt while others were too rigid or short-sighted to find local solutions. A feature of human culture is its remarkable ability to adapt rapidly. When faced with challenges, resilience, creativity, and ingenuity lead to cultural innovation and change. This is what we can see, even in our own times, during the period of environmental stress.

Millet. *This hardy grain, cultivated for its resistance to drought, persists in the desert environment of present-day western Pakistan.*

QUESTIONS FOR ANALYSIS

- What technological innovations resulted from the drought in the Indus Valley? Why?
- Imagine that the climate during the third millennium BCE had not changed. How do you think this might have affected the development of ancient Egypt?
- How has our understanding of global climate changed the way we study prehistory?

Explore Further

Wolfgang Behringer, *A Cultural History of Climate* (2010).

Barbara Bell, "The Dark Ages in Ancient History. 1. The First Dark Age in Egypt," *American Journal of Archaeology*, vol. 75, No. 1 (January, 1971), pp. 1–26.

Max Weiss et al, "The Genesis and Collapse of Third Millennium North Mesopotamian Civilization," *Science*, New Series, vol. 261, No. 5124 (August 20, 1993), pp. 995–1004.

based on agriculture, the herding of cattle for meat and milk, the use of the plough, and the use of wheeled vehicles and metal tools and weapons, mainly of copper. The most characteristic objects associated with this shared culture are the Corded Ware pots—so-called from the cords used to impress lines on their surfaces (see Map 2.7). The fact that this new economy was found from Ukraine in the east to the Low Countries in the west is evidence of the much-improved communications that linked and united previous disparate and widely separated regions.

Increasing communication, exchange, and mobility among the European communities led to increasing wealth but also sparked organized warfare over frontier lands and valuable resources. In an ironic twist, the integration of local communities led to greater friction and produced regional social stratification. The first sign of an emerging warrior culture was the appearance of drinking cups. (See Primary Source: The Male Warrior Burials of Varna and Nett Down.) The violent men who now protected their communities received ceremonial burials complete with their own drinking cups and weapons. Archaeologists have found these warrior burials in a swath of European lands extending from present-day France and Switzerland to present-day central Russia. Because the agricultural communities now were producing surpluses that they could store, residents had to defend their land and resources from encroaching neighbors.

Stonehenge. *This spectacular site, located in the Salisbury Plain in Wiltshire in southwestern England, is one of several such megalithic structures found in the region. Constructed by many generations of builders, the arrangement of the large stone uprights enabled people to determine precise times in the year through the position of the sun. Events such as the spring and autumn equinoxes were connected with agricultural and religious activities.*

An aggressive culture was taking shape based on violent confrontations between adult males organized in "tribal" groups. War cultures arose in all western European societies, marked by the universal presence of a new drinking instrument, the "bell beaker"—so named by archaeologists because it resembled an inverted bell. Armed groups carried these cups across Europe, using them to swig beer and mead distilled from grains, honey, herbs, and nuts. As beer drinking spread, many local variations on beer mugs appeared, again illustrating the constant interplay between external communication and local forces.

Corded Ware pots. *Traded across northern Europe, this pottery is known for its ornamental grooves, made when twisted cords were pressed into the wet clay.*

As new tools and weapons spread across Europe, the region adopted similar cultural practices. The twin pillars of agriculture and metalworking, initially in copper, became the supports of daily life almost everywhere. At the same time, though, a split between Europe's eastern and western flanks occurred: in the millennium following 2500 BCE, warriors in western Europe became more combative in battling for territory and resources.

Warfare had the ironic effect of accentuating the borrowing among the region's competing peoples. After all, the violent struggles and emerging kinship groups fueled a massive demand for weapons, alcohol, and horses. Warrior elites borrowed from Anatolia the technique of combining copper with tin to produce harder-edged weapons made of the alloy bronze. Soon smiths were producing them in bulk—as evidenced by hoards of copper and bronze tools and weapons from the period found in central Europe. Traders used the rivers of central and northern Europe to exchange their prized metal products, creating one of the first commercial networks that covered the landmass.

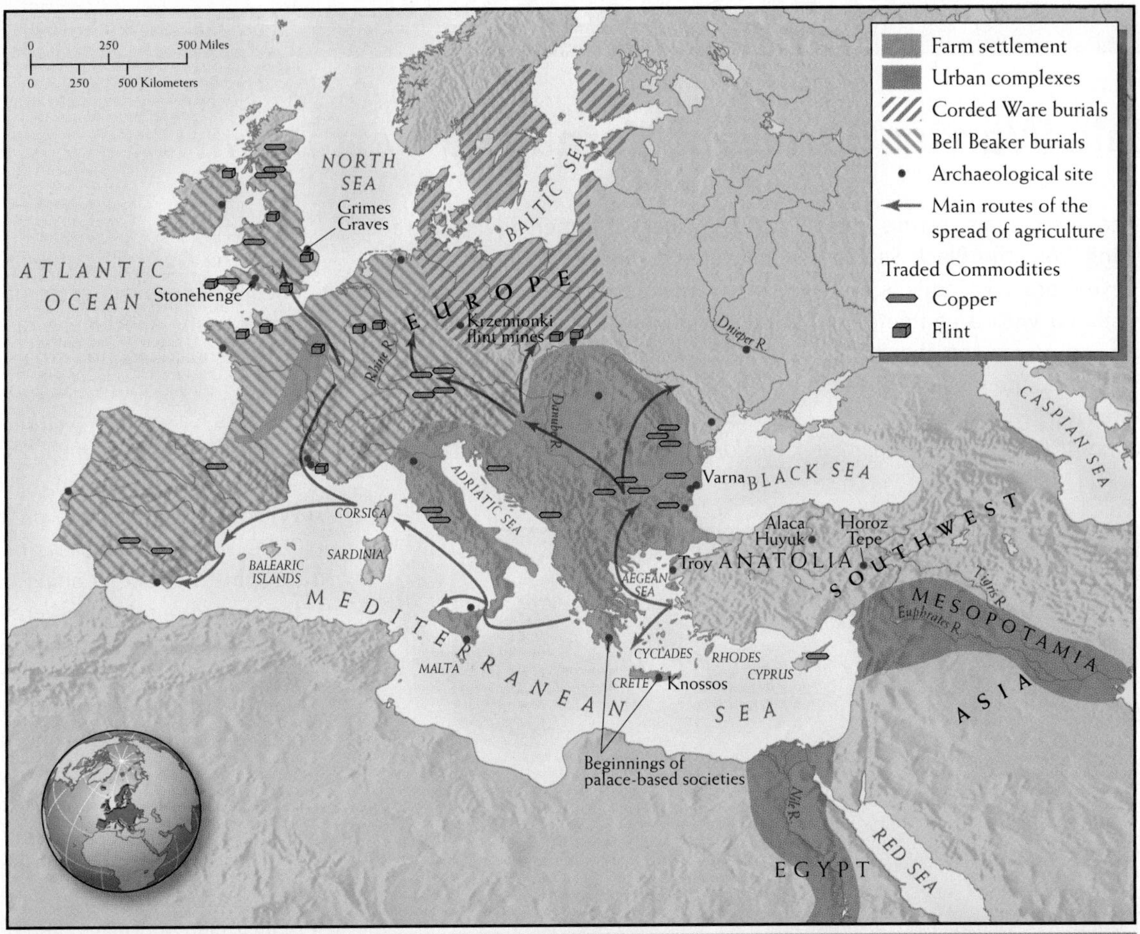

MAP 2.7 | Settlements on the Margins: The Eastern Mediterranean and Europe, 5000–2000 BCE

Urban societies in Southwest Asia had profound influences on peripheral societies.

- What three peripheral worlds did the urban societies of Southwest Asia influence?
- In what ways did the spread of flint and copper tools and weapons transform Aegean and European societies?
- How did agriculture spread from Southwest Asia to these worlds?

Constant warfare propelled Europe to become an innovative frontier society. The culture of violence and conflict that now drove a basic agricultural economy had two significant effects: it integrated European kinship-based oral societies in a realm of their own, and it separated them from the Mediterranean societies—an ordered world of palaces, scribes, and well-disciplined commoners.

CONCLUSION

Over the fourth and third millennia BCE, the world's social landscape changed in significant ways. In a few key locations, where giant rivers irrigated fertile lands, complex human cultures began to emerge. These areas experienced all the advantages and difficulties of expanding populations: occupational specialization; social hierarchy; rising standards of living; sophisticated systems of art and science; and centralized production and distribution of food, clothing, and other goods. Ceremonial sites and trading crossroads became cities that developed centralized religious and political systems. As scribes, priests, and rulers labored to keep complex societies together, the differences between country folk and city dwellers sharpened. In effect, urbanization was an example of the many ways in which societies were becoming more complex and stratified. Social distinctions also affected the roles of men and women, as urban families began to differ from kinship groups in the countryside.

PRIMARY SOURCE

The Male Warrior Burials of Varna and Nett Down

Burials of elite individuals across the region stretching from the Black Sea to the Atlantic reveal precious objects and weapons associated with a competitive warrior culture. At Varna, on the Black Sea coast of Bulgaria, the lifestyle of the "big men" associated with a farming village from around 4000 BCE came to light in 1972 when a farmer driving a tractor uncovered an ancient cemetery. The burials at Varna may represent a powerful and well-connected settlement, since most other contemporary sites do not display such high levels of wealth. The grave of a man who died at about age forty-five (pictured here), large pots used for drinking and storage were found. More striking were the 990 gold objects: most were decorative devices sewn onto his clothing, but others included bracelets on both arms, a necklace, and small gold-handled axe. The weapons buried with him—daggers, axes, and spearheads, and points—were made of flint.

Another burial—from Nett Down in Wiltshire, England, and dating to around 2500 BCE—reveals a less developed culture. In this case, a small tomb cut into the chalk ground and covered with a small mound of earth contained a young male warrior. He was buried with the two most significant objects connected with his life: a bronze dagger and, by his hands, a large bell beaker. No gold or precious metal ornaments accompanied the man, who was clearly part of a poorer society than Varna's. As one scholar has remarked, "the grave neatly encapsulates the ideal male image of drinking and fighting."

QUESTIONS FOR ANALYSIS

- Most individual burials contain male bodies. What does this fact tell us about men's roles in these evolving patriarchal societies?
- When we compare these sites to those in Egypt and China, what can we learn about the importance of burying the dead across these societies?

Although the riverine cultures shared basic features, each one's evolution followed a distinctive path. Where there was a single river—the Nile or the Indus—the agrarian hinterlands that fed the cities lay along the banks of the mighty waterway. In these areas cities were small; thus the Egyptian and Harappan worlds enjoyed more political stability and less rivalry. In contrast, cities in the immense floodplain of the Tigris and Euphrates needed large hinterlands to sustain their populations. Because of their growing power and need for resources, Mesopotamian cities vied for preeminence, and

"Bell beaker" pottery. *Named for their characteristic inverted bell shape, these cups were carried across western Europe by tribes who primarily used the vessels to consume alcoholic beverages like beer or mead.*

their competition often became violent. (As we will see in Chapter 3, a similar pattern emerged after 1500 BCE in China, where the Yellow and Yangzi river environments facilitated the rapid expansion of Chinese settlements into cities.)

Cities stood at one end of the spectrum of social complexity. At the other end, in most areas of the world, people still lived in simple, egalitarian societies based on hunting, gathering, and basic agriculture—as in the Americas and sub-Saharan Africa. In between were worlds such as Anatolia, Europe, and large parts of China, where towns emerged and agriculture advanced—but not with the leaps and bounds of the great riverine cultures. Beyond these frontiers, farmers and nomads survived as they had for many centuries. Some of them, as in the Aegean, forged warrior societies. Elsewhere, as in the borderlands between Mesopotamian city-states, people created thriving trading networks.

In spite of these global differences, changes in climate affected everyone and could slow or even reverse development. How—and whether—cultures adapted depended on local circumstances. As the next chapter will show, the human agents of change often came from the fringes of larger settlements and urban areas.

TRACING THE GLOBAL STORYLINES

AFTER YOU READ THIS CHAPTER

FOCUS ON: ***Societies in the Great River Basins***

Mesopotamia

- Peoples living along the **Tigris River** and **Euphrates River** control floodwaters and refine irrigation techniques.
- Mesopotamians establish the world's first large cities, featuring powerful rulers, social hierarchies, and monumental architecture.
- Mesopotamia is the birthplace of writing.

Indus Valley

- South Asian peoples harness the **Indus River** and create cities like Harappa and Mohenjo Daro.

Egypt

- Peoples of Egypt use **Nile River** waters to irrigate their lands and create a bountiful agriculture.
- Egyptian rulers known as pharaohs unify their territory, establish a powerful state, and develop a vibrant economy.
- Egyptians build magnificent burial chambers (pyramids) and worship a pantheon of gods.

East Asia

- Peoples dwelling in the basins of the **Yellow River** and the **Yangzi River** control the waters' flow and expand agriculture.
- These people develop an elaborate culture, which scholars later label Yangshao and Longshan, respectively.

Review and research materials are available on **StudySpace:** wwnorton.com/studyspace

CHRONOLOGY

Southwest Asia and Egypt
- Earliest Sumerian cities appear in Mesopotamia **3500 BCE**

South Asia

East Asia
- Yangshao culture thrives along Yellow River **5000 BCE**

Europe and the Mediterranean

The Americas
- Chicama Valley culture thrives on Pacific Coast of South America **3500 BCE**
- Tehuacan Valley in Mexico thrives **3500 BCE**

Sub-Saharan Africa
- Dense village life along many lakes and rivers **3500 BCE**

Inner and Central Asia
- Spread of nomadic pastoralism begins **3500 BCE**

5000 BCE — **4000 BCE**

KEY TERMS

bronze *p. 45*

city *p. 50*

city-state *p. 52*

cult *p. 53*

palace *p. 53*

river basins *p. 44*

scribes *p. 55*

social hierarchies *p. 52*

temple *p. 53*

territorial state *p. 58*

urban-rural divide *p. 45*

STUDY QUESTIONS

1. **Describe** how cities in Mesopotamia, the Indus Valley, and Egypt differed from small village communities across the globe. Why did cities emerge in relatively few places between 3500 and 2000 BCE?
2. **Define** *pastoralism*. Where in Afro-Eurasia did this form of social organization develop and thrive?
3. **Identify** shared characteristics among urbanites in Mesopotamia, the Indus Valley, and Egypt. What features distinguished each from the others?
4. **Compare and contrast** city-state structures in Egypt and Mesopotamia. Why was Egypt more politically unified than Mesopotamia?
5. **Analyze** the influence of long-distance trade on the political and economic development of urban societies in Egypt, Mesopotamia, and the Indus Valley. How did contacts with other people influence each society?
6. **Compare and contrast** the ways in which early writing emerged in the urban societies between 4000 and 2000 BCE. How did each use this new technology? How common was literacy?
7. **Explain** how the rise of cities represented a leap forward in complexity in human history. How did urban dwellers shape political, economic, and cultural developments in their region?
8. **Explain** East Asia's relative physical isolation from other Afro-Eurasian societies during this period. To what extent did this isolation shape social development in this region between 4000 and 2000 BCE?
9. **Identify** shared characteristics of European, Anatolian, and Aegean settlements between 3500 and 2000 BCE. How did settlements in these regions on the margins differ from urban settlements in river basins?

First Dynasty emerges in Egypt **3100 BCE**

Sargon's Akkadian territorial state in Mesopotamia **2334–2103 BCE**

Old Kingdom Egypt **2649–2152 BCE**

Cities appear in Indus Valley **2500 BCE**

Longshao Culture emerges in Yellow River Valley **5000–2000 BCE**

Fortified villages in the Aegean **2500 BCE**

Stonehenge constructed **2000 BCE**

3000 BCE **2000 BCE**

BEFORE YOU READ THIS CHAPTER

GLOBAL STORYLINES

- Climate change leads to the collapse of river-basin societies.
- Herders and pastoral nomads migrate into riverine societies, utilizing horse-drawn chariot warfare to challenge traditional ruling elites and conquer surrounding states.
- Large territorial states arise, led by charismatic rulers who expand boundaries, create more competition and trade, and wage warfare.
- Microsocieties emerge in other parts of the world based on expanding populations and increased trade.

CHAPTER OUTLINE

3

Nomads, Chariots, Territorial States, and Microsocieties, 2000–1200 BCE

FOCUS QUESTIONS

- How did the interaction of nomadic groups and settled people change the political and cultural landscape of Afro-Eurasia during the second millennium BCE?
- What were the direct and indirect effects of drought on the organization of societies?
- How did political and cultural developments in South Asia differ from Southwest and East Asia during this period?
- To what extent did political developments follow similar trajectories in East and Southwest Asia?
- How were microsocieties similar and different from territorial states?

Around 2200 BCE, the Old Kingdom of Egypt collapsed. Evidence for its ruin includes a history of numerous ineffective rulers in Memphis, imprecise workmanship on pyramids, and many incomplete funerary and temple structures. Yet the collapse did not occur because of incompetent rulers or a decline in the arts and sciences. The Old Kingdom fell because of radical changes in climate—namely, a powerful warming and drying trend that blanketed Afro-Eurasia between 2200 and 2150 BCE. The Mesopotamians and Harappans were as hard hit as the Egyptians. In Egypt the environmental disaster yielded a series of low Niles because the usual monsoon rains did not arrive to feed the river's upper regions, particularly the Blue Nile arising in the mountains of Ethiopia. (For the impact of climate change in the river-basin cultures, see the Current Trends in World History box, page 76, in the previous chapter.)

Documents from this period reveal widespread suffering and despair. Indeed, people who had enjoyed prosperity and good government for centuries now lived in utter disbelief that the world had been turned upside down and that the wicked triumphed over the virtuous. Consider the following tomb inscription: "All of Egypt was dying of hunger to such a degree that everyone had come to eating his children." Or another: "The tribes of the desert have become Egyptians everywhere. . . . The plunderer is everywhere, and the servant takes what he finds."

Settled societies were not alone in their losses. Herders and pastoral nomads also felt the pinch. As these outsiders pressed upon permanent settlements in search of sustenance, the governing structures in Egypt, Mesopotamia, and the Indus Valley collapsed. The pioneering city-states may have created unprecedented differences between elites and commoners, between urbanites and rural folk, but everyone felt the effects of this disaster.

This chapter focuses on two related developments. The first is the effect of climate change on the peoples of Afro-Eurasia, the early consequences of which were decisively negative: famines occurred, followed by political and economic turmoil; the old order gave way; river-basin states in Egypt, Mesopotamia, and the Indus Valley collapsed. Herders and pastoral nomads, driven from grazing areas that were drying up, forced their way into the heartlands of these great states in pursuit of better-watered lands. Once there, they challenged the traditional ruling elites. They also brought with them an awesome new military weapon—the horse-drawn chariot, which is the second focus of this chapter. Chariots brought a type of warfare that would dominate the plains of Afro-Eurasia for a half a millennium. The nomads' advantage proved only temporary, however. Soon the Egyptians, Mesopotamians, Chinese, and many others learned from these challengers: they assimilated some of the newcomers into their own societies and drove others away, adopting the invaders' most useful techniques, especially mastering the military usages of chariotry.

We must note that the rise of highly centralized polities does not tell the entire story of this period; thus the chapter also examines worlds apart from the expanding centers of population and politics. The islanders of the Pacific and the Aegean, as well as peoples living in the Americas, did not interact with one another with such intensity—and therefore their political systems evolved differently. In these locales, microsocieties were the norm.

NOMADIC MOVEMENT AND THE EMERGENCE OF TERRITORIAL STATES

At the end of the third millennium BCE, drought and food shortages led to the overthrow of ruling elites throughout central and western Afro-Eurasia. Walled cities could not defend their hinterlands. Trade routes lay open to predators, and pillaging became a lucrative enterprise. More immediately threatening were those herders living in close proximity to settled agriculturalists, whom we have called **transhumant migrants.** (See Chapter 1 for the distinction between pastoral nomads and transhumant migrants.) From the borderlands of the Iranian plateau and the Arabian Desert herders advanced on the populated areas, searching for food and resources. Similar migrations occurred in the Indus River valley and the Yellow River valley. (See Map 3.1.)

Environmental changes compelled humans across Afro-Eurasia to adapt or perish. When and where the pastoral nomads and transhumant herders managed to adjust to the dry conditions, they prompted the rise of new, larger, and expansionist territorial states from pharaonic Egypt and Mesopotamia to Vedic South Asia and Shang China. Using **chariots** (two-wheeled horse-drawn vehicles used in warfare and later in processions and races), the horse-mounted nomads introduced technologies that led to new forms of warfare whose spread transformed the Afro-Eurasian world. Moreover, the new rulers' innovations in state building and governance enabled people to rebuild their communities and to flourish in the changed climate.

Nomadic and Transhumant Migrations

Desperate for secure water sources and pastures, many transhumant herders and pastoralists migrated onto the highland plateaus bordering the Inner Eurasian steppes. From there, some continued into the more populated river valleys and soon were competing with the farming communities over space and resources. They also streamed in from the western and southern deserts in Southwest Asia in modern-day inner Syria and Arabia.

These migrants settled in the agrarian heartlands of Mesopotamia, the Indus River valley, the highlands of Anatolia, Iran, China, and Europe. After the first wave of newcomers, more migrants arrived by foot or in wagons pulled by draft animals. Some sought temporary work; others settled permanently. They brought horses and new technologies that were useful in warfare; religious practices and languages; and new pressures to feed, house, and clothe an ever-growing population.

HORSES AND CHARIOTS Although the hard-riding pastoral nomads contributed much to settled societies (they linked cities in South Asia and China for the first time, enhanced trade, and maintained peace), they could not control what the elites whom they disrupted wrote about them. Those who lost power described the nomadic warriors as "barbaric," portraying them as cruel enemies of "civilization." Yet what we know of these nomads today suggests that they were anything but barbaric.

Perhaps the most vital breakthroughs that nomadic pastoralists transmitted to settled societies were the harnessing of horses and the invention of the chariot. On the vast steppe lands north of the Caucasus Mountains, during the late fourth millennium BCE, settled people had domesticated horses in their native habitat. Elsewhere, as on the northern steppes of what is now Russia, horses were a food source. Only during the late third millennium

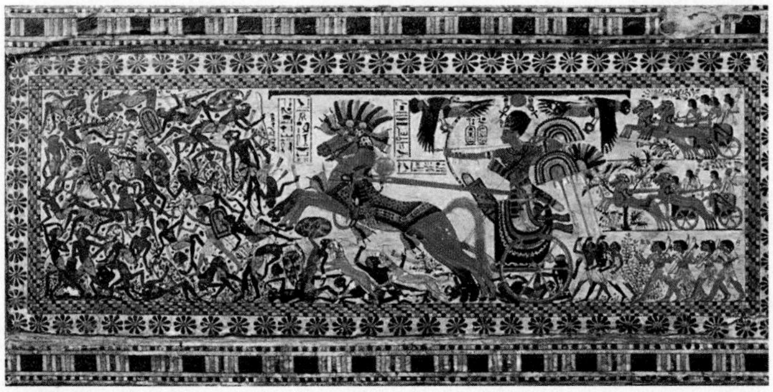

War Chariots. Upper left: *A large vase typical of Mycenaean art on the mainland areas of Greece. The regular banding and presentation of scenes reflect a society that is more formally ordered and rigidly hierarchical than that on Minoan Crete. Note the presence of the horse-drawn chariot. Possessing this more elaborate means of transport and warfare characterized the warrior elites of Mycenaean society and linked them to developments over wide expanses of Afro-Eurasia at the time.* Bottom left: *This wooden chest covered with stucco and painted on all sides with images of the Egyptian pharaoh in his war chariot was found in the fabulously wealthy tomb of Tutankhamun in the Valley of the Kings in Egypt. The war chariot was introduced into Egypt by the Hyksos. By the reign of Tutankhamun in the New Kingdom, depictions of the pharaoh single-handedly smiting the enemy from a war chariot drawn by two powerful horses were common.* Upper right: *The Shang fought with neighboring pastoral nomads from the central Asian steppes. To do this, they imported horses from central Asia and copied the chariots of nomads they had encountered. This gave Shang warriors devastating range and speed for further conquest.*

BCE did people harness them with cheek pieces and mouth bits, signaling their use for transportation. Horses can outrun other draft animals, but harnessing them for pulling is complicated. Unlike cattle or donkeys, which stretch their necks ahead when walking, a horse raises its head. So the drivers needed headgear to control their steeds' speed and direction. In tombs scattered around the steppe, archaeologists have found parts of horse harnesses made from wood, bone, bronze, and iron. These reveal the evolution of headgear from simple mouth bits to full bridles with headpiece, mouthpiece, and reins.

Sometime around 2000 BCE, pastoral nomads beyond the Mesopotamian plain to the north in the mountains of the Caucasus joined the harnessed horse to the chariot. The invention of the chariot yoked to agile, speedy, and highly trained horses transformed warfare. Pastoralists lightened chariots so their warhorses could pull them faster. They were so light that an empty one could be lifted by one hand. Such techniques included spoked wheels made of special wood and bent into circular shapes, wheel covers, axles, and bearings—all produced by settled people. But there was even more adaptation: durable metal went into the chariot's moving parts, first bronze and later iron. A cluster of more than twenty settlements of steppe nomads, based in the area to the east of the Ural Mountains, led the way in making bronze weapons and chariot parts. Farther south, craftsmen working out of urban settlements fashioned true tin-bronze weapons and utensils and imported horses and chariots from the steppe peoples.

The next innovation in the chariot was the use of iron. Initially iron was a decorative and experimental metal, and all tools and weapons were bronze. Iron's hardness and flexibility, however, eventually made it more desirable for reinforcing moving parts and protecting wheels. Similarly, solid wood wheels that were prone to shatter ceded to spokes and hooped bronze (and, later, iron) rims. Thus the horse chariots were the result of a creative combination of innovations by both nomadic and agrarian peoples. These innovations—combining new engineering skills, metallurgy, and animal domestication—and their ultimate diffusion revolutionized the way humans made war.

The horse chariot slashed travel time between capitals and overturned the machinery of war. Slow-moving infantry now

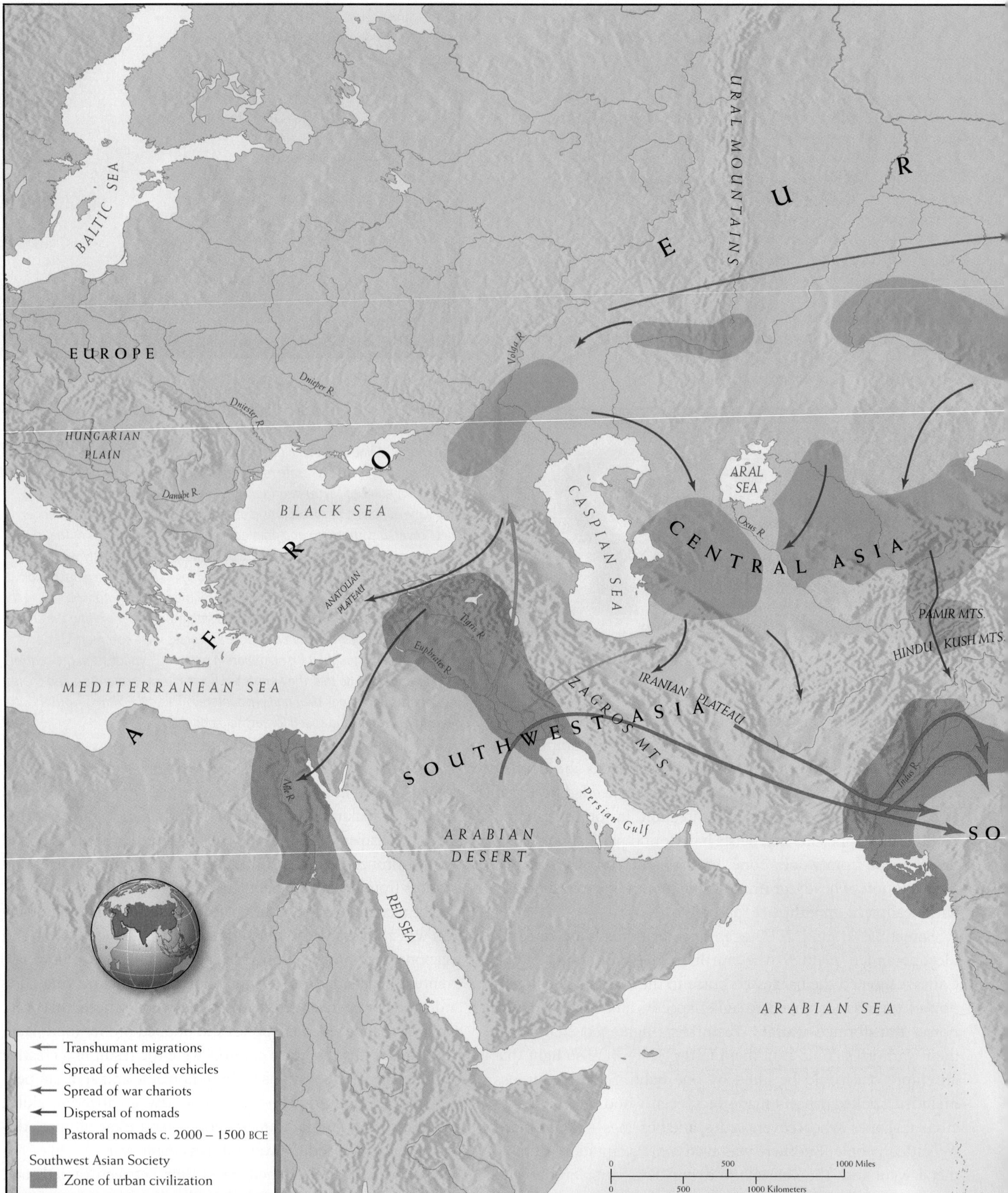
BALTIC SEA
URAL MOUNTAINS
E U R
EUROPE
Volga R.
Dnieper R.
Dniester R.
HUNGARIAN PLAIN
Danube R.
BLACK SEA
A F R O
CASPIAN SEA
ARAL SEA
Oxus R.
CENTRAL ASIA
ANATOLIAN PLATEAU
Tigris R.
Euphrates R.
PAMIR MTS.
HINDU KUSH MTS.
MEDITERRANEAN SEA
IRANIAN PLATEAU
ZAGROS MTS.
SOUTHWEST ASIA
Nile R.
Indus R.
Persian Gulf
SO
ARABIAN DESERT
RED SEA
ARABIAN SEA
Transhumant migrations
Spread of wheeled vehicles
Spread of war chariots
Dispersal of nomads
Pastoral nomads c. 2000 – 1500 BCE
Southwest Asian Society
Zone of urban civilization
0 500 1000 Miles
0 500 1000 Kilometers

MAP 3.1 | Nomadic Migrations in Afro-Eurasia, 2000–1000 BCE

- According to this map, what parts of the world did pastoral peoples migrate from?
- What areas did they move into?
- What regions did they bring into closer connection?
- How did nomadic pastoral migrations affect settled, agriculture-based societies?

ceded to battalions of chariots. Each vehicle carried a driver and an archer and charged into battle with lethal precision and ravaging speed. In fact, the mobility, accuracy, and shooting power of warriors in horse-drawn chariots tilted the political balance. For after the nomads perfected this type of warfare (by 1600 BCE), they challenged the political systems of Mesopotamia and Egypt and soon became central to the armies of Egypt, Assyria, Persia, the Vedic kings of South Asia, and the Zhou rulers in China, and to local nobles as far west as Italy, Gaul, and Spain. Mounted archers and spearmen first played a prominent role in the Assyrian army under Sargon II, who depended on the chariots' greater mobility while fighting in mountainous landscapes. Later, the Persians added a deadly feature to the chariot by projecting a long, curved scythe blade at the center of each wheel. Only with the arrival of cheaper armor made of iron (after 1000 BCE) could foot soldiers (in China, armed with crossbows) recover their military importance. And only after states developed cavalry units of horse-mounted warriors did chariots lose their decisive military advantage. For much of the second millennium BCE, then, charioteer elites prevailed in Afro-Eurasia.

For city dwellers in the river basins the first sight of horse-drawn chariots must have been terrifying, but they knew that war making had changed and they scrambled to adapt. The pharaohs in Egypt probably copied chariots from nomads or neighbors, and they came to value them highly. For example, the young pharaoh Tutankhamun (r. c. 1336–1327 BCE) was a chariot archer who made sure his war vehicle and other gear accompanied him in his tomb. A century later the Shang kings of the Yellow River valley, in the heartland of agricultural China, likewise were entombed with their horse chariots.

The Emergence of Territorial States

While nomad and transhumant populations toppled the riverine cities in Mesopotamia, Egypt, and China, the turmoil that ensued sowed seeds for a new type of regime: the territorial state. (See Map 3.2.) Breaking out of the urban confines of its predecessors, the **territorial state** exerted power over distant hinterlands. In this way, it represented the chief political innovation of this new era: the centralized kingdom, organized around charismatic rulers. The new rulers of these territorial states also enhanced their stability by devising rituals for passing the torch of command from one generation to the next. People no longer identified themselves as residents of cities; instead, they felt allegiance to large territories, rulers, and broad linguistic and ethnic communities. While never formalized, these territories for the first time had borders that extended beyond individual cities, and their residents felt a shared identity.

Territorial states differed from the city-states that preceded them. The city-states of the riverine societies, organized around the temple and palace, were autonomous **polities** (politically organized communities or states) without clearly defined hinterlands. In contrast, the new territorial states in Egypt, Mesopotamia, and China based their authority on monarchs, widespread bureaucracies, elaborate legal codes, large territorial expanses, definable borders, and ambitions for continuous expansion. Although power still emanated from central cities, new ruling groups also appeared in these areas. The once-marginalized peoples of the Syrian Desert (the Amorites) and of the northern steppe lands and Anatolia (the Hittites) now held power. Their drive to conquer and expand replaced the earlier models of competition and coexistence. Territorial states also emerged in Greece and the Aegean, where the newcomers who took power adopted local ways more completely. Other regions went through similar processes, but more slowly; they would not see state formation for a few more centuries. In one fundamental way, the South Pacific, the Aegean, Europe, and the Americas were different from the lands stretching from North Africa to South Asia: because they were less densely populated, they experienced less rivalry and less conflict over borders.

THE RISE OF TERRITORIAL STATES IN EGYPT AND SOUTHWEST ASIA

Climatic change, invasions by pastoral nomads, and the use of war chariots transformed the city-states of Egypt and Southwest Asia. They brought an end to regimes like Old Kingdom Egypt and the many states occupying the Mesopotamian floodplain. But, as inhabitants of these areas assimilated the newcomers or drove out those who resisted assimilation, new states came to the fore. Thus the second millennium BCE divides into two distinct phases. The first phase, roughly 2000 to 1600 BCE, resembled what had gone before: small kingdoms, organized by territorial and ethnic identities, dominated the landscape from the Aegean Sea through Mesopotamia and Iran. The most powerful kingdoms were Babylonia in Mesopotamia and the Middle Kingdom in Egypt. A second, more radical phase occurred after 1600 BCE, when a renewed wave of nomadic migrations and conquests undermined these fledgling but unstable territorial kingdoms. After an agonizing century of turmoil, the balance of power shifted and a new group of expansionist states emerged. From their urban capitals, they commanded vast hinterlands, claimed definable territories, and consolidated common cultures. The most powerful of the second period were New Kingdom Egypt, the Hittites of Anatolia, Babylonian Amorites, and the Kassites of Mesopotamia.

All across Southwest Asia the war chariot became the decisive instrument of war. The Hittites were especially noted for the skill of their charioteers. Hittite horses already were being

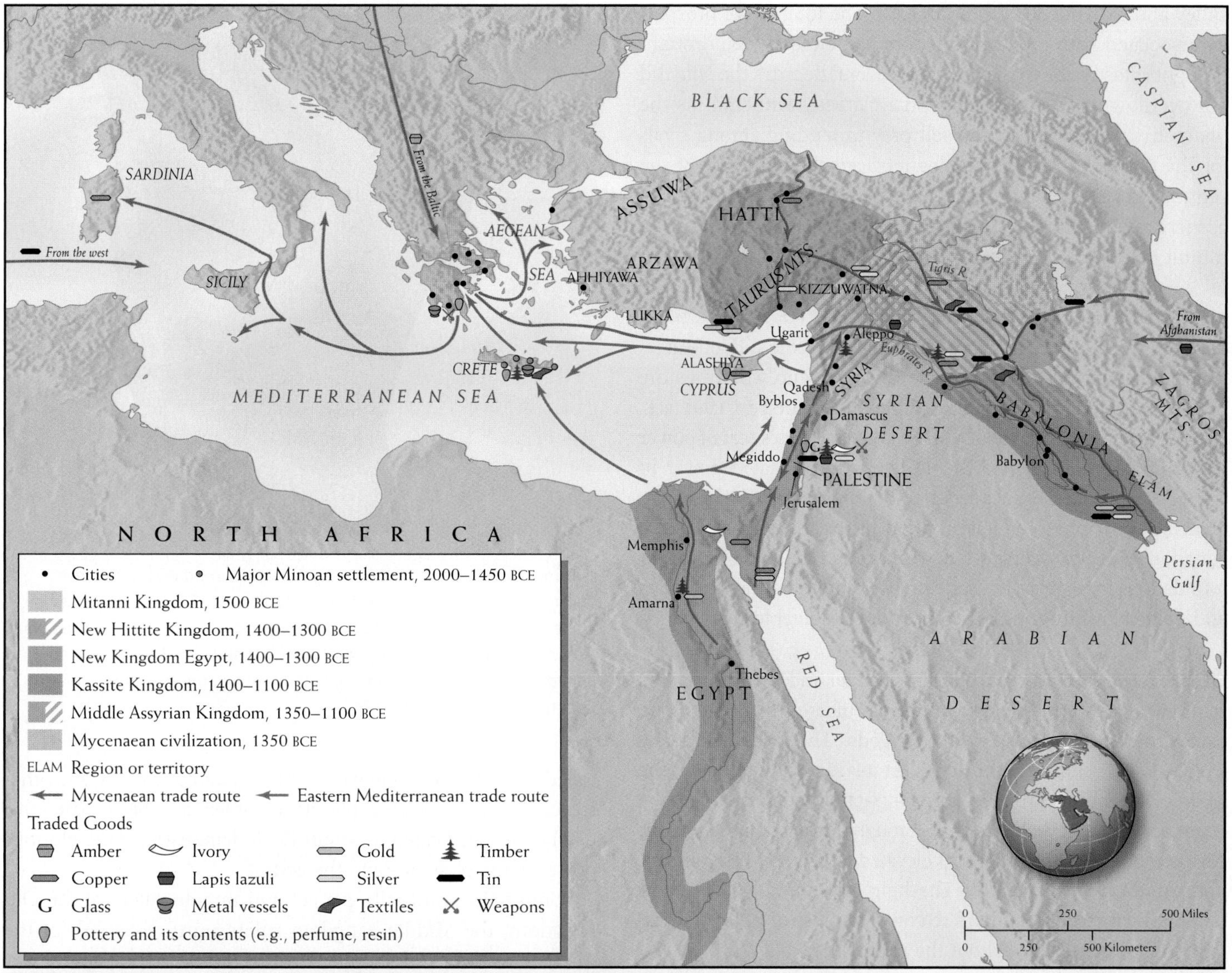

MAP 3.2 | Territorial States and Trade Routes in Southwest Asia, North Africa, and the Eastern Mediterranean, 1500–1350 BCE

- What were the major trade routes and the major trading states in Southwest Asia, North Africa, and the Eastern Mediterranean during this time?
- What were the major trade goods?
- Did trade enhance peaceful interactions among the territorial states?

exploited for their speed and strength by the early second millennium. And a cuneiform text from the Hittite capital captures the attention its rulers gave to their preparations for chariot warfare. The text, a detailed manual of a horse trainer, describes the training regime for chariot horses that took place over the course of 150 days. Its methods are still in place today.

In this second period the entire region was marked by competition between well-balanced military kingdoms. Although there was much quarreling and some warfare, shrewd statecraft and international diplomacy kept the peace for many centuries. Not so fortunate were the smaller kingdoms, such as the Syro-Palestinian states, squeezed between the major powers. They were trapped in buffer zones between the regions that the territorial powers dominated.

Egypt

The first of the great territorial kingdoms of this era arose from the ashes of chaos in Egypt. There the pharaohs of the Middle Kingdom and, later, the New Kingdom reunified the river valley and expanded south and north. The long era of prosperity associated with the Old Kingdom had ended when drought brought catastrophe to the area. For several decades the Nile did not overflow its banks, and Egyptian harvests withered. As the pharaohs lost legitimacy and fell prey to feuding among rivals for the throne, regional notables replaced the authority of the centralized state. Egypt, which had been one of the most stable corners of Afro-Eurasia, would endure more than a century of tumult before a new order emerged.

MIDDLE KINGDOM EGYPT (2040–1640 BCE) Around 2050 BCE, after a century of drought, the Nile's floodwaters returned to normal. Crops grew again. But who would restore order and reunite the kingdom? From about 2061 to 1991 BCE, two rulers at Thebes (far south of the Old Kingdom's seat of power in Memphis), both named Mentuhotep, consolidated power in Upper Egypt and began new state-building activity. They ushered in a new phase of stability that historians call the Middle Kingdom. For 350 years, the new pharaonic line built on earlier foundations to increase the state's power and to develop religious and political institutions far beyond their original forms.

GODS AND KINGS Once again spiritual and worldly powers reinforced each other in Egypt. Just as rulers of this new phase came from the margins, so did its gods. The Twelfth Dynasty (1985–1795 BCE), with its long list of kings, dominated the Middle Kingdom partly because its sacred order replaced the chaos that people believed had brought drought and despair. Amenemhet I (1985–1955 BCE) elevated a formerly insignificant god, Amun, to prominence. The king capitalized on the god's name, which means "hidden," to convey a sense of his own invisible omnipresence throughout the realm.

Because Amun's attributes were largely hidden, believers in other gods were able to embrace his cult. Amun's cosmic power appealed to those in areas that had recently been impoverished. As the pharaoh elevated the cult of Amun he unified the disparate parts of his kingdom, further empowering Amun—as well as his worldly sponsor, the pharaoh. In this way Amun eclipsed all the other gods of Thebes. Merging with the formerly omnipotent sun god Re, the deity now was called Amun-Re: the king of the gods. Because the power of the gods and kings was intertwined, Amun's earthly champion (the king) enjoyed enhanced legitimacy as the supreme ruler. The cult was more than a tool of political power, however: it also had a strong spiritual impact on the pharaoh and on Egyptian society.

ROYAL SPLENDOR AND ROYAL CARE While gods and kings allied, Middle Kingdom rulers tapped into their kingdom's bounty, their subjects' loyalty, and the work of untold slaves and commoners to build the largest, longest-lasting public works project ever undertaken. For 2,000 years, Egyptians and slaves toiled to erect monumental gates, enormous courtyards, and other structures in a massive temple complex at Thebes (present-day Luxor). Dedicated to Amun-Re, it demonstrated the glorious power of the pharaohs and the gods.

Amun. *This sculpture of the head of the god Amun was carved from quartzite during the Eighteenth Dynasty, around 1335 BCE. At Thebes in Upper Egypt, a huge temple complex was dedicated to the combined god Amun-Re. The powerful kings of the Middle and New Kingdoms each added a courtyard or a pylon, making this one of the largest religious structures in the ancient world.*

Unlike the spiritually perfect and remote rulers of the Old Kingdom, the Middle Kingdom rulers nurtured a cult of the pharaoh as the good shepherd whose prime responsibility was to fulfill the needs of his human flock. By instituting charities, offering homage to gods at the palace to ensure regular floodwaters, and performing ceremonies to honor their own generosity, the pharaohs portrayed themselves as the stewards of their people.

MERCHANTS AND TRADE NETWORKS Prosperity gave rise to an urban class of merchants and professionals who used their wealth and skills to carve out places for their own leisure and pastimes. Indoors they indulged in formal banquets with professional dancers and singers, and outdoors they honed their skills in hunting, fowling, and fishing. What was new was that they did not depend on the kings for such benefits. In a sign of their upward mobility and autonomy, some members of the middle class constructed tombs filled with representations of the material goods they would use in the afterlife as well as the occupations that would engage them for eternity. During the Old Kingdom, this privilege had been the exclusive right of the royal family and a few powerful nobles.

Centralized and reforming kingdoms also expanded their trade networks. Because the floodplains had long since been deforested, the Egyptians needed to import massive quantities of wood by ship. Most prized were the cedars from Byblos (a city in the land soon known as Phoenicia, roughly present-day Lebanon), which artisans crafted into furniture for the living and coffins for the dead. Superb examples remain from the tombs of nobles and pharaohs. Commercial networks extended south through the Red Sea as far as present-day Ethiopia; traders brought back precious metals, ivory, livestock, slaves, and exotic animals such as panthers and monkeys to enhance the pharaoh's palace. Expeditions to the Sinai Peninsula searched for copper and turquoise. Egyptians looked south for gold, which they prized for personal and architectural ornamentation. To acquire it they crossed into Nubia, where they met stiff resistance; eventually the Egyptians colonized Nubia to broaden their trade routes and secure these coveted resources. As part of their colonization, a series of forts extended as far south as the second cataract of the Nile River. (See Map 2-5 in Chapter 2.)

HYKSOS INVADERS AND NEW FOUNDATIONS Pharaonic peace brought prosperity, but it did not ensure uninterrupted pharaonic rule. Now Egypt found itself open to migration and foreign invasion, coming once again from the margins. First, the very success of the new commercial networks lured pastoral nomads who were searching for work. Later, a new people from Southwest Asia attacked Egypt, initially destabilizing the kingdom but ultimately putting it on stronger foundations.

Sometime around 1640 BCE a western Semitic-speaking people, whom the Egyptians called the Hyksos ("Rulers of Foreign Lands"), overthrew the unstable Thirteenth Dynasty. The Hyksos had mastered the art of horse chariots. Thundering into battle with their war chariots and their superior bronze axes and composite bows (made of wood, horn, and sinew), they easily defeated the pharaoh's foot soldiers. Yet the victors did not destroy the conquered land; instead, they ruled over it. By adopting Egyptian ways, they also reinforced them. The Hyksos settled down and ruled as the Fifteenth Dynasty, asserting control over the northern part of the country and transforming the Egyptian military force.

Luxury imports. *Crafted with lapis from the east and gold from the south, these amulets and other treasures from King Tut's tomb demonstrate the impact that trade had upon Egyptian religious and visual culture.*

After a century of political conflict, an Egyptian who ruled the southern part of the country, Ahmosis (r. 1550–1525 BCE), successfully used the Hyksos weaponry—horse chariots—against the invaders themselves and became pharaoh. The Egyptian rulers had learned an important lesson from the invasion: they had to vigilantly monitor their frontiers, for they could no longer rely on deserts as buffers. Ahmosis assembled large, mobile armies and drove the "foreigners" back. Diplomats followed in the army's path, as the pharaoh initiated a strategy of interference in the affairs of small kingdoms in the Levant. Such policies laid the groundwork for statecraft and an international diplomatic system that future Egyptian kings would use to dominate the eastern Mediterranean world.

The migrants and invaders from the west introduced new techniques that the Egyptians adopted to consolidate their power. These included bronze working (which the Egyptians had not perfected), an improved potter's wheel, and a vertical loom. In addition, South Asian animals such as humped zebu cattle, as well as vegetable and fruit crops, now appeared on the banks of the Nile for the first time.

Of course, the most significant innovations pertained to war: the horse and chariot, the composite bow, the scimitar (a sword with a curved blade), and other weapons from western Eurasia. These weapons transformed the Egyptian army from a standing infantry to a high-speed, mobile, and deadly fighting force. As Egyptian troops extended the military frontier as far south as the fourth cataract of the Nile River, the kingdom now stretched from the Mediterranean shores to Ethiopia.

NEW KINGDOM EGYPT By the beginning of the New Kingdom (1550–1069 BCE), Egypt was projecting its interests outward: it defined itself as a superior, cosmopolitan society with an efficient bureaucracy run by competent and socially mobile individuals. For 100 years Egypt expanded its control southward into Nubia, a source of gold, exotic raw materials, and manpower. Historians identify this expansion most strongly with the reign of Egypt's most powerful woman ruler, Hatshepsut. She served as regent for her young son, Thutmosis III, who came to the throne in 1479 BCE. When he was seven years old she proclaimed herself "king," ruling as co-regent until she died. During her reign there was little military activity, but trade contacts into the Levant and Mediterranean and southward into Nubia flourished.

Hatshepsut. *The only powerful queen of Egyptian pharaonic history was Hatshepsut, seen here in a portrait head created during her reign. Because a woman on the throne of Egypt would offend the basic principles of order (ma'at), Hatshepsut usually portrayed herself as a man, especially late in her reign. This was reinforced by the use of male determinatives in the hieroglyphic renditions of her name.*

Thutmosis III (r. 1479–1425 BCE) launched another expansionist phase that lasted for 200 years. Spreading northeastward into the Levant, under his rule the Egyptians collided with the Mitanni and the Hittite kingdoms. At the Battle of Megiddo (1469 BCE), the first recorded chariot battle in history, Thutmosis III, whose army employed nearly 1,000 war chariots, defeated his adversaries and established an Egyptian presence in Palestine. Two centuries later, in 1274 BCE, Egypt's most notable pharaoh, Ramses II (r. 1279–1213 BCE), engaged in what historians regard as the greatest chariot battle in world history. More than 6,000 chariots fought to a draw on the plains of what is present-day Syria for control of the Fertile Crescent.

Anatolia and the Rise of the Hittites

Anatolia was an overland crossroads that linked the Black and Mediterranean seas. Like other plateaus of Afro-Eurasia it had high tablelands, was easy to traverse, and was hospitable to large herding communities. Thus during the third millennium BCE Anatolia had become home to numerous polities run by indigenous elites. These societies combined pastoral lifeways, agriculture, and urban commercial centers. Before 2000 BCE, peoples speaking Indo-European languages began to enter the plateau, probably coming from the steppe lands north and west of the Black Sea. The newcomers lived in fortified settlements and often engaged in regional warfare, and their numbers grew. Splintered into competing clans, they fought for regional supremacy. They also borrowed extensively from the cultural developments of the Southwest Asian urban cultures, especially those of Mesopotamia.

THE OLD AND NEW HITTITE KINGDOMS (1800–1200 BCE) In the early second millennium BCE chariot warrior groups, which were the most powerful of the competing communities in Anatolia, grew even more powerful on the commercial activity that passed through Anatolia. Chief among them were the Hittites, who became unified during the seventeenth century BCE under Hattusilis I.

After securing his base in Anatolia, Hattusilis turned his attention to the east, crossed the Taurus Mountains, and defeated the kingdom that controlled all of northern Syria. In 1595 BCE, Hattusilis and his son Mursilis I marched even farther, campaigning along the Euphrates River as far as the city of Babylon, which they sacked. The Hittites enjoyed another period of political and military success two centuries later under the great king Suppilulimua I (r. 1380–1345 BCE), who restored Hittite glory in Southwest Asia from the Euphrates in the east to Syria in the south. As noted earlier, at Qadesh they met the Egyptians in what some experts regard as the greatest battle in ancient times, one that involved a vast number of chariots. Because the Hittites controlled much of the territory between Mesopotamia and the Nile, their rulers were crucial in maintaining the region's balance of power.

Mesopotamia

In Mesopotamia, as in Egypt and Anatolia, the intervention of mobile pastoral peoples led to the emergence of new states. Here, too, drought was devastating. Harvests shrank, the price of basic goods rose, and the social order broke down. Already short of agricultural produce, the towns of southern Mesopotamia suffered invasions by transhumant migrants from two directions: the Zagros Mountains and the Syrian Desert. These herders, who did not use horses or chariots, were seeking grazing lands to replace those swallowed up by the expanding deserts. As elsewhere in Afro-Eurasia, environmental changes were altering the human landscape.

A millennium of intense cultivation, combined with severe drought, had ruined the land's productivity. The rich alluvial soil lost more and more nutrients, while at the same time salt water from the Persian Gulf seeped into the marshy deltas and contaminated the water table (the underground level at which water can reliably be found). As the main branch of the Euphrates River shifted to the west, large areas of previously arable land no longer received sufficient water for cultivation. As a result, many of the ancient cities lost access to their fertile agrarian hinterlands and withered away. All these alterations pushed Mesopotamia's center of political and economic gravity northward, away from the silted, marshy deltas of the southern heartland.

NOMADIC AND TRANSHUMANT MIGRATION TO MESOPOTAMIAN CITIES The conquerors of Mesopotamian cities were the Amorites, a name given them by their vanquished urban dwellers and taken from the Akkadian word for "west," *Amurru*. City dwellers were scornful of these rustic folk, as the following poetry makes clear. It states that the Amorite is

> *a tent-dweller, [buffeted] by wind and rain, [who offers no] prayer,*
> *He who dwells in the mountains, [knows not] the places [of the gods];*
> *A man who digs up mushrooms at the foot of the mountain, who knows no submission,*
> *He eats uncooked meat,*
> *In his lifetime has no house,*
> *When he dies, he will not be buried;*
> *My girlfriend—why would you marry Martu?!*
> *(Klein, "The Marriage of Martu," 89)*

Transhumant herders may have been "foreigners" in the cities of Mesopotamia, but they were not strangers to them. Speaking a related Semitic language, they had always played an important role in Mesopotamian urban life and knew the culture of its city-states. These rural folk wintered in villages close to the river to water their animals, which grazed on fallow fields. In the scorching summer, they retreated to the cooler highlands. Their flocks provided wools for the vast textile industries of Mesopotamia, as well as leather, bones, and tendons for other crafted products. In return, the herders purchased crafted products and agricultural goods. They also paid taxes, served as warriors, and labored on public works projects. Yet despite being part of the urban fabric, they had few political rights within city-states.

As scarcities mounted, transhumant peoples began to press in upon settled communities more closely. Finally, in 2004 BCE, Amorites from the western desert joined allies from the Iranian plateau to bring down the Third Dynasty of Ur (which had controlled all of Mesopotamia and southwestern Iran for more than a century). As in Egypt, a century of political instability followed the demise of the old city-state models. Here, too, it was pastoral folk who finally restored order, increasing the wealth of the regions they conquered and helping the cultural realm to flourish. They founded the Old Babylonian dynasty centered in the city of Babylon, near modern Baghdad, around 2000 BCE; they also expanded trade and founded new kinds of political communities: territorial states with dynastic ruling families and well-defined frontiers. This was yet another example of the contribution of mobile communities to settled societies.

RESTORED ORDER AND CULTURE Restored order and prosperity enabled the new kings of Babylonia to nourish a vibrant intellectual and cultural milieu. These rulers commissioned public art and works projects and promoted institutions of learning. The court supported workshops for skilled artisans such as jewelers and sculptors, and it established schools for scribes, the transmitters of an expanding literary culture.

Now the Babylonians and their successors, the Kassites (1475–1125 BCE), reproduced the cultural achievements of earlier Mesopotamia. To dispel their image as rustic foreigners and to demonstrate their familiarity with the region's core values, they studied the oral tales and written records of the earlier Sumerians and Akkadians. Scribes copied the ancient texts and preserved their tradition. Royal hymns, for instance, continued the Sumerian language that had not been spoken for centuries. These hymns portrayed the king as a legendary hero of quasi-divine status.

Heroic narratives about legendary founders, based on traditional stories about the rulers of ancient Uruk, served to legitimize the new rulers. These great poems constituted the first epic narratives of human—as opposed to godly—achievement. Written in the Old Babylonian dialect of the Semitic Akkadian language, they identified the history of a people with their king, and their wide circulation helped to unify the kingdom. The most famous was the *Epic of Gilgamesh* (see Primary Source: *The Epic of Gilgamesh*), one of the earliest surviving works of literature. This story (composed more than a millennium earlier in the Sumerian language) narrated the heroism of the legendary king of early Uruk, Gilgamesh. Throughout the ages, scribes of royal courts preserved the tradition for future generations to venerate the idea of the benevolent king. It stands out as an example of how the Mesopotamian kings continually invested in cultural production in order to explain important political relations, unify their people, and distinguish their subjects from those of other kingdoms.

TRADE AND THE RISE OF A PRIVATE ECONOMY With restored prosperity came a shift away from economic activity dominated by the city-state and toward independent private ventures. The new rulers designated private entrepreneurs rather than state bureaucrats to collect taxes. People paid taxes in the form of commodities such as grain, vegetables, and wool, which the entrepreneurs exchanged for silver. They, in turn, passed on the silver to the state after pocketing a percentage for their profit.

Gilgamesh *This terra-cotta plaque in the Berlin Museum is one of the very few depictions of Gilgamesh (on the left wielding the knife) and his sidekick, Enkidu. It illustrates one of the episodes in their shared adventures, the killing of Humwawa, the monster of the Cedar Forest. The style of the plaque indicates that it was made during the Old Babylonian period, between 2000 and 1600* BCE.

This process generated more private activity and wealth, and more revenues for the state.

Mesopotamia at this time was a crossroads for caravans leading east and west. When the region was peaceful and well governed, the trading community flourished. The ability to move exotic foodstuffs, valuable minerals, textiles, and luxury goods across Southwest Asia won Mesopotamian merchants and entrepreneurs a privileged position as they connected producers with distant consumers. Merchants also used sea routes for trade with the Indus Valley. Before 2000 BCE, mariners had charted the waters of the Red Sea, the Gulf of Aden, the Persian Gulf, and much of the Arabian Sea. Now, during the second millennium BCE, shipbuilders figured out how to construct larger vessels and to rig them with towering masts and woven sails—creating truly seaworthy craft that could carry bulkier loads. Of course, shipbuilding required wood (particularly cedar from Phoenicia) as well as wool and other fibers (from the pastoral hinterlands) for sails. Such reliance on imported materials reflected a growing regional economic specialization and an expanding sphere of interaction across western Afro-Eurasia.

Doing business in Mesopotamia was profitable but also risky. If harvests were poor, cultivators and merchants could not meet their tax obligations and thus incurred heavy debts. The frequency of such misfortune is evident from the many royal edicts that annulled certain debts as a gesture of tax relief. Moreover, traders and goods had to pass through lands where some hostile rulers refused to protect the caravans. Thus taxes, duties, and bribes flowed out along the entire route. If goods reached their final destination, they yielded large profits; if disaster struck, investors and traders had nothing to show for their efforts. As a result, merchant households sought to lower their risks by formalizing commercial rules, establishing insurance schemes, and cultivating extended kinship networks in cities along trade routes to ensure strong commercial alliances and to gather intelligence. They also cemented their ties with local political authorities. Indeed, the merchants who dominated the ancient city of Assur on the Tigris pumped revenues into the coffers of the local kingdom in the hope that its wealthy dynasts would protect their interests.

MESOPOTAMIAN KINGDOMS The new rulers of Mesopotamia also changed the organization of the state. Herders-turned-urbanite rulers mixed their own nomadic social organization with that of the once-dominant city-states to create the structures necessary to support much larger territorial states.

The basic social organization of the Amorites, out of which the territorial state evolved, was tribal, dominated by a ruling chief and based on clans, each claiming descent from a common ancestor. Although clans drew a sharp line between themselves and all who were not kin, they did allow intermarriage and adoption. Even the many Amorites who had given up their nomadic ways and settled in the cities remained conscious of their genealogical roots, and their new territorial polities honored identification with the clan and tribe.

The evolution of the new territorial states of Southwest Asia occurred in three stages. First, chieftains became kings. Second, the new kings turned their authority—which in the tribe had depended on personal charisma and battlefield prowess—into an alliance with wealthy merchants in exchange for revenues and political support. Third, royal status became hereditary. This practice of hereditary succession replaced the tribal system under which influential community leaders had selected the

PRIMARY SOURCE

The Epic of Gilgamesh

Gilgamesh, an early ruler of ancient Uruk, was the supreme hero of Mesopotamian legend. He was a successful ruler, boastful and vain, as well as a courageous adventurer and a devoted friend to his companion Enkidu. The Gilgamesh epic, constructed in the early second millennium BCE from numerous stories, is the oldest piece of world literature. It portrays a tragic hero who is obsessed with glory and whose quest for immortality ends in failure. The following excerpt tells of his anguish on his fruitless journey to gain immortal life. He is speaking to an alewife (a woman who keeps an alehouse) as he continues to deny his humanity and the inevitability of death.

The alewife spoke to him, to Gilgamesh,
"If you are truly Gilgamesh, that struck down the Guardian,
Destroyed Humbaba, who lived in the Pine Forest,
Killed lions at the mountain passes,
Seized the Bull of Heaven who came down from the sky, struck him down,
Why are your cheeks wasted, your face dejected,
Your heart so wretched, your appearance worn out,
And grief in your innermost being?
Your face is like that of a long-distance traveler,
Your face is weathered by cold and heat . . .
Clad only in a lion skin you roam open country."
Gilgamesh spoke to her, to Siduri the alewife,
"How could my cheeks not be wasted, my face not dejected.
Nor my heart wretched, nor my appearance worn out,
Nor grief in my innermost being,
Nor my face like that of a long-distance traveler,
My friend whom I love so much, who
Experienced every hardship with me,
Enkidu, whom I love so much, who experienced every hardship with me—
The fate of mortals conquered him! Six days and seven nights I wept over him,
I did not allow him to be buried, until a worm fell out of his nose.
I was frightened and . . .
I am afraid of Death, and so I roam open country.
The words of my friend weigh upon me.
I roam open country for long distances; the words of my friend
Enkidu weigh upon me.
I roam open country on long journeys.
How, O how, could I stay silent, how O how could I keep quiet
My friend whom I love has turned to clay:
Enkidu my friend whom I love has turned to clay.
Am I not like him? Must I lie down too,
Never to rise, ever again?"

QUESTIONS FOR ANALYSIS

- What lines of the passage reveal how Gilgamesh feels about the death of Enkidu? Why does he feel that way?
- What does this passage tell us about human relationships and human nature during this period? What does it tell us about rulers and their relationship with their gods?

Source: "The Epic of Gilgamesh" from Myths from Mesopotamia: Creation, The Flood, Gilgamesh and Others, *pp. 100–101, trans. Stephanie Dalley. © Stephanie Dalley 1989. Reprinted with permission of Oxford University Press.*

leaders. Even in the new system, though, kings could not rule without the support of nobles and merchants.

Over the centuries, powerful Mesopotamian kings continued to expand their territories. They subdued weaker neighbors, coaxing or forcing them to become **vassal states**—that is, allies who had to pay tribute in luxury goods, raw materials, and manpower as part of a broad confederation of polities under the kings' protection. Control over military resources (access to metals for weaponry and, later, to herds of horses for pulling chariots) was necessary to gain dominance, but it was no guarantee of success. The ruler's charisma also mattered. This emphasis on personality explains why Mesopotamian kingdoms were strong for certain periods under certain rulers, but vulnerable to rivals and neighbors under other rulers. It also distinguished them from Middle Kingdom Egypt and Hittite Anatolia, territorial states where power was more institutionalized and durable.

The most famous Mesopotamian ruler of this period was Hammurapi (or Hammurabi) (r. 1792–1750 BCE), who ascended the throne as the sixth king of Old Babylonia's First Dynasty. Continuously struggling with powerful neighbors, he sought to centralize state authority and to create a new legal order. Using

Hammurapi's Code. *The inscription on the shaft of Hammurapi's Code is carved in a beautiful rendition of the cuneiform script. Because none of the laws on the code were recorded in the thousands of judicial texts of the period, it is uncertain if Hammurapi's Code presented actual laws or only norms for the proper behavior of Babylonian citizens.*

diplomatic and military skills to become the strongest king in Mesopotamia, he made Babylon his capital and declared himself "the king who made the four quarters of the earth obedient." He implemented a new system to secure his power, appointing regional governors to manage outlying provinces and to deal with local elites.

Hammurapi's image as ruler imitated that of the Egyptian pharaohs of the Middle Kingdom. The king was shepherd and patriarch of his people, responsible for proper preparation of the fields and irrigation canals and for his followers' well-being. Such an ideal recognized that being king was a delicate balancing act. While he had to curry favor among powerful merchants and elites, he also had to meet the needs of the poor and disadvantaged—in part to avoid a reputation for cruelty, and in part to gain a key base of support should the elites become dissatisfied with his rule.

Hammurapi elevated this balancing act into an art form, encapsulated in a grand legal code—**Hammurapi's Code**. It began and concluded with the rhetoric of paternal justice. For example, he concluded by describing himself as "the shepherd who brings peace, whose scepter is just. My benevolent shade was spread over my city, I held the people of the lands of Sumer and Akkad safely on my lap."

Hammurapi's Code was in fact a compilation of more than 300 edicts addressing crimes and their punishments. One theme rings loud and clear: governing public matters was man's work, and upholding a just order was the supreme charge of rulers. Whereas the gods' role in ordering the world was distant, the king was directly in command of ordering relations among people. Accordingly, the code elaborated in exhaustive detail the social rules that would ensure the kingdom's peace through its primary instrument—the family. The code outlined the rights and privileges of fathers, wives, and children. The father's duty was to treat his kin as the ruler would treat his subjects, with strict authority and care. Adultery, which represented the supreme violation of this moral code, was a female crime. Any woman found with a man who was not her husband would be bound and thrown into the river, and likewise her lover.

Hammurapi's Code also divided the people in the Babylonian kingdom into three classes: each member was a free person (*awilum*), a dependent (*mushkenum*), or a slave (*wardum*). Each had an assigned value and distinct rights and responsibilities. In this way, Hammurapi's order stratified society while also pacifying the region. By the end of his reign, Hammurapi had established Babylon as the single great power in Mesopotamia and had reduced competitor kingdoms to mere vassals. Following his death, his sons and successors struggled to maintain control over a shrinking domain for another 155 years in the face of internal rebellions and foreign invasions. In 1595 BCE, Babylon fell to the Hittite king Hattusilis I.

KASSITE RULE As a crossroads for Afro-Eurasia, Mesopotamia continued both to benefit from and be threatened by the arrival of nomadic and transhumant migrants. The Kassites, for instance, who came from the Zagros Mountains, had entered southern Mesopotamia from the Iranian plateau. Arriving in the river valley as agricultural laborers as early as 2000 BCE, they integrated themselves into Babylonian society by becoming bureaucrats associated with the temple. Once entrenched, they were well placed to fill the power vacuum when the Hittites destroyed the First Dynasty of Babylon. By 1475 BCE, Kassite rulers had reestablished order in the region. Over the next 350 years they brought all of southern Mesopotamia under their control, creating one of the great territorial states within an emerging network of states from North Africa to Southwest Asia.

The Kassites presided over a golden age based on trade in such precious commodities as horses, chariots, and lapis lazuli, which they exchanged for gold, wood, and ivory. Like earlier immigrant communities to this ancient land, the Kassites absorbed the traditions and institutions of Mesopotamia. Even more than their predecessors, they strove to preserve the past

ANALYZING GLOBAL DEVELOPMENTS

Climate Change and the Collapse of Riverine Societies

The three great riverine societies discussed in Chapter two (Egypt, Mesopotamia, and the Indus Valley) collapsed at around the same time. The collapse in Egypt and Mesopotamia was almost simultaneous (roughly between 2200 BCE and 2100 BCE). In contrast, while the collapse was delayed in the Indus Valley for approximately 200 years, when it came, it virtually wiped out the Harappan state and culture. At first historians focused on political, economic, and social causes, stressing bad rulers, nomadic incursions, political in-fighting, population migrations, and the decline of long-distance trade. In more recent times, however, a group of scientists—paleobiologists, climatologists, sendimentationists, and archaeologists—have studied these societies and found convincing evidence that a truly radical change in the climate—a two-hundred year long drought spreading across the Afro-Eurasian land mass—was a powerful factor in the collapse of these cultures. But how can these researchers know so much about the climate 4,000 years ago? The following table assembles the evidence for their assertions, drawing on their scholarly studies on Egypt, Mesopotamia, and the Indus Valley.

QUESTIONS FOR ANALYSIS

- Why did more standard historical explanations for the collapse of the large riverine societies precede the more recent emphases on climate change?
- Few scholars, even those cited in this footnote, are willing to regard climate change as the overwhelming factor in the collapse of these riverine societies. Why do you think that this is the case?
- On the basis of your reading of this note, do you think that the evidence for climate change is convincing for all three societies? Which ones are the more persuasive, which the less convincing?

Riverine Society	Date of Collapse	Climatological Evidence	Archaeological Evidence	Literary Evidence
Egypt	The Old Kingdom collapsed and ushered in a period a notable political instability, the First Intermediate Period (2184–2055 BCE).	Sedimentation studies reveal markedly lower Nile floods and an invasion of sand dunes into cultivated areas.	Much of the sacred sites of the Old Kingdom and their artwork is believed to have been destroyed in this period, due to the political chaos.	An abundant literary record is full of tales of woe and poetry and stelae, calling attention to famine, starvation, low Nile floods, even cannibalism.
Mesopotamia	The last effective ruler of the Kingdom of Akkad (2334–2193) was Naram Sin (r. 2254–2218).	Around 2100 BCE, inhabitants abruptly abandoned the Haabur drainage basin, whose soil samples reveal marked aridity as determined by the existence of fewer earthworm holes and wind-blown pellets.	Teil Leilan and other sites indicate that the large cities of this region began to shrink around 2200 BCE and were soon abandoned, and remained unoccupied for 300 years.	Later UR III scribes described the influx of northern "barbarians" and noted the construction of a wall, known as the Repeller of the Amorites, to keep these northerners out.
Indus Valley and the Harappan Society	Many of the Harappan peoples migrated eastward, beginning around 1900 BCE, leaving this region largely empty of people.	Hydroclimatic reconstructions show that precipitation began to decrease around 3000 BCE, reaching a low in 2000 BCE, at which point the Himalayan rivers stopped incising. Around 1700 BCE the Ghaggar-Hakra rivers dried up.	Major Harappan urban sites began to shrink in size and lose their urban character between 1900 and 1700 BCE.	No literary source material because the Harappan script has still to be deciphered.

Sources: Barbara Bell, "The Dark Ages in Ancient History," American Journal of Archaeology, *vol. 75, No. 1 (January, 1971), pp. 1–26; Max Weiss et al., "The Genesis and Collapse of Third Millennium North Mesopotamian Civilization,"* Science, New Series, *vol. 261, No. 5124 (August 20, 1993), pp. 995–1004; H. M. Cullen et al., "Climate Change and the Collapse of the Akkadian Empire,"* Geology, *Vol. 28, No. 4, April 2000, pp. 379–82; Liviu Giosan et al., "Fluvial Landscapes of the Harappan Civilization,"* Proceedings of the National Academy of Science, *published online, May 29, 2012; and Karl W. Butzer, " Collapse, Environment, and Society,"* Proceedings of the National Academy of Science, *published online, March 6, 2012, Vol. 109, No. 10, pp. 3632–39. For a general overview of climate change and historical studies the reader should consult Wolfgang Behringer,* A Cultural History of Climate *(2010).*

Akhenaten. *The pharaoh Amenhotep IV changed his name to Akhenaten to reflect his deep devotion to Aten, the god of the sun disk. The art of the period of his reign, like his religion, challenged conventions. In it, the faces of the king and queen, as well as their bodies, were extremely elongated and distorted. Some scholars think that this distortion reflects a condition that the king himself suffered from.*

and transmit its institutions to posterity. Although very little remains of their own language and customs (apart from their personal names), with thoroughness and dedication the Kassite scribes translated much of the older Sumerian literature into Akkadian. They revised and compiled texts into standard editions, from which scholars have recovered a Babylonian creation myth called the Enuma Elish. In their determination to become even more Babylonian than the Babylonians, the Kassites saved a treasure trove of historical literature and cultural practices for later generations. During the subsequent period of the Community of Major Powers, the Kassites served as the crucial link between Egypt, Anatolia, and southwestern Iran.

The Community of Major Powers (1400–1200 BCE)

Between 1400 and 1200 BCE, the major territorial states of Southwest Asia and Egypt perfected instruments of international diplomacy that have stood the test of time and inspired later leaders. The leaders of these powers learned to settle their differences through treaties and diplomatic negotiations rather than on the battlefield. Each state knew its place in the political pecking order. It was an order that depended on constant communication—the foundation of what we now call diplomacy. In fact, a remarkable cache of 300 letters discovered at the present-day Egyptian village of Amarna, beneath which Egyptologists discovered the remains of the capital city of the New Kingdom pharaoh Akhenaten, offers intimate views of these complex interactions. Most are letters from the Egyptian king to his subordinates in the vassal states of Palestine, but others are from Akhenaten and his father to the Babylonian, Mitanni, Middle Assyrian, Kassite, and Hittite kings. Many of these letters are in a dialect of Akkadian (used by the Babylonian bureaucrats) that served as the diplomatic language of the era. This correspondence reveals a delicate balance, constantly shifting, among competing kings who were intent on maintaining their status and who knew that winning the loyalty of the small buffer kingdoms was crucial to political success.

Formal treaties brought an end to military eruptions and replaced them with diplomatic contacts. In its more common form, diplomacy involved strategic marriages and the exchange of specialized personnel to reside at the court of foreign territorial states. Gifts also strengthened relations among the major powers and signaled a ruler's respect for his neighbors. Rulers had to acknowledge the gesture by reciprocating with gifts of equal value.

The foundations of power were not always durable, however. Building the state system was ultimately the task of those at the bottom of the social pyramid, and the ruling classes' reliance on them for power and political authority was a weakness of these regimes. Commoners remained tied to the land, which sometimes belonged to communities or institutions, not individual families. They paid taxes to the state, performed labor required by the state for public works (such as irrigation or building projects), and served as foot soldiers. The collapse of the international age had many causes, but one factor was the disintegration of the social fabric as workers could not pay their taxes or fled their communities rather than fight in the rulers' armies.

NOMADS AND THE INDUS RIVER VALLEY

Late in the third millennium BCE, drought ravaged the Indus River valley as it did other regions. By 1700 BCE, the population of the old Harappan heartland had plummeted. Here, too, around 1500 BCE, yet another group of nomadic peoples, calling themselves Aryans ("respected ones"), wandered out of their homelands in the steppes of Inner Eurasia. In contrast to Egypt, Anatolia, and Mesopotamia, these pastoral nomads did not immediately establish large territorial states. Crossing the northern highlands of central Asia through the Hindu Kush,

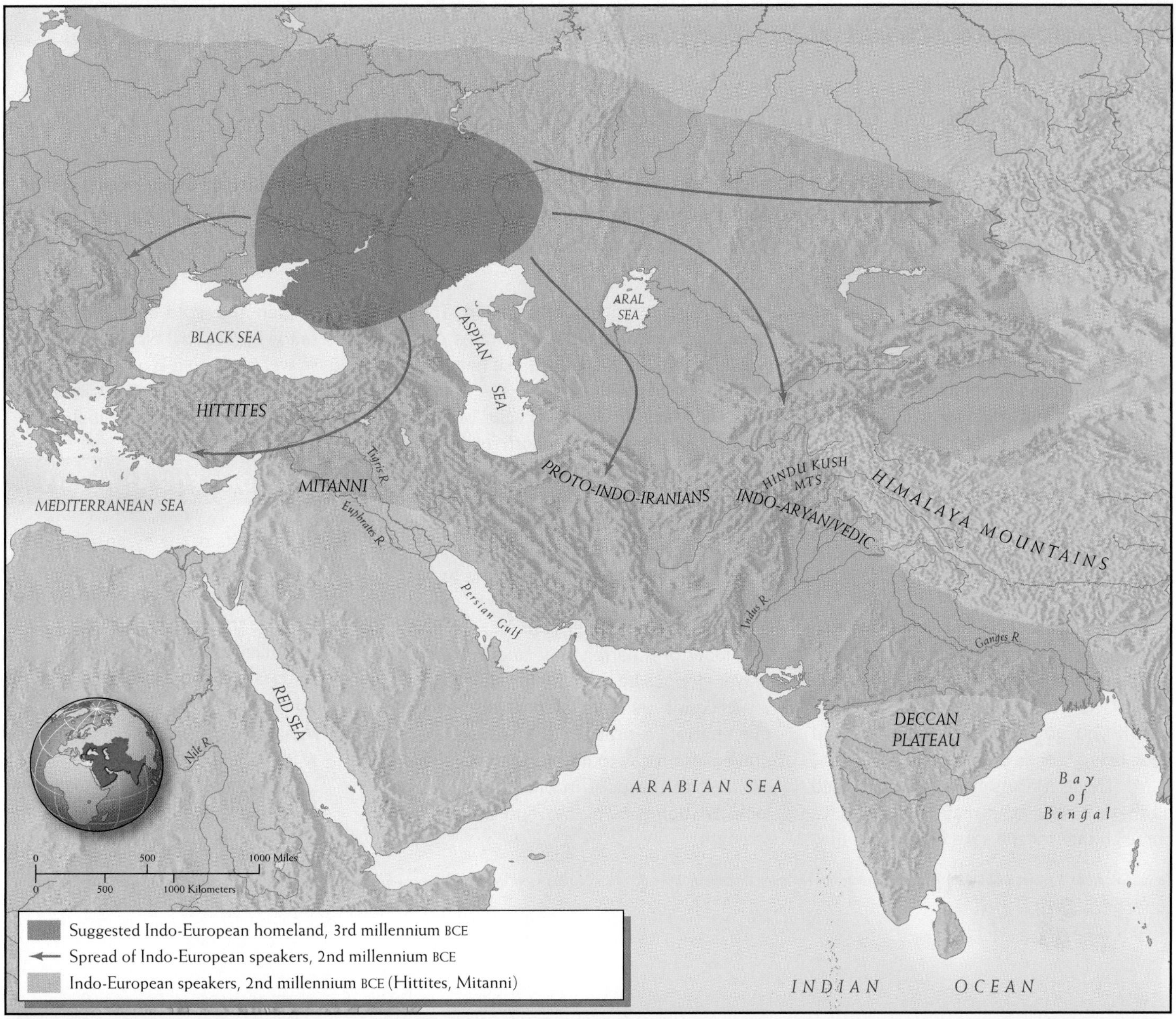

MAP 3.3 | Indo-European Migrations, 2nd Millennium BCE

- Where did the Indo-European migration originate?
- Where did Indo-European migrations spread to during this time?
- How did widespread drought push or draw the migrants into more settled agricultural regions, such as the Indus Valley?

they were a sight to behold. They descended into the fertile Indus River basin (see Map 3.3) with large flocks of cattle and horses, singing chants called Rig Veda as they sacrificed some of their livestock to their gods. Known collectively as the Veda ("knowledge"), these hymns served as the most sacred texts for the newcomers, who have been known ever since as the **Vedic people**. They also arrived with an extraordinary language, Sanskrit (perhaps prophetically labeled "perfectly made"). It is one of the earliest known Indo-European languages, which were a source for virtually all of the European languages, including Greek, Latin, English, French, and German. (See Current Trends in World History: How Languages Spread—The Case of Nomadic Indo-European Languages.)

Like other nomads from the northern steppe, they brought domesticated animals—especially horses, which pulled their chariots and established their military superiority. Not only

PRIMARY SOURCE

Vedic Hymns to the Chariot Race of the Gods

There are no extant accounts of the Vedic people's chariot races and festivals, despite the centrality of these events to their culture. However, scholars have translated Vedic hymns praising the chariot races of gods. The following hymn portrays the Maruts—the storm gods under the direction of Indra—as skilled charioteers.

1. The Maruts charged with rain, endowed with fierce force, terrible like wild beasts, blazing in their strength, brilliant like fires, and impetuous, have uncovered the (rain-giving) cows by blowing away the cloud.

2. The [Maruts] with their rings appeared like the heavens with their stars, they shone wide like streams from clouds as soon as Rudra, the strong man, was born for you, O golden-breasted Maruts, in the bright lap of Prisni.

3. They wash their horses like racers in the courses, they hasten with the points of the reed on their quick steeds. O golden-jawed Maruts, violently shaking [your jaws], you go quick with your spotted deer, being friends of one mind.

4. Those Maruts have grown to feed all these beings, or, it may be, [they have come] hither for the sake of a friend, they who always bring quickening rain. They have spotted horses, their bounties cannot be taken away, they are like headlong charioteers on their ways.

5. O Maruts, wielding your brilliant spears, come hither on smooth roads with your fiery cows [clouds] whose udders are swelling; [come hither], being of one mind, like swans toward their nests, to enjoy the sweet offering.

6. O one-minded Maruts, come to our prayers, come to our libations like [Indra] praised by men! Fulfill [our prayer] like the udder of a barren cow, and make the prayer glorious by booty to the singer.

7. Grant us this strong horse for our chariot, a draught that rouses our prayers, from day to day, food to the singers, and to the poet in our homesteads luck, wisdom, inviolable and invincible strength.

8. When the gold-breasted Maruts harness the horses to their chariots, bounteous in wealth, then it is as if a cow in the folds poured out to her calf copious food, to every man who has offered libations.

QUESTIONS FOR ANALYSIS

- What parts of the hymn give clues about how the charioteers' horses looked and were cared for?
- How do the images relating rain-filled clouds to cows reflect the pastoral roots of the Vedic nomads?
- What kinds of gods were the Maruts, and what was their heavenly job when racing on horse chariots?

Source: Mandala II, Hymn 34, in Vedic Hymns, translated by Hermann Oldenberg, in vol. 32 of Sacred Books of the East, *edited by F. Max Müller (1897; reprint, New Delhi: Motilal Banarsidass, 1979), pp. 295–96.*

were the Vedic people superb horse charioteers, but they were also masters of copper and bronze metallurgy and wheel making. Their expertise in these areas allowed them to produce the very chariots that transported them into their new lands.

Like other Indo-European-speaking groups, the Vedic peoples were deeply religious. They worshipped a host of natural and supernatural deities, the most powerful of which were the sky god and the gods that represented horses. They were confident that their chief god, Indra (the deity of war), was on their side. The Vedic people also brought elaborate rituals of worship, which set them apart from the indigenous populations. (See Primary Source: Vedic Hymns to the Chariot Race of the Gods.) But, as with many Afro-Eurasian migrations, the outsiders' arrival led to fusion as well as to conflict. While the native-born peoples eventually adopted the newcomers' language, the newcomers themselves took up the techniques and rhythms of agrarian life.

The Vedic people used the Indus Valley as a staging area for migrations throughout the northern plain of South Asia. As they mixed agrarian and pastoral ways and borrowed technologies (such as iron working) from farther west, their population expanded and they began to look for new resources. With horses, chariots, and iron tools and weapons, they marched south and east. By 1000 BCE, they reached the southern foothills of the Himalayas and began to settle in the Ganges River valley. Five hundred years later, they had settlements as far south as the Deccan plateau.

Each wave of occupation involved violence, but the invaders did not simply dominate the indigenous peoples. Instead, the confrontations led them to embrace many of the ways of the vanquished. Although the Vedic people despised the local rituals, they were in awe of the inhabitants' farming skills and knowledge of seasonal weather. These they adapted even as they continued to expand their territory. They moved into huts constructed from mud, bamboo, and reeds. They refined the already sophisticated production of beautiful carnelian stone beads, and they further aided commerce by devising standardized weights. In addition to raising domesticated animals, they sowed wheat and rye on the Indus plain, and they learned to plant rice in the marshy lands of the Ganges River valley. Later they mastered the use of plows with iron blades, an innovation that transformed the agrarian base of South Asia.

The turn to settled agriculture was a major shift for the pastoral Vedic people. After all, their staple foods had always been dairy products and meat, and they were used to measuring their wealth in livestock (horses were most valuable, and cows were more valuable than sheep). Moreover, because they could not breed their prized horses in South Asia's semitropical climate, they initiated a brisk import trade from central and Southwest Asia.

As the Vedic people adapted to their new environment and fanned out across uncharted agrarian frontiers, their initial political organization took a somewhat different course from those of Southwest Asia. Whereas competitive kingdoms dominated the landscape there, in South Asia competitive, balanced regimes were slower to emerge. The result was a slower process of political integration.

Indra with Buddha. *The Vedic people worshipped their gods by sacrificing and burning cows and horses and by singing hymns and songs, but they never built temples or sculptured idols. Therefore we do not know how they envisioned Indra and their other gods. However, when Buddhists started to make images of Buddha in the early centuries* CE, *they also sculpted Indra and Brahma as attendants of the Buddha. Indra in Buddhist iconography evolved into Vajrapani, the Diamond Lord. In this plate, the one on the left holding a stick with diamond-shaped heads is Indra/Vajrapani.*

RISE OF THE SHANG STATE (1600–1045 BCE)

Climatic change affected East Asia much as it had central and Southwest Asia. As Chapter 2 detailed, this was a time of cultural integration among agricultural communities along the Yellow and Yangzi rivers. Chinese lore says that during this era a mythological Yu the Great brought the rivers under control and founded the Xia dynasty. While evidence for such a kingdom is sketchy, archaeological and other evidence confirms the emergence, around 1800 BCE, of small states, and of a territorial polity called Shang, around 1600 BCE, located in northeastern China. (See Map 3.4.)

Like the ruling families in Southwest Asian societies, the Shang handed down their own foundation myths to unify the state. Stories supposedly written on bamboo strips and later collected into what historians call the "Bamboo Annals" tell of a time at the end of the Xia dynasty when the sun dimmed, frost and ice appeared in summer, and a long drought followed heavy rainfall and flooding. According to Chinese mythology, Tang, the first ruler of the Shang dynasty, defeated a despotic Xia king and then offered to sacrifice himself so that the drought would end. Tang survived, however, and proved to be a just and moral ruler who strengthened his state and unified his people.

As in South Asia, the Shang political system gradually became more centralized from 1600 to 1200 BCE. Much like the territorial kingdoms of Southwest Asia, the Shang state did not have clearly established borders. To be sure, it faced threats—but not in the form of rival territorial states encroaching on its peripheries. Thus it had little need for a strongly defended permanent capital, though its heartland was called Zhong Shang, or "center Shang." Its capital moved as its frontier expanded and contracted. This relative security is evident in the Shang kings' personalized style of rule, as they made regular trips around the country to meet, hunt, and conduct military

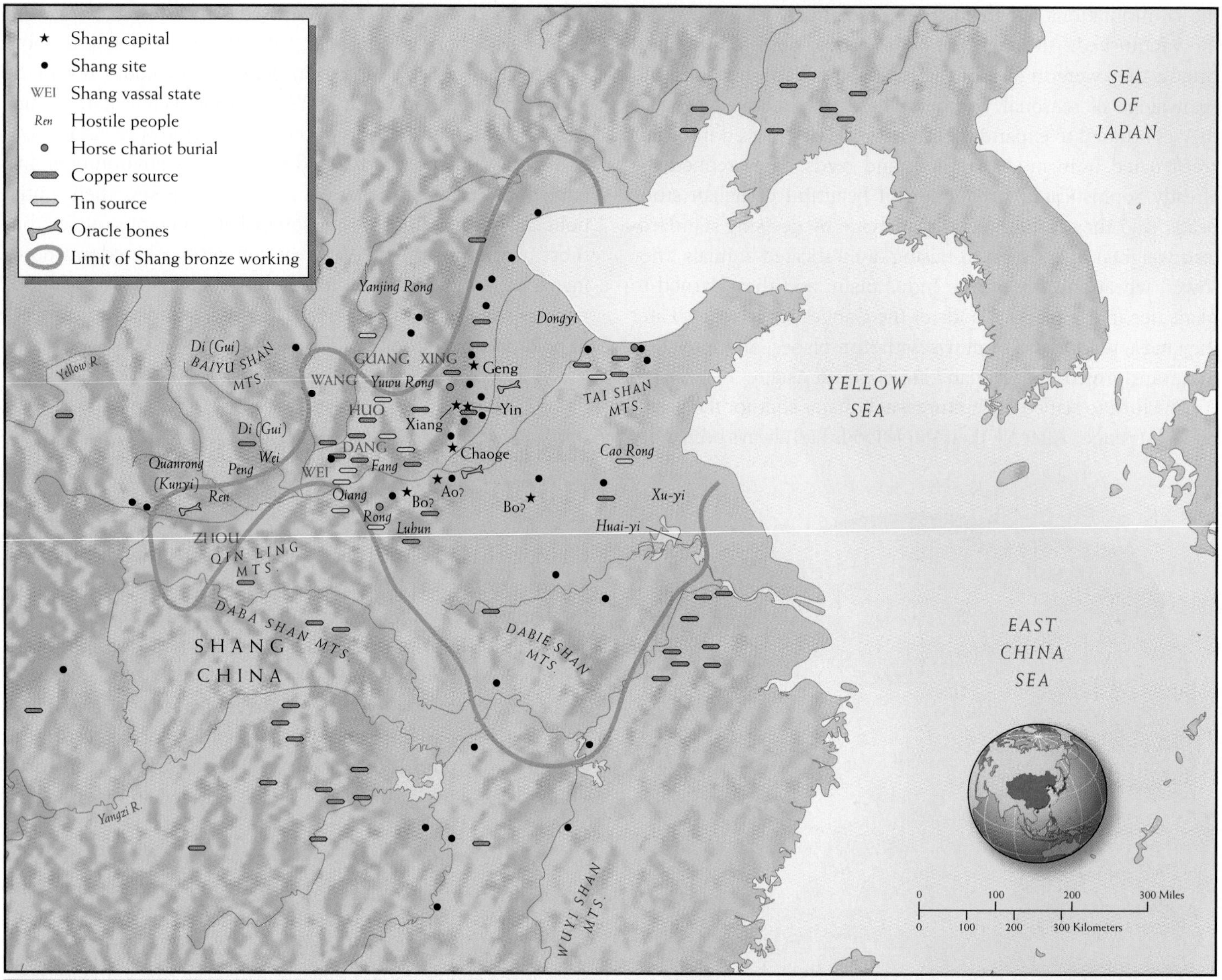

MAP 3.4 | Shang Dynasty in East Asia

- Based on analyzing this map, what raw materials were the most important to the Shang state?
- Why were there so many Shang capitals?
- Why were there no clear territorial boundaries for the Shang state?

campaigns with those who owed allegiance to them. Yet, like the territorial kingdoms of Southwest Asia, the Shang state had a ruling lineage (a line of male sovereigns descended from a common ancestor) that was eventually set down in a written record. (See Primary Source: Sima Qian on the Ruler's Mandate from Heaven to Rule.)

State Formation

The Shang built on the agricultural and riverine village cultures of the Longshan peoples, who had set the stage for an increasingly centralized state, urban life, and a cohesive culture (see Chapter 2). The Shang did not evolve out of city-states as occurred in Mesopotamia and Egypt. Rather, as the population increased and the number of village conflicts grew, it became necessary to have larger and more central forms of control. The Shang polity emerged to play that governmental role.

The Shang culture was built on four elements that the Longshan peoples had already introduced. These were a metal industry based on copper; pottery making; walled towns; and divination using animal bones. To these foundations the Shang dynasty added hereditary rulers whose power derived from

PRIMARY SOURCE

Sima Qian on the Ruler's Mandate from Heaven to Rule

Sima Qian was the first great historian in ancient China. He later had as much influence in East Asia as Herodotus, the first Greek historian, had in Greece and Rome. The excerpt below presents the transition from Xia ("Hsia") dynasty to Shang ("T'ang") dynasty as an example of the transfer of the ruler's heavenly mandate.

After Emperor K'ung-chia was enthroned, he delighted in following ghosts and spirits and engaging in licentious and disorderly actions. The prestige of the Hsia-hou Clan declined and the feudal lords rebelled against him.

Heaven sent down two dragons, a male and a female. K'ung-chia was not able to care for them and he lost the support of the Huan-lung (Dragon Raising) Clan. The Yao-t'ang Clan was already in decline, [but] among their descendants one Liu Lei learned the technique of taming dragons from the Huan-lung Clan and thus obtained service with K'ung-chia. K'ung-chia bestowed on him the *cognomen* Yü-lung (Dragon Tamer) and conferred on him the people descended from the Shih-wei [Clan]. The female dragon died and Liu Lei fed it to the Hsia-hou, the Hsia-hou sent [someone] to demand [more of it], and, fearing [that he would be punished], Liu Lei moved on.

When K'ung-chia passed away, his son Emperor Kao was enthroned. When Emperor Kao passed away his son Emperor Fa was enthroned. When Fa passed away, his son Emperor Lu-k'uei was enthroned. He was known as Chieh.

From K'ung-chia's time to the time of Emperor Chieh, the feudal lords had revolted many times against the Hsia. Chieh did not engage in virtuous [government] but in military power and [this] hurt the families of the hundred cognomens. The families of the hundred cognomens were not able to bear him.

Chieh then summoned T'ang and jailed him in Hsia-t'ai. After a while he freed him. T'ang cultivated his virtue and the feudal lords all submitted to T'ang. T'ang then led troops to attack Chieh of Hsia. Chieh fled to Ming-t'iao and subsequently was exiled and died there. Before he died he said to someone, "I regret failing to kill T'ang in Hsia-t'ai; that is what has brought me to this."

T'ang then ascended the throne of the Son of Heaven and received the world's homage in the Hsia's place. T'ang enfeoffed [made vassals or subjects] the descendants of the Hsia. In the Chou dynasty they were enfeoffed at Ch'i.

QUESTIONS FOR ANALYSIS

- What role did morality play in Sima Qian's description of the transfer of the Xia ruler's mandate from heaven to the Shang dynasty?
- How do the references to feuding illustrate the type of society that China had at this time?

Source: Ssu-ma Ch'ien, "Sima Qian on the Ruler's Mandate," from The Grand Scribe's Records, *ed. William H. Nienhauser Jr. Reprinted with permission of Indiana University Press.*

their relation to ancestors and gods; large-scale metallurgy; written records; tribute; and rituals that enabled them to commune with ancestors and foretell the future. By combining all of these elements the Shang strengthened and brought into existence a wealthy and powerful elite, notable for its intellectual achievements and remarkable aesthetic sensibilities. It became the preeminent society in China during the the second millennium BCE.

Two key elements to Shang success were the emergence of written records and new advances in metallurgy. Bureaucrats used written records to oversee a large and expanding population. Evidence for the importance of writing and written records comes from oracle-bone inscriptions, which were first discovered and translated beginning in 1899 CE and constitute some of the earliest writing in China. Equally significant were advances in metallurgy, the beginnings of which appeared in northwestern China. Pre-Shang sites here reveal that casting techniques were already in use as early as 1800 BCE. Because copper and tin were available from the North China plain, only short-distance trade was necessary to obtain the resources that a bronze culture needed. Access to copper and tin, and to new metallurgy technology, eventually gave the Shang a huge advantage and unprecedented power over their neighbors.

The Shang used copper, lead, and tin to produce bronze, from which they made weapons, fittings for chariots, and ritual vessels. The technique involved the use of hollow clay molds to hold the molten metal alloy, which, when removed after the liquid had cooled and solidified, produced firm bronze objects. The casting of modular components that artisans could assemble later promoted increased production and permitted the elite to make extravagant use of bronze vessels for burials. For example, archaeologists have unearthed a tomb at Anyang containing one enormous 1,925-pound bronze vessel; the Shang workshops

Bronze. *At the height of the Shang state, circa 1200 BCE, its rulers erected massive palaces at the capital of Yin, which required bronze foundries for its wine and food vessels. In these foundries, skilled workers produced bronze weapons and ritual objects and elaborate ceremonial drinking and eating vessels, like the one pictured.*

had produced it in 1200 BCE. Another Anyang tomb from the same period contained 3,500 pounds of cast bronze.

The bronze industry of this period shows a high level not only of material culture (the physical objects produced) but also of cultural development and aesthetic sensibility. Artisans skilled in the production of bronze produced ewers, tureens, boxes, and all manner of weapons; decorated jade, stone, and ivory objects; and wove silk on special looms. The bronzes were of the highest quality, decorated as they were with geometrical and animal designs featuring elephants, rams, tigers, horses, and more. Since Shang metalworking required extensive mining, it necessitated a large labor force, efficient casting, and a reproducible artistic style. Although the Shang state highly valued its artisans, it treated its copper miners as lowly tribute laborers.

By controlling access to tin and copper and to the production of bronze, the Shang kings prevented their rivals from forging bronze weapons and thus increased their own power and legitimacy. With their superior weapons, Shang armies by 1300 BCE could easily destroy armies wielding wooden clubs and stone-tipped spears. Moreover, rulers enhanced their power by hiring artisans to record their feats for posterity. Shang workers produced large and small bronze vessels on which they delicately inscribed images of important events—particularly those telling of rulers in significant roles, such as a battle, a wedding, the birth of an heir, or an astrological sighting.

Chariots entered the Central Plains of China together with nomads from the north around 1200 BCE, more than 500 years after the Hittites had used these vehicles to dominate much of Southwest Asia. Although upper classes quickly assimilated, they were not at first used extensively for military purposes and never achieved the military importance in China that they did elsewhere in Afro-Eurasia. The lesser use of chariots in the Shang era may have been because the large Shang infantry forces were able to awe their enemies. In Shang times, the chariots' primary purposes were hunting and markers of high status, though in fact Chinese chariots were much better built than those of their neighbors, having been improved by adding bronze fittings and harnesses. They were also larger than most of those in use in Egypt and Southwest Asia, accommodating three men standing in a box mounted on 18 or 26 spoke wheels. As symbols of power and wealth, chariots were often buried with their owners,

Rather than employ chariots to defend and expand their borders with neighboring states and pastoral nomads on the central Asian steppes, the Shang created armies composed mainly of foot soldiers, armed with axes, spears, arrowheads, shields, and helmets, all made of bronze. These forces prevailed at first, but eventually they lost ground and the Shang territorial domain shrank until the regime was unable to resist invasion, in 1045 BCE, from its western neighbor and former tributary, the Zhou, who may have employed chariots in overcoming the much larger Shang armies.

As a patchwork of regimes, East Asia did not rise to the level of military-diplomatic jostling of Southwest Asia. Other large states developed alongside the Shang. These included relatively urban and wealthy peoples in the southeast and more rustic peoples bordering the Shang. The latter traded with the former, whom they knew as the Fang—their label for those who lived in non-Shang areas. Other kingdoms in the south and southwest also had independent bronze industries, with casting technologies comparable to those of the Shang.

Agriculture and Tribute

The Shang dynasts also understood the importance of agriculture for winning and maintaining power, so they did much to promote its development. In fact, the activities of local governors and the masses revolved around agriculture. The rulers controlled their own farms, which supplied food to the royal family, craftworkers, and the army. New technologies led to increased food production. Farmers drained low-lying fields and cleared

PRIMARY SOURCE

The Oracle Bone

About 3,000 years old, the oracle bone below dates from the Shang dynasty reign of King Wu Ding (c. 1200 BCE). Oracle bones enabled diviners to access the other world and provided the ruler with important information about the future. Shang kings often used divination to make political or military decisions and to predict the weather.

A partial translation of the left-hand side of this oracle bone reads:

[Preface:] Crack making on *gui-si* day, Que divined:
[Charge:] In the next ten days there will be no disaster.
[Prognostication:] The king, reading the cracks, said, "There will be no harm; there will perhaps be the coming of alarming news."
[Verification:] When it came to the fifth day, *ding-you*, there really was the coming of alarming news from the west. Zhi Guo, reporting, said, "The Du Fang [a border people] are besieging in our eastern borders and have harmed two settlements." The Gong-fang also raided the fields of our western borders.

QUESTIONS FOR ANALYSIS

- What political or military decision do you think King Wu Ding might have made in response to the "alarming news"?
- Why did Shang kings rely on oracle bones?

Source: This translation follows, with slight modifications by Bryan W. Van Norden, David N. Keightley, Sources of Shang History *(Berkeley: University of California Press, 1978), p. 44.*

forested areas to expand the cultivation of millet, wheat, barley, and possibly rice. Their implements included stone plows, spades, and sickles. In addition, farmers cultivated silkworms and raised pigs, dogs, sheep, and oxen. To best use the land and increase production, they tracked the growing season. And to record the seasons, the Shang developed a twelve-month, 360-day lunar calendar; it contained leap months to maintain the proper relationship between months and seasons. The calendar also relieved fears about events such as solar and lunar eclipses by making them predictable.

As in other Afro-Eurasian states, the ruler's wealth and power depended on tribute from elites and allies. Elites supplied warriors and laborers, horses and cattle. Allies sent foodstuffs, soldiers, and workers and "assisted in the king's affairs"—perhaps by hunting, burning brush, or clearing land—in return for his help in defending against invaders and making predictions about the harvest. Commoners sent their tribute to the elites, who held the land as fiefs from the king. (Fiefs were grants, usually of land and occasionally of office, by kings and lords to subordinates.) Farmers transferred their surplus crops to the elite landholders (or to the ruler if they worked on his personal landholdings) on a regular schedule.

Tribute could also take the form of turtle shells and cattle scapulas (shoulder blades), which the Shang used for divination (see below). Divining the future was a powerful way to legitimate royal power—and then to justify the right to collect more tribute. By placing themselves symbolically and literally at the center of all exchanges, the Shang kings reinforced their power over others.

Shang Society and Beliefs

The advances in metalworking and agriculture gave the state the resources to create and sustain a complex society. The core

CURRENT TRENDS IN WORLD HISTORY

How Languages Spread: The Case of Nomadic Indo-European Languages

Linguistics, or the study of language, is an important tool in world history. Language arose independently in a number of places around the world. All languages change with time, and their divergence from a mother tongue serves as a tool in determining at what point different languages, like German or French, broke apart. Scholars call related tongues with a common origin "language families." Even though members of the same language family diverged over time, they all share grammatical features and root vocabularies.

While technically there are more than 100 language families, a much smaller number have influenced vast geographic areas. For example, the *Altaic* languages spread from central Asia to Europe. The *Sino-Tibetan* language family includes Mandarin, the most widely spoken language in the world. The *Uralic* family, which includes Hungarian and Finnish, occurs mainly in Europe. The *Afro-Asiatic* language family contains several hundred languages spoken in North Africa, sub-Saharan Africa, and Southwest Asia, Hebrew and Arabic among them.

One language family that linguists have studied extensively, and the one with the largest number of speakers today, is *Indo-European*. It was identified by scholars who recognized similarities in grammar and vocabulary among classical Sanskrit, Persian, Greek, and Latin. Living languages in this family include English, Irish, German, Norwegian, Portuguese, French, Russian, Persian, Hindi, and Bengali. For the past 200 years, comparative linguists have sought to reconstruct Proto-Indo-European, the parent of all the languages in the family. They have drawn conclusions about its grammar, hypothesizing a highly inflected language with different endings on nouns and verbs according to their use. They have also made suggestions about its vocabulary. For example, after analyzing patterns of linguistic change, scholars have proposed that the basic Indo-European root that means "horse"—in Sanskrit, *a´sva*; Persian, *aspa*; Latin, *equus*; and Greek, *hippos* (*íppoβ*)—is *ekwo-.

Table 3.1 demonstrates the similarity of words in some of the major Indo-European languages. We have emphasized numbers, which are especially stable in language systems because people do not like to change the way they count. We have also provided the equivalents in two Semitic languages (Arabic and Hebrew) to show how different these basic words are in another language family (the Afro-Asiatic).

Attempts to locate the homeland of the original speakers of Proto-Indo-European involve mapping the reconstructed vocabulary onto a matching geography. For example, some of the vocabulary contains words for "snow," "mountain," and "swift river," as well as for animals that are not native to Europe, such as "lion," "monkey," and "elephant." Other words describe agricultural practices and farming tools that date back as far as 5000 BCE. Many linguists believe that nomadic and pastoral peoples of the Eurasian steppes took this language—along with their precious horses and chariots—as far as the borderlands of what is now Afghanistan and eastern Iran.

Migration is only one of the possible reasons that languages move and change over vast areas and periods of time. Other influential factors are invasions, climatic conditions, natural resources, and ways of life.

QUESTIONS FOR ANALYSIS

- What relationships does Table 3.1 suggest among the Semitic languages and the Indo-European languages?
- How does the study of linguistics enhance our understanding of human geography?

Explore Further

David W. Anthony, *The Horse, the Wheel, and Language: How Bronze-Age Riders from the Eurasian Steppes Shaped the Modern World* (2007).

Joseph T. Shipley, *The Origins of English Words: A Discursive Dictionary of Indo-European Roots* (2001).

organizing principle of Shang society was familial descent traced back many generations to a common male ancestor. Grandparents, parents, sons, and daughters lived and worked together and held property in common, but male family elders took precedence. Women from other patrilines married into the family and won honor when they became mothers, particularly of sons.

The death ritual, which involved sacrificing humans to accompany the deceased in the next life, also reflected the importance of family, male dominance, and social hierarchy. Members of the royal elite were often buried with full entourage, including wives, consorts, servants, chariots, horses, and drivers. The inclusion of personal slaves and servants indicates a belief that the familiar social hierarchy would continue in the afterlife. Modern Chinese historians have described the Shang as a "slave society," but the basis of its economy was not slave labor. Instead, the driving force was the tribute labor (in particular, metalworking and farming) of the commoners who constituted most of society.

The Shang state was a full-fledged theocracy: it claimed that the ruler at the top of the hierarchy derived his authority through guidance from ancestors and gods. The Shang rulers practiced **ancestral worship**, which was the major form of

TABLE 3.1 | Similarity of Words in Some Major Indo-European Languages

	WORDS OF COMMON ORIGIN IN INDO-EUROPEAN LANGUAGES						SEMITIC LANGUAGES	
	SANSKRIT	HINDI	GREEK	LATIN	FRENCH	GERMAN	ARABIC	HEBREW
Numbers								
one	eka	ek	hen	unus	un	ein	wahid	ehad
two	dva	do	duo	duo	deux	zwei	ithnin	shnayim
three	tri	teen	treis	tres	trois	drei	thalatha	shlasha
four	catur	chār	tessara	quattuor	quatre	vier	arba'a	arba'a
five	pañca	pānch	penta	quinque	cinq	fünf	khamsa	hamisha
ten	daśa	das	deka	decem	dix	zehn	ashra	asara
hundred	śata	sau	hekaton	centum	cent	hundert	mi'a	me'a
Other common words								
father	pitṛ	pitā	pater	pater	père	vater	abu	aba
mother	mātṛ	mātā	mêter	mater	mère	mutter	umm	em
son	sūnu	betā	huios	filius	fils	sohn	ibn	ben
heart	hṛdaya	dil	kardia	cor	coeur	herz	qalb	lev
foot	pada	pair	pous	pes	pied	fuss	qadam	regel
god	deva	dev	theos	deus	dieu	gott	Allah	yahweh

religious belief in China during this period. Ancestral worship involved performing rituals in which the rulers offered drink and food to their recently dead ancestors with the hope that they would intervene with their more powerful long-dead ancestors on behalf of the living. In finding ritual ways to communicate with ancestors and foretell the future, rulers relied on **divination**, much as did the rulers in Mesopotamia at this time. The technique involved diviners applying intense heat to the shoulder bones of cattle or to turtle shells and interpreting the cracks that appeared on these objects as auspicious or inauspicious signs from the ancestors regarding royal plans and actions. (See Primary Source: The Oracle Bone.) On these bones scribes subsequently inscribed the queries asked of the ancestors to confirm the diviners' interpretations. Thus, Shang writing began as a dramatic ritual performance in which the living responded to their ancestors' oracular signs.

The oracle bones and tortoise shells also offer an invaluable window into the concerns and beliefs of the elite groups of these very distant cultures and often reveal to researchers how similar the worries and interests of these people were to our own concerns. The questions that would seem to have been put to diviners most frequently as they inspected bones and shells were about the weather, hardly surprising in communities so dependent on growing seasons and good harvests; about family health and well-being; and especially about the prospects of having male children, who would extend the family line.

In Shang theocracy, because the ruler was the head of a unified clergy and embodied both religious and political power, no independent priesthood emerged. Diviners and scribes were subordinate to the ruler and the royal pantheon of ancestors he represented. (Unlike in Mesopotamia and Egypt, rulers never entrusted diviners with independent action.) Ancestor worship sanctified Shang control and legitimized the rulers' lineage, ensuring that the ruling family kept all political and religious power.

Moreover, in the process of scribes and priests using their script on oracle bones for the Shang king, a predictable evolution took place. The Shang archaic script of primary images tied to sounds and phonetic compounds evolved into the formal, character-based writing that has endured to the present in East Asia. This character-based writing has set China (and later Japan, Korea, and Vietnam) apart from the societies in Mesopotamia and the Mediterranean that rely on syllable- and alphabet-based writing systems. (See Current Trends in World History: How Languages Spread: The Case of Nomadic Indo-European Languages.)

Because the Shang gods were ancestral deities, the rulers were deified when they died and ranked in descending chronological order. The primary Shang deity was Di, the High God (Shangdi), who was the founding ancestor of the Shang royal family. Still, Shang rulers when they became gods were thought to be closer to the world of humans than the supreme Egyptian and Mesopotamian gods, and they served to unite the world of the living with the world of the dead. Much as the Egyptians believed their pharaohs (supposedly born of human mothers and godlike fathers) ascended into heaven after their deaths, so the Shang believed their kings moved into a parallel other world when they died.

THE SOUTH PACIFIC (2500 BCE–400 CE)

As Afro-Eurasian populations grew, and migration and trade brought cultures together, some peoples took to the waters in search of opportunities or refuge. By comparing the vocabularies and grammatical similarities of languages spoken today by the tribal peoples in Taiwan, the Philippines, and Indonesia, we can trace the ancient Austronesian-speaking peoples back to coastal South China in the fourth millennium BCE. A first wave of migrants reached the islands of Polynesia. A second wave from Taiwan around 2500 BCE again reached Polynesia and then went beyond into the South Pacific. By 2000 BCE these peoples had replaced the earlier inhabitants of the East Asian coastal islands, the hunter-gatherers known as the Negritos, who had migrated south from the Asian landmass around 28,000 BCE, during an ice age when the coastal Pacific islands were connected to the Asian mainland.

Austronesian Canoe. *Early Austronesians crossed the Taiwan Straits and colonized key islands in the Pacific using double-outrigger canoes from sixty to one hundred feet long equipped with triangular sails. In good weather, such canoes could cover more than 120 miles in a day.*

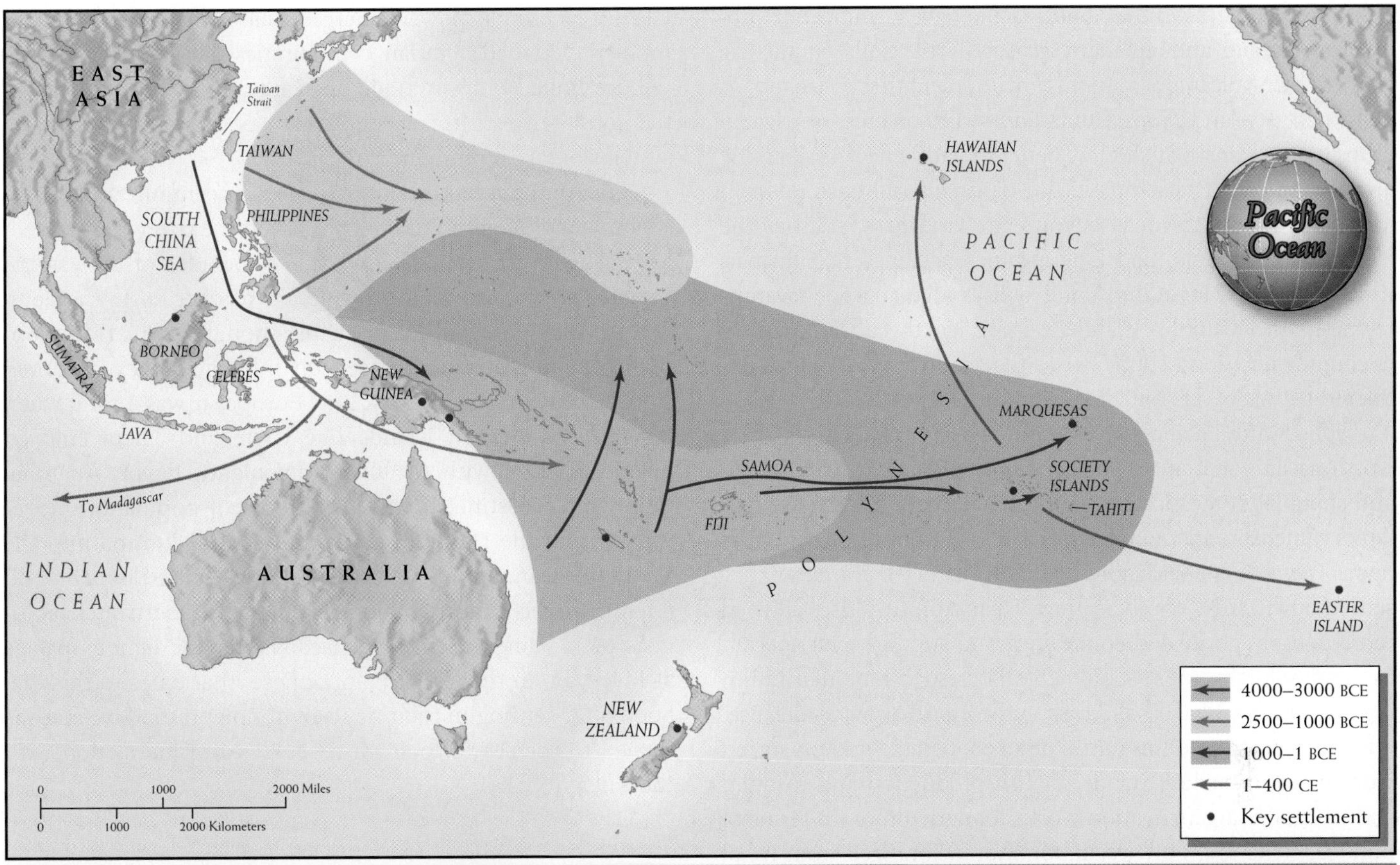

MAP 3.5 | Austronesian Migrations

- Where did the Austronesian migrants come from?
- What were the boundaries of their migration?
- Why, unlike other migratory people during the second millennium, did Austronesian settlers in Polynesia become a world apart?

Seafaring Skills

Using their remarkable double-outrigger canoes, which were 60 to 100 feet long and bore huge triangular sails, the early Austronesians crossed the Taiwan Straits and colonized key islands in the Pacific. Their vessels were much more advanced than the simple dugout canoes used in inland waterways. In good weather, double-outrigger canoes could cover more than 120 miles in a day. The invention of a stabilization device for deep-sea sailing sometime after 2500 BCE triggered further Austronesian expansion into the Pacific. By 400 CE, these nomads of the sea had reached most of the South Pacific except for Australia and New Zealand.

Their seafaring skills enabled the Austronesians to monopolize trade wherever they went (as the Phoenicians did during the first half of the first millennium BCE). Among their craftworkers were potters, who produced distinctive Lapita ware (bowls and vessels) on offshore islets or in coastal villages. Archaeological finds reveal that these canoe-building people also conducted inter-island trade in New Guinea after 1600 BCE, reaching Fiji, Samoa, and Tonga according to the evidence from pottery fragments and the remains of domesticated animals.

Environment and Culture

Pottery, stone tools, and domesticated crops and pigs characterized Austronesian settlements throughout the coastal islands and in the South Pacific. These cultural markers reached the Philippines from Taiwan. By 2500 BCE, according to archaeologists, the same cultural features had spread to the islands of Java, Sumatra, Celebes, Borneo, and Timor. Austronesians arrived in Java and Sumatra in 2000 BCE; by 1600 BCE they were in Australia and New Guinea, although they failed to penetrate the interior, where descendants of the indigenous peoples still live. The Austronesians then ventured farther eastward into the South Pacific, apparently arriving in Samoa and Fiji in 1200 BCE and on mainland Southeast Asia in 1000 BCE. (See Map 3.5.)

Equatorial lands in the South Pacific have a tropical or subtropical climate and, in many places, fertile soils containing nutrient-rich volcanic ash. In this environment the Austronesians cultivated dry-land crops (yams and sweet potatoes), irrigated crops (more yams, which grew better in paddy fields or in rainy areas), and tree crops (breadfruit, bananas, and coconuts). In addition, colonized areas beyond the landmass, such as the islands of Indonesia, had labyrinthine coastlines rich in maritime resources, including coral reefs and mangrove swamps teeming with wildlife. Island hopping led the adventurers to encounter new food sources, but the shallow waters and reefs offered sufficient fish and shellfish for their needs.

In the South Pacific, the Polynesian descendants of the early Austronesians shared a common culture, language, technology, and stores of domesticated plants and animals. These later seafarers came from many different island communities (hence the name *Polynesian,* "belonging to many islands"), and after they settled down, their numbers grew. Their crop surpluses allowed more densely populated communities to support craft specialists and soldiers. Most settlements boasted ceremonial buildings to promote local solidarity and forts to provide defense. On larger islands, communities often cooperated and organized workforces to enclose ponds for fish production and to build and maintain large irrigation works for agriculture. In terms of political structure, Polynesian communities ranged from tribal or village units to multi-island alliances that sometimes invaded other areas.

The Austronesians reached the Marquesas Islands, strategically located for northern and southern exploration, in the central Pacific around 200 CE. Over the next few centuries, some moved on to Easter Island to the south and Hawaii to the north. The immense thirty-ton stone structures on Easter Island represent the monumental Polynesian architecture produced after their arrival. In separate migrations they traversed the Indian Ocean westward and arrived at the island of Madagascar by the sixth century CE. Along the way, they transmitted crops such as the banana to East Africa.

The expansion of East Asian peoples throughout the South Pacific and their trade back and forth did not, however, integrate the islands into a mainland style culture. Expansion could not overcome the tendency of these **microsocieties**, dispersed across a huge ocean, toward fragmentation and isolation.

MICROSOCIETIES IN THE AEGEAN WORLD

In the region around the Aegean Sea, the islands and the mainland of present-day Greece—in short, the island world of the eastern Mediterranean—initially resembled that of the South Pacific. No single power emerged before the second millennium BCE. Settled agrarian communities developed into local polities linked only by trade and culture. Fragmentation was the norm—in part because the landscape had no great riverine systems or large common plain.

As an unintended benefit of the lack of centralization, there was no single regime to collapse when the droughts arrived. Thus, in the second millennium BCE, peoples of the eastern Mediterranean did not struggle to recover lost grandeur. Rather, they enjoyed a remarkable though gradual development, making advances based on influences they absorbed from Southwest Asia, Egypt, and Europe. It was a time when residents of Aegean islands like Crete and Thera enjoyed extensive trade with the Greek mainland, Egypt, Anatolia, Syria, and Palestine. It was also a time of population movements from the Danube region and central Europe into the Mediterranean. Groups of these migrants settled in mainland Greece in the centuries after 1900 BCE; modern archaeologists have named them Mycenaeans after the famous palace at Mycenae, in the Greek Peloponnese, that dates to this era. Soon after settling in their new environment, the Mycenaeans turned to the sea to look for resources and interaction with their neighbors.

Seaborne Trade and Communication

At the outset, the main influence on the Aegean world came from the east by sea. As the institutions and ideas that had developed in Southwest Asia moved westward, they found a ready reception along the coasts and on the islands of the Mediterranean. These innovations followed the sea currents, moving up the eastern seaboard of the Levant, then to the island of Cyprus and along the southern coast of Anatolia, and then westward to the islands of the Aegean Sea and to Crete. Trade was the main source of eastern influences, with vessels carrying cargoes from island to island and up and down the commercial centers along the coast. (See Map 3.6.)

The Mediterranean islands were important hubs that linked the mainland peoples of western Asia and Europe with the islanders. They also served as a springboard from which eastern influences shot northward into Europe. By 1500 BCE, the islands were booming. Trade centered on tin from the east and readily available copper, both essential for making bronze (the primary metal in tools and weapons). Islands located in the midst of the active sea-lanes flourished. Because Cyprus straddled the main sea-lane, it was a focal point of trade. It also had large reserves of copper ore, which started to generate intense activity around 2300 BCE. By 2000 BCE, harbors on the southern and eastern sides of the island were shipping and transshipping goods, along with copper ingots, as far west as Crete, east to

Seaborne Trade. *The size of the seaborne trade is revealed most spectacularly in the shipwrecks recovered by underwater archaeologists. One of these ships, sunk off the southern coast of Anatolia around 1325 BCE, was transporting ten tons of copper in 354 oxhide-shaped ingots, as well as more than 100 amphorae (large, two-handled jars) containing all kinds of high-value commodities.*

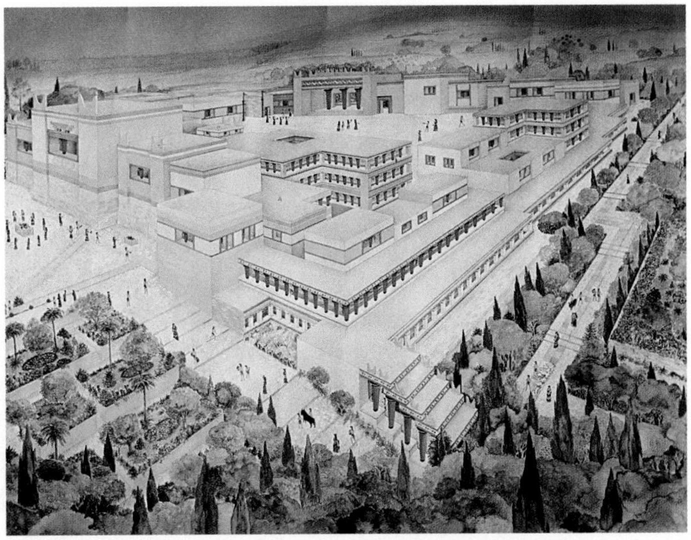

Palace at Knossos. *An artist's reconstruction of the Minoan palace at Knossos on Crete. This complex, the largest such center on the island, covered more than six acres and contained more than 1,300 rooms. Its main feature was a large, open-air central courtyard, around which were arranged the storage, archive, ritual, and ceremonial rooms. Rather than the complex cities that would emerge later, the urbanized centers on Crete were represented by these large complexes, similar to palace complexes in contemporary Levantine sites.*

the Euphrates River, and south to Egypt. So identified was this island with the metal that the English word *copper* is derived from "Cyprus."

Crete, too, was an active trading node in the Mediterranean, with networks reaching as far east as Mesopotamia. Around 2000 BCE, a large number of independent palace centers began to emerge on Crete, at Knossos and elsewhere. Scholars have named the people who built these elaborate centers the Minoans, after the legendary King Minos who may have ruled Crete at this time. The Minoans sailed back and forth across the Mediterranean, and by 1600 BCE they were colonizing other Aegean islands as trading and mining centers. The Minoans' wealth soon became a magnet for the Mycenaeans, their mainland competitors, who took over Crete around 1400 BCE.

Minoan Culture

As the island communities traded with the peoples of Southwest Asia, they borrowed some ideas but also kept their own cultural traditions. In terms of borrowing, the monumental architecture of Southwest Asia found small-scale echoes in the Aegean world—notably in the palace complexes built on Crete between 1900 and 1600 BCE (the most impressive was at Knossos). Unlike in Mesopotamia or Egypt, however, microsocieties or small-scale insular communities remained the norm for human organization on these Aegean islands.

In terms of a distinctive cultural element, worship on the islands focused on a female deity, the "Lady," but there are no traces of large temple complexes similar to those in Mesopotamia, Anatolia, and Egypt. Nor, apparently, was there any priestly class of the type that managed the temple complexes of Southwest Asian societies. Moreover, it is unclear whether these societies had full-time scribes.

There was significant regional diversity within this small Aegean world. On Thera, a small island to the north of Crete, archaeologists have uncovered a splendid trading city—one that was not centered on a major palace complex—in which private houses had bathrooms with toilets and running water and rooms decorated with exotic wall paintings. One painting depicted a flotilla of pleasure, trading, and naval vessels. On Crete, the large palace-centered communities controlled centrally organized societies of a high order of refinement. Confident in their wealth and power, the sprawling palaces had no fortifications and no natural defenses. They were light, airy, and open to their surrounding landscapes.

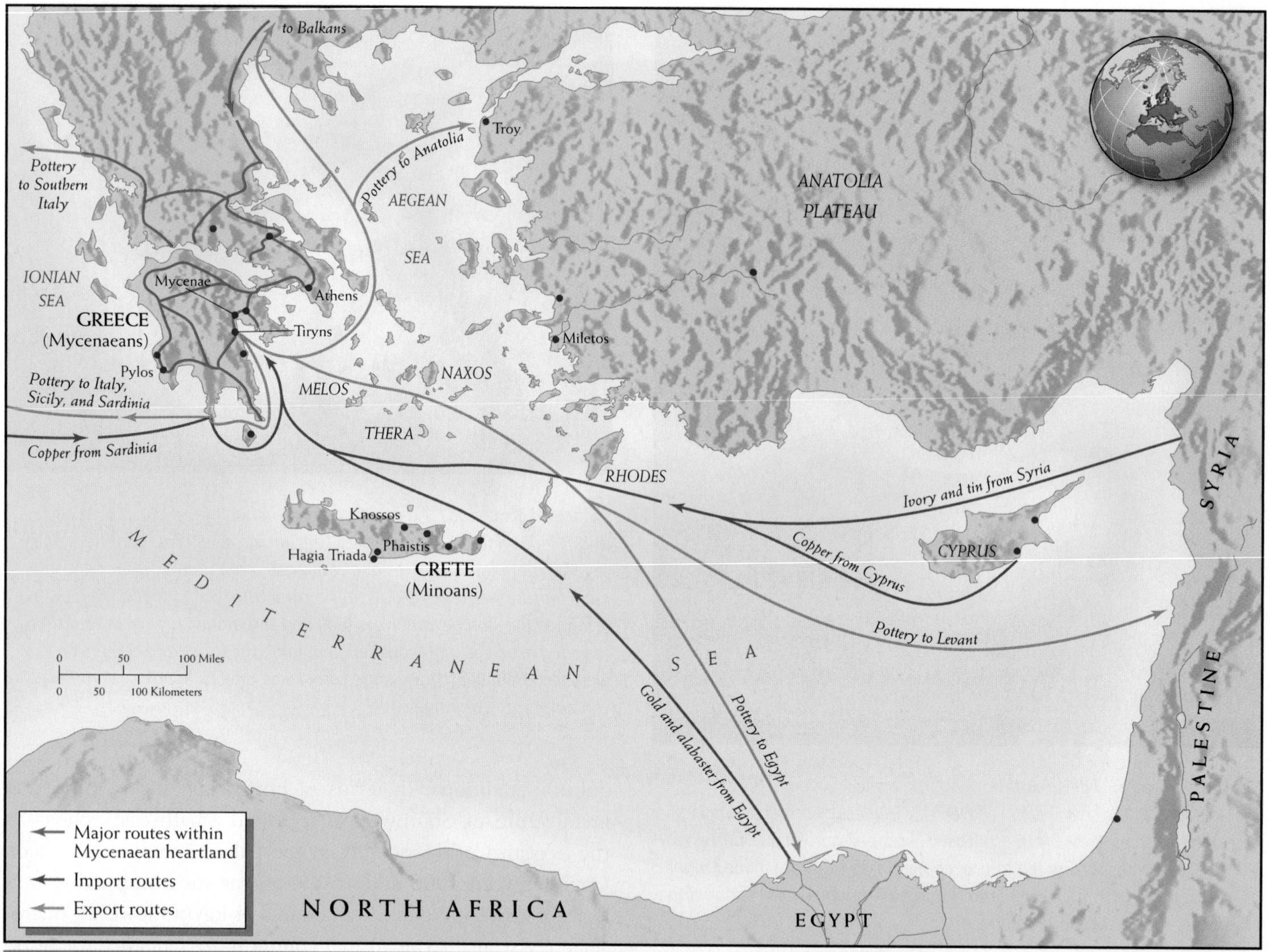

MAP 3.6 | Trade in the Eastern Mediterranean World

- What were the major commodities that were traded in the eastern Mediterranean?
- Why did trade originally move from east to west?
- What role did geographic location play in terms of the Mycenaeans' eventually conquering the Minoans?

Mycenaean Culture

When the Mycenaeans migrated to Greece from central Europe, they brought their Indo-European language, their horse chariots, and their metalworking skills. Their move was gradual, lasting from about 1850 to 1600 BCE, but ultimately they dominated the indigenous population. Known for their exceptional height, they maintained their dominance with their powerful weapon, the chariot, until 1200 BCE. Indeed, horse chariots were important in their mythology and cultural tradition. The battle chariots and festivities of chariot racing described in the epic poetry of Homer (which date from after the collapse of Mycenaean societies) express memories of glorious chariot feats that echo Vedic legends from South Asia (see p. 102).

The Mycenaeans were more war oriented than the peaceful, seafaring Minoans, and they possessed a less refined material culture: it emphasized displays of weaponry, portraits of armed soldiers, and illustrations of violent conflicts. The main palace centers at Tiryns and Mycenae were the hulking fortresses of warlords surrounded by rough-hewn stone walls and strategically located atop large rock outcroppings. The Mycenaeans amassed an amazing amount of wealth and carried some of it to their graves. Their tombs contain many gold vessels and decorations; most ostentatious were the gold masks. The many amber

Aegean Fresco. *This is one of the more striking wall paintings, or frescoes, discovered by archaeologists in the 1970s and 1980s at Akrotiri on the island of Thera (Santorini) in the Aegean Sea. Its brilliant colors, especially the blue of the sea, evoke the lively essence of Minoan life on the island. Note the houses of the wealthy along the port and the flotilla of ships that reflects the seaborne commerce that was beginning to flourish in the Mediterranean in this period.*

beads indicate that the warriors had contacts with inhabitants of the coniferous forest regions in northern Europe.

Southwest Asian economic and political structures shaped the coastal sites where the Mycenaeans settled, such as Tiryns and Pylos. Massive stone fortresses and fortified palaces dominated these urban hubs. A preeminent ruler (*wanax*) stood atop a complex bureaucratic hierarchy; numerous subordinates aided him, including slaves. At the heart of the palace society were scribes, who recorded the goods and services allotted to local farmers, shepherds, and metalworkers, among others. (See Primary Source: Linear A and B—Writing in the Early Mediterranean Worlds.)

Mycenaean expansion eventually overwhelmed the Minoans on Crete. The Mycenaeans also created colonies and trading settlements, reaching as far as Sicily and southern Italy. In this fashion, the trade and language of the early Greek-speaking peoples created a veneer of unity linking the dispersed worlds of the Aegean Sea.

At the close of the second millennium BCE, the eastern Mediterranean faced internal and external convulsions that ended the heyday of these microsocieties. Most notable was a series of migrations of peoples from central Europe who moved through southeastern Europe, Anatolia, and the eastern Mediterranean (see Chapter 4). The invasions, although often destructive, did

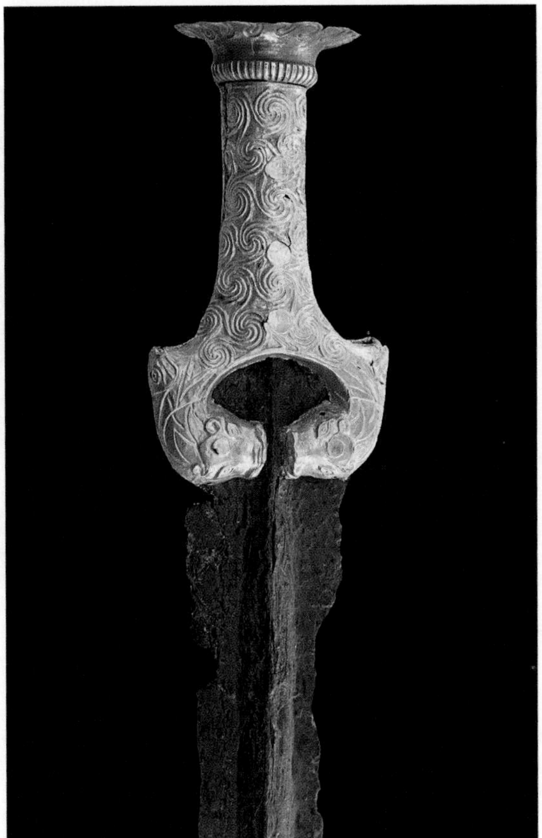

Mycenaean Sword. *The hilt and engraved gold pommel of a sword from the regal burials at the site of Mycenae. The presence of this weaponry, both depicted in the art of the period and preserved in artifacts buried with the dead, was typical of a violent society with a warrior elite. The riveted hilt and the bronze sword blade are of a kind found widely distributed in the Mediterranean, following the patterns of Mycenaean trade routes.*

PRIMARY SOURCE

Linear A and B—Writing in the Early Mediterranean Worlds

On the island of Crete and on the mainland of Greece, scribes working in the palace-centered societies kept records on clay tablets in two scripts that were linear. Linear A script, apparently written in Minoan, has not yet been deciphered. Linear B was deciphered in the 1950s and proved that, contrary to what almost all classical scholars had assumed, the Linear B tablets were the work of speakers of Mycenaean—an early form of Greek.

Massive numbers of these clay tablets have survived. Noting every detail of the goods and services that the palace bureaucracy managed, they contain lists short and long of persons or things—about as interesting as modern grocery lists. The following tablet from Pylos on the Greek mainland notes how much seed grain the bureaucrats were distributing to rural landholders who were dependent on the ruler:

The plot of Qelequhontas: this much seed: 276 l. of wheat

R. slave of the god, holds a lease: so much seed: 12 l. of wheat

W. the priest holds a lease: so much seed: 12 l. of wheat

Thuriatis, female slave of the god, dependant of P. the old man: so much seed: 108 l. of wheat

The plot of Admaos, so much seed: 216 l. of wheat. . . .

T. slave of the god, holds a lease: so much seed: 32 l. of wheat

The plot of A . . . eus, so much seed: 144 l. of wheat. . . .

The plot of T. slave of the god, holds a lease: 18 l. of wheat

The plot of R., so much seed: 138 l. of wheat. . . .

The plot of Aktaios, so much seed: 384 l. of wheat. . . .

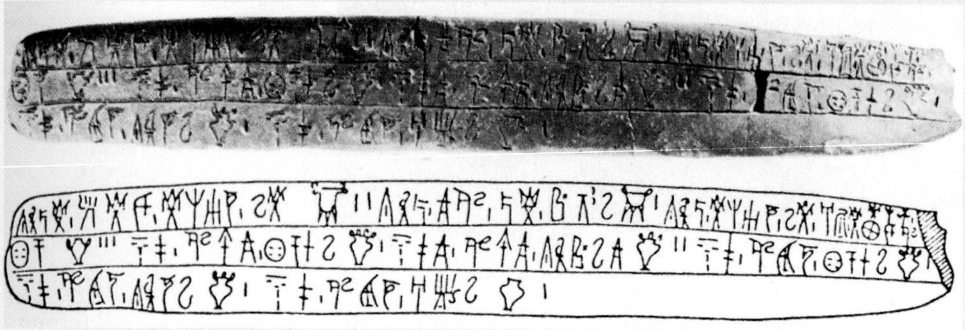

This is an example of the earlier Linear A script, used to write the non-Greek language of the Minoans. Because evidence of the script has appeared only on the island of Crete, scholars believe the early Minoan palace centers were its sole users (probably for keeping records). This example came from the small palace site at Hagia Triada.

This is a typical Linear B document inscribed on clay with linear marks representing syllables and signs. The clay tablet was stored in a palace archive. This tablet came from the excavated Mycenaean palace at Pylos on the mainland of Greece.

QUESTIONS FOR ANALYSIS

- Notice that all the people identified in this passage are going to plant wheat. How does this underscore the blending of agriculture with war making in the aggressive Mycenaean society?
- What does this document suggest is the function of writing in these societies?

Source: M. Ventris and J. Chadwick, Documents in Mycenaean Greek, *2nd ed. (Cambridge: Cambridge University Press, 1973), doc. 116.*

not extinguish but rather reinforced the creative potential of this frontier area. Following the upheaval at the close of the millennium, a new social order emerged that was destined to have an even greater brilliance and influence. Because theirs was a closed maritime world—in comparison with the wide-open Pacific—the Greek-speaking peoples around the Aegean quickly reasserted dominance in the eastern Mediterranean that the Austronesians did not match in Southeast Asia or Polynesia.

EUROPE—THE NORTHERN FRONTIER

The transition to settled agriculture and the raising of domesticated animals took longer in western Afro-Eurasia than in the rest of the landmass. Two millennia passed, from 5000 to 3000 BCE, before settled agriculture became the dominant economic form in Europe. In many broad areas, hunters and gatherers clung to their traditional ways. Even this frontier, however, saw occasional visits from peoples driving horse chariots during the second millennium.

Forbidding evergreen forests dominated the northern area of the far western stretches of Europe, and the area's sparse population was slow to implement the new ways. The first agricultural communities were frontier settlements where pioneers broke new land. Surrounded by hunting and foraging communities, these innovators lived hard lives in harsh environments, overcoming their isolation only by creating regional alliances. Such arrangements were too unstable to initiate or sustain long-distance trade. These were not fertile grounds for creating powerful kingdoms.

The early European cultivators adopted the techniques for controlling plants and animals that Southwest Asian peoples had developed. But rather than establishing large, hierarchical, and centralized societies, the Europeans used these techniques to create self-sufficient communities. They did not incorporate the other cultural and political features that characterized the societies of Egypt, Mesopotamia, and the eastern Mediterranean. Occasional innovations such as the working of metal (initially, copper), the manufacture of pottery, and the use of the plow had little impact on local conditions. Throughout this period, Europe was hardly a developed cultural center. Instead, it was a wild frontier.

Two significant changes affected the northern frontier: the domestication of the horse, and the emergence of wheeled chariots and wagons. Both became instruments of war, and both promoted adaptation to the steppe lands of inner and central Europe, where pasturing animals in large herds proved profitable. The success of this horse culture led to the creation of several new frontiers, including those of agriculturally self-sustaining communities.

The new agriculturalists faced constant challenges not just within Europe but also to the east, as they entered the rolling grasslands of central Eurasia. Their attempts to enter this zone usually met overpowering resistance by fierce men on horseback. The inhabitants of the steppe lands north of the Black Sea gradually shifted from a primitive agriculture to an economy based on the herding of animals. In this zone, the domestication of the horse fostered a highly mobile culture in which whole communities moved on horseback or by means of large wheeled wagons. Because these pastoral nomads regularly sought out the richer agricultural lands in central Europe, there was constant hostility between the two worlds.

These struggles among settlers, hunter-gatherers, and nomadic horse riders bred cultures with a strong warrior ethos. The fullest development of this mounted horse culture occurred in the centuries after 1000 BCE, when the steppe-land Scythian peoples engaged in rituals (such as drinking blood) that forged bonds of blood brotherhood among warriors and heightened their aggressive behavior. This rough-and-tumble frontier gave its people an appetite to borrow more effective means of waging war. Europeans desired the nomadic people's weaponry, and

Steppe Horse Culture. *This gold comb from the early fourth century BCE is decorated with a battle scene from a Scythian heroic epic and illustrates the fascination of these European peoples with horses, weapons, and warfare.*

over time their interactions with the horsemen included trade as well as violence. As a result of the trading contacts, Europeans adopted horses and finer metalworking technologies from the Caucasus. Of course, such trade made their battles even more lethal. And while the connections between this frontier zone and other parts of the Afro-Eurasian world began to multiply, it was still too dispersed and unruly to develop integrated kingdoms. At a time when the rest of Afro-Eurasia was developing an interrelated network of large territorial states, Europe remained a land of war-making, small chieftainships.

EARLY STATES IN THE AMERICAS

Across all the Americas, river valleys and coasts sheltered villages and towns drawing sustenance from the rich resources in their hinterlands. Hunting and gathering was still the main lifeway here. But without beasts of burden or domesticated animals to carry loads or plow fields, local communities produced limited surpluses. Local trade involved only luxuries and symbolic trade goods, such as shells, feathers, hides, and precious metals and gems.

In the Central Andes, however, archaeologists have found evidence of early state systems that transcended local communities to function as confederations, or alliances of towns. These were not as well integrated as many of the territorial states of Southwest Asia, the Indus Valley, and China; they were more like settlements in Europe and the eastern Mediterranean, where towns traded basic goods and in some cases cooperated to resist aggressors.

The region's varied ecology promoted the development of such confederations. Along the arid coast of what is now Peru, fishermen harvested the currents teeming with large and small fish; this was a staple that, when dried, was hardly perishable and easy to transport. The rivers flowing down from the Andean mountains fanned out through the desert, often carving out basins suitable for agriculture. And where the mountains rose from the Pacific, rainfall and higher altitudes favored extensive pasturelands. Here roamed wild llamas and alpacas—difficult as beasts of burden, but valued for their wool in textile production. Such ecological diversity within a limited area promoted greater trade among subregions and towns. Indeed, the interchange of manioc (root of the cassava plant), chili peppers, dried fish, and wool gave rise to the commercial networks that could support political ones.

Communities on the coast, in the riverbeds, or in the mountain valleys were small but numerous. They took shape around central plazas, most of which had large platforms with special burial chambers for elders and persons of importance. Clusters of dwellings surrounded these centers. Much of what we know about political and economic transactions among these communities—as well as long-distance trade and statecraft—comes from the offerings and ornaments left in the burial chambers. Painted gourds, pottery, and fine textiles illustrate the increasing contact among cultures, often bound in alliances. For instance, marriage between noble families could strengthen a pact or confederation.

Cerro Sechin Artifact. *This stele of a warrior brandishing a club was discovered in the Casma Valley in present-day Peru and is a good example of the many striking stone sculptures found in this area.*

One early site known as Aspero reveals how a local community evolved into a form of chiefship, with a political elite and diplomatic and trading ties with neighbors. Temples straddled the top of the central platform, and the large structure at the center boasted lavish ornamentation. Also, there is evidence that smaller communities around Aspero sent crops (fruits) and fish (anchovies) as part of an intercommunity system of mutual dependence.

Not all politics among the valley peoples of Peru consisted of trade and diplomacy, however. In the Casma Valley near the Pacific coast, a clay and stone architectural complex at Cerro Sechín has revealed a much larger sprawl of dwellings and plazas dating back to 1700 BCE. Around the community's central structure stood a wall composed of hundreds of massive stone tablets, carved with ornate etchings of warriors, battles, prisoners, executions, and human body parts. The warriors' clothing is simple and rustic, and the main weapon resembles a club. Clearly, warfare accompanied the first expressions of statecraft in the Americas.

CONCLUSION

The second millennium BCE was an era of migrations, warfare, and kingdom building in Afro-Eurasia. Whereas riverine societies had flourished in the fourth and third millennia BCE in Mesopotamia, Egypt, and the Indus Valley, now droughts and deserts shook the agrarian foundations of their economies. Old states crumbled; from the steppes and plateaus nomadic pastoralists and transhumant herders descended in search of food, grazing lands, and plunder. As transhumant herders pressed into the riverine societies, the social and political fabric of these communities changed. Likewise, horse-riding nomads from steppe communities in Inner Eurasia conquered and settled in the agrarian states, bringing key innovations. Foremost were the horse chariots, which became a military catalyst sparking the evolution from smaller states to large kingdoms encompassing crowded cities and vast hinterlands. The nomads and herders also adopted many of the settled peoples' beliefs and customs. On land and sea, migrating peoples created zones of long-distance trade that linked agrarian societies.

The Nile Delta, the basin of the Tigris and Euphrates rivers, the Indus Valley, and the Yellow River basin were worlds apart before 2000 BCE. Now trade and conquest brought many of these societies into closer contact, especially those in Southwest Asia and the Nile River basin. Here, the interaction even led to an elaborate system of diplomatic relations. The first territorial states appeared in this millennium, composed of communities living under common laws and customs. An alliance of farmers and warriors united agrarian wealth and production with political power to create and defend extended territories. The new arrangements overshadowed the nomads' historic role as predators and enabled them to become military elites. Through taxes and drafted labor, villagers repaid their rulers for local security and state-run diplomacy.

The rhythms of state formation differed where regimes were not closely packed together. In East Asia, the absence of strong rivals allowed the emerging Shang dynasty to develop more gradually. Where landscapes had sharper divisions—as in the island archipelagos of the South China Sea, or in Europe—small-scale, decentralized microsocieties emerged. This was true above all in the Americas, where the lack of wheeled vehicles and horses made long-distance communication much more challenging—and inhibited rulers' territorial ambitions. Here, too, microsocieties were the norm. But fragmentation is not the same as isolation. Even peoples on the fringes and the subjects of microsocieties were not entirely secluded from the increasing flows of technologies, languages, goods, and migrants.

AFTER YOU READ THIS CHAPTER

Review and research **StudySpace:** wwnorton.com/studyspace

TRACING THE GLOBAL STORYLINES

FOCUS ON: ***The Emergence of Territorial States***

EGYPT AND SOUTHWEST ASIA

- Invasions by nomads and transhumant herders lead to the creation of larger territorial states: New Kingdom Egypt, Hittites, Babylonia, and Kassites.
- A centuries-long peaceful era, "The Community of Major Powers," emerges among the major states as the result of shrewd statecraft and diplomacy.

INDUS RIVER VALLEY

- Migratory Vedic peoples from the steppes of Inner Eurasia use charioteer technology and rely on domesticated animals to spread out and begin integrating the northern half of South Asia.

SHANG STATE (CHINA)

- Shang dynasts promote improvements in metalworking, agriculture, and the development of writing, leading to the growth of China's first major state.

MICROSOCIETIES

- Substantial increases in population, migrations, and trade lead to the emergence of microsocieties among peoples in the South Pacific (Austronesians), the Aegean world (Minoans and Mycenaeans), and the Americas, while Europe remains a land of war-making small chieftanships.

CHRONOLOGY

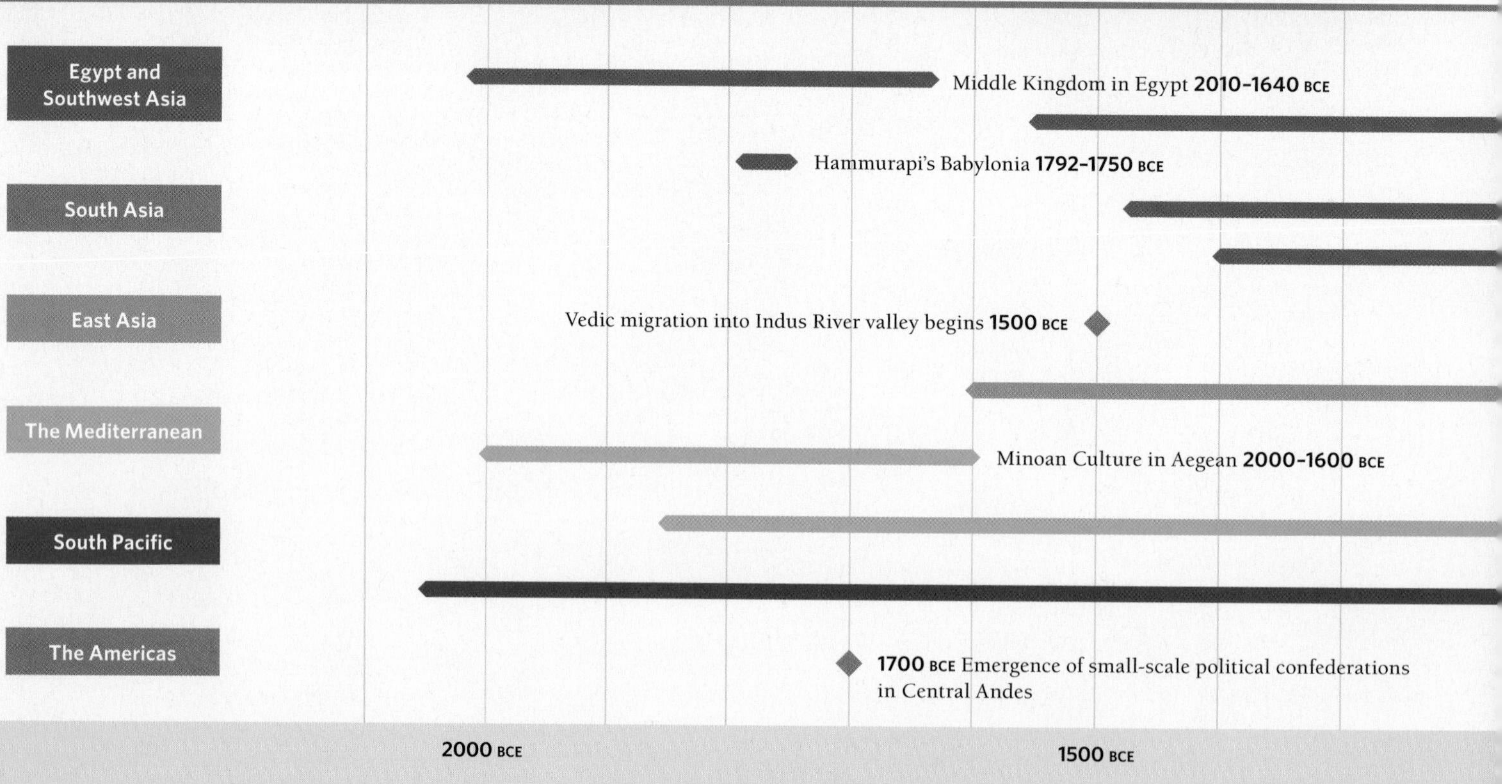

KEY TERMS

ancestral worship p. 108

chariots p. 86

divination p. 109

Hammurapi's Code p. 98

microsocieties p. 112

polities p. 90

territorial state p. 90

transhumant migrants p. 86

vassal states p. 97

Vedic people p. 101

STUDY QUESTIONS

1. **Explain** the differences between nomadic pastoral and transhumant migrations. How did each shape Afro-Eurasian history during the second millennium BCE?
2. **Analyze** the impact of the domestication of horses on Afro-Eurasia during this period. How did this development affect both nomadic and settled societies?
3. **Define** the term *territorial state*. In what areas of Afro-Eurasia did this new form of political organization emerge and thrive?
4. **Compare and contrast** political developments in Mesopotamia and Egypt during this period. To what extent did outside groups influence each region?
5. **Identify** the great territorial states of western Asia and North Africa during the second half of the second millennium BCE, and describe their relationships with one another. How did they pioneer international diplomacy?
6. **Compare and contrast** Austronesian and Indo-European migrations. What impact did each people have on the regions they settled?
7. **Describe** the Shang state in East Asia. How was it similar to and different from the territorial states of western Afro-Eurasia?
8. **Compare and contrast** the islands of the South Pacific to those in the eastern Mediterranean. Why were societies in the South Pacific more fragmented and isolated than those in the eastern Mediterranean?
9. **Explain** why early state structures were smaller and less integrated in Europe and the Central Andes than the territorial states that arose elsewhere. How similar and different were the early state structures in Europe and the Central Andes?

New Kingdom in Egypt **1550–1070 BCE**

Kassite rule in Mesopotamia **1475–1125**

Community of Major Powers—**1400–1200 BCE**

Vedic migration into Ganges River valley begins **1000 BCE**

Shang State **1600–1046 BCE**

Mycenaean culture in Greece and Aegean **1850–1200 BCE**

Austronesian migrations **2500 BCE–500 CE**

1000 BCE **500 CE** **1 CE**

BEFORE YOU READ THIS CHAPTER

GLOBAL STORYLINES

- Climate change, nomadic migrations, and invasions from neighboring states lead to the collapse of territorial states across Afro-Eurasia.
- The first great empires emerge in Southwest Asia, based on innovations in warfare, administration, commerce, metallurgy (iron), and agricultural production.
- South Asia and smaller borderland societies like the Greeks, Phoenicians, and Israelites innovate and build common cultures in nonpolitical ways.

CHAPTER OUTLINE

FOCUS QUESTIONS

- What factors led to the rise of early empires in Southwest Asia?
- How were empires different from earlier territorial states?
- How did empires extend their influence across vast regions?
- How did the emergence of empires affect peoples on their peripheries?
- To what extent, in the absence of empires, did political, economic, and cultural integration occur in East and South Asia?

4

First Empires and Common Cultures in Afro-Eurasia, 1250–325 BCE

Sennacherib—ruler of the Assyrian Empire early in the seventh century BCE—writes that at the end of one successful campaign he took "200,150 people, great and small, male and female, horses, mules, asses, camels, and sheep without number. I brought away from them and counted them my spoil." Those who resisted were dragged back to Assyria and forced to labor on Sennacherib's expanding, magnificent capital, Nineveh, and toiled on the immense irrigation works to open up new agricultural frontiers.

The booty that Sennacherib took away was unheard of in earlier ages. The immensity of the conquest highlights the arrival of a new era that involved states with even larger geographical, political, economic, and cultural ambitions and achievements. In fact, the prosperity and bounty of the first millennium BCE were the fruits of a spasm of disorder across Afro-Eurasia that swept away almost all of the territorial states described in Chapter 3. As these states collapsed, their successors were replacements, not descendants. The key factor shaping human development now was warfare spurred by military innovation.

Some of the warrior/political leaders of this era came from the fringes of formerly powerful empires and city-states, driven to challenge the centers of power when radical changes in climate made their home territories less viable. They established hybrid societies in Assyria, Persia, Vedic parts of South Asia, and Zhou China where new imperial ideologies and religious beliefs were elaborated in support of the new states. Under the protection of fierce warriors, cities and hinterlands came together under a single ruler. Farming yields increased and populations grew. The expansion of territorial power via conquest contributed to the integration of increasingly larger states, some of which became the first empires. Also, on the fringes of formerly great empires microsocieties arose and made significant contributions to human development: the seafaring Phoenicians provided Afro-Eurasia a simplified alphabet, the Israelites espoused a strict monotheism, and Greek city-states came to the fore and even began to challenge the power of the Persian Empire.

FORCES OF UPHEAVAL AND THE RISE OF EARLY EMPIRES

Although the new, bigger states built on the achievements of earlier complex societies, they also developed in response to new forces. A decisive first factor was *climate change*. Beginning around 1200 BCE prolonged drought gripped Afro-Eurasia, causing profound social upheavals and migrations and utterly destroying settled societies and long-established governments. Drought also forced nomadic and seminomadic populations that had lived at the edge of settled societies out of their home territories and into the lands of the settled communities. Many regions that had enjoyed rapid population growth now found themselves unable to support such large numbers, forcing peoples to leave their homes in search of food and fertile land. (See Map 4.1.) Renewed migrations disrupted urban societies and destroyed the administrative centers of kings, priests, and dynasties, leaving the way open for new states to develop, but only after many centuries of turmoil and economic decline.

A second factor, bound up with climate change, was the violent *movement of peoples*. Invaders, moving out of loosely organized peripheral societies, assaulted the urban centers and territorial kingdoms of mainland Greece, Crete, Anatolia, Mesopotamia, and Egypt, causing the collapse of many of these once-powerful states. Marauders from the Mediterranean basin and the Syrian desert upset the diplomatic relations and the elaborate system of international trade that had linked Southwest Asia and North Africa. In East Asia, nomads from the steppes of Inner Eurasia tangled with the Shang authorities in the Yellow River valley and eventually overwhelmed the regime. In the Indus Valley, waves of nomads pressed down from the northwest, lured by fertile lands to the south. Once there, they became an agrarian folk. The process of settling down took centuries, but by the time of Alexander the Great (see Chapter 6) the splendor of India had become legendary.

The mingling of nomadic and settled societies provided opportunities for ambitious men to expand the old territorial kingdoms or to create new states that went on to conquer other kingdoms. Gradually, a new political organization came into being: the empire. (An **empire** is a group of states or different ethnic groups under a single sovereign power.) Empires connected distant regions through common languages, unifying political systems, and shared religious beliefs. Most regions did not experience the rise of empire. The peoples of South Asia were united less through shared political systems than through shared cultures and religious beliefs. Trade also united regions. For example, the commercial activities of coastal cities such as Byblos and Tyre on the eastern shore of the Mediterranean reached as far as—and sometimes farther than—the empires' military conquests. There were great variations within and across Afro-Eurasia.

The third factor, *technological change*, was crucial in reconstructing communities that had been devastated by drought and violent population movements. Pack camels, seaworthy vessels, iron tools for cultivation, and iron weapons for warfare facilitated the rise of empires. The first-millennium empires were centralized and militarized states that used force to expand their boundaries, and here the role of changing technology was significant.

Pack Camels

The camel became the chief overland agent of change during this period, helping to open up trade routes across the Syrian and Arabian deserts. The fat stored in camels' humps allows them to survive long journeys and harsh desert conditions, and thick pads under their hoofs enable them to walk smoothly over sand. First to be domesticated was the one-humped camel called the *dromedary*, a camel native to the Sahara Desert. Other peoples, probably in central Asia, later domesticated the bigger, two-humped Bactrian camel. A stockier and hardier animal, it was better able than the dromedary to survive the scorching heat of northern Iran and the frozen winters along the route from China that later became the Silk Road (so named because silk was a major product carried along this route).

New Ships

New shipbuilding technologies had been developing rapidly since 1600 BCE and now were making a significant impact. Boats that had once been designed for limited transport on rivers

Camels. *Dromedary camels (left) are good draft animals for travel and domestic work in the deserts of Arabia, Afghanistan, and India. Two-hump camels (right) are much bigger than dromedary camels. They are more suited to the extreme dry and cold weather in Iran and central Asia.*

and lakes and along shorelines could now be built stronger and bigger for sailing on seas. These new, truly seafaring ships boasted larger and better-reinforced hulls, and stronger masts and rigging that allowed billowing sails to harness wind power effectively. These innovations, along with smaller ones in steering and ballast (among others), propelled bold mariners to venture out across large bodies of open water like the Mediterranean Sea.

Iron

Although far more abundant than the tin and copper used to make bronze, iron is harder to extract from ore and to fabricate into useful shapes. (**Iron** is a malleable metal found almost everywhere in the world; it became the most important and widely used metal in world history from this time onward.) To make iron implements, metalworkers learned to apply intense heat to soften the ore and remove its impurities. Subsequently they discovered that by adding carbon to the iron they could make an early form of steel. When the technology to smelt and harden iron advanced, iron tools and weapons replaced those made of bronze. The ability to use iron was a staggering breakthrough that leaped across territorial and cultural borders.

Iron also helped cause a revolutionary shift in agrarian techniques. Innovators learned to tip their plowshares with forged-iron edges that they could easily shape and resharpen. With the iron-tipped plow, for instance, cultivators could clear the dense jungle of the Ganges plain and till the topsoil to keep it weed-free and to enhance its quality. Increasingly, farmers did not have to rely on floods to restore layers of rich soil to their fields. Instead, they could break the sod and turn it over to bring up fertile subsoils. The effects of this transformation drove the agrarian frontier far beyond the traditional floodplains of riverbank settings. Agricultural developments thus provided the technological basis for supporting larger, more integrated societies linked by roads and canals.

The final developments driving change were *innovations in military and administrative control*. Indeed, the expansion of the first empires depended on military might. With an army wielding the most advanced weapons and armor, the Assyrian king led annual campaigns to establish his control over the countryside. Deportations were another strategy to break resisters' unity, to provide slave labor in parts of the empire that needed manpower, and to integrate the realm. Throughout the 300 years of their rule, the Assyrians constructed an infrastructure of roads, garrisons, and relay stations throughout the entire territory, making it easier to communicate and to move troops. Moreover, they made subject peoples send tribute in the form of grains, animals, raw materials, and people in addition to precious goods such as gold and lapis lazuli, which they used to build imperial cities and to enrich the royal coffers. In later centuries these practices would become common among empires, with varying degrees of brutality as a method of control.

THE ENVIRONMENTAL CRISIS IN SOUTHWEST ASIA AND GREECE

The drought that descended on the Afro-Eurasian landmass in 1200 BCE swept away most of the states that had been dominant in the second millennium BCE. All across Afro-Eurasia societies entered a two-century period of decline: artistic representation and large-scale construction diminished, urban centers ceased to exist, trading and shipping ebbed, record keeping and much

NORTH SEA
BALTIC SEA
EUROPE
Dnieper R.
Dniester R.
Volga R.
Danube R.
BLACK SEA
CASPIAN SEA
MYCENAEANS
AEGEAN SEA
Troy
Tiryns
CRETE
ANATOLIA
CYPRUS
HITTITES
MITANNI
Nineveh
Ashur
Tigris R.
Euphrates R.
SYRIAN DESERT
LEVANT
ELAMITES
ZAGROS MTS.
IRANIAN
Tyre
Jericho
Jerusalem
Babylon
SOUTHWEST ASIA
Persian Gulf
MEDITERRANEAN SEA
NORTH AFRICA
AFRO
EGYPT
Amarna
Thebes
Nile R.
NUBIA
RED SEA
ARABIAN PENINSULA
SAHARA
Sub-Saharan periphery: Increased population and gradual adoption of agriculture
Niger R.
SUB-SAHARAN AFRICA
Tropical woodlands: Yams and palm nuts cultivated
ATLANTIC OCEAN
Congo R.
Lake Victoria
Urban cores
Vedic settlement by 900 BCE
Nomadic incursions (sea peoples
Nomadic incursions (pastoralists
Destroyed site
City

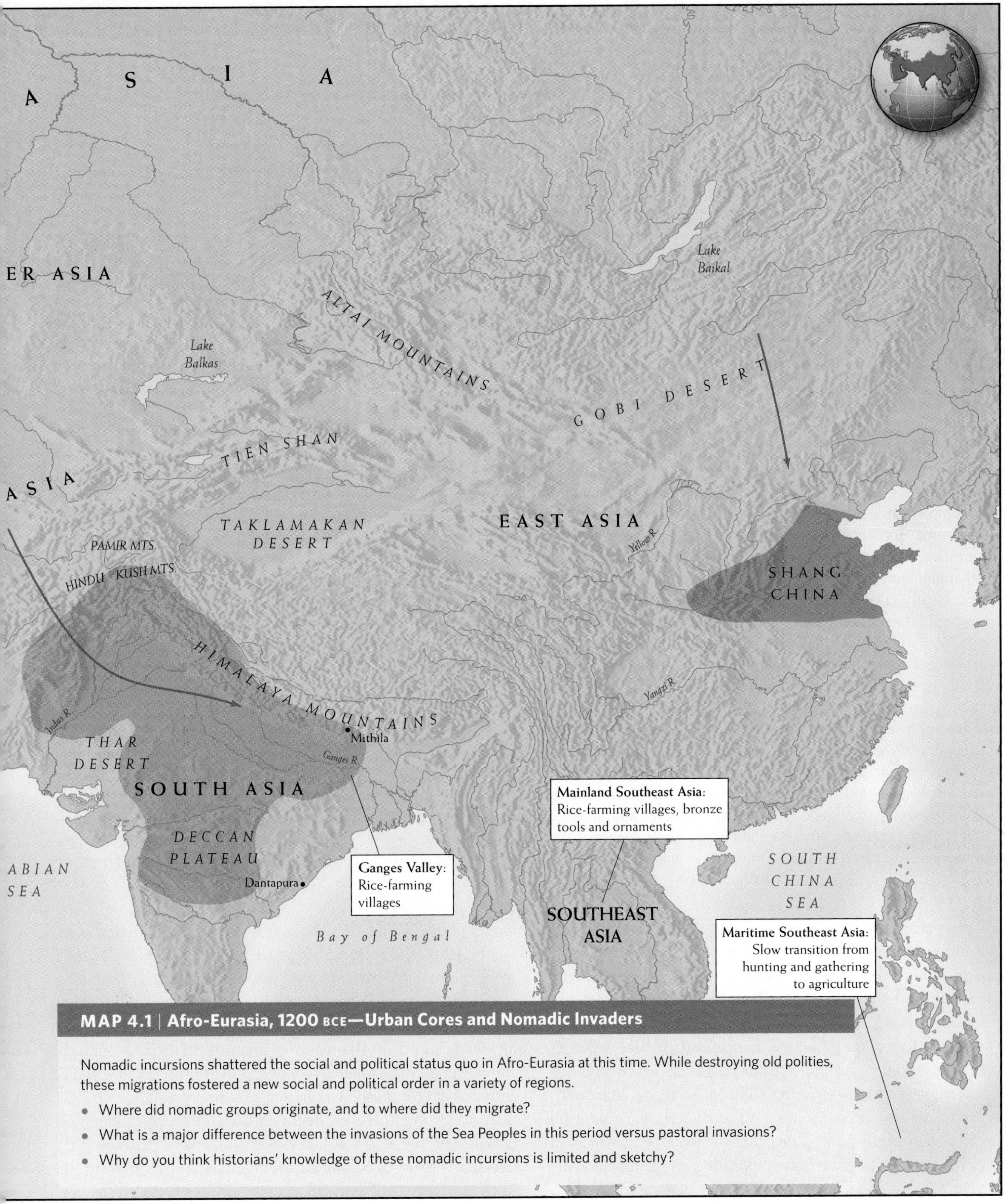

MAP 4.1 | Afro-Eurasia, 1200 BCE—Urban Cores and Nomadic Invaders

Nomadic incursions shattered the social and political status quo in Afro-Eurasia at this time. While destroying old polities, these migrations fostered a new social and political order in a variety of regions.

- Where did nomadic groups originate, and to where did they migrate?
- What is a major difference between the invasions of the Sea Peoples in this period versus pastoral invasions?
- Why do you think historians' knowledge of these nomadic incursions is limited and sketchy?

CURRENT TRENDS IN WORLD HISTORY

Big Forces in Early Empires

Conflict has always been a part of the human condition. But organized warfare and the use of "big force"—that is, large, well-disciplined armies—appears only with the formation of complex societies. The military units created in these complex societies became crucial vehicles for expanding the lands and peoples under the control of single states and broadcasting the influence of these states well beyond the territories that they controlled militarily. The field of comparative empires has become one of the hottest in world history because it allows for large-scale comparisons.

Evidence for intermittent conflict among the city states of Sumer in the fourth millennium BCE and in Old Kingdom Egypt (2649–2152 BCE) shows that local populations were drafted into a common army when needed. Permanent forces, first recorded in the Old Akkadian period in the third millennium BCE, were used to forge unity, dominate trade routes, and repel threatening "barbarians." Over the next two millennia, across the full extent of Afro-Eurasia, the technologies and structure of war machines developed along similar paths, leading to large standing armies equipped with new and improved weapons, marked by continual innovation and addition of new capabilities.

The earliest armies of Sumer were soldiers on foot arranged in a boxlike (*phalanx*) formation. The men were protected by the same types of leather capes and helmets and carried the same large shields to deflect spears and arrows. This mass-formation fighting of infantry that was enabled by uniform training, uniform armaments, and state provisioning became the norm for land forces in Egypt, Assyria and, later, the Greek city-states. By the early second millennium BCE, horse-drawn chariots were added to the force, giving mobility and the potential of surprise to an ever-larger infantry force (see Chapter 3). Mounted cavalry was introduced late in the middle of the first millennium BCE in Assyria when fighting in mountainous terrain rendered the chariot impractical. Camels, long used as pack animals, were also used in warfare, primarily by Arab tribesmen conscripted into the Assyrian army. And elephants were one of the four components of the South Asian Vedic armies, combined with cavalry, infantry, and chariots into a highly effective fighting force.

Even before the rise of complex societies and large military forces, the weapons of warfare had been those of the hunter: bows and arrows, spears, and slings. Like these weapons, knives, daggers, axes, and maces were also incorporated into armies and were wielded by infantries in hand-to-hand combat. The compound bow, first used in warfare by the Sumerians, was refined by the Assyrians into a powerful projectile that could achieve an arc of more than 200 yards, raining destruction down on the opposing infantry. Although bronze was the most important metal for weapons, the introduction of iron toward the end of the second millennium BCE expanded the availability of metal for these state war machines. Since war was often conducted to acquire land, cities had to be conquered by force. Battering rams, first documented in Egypt, were added to mobile siege machines; towers supporting archers are pictured on the Assyrian stone sculptures. Levers and breaking bars as well as tunneling were used to undermine the integrity of the walls. And scaling ladders were thrown against the fortification for the final assault.

In China, the same elements of infantry, chariots, and archers were at the core of the army from as early as the Shang dynasty. While their original goal was to capture prisoners needed for sacrifice to the ancestors, soon defensive forces were needed to protect them against their neighbors. The Zhou gradually defeated the Shang through their superior forces and more ingenious and agile tactics. A fundamental advance was made with the invention around 475 BCE of the crossbow, a far more powerful personal killing machine, and

else disappeared. Communities were smaller, technically simpler, impoverished, illiterate, and more violent.

The lands bordering the eastern Mediterranean suffered grievously, and the evidence gathered there leaves no doubt that climate change was a major underlying cause. In Egypt low Nile floods forced the pharaohs to spend their time securing food supplies and repelling Libyans from the desert and Sea People marauders who were drawn toward a region known for its abundant resources. From Hattusas, the Hittite capital on the Anatolian plateau, kings dispatched envoys to the rulers of all of the major agricultural areas, pleading for grain shipments to save their starving people, noting that their needs were "a matter of life and death." Apparently the pleas fell on deaf ears, for the Hittites were forced to move their capital from Anatolia to northern Syria where food was more plentiful. Even this move did not save the empire, which soon collapsed, its capital burned to the ground. The Mycenaeans were particularly hard hit, living in one of the marginal areas of the Greek mainland and dependent for their livelihood on exporting olives, wine, and timber. Diminished rains made it impossible for farmers there to export these products and led to the disintegration of their culture. As a result the Greek mainland experienced a 400-year period of economic decline, vividly captured by the Athenian historian Thucydides, writing in the fifth century BCE.

the torsion catapult, which threw both heavy projectiles and fiery masses onto the enemy. From the beginning, the techniques and technologies of war were rapidly shared across cultural boundaries as a natural result of adapting and improving on the achievements of the enemy. What mattered most for success was the ability to integrate and coordinate the increasing number of elements that went into a fighting force. The Persians learned at the hands of the Greeks that numbers and sheer firepower could not overcome agility, communication, and integration.

Toward the end of the second millennium BCE, new forms of force were appearing not just on land but also on the sea. The construction of purpose-built ships for the conduct of war on water—the world's first "battleships"—occurred over the course of the eighth century BCE in the eastern Mediterranean. These special ships were built mainly by the Phoenician and the Greek city-states whose livelihood depended on commerce on the high seas. They were not designed like the slow-sailing bulky ships used for the transport of large cargoes but were sleek and slim—about 120 feet long and only 15 feet wide—with little room for anything other than the men rowing them. With up to 170 rowers, they were designed and constructed for speed and power. They had no purpose other than the deliberate sinking of other ships. At first, the rowers were arranged in ships with two banks (called *biremes* by the Greeks) and later with three (called *triremes*). They were armed with bronze "beaks" or rams that were used to cave in the sides of enemy ships. These ships were costly to construct, to man, to provision, and to command. As with the maintenance, training, and arming of large land forces, only relatively wealthy states and governments could afford to mount this kind of power on the high seas. The creation of large standing armies, innovations in weaponry like the crossbow, and the appearance of the first ever battleships transformed the nature of warfare during this period when the world's first empires emerged.

Early Sumerian Infantry. *Dating back to 2400 BCE, this panel from the Syrian Temple of Ishtar illustrates the victorious homecoming of foot-soldiers with battle-axes in hand.*

QUESTIONS FOR ANALYSIS

- In terms of using "Big Forces," what made some states or empires more successful than others?
- Why is it useful for historians to compare empires? What other ways could you compare empires in addition to "Big Forces?"

Explore Further

Pierre Briant, *From Cyrus to Alexander: A History of the Persian Empire* (2002).

Harold M. Tanner, *China: A History: From Neolithic Cultures through the Great Qing Empire (10,000 BCE–1799 CE),* (2009).

Looking back on a dismal past, he remembered a dark age "without commerce, without communications by land or sea, cultivating no more acreage than the necessities of life demanded, destitute of capital, building no large towns or attaining any form of greatness" (*History of the Peloponnesian War*, p. 3).

THE NEO-ASSYRIAN EMPIRE

The story of the rise of empires begins in Southwest Asia with the Neo-Assyrian Empire (911–612 BCE), successor to the "Old" and "Middle" Assyrian states of the second millennium. The Neo-Assyrians perfected techniques of imperial rule that others imitated and that ultimately became standard in many ancient and modern empires. In particular the Neo-Assyrian state revealed the raw military side of imperial rule: constant and harsh warfare, brutal exploitation of subjects, and an ideology that glorified imperial masters and justified the subjugation and harsh treatment of subjects. In this regard the Neo-Assyrians were legendary for their ruthless efficiency, reliance on terror (such as cutting off ears, lips, and fingers; castration; and mass executions), deportations, and intimidation to crush their adversaries.

Neo-Assyrian rulers had ambitions beyond governing their own people: they also wanted to subordinate peoples in

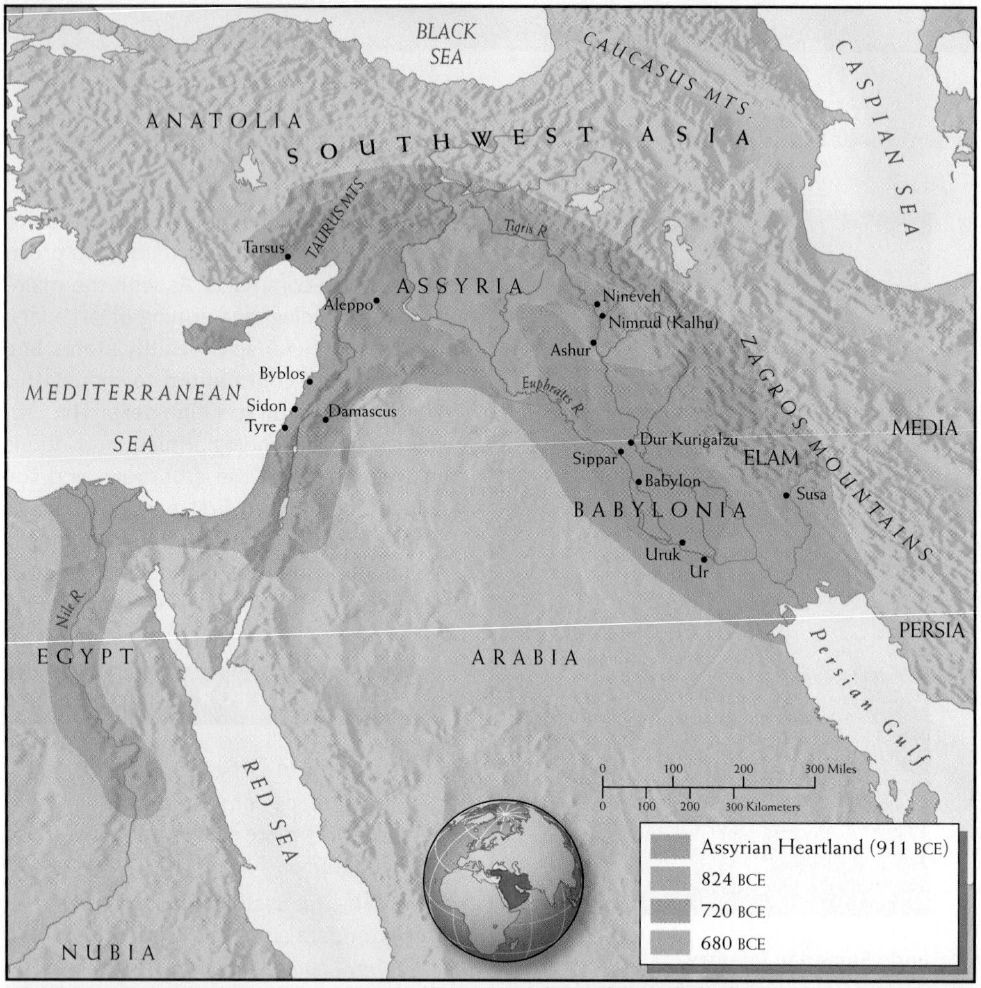

MAP 4.2 | The Neo-Assyrian Empire

The Neo-Assyrians built the first strong regional empire in Afro-Eurasia. In the process, they faced the challenge of promoting order and stability throughout their diverse realm.

- Where did the Neo-Assyrian Empire expand?
- Which parts of the empire were "the Land of Ashur," and which were "the Land under the Yoke of Ashur"?
- Why do you think expansion after 720 BCE led to the empire's destruction?

distant lands and control their resources, trading cities, and trade routes. They succeeded by the mid-seventh century BCE with the conquest of Southwest Asia and parts of North Africa, including Egypt (see Map 4.2).

Expansion into an Empire

The heartland of Assyria cradled the ancient cities of Ashur and Nineveh on the upper reaches of the Tigris River. By the ninth century BCE the Assyrian state had become strong enough to expand westward; by 824 BCE it dominated the lands and peoples all the way to the Mediterranean, controlling trade and tribute from the entire area.

The Assyrians had several advantages. First, their armies were hardened and disciplined professional troops led by officers who rose high in the ranks because of their merit, not their birth. In addition, they perfected the combined deployment of infantry and cavalry (horse-mounted warriors equipped with iron weapons) together with horse-drawn chariots armored with iron plates and carrying expert archers. The Assyrians were also skilled siege warriors, using iron to build massive wheeled siege towers and to cap their battering rams. No city walls could stand against them for long. Finally, the Assyrian armies were massive. At the height of their power in the ninth century BCE, the rulers sent 120,000 soldiers on the annual campaign to the west. (In contrast, Chinese armies would not reach this scale for another 500 years.)

Assyrian expansion provoked fierce but ultimately futile opposition, particularly from the small independent states in the west. Resisting populations were devastated—they were relocated through forced deportations, and their lands were annexed. The Assyrian state grew even more ambitious when a talented military leader usurped the throne. Tiglath Pileser III (r. 745–728 BCE) reorganized the Assyrian state to centralize power in royal hands and thus prepare for a second phase of imperial expansion and consolidation. He took away the nobles' rights to own and inherit land and other wealth, and he replaced hereditary provincial governors with appointed officials whom the center of the empire controlled. He also reinstated aggressive, expansionary annual military campaigns. But the destruction and mass deportations carried out by his armies intensified the conquered peoples' hatred of the Assyrians.

Integration and Control of the Empire

A unique imperial structure, deportations, and the labors of subjugated peoples, and a belief that empires worked, at least

Tiglath Pileser III. *The walls of the Assyrian palaces were lined with stone slabs carved with images of the victories of the king. This fragmentary slab from the palace of Tiglath Pileser III originally decorated the wall of his palace at Nimrud. It shows the inhabitants and their herds being forced to leave after the defeat of their town by the Assyrians. Below is Tiglath Pileser III, shaded by his royal umbrella, in his war chariot.*

for the imperialists, were the defining features of the Neo-Assyrian Empire. While they were hugely important to the success of the empire, they also contributed to its ultimate failure.

STRUCTURE OF THE EMPIRE The Assyrian rulers divided their empire into two parts and ruled them in different ways. The core, which the Assyrians called the "Land of Ashur," included the lands between the Zagros Mountains and the Euphrates River. The king's appointees governed these interior lands, whose inhabitants had to supply food for the temple of the national god Ashur, manpower for the god's residence in the city of Ashur, and officials to carry out the state's business.

The other area, known as "the Land under the Yoke of Ashur," lay outside of Assyria proper. Its inhabitants were not considered Assyrians; rather, their local rulers held power as subjects of Assyria. Instead of supplying agricultural goods and manpower, these subordinated states had the greater burden of delivering massive amounts of tribute in the form of gold and silver. This wealth went directly to the king, who used it to pay for his extravagant court and ever-increasing military costs. After the reforms of Tiglath Pileser III, even more lands were incorporated into the Land of Ashur proper. While this eliminated the oppressive need for the inhabitants of these lands to pay tribute, the empire continued to harshly administer its programs of forced Assyrianization. (Many empires in later centuries, including the Persian, Roman, and even the modern-day British and French empires, would use this strategy to assimilate subject peoples to the values of the conquerors.)

DEPORTATION AND FORCED LABOR In the empire's early years, the army comprised Assyrians who went to war on annual summer campaigns. Later, when campaigning became year-round, the army grew to several hundred thousand men mobilized to protect and extend the imperial holdings. These forces included not only Assyrians but also men from the conquered peoples. By the seventh century BCE, the Assyrians assigned different ethnic groups to specialized military functions: Phoenicians from the Levant provided ships and sailors for battle in the Mediterranean, Medes from the Iranian plateau served as the king's bodyguards, and charioteers from Israel subdued rebellious western provinces.

To accomplish its goals, the Assyrian state needed huge labor forces for agricultural work and for enormous building projects. Since so many Assyrians served in the army, the state recruited most agricultural and construction workers from conquered peoples. Over three centuries the Neo-Assyrian state relocated more than 4 million people—a practice that not only supported its stupendous work projects but also undermined local resistance efforts.

ASSYRIAN IDEOLOGY AND PROPAGANDA The Neo-Assyrian Empire put forth an imperial ideology to support and justify its system of expansion, exploitation, and inequality. (An **ideology** is the dominant set of ideas of a widespread culture

Capture of an Egyptian City. *This stone panel from the North Palace in Nineveh shows warriors scaling walls with ladders during Ashurbanipal's campaign against Egypt (mid-seventh century BCE).*

PRIMARY SOURCE

The Banquet Stele of Assurnasirpal II

Starting in the third millennium BCE, the rulers of Mesopotamia used architecture to signal their power to their subjects. When a change of dynasty or other reorganization of power occurred, rulers would build new palaces or even move their capital city. In the ninth century, Assurnasirpal II established Assyria as an imperial power that intended to expand and consolidate its economic and political control of surrounding peoples. After moving the capital and building a new palace and royal precinct, he called all of the empire's peoples to a ten-day celebration. This remarkable event was commemorated by an inscribed stele (a stone pillar) that he erected next to the throne room.

(102) When Ashur-nasir-apli, king of Assyria, consecrated the joyful palace, the palace full of wisdom, in Kalach [and] invited inside Ashur, the great lord, and the gods of the entire land; 1,000 fat oxen, 1,000 calves [and] sheep of the stable, 14,000 . . . -sheep which belonged to the goddess Ishtar my mistress, 200 oxen which belonged to the goddess Ishtar my mistress, 1,000 . . . -sheep, 1,000 spring lambs, 500 *ayalu*-deer, 500 deer, 1,000 ducks [*iṣṣūrū rabûtu*], 500 ducks [*usū*], 500 geese, 1,000 wild geese, 1,000 *qaribu*-birds, 10,000 pigeons, 10,000 wild pigeons, 10,000 small birds, 10,000 fish, 10,000 jerboa, 10,000 eggs, 10,000 loaves of bread, 10,000 jugs of beer, 10,000 skins of wine, 10,000 containers of grain [and] sesame, 10,000 pots of hot . . . , 1,000 boxes of greens, 300 [containers of] oil, 300 [containers of] malt, 300 [containers of] mixed *raqqatu*-plants, 100 [containers of] *kudimmus*, 100 [containers of] . . . , 100 [containers of] parched barley, 100 [containers of] *ubuḫšennu*-grain, 100 [containers of] fine *billatu*, 100 [containers of] pomegranates, 100 [containers of] grapes, 100 [containers of] mixed *zamrus*, 100 [containers of] pistachios, 100 [containers of] . . . , 100 [containers of] *ionions*, 100 [containers of] garlic, 100 [containers of] *kunipḫus*, 100 *buncbes* of turnips, 100 [containers of] *ḫinḫinu*-seeds, 100 [containers of] *giddū*, 100 [containers of] honey, 100 [containers of] ghee, 100 [containers of] roasted *abšu*-seeds, 100 [containers of] roasted *šu'u*-seeds, 100 [containers of] *karkartu*-plants, 100 [containers of] *tiatu*-plants, 100 [containers of] mustard, 100 [containers of] milk, 100 [containers of] cheese, 100 bowls of *mīzu*-drink, 100 stuffed oxen, 10 homers of shelled *dukdu*-nuts, 10 homers of shelled pistachios, 10 homers of . . . , 10 homers of *ḫabbaququ*, 10 homers of dates, 10 homers of *titip*, 10 homers of cumin, 10 homers of *saḫūnu*, 10 homers of . . . , 10 homers of *andaḫšu*, 10 homers of *šišanibu*, 10 homers of *simberu*-fruit, 10 homers of *ḫašú*, 10 homers of fine oil, 10 homers of fine aromatics, 10 homers of . . . , 10 homers of *naṣṣabu*-gourds, 10 homers of *zinzimmu*-onions, 10 homers of olives; when I consecrated the palace of Kalach, 47,074 men [and] women who were invited from every part of my land, 5,000 dignitaries [and] envoys of the people of the lands Suhu, Hindanu, Patinu, Hatti, Tyre, Sidon, Gurgumu, Malidu, Hubushkia, Gilzanu, Kumu, [and] Musasiru, 16,000 people of Kalach, [and] 1,500 *zarīqū* of my palace, all of them—altogether 69,574 [including] those summoned from all lands and the people of Kalach—for ten days I gave them food, I gave them drink, I had them bathed, I had them anointed. [Thus] did I honour them [and] send them back to their lands in peace and joy.

QUESTIONS FOR ANALYSIS

- What does the extensive list of food and drink listed in the text tell the reader about the size and geographical reach of the empire and the role of trade in it?
- What techniques, as reflected in the text of the Banquet Stele, did Assurnasirpal use to build loyalty among his subjects?

Source: Assyrian Royal Inscriptions, Part 2: From Tiglath-pileser I to Ashur-nasir-apli II, *compiled and translated by Albert Kirk Grayson, vol. 2 of* Records of the Ancient Near East, *edited by Hans Goedicke (Wiesbaden: Otto Harrassowitz, 1976), pp. 175–76.*

or movement.) Even in the early stages of expansion, Assyrian inscriptions and art expressed a divinely determined destiny that drove the regime to expand westward toward the Mediterranean Sea. The national god Ashur had commanded all Assyrians to support the forcible growth of the empire, whose goal was to establish and maintain order and keep an ever-threatening cosmic chaos at bay. Only the god Ashur and his agent, the king, could bring universal order. The king conducted holy war to transform the known world into the well-regulated Land of Ashur, intensifying his campaign of terror and expansion with elaborate propaganda. This propaganda, based on a detailed historical record of countless military and political victories, proclaimed that Assyria's triumph was inevitable. Its main focus was the nobles, whom the king and the empire relied on for support.

The rulers devised three mutually reinforcing types of propaganda. First, they used elaborate architectural complexes to

The Annals of Ashurbanipal. *This baked clay faceted cylinder carries a portion of the annals of Ashurbanipal. It was found at Nineveh along with thousands of other tablets preserved in his famous library. The annals of Ashurbanipal were detailed, almost novelistic accounts of his military and civic achievements. Unlike earlier annals, there is first-person discourse, indirect discourse, flashbacks, and lively description of events and places.*

stage ceremonial displays of pomp and power (as in Egypt and China). Second, they made sure that different types of texts glorified the king and the empire. These texts were recited at state occasions, inscribed on monuments, written in annals about the kings' military campaigns and achievements, and buried at propitious places in public buildings, where only the eyes of Ashur could view them. (See Primary Source: The Banquet Stele of Assurnasirpal II.) Third, state officials placed images glorifying the king and the Assyrian army on palace walls. These images depicted the army's force, showing all who resisted being smashed into submission—their towns burned; their men killed, impaled on stakes, or flayed; and their women and children deported along with any male survivors.

The commitment to record the regime's triumphal events was evident not only on palace walls but also in a uniquely Assyrian literary form called **annals** (historical records arranged year-by-year). Constituting a milestone in human history, these documents illustrate how communication and writing promoted the formation of organized states. Court scribes inscribed the annals on stone slabs, tablets, and clay cylinders, detailing each campaign in the yearly report of the king's achievements. These written compositions, like the images, never gave any indication that the Assyrians did or could lose a battle.

Assyrian Social Structure and Population

The Assyrians' iron-fisted rule rested on a rigid social hierarchy. Alone at the top was the king, who as the sole agent of the god Ashur conducted war to expand the Land of Ashur. Below were the state's military elites, handsomely rewarded through gifts of land, silver, and exemptions from royal taxes. Over time, they became the noble class and intimates of the king, replacing the older landed elites who lost their resources after Tiglath Pileser III reorganized the empire's landholdings. Elites often controlled vast estates that included both the land and the local people who worked it. The throne and the elites owned the most populous part of the society, the peasantry, in which various categories of workers had differing privileges. Those who were enslaved because they could not pay their debts were allowed to marry nonslave partners, conduct financial transactions, and even own property with other slaves attached. In contrast, foreigners who were enslaved after being captured had no rights—they were forced to do hard manual labor on the state's monumental building projects. Those who were forcibly relocated were not slaves but became attached to the lands that they had to work. Families were small and lived on modest plots of land, where they raised vegetables and planted vineyards.

Women in Assyria were far more restricted than their counterparts in the earlier periods of Sumerian and Old Babylonian Mesopotamia (see Chapter 3). Under the Assyrians' patriarchal social system, women had almost no control over their lives. Because all inheritance passed through the male line, it was crucial that a man be certain of the paternity of the children borne by his wives. As a result, all interactions between men and women outside of the family were highly restricted. The Middle Assyrians introduced the practice of veiling in the thirteenth century BCE, requiring it of all respectable women. Indeed, prostitutes who serviced the men of the army and worked in the taverns were forbidden to wear the veil, so that their revealed faces and hair would signal their disreputable status. Any prostitute found wearing the veil would be dragged to the top of the city wall, stripped of her clothing, flogged, and sometimes even killed.

The queens of Assyria obeyed the same social norms, but their lives were more comfortable and varied than the commoners'. They lived in a separate part of the palace with servants who were either women slaves or eunuchs (castrated males). Though Assyrian queens rarely wielded genuine power, they enjoyed respect and recognition, especially in the role of mother of the king. In fact, a queen could serve as regent for her son if the king died while his heir was still a child. Such was the case of Sammuramat, who served as regent from 810 to 806 BCE, successfully ruling the empire until her son came of age.

The Instability of the Assyrian Empire

At their peak, the Assyrians controlled most of the lands stretching from Persia to Egypt. This was an awesome feat, but the empire was unstable nonetheless. Assyrian commanders had to position occupying armies far and wide to keep subjects in line; and as the propaganda machine ramped up, so did discontent among the nobility. Once a successful rebellion challenged the Assyrian worldview of invincibility, the empire's fall was inevitable. Although successor states temporarily filled the Assyrian political vacuum, the three-millennia-long culture of Mesopotamia was dead. In 612 BCE, the Neo-Assyrian Empire collapsed as Nineveh was conquered.

THE PERSIAN EMPIRE

After a brief interlude of Neo-Babylonian rule, the Persians reasserted imperial power in Southwest Asia. They created a gentler form of imperial rule, based more on persuasion and mutual benefit than on raw power. A nomadic group speaking an Indo-Iranian language, the Persians had arrived on the Iranian plateau from central Asia during the second millennium and gradually spread to the plateau's southwestern part. These expert horsemen shot arrows with deadly accuracy while whirling on horseback in the midst of battle. After Cyrus the Great (r. 559–529 BCE) united the Persian tribes, his armies defeated the Lydians in southwestern Anatolia and took over their gold mines, land, and trading routes. He next overpowered the Greek city-states on the Aegean coast of Anatolia.

In building their immense empire, the Persians, whose ancestors were pastoralists and had no urban traditions to build on, adapted the ideologies and institutions of the Babylonians (see Chapter 3), the Assyrians, and the indigenous Elamites, modifying them to fit their own customs and political aims. This process gave rise to uniquely Persian institutions that undergirded the new empire, which would last until the arrival of Alexander the Great in 331 BCE.

The Integration of a Multicultural Empire

From their base on the Iranian plateau, over the next 200 years the Persian rulers developed an enormous empire that reached from the Indus Valley to northern Greece and from central Asia to the south of Egypt. (See Map 4.3.) Cyrus presented himself as a benevolent ruler who claimed to have liberated his subjects from the oppression of their own kings. He pointed to his victory in Babylon as a sign that the city's gods had turned against its king as a heretic. According to the cuneiform text known as the Cyrus cylinder, the Babylonians greeted him "with shining faces." At the same time, Cyrus released the Jews from their fifty-year captivity in Babylon. They, too, considered him a savior who, having freed them on the orders of their God, allowed them to return to Jerusalem and rebuild their temple. Even the Greeks, who later defeated the Persians, saw Cyrus as a model ruler.

Cyrus the Great. *This great Genius with four wings was preserved in the doorjamb of Gate R at the palace of Cyrus the Great at Pasargadae. When Cyrus forged the Persian Empire from Media, Assyria, Babylonia, and Egypt, there was no coherent imperial imagery to represent the new political entity. His court artists borrowed freely from the realms that he had brought into his empire. The image is a combination of features borrowed from Egypt (the headdress), Assyria (low-relief representation on a stone slab and the four wings), and Babylonia (the long garment).*

Following Cyrus's death on the battlefield, Darius I (r. 521–486 BCE) put the new empire on a solid footing. First he suppressed revolts across the lands, recording this feat on a monumental rock relief overhanging the road to his capital, Persepolis. (See Primary Source: Beisitun Inscription.) Then he conquered territories held by seventy different ethnic groups, stretching from the Indus River in the east to the Aegean and Mediterranean seas in the west, and from the Black, Caspian,

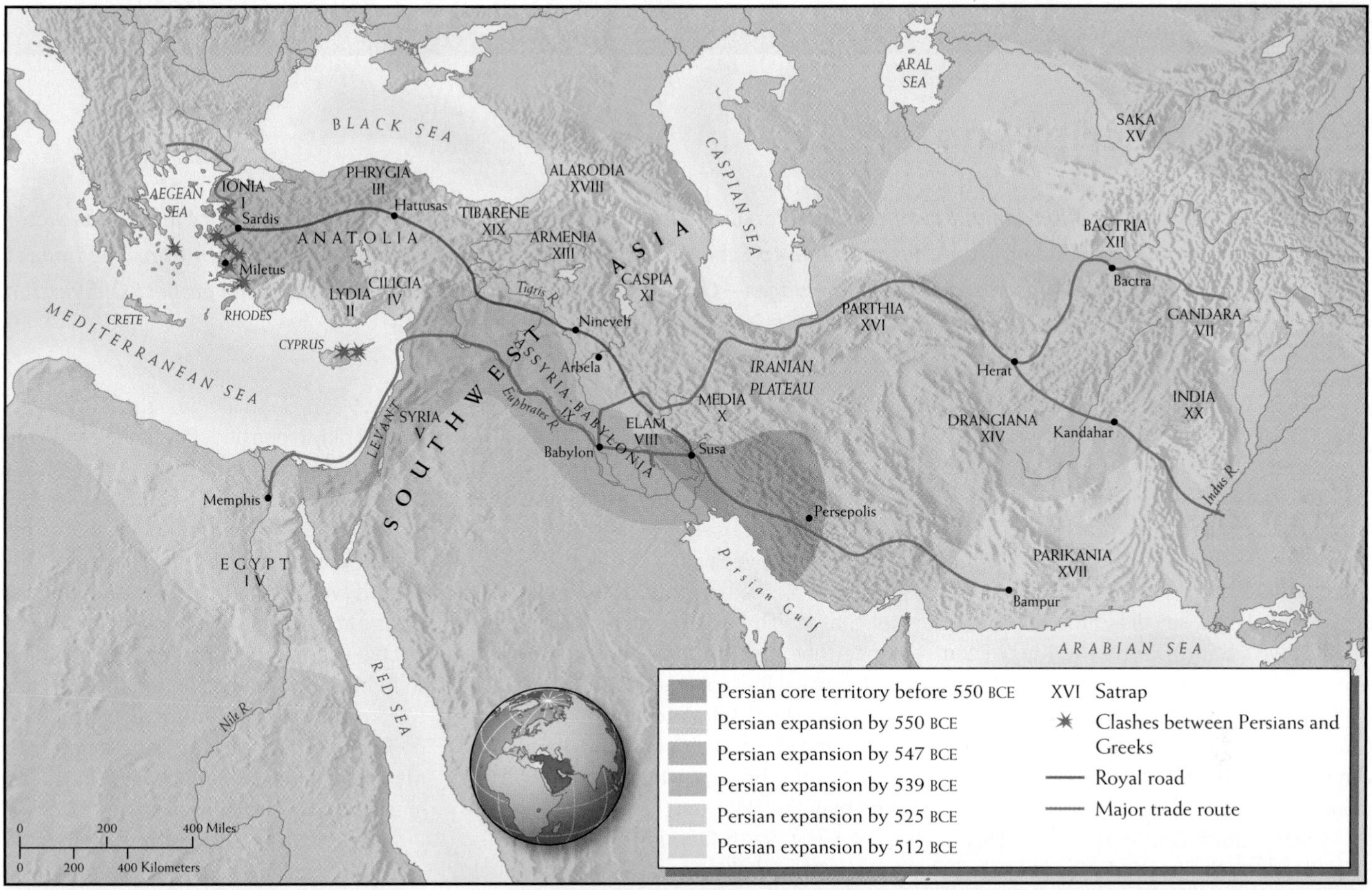

MAP 4.3 | The Persian Empire, 550–479 BCE

Starting in the sixth century BCE, the Persians succeeded the Assyrians as rulers of the large regional empire of Southwest Asia and North Africa. Compare the Persian Empire's territorial domains to those of the Neo-Assyrian Empire in Map 4.2.

- Geographically, how did the Persian Empire differ from the Neo-Assyrian state?
- Analyzing the map, how many Persian satrapies existed, and what role do you think they played in the success of the Persian Empire?
- How does geography help explain why the Greeks were able to defeat the Persians twice?

and Aral seas in the north to the Nile River in the south. To manage this huge domain, Darius introduced dynamic administrative systems that enabled the empire to flourish for another two centuries. Its new bureaucracy combined central and local administration and made effective use of the strengths of local tradition, economy, and rule—rather than forcing Persian customs on subject people via rigid central control (as the Assyrians had done).

This empire was both centralized and multicultural. The Persians believed that all subject peoples were equal; the only requirement was to be loyal to the king and pay tribute—which was considered an honor, not a burden. Although local Persian administrators used local languages, Aramaic (a dialect of a Semitic language long spoken in Southwest Asia) became the empire's official language because many of its literate scribes came from Mesopotamia. They wrote Aramaic on parchment or papyrus in an alphabetic script, and its use spread quickly.

Much like Tiglath Pileser III of Assyria, Darius understood that he could not expand the empire without reorganizing and centralizing. To bring the wealth of the provinces to the imperial center he established a system of provinces, or satrapies, each ruled by a satrap (a governor) who was a relative or a close associate of the king. The local bureaucrats and officials who administered the government worked under close monitoring by military officers, central tax collectors, and spies (the so-called eyes of the king), who enforced the satraps' loyalty. Further, Darius established a system of fixed taxation and formal tribute allocations; when needed, he also instituted economic reforms. Moreover, he promoted trade throughout the empire by building roads, establishing a standardized

PRIMARY SOURCE

Beisitun Inscription

To commemorate his consolidation of power over the Persian state, Darius I commissioned a pictorial relief of himself as victor high above the main road leading from Mesopotamia to Ecbatana (the modern city of Hamadan) in western Iran. The images are surrounded by a long text inscribed in three languages—Old Persian, Akkadian, and Elamite. This is the earliest Old Persian inscription; it is a version of cuneiform script that Darius devised especially for this occasion.

4.31–2. Saith Darius the King: These IX kings I took prisoner within these battles.

4.33–6. Saith Darius the King: These are the provinces which became rebellious. The Lie made them rebellious, so that these [men] deceived the people. Afterwards Ahuramazda put them into my hand; as was my desire, so I did unto them.

4.36–40. Saith Darius the King: Thou who shalt be king hereafter, protect thyself vigorously from the Lie; the man who shall be a Lie-follower, him do thou punish well, if thus thou shalt think, "May my country be secure!"

4.40–3. Saith Darius the King: This is what I did; by the favor of Ahuramazda, in one and the same year I did [it]. Thou who shalt hereafter read this inscription, let that which has been done by me convince thee; do not thou think it a lie.

4.43–5. Saith Darius the King: I turn myself quickly to Ahuramazda, that this [is] true, not false, [which] I did in one and the same year. . . .

4.52–6. Saith Darius the King: Now let that which has been done by me convince thee; thus to the people impart, do not conceal it: if this record thou shalt not conceal, [but] tell it to the people, may Ahuramazda be a friend unto thee, and may family be unto thee in abundance, and may thou live long!

4.57–9. Saith Darius the King: If this record thou shalt conceal, [and] not tell it to the people, may Ahuramazda be a smiter unto thee, and may family not be to thee!

4.59–61. Saith Darius the King: This which I did, in one and the same year by the favor of Ahuramazda I did; Ahuramazda bore me aid, and the other gods who are.

4.61–7. Saith Darius the King: For this reason Ahuramazda bore aid, and the other gods who are, because I was not hostile, I was not a Lie-follower, I was not a doer of wrong—neither I nor my family. According to righteousness I conducted myself. Neither to the weak nor to the powerful did I do wrong. The man who cooperated with my house, him I rewarded well; whoso did injury, him I punished well.

4.67–9. Saith Darius the King: Thou who shalt be king hereafter, the man who shall be a Lie-follower or who shall be a doer of wrong—unto them do thou not be a friend, [but] punish them well.

4.69–72. Saith Darius the King: Thou who shalt hereafter behold this inscription which I have inscribed, or these sculptures, do thou not destroy them, [but] thence onward protect them; as long as thou shalt be in good strength!

Darius's Relief at Beisitun. *At Beisitun, high above the Royal Road through the Zagros Mountains, Darius carved a relief commemorating his victories over Gaumata (the false Smerdis) and nine rebel kings. The kings are roped together at the neck, and Gaumata lies under Darius's feet. Above the rebels is a winged disk, probably representing the god Ahura Mazda. Darius had his scribes develop a version of cuneiform script to represent Old Persian. In a trilingual inscription (Old Persian, Elamite, and Akkadian) he recorded this victory, which consolidated and expanded the empire founded by Cyrus. This inscription provided the key for deciphering Babylonian cuneiform.*

QUESTION FOR ANALYSIS

- Throughout the millennia, local and imperial rulers on the Iranian plateau used rock reliefs such as the Beisitun inscription to project their power and to mark boundaries. Who would see these monuments, and what messages would they receive?

Source: Roland G. Kent, Old Persian: Grammar, Texts, Lexicon, *2nd rev. ed. (New Haven: American Oriental Society, 1953), pp. 131–32.*

currency including coinage, and introducing standard weights and measures.

Zoroastrianism, Ideology, and Social Structure

Like the Assyrians, the Persians established their ideology of kingship on religious foundations. They believed that the supreme god, Ahura Mazda, appointed the monarch as ruler over all peoples and lands of the earth and charged him with maintaining a perfect order from which all would benefit. Unlike their Mesopotamian neighbors, the Persians drew their religious ideas from their pastoral and tribal roots (which reflected the same traditions of warrior and priestly classes as those preserved in the Vedic texts of the Indus Valley; see Chapter 3).

Zoroaster (also known as Zarathustra), who most likely lived sometime after 1000 BCE in eastern Iran, was responsible for crystallizing the region's traditional beliefs into a formal religious system. The eastern tribes of the Iranian plateau spread the ideas of **Zoroastrianism** to the Iranian peoples living in the west, and Zoroastrianism ultimately became the religion of the entire empire. The main source for the teachings of Zoroaster is the Avesta, a collection of holy works initially transmitted orally by priests and then, according to legend, written down in the third century BCE.

Zoroaster's teachings tried to wean the Iranian faithful away from their earlier animistic beliefs that led them to see all objects, alive and dead, as possessing life and vitality. In a radical change, Zoroaster promoted belief in the god Ahura Mazda, who had created the world and all that was good. (Though rare, monotheism also existed during this time in Judah; it had briefly been the official religion of Egypt, when Akhenaten imposed worship of Aten, the sun.) Persians came to believe that the universe was dualistic: Ahura Mazda was good and capable only of good, whereas his adversary, Ahiram, was deceitful and wicked. The Persians saw these two forces as engaging in a cosmic struggle for control of the universe.

Unlike the fatalistic religions of Mesopotamia, Zoroastrianism treated humans as capable of choosing between good and evil. Their choices had consequences: rewards or punishments in the afterlife. Strict rules of behavior determined the fate of each individual. For example, because animals were good, they deserved to be treated well. Intoxicants, widely used in tribal religions, were forbidden. Also, there were strict rules for treatment of the dead. For example, to prevent death from contaminating the sacred elements of earth, fire, and water, it was forbidden to bury, burn, or drown the deceased. Instead, people left corpses out for beasts and birds of prey to devour.

Persian kings enjoyed absolute authority. In return, they were expected to follow moral and political guidelines that reflected Zoroastrian notions of ethical behavior. As the embodiment of the positive virtues that made them fit to hold power, they were to display insight and the ability to distinguish right from wrong so that they could preserve justice and maintain social order. In addition, kings had to show physical superiority that matched their moral standing. They had to be expert horsemen and peerless in wielding bows and spears. These were qualities valued by all Persian nobles, who revered the virtues of their nomadic ancestors. As the ancient Greek historian Herodotus tells us, Persian boys were taught three things only: "to ride, to shoot with the bow, and to tell the truth."

The Persian social order included four diverse groups: a ruling class of priests, nobles, and warriors; an administrative and commercial class consisting of scribes, bureaucrats, and merchants; and two laboring groups of artisans and peasants. Each group had a well-defined role. Priests maintained the ritual fire in temples, nobles administered the state by paying taxes and performing appropriate duties, warriors protected and expanded the empire, bureaucrats kept records, merchants secured goods from distant lands, artisans rendered raw materials into symbolic form, and peasants grew the crops and tended the flocks that fed the imperial machine.

Panel from the Palace of Darius. *The Palace of Darius at Susa was elaborately decorated with glazed bricks. This panel shows human-headed winged lions in a heraldic seated posture. Above them is a winged disk with tendrils and a human bust. This symbol, which borrows from Assyrian and Egyptian imagery, is thought to represent the Zoroastrian god Ahura Mazda.*

Persian Water-Moving Technique. *The Persians perfected the channeling of water over long distances through underground channels called* qanats. *This technique, an efficient way to move water without evaporation, is still used today in hot, arid regions. In this example near Yazd, in central Iran, the domed structure leading to the underground tunnel is flanked by two brick towers called "badgir," an ancient form of air conditioning that cools the water using wind (bad in Persian).*

Surrounding the king was the powerful Persian hereditary nobility. These men had vast landholdings and often served the king as satraps or advisers. Also close to the king were wealthy merchants who directed trade across the vast empire. In turn, the king was obligated to take his wives only from these families and to exempt them from certain taxes. To consolidate his hold on the throne, Darius reduced the aristocrats' political power. By controlling all appointments, he essentially made the nobles his puppets, but he let them keep their high status in a society in which birth and royal favor counted for everything.

Royal gifts solidified the relations between king and nobles, reinforcing the king's place at the top of the political pyramid. In public ceremonies he presented gold vessels, elaborate textiles, and jewelry to reward each recipient's loyalty and demonstrate dependence on the crown. Any kind of failure would result in the withdrawal of royal favor. Should such failures be serious or treasonous, the offenders faced torture and death.

Public Works and Imperial Identity

The Persians engaged in large-scale road building and constructed a system of rapid and dependable communication. The key element in the system was the Royal Road, which followed age-old trade routes some 1,600 miles from western Anatolia to the heart of the empire in southwestern Iran, continuing eastward across the northern Iranian plateau and into central Asia. Traders used the Royal Road, as did the Persian army; subjects took tribute to the king, and royal couriers carried messages to the satraps and imperial armies over this road. As the Assyrians had done, the Persians placed way stations with fresh mounts and provisions along the route.

In addition to the Royal Road, the Persians devised other ways to connect the far reaches of the empire with its center. Darius oversaw the construction of a canal more than fifty miles long linking the Red Sea to the Nile River. One of the Persians' most ingenious contributions was the invention of *qanats*, underground tunnels through which water flowed over long distances without evaporating or being contaminated. (Later adopted by many cultures, this type of system moves water under arid lands even today.) Laborers from the local populations toiled on these feats of engineering as part of their obligations as subjects of the empire.

Until Cyrus's time, the Persians had been pastoral nomads who lacked traditions of monumental architecture, visual arts, or written literature or history. Cyrus began to define a Persian court style, but Darius was most responsible for promoting visual and physical expressions that were uniquely Persian. The vast capital at Persepolis expressed this new imperial identity. On the highland plain near Cyrus's capital at Pasargadae, Darius built an immense complex that complemented the administrative center at Susa in the lowlands. Skilled craftsmen from all

Persepolis. *In the highland valley of Fars, the homeland of the Persians, Darius and his successors built a capital city and ceremonial center at the site of Persepolis. On top of a huge platform, there were audience halls, a massive treasury, the harem, and residential spaces. The building was constructed of mudbrick. The roof was supported by enormous columns projecting the images of bulls.*

over the empire labored on the complex, blending their distinct cultural influences into a new Persian architectural style. Darius erected his city, designed for celebrations and ceremonies, on a monumental terrace covering more than thirty acres. Into the cliffs behind it, he and his successors cut their eternal resting places in the living rock. Persepolis was also an important administrative hub where archaeologists have found more than 30,000 cuneiform tablets detailing the workings of the bureaucracy of the great empire.

The Persians used monumental architecture with grand columned halls and huge open spaces to provide reception rooms for thousands of representatives bringing tribute from all over the empire and as a way to help integrate subject peoples by connecting them to one central, imperial authority. In the royal palace, three of the columned halls stood on raised platforms accessed via processional stairways that were lined with elaborate images of subjects bringing gifts and tribute to the king. This was a highly refined program of visual propaganda, with the carved images showing the Persian Empire as a society of diverse but obedient peoples. The carvings on the great stairway of Persepolis offer a veritable ethnographic museum frozen in stone. Each group brings distinctive tribute—the Armenians present precious metal vessels, the Lydians from Anatolia carry gold armlets and bowls, the Egyptians offer exotic animals, and the Sogdians from central Asia lead proud horses. Gateway figures and protective relief images copied from the palaces of Assyria represent the grandeur of the occasion and the power of the king.

IMPERIAL FRINGES IN WESTERN AFRO-EURASIA

A very different world emerged on Afro-Eurasia's western edges, well beyond the reach of the Neo-Assyrian and Persian empires. Although their powerful neighbors affected them, these western people retained their own languages, beliefs, and systems of rule. Their communities were smaller than those in Southwest Asia, and their compactness and intimacy enabled them to project a unique kind of power and influence.

Migrations and Upheaval

Beginning around 1200 BCE, as the full effects of drought struck this area, new waves of Indo-European-speaking peoples inhabiting the Danube River basin in central Europe became dynamic historical actors. Previously this area's dynamism had come from the outside, but two key factors reversed this trend. These were a rapid rise in population and the development of local natural resources, including metallurgy in a new metal, iron. By the end of the second millennium BCE, this surplus population, armed with its new metal weapons, moved in large groups back down the Danube into southeastern Europe, the Aegean, and the eastern Mediterranean. Advancing even into Southwest Asia, the invaders brought turmoil to the peoples living there. These huge movements weakened the power of empires and regimes in the region, increased the value of mobility as peoples

The King and His Courtiers. *Leading to the Apadana (reception hall) are two monumental staircases that are faced with low-relief representations of the king and his courtiers, as well as all of the delegations bringing tribute to the center of the empire. The lion attacking the bull is a symbolic rendering of the forces of nature. Above the central plane is the winged disk of Ahura Mazda and the human-headed lion griffins.*

vied for resources, and opened new frontiers for the development of smaller, more innovative communities.

The ultimate blow to already weakened imperial states came from the fringe in the form of armed invasions that caused the collapse of even the most highly developed societies in the region. The first to fall were the Hittites, who had once dominated the central lands of what is today Turkey. Once the invaders reached the Mediterranean, they mainly used boats for transportation. These dynamic communities are sometimes known as the Sea Peoples. The Egyptians knew them as the Peleset, and only by marshalling all the resources of their land did the pharaohs manage to repel them. Outside Egypt, states and kingdoms suffered heavily from their ravages. The Sea Peoples settled along the southern coast of the Levant, where they became known as the Philistines.

In the Mediterranean, the Sea Peoples' intrusion shook the social order of the Minoans on the island of Crete (see Chapter 3). Agricultural production declined and. as the palace-centered bureaucracies and priesthoods of the second millennium BCE vanished, more violent societies emerged that relied on the newcomers' iron weapons. This was the culture of warrior-heroes described in the *Iliad,* an epic poem about the Trojan War composed centuries after the events it relates. It was based on oral tales passed down and embellished for generations. (See Primary Source: War in Homer's *Iliad.*)

For the long-established kingdoms and states of Southwest Asia and the Mediterranean, these rapid transformations were destructive and traumatic. But they were also creative because they shattered traditional ways of doing things, wiping the social slate clean. In fact, violent change and the emergence of new powers at the margins were the first steps toward completely new patterns of human relations.

Persia and the Greeks

Among the different small-scale societies that emerged in Persia's shadow, the Greeks perhaps offer the best example of the energy and dynamism of these new communities. In areas of contact with the Persian Empire, Greek-speaking people in different cities sometimes cooperated with the Persians, even borrowing their ideas, but sometimes strongly resisted them.

In 499 BCE, some Greek city-states and others in the eastern Mediterranean revolted against the Persians, who claimed control over the Greek islands and mainland. During the five-year struggle, some Greek communities sided with the Persians and suffered condemnation by other Greeks for doing so. On the mainland, farther away from the contact zone, most Greek cities resisted the Persian king's authority. So, in 492 BCE, Darius sent his fleet to subdue Athens and Sparta on the mainland, but the ships were destroyed in a storm. Two years later, Darius and his vast army invaded mainland Greece but suffered a humiliating defeat at the hands of the much smaller force of Athenians at Marathon, near Athens. The Persians retreated and waited another decade before challenging their western foe again. Meanwhile, however, Athens was becoming a major sea power.

Under the leadership of Themistocles in the 480s BCE and exploiting newfound silver mines, Athens became a naval power whose strength was its fleet of triremes (battleships). This shift

PRIMARY SOURCE

War in Homer's *Iliad*

The great epic poem called the* Iliad*—about the war that took place at Ilium, a Greek name for the city of Troy—was attributed by the later Greeks to a poet named Homer. However, the written text is actually the result of generations of oral singers who composed different versions of this story in the ninth and eighth centuries BCE. The story takes place on the plains in front of Troy, and it focuses on a few prominent warriors—such as Achilles and Odysseus on the side of the Achaeans (the Greeks, also called Akhaians), and Hector and Paris (the son of Priam, king of Troy) on the Trojans' side. Historians debate the historical reality of the story, but almost all agree on the site of the ancient city it describes.

The son of Priam wearing a gleaming breastplate
let fly through the lines but his sharp spear missed
and he hit Leucus instead, Odysseus' loyal comrade,
gouging his groin as the man hauled off a corpse—
it dropped from his hands and Leucus sprawled across it.
Enraged at his friend's death Odysseus sprang in fury,
helmed in fiery bronze he plowed through the front
and charging the enemy, glaring left and right
he hurled his spear—a glinting brazen streak—
and the Trojans gave ground, scattering back,
panicking there before his whirling shaft—
a direct hit! Odysseus struck Democoon,
. . . speared him straight through one temple
and out the other punched the sharp bronze point
and the dark came swirling thick across his eyes—
down he crashed, armor clanging against his chest.
And the Trojan front shrank back, glorious Hector too
as the Argives yelled and dragged away the corpses,
pushing on, breakneck on. But lord god Apollo,
gazing down now from the heights of Pergamus,
rose in outrage, crying down at the Trojans,
"Up and at them, you stallion-breaking Trojans!
Never give up your lust for war against these Argives!
What are their bodies made of, rock or iron to block
your tearing bronze? Stab them, slash their flesh!

■ ■ ■

Now a jagged rock struck Amarcineus's son
Diores against his right shin, beside the ankle.
Pirous son of Imbrasus winged it hard and true,
the Thracian chief who had sailed across from Aenus . . .
the ruthless rock striking the bones and tendons
crushed them to pulp—he landed flat on his back,
slamming the dust, both arms flung out to his comrades,
gasping out his life. Pirous who heaved the rock
came rushing in and speared him up the navel—
his bowels uncoiled, spilling loose on the ground
and the dark came swirling down across his eyes.
But Pirous—
Aetolian Thoas speared *him* as he swerved and sprang away,
the lancehead piercing his chest above the nipple
plunged deep in his lung, and Thoas, running up,
wrenched the heavy spear from the man's chest,
drew his blade, ripped him across the belly,
took his life but he could not strip his armor.
And now . . .
no man who waded into that work could scorn it any longer,
anyone still not speared or stabbed by tearing bronze
who whirled into the heart of all that slaughter—
not even if great Athena led him by the hand,
flicking away the weapons hailing down against him.
That day ranks of Trojans, ranks of Achaean fighters
sprawled there side-by-side, facedown in the dust.

QUESTIONS FOR ANALYSIS

- What does this selection reveal about the style of combat and the weapons used in this period?
- More important, what do the poet's words tell us about how violence connects gods, humans, social identity, and personal relationships?
- What can we surmise about the cultures from which these soldiers come?

Source: "The Truce Erupts in War" from The Iliad *by Homer, translated by Robert Fagles,*

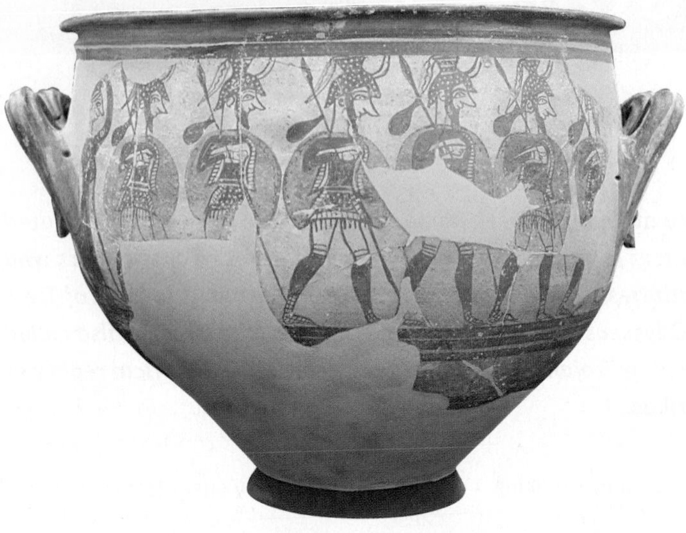

Mycenaean Arms and Armor. *A Mycenaean vase that illustrates the central role of arms and war to the societies on mainland Greece in the period down to 1200 BCE. The men bear common suits of armor and weapons—helmets, corsets, spears, and shields—most likely supplied to them by the palace-centered organizations to which they belonged. Despite these advantages, they were not able to mount a successful defense against the land incursions that destroyed the Mycenaean palaces toward the end of the thirteenth century BCE.*

in power had a significant effect on the subsequent relationship between Greeks and Persians. When the two forces met again in 480 BCE, the Persians lost the pivotal naval battle at Salamis. A year later, they suffered a decisive defeat on land and eventually lost the war. (But in a way that was typical of the intertwined relationships between the two cultures, Themistocles, the hero of Salamis, later finished his career in the service of the Persian king.)

Persian military defeats changed the balance of power. For the next 150 years Persia lost ground to the Greeks, who gradually regained territory in southeastern Europe and western Anatolia. During this time, palace intrigues and rebellions throughout the empire preoccupied the Persian court. The Greek historian Xenophon wrote that "whereas the king's empire was strong in that it covered a vast territory with large numbers of people, it also was weak because of the need to travel great distances and the wide distribution of its forces, making it vulnerable to a swift attack." In the end, the fatal blow against Persian rule came from the most remote Greek outpost in the eastern Mediterranean—Macedonia. Its armies, led by Alexander the Great, later ranged as far as India in their quest for empire (see Chapter 6).

The Phoenicians

Certain peoples living on the borderlands of large empires, such as the Phoenicians, coexisted with and flourished under imperial rule, while maintaining some political and economic autonomy. Particularly successful were those on the western edges of the emerging Assyrian and later Persian empires. (See Map 4.4.)

Living in the region of modern-day Lebanon were the Chanani (called "Canaanites" in the Bible). We know these entrepreneurial people by the name that the Greeks gave them—Phoenicians ("Purple People")—because of an expensive purple dye that they manufactured and traded. A mixture of the local population and the more recently arrived Sea Peoples, these traders preferred opening up new markets and new ports to subduing frontiers. Their coastal cities were ideally situated to develop trade throughout the entire Mediterranean basin.

The Sea Battle at Salamis. *A modern artist's reconstruction of the sea battle at Salamis in which the Greek ships led by Athens defeated a large invading fleet commanded by King Xerxes of Persia. The trireme—so-called because of its three banks of oars—was the state-of-the-art battleship of the time. Drawing on their long experience of sailing on the Mediterranean and using the fleet of triremes built under Themistocles, the Athenians gained a critical victory over the Persians and asserted ascendancy over the eastern Mediterranean.*

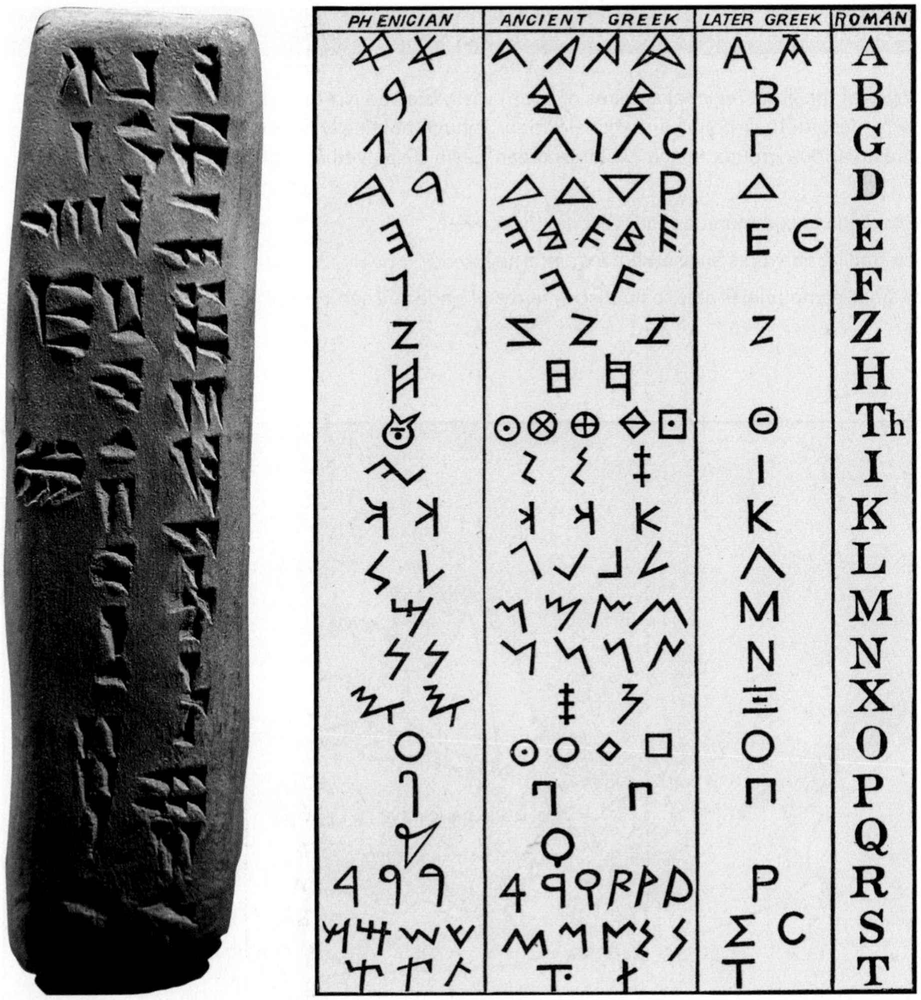

The Phoenician Alphabet. Left: *The first alphabet was written on clay tablets using the cuneiform script. It was developed by Phoenician traders who needed a script that was easy to learn so that they could record transactions without specially trained scribes. This tablet was found at the port town of Ugarit (Ras Shamra) in Syria and is dated to the fourteenth century* BCE. Right: *The forms of the letters in the Phoenician alphabet of the first millennium* BCE *are based on signs used to represent the Aramaic language. These Phoenician letters were then borrowed by the ancient Greeks. Our alphabet is based on that used by the Romans, who borrowed their letter forms from the later Greek inscriptions.*

Inland stood an extraordinary forest of massive cedars—perfect timber for making large, seaworthy craft, and a highly desirable export to the treeless heartlands of Egypt and Mesopotamia.

The innovations in shipbuilding and seafaring enabled the Phoenicians to sail as far west as present-day Morocco and Spain, carrying huge cargoes of such goods as timber, dyed cloth, glassware, wines, textiles, copper ingots, and carved ivory. Their trading colonies all around the southern and western rims of the Mediterranean (including Carthage in modern-day Tunisia on the North African coast) became major ports that shipped goods from interior regions throughout the Mediterranean.

During the eighth and seventh centuries BCE, the Assyrians expected the Phoenicians to supply the empire with special commercial services and, in return, allowed them autonomy in their business activities. In addition, the Assyrian kings signed treaties requiring the Phoenicians to pay tribute with luxury goods in return for granting some political autonomy. As the Phoenician merchants sent out waves of ships to other ports full of goods from the east, they brought back exotic luxuries for the Assyrian elites to enjoy. At the same time, Greek merchants established colonies on the northern rim of the Mediterranean. The competition and interaction of the two groups facilitated the transmission across the Mediterranean of many ideas from the advanced cultures of Southwest Asia.

The Phoenicians absorbed Mesopotamian religious and cultural elements such as gods, laws, units of measurement, and science, but the Phoenicians themselves developed an innovation that revolutionized communication and commerce: the alphabet. Introduced in the second millennium BCE in the western Levant, this new method of writing arrived in the west in 800 BCE, probably through Greek traders working in Phoenician centers. The alphabet allowed educated men to communicate directly with one another, dramatically reducing the need for professional scribes.

The Israelites and Judah

To the south of the mountains of Lebanon, the homeland of the Phoenicians, another minor region extended to the borderlands of Egypt. In this narrow strip of land between the Mediterranean Sea to the west and the desert to the east, an important

MAP 4.4 | The Mediterranean World, 1000–400 BCE

Peoples on the fringes of the great regional empires of Southwest Asia and North Africa had strong influences beyond their borders, despite their political marginalization. Though politically dwarfed by the Neo-Assyrian and Persian empires, various groups in the Mediterranean basin displayed strong cultural and economic power.

- What were the borderland communities and what did they trade?
- How far did their trading networks and settlement patterns extend?
- Why were such small communities able to flourish in terms of trade and settlement?

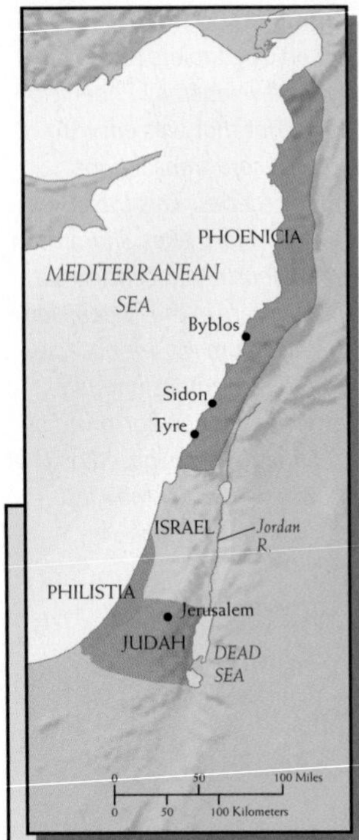

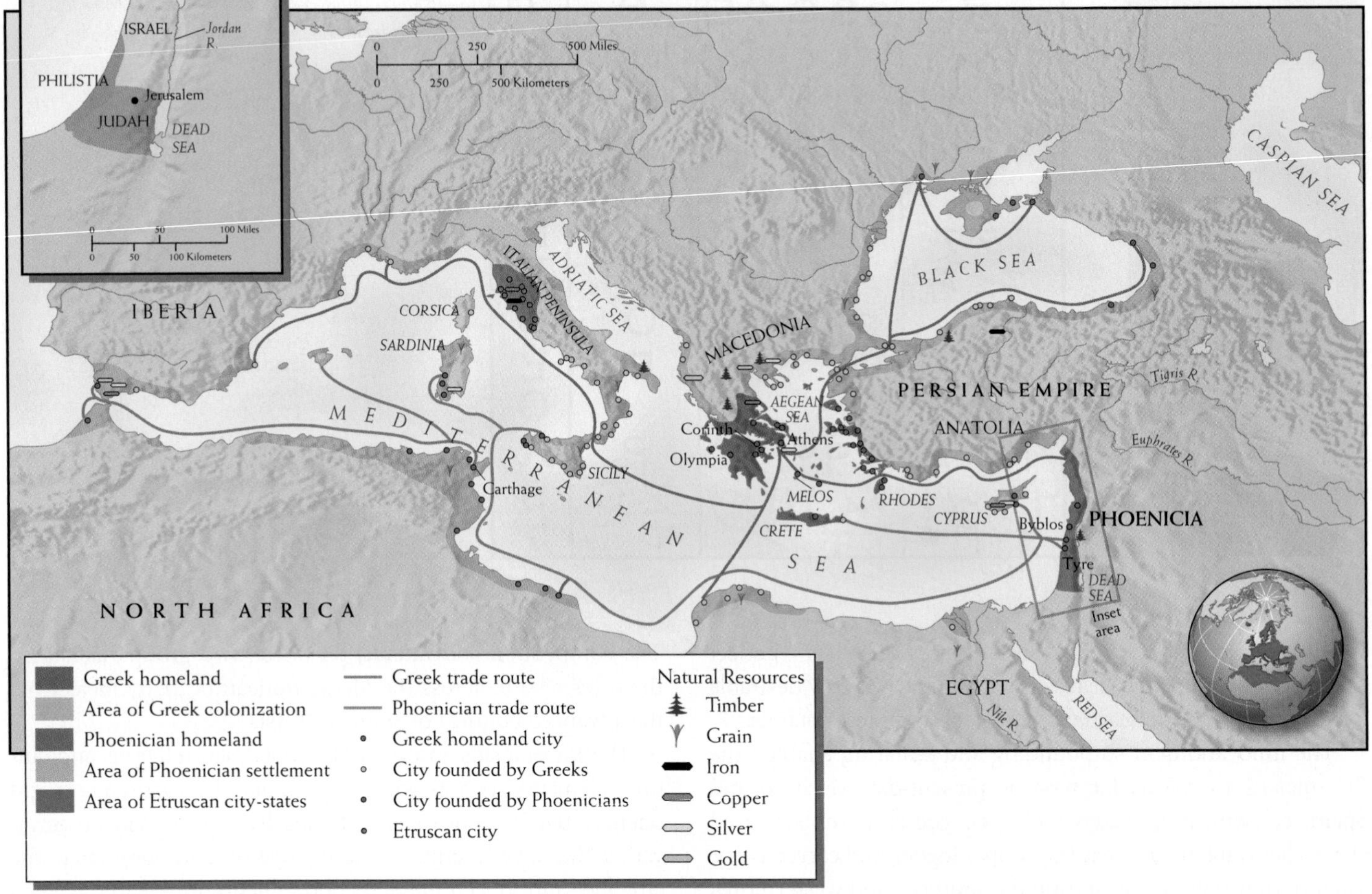

microsociety emerged, one that was to have an impact on world history that was out of proportion to its population and the geographic size of its homeland. The Israelites were less oriented to the Mediterranean and to seafaring than the Phoenicians. Their hybrid society mixed their local culture with social, economic, and religious forms commonly found across southwest Asia and Egypt.

THE ISRAELITES We do not know much that is certain about Israelite origins. Their own later stories emphasized beginnings in Mesopotamia to the east, and origins of the patriarch Abraham from the city of Ur on the Euphrates River. We can also see Mesopotamian influences on the early Israelites in a number of ways, from shared stories like devastating floods that destroyed all of humanity to similarities in Hebrew law to principles in Hammurapi's Code, and a range of shared deities, values, and customs. Later stories also emphasized connections with Egypt of the pharaohs to the west and the mass movement of a captive Israelite population out of Egypt under Moses. All that scholars can state with reasonable certainty is that material signs of a local regional culture began to emerge in the area of present-day Israel between 1200 and 1000 BCE, culminating with the emergence of a state in the form of a kingdom centered at Jerusalem under King David (c. 1000–960 BCE). The kingdom that David and his successor Solomon (c. 960–930 BCE) established around Jerusalem, centered on the great temple that Solomon built in the city, did not last long. Because of internal disputes, it fragmented immediately after Solomon's reign into a tiny northern kingdom, Israel, and a small southern one, Judah.

MONOTHEISM AND PROPHETS Within the microstate founded by David and Solomon, profound religious and cultural changes took place. A single great temple in Jerusalem now outranked all other shrines in the land. Especially among the educated upper classes linked to the temple, an absolute priority focused on one god, YHWH, over other regional deities. For a long time, however, this emphasis was relative, what modern scholars call *henotheism*: the ascendancy and power of one god over other spirits and deities that still exist. Gradually, however, there was a move to true *monotheism*: the acceptance of only one god to the exclusion of all others. What little evidence there is indicates that this process was in place by the seventh century BCE, when YHWH was so dominant compared to the few remaining earlier deities that he was mostly unchallenged. The long transition to monotheism, however, did not take place without quarrels and resistance, because it was a contentious process centered on prophetic figures. The **prophets** were freelance religious men of power who found themselves in opposition to the formal power of the kings and priests of the temple in Jerusalem.

The most ferocious of these prophets, men like Isaiah (c. 720s BCE), Ezra (c. 600s BCE), and Jeremiah (c. 590s BCE), were central to the formation of the Israelites' monotheistic religion. They did not shrink from threatening divine annihilation for groups that opposed the new idea of one temple, one god, and one moral system to the exclusion of all others. On one occasion, the prophet Ezra thundered: "Whoever will not obey the law of your God and the law of the king, let judgment be rigorously executed upon him, be it death, banishment, confiscation of property, or imprisonment" (Ezra 7:26 New English Bible). The moral preaching, exhortations, and threats of these men marked the high point of a long and difficult battle to defeat the religious diversity to which many people were accustomed. But prevail they did. They were part of a movement to enforce belief in a single, all-powerful god and his strict social and moral codes that governed the daily lives of all members of the community. These laws came to be enshrined in the Torah, a series of books that encapsulated the laws governing all aspects of life, including family and marriage, food, clothing, sex, and worship. The whole of it was formulated as a "contract" between all these people and their one and only god. They alone were his people.

The monotheism of the Israelites was to have far-reaching and long-lasting historical consequences, in part because Jewish peoples scattered far and wide throughout Afro-Eurasia and in part because of its influence in Christianity and Islam.

FOUNDATIONS OF VEDIC CULTURE IN SOUTH ASIA (1500–600 BCE)

In South Asia, it was language and belief systems, not political conquests, that brought people together. People moved in greater numbers and covered longer distances in this period, and in doing so, they created new mechanisms of integration. The Indo-European-speaking peoples who began to enter South Asia through the passes in the Hindu Kush Mountains in the middle of the second millennium BCE eventually occupied the whole of what are today Pakistan, Bangladesh, and northern India (see Chapter 3). Here their populations expanded and created a flourishing culture. Unlike societies in Mesopotamia and Egypt, the new rulers in this region did not have previous states on which to found their power. Floods and earthquakes had weakened the earlier Harappan urban centers in the Indus River valley (see Chapter 2), and its urban culture had died out several centuries before the new peoples streamed in from the northwest.

Social and Religious Culture

The men and women who migrated into the northern lands of South Asia were illiterate, chariot-riding, and cattle-keeping pastoral peoples who lacked experience of cities and urban life. They brought with them, however, much-beloved and elaborate rituals, mainly articulated in hymns, rhymes, and explanatory texts, called **Vedas** (Sanskrit for wisdom or knowledge), which they retained as they entered a radically different environment and which they relied on to provide a foundation for assimilating new ways. These hymns reflected their earlier lives on the plains of central Asia and were infused with images of animals and gods. In some of these Vedic poems storms "gallop" across the heavens, and thunder sounds like the "neigh of horses." The rituals that the people brought with them involved sacrificing cattle, horses, and sheep to their gods and gathering together at festivities to sing hymns, make animal sacrifices, burn *ghee* (clarified butter) for the gods, and share banquets. Priests conducted these ceremonies, receiving payment in cows. The Vedas became sacred religious works and were eventually written down in Sanskrit.

The Indo-European-speaking migrants encountered indigenous people who either lived in agricultural settlements or were herders like themselves. The newcomers allied themselves with some of the locals, who showed them how to live in their new environment. They made enemies of others, fighting with them for territory and dominance. In their interaction with peoples with different cultural practices and languages, the Vedic migrants kept their own language and religious rituals but also absorbed local words and deities. Allies and defeated enemies who became part of their society had to accept Vedic culture. By the middle of the first century BCE, the Vedic peoples covered all of what is now northern India, and their language and rituals had become dominant in their new land.

Even though the Vedic migrants changed the social and cultural landscape of the region, they did not give it political coherence by creating a single, unified regional kingdom. (See Map 4.5.) This world became integrated through a shared Vedic culture.

Material Culture

Initially, the material culture of Vedic society was rudimentary. Even chiefs and elite warriors enjoyed few luxuries. Early trade was not based on imported luxuries but on horses, which had to come in from the northwest beyond the Hindu Kush because local environmental factors prevented their successful breeding or training. The ruling elite never gave up its preoccupation with fine horses. To make their trade in these resplendent war mounts easier, they created a long-distance route across the North Indian plain that stretched from the Khyber Pass to the lower Ganges. Symbolic of the tremendous continuing significance of the horse to the ruling elites of Vedic society was the *ashvamedha* or horse sacrifice later found in the period of the kings. In this ritual, the king's horse was consecrated and then allowed to roam for a year over land that then became the king's land. At the end of the year, the horse was sacrificed in a great ceremony.

As the Vedic people entered the fertile river basins, they gradually settled down as cultivators of the land and herders of animals. Their turn to agriculture could hardly have been easy, but they were aided by learning plowing from local farmers and gaining access to excellent iron ore. The iron plow was crucial for tilling the Ganges plain and transforming the Deccan plateau into croplands. In the drier north, the Vedic people grew wheat, barley, millet, and cotton; in the wet lowlands, they cultivated rice paddies. Farmers also toiled to produce tropical crops such as sugarcane and spices like pepper, ginger, and cinnamon. With these new crops, the Vedic people transformed a sparsely populated region into a crowded domain.

As farming became the dominant way of life and urban settlements stretched out across the region, trade blossomed via river and land routes. Trade between settlements developed as the agricultural surpluses grew; grain was transported to towns to feed them. Artisans pressed sugarcane into sugar in the cities, and merchants sold the finished product back to people in the agricultural villages.

Splintered States

The region's social and economic integration offered a stark contrast to its political fragmentation. In the process of fanning out from the Punjab (the region of the five tributaries of the Indus River) and settling in the plain between the Ganges and Yamuna Rivers, the Vedic peoples created small regional governments and chieftainships. And as much as they fought with the indigenous peoples, they fought even more fiercely among themselves. Such aggression reinforced the importance of warriors and elevated the worship of the gods of war (Indra) and fire (Agni). The elite warriors battled one another and the farmers for land and other resources, just as occurred in the Mycenaean societies, in the tribal societies of the Iranian plateau, and in Zhou China.

Their chieftainships eventually became small kingdoms with inhabitants bound to each other through lines of descent from a common ancestor. They traced their family descent or lineage through blood ties, alliances by means of marriage, and by invented family relations. Earliest Vedic society had two main lineages: the lunar lineage and the solar lineage. Each had its own creation myth, ancestors, language, and rituals. The lineages included many clans (a **clan** is a social group comprising many households, claiming descent from a common ancestor) in which seniority determined one's power and importance. The Vedic peoples absorbed many local clans into their own lineages. Clans that adopted the Vedic culture became part of the lineage (through marriage or made-up ties) and were considered insiders. In contrast, clans that had other languages and rituals were considered to be uncivilized outsiders.

As Vedic society expanded, the clans of the solar lineage usually stayed together in the same area. In contrast, the clans of the lunar lineage split into many branches; some migrated east to the Ganges River valley and others south to the northern Deccan plain. Though separated by distance, the clans maintained their relationship through marriage. Inside these kin-bound clan structures, each member had a well-defined place in the political and social order.

Once urban society and states arose, these lineages no longer dominated the social structure, but they lived on in two major epics that recounted the earlier events of the Vedic people. The *Mahabharata* relates the last phase of the lunar lineage, and the *Ramayana* focuses on a hero of the solar lineage. Later rulers continued to draw on the memory of these two ancient lineages,

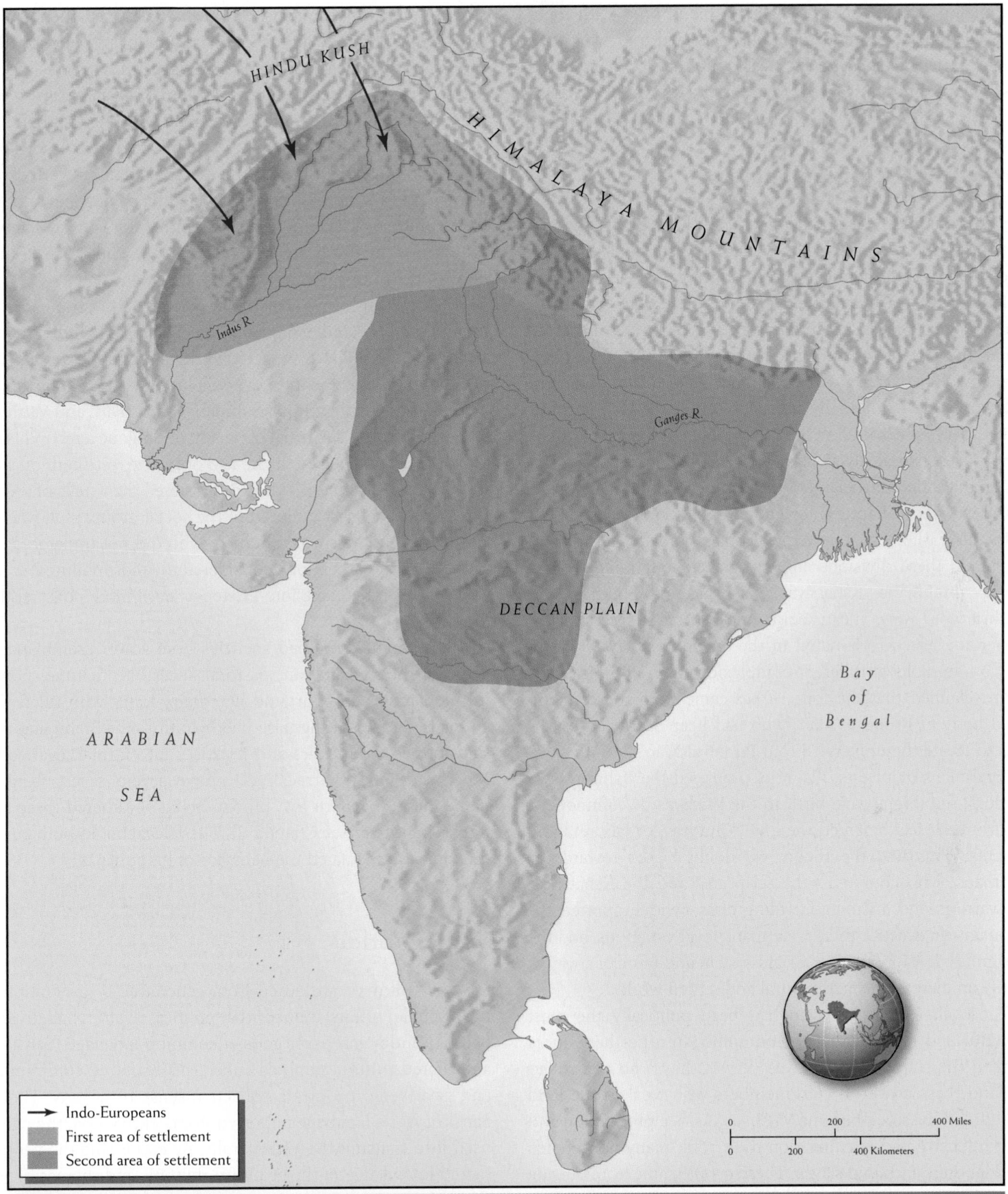

MAP 4.5 | South Asia, 1500–400 BCE

- Where did the Indo-Europeans originally come from?
- What enabled Vedic culture to spread so rapidly?
- What kept it from spreading further?

legitimizing their regimes by claiming blood links with them. These kinship communities gradually formed into what were known as *mahajanapada* or "great communities." Sixteen of these great communities were found in the Ganges River basin.

Varna in a Stratified Society

The Vedic peoples who spread across South Asia had originally been herding communities in which few social distinctions other than age and gender were important. As these peoples settled down, became farmers, and created state structures, their societies became more complex and hierarchical. In particular, the rise of settled agriculture after 1000 BCE led to a great divide between those who controlled the land and those who worked it. As these divisions developed, the Vedic peoples created a unique social system based on rigid distinctions of status. These social divisions described the specific strata that carried out different social, political, and economic functions in South Asia. (See Chapter 5 for more discussion.)

In this earlier era, the Vedic peoples used the term *varna* to refer to these divisions and recognized four ranked social groups—Brahmans, Kshatriyas, Vaishyas, and Shudras. The Sanskrit word *varna* means color, and its uses suggest that the four-group system originated in the encounter between clans and communities of different complexions and cultures. Vedic hymns claimed that the four *varnas* came from the dismembered body of Primeval Man, who had been sacrificed by the gods to create the universe. From Primeval Man's mouth came the Brahmans or priests; his arms produced the Kshatriyas or warriors; the thighs gave birth to the Vaishyas or commoners; and from the feet emerged the lowly Shudras, or laborers and servants. This was the theory, no doubt biased toward the Brahmans, who composed the scriptures and the Kshatriyas, the warriors and aristocratic ruling class, who supported the Brahmans. In practice there were many local variations, and the four-group division was less a rigid system and more of a way to stratify an increasingly agricultural and settled world.

Those clan members who had been politically the most powerful and had led their communities into northern India claimed the status of Kshatriyas. It was they who controlled the land. Less powerful clan members who worked the land and tended livestock became Vaishyas. As rice production and labor-intensive paddy cultivation took hold, many households hired laborers and used slaves. These people came from outside the Vedic lineages and became known as Shudras ("the small ones"). They constituted the lowest *varna*. The priests or Brahmans claimed the highest status, for they performed the rituals and understood the religious principles without which life was believed to be unsustainable. Only they were thought to be able to commune with the gods, a skill that many regarded as their most coveted talent. Some of these Brahmans functioned as priests for the chiefs, and some were sages who lived as ascetics (individuals who deny themselves comforts) in forests, where they discussed philosophical questions with their students. In addition, Brahmans and Kshatriyas reinforced each other's high status. Brahmans performed the sacrifices that converted warriors into kings, and kings reciprocated by paying fees and gifts to the Brahmans. The rest (Vaishyas and Shudras) were left with the tasks of assuring the sustenance of the elite. (See Primary Source: Becoming a Brahman Priest.)

Of the many ways in which societies have stratified their members and accorded higher or lower statuses to individuals—mainly in the modern western world through class, race, and gender—the Vedic peoples overwhelmingly stressed birth. The three higher social groups (Brahmans, Kshatriyas, and Vaishyas) were twice born. The ritual of having undergone a second birth, which usually occurred at the age of twelve, set them off from the Shudras. Brahmans, who administered the rituals of second birth, were the least polluted of the social groups, followed by Kshatriyas and Vaishyas. Shudras, who did not undergo a second birth, were, therefore, considered the most polluted. A fifth social group later came into existence, even more polluted than the rest.

These highly stratified societies bore scant resemblance to those of their egalitarian, pastoral ancestors. In time, powerful monarchies arose around hereditary kings who ruled with councils of elders. Kings also had help from the Brahmans, who transformed social rules and practices into formal legal codes. Much later (c. 100 BCE–100 CE) one or several sages, using the name Manu (Sanskrit for "human being"), gathered these laws into a single text (see Chapter 8). These legal books both guided the king and regulated the behavior of his subjects.

Vedic Worlds

A Vedic culture, transmitted from generation to generation by the Brahman priests, unified what political rivalries had divided. Belief in Indra and other gods, a common language (Sanskrit), and shared cultural symbols linked the dispersed communities and gave Vedic peoples a collective sense of destiny. Though Sanskrit was a language imported from central Asia, the people used it to transmit the Vedas orally. By expressing the people's sacred knowledge in the beautiful rhythms and rhymes of Sanskrit, the Vedas effectively passed on their culture from one generation to the next.

As the priests of Vedic society, the Brahmans were responsible for memorizing every syllable and sound of the Vedic works. These included commentaries on sacred works from

PRIMARY SOURCE

Becoming a Brahman Priest

When the Vedic people became farmers, many of them started to question the validity of sacrificing cows, the draft animals valued for their use in cultivation. Around the seventh century BCE, some thinkers abandoned Vedic rituals and chose to live simply in forests as they debated the meaning of life and the structure of the universe. Those sages were Brahman rishi, highly respected priests. However, not every one of the famous Brahmans was born a Brahman.

1. Satyakâma, the son of Gabâlâ, addressed his mother and said: 'I wish to become a Brahmakârin [religious student], mother. Of what family am I?'

2. She said to him: 'I do not know, my child, of what family thou art. In my youth when I had to move about much as a servant [waiting on the guests in my father's house] I conceived thee. I do not know of what family thou art. I am Gabâlâ by name, thou art Satyakâma [Philalethes]. Say that thou art Satyakâma Gâbâla.'

3. He going to Gautama Hâridrumata said to him, 'I wish to become a Brahmakârin with you, Sir. May I come to you, Sir?'

4. He said to him: 'Of what family are you, my friend?' He replied: 'I do not know, Sir, of what family I am. I asked my mother, and she answered: "In my youth when I had to move about much as a servant, I conceived thee. I do not know of what family thou art. I am Gabâlâ by name, thou art Satyakâma," I am therefore Satyakâma Gâbâla, Sir.'

5. He said to him: 'No one but a true Bráhmana would thus speak out. Go and fetch fuel, friend, I shall initiate you. You have not swerved from the truth.'

Having initiated him, he chose four hundred lean and weak cows, and said: 'Tend these friend.'

He drove them out and said to himself. 'I shall not return unless I bring back a thousand.' He dwelt a number of years [in the forest], until the cows became a thousand.

QUESTIONS FOR ANALYSIS

- Satyakama became a well-known Brahman teacher after his study. Judging from this story, was he born a Brahman?
- At that time, how did the rishis and their disciples survive in the forest areas when thinking and studying?

Source: The Upanishads, *translated by F. Max Müller, vol. 1 of* Sacred Books of the East, *edited by F. Max Müller (1900; reprint, New Delhi: Motilal Banarsidass, 1981), pp. 60–61.*

early nomadic times, as well as new rules and rituals explaining the settled, farming way of life. The Vedas promoted cultural unity and pride through common ritual practices and support for hereditary *raja* kingdoms. The main body of Vedic literature includes the four Vedas: Rig-Veda, Sama-Veda, Yajur-Veda, and Atharva-Veda. The Rig-Veda, the earliest text, is a collection of hymns praising the gods, including Indra (god of war), Agni (god of fire), and Varuna (god of water). Indra stands out as the most powerful and important, as he is the one who set the order of the universe and made life possible. The Sama-Veda is a textbook of songs for priests to perform when making ritual sacrifices; most of their stanzas also appear in the Rig-Veda. The Yajur-Veda is a prayer book for the priest who conducted rituals for chariot races, horse sacrifices, or the king's coronation. The Atharva-Veda includes charms and remedies; many address problems related to agriculture, a central aspect of life. Although the Vedic period left no impressive buildings and artifacts, it created a wealth of thinking about cosmology and human society. In this way, it laid the religious foundations for coming generations.

During the middle of the first millennium BCE, thinkers (mostly Brahman ascetics dwelling in forests) felt that the Vedic rituals no longer provided satisfactory answers to the many questions of a rapidly changing society. The result was a collection of works known as the Upanishads, or the supreme knowledge, which expanded the Vedic cultural system. Taking the form of dialogues between disciples and a sage, the Upanishads explored questions of deep concern at that time. Out of these dialogues came a set of lessons that offered insights into the ideal social order, and a script and eventually a canon to be shared beyond local communities.

The Upanishads teach that people are not separate from each other but belong to an integrated cosmic universe called Brahma. While the physical world is always changing and is filled with chaos and illusion, *atman*, the eternal being, exists in all people and all creatures. Atman's presence in each living being makes all creatures part of a universal soul. While all living beings must die, the atman guarantees eternal life, ensuring that souls are reborn and transmigrate into new lives. This cycle continues with humans as they are either reborn as humans or as other living creatures, like cows, insects, or plants. These unique Vedic views of life and the universe were passed along as principles of faith, bringing spiritual unity to the northern half of South Asia. Unlike the societies of Southwest Asia and North Africa, here in the kingdoms of the Indus Valley and the Ganges plain the common Vedic culture—rather than larger political units—was the unifying bond.

THE EARLY ZHOU EMPIRE IN EAST ASIA (1045–771 BCE)

Drought reshaped the political map of East Asia in much the same way that it altered power alignments in Southwest Asia. Here, too, a radical change in the climate was a major factor in the demise of a powerful state, the Shang, and the rise of a successor regime, the Zhou. East Asia's environmental crisis had its origins on the plains of central Asia where the more arid conditions that were sweeping across the Afro-Eurasian landmass resulted in powerful hot and dry winds carrying immense quantities of dust onto the North China plain. The dust storms reduced the soil's ability to retain moisture and led to a sharp decline in soil fertility. As in countless other parts of Afro-Eurasia, peoples went in search of more fertile soils and more reliable harvests. Conflicts were inevitable. One of the groups on the move were the Zhou peoples, who by the twelfth century BCE were settled on the periphery of the Shang state in the valley of the Wei River, located in northwestern China, one of the Yellow River's most important tributaries. Their migration brought them into direct conflict with the Shang, already in political decline. Although the Zhou had been only a minor state during the height of Shang power, the two peoples traded and often were allies to fend off raiders from the northwest. Over time, the appearance of a dynamic leader, King Wu, and the need to find more resources emboldened the Zhou to challenge the Shang for supremacy in North China. At a battle in 1045 BCE, the Zhou prevailed. King Wu owed his success to being able to amass an army of 45,000 troops and employ superior weaponry, including dagger axes, bronze armor, and 300 war chariots. These were small numbers by Southwest Asian standards, but overwhelming in East Asia. (See Map 4.6.)

Zhou Chariots. *After swearing allegiance to the Shang, the Zhou assembled superior military forces in the northwest, in part by emulating Shang chariots. The Zhou subsequently used their own chariots and archers to defeat the Shang in about 1045 BCE. The regional lords who owed allegiance to the Zhou king distinguished themselves in the aristocratic hierarchy by using chariots for travel and battle.*

Integration through Dynastic Institutions

When the Zhou took over from the Shang, their new state consisted of a patchwork of more than seventy small states, whose rulers, however, accepted the overarching authority of the Zhou kings. To solidify their power, the Zhou copied the Shang's patrimonial state structure, centered on ancestor worship in which the rulers' power passed down through genealogies of male ancestors reaching back to the gods. (A **genealogy** is a history of descent of a person or a family from a distant ancestor.) On such foundations, the Zhou crystallized the dynastic principle and though one dynasty succeeded another, the result was that the Chinese fostered one of the most long-lived dynastic systems in world history. Thirty-nine Zhou kings followed one after the other, mostly in an orderly father-to-son succession, over a span of eight centuries, and they in turn were succeeded by new dynasties..

Even though the Zhou drew heavily on Shang precedents, their own innovations produced some of the most significant contributions to China's distinctive cultural and political development. Regarding all those whom they governed as a single people, the Zhou employed the term *Huaxia*, or Chinese, when referring to their subjects. They also claimed that even though more than seventy states existed at this time, their territories were at heart unified, naming their lands *Zhongguo*, which at the

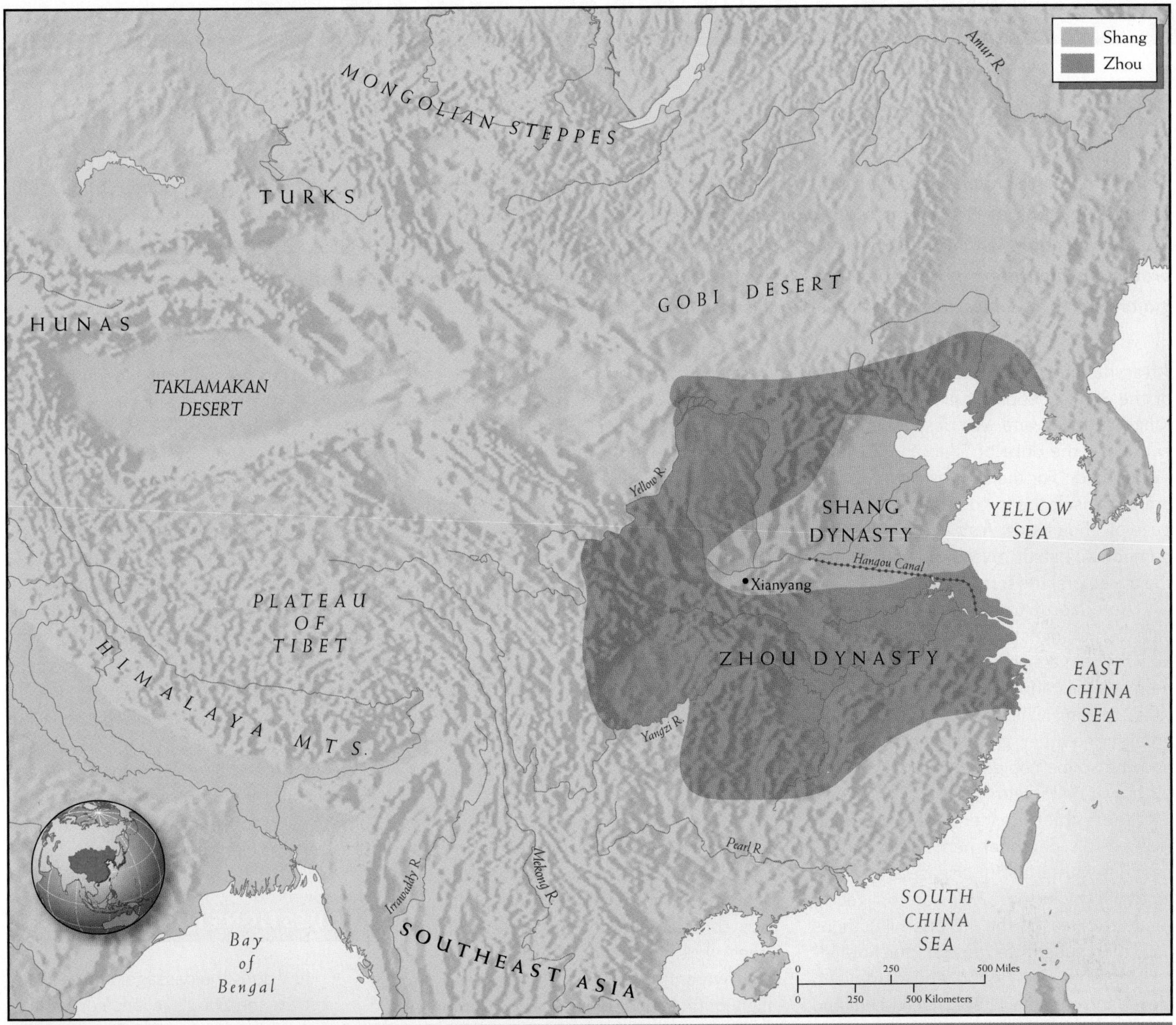

MAP 4.6 | The Zhou Dynasty, 2200–256 BCE

Toward the end of the second millennium BCE, the Zhou state supplanted the Shang dynasty as the most powerful political force in East Asia. Using the map above, compare and contrast the territorial reach of the Zhou state with that of the Shang.

- In what direction did the Zhou state expand the most dramatically?
- Why do you think this was the case?
- How did the Zhou integrate their geographically large and diverse state?

time meant "the central states" but later came to be called "the middle kingdom," a term that the Chinese used thereafter right down to present times to refer to their state. Moreover, the Zhou kings of this middle kingdom, in addition to being required to rule justly, believed that they had a duty to extend their culture to "less civilized" peoples living in outlying regions.

Zhou Succession and Political Foundations

Although smaller in size, the Zhou expanded their dynasty in many similar ways to those in Southwest Asia. King Wu (r. 1049–1043 BCE) and his successors expanded north toward what is now Beijing and south toward the Yangzi River valley.

PRIMARY SOURCE

Zhou Succession Story

Chinese lore often glamorized the early Zhou dynasty as an era of sage rulers such as King Wu and the Duke of Zhou (Chou). The* Shangshu (Book of History) *account, however, shows that the transition of power from the founder, King Wu, to the Duke of Zhou was fraught with difficulty—as was often the case in early states. It reveals how the Duke of Zhou tried simultaneously to protect his reputation as regent to King Wu's young son and to preserve Zhou rule. This document also represents one of the first major efforts in Chinese history to provide a historical narrative of events.

After he had completed the conquest of the Shang people, in the second year, King Wu fell ill and was despondent. The two lords, the duke of Shao and Tai-kung Wang, said, "For the king's sake let us solemnly consult the tortoise oracle." But the duke of Chou [King Wu's younger brother, named Tan] said, "We must not distress the ancestors, the former kings."

The duke of Chou then offered himself to the ancestors, constructing three altars within a single compound. . . . Then he made this announcement to the Great King, to King Chi, and to King Wen, his great grandfather, grandfather, and father, and the scribe copied down the words of his prayer on tablets:

"Your chief descendant So-and-so [King Wu's personal name is tabooed] has met with a fearful disease and is violently ill. If you three kings are obliged to render to Heaven the life of an illustrious son, then substitute me, Tan, for So-and-so's person. I am good and compliant, clever and capable. I have much talent and much skill and can serve the spirits. . . ."

Then he divined with three tortoises, and all were auspicious. He opened the bamboo receptacles and consulted the documents, and they too indicated an auspicious answer. The duke of Chou said to the king, "According to the indications of the oracle, you will suffer no harm."

[The king said,] "I, the little child, have obtained a new life from the three kings. I shall plan for a distant end. I hope that they will think of me, the solitary man."

After the duke of Chou returned, he placed the tablets containing the prayer in a metal-bound casket. The next day the king began to recover.

[Later, King Wu died and was succeeded by his infant son, King Ch'eng. The duke of Chou acted as regent and was slandered by King Wu's younger brothers, whom he was eventually forced to punish.]

In the autumn, when a plentiful crop had ripened but had not yet been harvested, Heaven sent great thunder and lightning accompanied by wind. The grain was completely flattened and even large trees were uprooted. The people of the land were in great fear. The king and his high ministers donned their ceremonial caps and opened the documents of the metal-bound casket and thus discovered the record of how the duke of Chou had offered himself as a substitute for King Wu. . . . .

The king grasped the document and wept. "There is no need for us to make solemn divination about what has happened," he said. "In former times the duke of Chou toiled diligently for the royal house, but I, the youthful one, had no way of knowing it. Now Heaven has displayed its terror in order to make clear the virtue of the duke of Chou. I, the little child, will go in person to greet him, for the rites of our royal house approve such action."

When the king came out to the suburbs to meet the duke of Chou, Heaven sent down rain and reversed the wind, so that the grain all stood up once more. The two lords ordered the people of the land to right all the large trees that had been blown over and to earth them up. Then the year was plentiful. (*Chin t'eng.*)

QUESTIONS FOR ANALYSIS

- How does the passage demonstrate the Zhou's reliance on male ancestor worship?
- What do the direct speeches tell us about the place of divination in Zhou politics?

Source: Translated in Burton Watson, Early Chinese Literature *(New York: Columbia University Press, 1962), pp. 35–36.*

(See Primary Source: Zhou Succession Story.) Seeking to retain the allegiance of the lords of older states and to gain the support of new lords, whom they appointed in annexed areas, Zhou kings rewarded their political supporters with lands that they could pass on to their descendants. As the Zhou expanded their territory, their new colonies often consisted of garrison towns where the Zhou colonizers lived surrounded by fields inhabited by local farmers. As under the Shang, Zhou regional lords were expected to supply military forces as needed, pay tribute, and appear at the imperial court to pledge their continuing allegiance.

The Zhou "Mandate of Heaven" and the Justification of Power

In addition to promoting a Chinese ethnic and political identity, the Zhou rulers also introduced what was to prove one of East Asia's most enduring political doctrines—the concept of the mandate of heaven. They did so by asserting that their moral superiority justified taking over Shang wealth and territories and that heaven had imposed a moral mandate on them to replace the Shang and return good governance to the people. At first they presented the **mandate of heaven** as a religious compact between the Zhou people and their supreme god in heaven (literally the "sky god"), but over time Zhou kings and the court detached the concept from the sky god and made it into a freestanding and fundamental Chinese political doctrine. The Zhou argued that since worldly affairs were supposed to align with those of the heavens, heavenly powers conferred legitimate rights to rule only on their chosen representative. In return, the ruler was duty-bound to uphold heaven's principles of harmony and honor. Any ruler who failed in this duty, who let instability creep into earthly affairs, or who let his people suffer, would lose the mandate. Under this system, it was the prerogative of spiritual authority to withdraw support from any wayward ruler and to find another, more worthy one. In this way, the Zhou sky god legitimated regime change.

In using this creed the Zhou rulers had to acknowledge that any group of rulers, even they themselves, could be ousted if they lost the mandate of heaven because of improper practices. *The Book of Odes*, written in the Zhou period, clearly intoned this caution, "the mandate is not easy to keep," as did a Zhou poem, "it is not easy to be king." Moreover, after the Zhou overturned the Shang line of succession, rulers were no longer considered gods. From that point on, dynastic legitimacy depended on ruling in accordance with the principles of good governance and upright behavior. Unlike the theocracies of Southwest Asia and the later emperors of Japan, China's rulers created an empire based more on politics, military power, and morality than on religious legitimacy. This concept of the mandate of heaven would be used by the Chinese Dynasties to justify their rule all the way down into the twentieth century, making it along with the tradition of hereditary rule two of the most important cultural characteristics developed during early Chinese history.

The early Zhou kings contended that heaven favored their triumph because the last Shang kings had been evil men whose policies brought pain to the people through waste and corruption. Thereafter, the mandate became a political tool. It was a compelling way to defend continuity of political institutions, if not rulers, in the name of preserving a natural order. It also helps explain why each change in power did not bring about an abrupt overhaul of political and cultural institutions.

A century after the Zhou had seized power, King Mu (r. 956–918 BCE) began a series of reforms that strengthened the powers of the state at a time when its authority was under severe challenge. In the years leading up to Mu's ascension to the throne, the Zhou had suffered many setbacks. The most ominous was the defeat of the Zhou armies in a battle against a large tributary neighbor on the state's southeastern border. Not only were the Zhou's famous six armies routed but King Zhao was also killed. With the royal house in obvious decline, poets began to compose satires that poked fun at it, and critics wondered whether the Zhou had lost the mandate of heaven. King Mu turned first to the military, bringing in more competent leaders and reinvigorating the spirit of the forces. Next came the civil bureaucracy, where he restructured the court and military by appointing officials, supervisors, and military captains who were not related to him, and he instituted a formal legal code. These changes, created a need for bureaucratic records, including archives of appointments and legal verdicts. Increasingly, a pool of scribes and scholars joined the entourage of royal diviners, using their mastery of writing to find patrons at court and among regional powers. Through their powerful rhetoric, they tied many of the new changes to the early Zhou founding myth.

One of the duties and privileges of the king was to create a royal calendar. This official document defined times for undertaking agricultural activities and celebrating rituals, But unexpected events such as solar eclipses or natural calamities threw into question the ruling house's mandate. Since rulers claimed that their authority came from heaven, the Zhou made great efforts to gain accurate knowledge of the stars and to perfect the astronomical system on which they based their calendar. Advances in astronomy and mathematics enabled Zhou astronomers to precisely calculate the length of a lunar month (29.53 days) and measure the length of the solar year (365.25 days). But a year of twelve lunar months is 354.36 days long. To resolve the discrepancy, the Zhou occasionally inserted a leap month. Scribes dated the reigns of kings by days and years within a repeating sixty-year cycle, which matched the cosmological interaction between heaven and earth.

Zhou legitimacy also derived indirectly from Shang material culture through the use of bronze ritual vessels, statues, ornaments, and weapons. As the Zhou emulated the Shang's large-scale production of ceremonial bronzes, they developed an extensive system of bronze metalworking that required a large force of tribute labor. Many of its members were Shang, who were sometimes forcibly transported to new Zhou towns to produce the bronze ritual objects, which were

Zhou Wine Vessel. *Under the Zhou, bronze metallurgy depended on a large labor force. Many workers initially came from Shang labor groups, who were superior to the Zhou in technology. The use of bronze, such as for this wine vessel, exemplified dynastic continuity between the Shang and Zhou.*

then sold and distributed across the lands, symbolizing Zhou legitimacy.

Social and Economic Transformation

As the Chinese social order became more integrated, it also became more class-based. Directly under the Zhou ruler and his royal ministers were the hereditary nobles, divided into five ranks. These regional lords had landholdings of different sizes but under the powerful tributary state they all owed allegiance to the Zhou king. They paid tribute and taxes and supplied warriors to fight in the king's army and laborers to clear land, drain fields, and do other work. They periodically appeared at court and took part in complex rituals to reaffirm their allegiance to the king. Below the regional lords were high officers at the Zhou court, as well as ministers and administrators who supervised the people's work. A military **caste** of aristocratic warriors stood at the bottom of the noble hierarchy.

Occupational Groups and Family Structures

Initially, most of the population worked as farmers on fields owned by great landholding families. Some commoners were artisans, such as those who produced valuable bronze ritual vessels, or weavers who spun delicate silk textiles. Over time, an elaborate ladder of occupational strata arose. This system divided people by function: landholders who produced grain, growers of plants and fruit trees, woodsmen, breeders of cattle and chickens, artisans, merchants, weavers, servants, and those with no fixed occupation. The central government apparently controlled how each group did its work—for example, telling landholders what crops to plant, when to harvest, and when to irrigate. Although reports of these efforts may overstate the government's reach, the Chinese state played a major role in uniting the region's diverse peoples in ways that none of Afro-Eurasia's other great regimes did.

One important method of integration was the political and legal use of family structures. In their patrilineal society, the Zhou established strict hierarchies for both men and women. Both art and literature celebrated the son who honored his parents. Men and women had different roles in family and ceremonial life. On landholdings, men farmed and hunted, while women produced silk and other textiles and fashioned them into clothing. Wealth increasingly trumped gender and class distinctions, however. In particular, rich women high in the Zhou aristocracy enjoyed a greater range of actions than other women. And wealthy merchants in emerging cities challenged the authority of local lords.

TECHNOLOGICAL DEVELOPMENT What has been remarkable about China throughout history is how its integration progressed in small steps, not in a single triumphal bound. Zhou achievements likewise were incremental, rooted in a transformation of the countryside as both princes and peasants began expanding the agrarian frontier inland. Wooden and, much later, iron plows enabled farmers to break the hard sod of lands beyond the river basins, and over time cultivators learned the practice of field rotation to prevent soil nutrients from being exhausted. A great advance occurred in the middle of the first millennium BCE as regional states organized local efforts to regulate the flow of the main rivers. They built long canals to promote communication and trade, and they dug impressive irrigation networks to convert arid lands into fertile belts. (Some of these systems remain in use today.) This slow agrarian revolution enabled the

ANALYZING GLOBAL DEVELOPMENTS

City-States to Empires: Growth in Scale: Mesopotamia

Dramatic developments in urban growth, agricultural production, military innovations, and governance in Southwest Asia in this period led to the emergence of the largest states known to that time, which we have called the first empires. Larger than either city-states or territorial states, empire represented a quantum leap in scale and size. In four distinct periods between 2900 BCE–350 BCE, this region was transformed from being governed by city-states, each covering less than 4 square miles with 30,000 people, to large-scale empires covering 3,000,000 square miles and governing 35,000,000 people. The Achaemenid Empire (540–330 BCE) rivaled the Roman and Han Empires in terms of its size and scale.

QUESTIONS FOR ANALYSIS

- By what scales of magnitude did each stage of empires increase? Were the rough How much larger were the empires than the world's first states?
- When did the biggest leaps in development between stages occur?
- By what sort of mechanisms did these very large states come about?

State/Empire	Est. area (sq. miles)	Est. population	Notes
STAGE ONE: City States (2900–2100 BCE)			
Ur, Uruk and Nipur	1–4	20–30,000 people	*Uruk was largest city-state for 2,000 years.*
STAGE TWO: First Small Empire (c. 1800–1600 BCE)			
The Babylonian empire	65,000	200,000 people	*The city of Babylon was possibly the largest in the world, with 150,000 people.*
STAGE THREE: First Large-Scale Empires (c.910–540 BCE)			
The Neo-Assyrian Empire (c.910–625 BCE)	540,000	15,000,000 people	*Major cities included Kalhu, Nineveh, and Assur.*
The Neo-Babylonian Empire (c. 625–540 BCE)	200,000	15,000,000 people	*Babylon remained the largest city in the world, surrounded by 8–9 miles of walls.*
STAGE FOUR: The Largest Empire in the Ancient World (c. 540–330 BCE)			
Achaemenid Empire	3,000,000	35,000,000 people	*Largest empire ever (measured as percentage of global population).*

Sources: T. Boiy, Late Achaemenid and Hellenistic Babylon; *Pierre Briant,* Histoire de l'empire perse, *Paris, Fayard, 1996; Amélie Kuhrt,* The Ancient Near East, 3000–330 BCE, *2 vols.,1995; London, RKP, J. N. Postgate,* Early Mesopotamia: Society and Economy at the Dawn of History, *London-New York, Routledge, 1992; M. Roaf,* Cultural Atlas of Mesopotamia and the Ancient Near East, *New York, Facts on File, 1990; W. Scheidel, "The Dynamics of Ancient Empires"; Marc van de Mieroop,* A History of the Ancient Near East, ca. 3000–323, *2. ed., Oxford, Blackwell, 2007;* The Ancient Mesopotamian City, *Oxford, Clarendon Press, 1997.*

Chinese population to soar, reaching perhaps 20 million by the late Zhou era.

Under the Zhou, landowners and rulers organized the construction of dikes and irrigation systems to control the floodplain of the Yellow River and Wei River valley surrounding the capital at Xianyang (present-day Xi'an). For centuries, peasants labored over this floodplain and its tributaries—building dikes, digging canals, and raising levees as the waters flowed to the sea. When their work was done, the bottom of the floodplain was a latticework of rich, well-watered fields, with carefully manicured terraces rising in gradual steps to higher ground. This enormous undertaking was the work of many generations. Eventually, irrigation works grew to such a scale that they required management by the Zhou dynasts, centered in the Wei River valley, and their skilled engineers. The engineers also designed canals that connected rivers and supported commerce and other internal exchanges. Tens of thousands of workers spent countless days digging these canals, paying tribute in the form of labor. As we have seen, other dynasties in Afro-Eurasia also produced massive building works through forced labor.

Increasingly, the canals linked China's two breadbaskets: the wheat and millet fields in the north, and the rice fields in the south. And as with the Yellow River in the north, engineers controlled the Yangzi River in the south. So wealthy was China that its influence even reached the distant steppe lands to the north and west. Nomads in mountainous areas or on the Zhou frontiers, who often fought with the Zhou ruler and his regional lords, now depended on trade with the fertile heartlands. In return for their pastoral produce the Zhou received textiles, metal tools and weapons, and luxury items.

Limits and Decline of Zhou Power

At its center the Zhou state had great influence, but its power elsewhere was limited. Unlike Assyria and Persia, it never evolved into a regional power or became a territorial empire. The dynasty relied instead on culture (its bronzes) and statecraft (the mandate of heaven) to maintain its leadership among competing powers and lesser principalities. Rather than having absolute control of an empire, the Zhou state stood first among many regional economic and political allies.

The Zhou dynasty ruled over a much larger territory than the Shang did, but it was not highly centralized. Instead, it expected regional lords (who in this regard resembled Persian satraps) to hold the provinces in line. Military campaigns continued to press into new lands or to defend Zhou holdings from enemies. Rulers attempted to keep neighbors and allies in line by giving them power, protecting them from aggression, and continuing the tried-and-true method of intermarriage between dynastic family members and local nobles. But their subordinates had more than autonomy. They also had genuine resources that they could turn against the dynasts at opportune moments. The power of the Zhou royal house over its regional lords declined in the ninth and eighth centuries BCE. In response, the Zhou court at its impressive capital at Xianyang introduced ritual reforms with grandiose ceremonies featuring larger, standardized bronze vessels. Yet even this move could not reverse the regime's growing political weakness in dealing with its steppe neighbors and internal regional lords. For the most part, the Zhou court became a theatrical state, hoping that impressive rituals would conceal its lack of military might.

The facade began to crumble as wars, social dislocations, and changes in landholding shook the system's social and political foundations. The Zhou dynasts managed to cling to their authority until 771 BCE, when northern steppe invaders forced them to flee their western capital. The Zhou dynastic period, like the Shang, was later idealized by Chinese historians as a golden age of wise kings and officials. Though the Mesopotamian and Persian superpowers were capable of greater expansion during this period, China was sowing the seeds of a more durable state.

CONCLUSION

Upheavals in the territorial states of Afro-Eurasia led to the emergence of more extensive political powers—in Mesopotamia, Persia, and China—during the first half of the first millennium BCE. For seven centuries, both the Assyrian Empire based in Mesopotamia and the Persian Empire based in Iran were superpowers whose reach continued to grow. These first empires expanded territorial states far beyond their "ethnic" or linguistic homelands and, in so doing, brought more extensive interactions and exchanges to parts of Afro-Eurasia. Driving these events were changes in climate, invasions by nomadic peoples, new weapons, trade, and new administrative strategies and institutions.

The Assyrian and Persian empires differed in fundamental ways from the earlier city-states and territorial states of this area. Assyrians and Persians created ideologies, political institutions, economic ties, and cultural ways that extended their power across vast regions. Indeed, their strong imperial institutions enabled them to exploit human and material resources at great distances from the imperial centers.

But there were other models of expansion that did not yield political empires, at least at first. In the Vedic world of the Indus Valley and Ganges plain, shared values and revered texts did not lead even to a single major state. The unparalleled degree of integration across northern South Asia was cultural and economic rather than political. Centuries would pass before a regime would layer a state over this shared cultural world.

In China as well, a core of cultural and political beliefs developed. As in Persia and the Indus Valley and Ganges plain, shared ideas and values spanned a wide geographic area. But unlike in Vedic South Asia, a powerful dynastic political system emerged in China when the Zhou rulers began integrating diverse peoples and territories. Their rule could not last, however. Although the Zhou transformed China, they could not overcome the power of local nobles or fully protect the western frontier from nomadic attacks. Thus the regime never developed military and fiscal powers as great as those of the Southwest Asian empires. Nevertheless, Zhou efforts did implant the foundations of a political and ruling culture that enabled later imperial rulers to achieve success.

Empire building did not occur everywhere. The majority of the world's people still lived in smaller political groupings. Even within Afro-Eurasia, some areas were completely untouched. And even where the Assyrian and Persian rulers, soldiers, and traders came into contact with certain groups, they did not necessarily crush them. For example, the nomadic peoples of the northern steppes and the southern desert locations throughout Afro-Eurasia continued to be autonomous. But fewer and fewer were untouched by the technological, cultural, and political pulses of empires.

The peoples living on the eastern Mediterranean shore, in the Vedic society of South Asia, and in the Zhou kingdom of China made lasting contributions to the cultural and religious history of humanity. The Phoenicians traversed the whole of the Mediterranean basin and spread their simplified alphabet. From the land of Judah, a budding monotheism sprouted. Late Vedic South Asia spun out the concept of cyclic universal time in the form of reincarnation. And in late Zhou China, an ideal of statecraft and social order took shape. All evolved into powerful cultural forms that in time spread their influences far beyond their sites of origin.

TRACING THE GLOBAL STORYLINES

AFTER YOU READ THIS CHAPTER

Review and research on **STUDYSPACE:** wwnorton.com/studyspace

FOCUS ON: ***First Empires and Smaller States***

ANCIENT NEAR EAST

- Neo-Assyrians use raw military power and massive population relocations to build and maintain the world's first empire.
- Persians rely on persuasion and tolerance to build a cosmopolitan empire.

MEDITERRANEAN WORLD

- Greeks, Phoenicians, and Israelites show the advantages of small-scale states with innovations in writing, trading, and religious thought.

SOUTH ASIA

- Vedic peoples build a unified common culture through religious and economic ties.

CHINA

- Zhou dynasty constructs a powerful tributary state and legitimates its rule via the mandate of heaven doctrine (good governance and upright behavior = legitimate rule).

CHRONOLOGY

Southwest Asia and Northern Africa

Neo-Assyrian Empire **950–612 BCE**

The Mediterranean

Vedic culture develops **1500–600 BCE**

East Asia

Zhou state **1045–221 BCE**

1100 BCE | **1000 BCE** | **900 BCE**

KEY TERMS

annals *p. 133*

caste *p. 154*

clan *p. 146*

empire *p. 124*

genealogy *p. 150*

ideology *p. 131*

iron *p. 125*

mandate of heaven *p. 153*

prophets *p. 145*

Vedas *p. 145*

Zoroastrianism *p. 137*

STUDY QUESTIONS

1. **Migrating populations** paved the way for greater cultural integration across Afro-Eurasia after 1200 BCE. Where did the migrants come from, and where did they move? How did they shape the regions in which they settled?

2. **Compare and contrast** the statecraft of the Neo-Assyrian and Persian empires. How did each try to integrate their multicultural empires?

3. **Analyze** the role of the fringe societies in the Aegean and Levant in western Afro-Eurasia during the first millennium BCE. How did they contribute to the cultural and religious history of humanity?

4. **Explain** the function of hereditary status, clans, and religious beliefs in Vedic society in South Asia during the first millennium BCE. To what extent did these beliefs and values maintain a culturally integrated and distinct world in the absence of political unity?

5. **Compare and contrast** the Zhou state to the regional empires in western Afro-Eurasia in the second millennium BCE. What legacies did each leave?

6. **Compare and contrast** the role of the state in facilitating regional integration in East Asia, South Asia, and western Afro-Eurasia.

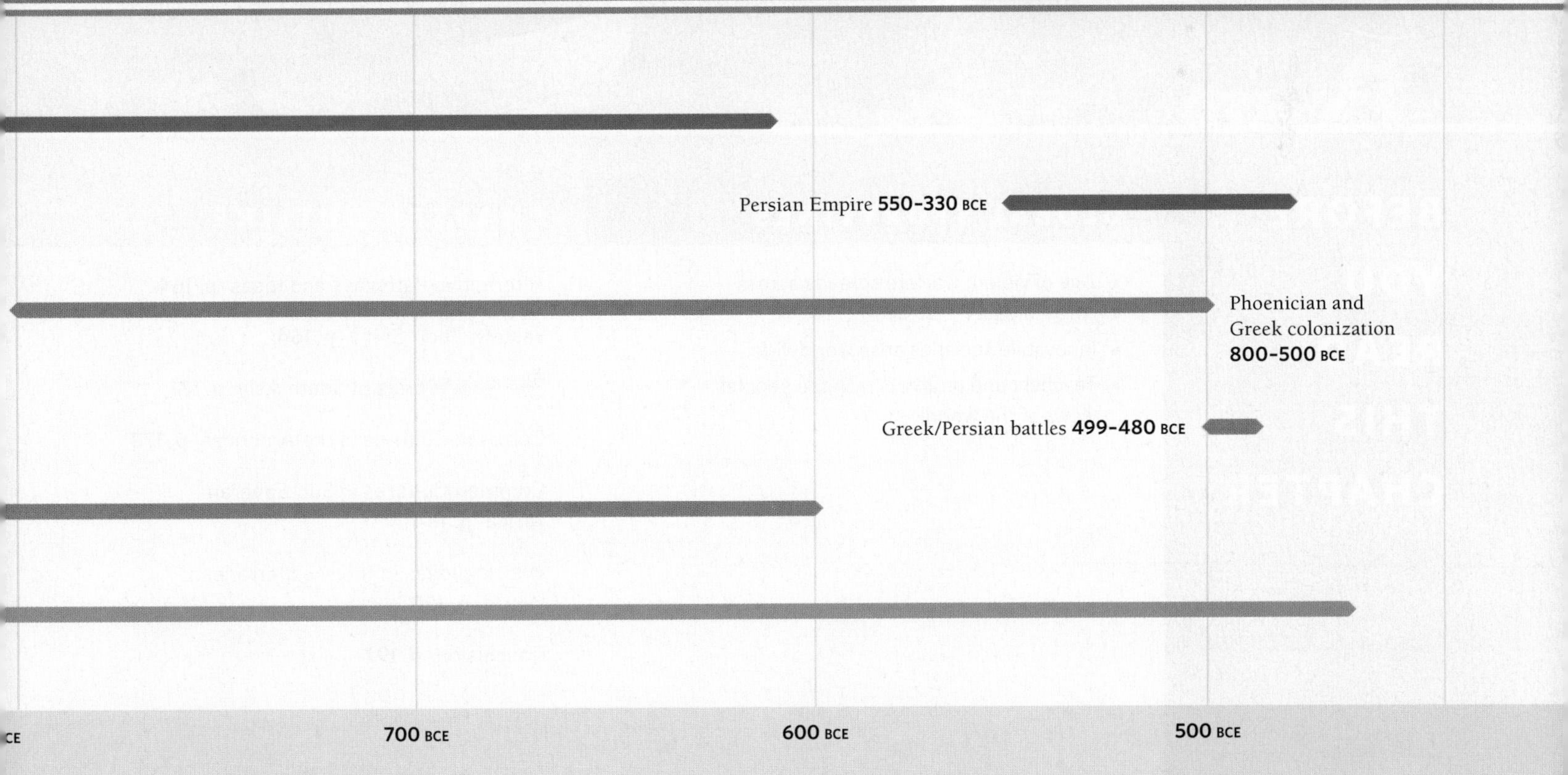

BEFORE YOU READ THIS CHAPTER

GLOBAL STORYLINES

- Age of violent warfare spreads across Afro-Eurasia.
- Innovative societies arise worldwide.
- Teachers and prophets reshape peoples' views of the world.

CHAPTER OUTLINE

5

Worlds Turned Inside Out, 1000–350 BCE

FOCUS QUESTIONS

- How did "second-generation" societies create alternative new orders?
- How did political, military, economic, and social transformations encourage new beliefs and dissident thinkers across Afro-Eurasia?
- What role did teachers and prophets play in creating new concepts of being human and part of a larger community?
- How did cultural integration occur in the Americas and sub-Saharan Africa in the absence of political unity?
- Why do many modern thinkers consider this period the axial age?

A struggle for power and territory gripped societies from China to Africa. It turned the sixth century BCE into an age of violent upheaval and resulted in profound societal and intellectual breakthroughs. In the midst of these changes, Master Kong Fuzi of China instructed his disciples on how to govern, saying: "Guide them by edicts, keep them in line with punishments, and the people will stay out of trouble but will have no sense of shame. Guide them by virtue, keep them in line with the rites, and they will, besides having a sense of shame, reform themselves" (Confucius, *The Analects*, II, 3).

Master Kong, also known as Confucius, represented a new breed of influential leaders—teachers and thinkers, not kings, priests, or warriors. Instead of fighting wars of conquest, they conducted wars of ideas. At the same time, it was the convulsions around them—incessant warfare, population growth, and the emergence of new cities—that motivated the search for new insights and solutions. By viewing the world in new ways, they sought to lead societies out of turbulence. Their arsenal: words. Their strategy: instruction. These teachers strove to instruct rulers on how to govern justly, and to show ordinary individuals how to live

ROCKY MOUNTAINS
NORTH AMERICA
NOMADIC HUNTERS
Great Lakes
Mississippi R.
St. Lawrence R.
ATLANTIC OCEAN
Gulf of Mexico
OLMEC
MESOAMERICA
WEST INDIES
SAHEL
Amazon R.
NOMADIC HUNTERS
ANDES MOUNTAINS
PACIFIC OCEAN
CHAVÍN
SOUTH AMERICA
NOK State
SLAVS People
0 1000 2000 Miles
0 1000 2000 Kilometers

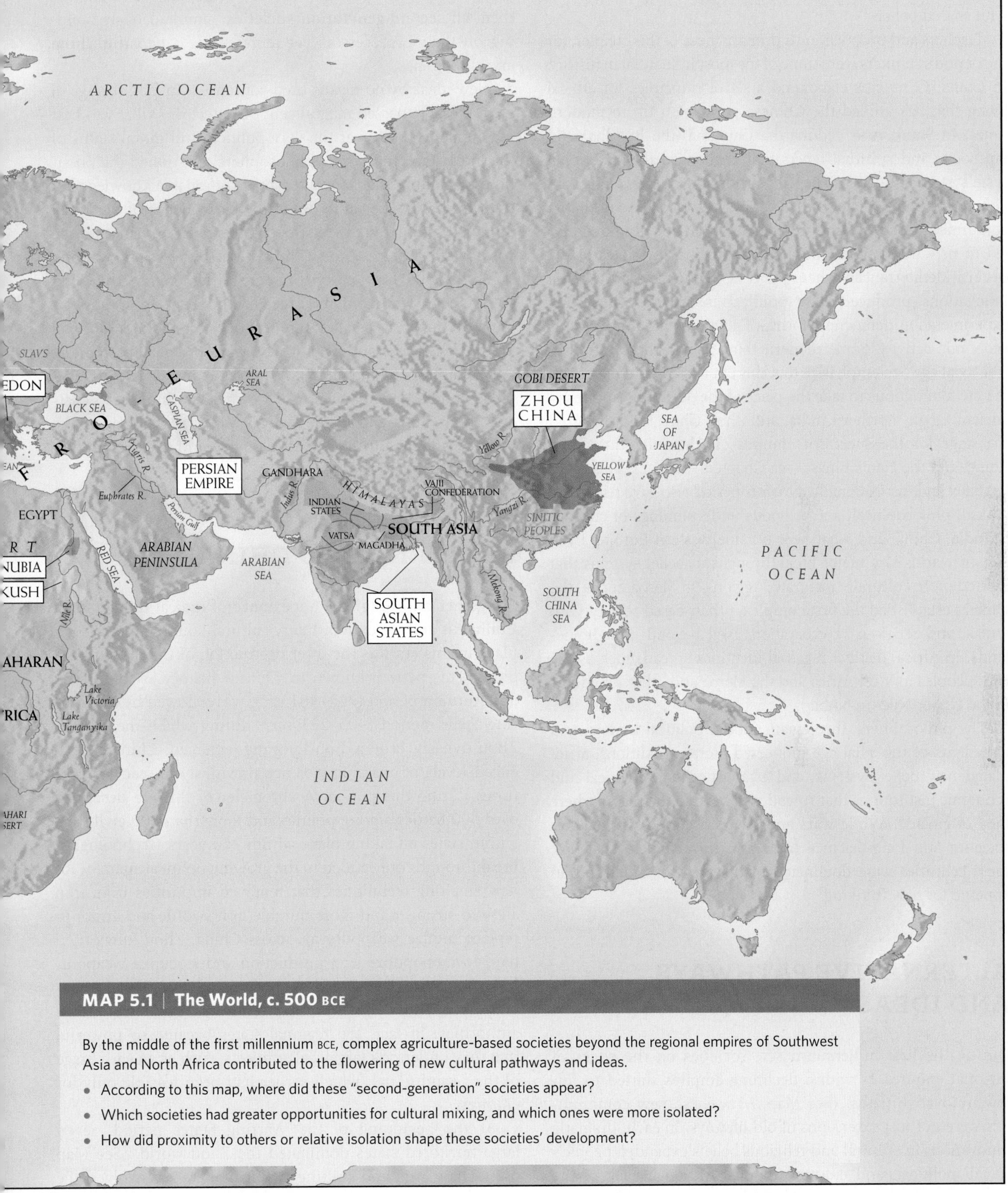

MAP 5.1 | The World, c. 500 BCE

By the middle of the first millennium BCE, complex agriculture-based societies beyond the regional empires of Southwest Asia and North Africa contributed to the flowering of new cultural pathways and ideas.

- According to this map, where did these "second-generation" societies appear?
- Which societies had greater opportunities for cultural mixing, and which ones were more isolated?
- How did proximity to others or relative isolation shape these societies' development?

ethically. In doing so, they began to integrate regional worlds with shared beliefs.

Teachers and prophets are a primary focus of this chapter, for the period's thinkers were some of the most influential in history. In China, Confucius elaborated a set of principles for ethical living that has guided the Chinese population up to modern times. In South Asia, Siddhartha Gautama (the Buddha) laid out social and spiritual tenets that challenged the traditional caste system and the privileged warrior and priestly classes. In Greece, Socrates, Plato, and Aristotle described a world that conformed to natural and intelligible laws. New thinking also led to new institutions, most notably in the city-states of the eastern Mediterranean where political, economic, and cultural innovations produced new political institutions, including experiments in democratic forms of government, and vigorous economic activity. Some modern thinkers call these centuries "the axial age," to emphasize that this era witnessed the creation of new foundations to take the place of the declining empires of ancient Egypt, northern India, and Zhou China, and prepared the stage for the successor empires of Alexander the Great, Rome, and the Han Chinese (see Chapters 6 and 7). This intellectually and institutionally dynamic period also gave rise to the ethical, philosophical, and religious underpinnings of cultures in India, China, and what later became western Europe. Even distant worlds saw major breakthroughs in belief systems that created more culturally integrated regions. In Mesoamerica, the Olmecs established the first complex, urban-based society, with artistic and religious reverberations well beyond their homelands. In Africa, distinct regional identities spread, such as the Nok peoples in West Africa and the Meroe and other kingdoms in the Upper Nile (in Nubia).

The philosophers, theologians, poets, political leaders, and merchants of the axial age pioneered literary traditions, articulated new belief systems, and established new political and economic institutions that spread well beyond the places where they originated. While wars and havoc occurred within their societies and long-distance trade and travel linked societies, these centuries were dominated by a search for order and an appetite for new thinking.

ALTERNATIVE PATHWAYS AND IDEAS

During the first millennium BCE, societies on the edges of regional empires or within declining empires started to follow innovative paths. (See Map 5.1.) These new communities were not just extensions of old lifeways. In each, dramatic innovations in cultural and religious beliefs expanded people's social, political, and cultural options. Although each of the cultures was clearly different from the others, we might call them all **second-generation societies**, simultaneously building on their predecessors yet representing a departure from ancient legacies.

New ideas by no means bred consensus. In fact, the age of great ideas witnessed magnificent disputes over what was best for humanity, and over the very political and moral status of the individual. In Greece, philosophers questioned the possibility of gaining and transmitting true or reliable knowledge of the world. They began to doubt the permanence of the social order and pondered the relationship between humans and the cosmos. In Eastern Zhou China, beset by constant warfare, sages debated how best to restore order; some advocated engagement while others urged withdrawal from government. In the Ganges Valley, thinkers questioned the traditional Brahmanic rituals and sought new ways of behaving morally and attaining enlightenment. Whereas many Greek philosophers endorsed skepticism for its own sake, thinkers in Eastern Zhou China and in the Ganges Valley at the time of the Buddha sought ultimate truths that would yield a unitary vision of state and society.

EASTERN ZHOU CHINA

Altogether critical for the appearance of radical thinkers like Confucius and the extraordinary cultural flourishing that took place in this era was the utter destruction of the old political order. This period, known in Chinese history as the Spring and Autumn period (722–481 BCE), was followed by the Warring States period (403–221 BCE), during which the Eastern Zhou dynasty, centered on Luoyang, emerged. China experienced levels of anarchic violence previously unseen for centuries during this period. A chronicler of this era described over 500 battles among polities and more than 100 civil wars within states all taking place within 260 years. Technological breakthroughs only added to the growing political anarchy, for new smelting techniques that removed impurities from iron allowed stronger and more durable iron swords and armor to replace bronze weaponry all across China. Zhou kings tried hard to monopolize iron production and stockpile weapons, but to no avail. The spread of cheaper and more lethal weaponry shifted influence from the central government to local authorities. In fact, the regional states became so powerful that they undertook large-scale projects, such as an early stage of the Grand Canal, which earlier had been feasible only for empires.

At the beginning of the Warring States period, seven large territorial states dominated the Zhou world. (See Map 5.2.) Their wars and shifting political alliances involved the

Bronze Spearhead. *Although bronze weaponry gave way to stronger iron swords and armor during the Warring States era, stylized bronze spearheads were still prized by Zhou kings and regional lords.*

mobilization of armies and resources on an unprecedented scale (far surpassing the Assyrian armies at the height of their power). Qin, the greatest state, which ultimately replaced the Zhou dynasty in 221 BCE, fielded armies that combined huge infantries in the tens of thousands with lethal cavalries and even more lethal legions of skilled archers using state-of-the-art crossbows. To ensure that the Qin war machine could match all threats, the preparation to defend the Chinese heartland even crossed into the otherworld. Some 7,000 artisans and workers prepared thousands of ornate, carefully made terra-cotta warriors and horses, which the Qin buried in precise military formations within the tomb of the first Qin emperor to help him in the expected wars he would face in the next life.

Overall, the conception of central power changed dramatically during this era, as royal appointees replaced hereditary officeholders. By the middle of the fourth century BCE, power was so concentrated in the major states' rulers that each began to call himself "king." Moreover, the Warring States would form coalitions if one of them became too strong. Despite the incessant warfare, scholars, soldiers, merchants, peasants, and artisans thrived in the midst of an expanding agrarian economy and interregional trade.

New Ideas and the "Hundred Masters"

Out of this extreme political and social turmoil came new visions that were to dominate Chinese thinking about man's and woman's place in society and provide the intellectual and philosophical underpinnings for the creation of the world's longest-lasting imperial system. The establishment of the Qin state in 221 BCE and the proclamation of an emperor (*huangdi*) in place of a king (*wang*) produced a succession of Chinese dynasties and emperors that, except for several periods of disunion, lasted for two millennia down to February 12, 1912, when China's last monarch abdicated in favor of the Chinese Republic. What is even more striking about the background to this starting point for imperial splendor is that it was often the losers among the political elites, seeking to replace their former advantages with status gained through new types of service, who sparked this intellectual creativity. Important teachers emerged, each with disciples. The most prominent of the "hundred masters" of the age was **Confucius** (551–479 BCE); others either expanded on Confucian thought or formulated opposing ideas about human nature and the role of government. Their philosophies constitute the Hundred Schools of Thought.

CONFUCIUS Confucius was very much the product of his times. Born in the state of Lu at a time when Zhou power was crumbling, and at first a mere hanger-on at court, he looked back to earlier, for him halcyon, days of the Zhou dynasty for moral and political inspiration. Believing that the founders of the Zhou dynasty had established ideals of good government and principled action, but seeing only division and war among rival states all around him, he set out in search of an enlightened ruler, much as we shall see the Buddha doing in South Asia. He returned home in despair in 484 BCE. Yet, though he died a discouraged man, his teachings, drawn from his unrivaled knowledge of the high traditions of Chinese thought, resonated in this turbulent age and beyond.

Confucius's teachings stemmed first and foremost from his belief that human beings behaved ethically, not in order to save their souls or to gain a place in heaven as philosophers and priests elsewhere believed, but because it was in their human makeup to do so. Humanity's natural tendencies, if left alone, produced harmonious existence. Confucius saw the family, and notably filial submission, as the locus from which proper ethical action, including loyalty to the state and rulers, sprang. His idea of modeling the state on the patriarchal family—that is, the ruler respecting heaven as if it were his father and protecting his subjects as if they were his children—became a bedrock principle of his thinking and the foundation of Chinese political thought. Although he regarded himself purely as a transmitter of ancient wisdom, in reality he established many of the major guidelines for Chinese thought and action. The first of

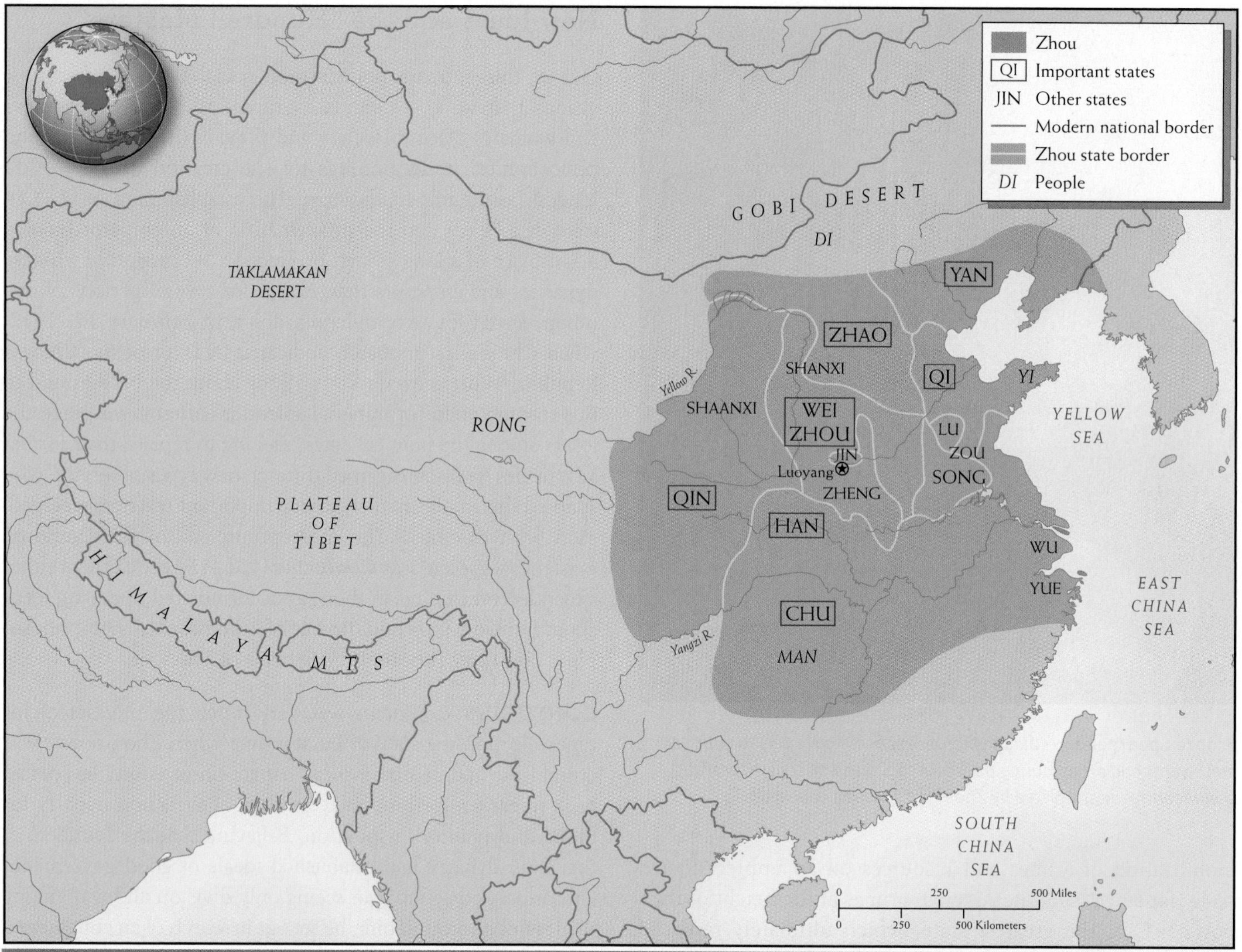

MAP 5.2 | Zhou China in the Warring States Period

The Warring States period witnessed a fracturing of the Zhou dynasty into a myriad of states.

- Find the Zhou capital of Luoyang on the map. Where was it located relative to the other key states?
- What about this map tells us why diplomacy was so important during this period?
- What does this map tell us about the relationships between "civilized" and "barbarian" peoples in East Asia?
- How do you think so many smaller polities could survive when they were surrounded first by seven and then by three even larger and more powerful states (Qin, Qi, and Chu)?

his guidelines was respect for the pronouncements of scholar-teachers—persons of learning like himself. The second was a commitment to a broad education—one that befitted a strong but benevolent state. The third was an insistence on providing training for all who were highly intelligent and willing to work, whether noble or humble in birth. Any man could gain the learning to become a gentleman of the ruling class. Confucius's philosophy stressed schooling for whoever wanted to learn. He also stressed that "the best educated men should serve in government," which was a dramatic departure from past centuries, when only nobles were believed capable of ruling. Nonetheless, Confucius's distinctions between gentlemen-rulers and commoners continued to support a social hierarchy, although an individual's position in that hierarchy would now rest on education rather than on birth.

Confucius's ethical teachings and cultural ideas, as found much later in the *Analects*, were passed down by his followers from generation to generation and had a decisive influence on the

Qin Warriors. *Terra-cotta warriors were buried with the Qin emperor in the expectation that they would join in his military campaigns in the next life. For such battles the emperor was to have at his disposal over 8,000 soldiers, 130 chariots with 520 horses, and 150 cavalry horses to accompany his soul as he passed from this world to the next, intimidating his rivals along the way. These reproduced warriors and horses were quite modest in number, but they symbolically evoked the massive scale of the Qin armies above ground. In the real world, the Qin mobilized millions of peasants in the northwest for their military campaigns and complemented them with hundreds of thousands of horses to produce the most devastating military force yet seen on earth before the famed Roman legions.*

scholar-officials who came after him. In his effort to persuade society to reclaim the lost ideals of the early Zhou, Confucius proposed a moral framework stressing correct performance of ritual (*li*) based on practices from an earlier, more enlightened age, responsibility, loyalty to the family (*xiao*), and perfection of moral character to become a "superior man" (*junzi*)—that is, a man defined by benevolence and goodness rather than by the pursuit of profit. Confucius believed that a society of such superior men would not need coercive laws and punishment to achieve order.

MO DI One competing school of thought, later called Mohism, derived from the teachings of Mozi, also known as Mo Di (c. 479–438 BCE). Even less is known of his life than of Confucius's, but recent studies have suggested that as a craftsman-builder he became for a time the most articulate exponent of China's lower and middling classes. Extolling hard work and spurning what he regarded as distracting diversions such as music and philosophical ruminations, he favored a simple life and called on his followers to engage in useful and profitable occupations. He believed that each man should feel obligated to all other people, not just to his own family and friends. He emphasized practical concerns of good government: promoting social order, ensuring material benefits for its people, and supporting population growth. He opposed wars of conquest, arguing that they wasted life and resources and interfered with productivity and the fair distribution of wealth; but he recognized the need for strong urban defenses to keep out marauders. For at least two centuries, his utilitarian philosophy found many enthusiastic followers, and although his school of thought was soon superseded, his views of practical statecraft and efficient government remained a part of the classical canon, along with Legalism, or Statism, which emerged as the dominant credo of the Qin empire (discussed in Chapter 7).

LAOZI AND ZHUANGZI Another key philosophy was **Daoism**, which diverged sharply from Confucius and his followers by scorning rigid rituals and social hierarchies. Its ideas originated with a Master Lao (Laozi, "Old Master"), who—if he actually existed—may have been a contemporary of Confucius. His sayings were collected in *The Daodejing*, or *The Book of the Way and Its Power* (c. third century BCE), which in time became the subject of more commentaries and more translations than any other Chinese work. His book was then elaborated by Master Zhuang (Zhuangzi, c. 369–286 BCE). Daoism stressed the *dao* (the Way) of nature and the cosmos: the best way to live was to follow the natural order of things. Its main principle was *wuwei*, "doing nothing": what mattered was spontaneity, noninterference, and acceptance of the world as it is, rather than attempting to change it through politics and government. In Laozi's vision, the ruler who interfered least in the natural processes of change was the most successful. Zhuangzi focused on the enlightened individual living spontaneously and in harmony with nature, free of society's ethical rules and laws and viewing life and death simply as different stages of existence. (See Primary Source: Warring Ideas: Confucianism versus Daoism—On the Foundations of Government.)

XUNZI AND HAN FEI **Legalism**, or Statism, another view of how best to live an orderly life, grew out of the writings of Master Xun (Xunzi, 310–237 BCE) toward the end of the Warring States period. He believed that men and women were innately bad and therefore required moral education and authoritarian control. In the decades before the Qin victory over the Zhou, the Legalist thinker Han Fei (280–233 BCE) agreed that human nature was primarily evil. He imagined a state with a ruler who followed the Daoist principle of *wuwei*, detaching himself from everyday governance—but only after setting an unbending standard (strict laws, accompanied by harsh punishments) for judging his officials and people. For Han Fei, the establishment and uniform application of these laws would keep people's evil nature in check. As we will see in Chapter 7, the Qin state, before it became the dominant state in China, systematically followed the Legalist philosophy.

PRIMARY SOURCE

Warring Ideas: Confucianism versus Daoism—On the Foundations of Government

Though both Confucians and Daoists viewed the world of political power as perilous, their competing teachings offered regional Chinese rulers a choice in political philosophies.

Confucius wanted to end the chaos of the times and restore order by promoting education, moral behavior, and the performance of ritual. He thought that cooperation rather than conflict, ethical behavior rather than reckless actions, merit rather than heredity, and concern with the welfare of others rather than self-aggrandizement should be the basis of society and government. Not as interventionist as other schools of thought, the Confucians opposed autocracy and appealed to the mandate of heaven as the "voice of the people." Not as laissez-faire as the Daoists, the Confucians prioritized strict ritual as a philosophy of behavior that would lead to cultural solidarity even in times of political chaos. The Daoists' rejoinder charged that the Confucians were, in effect, shutting the barn door after the horses had already escaped. A natural morality had once been the rule in small villages; a true morality was now the social exception, betrayed in practice by the moral hypocrisy of Confucian officials in the capital.

Initially, Confucius's call for moral rigor had little appeal to those in power. But some saw the attractions of his beliefs after they realized that a tyrannical government that punished its citizens harshly could be brought down by a peasant rebellion. In one exchange with a student, Confucius described the core foundations of government:

> Zigong asked about government. The Master said, "Sufficient food, sufficient military force, the confidence of the people." Zigong said, "If one had, unavoidably, to dispense with one of these, which of them should go first?" The Master said, "Get rid of the military." Zigong said, "If one had, unavoidably, to dispense with one of the remaining two, which should go first?" The Master said, "Dispense with food: Since ancient times there has always been death, but without confidence a people cannot stand."
> (*Analects* 12.7)

Many individuals who sought power were drawn more to Daoism, whose teachings warned that overly assertive rulers could ruin the state. Thus, the *Daodejing* (*The Book of the Way and Its Power*), a famous Daoist work attributed to Master Lao (Laozi), argued that political and social intervention was futile and that long-term rule should be based on "doing nothing" (*wuwei*); that is, letting everything take its natural course without premeditated human intervention:

> If one desires to take the empire
> and act on it,
> I say that he will not succeed.
> The empire is a sacred vessel,
> That cannot be acted upon.
> In being acted upon, it is harmed;
> And in being grasped, it is lost.
> Thus the sage rejects the excessive,
> the extravagant,
> the extreme.
> (*The Book of the Way and Its Power*, Vol. 1, p. 86)

QUESTIONS FOR ANALYSIS

- What elements of Confucius's teaching emphasized moral rigor and, when applied to government, would enable it to win "the confidence of the people"?
- Why did Confucius believe that a cruel tyrant could not remain in power for very long?
- Why did the Legalists find Daoism more appealing than Confucianism as a practical and moral philosophy?

Source: Excerpts from Analects *and* The Book of the Way and Its Power *from* Sources of Chinese Tradition, *vol. 1, ed. William Theodore de Bary and Irene Bloom,*

Scholars and the State

What emerged from all this activity was a foundational alliance of scholars and the state that was destined to become a vital feature of Chinese society through many centuries. Scholars became state functionaries dependent on the rulers' patronage. In return, rulers recognized the scholars' expertise in matters of punishment, ritual, astronomy, medicine, and divination. Philosophical deliberations, which tended to view the world as static, focused on the need to maintain order and stability by preserving the state. (In contrast, philosophers and priests in Greece and South Asia did not exclusively serve the state or a particular ruler, so they freely speculated on a far broader range of issues.) The bonds that rulers forged with their scholarly elites distinguished governments in Warring States China from the other Afro-Eurasian polities.

The growing importance of statecraft and philosophical discourse promoted the use of writing. In fact, even though the Chinese script was not standardized until 221 BCE, its use in the philosophical debates raging across states and regions helped foster cultural unity at a time of intellectual pluralism (diversity of thinking). As scholar-diplomats and scribes debated the best methods for creating stable and harmonious societies, some 9,000 to 10,000 graphs or signs became required for writing. The elevated influence that scholar-bureaucrats enjoyed in these debates set China apart from other societies of this period. The ideas of Confucianism, Daoism, and Legalism provided them with a rationale for their crucial role in empire building.

Shang Yang of Qin. *An important statesman of Qin during the Warring States period, Shang Yang introduced administrative reforms that enhanced the power of the central government.*

Innovations in State Administration

Although the most durable new developments in China in this era occurred in the realm of ideas, important innovations also took place in politics and economics. In the political arena, the Spring and Autumn period saw regional rulers enhance their ability to obtain natural resources, to recruit men for their armies, and to oversee conquered areas. This trend continued in the Warring States period, as the major states created administrative districts with stewards, sheriffs, and judges and a system of registering peasant households to facilitate tax collection and army conscription. The officials were drawn from the *shi*, who under the Western Zhou had been knights but were now bureaucrats in direct service to the ruler. Confucius and other classical masters called them "gentlemen" or "superior men" (*junzi*) and considered them partners of the ruler in state affairs. Officials were paid in grain and sometimes received gifts of gold and silver, as well as titles and seals of office, from the ruler.

Of all the ministers who sought to enhance the central government, none was more successful than Shang Yang of Qin. His reforms positioned the Qin domain to become the dominant state of its time. Dividing the state into administrative districts and appointing their magistrates, vice magistrates, military commanders, and overseers, he extended the ruler's authority into the hinterland and used the districts for universal military recruitment. He divided the land into blocks for individual households to farm, and he introduced a head tax. Those who distinguished themselves in war (as determined by the number of enemy killed in battle) earned titles and land; conversely, nobles who failed to distinguish themselves in war were stripped of status and honors. Shang Yang introduced a harsh penal code that stressed collective responsibility (for example, those who harbored criminals had their bodies cut in two). The legal code applied equally to government officials and peasants, with severe punishments for violent crimes, theft, use of nonstandard weights and measures, and wrongdoing in office.

Innovations in Warfare

The most successful states in China ruled over millions of people, and by 221 BCE they boasted million-man armies. (Contrast this with Athens, the most powerful city-state in the Mediterranean: with a population of 250,000, it could field an army of just 20,000 men. Only Rome, later to become a mega-state, could ultimately match China's scale.) With administrative reform came reforms in military recruitment and warfare. As noted above, one purpose of registering the rural population was to guarantee their military service.

In earlier battles, nobles had let fly their arrows from chariots while conscripted peasants fought beside them on the bloodstained ground. Now the Warring States relied on massed infantries of peasants bearing iron lances who fought fiercely and to the death, unconstrained by their relationships with nobles. War now involved huge state armies containing as many as 1,000,000 commoners in the infantry, supported by 1,000 chariots and 10,000 bow-wielding cavalrymen. During the Spring and Autumn period, one state's entire army would face another state's; now, during the Warring States period, armies could divide into separate forces and wage several battles simultaneously.

Armies also boasted elite professional troops wearing heavy iron armor and helmets, brandishing iron weapons, and wielding the recently invented crossbow. The crossbow's tremendous power, range, and accuracy, with its ingenious trigger mechanism, enabled archers to easily kill lightly armored cavalrymen or charioteers at a distance. The technology of siege warfare also advanced in response to the growing presence of defensive walls along frontiers and around towns. Enemy armies used counterweighted siege ladders (the Chinese called them "cloud ladders") to scale urban walls or dug tunnels under them; defenders often pumped smoke into the tunnels to thwart the attackers. The rhythms of warfare also changed. Rather than lasting through an agricultural season, campaigns now stretched over a year or longer. As commanders strategized over which troops to place where, which terrain was best suited for battle, and how to outmaneuver opposing armies, military action and thought became increasingly sophisticated.

Knife Coin. *Zhou dynasty coins, like the later Han coin shown here, were made of bronze and produced in a variety of shapes, some resembling spades and knives, depending on the region. Each of the Warring States had its own currency.*

Economic, Social, and Cultural Changes

Rather than draining the economy, the incessant warfare of both the Spring and Autumn period and the Warring States period spurred China's economic growth to remarkable heights. As an agricultural revolution on the North China plain along the Yellow River led to rapid population growth, the inhabitants of the Eastern Zhou reached approximately 20 million. Demographic changes also affected the environment. As more people required more fuel, deforestation—particularly on the North China plain—led to erosion of the fields. In addition, many animals were hunted to extinction; others, like the elephant, found their open range sharply curtailed. Many inhabitants migrated south to domesticate the marshes, lakes, and rivers of the Yangzi River delta; here they created new arable frontiers out of former wetlands, thus averting the ecological disaster that swept through northern China.

Eventually, such population pressures on arable land set in motion a vicious and tragic economic cycle for Chinese peasants. The shortage of cultivable land eventually pushed agricultural technology, based largely on peasant manual labor, to its limits. The agrarian methods of the time could produce only so much food. Agricultural growth was the result of ever-attentive peasant farmers tilling the fields of North and South China. From the late Zhou forward, they produced more rice and wheat than anyone else on earth, but they also created families with an unprecedented number of mouths to feed. The long-term economic result was a declining standard of living for massive numbers of Chinese peasants. In the meantime,

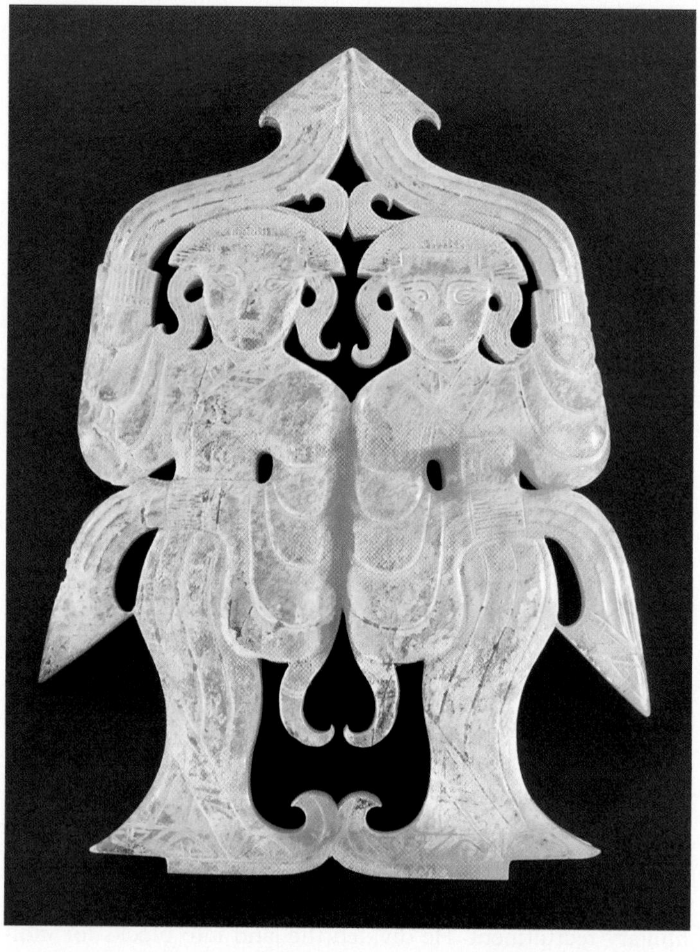

Pendant. *Gender relations became more inflexible because of male-centered kinship groups. Relations between the sexes were increasingly ritualized and were marked by heavy moral and legal sanctions against any behavior that appeared to threaten the purity of powerful lineages. This pendant depicts two women who formed a close relationship with each other in the "inner chambers" of their homes.*

the search for food propelled farmers into new frontiers at the expense of the wetlands. When this frontier hit its limits—which it did, invariably—Chinese families faced terrible food shortages and famines.

Nevertheless, in the short term, economic changes began in the Spring and Autumn period when some rulers gave peasants the right to own their land in exchange for taxes and military service. Because the peasants now could enjoy the benefits of their own labor, their productivity increased. Innovations in agricultural technologies also raised productivity, through crop rotation (millet and wheat in the north, rice and millet in the south) and the use of iron plowshares harnessed to oxen to prepare fields.

With larger harvests and advances in bronze and iron casting came trade in surplus grain, pottery, and ritual objects—the beginning of a market economy. Grain and goods traveled along roads, rivers, and canals. Peasants continued to barter, but elites and rulers used minted coins. In addition, rulers and officials applied their military and organizational skills for public projects, undertaking irrigation, building canals and dikes, and draining low-lying lands to open more acreage for agriculture.

Economic growth helped the rulers attain a high level of cultural sophistication, as reflected in their magnificent palaces and burial sites. At the same time, social relations became more fluid as commoners gained power and aristocrats lost it. In Qin, for example, peasants who served in the ruler's army were rewarded for killing enemy soldiers; their military success could win them land, houses, slaves, and a change in status. Officials also received lands and gifts that enhanced their status and wealth. Officials, ministers, and diplomats traveled far and wide during this period, but peasants had to keep toiling in their fields and villages, leaving them only to fight in the ruler's army.

While class relations had a revolutionary fluidity, gender relations became more rigid for elites and nonelites alike as male-centered kinship groups grew. The resulting separation of the sexes and male domination within the family affected women's position. An emphasis on monogamy, or at least the primacy of the first wife over additional wives and concubines, also emerged. Relations between the sexes became increasingly ritualized and constrained by moral and legal sanctions against any behavior that appeared to threaten the purity of authoritarian male lineages.

Archaeological evidence reveals that commoners and elites alike tried to restore stability in their lives through religion, medicine, and statecraft. The elites' rites of divination to predict the future and medical recipes to heal the body found parallels in the commoners' use of ghost stories and astrological almanacs to understand the meaning of their lives and the significance of their deaths. Elites recorded their political discourses on wood and bamboo slips, tied together to form scrolls. They also prepared military treatises, arts of persuasion, ritual texts, geographic

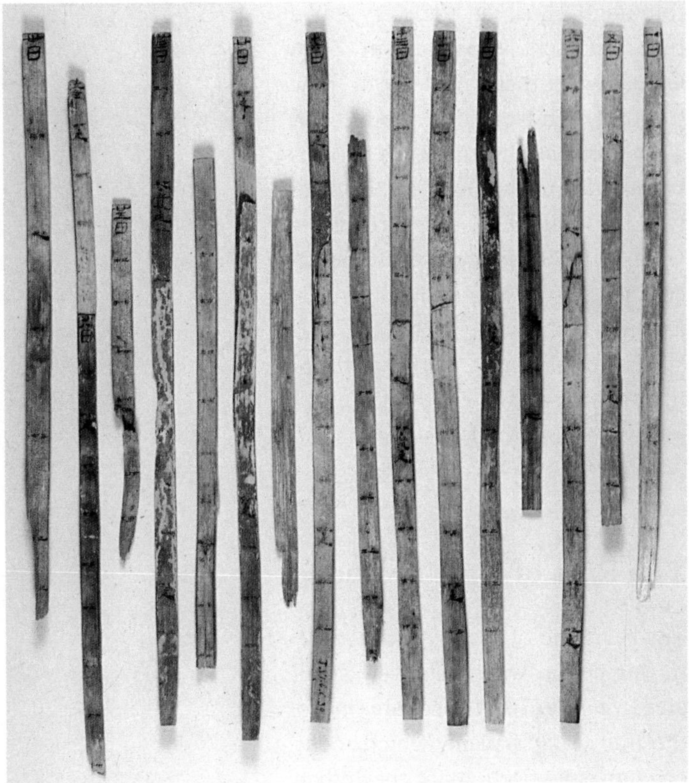

Chinese Calendar. *This Han-period calendar for 63 BCE is formed from sixteen slips of wood with handwritten characters; each begins with day one, day two, and so on; the calendar is to be read from right to left.*

works, and poetry in this way. Social changes were evident as well, as in commoners purchasing bronze metalwork whereas previously only Zhou rulers and aristocrats could afford to do so.

Even with the endless cycles of warfare and chaos—or perhaps because of them—many foundational beliefs, values, and philosophies for later dynasties sprang forth during the Spring and Autumn and Warring States periods. By the middle of the first millennium BCE, China's political activities and innovations were affecting larger numbers of people, spread over a much broader area, than comparable developments in South Asia and the Mediterranean.

THE NEW WORLDS OF SOUTH ASIA

The peoples of South Asia, like those in China, also saw their world transformed, and they too engaged in new thinking about just and stable political orders. Whereas in China incessant warfare and violence brought teachers and intellectuals like Confucius to the fore, in South Asia population migration and bringing new lands under cultivation produced new thinking. Thus, at the very same time that scholar-officials in Zhou China were theorizing about how to govern and make economic and social innovations, the Vedic peoples who settled in the Ganges valley and were assimilating earlier residents were themselves forging new political institutions, economic activities, and ways of viewing the natural and supernatural worlds. In this environment thinkers like the Buddha and Mahariva fashioned an axial age in South Asia.

The Rise of New Polities

The heartland of South Asian activity in this period was a relatively small area roughly 70,000 square miles, the mid-Ganges plain, which today encompasses portions of the Indian states of Uttar Pradesh and Bihar and the southern tip of the country of Nepal. This was the region into which waves of Vedic peoples migrated around 600 BCE, clearing land, establishing new cities and trade routes, expanding rice cultivation, and experimenting with new political forms. (See Chapter 4.) A monsoon region with abundant rainfall, the area was eminently suitable for cultivating rice farming (whereas the best Indus Valley crops were wheat and barley). The migrants cleared land by setting fire to the forests and using iron tools—fashioned from ore mined locally—to remove what was left of the jungle. (See Map 5.3.)

Two major kinds of states appeared in the mid- and lower Ganges plain: those ruled by hereditary monarchs, and those ruled by an elected elite, or oligarchies. (An **oligarchy** is a clique of privileged rulers.) As described in Chapter 4, the South Asian oligarchies were led by warriors and officials called

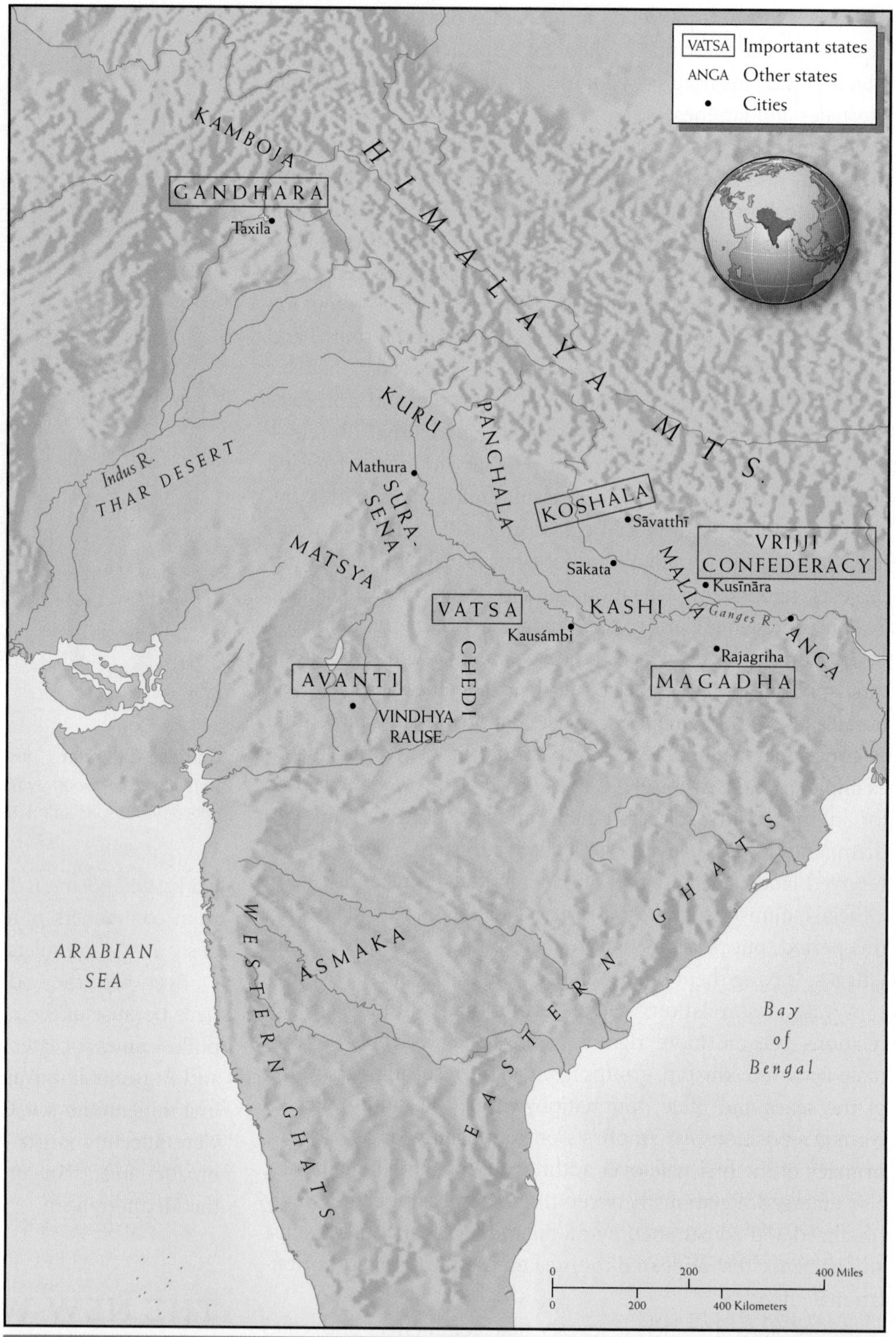

MAP 5.3 | Sixteen States in the Time of the Buddha in South Asia

South Asia underwent profound transformations in the first millennium BCE that reflected growing urbanization, increased commerce, and the emergence of two types of states: monarchies and oligarchies.

- Where did the new states and cities appear?
- What geographic and environmental features encouraged social and cultural integration?
- According to this map, what other regions had influence on South Asia, and where might South Asian culture spread?

collectively as a social group the Kshatriya. Both the rulers of the kingdoms and citizens of the Kshatriya republics assumed the title *raja*, usually translated as "king." Kshatriya oligarchs controlled the land and other resources and oversaw slaves and alien workers. fulfilling similar duties as the hereditary kings.

Evolution of the Caste System

In the kingdoms and oligarchic cities of northern India, a system of hierarchy, rigidly based on birth and occupation, evolved alongside the older *varnas* (described in Chapter 4). Later, in the sixteenth century, when the Portuguese came into contact with South Asians, they called these social groupings **castes**—a term that has served ever since to describe and categorize the groupings representing social, political, and economic differences in South Asia. While the *varna* remained the primary basis for ranking the social order, its actual functioning came to depend on a wide range of occupational groups defined by birth. This expansion of the caste system to include professional groups and the hardening of the lines of divisions between social groups during this period remains a prominent feature in Indian society today. The newer caste system emerged out of a booming agriculture that multiplied the number of professions and provided work for all manner of traders and artisans. Thus, as Vedic society became more complex, so did the caste system. Each of the occupational groups established its own subcaste, called *jatis* (the Sanskrit word for birth); each of the *jatis* stressed kinship ties and created its own religious rituals. The occupational subcastes were not only organized on the basis of profession but even by product. For example, a carpenter *jati* was more prestigious than a blacksmith *jati*, and farmers viewed leather tanners as literally untouchable. Social hierarchies layered cities as well as the countryside. In the emerging urban centers, traders were regarded as "purer" than artisans, while those making gold utensils had higher status than those making copper or iron products. Yet members of each group colluded to contain internal competition, and they closed ranks to preserve their status. Subcastes monopolized skills and resources by banning intermarriage, thereby preventing other groups from accessing their knowledge. Even when outsiders joined the Vedic landowners' farming economy as laborers, tenants, or cultivators, they maintained their communal structure by restricting marriage to within the group.

Religion served to buttress the caste system and maintain hierarchies. Brahmanical texts invoked the principle of purity and pollution to rank castes and to hinder movement between castes. To fortify this deeply hierarchical order, occupations were made hereditary, and taboos were placed on intermarriage and interdining. These injunctions ensured that individuals did not move out of their inherited caste occupation. Nonetheless, a caste as a group could move upward over time by acquiring wealth and power, and therefore claim a purer caste status than those jatis previously above them.

Brahman Recluse. *When Buddhists started to tell stories in sculptures and paintings, Brahmans were included when appropriate. This character in Gandharan Buddhist art probably represents a Brahman who lived as a recluse, instead of as a priest. He is not shaved or dressed, but his expression is passionate.*

New Cities and an Expanding Economy

Supported by rice agriculture, cities began to emerge on the Ganges plain around 500 BCE and in turn became centers of commercial exchange and a robust intellectual life. Some, such as Shravasti and Rajagriha, also thrived as artisanal centers. Others in the northwest, like Taxila (on the border between present-day Pakistan and Afghanistan), engaged in trade with Afghanistan and the Iranian plateau.

LIFE IN THE NEW CITIES These cities were dominated by new men and women—bankers, merchants, and teachers, whose occupations did not fit easily into the old caste system and whose lifestyles often shocked nearby villagers. Precisely laid-out streets were crowded with vendors, and well-heeled residents employed elephants and horse-drawn chariots to move them about. Alleys leading from the main streets zig-zagged between houses built with pebbles and clay. Although city expansion was often haphazard, civic authorities showed great interest in sanitation. The many squares dotting each city had garbage bins, and dirty water drained away in deep sink wells underground. Streets were graded so that rainfall would wash them clean. The important city of Shravasti may have contained as many as 200,000 inhabitants. Because most cities of this period have been continuously inhabited, they are difficult sites for archaeologists to explore. Taxila, located in the far northwest and destroyed in the fifth century CE, proved an exception: excavated in the twentieth century, it shed light on urban life in early South Asia. Taxila did not have the well-planned streets and water drainage of a center like Mohenjo Daro, an opulent Indus city (see Chapter 2); Taxila's building materials were simpler. But civic consciousness produced a hygienic and healthy urban environment. City officials arranged to have garbage taken out of town and dirty water routed to sink wells.

The new cities offered exciting opportunities for those who were adventurous. Rural householders who moved into them prospered by importing rice and sugarcane from villages to sell in the markets; they then transported manufactured goods such as sugar, salt, and utensils back to their villages. Those who already possessed capital became bankers who financed trade and industry. The less affluent turned to craftwork, fashioning textiles, tools such as needles, fine pottery, copper plates, ivory decorations, and gold and silver utensils. Other professions included physicians, launderers, barbers, cooks, tailors, and entertainers. The elaborate division of labor suggests high degrees of specialization and commercialization.

Coins came into use in these cities at about the same time as they appeared in Greece and China. Traders and bankers established municipal bodies that issued the coins and vouched for their worth. Made of silver, the coins had irregular shapes but specific weights, which determined their value; they also were punch-marked, or stamped with symbols of authority on one side.

UNEQUAL OPPORTUNITIES The new cities were melting pots of considerable social mobility—despite the rigid caste system. Yet the opportunities that they provided for social mobility did not ensure success for everyone. Many who lost their land and livelihood came in search of work, and some fared better than others. As a whole, city dwellers had more material wealth, but their lives were far more uncertain. In addition, urban life created a new social grouping: those who did the dirtiest jobs, such as removing garbage and sewage, and were therefore viewed as physically and ritually impure "untouchables." They were thought to be so polluting that a daughter of a decent householder was expected to wash her eyes after seeing one. Even though their work kept the cities clean, they were forced to live in shantytowns outside the city limits.

Some untouchables were dissatisfied with their fate. At a time when thinkers were questioning all types of authority,

Taxila. (Left) *Taxila became the capital of Gandhara, a kingdom located in what is today northern and eastern Pakistan, at the time that it was occupied by the Persian Empire in the fifth century BCE. Dharmarajika was one of the most important monasteries. The walkway around the stupa, a moundlike structure containing Buddhist relics, was covered with glass tiles, and the stupa itself was decorated with jewels.* (Right) *This corner of a stupa exhibits a variety of the architectural styles that prevailed in Gandharan art at its height. Both square and round columns are topped covered by Corinthian capitals. The right arch gate shows the style of Sanchi, the famous stupa in central India.*

some of the outcastes joined dissident sects. As the turbulence in the new cities affected even the most abject of their inhabitants, they became receptive audiences for those challenging the Vedic rituals and Brahman priests.

Brahmans, Their Challengers, and New Beliefs

Wise men looked at the urban life around them and the increasing levels of social violence and decried what they saw. For Brahman priests, as the keepers of the Vedic religious rituals, mingling was a problem: castes mixing indiscriminately, they felt, polluted society. Moreover, lowborn persons grasped at higher status by acquiring wealth or skill. Even worse, as people learned to write they threatened the Brahman priests' inherited monopoly of oral traditions. When an alphabetic script appeared around 600 BCE, it made sacred knowledge more accessible and thus undermined the Brahmans' ability to control the definition of right and wrong and the moral legitimacy of their order. Formerly all of Vedic literature had been memorized, and only the brightest Brahmans could master the tradition. To the Brahmans, nothing about the cities seemed good.

Frightened by these conditions, Brahmans sought to strengthen their relationships with the *rajas* by establishing the idea of a king endowed with divine power. Kingship had been unnecessary according to Brahmanic scripts in a long-ago golden age; a moral code and priests to uphold it were enough to keep things in order. Over time, though, the world deteriorated and the pure mixed with the impure, until many inhabitants spoke of "fish eating fish" to refer to the practice of individuals killing each other for wealth. According to Brahmanic writings, the gods then decided that people on earth needed a king to maintain order. The gods selected Manu ("Man"), but Manu did not want to accept the difficult job. To win his consent, the gods promised him one-tenth of the grain harvest, one-fiftieth of the cattle, one-quarter of the merits earned by the good behavior of his subjects, and the most beautiful woman in his domain. In this Brahmanic account, royal power has a divine origin: the gods chose the king and protected him. Moreover, priests and Vedic rituals were essential to royal power, since kingly authority was validated through religious ceremonies carried out by Brahman priests. Another Brahmanic account conveys this point, relating a story in which the priests themselves magically create a king, whose "birth" wins divine celebration and approval. (See Primary Source: Warring Ideas: The Buddha versus the Brahmans—On the Origin of the King.)

This emphasis on divine kingship solved some problems but created new ones. The Brahmans' claim to moral authority caused resentment among the Kshatriyas—especially those in the oligarchic republics, whose leaders did not assert divine power. Merchants and artisans also chafed at the Brahmans' claims to superiority. Such resentments provoked challenges to the Brahmans' domination. Some thinkers in South Asia (like those in China and in the Greek cities experiencing similar upheavals around this time) believed that they were in an age of acute crisis because their culture's ancient harmony had been lost. And like many scholars and philosophers elsewhere in this era, a new group of South Asian scholars and religious leaders developed their own answers to questions about human existence.

DISSIDENT THINKERS Dissident South Asian thinkers challenged the Brahmans' worldview by refusing to recognize the gods that populated the Vedic world. Some of these rebels sprang from inside the Vedic tradition; though Brahmans, they rejected the idea that sacrificial rituals pleased the gods. To them, God was a universal concept, not a superhuman creature. Also, they felt that the many cows that priests slaughtered for ritual sacrifices could serve more practical uses, such as plowing the land and producing milk. Their discussions and teachings about the universe and life were later collected in the Upanishads (see Chapter 4).

Other dissidents came from outside the Vedic tradition. Consider the Buddha and Mahavira, who both came from the middle Ganges region, where a pastoral economy and rituals of cattle sacrifice were nonexistent. Here people had never spoken Brahmanical Sanskrit and never had a Brahman caste in their communities. But they, too, challenged the Brahmans, though some adopted and developed ideas expressed in the Upanishads.

MAHAVIRA AND JAINISM Jainism and Buddhism were the two most influential schools outside the Vedic tradition that set themselves against the Brahmans. In the sixth century BCE, Vardhamana Mahavira (c. 540–468 BCE) popularized the doctrines of **Jainism**, which had emerged in the seventh century BCE. Born a Kshatriya in an oligarchic republic, Mahavira left home at age thirty to seek the truth about life; he spent twelve years as an **ascetic** (one who rejects material possessions and physical pleasures) wandering throughout the Ganges Valley before reaching enlightenment. He taught that the universe obeys its own everlasting rules and cannot be affected by any god or other supernatural being. He also believed that the purpose of life is to purify one's soul through asceticism and to attain a state of permanent bliss. The Jains' religious doctrines emphasized asceticism over knowledge: strict self-denial enabled one to avoid harming other creatures and thereby purify the soul. Moreover, the doctrine of *ahimsa* ("no hurt") held that every living creature has a soul. Killing even an ant would lead one to an unfavorable rebirth and further away from permanent bliss. Therefore, believers had to watch every step to avoid inadvertently becoming a murderer.

PRIMARY SOURCE

Warring Ideas: The Buddha versus the Brahmans—On the Origin of the King

THE ELECTION OF A KING

This passage is from one of the earliest Buddhist texts,* Dialogues of the Buddha. *Here the Buddha explains to one of his disciples, Vāseṭṭha, how the state and king came into being. Early human beings were pure, but they became greedy and chaotic. As a result they elected one person as king to maintain order. They rewarded the chosen one, called the Great Elect, with a share of their rice. (Note that in this account the people themselves choose the king. Unlike the Brahmanic account that follows, there is no mention of priests or gods.)

When they had ceased rice appeared, ripening in open spaces, without powder, without husk, pure, fragrant and clean grained. Where we plucked and took away for the evening meal every evening, there next morning it had grown ripe again. Where we plucked and took away for the morning meal, there in the evening it had grown ripe again. There was no break visible. Enjoying this rice, feeding on it, nourished by it, we have so continued a long long while. But from evil and immoral customs becoming manifest among us, powder has enveloped the clean grain, husk too has enveloped the clean grain, and where we have reaped is no re-growth; a break has come, and the rice-stubble stands in clumps. Come now, let us divide off the rice fields and set boundaries thereto! And so they divided off the rice and set up boundaries round it.

Now some being, Vāseṭṭha, of greedy disposition, watching over his own plot, stole another plot and made use of it. They took him and holding him fast, said: Truly, good being, thou hast wrought evil in that, while watching thine own plot, thou hast stolen another plot and made use of it. See, good being, that thou do not such a thing again! Ay, sirs, he replied. And a second time he did so. And yet a third. And again they took him and admonished him. Some smote him with the hand, some with clods, some with sticks. With such a beginning, Vāseṭṭha, did stealing appear, and censure and lying and punishment became known.

Now those beings, Vāseṭṭha, gathered themselves together, and bewailed these things, saying: From our evil deeds, sirs, becoming manifest, inasmuch as stealing, censure, lying, punishment have become known, what if we were to select a certain being, who should be wrathful when indignation is right, who should censure that which should rightly be censured and should banish him who deserves to be banished? But we will give him in return a proportion of the rice.

Then, Vāseṭṭha, those beings went to the being among them who was the handsomest, the best favoured, the most attractive, the most capable and said to him: Come now, good being, be indignant at that whereat one should rightly be indignant, censure that which should rightly be censured, banish him who deserves to be banished. And we will contribute to thee a proportion of our rice.

And he consented, and did so, and they gave him a proportion of their rice.

Since land could not be cultivated without killing insects, the extreme nonviolence of Jainism excluded the peasants. Instead, it became a religion of traders and other city dwellers. Mahavira's followers originally transmitted his teachings orally; but a thousand years after his death they wrote them down. The strictly nonviolent doctrine, though originally intended only for followers of Jainism, has profoundly affected the inhabitants of South Asia down to modern times.

BUDDHA AND BUDDHISM The most direct challenge to traditional Brahmanic thinking came from Siddhartha Gautama (c. 563–483 BCE), usually called the **Buddha**, or the Enlightened One. He was a contemporary of Mahavira as well as of Confucius. The Buddha not only objected to Brahmanic rituals and sacrifices but also denied their underlying **cosmology** (a branch of metaphysics devoted to understanding the order of the universe) and their preference for kingship that kept the priestly class in power. His teachings provided the peoples of South Asia and elsewhere with alternatives to established social and religious traditions. In this respect, Buddhism in South Asia functioned much like Confucianism in China.

Gautama was born into a comfortable life, the son of a highly respected Kshatriya in a small oligarchic community nestled in the foothills of the Himalayas. Yet, at the age of twenty-nine, he walked away from everything, leaving behind a respected and loving father, a wife, and a few-days-old son. Family and friends wept as he donned a robe and shaved his head and beard to symbolize the ascetic life that he intended to pursue. Legend has it that he concluded that the life that he and most others were destined to live would consist of little more than endless

A KING SELECTED BY BRAHMANS AND ENDORSED BY GODS

Several stories about the beginning of monarchy are preserved in Brahmanic Hindu literature. The story of Prithu tells of the mutual dependence of the king and Brahman priests, who selected the king and guaranteed the gods' endorsement of him. Initially a king named Vena refused to worship gods, so the Brahmans killed him. Then they created a new king, Prithu, who followed all the rituals.

Afterwards (after the Brahmans killed the vicious king Vena who refused to worship gods) the Munis (Brahmans) beheld a great dust arise, and they said to the people who were nigh, "What is this?" and the people answered and said, "Now that the kingdom is without a king, the dishonest men have begun to seize the property of their neighbors. The great dust that you behold, excellent Munis, is raised by troops of clustering robbers, hastening to fall upon their prey." The sages, hearing this, consulted, and together rubbed the thigh of the king, who had left no offspring, to produce a son. From the thigh, thus rubbed came forth a being of the complexion of a charred stake, with flattened features, and of dwarfish stature. "What am I to do?" cried he eagerly to the Munis. "Sit down" (Nishida), said they; and thence his name was Nishada. His descendants, the inhabitants of the Vindhya mountain, are still called Nishadas, and are characterized by the exterior tokens of depravity. By this means the wickedness of Vena was expelled; those Nishadas being born of his sins, and carrying them away. The Brahmans then proceeded to rub the right arm of the king, from which friction was engendered the illustrious son of Vena, named Prithu, resplendent in person, as if the blazing deity of Fire had been manifested.

There then fell from the sky the primitive bow (of Mahadeva) named Ajagava, and celestial arrows, and panoply from heaven. At the birth of Prithu all living creatures rejoiced; and Vena, delivered by his being born from the hell named Put, ascended to the realms above. The seas and rivers, bringing jewels from their depths, and water to perform the ablutions of his installation, appeared. The great parent of all, Brahma, with the gods and the descendants of Angiras (the fires), and with all things animate or inanimate, assembled and performed the ceremony of consecrating the son of Vena. Beholding in his right hand the (mark of the) discus of Vishnu, Brahma recognized a portion of that divinity in Prithu, and was much pleased; for the mark of Vishnu's discus is visible in the hand of one who is born to be universal emperor (chakravarti). One whose power is invincible even by the gods.

QUESTIONS FOR ANALYSIS

- After the Vedic peoples migrated into the mid-Ganges plain, rice cultivation and feuding characterized their society. How does the Buddha's story about the election of the first king reflect this social history?
- How does the Brahmans' story underscore the role of the priests in upholding the monarchy? Why do you suppose the Brahman priests were so concerned that the king worship gods and follow traditional rituals?

Source: Dialogues of the Buddha, Part iii, *vol. 4 of* Sacred Books of the Buddhists, *translated by T. W. Rhys David and C. A. F. Rhys David (London: Oxford University Press, 1921), pp. 87–88;* Vishnu Purana, *translated from Sanskrit by H. H. Wilson (1st ed. 1840, 3rd ed. Calcutta: Punthi Pustak, 1961), pp. 83–84.*

episodes of suffering, beginning with the pain of childbirth, followed by aging, illness, disease, and death; afterward, reincarnated beings would experience more of the same. Yet he was no dropout or deserter, for he was full of faith that his search for *nirvana*—enlightenment and the absence of pain—would succeed.

Success eluded him for six years, however. At a fateful moment, he remembered a trance of ecstasy that he had experienced as a child and realized that this mystical moment showed him the way forward. Humans, he now understood, did not need to punish their bodies, for they had built-in capacities to achieve happiness and repose. The ascetics with whom he had lived had stressed avoiding and depriving the body. But, in truth, *nirvana* came not through denial but by keeping a positive state of mind. Repose could be attained only by finding a middle ground between self-indulgence and self-denial.

The Buddha's wanderings and ascetic life led him to create a new credo, which his teachings expressed as the Four Truths: (1) life, from birth to death, is full of suffering; (2) all sufferings are caused by desires; (3) the only way to rise above suffering is to renounce desire; and (4) only through adherence to the Noble Eightfold Path can individuals rid themselves of desires and thus reach a state of contentment, or *nirvana*. The elements of the Eightfold Path represent wisdom (right views and right intentions), ethical behavior (right conduct, right speech, and right livelihood), and mental discipline (right effort, right thought, and right meditation). Because these principles were simple and clear, the Four Truths, as they became known, had a powerful appeal. The teachings of the Four Truths and the Noble

The Buddha's Footprints. *Before his followers came to regard Buddha as a god, they were reluctant to make an idol of him—the footprints were an early representation of Buddha. They were carved in a limestone panel in a first-century* BCE *stupa in India.*

Eightfold Path combined represent the Buddhist *dharma*—the basic doctrine shared by Buddhists of all sects. This teaching also signified a dramatic shift in thinking about humanity and correct behavior. Like the teachings of Mahavira, the Buddha's doctrines left no space for deities to dictate human lives, a theme stressed in classical Brahmanic thinking. Buddha's logical explanation of human suffering and his guidelines for renouncing desire appealed to many people, for it set forth tenets by which its followers strove to live virtuously and to take some measure of control and responsibility for their own lives.

Buddhism's appeal becomes more understandable in the context of reincarnation of the soul, a concept initiated in the Upanishads and widely accepted by the people of South Asia. If life itself is suffering, and if death leads simply to rebirth into another life, then the cycle of rebirth brings only pain. Attaining *nirvana* through meditation and living virtuously was the sole means of achieving liberation from life's troubles.

Like other dissident thinkers of this period, the Buddha delivered his message in a vernacular dialect of Sanskrit that all could understand. His many followers soon formed a community of monks called a *sangha* ("gathering"). The Buddha and his followers wandered from one city to another on the Ganges plain, where they found large audiences as well as the alms needed to sustain the expanding *sangha*. In fact, the Buddha's most influential patrons were urban merchants. And in struggles between oligarchs and kings, the Buddha sided with the oligarchs—reflecting his upbringing in an oligarchic republic. He inevitably aroused opposition from the Brahmans, who favored monarchical government. While the Buddha himself did not seek to erase the caste hierarchy, the *sangha* provided an escape from its oppressive aspects and the prestige that it afforded the Brahmans. Although Mahavira and the Buddha did not erase the Brahmans' spiritual authority or dismantle the caste hierarchy, nevertheless they established independent enclaves that carried out religious, scholarly, and social activities based on their own doctrines.

COMMON CULTURES IN THE AMERICAS

Although peoples living in the Americas during what we have termed the axial age in Eurasia and North Africa did not have immense cities, elaborate written texts, domesticated animals, and the other ingredients that underlay the radical new ideas of this era elsewhere, political and intellectual leaders among the Chavín peoples of the Andes and the Olmecs of Mesoamerica provided answers to many of the same questions that were perplexing Eurasians and North Africans. Their insights also left a profound imprint on their communities and on future generations. Of course, because we do not have the impressive documentary record that exists for Eurasian and North African written texts, our knowledge of their beliefs has to be based primarily on archaeological remains.

The Chavín in the Andes

In a world of extreme localization and diversity, the steep mountainsides and deep fertile valleys of the Andes Mountains became the home of a distinctive people called the Chavín. In what is now northern Peru, farmers and pastoralists began to share a common belief system around 1400 BCE. With time, their artistic influence and spiritual principles touched a broad expanse of Andean folk. Like the peoples of South Asia, the Chavín were united by culture and faith more than by any political structure.

The Chavín peoples literally organized their societies vertically. Communities and households spread their trading systems up the mountainsides: valley floors yielded tropical and subtropical produce; the mountains supported maize and other crops; and in the highlands, potatoes became a staple and llamas produced wool and dung (as fertilizer and fuel) and, eventually, served as beasts of burden. Llamas could not transport humans, however, so the Chavín migratory and political reach remained limited. No empire would emerge in the Andes for another millennium.

The ecological diversity of the Chavín societies enabled them to find all necessities close at hand, but they did undertake some long-distance trade—mainly in dyes and precious stones, such as obsidian. By 900 BCE, the Chavín were erecting elaborate stone carvings, using advanced techniques to weave fine cotton textiles, and making gold, silver, and copper metal goods. Scholars have found evidence that by 400 BCE trade in painted textiles, ceramics, and gold objects spanned the Pacific coast, the Andean highlands, and the watershed eastward to the tropical rainforests of the Amazon basin.

What unified the fragmented Chavín communities was a shared artistic tradition reflecting devotion to powerful deities. Their spiritual capital was the central temple complex of Chavín de Huántar, in modern Peru's northeastern highlands. The temple boasted a U-shaped platform whose opening to the east surrounded a sunken, circular plaza; from its passageways and underground galleries, priests could make dramatic entrances during ceremonies. The priests took hallucinogenic drugs, which believers felt enabled them to become jaguars—the region's most dangerous predator—and to commune with the supernatural. Pilgrims brought tribute to Chavín de Huántar, where they worshipped and feasted together.

The Chavín drew on influences from as far away as the Amazon and the Pacific coast as they created devotional cults that revered wild animals as representatives of spiritual forces. Carved stone jaguars, serpents, and hawks, baring their large fangs and claws to remind believers of nature's powers, dominated the spiritual landscape. The "Smiling God" at Chavín de Huántar, El Lanzón, shaped from a slab of white granite fifteen feet high, had a human form but a fanged, catlike face, hair of writhing snakes, feet ending with talons, and hands bristling with claws. This supernatural image dominated an awe-inspiring stage: dimly lit from above so that his face would glow from the reflection of polished mirrors, the god stood over a canal, and the vibrations and deep rumbling sounds of the rushing water below conveyed a sense of spiritual forces. Though they borrowed from neighbors and refined existing sculptural techniques, the Chavín created the first great art style of the Andes. Their cult gave way around 400 BCE to local cultural heirs, but some elements of it survived in successor religions adopted by stronger states to the south.

The Olmecs in Mesoamerica

Further to the north, in Mesoamerica, the first complex society emerged around 1500 BCE between the highland plateaus of central Mexico and the Gulf Coast around modern-day Veracruz. (See Map 5.4.) The **Olmecs** are an example of a first-generation community that created new political and economic institutions while contemplating

El Lanzón. *The Chavín excelled at elaborate stone carvings with complex images of their deities. This image of El Lanzón is a good example. At the center of one of the Chavín peoples' greatest temples is this massive gallery with a giant monument in the middle, etched with images of snakes, felines, and humans combined into one hybrid supernatural form. Observe the hands and feet with claws and the eyebrows that turn into serpents. The rendering on the right makes it easier to see the details on the actual object.*

CURRENT TRENDS IN WORLD HISTORY

Prophets and the Founding Texts: Comparing Confucius and the Buddha

World history offers many opportunities to compare one society with another, and this chapter, with its emphasis on teachers, prophets, and intellectuals in what we have called an axial age provides an unparalleled moment to contrast the lives and the ideals of central figures whose teachings spiritual movements, legal and political systems, and long-lasting traditions endured for centuries. In Confucianism and Buddhism, we find key leaders who inspired belief systems that were subsequently named for them.

Confucius (551–479 bce) was one of the ancient world's great innovators. Born in China, he elaborated a code of behavior that valued individual performance of traditional rituals and governmental morality based on correct social relationships, sincerity, and justice. Seeing division and war among rival states, he wished to restore order by promoting education, moral behavior, and the performance of ritual.

Over the centuries the method and substance of his teaching, with many revisions, became the mainstream value system of imperial China. His idea of modeling the state on the patriarchal family—that is, the ruler should respect the heaven as if it were his father and protect his subjects as if they were his children—became the foundation of Chinese political theory. Confucius wanted people to perform the rituals bequeathed by the early Zhou and to emulate the sages who had ordered the world according to principles of civility and culture.

Chinese philosophers did not always agree on how to interpret Confucius's ideas. Representing one school of Confucianists, Mencius (372–289 BCE) held that while recognizing the tendency of people to be led astray by worldly appetites and ambitions, he still believed in the inherent goodness of human nature. To recover that innate goodness required moral training. But according to Xunzi (310–237 BCE), Confucius saw humans as evil and lacking an innate moral sense. They therefore had to be controlled by education, ritual, and custom.

Nevertheless, both Mencius and Xunzi embraced Confucius's dictum that people were perfectible through education and the practice of proper conduct. All Confucians, whether pessimists or optimists, viewed moral cultivation through education as the heart of the civilizing process, and they ensured that his ideas remained a vital force throughout Chinese history.

The teachings of the **Buddha** (c. 563–483 BCE), like those of Confucius, had far-reaching influence. The two thinkers were roughly contemporary, and both formulated their ideas in response

profound questions about the nature of humanity and the world beyond.

The culture of the Olmecs, a name meaning "inhabitants in the land of rubber"—one of their staples—sprang up from local village roots. The region's peoples formed a loose confederation of villages scattered from the coast to the highlands, mainly nestling in river valleys and along the shores of swampy lakes. Their residents traded with one another, shared a common language, and worshipped the same gods. Around 1500 BCE, the residents of hundreds of hamlets began to develop a single culture and to spread their beliefs, artistic achievements, and social structure far beyond their heartland.

At the core of Olmec culture were its decentralized villages, which housed hundreds—possibly thousands—of households apiece. In these settlements productive subsistence farmers cultivated most of the foodstuffs their communities needed (especially maize, beans, squash, and cacao), while shipping lightweight products including ceramics and precious goods (such as jade, obsidian, or quetzal feathers, used to create masks and ritual figurines) to other villages. Most of the precious objects were for religious purposes rather than everyday consumption.

CITIES AS SACRED CENTERS Despite their dispersed social landscape, the Olmec peoples created shared belief systems, a single language, and a priestly class who ensured that villagers followed highly ritualized practices. Their primary cities, including San Lorenzo, La Venta, and Tres Zapotes, were not large compared to the urban centers of Afro-Eurasia, but they were religious and secular hubs. They were built around specialized buildings that featured massive earthen mounds, platforms, palaces, and capacious plazas.

The rulers of San Lorenzo, for instance, constructed a city of terraces and ridges on a plateau high above the Chiquito River. Their vassals used baskets to haul more than 2.3 million cubic feet of soil to lay out the enormous central platform, two football fields in length, upon which palaces and workshops rose. All around the courtyards and paths were massive stone monuments—colossal heads, jaguar sculptures, and basalt thrones—as well as clusters of large wooden busts. These vast sculpture gardens depicted the human rulers and deities to whom the Olmecs paid homage and offered sacrifice. Artificial lagoons and channels crisscrossed the precinct. Beneath these mounds archaeologists have found axes, knives to social chaos and degeneration. The Buddha presented a vision of society that challenged the Brahmanic order. Buddhism shaped the views of life and death and the scheme of time and space of the universe in South Asia. It also had a profound impact on peoples outside the region and even replaced Confucianism as the dominant religion in China for a few hundred years.

The Buddha offered a logical approach in the form of a unified system underlying the universe, instead of invoking divine intervention, to understand the universe and social life at a time of rapid political development. He believed that the universe and individual lives go through eternal cycles of birth, death, and rebirth, and he elaborated the concept of *karma* ("fate" or "action"), a universal principle of cause and effect. The birth of every living being, human or animal, reflects actions taken in his or her past lives. Karma embodies the sins and merits of each individual, establishing his or her status in the current life. In turn, deeds in the current life affect that karma and thus determine suffering and happiness in the next life. Buddhist believers therefore focused on the consequences of their actions: through their own behavior, they could attain better future lives.

Confucianism and Buddhism, much like the Vedic, Brahmin, and Judaic faiths discussed in Chapter 4, emerged in times of great turmoil. All the faiths were first transmitted orally; later, adherents created a written record to spread them more widely. But Buddhism and Confucianism stand out in that they have founders whose identification with their belief systems remains their most defining characteristic: the Buddha as an enlightened one, and Confucius as a sage. We will see this phenomenon again with the rise of Christianity (from the teachings of Jesus) and Islam (from the teachings of Muhammad) as we continue our discussion of universalizing religions.

QUESTIONS FOR ANALYSIS

- What is the reward for good moral behavior for Confucius? For Buddha?
- What are the major similarities and differences between these two traditions?

Explore Further

David Schaberg, *A Patterned Past: Form and Thought in Early Chinese Historiography* (2002).

Karen Armstrong, *Buddha* (2001).

Lothar von Falkenhausen, *Chinese Society in the Age of Confucius (1000-250 BC): The Archaeological Evidence* (2006).

of sharpened obsidian, other tools, and simple yet breathtaking figurines made most often of jade, buried as tokens for those who dwelled in the supernatural world. San Lorenzo was not a capital city with rulers and laws that controlled territorial domains. Rather, it was a devotional center whose monumental architecture and art had widespread influence reaching as far as the Olmec hinterlands.

Paying homage to their gods and rulers was part of the Olmecs' daily life. While devotional activity occurred on lakeshores, in caves, on mountaintops, and in other natural settings, it occurred above all in the primary cities. In La Venta, huge pits (one was thirteen feet deep and seventy-five feet wide) contained massive offerings of hundreds of tons of serpentine carved blocks. Olmec art speaks to the powerful influence of devotion on creativity. (See Primary Source: Olmec Art as Ideology.) Many images featured representations of natural and supernatural entities—not just snakes, jaguars, and crocodiles, but also certain humans called **shamans**, whose powers supposedly enabled them to commune with the supernatural and to transform themselves wholly or partly into beasts (also evident in images at Chavín sites). A common figurine is the "were-jaguar," a being that was part man, part animal. Shamans representing jaguars invoked the Olmec rain god, a jaguarlike being, to bring rainfall and secure the land's fertility. Indeed, the Olmecs' ceremonial life revolved around agricultural and rainfall cycles. Evidence of a shared iconography throughout the heartland suggests an integrated culture that transcended ecological niches.

CITIES AS ATHLETIC HUBS The Olmecs' major cities were not just devotional centers but also athletic hubs, where victorious teams paid homage to their deities. Intricate ball courts had room on the sidelines for fans to applaud and jeer at the sweating contestants, who struggled to bounce hard rubber balls off parallel sidewalls and their bodies and into a goal. Noble players, bearing helmets and heavy padding, could touch the six-pound rubber ball only with their elbows, hips, knees, and buttocks, and they were honored when they knocked the ball through the stationary stone hoop. Massive sculptures of helmeted heads carved out of volcanic basalt suggest monuments to famous ballplayers. At La Venta, a huge mosaic made out of greenstone served as an elegant ball court; at its center was a portal that was thought to open into the otherworld.

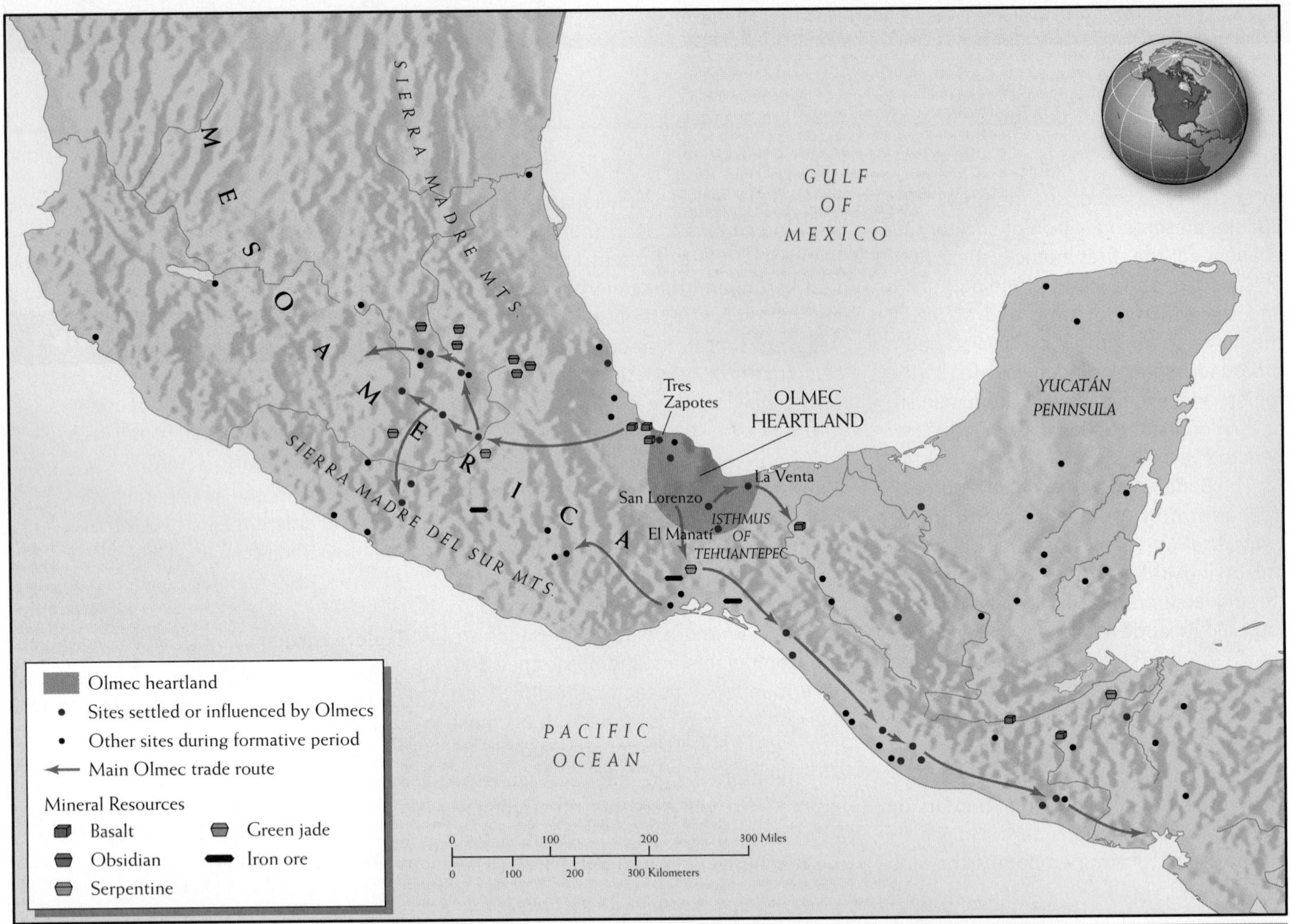

MAP 5.4 | The Olmec World

The Olmecs had a strong impact on Mesoamerica's early cultural integration.

- According to this map, how did they influence people living beyond the Olmec heartland?
- What factors limited the extent of Olmec influence?
- Why do you think the Olmecs never developed a politically unified regional empire?

Olmec archaeological sites are filled with the remains of game equipment and trophies, some of which were entombed with dead rulers so they could play ball with the gods in the otherworld. Ritual ball games, for all their entertainment value, were integral to Olmec devotional culture. It was in honor of the powerful rain god that players struggled to win.

What added to the thrill of the ball court was that they were dangerous places associated with water and agricultural fertility, for an equally important aspect of devotional culture was human sacrifice. Indeed, it is likely that athletics and sacrifice were blended in the same rituals. Many monuments depict a victorious and costumed ballplayer (sporting a jaguar headdress or a feathered serpent helmet) atop a defeated, bound human, though scholars are not sure whether the losers were literally executed. Rainmaking rites also included human sacrifice, which involved executing and dismembering captives. At El Manatí, offering sites alongside a spring and a boggy lakeshore have yielded the bones of children slaughtered for the gods. Across the Olmecs' artistic landscape are representations of human victims fed to the gods and to the rulers who embodied them.

MAN, NATURE, AND TIME The Olmec cosmology assumed a relationship between the natural and supernatural worlds. Olmec

PRIMARY SOURCE

Olmec Art as Ideology

Olmec ideology emphasized ties among the natural, supernatural, and human worlds. It also sought to influence and possibly convert the Olmecs' neighbors. Known primarily for their monumental architecture and artwork, Olmec craftworkers also made portable objects and miniature figures that unified their belief systems and could be transported over long distances to expand the spiritual frontier of Olmec belief throughout Mesoamerica.

One of the most famous surviving portable spiritual icons, called "Young Lord," combines many of the basic elements of Olmec belief into a single, beautiful jade figurine. Standing about two feet tall, Young Lord was a diplomatic artifact, intended to spread the influence of a complex belief system far and wide. His pose is rigid and tall, like that of a ruler who serves as the turning point to join earthly and supernatural worlds. Holding two scepters against his chest, and himself carved in the form of a scepter, he conveys power and influence. (A scepter is a staff or baton signifying authority.)

Young Lord is fierce. The delicate incisions around his body represent ceremonial practices—rituals that he oversees and that enable him to exercise shamanic powers over believers. His face, for instance, wears a mask that evokes classic Olmec shamanic images: a snarling mouth like a jaguar's, and a nose like an eagle's beak. The mask and its carvings suggest that this lord is capable of transforming into a jaguar or a bird of prey to conduct sacrificial rites. Extensive incisions all over his body reinforce this point.

The incisions or scars emphasize bloodletting and human sacrifice, and they underscore the importance of the scepters, which can be used to draw blood. These sacrifices were intended to please the forces of the supernatural world, which would reward believers with rain. In fact, images of ritual performers and victims cover Young Lord's arms and hands. Adorning his legs are figures of serpentlike creatures, monsters with gaping jaws, fangs, and forked tongues.

The statue as a whole is divided horizontally into three, signifying the three layers of the cosmos—the supernatural, the terrestrial, and the underworld—which Young Lord has the power to travel among as he brings messages to believers and nonbelievers alike. This is a powerful image, one meant to drive home the authority of Olmec rulers to their subjects and neighbors.

QUESTIONS FOR ANALYSIS

- What wild beings do the carvings on Young Lord represent? What characteristics of each one would have led the Olmecs to use them as symbols?
- What do the symbols reveal about spiritual aspects of Olmec society?

culture was saturated with belief in the power of supernatural forces and with tales of shamans controlling the supernatural. But the Olmecs were hardly a simple, superstitious folk; in fact, their conviction that the supernatural pervaded the natural world drove them to systematically observe the natural world so that they could discover godly meanings. There was no hard-and-fast line between what we now call "faith" and "science." The way that rulers reckoned time reflects this belief system, for they were convinced that the gods defined calendric passages—thus the seasons and crucial rainfall patterns. Priests, charting celestial movements, devised a complex calendar that marked the passage of seasons and generations. As in China and Mesopotamia, a cultural flowering encouraged priests and scholars to study and accurately chart the rhythms of the terrestrial and celestial worlds.

A WORLD OF SOCIAL DISTINCTIONS Daily labor kept Olmecs busy. The vast majority worked the fertile lands as

Olmec Head. *At La Venta, in Tabasco State in Mexico, four colossal heads rest on the ground, remnants of a field of monumental figures that once ornamented this Olmec site. Nine feet high and weighing up to twenty tons, the heads are the source of much speculation. Carved from single boulders, they are thought to be portraits of great kings or legendary ballplayers. Each head bears distinctive elements in homage to its subject.*

part of household units, with children and parents toiling in the fields with wooden tools, fishing in streams with nets, and hunting turtles and other small animals. Most Olmecs had to juggle the needs of their immediate families, their village neighbors, and the taxes imposed by rulers.

Unlike many decentralized agrarian cultures that were simple and egalitarian, the Olmecs developed an elaborate cultural system marked by many tiers of social rankings. The priestly class, raised and trained in the palaces at La Venta, San Lorenzo, and Tres Zapotes, directed the exchanges of sacred ritual objects among farming communities. Because these exchanges involved immense resources, the wealthy ruling families had to be involved—an association that buttressed their claim to be the descendants of divine ancestors. At the same time, by controlling trade in precious secular goods they added to their fortunes. As ruling families blurred the line between the everyday and the religious, they legitimized their power and gained access to vast resources.

Alongside the priestly elite, a secular one emerged composed of chieftains who supervised agrarian transactions, oversaw artisans, and accepted villagers' tribute. They set up workshops, managed by foremen, where craftworkers created pots, painted, sculpted, and wove. Some of their work featured stones and gems imported from surrounding villages. The highest-ranking chieftains commanded villages scattered over the approximate area of a territorial state (such as current-day Veracruz in Mexico).

The combination of an integrated culture and a complex social structure gave the Olmecs a degree of cohesion unprecedented in the Americas. Ultimately their influence radiated well beyond their heartland through trade. As the Olmecs' arts expanded, so did their demand for imported obsidian and jade, seashells, plumes, and other precious goods. The Olmecs themselves exported rubber (made by combining different latexes from trees and vines into a tough but pliable material—just right for a playing ball!), cacao, pottery, ceramics, figurines, jaguar pelts, and crocodile skins all throughout Mesoamerica. Importing and exporting were probably in the hands of a merchant class, about which scholars know little. The Olmecs also conveyed their belief system to neighbors—if not to convert them, at least to influence them and reinforce a sense of superiority. Without an urge to conquer or colonize, the Olmecs nonetheless shaped the social development of much of Mesoamerica.

THE LOSS OF CENTERS The breakdown of the Olmec culture is shrouded in mystery. The decline was abrupt in some centers and drawn out in others. At La Venta, the altars and massive basalt heads were defaced and buried, indicating a dramatic shift. Yet there is little evidence of a spasm of war, a peasant uprising, a population shift, or conflict within the ruling classes. Indeed, in many parts of the heartland, the religious centers that had been the hubs of the Olmec world were abandoned but not destroyed. Much of the Olmec hinterland remained heavily populated and highly productive.

Apparently the machinery for drawing resources into Olmec capitals eventually failed. As the bonds between rulers and subjects weakened, so did the exchange of ritual objects that had enlivened the Olmec centers and made them magnets for obedience and piety. Olmec hierarchies then collapsed. Without a sacred elite to transmit the belief system, it too faded. What was left of the Olmec heritage passed on to other Mesoamericans—especially those of the central plateaus and the tropical lowlands of the Yucatán peninsula.

COMMON CULTURES IN SUB-SAHARAN AFRICA

In Africa, too, widespread common cultures emerged in this era in a number of favorable locations. Yet to understand these communities it is essential first of all to describe the climate

The Las Limas Monument. *The were-jaguar was an important figure in the pantheon of Olmec deities. This sculpture represents a youth holding a limp were-jaguar baby. We do not know what these figures represented exactly—most likely they refer to spiritual journeys. Some have argued that this monument harkens to child sacrifice.*

and geography of Africa because these forces played a critical role in cultural formation. Climatically, Africa's most significant historical development at this time was the continued desiccation of the northern and central landmass, and the sprawl of the great Sahara Desert as its primary geographical and population barrier. (See Map 5.5.) Large areas that had once supported abundant plant and animal life, including human settlements, now became sparsely populated. As a result, the African peoples began to coalesce in a few locations. Most important was the Nile Valley, which may have held more than half of the entire population at this time.

The Four Zones

Climatic change divided Africa from the equator northward to the Sahara Desert into four zones. The first zone was the Sahara itself, which never completely emptied out despite its extreme heat and aridity. Its oases supported pastoral peoples, like the ancestors of the modern Tuareg tribal communities, who raised livestock and promoted contacts between the northern and western parts of the landmass. South of the Sahara was the Sahel, literally the "coast" (Arabic *sahil*) of the great ocean of sand. In time, some of Africa's great commercial cities, like Timbuktu, would arise here; but in the first millennium BCE no city of great size made an appearance.

The next zone was the Sudanic savanna, an area of high grasslands stretching from present-day Senegal along the Atlantic Ocean in the west to the Nile River and the Red Sea in the east. Many of West Africa's kingdoms emerged there because the area was free of the tsetse fly, which was as lethal to animals as to humans, killing off cattle, horses, and goats. The fourth zone comprised the western and central African rain forests, a sparsely populated region characterized by small-scale societies.

Although there was contact across the Sahara, Africa below the Sahara differed markedly from North Africa and Eurasia. It did not develop a plow agriculture; instead, its farmers depended on hoes. Also, except in densely populated regions, land was held communally and never carried as much value as labor. African peoples could always move into new locations. They had more difficulty finding workers to turn the soil.

Distinctive and widespread common cultures that would characterize certain parts of sub-Saharan Africa from 1000 CE onward were only beginning to emerge during the first millennium BCE. In the savanna, millet and sorghum were the primary food crops; in the rain forests, yams and other root crops predominated. Relatively large populations inhabited the Sudanic savanna, the sole area for which substantial historical records exist. Here, in fact, a way of life that we can call Sudanic began to crystallize.

These peoples were not completely dependent on their feet to get around (as were their counterparts in the Americas). They had domesticated several animals, including cattle and goats, and even possessed small horses. Although their communities were scattered widely across Africa, they had much in common. For example, they all possessed a cosmology dominated by a high god, polities led by sacred kings, and burial customs of interring servants alongside dead rulers to serve them in the afterlife. These peoples were skilled cultivators and weavers of cotton, which they had domesticated. Archaeologists and historians used to believe that the Sudanic peoples borrowed their institutions, notably their sacred kingships, from their Egyptian neighbors; but linguistic evidence and their burial customs indicate that the Sudanic communities developed these practices independently.

Nubia: Between Sudanic Africa and Pharaonic Egypt

One of the most highly developed locations of common culture in sub-Saharan Africa was Nubia, a region lying between the first Nile cataract (a large waterfall) and the last (near where the Blue and White Niles come together). From at least the fourth millennium BCE onward, peoples in this region had contact with both the northern and southern parts of the African landmass. It was one of the few parts of sub-Saharan Africa known to the outside world. The Greek poet Homer described its inhabitants as "the remotest nation, the most just of men; the favorites of the gods."

The first of the important Nubian states was Kush. It flourished between 1700 and 1500 BCE between the first and third cataracts and had its capital at Kerma. Because of its close proximity to Egypt it adopted many Egyptian cultural and political practices, even though it was under constant pressure from the northern

ANALYZING GLOBAL DEVELOPMENTS

"Axial Age" Thinkers and Their Ideas

In the mid-twentieth century, the German philosopher Karl Jaspers invented the term "axial age" to describe the importance of ideas that originated in the first millennium BCE. These thinkers and their ideas are characterized as "axial" because: 1) they were a pivot point, or axis, that seemed to turn the world in a new direction, 2) they occurred along an East-West axis stretching from the Mediterranean to East Asia, and 3) they are central to ethical thought even down to the present day. These axial age philosophers were both the product of, and a challenge to, the societies from which they came—in other words, they were spurred by complex social and political contexts to develop their new ideas, but these new ideas in many ways critiqued and offered alternatives to the status quo. The chart below does not represent every axial age tradition, but is meant to draw into relief the relationship between the innovative thinker, his historical context, and the tenets of the new belief system.

QUESTIONS FOR ANALYSIS

- What connections, if any, do you see between the geo-political situation of a society and the axial age philosophy that sprang from that region? In what ways does each philosopher support or challenge the status quo?
- Jaspers was particularly impressed that societies he understood as being disconnected from one another would develop philosophical ideas so similar. How might the temporal and geographic relationship of the philosophers listed on the chart be explained? How does connectivity or disconnectivity impact the development of these ideas? What might account for similarities and differences in these "axial age" philosophies?
- What are the similarities and differences in how these philosophers' ideas were transmitted through time?

Thinker	Philosophy	Core Text	Historical Context	Central Tenet	Exemplary Sayings
Zoroaster, (1000–600 BCE)	Zoroastrianism	Avesta, the most sacred part of which is the Gathas, seventeen Middle Persian hymns purportedly written by Zoroaster himself	Southwest Asia, based in eastern Iranian nomadic culture, eventually becoming the central religion of Persian Empire	**Dualistic ethical system,** a world order based on the cosmic struggle between Ahura Mazda, the god of light, and Angra Mainyu, the god of destruction. Humans must choose between good and evil with reward or retribution doled out in the afterlife.	**On dualism:** "There [are] . . . two spirits [present] in the primal [stage of one's existence], twins who have . . . [manifested themselves as] the two [kinds] of dreams, . . . thoughts and words, . . . [and] actions, the better and the evil." (30.3) **On rewards:** "Brilliant things . . . will be for the person who comes to the truthful one. But a long period of darkness, foul food, and the word "woe"—to such an existence your religious view will lead you, O deceitful ones, of your own actions." (31.20)
Ezekiel (6th century BCE) and Isaiah, among other Jewish writers and prophets	Judaism	The Hebrew Bible, whose second part, Nevi'im, contains the writings of the prophets	Southwest Asia, with origins in Mesopotamian tribal cultures, eventually spreading to the early empires of Egypt and the Levant	A strict monotheistic tradition which dictates that its followers are the chosen people and have entered a **covenant,** or contractual relationship, with their god	**On monotheism:** "I am the first and I am the last; besides me there is no god." (Isaiah 44:6) **On the covenant:** "[. . .] I will make a new covenant . . . not like the covenant which I made with their fathers . . . to bring them out of the land of Egypt, my covenant which they broke, though I was their husband, says the Lord." (Jeremiah 31:31-32)

Sources: H. Humbach and I. Ichaporia, The Heritage of Zarathustra (Heidelberg, 1994); *Helmut Humbach "Gathas, i. Texts"* Encyclopedia Iranica *(2000) Vol. X, Fasc. 3, pp. 321–327; William W. Malandra, "Gathas, ii. Translations,"* Encyclopedia Iranica *(2000) Vol. X, Fasc. 3, pp. 327–330;* Thomas G. West and Grace Starry West, Four Texts on Socrates (Cornell, 1984); D.C. Lau's translation of Analects in H. James, ed. Norton Anthology of World Literature, Vol. 1 (Norton, 2002), pp. 820–830; The Dhammapada, translated by Juan Mascaro (Penguin, 1973); New Oxford Annotated Bible with Apocrypha, Revised Standard Version (Oxford).

powerhouse. Its successor states had to move farther south, up the Nile, to keep free from the powerful Egyptians; the kingdom's capitals were repeatedly uprooted and relocated upriver.

Nubia's historical connection to Egypt was obvious: it was Egypt's corridor to sub-Saharan Africa; a source of ivory, gold, and slaves; and an area that Egyptian monarchs wanted to dominate. The Egyptians called the region Kush, the name that later historians gave to the various regimes that flourished there. To the Egyptians, Kush was a land and the Kushites a people to be exploited. It was not a location that the Egyptians wished

Thinker	Philosophy	Core Text	Historical Context	Central Tenet	Exemplary Sayings
Buddha (ca. 563–483 BCE)	Buddhism	Dhammapad, verse sayings of the Buddha, which were recorded in the 3rd century BCE	India, as a challenge to Kshatriya oligarchy and the caste system of the Vedic society	An ethical system governed by the **Four Noble Truths:** 1. Life is suffering 2. Suffering is rooted in attachment 3. Escape suffering by escaping attachment 4. Escape attachment via the **Eight-fold Path**	**On the Eight-fold Path:** The best of the paths is the path of eight. The best of the truths, the four sayings. The best of states, freedom from passions. The best of men, the one who sees. (*Dhammapada,* 273) **On extremes:** "He who lives not for pleasures, and whose soul is in self-harmony, who eats and fasts with moderation, and has faith and the power of virtue—this man is not moved by temptations, as a great rock is not shaken by the wind. (8)
Confucius (551–479 BCE)	Confucianism	*Analects,* Confucius' dialogues with state leaders and students that were most likely recorded centuries later	China, during political turmoil towards the end of the Spring and Autumn Period (722–481 BCE)	A code of moral behavior, as exemplified in the *junzi* (gentleman or superior man), centered on: 1. ***ren*** (benevolence) 2. ***li*** (proper ritual) 3. ***xiao*** (filial piety)	**On virtue:** "The rule of virtue can be compared to the Pole Star which commands the homage of the multitude of stars without leaving its place." (II.1) **On respect:** "Duke Ai asked: 'What must I do before the common people will look up to me?' Confucius answered: 'Raise the straight and set them over the crooked and the common people will look up to you." (II.19)
Socrates (469–399 BCE)	Greek Philosophy	Dialogues recorded in the contemporary work of his students, especially Plato, and a collection of his sayings published later on	Greece, during a period of Greco-Persian conflict and inter-city-state wars	Ethical code that encourages self-discovery through knowledge, the recognition of the limits to one's own faculties, and the questioning of authority to find truth	**On self-discovery:** "The unexamined life is not worth living for a human being." (*Apology* 38a) **On wisdom:** "I am wiser than this human being, for probably neither of us knows anything noble and good; but he supposes he knows something, when he does not know; while I, just as I do not know, do not even suppose that I do." (*Apology* 21d).
Jesus (6/4 BCE–ca. 30 CE)	Christianity	Sayings later known through canonical and non-canonical Christian Gospels, first put in writing in the late 1st century CE	Judea under Roman imperial rule, later spreads throughout the Indo-Mediterranean	God's personal relationship with humanity mediated by His son, Jesus, whose suffering expiates human sins and grants eternal life to believers	**On ethical thought:** "Blessed are you poor, for yours is the kingdom of God; Blessed are you that hunger now, for you shall be satisfied . . . Love your enemies, do good to those who hate you. . . . " (Luke 6:20-38) **On Judaism:** "'Love the Lord your God. . . . ' This is the first . . . commandment. And the second is like it: 'Love your neighbor as yourself.' All the Law and the Prophets hang on these two commandments." (Matthew 22:37-40)

to reside in. Their chroniclers best described the Egyptian view of the territory and the people, referring to it repeatedly as "miserable Kush." The best known of the Egyptian conquerors was Ramses II, who left his imprint on Nubian culture with his magnificent monuments at Abu Simbel. Historians have long stressed such connections with Egypt, but only recently have scholars determined just how deeply the Nubian peoples were influenced by the cultures of sub-Saharan Africa.

Building on the foundations of earlier kings that had ruled Nubia, the Meroe kingdom arose in the fourth century BCE

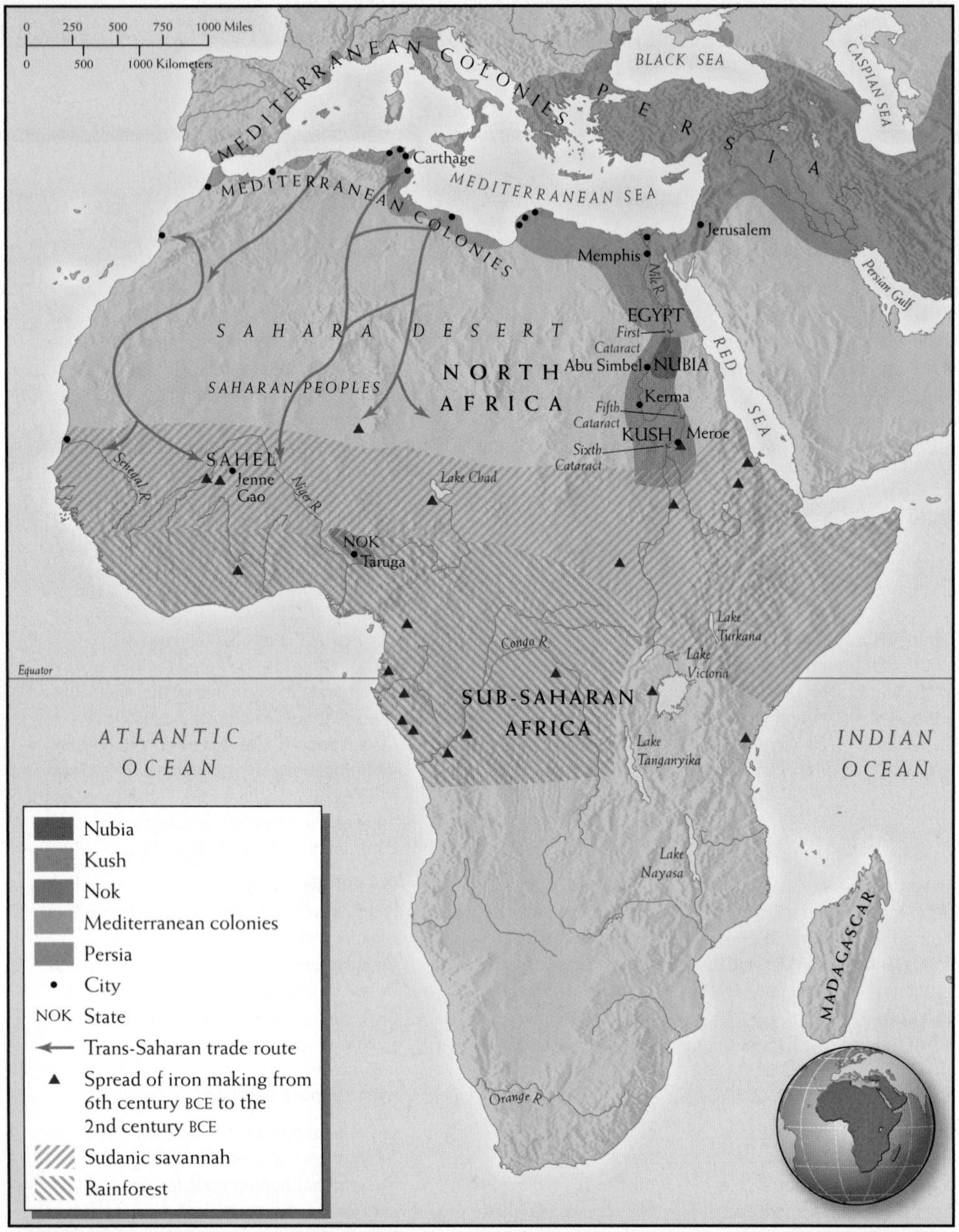

MAP 5.5 | Africa, 500 BCE

The first millennium BCE was a period of cultural, economic, and political integration for North and sub-Saharan Africa.

- According to this map, what effect did the Mediterranean colonies have on Africa?
- What main factor integrated Kush, Nubia, and Egypt?
- Does the map reveal a relationship between the rise of Sudanic culture and the spread of ironworking? If so, what is it?

and flourished until 300 CE. Its rulers were influenced by the pharaonic culture, adapting hieroglyphs, erecting pyramids in which to bury their rulers, viewing their kings as divine, and worshipping the Egyptian god Amun. However, Meroe was equally a part of the Sudanic savanna lifeway—as evidenced by the distinctiveness of the language and the determination of its inhabitants to retain political autonomy from Egypt, including, if necessary, moving farther south out of the orbit of Egypt and more into the orbit of Sudanic polities. Although they called their kings pharaohs, the influential leaders of Meroe selected them from among the many members of the royal family, attempting to ensure that their rulers were men of proven talents. In addition, the Nubian states had close commercial contacts with other merchants and commercial hubs in Sudanic Africa.

Meroe soon became a thriving center of production and commerce. Its residents were especially skilled in iron smelting and the manufacture of textiles, and their products circulated widely throughout Africa. The capital city itself covered a square mile; at its center was a royal complex surrounded by a wall 300 yards long and half again as wide. The city featured monumental and highly decorated buildings that were constructed, according to local custom, not of stone but of mud bricks.

West African Kingdoms

Meroe was not the only sacred kingship in the Sudanic savanna lands. Similar polities thrived in West Africa, among peoples living in the Senegal River basin and among the Mande peoples living inland around the western branch of the Niger River. They established settlements at such places as Jenne and Gao, which eventually became large trading centers. Here, artisans smelted iron ore and wove textiles, and merchants engaged in long-distance trade.

Even more spectacular was the Nok culture, which arose in the sixth century BCE in an area that is today the geographical center of Nigeria. Though slightly south of the savanna lands

PRIMARY SOURCE

Reconstructing the History of Preliterate African Peoples

Traditionally, historians have relied on written records and thus have had difficulty reconstructing the history of preliterate societies. Sources that now aid in understanding preliterate African groups include art, pottery, linguistic analysis, oral traditions, and many other elements. Here are two such vital historical sources.

The first is Nok terra-cottas. Discovered in the central region of modern-day Nigeria, the figurines probably were created in the Common Era but are part of a vibrant culture that dates back to the fifth century BCE.

Nok Figurine

The second source, Kush burial pyramids, comes from the sub-Saharan kingdom of Meroe, by no means a preliterate society but one that has many important nonwritten sources. Meroe flourished for nearly a millennium from around the fourth century BCE to the fourth century CE. Its predecessor kingdoms, referred to as the kingdoms of Kush, were located between the first and third Nile cataracts. The first kingdom of Kush existed between 1700 and 1500 BCE. A second powerful Kushitic state arose around 1000 BCE, and its most dynamic dynasty even overpowered Egypt, creating Egypt's "black pharaohs" dynasty, Egypt's twenty-fifth dynasty. Later, when Egyptian power was again ascendant, the peoples of Nubia moved even farther south to establish the kingdom of Meroe. Although Meroe continued to be deeply influenced by the culture and political forms of Egypt, its peoples spoke a different language from the Egyptians, a Nilo-Saharan language.

Nubia's close contact with Egypt led to profound and obvious influences—for example, the use of the term *pharaoh* to refer to the king, borrowed religious beliefs, and the use of hieroglyphs. Like the Egyptians, the Kushitic and Meroitic peoples buried their kings in pyramids and wrote texts on the walls of these burial chambers about what constituted an orderly and good life. The Meroitic peoples had a powerful priestly class, like the ancient Egyptians, but they retreated up the Nile to be independent of Egyptian rule. Scholars with the same archaeological and linguistic training as students of ancient Egypt (known as Egyptologists) have studied the Nubian cultures, but their studies have taken place more recently than those of ancient Egypt and have not yet yielded as much information.

QUESTIONS FOR ANALYSIS

- How do the Nok terra-cottas help scholars understand the very ancient culture of West Africa?
- Do they provide insight into the artistic abilities of the people living in this region?
- What can they tell us about how people dressed and how they looked?
- Can you see the Egyptian influence in the photograph of the Kush burial pyramids?

Burial Pyramids. *Dated between 300 BCE and 300 AD, these tombs are located in the Royal Necropolis of the ancient Kingdom of Kush.*

The Temple of Ramses II. *The temple of Ramses II at Abu Simbel was constructed during the reign of Ramses II between 1304 and 1237 BCE. It was cut out of the rock and featured four colossal statues of the king, each of which was sixty-five feet high. When the Aswan High Dam was built in the 1960s, the monument had to be cut into large stone slabs and moved to higher ground so that it would not be submerged under the waters of Lake Nasser, which the High Dam formed.*

of West Africa, it was (and still is) in regular contact with that region. At Taruga, near the present-day village of Nok, early iron smelting occurred in 600 BCE. Taruga may well have been the first place in western Africa where iron ores were smelted. Undeniably, ironworking was significant for the Nok peoples, who moved from using stone materials directly to iron, bypassing bronze and copper. They made iron axes and hoes, iron knives and spears, and luxury items for trade. This region in West Africa was also home to the Bantu-speaking peoples destined to play a major role in the history of the landmass. Around 300 BCE, small Bantu groups began to migrate southward into the equatorial rain forests, where they cleared land for farming; from there, some moved on to southern Africa. (See Chapter 8 for a discussion of the Bantu peoples.)

Nok has achieved its historical fame not for its iron-smelting prowess but for its magnificent terra-cotta figurines, discovered in the 1940s in the tin-mining region of central Nigeria. These naturalistic figures, whose features bear a striking resemblance to those of the region's modern inhabitants, date to at least 500 BCE. They were altarpieces for a cult associated with the land's fertility. Placed next to new lands that were coming into cultivation, they were believed to bless the soil and enhance its productivity. (See Primary Source: Reconstructing the History of Preliterate African Peoples.)

Although most sub-Saharan African communities lived in small-scale dispersed communities, in several locations, notably Nubia and West Africa, larger, common cultures based on shared beliefs and political institutions arose. The ability of these societies to produce more food and sustain larger settled communities ultimately caused the sub-Saharan population to triple in this period. As in the Americas, these lifeways proved durable.

WARRING IDEAS IN THE MEDITERRANEAN WORLD

The widespread migrations that convulsed southern Europe and Southwest Asia around 1200 BCE (see Chapter 4) also brought marauding armed bands into the well-settled regions of the Mediterranean. The combined impact of large population movements and social destruction radically transformed social organizations and cultures throughout the region. Thus, the first millennium BCE in the Mediterranean was a time of political, economic, and social changes, all of which stimulated new thinking and saw the creation of new political and economic institutions (just as in Eastern Zhou China and Vedic South Asia; see Map 5.6).

New Thinking and New Societies at the Margins

The violent upheavals that tore through the borderland areas of the northern Levant, the coastal lands of Anatolia, the islands of the Aegean and Mediterranean seas, and mainland Greece freed these peoples from the domination of Assyria and Persia. More on their own than ever before, these borderland communities could explore new cultural ideas and create new social and political organization. Thus, around 1000 BCE, these second-generation societies mixed the old and the new, devising new ways of organizing themselves.

Seaborne peoples from around the Mediterranean Sea basin—Phoenicians, Greeks, Cretans, Cypriots, Lydians, Etruscans, and many others—carried not just trade goods but also ideas about the virtues of self-sufficient cities whose inhabitants shared power more widely (even more democratically) than before. Inventions

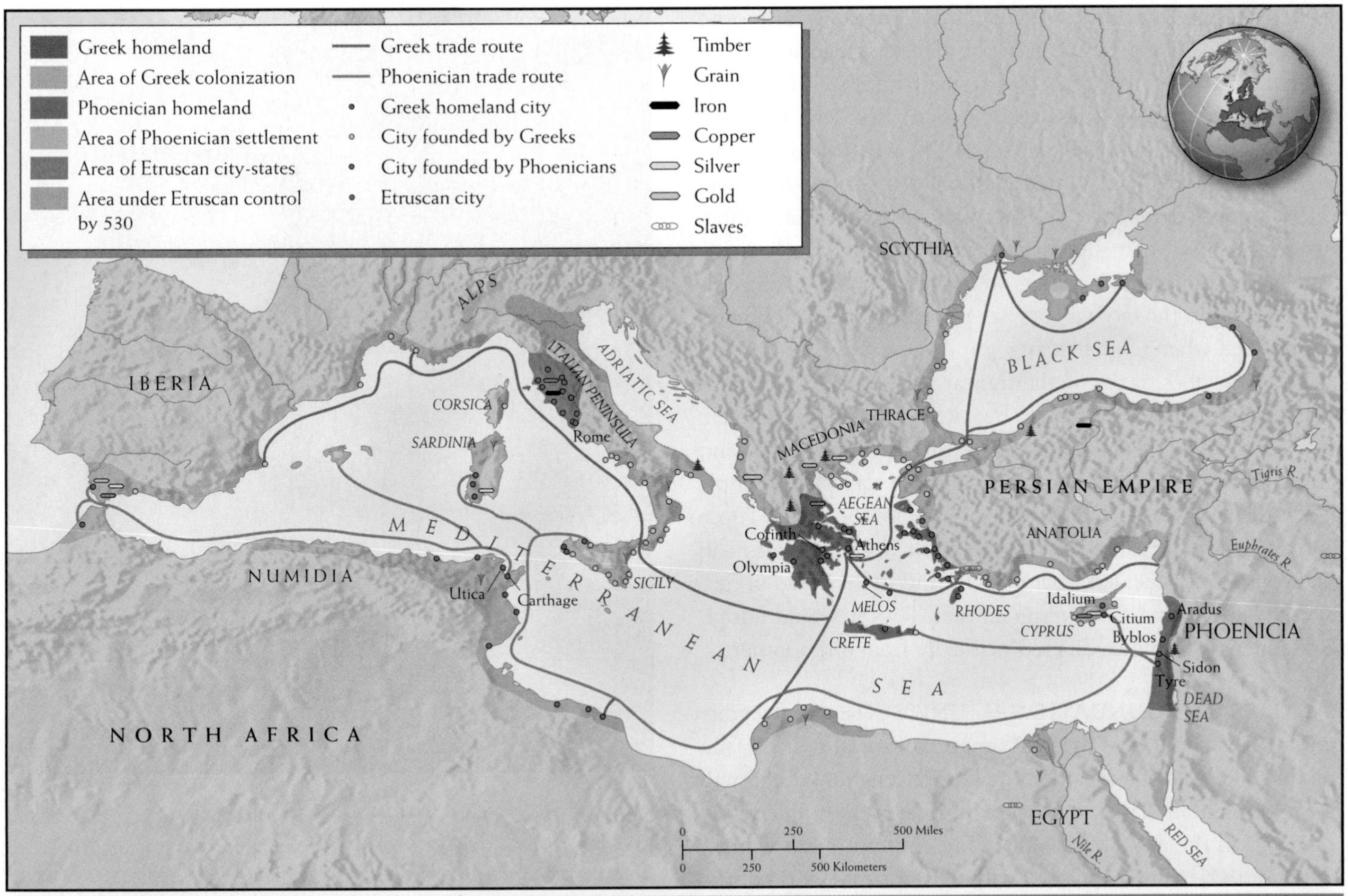

MAP 5.6 | The Mediterranean World

- What were the main goods traded in the Mediterranean world in this period?
- What areas did the Greeks and Phoenicians control, and what was their main settlement pattern?
- How do you think a small country like Phoenicia was able to extend its reach so dramatically?

that proved valuable in one place, such as the use of money and the alphabet, spread rapidly; the result was an unprecedented degree of intercommunication among diverse communities.

A New World of City-States

New ways of thinking about the world burst forth in the ninth and eighth centuries BCE, as order returned to the eastern Mediterranean and the population rebounded. The peoples who were clustered in more concentrated settlements at this time did not revive the old palace and temple organizations of the Mycenaeans and Minoans (see Chapter 3). Instead, they created something quite novel: city-states that, unlike those of earlier Mesopotamia, were governed not by semidivine monarchs but by their citizens. They also unleashed powerful waves of cultural innovation and economic activity.

SELF-GOVERNMENT AND DEMOCRACY The self-governing city-state was a new political form that profoundly influenced the Mediterranean region. First found among the Phoenicians (see Chapter 4) and in their settlements such as Carthage but ultimately associated with the Greeks, these new urban communities had multiplied throughout the Mediterranean by the sixth century BCE. The new urban entity was known by the Phoenicians as a *qart*, the Greeks as a *polis*, and the Romans as a *civitas*. Unlike the great urban centers in the Southwest Asian empires, the new city-states were not organized by an elite class of scribes or run by directives from high priests and monarchs.

The new principles of rulership were revolutionary. Ordinary residents, or "citizens," of these cities—such as Athens, Thebes, Sparta, or Corinth among the Greeks; Rome and Praeneste among the early Latins; Carthage and Gadir (modern-day Cádiz in Spain) among the western Phoenicians—governed themselves and selected their leaders. Their self-government took various forms. One kind was rule by a popularly approved political head of the city, whom the Greeks called a *tyrannis* ("tyrant"). Another was rule by a small number of wealthy and powerful citizens—the *oligoi,* meaning "the few" in Greek (hence "oligarchs" and "oligarchies"). The most inclusive type of government involved all free adult males in a city—in Greek, a *dēmokratia* ("democracy"). The wealthiest landowners often formed the power elite, but farmers, craftworkers, shopkeepers, merchants, soldiers, and traders were the backbone of the citizenry. They ran the city's affairs, set priorities for development, and decided when to go to war.

The new cities of the Mediterranean basin became communities of adult male citizens, other free persons (including women, who could not vote or hold office), foreign immigrants, and large numbers of unfree persons (including slaves and people tied to the land who could not vote or fight for the polis). Those enjoying full citizenship rights—the adult freeborn males—in each community decided what tasks the city-state would undertake and what kind of government and laws it would adopt. Consequently, the cities differed markedly from one another.

FAMILIES AS FOUNDATIONAL UNITS The small family unit, or household, was the most important social unit. In fact, thinkers like Aristotle regarded the state as a natural outgrowth of the household. Thus, the free adult male was fully entitled to engage in the city's public affairs. In contrast, adult women of free birth remained enclosed within the private world of the family and had no standing to debate policy in public, vote, or hold office. Women who did carry on intelligent conversations with men in public about public matters were criticized. Spartan women were a partial exception to these rules, and their unusual behavior—such as exercising in the nude in public (as did men) or holding property in their own right—evoked humor and hostility from men in the other Greek city-states.

COMPETITION AND ARMED WAR Because there were no centralized governments to control residents' actions and thoughts, the city-states were freewheeling and competitive places, sometimes bloodily so. Their histories relate violent rivalries between individuals, social classes, and other groups. Among the larger Greek city-states, only Sparta avoided most of this internal strife, achieving greater calm by means of rigorous social discipline and military organization that cut off the city from many external influences. The Spartans rejected coined money and chattel slavery (see below), thereby avoiding the "corruption" of cities with more mercantile interests. However successful it was as a military state, Sparta seemed to the other Greeks to be a very unusual polis.

Competition for honor and prestige was a value that shaped behavior in the city-states. This extreme competitive ethic found a benign outlet in organized sporting events. Almost from the moment that Greek city-states emerged, athletic contests sprang

Hetaira. *The painting on this vase by the artist Oitos is of a "companion" woman—called by the Greeks an* hetaira*—putting on a sandal. Proper Greek women were protected and kept within their households; they were modest and always fully clothed. Women who were so bold as to be out in public, talking and otherwise associating with men—like the woman portrayed here—were deemed immoral. The artist therefore had no problem portraying this* hetaira *in the nude.*

up—both on a small scale as an essential part of each city's life and in centralized events in which all Greeks could participate. The greatest competitions were the Olympic Games, which began in 776 BCE at Olympia in southern Greece.

The competitive spirit among communities took the destructive form of armed conflicts over borderlands, trade, valuable resources, religious shrines, and prestige. Wars of one sort or another were characteristic of city-state relations (as they were among states in Eastern Zhou China and Vedic South Asia during the same period). The incessant battles fueled new developments in military equipment, such as the heavy armor that gave its name to the hoplites, or infantrymen, and in tactics, such as the standard block-like configuration (which the Greeks called a *phalanx*) in which the regular rank and file fought. These wars were so destructive that they threatened to destabilize the city-states' world. The bigger the states and the more resources they had, the more likely they were to engage in warfare, even to the detriment of their own people. The most famous conflict was the Peloponnesian War (431–404 BCE) between Athens and Sparta. It dragged on for decades, eating away the resources

Hoplites. *Most battles between Greek city-states took place on land between massed formations of infantrymen, or "hoplites"* (hoplon *meaning shield). Serving the community in this way defined one's right to citizenship or membership in the city. Since hoplites wore the same armor and contributed equally to the battle line, the nature of hoplite warfare helped to define the democratic ethos of the individual citizen.*

of the two great polities and their allies. Sparta finally won the war, but only at the cost of destroying its own traditional social culture. In the end, everyone lost.

Economic Innovations and Population Movement

Economic innovations (the alphabet, coins, and the central marketplace) facilitated trade among the fragmented Mediterranean communities. As a result, the city-states enjoyed accelerated economic growth in the ninth and eighth centuries BCE. Even more spectacular was the speed with which they established colonies wherever they found resources and trade. The city-states' superior military technology, developed and tested in conflicts among themselves, enabled them to defeat local resistance. Moreover, through trade and colonization the Mediterranean peoples acquired as slaves the inhabitants of frontier communities to the north. The slaves' labor further contributed to the city-states' wealth and growth.

FREE MARKETS AND MONEY-BASED ECONOMIES Without a top-down bureaucratic and administrative structure, residents of the new cities had to devise other ways to run their affairs. They developed open trading markets and a system of money that enabled buyers and sellers to know the precise value of commodities so that exchanges were efficient. The Greek historian Herodotus, who journeyed widely in the mid-fifth century BCE, observed that the new city-states had at their center a marketplace (*agora*), a large open area where individuals bought and sold commodities. He found no such great open public commercial spaces in Egypt or Babylonia.

Soon most transactions required money rather than barter or gift exchange. Coins also bought services, perhaps at first to hire mercenary soldiers. In the absence of large bureaucracies, the Mediterranean cities relied on money to connect the producers and buyers of goods and services. By the end of the fifth century BCE the Greek city-states were issuing a striking variety of coins, and other peoples such as the Phoenicians, Etruscans, and Persians were also using them. (During the same period, money developed independently and saw common use in Vedic South Asia and Eastern Zhou China.)

TRADE AND COLONIZATION The search for silver, iron, copper, and tin drove the first traders westward across the Mediterranean. By about 500 BCE the Phoenicians, Greeks, and others from the eastern Mediterranean had planted new city-states around the shores of the western Mediterranean and the Black Sea. Once established, these colonial communities

The Agora. *The agora, or central open marketplace, was one of the core defining features of Mediterranean city-states. At its center, each city had one of these open-air plazas, the heart of its commercial, religious, social, and political life. When a new city was founded, the agora was one of the first places that the colonists measured out. The large, rectangular, open area in this picture is the agora of the Greek colonial city of Cyrene (in modern-day Libya).*

became completely independent, and they transformed the coastal world. City-based life became common from southern Spain and western Italy to the Crimea on the Black Sea.

With amazing speed, seaborne communications spread a Mediterranean-wide urban culture that bolstered the region's wealthy and powerful elites. Found among the local elites of Tartessos in southern Spain, the Gallic chiefs in southern France, and the Etruscan and Roman nobles of central Italy, the new aristocratic culture featured similar public displays of wealth: richly decorated chariots, elaborate armor and weapons, high-class dining ware, elaborate houses, and public burials. From one end of the Mediterranean to the other, as well as to the Black Sea, the city-state communities developed a culture founded on alphabetic scripts, market-based economies, and private property.

CHATTEL SLAVERY The explosion of buying and selling produced an ethos in which everything that the city dwellers needed, even human beings, took on a monetary value. Treating men, women, and children as objects of commerce, to be bought and sold in markets, created something novel—a new form of slavery called **chattel slavery**. This commercial slavery spread quickly. Where dangerous and exhausting tasks such as mining required extra labor, the freeborn citizens purchased slave laborers. In Athens, the largest and most economically powerful Greek city-state, slaves may have constituted up to a quarter of the population. They were essential to every one of the new city-states, providing manual and technical labor of all kinds and producing the agricultural surpluses that supported the urban population.

ENCOUNTERS WITH FRONTIER COMMUNITIES The forces that transformed the Mediterranean region's mosaic of urban communities and surrounding rural areas also affected those in northern and central Europe. Whether they wished it or not, diverse tribes and ethnic groups, such as the Celts and Germans in western Europe and the Scythians to the north of the Black Sea, who were living in nomadic bands, isolated settlements, and small villages became integrated into the expanding cities' networks of violence, conquest, and trade.

Increasingly drawn to the city-states' manufactured goods—money, wine, ornate clothing, weapons—these tribal peoples became an armed threat to the region's core societies. Seeking to acquire the desired commodities through force rather than trade, frontier peoples convulsed the settled urban societies in wave-like incursions between 2200 and 2000 BCE, 1200 and 1000 BCE, and 400 and 200 BCE. Called "barbarians" (the Greeks' mocking name for foreigners unable to speak their language), the invaders actually were not much different from the Phoenicians or Greeks—who themselves had sought new homes and a better future by migrating. In colonizing the Mediterranean, they too had dispossessed the original inhabitants. The Celts, Gauls, Germans, Scythians, and other northerners came to the Mediterranean first

Mediterranean Coins. *From the sixth century BCE onward, money in the form of precious metal coins began spreading through the city-states of the Mediterranean, beginning with the Greek city-states in the western parts of what is today Turkey, then spreading to the other Greek poleis and beyond. On the left here is the classic tetradrachm (four-drachma piece) coin of Athens with its owl of the goddess Athena; on the right is a silver coin of shekel weight produced by the city of Carthage in the western Mediterranean.*

as conquerors. Later, when Mediterranean empires grew more powerful and could keep them at bay, they were imported as slaves. Regarding these outsiders as uncivilized, the Greeks and western Phoenicians seized and colonized their lands—and sold the captives as commodities in their marketplaces.

New Ideas

New ways of thinking about the world emerged from the competitive atmosphere that the Greek city-states fostered. Moreover, since there were very few top-down controls (as in the kingdoms of Southwest Asia), citizens had to devise methods for managing their own affairs. In the absence of monarchical or priestly rule, ideas were free to arise, circulate, and clash. Individuals argued publicly about the nature of the gods, the best state, what is good, and whether to wage war. There was no final authority to give any particular idea a final stamp of approval and force its acceptance.

NATURALISTIC SCIENCE AND REALISTIC ART In this atmosphere, some daring thinkers developed novel ways of perceiving the cosmos and representing the environment. Rather than seeing everything as the handiwork of all-powerful deities, they took a naturalistic view of humans and their place in the universe. Consider their art, which idealized the natural world. Artists increasingly represented humans, objects, and landscapes not in abstract or formal ways but in "natural" ways, as they appeared to the human eye. Even their portrayals of gods became more humanlike. Later, these objective and natural views of humans and nature turned into ideals, the highest of which was the unadorned human figure: the nude became the centerpiece of Greek art.

The public display of the uncovered human body, in both art and everyday life (notably in men's athletic training and competition), signaled the sharp break between the moral codes of the older, traditional societies of the East and those of the revolutionary cities of the Mediterranean. Vase painters such as Exekias signed their works and became known as individual artists. Sculptors like Praxiteles also became famous. No less assertive were creative writers, such as the poets Archilochus and Sappho, who wrote lyrics exploring their own emotions—a clear manifestation of the new sense of the individual being freed from the restraints of an autocratic state or a controlling religious system.

NEW THINKING AND GREEK PHILOSOPHERS Armed with their own ideas and this borrowed knowledge, thinkers in cities such as Miletus and Ephesus did not accept traditional explanations of how and why the universe worked. Rather than focusing on gods, they looked to nature as constituting some fundamental substance (usually one of the traditional elements: earth, air or breath, fire, or water). Thales (c. 636–546 BCE) believed that water was the primal substance from which all other things were created.

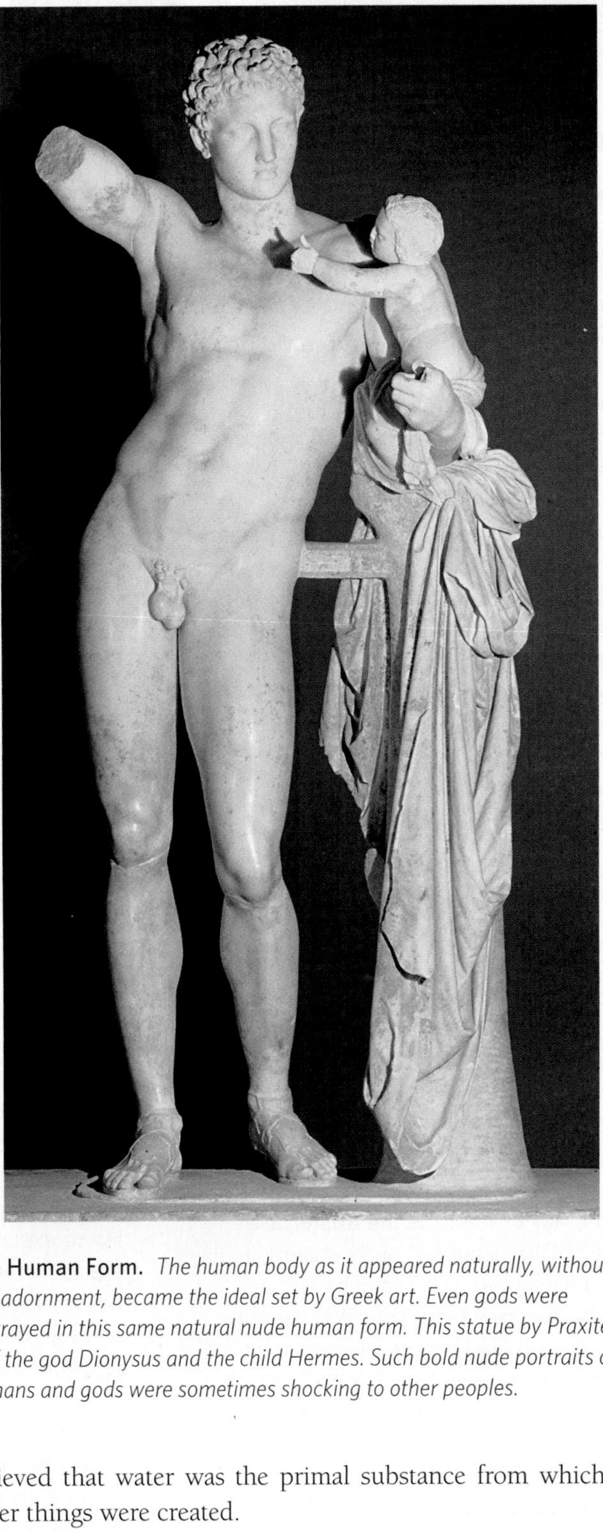

The Human Form. *The human body as it appeared naturally, without any adornment, became the ideal set by Greek art. Even gods were portrayed in this same natural nude human form. This statue by Praxiteles is of the god Dionysus and the child Hermes. Such bold nude portraits of humans and gods were sometimes shocking to other peoples.*

As each thinker competed to outdo his peers in offering persuasive and comprehensive explanations, theories became ever more radical. Men like Xenophanes (c. 570–480 BCE), from the city of Colophon, doubted the very existence of gods as they had been portrayed. He asserted instead that only one general divine aura suffused all creation. He pointed out that each ethnic group in fact produced images of gods that resembled themselves: Ethiopians represented their gods with dark skins

PRIMARY SOURCE

Warring Ideas: Plato versus Aristotle—On Gaining Knowledge of the Essence of the World

Great debates raged among Greek thinkers during the fifth and fourth centuries BCE over the essence of the world and how humans can have knowledge of it. Rejecting the existence of creator gods and goddesses, they sought explanations elsewhere. Some looked to the material world (in primary substances like water), while others turned to abstractions.

The Greek philosopher and mathematician Pythagoras suggested that numbers were the basis of everything. Some later thinkers, notably Plato, took this argument further and argued that all existence—and therefore all human knowledge—is based on absolute concepts that are like numbers, existing independent of time and place. Each of them Plato called an idea, a word whose meanings in Greek include "shape," "form," and "appearance." In a number of Plato's dialogues, his teacher, Socrates, tries to explain this theory:

> **Socrates:** I am going to try to explain to you the theory of causes that I myself have thought out. . . . I assume that you admit the existence of absolutes like "beauty" and "good" and "size" and the rest. If you admit that these absolutes exist, then I can hope with their help to show you what causes are. . . . I remain obstinately committed . . . to the explanation that the one thing that causes a thing to be "beautiful," for example, is the existence in it of "the beautiful" or its sharing in "the beautiful"[;] . . . and so, is it not also the case that things that we call "big" are big because they share the idea of "bigness" and similarly that things that we call "small" are small because they share in the idea of "smallness"? [Socrates then dismisses the claim that in calling things "tall" or "small" we are simply describing them in relation to other things.]
>
> **Phaedo:** I believe that Socrates has persuaded us of these matters and that we have agreed that these different ideas do exist; and he has also persuaded us that the reason why specific things in our world are named after these ideas is that they share in the existence of the specific idea. (*Phaedo* 99d–102b)

Still other thinkers drew on some of the first Greek philosophers of the sixth century BCE to argue that the basis of all existing things was, quite simply, other things. They rejected the proposal that all things we perceive with our senses are poor copies of permanent ideas of them that exist in a separate, unchangeable realm. Human knowledge, they argued, was in fact acquired through careful observation of existing things and through meticulous collection of data about them. Thus in the following passage Aristotle rejects Plato's concept of ideas:

> As for the followers of Plato who claim that "ideas" (or "shapes") are the causes or origins of all things, this too is objectionable. First of all, in their struggle to find causes for things that exist in our world of sense perceptions, they simply introduce as many new things into the equation as they are attempting to explain[;] . . . so their "ideas" are as many . . . as the things whose causes they are seeking to explain and for which reason they were led to invent these ideas. They must do this because they must create an idea to match every substance that exists in our real everyday world . . . and also one in the realm of the eternal heavenly entities. Not one of the arguments by which they try to demonstrate that these ideas actually exist can demonstrate or prove their claim. From some of their arguments, indeed, no real conclusions follow. From other arguments of theirs it only follows that there must be ideas of things for which they themselves hold no such ideas can exist. (*Metaphysics* 1.9, 990a–b)

In other works Aristotle put forth his own views about how to gain reliable knowledge of the world:

> All teaching and learning by means of rational argument is based on our existing knowledge and observations; . . . and I think that we have reliable knowledge of each thing . . . when we think that we have found the cause because of which that thing exists—what is the cause of that thing and of nothing else, with the result that this thing or this fact cannot be other than it is. That this is real knowledge of something is very clear. . . . We know what we do by demonstration, by showing that it is true. By demonstration I mean an argument that produces real knowledge, . . . all of which is based on a knowledge and observation of facts and things. . . . But I also say that not all real knowledge can in fact be demonstrated or proved. (*Posterior Analytics* 1.1–3, 71a–72b)

QUESTIONS FOR ANALYSIS

- How do our modern attitudes toward what we know and how we know it reflect these two approaches?
- What might have provoked Plato and Aristotle to advance such different concepts of knowledge?
- Where else might such factors be linked to major developments of the time (e.g., South or East Asia)?

Source: Plato, Phaedo, *99d–102b; Aristotle,* Metaphysics, *1.9 = 990a–b;* Posterior Analytics, *1.1–3 = 71a–72b. All translations are by Brent Shaw.*

and broad noses, while Thracians depicted theirs as blue-eyed redheads. Such variation in beliefs about divine attributes suggested that the gods existed only in the human imagination.

Some thinkers proposed that the real world had a physical, tangible basis. Among them was Democritus (c. 460–370 BCE), who claimed that everything comprised small and ultimately indivisible particles. Democritus called them *atoma* ("uncuttables"), or atoms. Even more radical were thinkers like Pythagoras, who devoted himself to the study of numbers (although the famous Pythagorean Theorem had already been discovered by Babylonian priests and mathematicians). Prefiguring the modern digital revolution, he held that a wide range of physical phenomena, like musical sounds, was in fact based in numbers.

The competition among ideas led to a more aggressive mode of public thinking. The Greeks called it *philosophia* ("love of wisdom"), and the professional thinkers who were good at it *philosophoi* ("philosophers"). Some of the earliest recorded debates addressed the nature of the cosmos, the environment, and the physical elements of human existence. By the fifth century BCE, philosophers were focusing on humans and their place in society. Finally, some thinkers tried to describe an ideal state, possessing harmonious relationships and being free from corruption and political decline.

Socrates (469–399 BCE), a philosopher in Athens, encouraged people to reflect on ethics and morality. He stressed the importance of honor and integrity as opposed to wealth and power (just as Confucius had done in Eastern Zhou China and the Buddha in Vedic South Asia). **Plato** (427–347 BCE), a student of Socrates, presented Socrates's philosophy in a series of dialogues (much as Confucius's students had written down his thoughts). In *The Republic,* Plato envisioned a perfect city that philosopher-kings would rule. He thought that if fallible humans could imitate this model city more closely, their polities would be less susceptible to the decline that was affecting the Greek city-states of his own day. This belief was an outgrowth of his more general theory of "ideas"—eternal and perfect models of abstract concepts and material objects—that are imperfectly copied in the real world. (See Primary Source: Warring Ideas: Plato versus Aristotle—On Gaining Knowledge of the Essence of the World.)

In the next generation, Plato's most famous pupil answered the same question differently. Deeply interested in the natural world, **Aristotle** (384–322 BCE) believed that by collecting all the facts one could about a given thing—no matter how imperfect—and studying them closely, one could achieve a better understanding. His main idea was that the interested inquirer can find out more about the world by collecting as much evidence as possible about a given thing and then making deductions from these data about general patterns. This was in stark contrast to Plato's claim that everything a person observes is in fact only a flawed copy of the "real" thing that exists in a thought-world of abstract patterns accessible only by pure mental meditation—completely the opposite of Aristotle's method. Following his approach, Aristotle collected evidence from more than 150 Greek city-states, and in *The Politics* he proposed institutional responses and codes of moral conduct that would allow urban communities to function better. But neither Plato nor Aristotle was able to preserve the city-state as the exemplary civilized society. During their lives the world of the independent city-state was to change dramatically, as new forms of bigger states emerged and became dominant.

CONCLUSION

Afro-Eurasia's great river-basin areas were still important in the first millennium BCE, but their time as centers of world cultures was passing. Now they yielded some of their leadership to regions that had been on the fringes, giving way to a generation of cultural and intellectual flourishing in search of alternative, new orders. Within the city-state in the Mediterranean world, the territorial states in China, and the kingdoms and oligarchies in urbanizing South Asia great social and intellectual dynamism occurred.

During this period influential thinkers came to the fore with perspectives quite different from those of the river-basin civilizations. The Greek philosophers offered new views about nature, their political world, and human relations and values—all based on secular rather than religious ideas. In South Asia, dissident thinkers challenged the Brahmanic spiritual and political order, and the Buddha articulated a religious belief system that was much less hierarchical and more positive, and provided for more individual self-control than its Vedic predecessor. In China, the political instability of the Warring States period propelled scholars such as Confucius to engage in political debate, where they stressed respect for social hierarchy.

Even where contacts with other societies were less intense, innovation occurred. In the Americas, the Olmecs developed a worldview in which mortals had to appease angry gods through human sacrifice and elaborate temples where many peoples could pay homage to the same deities. In sub-Saharan Africa, settled pockets devised complex cultural foundations for community life. The Mediterranean and Egyptian cultures continued to expand their influence up the Nile through Nubia and into sub-Saharan Africa. A spectacular example of sub-Saharan and Egyptian synthesis was the culture of Meroe. And in West Africa, the Nok peoples promoted interregional trade and cultural contact as they expanded their horizons.

As the world was coalescing into culturally distinct regions, all the ideas newly forged in Afro-Eurasia, the Americas, and sub-Saharan Africa would endure. No matter where they were created, they had a continuing impact on societies that followed.

AFTER YOU READ THIS CHAPTER

Review and research on **STUDYSPACE:** wwnorton.com/studyspace

TRACING THE GLOBAL STORYLINES

FOCUS ON: ***Innovative Societies***

CHINA

- Multistate system emerges from warfare, revolutionizing society and thought.
- Confucius and the hundred masters outline new ideals of governing and living.

SOUTH ASIA

- Small monarchies and urban oligarchies emerge after the Vedic peoples' migrations and rule over societies organized around the caste system.
- Dissident thinkers like Mahavira and the Buddha challenge Brahman priests and the caste system.

THE AMERICAS

- Olmecs and Chavín peoples produce increasingly hierarchical societies and connect villages via trade.
- Large-scale common cultures emerge.

SUB-SAHARAN AFRICA

- Expansion of the Sahara Desert and population explosion cause people to coalesce in a few locations.
- Early signs of a common culture appear across the savannah Sudanic region.

THE MEDITERRANEAN WORLD

- Independent city-states emerge from social destruction and facilitate revolutionary principles in rulership, commerce, and thought.
- Thinkers like Democritus, Plato, and Aristotle challenge conventions and encourage public discourse about the role of the individual in society and the way the universe works.

CHRONOLOGY

The Americas

Sub-Saharan Africa

South Asia

The Mediterranean

East Asia

1500 BCE

1000 BCE

KEY TERMS

Aristotle *p. 197*

ascetic *p. 175*

Buddha *p. 176*

caste *p. 173*

chattel slavery *p. 194*

Confucius *p. 165*

cosmology *p. 176*

Daoism *p. 167*

Jainism *p. 175*

Legalism *p. 167*

oligarchy *p. 172*

Olmecs *p. 179*

Plato *p. 197*

second-generation societies *p. 164*

shamans *p. 181*

Socrates *p. 197*

STUDY QUESTIONS

1. **Explain** the "war of ideas" that occurred during the first millennium BCE in China. How did Confucianism and Daoism influence political developments during the Warring States period?

2. **Analyze** the impact of commerce and urbanization on the Brahman order in South Asia at this time. Why were urban audiences receptive to Buddhist and other challenges to Brahman concepts?

3. **Compare and contrast** Buddhist and Confucian philosophies. What problems and issues did they address, and what solutions did they propose?

4. **Explain** the broad cultural features that characterized Olmec and Chavín societies in the Americas in the first millennium BCE. To what extent did each cultural group leave an imprint on its region?

5. **Analyze** the extent to which diverse sub-Saharan peoples were connected to one another and to the larger world during this period. What processes brought groups together, and what kept them apart?

6. **Describe** the political and economic innovations in the Mediterranean world in the first millennium BCE. What impact did these ideas have on peoples living on the periphery of that world?

7. **Compare and contrast** the Greek philosophers Socrates, Plato, and Aristotle with Confucius in China and the Buddha in South Asia. What was similar and what was different in their proposals for creating a better world?

8. **Explain** how second-generation societies created new cultural and social pathways and ideas in Afro-Eurasia in the first millennium BCE. What alternative approaches to philosophy, economics, and religion emerged in East Asia, South Asia, and western Afro-Eurasia?

Olmec culture emerges and diffuses through Mesoamerica **1500–400 BCE**

Chavin culture flourishes in Central Andes of South America **1400–400 BCE**

Nok culture in West Africa **600 BCE**

Meroe Kingdom in Nubia, **4th century BCE–3rd century CE**

Cities, states, and caste system emerge **600 BCE**

Siddhartha Gautama develops Buddhist principles **563–438 BCE**

City states flourish **c. 800–400 BCE**

Socrates, Plato, and Aristotle teach in Athens **5th and 4th centuries BCE**

Spring and Autumn period of Zhou Dynasty **722–481 BCE**

Warring State period **403–221 BCE**

Age of the Hundred Masters **c. 600 BCE–c. 200 BCE**

500 BCE **300 BCE**

BEFORE YOU READ THIS CHAPTER

GLOBAL STORYLINES

- Two broad cultural movements, Hellenism and Buddhism, link diverse populations across Afro-Eurasia.
- Conquests by Alexander the Great and the influence of his successor states spread Hellenism across Southwest Asia and into South Asia, where it begins the gradual process of cultural and political integration.
- The Mauryan Empire accelerates the integration of South Asia and helps Buddhism spread throughout that region and into central and East Asia via the Silk Road.

CHAPTER OUTLINE

6

Shrinking the Afro-Eurasian World, 350 BCE–250 CE

FOCUS QUESTIONS

- How did Hellenism and Buddhism link diverse populations across Afro-Eurasia?
- How did political expansion and integration facilitate economic and cultural exchanges between different parts of the Afro-Eurasian world?
- How did pastoral people influence economic, political, and cultural developments across Afro-Eurasia?
- To what extent were economic and political developments in China, South Asia, and the Mediterranean similar and different?
- How did merchants move goods across the Afro-Eurasian landmass?

In the blistering August heat of 324 BCE, at a town on the Euphrates River that the Greeks called Opis (not far from modern Baghdad), Alexander the Great's crack Macedonian troops declared that they had had enough. They had been fighting far from their homeland for more than a decade. They had marched eastward from the Mediterranean, forded wide rivers, traversed great deserts, trudged over high mountain passes, and slogged through rain-drenched forests. Along the way they had defeated massive armies, including those armed with fearsome war elephants. Some had taken wives from the cities and tribes they vanquished, so the army had become a giant swarm of ethnically mixed families. This was an army like no other. It did more than just defeat neighbors and rivals—it forcefully connected entire worlds, bringing together diverse peoples and lands.

Conquering in the name of building a new world, however, was not what the soldiers had bargained for. They loved their leader, but many thought he had gone too far. They had lost companions and grown weary of war. Some had mutinied at a tributary of the Indus, halting Alexander's advance into South Asia. Now they threatened to desert him altogether. Summoning up their courage, they voiced these resentments to their supreme commander. Alexander's response was immediate and inspired. In persuading his troops not to desert him, he evoked the astounding military triumphs and historic achievement they had accomplished: establishing his personal rule from Macedonia to the Indus Valley. This far-reaching political vision came to a sudden end with Alexander's death a year later, when he was thirty-two years old. Even in his short lifetime, though, he set in motion cultural and economic forces that would transform Afro-Eurasia.

During this period two broad cultural movements came to link diverse populations across wide expanses of the Afro-Eurasian landmass: Hellenism and Buddhism. They constitute the central subject of this chapter. In both cases new empires and broad trade routes created the circuits through which—and beyond which—new cultures flowed. Imperial conquests and long-distance trade laid the foundations for widespread cultural systems that were far more enduring than the empires themselves. Alexander's armies forged only a fleeting political regime, though an enormous one, extending all the way from the Greek homeland to northern India, enabling a Greek-infused culture that we call Hellenism to stretch over the regions of conquests, and beyond. Although this movement did not eradicate local cultures, it provoked profound shifts in them. In the process, many of the world's regions, from China to Africa, became more integrated.

One region where Hellenism had a profound impact was South Asia, where it initiated a process of gradual political integration and religious change. The result: an equally powerful cultural movement, Buddhism, spread outward from its founding in South Asia (see Chapter 5) to become the world's most expansive religious system. It, too, had a political agent: the Mauryan dynasty of South Asia, indirectly influenced by Alexander's triumphs, whose powerful armies and legions of magistrates and monks spread the religion of the Buddha throughout South Asia, laying the groundwork for its expansion beyond. Dynastic empires, therefore, created the political latticework and institutions through which cultural influences grew and extended like vines spreading into regions far from their roots.

POLITICAL EXPANSION AND CULTURAL DIFFUSION

Alexander's bloody campaigns made for legendary drama. But from a long-term perspective, it was their cultural effects that were more dramatic. His armies transformed Afro-Eurasia. They promoted the establishment of culturally Greek-oriented communities across Afro-Eurasia. For at least five centuries after Alexander's short-lived rule, Hellenistic culture reverberated from Rome in the west all the way to the Ganges in the east.

Hellenism—a term derived from the Greeks' name for themselves, *Hellēnes*—was a new phenomenon. It involved the process by which the individual cultures of the Greek city-states gave way to a uniform culture stressing the common identity of all who embraced Greek ways. This culture had common features of language, art, architecture, drama, politics, philosophy, and much more, to which anyone anywhere in the Afro-Eurasian world could have access. By diffusing well beyond its homeland, it brought worlds together: its influence spread from Greece to all shores of the Mediterranean, into parts of sub-Saharan Africa, across Southwest Asia, and through the Iranian plateau into central and South Asia. It even had echoes in China. Like "Americanization" in the modern world, Hellenism took the attractive elements of one culture—its language, its music, its modes of dress and entertainments—and made these parts of a new global culture.

Alexander not only conquered but also laid the foundations for state systems and introduced institutional stability for trading systems. Instead of plundering, governments under his rule promoted trade. With their fear of attack reduced, cities could thrive. In effect, major commercial arteries replaced the early passageways that had carried small bands of traders. Political expansion facilitated all kinds of exchanges within the Afro-Eurasian world. One consequence was the emergence of the **Silk Road**, an artery that for nearly a thousand years was the primary commercial network linking East Asia and the Mediterranean world. This trade route extended over 5,000 miles and took its name from the huge quantities of precious silk that passed along it.

We cannot make sense of Alexander and the Hellenistic cultural movement or the spread of Buddhism without acknowledging the important ways in which distinct parts of the Afro-Eurasian world were already in contact. Alexander's conquests did not take arbitrary pathways, because earlier long-distance trade and cross-cultural exchanges had laid the trails for them. Similarly, Buddhism spread along preexisting trade routes. Slowly a new idea took hold: common cultures and shared commodities could integrate the Afro-Eurasian world. Merchants joined with monks and administrators in connecting widespread parts of Afro-Eurasia, enabling busy sea-lanes and the Silk Road to flourish. Merely a few centuries after the conquests of Alexander and Mauryan kings, the world looked very different from the realms their armies had traversed.

THE EMERGENCE OF A COSMOPOLITAN WORLD

The armed campaigns of a minor Greek people, the Macedonians, and their leader, Alexander the Great, began a drive for empire from the west. Alexander's novel use of new kinds of armed forces in a series of lightning attacks on the Persian Empire further undermined barriers that separated the Mediterranean world from the rest of Southwest Asia. The massive transfers of wealth and power resulting from his conquests transformed the Mediterranean into a more unified world of economic and cultural exchange. (See Map 6.1.)

Conquests of Alexander the Great

Historians and biographers have filled libraries with books about **Alexander the Great** (356–323 BCE), yet he still remains one of the most intriguing figures in world history. Alexander came from the frontier state of Macedonia to the north of Greece and commanded a highly mobile force armed with advanced military technologies that had developed during the incessant warfare among Greek city-states (see Chapter 5).

Under Alexander's predecessors—especially his father, Philip II—Macedonia had become a large ethnic and territorial state. Philip had unified Macedonia and then gone on to conquer neighboring states. Importantly, Macedonia boasted gold mines that could finance his new military technology and a disciplined, full-time army. The costs of heavily armored infantry in closely arrayed phalanxes, allied with large-scale shock cavalry formations, were supported not just from the mines' substantial income but also from the enormous profits of a slave trade that passed directly through Macedonia. By the early 330s BCE, Philip had crushed the Greek city-states to the south, including Athens. After Philip's assassination, his son Alexander used this new military machine in a series of daring attacks on the apparently invincible power of the Persian Empire and its king, Darius III.

Like many other successful conquerors, Alexander owed much of his success to a readiness to take risks. In his initial forays into Southwest Asia he outpaced and outflanked his adversaries, repeatedly taking them by surprise. Through these rapid assaults he brought under the rule of his Greek-speaking elites all the lands of the former Persian Empire, which extended from Egypt and the shores of the Mediterranean to the interior of what is now Afghanistan, and as far as the Indus River valley even farther to the east. (See Primary Source: Clash of Empires: The Battle of Gaugamela.)

The result of this violent rampage was hardly an empire, given that Alexander did not live long enough to establish institutions to hold the distant lands together. But his military campaigns continued a process that the Persians had already set in motion of smashing barriers that had separated peoples on the eastern and western ends of Afro-Eurasia. The conqueror saw himself as a new universal figure, a bridge connecting distant cultures. He demonstrated this vision in his choice of Roxana, the daughter of a Bactrian chief from central Asia, as a wife.

Battle of Issus. *Mosaic of the Battle of Issus between Alexander the Great of Macedon and Darius, the king of Persia (found as a wall decoration in a house at Pompeii in southern Italy). Alexander is the bareheaded figure to the far left; Darius is the figure to the right, gesturing with his right hand. The men represent two different types of warfare. On horseback, Alexander leads the cavalry-based shock forces of the Macedonian Greeks, while Darius directs his army from a chariot in the style of the great kings of Southwest Asia.*

Alexander's conquests exposed Syria, Palestine, Egypt, and Mesopotamia to the commodities of the Mediterranean, to money-based economies (both Philip and Alexander issued gold coins to pay for their invasions), and to cultural ideas associated with the Greek city-states. Alexander founded dozens of new cities named after himself, the most famous of which was Alexandria in Egypt.

One of Alexander's most significant acts involved seizing the accumulated wealth that the Persian kings stored in their immense palaces, especially at Persepolis, and dispersing it into the money economies of the Mediterranean city-states. This massive redistribution of wealth (like the post-Columbian exploitation of the Americas; see Chapters 12 and 13) fueled a widespread economic expansion in the Mediterranean.

Alexander's Successors and the Territorial Kingdoms

Alexander died in Babylon at age thirty-two, struck down by overconsumption of alcohol and other excesses that matched his larger-than-life personality and reflected the war culture of Macedonian warriors. His death in 323 BCE brought on the collapse of the regime he had personally held together. The conquered lands fragmented into large territories over which his generals squabbled for control.

Alexander's generals, his successors—Seleucus, Ptolemy, Antigonus, Lysimachus, and others—did not think of themselves

NORTH SEA
GERMANIC PEOPLES
BALTIC PEOPLES
CELTIC PEOPLES
CONQUESTS OF ALEXANDER THE GREAT, 323 BCE
GREEK CITY STATES
GREEK CITY STATES
GREEK CITY STATES
SCYTHIAN STEPPES
ARAL SEA
CASPIAN SEA
CAUCASIAN PEOPLES
BLACK SEA
Massilia
Rome
Pella
Byzantium
MACEDONIA
Troy
Ancyra
Gordium
Sardis
Delphi
Athens
Sparta
Syracuse
Carthage
CARTHAGE
RHODES
MEDITERRANEAN SEA
Antioch
Tigris R.
Euphrates R.
Gaugamela
Ecbatana
SELEUCID EMPIRE
Tyre
Seleucia
Babylon
Susa
Jerusalem
Alexandria
Memphis
Siwa Oasis
Persepolis
Persian Gulf
Merv
Aï Khanoum
Bukh
ARABS
PTOLEMAIC EMPIRE
Nile R.
RED SEA
ARABIAN PENINSULA
SAHARA DESERT
KUSH
SAHARAN PEOPLES
Niger R.
SUB-SAHARAN AFRICA
NOK
Congo R.
ATLANTIC OCEAN
BANTUS
IND
MADAGASCAR
KALAHARI DESERT
0 500 1000 Miles
0 500 1000 Kilometers

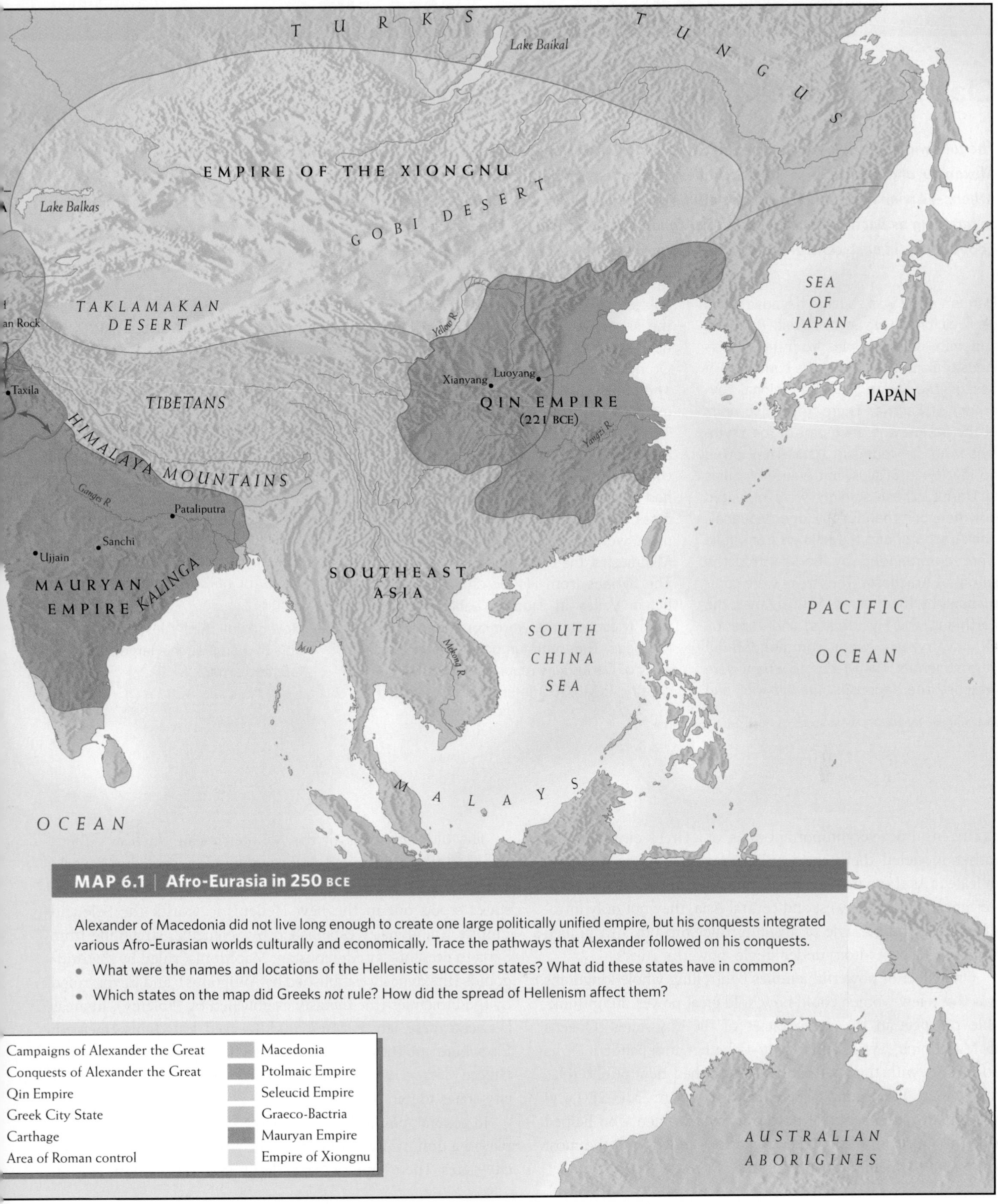

MAP 6.1 | Afro-Eurasia in 250 BCE

Alexander of Macedonia did not live long enough to create one large politically unified empire, but his conquests integrated various Afro-Eurasian worlds culturally and economically. Trace the pathways that Alexander followed on his conquests.

- What were the names and locations of the Hellenistic successor states? What did these states have in common?
- Which states on the map did Greeks *not* rule? How did the spread of Hellenism affect them?

PRIMARY SOURCE

Clash of Empires: The Battle of Gaugamela

The following passage, taken from the Greek historian Arrian, delineates the makeup of Darius's army as it prepared to confront Alexander and his forces in 331 BCE. In describing the size of the army—much larger than that of the largest Greek city-state, Athens—Arrian mentions the various ethnic groups of the Persian Empire that contributed troops. Contingents came from lands as far-flung as Bactria (near modern-day Afghanistan), Scythia (the broad area stretching from Ukraine to Kazakhstan), Armenia, Cappadocia (in east-central Turkey), and Caria (in southwestern Turkey), as well as from lands close to the Red Sea.

Darius's army was so large because it had been reinforced with Sogdians, with Bactrians, and with Indian peoples from the borderlands of Bactria, all under the command of Bessus, the satrap [i.e., the regional governor] of Bactria. There were also units of the Sakai—who were part of the Scythians who are found in Asia. They owed no loyalty to Bessus, but were still allies of Darius. These soldiers were mounted bowmen commanded by one Mauaces. The Arachotoi and the hillmen from India were commanded by Barsaentes, the satrap of Arachosia. The Areioi were commanded by their satrap, Satibarzanes; the Parthians, the Hyrcanians, and Tapeiroi, all cavalrymen, were commanded by Phrataphernes. The Medes, to whom were attached the Kadousioi, the Albanoi, and Sakesinai, were commanded by Atropates the Mede. All the units from the lands near the Red Sea were commanded by Orontobates, Ariobarzanes, and Orxines. The Ouxioi and Sousianoi were commanded by Oxathres, son of Aboultius. The men from Babylon, to whom were attached the Siracenioi and Carians, were commanded by Boupares—these Carians had been resettled in the empire by a mass transfer of their people. The Armenians were commanded by Orontes and Mithraustes; the Cappadocians, by Ariaces. The Syrians from Hollow Syria [i.e., the Bekáa Valley in modern Lebanon] and from Mesopotamia were commanded by Mazaeus. The total number of men in the army of Darius was reported to be 40,000 cavalry, 1,000,000 infantry, 200 scythed chariots [i.e., war chariots with blades mounted on both ends of the axle], and some war elephants—the Indians who came from this side of the Indus River had about fifteen of them.

QUESTIONS FOR ANALYSIS

- How many ethnic groups can you identify in this passage?
- What does Darius's command of so many ethnic loyalties tell us about the nature of the Persian Empire?
- How do you think Alexander was able to defeat such a large and talented army?

Source: Arrian, The History of Alexander *3.8; translated by Brent Shaw.*

as citizens, even very important ones, of a Greek city-state, but rather modeled themselves on the regional rulers they had defeated. As these men installed kingdoms in the eastern Mediterranean and Southwest and central Asia, they not only introduced Alexander's style of absolute rulership but also unified large blocks of territory under single, powerful rulers.

One effect of powerful families controlling whole kingdoms was that a few women could now hold great power, an unthinkable prospect in the democracies of the city-states. Queens in Macedonia, Syria, and Egypt—whether independent or as co-regents with their husbands—established new public roles for women. For example, Berenice of Egypt (c. 320–280 BCE) was the first in a series of powerful royal women who helped rule the kingdom of the Nile, a line that ended with the most famous of them all, Cleopatra, in the 30s BCE.

The old city-states of the Mediterranean, such as Athens and Corinth, still thrived, but now they functioned in a world dominated by much larger power blocs. Three large territorial states stood out in the new Hellenistic world: the Seleucid Empire (the dynasty established by Seleucus), stretching from Syria to present-day Afghanistan; Macedonia, ruled by the Antigonids (the dynasty established by Antigonus); and Egypt, ruled by the Ptolemies (the dynasty established by Ptolemy). In areas between these larger states, middle-sized kingdoms emerged. Elsewhere, polities banded together to survive; on mainland Greece, larger confederations forced previously independent city-states to join them.

In general, political states coalesced into larger units that displayed a uniformity unknown in the governments of the earlier city-states. Their impulse to standardization is evident not just in

Berenice. *Portrait head of Berenice, wife and consort of Ptolemy I, the first Macedonian king of Egypt after its conquest by Alexander the Great. Berenice was one of the women who, as queens of huge empires, wielded power and commanded wealth in their own right.*

politics but in every aspect of daily life. Unlike the early empires described in Chapter 4, which subordinated neighbors as colonies or tribute states, these kingdoms integrated neighboring peoples as fellow subjects. They believed that their cultural assets merited dissemination across broader geographic areas.

Competition in war remained an unceasing fact of life, but the wars among the kingdoms of Alexander's successors were broader in scope and more complex in organization than ever before. At the same time, their relative parity in strength meant a near-constant state of wars between the new kings that never achieved very much. After all, every large state had access to essentially the same advanced military technology: rulers went into the marketplace and acquired the highly trained soldiers, mercenaries, generals, and military advisers required to run their armies. After battles that killed tens of thousands, and severely injured and wounded hundreds of thousands more, the three major kingdoms—and even the minor ones—remained largely unchanged.

The great powers therefore settled into a centuries-long game of watching one another and balancing threats with alliances. What emerged was a fierce competition that dominated international relations, in which diplomacy and treaty making sometimes replaced actual fighting. This was an equilibrium reminiscent of the first age of international interstate relations in the second millennium BCE (see Chapter 3). Long periods of peace began to grace the intervals between the new kingdoms' violent and destructive wars.

Hellenistic Culture

Just as broad uniformity in politics and war trumped the small size and diversity of the old city-state, so the individual city-state cultures now gave way to a homogenized Hellenistic culture. Following the existing commercial networks, this uniform Greek culture spread rapidly through the entire Mediterranean basin and beyond. It was an alluring package, and ruling elites in all regions that encountered it fell under its powerful spell.

Hellenistic culture included philosophical and political thinking, secular disciplines ranging from history to biology, popular entertainment in theaters, competitive public games, and art for art's sake in all kinds of media. No other society at the time had such a complete package of high culture; hence its widespread appeal and diffusion. Archaeologists have found a Greek-style gymnasium and theater in the town of Aï Khanoum in modern Afghanistan, and adaptations of Greek sculptures made at the order of the Vedic king Sandrakottos (better known as Chandragupta; see below). We also know of Carthaginians in North Africa who became "Greek" philosophers, and Gallic and Berber chieftains, from the far west of France and North Africa, who had fine Greek-style drinking vessels buried with them.

COMMON LANGUAGE The core element of Hellenism was a common language, known as *koine* or "common" Greek. It replaced the city-states' numerous dialects with an everyday form that people anywhere could understand and quickly became the international language of its day.

Most peoples who came into contact with Hellenistic culture accepted the benefits that it afforded in expanding a network of communication and exchange. Peoples in Egypt, Judea, Syria, and Sicily, who all had distinct languages and cultures, could now communicate more easily with one another, and enjoy the same dramatic comedies and new forms of art and sculpture. Despite pockets of resistance, the Hellenizing movement was remarkably successful in spreading a shared Greek culture throughout the Mediterranean world and into Southwest Asia.

COSMOPOLITAN CITIES Much as Athens had been the model city of the age of the Greek city-state, Alexandria in Egypt became exemplary in the new age. Whereas fifth-century BCE Athens had zealously maintained an exclusive civic identity, Alexandria was a multiethnic city built from scratch by immigrants, who rapidly totaled half a million as they streamed in from all over the Mediterranean and Southwest Asia seeking new opportunities. Members of its dynamic population, representing dozens of Greek and non-Greek peoples, communicated in the common language that supplanted their original dialects. Soon a new urban culture emerged to meet the needs of so

PRIMARY SOURCE

The Cosmopolitan City of Alexandria

According to legend, Alexander selected the site of Alexandria and named the city after himself. As a result of his personal influence and its strategic location, Alexandria attracted an immense and diverse immigrant population from the entire Mediterranean world. In the following description, the Greek geographer Strabo—writing later during the time of the Roman Empire—emphasizes the city's function as an enormous entrepôt for trade and commerce across Afro-Eurasia. (Entrepôts are transshipment centers where seafaring vessels unload their cargoes and then send them elsewhere, by sea or by land.)

As for the Great Harbor at Alexandria, it is not only wonderfully well closed in and protected by artificial levees and by nature, it is also so deep that even the largest ships can be moored right at the stairs along its quayside. This Great Harbor is divided up into several minor harbors. . . . Even more exports are handled than imports. Anyone who might happen to be at Alexandria and at Dichaiarchia [the large Italian port on the Bay of Naples] would easily see for himself that the cargo ships sailing from here are bigger and more heavily laden. . . . The city itself is crisscrossed by streets that are wide enough for riding horses and driving chariots, and intersected by two main roads very much broader than the others. Its streets and avenues cut across each other at right angles. The city also boasts exceedingly beautiful public parks and its royal quarters take up a quarter, perhaps even a third of the whole city. . . . In earlier times, not even twenty ships would dare to go as far as the Arabian Gulf and manage to get a look outside its straits. But now large fleets of ships are sent out as far as India and to the furthest lands of the Ethiopians, from which the most valuable cargoes are brought to Egypt and then sent out again to other regions of the world. Double charges are collected on these shipments—both when they come in and when they go out—and the duties are especially high on luxury goods . . . for Alexandria alone does not just receive trade goods of this kind from all over the world, but it also furnishes supplies to the whole of the world outside.

Source: Strabo, Geography *17.1.6, 7, 8, 13; translated by Brent Shaw.*

QUESTIONS FOR ANALYSIS

- According to this passage, what features of the site made Alexandria well suited as a center for sea trade and a destination for immigrants?
- By Strabo's time, Alexandria was the second-largest city in the Mediterranean, surpassed only by Rome. How does this passage reflect the role of trade in its development?
- The passage indicates that Alexandria exported more than it imported. In what way does this indicate the city's role as a cosmopolitan entrepôt?

diverse a population. (See Primary Source: The Cosmopolitan City of Alexandria.)

The culture of the Hellenistic movement took the place of local art forms. In the previous city-state world, comic playwrights had written plays for their individual cities and local cultures, highlighting familiar languages, foibles, problems, and politicians. In contrast, entertainment in the more widely connected world had to appeal to bigger audiences and a greater variety of people. Plays were now staged in any city touched by Greek influence, and they were understood in any environment. Distinctive regional humor and local characters gave way to dramas populated by stock characters of standard sit-coms that any audience could identify with: the miser, the old crone, the jilted lover, the golden-hearted whore, the boastful soldier, the befuddled father, the cheated husband, the rebellious son. At performances throughout the Mediterranean basin, laughter would be just as loud in Syracuse on the island of Sicily as in Scythopolis in the Jordan Valley of Judea.

Ways of thinking changed to match this unified world. The new ideas reflected the fact that individuals were no longer citizens of a particular city (*polis*); instead they were the first "cosmopolitans," that is, citizens (*polites*) belonging to the whole world or "universe" (*kosmos*). The new political style was relentlessly cosmopolitan, radiating out of cities not just into nearby hinterlands but also to distant (and often rivalrous) cities.

Kingdoms and states by now had become so enormous that individuals could relate to political style only through the personality of kings or rulers and their families. Rulership was personality, and personality and style united large numbers of subjects. For example, Demetrius Poliorcetes, the ruler of Macedonia, wore high-platform shoes and heavy makeup, and he decorated his elaborate, flowing cape with images of the

The Theater at Syracuse. *The great theater in the city-state of Syracuse in Sicily was considerably refurbished and enlarged under the Hellenistic kings. It could seat 15,000 to 20,000 persons. Here the people of Syracuse attended plays written by playwrights who lived on the far side of their world, but whose works they could understand as if the characters were from their own neighborhood. In the common culture of the Hellenistic period, plays deliberately featured typecast characters and situations, thereby broadening their audience.*

sun, the stars, and the planets. In the presence of a powerful and solitary sun king like Demetrius, ordinary individuals felt small, inconsequential, and isolated. In response, an obsessive cult of the self arose, as Hellenistic religion and philosophy increasingly focused on the individual and his or her place in the larger world.

PHILOSOPHY AND RELIGION Growing concern with the individual self found expression in many ways. Consider the Athenian philosopher Diogenes (c. 412–323 BCE). He sought self-sufficiency and freedom from society's laws and customs, rejecting cultural norms as human-made inventions not in tune with nature and therefore false. He masturbated in public to "relieve himself" (it was, after all, a "natural need"), as well as to show disdain for what he considered to be the city's artificial sexual mores. He lived with no clothing in a wooden barrel in the public square, or *agora*, of Athens, with his female companion in her own barrel beside him. Other teachers also rejected the values of the city-state, although with more finesse and less contentiousness than Diogenes. Nonetheless, all recognized the need for a new orientation now that the world of the city-state, with its face-to-face relationships, had vanished.

The teacher Epicurus (c. 341–279 BCE), founder of a school in Athens that he called The Garden, likewise emphasized the self. He envisioned an ideal community centered on The Garden and stressed the importance of sensation, saying that pleasurable sensations were good and painful sensations were bad. Epicurus taught his students to pursue a life of contemplation and ask themselves, "What is the good life?" Known as Epicureans, his followers struggled to develop a sense of "not caring" (*ataraxia*) about worries—like threats to personal health or the challenges of coping with excessive wealth—in order to find peace of mind. In Epicurus's cult, none of the social statuses of the old city-state had more value than any other: women, slaves, and others in the underclass were equally welcome in The Garden as worshippers.

Epicurus and his new ideas acquired followers throughout the Mediterranean, but they were hardly alone. Unrestrained by the controls of any one city-state, other cults and schools of philosophy emerged. Of these, Stoicism was perhaps the most widespread. A man named Zeno (c. 334–262 BCE), from the island of Cyprus, initiated it, and other cosmopolitan figures across the Hellenistic world—from Babylon in Mesopotamia to Sinope on the Black Sea—developed its beliefs. Their mission was to help individuals understand their place in the cosmos. Zeno put forth his ideas in the Stoa Poikilē, a decorated and roofed colonnade that opened onto the central marketplace in Athens and gave his followers their name. For the Stoics, everything was grounded in nature itself, which they saw as the ultimate, permanent world. They regarded cities and kingdoms as human-made things, important but transient. Being in tune with nature and living a good life required understanding the rules of the natural order and being in control of one's passions, and thus indifferent to pleasure and pain.

Greek colonial control of other lands transformed long-established religions, and then re-exported them throughout the Mediterranean. The Greeks in Egypt drew on the indigenous cult of Osiris and his consort, Isis (formerly a vital element in

The Painted Stoa. *An artist's reconstruction of the Stoa Poikilē, or "Painted Stoa," in the city-state of Athens of the fourth century* BCE. *In the manner of a modern-day strip mall, this business and administrative center ran along the northern side of the agora, or central business and marketplace of the city. Philosophers and their students would hang out at the Stoa, lounging in the shaded areas under the colonnade as they debated the ideas flowing into Athens from all over the Hellenistic world. The painted wall decoration behind the columns (from which the Stoa received its name) depicts the Battle of Marathon.*

pharaonic temple rituals; see Chapter 2), to fashion a new narrative about Osiris's death and rebirth that represented personal salvation from death. Isis became a supreme goddess whose "excellencies" or "supreme virtues" encompassed the powers of dozens of other Mediterranean gods and goddesses. Believers experienced personal revelations and out-of-body experiences (*exstasis*, "ecstasy"). A ritual of dipping in water (*baptizein*, "to baptize") marked the transition of believers, "born again" into lives devoted to a "personal savior" who delivered an understanding of a new life by direct revelation. These new beliefs, like the worship of Isis, emphasized the spiritual concerns of humans as individuals, rather than the collective worries of towns or cities.

HELLENISM AND THE ELITES The appeal of this new, high Greek culture to elites in widely dispersed communities along the major communication routes became almost irresistible. Social elites sought to enhance their position by adopting Hellenistic culture, the only one that had standing above the level of local values. Syrian, Jewish, and Egyptian elites in the eastern Mediterranean adopted this attitude, as well as Roman, Carthaginian, and African elites in the western Mediterranean. Early Roman high culture was itself a form of Greek culture. Secular plays, philosophy, poetry, competitive games, art, and the writing of history followed, all based on Greek forms or local imitations. North African kings similarly decked themselves out in Greek dress, built Greek-style theaters, imported Greek philosophers, and wrote history. Now they, too, had "culture."

The Hellenistic influences penetrated deeply into sub-Saharan Africa, where the kingdom of Meroe (see Chapter 5), already influenced by pharaonic forms, now absorbed characteristics of Greek culture as well. It is not surprising that Greek influences were extensive at Meroe, because continuous interaction with the Egyptians also exposed its people to the world of the Mediterranean. Both Meroe and its rival, Axum, located in the Ethiopian highlands, used Greek stelae to boast of their military exploits. Moreover, the Greek historian Herodotus mentions that the citizens of Meroe "worshipped Zeus and Dionysus alone of the gods, holding them in great honor. There is an oracle of Zeus there, and they make war according to its pronouncements." The rulers of Meroe, understanding the advantages of the Greek language, employed Greek scribes to record their accomplishments on the walls of Greek-Egyptian temples. In this way, Meroe developed a remarkable mix of Greek, Egyptian, and African cultural and political elements.

Jewish Resistance to Hellenism

Not every community succumbed to the allure of Hellenism. The Jews in Judea, squeezed between Egypt and the superstates of Mesopotamia, offer a striking case of resistance to its universalizing forces. The Jews had a long schooling in surviving and resisting foreign rule, having been conquered by the Assyrians and the Babylonians (see Chapter 4). After the Persians defeated Babylon, a royal edict of restoration issued by the Persian monarch Cyrus led to the integration of Judea—now a province—into the Persian Empire. As the Jews who had once been forced to move to Babylon returned to Judea, the process of rebuilding Jerusalem began.

All this rebuilding of Jewish society occurred under the administration of another great Southwest Asian empire—that of the Persians, who tolerated local customs and beliefs. It took Alexander's lightning defeat of the Persian Empire in the 330s BCE to introduce a shocking new openness to the cultural innovations of the Mediterranean world.

While some parts of the Jewish ruling elite began to adopt Greek ways—to wear Greek clothing, to introduce the culture of the gymnasium with its cult of male nudity, to produce images of gods as art—others rejected the push. Those who spurned assimilation rebelled against the common elements of Hellenism—its language, music, gymnasia, nudity, public art, and secularism—as being deeply immoral and threatening to their beliefs. Ultimately, this resistance led to a full-scale armed revolt, headed up by the family of the Maccabees, in 167 BCE, provoked when Syrian overlords, the Seleucids, forbade the practice of Judaism and profaned the Jews' temple. Though the Maccabees succeeded in establishing an independent Jewish state centered on the temple in Jerusalem, they did not entirely overcome the impact of the new universal culture. By the beginning of the first century BCE, descendants of the Maccabees were calling themselves kings, minting coins with Greek legends, and presiding over a largely secular kingdom. Moreover, a huge Jewish society in the Hellenistic city of Alexandria in Egypt embraced the new culture. Scholars there produced a Bible in koine Greek, and historians (such as Jason of Cyrene) and philosophers (such as Philo of Alexandria) wrote in Greek, imitating Greek models.

The Hellenistic World and the Beginnings of the Roman Empire

Other cities were less reluctant than Jerusalem to follow Hellenistic ways. Early on, the Romans saw the Greek model as offering opportunities to increase their own importance. In the 330s and 320s BCE, when Alexander was uniting the eastern Mediterranean, a city-state on the Tiber River in central Italy took the first critical military actions to unify Italy; eventually it would bring together the rest of the Mediterranean and parts of Southwest Asia. Rather than beginning as a kingdom like Macedonia, Rome went from being a city-state to flourishing as a large territorial state. During this transformation it adopted significant elements of Hellenistic culture: Greek-style temples, elaborately decorated Greek-style pottery and paintings, and an alphabet based on that of the Greeks.

The Roman elites saw immersion in Greek culture and language as a way to appear to the rest of the world as "civilized." Yet the Roman elites did not accept this notion without resistance, worry, and debate. Consider the conservative Roman senator Cato the Elder (234–149 BCE), who struggled with the tensions that these changes involved. Although he was devoted to the Roman past, the Latin language, and the ideal of small-scale Roman peasant farmers and their families, he embraced many Hellenistic influences. He wrote a standard manual for the new economy of slave plantation agriculture (see below), invested in shipping and trading, learned Greek rhetoric (both speaking and writing the language), added the genre of history to Latin literature, and much more. Indeed, Cato blended an extreme devotion to tradition, manifested in his public statements, with bold innovations in most aspects of his daily life.

Carthage

In contrast to Rome, which assimilated Greek ways to elevate its status in the Mediterranean world, cities that were prosperous and already well integrated into the world economy welcomed Hellenistic culture because it facilitated communication and exchange. When these influences reached the great city of Carthage (in the area of present-day Tunisia), its residents adopted them without fanfare but with much success.

Not only did Carthaginian merchants trade with other Phoenician colonies in the western Mediterranean, but the city's ruling families took control over western Sicily and Sardinia. Remains of pottery and other materials demonstrate that the Carthaginians' trading contacts extended far beyond other Phoenician settlements to towns of the Etruscans and the Romans in Italy, to the Greek trading city of Massilia (modern Marseilles) in southern France, and to Athens in the eastern Mediterranean. In addition, the Carthaginians expanded their commercial interests into the Atlantic, moving north along the coast of Iberia and south along the coast of West Africa—which the commander Hanno explored and colonized. Pushing their influence even farther, they established a trading post at the island of Mogador more than 600 miles down the Atlantic coast of Africa.

Carthaginian culture (or Punic culture, to use the Romans' name for the people with whom they would soon be at war; see Chapter 7) took on important elements of Hellenistic culture. For example, some Carthaginians went to Athens to become

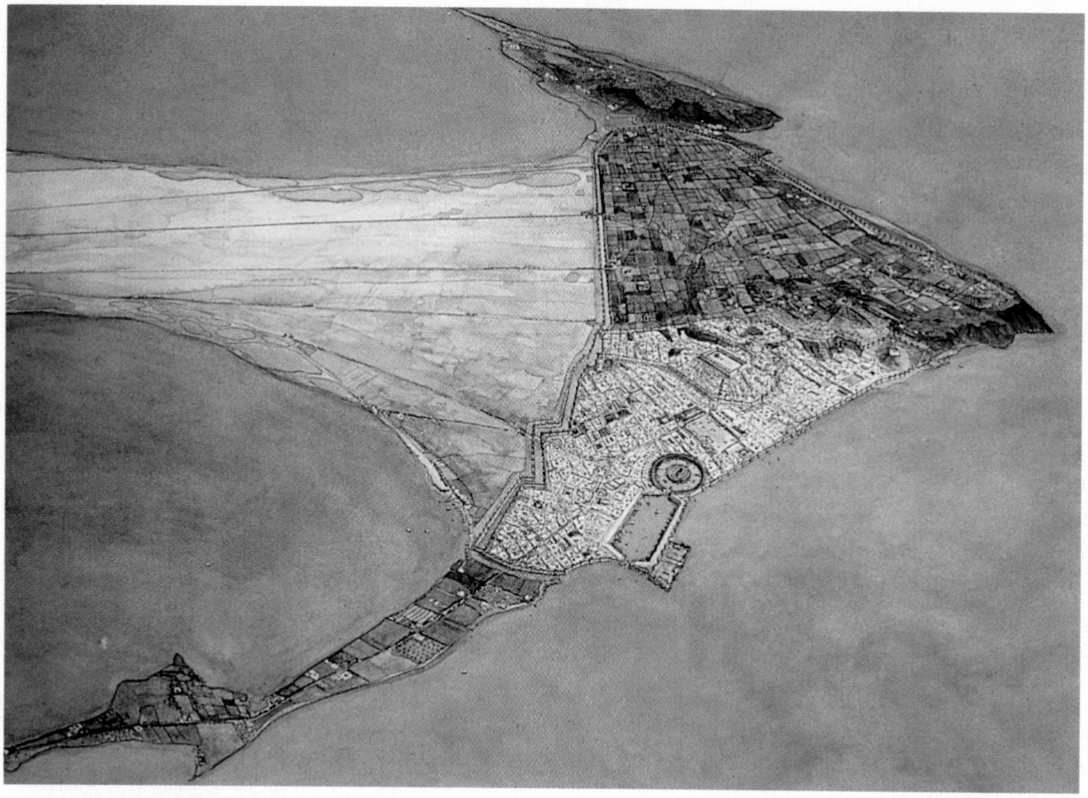

Aerial View of Punic Carthage. *Carthage was located on a promontory in the Bay of Tunis. In the lower foreground of this artist's reconstruction is a rectangular area of water and above it a circular-shaped one. These were the two major harbors of Carthage—the rectangular one was the commercial port and the circular one was the military harbor. Above these harbors are the main market square and the high central point, named the Byrsa. To the left is the twenty-mile-long wall that defended the city on its land side.*

philosophers. Also, the design of their sanctuaries, temples, and other public buildings reveals a marriage of styles: Greek-style pediments and columns mixed with Punic designs and measurements, and local North African motifs and structures added to the mix. The splendid jewelry that Phoenician women adorned themselves with reflected styles from Egypt, such as ornate necklaces of gold and earrings of lapis lazuli, but coinage and innovative ideas on political theory and warfare came from the Greek city-states.

Economic Changes: Plantation Slavery and Money-Based Economies

The main economic innovation that accompanied unification of the Mediterranean world was the use of large numbers of slaves in agricultural production—especially in Italy, Sicily, and North African regions close to Carthage. After all, Alexander's conquests and Rome's political rise had produced unprecedented wealth for a small elite. These men and women used their riches to acquire huge tracts of land and to purchase slaves (either kidnapped individuals or conquered peoples) on a scale and with a degree of managerial organization never seen before.

The slave plantations, wholly devoted to producing surplus crops for profit, became one of the engines driving a new Mediterranean economy. The estates created vast wealth for their owners—though at a heavy price to others, as reliance on slave labor now left the free peasants who used to work the fields with no option but to move into overcrowded cities, where employment was hard to find. The sudden importation of so many slaves to work in harsh conditions also had unanticipated outcomes. Between 135 and 70 BCE, authorities on Sicily and in southern Italy faced several massive slave uprisings, the largest and most dangerous of them led by the slave gladiator Spartacus in the late 70s. These were among the greatest slave wars in world history. The superior military force of the Roman state prevailed in all three wars, and the rebels were finally defeated. But the political repercussions of the wars had a fundamental impact in the subsequent political crises that transformed the Roman state.

The circulation of money reinforced the effects of forced labor. With more cash in the economy, wealthy landowners, urban elites, and merchants could more easily do business. The increasing use of Greek-style coins to pay for goods and services (in place of barter) promoted the importation of commodities such as wine from elsewhere in the Mediterranean. As coined money became even more available, it led to even more commercial exchanges. The forced transfer of precious metals to the Mediterranean from Southwest Asia by Alexander's conquests was so large that it actually caused the price of gold to fall. In the west, Carthage now began to mint its own coins—at first mainly in gold, but later in other metals. Rome moved to a money economy at the same time. By the 270s and 260s BCE, the Romans were issuing coins on a large scale under the pressures of their first war with Carthage (264–241 BCE). By the end of the third

Early Roman Coin. *Coins like this one were the standard means by which the state paid its expenditures; they later were widely used in ordinary commercial dealings. This coin features the prow of a ship with an "evil eye" decoration and armed beak for ramming other ships. The legend ROMA at the bottom signals that Rome is a state with the power and autonomy to have its own money.*

century, even borderland peoples such as the Gauls had begun to mint coins, imitating the galloping-horse images found on Macedonia's gold coins. So, too, did kingdoms in North Africa, where the coins of kings Massinissa and Syphax bore the same Macedonian royal imagery. By the end of this period, inhabitants of the entire Mediterranean basin and surrounding lands were using coins to buy and sell all manner of commodities.

To pay for the goods that satisfied their newly acquired tastes, Celtic chieftains in the regions encompassing modern-day France began selling their own people in the expanding slave markets of the Mediterranean. Slavery and slave trading also became central to the economies of the Iberian Peninsula—especially in the hinterlands of large river valleys like the Ebro, where local elites founded urban centers imitating Greek styles.

Roman Slaves. *One of the most profitable occupations for peoples living beyond the northwestern frontiers of the Roman Empire, in what was called Germania, was providing bodies for sale to Roman merchants. In this relief, we see chained German prisoners whose fate was to become slaves in the empire. This stone picture supported columns in front of the headquarters of the Roman fortress at Mainz-Kästrich.*

CONVERGING INFLUENCES IN CENTRAL AND SOUTH ASIA

The mountains of what we know today as Afghanistan are formidable but not impenetrable. The passes between the high plateau of Iran to the west and the towering ranges of Tibet to the east are pinched like the narrow neck of an hourglass—but they offer the shortest route through the mountains.

By crossing these passes, Alexander's armies expanded the routes between the eastern and western portions of Afro-Eurasia, fashioned a land bridge that has remained open to this day, and brought about massive political and cultural changes in central and South Asia. These routes created avenues for unprecedented cross-cultural exchange that eventually remapped entire regions. Conquerors moved from west to east (like Alexander), from east to west (like the later nomads from central Asia), and from north to south, through the mountains, into the rich plains of the Indus and Ganges river valleys. At the same time, South Asian trade and religious influences moved northward toward routes running west to east along what became known as the Silk Road.

Influences from the Mauryan Empire

Alexander's brief occupation of the Indus Valley (327–325 BCE) paved the way for one of the largest empires in South Asian history, quite possibly larger, though not more long lasting than the Mughal Empire, which came into existence in the sixteenth century. (See Chapter 11.) Before the arrival of Alexander's forces, South Asia had been a conglomerate of small warring states. Its political instability came to an abrupt halt when, in 321 BCE, an ambitious young man named Chandragupta Mori, inspired by Alexander, ascended the throne of the Magadha kingdom and launched a series of successful military expeditions in what is now northern India.

The Bolan Pass. *The formidable Bolan Pass separated India from the highland of Baluchistan. It was both an artery for transportation and a strategic military position.*

THE REGIME OF CHANDRAGUPTA Magadha, located on the lower Ganges plain, had great strategic advantages over other states. For one thing, it contained rich iron ores and fertile rice paddies. Moreover, on the northeast Deccan plateau ample woods supported herds of elephants, the mainstay of the potent Magadha mobile military forces. The Mori family, or Mauryans, did not start out as a distinguished ruling family, but economic strength and military skill elevated them over their rivals. Alexander's retreat created a momentary political vacuum that gave the Mauryans an opportunity to extend the dynasty's claims to northwestern regions of South Asia that had previously been controlled by the Persian Empire.

Chandragupta's Mauryan Empire constituted South Asia's first empire and served as a model for later Indian empire-builders. The contemporary Greek world knew this empire as "India," stretching from the Indus River eastward. Indeed, the Mauryan regime began to etch out the territorial contours of what would become, many centuries later, modern India.

Chandragupta (r. 321–297 BCE), though of lowly origins, probably from the Vaishya caste, grew up in the Punjab region observing Alexander and his forces and aspiring to be an equally powerful military and political leader. When Alexander withdrew his forces from northern India, Chandragupta inserted himself into the political vacuum created by the Greek withdrawal. After supplanting the Nanda monarchy in Magadha, he used his military resources to reach westward beyond the Ganges plain into "Five Rivers," the area around the upper stream of the Indus where four tributaries join it. Here he pushed up to the border with the Seleucid kingdom, the largest successor kingdom of Alexander's empire, based in Mesopotamia. Its king, Seleucus Nicator, fretted about his neighbor's challenge and invaded Mauryan territory—only to face Chandragupta's impregnable defenses. Soon thereafter, a treaty between the two powers gave a large portion of Afghanistan to the Mauryan Empire. Yet, even after being incorporated into the Mauryan Empire, this territory remained Greek-speaking for centuries, and some **garrison towns** developed into genuine Greek-style city-states. The treaty yielded a round of gift exchanges and diplomacy. One of the daughters of Seleucus went to the Mauryan court at Pataliputra, accompanied by a group of Greek women. Seleucus also sent an ambassador, Megasthenes, to Chandragupta's court. Megasthenes lived in South Asia for years, gathering observations on life there in a book titled *Indica*, from which much information about the Mauryan Empire has been learned. In return the Mauryans sent Seleucus many South Asian valuables, including hundreds of elephants, which the Greeks soon learned to use in battles.

Megasthenes's *Indica* depicted a well-ordered and highly stratified society divided into seven groups: philosophers, farmers, soldiers, herdsmen, artisans, magistrates, and councillors. People respected the boundaries between groups and honored rituals that reinforced their identities: members of different groups did not intermarry or even eat together. Megasthenes also noted the ways in which rulers integrated the region—for example, with extensive roads connecting major cities. These arteries were lined with trees and were provided with mileage stones. If these roads helped traders, they also enabled the ruler's troops to march around his dominions. According to Megasthenes, soldiers were a profession separate from the rest of the population. This surprised the Greek observer, who was more accustomed to the idea of the military closely integrated into civil society. Mauryan troops did not pretend to work when there was no war. They constituted a standing force of immense proportions, ready to obey their commander. This military force was huge, boasting cavalry divisions of mounted horses, war elephants, and scores of infantry. Most of the fighters evolved into a warrior caste of their own.

THE REGIME OF AŚOKA The Mauryan Empire reached its height during the reign of the third king, Aśoka (r. 268–231 BCE), Chandragupta's grandson. Aśoka lands comprised almost all of South Asia; only the southern tip of the peninsula remained outside his control. In 261 BCE, Aśoka waged the dynasty's last campaign: the conquest of Kalinga, a kingdom on the east coast of the South Asian peninsula by the Bay of Bengal. It was a gruesome and despicable operation. The Mauryan army triumphed, but at a high price: about 100,000 soldiers died in battle, many more perished in its aftermath, and some 150,000 people endured forcible relocation. Aśoka himself, when he learned of the devastation, was shocked and appalled at his own handiwork. Overcome by remorse, he vowed to cease inflicting pain on his people and pledged to follow the peaceful doctrines of Buddhism. While in this state of guilt, he issued a famous edict renouncing brutal ways.

Although his grandfather, Chandragupta, was a Jain, and his father an Ajavika, an ascetic sect that arose at the same time as Jainism and Buddhism, Aśoka was a faithful follower and patron of Buddhism. In fact, the Kalinga campaign deepened his devotion to Buddhism, which informed his edict on peace. (See Primary Source: Aśoka's Kalinga Edict.) Following the conquest of Kalinga, Aśoka claimed that henceforth his conquests would only be religious conquests. All over his domain he built **stupas**, or dome monuments, marking the burial sites of relics of the Buddha.

In his Kalinga edict Aśoka proclaimed his intention to rule according to the Indian concept of ***dhamma*** (a vernacular form of the Sanskrit word *dharma*), a term widely known in the empire and understood to mean tolerance of others, obedience to the natural order of things, and respect for all of earth's life forms. Dhamma, or dharma, was to apply to everyone, including the priestly Brahmans, Buddhists, members of other religious sects, and even Greeks. It became an all-encompassing moral code that all religious sects in South Asia accepted. With dhamma as a unifying symbol, Aśoka required all people, whatever their religious practices and cultural customs, to consider themselves his subjects, to respect him as their father, and to conform to his moral code—starting with the precept that people of different religions or sects should get along with each other. He also praised the benefits of agrarian progress and banned large-scale cattle sacrifice as detrimental to agriculture. Meanwhile,

Left: *Stupa at Sarnath; right: Lion Pillar.*

CURRENT TRENDS IN WORLD HISTORY

Building Roads: Early Highways for Communication, Trade, and Control

World historians have become fascinated with the history of roads because they provide insight into the way nations and empires functioned, and they allow us to study transnational forces that cross borders like trade, migration, and the spread of ideas. Indeed, reliable communications and regular trade were among the most important forces that enabled the great regions of the world to be linked. If rivers and seas offered natural waterways to meet this demand, roads were the man-made answer that enabled soldiers, traders, and travelers to cross great stretches of land or go around high mountain ranges more quickly. Road building required huge financial and labor resources. Only empires had the incentives and resources to build large-scale roads and the networks that fed into them; these roads would aid in the empire's rule over their domain and in gathering the revenue that came from transregional trade.

The Persian (Achaemenid) empire was the largest state in the Afro-Eurasian world, which necessitated efficient communications over vast distances and terrain that was varied and forbidding. The problems were overcome by the construction of many "great" or "royal" roads across the empire to connect the royal capitals where the king resided from time to time. One of the best-known great roads connected the far western coast at Sardis in Asia Minor (present-day Turkey) with the heartland of the Persian empire around Susa (southern Iran) in the east, more than 1,700 miles away. The great roads featured way stations, supply depots, relays of horses and other pack animals, and state personnel, all to enable the local governors or satraps of the emperor to dispatch men and missions to the King of Kings.

If the royal Persian road communications system was a marvel of its age, the roads of the Roman Empire are rightly renowned for their extent and quality of construction. At its height, the empire boasted about 250,000 miles of roads; about 55,000 miles were of the formal stone-paved quality that most impresses us today. They were formally called "public roads" and were open to travel by anyone. Provincial, city, and municipal officials were in charge of upkeep. High standards of construction were imposed for the main paved highways—land was leveled and roadbeds were built up of layers of hard-packed sand and gravel, with careful gradients that allowed for drainage. The top layer was paved with heavy flagstones that provided long life.

It is easy to underestimate the amount of hard work and engineering required to construct the roadbeds, drainage, and bridges. The work and materials required to construct one major road in Italy, the Via Appia (the "Appian Way"), would be several times that required to build the great pyramids in Egypt. The major roads were marked with milestones that informed the traveler about the distance from the point of departure or to the next major town (5,000 or so of these have survived). The English word "mile" comes from the Roman *milia passuum* (slightly less than our mile in length). The system of roads allowed the Roman state to maintain a public relay service called the *cursus publicus* along which imperial officials and units of the army, as well as information, could move efficiently and predictably from one part of the empire to another.

One of the singular achievements of the Qin dynasty was the building of a road

he warned the "forest people," the hunters and gatherers living beyond the reach of government, to avoid making trouble and to be wary of his anger.

To disseminate the ideals of dhamma, Aśoka regularly issued decrees, which he had chiseled on stone pillars and boulders in every corner of his domain, selecting locations where people were likely to congregate and where they could hear the words as read to them by the few who were literate. Occasionally he also issued edicts to explain his Buddhist faith. All were inscribed in local languages. While most of his decrees were in dialects of Sanskrit, those published in northwestern regions were in Greek or in Aramaic, the administrative script of old Persia. Aśoka's legal pronouncements helped legitimize the Greek-speaking population that had arrived with Alexander and now resided in Greek-style towns.

One of these pillars, known as the eleventh major rock edict, provides a sense of the ideology that Aśoka promoted and the meaning of the term, dhamma, that he wanted all to live by. "There is no gift comparable to the gift of dhamma, the praise of dhamma, the sharing of dhamma, the fellowship of dhamma. This is good behavior toward slaves and servants, obedience to mother and father, generosity towards friends, acquaintances and relatives, and towards brahmans, and abstention from killing human beings. . . . By doing so, there is gain in this world and in the next there is infinite merit." (Keay, *India*, pp. 94–95).

Aśoka hoped that dhamma would function as a unifying ideology, binding together an immense landmass and diverse people. The Mauryan Empire at its height encompassed 3,000,000 square miles, including all of what is today Pakistan, much of what is Afghanistan, the southeastern part of Iran, and the whole of the system to create sufficient infrastructure to unify its far-flung empire. The Qin network of roads connected the capital at Xianyang to every part of the country. The Qin used peasants, soldiers, and some slaves as forced laborers to build new roads and widen existing ones, so that troops could move quickly and easily to put down revolts anywhere in the empire. These roads were expanded under the succeeding Han dynasty to facilitate travel not only for the military, but also for merchants and commoners.

The road system of Qin and Han China paralleled the Persian royal roads and the Roman road network in scale and magnitude. By 100 BCE, many roads were wide, surfaced with stone, and lined with trees; steep mountains were traversed by stone-paved stairways with broad treads and low steps. By the end of the sixth century CE, the internal road network, not counting the Silk Road from the Han and Tang capital of Chang'an to Central Asia, had grown to encompass some 25,000 miles.

Similarly, the Inca (Tawantinsuyu) in the Americas were able to connect the far-flung parts of their large empire in the Andean highlands by the construction of a complex network of roads based on two great north-south trunk roads that ran parallel to the Pacific coast from modern Ecuador to modern Argentina. The backbone of the system, called the Qahpag Ñan or the Beautiful Road, was 3,700 miles long. The two big highways knit together an immense system of about 25,000 miles of roads. Traversing some of the most difficult mountainous terrain on the planet, the Inca roads had to vary considerably in size and design to function, punctuated with stone bridges and impressive hanging bridges constructed of rope that bridged deep canyons. This ingeniously engineered system of travel ways enabled the Inca—like other world empires—to control an empire of daunting geographic disparity.

Inca Road System. *This extraordinarily advanced transportation network provided the Incas access to over one million square miles of territory. Pictured here is the famous Inca Trail to Machu Picchu, which winds through the Andes Mountains.*

QUESTIONS FOR ANALYSIS

- What political and geographical motives did empires have to build road systems?
- What sort of people benefited most from these road systems? Who actually built the roads?

Explore Further

Liu, Xinru, *The Silk Road in World History* (2010).

Wood, Francis, *The Silk Road: Two Thousand Years in the Heart of Asia* (2004).

Indian subcontinent except for the lands at the southern tip. Its extraordinarily diverse geography consisted of jungles, mountains, deserts, and floodplains, and its equally disparate population of 50 to 60 million inhabitants was made up of pastoralists, farmers, forest dwellers, merchants, artisans, and religious leaders. No wonder that the early twentieth-century world historian H. G. Wells, in his 1922 *Short History of the World*, called Aśoka "one of the greatest monarchs the world has ever seen," and later historians have marveled at his achievements. Yet his empire, which had an elaborate administrative structure that stretched all the way from the capital at Pataliputra into small villages, did not last long after Aśoka's death in 231 BCE.

The works of art during his reign celebrated the copious cultural and economic exchanges among Greeks, Persians, and Indians. The most famous of these works was the edict pillar that Aśoka erected in Sarnath at the Deer Garden, where the Buddha gave his first sermon. Atop the pillar, four lions sat facing four directions. Beneath the four lions were four wheels representing universal rule; they were separated by a bull, a horse, elephants, and another lion. The majestic images of lions, animals not found in the Ganges plain, represented an Indian version of the Persian royal symbol. Its artistic technique displayed Greek influence in a vivid, animated style.

The Seleucid Empire and Greek Influences

Alexander's military thrust into Asia reached as far as the Punjab. There he defeated several rulers of Gandhara in 326 BCE. In the course of this campaign he planted many garrison

PRIMARY SOURCE

Aśoka's Kalinga Edict

After the Kalinga war, Aśoka issued an edict to express his regret at the miseries it had caused his people. From this edict, we can tell that Aśoka ruled a country of many different cultures and religions.

Beloved of the Gods, is that those who dwell there, whether brahmans, *śramanas*, or those of other sects, or householders who show obedience to their superiors, obedience to mother and father, obedience to their teachers and behave well and devotedly towards their friends, acquaintances, colleagues, relatives, slaves, and servants suffer violence, murder, and separation from their loved ones. Even those who are fortunate to have escaped, and whose love is undiminished [by the brutalizing effect of war], suffer from the misfortunes of their friends, acquaintances, colleagues, and relatives. This participation of all men in suffering weighs heavily on the mind of the Beloved of the Gods. Except among the Greeks, there is no land where the religious orders of brahmans and *śramanas* are not to be found, and there is no land anywhere where men do not support one sect or another. Today if a hundredth or a thousandth part of those people who were killed or died or were deported when Kalinga was annexed were to suffer similarly, it would weigh heavily on the mind of the Beloved of the Gods.

The Beloved of the Gods believes that one who does wrong should be forgiven as far as it is possible to forgive him. And the Beloved of the Gods conciliates the forest tribes of his empire, but he warns them that he has power even in his remorse, and he asks them to repent, lest they be killed. For the Beloved of the Gods wishes that all beings should be unharmed, self-controlled, calm in mind, and gentle.

The Beloved of the Gods considers victory by *Dhamma* to be the foremost victory. And moreover the Beloved of the Gods has gained this victory on all his frontiers to a distance of six hundred *yojanas* [i.e., about 1,500 miles], where reigns the Greek king named Antiochus, and beyond the realm of that Antiochus in the lands of the four kings named Ptolemy, Antigonus, Magas, and Alexander; and in the south over the Colas and Pāndyas as far as Ceylon. Likewise here in the imperial territories among the Greeks and the Kambojas, Nābhakas and Nābhapanktis, Bhojas and Pitinikas, Andhras and Pārindas, everywhere the people follow the Beloved of the Gods' instructions in *Dhamma*. Even where the envoys of the Beloved of the Gods have not gone, people hear of his conduct according to *Dhamma*, his precepts and his instruction in *Dhamma*, and they follow *Dhamma* and will continue to follow it.

What is obtained by this is victory everywhere, and everywhere victory is pleasant. This pleasure has been obtained through victory by *Dhamma*—yet it is but a slight pleasure, for the Beloved of the Gods only looks upon that as important in its results which pertains to the next world.

This inscription of *Dhamma* has been engraved so that any sons or great grandsons that I may have should not think of gaining new conquests, and in whatever victories they may gain should be satisfied with patience and light punishment. They should only consider conquest by *Dhamma* to be a true conquest, and delight in *Dhamma* should be their whole delight, for this is of value in both this world and the next.

QUESTIONS FOR ANALYSIS

- Why would Aśoka refer to himself as "the Beloved of the Gods"? Whose gods might he be referring to?
- Aśoka was a follower of Buddhism, which held that mortals passed through cycles of life, death, and rebirth. What parts of this passage reflect that belief?
- Aśoka promises to rule his people with *dhamma* (*dharma* in Sanskrit). Whereas Buddhist doctrine considers *dharma* to encompass religious teachings that guided the Buddha's followers, Aśoka's *dhamma* refers to a general moral standard that applied to all religious and ethnic communities—Buddhists or not. Why do you suppose he emphasizes this broader meaning?

Source: Romila Thapar, Aśoka and the Decline of the Maurya, *2nd ed. (1973), 255–57.*

towns—especially in eastern Iran, northern Afghanistan, and the Punjab, where he needed to protect his easternmost territorial acquisition. These towns were originally stations for soldiers, but they soon became centers of Hellenistic culture. Many of these outposts, such as those at Ghazni, Kandahar, Kapisi, and Bactra (modern Balkh), displayed the characteristic features of a Greek polis: a colonnaded main street lined by temples to patron gods or goddesses, a theater, a gymnasium for education, an administrative center, a marketplace. After Alexander's death, Seleucus Nicator (358–281 BCE), ruler of the Hellenistic successor state in this area, built more of these Greek garrison towns. Seleucus, who also controlled Mesopotamia, Syria, and Persia,

Elephant Cavalry. *As shown by this terra-cotta statuette from 200 BCE, elephant cavalry was an important component of the Greek military. In their exchanges with India, Hellenistic states requested numerous elephants for their armies.*

named sixteen cities "Antioch" after his father, five "Laodicea" after his mother, nine "Seleucia" after himself, three "Apamea" after his wife Apama, and one "Stratonicea" after another wife.

Most of the Greek invaders integrated themselves into the local societies. Once the soldiers realized they would be spending their lives far from their homeland, they married local women and started families. Bringing their own customs to the local populations, they established institutions familiar to them from the polis. Greek was the official language; but because local women used their own languages in daily life, subsequent generations were bilingual. For centuries the traditional Greek institutions—especially Greek language and writing—survived many political changes and much cultural assimilation, providing a common basis of engagement in a long zone stretching from the Mediterranean to South Asia.

The Kingdom of Bactria and the Yavana Kings

Hellenistic influences were even more pronounced in the Seleucid successor regimes of central Asia of the late third century BCE. The Seleucid state had taken over the entirety of the former Persian empire, including its central Asian and South Asian territory. The Hellenistic kingdom of Bactria broke away from the Seleucids around 200 BCE to establish a strong state that included the Gandhara region in modern Pakistan. As Mauryan power receded from the northwestern part of India, the Bactrian rulers extended their conquests into this area. Because the cities that the Bactrian Greeks founded included many Indian residents, they have been called "Indo-Greek." Those in Gandhara incorporated familiar features of the Greek polis, but inhabitants still revered Indian patron gods and goddesses.

Hellenistic Bactria served as a bridge between South Asia and the Greek world of the Mediterranean. Among the goods that the Bactrians sent west were elephants, which were vital to the Greek armies there. Not only did the Bactrian Greeks revive the cities in India left by Alexander but they also founded new Hellenistic cities in the Gandhara region. The Greek king Demetrius, who invaded India around 200 BCE, entrusted the extension of his empire in the northern region of India to his generals, many of whom became independent rulers after his death. Sanskrit literature refers to these Greek rulers as the Yavana kings—a word derived from "Ionia," a region whose name applied to all those who spoke Greek or came from the Mediterranean.

Remains of a Greek garrison town, unearthed under the site of the ancient city of Samarkand in Uzbekistan, attest to the strength of these Hellenistic influences. In the 1960s, archaeologists at Aï Khanoum on the Oxus River (now the Amu) in present-day Afghanistan were stunned to find the ruins of nearly an entire Greek city. Miraculously, Aï Khanoum had avoided the devastations that befell so many other Hellenistic cities in this region. It was clearly an administrative center, if not the capital city, of the Bactrian state. The Greek-style architecture and inscriptions indicate that the original residents were soldiers from Greece. Following the typical pattern, they married local women and established the basic institutions of a Greek polis.

Aï Khanoum's characteristic Greek structures included a palace complex, a gymnasium, a theater, an arsenal, several temples, and elite residences. Featuring marble columns with Corinthian capitals, the palace contained an administrative section, storage rooms, and a library. A main road divided the city into lower and higher parts, with the main religious buildings located in the lower city. Though far from Greece, the elite Greek residents read poetry and philosophy and staged Greek dramas in the theater. Grape cultivation supported a wine festival associated with the god Dionysus. The remains of various statues indicate that the residents not only revered the Greek deity Athena and the demigod Heracles but also paid homage to the Zoroastrian religion.

Perhaps the most adept ruler at mingling Greek and Indian influences was Menander, the best-known Yavana city-state king

Three Coins. Top: *Wearing an elephant cap, Demetrius of Bactria titled himself the king of Indians as well as Greeks. On the other side of the coin is Hercules.* Middle: *The king Menander is remembered by Buddhists for his curiosity about their theology. His image appears on one side of the coin with a Greek legend of his name and title. On the other side, Athena is surrounded by Kharoshthi script, an Indian type of writing.* Bottom: *The Scythian king Maues used Greek to assert his position as "King of Kings" on one side of his coin. On the other side, the goddess Nike is surrounded by Kharoshthi letters.*

of the mid-second century BCE. Using images and legends on coins to promote both traditions among his subjects, Menander claimed legitimacy as an Indian ruler who also cultivated Greek cultural forms. The face of his coins bore his regal image surrounded by the Greek words *Basileus Sōtēr Menandros* ("King, Savior, Menander"). The reverse side featured the Greek goddess Athena and the king's title in the local Pakrit language. These legacies persisted long after the Hellenistic regimes collapsed, because they remained essential to communication and trade around the rim of the Indian Ocean.

Nomadic Influences of Parthians and Kushans

The political domination that Alexander's successor kingdoms and some smaller independent kingdoms enjoyed in much of central and Southwest Asia was, nevertheless, short-lived. Nomadic peoples who had always been powerful in this region quickly reasserted themselves and their way of life; yet in doing so they assimilated many Hellenistic influences. (See Map 6.2.) First to feel the impact of the nomads was the Seleucid state in Iran. Having lost control of Bactria, it now came under relentless pressure from nomadic peoples living on the steppes to the north. The first to prey on them were the horse-riding Parthians, who wiped out the Greek kingdoms in Iran. The Parthians then extended their power all the way to the Mediterranean, where they would ultimately face the forces of the Roman Empire.

THE PARTHIANS The Parthian people had moved south from present-day Turkmenistan and settled in the region comprising the modern states of Iraq and Iran. Unlike the Persians before them, the Parthians had a social order founded on nomadic pastoralism and a war capability based on technical advances in mounted horseback warfare. Reliance on horses made their style of fighting highly mobile and ideal for warfare on arid plains and deserts. They perfected the so-called Parthian shot: the arrow shot from a bow with great accuracy at long distance and from horseback at a gallop. On the flat, open plains of Iran and Iraq, the Parthians had a decisive advantage over slow-moving, cumbersome mass infantry formations that had been developed for war in the Mediterranean. Eventually the expansionist states of Parthia and Rome became archenemies: they confronted each other in Mesopotamia for nearly four centuries. In spite of the conflicts between Romans and Parthians, Hellenistic caravan cities on the Roman Empire's eastern frontier continued to trade with the east, and Greek remained the essential language for commercial activities from the eastern shore of the Mediterranean all the way to Afghanistan.

In the second century BCE, a vast nomadic tribal confederacy called the Xiongnu became dominant in the East Asian steppe lands. While consolidating their power, the Xiongnu drove many other pastoral groups out of their homelands. Meanwhile, the Parthians, who had supplanted the Greek Seleucids in Iran, entered the Indus Valley from the northwest, through the mountain passes of Baluchistan.

THE KUSHANS Even more dynamic and powerful than the Xiongnu were the Yuezhi-Kushans, who appeared as a political force around 50 CE. Led by their chief, the Yuezhi unified the region's tribes and established the Kushan dynasty in Afghanistan and the Indus River basin. The Kushans' empire embraced a

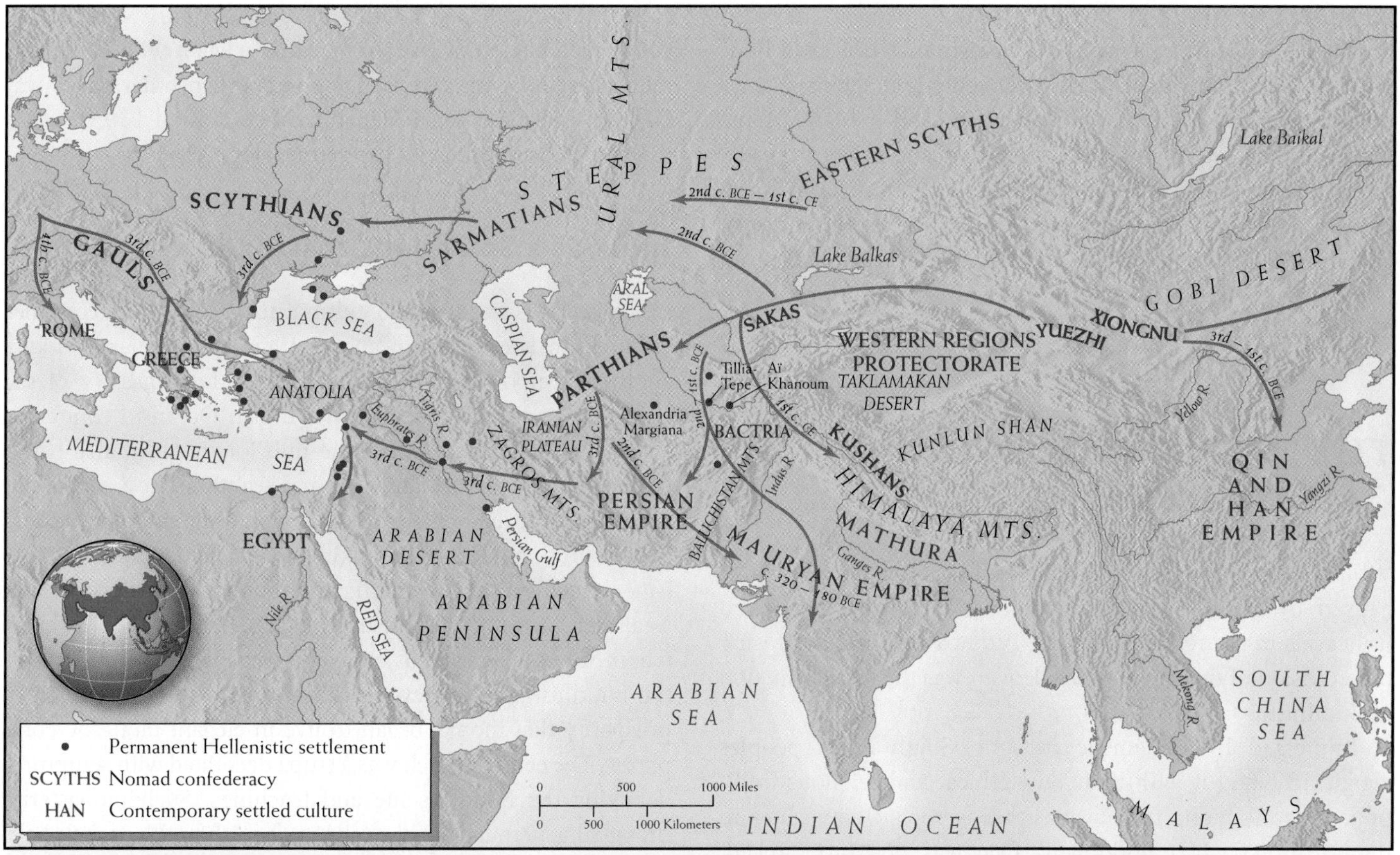

MAP 6.2 | Nomadic Invasions, 350 BCE–100 CE

Interaction between nomadic and settled societies was a major engine of change in Afro-Eurasia in the first millennium BCE.

- According to the map, where did most of the nomadic and settled societies come from? What were their two primary destinations?
- How did this interaction shape cross-cultural processes (the spread and diffusion of goods, peoples, and ideas)?

large and diverse territory and was critical in the formation of the Silk Road.

Like the Parthians, the Kushans had been an illiterate people, but they adopted Greek as their official language. The face of the second Kushan king to rule South Asia, Wima Kadphises, is featured on a gold coin surrounded by Greek legends. The reverse side shows the Hindu god Shiva with his cow. Until the end of the Kushan Empire in the early third century CE, Greek letters continued to appear on Kushan coins. Their rulers kept alive the influence of Hellenism in an area strategically located on the Silk Road, even though by this time few fluent speakers of Greek were left in the population. Mediterranean traders arriving in the Kushan markets to purchase silks from China, as well as Indian gemstones and spices, conducted their transactions in Greek. The coins they used—struck to Roman weight standards (themselves derived from Greek coinage) and inscribed in Greek—served their needs perfectly.

Although these diverse nomadic groups did not undermine local cultural traditions or the Hellenistic heritage, they introduced a powerful new ingredient: the culture of the warhorse. The proud Kushans carried their horse-riding skills into India and, in spite of the hot climate, continued to wear their trademark cone-shaped leather hats, knee-length robes, trousers, and boots. Since the time of the Vedic invaders (see Chapter 3), horses had been valued imports into the region—and under the Kushans they became the most prestigious status symbol of the ruling elite. At the same time, the Kushans began consuming exotic goods that arrived from as far east as China and as far west as the Mediterranean. Their rule also stabilized the trading routes through central Asia that stretched from the steppes in the east to the Parthian Empire in the west. This would become a major segment of the Silk Road.

The Kushans also courted the local population by patronizing local religious cults. In Bactria, where they encountered the shrines of many different gods, the Kushan kings had their coins cast with images of various deities. They also donated generously to shrines of Zoroastrian, Vedic, and Buddhist cults. Around Kushan political centers, religious shrines mushroomed and sculptural works reached a high artistic level. Kushan kings also built royal dynastic shrines, beside which they placed statues of themselves as patrons of the local deities. Governors and generals followed their example of patronizing local religions, as did traders, artisans, and other city-dwellers. Wealth flowed into religious institutions, especially Buddhist monasteries.

THE TRANSFORMATION OF BUDDHISM

While South Asia was undergoing political and social change caused by these encroaching nomads, it also experienced upheavals in the religious sphere. Perhaps the most surprising repercussion of the spread of Hellenism was the transformation of Buddhism.

Impressed by Hellenistic thought, South Asian peoples sought to blend it with their own ethical and religious traditions. Begun among the Yavana (that is, Greek) city-states in the northwest, where Buddhism's sway was most pronounced, Buddhism rapidly spread to other regions that were experiencing the same currents of change. (See Primary Source: Sâgala: The City of the Gods.) For example, the Yavana king Menander went beyond claiming that the Buddha was an inspired ethical philosopher. Instead, he held that the Buddha was a god. He reached this conclusion by a discussion with a Buddhist sage named Nagasena. Menander asked many questions about Buddhist ideas and beliefs and Nagasena explained away all his doubts in a conversation recorded in a Buddhist text called *Milindapunha* (*Questions of King Milinda*). Nonetheless, the transformation of Buddhism into a religion with Hellenistic influences and with wide-ranging support in other states was far from complete when Menander died around 130 BCE. (See Chapter 8 for Buddhism's further development.)

India as a Spiritual Crossroads

Hellenism was not the sole cultural movement to affect other cultures. In addition to nomad settlers, new seafarers added another layer of cultural change. The latter's mastery of the monsoon trade winds opened the Indian Ocean to commerce (see below) and made India the hub for long-distance ocean traders and travelers. Many land and sea routes now seemed to converge on India, rendering the region a melting pot of ideas and institutions. From the mixing of the influences of Hellenism, nomadism, and seafaring a profoundly transformed and wealthier form of Buddhism emerged. Under the Kushans, whom we noted earlier as energetic patrons of many religions, the Buddhist *sangha* grew so rich through India's commercial prosperity that monks began to live in elegant monastic complexes. The center of each was a stupa decorated with sculptures depicting the Buddha's life and teachings. Such monasteries provided generously for the monks, furnishing them with halls where they gathered and worshipped and rooms where they meditated and slept. And Buddhist monasteries were also open to the public as places for worship.

The New Buddhism: The Mahayana School

The mixing of new ways—nomadic, Hellenistic, Persian, and Mesopotamian—with traditional Buddhism produced a spectacular spiritual and religious synthesis: **Mahayana Buddhism**.

Buddhist Cave Temple at Ajanta. *Buddhists excavated cave temples along the trade routes between ports on the west coast of India and places inland. Paintings and sculptures from Ajanta became the models of Buddhist art in central Asia and China.*

PRIMARY SOURCE

Sâgala: The City of the Gods

The Indo-Greek king Menander was a famous patron of Buddhism, as described in the* Questions of King Milinda. *The book, written in Pāli, a northwestern dialect of Sanskrit, begins with a description of the kingdom of Milinda (Menander) located in the country of Yonakas, the Pāli name for Greeks. This kingdom, according to the following passage, is a center of prosperous trade and people of many creeds, with a city called Sâgala whose glory rivals that of "the city of the gods."

Thus hath it been handed down by tradition—There is in the country of the Yonakas a great centre of trade, a city that is called Sâgala, situated in a delightful country well watered and hilly, abounding in parks and gardens and groves and lakes and tanks, a paradise of rivers and mountains and woods. Wise architects have laid it out, and its people know of no oppression, since all their enemies and adversaries have been put down. Brave is its defence, with many and various strong towers and ramparts, with superb gates and entrance archways; and with the royal citadel in its midst, white walled and deeply moated. Well laid out are its streets, squares, cross roads, and market places. Well displayed are the innumerable sorts of costly merchandise with which its shops are filled. It is richly adorned with hundreds of almshalls of various kinds; and splendid with hundreds of thousands of magnificent mansions, which rise aloft like the mountain peaks of the Himâlayas. Its streets are filled with elephants, horses, carriages, and foot-passengers, frequented by groups of handsome men and beautiful women, and crowded by men of all sorts and conditions, Brahmans, nobles, artificers, and servants. They resound with cries of welcome to the teachers of every creed, and the city is the resort of the leading men of each of the differing sects. Shops are there for the sale of Benares muslin, of Kotumbara stuffs and of other cloths of various kinds; and sweet odours are exhaled from the bazaars, where all sorts of flowers and perfumes are tastefully set out. Jewels are there in plenty, such as men's hearts desire, and guilds of traders in all sorts of finery display their goods in the bazaars that face all quarters of the sky. So full is the city of money, and of gold and silver ware, of copper and stone ware, that it is a very mine of dazzling treasures. And there is laid up there much store of property and corn and things of value in warehouses—foods and drinks of every sort, syrups and sweetmeats of every kind. In wealth it rivals Uttara-kuru, and in glory it is as Âlakamandâ, the city of the gods.

QUESTIONS FOR ANALYSIS

- The city Sâgala is in the country of the Yonakas, that of the Greeks. Judging from the references to elephants, horses, and the Himalayas, where approximately would it have been located?
- What kinds of people lived there?
- Why do you suppose Buddhist ideas found easy acceptance there?

Source: The Questions of King Milinda, *translated by T. W. Rhys Davis (1890; reprint, Delhi: Motilal Banarsidass, 1975), 2–3.*

For at least a hundred years, Buddhist scholars had debated whether the Buddha was a god or a wise human being. The Mahayana Buddhists resolved this dispute in the first two centuries of the Common Era with a ringing affirmation: the Buddha was indeed a deity. Yet Mahayana Buddhism was worldly and accommodating, a spiritual pluralism that positioned Indian believers as a cosmopolitan people—welcoming contacts with peoples from other parts of Afro-Eurasia and laying the spiritual foundations for a region that had become a crossroads of world cultures.

As Buddhism adapted to external impulses, Mahayana Buddhism appealed especially to foreigners and immigrants who traded or settled in India. It made the Buddha easier to understand. The Buddha's preaching had stressed life's suffering and the renunciation of desire to end suffering and achieve *nirvana*. This was a tough road to a better life. As we saw in Chapter 5, those who did not believe in reincarnation found it difficult to understand the appeal of *nirvana*. Newcomers such as migrants or traders saw no attraction in a belief that life consisted of painful cycles of birth, growth, death, and rebirth. This sharp dichotomy between a real world of hardship and the Buddha's abstract one of *nirvana* gave way to the Mahayana Buddhists' vision that **bodhisattvas**, enlightened demigods, ready to reach *nirvana*, delayed doing so to help others attain it. They prepared "Buddha-lands"—spiritual halfway points—to welcome deceased devotees

ANALYZING GLOBAL DEVELOPMENTS

The Cosmopolitan World of the *Periplus Maris Erythraei*

Periplus Maris Erythraei, or *Periplus of the Red Sea,* was a first-century BCE handbook that offered advice to merchants traveling and trading along two major, connected routes: one that scaled the African coast from the Red Sea ports of Egypt and the other that travelled eastward to India in the Arabian Sea. A shrewd trader, keen observer, and experienced navigator, the author catalogued the navigable routes, listed marketable goods at each port, and even recorded anthropological insights on the inhabitants of the far-flung regions he encountered.

The author's voyage began in the Red Sea port of Berenice and moved southward to the tribal countries of modern-day Sudan and Eritrea. To the east, he found the placid waters of the Gulf of Aden and the frankincense of the Arabian coast. Though Indian products like rice and ghee were widely sold in Arabian market towns, the Indian port of Barygaza remained the most sought-after port of the time, despite its rugged coast, uneven sea bottom, and tidal waves. An important node in the Afro-Eurasian trade network, Barygaza proved to be a curious mix of the exotic and the familiar in the author's eyes, with its vendors hawking everything from Chinese silks to old Greek coins. Pragmatic in tone, the *Periplus* and its display of economic opportunity cannot help but dazzle even modern readers. The following table gives an overview of a few important ports in the *Periplus*, as well as a taste of the ancient world.

QUESTIONS FOR ANALYSIS

- What do the author's highly specific descriptions of imports and exports suggest about the types of goods that were traded along this route? What might these commodities imply about the socio-economic status of the Greek trader and the status of the consumers of the goods that moved along these routes?
- What are some apparent patterns or commonalities in the goods that these market towns import? In the goods that they export? What goods exported at some of these ports are imported at other ports listed in the *PME*'s itinerary? What does that suggest about the nature of trade along this overseas route?
- What other specific types of evidence might help you interpret the nature of the trade that took place on these overseas routes? In what ways might that evidence complete, or even add complexity to, the snapshot of trade offered by a periplus such as this one for Red Sea trade?

	Port	Exports	Imports	Gifts for Rulers
Southern Arabia	Muza (Sect. 24)	myrrh, white marble, stacte (sweet spice for ancient Hebrew incense)	purple cloth; Arab-sleeved clothing, with no adornment, with checks, or interwove with gold thread; herbs cyperus and saffron; blankets, with traditional local adornment or none; girdles with shaded stripes; ungent; money, considerable amount; wine; grain	horses, pack mules, expensive clothing, goldware, embossed silverware, copperware

Source: Casson, Lionel. The Periplus Maris Erythraei: Text with Introduction, Translation, and Commentary *(1989).*

not yet ready to release desires and to enter *nirvana*. In this fashion the universe of the afterlife in Mahayana Buddhism was colorful and pleasant, presenting an array of alternatives to the harsh real existence of worldly living.

Mahayana ("Great Vehicle") Buddhism enabled all individuals—the poor and powerless as well as the rich and powerful—to move from a life of suffering into a happy existence. The new Buddhist brokers—the bodhisattvas—were effective instruments for helping all classes find their way to heaven. One of these bodhisattvas, Avalokiteshvara, proclaimed his willingness to stay in this world to guide people out of trouble—especially those who traveled in caravans and had the misfortune of running into murderous robbers, or those who had to navigate unwieldy ships through violent storms. As Avalokiteshvara guided and protected the living more than he appeased the dead, lay followers, especially traveling merchants, invoked him constantly and spread his cult along trade routes.

Just as Buddhism absorbed outside influences and became more appealing, it also inspired a new genre of literature dealing with the Buddha and the bodhisattvas. Buddhist texts written in Sanskrit disseminated the life of the Buddha and his message far and wide, reaching far corners of Asia. Aśvaghosa

	Port	Exports	Imports	Gifts for Rulers
East Africa	Opone (Sect. 13)	cinnamon, frankincense, cassia (Chinese cinnamon), better-quality slaves, tortoise shell	grain, rice, ghee, sesame oil, *monache* and *sagmatogene* (India cotton cloth), girdles, Indian cane sugar	
Persia	Omana, Apologos (Sect. 36)	purple cloth; native clothing; slaves; wine; dates; *madarate* (local sewn boats); pearls, in quantity but inferior to Indian	copper, teakwood beams, saplings, logs of sissoo (rosewood), ebony, frankincense from Kane	
Western India	Barygaza (Sect. 14, 47-8)	grain, rice, ghee, sesame oil, *monache* and *sagmatogene* (Indian cotton cloth), girdles, cane sugar, onyx, agate, molochinon (?), nard, costus, bedellium, ivory, lykion, Chinese [sc. silk] cloth, long pepper	Italian, Laodicean, and Arabian wine; copper, tin, lead; coral, peridot; printed and plain clothing; multicolored girdles, eighteen inches wide; storax, yellow sweet clover; raw glass; Roman money, gold and silver, which commands an exchange at some profit against the local currency; inexpensive ungent	slave musicians, beautiful girls for concubinage, precious silverware, fine wine, expensive clothing with no adornment, choice ungent
Eastern India	Ganges (Sect. 63-4)	malabathron; Gangetic nard; pearls; cotton garments of the very finest quality, the so-called Gangetic; *kaltis* (gold coins); finest tortoise shell; silk floss; yarn		

(c. 80–c. 150 CE), a great Buddhist thinker and the first known Sanskrit writer, wrote a biography of the Buddha. This work, known as the Buddhacarita, set the Buddha's life story within the commercial urban environment of the Kushan Empire (instead of in the rural Shakya republic in the Himalaya foothills, where he had actually lived). Aśvaghosa said that the Buddha was born as a prince into a life of extreme luxury and only became aware of human suffering after experiencing heavenly revelations. To escape his mundane life, the young prince left home in the middle of the night, riding on a white horse. This largely fictive version of the Buddha's life story spread rapidly throughout India and beyond, introducing Buddha and his teachings to many potential converts.

Cultural Integration

The colorful images of Sanskrit Buddhist texts of the first centuries CE gave rise to a large repertoire of Buddhist sculptural art and drama. On Buddhist stupas and shrines, artisans carved scenes of the Buddha's life, figures of bodhisattvas, and statues of patrons and donors. Buddhist sculptures from the northern Kushan territory, fashioned from gray schist rock, are called

Gandharan art. Those from the central region of India, created mainly from local red sandstone, are called Mathuran art. Gandharan Buddhist art shows strong Greek and Roman influences, whereas the Mathuran style evolved from the carved idols of South Asian folk gods and goddesses.

Despite their stylistic differences, the schools shared themes and cultural elements. Inspired by Hellenistic art and religious tradition, both took the bold step of sculpting the Buddha and bodhisattvas in realistic human, rather than symbolic, form (such as a bodhi tree, which symbolizes Buddha's enlightenment). Though the Buddha wore no decorations because he had cut off all links to the world, bodhisattvas were dressed as princes because they were still in this world, generously helping others. What was important was bringing the symbolic world of Buddhism closer to the people.

Buddhist art reflected a spiritual system that appealed to people of diverse cultural backgrounds. Consider the clothes of the patron figures. For male and female figures alike, the garments were simple and well adapted to tropical climates. Those indigenous to the semitropical land had nude upper bodies and, a wrapping like the modern *dhoti* or loincloth on their lower bodies. Jewelry adorned their headdresses and bodies. By contrast, the nomadic patron figures wore traditional cone-shaped leather hats, knee-length robes, trousers, and boots. Figures with Greek clothing demonstrate continuing Hellenistic influence, and those wearing Roman togas reveal imperial Rome's influence. The jumble of clothing styles illustrates that Buddhist devotees could share a faith while retaining their ethnic or regional differences.

The many peoples living under Kushan rule shared important cultural traits. They preferred Hellenistic or pseudo-Hellenistic architecture, particularly favoring columns, and they reveled in Greek music and dance. We can recognize many of their musical instruments, such as the lyre (a small version of the harp), the flute, cymbals, drums, and the xylophone. In their carvings, grape and grape-leaf motifs celebrated wine's intoxicating pleasures; those found near Buddhist shrines often highlighted festive drinking scenes. The story of the Buddha also celebrated the horse, an important nomadic cultural symbol. Under the Kushans, Buddhist monasteries were cosmopolitan organizations where Greco-Roman, Indic, and steppe nomadic cultural themes blended together. The monasteries also welcomed traders converging on India, bringing incense and jewels to decorate bodhisattvas and stupas.

Buddhas. *The bronze Buddha on the left often strikes viewers as a Christlike figure. Greco-Roman influence on the iconography of Buddha was probably responsible for the Gandharan-style attire and facial expression of Buddhas and bodhisattvas. The Mathuran Buddha of Gupta times (right) is more refined than the Buddhas of the Kushan era. The robe is so transparent that the artist must have had very fine silk in mind when sculpting it.*

THE FORMATION OF THE SILK ROAD

In the first century BCE, trade routes stretching from China to central Asia and westward had merged into one big route. It has famously been known as the Silk Road. Though caravans transported many commodities, it was silk that brought about the commercial integration of the Afro-Eurasian world. Traders traveled segments of the route, passing their goods on to others who took them farther along the road and, in turn, passed them on again. The Silk Road owed much to earlier overland routes through which merchants had exchanged frankincense and myrrh from the Arabian Peninsula for copper, tin, iron, gemstones, and textiles. (See Map 6.3.)

The expansion of commerce between the Mediterranean and South Asia reinforced a frenetic rise in commercial activity within each region. Over land and across the seas, traders loaded textiles, spices, and precious metals onto the backs of camels and into the holds of oceangoing vessels destined for distant markets.

A New Middle Ground

The effects of long-distance exchanges altered the political geography of Afro-Eurasia. Egypt and Mesopotamia faded as sources of innovation and knowledge, becoming instead crossroads for peoples on either side of them. The former borderlands emerged as new imperial centers. What we now call the Middle East literally became a commercial middle ground between the Mediterranean and India.

East Asia, principally China, finally connected with the Mediterranean via central and South Asia. Through China, whose traders penetrated Bali and other Indonesian islands, connections developed with Japan, Korea, and Southeast Asia. But China remained politically and culturally a mysterious land to those from the Mediterranean. Although Alexander had marched as far east as the Indus Valley, the Himalayas and Pamir Mountains kept the Chinese insulated. Products made of silk—a word derived from *Sēres,* the Greek and Roman name for the people of northwestern China—revealed to the Greeks and Romans that an advanced society lay far to the east, though the Greeks and Romans knew little more about it.

Nomads, Frontiers, and Trade Routes

The horse-riding nomads of Inner Afro-Eurasia made long-distance trade possible. As pioneers in a slow but powerful transformation of Afro-Eurasian trade in the second millennium BCE, they responded to the drying out of their homelands by sending out conquering armies that linked entire regions and facilitated trade and interactions between distant communities (see Chapter 3).

One other advantage proved crucial to the interactions of nomads with other populations. Because of their movements from place to place, they were exposed to—and acquired resistance to—a greater variety of microbes than settled peoples did. Their relative immunity to disease made them ideal agents for linking distant settled communities.

Even more important were the ways in which nomads raced into political vacuums and installed new regimes that would link northwest China and the Iranian plateau. At a time when chariots appeared in central Asia, pastoral peoples began to link the North China plain with Turkestan (Xinjiang), Mongolia, and Manchuria. Around 600 BCE horse-riding nomads on the steppe became skilled archers on horseback whose advantages in fighting emboldened them to range farther from their homelands. These long-distance marauders eventually learned the skills of mediating between cultures, blending terror and traffic to bring diverse Afro-Eurasian worlds together. Early on, the most important of these nomadic peoples were the Xiongnu (Hsiung-nu) pastoralists, originally from the eastern part of the Asian steppe in modern Mongolia. By the third century BCE their mastery of bronze technology made them the most powerful nomadic community in the area. But as their power waned, a new empire, that of the Kushans, arose in their place. In addition to being fearsome warriors, the Kushans played the key role in making the Silk Road available to merchants, for both the land routes linking the Roman trading city of Palmyra to central Asia and the sea routes carrying ships from the Red Sea to ports on the western coast of India had to pass through the Kushan Empire. At the eastern end of this chain of political and commercial contacts, the Chinese state was also beginning to protect outposts and frontiers, enabling caravans to move more easily. Chinese silk textiles were reaching the Roman market, and glassware from the Mediterranean, incense from the Arabian Peninsula, and gemstones from India were reaching China. The Silk Road now connected the Mediterranean and the Pacific coasts.

Early Overland Trade and Caravan Cities

As nomads moved southwestward, they produced a new kind of commercial hub: the **caravan city**. Established at strategic locations (often at the edges of deserts or in oases) these cities became locations where vast trading groups assembled before beginning their arduous journeys. Some caravan cities originating as Greek garrison towns became centers of Hellenistic culture, displaying such staples of the polis as public theaters. Even those founded by Arab traders had a Hellenistic tinge, as local traders often

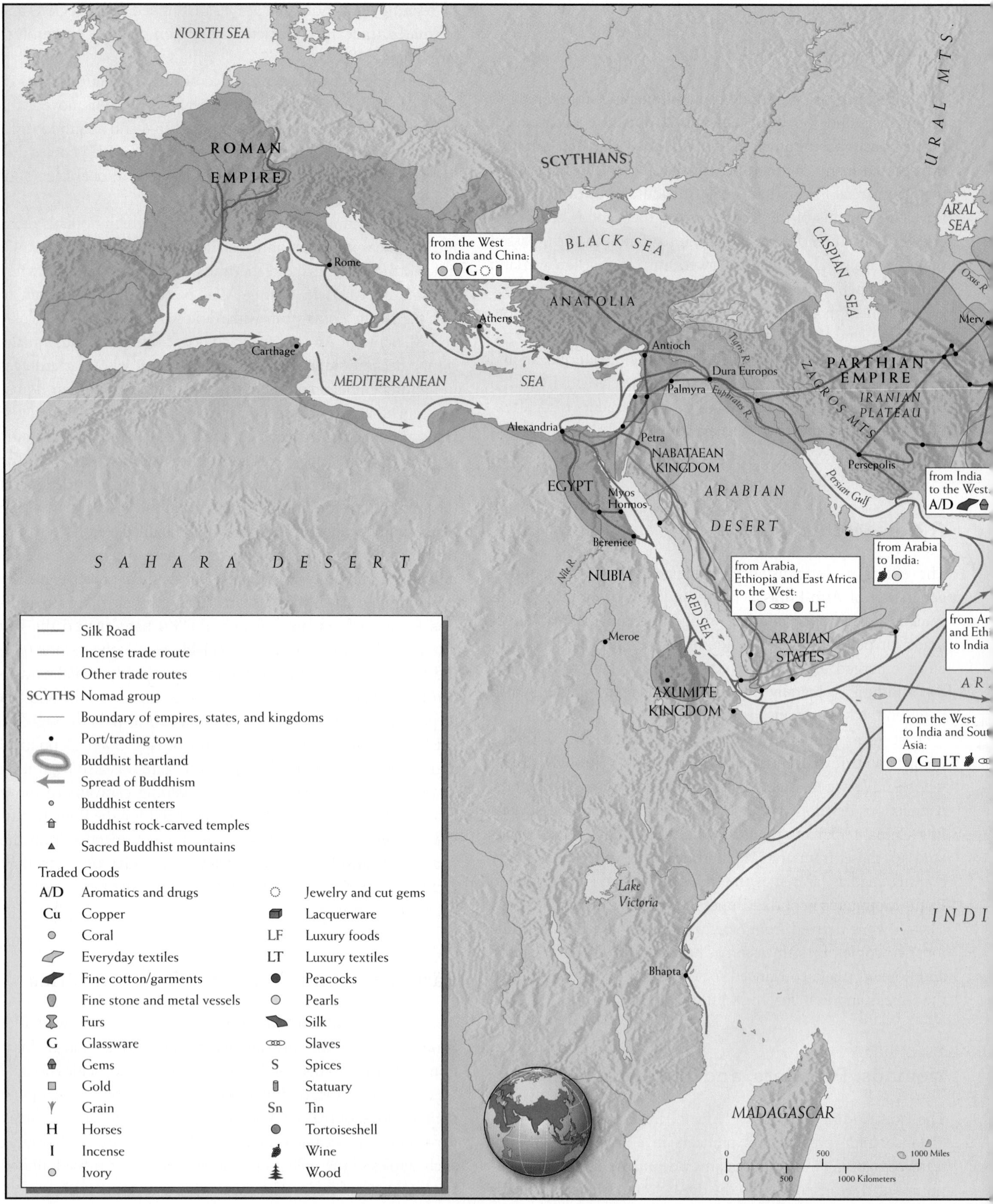
NORTH SEA
ROMAN EMPIRE
SCYTHIANS
URAL MTS.
ARAL SEA
BLACK SEA
CASPIAN SEA
from the West to India and China:
G
Rome
ANATOLIA
Athens
Carthage
Antioch
Tigris R.
Dura Europos
Palmyra
Euphrates R.
PARTHIAN EMPIRE
IRANIAN PLATEAU
ZAGROS MTS.
Merv
Oxus R.
MEDITERRANEAN SEA
Alexandria
Petra
NABATAEAN KINGDOM
Persepolis
Persian Gulf
from India to the West:
A/D
EGYPT
Myos Hormos
ARABIAN DESERT
Berenice
from Arabia to India:
SAHARA DESERT
Nile R.
NUBIA
from Arabia, Ethiopia and East Africa to the West:
I LF
RED SEA
Meroe
ARABIAN STATES
AXUMITE KINGDOM
from the West to India and South Asia:
G LT
Lake Victoria
Bhapta
MADAGASCAR
INDI
Silk Road
Incense trade route
Other trade routes
SCYTHS Nomad group
Boundary of empires, states, and kingdoms
Port/trading town
Buddhist heartland
Spread of Buddhism
Buddhist centers
Buddhist rock-carved temples
Sacred Buddhist mountains
Traded Goods
A/D Aromatics and drugs
Cu Copper
Coral
Everyday textiles
Fine cotton/garments
Fine stone and metal vessels
Furs
G Glassware
Gems
Gold
Grain
H Horses
I Incense
Ivory
Jewelry and cut gems
Lacquerware
LF Luxury foods
LT Luxury textiles
Peacocks
Pearls
Silk
Slaves
S Spices
Statuary
Sn Tin
Tortoiseshell
Wine
Wood
0 500 1000 Miles
0 500 1000 Kilometers

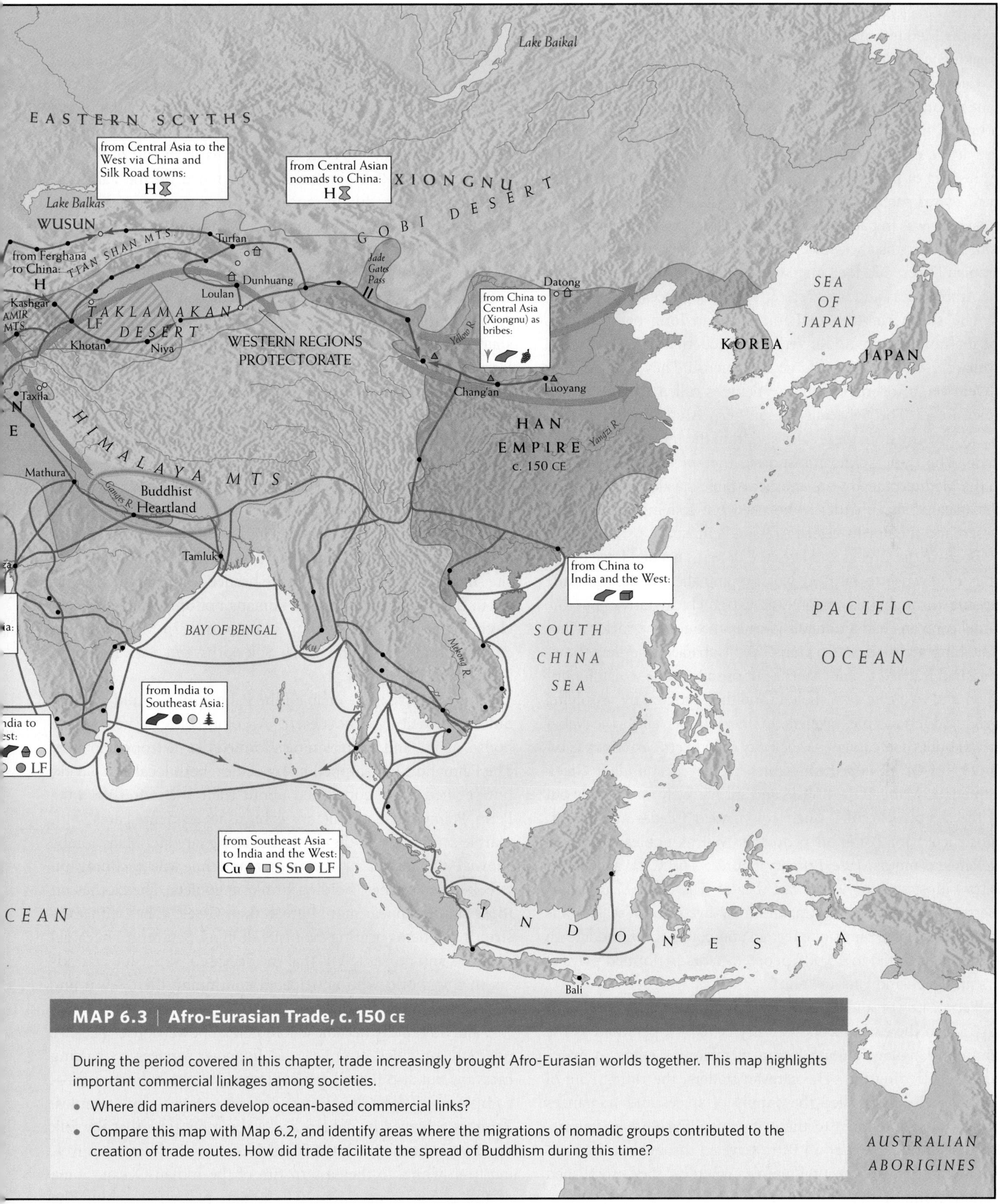

MAP 6.3 | Afro-Eurasian Trade, c. 150 CE

During the period covered in this chapter, trade increasingly brought Afro-Eurasian worlds together. This map highlights important commercial linkages among societies.

- Where did mariners develop ocean-based commercial links?
- Compare this map with Map 6.2, and identify areas where the migrations of nomadic groups contributed to the creation of trade routes. How did trade facilitate the spread of Buddhism during this time?

admired Greek culture and had frequent commercial interactions with the Mediterranean world. They wrote in Greek, sometimes speaking it in addition to their native tongues.

Caravan cities were among the most spectacular and resplendent urban centers of this era. They often emerged at the end points of major trade arteries. One such end point for traders was at the extreme southwestern tip of the Arabian Peninsula, in the area of present-day Yemen. The area was a wonder of its own, a vivid patch of green at the end of 1,200 miles of desert. Its prosperity was in part due to its role as a major gathering place—both for long-distance spice traders heading north through the Arabian Desert and for sailors whose ships traveled the Red and the Arabian seas and later crossed the Indian Ocean.

The southern Arabian Peninsula had long been famous for its frankincense and myrrh, products that the Greeks and Romans used to make perfume and incense. They reached their buyers via an overland route sometimes called the Incense or Spice Road. The Sabaeans of southern Arabia became fabulously wealthy from these sales and from the Indian Ocean spice trade. The traders who transported the spices and fragrances to the Mediterranean were another Arabic-speaking people: the Nabataeans, sheepherders who eked out a living in the Sinai Desert and the northwestern Arabian Peninsula.

Because the Greeks and later the Romans needed large quantities of incense to burn in worshipping their gods, the trade passing through this region was extremely lucrative. But the camel caravans had a difficult journey through the rock ravines stretching across desert regions. The Nabataean herders, however, had learned to cut cisterns out of solid stone to catch rainwater and to create cave shelters and they profited by supplying water and food to the travelers. In one of these valleys the Nabataeans built their capital—a rock city called Petra, or "Rock City" ("rock" in Greek is *petros*)—which displayed abundant Greek influences. Many of the houses and shrines were cut directly out of the steep rock cliffs. Their colonnaded facades and tombs, constructed for common people as well as nobles, projected Hellenistic motifs. (See Primary Source: The Caravan City of Petra.) Most striking was a vast theater. The entire structure—the stage platform, orchestra, and forty-five rows of seats—was carved out of the sandstone terrain and could accommodate an audience of 6,000 to 10,000 people. Actors performed plays at first in Greek and later in Latin.

Petra's power and wealth lasted from the mid-second century BCE to the early second century CE. Greek persisted as the common language among Petran merchants seeking to maintain their trading ties. The caravan traders, the ruling elite of the rock city, controlled the supply of spices and fragrances from Arabia and India to the ever-expanding Roman Empire. Nabataean traders based in Petra traveled throughout the eastern Mediterranean, erecting temples wherever they established trading communities.

The Western End of the Silk Road: Palmyra

As trading hubs proliferated in central Asia, similar commercial cities thrived in Southwest Asia as well. They soon overshadowed the older political or religious capitals. With Petra's decline during the Roman period, another settlement became the most important caravan city at the western end of the Silk Road: Palmyra. Rich citizens of Rome relied on the Palmyran traders to procure luxury goods for them, importing Chinese silks for women's clothing and incense for religious rituals, as well as gemstones, pearls, and many other precious items.

Administered by the chiefs of local tribes, Palmyra had considerable autonomy even under formal Roman control. Although the Palmyrans used a Semitic dialect in daily life, for state affairs and business they used Greek. Their merchants had learned Greek when the region came under Seleucid rule, and it remained useful when doing business with caravans from afar, long after the political influences of Hellenism had waned. Palmyran traders handled many kinds of textiles, including cotton from India and cashmere wool from Kashmir or the nearby central Asian highlands. The many silk textiles discovered at this site were products of Han China (see Chapter 7), indicating that the Silk Road had reached the Mediterranean by the first century CE. While the local leaders retained some of the exquisite silks for themselves, most were headed to wealthier consumers in the Mediterranean. The Romans not only purchased silk cloth but also had it woven to order in eastern Mediterranean cities such as Beirut and Gaza. Silk yarns and dyes have also been found at Palmyra.

This lucrative trade enabled the Palmyrans to build a splendid marble city in the desert. A colonnade, theater, senate house, agora, and major temples formed the metropolitan area. The Palmyrans worshipped many deities, both local and Greek, but seemed most concerned about their own afterlife. Like Petra, Palmyra had a cemetery as big as its residential area, with marble sculptures on the tombs depicting city life. Many tombs showed the master or the master and his wife reclining on Greek-style couches, holding drinking goblets. The clothes on those statues appear more Iranian than Greek: robes with wide stripes and hems bearing exquisite designs. Sculptures of camel caravans and horses tell us that the deceased were caravan traders in this world who anticipated continuing their rewarding occupation in the afterlife.

Palmyra rapidly became a commercial powerhouse. The city not only provided supplies and financial services to passing caravans but also hosted self-contained trading communities—complexes of hostels, storage houses, offices, and temples. Palmyra achieved its golden age at the same time that the Silk Road was the major route for silk and other luxuries traveling from China to the eastern rim of the Indian Ocean. Some of the goods went across the Iranian plateau, reaching the

PRIMARY SOURCE

The Caravan City of Petra

Petra was a city cut out of the pink rock cliffs in the valley between the Dead Sea and the Red Sea. The Nabataeans built the city to host traders from west and east; from here, caravans headed out to trading centers in the Mediterranean and on the Iranian plateau. Petra's good fortune ran out under the Roman Empire when the silk trade favored another caravan city, Palmyra. Yet even today the rock structure of the city shining in the sun is an imposing sight, as this account by a modern traveler makes vividly clear.

When one descends into the valley from the surrounding heights towards the place where the river has cut for itself a passage between the dark-red rocks, one seems to be gazing at some large and fantastic excrescence—a piece of reddish-mauve raw flesh set between the gold of the desert and the green of the hills. It is a most extraordinary sight, which becomes even more extraordinary when the cavalcade slowly descends into the river valley, and the rocky walls of the ever-narrowing gorge tower up to the right and left, speckled with red, orange, mauve, grey, and green layers. Wild and beautiful they are, with their contrasts of light and shade; the light blinding, the shadows black. And there is seldom even anything to remind the visitor that this gorge served for centuries as a main road, trodden by camels, mules, and horses, and that along it rode Bedouin merchants who must have felt like ourselves its horror and its mystic fascination. Yet suddenly one may be confronted with the façade of a tomb-tower with dog-tooth design, or with an altar set high up on one of the vertical walls, bearing a greeting or prayer to some god, inscribed in the Nabataean tongue. Our caravan advanced slowly along the gorge, until an unexpected bend disclosed to us an apparition sparkling pinky-orange in the sun, which must once have been the front of a temple or tomb. Elegant columns joined by fascinating pediments and arches form the frames of the niches in which its statues stand. All this rose up before us dressed in a garb of classicism yet in a style new and unexpected even by those well acquainted with antiquity. It was as though the magnificent scenery of some Hellenistic theatre had appeared, . . . chiselled in the rock.

Petra. *This beautiful building is known as El-Khaznah, or The Treasury, at Petra. The wealth created by the region's long-distance trade is manifest in the magnificent buildings at the center of the city. Both the face of the building and its interior are cut out of the sandstone rock that forms the cliffs surrounding Petra.*

QUESTIONS FOR ANALYSIS

- What features in the description of Petra and the monuments in and around the city suggest that it hosted a variety of cultures with different art forms?
- Imagine being part of a caravan arriving in bustling Petra via the route described here. What feelings would the atmosphere evoke in you?

Source: M. Rostovtzeff, Caravan Cities *(Oxford: Clarendon Press, 1932), 42–43.*

Palmyran Tomb Sculpture. *This tombstone relief sculpture shows a wealthy young Palmyran, attended by a servant—probably a household slave. Palmyra was at the crossroads of the major cultural influences traversing Southwest Asia at the time. The style of the clothing—the flowing pants and top—and the couch and pillows reflect the trading contacts of the Palmyran elite, in this case with India to the east. The hairstyle and mode of self-presentation signal influences from the Mediterranean to the west.*

Mediterranean via Syria's desert routes. Another artery went through Afghanistan, the Indus, and the west coast of India, then across the Indian Ocean to the Red Sea.

Reaching China along the Silk Road

China was the ultimate end and beginning point of the Silk Road. Its flourishing economy owed much to the fact that Chinese silks were the most sought-after commodity in long-distance trade. As thousands of precious silk bales made their way to Indian, central Asian, and Mediterranean markets, silk became the ultimate prestige commodity of the regions' ruling classes. But the exchange between eastern and western portions of the Silk Road was increasingly mediated by Persian, Xiongnu, Kushan, and other middlemen at the great oases and trading centers that grew up in central Asia. Local communities took profitable advantage of the silk trade from China based on their increased knowledge and contacts.

THE SILK ECONOMY Not only was silk China's most valuable export, but it also served as a tool in diplomacy with the nomadic kingdoms on China's western frontiers and in underwriting the Chinese armies. The country's rulers used silk to pay off neighboring nomads and borderlanders, buying both horses and peaceful borders with the fabric. During the Zhou dynasty, it served as a precious medium of exchange and trade.

Silk has always been prized as a material for clothing; as a filament made by spinning the protein fibers extracted from the cocoons of silkworms, it is smooth yet strong. Whereas cloth spun from hemp, flax, and other fibers tends to be rough, silk looks and feels rich. Moreover, it is cool against the skin in hot summers and warm in the winter. Silk also has immense tensile strength, being useful for bows, lute strings, and fishing lines. Artisans even spun it into a tight fabric to make light body armor or light bags for transporting liquids (particularly useful for traders crossing arid expanses). Before the Chinese invented paper, silk was a popular writing material that was more durable than bamboo or wood. Brush writing on silk was the medium of choice for correspondence, maps, and illustrations and important texts written on silk often joined other funerary objects in the tombs of aristocratic lords and wealthy individuals.

Because of reforms in the Warring States period, economic life in China after 300 BCE centered increasingly on independent farmers producing commercial crops for the marketplaces along land routes as well as rivers, canals, and lakes. As this market economy grew, merchants organized themselves into influential family lineages and occupational guilds. Now power shifted away from agrarian elites and into the hands of urban financiers and traders. The latter benefited from the improvement in roads and waterways, which eased the transportation of grain, hides,

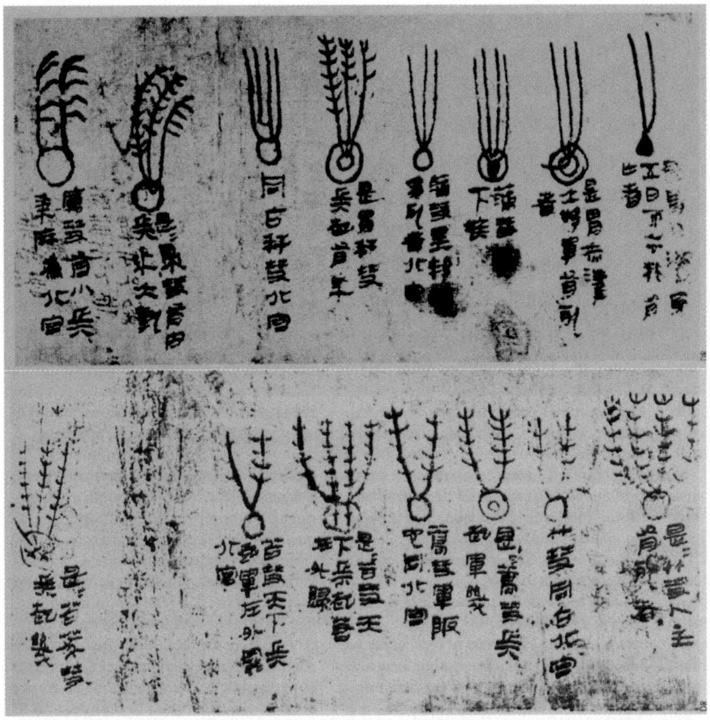

Silk Texts. *Before the invention of paper, silk was widely used as writing material because it was more mobile and durable than bamboo or wood for correspondence, maps, illustrations, and important texts included as funerary objects in the tombs of aristocrats. The Mawangdui silk texts shown here are from a Hunan tomb that was closed in 168* BCE *and opened in 1973.*

horses, and silk from the villages to the new towns and cities. Bronze coins of various sizes and shapes (such as the spade-shaped money of several semiautonomous Warring States; see photo in Chapter 5), as well as cloth and silk used in barter, also spurred long-distance trade. By the second century BCE, wealthy merchants were ennobled as local magnates and wore clothing that marked their official status. As commerce further expanded, regional lords opened local customs offices along land routes and waterways to extract a share of the money and products for themselves.

THE EXPANSION OF TRADE Though China still had little intellectual interaction with the rest of Afro-Eurasia, its commercial exchanges skyrocketed due to the Silk Road trade. Southern silk was only the first of many Chinese commodities that reached the world beyond the Taklamakan Desert. China also became an export center for lacquer, hemp, and linen. From Sichuan came iron, steel, flint, hard stone, silver, and animals, while jade came from the northwest. At the same time, China was importing Mediterranean, Indian, and central Asian commodities.

Despite its early development of commerce, China still had no major ports that could compare to the oasis hub of Palmyra. Internal, interregional trade predominated, and it fed into the Silk Road through decentralized networks. Most cities in the landlocked north were administrative centers where farmers and traders gathered under the regional states' political and military protection. The larger cities had gates that closed between sunset and sunrise; during the night, mounted soldiers patrolled the streets. Newer towns along the southeastern seacoast still looked upriver to trade with inland agrarian communities, which also produced silk for export. Facilitating oceanic trade did become more of a concern for the state during this period. For example, merchant ships now enjoyed the protection of military boats, able to cover seventy-five miles in a day and carry fifty soldiers and supplies for a three-month voyage. It would not be until later, during the sixth and seventh centuries CE, that China would become the site of massive trading centers.

The Spread of Buddhism along the Trade Routes

Silk traders were not the only individuals who traversed Afro-Eurasian trade arteries. Monks also traveled these roads to spread the word of new religions. The chief expansionist faith in this period came out of India, inspired in part by the successful spread of Hellenism. The Buddha was no longer just a sage departed to the state of nirvana; he was also a god whom people could worship like any Greek deity.

Under Kushan patronage during the first centuries CE, Buddhism reached out from India to China and central Asia, following the Silk Road. Monks from the Kushan Empire accompanied traders to Luoyang, the eastern capital of the Han Empire. There they translated Buddhist texts into Chinese and other languages, aided by Chinese converts who were also traders. Buddhist ideas were slow to gain acceptance everywhere they proselytized. It took several centuries, and a new wave of nomadic migrations, for Buddhism to take root in China.

Buddhism fared less well when it followed the commercial arteries westward. Although Buddhists did gain some followers in the Parthian Empire, the religion never became established on the Iranian plateau and made no further headway toward the Mediterranean. The main barrier was Zoroastrianism, which had been a state religion in the Persian Empire during the fifth and fourth centuries BCE (see Chapter 4); by the time Buddhism began to spread, Zoroastrianism had long been established in Iran. Iranian Hellenism had done little to weaken the power of Zoroastrianism, whose adherents formed city-based religious communities affiliated primarily with traders, who continued to adhere to their own faith while traveling along the Silk Road and therefore did nothing to help Buddhism spread westward.

TAKING TO THE SEAS: COMMERCE ON THE RED SEA AND INDIAN OCEAN

Although land routes were the tried-and-true avenues for migrants, traders, and wayfarers, they carried only what could be borne on the backs of humans and animals. Travel on them was slow, and they were vulnerable to marauders. With time, some risk takers found ways of traversing waterways—eventually on an unprecedented scale and with an ease unimaginable to earlier merchants. These risk takers were Arabs, from the commercial middle ground of the Afro-Eurasian trading system.

Arab traders had long carried such spices as frankincense and myrrh to the Egyptians, who used them in religious and funerary rites, and later to the Greeks and Romans. Metals such as bronze, tin, and iron passed along overland routes from Anatolia, as did gold, silver, and chlorite from the Iranian plateau. Gold, ivory, and other goods from the northern part of India passed through Taxila (the capital of Gandhara) and the Hindu Kush Mountains into Persia as early as the sixth century BCE. Following the expansion of the Hellenistic world, however, ships increasingly conducted long-distance trade. They sailed down the Red Sea and across the Indian Ocean as they carried goods between the tip of the Arabian Peninsula and the ports of the Indian landmass.

Arab seafarers led the way into the Indian Ocean, forging links that joined East Africa, the eastern Mediterranean, and the Arabian Peninsula with India, Southeast Asia, and East Asia. Such voyages involved longer stays at sea and were far more dangerous than sailing in the Mediterranean. Yet by the first century CE, Arab and Indian sailors were transporting Chinese silks, central Asian furs, and fragrances from Himalayan trees across the Indian Ocean. The city of Alexandria in Egypt soon emerged as a key transit point between the Mediterranean Sea and the Indian Ocean. Boats carried Mediterranean exports of olives and olive oil, wine, drinking vessels, glassware, linen and wool textiles, and red coral up the Nile, stopping at Koptos and other port cities, from which camel caravans took the goods to the Red Sea ports of Myos Hormos and Berenice. For centuries, Mediterranean merchants had considered the Arabian Peninsula to be the end of the Spice Road. But after Alexander's expedition and the establishment of colonies between Egypt and Afghanistan, they began to value the wealth and opportunities that lay along the shores of the Indian Ocean.

Arab sailors who ventured into the Indian Ocean benefited from new navigational techniques, especially celestial bearings (using the position of the stars to determine the position of the ship and the direction to sail). They used large ships called *dhows*, whose sails were rigged to easily capture the wind; these forerunners of modern cargo vessels were capable of long hauls in rough waters. Beginning about 120 BCE, mariners came to understand the seasonal rain-filled monsoon winds, which blow from the southwest between October and April and then from the northeast between April and October—knowledge that propelled the maritime trade connecting the Mediterranean with the Indian Ocean.

Mariners accumulated the new sailing knowledge in books—each called a ***periplus*** ("sailing around")—in which sea captains recorded the landing spots and ports between their destinations, as well as their precious cargoes. From such books, for example, we learn that trading ships left the southern Arabian coast with the monsoon winds behind them, heading for the entrepôts (trading centers) of India. Barbaricum, at the mouth of the Indus, was the first Indian port reached from the west. On their arrival, traders unloaded linen textiles, red coral, glassware, wine, and money from the Mediterranean and Egypt, as well as frankincense and storax, aromatic gum resins from Southwest Asia. These cargoes were headed to the upper Indus region of the Punjab and Gandhara. While at harbor in India, traders loaded their ships with treasures from the east: fragrances or spices from the Himalayas and India, such as costus root and bdellium, turquoise from Khorasan in Iran, lapis lazuli from Badakhshan in Afghanistan, indigo dye and cotton textiles from India, furs from central Asia, and silk textiles and yarn from China.

By now, the revolution in navigational techniques and knowledge had dramatically reduced the cost of long-distance shipping and multiplied the ports of call around large bodies of water. Some historians have argued that there were now two Silk Roads: one by land and one by sea.

CONCLUSION

Alexander's conquests were awesome in their scale and brilliant in their execution. But his empire was as transitory as it was huge. Though it crumbled upon his death, it had effects more profound than those of any military or political regime that preceded it. Alexander's armies ushered in an age of thinking and practices that transformed Greek achievements into a common culture—Hellenism—whose influences, both direct and indirect, touched far-flung societies for centuries thereafter.

This Hellenistic movement was most strongly represented by a common, simpler Greek language, which linked culture, institutions, and trade. However, many Greek-speaking peoples and their descendants in parts of Southwest and central Asia integrated local cultural practices with their own ways, creating diverse and rich cultures. Thus the influences of culture flowed both ways. The economic story is equally complex. In many respects, Alexander and his successors followed pathways established by previous kingdoms and empires. If anything,

Alexander's successors helped strengthen and expand the existing trade routes and centers of commercial activity, which ultimately led to the creation of the Silk Road.

Although the effects of this Hellenistic age lasted longer than most cultural systems and had a wider appeal than previous philosophical and spiritual ideas, they did not sweep away everything before them. Indigenous peoples accommodated to this movement or fought against it with all their might, fearing the loss of their own cultural identities. Others took from the new common culture what they liked and discarded the rest. Some Romans admired its achievements and steeped themselves in it while fashioning their own Latin-based culture. Eventually, they created an imperial polity that outdistanced Alexander's. In North Africa, the commercially talented Carthaginians saw some of these Greek means of expression as useful for new elites like themselves.

Of all those exposed to Hellenistic thinking, the South Asian peoples produced the most varied responses because they represented a multitude of cultures. The immediate successor to Alexander's military was the Mauryan Empire, which established its dominion over almost all of South Asia and even some of central Asia for close to a century and a half. Once it had passed out of existence, South Asia was opened up more decisively than before to currents moving swiftly across Afro-Eurasia, including the institutions and cultures of steppe nomads, seafarers, and Hellenists. The most telling South Asian responses occurred in the realm of spiritual and ethical norms, where Buddhist doctrines evolved toward a full-fledged world religious system.

Greater political integration helped fashion highways for commerce and enabled the spread of Buddhism. Nomads left their steppe lands and exchanged wares across great distances. As they found greater opportunities for business, their trade routes shifted farther south, radiating out of the oases of central Asia. Eventually merchants, rather than the trading nomads, seized the opportunities provided by new technologies, especially in sailing and navigation. These commercial transformations connected distant parts of Afro-Eurasia. Accompanying the spread of Greek ways was the opening of trade. Alexander's campaigns had followed some of the trade routes east, and his conquests opened up permanent channels of exchange. In the wake of his conquests, the Silk Road and new sea-lanes connected ports and caravan cities from North Africa to South China, created new social classes, produced new urban settings, supported powerful new polities, and transported Buddhism to China, where it would ultimately proliferate on an even grander, more lasting scale than it did in South Asia.

AFTER YOU READ THIS CHAPTER

Review and research materials are available on **STUDYSPACE:** wwnorton.com/studyspace

TRACING THE GLOBAL STORYLINES

FOCUS ON: ***Forces that Unify Afro-Eurasia***

THE MEDITERRANEAN WORLD

- The spread of Hellenism around the Mediterranean via Alexander's conquests leads to a common language, cosmopolitan cities, new types of philosophy and religion, plantation slavery, and money-based economies.

CENTRAL AND SOUTH ASIA

- Alexander's withdrawal from the Indus Valley leads to the creation of the Mauryan Empire, which integrates the northern half of India.
- The Seleucid and Bactrian kingdoms further solidify the spread of Hellenism into central Asia.

TRANSFORMATION OF BUDDHISM

- The combined influences of Hellenism, nomadism, and Arab seafaring culture transform Buddhism into a world religion.

FORMATION OF THE SILK ROAD

- Nomadic warriors from central Asia complete the final links of the overland Silk Road, strengthening the ties that joined peoples across Afro-Eurasia.
- Overland traders use camels to carry spices, transport precious metals, and convey Buddhist thought along the Silk Road into China.
- Seafaring Arab traders use new navigation techniques and larger ships called dhows to expand the transport of Silk Road commodities to the Mediterranean world via the Indian Ocean.

CHRONOLOGY

Southwest Asia and Egypt

- Conquests of Alexander the Great **334–323 BCE**
- Emergence of Hellenistic successor states **323 BCE**

The Mediterranean

- Expansion and clash of Rome and Carthage **330 BCE–200 BCE**

Central and South Asia

- Mauryan Empire **321–184 BCE**

East Asia

- Warring States period **401–223 BCE**

350 BCE | 300 BCE | 250 BCE | 200 BCE | 150 BCE | 100 BCE

KEY TERMS

Alexander the Great p. 203

bodhisattva p. 223

caravan city p. 230

dhamma p. 215

garrison towns p. 214

Hellenism p. 202

Mahayana Buddhism p. 222

periplus p. 234

Silk Road p. 202

stupa p. 215

STUDY QUESTIONS

1. **Analyze** the impact of Alexander's conquest on the Afro-Eurasian world. How did his military pursuits, and those of his successors, bring together various worlds?

2. **Describe** the influence of Hellenism on societies outside the Greek homeland. What aspects of Hellenistic culture held broad appeal for diverse groups?

3. **Compare and contrast** Judean, Roman, and Carthaginian responses to Hellenistic influences. How receptive was each society to Greek cultural influences?

4. **Explain** how South Asia became a melting pot for the intellectual, political, and economic currents sweeping across Afro-Eurasia between 350 BCE and 250 CE. How did this development affect Buddhist doctrine?

5. **Analyze** the extent to which long-distance trade routes connected societies during this period. Which societies were involved? How did commercial linkages affect them?

6. **Analyze** the influence of nomadic pastoral groups in Afro-Eurasia during this period. What role did they play in integrating cultures and economies?

7. **Explain** how interregional contacts transformed Buddhism. How did it expand across a variety of cultures?

8. **Explain** how art, architecture, and other forms of material culture in Afro-Eurasian societies reflected broader patterns of cultural, political, and economic integration during this period. In particular, how did caravan cities reflect new cultural configurations?

Parthian State **240 BCE–224 CE**

Spread of plantation and money-based economies

Kushan State **1st–3rd centuries**

Transformation of Buddhism begins **1st century**

Growth of market economy

50 BCE | 1 CE | 50 CE | 100 CE | 150 CE | 200 CE | 250 CE

BEFORE YOU READ THIS CHAPTER

GLOBAL STORYLINES

- At both ends of Afro-Eurasia two great empires rise, flourish, and fall at roughly the same time.
- Han China and imperial Rome exercise greater power over more people and larger expanses of territory than any previous state.
- The two empires create long-lasting foundations for China and Christendom.

CHAPTER OUTLINE

7

Han Dynasty China and Imperial Rome, 300 BCE–300 CE

FOCUS QUESTIONS

- How did the Roman and Han empires differ from earlier large states?
- How did the Qin, Han, and Romans build their empires?
- What new cultural identities emerged in the Roman and Han empires?
- To what extent were the policies and institutions that integrated the Roman Empire similar to those of Han dynasty China?
- What were the limits on the Han and Roman Empires?

In third century BCE China, the Eastern Zhou state of Qin absorbed the remaining Warring States (see Chapter 5) and set the stage for the epic Han dynasty. The chief minister of the Qin state, Li Si, urged his king to dispense with niceties and to seize opportunities: a man who aimed at great achievements must exploit the advantages offered to him. By combining his fearsome armies and his own personal virtues, the king could sweep away his rivals as if dusting ashes from a kitchen hearth—he could eliminate them all. In this way he could establish a truly imperial rule and unify the entire world. "This is the one moment in ten thousand ages," Li Si whispered. The king listened carefully. He followed the advice. He laid the foundations for a mighty empire.

The Qin Empire was an important transitional empire, but it was not meant to endure, and it collapsed in 207 BCE. The Han Empire took its place, becoming one of the most successful dynasties in Chinese history. Following the Qin model, the Han defeated other regional groups and established the first long-lasting Chinese empire. Subjects of the Han basked in a society whose landholding elites, free farmers, trained artisans, itinerant traders, and urban merchants were building a society that, unlike the allegedly cruel Qin state, would emulate the statecraft ideals of antiquity.

At the other end of Afro-Eurasia another great state, imperial Rome, also met its rivals in war, emerged victorious, and consolidated its power into a vast empire. The Romans achieved this feat by using violent force on a scale hitherto unseen in their part of the globe. The result was a state of huge size, astonishingly unified and stable. Living in the Roman Empire in the mid-70s CE, a man of middle rank, Pliny the Elder, could write glowingly about the unity of the imperial state. In his eyes, all the benefits that flowed from its extensive reach derived from the boundless greatness of a peace that joined diverse peoples under one benevolent emperor.

The Han and the Roman states were not new because they found new ways to plow resources into big armies and civil bureaucracies or in the new reasons that rulers gave for their rulership. First, they were novel in becoming true globalizing empires based on their geographical size, their population size, and their efforts not just to rule over their neighbors and those they conquered but to fully incorporate those peoples into their empires and to rule directly over them. Second, they transcended the limits of previous territorial kingdoms and the first empires by deploying resources and reasons of state in new ways. They concentrated military power in professionalized military elites that owed allegiance above all to the state, not to its ruler. They modernized tax collecting to support large-scale killing machines—that is, armies. They wrote laws and codes for their subjects. And they promoted the idea that the state should support schooling, the arts, architecture, and a learned society as ways to bring peace and prosperity. Ever since, we have come to associate the ideal of empire with these two founders at either end of Afro-Eurasia.

Just as we see these empires as models for world history, we must understand how they were built—for they did not emerge as the inevitable consequences of destiny. They were crafted of a delicate mixture of coercion, coaxing, and convincing—and not just to prove that empires were exalted and enjoyed benefits that faraway neighbors did not. They actually had to deliver on these promises in order to endure. These were no short-lasting conquerings, like Alexander the Great's. They had the institutional muscle to outlive any particular ruler.

CHINA AND ROME: HOW EMPIRES ARE BUILT

Afro-Eurasia had seen empires come and go, emerging out of territorial kingdoms to exercise their power over neighboring states as clients, often demanding tribute in return for protection. The Romans and the Han took imperial expansion to the next level: not content to exercise influence over neighbors, they wanted to incorporate them fully into their realm. What distinguished these two from their predecessors was their commitment to integrating conquered neighbors and rivals into their worlds—by extending laws, offering systems of representation, exporting belief systems, colonizing lands, and promoting trade within and beyond the empires. In effect, subject peoples became members of empires, not just the vanquished. Those who resisted not only waved away the benefits of living under an imperial mantle but also became the targets for awesome and relentless armies.

Empire and Cultural Identity

The existence of these two vast imperial states meant that at least one out of every two human beings in Afro-Eurasia now fell directly under the control of China or Rome. What did it mean to live under the imperial umbrella of these giants?

To be "Han Chinese" meant that elites shared a common written language based on the Confucian classics, which qualified them for public office. It also meant that commoners from all walks of life shared the elites' belief system based on ancestor worship, ritual practices stressing appropriate decorum and dress for each social level, and a view that the Han as an agrarian-based empire was a small-scale model of the entire cosmos. Those who lived beyond the realm of the Han were considered uncivilized.

In the fifth century BCE, being Roman meant being a citizen of the city of Rome, speaking Latin (the regional language of central Italy), and eating and dressing like Latin-speaking people. By the late second century BCE, however, the concept of citizenship expanded to include anyone who had formal membership in the larger territorial state that the Romans were building.

By the beginning of the third century CE, even this bigger view was no longer true. Now being Roman meant simply being a subject of the Roman emperors. This identity became so deeply rooted that when the western parts of the empire disintegrated two centuries later, the inhabitants of the surviving eastern parts—who had no connection with Rome, did not speak Latin, and did not dress or eat like the original Romans—still considered themselves "Romans" in this broader sense.

Patterns of Imperial Expansion

Despite their similarities, the empires reflected different patterns of development, types of public servants, and ideals for the best kind of government. For example, whereas the civilian magistrate and the bureaucrat were typical of the Han Empire,

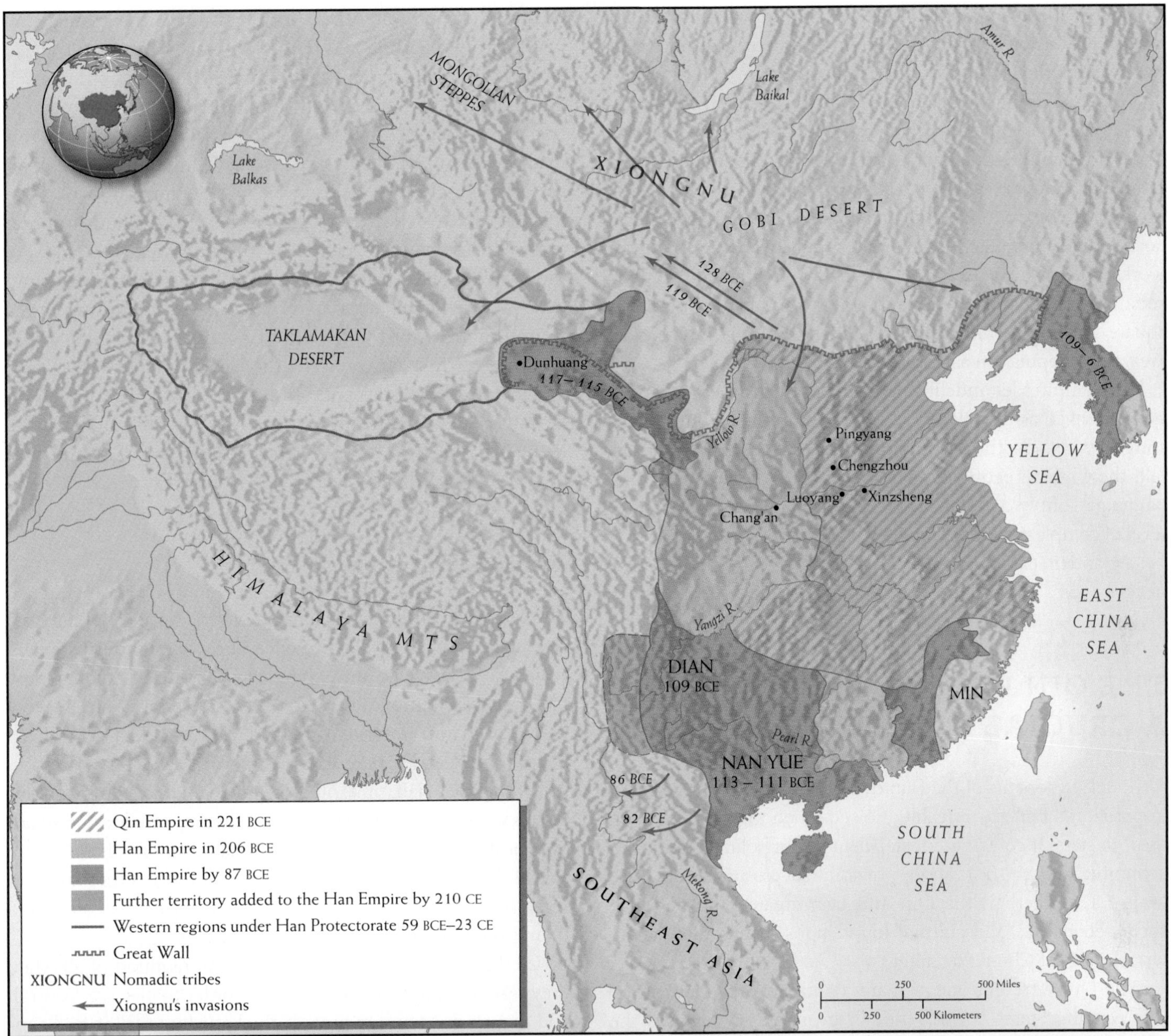

MAP 7.1 | East Asia, 206 BCE–220 CE

Both the Qin and the Han dynasties consolidated much of East Asia into one large regional empire.

- According to the map, what physical features imposed a limit to this territorial expansion?
- Why was the great wall so long and why was it placed facing north?
- What impact did the pastoral Xiongnu have on each empire's effort to consolidate a large territorial state?
- According to your reading, why did the Han expand their influence farther west than the Qin?

the citizen, the soldier, and the military governor stood for the Roman Empire. In China, dynastic empires fashioned themselves according to the models of past empires. The Chinese treated imperial culture as an ideal descended from the past that had to be emulated in the present. By contrast, Rome began as a collectively ruled city-state and pursued a pragmatic road to domination of its world as if creating something anew. Only by a long, sometimes violent process of trial and error did the Romans achieve a political system of one-man rule by emperors. Nonetheless, they, like the Chinese, were strongly traditional.

They also idealized their ancestors. But what characterized Roman expansion and empire building was a process of continual experimentation, innovation, and adaptation.

The new empires united huge landmasses and extraordinarily diverse populations. For example, the scale of the Han dynasty was unprecedented. A land survey by the imperial government in 2 CE revealed a registered population of 12,233,062 households, or around 58 million people. These households paid taxes, provided military recruits, and supplied laborers for public works. At its height, the Han Empire covered some 3 million square miles in China proper and, for a while, another 1 million square miles in central Asia. The Roman Empire governed an area and a population as great as those of Han China.

Both empires left indelible legacies; following their collapses, both survived as models. Successor states in the Mediterranean sought to become the Second Rome, and after the Han dynasty fell, the Chinese people always identified themselves and their language simply as "Han." Both empires raised life to a new level of complexity—now people could share a common identity on a grander scale than ever before. It was a vision that would never be lost.

THE QIN DYNASTY AS A CRUCIAL FORERUNNER

Although exponents of the Han dynasty boasted of the regime's imperial uniqueness, in reality it owed much to its predecessor, the Qin state. It contributed vital elements of political unity and economic growth to its more powerful successor regime. (See Map 7.1.) Together, the Qin and Han created the political, social, economic, and cultural foundations that would characterize imperial China thereafter.

The Qin were but one of many militaristic regimes during the Warring States period, though in many ways it was the most warlike of them. What enabled the Qin to prevail over rivals was not its taste for violence, but a decision to expand southwestward from its base in the Wei valley into the Sichuan region, a vast area, twice the size of its home territory and remarkable for rich mineral resources and fertile soils. There, in the fourth century, a full century before the Qin became all-powerful, its leaders used a dynamic merchant class and an expanding silk trade to spur economic growth. Its myriad public works turned the region into the rice bowl of China. By the time that King Zheng ascended the throne at the age of fourteen in 247 BCE, the Qin were prepared to defeat the remaining Warring States and unify an empire that covered roughly two-thirds of modern China. It did so between 230 and 221 BCE, ending one of the most violent periods in Chinese history. With the help of able ministers and generals and a large conscripted army, as well as a system of taxation that financed all-out war, King Zheng assumed the mandate of heaven from the Zhou and unified the states into a centralized empire. Having accomplished this feat, he declared himself Shi Huangdi, or "First August Emperor," in 221 BCE (much as Rome's first emperor also called himself Augustus). In this instance Zheng harkened back to the China's mythical emperors of great antiquity. He took the title of emperor (*di*), a term that had meant ancestral ruler in Shang and Zhou, in order to exalt his dynasty over that of the Zhou and the rulers of the Warring States, all of whom had called themselves kings (*wang*). He and his supporters went further, boasting that a second, and a third, and indeed countless emperors would succeed the first emperor for thousands and ten thousands of generations without end. To further consolidate his power he forced the defeated rulers and their families to move to Xianyang, the Qin capital—where, under his watchful eye, they would be unable to gather rebel armies.

Administration and Control

The First August Emperor parceled out the territory of his massive state into thirty-six provinces or **commanderies** (*jun*), which he subdivided into counties (*xian*). Each commandery had a civilian and a military governor answering to an imperial inspector. These reforms provided China with a centralized bureaucracy and a hereditary emperor that later dynasties, including the Han, inherited. Crucial to this administrative strategy were requirements that regional and local officials answer directly to the emperor and that he could dismiss them at will. Moreover, he made sure that civilian governors did not serve in their home areas—a calculated move that prevented them from building up power for themselves.

Clerks registered the common people, required of all when they reached sixteen or seventeen, in order to observe, control, and punish them and to provide the basis for taxation and conscription. All able-bodied males had to serve in the army and work on public projects: building border walls, imperial roads, canals, and huge palaces in the capital. Although imperial rule was harsh, and censorship was rife, these practices imposed a social order that had been lacking during nearly two and a half centuries of warfare and chaos.

To further unify the varied systems surviving from the Warring States period, the Qin emperor established standard weights and measures, as well as a standard currency. Circular copper coins with square holes in the center (to string them together) replaced the old coins shaped like miniature spades or knives.

The Qin extended China's boundaries in the northeast to the Korean Peninsula, in the south to present-day Vietnam, and in the west into central Asia. The chief minister of the Qin Empire, Li Si, enacted harsh decrees to unify the Central Plain states.

Intellectual Censorship. *This seventeenth-century painting depicts the infamous "Burning of the Books and Burying of the Scholars" edict. As luck would have it, even the state-approved texts were destroyed a mere six years later, during the fall of the dynasty and sack of the capitol.*

Li Si subscribed to the principles of Legalism developed during the Warring States period. This philosophy valued written law codes, administrative regulations, and inflexible punishments more highly than rituals and ethics (which the Confucians emphasized) or spontaneity and the natural order (which the Daoists stressed). Determined to bring order to a turbulent world, Li Si' s strict laws and regulations, as well as harsh punishments, were applied to everyone regardless of rank or wealth. Punishments included beheading, mutilation by cutting off a person's nose or foot, tattooing, shaving off a person's beard or hair, hard labor, and loss of office and rank. After registering people in groups of five and ten, officials made them all responsible for one another—and subject to punishment for any crime that any one of them might commit.

Qin Coin. *After centuries of distinctive regional currencies, the Qin created this standardized bronze coin as part of its general unification policy.*

Small Seal Script. *Under the Qin, the "large seal" script of the Zhou dynasty was unified and simplified to produce a style of calligraphy still used today.*

The Qin also improved communication systems. They constructed roads radiating out from their capital to all parts of the empire. These immense thoroughfares had lanes to accommodate vehicles, pedestrians, animals, and soldiers. Their thick embankments of soil bristled with reinforcing metal poles and pine trees to check erosion. Officials required vehicles to have a standard axle length so that all wheels would fit in the same dirt ruts. Still, the dust and stench were nearly unbearable as travelers journeyed along the hundreds of miles from local towns and villages to the capital and back. After several days of travel, merchants would be lucky if their wares and goods survived undamaged.

Just as crucial was the Qin effort to standardize writing. Banning regional variants in written characters, which had characterized the Warring States period, the Qin required scribes and ministers throughout the empire to adopt the "small seal script," a revised form of writing that resembled the pictographic forms carved on ancient Shang oracle bones (see Chapter 3). Its simpler characters evolved into the less complicated style of bureaucratic writing known as "clerical script" that was prominent during the Han dynasty.

The Qin then used this standard type of writing to disseminate their vision of the state. Standardization also eliminated troublesome ideas that might disturb the new imperial unity. In 213 BCE, a Qin decree ordered officials to confiscate and burn all books in private possession, except for technical works on medicine, divination, and agriculture. In addition, the court prosecuted teachers who used outlawed classical books, including some Confucian works that troublemakers could cite to criticize the Qin regime. Education and learning were now under the exclusive control of state officials. (See Primary Source: A Qin Legal Document: Memorial on the Burning of Books.)

Although critics later described the Qin period as brutal and immoral, even the most outspoken of these writers, Sima Qian, grand historian of the Han, conceded that the people living under Qin rule "were initially delighted. . . . The mountains were free of robbers and bandits, and each family had what it needed."

Economic and Social Changes

The agrarian empire of the Qin yielded wealth that the state could tax, and increased tax revenues meant more resources

PRIMARY SOURCE

A Qin Legal Document: Memorial on the Burning of Books

When the first Qin emperor came to power, his minister, Li Si, devised a policy to enhance state power through a unified political ideology. Any traditions of learning that differed from the Qin orthodoxy were targets for elimination. The most serious threat to Qin power came from the Five Classics (said to have been compiled by Confucius), which stressed moral rectitude, personal character, and political responsibility while holding office. Such texts were an affront to imperial power, Li thought, so he called for their destruction and the execution of scholars who defended them in public.

In earlier times the empire disintegrated and fell into disorder, and no one was capable of unifying it. Thereupon the various feudal lords rose to power. In their discourses they all praised the past in order to disparage the present and embellished empty words to confuse the truth. Everyone cherished his own favorite school of learning and criticized what had been instituted by the authorities. But at present Your Majesty possesses a unified empire, has regulated the distinctions of black and white, and has firmly established for yourself a position of sole supremacy. And yet these independent schools, joining with each other, criticize the codes of laws and instructions. Hearing of the promulgation of a decree, they criticize it, each from the standpoint of his own school. At home they disapprove of it in their hearts; going out they criticize it in the thoroughfare. They seek a reputation by discrediting their sovereign; they appear superior by expressing contrary views, and they lead the lowly multitude in the spreading of slander. If such license is not prohibited, the sovereign power will decline above and partisan factions will form below. It would be well to prohibit this.

Your servant suggests that all books in the imperial archives, save the memoirs of Qin, be burned. All persons in the empire, except members of the Academy of Learned Scholars, in possession of the *Classic of Odes,* the *Classic of Documents,* and discourses of the hundred philosophers should take them to the local governors and have them indiscriminately burned. Those who dare to talk to each other about the *Odes* and *Documents* should be executed and their bodies exposed in the marketplace. Anyone referring to the past to criticize the present should, together with all members of his family, be put to death. Officials who fail to report cases that have come under their attention are equally guilty. After thirty days from the time of issuing the decree, those who have not destroyed their books are to be branded and sent to build the Great Wall. Books not to be destroyed will be those on medicine and pharmacy, divination by the turtle and milfoil, and agriculture and arboriculture. People wishing to pursue learning should take the officials as their teachers.

QUESTIONS FOR ANALYSIS

- According to Li Si, how would the burning of classic texts help the Qin emperor keep "a unified empire" and "sole supremacy"?
- What types of books were still acceptable? Why would the first Qin emperor want to keep these practical works alive?

for imposing order. The government issued rules on working the fields, taxed farming households, and conscripted laborers to build irrigation systems and canals so that even more land could come under cultivation. Unlike the Greek city-states and the Roman Empire, which relied on slave labor for many large-scale tasks in city and countryside, the Qin and the Han dynasties relied much more on free farmers and conscripted their able-bodied sons into their huge armies. Free to work their own land, and paying only a small portion of their crops in taxes, peasant families were the economic bedrock of the Chinese empire.

Agricultural surpluses fueled long-distance commerce—the source of even more wealth and revenues. A class of merchants turned China's cities into dynamic regional market centers. Merchants peddled foodstuffs as well as weapons, metals, horses, dogs, hides, furs, silk, and salt—all produced in different regions. Moreover, the new roads and canals not only aided soldiers' movements but also promoted commerce, carrying both goods and tax revenues from commanderies far and wide. Nonetheless, because the central government valued the production of crops and goods over trade, it imposed ever-higher taxes on goods in transit and in the markets.

Nomads and the Qin along the Northern Frontier

Both the Qin dynasty and, later, the Han dynasty grappled with the need to expand and defend their borders. After the Qin united the Warring States into an empire, it started looking beyond to the north and west where it encountered nomadic warrior peoples—especially the proud Xiongnu discussed in Chapter 5, who dominated the steppes to the north and west of China.

Relations between nomadic peoples and the settled Chinese teetered in a precarious balance until 215 BCE, when the Qin Empire pushed north into the middle of the Yellow River basin, seizing pasturelands from the Xiongnu and opening the region up for settlement. Qin officials built roads into these areas and employed conscripts and criminals to create a massive defensive wall that covered a distance of 3,000 miles along the northern border (the beginnings of the Great Wall of China—though north of the current wall, which was constructed more than a millennium later). In 211 BCE the Qin settled 30,000 colonists in the steppe lands of Inner Eurasia.

The Qin Debacle

Despite its military power, the Qin dynasty collapsed quickly. Its rule weighed heavily on taxpayers, and its constant warfare consumed massive tax revenues and huge numbers of laborers. When desperate conscripted workers mutinied in 211 BCE, they found allies in descendants of Warring States nobles, local military leaders, and influential merchants. The rebels swept up thousands of supporters with their call to arms against the "tyrannical" Qin. Shortly before the First Emperor died in 210, even the educated elite joined former lords and regional vassals in revolt. The second Qin emperor committed suicide early in 207, and his weak successor surrendered to the leader of the Han forces later that year. The resurgent Xiongnu confederacy also reconquered their old pasturelands as the dynasty fell.

In the civil war that followed, an unheralded commoner and former policeman named Liu Bang (r. 206–195 BCE) declared himself prince of his home area of Han. In 202 BCE, Liu proclaimed himself the first Han emperor. Emphasizing his peasant origins, Liu demonstrated his initial disdain for intellectuals by urinating into the hat of a court scholar. But he quickly learned that power would be better served through good manners. Confucian scholars loyal to the Han soon were busy justifying Liu Bang's victory by depicting his Qin predecessors as cruel dynasts and ruthless despots. The scholar Jia Yi (c. 200–168 BCE) rhetorically claimed that the Qin fell "because the ruler lacked moral values." (See Primary Source: Jia Yi on the Faults of the

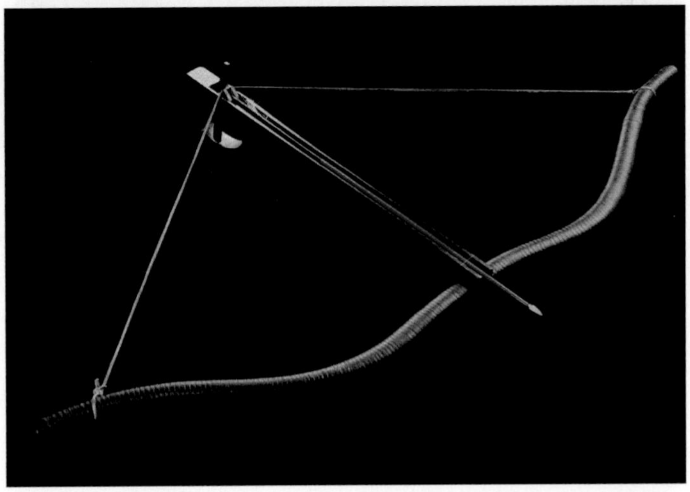

Qin Archer and Crossbow. *This kneeling archer (top) was discovered in the tomb of the First Emperor. Notice his breastplate. The wooden bow he was holding has disintegrated, but a replica appears below. The bronze arrowhead and trigger mechanism in this reproduction were found with the terra-cotta army.*

PRIMARY SOURCE

Jia Yi on "The Faults of the Qin"

After the Qin dynasty disintegrated, Confucians sought to explain the fall of so strong a military power that had unified China just fourteen years before. Jia Yi tied the dynasty's collapse to its autocratic rule and mean-spirited policies. Rather than blame the imperial system itself, Jia blamed the immorality of the Qin penal code and the first Qin emperor's totalitarian policies for his loss of the mandate of heaven. If the Qin had ruled according to Confucian teachings and ritual guidelines, Jia contended, the dynasty would have endured.

[Later] when the First Emperor ascended [the throne] he flourished and furthered the accomplishments of the six generations before him. Brandishing his long whip, he drove the world before him; destroying the feudal lords, he swallowed up the domains of the two Zhou dynasties. He reached the pinnacle of power and ordered all in the Six Directions, whipping the rest of the world into submission and thus spreading his might through the Four Seas. . . . He then abolished the ways of ancient sage kings and put to the torch the writings of the Hundred Schools in an attempt to keep the people in ignorance. He demolished the walls of major cities and put to death men of fame and talent, collected all the arms of the realm at Xianyang and had the spears and arrowheads melted down to form twelve huge statues in human form—all with the aim of weakening his people. Then he . . . posted capable generals and expert bowmen at important passes and placed trusted officials and well-trained soldiers in strategic array to challenge all who passed. With the empire thus pacified, the First Emperor believed that, with the capital secure within the pass and prosperous cities stretching for ten thousand *li*, he had indeed created an imperial structure to be enjoyed by his royal descendants for ten thousand generations to come.

Even after the death of the First Emperor, his reputation continued to sway the people. Chen She was a man who grew up in humble circumstances in a hut with broken pots for windows and ropes as door hinges and was a mere hired field hand and roving conscript of mediocre talent. He could neither equal the worth of Confucius and Mozi nor match the wealth of Tao Zhu or Yi Dun, yet, even stumbling as he did amidst the ranks of common soldiers and shuffling through the fields, he called forth a tired motley crowd and a mob of several hundred to turn upon the Qin. Cutting down trees to make weapons, and hoisting their flags on garden poles, they had the whole world come to them like gathering clouds, with people bringing their own food and following them like shadows. These men of courage from the East rose together, and in the end they defeated and extinguished the House of Qin.

. . . Qin, from a tiny base, had become a great power, ruling the land and receiving homage from all quarters for a hundred-odd years. Yet after they had unified the land and secured themselves within the pass, a single common rustic could nevertheless challenge this empire and cause its ancestral temples to topple and its ruler to die at the hand of others, a laughingstock in the eyes of all. Why? Because the ruler lacked humaneness and rightness; because preserving power differs fundamentally from seizing power.

QUESTIONS FOR ANALYSIS

- According to the reading, what specific steps did the Qin emperor take that were mean-spirited and autocratic?
- What details in this reading help you to imagine the peasant rebellion? What did the peasants use for weapons? What was their typical dwelling like?
- Why would Jia Yi want to preserve imperial government after the Qin had been so cruel?

Qin.) Under the cover of receiving the mandate of heaven, the Han portrayed the Qin as evil; yet at the same time they adopted the Qin's bureaucratic system. In reality—as we can see from a cache of Qin penal codes and administrative ordinances, written on some 1,000 bamboo slips—Qin laws were no crueler than those of the Han.

THE HAN DYNASTY

The Han dynasty, which lasted 400 years (206 BCE–220 CE), became China's formative empire and ultimately oversaw an unprecedented blossoming of peace and prosperity. (See Map 7.2.) Its armies swelled with some 50,000 crossbowmen who

Emperor Wu. *This idealized representation of Emperor Wu (156–87 BCE, r. 141–87 BCE) welcoming a man of letters was one of a series of seventeenth-century silk paintings of Chinese emperors.*

brandished mass-produced weapons made from bronze and iron. Armed with the crossbow, foot soldiers and mounted archers extended Han imperial lands in all directions. Following the Qin practice, the Han also relied on a huge conscripted labor force for special projects such as building canals, roads, and defensive walls.

The first part of the Han dynastic cycle, known as the Western (or Former) Han dynasty (206 BCE–9 CE), brought economic prosperity and the expansion of empire. This was especially the case under Emperor Wu or Wudi, who presided over one of the longest and most eventful reigns in Chinese history (r. 140–87 BCE). Although he was known as the "Martial Emperor" because of the state's many military campaigns, Emperor Wu rarely inspected his military units and never led them in battle. Historians have differed in their opinion of his influence. Some regard him as the most dynamic of the Han monarchs, while others view him as a mere delegator of power, who chose wise subordinates and allowed them to make policy. Undoubtedly he endeavored to cultivate the Daoist principle of *wuwei*, translated as letting things be, that is a policy of laissez-faire, striving to remain aloof from day-to-day activities and permitting the empire to function on its own as if it did not require intervention. Still, he used a stringent penal code to eliminate powerful officials who got in his way. In a single year, his court system prosecuted over a thousand such cases. (See Primary Source: Han Legal Philosophy from Dong Zhongshu.) A usurper tried to introduce land reforms and took power from 9 to 23 CE, but he lost control to a coalition of landowners and peasants who restored the Han dynasty to power. Thereafter, the Han reconsolidated the empire as the Eastern (or Later) Han dynasty (25–220 CE) and moved the capital slightly eastward from Chang'an to Luoyang on the North China plain.

Out of the experience of the Han, the Chinese produced a political narrative known as the **dynastic cycle**. In this scheme, influential families would vie for supremacy. Upon gaining power, they legitimated their authority by claiming to be the heirs of previous grand dynasts and by preserving or revitalizing the ancestors' virtuous governing ways. As a consequence, the Chinese empire was, in the minds of the Chinese at least, different from all other empires. Other empires, such as the Roman or the Persian, rose and fell. The Chinese empire did not, since heaven would grant its mandate to anyone who could keep the empire going. Indeed, the imperial continuity established by the Han was extraordinarily long-lasting, enduring more than 2,000 years until 1911.

Foundations of Han Power

The Han and Roman empires relied on political institutions, ideological supports, and control of economic assets to maintain power. Yet they differed in their use of civil bureaucracy, the military, and ideologies to ensure their subjects' consent. Undergirding the Han Empire was the tight-knit alliance between the imperial family and the new elite—the scholar-gentry class—who shared a determination to impose order on the Chinese population.

POWER AND ADMINISTRATION Although the first Han emperors had no choice but to compromise with the aristocratic groups who had helped overthrow the Qin, in time the Han created the most highly centralized bureaucracy in the world, far more centralized than that of the Roman Empire. No fewer than 130,000 individuals staffed the central and local governments. That structure became the source of its enduring power. As under the Qin, the bureaucracy touched everyone because all males had to register, pay taxes, and serve in the military. The Han court also moved quickly to tighten its grip on regional administration. First it removed powerful princes, crushed rebellions, and took over the areas controlled by regional lords. According to arrangements instituted in 106 BCE by Emperor Wu, the empire consisted of thirteen provinces under imperial inspectors.

A civilian official and a commandant for military affairs shared the work of administering each commandery. These men shouldered immense responsibilities, far exceeding those of their

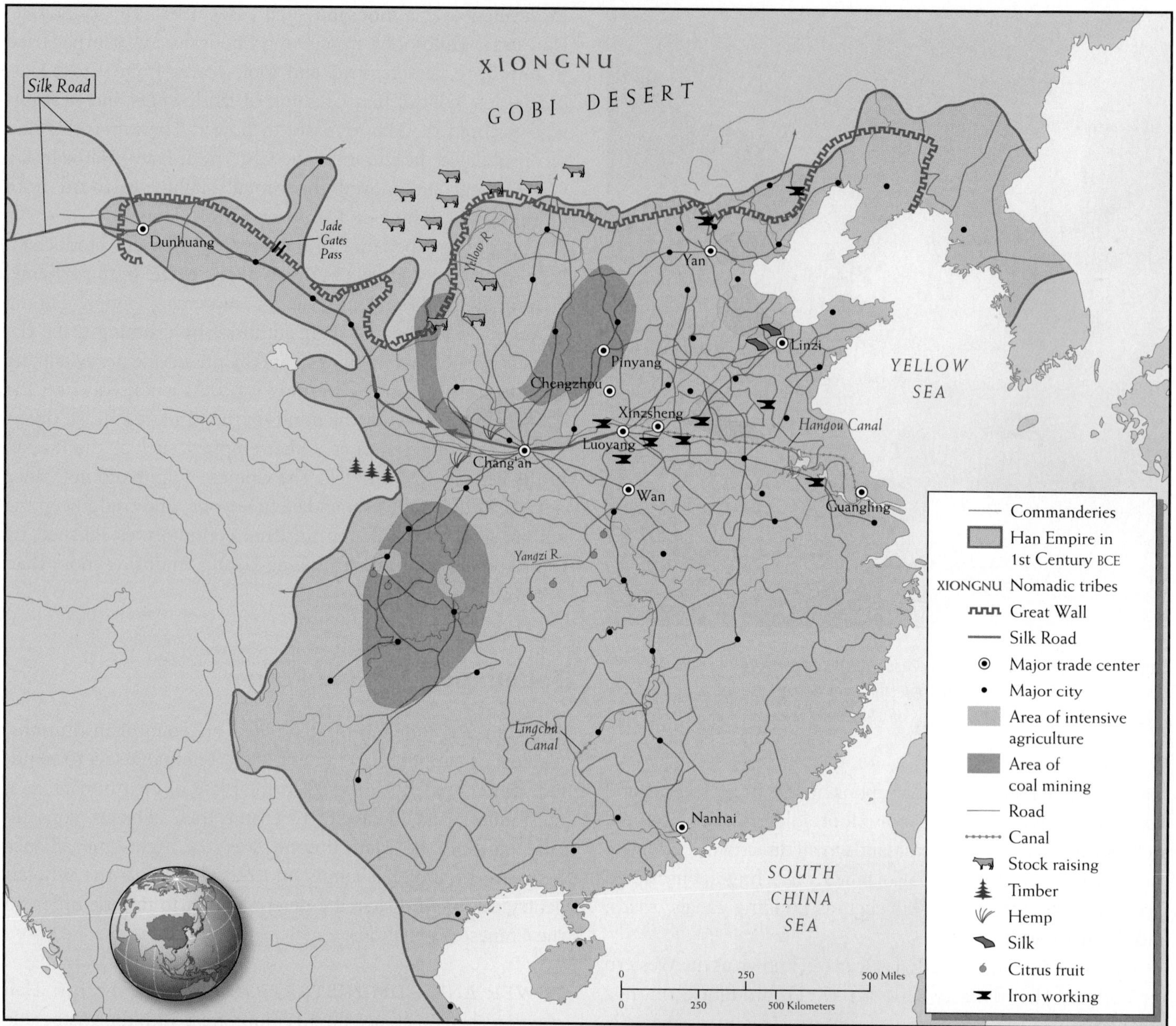

MAP 7.2 | *Pax Sinica:* The Han Empire in the First Century BCE

Agriculture, commerce, and industry flourished in East Asia under Han rule.

- According to the map, what were the main commodities that passed among the empire's regions?
- What type of administrative infrastructure integrated the vast domain?
- What Han policies contributed to this period of peace and prosperity?

counterparts in the Roman Empire. The commanderies covered vast lands inhabited by countless ethnic groups totaling millions of people. These officials, like their Roman equivalents, had to maintain political stability and ensure the efficient collection of taxes. However, given the immense numbers under their jurisdiction and the heavy duties they bore, in many respects the local administrative staff was still inadequate to the tasks facing them.

Government schools that promoted the scholar-official ideal became fertile sources for recruiting local officials. The Han established formal institutions of learning to ensure adequate numbers of well-trained bureaucrats. Emperor Wu founded a college for classical scholars in 136 BCE and soon expanded it into the Imperial University. By the second century CE it boasted 30,000 members, dwarfing the number of students in even

PRIMARY SOURCE

Han Legal Philosophy from Dong Zhongshu

The Qin legal system was considered brutal in its application of uniform punishments against criminals. Scholars claimed that the Qin punished all equally, regardless of the accused's motive or social status. Under the Han emperor Wu, Dong Zhongshu devised an ingenious way to humanize the Han penal code by using Confucian philosophy, so that jurists could consider the litigant's social status and personal motives behind allegedly criminal behavior. In essence, Dong as a Confucian argued that the spirit of the law took precedence over its letter when true justice was the goal.

At the time, there were those who questioned the verdict saying: "A had no son. On the side of the road, he picked up the child B and raised him as his own son. When B grew up, he committed the crime of murder. The contents of the accusation [against B] included [the fact that] A had concealed B [after the crime]. What should be the judgment regarding A?"

Tung Chung-shu passed judgment saying: "A had no son. He restored [B] to life and raised him [as his own son]. Although B was not A's natural son, who would think of seeing [B] as anyone but [A's] son? The *Poetry* [*Classic*] says: 'The mulberry-tree caterpillar has little ones, but the wasp raises them.' According to the intent of the *Annals*, a father must cover up for his son. A accordingly concealed B. The verdict: A does not deserve to be punished."

QUESTIONS FOR ANALYSIS

- Mulberry-tree caterpillars are silkworms. What does the use of this example in a classic text indicate about the importance of that creature to Chinese culture?
- Why would the Han penal code exonerate a stepfather for harboring his son even though the son had committed a serious crime?

Source: Pan Ku, Han-shu 3:1714 (chüan 30); quoted in Benjamin A. Elman, Classicism, Politics, and Kinship: The Ch'ang-chou School of New Text Confucianism in Late Imperial China *(Berkeley: University of California Press, 1990), p. 262.*

the very largest Roman training schools. Not only did students study the classics, but Han scholars also were naturalists and inventors. They made important medical discoveries, dealing with rational diagnoses of the body's functions and the role of wind and temperature in transmitting diseases. They also invented the magnetic compass and developed high-quality paper, which replaced silk, wood, and bamboo strips as media for communicating laws, ideas, rituals, and technical knowledge.

Increasingly, even local elites encouraged their sons to master the classical teachings of Confucianism. This practice not only guaranteed a future entry into the ruling class but also planted the Confucian classics at the heart of the imperial state.

CONFUCIAN IDEOLOGY AND LEGITIMATE RULE

Confucian thought slowly became the ideological buttress of the Han empire. Under Emperor Wu, the people's welfare was deemed the essential purpose of legitimate rule. (See Primary Source: Dong Zhongshu on Responsibilities of Han Rulership.) When the scholar-official Jia Yi wrote that "the state, the ruler, and the officials all depend on the people for their mandate," he was underscoring "the primacy of the people" in affirming the mandate of heaven. However, such principles did *not* imply that the people actually chose their own leaders, as in the Greek-city states (see Chapter 5). The people's only power was the ability to reject rulers who did not promote general well-being.

By 50 BCE, the *Analects* containing Confucius's sayings was widely promulgated and three Confucian ideals reigned as the official doctrine of the Han Empire: honoring tradition, respecting the lessons of history, and the emperor's responsibility to heaven. Scholars such as Dong now used Confucius's words to tutor the princes. By embracing such political ideals, the Han rulers established a polity based on the people's mandate and crafted a careful balance in which the officials provided a counterweight to the emperor's autocratic strength. Of course, when the interests of the court and the bureaucracy clashed, the emperor's will was paramount.

The New Social Order and the Economy

Part of the Han's genius was their ability to win the support of diverse social groups that had been squabbling for centuries.

PRIMARY SOURCE

Dong Zhongshu on Responsibilities of Han Rulership

Early Han dynasty officials sought to enhance the government's legitimacy by adding to the Legalist defense of an autocratic state with a Confucian view of the ruler as the moral and cosmological foundation of government and to laws. Thus the philosopher Dong Zhongshu offered a new theory to legitimize the Han dynasty, while criticizing the Qin's mismanagement of government. Under the guidance of Confucian officials, Dong argued, the imperial system would nourish the people and promote upright officials who would maintain the Han dynasty's mandate to govern, rather than ruling through fear and intimidation.

He who rules the people is the foundation of the state. Now in administering the state, nothing is more important for transforming [the people] than reverence for the foundation. . . . What do I mean by the foundation? Heaven, Earth, and humankind are the foundation of all living things. Heaven engenders all living things, Earth nourishes them, and humankind completes them. With filial and brotherly love, Heaven engenders them; with food and clothing, Earth nourishes them; and with rites and music, humankind completes them. These three assist one another just as the hands and feet join to complete the body. None can be dispensed with because without filial and brotherly love, people lack the means to live; without food and clothing, people lack the means to be nourished; and without rites and music, people lack the means to become complete. If all three are lost, people become like deer, each person following his own desires and each family practicing its own customs. Fathers will not be able to order their sons, and rulers will not be able to order their ministers. Although possessing inner and outer walls, [the ruler's city] will become known as "an empty settlement." Under such circumstances, the ruler will lie down with a clod of earth for his pillow. Although no one endangers him, he will naturally be endangered; although no one destroys him, he will naturally be destroyed. This is called "spontaneous punishment." When it arrives, even if he is hidden in a stone vault or barricaded in a narrow pass, the ruler will not be able to avoid "spontaneous punishment."

One who is an enlightened master and worthy ruler believes such things. For this reason he respectfully and carefully attends to the three foundations. He reverently enacts the suburban sacrifice, dutifully serves his ancestors, manifests filial and brotherly love, encourages filial conduct, and serves the foundation of Heaven in this way. He takes up the plough handle to till the soil, plucks the mulberry leaves and nourishes the silkworms, reclaims the wilds, plants grain, opens new lands to provide sufficient food and clothing, and serves the foundation of Earth in this way. He establishes academies and schools in towns and villages to teach filial piety, brotherly love, reverence, and humility, enlightens [the people] with education, moves [them] with rites and music, and serves the foundation of humanity in this way.

If these three foundations are all served, the people will resemble sons and brothers who do not dare usurp authority, while the ruler will resemble fathers and mothers. He will not rely on favors to demonstrate his love for his people nor severe measures to prompt them to act. . . . [W]hen the ruler relies on virtue to administer the state, it is sweeter than honey or sugar and firmer than glue or lacquer. This is why sages and worthies exert themselves to revere the foundation and do not dare depart from it.

QUESTIONS FOR ANALYSIS

- Count the number of times the following words appear in this reading: *fathers, sons, brothers, filial conduct.* What do these words tell us about Han officials' view of the proper relationship between rulers and subjects?
- How does this reading reflect the gender ideology of Han China?
- Why was the emperor so important in Dong Zhongshu's vision of Han political culture after the fall of the Qin? Was the law code actually made more humane in practice?

Source: "Responsibilities of Han Rulership" from Sources of Chinese Tradition, *Vol. 1, ed. William Theodore de Bary and Irene Bloom, © 1999 Columbia University Press. Reprinted with the permission of the publisher.*

They let aristocratic Qin survivors reacquire some of their former power and urged enterprising peasants who had worked the nobles' lands to become local leaders in the countryside. Successful merchants won permission to extend their influence in cities, and in local areas scholars found themselves in the role of masters when their lords were removed.

Out of a massive agrarian base flowed a steady stream of tax revenues and labor for military forces and public works. The Han court also drew revenues from state-owned imperial lands, mining, and mints; tribute flowed in from outlying domains; household taxes on the nobility; and surplus grains from wealthy merchants who were hungry for noble ranks,

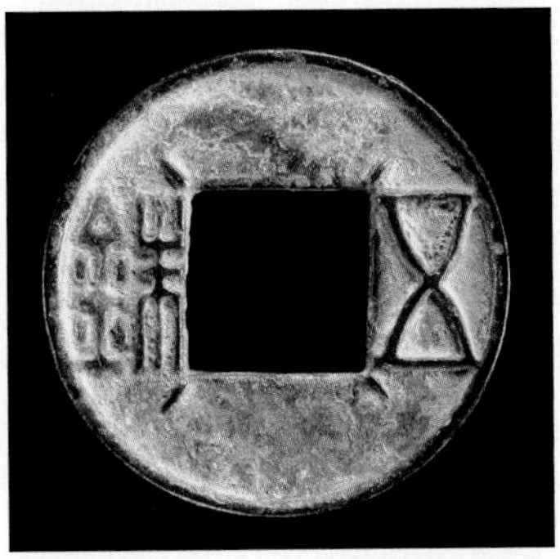

Wuzhu Coin. *This copper coin was issued by Emperor Xuandi during the Western Han Dynasty, 73–49* BCE. *Wuzhu, which means "five grains," refers to the weight of the coin (1 wuzhu = 5 grains = 4 grams). The wuzhu was in circulation until 621* CE.

official appointments, or smaller tax burdens. Emperor Wu established state monopolies in salt, iron, and wine to fund his expensive military campaigns. His policies promoted silk and iron production—especially iron weapons and everyday tools—and controlled profiteering through price controls. He also minted standardized copper coins and imposed stiff penalties for counterfeiting.

Laid out in an orderly grid, Han cities—particularly capitals—reflected their political functions. Bustling markets served as public areas. Carriages transported rich families up and down wide avenues (and they paid a lot for the privilege: keeping a horse required as much grain as a family of six would consume). Court palaces became forbidden inner cities, off-limits to all but those in the imperial lineage or the government. Monumental architecture in China announced the palaces and tombs of rulers rather than the sites of mass entertainment, like the Colosseum in Rome.

DAILY LIFE Wealthy families took pride in their several-story homes displaying richly carved crossbeams and rafters. They cushioned their floors with embroidered pillows, wool rugs, and mats. Fine embroideries hung as drapes, and screens in the rooms secured privacy. Families also sharply distinguished gender roles to increase the authority of the father figure. Women and children stayed cloistered in inner quarters, preserving the sense that the family patriarch's role was to protect mothers, wives, and children from a harsh society. But this did not deprive women from following careers of their own. Elite women, often literate, enjoyed respect as teachers and managers within the family while their husbands served as officials away from home. Ban Zhao, the younger sister of the historian Ban Gu (32–92 CE), serves as an example of an elite woman whose talents reached outside the home. She became the first female Chinese historian and lived relatively unconstrained. After marrying a local resident, Cao Shishu, at the age of fourteen, she was called Madame Cao at court. Subsequently she completed her elder brother's *History of the Former Han Dynasty* when he was imprisoned and executed. In addition to completing the first full dynastic history in China, Ban Zhao wrote *Lessons for Women*, in which she described the status of elite women and presented the ideal woman in light of her virtue, her type of work, and the words she spoke and wrote. Women who were commoners led less protected lives. Many worked in the fields, and some joined troupes of entertainers to sing and dance for food at the open markets.

Silk was abundant and available to all classes, though in winter only the rich wrapped themselves in furs while everyone else stayed warm in woolens and ferret skins. The rich also wore distinctive slippers inlaid with leather or lined with silk. No longer were wine and meat reserved only for festivals, leading critics to decry the debauches of the well-to-do. In the cooked-meat stalls of the markets, those who could afford them pushed and shoved to buy their piglets, dog cutlets, or chopped liver. These tasty foods came to the dinner tables of the wealthy on vessels fashioned with silver inlay or golden handles.

Entertainment for those who could afford it included performing animals, tiger fights, and foreign dancing girls. Some gambled, betting for high stakes at *liubo*, a board game that involved shaking bamboo sticks out of a cup. Live music was popular at private homes, and rich families kept their own

Model of a Han House. *Elite families in Chang'an and other Han cities typically lived in two-story houses with carved crossbeams and rafters and enclosed courtyards. The floors were covered with embroidered cushions, wool rugs, and mats for sitting. Screens were used for privacy. Women and children were cloistered in the inner quarters.*

orchestras, complete with bells and drums. Although events like these had occurred during the Zhou dynasty, they had marked only public ritual occasions.

SOCIAL HIERARCHY At the base of Han society was a free peasantry—farmers who owned and tilled their own land. The Han court upheld an agrarian ideal by honoring the peasants' productive labors, while subjecting merchants to a range of controls (including regulations on luxury consumption) and belittling them for not doing physical labor. Confucians and Daoists supported this hierarchy. Confucians envisioned scholar-officials as working hard for the ruler to enhance a moral economy in which profiteering by greedy merchants would be minimal. In reality, however, the first century of Han rule perpetuated powerful elites. At the apex were the imperial clan and nobles, followed, in order, by high-ranking officials and scholars, great merchants and manufacturers, and a regionally based class of local magnates. Below these elites, lesser clerks, medium and small landowners, free farmers, artisans, small merchants, poor tenant farmers, and hired laborers eked out a living. The more destitute became government slaves and relied on the state for food and clothing. At the bottom was a thin layer of convicts and private slaves.

Between 100 BCE and 200 CE, scholar-officials stood as the bulwark of imperial authority and legitimacy. In their official capacity, they linked the imperial center with local society. At first, their political clout and prestige complemented the power of landlords and large clans, but over time their autonomy grew as they gained wealth by acquiring private property. Following the fall of the Han, they emerged as the dominant aristocratic clans.

In the long run, the imperial court's struggle to limit the power of local lords and magnates failed. Rulers had to rely on local officials to enforce their rule, but those officials could rarely stand up to the powerful men they were supposed to be governing. And when central rule proved too onerous for local elites, they always had the option of rebelling. Local uprisings against the Han that began in 99 BCE forced the court to relax

Han Entertainment. *Han entertainment included dancing, particularly by foreign girls (top left), and acrobatics, for which the Chinese remain famous today (bottom left). Music was often played at the homes of rich families, who kept their own orchestras complete with bells and drums. Musical events became so popular, for both the entertainers (note the face in the Han statue on the right) and the entertained, that performances ceased being only somber ritual occasions.*

its measures and left landlords and local magnates as dominant powers in the provinces. Below these privileged groups, powerless agrarian groups turned to Daoist religious organizations that crystallized into potent cells of dissent.

RELIGION AND OMENS Under Emperor Wu, Confucianism took on religious overtones. Dong Zhongshu, Wu's chief minister, advocated a more activist Confucius. One treatise portrayed him not as a humble teacher but as an uncrowned monarch, and even as a demigod and a giver of laws, which differed from the more sober portrait of Confucius in the *Analects*.

Classical learning also informed popular religion. In the early Han world dominated by social elites, religion linked scholars and officials to the peasantry. Although classical learning remained the preserve of the Confucians at court, many local communities practiced forms of a remarkably dynamic popular Chinese religion.

Imperial cults, magic, and sorcery reinforced the court's interest in astronomical omens—such as the appearance of a supernova, solar halos, meteors, and lunar and solar eclipses. Unpredictable celestial events, as well as earthquakes and famines, were taken as signs of the emperor's lack of virtue, and powerful ministers exploited them to intimidate their ruler. A cluster of calamities, prodigies, and heavenly omens usually meant that the emperor had lost the mandate of heaven. At the same time, people of high and low social position alike took witchcraft very seriously, believing that its practitioners could manipulate natural events and interfere with the will of heaven. Thought about the supernatural affected imperial power, usually buttressing it but at other times promoting dissident leaders and movements. Han elites also took funerary rites very seriously: the rich ordered the finest wood for their coffins, and even the poor had at least their coffin lids painted.

Expansion of the Empire and the Silk Road

Empires seldom stand on shared political and cultural beliefs alone. More often, they survive by force. The Han Chinese were no exception to the general rule. Like their Roman counterparts, they created a ruthless military machine that was effective at expanding their borders and enforcing stability around the borderlands. Peace was good for business, specifically for creating stable conditions that allowed the safe transit of goods over the Silk Road.

Emperor Wu did much to transform the military forces. Following the Qin precedent, he again made military service compulsory. The number of men under arms was stunning: some 100,000 crack troops in the Imperial Guard were stationed in the capital, and more than a million in the standing army. In contrast, the armies of Athens, the largest of the Greek city-states, rarely exceeded 20,000 men; even the Roman field armies rarely exceeded 30,000, and the full standing army of the empire reached only 250,000 or so. The Han created armies on an entirely different scale.

EXPANDING BORDERS During the reign of Emperor Wu, Han control extended from southeastern China to northern Vietnam. Because of similar strife in the northeast, pro-Han Koreans could appeal for Han help against rulers in their internal squabbles. After Emperor Wu's expeditionary force defeated the Korean king, four Han commanderies sprang up in northern Korea. Incursions into Sichuan and the southwestern border areas were less successful, as both mountainous terrain and malaria hampered the Han armies. Nevertheless, a commandery took root in southern Sichuan in 135 BCE, and soon it opened trading routes to Southeast Asia.

THE XIONGNU, THE YUEZHI, AND THE HAN DYNASTY Mighty as this empire was, expansion invariably renewed conflicts along more extended borders. The Han's most serious military threat came from nomadic peoples in the north, especially the Xiongnu. The Han inherited from the Qin a symbiotic relationship with these proud, horse-riding nomads from outside the frontier's defensive wall. Merchants of the Han Empire brought silk cloth and thread, bronze mirrors, and lacquerware to the nomadic chiefs, exchanging them for furs, horses, and cattle.

At first, the Han suffered humiliating defeats at the hands of the Xiongnu. But as the regime grew more powerful, the tables turned. Under Emperor Wu, the Han launched offensive campaigns across the Mongolian steppe to drive back the raiders. Between 129 and 124 BCE, they repelled several Xiongnu invasions. In subsequent campaigns Han forces penetrated deep into Xiongnu territory, reaching as far as the northern Mongolian steppe. Eventually the Han armies split the Xiongnu tribes. The southern tribes surrendered, but the northern ones moved westward—toward the Mediterranean, where they eventually threatened the eastern flank of the Roman Empire.

THE CHINESE PEACE: TRADE, OASES, AND THE SILK ROAD The retreat of the Xiongnu (and other nomadic peoples) introduced a glorious period of peace and prosperity. Now China achieved a ***Pax Sinica*** (149–87 BCE) that was much like the ***Pax Romana*** (25 BCE–235 CE) in the west. Long-distance trade flourished, cities ballooned, standards of living rose, and the population surged. As a result of their military campaigns, Emperor Wu and his successors became monarchs enjoying tribute from distant vassal states. Normally the Han did not intervene in the domestic policy of such states unless they rebelled. Instead, the Han relied on trade and markets to induce their vassals to work within the tribute system and become prosperous satellite states.

Although clashes occurred between the nomadic Xiongnu and the settled Chinese, more often relations in the borderlands

Bronze Horsemen. *Two bronze horsemen holding Chi-halberds from the Later Han dynasty, circa second century CE. These statues were excavated in 1969 in Gansu along the Silk Road. Note the size and strength of these Ferghana horses from central Asia.*

produced benefits for both sides. After all, Han expansion coincided with the flourishing of the Silk Road, where Xiongnu nomads were key middlemen. When the Xiongnu were no longer a threat to the north, Emperor Wu expanded westward. By 100 BCE, he had extended the northern defensive wall from the Tianshan Mountains to the Gobi Desert. Along the wall stood signal beacons for sending emergency messages, and its gates opened periodically for trading fairs. The westernmost gate was called the Jade Gate, since jade from the Taklamakan Desert passed through it. Wu also built garrison cities at oases to protect the trade routes; farthest west was Dunhuang, which later become a culturally diverse center of Buddhist thought and activity.

It was expensive to maintain a strong military force in such a remote and barren country, so Wu established military and farming settlements in the semidesert region. The state even encouraged soldiers to bring their families to settle on the frontier. As warfare in these territories was relatively infrequent, soldiers could spend time digging wells, building canals, and reclaiming wastelands. Soon after its military power expanded beyond the Jade Gate, the Han government set up a similar system of oases on the rim of the Taklamakan Desert. With irrigation, oasis agriculture attracted many more settlers. Traders now could find food for themselves and fodder for their animals as the Xiongnu fled westward. Trade routes passing through deserts and oases now were safer and more reliable than the steppe routes, which they gradually replaced. These new desert routes would flourish for another century, until fierce Tibetan tribes challenged the distant Han frontiers.

Social Convulsions, a Usurper, and the Later Han Dynasty

Emperor Wu's dramatic military expansions required the stationing of soldiers in garrisons from central Asia to the Pacific and from Korea to Vietnam. But further conquests failed to bolster the state's coffers, and supporting the huge expenses of maintaining a gigantic army exhausted the imperial treasury. Wu raised taxes, which put a strain on small landholders and peasants—the bedrock of the empire. The strain continued after his death, and by the end of the first century BCE the Chinese empire was drained financially.

During this epoch large segments of the population suffered a dramatic economic blow, as natural disasters led to crop

The Jade Gate. *From the Jade Gate, the most significant pass on the Silk Road, foods, fruits, and religions of the "Western Regions" were introduced into central China during the Han dynasty. Chinese inventions, such as paper during the Later Han and then the compass and gunpowder, traveled in the opposite direction.*

failures. These worsened the plight of poor farmers, for their taxes were based not on their crop yield but on the size of their holdings. Unable to pay their taxes, many free peasants had to sell their land to large landholders; they then became tenant farmers and sometimes slaves. As local landlords rebuilt their power and their landholdings, they accumulated even more wealth, which enabled them to obtain classical educations and pursue careers as government officials. As a burgeoning population faced land shortages in the countryside, the social fabric of Han society finally tore apart. In desperation, the dispossessed peasants rebelled.

This crisis enabled a former Han minister and regent to a child emperor, Wang Mang (r. 9–23 CE), to take over the throne and establish a new dynasty. He believed that the Han had lost the mandate of heaven. In theory he enacted reforms to help the poor and he fostered economic activity by confiscating gold from wealthy landowners and merchants. His words seemed to favor the redistribution of excess land equitably on the basis of an ancient Mencian ideal of a "well-field" land system: all families would work their own parcels and share in cultivating a communal plot whose crops would become tax surplus for the state. His idealistic reforms failed miserably.

Natural Disaster and Rebellion

Wang Mang succumbed to a violent upheaval by peasants and large landholders against central authority. Bad luck also played a part. Up to 5 million Chinese lived along the great northern plain south of the Yellow River, whose course—unluckily for Wang—changed soon after he assumed power. In 11 CE, the river broke through its dikes. Rather than bending northward on the Central Plain, it flowed due southward toward the Yellow Sea.

This demographic catastrophe plunged the north part of China into famine and banditry; it would repeat itself several more times in Chinese history. Each time it changed course from north to south and then back again, "China's Sorrow," as the river was called, unleashed tremendous floods that caused mass death and vast migrations. Peasant impoverishment and revolt followed with chilling regularity. Researchers estimate that the floods of 11 CE affected some 28 million Chinese, or nearly half the total population.

Wang Mang's reforming regime was utterly unable to cope with a cataclysm of such magnitude. Rebellious peasants, led by Daoist clerics, used the disaster as a pretext to march on Wang's capital at Chang'an. The peasants painted their foreheads red and called themselves Red Eyebrows in imitation of demon warriors, and their leaders spoke to them through inspired religious mediums. By 23 CE they had overthrown Wang Mang. Wang's enemies attributed the natural disaster to the emperor's unbridled misuse of power. They created a history of legitimate Han dynastic power that Wang Mang had illegitimately overturned, and soon Wang became the model of the evil usurper.

The Later Han Dynasty

After Wang Mang's fall, problems of social, political, and economic inequalities fatally weakened the power of the emperor and the court. As a result, the Later Han dynasty (25–220 CE) followed a hands-off economic policy under which large landowners and merchants amassed more wealth and more property. Decentralizing the regime was also good for local business and long-distance trade, as the Silk Road continued to flourish. Chinese silk became popular as far away as the Roman Empire. In return, China received glass, jade, horses, precious stones, tortoiseshells, and fabrics.

By the second century CE, landed elites were enjoying the fruits of their success in manipulating the Later Han tax system. It granted them so many land and labor exemptions that the government never again firmly controlled its human and agricultural resources as Emperor Wu had. As the court refocused on the new capital in Luoyang, local power fell into the hands of great aristocratic families, who acquired even more privately owned land and forced free peasants to become their rent-paying tenants.

Such prosperity bred greater social inequity and a new source of turmoil. Pressure grew on tenants to pay high rents, on the remaining free peasants to pay most of the taxes, and on poor migrant workers to serve as laborers. As the Later Han state's power weakened, its ritual tasks became more formalized. The simmering tensions between landholders and peasants boiled over in a full-scale rebellion in 184 CE. Popular religious groups, such as the Red Eyebrows, championed new ideas among commoners and elites. Confucius was no longer an exemplary figure: the new models were a mythical Yellow Emperor, extolled as the

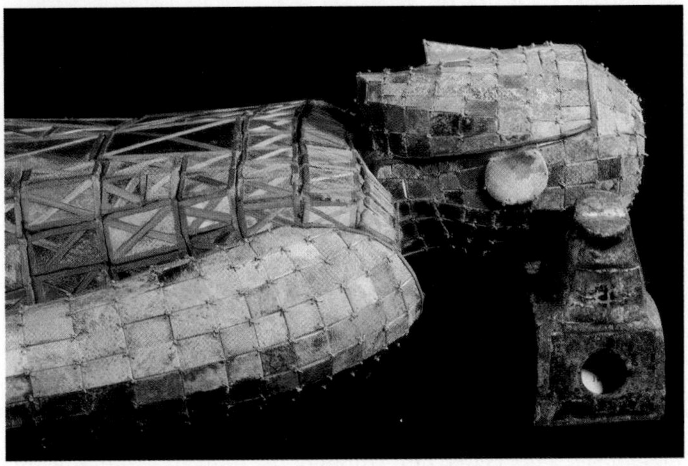

Jade Burial Shroud. *Shown here is the jade burial suit of Princess Tou Wan, late second century BCE.*

inventor of traditional Chinese writing and medicine; and the Daoist sage Master Laozi, the voice of naturalness and spontaneity. Laozi was now treated as a god. Although scholars scorned folk cults and magical practices, both commoners and local magnates in rural communities kept these beliefs alive.

At this propitious moment, Buddhist clerics from central Asia arrived in northern China preaching personal enlightenment for the elite and millenarian salvation for the masses. (A **millenarian movement** is a broad, popular upheaval calling for the restoration of a bygone moral age, often led by charismatic spiritual prophets.) Their message received a warm welcome from an increasingly hostile population. Yet the most powerful challenge to the Later Han came not from the Buddhists but from the Daoists. As Daoist masters challenged Confucian ritual conformity, they advanced their ideas in the name of a divine order that would redeem all people, not just elites. Officials, along with other political outcasts, headed strong dissident groups and eventually formed local movements. Under their leadership, religious groups such as the Yellow Turbans—so called because they wrapped yellow scarves around their heads—championed Daoist millenarian movements across the empire.

Proclaiming the Daoist millenarian belief in a future "Great Peace," the Yellow Turbans demanded fairer treatment by the Han state and equal distribution of all farmlands. As agrarian conditions got worse, a widespread famine ensued. It was a catastrophe that, in the rebels' view, demonstrated the emperor's loss of the mandate of heaven. The economy disintegrated when people refused to pay taxes and provide forced labor, and internal wars engulfed the dynasty. After the 180s CE, three competing states replaced the Han: the Wei in the northwest, the Shu in the southwest, and the Wu in the south. A unified empire would not return until three centuries later.

THE ROMAN EMPIRE

The other large empire of the time flexed its muscle at the other end of Afro-Eurasia. There, Rome became a great power ruling 60 to 70 million subjects. The Roman Empire at its height encompassed lands from the highlands of what is now Scotland in Europe to the lower reaches of the Nile River in modern-day Egypt and part of Sudan, and from the borders of the Inner Eurasian steppe in Ukraine and the Caucasus to the Atlantic shores of North Africa. (See Map 7.3.) It was comparable in size to Han dynasty China.

Whereas China dominated an enormous and unbroken landmass, the Roman Empire dominated lands around the Mediterranean Sea. Like Han China, though, the Romans acquired command over their world through an unprecedented exercise of violence. By the first century CE, almost unceasing wars against their neighbors had enabled the Romans to forge an unparalleled number of ethnic groups and minor states into a single, large political state. (See Current Trends in World History: Empires, Allies, and Frontiers.) This achievement was so striking that the Jewish historian and general Josephus, writing in the 90s CE, saw the empire as the unchallengeable work of God on earth. We can easily see how the Latin word that the Romans used to designate command over their subjects—*imperium*—became the source for the English words *empire* and *imperialism*.

Foundations of the Roman Empire

The emergence of Rome as a world-dominating power was a surprise. Although the Romans might have looked to the Persians or to Alexander the Great for imperial models, they did not. And unlike the Han, they had no great direct imperial ancestors. Down to the 350s BCE, the Romans were just one of a number of Latin-speaking communities in Latium, a region in the center of the Italian peninsula. Although Rome was one of the largest urban centers there, it was still only a city-state that had to ally with other towns for self-defense. However, Rome soon began an extraordinary phase of military and territorial expansion, and by 265 BCE it had taken control of most of the peninsula. At least two factors contributed to this achievement: a migration of foreign peoples, and the Romans' own military and political innovations.

POPULATION MOVEMENTS Between 450 and 250 BCE, migrations from northern and central Europe brought large numbers of Celts to settle in lands around the Mediterranean Sea. They convulsed the northern rim of the Mediterranean, staging armed forays into lands from what is now Spain in the west to present-day Turkey in the east.

One of these migrations involved dozens of Gallic peoples in a series of violent incursions into northern Italy that ultimately—around 390 BCE—led to the seizure of Rome. The important result for the Romans was not their city's capture, but the permanent dislocation that the invaders inflicted on the city-states of the Etruscans, who until then had dominated the Italian peninsula. The Etruscans survived and, with great effort, drove the invading Gauls back northward. But the Etruscan cities never recovered their ability to dominate other peoples in Italy, including the Romans. Thus the Gallic migrations removed one of the most formidable roadblocks to Roman expansion in Italy.

MILITARY INSTITUTIONS AND THE WAR ETHOS Rome's unparalleled expansion could not have occurred without the unique military and political institutions that it developed. Basically, the Romans were more successful and more

War Elephants. *There are no contemporary illustrations of the elephants that Hannibal brought when he invaded Italy in 217 BCE. Hannibal was influenced by the Hellenistic armies in the east who had borrowed the idea of war elephants, and the elephants themselves, from Indian rulers. This painting, by an artist from the school of the Renaissance painter Raphael, highlights the terrifying aspect of the elephants and reduces the human warriors to bit players. In fact, the elephants were not decisive in the winning of any major battle in Italy in the Second Roman-Carthaginian War. Hannibal won them all by superior generalship.*

efficient in killing other humans than any other people in their part of the world. They achieved unassailable military power by organizing the communities that they conquered in Italy into a system that generated huge reservoirs of manpower for their army. This development began between 340 and 335 BCE, when the Romans faced a concerted attack by their fellow Latin city-states. By then, the Latins were viewing Rome not as an ally in a system of mutual defense but as a growing threat to their own independence. After overcoming the nearby Latins, the Romans charged onward to defeat one community after another in Italy. Their main demand of all defeated enemies was to provide men for the Roman army every year. The result was a snowball-like accumulation of military manpower.

By 265 BCE, Rome controlled the Italian peninsula. It next entered into three great wars with the Carthaginians, the major power centered in the northern parts of present-day Tunisia. The First Punic War (264–241 BCE) was a prolonged naval battle over the island of Sicily. With their victory, the Romans acquired a dominant position in the western Mediterranean. The Second Punic War (218–201 BCE), however, revealed the real strength and might of Roman arms. The Carthaginian general Hannibal realized that if his troops were to have any hope of victory, they would have to attack the Italian peninsula itself. The new Roman military system, however, made a Roman victory almost certain. Whereas the Carthaginians' resources were those of a large city-state, by this time Rome was more like a modern nation-state drafting manpower from a huge population. After the heroic feat of crossing the Pyrenees and the Alps with his war elephants, Hannibal entered Italy with a force of only about 20,000 soldiers. In contrast, Rome could draw on reserves of more than 750,000 men. With those numbers, Roman commanders could afford to lose battles—which they proceeded to do, suffering casualties of about 60,000 to 80,000 dead in three great encounters with the Carthaginian general—and still win the war. They finally did so in 201 BCE. In the end, not even a strategic and tactical genius like Hannibal could prevail against the Roman military system. In a final war of extermination, waged between 150 and 146 BCE, the Romans used their overwhelming advantage in manpower, ships, and other resources to bring the five-centuries-long hegemony of Carthage in the western Mediterranean to an end.

In addition to their overwhelming advantage in manpower, the Romans cultivated an unusual **war ethos**. A heightened sense of honor drove Roman men to push themselves into battle again and again, and never to accept defeat. They were educated to imitate the example of soldiers like Marcus Sergius. Wounded twenty-three times in battle, Sergius was crippled in both hands and both feet. In the war with Hannibal he lost one hand but continued to serve, using a false right hand made out of iron. He was twice taken prisoner by Hannibal, each time escaping despite being kept in chains. Going into action four times with his artificial hand tied to the stump of his arm, Sergius helped to rescue major Roman cities from Carthaginian sieges—and twice the horse that he was riding was cut out from under him. Such men set a high standard of commitment to war. What also

NORTH SEA
BALTIC
BRITANNIA
Londinium
0 250 500 Miles
0 250 500 Kilometers
ATLANTIC OCEAN
GERMANIA INFERIOR
GERMANI
BELGICA
GALLIA LUGDUNENSIS
DECUMATES
Rhine R.
AGRI
RAETIA
GERMANIA SUPERIOR
GALLIA AQUITANIA
NORICUM
PANNONIA
GALLIA NARBONENSIS
DALMATIA
LUSITANIA
TARRACONENSIS
ITALIA
ADRIATIC SEA
CORSICA
Rome
Corduba
SARDINIA
BAETIA
MEDITERRANEA
MAURETANIA TINGITANA
SICILIA
MAURETANIA CAESARIENSIS
Carthage
Syracusa
NUMIDIA
AFRICA
GAETULI
GARAMANTES
Mediterranean Sea current
Roman expansion to 201 BCE
Roman expansion 201–100 BCE
Roman expansion 100–44 BCE
Roman expansion 44 BCE–14 CE
Roman expansion 14–96 CE
Roman expansion 96–106 CE
GALLIA Roman province
AGRI Roman region
Roman provincial capital

MAP 7.3 | Roman Expansion to 120 CE

Roman expansion continued for several centuries before reaching its peak in the second century CE.

- According to the map, what were the first provinces to fall under Rome's power? What were the last two?
- Why did the Romans not expand their empire farther into eastern Europe or Southwest Asia?
- What were the geographic limits to Rome's expansion?

CURRENT TRENDS IN WORLD HISTORY

Empires, Allies, and Frontiers

Both the Han and the Roman empires faced threats on their frontiers and used allies as well as their own military prowess to counter such threats. Keeping good relations with frontier allies was essential to the statecraft of empires. It could also yield important intelligence for rulers in capitals.

THE HAN

Consider how the Han dealt with their enemies, the Xiongnu. Emperor Wu sent a special envoy to the Yuezhi, whom he thought would be willing to ally with him against the Xiongnu. His emissary was Zhang Qian, who had volunteered to undertake the journey into the dangerous steppe. In 139 BCE, Zhang set out with a group of 100 people; one was a former slave from the steppe, Ganfu, who guided the travelers and used his bow to kill wild animals when they ran out of food. Aware of the envoy's purpose, the Xiongnu chief detained the group when they tried to pass through his territory. The Xiongnu kept Zhang Qian for ten years, during which time he married a Xiongnu woman and had children. Zhang learned much of steppe life and geography, but he did not forget his mission; together with Ganfu, he eventually managed to escape. At last, they reached the Yuezhi camp on the northern bank of the Oxus River.

Unfortunately, Zhang Qian did not succeed in enlisting the support of the Yuezhi. Their surviving leaders had little inclination to return to the steppe to again battle the fierce Xiongnu, especially as they could see before them the fertile Bactrian plain dotted with Hellenistic cities (see Chapter 6). Zhang Qian accompanied the Yuezhi court in touring the land of Bactria. After consuming a year in futile negotiations with the Yuezhi leaders, Zhang set out for home, bearing much information about the cultures and products of Bactria and regions beyond, including India and Persia. He finally reached Chang'an, the Han capital, thirteen years after beginning his expedition. Although he had failed in his diplomatic mission, Zhang had collected invaluable information for Wudi about the frontier areas in central Asia.

THE ROMANS

The Romans also had to deal with their frontiers. To the north they contended with "barbarians," and to the east they ran up against the powerful kingdoms of the Parthians and the Sasanians. But the Romans did have occasional contacts with kingdoms far to the east. For example, in the reign of Augustus (r. 27 BCE–14 CE) an embassy came from Poros, a king in India. In a letter that his ambassadors carried, Poros described himself as the king over 600 other kings, and he offered any help that the emperor Augustus might want of him. With the letter came gifts carried by eight slaves, naked except for their scented loincloths: a "freak," a number of large snakes, a huge turtle, and a partridge larger than a vulture.

Although embassies of this sort did bring information from far afield, Rome knew little of communities outside the empire to the east except for the peoples and provinces of the Parthian and Sasanian empires, which were closest to its frontiers. Most of this knowledge was very local in nature, gained not through formal channels but in contacts between the two

propelled Roman soldiers was an unusual regime of training and discipline, in which minor infractions of duty were punishable by death (in Greek armies, by contrast, misconduct merely drew fines). Disobedience by a whole unit led to a savage mass punishment, called "decimation," in which every tenth man was arbitrarily selected and executed. For men like Sergius, marching out to war in annual spring campaigns in the month dedicated to Mars (still called March today), the Roman god of war, had an almost biological rhythm.

With an unrelenting drive to war, the Romans continued to draft, train, and field extraordinary numbers of men for combat. Soldiers, conscripted at age seventeen or eighteen, could expect to serve for up to ten years at a time. With so many young men devoted to war for such long spans of time, a war ethos became deeply embedded in the ideals of every generation. After 200 BCE the Romans unleashed this successful war machine on the kingdoms of the eastern Mediterranean—with devastating results. In one year, 146 BCE, the Romans achieved the final extermination of what was left of Carthage in the west—killing all its adult males and selling all its women and children into slavery—and the parallel obliteration of the great Greek city-state of Corinth in the east. Their monopoly of power over the entire Mediterranean basin was now unchallenged.

Roman military forces served under men who knew they could win not just glory and territory for the state, but also enormous rewards for themselves. They were talented men driven by burning ambition, from, in the 200s BCE, Scipio Africanus, the conqueror of Carthage (a man who claimed that he personally states over military or territorial problems or from merchants and other travelers. Diplomacy did exist, but the Roman Empire had no centralized office to manage intelligence reports.

More important than statecraft were exchanges along the Silk Road that brought news, rumors, and impressions of distant empires. The Chinese were the source of the most expensive item in the Roman Empire: the highly valued commodity silk. But in Roman eyes, the Chinese were still very remote and unknown. As Pliny the Elder wrote, "Though mild in character, the Chinese still resemble wild animals in that they shun the company of the rest of humankind, and wait for trade to come to them." Although connected, the two empires that so dominated their own worlds were still worlds apart.

Zhang Qian. *This painting shows Zhang Qian crossing the Yellow River during his journey to the Yuezhi. Although he failed to forge an alliance for Emperor Wu, he returned home with valuable information about frontier areas of central Asia.*

QUESTIONS FOR ANALYSIS

- Compare and contrast the ways in which the Hans and Romans dealt with enemies on the fringes of their respective empires.
- What makes frontier zones useful for the study of world history?

Explore Further

Loewe, Michael. *The Government of Qin and Han Empires: 221 BCE–220 CE* (2006).

Wells, Peter S. *The Barbarians Speak: How the Conquered Peoples Shaped Roman Europe* (1999).

communicated with the gods), to Julius Caesar, the great general of the 50s BCE. A man of prodigious abilities, the greatest orator of his age, and a writer of boundless persuasion, Julius Caesar (100–44 BCE) allegedly could dictate seven letters simultaneously while attending to other duties. He was also a mass killer who kept an exact body count: he knew that he had killed precisely 1,192,000 of the enemy in his wars. And that number did not include his fellow citizens, whose murders during civil wars he refused to acknowledge or add to the total. The eight-year-long cycle of his wars in Gaul (modern-day France and the Rhine valley) was one of the most murderous of his expeditions. By Caesar's own estimation, his army killed more than 1 million Gauls and enslaved another million. The Western world had never witnessed war on this scale; it had no equal anywhere, except in China.

POLITICAL INSTITUTIONS AND INTERNAL CONFLICT

The conquest of the Mediterranean placed unprecedented power and wealth into the hands of a few men in the Roman social elite. The rush of battlefield successes had kept Romans and their Italian allies preoccupied with the demands of army service overseas. Once this process of territorial expansion slowed, social and political problems that had been lying dormant began to resurface.

Following the traditional date of its foundation in 509 BCE, the Romans had lived in a state that they called the "public thing," or *Res publica* (hence, the modern word "republic"). In this state, policy and rules of behavior issued from the Senate—a body of permanent members, 300 to 600 of Rome's most powerful and wealthy citizens—and from popular assemblies of the citizens.

Roman Farmers and Soldiers. *In the late Republic most Roman soldiers came from rural Italy, where small farms were being absorbed into the landholdings of the wealthy and powerful. In the empire, soldiers were recruited from rural provincial regions. They sometimes worked small fields of their own and sometimes worked the lands of the wealthy—like the domain in the Roman province of Africa (in modern-day Tunisia) that is depicted in this mosaic.*

Every year the citizens elected the officials of state, principally two consuls who held power for a year and commanded the armies. In addition, the people annually elected ten men who, as tribunes of the plebs ("the common people"), had the special task of protecting their interests against those of the rich and the powerful. In severe political crises, the Romans sometimes chose one man to hold absolute power over the state; his words, or *dicta,* were law—so he was called a *dictator*. (Under a similar device in China, centrally designated overlords were charged with stabilizing unruly provinces.) Ordinarily the dictator could hold those powers for no longer than six months. The problems with using these institutions, originally devised for a city-state, to rule a Mediterranean-sized empire became glaringly apparent by the second century BCE.

Rome's power elite exploited the wealth from its Mediterranean conquests to acquire huge tracts of land in Italy and Sicily, and then they imported enormous numbers of slaves from all around the Mediterranean to work them. This process drove the free citizen farmers, the backbone of the army, off their lands and into the cities. The result was a severe agrarian and recruiting crisis. In 133 and 123–121 BCE two tribunes, the brothers Tiberius and Gaius Gracchus, tried to institute land reforms guaranteeing to all of Rome's poor citizens a basic amount of land that would qualify them for army service. But political enemies assassinated both men. Thereafter, poor Roman citizens looked not to state institutions but to army commanders, to whom they gave their loyalty and support, to provide them with land and a decent income. These generals became increasingly powerful and started to compete with one another, ignoring the Senate and the traditional rules of politics. As they sought control of the state and their supporters took sides, a long series of civil wars began in 90 BCE. The tremendous resources built up during the conquest of the Mediterranean were now turned inward by the Romans on themselves. These civil wars, lasting down to the late 30s BCE, threatened to tear the empire to pieces from the inside.

Emperors, Authoritarian Rule, and Administration

It is ironic that the most warlike of all ancient Mediterranean states was responsible for creating the most pervasive and long-lasting peace of its time—the *Pax Romana* ("Roman Peace"; 25 BCE–235 CE). Worn out by half a century of savage civil wars, by the 30s BCE the Romans, including their warlike governing elite, were ready to change their values. They were now prepared to embrace the virtues of peace.

But political stability came at a price: authoritarian one-man rule. Peace depended on the power of one man who possessed enough authority to enforce an orderly competition among Roman aristocrats. Ultimately, Julius Caesar's adopted son, Octavian (63 BCE–14 CE), would reunite the fractured empire and emerge as undisputed master of the Roman world. Octavian concentrated immense wealth and the most important official titles and positions of power in his own hands. To signal the transition to a new political order in which he alone would control the army,

Julius Caesar. *This full-size statue represents Caesar as a high-ranking Roman army commander and conveys some of the power and influence that a charismatic military and political leader like Caesar had over both soldiers and citizen voters. Caesar belonged to a generation of Roman politicians who were immensely attentive to their public images.*

the provinces, and the political processes in Rome, he assumed a new name, Augustus ("the Revered One"). He also assumed a series of titles: *imperator,* or "commander in chief" (compare the English word *emperor*); *princeps,* or "first man" (whence the English *prince*); and *caesar* (pronounced "kaisar" in Latin and the source of the words *tsar* in Russian and *kaiser* in German). Augustus became the first of dozens of men who, over the next five centuries, were to rule over Rome's vast dominions as emperors.

Rome's subjects tended to see these emperors as heroic or semidivine beings in life, and to think of the good ones as becoming gods on their death. This propensity to deify good emperors prompted the Emperor Vespasian's famous deathbed joke: "Dear me, I think I'm turning into a god!" Yet emperors were always careful to present themselves as civil rulers whose power ultimately depended on the consent of Roman citizens and the might of the army. They contrasted themselves with the image of "king," or absolute tyrannical ruler, whom the Romans for centuries had learned to detest. The emperors' powers were nevertheless immense. Moreover, many of them deployed their powers arbitrarily and whimsically, exciting a profound fear of emperors in general. One such emperor was Caligula (r. 37–41 CE), who presented himself as a living god on earth, engaged in casual incest with his sister, and kept books filled with the names of persons he wanted to kill. His violent behavior was so erratic that people thought he suffered from serious mental disorders; those who feared him called him a living monster.

Being a Roman emperor was a high-wire act that required finesse and talent, and few succeeded at it. Of the twenty-two emperors who held power in the most stable period of Roman history (between the first Roman emperor, Augustus, and the early third century CE), fifteen met their end by murder or suicide. As powerful as he might be, no individual emperor alone could govern an empire of such great size and population, encompassing a multitude of languages and cultures. He needed institutions and competent people to help him. In terms of sheer power, the most important institution was the army. So the emperors systematically transformed the army into a full-time professional force. Men now entered the imperial army not as citizen volunteers but as paid experts who signed up for life and swore loyalty to the emperor and his family. And it was part of the emperor's image to present himself as a victorious battlefield commander, inflicting defeat on the "barbarians" who threatened the empire's frontiers. Such a warrior emperor, like Trajan, was a "good" emperor.

For most emperors, however, governance was largely a daily chore of listening to complaints, answering petitions, deciding court cases, and hearing reports from civil administrators and military commanders. By the second century CE, the empire encompassed more than forty provinces or administrative units; as in Han China, each had a governor appointed or approved by the emperor. In turn, these governors depended on lower-ranking officials. Compared with the Chinese imperial state, however, which had its ranks of senior and junior officials, the Roman empire of this period was relatively understaffed in terms of central government officials. The emperor and his provincial governors had to depend very much on local help, sometimes aided by elite slaves and freedmen (former slaves) serving as government bureaucrats. With these few full-time assistants and an entourage of friends and acquaintances, the governor was expected to guarantee peace and collect taxes for his province. For many essential tasks, though, especially the collection of imperial taxes, even these helpers were insufficient. Thus the state had to rely on private companies, a measure that set up a tension between the profit motives of the publicans (the men in the companies that took up government contracts) and expectations of fair government among the empire's subjects.

Symbols of Roman Power. *Imperial power was conveyed to the people through highly symbolic public art. In this relief from Sant' Omobono in Rome, which dates to the third century BCE, the winged figures to the left and right of the military shield represent the idea of Victory; the eagle on the shield, holding lightning bolts in its claws, represents brute power; and the garland at the top of the shield represents the wealth and rewards of empire. These symbols of power have been adopted by many modern states in the West.*

Town and City Life

Above all, the emperor counted on local elites to see him as a presence that guaranteed the stability of their world and their personal well-being. Because of the conditions of peace and the unusual concentration of wealth that imperial unity generated, core areas of the empire—central Italy, southern Spain, northern Africa, and the western parts of present-day Turkey—had surprising densities of urban settlements.

A Roman Town. *Roman towns featured many of the standard elements of modern towns and cities. Streets and avenues crossed at right angles; streets were paved; sidewalks ran between streets and houses. The houses were often several stories high and had wide windows and open balconies. All these elements can be seen in this street from Herculaneum, nicely preserved by the pyroclastic flow that ran down the slopes of nearby Mount Vesuvius when its volcano erupted in August of 79 CE, burying the town and its inhabitants.*

MUNICIPALITIES Inasmuch as these towns imitated Roman forms of government, they provided the backbone of local administration for the empire. (See Primary Source: Municipal Charter of a Roman Town.) This system of municipalities would become a permanent legacy of Roman government to the Western world. Some of our best records of how these towns operated come from Spain, which later flourished as a colonial power that exported Roman forms of municipal life to the Americas.

Remarkable physical records of such towns come from Pompeii and Herculaneum in southern Italy. Both towns were almost perfectly preserved by the ash and debris that buried them following the explosion of a nearby volcano, Mount Vesuvius, in 79 CE. Towns often were walled, and inside those walls the streets and avenues ran at right angles. A large, open-air, rectangular area called the *forum* dominated the town center. Around it clustered the main public buildings: the markets, the main temples of principal gods and goddesses, and the building that housed city administrators. Residential areas featured regular blocks of houses, usually roofed with bright red tiles, close together and fronting on the streets. Larger towns like Ostia, the port city of Rome, contained large apartment blocks that were not much different from the four- and five-story buildings in any modern city. In the smaller towns, sanitary and nutritional standards were reasonably good. Human skeletons discovered at Herculaneum in the 1970s revealed people in good health, with much better teeth than many people have today—a difference we can explain largely by the lack of sugar in their diet.

ROME The imperial metropolis of Rome was another matter. With well over a million inhabitants, it was an almost grotesque exaggeration of everything good and bad in Roman city life.

A Roman Municipal Charter. *This bronze tablet inscribed in Latin is part of a group of six bronze tablets discovered in 1981 at the Roman town of Irni, near modern Molino del Postero, in southern Spain. Charters like this one, set up for public display in the forum or central open area of the town, displayed regulations for the conduct of public life in a Roman town, from rules governing family inheritance and property transfers to the election of town officials and definitions of their powers and duties. For some of these rules, see the Primary Source box on the facing page.*

(The only other urban centers of comparable size at the time were Xianyang and Chang'an—the Qin and Han capitals, respectively—each with a population of between 300,000 and 500,000.) Rome's inhabitants were privileged, because there the emperor's power and state's wealth guaranteed them a basic food supply. Thirteen huge and vastly expensive aqueducts provided a dependable daily supply of water, sometimes flowing in from great distances. Most adult citizens regularly received a free, basic amount of wheat (and, later, olive oil and pork). But living conditions were often appalling, with people jammed into ramshackle high-rise apartments that threatened to collapse on their renters or go up in flames. And people living in Rome constantly complained of crime and violence. Even worse was the lack of sanitary conditions—despite the sewage and drainage works that were wonders of their time. Rome was disease-ridden; its inhabitants died from infection at a fearsome rate—malarial infections were particularly bad—so the city required a substantial input of immigrants every year just to maintain its population.

MASS ENTERTAINMENT Every self-respecting Roman town had at least two major entertainment venues. One was an adoption from Hellenistic culture: a theater devoted to plays, dances, and other popular events. The other was a Roman innovation that combined two of these horseshoe-shaped theaters into a single, more elaborate structure called an amphitheater. A much larger seating capacity than in a regular theater surrounded the oval performance area at its center. The emperors Vespasian and Titus completed the Flavian Amphitheater in Rome and dedicated it in 80 CE. It is the vast structure that we know today as the Colosseum, after the colossal statue of the emperor Nero that used to stand beside it. It was a state-of-the-art facility whose floor area, the arena, could handle elaborate hunts of exotic wild animals such as giraffes and elephants. The arena could also be flooded to stage naval battles between hostile fleets, much to the delight of the audience, or it could provide a venue for a Roman invention, gladiatorial games. In these expensive public entertainments, heavily armed and well-trained men—most of them slaves and prisoners of war, but sometimes free men who volunteered—fought each other, wounding or killing for the enjoyment of the huge crowds of appreciative spectators.

Westerners tend to think of these structures for public entertainment as ordinary and normal. Seen from a contemporary Chinese perspective, however, they were strange and unusual. Among the Han, local elites and the imperial family created gigantic palace complexes complete with hunting parks to impress and amuse themselves, not the general public. In contrast, the public entertainment facilities of a Roman town reflected attitudes that stressed the importance of citizens in town life.

Social and Gender Relations

Even more significant than political forums and game venues were the personal relations that linked the rich and powerful with the mass of average citizens. Men and women of wealth and high social status acted as **patrons**, protecting and supporting

PRIMARY SOURCE

Municipal Charter of a Roman Town

Town governments in the Roman Empire followed standard rules and regulations that developed during the Roman conquest of Italy. In 1981, detailed copies of some of these regulations came to light in southern Spain at Molino del Postero (called Irni in Roman times). The Roman governor of Spain in 81 CE had the rules incised on ten plates of bronze for public display in the town's forum. By following these and other rules, the residents of a Spanish community learned how to govern themselves as the Romans did (see a Roman municipal charter on the facing page).

XIX ON AEDILES: The aediles [the two town business managers] . . . are to have the right and power of managing the grain supply, the sacred buildings, the sacred and holy places, the town and its roads and neighborhoods, the drains and sewers, the baths, the marketplace, and of checking weights and measures; and also of setting a night watch if the need arises.

XX CONCERNING THE RIGHT AND POWER OF QUAESTORS: The quaestors [the two town financial officers] . . . are to have the right and power of collecting, spending, storing, administering, and managing the common funds of the municipality at the discretion of the duumviri [the two town mayors]. And they are allowed to have the public slaves belonging to the municipality to help them.

XXI HOW ROMAN CITIZENSHIP IS ACQUIRED IN THE MUNICIPALITY: When those who are senators, decurions [town councillors], or conscripted town councillors who have been or are chosen as town magistrates according to the terms of this law, have completed their term of office, they are to become Roman citizens, along with their parents and wives and any children who have been born out of legal marriages and who are in the power of their parents, and likewise grandsons and granddaughters born to a son. . . .

XXVIII CONCERNING THE FREEING OF SLAVES BEFORE THE MAYORS: If any citizen of the municipality of Flavian Irni . . . in the presence of a duumvir [mayor] of that municipality in charge of the administration of justice sets free his male or female slave from slavery into freedom or orders him or her to be free . . . then any male slave who has been manumitted or ordered to be free in this way is to be free, any female slave who has been manumitted or ordered to be free in this way is also to be free. . . . Someone who is under twenty years of age may manumit his or her slave only if the number of town councillors necessary for decrees passed under this law to be valid decides that the grounds for said manumission are proper.

QUESTIONS FOR ANALYSIS

- What were some of the titles of civil servants in a typical Roman town or municipality?
- According to this charter, what different types of people were part of the normal social structure?
- In what ways could certain inhabitants of towns such as Irni become Roman citizens?
- Why would making small towns uniform in design and function be important to the Roman Empire?

Source: J. González, "The Lex Irnitana: A New Copy of the Flavian Municipal Law," from Journal of Roman Studies, *Vol. 76 (1986). Reprinted with permission of the Society for the Promotion of Roman Studies. Translated by Brent Shaw.*

dependents or "clients" from the lower classes. From the emperor at the top to the local municipal man at the bottom, these relationships were reinforced by generous distributions of food and entertainments from wealthy men to their people. The bonds between these groups in each city found formal expression in legal definitions of patrons' responsibilities to clients; at the same time, this informal social code raised expectations that the wealthy would be public benefactors. For example, a senator, Pliny the Younger, constructed for his hometown a public library and a bathhouse; supported a teacher of Latin; and established a fund to support the sons and daughters of former slaves. The emperors at the very top were no different. Augustus documented the scale of his gifts to the Roman people in his autobiography, gifts that exceeded hundreds of millions of sesterces (a small silver or bronze coin) in expenditures from his own pocket. A later emperor, Trajan, established a social scheme for feeding the children of poor Roman citizens in Italy—a benefaction that he advertised on coins and in pictures on arches in Beneventum and in other towns in Italy.

The essence of Roman civil society, though, involved the formal relationships governed by Rome's laws and courts. By the last century BCE, the Roman state's complex legal system

Aqueduct. *The Romans built aqueducts to transport to Rome the huge amounts of water needed for the city's population of over a million. The idea soon spread to the provinces, where these structures were built to bring water to Roman-style cities developing in the peripheral regions of Roman rule. This aqueduct at Segovia in modern Spain is one of the best preserved.*

North African Amphitheater. *This huge amphitheater is in the remains of the Roman city of Thysdrus in North Africa (the town of el-Jem in modern-day Tunisia). The wealth of the Africans under the empire enabled them to build colossal entertainment venues that competed with the one at Rome in scale and grandeur.*

featured not only a rich body of written law but also institutions for settling legal disputes and a growing number of highly educated men who specialized in interpreting the law. The apparatus of Roman law eventually appeared in every town and city of the empire, creating a deeply entrenched civil culture. It is no surprise that this legal infrastructure persisted long after the empire's political and military institutions had disappeared.

Municipal charters and civil laws—as well as secular philosophers and, later, Christian writers—placed the family at the very foundation of the Roman social order. The authoritarian *paterfamilias* ("father of the family") headed the family. Legally speaking, he had nearly total power over his dependents, including his wife, children, grandchildren, and the slaves whom he owned. Imperial society heightened the importance of the basic family unit of mother, father, and children in the urban centers. As in Han dynasty China, the Roman state regularly undertook a census, rigorously counting the empire's inhabitants and assessing their property for tax purposes—a process that underscored the family as the core unit of society.

This system might seem to place women under the domineering rule of fathers and husbands. That is certainly the picture presented in the repressive laws that Roman men drafted and in the histories that Roman men wrote. But compared with women in most Greek city-states, Roman women, even those of only modest wealth and status, had much greater freedom of action and much greater control of their own wealth and property. (See Primary Source: Birthday Invitation of Claudia Severa.) Thus Terentia, the wife of the Republican senator Cicero (and who also reminds us of Ban Zhao, the female Han historian discussed earlier), bought and sold properties on her own, made decisions regarding her family and wealth without consulting her husband (much to his chagrin—he later divorced her), and apparently fared well following her separation from Cicero. Her behavior was normal for a woman of her status: she was well educated, literate, well connected, and in control of her own life—despite what the laws and ideas of Roman males might suggest. The daily lives of ordinary women that we know of from papyrus documents found in the Roman province of Egypt, for example, show them buying, selling, renting, and leasing with no sign that the legal constraints subjecting them to male control had any significant effect on their dealings.

Economy and New Scales of Production

Rome achieved staggering transformations in the production of agricultural, manufactured, and mined goods. Public and private demand for metals, for example, led the Romans to mine lead, silver, and copper in Spain in operations so massive that traces of the air pollution they generated remain in ice core samples taken from Greenland today (See Analyzing Global Developments: Great Empires Compared: The Han, the Roman, and the British Empire after World War I.) Evidence from Mediterranean shipwrecks similarly indicates a seaborne trade on an unprecedented

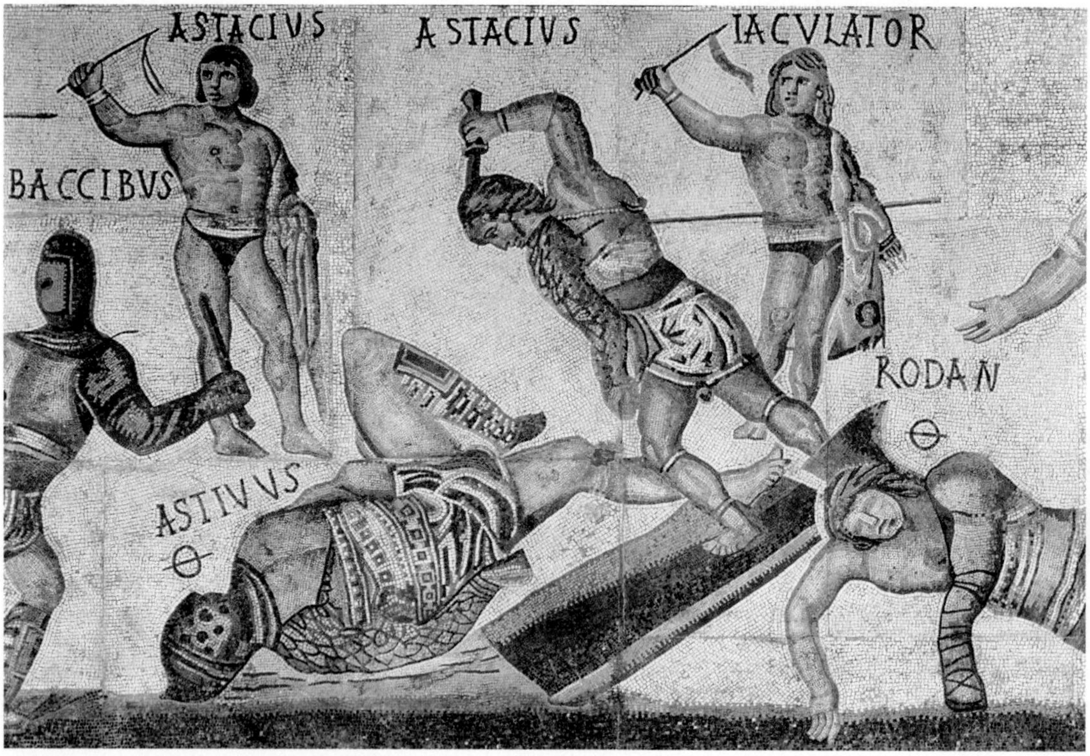

Roman Gladiators. *In this brilliant mosaic from Rome, we see two gladiators at the end of a full combat in which Astacius has killed Astivus. The Greek letter theta, or "th" (the circle with crossbar through it), beside the names of Astivus and Rodan indicates that these men are dead—*thanatos *being the Greek word for "death."*

scale. The area of land surveyed and cultivated rose steadily throughout this period, as Romans reached into arid lands on the periphery of the Sahara Desert to the south and opened up heavily forested regions in present-day France and Germany to the north. (See Map 7.4.)

The Romans also built an unprecedented number of roads to connect far-flung parts of their empire. Although many roads did not have the high-quality flagstone paving and excellent drainage exhibited by highways in Italy, such as the Via Appia, most were systematically marked by milestones (for the first time in this part of the world) so that travelers would know their precise location and the distance to the next town. Also for the first time, complex land maps and itineraries specified all major roads and distances between towns. Adding to the roads' significance was their deliberate coordination with Mediterranean sea routes to support the smooth and safe flow of traffic, commerce, and ideas on land and at sea.

The mines produced copper, tin, silver, and gold—out of which the Roman state produced the most massive coinage known in the Western world before early modern times. Coinage facilitated the exchange of commodities and services, which now carried standard values. Throughout the Roman Empire, from small towns on the edge of the Sahara Desert to army towns along the northern frontiers, people appraised, purchased, and sold goods in coin denominations. Taxes were assessed and hired laborers were paid in coin. The economy in its leading sectors functioned more efficiently because of the production of coins on an immense scale (paralleled only by the coinage output of Han dynasty China and its successors).

Roman mining, as well as other sizable operations, relied on chattel slaves—human beings purchased as private property. The massive concentration of wealth and slaves at the center of the Roman world led to the first large-scale commercial

Roman Roads. *Like Qin and Han China, the Roman Empire was characterized by large-scale road building, which began as early as the late fourth century* BCE*. Roads eventually connected most land areas and larger urban centers in the empire, considerably easing ordinary travel, as well as trade and commerce. Here we see part of the Via Appia, the great highway that connected Rome with the southern parts of Italy.*

PRIMARY SOURCE

Birthday Invitation of Claudia Severa

The ability to write in Latin became so widespread under the Roman Empire that even its frontier areas could boast basic literacy. Excavations of a Roman army base at Vindolanda, in northern England, have unearthed a cache of documents written on thin sheets of wood. These reveal the normal use of Latin writing for everyday activities late in the first century CE. Officers' wives were just as skilled in writing as the men. One of these elite women, Claudia Severa, sent a letter inviting a good friend (whom she addresses affectionately as "sister") to her birthday party. The elegant handwriting on several documents is almost certainly that of Claudia herself. The second letter is her friend's reply.

[Address on the outside:] To Sulpicia Lepidina, wife of Cerialis, from Severa.
[Claudia Severa to her Lepidina, Greetings!]

My sister, I am sending an invitation to you to attend my birthday festivities on the third day before the Ides of September [September 11 in our calendar]—just to make sure that you come to visit us. Your presence will make the day all the more enjoyable for me. Please convey my greetings to your Cerialis [i.e., Lepidina's husband]. My Aelius and our little son send him their warmest greetings.

I await your arrival, my sister.

I bid you goodbye, my sister, my dearest soul. Be well.

[Sulpicia Lepidina to Claudia Severa] Greeting.

Just as I had told you, my sister, and had promised that I would ask your Brocchus [i.e., Claudia Severa's husband, Aelius Brocchus] for permission to come to visit you, he replied to me that I was, of course, always most welcome to come. . . . [I shall try] to come to you by whatever way I can, for there are certain things that we must do . . . on which matter you will receive a letter from me so that you will know what I am going to do. . . .

Farewell, my sister, my dearest and most-desired soul . . .

QUESTIONS FOR ANALYSIS

- What does the writing of letters in Latin at this far edge of the empire tell us about Roman culture?
- Sulpicia mentions asking Claudia's husband for permission to visit Claudia. Why would she do this? Do you think it indicates that the women's husbands were of different military rank, or that Sulpicia was merely following Roman social customs for women—or both? Or something else?
- What does the very existence of these letters tell us about Roman women?

Source: Alan K. Bowman and J. David Thomas, with contributions by J. N. Adams, The Vindolanda Writing-Tablets (Tabulae Vindolandenses II) *(London: British Museum Press, 1994), nos. 291 and 292, pp. 256–62. Translated by Brent Shaw.*

plantation agriculture, along with the first technical handbooks on how to run such operations for profit. These estates specialized in products destined for the big urban markets: wheat, grapes, and olives, as well as cattle and sheep. Such developments rested on a bedrock belief that private property and its ownership were sacrosanct. In fact, the Roman senator Cicero argued that the defense and enjoyment of private property constituted basic reasons for the existence of the state. (See Primary Source: Cicero on the Role of the Roman State.) Roman law more clearly defined and more strictly enforced the rights of the private owner than any previous legal system had done. The extension of private ownership of land and other property to regions having little or no prior knowledge of it—Egypt in the east, Spain in the west, the lands of western Europe—was one of the most enduring effects of the Roman Empire.

Religious Cults and the Rise of Christianity

The world of gods, spirits, and demons that characterized earlier periods remained hugely important. But if there was any religion of empire, it was **Christianity**. Its foundations lay in a direct confrontation with Roman imperial authority: the trial of Yeshua ben Yosef (Joshua son of Joseph). He preached the new doctrines of what was originally a sect of Judaism, and we know him today by the Greek form of his name, Jesus. A Roman governor, Pontius Pilatus, tried Jesus in a typical Roman provincial trial; he was found guilty of sedition and executed, along with two bandits, by a standard Roman penalty—crucifixion.

We know of Jesus only after his death. No reference to him survives from his own lifetime. Two years after the crucifixion,

ANALYZING GLOBAL DEVELOPMENTS

Great Empires Compared: The Han, the Roman, and the British Empire after World War I

The Roman and Han empires were the most powerful and extensive empires that the world had known at the time, and because of their grandeur and accomplishments, they remained part of the European and Chinese historical traditions. Even the British imperialists, who, as the following table demonstrates, ruled over much larger populations than the Romans and the Han Chinese, though with lesser military forces, often compared their empire to that of the Romans. We have added the Qing Empire at its height at the end of the nineteenth century because it rivaled the British Empire in so many respects.

QUESTIONS FOR ANALYSIS

- If you compare the modern-day British Empire with the empires of the Romans and the Han Chinese, what differences stand out in terms of land area and total population? How can we explain some of these differences?
- Can you explain why the Han Empire and the Qing Empire had much larger armies than the Roman and British empires?
- What does the population data on cities suggest about the place of cities in early world history versus modern world history?

Maximum Land Area	
Roman Empire	970,000 square miles, mainly land based
Han Empire	4,000,000 square miles, mainly land based
British Empire	1,800,000 square miles, largely sea-borne
Qing Empire	3,500,000 square miles, largely land based
Total Population	
Roman Empire	c. 60,000,000 (c. one-eighth of the Afro-Eurasian population)
Han Empire	c. 59,000,000 (c. one-eighth of the Afro-Eurasian population)
British Empire	459,307,735 (c. one-quarter of the world's population)
Qing Empire	450,000,000 (c. one-quarter of the world's population)
Size of the Military Forces	
Roman Empire	400,000
Han Empire	1,000,000
British Empire	330,000
Qing Empire	1,000,000

Largest Cities	
ROMAN EMPIRE	
Rome	1,100,000
Alexandria	600,000
Carthage	400,000
Athens	300,000
Antioch	250,000
HAN EMPIRE	
Chang'an City	1,000,000
Luoyang City	400,000
BRITISH EMPIRE IN 1920	
London	7,488,000
Calcutta	1,328,000
Bombay	1,176,000
Glasgow	1,052,000
Birmingham	922,000
Cairo	791,000
QING EMPIRE IN 1910	
Beijing	1,100,000
Guangzhou	739,000
Yangzhou	567,300
Shanghai	444,318

Sources: Ping-Ti Ho, Studies on the Population of China, 1368–1953 *(Cambridge, Mass.: Harvard University Press, 1959); Susan Naquin,* Peking: Temples and City Life, 1400–1900 *(Berkeley: University of California Press, 2000); Tim Cornelland and John Matthews,* Atlas of the Roman World *(New York: Checkmark Books, 1982); Greg Woolf,* Rome: An Empire's Story *(New York: Oxford University Press, 2012).*

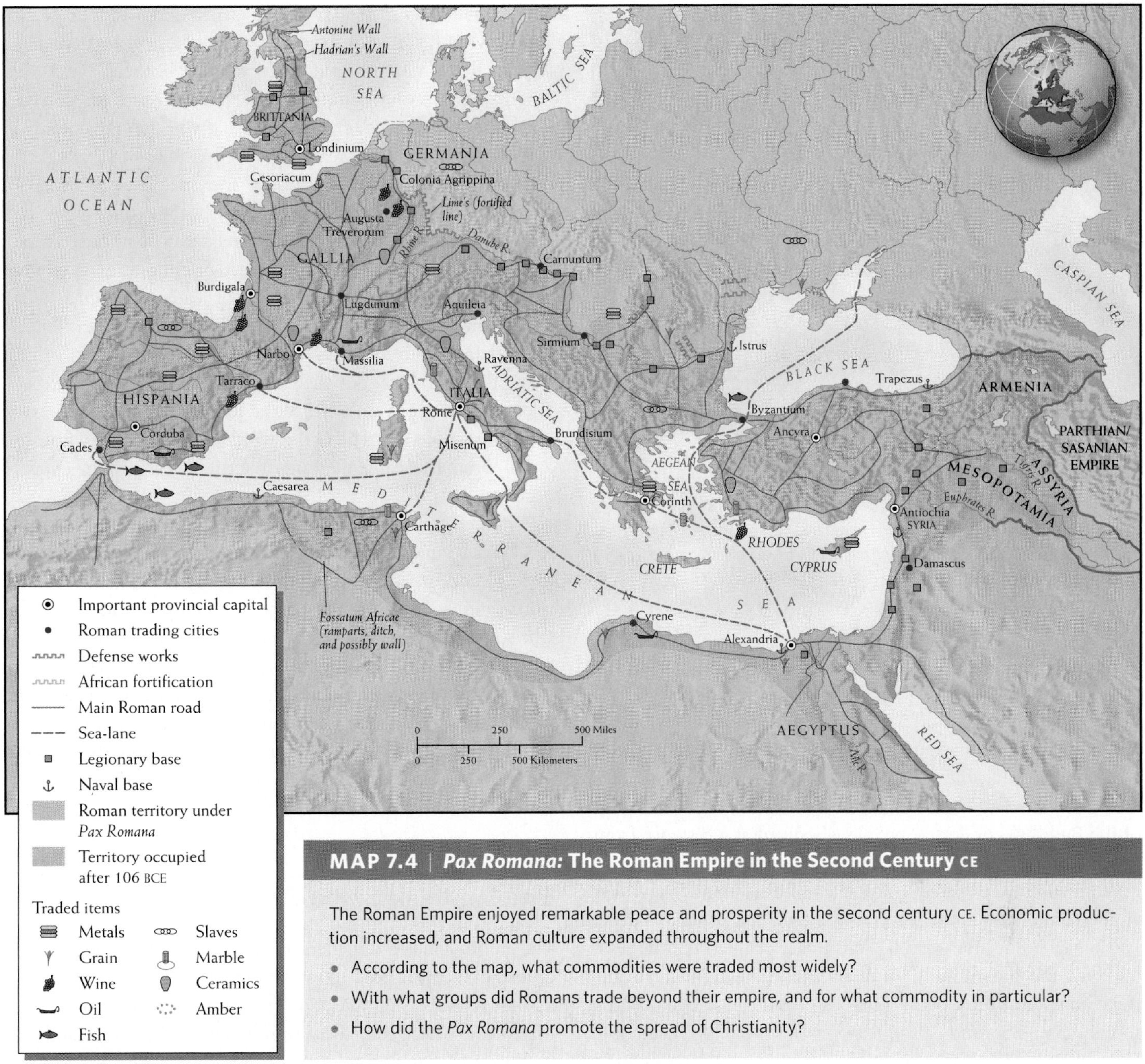

MAP 7.4 | *Pax Romana:* The Roman Empire in the Second Century CE

The Roman Empire enjoyed remarkable peace and prosperity in the second century CE. Economic production increased, and Roman culture expanded throughout the realm.

- According to the map, what commodities were traded most widely?
- With what groups did Romans trade beyond their empire, and for what commodity in particular?
- How did the *Pax Romana* promote the spread of Christianity?

Paul of Tarsus, a Jew and a Roman citizen from southeastern Anatolia, claimed to have seen Jesus in full glory outside the city of Damascus. Paul and the communities to whom he preached between 40 and 60 CE were the first to call Yeshua "Jesus." They also referred to him as "the Christ"—*ho Christos*—or the Anointed One (i.e., the Messiah), and thought of him as a god.

Paul had not been one of Jesus's original disciples. Only much later did four of those men—Matthew, Mark, Luke, and John—write about his life and record his sayings in accounts that came to be called the Gospels. (That early English word translates their name in the original Greek, *Evangeliai*, or "Good News.") The Gospels all sought to tell the world not what Jesus had said, but who he had been. They served as answers to the question that Jesus reportedly asked his disciples a few months before he died: "Who do people say that I am?" (Mark 8:27).

Jesus's preachings could not have been more Jewish. He taught that God is the father of his people—sinners who are always liable to fall away. But God is like a good shepherd to them. Scrambling down dangerous ravines, the good shepherd seeks those who have gone astray, joyfully carrying home on his shoulders even a single lost lamb (see John 10:1–18). We have already met the image of the great king as shepherd of his

Coin Hoard. *The use of coins for a wide spectrum of economic exchanges became common in the Roman Empire. Looking at the batches buried for safekeeping gives us an idea of the range of coins in circulation at any one time. This coin hoard was found near Didcot in Oxfordshire, England. Buried about 165 CE, it contained about 125 gold coins minted between the 50s and 160s CE and represents the equivalent of about eleven years' pay for a Roman soldier. Gold coins were used for expensive transactions or to store wealth. Most ordinary purchases or payments were made with silver or brass coins.*

people in both Egypt and Mesopotamia (see Chapter 3). With Jesus, this ancient image took on a new, personal closeness. Not a distant monarch but a preacher, Jesus had set out on God's behalf to gather a new, small flock. Jesus's teachings (like those of the Buddha) comforted people who lived at a distance from power, such as scholars, merchants, and farmers.

To his followers, Jesus was a man who had slowly revealed an awesome, hidden identity. He was crucified not for what he had preached but for what he (or others) claimed that he was. Through the preaching of Paul in Greek and the textual portraits painted in the Gospels, also in Greek, this image of Jesus rapidly spread beyond Palestine (where Jesus had preached only to Jews and only in the local language, Aramaic) and entered the religious bloodstream of the Mediterranean. Core elements of Jesus's message, such as the special responsibilities of the well-off for the poor and the promised eventual empowerment of "the meek," appealed to huge numbers of ordinary persons in the wider Mediterranean world. But it was the apostle Paul who was especially responsible for reshaping this message for a wider audience. While Jesus directed his teachings to villagers and peasants, Paul's writing and preaching dealt with a world heavily populated by slaves. For him, God was a father figure who set converts free and embraced them as His children. This new message was immediately accessible to the dwellers of the towns and cities of the Roman Empire.

Just half a century after Jesus's crucifixion, the followers of Jesus saw in his life not the wanderings of a Jewish charismatic teacher but a moment of head-on conflict between "God" and "the world." (A **charismatic** is a person who uses his personal strengths or virtues, often laced with a divine aura, to command followers.) Thus, the preaching that his followers brought to confront this world was no longer the preaching of a man. It was the message of a divine being—who, for thirty years half a century before, had moved (largely unrecognized) among human beings. The followers formed a church: a permanent gathering committed to the charge of leaders chosen by God and by their fellow believers. For these leaders and their followers, death—death for Jesus—was the hallmark of their faith. In dying they witnessed for the faith. Indeed, the defining experience for Christians was that of the Roman trial and the idea of "witnessing" to God. The Greek word *martus* means a witness in a trial. From this came the English term *martyr* and the concept of martyrdom.

The persecutions of Christians were sporadic and intensely local. Like imperial power itself, persecutions were responses to local concerns. Not until the emperor Decius, in the mid-third century CE, did the state direct an empire-wide attack on Christians. And that attempt failed. Decius died within the year, and Christians interpreted their persecutor's death as evidence of the hand of God in human affairs. By the last decades of the third century, Christian communities of various kinds, reflecting the different strands of their movement through the Mediterranean as well as the local cultures in which they settled, were present in every society in the empire.

The Limits of Empire

The empire labeled outsiders as those whom it excluded, and a crucial part of this process was the exercise of force in extending its borders. (See Map 7.5.) The limitations of Roman force determined who belonged in the empire and was subject to it, and who was outside it and therefore excluded. To the west the Romans pushed their authority to the shores of the Atlantic Ocean, and to the south they drove it to the edges of the Sahara Desert. In both cases, there was little more useful land available to dominate. To the east and north, however, things were different.

On Rome's eastern frontiers, powerful Romans such as Marcus Crassus in the mid-50s BCE and Mark Antony in the early 30s BCE wished to imitate the achievements of Alexander the Great and conquer the arid lands lying east of Judea and Syria. But they failed miserably, stopped by the Parthian Empire and their successors the Sasanian Empire (see Chapter 6 for a full discussion of the Parthians and Chapter 8 for more on the Sasanians). The Sasanians expanded the technical advances

PRIMARY SOURCE

Cicero on the Role of the Roman State

Whereas Greek thinkers debated ethics and morals, the role of the good life, and the nature of the universe, Romans deliberated more about the nature of government and the role of the state. This focus reflects their pragmatic attitudes and their possession of a huge empire. In the following passage, Marcus Tullius Cicero, one of the leading Roman politicians from the 60s to the 40s BCE, discusses how any man who holds public office in the Roman state has a duty to defend the state's main function.

That man who undertakes responsibility for public office in the state must make it his first priority to see that every person can continue to hold what is his and that no inroads are made into the goods or property of private persons by the state. It was a bad policy when Philippus, when he was tribune of the plebs [about 104 BCE], proposed an agrarian reform law. When his law was defeated, he took the defeat well and was moderate in his response. In the debates themselves, however, he tried to curry popular favor and acted in a bad way when he said, "In our community there are not more than two thousand men who have real property."

That speech ought to be condemned outright for attempting to advocate equality of property holdings. What policy could be more dangerous? It was for this very reason—that each person should be able to keep his own property—that states and local governments were founded. Although it was by the leadership of nature herself that men gathered together in communities, it was for the hope of keeping their own property that they sought the protection of states. . . .

Some men want to become known as popular politicians and for this reason they engage in making revolutionary proposals about land, with the result that owners are driven from their homes and money lent out by creditors is simply given free to the borrowers with no need for repayment. Such men are shaking the very foundations of the state. First of all, they are destroying that goodwill and sense of trust which can no longer exist when money is simply taken from some people and given to others [by the state]. And then they take away fairness, which is totally destroyed if each person is not permitted to keep what is his own. For, as I have already said, it is the peculiar function of the state and of local government to make sure that each person should be able to keep his own things freely and without any worry.

Source: De Officiis (On Duties), *2.21.73, 22.78; translated by Brent Shaw.*

QUESTIONS FOR ANALYSIS

- According to Cicero, what is the main function of the Roman state and the main reason men "sought the protection of states"?
- How does the protection of private property rights affect the claims that citizens had on their rulers?
- And how does this differ from the role of the state in contemporary Han dynasty China?

in mounted horseback warfare that the Parthians had used so successfully in open desert warfare against the slow-moving Roman mass infantry formations. King Shapur I (Shabuhr), their greatest monarch, exploited the weaknesses of the Roman Empire in the mid-third century, even capturing the Roman emperor Valerian. As successful as Parthians and Sasanians were in fighting the Romans, however, they could never challenge the Romans' sway over Mediterranean lands. Their decentralized political structure limited their coordination and resources, and their horse-mounted style warfare was ill-suited to fight around the more rocky and hilly environments of the Mediterranean world. In the lands across the Rhine and Danube, to the north, environmental conditions largely determined the limits of empire. The long and harsh winters, but excellent soil and growing conditions, produced hardy populations clustered densely across vast distances. These illiterate, kin-based agricultural societies had changed little since the first millennium BCE. And because their warrior elites still engaged in armed competitions, war and violence characterized their connections with the Roman Empire. As the empire fixed its northern frontiers along the Rhine and Danube rivers, two factors determined its relationship with the Germans and Goths on the rivers' other side. First, these small societies had only one big commodity for which the empire was willing to pay: human bodies. So

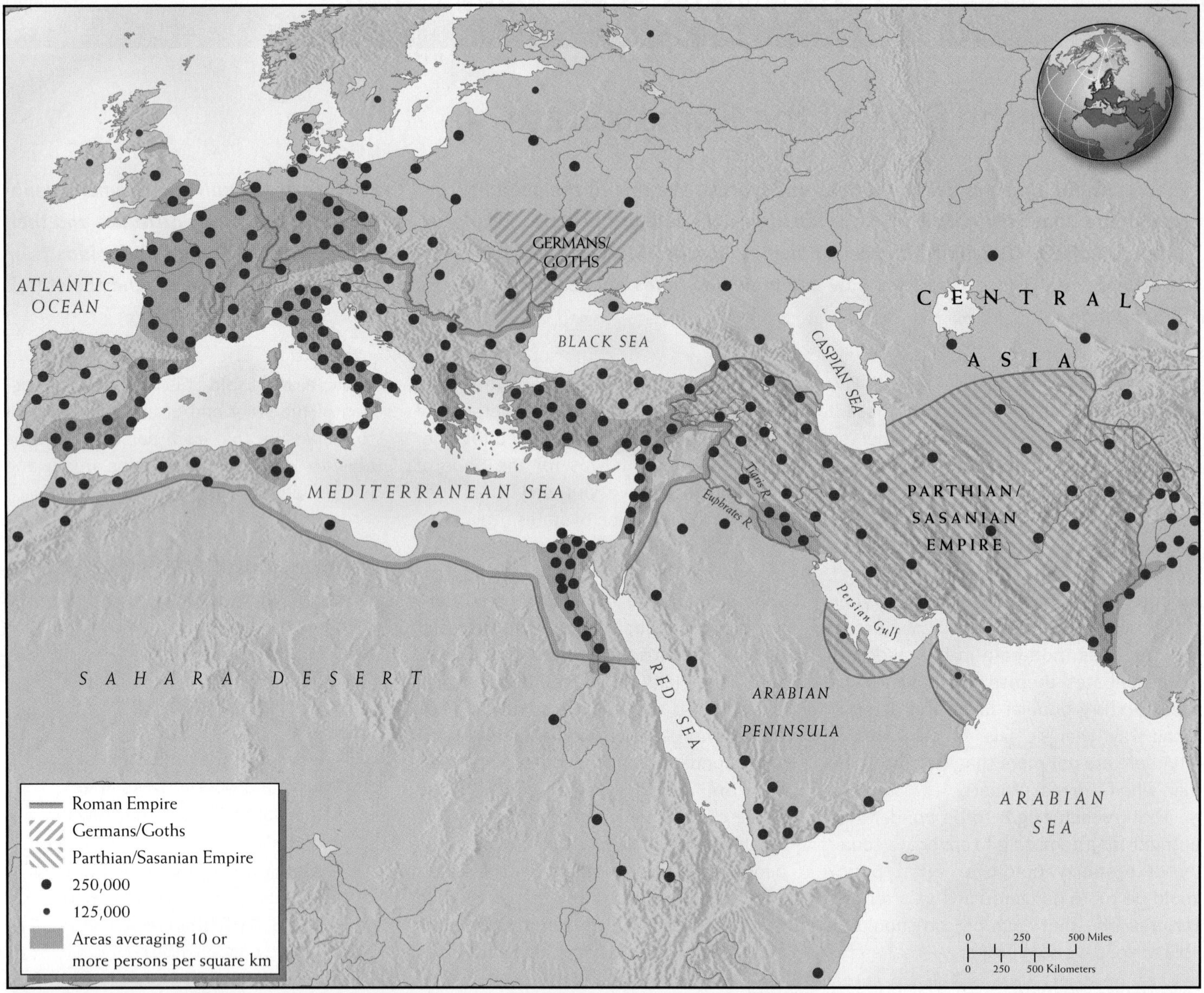

MAP 7.5 | Population of Roman World in 362 CE

Roman frontiers at the northern and eastern limits of the empire were persistent sources of anxiety and concern for imperial leaders. While not as densely populated as the Roman Empire, these regions contained large population centers as well.

- Name some of the major groups of peoples that lived just beyond Roman rule in the areas of eastern Europe and Southwest Asia.
- What were the geographical limits of the Roman Empire?
- According to your reading, why were Roman armies never able to subdue these neighboring peoples?

the slave trade out of the land across the Rhine and Danube became immense: gold, silver, coins, wine, arms, and other luxury items flowed across the rivers in one direction in exchange for slaves in the other. Second, their wars were unremitting, as every emperor faced the expectation of dealing harshly with the "barbarians." These connections, involving arms and violence, were to enmesh the Romans ever more tightly with the tribal societies. They even overlapped, as internal conflicts within the Roman Empire ultimately prompted increasing use of "barbarians" as soldiers and officers who served the empire. While the Han Empire had fallen by 300 CE, the Roman Empire would continue to exist politically for nearly two more centuries in which its history would become intertwined with the rise of Christianity, one of the world's universalizing religions.

Soldier versus Barbarian. *On the frontiers of the Roman Empire, the legionary soldiers faced the non-Roman "barbarians" from the lands beyond. In this piece of a stone-carved picture from the northwestern frontier, we see a civilized and disciplined Roman soldier, to the left, facing a German "barbarian"—hair uncut and unkempt, without formal armor, his house a thatched hut. Frontier realities were never so clear-cut, of course. Roman soldiers, often recruited from the "barbarian" peoples, were a lot more like them than was convenient to admit, and the "barbarians" were influenced by and closer to Roman cultural models than this picture indicates.*

CONCLUSION

China and Rome both constructed empires of unprecedented scale and duration, yet they differed in fundamental ways. Starting out with a less numerous and less dense population than China, Rome relied on slaves and "barbarian" immigrants to expand and diversify its workforce. While less than 1 percent of the Chinese population were slaves, more than 10 percent were slaves in the Roman Empire. The lifeblood of the Chinese rural economy was a huge population of free peasant farmers; this enormous labor pool, together with a remarkable bureaucracy, enabled the Han to achieve great political stability. In contrast, the millions of peasant farmers who formed the backbone of rural society in the Roman Empire were much more loosely integrated into the state structure. They never unified to revolt against their government and overthrow it, as did the mass peasant movements of Later Han China. By comparison with their counterparts in China, the peasants in the Roman Empire were not as well connected in their proximity or density, or as united in purpose. Here, too, the Mediterranean environment accented separation and difference.

By Chinese standards, the Roman Empire was relatively fragmented and underadministered. Moreover, philosophy and religion never underpinned the Roman state in the way that Confucianism buttressed the dynasties of China. Both empires, however, benefited from the spread of a uniform language and imperial culture. The process was more comprehensive in China, which possessed a single language that the elites used, a literary language based on classical Chinese, than in Rome, whose empire spanned a two-language world: Latin in the western Mediterranean, Greek in the east. Both states fostered a common imperial culture across all levels of society. Once entrenched, these cultures and languages lasted well after the end of empire.

Differences in human resources, languages, and ideas led the Roman and Han states to evolve in unique ways. In both places, however, the faiths of outsiders—Christians and Buddhists—eclipsed the classical and secular traditions that grounded their states' foundational ideals. Transmission of these new faiths benefited from expanded communications networks. The new religions added to the cultural mix that succeeded the Roman Empire and the Han dynasty.

At their height, both states surpassed their forebears by translating unprecedented military power into the fullest form of state-based organization. Each state's complex organization involved the systematic control, counting, and taxing of its population. In both cases, the general increase of the population, the growth of huge cities, and the success of long-distance trade contributed to the new scales of magnitude, making these the world's first two global empires. The Han would not be superseded in East Asia as the model empire until the Tang dynasty in the seventh century CE. In western Afro-Eurasia, the Roman Empire would not be surpassed in scale or intensity of development until the rise of powerful European nation-states more than a millennium later.

AFTER YOU READ THIS CHAPTER

Review and research materials are available on STUDYSPACE: wwnorton.com/studyspace

TRACING THE GLOBAL STORYLINES

FOCUS ON: *Comparing the Two Empires*

- Han China and imperial Rome assimilate diverse peoples to their ways and regard outsiders as uncivilized.
- Both empires develop professional military elites, codify laws, and value the role of the state (not just the ruler) in supporting their societies.
- Both empires serve as models for successor states in their regions.
- The empires differ in their ideals and the officials they value: Han China values civilian bureaucrats and magistrates; Rome values soldiers and military governors.

CHRONOLOGY

East Asia

Qin Empire **221–207 BCE**

Emperor Wu expands Han Empire **140–87 BCE**

The Mediterranean

Roman state expands through Italian peninsula **350–265 BCE**

Rome eliminates Carthage (Punic Wars) **265–146 BCE**

400 BCE | **300 BCE** | **200 BCE** | **100 BCE**

KEY TERMS

charismatic p. 272

Christianity p. 269

commanderies p. 242

dynastic cycle p. 247

millenarian movement p. 256

patrons p. 265

Pax Romana p. 253

Pax Sinica p. 253

war ethos p. 257

STUDY QUESTIONS

1. **Analyze** the impact of Xiongnu pastoralists on imperial policies of the Qin and Han dynasties. How did each dynasty counter the threat of nomadic incursions into its territorial heartlands?
2. **Explain** the influence of Confucian ideas during the Han dynasty. How did these ideas shape political and social hierarchies during this period?
3. **Describe** the process through which the Roman city-state created a vast empire in the Mediterranean world. How did Roman attitudes toward military service influence the empire's growth?
4. **Explain** the social and legal hierarchies that governed Roman urban life. To what extent did residents enjoy personal autonomy?
5. **Explain** the concepts of *Pax Sinica* and *Pax Romana*. How did Han and Roman leaders promote long periods of peace and prosperity in eastern and western Afro-Eurasia, respectively?
6. **Compare and contrast** the concept of emperor in the Han dynasty with that in the Roman Empire. What role did emperors play in the governing structure of their respective empires?
7. **Compare and contrast** the methods through which Han and Roman leaders enlisted their subjects' support. What emphasis did each state place on ideology, civil bureaucracy, and military organization?
8. **Compare and contrast** the labor systems in the Qin and Han dynasties with that of the Roman Empire. To what extent did each rely on forced labor?
9. **Compare and contrast** Roman strategies for promoting stability along its borders with those of the Han dynasty. How different were the threats that each empire faced from borderland peoples?

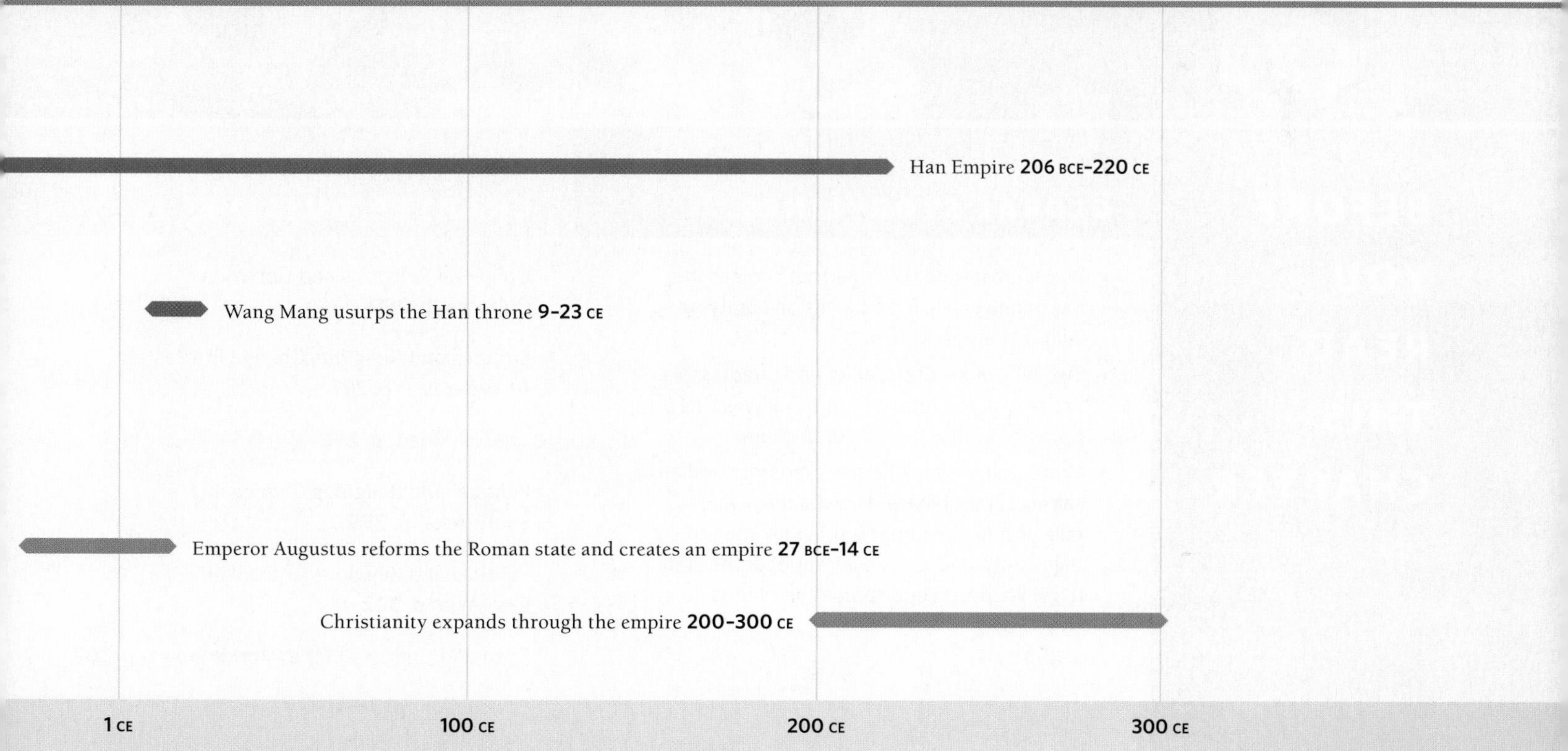

BEFORE YOU READ THIS CHAPTER

GLOBAL STORYLINES

- Afro-Eurasia and the Americas witness the rise of universalizing religions and unifying cultural beliefs.
- Two religions—Christianity and Buddhism—aspire to world missions and challenge the power of secular rulers and thinkers.
- While undermining Roman emperors, Indian satraps, and Chinese dynasts, these new religions also win important statesmen to their cause and use the authority of the state to gain converts and spread their faiths.

CHAPTER OUTLINE

8

The Rise of Universal Religions, 300–600 CE

FOCUS QUESTIONS

- How did Christianity and Buddhism shape Afro-Eurasian communities during this era?
- Where and why did universal religions have such a wide appeal?
- How was Hinduism similar to and different from Buddhism and Christianity?
- To what extent did common cultural outlooks develop in sub-Saharan Africa and the Americas?
- How did religious development bring worlds together and drive them apart during this era?

Around 180 CE, a humble group of seven men and five women stood trial before the provincial governor at Carthage. They claimed to be Christians, and their crime was refusal to worship the gods of the Roman Empire. The governor was unimpressed; his god was "the protecting spirit of our lord the emperor." One Christian retorted that his god was also an emperor, but that he could not be seen, for he stood "above all kings and all nations." There was an unbridgeable gap between the governor and the Christians. So the governor read out a death sentence, ordering their immediate execution. "Thanks be to God!" cried the Christians, and straightaway they were beheaded.

As the centuries unfolded, the tables would turn dramatically. Old ideas of the supremacy of an emperor-lord gave way to those of the Lord God as emperor. Previously, the impulse toward universalism, that is to say bringing everyone under the sway of a single ruler or a single religion, had come from ambitious empire builders, like Alexander the Great and the Roman emperors. Now, for the first time, religious leaders became the agents of universalist messages and worked to convert humanity to their belief systems. This period, which witnessed the bonding of religions to universal aspirations, spread religious tenets across the Afro-Eurasian landmass and gave religions, notably Christianity and Buddhism, a universalistic message and widespread appeal to diverse peoples and cultures. In this era spiritual and religious fervor, while it triggered new divides in the world, became an even more powerful force of integration than political ambitions. This advent of religions as global shapers of unity was anything but simple. They built on the expansive reach of the Roman and Han empires while at the same time reshaping the institutions of these states. They also profited from the closer commercial and intellectual connections between east and west. This chapter tells the story of how Christianity and Buddhism became universal religions that changed world history.

UNIVERSAL RELIGIONS AND COMMON CULTURES

From 300 to 600 CE, the entire Afro-Eurasian landmass experienced a surge of religious ferment. In the West, Christianity became the state faith of the Roman Empire. In India, Vedic religion (Brahmanism) evolved into a more formal spiritual system called Hinduism. In northern India, central Asia, and even China, Buddhism—originally a code of ethics—became a religion. Across much of the world, spiritual concerns integrated scattered communities into shared faiths.

Two faiths in particular aspired to universality in this era—Christianity and Buddhism. They were to be joined by Islam several centuries later. What made them universalistic in comparison with, say, Judaism, Hinduism, and traditional African religious beliefs was that they were not tied to a locality. Hinduism was the belief system of the peoples of South Asia. Judaism was tied to a specific ethnicity, while traditional African religious beliefs varied from people to people. In contrast, Christianity and Buddhism appealed to diverse populations (men and women, freeborn and slaves, rich and poor) and proved adaptable as they moved from one cultural and geographical area to another. They were promoted by energetic and charismatic missionizing agents and, despite their many and insistent demands, they provided a deep sense of community to their converts. In the case of Christianity, though to a lesser extent Buddhism, these religions also benefited from the support of powerful empires.

The new spirituality blossomed inside and also outside empires (see Map 8.1). In western Europe, Christianity continued to expand alongside a decaying Roman state. In the eastern Mediterranean, it inspired a revived Roman *imperium* at Byzantium. In India, Hinduism and Buddhism vied for cultural preeminence; in central Asia and China, Buddhism flourished as the old polities foundered.

The peoples living in sub-Saharan Africa and the Americas, too, reached beyond their local communities, creating common cultures across wider geographical areas. In Africa, the Bantu-speaking peoples, residing in the southeastern corner of present-day Nigeria, began to spread their way of life throughout the entire southern half of the landmass. Similarly, across the Atlantic Ocean, the Mayans established political and cultural institutions over a large portion of Mesoamerica.

A wide variety of societies experienced spiritual ferment. This does not mean that people became more excitable or more otherworldly; it means that religion touched more areas of society and in more demanding ways. People felt deeply about religion because it was through religious filters that they processed the meaning of what was important to them as individuals. They discussed issues of truth, loyalty, and solidarity in terms framed by spiritual leaders who claimed to know the truth about an invisible other world.

Consider how many questions in our own world are assumed to be answerable by science. In many respects, religion functioned in that age as science does in ours. It claimed to give clear answers about the nature of human beings, whom they should obey, and the degree of allegiance they owed to something unseen rather than to any ruler. Even more, as the case of the Christian martyrs showed, religion told them what they should die for.

As cultures shrugged off their older heritages, shared faith brought people together and enabled them to identify with people and places beyond their own local worlds. Some religious systems, such as Buddhism and Christianity, spread far and wide because they professed universal rules and principles to guide behavior that transcended place, time, and specific cultural practices; later, Islam would follow the same pattern (see Chapter 9).

Sharp distinctions between right and wrong also drew new lines between peoples. Religion became a wedge that drove worlds apart, as absolute conviction left little room for tolerance. Centuries of harmonious interaction offered few protections to neighbors now perceived to be "wrong" in their beliefs—and their errors could get them ostracized, exiled, or killed. For wrong beliefs were considered as dangerous as today's counterfeit medicines. Like noxious drugs, they had to be removed from circulation as quickly as possible. Conflict, even violence and religious persecution, accompanied this new sense of certainty.

Across Afro-Eurasia, universal religions were on the move. Religious leaders carrying written texts (books, scrolls, or tablets of wood or palm leaf) often traveled widely. Christians from Persia went to China. Buddhists journeyed from South Asia to Afghanistan and used the caravan routes of central Asia to reach China. In 643 CE, the Chinese Buddhist Xuanzang brought back to Chang'an (then the world's largest city) an entire library of Buddhist scriptures—527 boxes of writings and 192 birch-bark tablets—that he had collected on a pilgrimage to Buddhist holy sites in South Asia. He lodged them in the Great Wild Goose Pagoda and immediately began to translate every line into Chinese. Here was the "truth" of Buddhism for Xuanzang, similar to the way we accept information we find in a modern science textbook, and as exciting as a revelation when they reached distant China as when Buddhist thinkers had elaborated them in northern India, more than 5,000 miles away. Some Chinese Buddhists now referred to India as the "Central Kingdom."

Xuanzang. *This painting c. 900 CE, which survives in the caves of Dunhuang along the Silk Road, portrays the Chinese pilgrim Xuanzang accompanied by a tiger on his epic travels to South Asia to collect important Buddhist scriptures.*

EMPIRES AND RELIGIOUS CHANGE IN WESTERN AFRO-EURASIA

By the fourth century in western Afro-Eurasia, the Roman Empire was hardly the political and military juggernaut it had been 300 years earlier. Surrounded by peoples who coveted its wealth while resisting its power, Rome was fragmenting. Yet its endurance was a boon to the new religious ferment, which took hold in its rapidly changing political institutions. Although so-called barbarians eventually overran the western parts of the empire, in many ways those areas still felt "Roman." They looked to the new faith of Christianity to maintain continuity with the past, eventually founding a central church in Rome to rule the remnants of empire.

This Christian empire split almost from the start (see Map 8.2). In Rome's east, a powerful successor state appeared in the form of the Byzantine Empire based at Constantinople. Its claim to be the political arm of Christianity seemed more viable than that of the church based in Rome. But it faced a new foe still farther east. The Sasanian Empire of Persia, like the church at Rome and the Byzantine state, was unique. These states represented something unprecedented: they claimed the blessing of newer religions, Christianity and Zoroastrianism, and their rulers expected all subjects to worship the correct god in the correct manner. Those who did not were treated as outsiders, in both this life and the next—where hell awaited them.

The Rise and Spread of Christianity

Ironically, the most crucial change ever to befall the Roman Empire had little to do with distant frontier wars. Instead, it grew from a religious war fought, from the bottom up, in the peaceful and tightly administered towns that were the nerve centers of the Roman Mediterranean.

The rise of Christianity coincided with the appearance of a new figure in matters of spiritual belief: the **martyr**. Martyrs were people whom the Roman authorities executed for persisting in their Christian beliefs instead of submitting to traditional rituals or beliefs. Many of them were remarkable witnesses to their faith. In 203 CE, a well-to-do mother in her early twenties, Vibia Perpetua, faced a horrible punishment for refusing to sacrifice to the Roman gods. Denied the benefit of a human executioner, she and her companions were condemned to face wild beasts in the amphitheater of Carthage. The amphitheater is still there, north of modern Tunis. It is a mean, small place—not a gigantic stadium. The condemned and the spectators would have had eye contact with one another throughout the fatal encounter.

FOREST
NOMADIC
HUNTERS
NORTH
AMERICA
ROCKY MOUNTAINS
PLAINS
NOMADIC
HUNTERS
Great Lakes
Mississippi R.
St. Lawrence R.
ATLANTIC
OCEAN
Gulf
of
Mexico
Teotihuacán
MAYAN
CITY STATES
WEST INDIES
PACIFIC
OCEAN
Amazon R.
ANDES MOUNTAINS
CHAVIN
SOUTH
AMERICA
CELTIC
PEOPLES
GOTH
Qi
Tuoba
Hephthalites
Sasanian
Gupta
Eastern Roman
Mayan
VANDALS Kingdom
BANTU People
City
0
1000
2000 Miles
0
1000
2000 Kilometers

MAP 8.1 | Empires and Common Cultures from 300 to 600 CE

The period 300–600 CE was a time of tumultuous political change.

- Comparing this map with Map 6.3, which polities are new? Which polities have disappeared? Which ones have expanded or contracted?
- What historical factors are driving these changes in the political landscape?

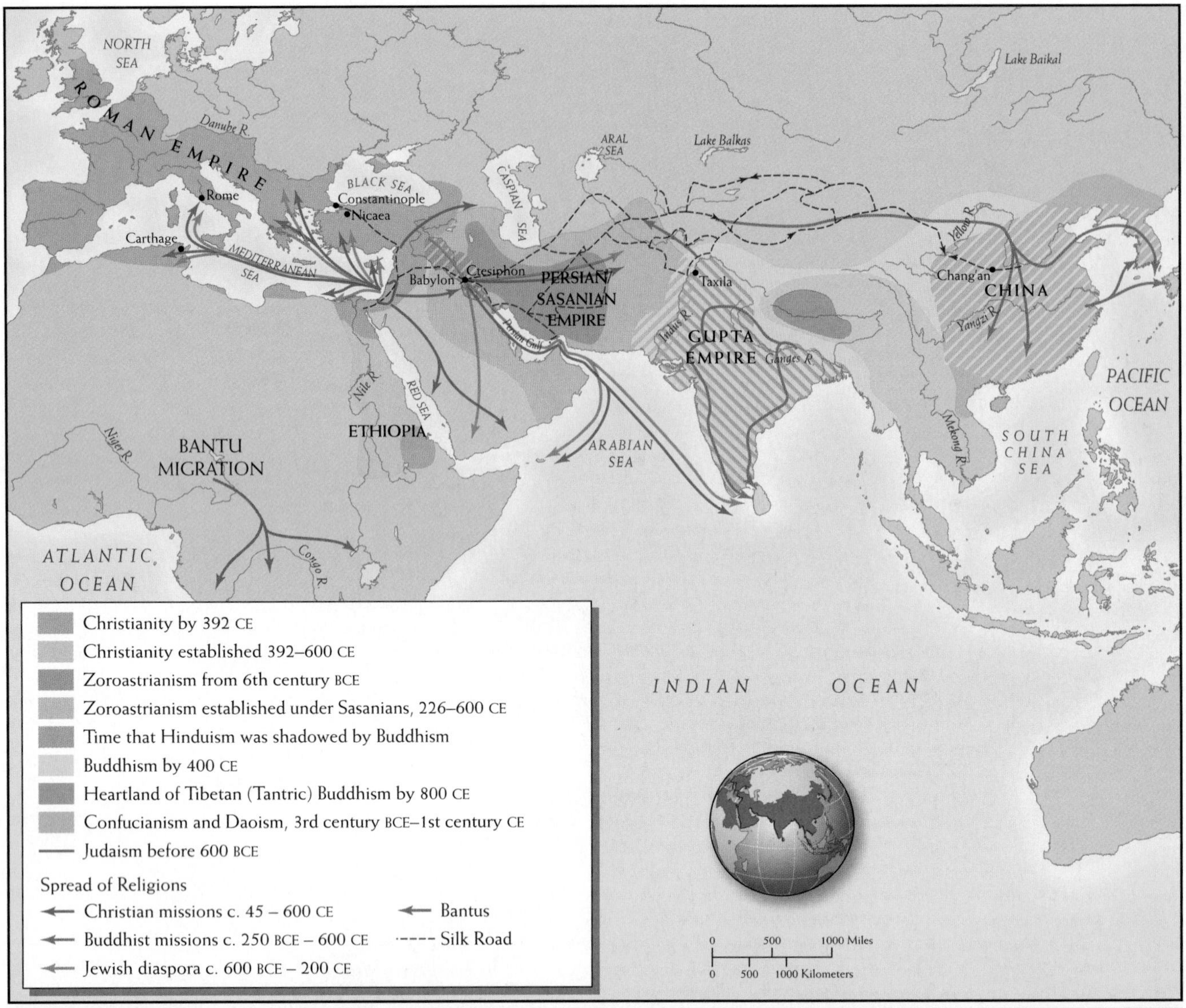

MAP 8.2 | The Spread of Universal Religions in Afro-Eurasia, 300–600 CE

The spread of universal religions and the shifting political landscape were intimately connected.

- Using Map 8.1, identify the major polities in Afro-Eurasia during this era. How did these political configurations differ from those in the era covered in Chapter 7?
- Compare and contrast Map 8.1 with Map 8.2. Where did Hinduism, Buddhism, and Christianity emerge, and where did they spread?
- How did the rise and fall of empires affect the expansion of universal religions?

Before her death, Perpetua dictated a prison diary that is unique in Roman literature. Here a woman speaks with a full religious message. She describes her relief at being allowed to have her baby stay with her: "My prison had suddenly become a palace, so that I wanted to be there rather than anywhere else." More important, she recounts powerful visions of the next world that fortify her with courage. Perpetua stepped every night into paradise, a place of peace and abundance: "I saw an immense garden, and in it a gray-haired man sat in a shepherd's garb; tall he was, and milking sheep. And around him were many thousands of people clad in white garments. He raised his head, looked at me and said: 'I am glad you have come, my child.'"

Other religions, including Judaism and later Islam, honored martyrs who died for their faith. But because Christianity claimed to be based directly on "the blood of martyrs," in the words of Tertullian (197 CE), martyrdom gained unusual significance in the early church. Moreover, the remembered heroism of women martyrs balanced the increasingly all-male leadership—bishops and clergy—of the institutionalized Christian church.

Christian Martyrs. *The Christian martyr Perpetua (left) came to be represented as an upper-class Roman matron with carefully covered hair. Set in a circle of bright blue, in the golden dome of a church, she looks out from a distant, peaceful Heaven. The detail from a mosaic found in a Roman circus in North Africa (right) shows a criminal tied to a stake and being pushed on a little cart toward a lunging leopard. Christian martyrs were treated much the same as criminals: they were executed—exposed to animals without even the "privilege" of suffering at the hands of a human executioner.*

RELIGIOUS DEBATE AND CHRISTIAN UNIVERSALISM

The spread of religious ideas in the Roman Empire changed the way people viewed their existence. Believing implied that an important "other" world loomed beyond the world of physical matter. Feeling contact with it gave worshippers a sense of worth; it guided them in this life, and they anticipated someday meeting their guides and spiritual friends there. The fervor for paradise was so potent that scarcely a century after Perpetua's execution, the Roman emperor Constantine believed that a vision sent by Christ had brought him military victory. Thereafter Constantine and his successors placed the awesome authority of the Roman state behind a Christian church that until then had been marginal and often persecuted.

No longer were the gods local powers to be placated by archaic rituals in sacred places. Many became omnipresent figures whom mortals could touch through loving attachment. As ordinary mortals now could hope to meet these divine beings in another, happier world, the sense of an afterlife glowed brighter.

Above all, gods now expected to be obeyed; and it was on the issue of obedience to God, rather than to a human ruler, that the Christians sparked a Mediterranean-wide debate on the nature of religion. Like the Jews, the Christians possessed divinely inspired scriptures that told them what to believe and do, even when those actions went against the empire's laws.

In their emphasis on texts, the Christians were moving with the times. After 200 CE, published writings circulated widely in the Roman world. By 300 CE, a revolution in book production had taken place. The scroll that all ancient readers had used (and that survives in the Torah scrolls of Jewish synagogues) gave way to the codex: separate pages bound together as a book (just like the book that you now have in your hand). Christians spoke of their scriptures as "a divine codex." Bound in a compact volume or set of volumes, this was the definitive Code of God's law.

THE CONVERSION OF CONSTANTINE Crucial in spurring Christianity's eastward expansion was the transformative experience of a man named **Constantine** (c. 280–337 CE). Born

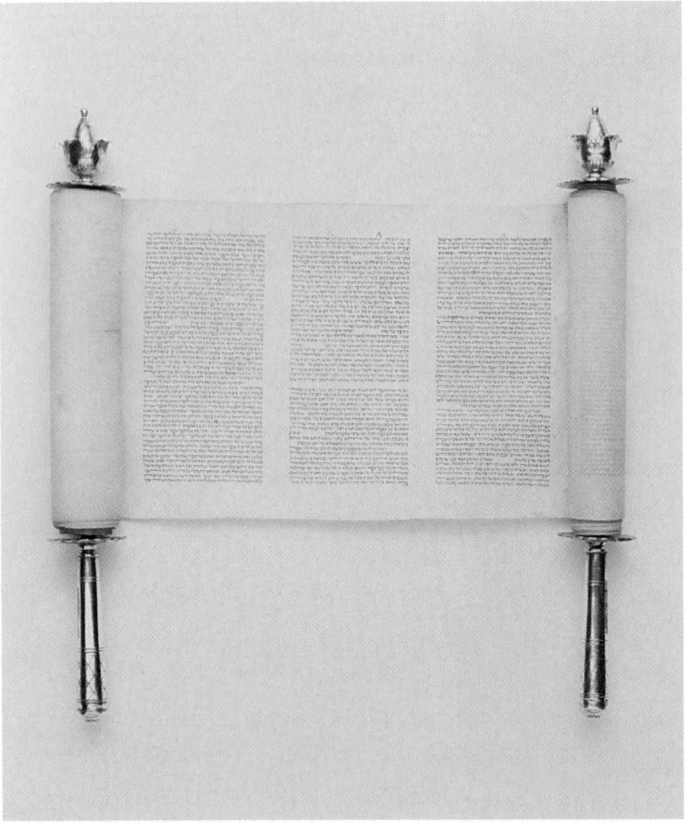

Scroll and Codex. *Constructed from carefully joined sheets of papyrus, the Torah scroll* (left) *is still used in modern synagogues as it was in the ancient world. The Christian Scriptures, however, took on an alternate yet no less labor-intensive form: the codex, or bound book. On the right is a page from a sixth-century account of the Last Supper in the Codex Purpureus Rossanensis.*

near the Danubian frontier, he belonged to a class of professional soldiers whose careers took them far from the Mediterranean. His troops proclaimed him emperor after the death of his father, the emperor Constantius. It was a time of political confusion when several claimants fought for power. In 312 CE, Constantine's armies closed in on Rome in his first bid to rule the Mediterranean heartlands.

Like earlier Roman emperors, Constantine looked for signs from the gods. Before the decisive battle for Rome, which took place for control of a strategic bridge, he supposedly had a dream in which he saw an emblem bearing the words "In this sign conquer." He was told to place this mysterious sign on his soldiers' shields. It took the form of an X (the Greek letter chi, representing a "ch" sound) placed over P (the Greek letter rho, or "r")—the first letters of the name of Christ. In the ensuing battle, the rival troops were routed and the rival emperor was pushed off the bridge and drowned. Thereafter, Constantine's visionary sign became known all over the Roman world.

The persecuted Christian church was the beneficiary of Constantine's vision, as he soon issued a proclamation exalting the work of Christian bishops and giving them significant tax exemptions, and, importantly, showered the favors of the Roman emperor on this religious group. The edict's effects were long-lasting, for it would be through the institutions and over the roads of the Roman Empire that Christianity would spread.

By the time that Constantine embraced Christianity, it had already made considerable progress within the Roman Empire. At the outset, it was only one of many different new sects competing for attention within the empire. It prevailed in the face of stiff competition and episodes of intense persecution from the imperial authorities largely because of the universalistic aspects of its message, the charisma of its holy men and women, the sacred aura surrounding its scriptural canon, and the fit that existed between its doctrines and popular preexisting religious beliefs and practices. The new religion made few distinctions. It appealed alike to rich and poor, city dwellers and peasants, slave and free, young and old, and men and women.

CHRISTIANITY IN THE CITIES After 312 CE, the large churches built in every major city, many with imperial funding, signaled Christianity's growing strength. These gigantic meeting halls often accommodated over a thousand worshippers. Called *basilicas* (from the Greek *basileus*, "king"), the solemn halls were modeled on Roman law-court buildings. But unlike ancient temples,

The Conversion of Constantine. *In this painting, the seventeenth-century artist Rubens uses "period" details for historical accuracy: the XP (the first letters of the name of Christ in Greek) in the sky; beneath them, the "dragon" standard of the Roman cavalry of the year 312 (the standard came from China and passed to Rome via the cavalry-nomads of central Asia); beside the dragon, the eagle of the traditional Roman standard.*

which housed the gods deep inside while the people worshipped outdoors, the basilicas were open to all. Those who entered found a vast space shimmering with the light of oil lamps playing on shining marble and mosaics. Rich silk hangings, swaying between rows of columns, increased the sense of mystery and directed the eye to the far end of the building—a semicircular apse furnished with particular splendor. Worshippers had come into a different world. This was heaven on earth.

And it was a very orderly heaven. The bishop and priests sat under the dome of the apse, which represented the dome of heaven. The bishop had a special throne, or *cathedra* (the Latin word for both a teacher's seat and a governor's throne). Low marble screens and especially vivid floor mosaics marked off the holy space around the bishop and clergy. (The church at Verona in Italy even had under-floor heating in this area!) Ordinary worshippers would stand, as a gesture of respect, while the bishop sat and preached.

Such churches became the new urban public forums, ringed with spacious courtyards where the city's poor would gather. In return for the tax exemptions that Constantine had granted them, the bishops were responsible for the metropolitan poor, becoming in effect their governors. Bishops also became judges, as Constantine turned their arbitration process for disputes between Christians into a kind of small claims court.

Basilica Interior. *The interior of a basilica was dominated by rows of ancient marble columns and was filled with light from upper windows, so that the eye was led directly to the apse of the church, where the bishop and clergy would sit under a dome, close to the altar.*

It was by such means—offering the poor shelter, quick justice, and moments of unearthly splendor in grand basilicas—that bishops throughout the Roman world secured a position that would last until modern times. And in their basilicas, "Rome" lived on for centuries after the empire had disappeared.

The Christian Empire

Christianity was spreading into the hinterlands of Africa and Southwest Asia, and these efforts required the breaking of language barriers. After around 300 CE, the Christian clergy in Egypt replaced hieroglyphs—which only a few temple priests could read—with a more accessible script based on Greek letters: it is known today as Coptic. With this innovation the Christian clergy brought the countryside and its local languages closer to the towns, and the towns closer to the countryside.

A similar pattern unfolded in Nubia and Ethiopia, as each developed its own scripts and language under Christian influence. And in the crucial corridor that joined Antioch to Mesopotamia, Syriac, an offshoot of the Semitic language Aramaic, became a major Christian language. Christianity also spread farther north, to Georgia in the Caucasus and to Armenia. Christian clergy created the written languages that are still used in those regions.

In 325 CE, Constantine summoned all the Christian bishops to a council at Nicaea (modern Iznik in western Turkey). Though their religion has since produced many denominations, all Christians still regard the Council of Nicaea as the foundational moment when their faith was summed up in a **creed** (from the Latin *credo,* "I believe"). It was a statement of religious belief formulated in technical, philosophical terms. It asked believers to balance three separate Gods in one supreme being—God "the father," "the son," and "the holy spirit." Also at Nicaea the bishops agreed to hold Easter, the day on which Christians celebrate Christ's resurrection from the tomb, on the same day in every church of the Christian world.

Constantine's legacy to the Christian Church was monumental. His conversion had happened in such a way that Christianity itself became the religion of the Roman Empire. Writing near the end of Constantine's reign, an elderly bishop in Palestine named Eusebius presented a vision of the new Christian Roman Empire that would have surprised the martyrs of Carthage, who had willingly died rather than recognize any "empire of this world." (See Primary Source: Eusebius: In Praise of "One Unity and Concord.") From the time of Constantine onward, many Christians around the eastern Mediterranean believed that Christianity, empire, and culture had flowed together into a new unity.

The Fall of Rome: A Takeover from the Margins

Soon, however, the Roman world began to fall apart (see Map 8.3). After 400 CE the western European provinces went their own way, as the presence of Roman armies and cities along the Rhine and Danube had blurred the boundary between Roman and non-Roman worlds.

WHO WERE THE BARBARIANS? The so-called barbarian invasions of the late fourth and fifth centuries CE were simply a more violent and chaotic form of a steady immigration of young fighting men from the frontiers of the empire. Today the term *barbarian* implies uncultivated or savage, but its core meaning is "foreigner" (with overtones of inferiority). Inhabitants of the western provinces had become used to non-Roman soldiers from across the frontiers, and for them *barbarian* was synonymous with "soldier." Soldiers could be destructive, but nobody feared that the presence of barbarians fighting in armies on Roman territory would bring the end of Roman culture.

THE GOTHS The popular image of bloodthirsty barbarian hordes streaming into the empire bears little resemblance to reality. In fact, it was the Romans' need for soldiers that drew the barbarians in. The process reached a crisis point when Gothic tribes petitioned the emperor Valens (r. 365–378 CE) to let them immigrate into the empire. Desperate for manpower, Valens encouraged their entrance. But the Roman authorities failed to feed their guests. It was a lethal combination of famine and anger at the breakdown of supplies—not innate bloodlust—that turned the Goths against Valens. When he marched against them on the flat plains outside Adrianople in the hot August of 378 CE, he was not seeking to halt a barbarian invasion. He was planning to teach a lesson in obedience to his new recruits. But the Goths had brought cavalry from the steppes, and its thunderous charge proved decisive. Valens and a large part of the Roman army of the East vanished in a cloud of red dust, trampled to death by the men and horses they had hoped to hire.

Even the most notorious invasions followed a similar pattern, drawn into the crumbling empire by its civil wars. These internal wars had long been a feature of Roman society, but the state could not survive this bout, constantly fed by "barbarian" recruits. The "fall" of the empire in western Europe was the result of a long process of overextension. Rome could never be as strong along its frontiers as it was around the Mediterranean, because those frontiers were too far away. Despite the famous Roman roads, travel time between the Rhine border and Rome was more than thirty days. Lacking the vast network of canals that enabled Chinese emperors to move goods and soldiers by

PRIMARY SOURCE

Eusebius: In Praise of "One Unity and Concord"

Eusebius (c. 263–339?) believed that the Roman Empire owed its success to divine providence. He viewed the birth of Christ during the rule of the emperor Augustus as no coincidence: it showed God's choice to come to earth at a time when the preaching of his message could coincide with a blessed era of peace and unity in the Roman world. Christianity had ridden to its favored position on the providential tide of a unified world empire. The excerpt below is from a speech commemorating thirty years of Constantine's rule.

Now formerly all the peoples of the earth were divided, and the whole human race cut up into provinces and tribal and local governments, states ruled by despots or by mobs. Because of this continuous battles and wars, with their attendant devastations and enslavements, gave them no respite in countryside or city. . . .

But now two great powers—the Roman Empire, which became a monarchy at that time, and the teaching of Christ—proceeding as if from a single starting point, at once tamed and reconciled all to friendship. Thus each blossomed at the same time and place as the other. For while the power of our Savior destroyed the multiple rule and polytheism of the demons [the old gods] and heralded the one kingdom of God to Greeks and barbarians and all men to the furthest end of the earth, the Roman Empire, now that the causes of manifold governments had been abolished, subdued the visible governments of, in order to merge the entire race into one unity and concord. . . .

Moreover, as One God and one knowledge of this God is heralded to all, one empire has waxed strong among men, and the entire race of mankind has been re-directed into peace and friendship as all acknowledged each other as brothers. . . . All at once, as if sons and daughters of one father, the One God, and children of one mother, true religion, they greeted and received each other peaceably, so that from that time the whole inhabited world differed in no way from a single well-ordered and related household. It became possible for anyone who pleased to make a journey and to leave home for wherever he might wish with all ease. Thus some from the East moved freely to the West, while others went from here [the East] back there, as easily as if traveling to their native lands.

QUESTIONS FOR ANALYSIS

- The elderly Eusebius was a bishop in Palestine, and as a younger man he had witnessed the persecution of Christians. Can you find evidence of this background in his praise of Constantine as the first Christian emperor, who fostered "one unity and concord" among "the whole human race"?
- Being patriarchal, Roman society highly valued the family unit. What lines in the excerpt reflect this outlook?
- What elements in the history of Christianity would have led Eusebius to emphasize its role as a unifying force in the Roman world?

Source: Eusebius, Tricennial Oration *16.2–7 [Jubilee Oration on the Thirtieth Year of the Reign of Constantine, delivered on July 25, 336], translated by H. L. Drake in* In Praise of Constantine: A Historical Study and New Translation of Eusebius' Tricennial Orations *(Berkeley: University of California Press, 1976), pp. 119–21.*

water, Roman power could survive in the north only at the cost of constant effort and high taxes. But after 400 CE the western emperors could no longer raise enough taxes to maintain control of the provinces.

In 418 CE, the Goths settled in southwest Gaul. Ruled by their own king, who kept his military in order, they suppressed the peasants' revolts that were occurring with alarming frequency. Though never as savage or widespread as the uprisings that had undermined the Han dynasty in China, they created a mood of emergency. Now the Roman landowners of Gaul and elsewhere anxiously allied themselves with the new military leaders rather than face social revolution and the raids of even more dangerous armies. The Goths came as allies of the aristocracy, not as enemies of Rome.

CONTINUITY IN CHANGE Romans and non-Romans also drew together because both suddenly confronted a common enemy. As happened many times in the history of Afro-Eurasia, a nomad confederation—in this case, that of the Huns—threatened the edge of western Europe. For twenty chilling years a single king, Attila (406–453 CE), imposed himself as sole ruler of all the Hunnish tribes. He was a harsh overlord who frightened the Germanic peoples even more than he frightened the Romans. The Romans had walls to hide behind—Hadrian's Wall, town

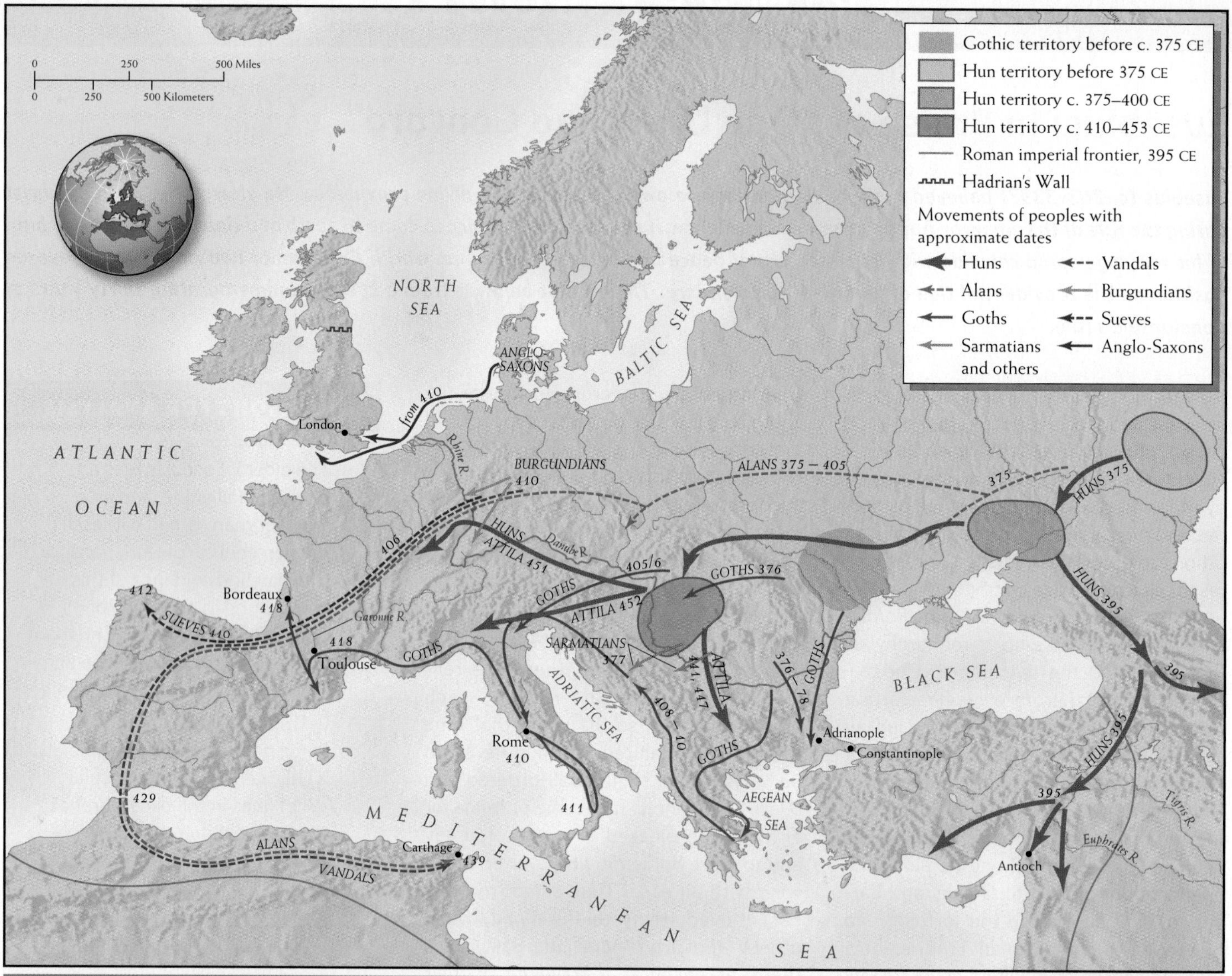

MAP 8.3 | Western Afro-Eurasia: War, Immigration, and Settlement in the Roman World, 375–450 CE

Invasions and migrations brought about the reconstitution of the Roman Empire at this time.

- Using the map, identify the people who migrated to or invaded the Roman Empire. Where were they from, and where did they go? How did they reshape the political landscape of western Afro-Eurasia?
- Considering these effects, was the Roman depiction of these groups as "barbarians" a fair assessment?

walls, villa walls, city walls. In the open plains north of the Danube, however, the Hunnish cavalry found only scattered villages and open fields, whose harvests they plundered on a regular basis.

Attila intended to be a "real" emperor. Having seized (perhaps from the Chinese empire) the notion of a "mandate of heaven"—in his case, a divine right to rule the tribes of the north—he fashioned the first opposing empire that Rome ever had to face in northern Europe. Its traces remain in the archaeology of Ukraine, Hungary, and central Europe. Spectacular jewelry of a Hunnish style, often bearing dragon motifs originating in China, reveals a true warrior-aristocracy. Rather than selling his people's services to Rome, Attila extracted thousands of pounds of gold coins from the Roman emperors in tribute. With Roman gold, he could dominate the barbarian world. The result: the Roman Empire in the west vanished only twenty years after his death. In 476 CE, the last Roman emperor of the west, a young boy named Romulus Augustulus (namesake of both Rome's founder and, as "Mini-Augustus," its first emperor) resigned to make way for a so-called barbarian king in Italy.

Rule from Rome was over, but not its legacies. Future rulers had to ally with the surviving Roman landowners of southern Europe, and among them the Goths felt fully at home. Their king called himself Alaric II, underscoring his connection to the man who had sacked Rome in 410 CE. At the same time, he enjoyed the warm support of the Roman landowners, some of whom claimed to be descendants of ancient Roman senators. Alaric II issued for them a simplified code of imperial law that owed nothing to the non-Roman world. It provided his Roman subjects with all that was necessary to maintain a Roman way of life in a world without an empire.

Now the sense of unity of the Roman Empire gave way to a sense of the continued unity of the church. The Catholic Church (*Catholic* meaning "universal") became the one institution to which all Christians in western Europe, Romans and non-Romans alike, felt that they belonged. As a result, the bishops of Rome emerged as popes—the symbolic head of the western churches. Rome became a spiritual capital instead of an imperial one. By 700 CE, the great Roman landowning families had vanished (unlike the more tenacious elites of China). Replacing them in the power structure were religious leaders with vast moral authority.

Byzantium, Rome in the East: The Rise of Constantinople

Elsewhere the Roman Empire was alive and well. From the borders of Greece to the borders of modern Iraq, and from the Danube River to Egypt and the borders of Saudi Arabia, the empire survived undamaged. Rich and self-confident, it saw itself as a more fortunate version of Old Rome.

Whatever we call it—whether by its modern name of Byzantium or simply the surviving empire of Rome—this was a highly centralized empire. All roads led to Constantinople. All decisions were made in the great palace. Gold from taxes and grain to feed the city arrived regularly. In fact, the speed of sea travel in the eastern Mediterranean facilitated this centralization. As long as emperors of Constantinople controlled the sea-lanes, they controlled the heart of their empire.

The new Roman empire of the East now had its own Rome. In 324 CE, a year before he assembled the Christian bishops at Nicaea, Constantine decided to build a grandiose city on the European side of the Bosporus—the waterway that separates Europe from Asia. He chose the site of the ancient Greek city of Byzantium and called it New Rome, but it soon took on the name "Constantine's City," or Constantinople.

Thereafter Constantinople grew explosively, becoming an even bigger and better Rome. It was one of the most spectacularly successful cities in Afro-Eurasia, soon boasting a population of over half a million and 4,000 new palaces. Every year, more than 20,000 tons of grain arrived from Egypt, unloaded on a dockside over a mile long. A gigantic hippodrome echoing Rome's Circus Maximus straddled the city's central ridge, flanking an imperial palace whose opulent, enclosed spaces stretched down to the busy shore. As in Rome, the emperor would sit in his imperial box, witnessing chariot races as rival teams careered around the stadium. The

Justinian and Theodora. *These portraits face each other on either side of the altar in the apse of the church of San Vitale at Ravenna. Both Justinian and Theodora are shown presenting lavish gifts. As emperor, Justinian heads the procession. On his left are the clergy; on his right are guards with Constantine's XP symbol on their shields and his lay advisers. Thus, both church and state line up behind their leader, the emperor. Theodora is more secluded. She is surrounded by ladies with veiled heads and by beardless eunuchs. The curtain is pulled back to enable Theodora to place her gift on the altar.*

The Hagia Sophia. *After the conquest of Constantinople by the Muslim Ottomans in 1453, the Hagia Sophia was made into a mosque by having minarets (slender, high towers) added to each corner. Otherwise, it looks exactly as it did in the days of Justinian. In modern times, it became the model for the domed mosques that appear all over the Islamic world.*

Hippodrome also featured displays of eastern imperial might, as ambassadors came from as far away as central Asia, northern India, and Nubia.

Constantinople had the resources of a world capital. Long after their western colleagues had been declared bankrupt, its emperors had a yearly budget of 8,500,000 gold pieces. No other state west of China had tax revenues so gigantic. It was a predominantly Greek city whose residents were proud to live under Roman law, a circumstance that made them "Romans." This was the Constantinople to which the future emperor Justinian came, as a young man from an obscure Balkan village, to seek his fortune. When he became emperor in 527 CE, he considered himself the successor of a long line of forceful Roman emperors—and he was determined to outdo them.

Most importantly, Justinian reformed the Roman laws. Within six years a commission of lawyers had created the *Digest:* a volume of 800,000 words that condensed the contents of 1,528 Latin law books. Its companion volume was the *Institutes,* a teacher's manual for schools of Roman law. These works were the foundation of what later ages came to know as "Roman law," followed in both eastern and western Europe.

Reflecting the marriage of Christianity with empire was the church of the Hagia Sophia at one end of the Hippodrome. Constructed on the spot where the city's old basilica church was destroyed during a riot, Hagia Sophia ("Holy Wisdom") must have astounded those who first entered it. The nave was twice the span of the former basilica—230 feet wide—and the new church was more than twice as high. The largest church built by Constantine, the basilica of Saint Peter in Rome, would have reached only as high as its lower galleries. Above all, the solemn straight lines of the traditional Christian basilica were transformed. Great cliffs of stone, sheathed in multicolored marble and supported on gigantic columns of green and purple granite, rose to a dreamlike height. Audaciously curved semicircular niches placed at every corner made the entire building seem to dance. And a spectacular dome lined with gleaming gold mosaics floated almost 200 feet above it all.

In later centuries Greek and non-Greek Christians of the east called Hagia Sophia "the eye of the civilized world." It represented the flowing together of Christianity and imperial culture that, for another 1,000 years, would mark the eastern Roman empire centered on Constantinople.

Sasanian Persia

Justinian had the misfortune of ruling an empire at the edge of Asia when Asia itself was changing dramatically (see Map 8.4). To begin with, the contacts between east and west were intensifying. The most unexpected reminder of this was a sudden onslaught of the bubonic plague—the grim gift of the Indian Ocean. One-third of the population of Constantinople died within weeks. Justinian himself survived, but thereafter he ruled an empire whose heartland was decimated.

Another reminder of growing interconnectedness was an escalating rivalry for territorial control. Justinian's empire

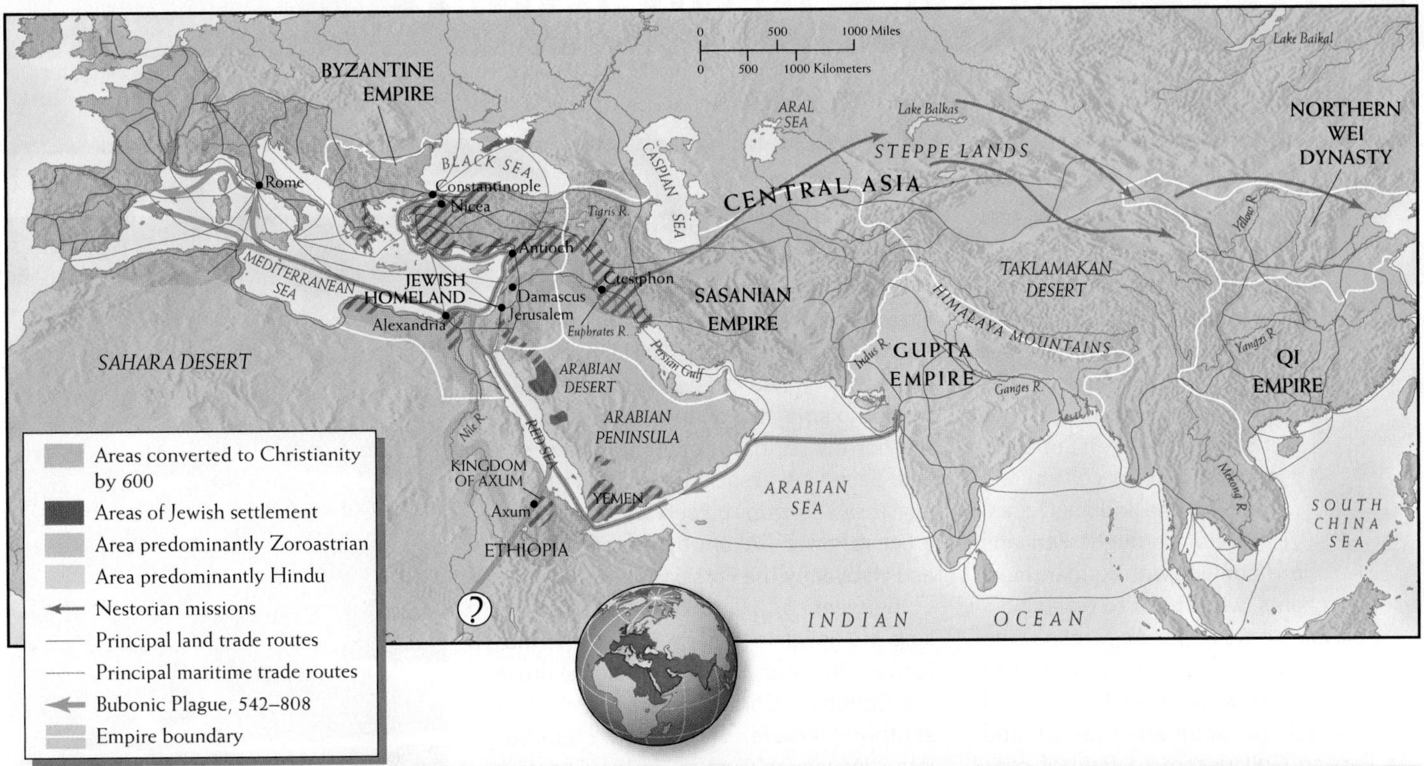

MAP 8.4 | Southwest Asia, 300–600 CE

Southwest Asia remained the crossroads of Afro-Eurasia in a variety of ways. Trade goods flowing between west and east passed through this region, as did universal religions. The question mark in eastern Africa indicates scholars' uncertainty about the origination of the plague.

- Using your finger, trace the principal trade routes and maritime routes. What were the areas of major religious influence? What was the relationship between trade routes and the areas of major religious influence?
- Then point out each area of religious influence. How did religious geography correspond to political geography?
- How was Southwest Asia affected by other regions, such as sub-Saharan Africa and central Asia, and how did it shape developments in these regions?

struggled with a formidable eastern rival for the control of Southwest Asia. Beginning at the Euphrates River and stretching for eighty days of slow travel across the modern territories of Iraq, Iran, Afghanistan, and much of central Asia, the Sasanian Empire of Persia encompassed all the land routes of western Asia.

KING OF KINGS OF ERAN AND AN-ERAN As we saw in Chapter 7, the Sasanians had replaced the Parthians as rulers of the Iranian plateau and Mesopotamia. Westerners called this domain the empire of Persia, but its precise title is more revealing of the Sasanians' universalistic aspirations: the Sasanian ruler called himself the "King of Kings of Eran and An-Eran"—"of the Iranian and non-Iranian lands." The ancient, irrigated fields of what is modern Iraq became the economic heart of this empire. Its capital, Ctesiphon, arose where the Tigris and the Euphrates rivers come close, only twenty miles south of modern Baghdad. Symbolizing the king's presence was a 110-foot-high vaulted arch decorated with rows of smaller, window-like arches, called the Great Arch of Khusro after Justinian's rival, Khusro I Anoshirwan (Khusro of the Righteous Soul).

As his name implied, Khusro Anoshirwan exemplified the model ruler: strong and just. His image in the east as an ideal monarch was as glorious as that of Justinian in the west as an ideal Christian Roman emperor. For both Persians and Arab Muslims of later ages, the Arch of Khusro was as awe-inspiring as Justinian's Hagia Sophia was to Christians.

As Khusro's reign unfolded, it became obvious that the **Sasanian Empire** was more than the equal of the Mediterranean empire of Rome, for it controlled the trade crossroads of Afro-Eurasia. (See Current Trends in World History: Religious Conflict in Imperial Borderlands.) But control of trade was only

CURRENT TRENDS IN WORLD HISTORY

Religious Conflict in Imperial Borderlands

World historians often study borderland areas because it is in these zones where they can see most clearly the effects of cultural interaction. One example is the borderlands of the Sasanian Empire, which through the Persian Gulf reached out to control the trade on the Indian Ocean. This effort brought Persians into conflict with Roman merchants, who strove to reach India from the Red Sea. As a result, the entire region bounded by present-day Ethiopia (at the western end of the Red Sea), Yemen (in southern Arabia), and the Persian Gulf became a field of conflict between the Roman and Sasanian empires.

Their clash took religious as well as commercial and political form. Both Axum (modern-day Ethiopia) and Himyar (modern-day Yemen) had embraced monotheism, expressed in the worship of a Most High God known as al-Rahmānā (the Merciful One). In Axum, this monotheism was Christian: Christ was the protector of its kings, and the Cross of Christ was their talisman in battle. In contrast, the leaders of Himyar and the southern coast of Arabia were Jewish, and they dismissed Jesus as a crucified sorcerer.

The kings of Axum occupied the African side of the southern end of the Red Sea, looking down from the foothills of the well-watered and populous mountains of Ethiopia. Their formidable warrior-kingdom stretched as far as the Nile to the northwest, south into equatorial Africa, and eastward across the Red Sea to southern Arabia and Yemen. Axum's rulers, who became Christian around 340 CE, celebrated their victories on gigantic granite obelisks; they were monuments to a God that was very much a god of battles.

Faced by the aggressive Christian kingdom of Axum, the Sasanians reached out to support the kings of Himyar, who since 380 CE had been Jewish. Thus two monotheisms faced each other across the narrow southern opening of the Red Sea. Each was associated with a rich and aggressive kingdom. Each was backed by a Great Power—Axum by Christian Rome and Himyar by the Persians.

Between 522 and 530 CE, a Jewish king of Himyar popularly known as Dhu-Nuwas (the Man with the Forelock) drove the Ethiopian Christian garrisons out of southern Arabia. He turned churches into synagogues (just as, in the Christian empire far to the north, many synagogues had been turned into churches). In 523 CE, the Christians of the oasis city of Najran were ordered to become Jewish. Those who refused to do so, Dhu-Nuwas burned on pyres of brushwood piled into a deep trench.

Swept by these rivalries, the Arabian Peninsula was no longer a world apart, shut off from "civilization" by its cruel deserts and by its inhabitants' nomadic lifestyle. Far from it. Arabia had become a giant soundboard that amplified claims about the pros and cons of Judaism and Christianity, argued over with unusual intensity for an entire century. The "nonaligned" Arabs of the intermediate regions (between southern Arabia and Mesopotamia) still worshipped their ancestral tribal gods. But they had heard much, of late, about Jews and Christians, Romans and Persians. Arab tribes around Yathrib (modern Medina) adopted Judaism and remained in touch with the rabbis of Galilee along the caravan routes of northern Arabia. Here was a new kind of borderland between empires and between religions. In fact, it would be from this borderland that a new religion and a new prophet would emerge. His name was Muhammad.

Crossing Boundaries. *This Iranian rock relief of a Roman king paying obeisance to a Sasanian ruler is an instance of cross-cultural interchange.*

QUESTIONS FOR ANALYSIS

- How did the geographical features of the Arabian Peninsula shape its religious development?
- What about borderlands makes them useful locations of analysis for world historians?

Explore Further

Fowden, Garth, *Empire to Commonwealth: The Consequences of Monotheism in Late Antiquity* (1993).

Yarshater, Ehsan, *Encyclopedia Iranica* (1982–).

The Great Arch. *For a Persian king-of-kings, the prime symbol of royal majesty was the great arch marking the entrance gate of his palace. Here, in a Middle Eastern tradition that reached back for millennia, the king would appear to his subjects to deliver judgment. This building was associated with Khusro I, who came to be remembered as an ideal ruler.*

part of the story. Christian forces also met their match in the form of Iranian armored cavalry, a fighting machine adapted from years of competition with the nomads of central Asia. These fearless Persian horsemen fought covered from head to foot in flexible armor (small plates of iron sewn onto leather) and chain mail, riding "blood-sweating horses" draped in thickly padded cloth. Their lethal swords were light and flexible owing to steel-making techniques imported from northern India. With such cavalry, Khusro sacked Antioch in 540 CE. The campaign was a warning, at the height of Justinian's glory, that Mesopotamia could reach out once again to conquer the eastern Mediterranean shoreline.

Under Khusro II the confrontation between Persia and Rome escalated into the greatest war that had been seen for centuries. Between 604 and 628 CE, Persian forces conquered Egypt and Syria and even reached Constantinople. Khusro II finally fell to the emperor Heraclius in a series of brilliant campaigns in northern Mesopotamia. Never had either empire reached so far into the heart of the other, and the effort exhausted both. For that reason, both fell easily to an Arab invasion only a few years later (see Chapter 9).

AN EMPIRE AT THE CROSSROADS In their confrontations with Rome, Khusro I and Khusro II had the benefit of several factors. Culturally, Southwest Asia was already more united than its political boundaries implied. The political frontier cut across an exuberant common zone where Syriac was the main language and Christianity was making inroads. The Sasanians themselves were devout Zoroastrians, but they were forbearing rulers. Indeed, Jews and Christians enjoyed a tolerance in Mesopotamia that no Christian emperor had extended to non-Christians within the Roman Empire. Protected by the King of Kings, the rabbis of Mesopotamia compiled the monumental Babylonian Talmud at a time when their western peers, in Roman Palestine, were feeling cramped under the Christian state.

But the Sasanian court not only was interested in western religions such as Christianity and Judaism. It also embraced offerings from northern India, including the *Pancantantra* stories (moral tales played out in a legendary kingdom of the animals), polo, and the game of chess. In this regard Khusro's was truly an empire of crossroads, where the cultures of central Asia and India met that of the eastern Mediterranean.

Christians flourished in the Sasanian Empire, establishing dynamic communities in northern Mesopotamia, at the head of the Persian Gulf, and along the trade routes of central Asia. Named by their enemies "Nestorian" Christians after Nestorius, a bishop of Constantinople, these members of the "Church of the East" exploited Sasanian trade and diplomacy to spread their faith more widely. As Nestorian merchants passed along the Silk Road, they settled numerous communities and even established monasteries and a church in Chang'an, China. Others operating out of the Persian Gulf founded colonies on the west coast of southern India. Although they were Nestorian Christians, these colonists asserted a special claim for themselves as having been converted by Thomas the Apostle, the companion of Jesus. The Christians of this part of India are still called "Saint Thomas Christians."

THE SILK ROAD

Simurgh, *the legendary dog-headed bird of Persian mythology, as shown on this seventh-century silver plate from Sasanian Persia, was a favored motif on textiles, sculptures, paintings, and architecture from the Byzantine Empire to Tang China.*

Crucial to growing interconnectedness was central Asia. Wending their way across its difficult terrains, a steady parade of merchants, scholars, and travelers transmitted commodities, technologies, and ideas between the Mediterranean worlds and China, and across the Himalayas into northern India, exploiting a series of commercial routes that have come to be known as the Silk Road.

The sharing of knowledge between the Mediterranean world and China began in earnest during the period when Christianity and Buddhism were spreading and when Vedic religion (Brahmanism) was developing a scholarly written tradition. Byzantium dispatched ambassadors from Constantinople to the nomads of eastern central Asia. In 568 CE these emissaries brought back glowing firsthand reports of the great empire of China.

Chinese observers likewise admired aspects of the eastern and western Roman empires. According to the historian Fan Ye, writing in the fifth century CE, "They have no permanent rulers, but when an extraordinary calamity visits the country, they elect a new king."

The great oasis cities of central Asia played a crucial role in the effective functioning of the Silk Road. While the Sasanians controlled Merv in the west, nomadic rulers became the overlords of Sogdiana and Tukharistan and extracted tribute from the cities of Samarkand and Panjikent in the east. The tribal confederacies in this region maintained the links between west and east by patrolling the Silk Road between Iran and China. They also joined north to south as they passed through the mountains of Afghanistan into the plains of northern India. As a result, central Asia between 400 and 600 CE was the hub of a vibrant system of religious and cultural contacts covering the whole of Afro-Eurasia. (See Map 8.5.)

The Sogdians as Lords of the Silk Road

Sogdians in the oasis cities of Samarkand and Panjikent served as human links between the two ends of Afro-Eurasia. Their religion was a blend of Zoroastrian and Mesopotamian beliefs, touched with Brahmanic influences. Their language was the common tongue of the early Silk Road, and their shaggy camels bore the commodities that passed through their entrepôts. Moreover, their splendid mansions (excavated at Panjikent) show strong influences from the warrior-aristocracy culture of Iran. The palace walls display gripping frescoes of armored riders, reflecting the revolutionary change to cavalry warfare from Rome to China. The **Sogdians** were known as far away as China as merchants. To the Chinese, they were persons "with honey on their tongues and gum on their fingers"—to sweet-talk money out of others' pockets and to catch every stray coin. (See Primary Source: A Letter from a Sogdian Merchant Chief.)

Through the Sogdians, products from western Asia and North Africa found their way to the eastern end of the landmass. Carefully packed for the long trek on jostling camel caravans, goods displaying Persian motifs—such as the legendary simurgh bird and prancing rams with fluttering ribbons—rode side by side with Roman glass from Mediterranean cities. Along with Sasanian silver coins and gold pieces minted in Constantinople, these exotic products found eager buyers as far east as China and Japan.

Buddhism on the Silk Road

Unstable political systems did not hinder the flow of ideas or commodities. Instead, the civil wars marking the end of the Han Empire rendered China more open to the cultures of its far western regions. South of the Hindu Kush Mountains, in northern India, nomadic groups made the roads into central Asia safe to travel, enabling Buddhism to spread northward and eastward via the mountainous corridor of Afghanistan into China. Buddhist monks were the primary missionary agents, the bearers of a universal message who traveled across the roads of central Asia, carrying holy books, offering salvation to commoners, and establishing themselves more securely in host communities than did armies, diplomats, or merchants.

Starting at Bamiyan, a valley of the Hindu Kush—where two gigantic statues of the Buddha, 121 and 180 feet in height, were hewn from the stone face of the cliff during the fourth and fifth centuries CE (and stood there for 2,500 years until dynamited by the Taliban in 2001)—travelers found welcoming cave monasteries at oases all along the way from the Taklamakan Desert to northern China. They also encountered five huge Buddhas carved from cliffs in Yungang. While those at Bamiyan stood tall with royal majesty, the Buddhas of Yungang sat in postures of meditation. Surrounding the Buddhas, over fifty caves sheltered more than 50,000 statues representing Buddhist deities and patrons. The Yungang Buddhas, seated just inside the Great

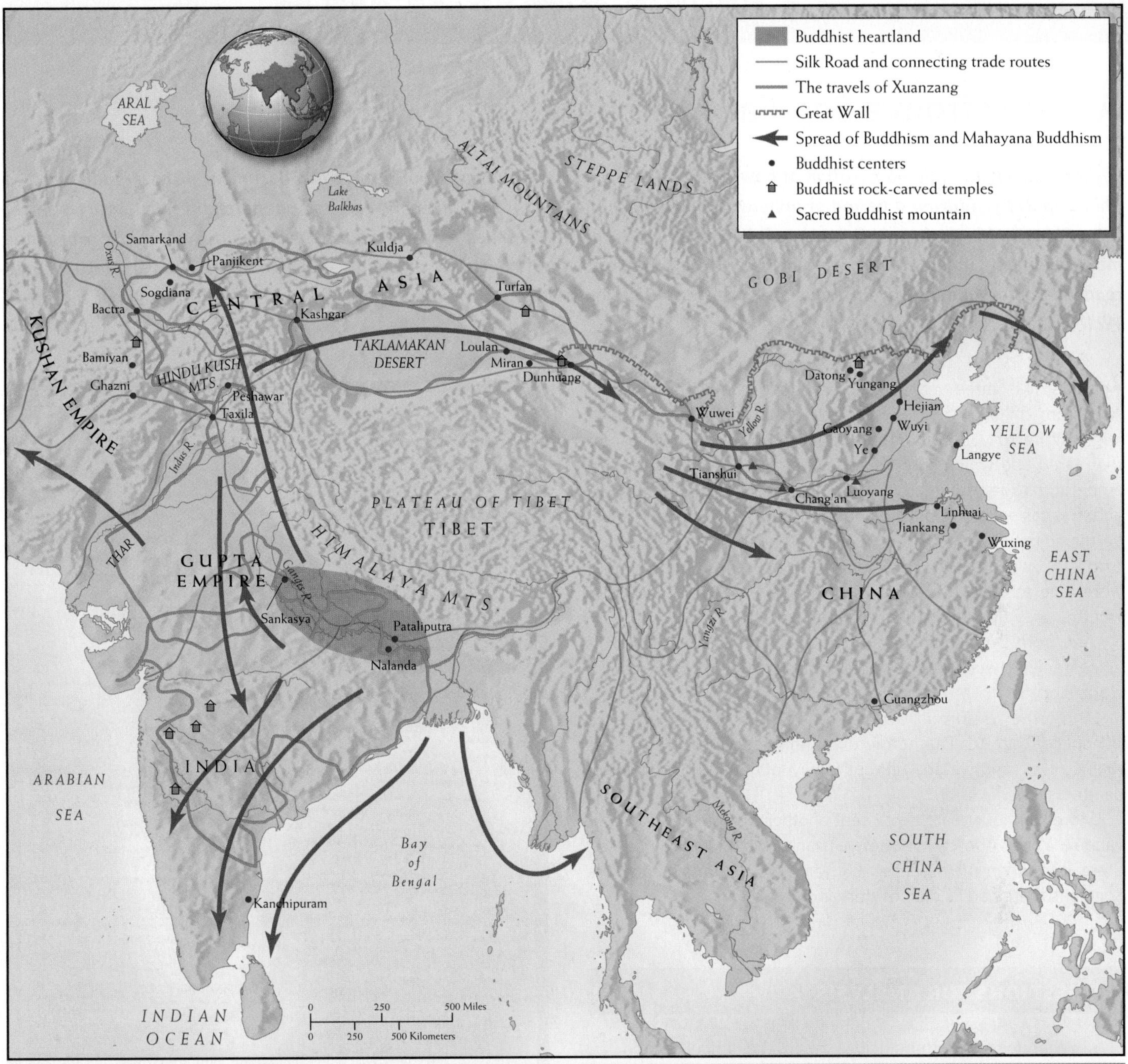

MAP 8.5 | Buddhist Landscapes, 300–600 CE

Buddhism spread from its heartland in northern India to central and East Asia at this time.

- Using your finger, trace the red lines of trade routes and then the green arrows showing the spread of Buddhism.
- According to the map, what role did increasingly extensive trade routes play in pushing this movement?
- What was the relationship among Buddhist centers and rock-carved temples, trade routes, and the spread of this universal faith?
- How did the travels of Xuanzang symbolize growing connections between East and South Asia?

Wall, welcomed travelers to the market in China and marked the eastern end of the central Asian Silk Road.

The Bamiyan and Yungang Buddhas, placed more than 2,500 miles apart, are a reminder that by now religious ideas were creating world empires of the mind. Religions such as early Christianity and Buddhism saw themselves as transcending kingdoms of this world: they were bringing a universal message contained in holy scriptures. And they enjoyed greater reach

PRIMARY SOURCE

A Letter from a Sogdian Merchant Chief

Perhaps the clearest demonstration of how the Sogdians linked the ends of Afro-Eurasia is a document discovered in western China. In 313 CE (during a period of upheaval following the fall of the Han dynasty), a Sogdian merchant chief wrote a letter from China to his partner in Samarkand, his homeland some 2,000 miles to the west. He describes a state of civil war made more violent by invading barbarian armies. He also describes the "business as usual" attitude of traders. The letter never reached Samarkand, however. It was among several Sogdian letters in a mailbag found in one of the guard posts of the Great Wall of China.

And sirs, it is three years since a Sogdian came from "inside" [i.e., from China]. And now no one comes from there so that I might write to you about the Sogdians who went inside, how they fared and which countries they reached. And, sirs, the last emperor, so they say, fled from Luoyang because of the famine and fire was set to his palace and to the city, and the palace was burnt and the city [destroyed]. Luoyang is no more, Ye is no more! And sirs, we do not know whether the remaining Chinese were able to expel the Huns [from] Chany'an, from China, or whether they took the country beyond. . . .

And from Dunhuang up to Jincheng . . . to sell, linen cloth is going [selling well?], and whoever has made cloth or woolen cloth. . . .

And, sirs, as for us, whoever dwells in the region from Ji[ncheng] up to Dunhuang, we only survive so long as the . . . lives, and we are without family, old and on the point of death. . . .

Moreover, four years ago, I sent another man named Artikhuvandak. When the caravan left Guzang, Wakhushakk . . . was there, and when they reached Luoyang . . . the Indians and the Sogdians there had all died of starvation.

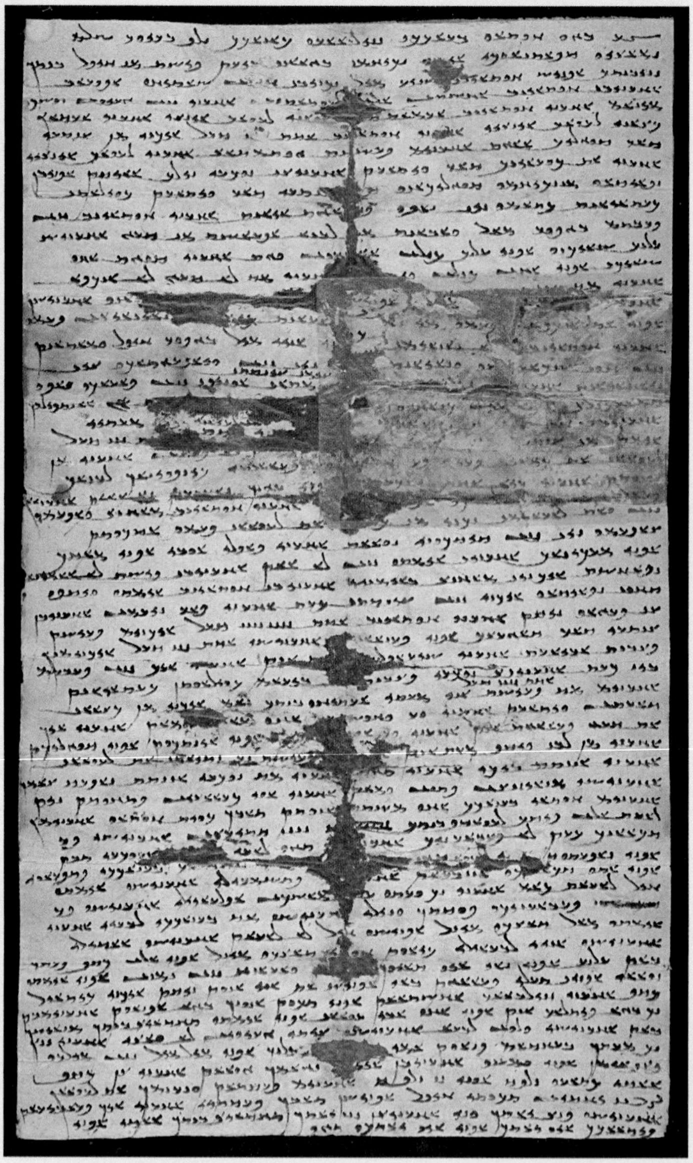

QUESTIONS FOR ANALYSIS

- What does the letter elucidate about the difficulties and dangers of trade along the Silk Road?
- What does it reveal about the fall of Luoyang—and about the way news traveled over long distances at this time?
- The letter seems to imply that cloth is in high demand in northern areas of China. How might this indicate the effects of civil war and invasions disrupting local agriculture and trade?

Source: Annette L. Juliano and Judith A. Lerner (eds.), Monks and Merchants: Silk Road Treasures from Northwest China Gansu and Ningxia, 4th–7th Century *(New York: Harry N. Abrams with the Asia Society, 2001), p. 49.*

Yungang Buddha. *This is one of the five giant statues of the Buddha in Yungang, created under the emperors of the Northern Wei, a dynasty built by nomads who invaded and occupied north China. Sitting at the foothills of the Great Wall, the Buddhas marked the eastern destination of the central Asian Silk Road.*

than the ponderous empires that *were* of this world—whether Roman or Chinese. Religion traveled light and traveled faster than did armies.

POLITICAL AND RELIGIOUS CHANGE IN SOUTH ASIA

South Asia, especially the area of modern India, also enjoyed a surge of religious enthusiasm during the Gupta dynasty, the largest political entity in South Asia from the early fourth to the mid-sixth century CE. (See again Map 8.5.) Its kings facilitated commercial and cultural exchange, much as the Roman Empire had done to the west. Chandragupta (r. c. 320–335 CE), calling himself "King of Kings, Great King," and his son expanded the Gupta territory to the entire northern Indian plain and made a long expedition to southern India.

The poetry during the reign of Chandragupta, a generous patron of the arts, expressed the widespread religious yearnings and popular sentiments of the age. Kalidasa, a prolific poet and playwright, for instance, worked with the motifs and episodes from two early epics, *Mahabharata* and *Ramayana* (see Chapter 4), to address new problems and to extol new virtues. In his and others' hands what had once been lyric dramas and narrative poems written to provide entertainment now served as collective memories of the past and underscored religious precepts of ideal behavior. The heroes and deeds that the poets praised served as models for kings and their subjects. Because these epics were intended to become part of the religious canon, they were rendered in classical Sanskrit.

These works preserve stories from ancient times and offer insights into those eras. Consider the original *Mahabharata* epic, which told of a king who left his court for an assertive woman of a forest society. In Kalidasa's accounting, what had been a saga of love and suffering becomes a morality play about holding to strict religious precepts. The main character, Sakuntala, portrayed as a shy girl who had been adopted by a forest holy man but who had neglected her religious duties, was made to suffer punishments and to live out her life in great misery. The moral of Kalidasa's story was that misfortune comes from failing to follow Brahmanical religious rules.

A Gold Coin of Chandra Gupta II. *The Gupta dynasty, based in the middle and lower Ganges plain, was known for its promotion of indigenous Indian culture. Here, Chandra Gupta II, the most famous king of the dynasty, is shown riding a horse in the style of the invaders from the central Asian steppes.*

The Transformation of the Buddha

During the Gupta period, the two main schools of Buddhism acquired universalistic features. Initially regarded as a contemplative ascetic (someone who chooses a simple, hard life of self-denial), the Buddha now came to be worshipped as a god.

The doctrines of both schools—the Mahayana or Greater Vehicle school; and the school of elders, the Hinayana or Lesser Vehicle school—became quite different from what the Buddha preached centuries earlier. As we saw in Chapter 5, the historical Buddha was a sage who was believed to enter *nirvana,* ending the pain of consciousness. In the earliest Buddhist doctrine, god and supernatural powers did not exist. But by 200 CE a crucial transformation had occurred: his followers started to view the Buddha as a god (see Chapter 6). **Mahayana (Greater Vehicle) Buddhism** also extended worship to the many bodhisattvas who bridged the gulf between the Buddha's perfection and the world's sadly imperfect peoples.

Some Buddhists fully accepted the Buddha as god but could not accept the divinity of bodhisattvas; these adherents belonged to the more monkish school of old-fashioned **Hinayana (Lesser Vehicle) Buddhism**, later called Theraveda in Ceylon and Southeast Asia. They rejected the Sanskrit canon on the supernatural power of bodhisattvas and remained loyal to the early Buddhist texts, which were probably based on the words of Buddha himself. Hinayana temples barred all colorful idols of the bodhisattvas and other heavenly beings; they only contained images of the Buddha.

It was especially in the Mahayana school that Buddhism became a universal religion, whose adherents worshipped divinities rather than recognizing them merely as great men. Spreading along the Silk Road, this new religion with claims to universality that rivaled those of Christianity, eventually appealed to peoples all over East Asia.

The religion's universalizing transformation also involved rituals that recognized powerful local spirits. Consider the observations of Faxian, a Chinese pilgrim to India around 400 CE. He described the city of Sankasya, where both Mayahana and Hinayana Buddhists took hold, as being home to a Buddhist *sangha* whose patron was "a white-eared dragon." Believing that it brought rain at propitious times to guarantee a good harvest, the Buddhists constructed a shrine in its honor and offered the dragon food each day. At the end of the summer rainy period, "the dragon appears in the form of a white-eared snake. Monks recognize him and offer some cheese in a copper bowl. . . . The snake then moves from the high seats to the low seats of the sangha, as if sending his regards to everyone. Then he disappears. This happens every year." This Buddhist ritual likely reflects the local agrarian lifestyle and traditions of propitiating spirits from the natural world.

The Hindu Transformation

During this period, the ancient Brahmanic Vedic religion also spread widely and became the dominant religion of South Asia. Because Buddhism and Jainism (see Chapter 5) had many devotees in cities and commercial communities, conservative Brahmans turned their attention to rural India and refashioned their religion, bringing it in accord with rural life and agrarian values. As a result of these changes, the Brahmanic religion emerged as the dominant faith in Indian society in the form of what we today call **Hinduism**. (Hinduism is a modern word coined from *Hindu*, the people who live in Hind, the Arabic word for India).

In the religion's new form, believers became vegetarians, forsaking the animal sacrifices that had been important to their earlier rituals. They abandoned long-held customs associated with pastoralists and nomads and even absorbed Buddhist and Jain practices, as they identified themselves with agrarian culture. Their new rituals were linked to self-sacrifice—denying themselves meat rather than offering up slaughtered animals to the gods, as they had done previously. Three major deities—Brahma, Vishnu, and Siva—formed a trinity representing the three phases of the universe—birth, existence, and destruction, respectively—and the three expressions of the eternal self, or *atma*.

Vishnu, who embodied the present, was the most popular of the three deities. Believers thought he revealed himself to the world in various avatars, or incarnations. One of these was Krishna, the dark-skinned cattle herder and charioteer of the ancient hero Arjuna in the epic poem *Mahabharata*, who also became a religious teacher to Arjuna. A central part of this epic revolves around the final battle between two warring

Hindu Statue. *This huge statue of a three-headed god in a cave on a small island near Mumbai (Bombay) represents the monotheistic theology of Hinduism. Brahma, the creator, Vishnu, the keeper, and Siva, the destroyer, are all from one atma, or the single soul of the universe.*

confederations of Vedic tribes. Arjuna, the best warrior of one of these confederations, holds back from the fray, unwilling to fight against his enemies because many of them are his cousins. At a crucial moment on the battlefield, Krishna intervenes, commanding him to slay his foes—even those related to him. Krishna reminds Arjuna that he belongs to the Kshatriyas, the warrior caste that has been put on earth to govern and to fight against the community's enemies. In the early rendition of this tale the episode takes up little space. But by the Gupta period the story had become a lengthy poem, *The Bhagavad Gita,* or "Song of the God." In this form it prescribed religious and ethical precepts or *dharma* for people in all walks of life and served as a major canon of Hindu spirituality.

Hindus also adopted the deities of other religions, even regarding the Buddha as an avatar of Vishnu. Thus the Hindu world of gods became larger and more accessible than the Vedic one, enabling more believers to share a single faith. Hindus did not wish to approach the gods only through sacrificial rituals at which Brahmans alone could officiate. They preferred to devote their passion and faith to an individual form of each of the great gods. For example, women, especially widows, tended to worship Krishna and kept a small idol of him in the home. This practice, which stressed personal devotion to gods, was called ***bhakti***. It attracted Hindus of all social strata, while the body of mythological literature wove the deities into an intriguing heavenly order presided over by the trinity of Brahma, Vishnu, and Siva as universal gods

During this period Buddhism and Hinduism lived side by side, competing for followers by building ornate temples and sculptures of gods and by holding elaborate rituals and festivals. Hindu temples and Buddhist monasteries also developed into centers of education, with both communities learning from each other.

Culture and Ideology Instead of an Empire

If Hinduism ordered the heavens, what then was to guide the political and social order on earth? Unlike China and Rome, India did not have a centralized empire that could establish a code of laws and an overarching administration. After the fall of the Mauryan Empire in the second century BCE (see Chapter 6), northern India came under the rule of distant rulers who had no contact with the people except to collect taxes and exact tariffs from their subjects. Even the considerably more powerful Gupta Empire (see below) did not extend its authority over the whole subcontinent or enjoy direct relations with the rural population. Instead, what emerged to unify South and even large parts of Southeast Asia was a distinctive form of cultural synthesis, based on Hindu spiritual beliefs and articulated in the Sanskrit language. Recently, scholars have called this cultural synthesis, which prevailed for a full millennium (300 to 1300 CE), the Sanskrit cosmopolis. Spearheading this development were priests and intellectuals, well versed in the Sanskrit language and literary and religious texts. As they carried Sanskrit far and wide, they enabled the language to eclipse even Poli, which had served for centuries as the linguistic vehicle for Buddhism and Buddhist polities. As Sanskrit spread, it stepped beyond religious scriptures and became the public language of politics. Kings and emperors used it to express the ideals of royal power and responsibility. Rulers issued inscriptions in it, recording their genealogies and their prestigious acts. Poets celebrated ruling dynasties and recorded important moments in the language. Although local languages retained their prominence in day-to-day administration and everyday life, kings delivered their speeches and issued their edicts in Sanskrit.

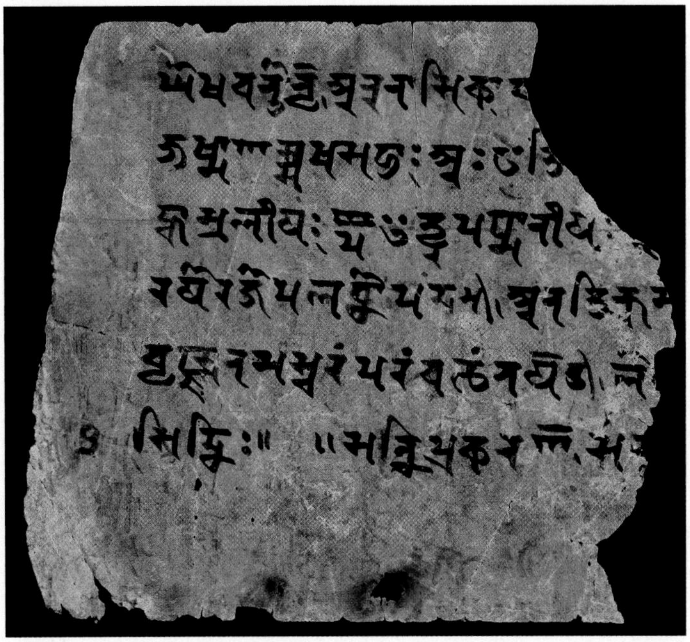

Sanskrit. *The widespread and enduring nature of this language is demonstrated in this thirteenth-century Sanskritic manuscript of Mongolian origin.*

THE CODE OF MANU The emergence of Sanskrit as the lingua franca of the elites in South and Southeast Asian societies also facilitated the spread of Brahmanism. Possessing an unparalleled knowledge of the language, Brahmans circulated their ideals on morality and society in Sanskritic texts, the most influential of which was the Code of Manu. This document is a discourse given by the sage, Manu, to a gathering of wise men, seeking answers on how to organize their communities after a series of floods has brought the people to their knees. The text, which originally took the form of more than 1,000 chapters and was later grouped into twelve subchapters, lays out a set of laws designed to address the problems of assimilating strangers into expanding towns and refining the caste order as the agricultural frontier expanded. In Hindu mythology, Manu ("Human") was the father of the human race, and the laws of Manu were held to apply to all persons no matter where they lived. Kingdoms might come and go, but the "true" order of society, summed up in the Laws of Manu, remained the same everywhere.

Above all, the **Laws of Manu** offered guidance for living within the caste system, whose origins lay centuries earlier. (See Primary Source: The Laws of Manu: Castes and Occupations.) The laws prescribed that every person had to marry within his or her caste and follow the caste's profession and dietary rules in order to perpetuate its status. Thus social and religious pressure, not government coercion, kept all individuals in orderly social groups. Though seemingly rigid, the Laws of Manu offered a way to cope with a constantly changing Indian society. In providing mechanisms for absorbing new groups into the caste system, it propelled Hinduism into areas beyond the reach of the state.

Caste System. *The dazzlingly diverse population of India, as depicted in this palace scene from a Gupta dynasty cavepainting, depended on the ancient caste system to lend it law and order.*

INTERNAL COLONIZATION Behind these developments was a remarkable movement of internal colonization, as settlers from northern India pushed southward into lands formerly outside the domain of the Brahmans. In these territories Brahmans encountered Buddhists and competed with them to win followers. The mixing of these two groups and the intertwining of their ideas and institutions ultimately created a common "Indic" culture organized around a shared vocabulary addressing concepts such as the nature of the universe and the cyclical pattern of life and death. Much of this mixing of ideas took place in schools, universities, and monasteries. The Buddhists already possessed large monasteries, such as Nalanda in northeast India, where 10,000 residential faculty and students assembled, and more than 100 smaller establishments in southeast India housing at least 10,000 monks. In these settings Buddhist teachers debated subjects like theology, theories about the universe, mathematics, logic, and botany. In response, the Brahmans established schools, called *maths*, where similar high intellectual topics were discussed and where Buddhist and Brahmanic Hindu ideas were fused.

The resulting Indic cultural unity covered around 1 million square miles (an area as great as the extent of the Roman Empire) and a highly diverse population. Although India was not one polity like China and did not adhere to one religious system as in the Christian Roman Empire and in medieval western Europe, it was developing a distinctive culture based on the intertwining of two shared major religious traditions. Outsiders recognized this new unity. Xuanzang, a Chinese Buddhist pilgrim, began his account of a visit to India in the 630s–640s CE by discussing the name *Indu*. For him and others, Indu (what we today call India) began after a traveler crossed the valley of the Hindu Kush from the northwest. Its other boundaries were oceans on three sides and the snowy Himalayas to the north. Although the region comprised more than seventy states, he found it to be culturally cohesive. Throughout this large land, Xuanzang observed, the Brahmans were the highest caste, so he suggested calling the territory "the land of the Brahmans." In short, he described an area of greatly diverse regimes, climates, and customs. But it was a unity nonetheless—possibly even a country.

POLITICAL AND RELIGIOUS CHANGE IN EAST ASIA

In the first century CE, Han China had been the largest state in the world, with as great a population as the Roman Empire had at its height. Its emperor ruled an area more than twice the size of the Roman Empire, extracted an annual income of millions of pounds of rice and bolts of cloth, and conscripted millions of

PRIMARY SOURCE

The Laws of Manu: Castes and Occupations

Brahmans compiled the Laws of Manu during the first or the second century CE, when the Kushans from the northern steppes ruled over much of South Asia. It was a time of constant social upheaval. Among the many law codes that appeared throughout Indian history, that of Manu (father of the human race) holds the most authority among Hindus because it is the most comprehensive. It describes the origins of the four castes and clearly designates the occupations that provide members of each with their livelihood.

87. But in order to protect this universe He, the most resplendent one, assigned separate (duties and) occupations to those who sprang from his mouth, arms, thighs, and feet.

88. To Brâhmanas he assigned teaching and studying (the Veda), sacrificing for their own benefit and for others, giving and accepting (of alms).

89. The Kshatriya he commanded to protect the people, to bestow gifts, to offer sacrifices, to study (the Veda), and to abstain from attaching himself to sensual pleasures;

90. The Vaisya to tend cattle, to bestow gifts, to offer sacrifices, to study (the Veda), to trade, to lend money, and to cultivate land.

91. One occupation only the lord prescribed to the Sûdra, to serve meekly even these (other) three castes.

QUESTIONS FOR ANALYSIS

- According to Hindu belief, the four castes sprang from "the mouth, arms, thighs, and feet" of "the most resplendent one." In what ways is it significant that the Brahman caste sprang from the mouth?
- What caste do soldiers belong to? What caste do farmers and merchants belong to? Which caste do you suppose represents the majority of the population?
- How are the different caste statuses reflected in the jobs that their members can take?

Source: The Laws of Manu, *I.87–91; translated by G. Bühler, vol. 25 of* The Sacred Books of the East *(Oxford: Clarendon Press, 1886), p. 24.*

workers whose families paid tribute through their labor. Later Chinese regarded the end of the Han Empire as a disaster just as great as western Europeans regarded the end of the Roman Empire. Successive generations recalled the centuries after the fall of the Han as a period marked by barbarization.

In reality, as with the Roman Empire, "barbarization" meant the opening up of a proud society to cultures along its margins. In post-Han China, new influences emanated from the Silk Road, the nomads' military talents, and the proselytizing of Buddhist monks from the so-called Western Regions (see again Map 8.5). Buddhism took much the same role as Christianity played in Rome, adapting to the Chinese empire and gaining popularity through imperial and elite patronage. Here Buddhism evolved into a Chinese religion, but one with universal appeal.

Northern and Southern China

After the fall of the Han in 220 CE, several small kingdoms—at times as many as sixteen of them—competed for the remembered glories of a large empire. Civil wars raged for roughly three centuries, a time called the Six Dynasties period, when no single state was able to conquer more than half of China's territory.

The most successful regime was that of the Tuoba, a people originally from Inner Mongolia. The Tuoba founded the **Northern Wei dynasty** in 386 CE, which lasted one and a half centuries and administered part of the Han territory. These "barbarian" rulers from northern China maintained many of their preconquest forms of state and society. Because they had lived for generations within the Chinese orbit as tributary states, they were "civilized" by imperial standards. They even maintained many Chinese traditions of statecraft and court life: they taxed land and labor on the basis of a census, conferred official ranks and titles, practiced court rituals, preserved historical archives, and promoted classical learning and the use of classical Chinese for record keeping and political discourse. Though they were nomadic warriors, they adapted their large standing armies to city-based military technology, which required dikes, fortifications, canals, and walls. Following the Qin and Han precedent, they drafted huge numbers of workers to complete such enormous projects as rebuilding a capital city at Luoyang.

Among the challenges facing the Northern Wei rulers was the need to consolidate authority over their own highly competitive nomadic people. One strategy, which they pursued with little success for nearly a century, was to make their own government more "Chinese." Under Emperor Xiaomen (r. 471–499 CE), for example, the Tuoba royal family adopted the Chinese family name of Yuan and required all court officials to speak Chinese and wear Chinese clothing. However, the Tuoba warrior families resisted these policies. They blatantly spoke their native tongues, shaved most of their heads and tied their remaining hair in pigtails, and continued wearing loose-fitting pants and shirts more typical of the warrior on horseback than the flowing gowns of urbane Han Chinese civilians riding in carts or walking the streets.

At the same time, the Wei rulers sought stronger relationships with the Han Chinese families of Luoyang that had not fled south. The Wei offered them more political power as officials in the Wei bureaucracy and more land. A key figure in this effort was the Dowager Empress Fang (regent 476–490 CE). As widows, such dowagers often held power over their young emperor sons and controlled their own property, or dower. Her most substantial initiative involved progressive land reforms: all young men—whether Han or Wei—who agreed to cultivate the land would receive two allotments, one at age eleven and one at fifteen, which they could pass on to their heirs. After age seventy, they would no longer have to pay taxes on it. But even this plan failed to bridge the cultural divides between the "civilized" Han Chinese of Luoyang and the "barbarian" Tuoba Wei because the latter showed no interest in farming.

The boldest attempt to unify northern China came under Emperor Xiaomen, who rebuilt the old Han imperial capital of Luoyang based on classical architectural models dating from the Han dynasty (see Chapter 7) and made it the seat of his government. To gain political legitimacy with the Han, members of the Wei court supported Buddhist temples and monumental cave sites in an appeal to their Tuoba roots while also honoring Confucian traditions dating to the ancient Zhou period. Emperor Xiaomen's untimely death cut short his efforts to unify the north, however. Several decades of intense fighting among military rulers followed, leading ultimately to the downfall of the Northern Wei dynasty.

Buddhism in China

By the third and fourth centuries CE, travelers from central Asia who had converted to Buddhism had become frequent visitors in the streets and temples of the competing capitals: Chang'an, Luoyang, and Nanjing. (See Primary Source: The Art of Religious Fervor in China.)

MADHYAMIKA BUDDHISM AND CULTURAL CHANGE

Spreading the increasingly universalizing faith required intermediaries, endowed with texts or codes, to convey its message. Kumarajiva (344–413 CE), a renowned Buddhist scholar and missionary, was the right man, in the right place, at the right time to spread Buddhism in China—where it already coexisted with other faiths. He was a bearer of exotic holy books (not unlike the Christian missionaries of the Roman Empire) and his influence on Chinese Buddhist thought was critical. Not only did he translate previously unknown Buddhist texts into Chinese, but he also clarified Buddhist terms and philosophical concepts. He and his disciples established a Mahayana branch known as **Madhyamika (Middle Way) Buddhism**, which used irony and paradox to show that reason was limited. For example, they contended that all reality was transient because nothing remained unchanged over time. They sought enlightenment by means of transcendental visions and spurned experiences in the material world of sights and sounds.

Kumarajiva represented the beginning of a profound cultural shift. After 300 CE Buddhism began to expand in northwestern China, taking advantage of imperial disintegration and the decline of state-sponsored Confucian classical learning. The Buddhists stressed devotional acts, such as daily prayers and mantras, which included seated meditations in solitude requiring mind and breath control, as well as the saving power of the Buddha and the saintly bodhisattvas who postponed their own salvation for the sake of others. They even encouraged the Chinese to join a new class—the clergy. The idea that persons could be defined by faith rather than kinship was not new in Chinese society (see Chapter 7), but it had special appeal in a time of unprecedented crisis. In the south, the immigrants from the north found that membership in the Buddhist clergy and monastic orders offered a way to restore their lost prestige.

Even more important, in the northern states—now part-Chinese, part-barbarian—Buddhism provided legitimacy. With Buddhists holding prominent positions in government, medicine, and astronomy, the Wei ruling houses could espouse a philosophy that was just as legitimate as that of the Han Chinese. As a Tuoba who ruled at the height of the Northern Wei, Emperor Xuanwu, for instance, was an avid Buddhist who made Mahayana Buddhism the state religion during his reign.

Buddhism, unlike Christianity, was not a universalizing religion that sought to be the same in all places and at all times. On the contrary, as the expression of a cosmic truth as timeless and varied as the world itself, Buddhism showed a high level of adaptability, easily absorbing as its own the gods and the wisdom of every country it touched, making it a different kind of universalizing religion.

PRIMARY SOURCE

The Art of Religious Fervor in China: The Pagoda

Religious fervor changed the visual environment of China. For example, the decorations on pottery and metal objects from this time show strong central Asian and Sasanian influences, transmitted primarily through Buddhism. The impact on architecture was even more striking. In India, Buddhists had adapted a form of dome-shaped tombs (called stupas) into shrines for housing relics of the Buddha. Now, in China, huge pagodas represented an attempt—mostly in wood—to imitate the stone and brick stupas of India. Regarded by Koreans and Japanese (and later by Westerners) as quintessentially Chinese, the pagoda was in fact a distant echo, on Chinese soil, of northern Indian Buddhism. Similarly, the complexes of cave temples at Longmen and Yungang reflect Indian and central Asian influences. In these ways, a universal religion created common artistic themes that stretched from central to East Asia.

One site that featured the work of central Asian artisans was the oasis city of Dunhuang. Located along the Silk Road, it contained a number of cave temples. Starting in 400 CE they were adorned with paintings and statues, and between the fifth and eighth centuries hundreds of them were decorated with wall paintings. Some illustrated Buddhist legends, and others depicted scenes of paradise. The caves were sealed in 1035 to save them from raids by Tibetans, and they have survived to this day. In 1900, the cave housing the great Buddhist library at Dunhuang was found unopened. The dry climate had preserved thousands of manuscripts, including Buddhist texts and works of popular literature.

QUESTIONS FOR ANALYSIS

- What do the architectural links from India to China, Japan, and Korea tell us about Buddhism?
- Why do you suppose the Dunhuang caves are essential to our understanding of Chinese Buddhism at this time?

Pagoda on Mount Song. *This is probably the earliest pagoda in China. The solid stone structure shows the influence of pagodas in the contemporary eastern part of India, such as the one in Mahabodhi Monastery in Bodhgaya.*

The Western Pure Land. *This mural painting of the Western Pure Land (a place where enlightenment is achieved) is from Dunhuang, close to the eastern end of the Silk Road. The facial features of the celestial beings and the art style are more Chinese than Indian. Lazulite blue, a pigment made from lapis lazuli from Badakshan, Afghanistan, is the dominant color here, as it is on all the cave art along the central Asian Silk Road.*

ANALYZING GLOBAL DEVELOPMENTS

One God, Two Communities: Comparing the Structures of Christianity and Judaism, 600 CE

Christianity emerged from Judaism in the first and second centuries CE and continues to share the same God and many of the same scriptures to this very day. Yet, despite these fundamental commonalities, what arose were two distinct religious communities, each with its own notions of God in relation to humanity. The following diagrams illustrate the major impact that Christian and Jewish understandings of the same God had upon the structures of their early religious institutions and their ability to grow and become universalizing.

Looking at the diagram, Judaism's institutional structure is flatter and simpler, and Christianity's is more hierarchical. One would think the more direct connection to God found in Judaism, with rabbis being the primary teachers of the Torah and overseeing most of the responsibilities at the synagogue, would make it more appealing and universalizing than Christianity, with its church's hierarchical structure composed of bishops, priests, monks, and nuns—but this was not the case.

QUESTIONS FOR ANALYSIS

- The diagram suggests that the people of Israel had a direct connection to God. What does the diagram suggest about the relationship of Christians to the same God? Why is this relationship important in understanding the structures of the two religions and their universalizing appeal?
- Martyrs, like Perpetua (discussed in the chapter), played a big role in both Christianity and Judaism (e.g. rabbis resisting Rome ca. 100 CE). Where would you place martyrs on this diagram and why? What role might martyrdom have played in the universalizing appeal of Christianity as opposed to Judaism?
- Based on your reading, what were the origins of the hierarchical structure of Christianity, and why would it actually aid in the growth of the religion?

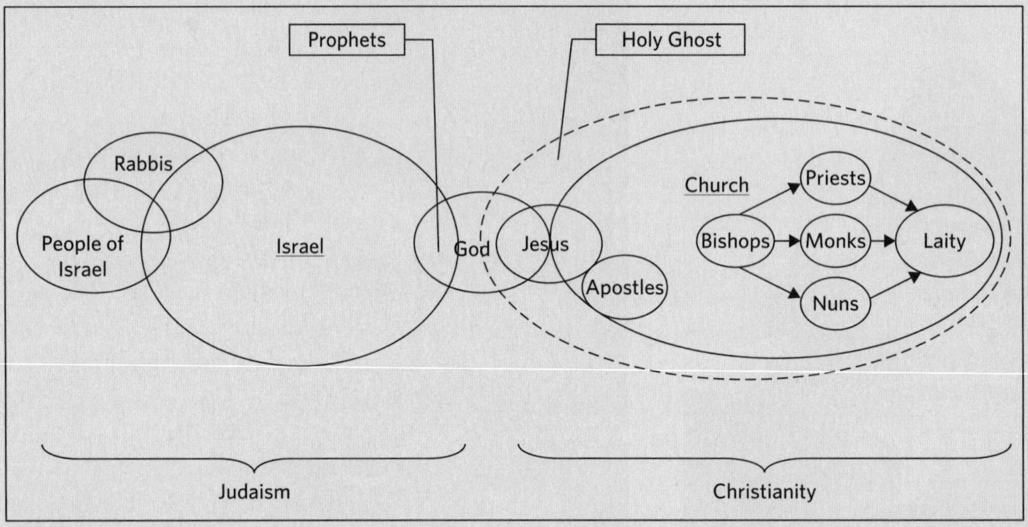

DAOISM, ALCHEMY, AND THE TRANSMUTATION OF THE SELF Daoism, a popular Chinese religion under the Han and a challenge to the Confucian state and its scholar-officials (see Chapter 7), lost its political edge and adapted to the new realities in this period of disunity. Two new traditions of Daoist thought flourished in this era of self-doubt. The first was organized, community oriented, and involved heavenly masters who as mortals guided local religious groups or parishes. Followers sought salvation through virtue, confession, and liturgical ceremonies. Through ecstatic initiation rites, often achieved via an "external alchemy," including the use of hallucinatory drugs, a new Daoist clergy also brought believers into contact with the divine.

A second Daoist tradition was more individualistic. In the Yangzi delta, personal expressions of religious faith emerged. For example, Ge Hong (283–343 CE) sought to reconcile Confucian classical learning with Daoist religious beliefs in the

Amitabha. *This exquisite tapestry is an illustration for the* Amitabha Sutra, *the "Sutra of the Western Pureland." Since the text was translated into Chinese by Kumarajiva in the fourth century* CE, *Amitabha has been one of the most popular bodhisattvas in China. A devotee who invokes the name of Amitabha ten times before death would be saved to this Western Pure Land, where the Seven Treasures decorated the quiet landscape.*

occult and magical. He focused on "internal alchemy"—the use of trance and meditation to control human physiology. Through such mental and physical exertions, an adept, both as believer and practitioner, believed that the soul could accumulate enough religious merit to prolong his life. A recommended set of nine body postures involved full chest breathing combined with extensive stretching to facilitate the healthy flow of Qi, the life force circulating throughout the body. Adepts complemented this extension of life via trance and physiological control by taking elixirs, boiling exquisite teas as medical beverages, and knowing the specific effects of herbs and minerals.

The concept of merit and demerit in Daoist circles echoed the Buddhist notion of karmic retribution (the cosmic assessment of one's acts in this life that determines one's rebirth into a better or worse next life; see Chapter 5). For the Daoists, however, eternal life was the ultimate goal, and not the Buddhists' ideal of release from the cycle of life, death, and rebirth.

By 400 CE China had more than 1,700 Buddhist monasteries and about 80,000 monks and nuns. By contrast, in 600 CE (after two centuries of monastic growth), Gaul and Italy—the two richest regions of western Europe—had, altogether, only 320 monasteries, many with fewer than thirty monks. Yet, in the two ends of Afro-Eurasia the principal bearers of the new religions were monks. Set apart from "worldly" affairs in their refuges, they enjoyed the pious support of royal courts and warriors whose lifestyles differed sharply from their own. It would be through their devoted faith in the divine and the support of secular rulers that these two universalizing religions would continue to grow, flourish, and revitalize themselves.

FAITH AND CULTURES IN THE WORLDS APART

In most areas of sub-Saharan Africa and the Americas, it was not easy for ideas, institutions, peoples, and commodities to circulate broadly. Thus we do not see the development of universalizing faiths. Rather, belief systems and their deities remained local.

This is not to say that sub-Saharan Africa and the Americas lacked the elements for creating communities of faith. Africans and Americans alike had prophetic figures who, they believed, communicated with deities and brought to humankind divinely prescribed rules of behavior. Moreover, peoples in both regions honored beliefs and rules that were passed down orally from generation to generation. These spiritual traditions guided behavior, established social customs, and determined people's fates. In fact, relationships with deities and spirits governed the calendar of rituals across these regions.

Bantus of Sub-Saharan Africa

Today, most of Africa south of the equator is home to peoples who speak some variant of more than 400 Bantu languages. Early Bantu history is shrouded in mystery. At present, scholars using oral traditions and linguistic evidence can trace the narrative of these peoples no further back than 1000 CE (see Map 8.6).

The first Bantu speakers lived in the southeastern part of modern Nigeria, where about 4,000 or 5,000 years ago they

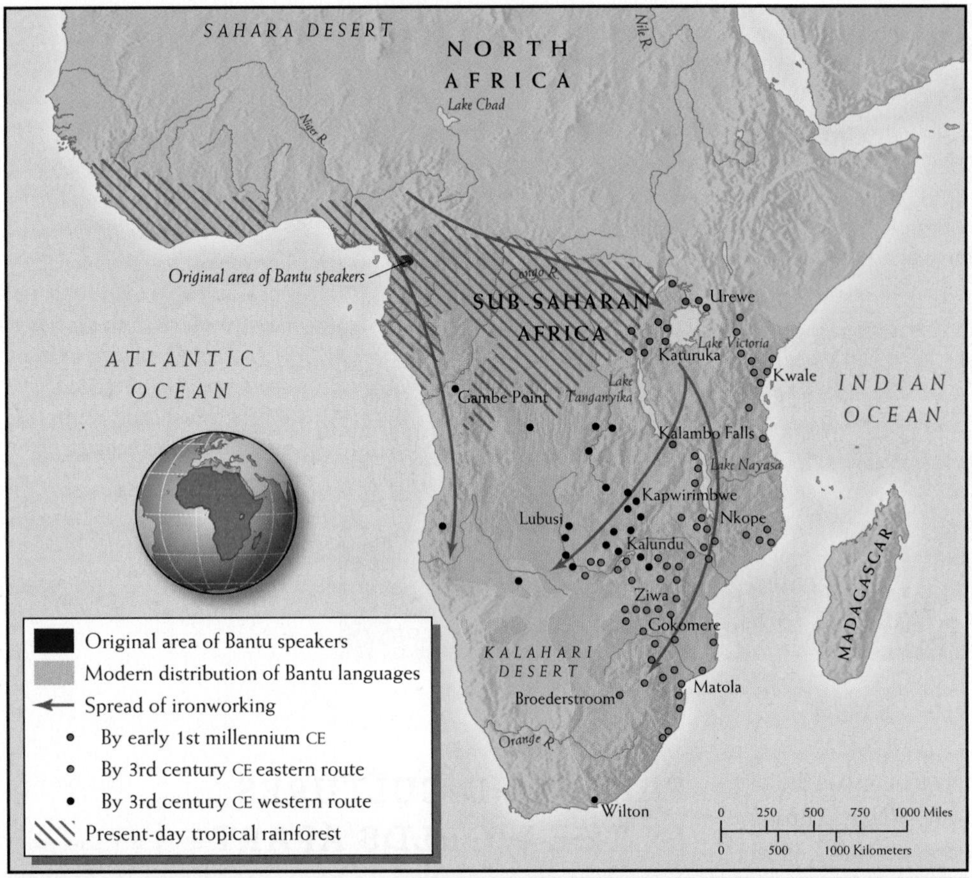

MAP 8.6 | Bantu Migrations

The migration of Bantu speakers throughout much of sub-Saharan Africa in the first millennium CE dramatically altered the cultural landscape.

- According to the map, where did the Bantu speakers originate? Where were the Bantu speakers' migrations?
- What skills did they have that enabled them to dominate the peoples already living there?
- Did the Bantu migrations create a common culture below the Sahara Desert during this time?

shifted from hunting, gathering, and fishing to practicing settled agriculture. The areas they spread into, being tropical rain forest, demanded an immense amount of work. To ready a new acre for cultivation required removing some 600 tons of moist vegetation, and the migrants brought to the task only simple tools (mainly machetes and billhooks). In fact, their most effective technique was controlled burning. Moreover, the African equatorial forests were almost totally devoid of food plants. So these peoples made do with woodland plants such as yams and mushrooms, as well as palm oils and kernels.

BANTU MIGRATIONS Following riverbeds and elephant trails, Bantu migrants traveled out of West Africa in two great waves. One group moved across the Congo forest region to East Africa, aided by their knowledge of iron smelting, which enabled them to use iron tools for agriculture. Because their new habitats supported a mixed economy of animal husbandry and sedentary agriculture, this group became relatively prosperous. The second wave of migrants moved southward through the rain forests in present-day Congo, eventually reaching the Kalahari Desert. They were not so fortunate. The tsetse fly–infested environment did not permit them to rear livestock, so they were limited to subsistence farming. These Bantus learned to use iron later than those who had moved to the Congo region in the east.

Precisely when the **Bantu migrations** began is unclear, but once under way the travelers moved with extraordinary rapidity. Genetic and linguistic evidence reveals that they swept all else before them, absorbing most of the hunting-and-gathering populations who originally inhabited these areas.

What enabled the Bantus to prevail and then to prosper was their skill as settled agriculturalists. They knew how to cultivate the soil, and they adapted their farming techniques to widely different environments. They thrived equally well in the tropical rain forests of the Congo River basin, the high grasslands around Lake Nyanza (former Lake Victoria), and the highlands of Kenya, even though they had to grow different crops in each location.

For the Bantu of the rain forests of central Africa (the Western Bantu), the introduction of the banana plant was decisive. The banana plant originated in tropical South and Southeast Asia and spread rapidly into many regions. Linguistic evidence suggests that it first arrived in the Upper Nile region and then traveled into the rest of Africa with small groups migrating from one favorable location to another; the earliest proof of its presence is a record from the East African coast dating to 525 CE. When it reached the equatorial rain forests, its adaptability to local conditions was unmatched. Not only did it provide more nutrients than the yam crop, but it better withstood heavy rainfalls. In addition, banana plantings required the clearing of fewer trees than yam cultivation and created an environment free of the anopheles mosquito, which carried malaria. Exploiting the benefits of banana cultivation, the Western Bantu filled up the equatorial rain forests of central Africa—perhaps as early as 500 CE, certainly by 1000 CE.

PRIMARY SOURCE

Instructions to a Young Man in West Africa

The words that were traditionally spoken to young men coming of age in the Cameroons in West Africa (an area where the Bantus likely originated) reflect the importance that families attached to being a strong and enterprising individual.

The grandfather gave an ivory bracelet and said:
"This elephant which I put on your arm, become a man of crowds,
a hero in war, a man with women
rich in children, and in many objects of wealth
prosper within the family, and be famous throughout the villages."

The grandmother gave a charm of success as a belt and said:
"Father, you who are becoming a man
Let toughness and fame be with you as this sap of the
[*Baillonella toxisperma*] tree is glued to this thread.
Become dominant, *a great man*,
a hero in war, who surpasses strangers and visitors;
prosper, Have us named!"

QUESTIONS FOR ANALYSIS

- Think about the Bantu speakers' environment. Why would a bracelet made from elephant tusk carry special meaning?
- How do the words and gifts (typically charms) offered reflect a belief that spirits inhabited the natural world?
- According to the chapter text, why did the sub-Saharan peoples organize themselves around "big men" rather than kings or other sorts of rulers?
- Have you ever had or attended a coming-of-age ceremony? Were certain words or gifts significant? Have you ever owned any good-luck charms? What were (or are) they?

Source: Jan Vansina, Paths in the Rainforests: Toward a History of Political Tradition in Equatorial Africa *(Madison: University of Wisconsin Press, 1990), pp. 73–74.*

BANTU CULTURES, EAST AND WEST Did these peoples create a common Bantu culture? Clearly, they could not establish the same political, social, and cultural institutions in widely different ecological zones. In the Great Lakes area of the East African savanna lands, where communication was relatively easy, the Bantu speakers developed centralized polities whose kings ruled by divine right. Mostly, however, they moved into heavily forested areas similar to those they had left in southeastern Nigeria. These locations supported a way of life that remained fundamentally unaltered for perhaps a millennium and a half, withstanding the later impact of the Atlantic slave trade and withering only under European colonialism in the twentieth century.

The western Bantu-speaking communities of the lower Congo River rain forests formed small-scale societies based on family and clan connections. They organized themselves socially and politically into age groups, the most important of which were the ruling elders. Within these age-based networks, individuals who demonstrated talent in warfare, commerce, and politics provided leadership.

Age-grading tended to impose certain rights and duties on different social groups based mainly on their physical age. Many such societies established three age grades for males and two for females. Males moved from (1) being children and learning male roles from older men, to (2) acquiring warrior status, when they defended the community, raided for livestock, and acquired new lands for the community, and then (3) becoming the politically ruling age grade—the elders. Females' age grades consisted of childhood and marriage. Bonds among age grades were powerful, and movement from one to the next was marked by meaningful and well-remembered rituals.

Lacking chiefs and kings, the loosely organized Bantu societies rallied around individuals of talent—so-called **big men**—whose abilities attracted followers and thereby promoted territorial expansion. Their courage, military valor, and wisdom won them many supporters, but rarely did their high positions pass along to offspring or relatives. Invariably, other dynamic individuals arose to compete for power. In the rain forest, land was abundant but labor was in short supply. Thus, individuals who could attract a large community of followers, marry many women, and sire many children could lead their bands into new locations and establish dominant communities.

Although dispersed, these rain forest communities embraced a common worldview. They believed that the natural world was inhabited by spirits, many of whom were their own heroic ancestors. These spiritual beings intervened in mortals' lives and required constant appeasement. Diviners helped men and women understand the spirits' ways, and charms warded off the misfortune that aggrieved spirits might wish to inflict. Diviners

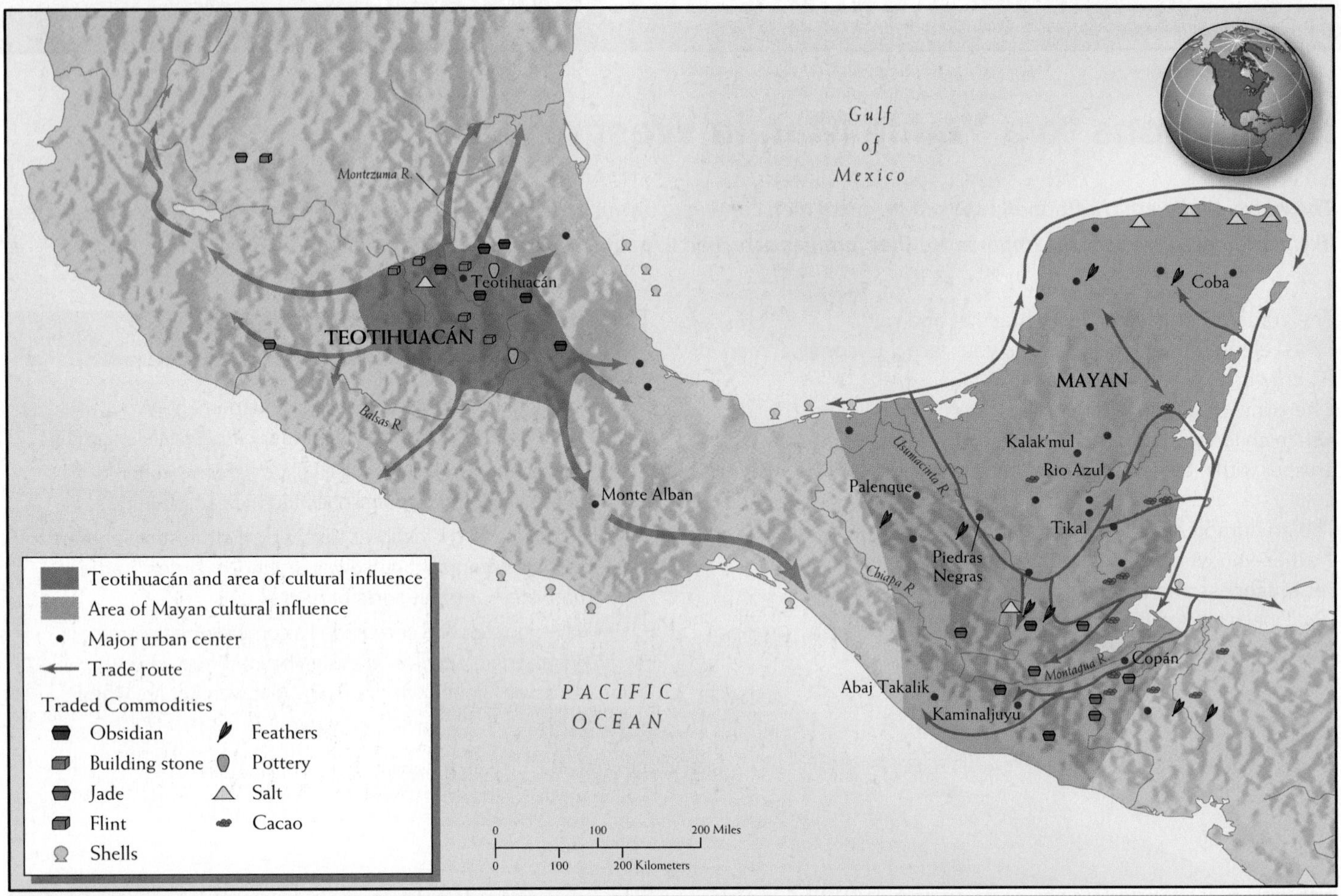

MAP 8.7 | Mesoamerican Worlds, 200–700 CE

At this time, two groups dominated Mesoamerica: one was located at the city of Teotihuacán in the center, and the other, the Mayans, was in the south.

- What commodities did these cultures trade? Look at the symbols for Traded Commodities in the map key, and find them all on the map.
- Judging by what you see, how did each group create a common culture in surrounding regions?
- To what extent do you believe the people of the Teotihuacán and Mayan worlds influenced each other?

and charms also protected against the injuries that living beings—witches and sorcerers—could inflict. In fact, much of the misfortune that occurred in the Bantu world was attributed to these malevolent forces. The Bantus believed their big men could control such forces and use them to punish opponents and reward friends. These beliefs survived unchallenged for well over a millennium. (See Primary Source: Instructions to a Young Man in West Africa.)

The Bantu migrations ultimately filled up more than half the African landmass and introduced settled agriculture throughout its southern part. They spread a political and social order based on family and clan structures that allowed considerable leeway for individual achievement—and maintained an intense relationship to the world of nature that they believed, for good or ill, was shot through with supernatural forces.

Mesoamericans

As in sub-Saharan Africa, the process of settlement and expansion in Mesoamerica differed from that in the large empires of Afro-Eurasia. Mesoamerica had no integrating artery of a giant river and its floodplain, and so it lacked the extensive resources that a state could harness for monumental ambitions. What Mesoamericans achieved was remarkable if we bear this in mind.

In the case of Teotihuacán, the first major community to emerge since the Olmecs (see Chapter 5), we see the growth of a city-state that ruled over a large, mountainous valley in the area of present-day Mexico (see Map 8.7). While it did not evolve into a territorial state, it traded and warred with neighboring peoples and created a smaller-scale common culture. In the case of the Mayans, on the other hand, we witness the emergence of a common culture that ruled over large stretches of Mesoamerica under a series of kingdoms built around ritual centers rather than cities. The Mayans aggressively engaged in warfare and trade, expanding their borders through tributary relationships. The extraordinary feature of Mayan society was that its people were defined not by a great ruler or a great capital city, but by their shared religious beliefs, worldview, and sense of purpose.

TEOTIHUACÁN Around 300 BCE, people in the central plateau and the southeastern districts of Mesoamerica where the dispersed villages of Olmec culture had risen and fallen (see Chapter 5) began to gather in larger settlements. Soon, political and social integration led to city-states. **Teotihuacán**, in the heart of the fertile valley of central Mexico, became the largest center of the Americas before the Aztecs almost a half-millennium later.

Fertile land and ample water from the valley's marshes and lakes fostered high agricultural productivity despite the inhabitants' technologically rustic methods of cultivation. The local food supply sustained a metropolis of between 100,000 and 200,000 residents, living in more than 2,000 apartment compounds lining the city's streets. At one corner rose the massive pyramids of the sun and the moon—the focus of spiritual life for the city dwellers. Marking the city's center was the huge royal compound, or Ciudadela; the grandeur and refinement of its stepped stone pyramid, the Temple of the Feathered Serpent, were famous throughout Mesoamerica. The feathered serpent was the anchor for their spiritual lives. It was a symbol of fertility, a deity that governed reproduction and life, often bearing powerful maternal features—despite the fearsome (to our eyes) appearance of the fangs and jaws, and the snakes that invariably writhed in the deity's grip. Its temple was the core of a much larger structure. From it radiated the awesome promenade known as the Street of the Dead, which culminated in the hulking Pyramid of the Moon. Here foreign warriors and dignitaries were mutilated, sacrificed, and often buried alive to consecrate the holy structure.

Teotihuacán was a powerful city-state. Its military muscle was imposing. After overwhelming or annexing its rivals, by 300 CE Teotihuacán controlled the entire basin of the Valley of Mexico. It dominated its neighbors and demanded gifts, tribute, and humans for ritual sacrifice. Its massive public architecture displayed art that commemorated decisive battles, defeated neighbors, and captured fighters.

Beyond the basin, though, the city's political influence was limited. Far more important was its cultural and economic diffusion, for Teotihuacán's merchants traded throughout Mesoamerica. Ceramics, ornaments of marine shells, and all sorts of decorative and valued objects (especially of green obsidian) made by Teotihuacano artisans traveled on the backs of porters for exchange far and wide. At the same time, Teotihuacán imported pottery, feathers, and other goods from distant lowlands.

This kind of expansion left much of the political and cultural independence of neighbors intact, with only the threat of force keeping them in check. But for some unknown reason

Teotihuacán. *The ruins of Teotihuacán convey the importance of monumental architecture to Aztec culture. In the foreground is the Plaza of the Moon, leading to the Street of the Dead, with the Pyramid of the Sun to the left. These massive structures were meant to confirm the importance of spiritual affairs in urban life.*

Quetzalcoatl. *The artisans of Teotihuacán decorated the sides of their monumental buildings with sculptures. Here, feathered serpents, denoting the god Quetzalcoatl, burst from the sides of a wall to stare menacingly at passers-by.*

that threat apparently waned, for late in the fifth century CE the city fell. Invaders burned it and smashed the carved figurines of the central temples and palaces, targeting Teotihuacán's institutional and spiritual core.

THE MAYANS Teotihuacán's power eventually spread as far as the Caribbean region of the Yucatán and its interior. Here the Mayan people arose and flourished from about 250 CE to their zenith in the eighth century. The **Mayans** have been a never-ending mystery to historians and archaeologists. They lived in an inhospitable region—hot, infertile, lacking navigable river systems, and vulnerable to hurricanes. Still, their communities, grouped into large settlements, conducted long-distance trade and produced stunning scientific and mathematical innovations. The Mayans were also great artists and builders, and it is largely from the remains of their prodigious constructions that scholars know much about them. Like the earlier Olmecs, the Mayans accomplished magnificent feats only to collapse, leaving their centers deserted for centuries and entire provinces utterly depopulated.

In contrast to the inhabitants of Teotihuacán (or Baghdad or Constantinople), the Mayans achieved greatness without founding a single great central metropolis. Instead, they established hundreds, possibly thousands, of agrarian villages scattered across present-day southern Mexico to western El Salvador. In this region of diverse ecological zones, people shared the same Mayan language. Villages were also linked through tribute payments, chiefly from lesser settlements to sacred towns. At their peak the Mayans may have numbered as many as 10 million—a figure that qualifies them as a "big" culture. Bigness in a cultural system without big cities made them unique.

MAYAN POLITICAL AND SOCIAL STRUCTURE The Mayans established a variety of kingdoms around major hubs and their hinterlands. Palenque, Copán, and Piedras Negras, for instance, embodied the model of a ritual center with hinterlands (similar in some respects to Mesopotamian city-states surrounded by transhumant societies; see Chapter 3). Such hubs were politically independent but culturally and economically interconnected. Some larger polities, such as Tikal and Kalak'mul, became sprawling centers with dependent provinces. Ambitious rulers in these larger states frequently engaged in hostilities with one another.

Thus a single culture encompassed about a dozen kingdoms that shared many features. Each was highly stratified, displaying an elaborate class structure. At the center was a shamanistic king who legitimated his position by extolling his lineage, which reached back to a founding father and, ultimately, the gods. While there was a vast pantheon of gods and each subregion had its own patron, there were some common features. There was a creator god and there were deities for rain, maize, war, and the sun—as well as of bees and midwifery. The importance of reproduction is evident, but the creation of humans was only one act in an eternal cycle of births, deaths, and renewals that constituted the entire population of the cosmos. Gods were neither especially cruel nor benevolent. They were just very

Palenque. *Deep in the Lacandon jungle lies the ruin of the Mayan city of Palenque. Its pyramid, on the left, overlooks the site; on the right, the Tower of the Palace shadows a magnificent courtyard where religious figures and nobles gathered. There is no mistaking how a city like Palenque could command its hinterland with religious authority.*

busy with the work, or dance, that sustained the axis connecting the underworld and the skies. What humans had to worry about was making sure that the gods got the attention and reverence they needed.

This was the job of Mayan rulers. Kings sponsored elaborate public rituals to reinforce their divine heritages, including ornate processions down their cities' main boulevards to pay homage to gods and their descendants, the rulers. Lords and their wives performed ritual blood sacrifice to feed their ancestors. Though there may have been a powerful priestly elite, the pillars of these societies were their scribes, legal experts, military advisers, and skilled artisans.

Most of the Mayan people remained tied to the land, which could sustain a high population only through dispersed settlements. In much of the region, the soil was poor and quickly exhausted. Limited water also prevented large-scale agriculture, as major rivers or irrigation systems were lacking. Mayans therefore employed a combination of adaptations to the ecology. Where possible they created terraces and drained fields for intensive cultivation. But in much of the region they relied on slash-and-burn agriculture, which pushed the arable frontier farther into the dense jungle. The result: a subsistence economy of diversified agrarian production. Villagers cultivated maize, beans, and squash, rotating them to prevent the depletion of soil nutrients. Where possible, farmers supplemented these staples with root crops such as sweet potato and cassava. Cotton was the basic fiber used for robes, dresses, and blouses; it frequently grew amid rows of other crops as part of a diversified mix.

MAYAN WRITING, MATHEMATICS, AND ARCHITECTURE Commerce connected the dispersed Mayan worlds, as did a common set of beliefs, codes, and values. Villagers spoke dialects of roughly the same language. Writing developed very early, though the Maya script was deciphered only recently. The advent of writing created an important caste of scribes who were vital to the society's integration. Rulers rewarded them with great titles and honors, as well as material comforts, for writing grand epics about dynasties and their founders, major battles, marriages, deaths, and sacrifices. Such writings taught generations of Mayan subjects that they shared common histories, beliefs, and gods—always associated with the narratives of ruling families.

The combination of writings and performances created a historic memory to serve rulers' power and to venerate the gods whose patronage they required. The best-known surviving text is the Popol Vuh, a "Book of Community." It narrates one community's creation myth, extolling its founders (twin heroes) and trials and tribulations—wars, natural disasters, human ingenuity—that enabled a royal genealogy to rule the Quiché Kingdom. It begins with the gods' creation of the earth, in this case the work of three water-dwelling plumed serpents. And it ends with the elaboration of rituals to which the kingdom's tribes must subscribe if they are to avoid losing their way, which had occurred several times throughout their history. One must note, however, in the use of Mayan "written" texts like the Popol Vuh, that they comprise narratives recited to later Spanish sources. They are not texts inscribed in the Classical Mayan era.

Wood Tablet. *This detail of a wood-carved tablet from a temple in the city of Tikal (c. 741 CE) is a fine example of the ornate form of scribal activity, which combined images and portraits with glyphs that tell a narrative.*

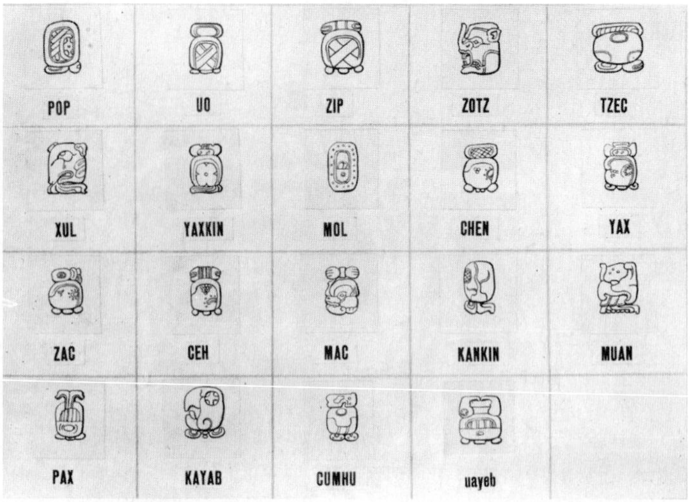

Mayan Pictograms. *The Mayans were famous for keeping records of time with an elaborate calendar. Pictograms, each with a separate image, represented the months of the year. All literate Mayans would have recognized this index.*

The Mayans also were skilled mathematicians, devising a calendar and studying astronomy. They charted regular celestial movements with amazing accuracy and marked the passage of time by precise lunar and solar cycles. Keen readers of the stars, the Mayans could map heavenly motions onto their sacred calendars and rigorously observe their rituals at the proper times. Indeed, the movement of the stars and the chronology of the calendar governed annual ritual cycles. Each change in the cycle had particular rituals, dances, performances, and offerings, including the offering of human blood to honor the gods with life's sustenance. The most sacred blood was drawn from ears, tongues, and the foreskins of penises, to open pathways to the gods through which "donors" could hear, speak, and participate in heavenly reproduction.

Here, then, was a world characterized by political divisions and often crippling warfare, but with common religious and cultural features. A common faith provided a powerful human resource that rulers could exploit. Cities reflected a ruler's ability to summon his subjects to contribute to the kingdom's greatness. Plazas, ball courts, terraces, and palaces sprouted out from neighborhoods in an early form of urban sprawl. Activity revolved around grand royal palaces and massive ball courts, where competing teams treated enthusiastic audiences to contests that were more religious ritual than game (see discussion of Olmec ball courts in Chapter 5). Moreover, rulers exhorted their people to build not just outward but upward. The Mayans excelled at building skyscrapers. In Tikal, for instance, surviving buildings include six steep and massive funerary pyramids featuring thick masonry walls and vaulted ceilings and chambers; the tallest temple soars above the treetops, more than 220 feet high. Embellishing the outsides are giant carvings and paintings, and deep within lie the crypts of royal family members. For example, the famous Bonampak site (in current-day southern Mexico) has a magnificent Temple of the Murals with the finest examples of Classical Mayan painting. These depict a series of events in precise detail—from an orchestra performing, to nobles discussing current affairs, to captured warriors being prepared for human sacrifice. The artwork dates from 790 CE. This kind of artwork likely adorned other Mayan centers as well.

MAYAN BLOODLETTING AND WARFARE The elites were obsessed with blood, for spilling it was a way to honor dynastic lineages as well as gods. This rite led to chronic warfare, especially among rival dynasties, the goal of which was to capture victims for the bloody rituals. Rulers also would shed their own blood at intervals set by the calendar. Royal wives drew blood from their tongues; men had their penises perforated by a stingray spine or sharpened bone. Such bloodletting was reserved for those of noble descent, with the aid of elaborately adorned and sanctified instruments; carvings and paintings portray blood cascading from rulers' mutilated bodies.

The spiral of warfare doomed the Mayans, especially after devastating confrontations between Tikal and Kalak'mul during the fourth through seventh centuries CE. With each outbreak, rulers drafted larger armies and sacrificed greater numbers of captives, and their resolve fueled the carnage. Crops perished. People fled. Food supplies dwindled. After centuries of misery, it must have seemed as if the gods themselves were abandoning the Mayan people.

As warfare engulfed the fractured Mayan communities and ruling households collapsed, entire states fell. The cycle of violence destroyed the cultural underpinnings of elite rule that had held the Mayan world together. There was no single catastrophic event, no great defeat by a rival power. The Mayan people simply abandoned their spiritual centers, and cities became ghost towns. As populations declined, jungles overtook temples. Eventually, the hallmark of Mayan unity—the ability to read a shared script—vanished.

CONCLUSION

The breakdown of two imperial systems—Rome around the Mediterranean, and Han China in East Asia—introduced an era in which religion and shared culture rather than military conquest and political institutions linked large areas of Afro-Eurasia.

The Roman Empire gave way to a new religious unity, first represented by Christian dissenters and then co-opted by the emperor Constantine. In western Europe, the sense of unity unlimited by imperial frontiers gave rise to a universal, or "Catholic," church—the "true" Christian religion that believers felt all peoples should share. In the eastern Mediterranean, where the Roman Empire survived, Christianity and empire coalesced to reinforce the feeling that true religion, high culture, and empire went hand in hand. Christians here held that beliefs about God and Jesus found their most correct expression within the eastern Roman Empire and in its capital, Constantinople.

Similarly, in East Asia, the weakening of the Han dynasty enabled Buddhism to dominate Chinese culture. Without a unified state in China, Confucian officials languished in obscurity, while Buddhist priests and monks enjoyed patronage from regional rulers, local warriors, and commoners. In India, too, a political vacuum allowed the unfolding of a new culture: the Brahman elites exploited population movements beyond the reach of traditional rulers as they established ritual forms for daily life on every level of society, while melding together aspects of their own Vedic faith with those of Buddhism to create a new Hindu synthesis.

Not all regions felt the spread of universalizing religions, however. In most of sub-Saharan Africa belief systems were much more localized. The same pattern emerged in the Americas, where long-distance transportation was harder and language systems had not yielded texts to share with nonbelievers. But spiritual life was no less profound. Here, it was the strong sense of a shared worldview, a shared sense of purpose, and a shared sense of faith that enabled common cultures to develop. Indeed, the Bantus and Mayans became large-scale common cultures—but ruled at the local level.

Thus, the period 300–600 CE saw the emergence of three great cultural units in Afro-Eurasia, each defined in religious terms: Christianity in the Mediterranean and Southwest Asia, Brahmanism in South Asia, and Buddhism in East Asia. They illustrated the ways in which peoples were converging under larger religious tents, while also becoming more distinct. Universal religions, whether Christian or Buddhist, and universal codes of behavior, such as the Brahmanic Laws of Manu, gave people a new way to define themselves and their loyalties.

But the pattern would soon change. As we will see, empire would return to East Asia in the form of the mighty Tang dynasty. And the zone stretching from Morocco to central Asia would find itself united in a gigantic imperial system fashioned by followers of the Prophet Muhammad.

TRACING THE GLOBAL STORYLINES

AFTER YOU READ THIS CHAPTER

FOCUS ON: *Religions and Regions*

Western and Eastern Europe and Southwest Asia

- Christianity moves from a minority, persecuted faith to a state religion in the Roman Empire.
- Both Christianity and South Asian religious tenets buttress the powerful Sasanian state based in Iran.

Sub-Saharan Africa and Mesoamerica

- Large parts of Africa and the Americas develop common cultures based on religious beliefs shared by large, widely dispersed groups.

South Asia and East Asia

- Brahmanism, or Hinduism, becomes the dominant religion among the Vedic peoples of South Asia.
- Buddhism spreads out of South Asia along the Silk Road through central Asia and into East Asia.

Review and research on STUDYSPACE: wwnorton.com/StudySpace

CHRONOLOGY

The Mediterranean and Southwest Asia

- Sasanian Empire flourishes in Iran and Mesopotamia **3rd–6th century**
- Emperor Constantine legalizes Christianity in Roman Empire **313**

Central Asia

- Buddhism spreads through central Asia **3rd–6th century**
- Sogdian merchant communities dominate Silk Road trade through central Asia

South Asia

- Transformation of Brahmanism to Hinduism begins **1st or 2nd century**
- Gupta Empire **320–550**

East Asia

Sub-Saharan Africa

- Bantu migrations from western Africa to south, central, and east

Mesoamerica

- Maya culture dominates Yucatán Peninsula and surrounding area **3rd–9th century**

1 CE | **100 CE** | **200 CE** | **300 CE** | **400 CE**

KEY TERMS

Bantu migrations *p. 308*

bhakti *p. 301*

big men *p. 309*

Constantine *p. 285*

creed *p. 288*

Hinayana (Lesser Vehicle) Buddhism *p. 300*

Hinduism *p. 300*

Laws of Manu *p. 302*

Madhyamika (Middle Way) Buddhism *p. 304*

Mahayana (Greater Vehicle) Buddhism *p. 300*

martyr *p. 281*

Mayans *p. 312*

Northern Wei dynasty *p. 303*

Sasanian Empire *p. 293*

Sogdians *p. 296*

Teotihuacán *p. 311*

STUDY QUESTIONS

1. **Describe** the connections between the growing power of Christianity and the political reconfiguration of the Roman Empire. What was the appeal of Christianity in the Roman Empire?
2. **Analyze** the Sasanian Empire's role in facilitating the spread of universal religions and the development of common cultures in Afro-Eurasia. How did the empire's geographic location support this cross-cultural dissemination?
3. **Explain** the role of Sogdians and other central Asian peoples in the dispersion of universal religions. How did they influence East Asian societies in particular?
4. **Describe** how Brahmanism (Vedic religion) evolved into Hinduism during this era. What factors contributed to this development?
5. **Identify** key changes in Buddhist thought and practice in South Asia at this time. How did these refinements aid the spread of this religious outlook beyond its homeland?
6. **Explain** the role of written texts in universalizing religion. How did these texts reshape social attitudes toward spiritual behavior and identity?
7. **Analyze** the ways in which political decentralization affected the growing popularity of Buddhist and other religious ideas in East Asia. To what extent did they challenge Confucian ideas on social and political organization?
8. **Analyze** the impact of Bantu migrations on the social and cultural geography of sub-Saharan Africa. What set of beliefs helped unite societies in this region?
9. **Compare and contrast** Mayan society with that of Teotihuacán. To what extent did each represent a common religious and cultural outlook in Mesoamerica at different times?
10. **Analyze** the extent to which universal religions brought worlds together and pushed them apart. How did religion create new cultural boundaries and rivalries in Afro-Eurasia at this time?

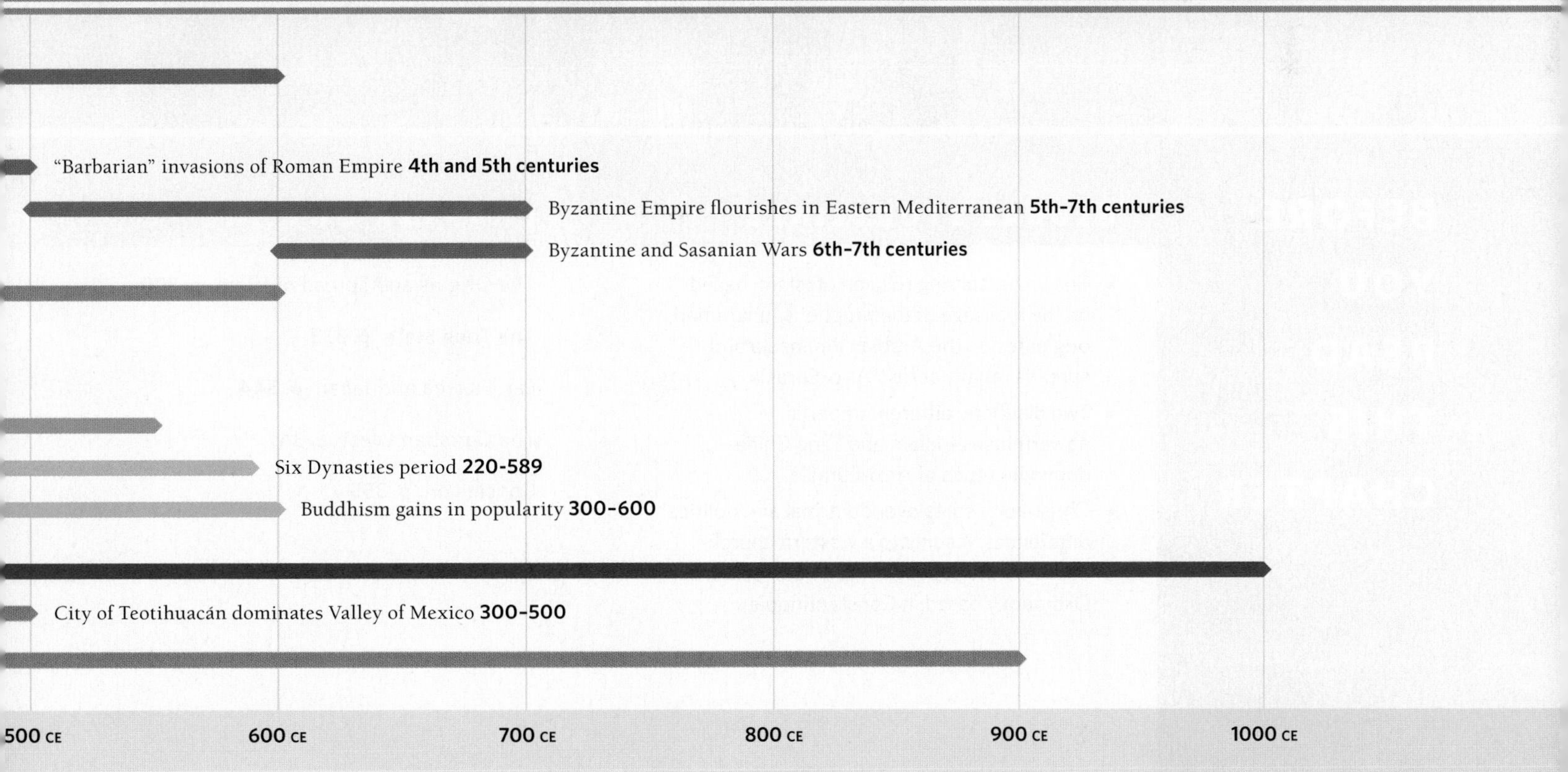

BEFORE YOU READ THIS CHAPTER

GLOBAL STORYLINES

- The universalizing religion of Islam, based on the message of the prophet Muhammad, originates on the Arabian Peninsula and spreads rapidly across Afro-Eurasia.
- Two distinctly different imperial powerhouses—Islam and Tang China—dominate much of Afro-Eurasia.
- Christianity splits over doctrinal and political differences, leading to a western church based on the papacy in Rome and Eastern Orthodoxy based in Constantinople.

CHAPTER OUTLINE

FOCUS QUESTIONS

- How did religion and empire reshape the cultural boundaries of Afro-Eurasia during this era?
- How and where did Islam, Buddhism, and Christianity spread?
- How did Islamic and East Asian empires organize their realms?
- What divisions emerged in the Islamic and Christian worlds?
- How did the growth and spread of empires and religions affect commercial and cultural exchange across Afro-Eurasia?

9

New Empires and Common Cultures, 600–1000 CE

In 754 CE, the Muslim caliph (ruler) al-Mansur decided to relocate his capital city. Islam was barely a century old, yet flourishing under its second dynasty, the Abbasids. Al-Mansur wanted to relocate power away from Damascus (the capital of Islam's first dynasty) to the Abbasids' home region on the Iranian plateau to signal its new dawn. After traveling the length of the Tigris and Euphrates rivers in search of a perfect site, the caliph decided to build his capital near an unimposing village called Baghdad.

He had good reasons for this selection. The site lay between Mesopotamia's two great rivers at the juncture of the canals that linked them. It was also a powerful symbolic location: close to the ancient capital of the Sasanian Empire, Ctesiphon, where the Arch of Khusro was still standing. It was also the site of earlier Sumerian and Babylonian power. By building at Baghdad, al-Mansur could reaffirm Mesopotamia's centrality in the world and exalt the universalizing ambitions of Islam. Within five years of laying the first brick, towering walls surrounded what soon became known as the "round city," so named because of the way in which the different segments radiated out from the administrative and religious center.

Al-Mansur's choice had enduring effects. As the new capital of Islam, Baghdad also became a vital crossroads for commerce. Overnight, the city exploded into a bustling world entrepôt. Chinese goods arrived by land and sea; commodities from Inner Eurasia flowed in over the Silk Road; and cargo-laden camel caravans wound across Baghdad's western desert, linking the capital with Syria, Egypt, North Africa, and southern Spain. In effect, the unity that the Abbasids imposed from Baghdad intensified the movement of peoples, ideas, innovations, and commodities.

Baghdad's eminence and prosperity reflected its role as the center of the Islamic world. Yet, while Islam was gaining ground in central Afro-Eurasia, Chinese might was surging in East Asia—powerfully under the Tang—and Christianity was striving to extend its domains and add to its converts. Unquestionably, however, the two imperial powerhouses of this period were Islam and Tang China, and they are the focus of this chapter.

Islam and Tang China were manifestly different worlds. The Islamic state had a universalizing religious mission: to bring humankind under the authority of the religion espoused by the Prophet Muhammad. In contrast, the Tang had no such grandiose religious aspirations, and while the ruling elite supported religious pluralism within China, they did not use Buddhism to expand their control into areas outside China. Instead, the Tang rulers expected that their neighbors would emulate Chinese institutions and pay tribute as symbols of respect to the greatness of the Tang Empire. As Islam's warriors and scholars crossed into Europe and as Chinese influences took deeper root in East Asia, religion and empire once again intertwined to serve as the social foundation across much of Afro-Eurasia.

Given the surge of religious energy across Afro-Eurasia, it was perhaps only a matter of time before a prophetic figure would arise among the Arabs. Christianity and Buddhism were laying claim to universal truths, spreading their faiths across wide geographic areas outside their places of origin, and competing groups now had to speak the language of universal religion. Only the Tang dynasty resisted the universalizing faiths, as Confucianism and Daoism withstood the upsurge of Chinese Buddhism—revealing that China would follow a different path by maintaining past traditions. In the seventh century, Arab peoples would become the makers of their own universal faith, which would join and jostle with predecessors in Afro-Eurasia.

THE ORIGINS AND SPREAD OF ISLAM

Islam began inside Arabia. Despite its remoteness and sparse population, by the sixth century CE Arabia was brushing up against exciting outside currents: long-distance trade, religious debate, and imperial politics. Byzantine and Sasanian imperial pressures already had intruded deeply into Arabia (see Chapter 8); commodities from Egypt, Syria, and Iraq circulated in local markets; and learned men debated the doctrines of Christianity and Judaism. The Hijaz—the western region bordering the Red Sea—knew the outside world through trading routes reaching up the coast to the Mediterranean. While one of the world's major universalizing faiths would be born in a remote region

Mecca. *At the great mosque at Mecca, which many consider the most sacred site in Islam, hundreds of thousands of worshippers gather for Friday prayers. Many are performing their religious duty to go on a pilgrimage to the holy places in the Arabian Peninsula.*

of Southwest Asia, Islam would quickly take advantage of the dynamic trade routes stretching across Southwest Asia and North Africa to spread its faith and political empire.

Mecca, in the Hijaz, was not an imposing place. A pre-Islamic poet wrote that its "winter and summer are equally intolerable. No waters flow . . . [and there is] not a blade of grass on which to rest the eye; no, nor hunting. [Here there are] only merchants, the most despicable of professions" (Peters, p. 23). Hardly more than a village of simple mud huts, Mecca's inhabitants sustained themselves less as traders than as caretakers of a revered sanctuary called the kaaba. They regarded this collection of unmortared rocks piled on top of one another as the dwelling place of deities, whom the polytheistic Meccans worshipped. Here a great prophet was born.

A Vision, a Text

In the early life of **Muhammad**, little suggested that momentous events would soon occur. Born in Mecca around 570 CE into a well-respected tribal family, he enjoyed only moderate success as a trader. Then came a revelation, which would convert this broker of commodities into a proselytizer of a new faith. In 610 CE, while Muhammad was on a month-long spiritual retreat in a cave near Mecca, he believed that God came to him in a vision and commanded him to recite these words:

> Recite in the Name of the Lord who createth,
> Createth man from a clot
> Recite: And thy Lord is the most Bounteous who teacheth by the pen
> Teacheth man that which he knew not.

Further revelations followed. The early ones were like the first: short, powerful, emphasizing a single, all-powerful God (Allah), and full of instructions for Muhammad's fellow Meccans to carry this message to nonbelievers. The words were eminently memorable, an important feature in an oral culture where poetry recitation was the highest art form. Muhammad's early preaching had a clear message. He urged his small band of followers to act righteously, to set aside false deities, to submit themselves to the one and only true God, and to care for the less fortunate—for the Day of Judgment was imminent. Muhammad's most insistent message was the oneness of God, a belief that has remained central to the Islamic faith ever since.

These teachings, compiled into an authoritative version after the Prophet's death, constituted the foundational text of Islam: the **Quran**. Its 114 chapters, known as suras, occur in descending order of length; the longest has three hundred verses and the shortest, a mere three. Accepted as the very word of God, they flowed without flaw through God's perfect instrument, the Prophet Muhammad. (See Primary Source: The Quran: Two Suras in Praise of God.) Like the Jewish Torah, the Christian Bible, and other foundational texts, this one proclaimed the tenets of a new faith to unite a people and to expand its spiritual frontiers. Its message already had universalist elements, though how far it was to be extended, whether just to the tribesmen living in the Arabian Peninsula or well beyond, was not at all clear at first.

Muhammad believed that he was a prophet in the tradition of Moses, other Hebrew prophets, and Jesus, and that he communicated with the same God that they did. As we have seen, Christian and Jewish communities existed in the Arabian Peninsula at this time. The city of Yathrib (later called Medina) held a substantial Jewish community. Just how deeply Muhammad understood the tenets of Judaism and Christianity is difficult to determine, but his professed indebtedness to their tradition is a part of Islamic belief.

The Move to Medina

Muslims date the beginning of the Muslim era from the year 622 CE. At this time Muhammad and a small group of followers, opposed by Mecca's leaders because of their radical religious tenets and their challenge to the ruling elite's authority, escaped to Medina. Known as the *hijra* ("breaking off of relations" or "departure"), the perilous 200-mile journey yielded a new form of communal unity: the *umma* ("band of the faithful").

The city of Medina had been facing tribal and religious tensions, and by inviting Muhammad and his followers to take up residence there, its elders hoped that his leadership and charisma would bring peace and unity to their city. Early in his stay Muhammad promulgated a document, the Constitution of Medina, requiring the community's people to refer all disputes to God and him. Medina thus became the birthplace of a new faith called **Islam** ("submission"—in this case, to the will of God) and a new community called Muslims ("those who submit"). Now the residents were expected to replace traditional family, clan, and tribal affiliations with loyalty to Muhammad as the one and true Prophet of God. From Medina the faithful broadcast their faith and their mission, at first mainly by military means, to the recalcitrants of Mecca and then to all of Arabia, and then later to the entire world. In this way, Islam joined Christianity in seeking to bring the whole known world under its authority.

Conquests

In 632 CE, in his early sixties, the Prophet passed away. Islam might have withered without its leader, but the movement remained

PRIMARY SOURCE

The Quran: Two Suras in Praise of God

These two suras from the Quran are relatively short, but they convey some of the essence of Muhammad's message. The Quran opens with a sura known as the fatiha ("of the opening"), which in its powerfully prayerlike quality lends itself to frequent recitation. Sura 87, "The Most High," provides a deeper insight into the nature of humanity's relationship with God.

THE FATIHA

In the Name of God the Compassionate the merciful
Praise be to God, Lord of the Universe,
The Compassionate, the Merciful,
Sovereign of the Day of Judgement!
You alone we worship, and to You alone we turn for help.
Guide us to the straight path,
The path of those whom You have favoured,
Not of those who have incurred Your wrath,
Nor of those who have gone astray.
(1.1-1.7)

THE MOST HIGH

In the Name of God, the Compassionate, the merciful
Praise the name of your Lord, the Most High, who has created all things and proportioned them; who has ordained their destinies and guided them; who brings forth the green pasture, then turns it to withered grass.
We shall make you recite our revelations, so that you shall forget none of them except as God pleases. He has knowledge of all that is manifest, and all that is hidden.
We shall guide you to the smoothest path. Therefore give warning, if warning will avail. He that fears God will heed it, but the wicked sinner will flout it. He shall burn in the gigantic Fire, where he shall neither die nor live. Happy shall be the man who purifies himself, who remembers the name of his Lord and prays.
Yet you prefer this life, although the life to come is better and more lasting.
All this is written in earlier scriptures; the scriptures of Abraham and Moses.
(87.1–87.19)

QUESTIONS FOR ANALYSIS

- What themes do these passages reveal about Islam's view of the relationship between God and mortals?
- Do you find any similarities to the tenets of Judaism and Christianity as you have encountered them in this volume?

vibrant thanks to the energy of the early followers—especially Muhammad's first four successors, the "rightly guided caliphs." The Arabic word *khalīfa* means "successor," and in this context it referred to Muhammad's successors as political rulers over Muslim peoples and the expanding state. Their breakthrough was to institutionalize the new faith. They set the new religion on the pathway to imperial greatness and linked religious uprightness with territorial expansion, empire building, and an appeal to all peoples.

Now Islam's expansive spiritual force galvanized its political authority. But what kind of polity would this be? Driven by religious fervor and a desire to acquire the wealth of conquered territories, Muslim soldiers embarked on military conquests and sought to found a far-reaching territorial empire. This expansion of the Islamic state was one aspect of the struggle that they called ***jihad***. From the outset Muslim religious and political leaders divided the world into two units: the *dar al-Islam* (or the world of Islam) and the *dar al-harb* (the world of warfare), seeking nothing less than world dominion. Within fifteen years Muslim soldiers had grasped Syria, Egypt, and Iraq—centerpieces of the former Byzantine and Sasanian empires that now became pillars undergirding an even larger Islamic empire. Mastery of desert warfare and inspired military leadership yielded these astonishing exploits, as did the exhaustion of the Byzantine and Sasanian empires after generations of warfare.

The Byzantines saved the core of their empire by pulling back to the highlands of Anatolia, where they had readily defensible frontiers. In contrast, the Sasanians gambled all on a final effort: they hurled their remaining military resources against the Muslim armies, only to be crushed. Having lost Iraq and unable to defend the Iranian plateau, the Sasanian Empire passed out of existence. The result: Islam acquired political foundations within a generation of its birth.

The Battle of Badr. *This image depicts the battle of Badr, which took place in 624 CE and marked the beginning of Muhammad's reconquest of Mecca from his new base in the city of Medina.*

An Empire of Arabs

Creating an empire and stabilizing it were two different things. We have seen some come and go, like Alexander's. Others had more stamina. How would Islam fare? After the assassination of the last of the "rightly guided caliphs," Ali, a political vacuum opened. At this point a branch of one of the Meccan clans, the Umayyads, laid claim to Ali's legacy. Having been governors of the province of Syria under Ali, this first dynasty moved the core of Islam out of Arabia to the Syrian city of Damascus. They also introduced a hereditary monarchy to resolve leadership disputes. These adaptable, cosmopolitan traders ruled from Damascus until the Abbasids overthrew them in 750 CE.

By then, the core practices and beliefs of every Muslim had crystallized as the five "pillars" of Islam, which found clear expression in the Quran. Building on long-standing Arabian customs and certain familiar Jewish practices, these pillars undergirded Islamic practice early in Muhammad's career as a prophet and gave the imperial system a doctrinal and legal structure and a broad appeal to diverse populations.

The five pillars of Islam established clear-cut demands on believers. Converts were expected to: (1) *adhere* to and repeat the phrase that there is no God but God and that Muhammad was His Prophet; (2) *pray* five times daily facing Mecca; (3) *fast* from sunup until sundown during the month of Ramadan; (4) *make* a pilgrimage to Mecca at least once in a lifetime if their personal resources permitted; (5) *pay* alms in the form of taxation that would alleviate the hardships of the poor.

There was, however, a political limit to Islam's welcoming embrace. Although tolerant of conquered populations, Umayyad dynasts did not permit non-Arabic-speaking converts to hold high political offices. Not until the overthrow of Umayyad rule did the "Arabs only" empire come to an end and non-Arab populations become incorporated into the Islamic core. This changed the nature of the emerging empire. For as the political center of Islam moved out of Arabia to Syria (at Damascus), and then with the Abbasids to Mesopotamia, ethnic and geographical diversity replaced what had been ethnic purity. Thus even as the universalizing religion strove to create a common spiritual world, it became more diverse within its political dimensions.

The Abbasid Revolution

As the Umayyad dynasts spread Islam beyond Arabia, some peoples resented the rulers' high-handed ways. For example, the central Asian province of Khurasan was home to many converts who chafed at their subordination to Arab peoples. Here, religious reformers and political dissidents stressed doctrines of religious purity and depicted the Umayyads as irreligious and politically repressive.

A coalition emerged under the Abbasi family, which claimed descent from the Prophet. Soon disgruntled provincial authorities and their military allies, as well as non-Arab converts, joined the movement. These individuals had embraced Islam and learned Arabic, only to discover that they were still second-class citizens. After amassing a sizable military force, the Abbasid coalition trounced the Umayyad ruler in 750 CE. Thereafter the center of the caliphate shifted to Iraq (at Baghdad; recall the opening anecdote about al-Mansur), signifying the eastward sprawl of the faith and its empire. It also represented a success for non-Arab groups within Islam without eliminating Arab influence at the dynasty's center—the capital, Baghdad, in Arabic-speaking Iraq.

Ultimately, conversion to Islam rested on the zeal of evangelizers and the faith's appeal to converts. Some turned to it for practical reasons, seeking reduced taxes or enhanced power.

Others, particularly those living in ethnically and religiously diverse regions, welcomed the message of a single all-powerful God and a single community united by a clear code of laws; they saw it as offering superior answers to thorny secular and spiritual questions. Not only did the Abbasids open Islam to Persian peoples, but they also embraced Greek and Hellenistic learning, Indian science, and Chinese innovations. In this fashion, Islam, drawing its original impetus from the teachings and actions of a prophetic figure, followed the trajectory of Christianity and Buddhism and became a faith with a universalist message and appeal. It owed much of its success to its ability to merge the contributions of vastly different geographic and intellectual territories into a rich yet unified culture (see Map 9.1).

THE CALIPHATE An early challenge for the Abbasid rulers was to determine how traditional, or "Arab," they could be and still rule so vast an empire. They chose to keep the bedrock political institution of the early Islamic state—the **caliphate**. Signifying both the political and spiritual head of the Islamic community, this institution had arisen as the successor to Muhammad's shining leadership. Although the caliphs exercised political and spiritual authority over the Muslim community, they did not inherit his prophetic powers. Nor were they authorities in religious doctrine. That power was reserved for religious scholars, called ***ulama***; some of these men were schooled in Islamic law, others were experts in Quranic interpretation, and still others were religious thinkers.

Imperial rule reflected borrowed practices from successful predecessors. The caliphates' leadership style was a mixture of Persian absolute authority and the royal seclusion of the Byzantine emperors who lived in palaces far removed from their subjects. Imperial Islam mingled absolute authority with decentralized power through its envoys in the provinces. This involved a delicate and ultimately unsustainable balancing act. As the empire expanded it became increasingly decentralized, enabling wily regional governors and competing caliphates in Spain and Egypt to grab power. The political result was an Islamic world shot through with multiple centers of power, nominally led by a weakened Abbasid

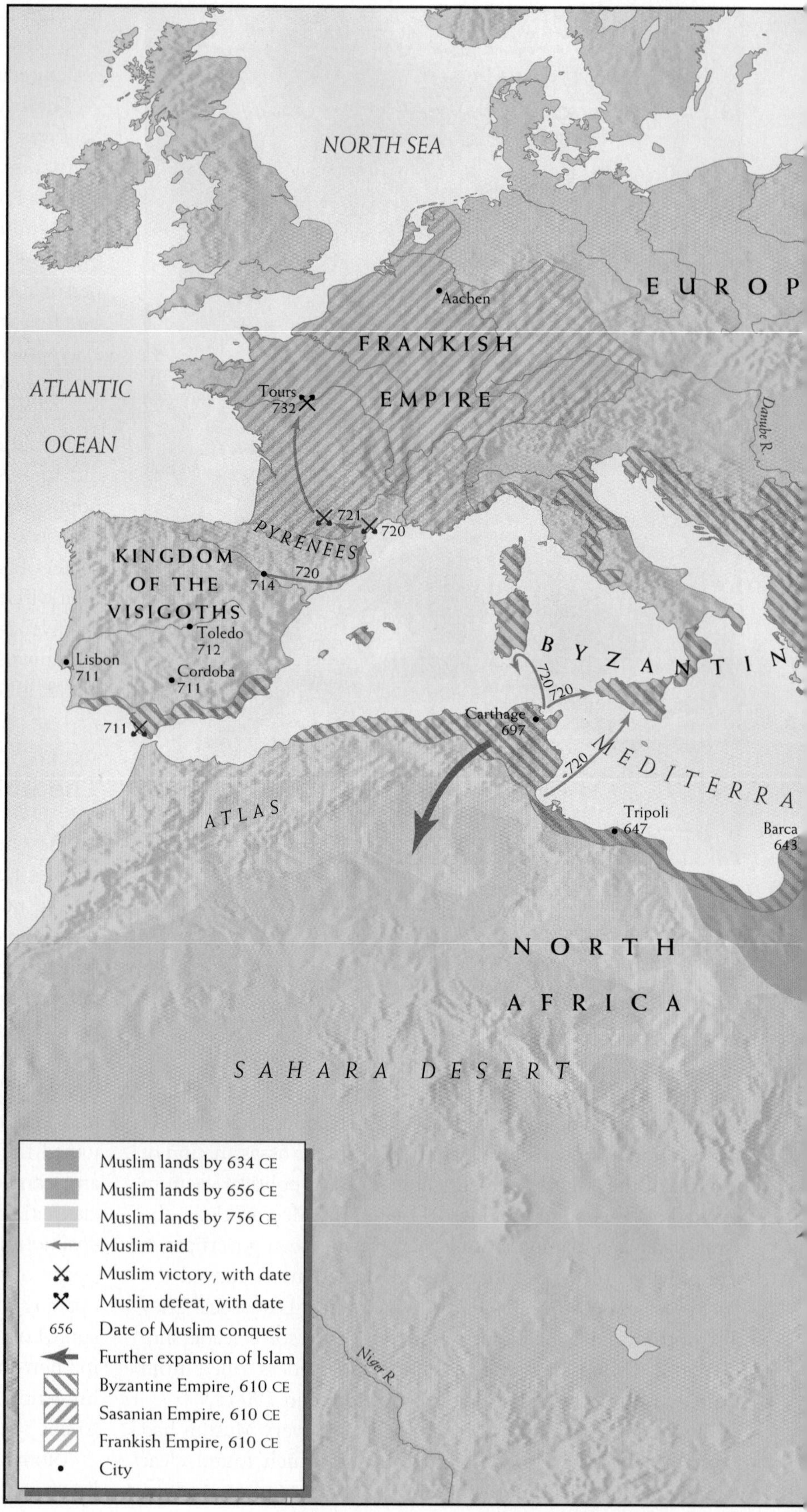

MAP 9.1 | The Spread of Islam during the First Millennium

Islam emerged in the Arabian Peninsula in the seventh century. Within 150 years, leaders of this religious community had conquered a vast amount of territory.

- What was the area of Muslim lands by 634 CE? By 756 CE?
- What were the limits to Muslim expansion during the first 150 years according to the map?
- How did Islam ultimately expand beyond these areas of conquest?

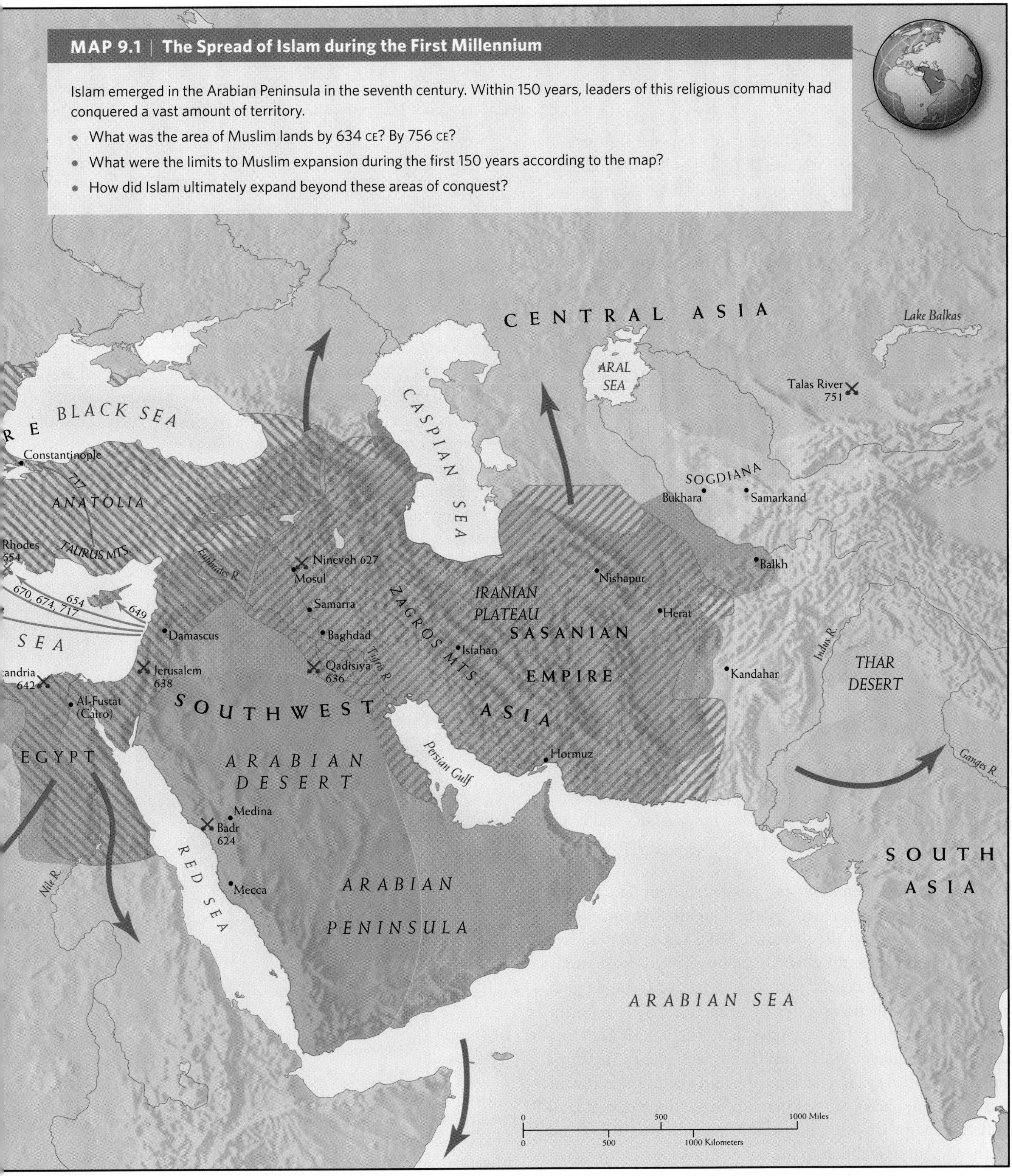

caliphate. Even as Islam's political center diffused, though, its spiritual center remained fixed in Mecca, where many of the faithful gathered to circle the kaaba and to reaffirm their devotion to Islam as part of their pilgrimage obligation.

THE ARMY The Abbasids, like all rulers, relied on force to integrate their empire. For imperial Islam (as for the Romans), exercising military power required marshalling warriors and soldiers from across Afro-Eurasia.

How "Arab" should the Muslim armies be? In the early stages, leaders had conscripted military forces from local Arab populations, creating citizen armies. But as Arab populations settled down in garrison cities, the Abbasid rulers turned to professional soldiers from the empire's peripheries. Now they recruited from Turkish-speaking communities in central Asia, and from the non-Arab, Berber-speaking peoples of North Africa and West Africans. Their reliance on foreign—that is, non-Arab—military personnel represented a major shift in the Islamic world. Not only did the change infuse the empire with dynamic new populations, but soon these groups gained political authority (just as the "barbarians" had done in the last centuries of the Roman Empire; see Chapters 6 and 8). Having begun as an Arab state and then incorporated strong Persian influence, the Islamic empire now embraced Turkish elements from the pastoral belts of central Asia.

ISLAMIC LAW (THE *SHARIA*) AND THEOLOGY In the Abbasid period, not just the caliphate but also Islamic law took shape. The ***sharia*** stands as the crucial foundation of Islam. It covers all aspects of practical and spiritual life, providing legal principles for marriage contracts, trade regulations, and religious prescriptions such as prayer, pilgrimage rites, and ritual fasting. It reflects the work of generations of religious scholars, rather than soldiers, courtiers, and bureaucrats. And it has remained vital throughout the Muslim world, independent of empires, to the present day.

Early Muslim communities prepared the ground for the *sharia,* endeavoring (guided by the Quran) to handle legal matters in ways that they thought Muhammad would have wanted. However, because the Quran mainly addressed family concerns, religious beliefs, and social relations (such as marriage, divorce, inheritance, dietary restrictions, and treatment of women) but not other legal questions, local judges exercised their own judgment where the Quran was silent. The most influential early legal scholar was an eighth-century Palestinian-born Arab, al-Shafi'i, who wanted to make the empire's laws entirely Islamic. He insisted that Muhammad's laws as laid out in the Quran, in addition to his sayings and actions as written in later reports (*hadith*), provided all the legal guidance that Islamic judges needed.

The triumph of scholars such as Shafi'i was deeply significant: it placed the *ulama,* the Muslim scholars, at the heart of Islam. *Ulama,* not princes and kings, became the lawmakers, insisting that the caliphs could not define religious law. Only the scholarly class could interpret the Quran and determine which *hadith* were authentic. The *ulama*'s ascendance opened a sharp division within Islam: between the secular realm, where caliphs and their representatives exercised power, and the religious sphere, where religious officials and scholars (judges, experts on Islamic jurisprudence, teachers, and holy men) exercised their authority.

GENDER IN EARLY ISLAM Pre-Islamic Arabia was one of the last regions in Southwest Asia where patriarchy had not triumphed. Instead, men still married into women's families and moved to those families' locations, as was common in tribal communities. Some women engaged in a variety of occupations and even, if they became wealthy, married more than one husband. But contact with the rest of Southwest Asia, where men's power over women prevailed, was already altering women's status in the Arabian Peninsula before the birth of Muhammad.

Muhammad's relations with women reflected these changes. As a young man, he married a woman fifteen years his senior—Khadija, an independent trader—and took no other wives before

Khadija. *The importance of women to the founding of Islam is apparent in this Ottoman miniature, which depicts Khadija* (left) *bearing witness to Gabriel* (center) *as he conveys God's will to Muhammad* (right). *Both wife and prophet are veiled in accordance with hadiths promoting female modesty and prohibiting representations of Muhammad, respectively.*

she died. It was Khadija to whom he went in fear following his first revelations. She wrapped him in a blanket and assured him of his sanity. She was also his first convert. Later in life, however, he took younger wives, some of whom were widows of his companions, and insisted on their veiling. He married his favorite wife, Aisha, when she was only nine or ten years old. An important figure in early Islam, she was the daughter of Abu Bakr, who became the first caliph after Muhammad's death. She became a major source for collecting Muhammad's sayings.

Hence, by the time Islam reached Southwest Asia and North Africa, where strict gender rules and women's subordinate status were entrenched, the new faith was adopting a patriarchal outlook. Muslim men could divorce freely; women could not. A man could take four wives and numerous concubines; a woman could have only one husband. Well-to-do women, always veiled, lived secluded from male society. Still, the Quran did offer women some protections. Men had to treat each wife with respect if they took more than one. Women could inherit property (although only half of what a man inherited). Infanticide was taboo. Marriage dowries went directly to the bride rather than to her guardian, indicating women's independent legal standing; and while a woman's adultery drew harsh punishment, its proof required eyewitness testimony. The result was a legal system that reinforced men's dominance over women but empowered magistrates to oversee the definition of male honor and proper behavior.

The Blossoming of Abbasid Culture

The arts flourished during the Abbasid period, a blossoming that left its imprint throughout society. Within a century, Arabic had superseded Greek as the Muslim world's preferred language for poetry, literature, medicine, science, and philosophy. Like Greek, it spread beyond native speakers to become the language of the educated classes.

Arabic scholarship now made significant contributions, including the preservation and extension of Greek and Roman thought and the transmission of Greek and Latin treatises to Europe. Scholars at Baghdad translated the principal works of Aristotle; essays by Plato's followers; works by Hippocrates, Ptolemy, and Archimedes; and the medical treatises of Galen. To house such manuscripts, patrons of the arts and sciences—including the caliphs—opened magnificent libraries.

The intense borrowing, translating, storing, and diffusing of written works brought worlds together. The Muslim world absorbed scientific breakthroughs from China and other areas, incorporated the use of paper from China, adopted siege warfare from China and Byzantium, and applied knowledge of plants from the ancient Greeks. From Indian sources, scholars borrowed a numbering system based on the concept of zero and units of ten—what we today call Arabic numerals. Arab mathematicians were pioneers in arithmetic, geometry, and algebra, and they expanded the frontiers of plane and spherical trigonometry.

Islam in a Wider World

As Islam spread and became decentralized, it generated dazzling and often competitive dynasties in Spain, North Africa, and points farther east. Each dynastic state revealed the Muslim talent for achieving high levels of artistry far from its heartland. As more peoples came under the roof provided by the Quran, they invigorated a broad world of Islamic learning and science. But growing diversity led to a problem: Islam's political structures could not hold its widely dispersed believers under a single regime. Although its polities shared many legal elements (especially those controlled by Islamic texts and its enforcers), in terms of secular power Islam was deeply divided—and remains so to this day (see Map 9.2).

DAZZLING CITIES IN SPAIN One extraordinary Muslim state arose in Spain under Abd al-Rahman III, al-Nasir (the Victorious; r. 912–961 CE), the successor ruler of a Muslim kingdom founded there over a century earlier. Abd al-Rahman brought peace and stability to a violent frontier region where civil conflict had disrupted commerce and intellectual exchange. His evenhanded governance promoted amicable relations among Muslims, Christians, and Jews, and his diplomatic relations with Christian potentates as far away as France, Germany, and Scandinavia generated prosperity across western Europe and North Africa. He expanded and beautified the capital city of Cordoba, and his successor made the Great Mosque of Cordoba one of Spain's most stunning sites.

The Great Mosque of Cordoba, known in Spanish as la Mezquita, is the oldest standing Muslim building on the Iberian Peninsula. It is a stirring tribute to the architectural brilliance and religious zeal of Iberia's Muslims. Conceived of in 785 CE by the Umayyad ruler Abd al-Rahman I, it was finished within a year of the laying of the foundations. It arose on a site with a rich cultural and political history. Here had existed a Roman temple and later a Gothic church, which after the Arab Muslim conquest housed both Muslim and Christian believers (the latter permitted by the Muslim conquerors to worship under the same roof). Convinced that this building could no longer accommodate the area's increasing Muslim population, Abd al-Rahman I sketched out the plan of the mosque. He commanded that it be built in the form of a perfect square. Its most striking features were alternating red and white arches, made of jasper, onyx, marble, and granite and fashioned from materials from the Roman temple and other buildings in the vicinity. These huge

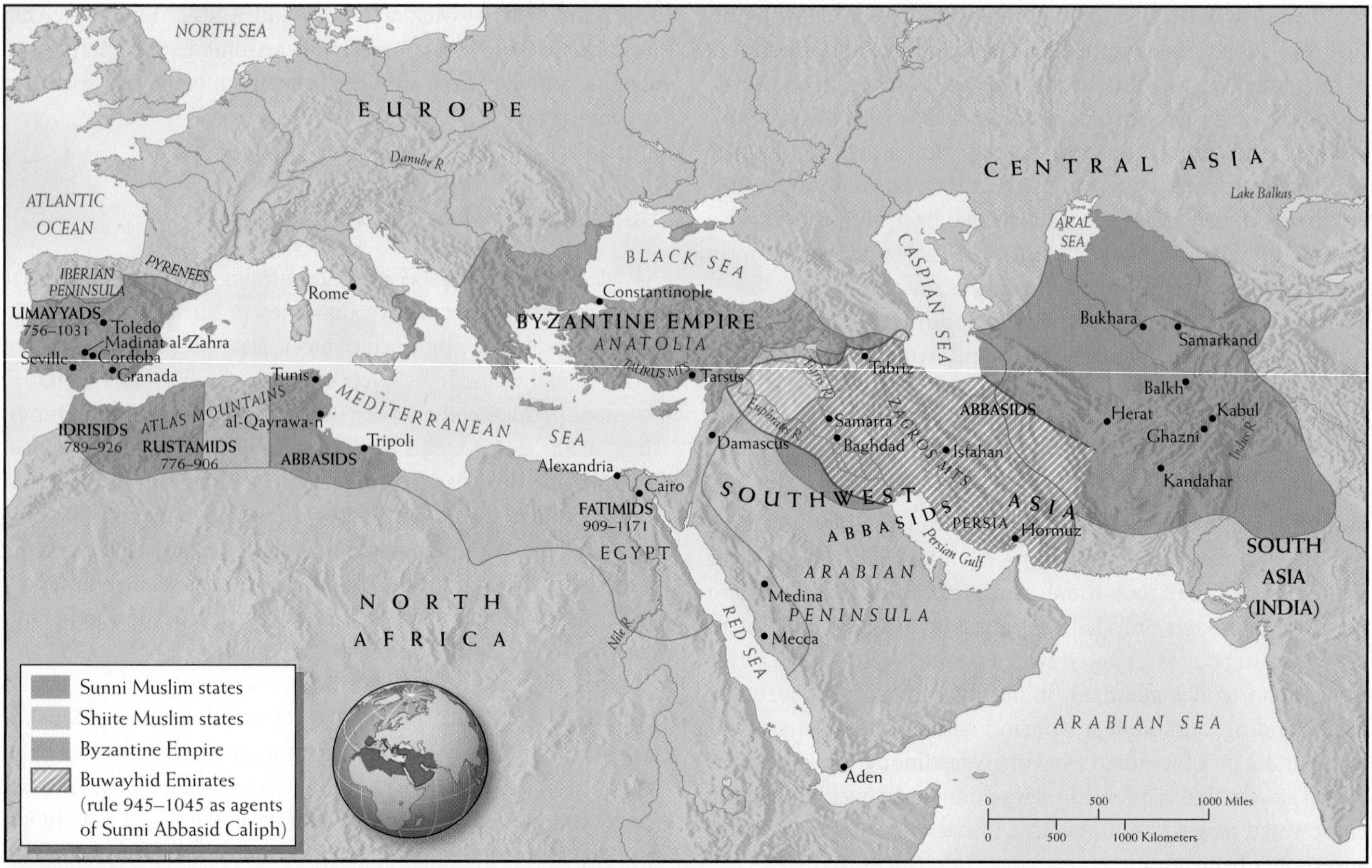

MAP 9.2 | Political Fragmentation in the Islamic World, 750–1000 CE

By 1000, the Islamic world was politically fractured and decentralized. The Abbasid caliphs still reigned in Baghdad, but they wielded very limited political authority. Looking at the map, first point to Baghdad and then point out all the areas under Abbasid control.

- What are the regions where major Islamic powers emerged?
- What areas were Sunni versus Shiite?
- Why were the Abbasids unable to sustain political unity in the Islamic world?

double arches hoisted the ceiling to forty feet and filled the interior with light and cooling breezes. Around the doors and across the walls Arabic calligraphy proclaimed Muhammad's message and asserted the superiority of Arabic as God's chosen language.

At this time, competition among rival rulers spurred artistic creativity. Soon the Islamic world resembled a series of dazzling lanterns, each vying to outdo the others in brilliance. When Abd al-Rahman III built an extravagant city, Madinat al-Zahra, next to Cordoba, his goal was to overshadow the splendor of Islam's most fabled cities, including Baghdad and al-Qayrawān (in northeastern Tunisia). He surrounded the city's administrative offices and mosque with verdant gardens of lush tropical and semitropical plants, tranquil pools, fountains that spouted cooling waters, and sturdy aqueducts that carried potable water to the city's inhabitants. Madinat al-Zahra was meant to be paradise on earth.

A CENTRAL ASIAN GALAXY OF TALENT The other end of the Islamic empire, 8,000 miles east of Spain, enjoyed an equally spectacular cultural flowering. In a territory where Greek culture had once sparkled and where Sogdians had become leading intellectuals, Islam was now the dominant faith and the source of intellectual ferment.

The Abbasid rulers in Baghdad delighted in surrounding themselves with learned men from this region. The Barmaki family, who for several generations held high administrative offices under the Abbasids, came from the central Asian city of Balkh. They had been Buddhists living under the serene gaze of the great carved Buddhas of Bamiyan (see Chapter 8). This family prospered under Islam and enjoyed remarkable influence in Baghdad. Loyal servants of the caliph, they made sure that all wealth and talent from the crossroads of Asia found their way to Baghdad, as they themselves had done.

The Great Mosque of Cordoba. *The great mosque of Cordoba was built in the eighth century by the Umayyad ruler Abd al-Rahman I and added to by other Muslim rulers, including al-Hakim II (who succeeded Abd al-Rahman III), considered by many historians to have been the most powerful and effective of the Spanish Umayyad caliphs.*

In turn, the Barmakis were devoted patrons of the arts. They promoted and collected Arabic translations of Persian, Greek, and Sanskrit manuscripts, and they encouraged central Asian scholars to enhance their learning by moving to Baghdad. One of their protégés, the Islamic cleric al-Bukhari (d. 870 CE), was Islam's most dedicated collector of *hadith,* which provided vital knowledge about the Prophet's life.

Others made notable contributions to science and mathematics. Al-Khwarizmi (c. 780–850 CE) modified Indian digits into Arabic numerals and wrote the first book on algebra. The renowned Abbasid philosopher al-Farabi (d. 950 CE), from a Turkish military family, also made his way to Baghdad, where he studied eastern Christian teachings. Although he considered himself a Muslim, he thought good societies would succeed only if their rulers implemented political tenets espoused in Plato's *Republic.* He championed a virtuous "first chief" to rule over an Islamic commonwealth in the same way that Plato had favored a philosopher-king.

In the eleventh century the Abbasid caliphate began to decline, weakening under overextension and the influx of outsider groups (the same problems the Roman Empire had faced). Scholars no longer trekked to the court at Baghdad. Yet the region's intellectual vitality remained strong, for young men of learning found patrons among local rulers. Consider Ibn Sina, known in the west as Avicenna (980–1037 CE). He grew to adulthood in Bukhara, practiced medicine in the courts of various Islamic rulers, and spent his later life in central Persia. Schooled in the Quran, Arabic secular literature, philosophy, geometry, and Indian and Euclidean mathematics, Ibn Sina was a master of many disciplines. His *Canon of Medicine* stood as the standard medical text in both Southwest Asia and Europe for centuries.

ISLAM IN SUB-SAHARAN AFRICA Islam also crossed the Sahara Desert and penetrated well into Africa, carried by traders and scholars (see Map 9.3); there merchants exchanged weapons and textiles for gold, salt, and slaves. Trade did more than join West Africa to North Africa. It also generated prodigious wealth, which allowed centralized political kingdoms to develop. The most celebrated was Ghana, which lay at the terminus of North Africa's major trading routes.

Of Ghana, scholars know little. The first to mention it was a Baghdadi scholar, who in the eighth century described it as "the land of gold." A century later, an Arab geographer wrote of Ghana, "the king of which is very powerful. In his country there are gold mines. Under his authority are other kingdoms . . . and gold is found in all of these regions" (Fage, p. 15). Although Muslim traders frequented the state, its rulers were not Muslims. Still, Ghana's pomp and power impressed visitors; in 1067–1068 CE, a geographer from the Muslim province of Andalusia in Spain, wrote of a resplendent king who heard "grievances against officials in a domed pavilion around which stand ten horses covered with gold-embroidered materials. Behind the king stand ten pages holding shields and swords decorated with gold and on his right are the sons of the (vassal) kings of his country wearing splendid garments and their hair plaited with gold" (Levtzion and Spaulding, p. 16). (See also Primary Source: Ghana as Seen by a Muslim Observer in the Eleventh Century.)

Ibn Sina. *Ibn Sina was a versatile scholar, most famous for his* Canon of Medicine.

Seafaring Muslim traders carried Islam into East Africa via the Indian Ocean. There is evidence of a small eighth-century Islamic trading community at Lamu, along the northern coast of present-day Kenya; and by the mid-ninth century other coastal trading communities had sprung up. They all exported ivory and, possibly, slaves. On the island of Pate, off the coast of Kenya, the inhabitants of Shanga constructed the region's first mosque. This simple structure was replaced 200 years later by a mosque capable of holding all adult members of the community when they gathered for their Friday prayers. By the tenth century, the East African coast featured a mixed African-Arab culture. The region's evolving Bantu language absorbed Arabic words and before long gained a new name, Swahili (derived from the Arabic plural of the word meaning "coast").

Opposition within Islam, Shiism, and the Rise of the Fatimids

Islam's whirlwind rise generated internal tensions from the start. It is hardly surprising that a religion that extolled territorial conquests and created a large empire in its first decades would also spawn dissident religious movements that challenged the existing imperial structures. Muslims shared a reverence for a basic text and a single God, but often had little else in common. Religious and political divisions only grew deeper as Islam spread into new corners of Afro-Eurasia. Once the charismatic prophet died, believers disagreed over who should take his place and how to preserve authority. Strains associated with selecting the first four caliphs after Muhammad's death left a legacy of protest; to this day, they represent the greatest challenge facing Islam's efforts to create a unified culture.

SUNNIS AND SHIITES The most powerful opposition movement arose in North Africa, lower Iraq, and the Iranian plateau. The questions that fueled disagreements were who should succeed the Prophet, how the succession should take place, and who should lead Islam's expansion into the wider world. The vast majority of Muslims today are **Sunnis** (from the Arabic word meaning "tradition"). They accept that the political succession to the Prophet through the four rightly guided caliphs and then to the Umayyad and Abbasid dynasties was the correct one. Dissidents, like the Shiites, contest this version. Over time the Sunnis and Shiites diverged even more than these political disputes would have indicated. Both groups had their own versions of the *sharia*, their own collections of *hadith*, and their own theological tenets.

Shiites ("members of the party of Ali"), among the earliest dissidents, felt that the proper successors should have been Ali, who had married the Prophet's daughter Fatima, and his descendants. Ali was one of the early converts to Islam and one of the band of Meccans who had migrated with the Prophet to Medina. The fourth of the rightly guided caliphs, he ruled over the Muslim community from 656 to 661 CE, dying at the hands of an assassin who struck him down as he was praying in a mosque in Kufa, Iraq. Shiites believe that Ali's descendants, whom they call *imams,* have religious and prophetic power as well as political authority—and thus should enjoy spiritual primacy. Shiism appealed to groups whom the Umayyads and Abbasids had excluded from power; it became Islam's most potent dissident force and created a permanent divide within Islam. Shiism was well established in the first century of Islam's existence.

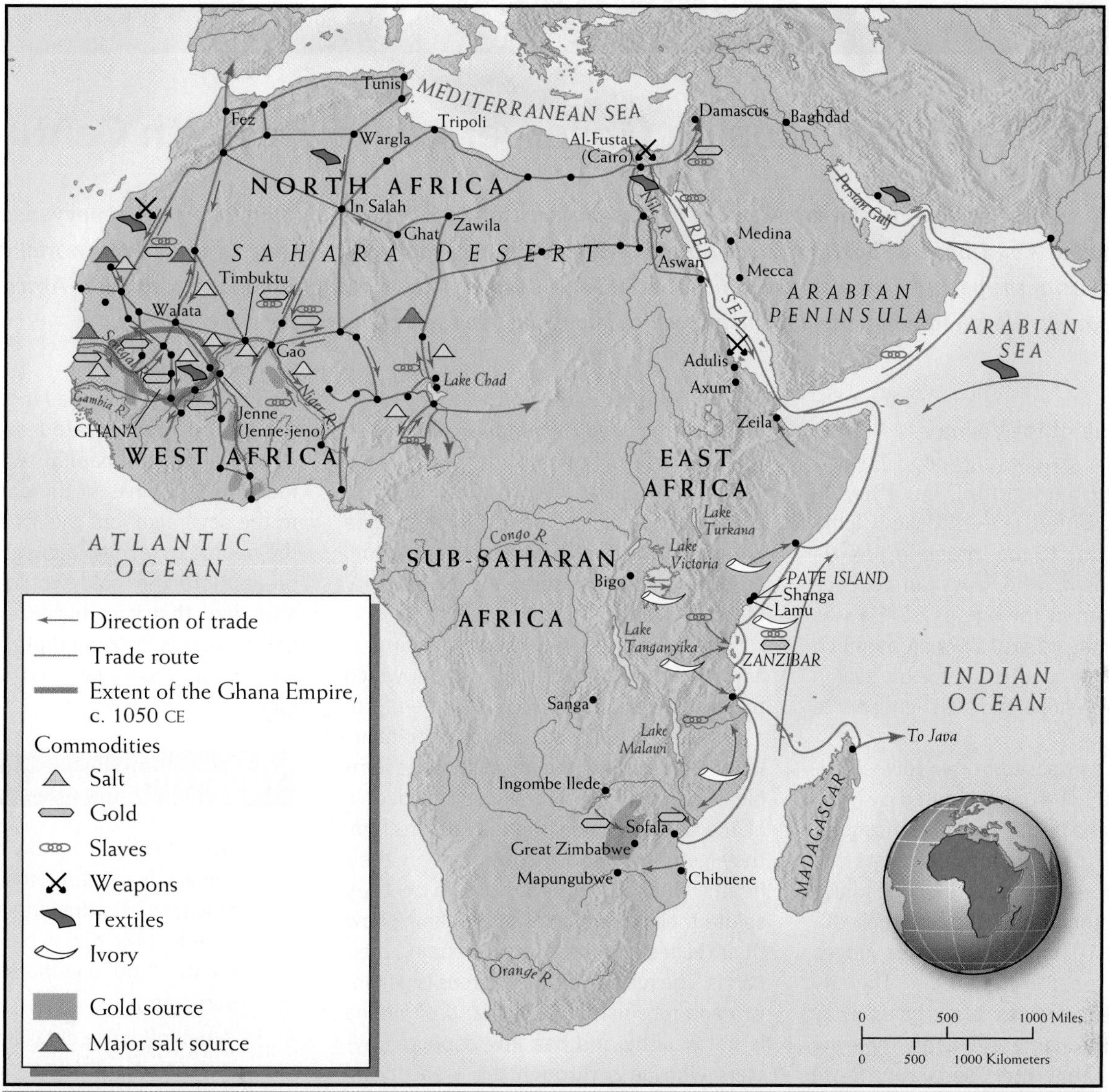

MAP 9.3 | Islam and Trade in Sub-Saharan Africa, 700–1000 CE

Islamic merchants and scholars, not Islamic armies, carried Islam into sub-Saharan Africa.

- Trace the trade routes in Africa, being sure to follow the correct direction of trade.
- According to the map key and icons, what commodities were Islamic merchants seeking below the Sahara?
- How did trade and commerce lead to the geographic expansion of the Islamic faith?

FATIMIDS After 300 years of struggling, the Shiites finally seized power. Repressed in Iraq and Iran, Shiite activists made their way to North Africa, where they joined with dissident Berber groups to topple several rulers. In 909 CE, a Shiite religious and military leader, Abu Abdallah, overthrew the Sunni ruler there. Thus began the Fatimid regime.

After conquering Egypt in 969 CE, the Fatimids set themselves against the Abbasid caliphs of Baghdad, refusing to acknowledge their legitimacy and claiming to speak for the whole Islamic world. The Fatimid rulers established their capital in a new city that arose alongside al-Fustat, the old Umayyad capital. They called this place al-Qahira (or Cairo), "the Victorious," and promoted its beauty. Early on they founded a place of worship and learning, the al-Azhar mosque, which attracted scholars from all over Afro-Eurasia and spread Islamic learning outward; they also built other elegant mosques and centers of learning. The Fatimid regime lasted until the late twelfth century, though its rulers made little headway in persuading the Egyptian population to embrace their Shiite beliefs. Most of the population remained Sunnis.

By 1000 CE Islam, which had originated as a radical religious revolt in a small corner of the Arabian Peninsula, had grown

PRIMARY SOURCE

Ghana as Seen by a Muslim Observer in the Eleventh Century

The following excerpt is from an eleventh-century manuscript written by a Muslim serving under the Umayyads in Spain. Its author, Abdullah Abu Ubayd al-Bakri, produced a massive general geography and history of the known world, as did many Muslim scholars of the period. This manuscript has special value because it provides information about West Africa, a region in which the Spanish rulers had great interest and into which Islam had been spreading for several centuries.

Ghana is the title of the king of the people. The name of the country is Aoukar. The ruler who governs the people at the present time—the year 460 AH (after the Hijra and 1067–68 CE)—is called Tenkamein. He came to the throne in 455 AH. His predecessor, who was named Beci, began his reign at the age of 85. He was a prince worthy of great praise as much for his personal conduct as for his zeal in the pursuit of justice and his friendship to Muslims. . . .

Ghana is composed of two towns situated in a plain. The one inhabited by Muslims is large and contains twelve mosques, in which the congregants celebrate the Friday prayer. All of these mosques have their imams, their muezzins, and their salaried readers. The city possesses judges and men of great erudition. . . . The city where the king resides is six miles away and carries the name el-Ghaba, meaning "the forest." The territory separating these two locations is covered with dwellings, constructed out of rocks and the wood of the acacia tree. The dwelling of the king consists of a chateau and several surrounding huts, all of which are enclosed by a wall-like structure. In the ruler's town, close to the royal tribunal, is a mosque where Muslims come when they have business with the ruler in order to carry out their prayers. . . . The royal interpreters are chosen from the Muslim population, as was the state treasurer and the majority of the state ministers. . . .

The opening of a royal meeting is announced by the noise of a drum, which they call a *deba*, and which is formed from a long piece of dug-out wood. Upon hearing the drumming, the inhabitants assemble. When the king's coreligionists [people of the same religion] appear before him, they genuflect and throw dust on their heads. Such is the way in which they salute their sovereign. The Muslims show their respect for the king by clapping their hands. The religion of the Negroes is paganism and fetishism. . . . The land of Ghana is not healthy and has few people. Travelers who pass through the area during the height of the agricultural season are rarely able to avoid becoming sick. When the grains are at their fullest and are ready for harvesting is the time when mortality affects visitors.

The best gold in the land comes from Ghiarou, a town located eighteen days' journey from the capital. All of the gold found in the mines of the empire belongs to the sovereign, but the sovereign allows the people to take gold dust. Without this precaution, the gold would become so abundant that it would lose much of its value. . . . It is claimed that the king owns a piece of gold as large as an enormous rock.

QUESTIONS FOR ANALYSIS

- From this excerpt, how much can you learn about the kingdom of Ghana? Try drawing a sketch of the region based on the description in the second paragraph.
- What influence did Islam have in the empire? What aspects of the excerpt reveal the extent of Islam's acceptance?
- What elements of Ghana most interested the author?

Source: Abou-Obeïd-el-Bekri, Description de l'Afrique septentrionale, *revised and corrected edition, translated by [William] Mac Guckin de Slane (Paris: A. Maisonneuve, 1965), pp. 327–31; translated from the French by Robert Tignor.*

into a vast political and religious empire. It had become the dominant political and cultural force in the middle regions of Afro-Eurasia. Like its rival in this part of the world, Christianity, it aspired to universality. But unlike Christianity, it was linked from its outset to political power. Muhammad and his early followers created an empire to facilitate the expansion of their faith while their Christian counterparts inherited an empire when Constantine embraced the new faith. A vision of a world under the jurisdiction of Muslim caliphs, adhering to the dictates of the *sharia,* drove Muslim armies, merchants, and scholars to territories thousands of miles away from Mecca and Medina. Yet the impulse to expand ran out of energy at the fringes of Islam's reach, creating political fragmentation within the Muslim world and leaving much of western Europe and China untouched. But it also had important internal consequences: Muslims were no longer the minority within their own lands, owing to the conversion of Christians, Jews, and other populations under Muslim emperors.

Jenne Mosque. *This fabulous mosque arose in the kingdom of Mali when that kingdom was at the height of its power. The mosque speaks to the depth and importance of Islam's roots in the Malian kingdom.*

Al-Azhar Mosque. *The mosque of al-Azhar is Cairo's most important ancient mosque. Built in the tenth century by the Fatimid conquerors and rulers of Egypt, it quickly became a leading center for worship and learning, frequented by Muslim clerics and admired in Europe.*

THE TANG STATE

The rise of the short-lived Sui Dynasty (589–618 CE) and the more durable Tang empire (618–907 CE) in China, and their impact on Korea and Japan, paralleled Islam's explosion out of Arabia and its impact throughout Afro-Eurasia. Once again the landmass had two centers of power, as Islam replaced the Roman Empire in counterbalancing the power and wealth of China.

However, this bipolar world differed significantly from that of the Roman and Han empires: in the centuries since their waning, Eurasian and African worlds had drawn much closer through trade, conversion, and regular political contacts. Now the two powerhouses competed for dominance in central Asia, sharing influences and even mobile populations that weaved back and forth across porous borders between Islamic and Chinese territories.

China was both a recipient of foreign influences and a source of influences on its neighbors. Indeed, it was becoming the hub of East Asian integration. Like the Umayyads and the Abbasids, the **Tang dynasty**, recovering the territory and confidence of the Han Empire, promoted a cosmopolitan culture. Under its rule Buddhism, medicine, and mathematics from India gave China's chief cities an international flavor. Buddhist monks from Bactria; Greeks, Armenians, and Jews from Constantinople; Muslim envoys from Samarkand and Persia; Vietnamese tributary missions from Annam; nomadic chieftains from the Siberian plains; officials and students from Korea; and monkish visitors from Japan all rubbed elbows in the streets of Chang'an and Luoyang. Ideas traveled east as well—notably to Korea and Japan, where Daoism and Buddhism made inroads. Similarly, Chinese statecraft, as expressed through the Confucian classics, struck the early Koreans and Japanese as the best model for their own state building.

Territorial Expansion under the Tang Dynasty

After the fall of the Han, China had faced a long period of political fragmentation (see Chapter 8). Ultimately, though, Tang rulers restored Han models of empire building. Their claims that an imperial system could outperform small states found a receptive audience in a populace fatigued by internal chaos. The Tang dynasty expanded the boundaries of the Chinese state and reestablished its dominance in East and central Asia.

A sudden change in the course of the Yellow River (not the first such environmental calamity; see Chapter 7) caused extensive flooding on the North China plain and set the stage for the emergence of the Tang dynasty. Revolts ensued as the population faced starvation. Li Yuan marched on Chang'an and took the throne for himself. He promptly established the Tang dynasty and began building a strong central government by doubling the number of government offices. By 624 CE the initial steps of establishing the Tang dynasty were complete. But the fruits of these gains slipped into the hands of Li Yuan's ambitious son Li Shimin, who forced his father to abdicate and took the throne in 627 CE.

The Army and Imperial Campaigning

An expanding Tang state required a large and professionally trained army, capable of defending far-flung frontiers and squelching rebellious populations. Toward these efforts the Tang built a military organization of aristocratic cavalry and peasant soldiers. The cavalry regularly clashed on the northern steppes with encroaching nomadic peoples, who also fought on horseback;

CURRENT TRENDS IN WORLD HISTORY

Green Revolutions in the Islamic World and Tang China, 300–600 CE

World historians often focus on the more famous Columbian Exchange to talk about how the sharing of foods between regions of the world created revolutions in diet. The Afro-Eurasian world underwent a food revolution of its own between 300 and 600 CE. New crops, especially food crops, leaped across political and cultural borders during this period, offering expanding populations more diverse and nutritious diets and the ability to feed increased numbers. Such was true of the Islamic world and Tang China in the eighth century. Now, however, it was India that replaced Mesopotamia as the source of a dazzling array of new cultigens. Most of them originated in Southeast Asia, made their way to India, and dispersed throughout the Muslim world and into China. These crops included new strains of rice, taro, sour oranges, lemons, limes, and most likely coconut palm trees, sugarcane, bananas, plantains, and mangoes. Sorghum and possibly cotton and watermelons arrived from Africa. Only the eggplant was indigenous to India. Although these staples spread quickly to East Asia, their westward movement was slower. Not until the Muslim conquest of Sindh in northern India in 711 CE did territories to the west fully discover the crop innovations pioneered in Southeast Asia.

India fascinated the Arabs, and they exploited its agricultural offerings to the hilt. Soon a revolution in crops and diet swept through the Muslim world. Sorghum supplanted millet and the other grains of antiquity because it was hardier, had higher yields, and required a shorter growing season. Citrus trees added flavor to the diet and provided refreshing drinks during the summer heat. Increased cotton cultivation led to a greater demand for textiles.

For over three hundred years, farmers from northwest India to Spain, Morocco, and West Africa made impressive use of the new crops. They increased agricultural output, slashed fallow periods, and grew as many as three crops on lands that formerly had yielded one. (See Map 9.4). As a result farmers could feed larger communities; even as cities grew, the countryside became more densely populated and even more productive.

The same agricultural revolution that was sweeping through South Asia and the Muslim world also took East Asia by storm. China received the same crops that Muslim cultivators were carrying westward. Rice was critical. New varieties entered from the south, and groups migrating from the north (after the collapse of the Han Empire) eagerly took them up. Soon Chinese farmers became the world's most intensive wet-field rice cultivators. Early- and late-ripening seeds supported two or three plantings a year. Champa rice, introduced from central Vietnam, was especially popular for its drought resistance and rapid ripening.

Because rice needs ample water, Chinese hydraulic engineers went into the fields to design water-lifting devices, which peasant farmers used to construct hillside rice paddies. They also dug more canals, linking rivers and lakes (see Map 9.5) and even drained swamps, alleviating the malaria that had long troubled the region. Their efforts yielded a booming and constantly moving rice frontier.

QUESTIONS FOR ANALYSIS

- Historians think of the eighteenth century as having produced an agricultural revolution. Are we justified in using the same term for this earlier period?
- How did the new crops change diets and contribute to population growth?

Explore Further

Watson, Andrew, *Agricultural Innovation in the Early Islamic World: The Diffusion of Crops and Farming Techniques, 700–1100* (1983).

at its height the Tang military had some 700,000 horses. At the same time, between 1 and 2 million peasant soldiers garrisoned the south and toiled on public works projects.

Much like the Islamic forces, the Tang's frontier armies increasingly relied on pastoral nomadic soldiers from the Inner Eurasian steppe. Notable were the Uighurs, Turkish-speaking peoples who had moved into western China and by 750 CE constituted the empire's most potent military force. These hard-riding and hard-drinking warriors galvanized fearsome cavalries, fired longbows at distant range, and wielded steel swords and knives in hand-to-hand combat. The Tang military also pushed the state into Tibet, the Red River valley in northern Vietnam, Manchuria, and Bohai (near Korea).

By 650 CE, as Islamic armies were moving toward central Asia, the Tang were already the region's new colossus. At the empire's height, Tang armies controlled more than 4 million square miles of territory—an area as large as the entire Islamic world in the ninth and tenth centuries. Once the Tang administrators brought South China's rich farmlands under cultivation (by draining swamps, building an intricate network of canals and channels, and connecting lakes and rivers to the rice lands), the state was able to collect taxes from roughly 10 million families, representing 57 million individuals. Most of these taxes took the form of agricultural labor, which propelled the expansion of cultivated frontiers throughout the south.

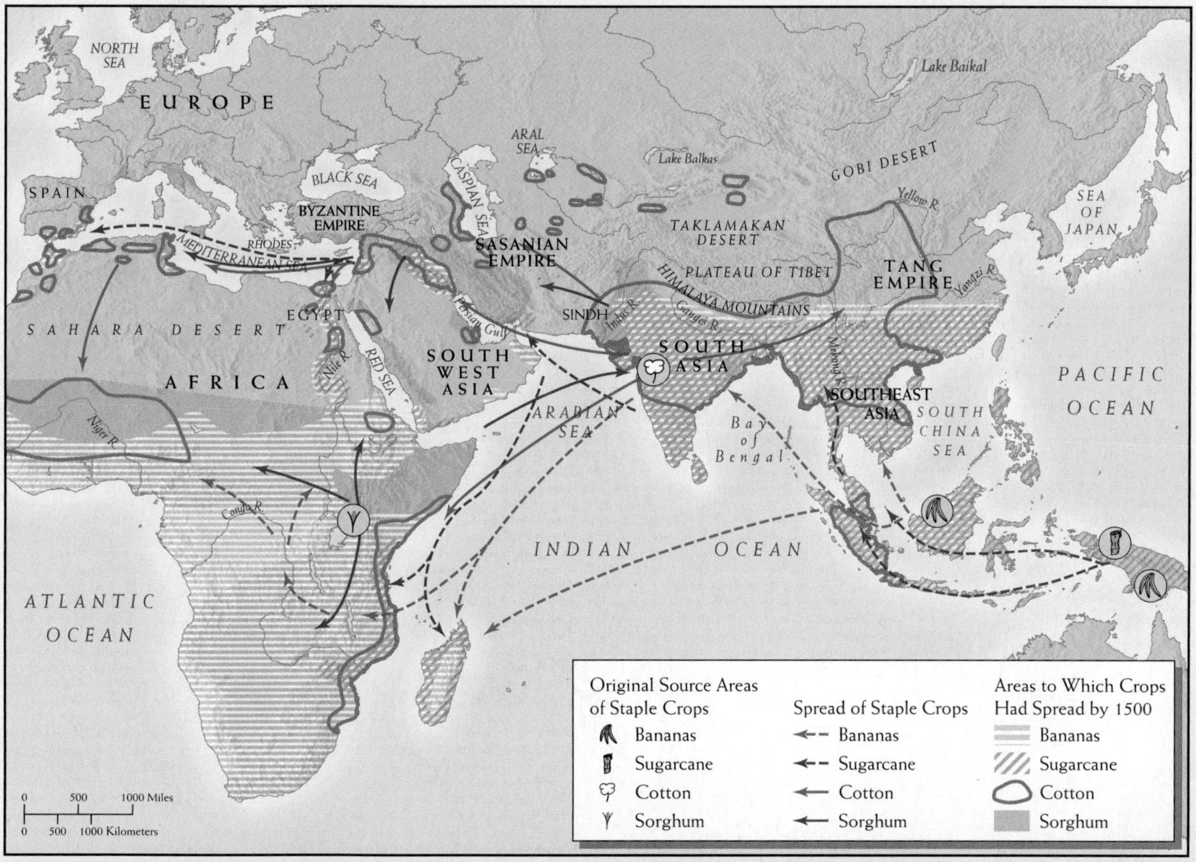

MAP 9.4 | Agricultural Diffusion in the First Millennium

The second half of the first millennium saw a revolution in agriculture throughout Afro-Eurasia. Agriculturalists across the landmass increasingly cultivated similar crops.

- Where did most of the cultigens originate? In what direction and where did most of them flow?
- What role did the spread of Islam and the growth of Islamic empires (see Map 9.1) play in the process?

In spite of the Abbasid Empire's precocious spread, China in 750 CE was the most powerful, most advanced, and best administered empire in the world (see Map 9.6). Korea and Japan recognized its superiority in every material aspect of life. Muslims were among the people who arrived at Chang'an to pay homage. Persians, Armenians, and Turks brought tribute and merchandise via the busy Silk Road or by sea, and other travelers and traders came from Southeast Asia, Korea, and Japan.

The peak of Chinese power occurred just as the Abbasids were expanding into Tang portions of central Asia. Rivalry brought these worlds together, but not peaceably. Muslim forces drove the Tang from Turkistan in 751 CE at the battle of Talas River, and their success emboldened groups such as the Sogdians and Tibetans to challenge the Tang in the west. As a result, the Tang gradually retreated into the old heartlands along the Yellow and Yangzi rivers. They even saw their capital fall to invading Tibetans and Sogdians. Thereafter misrule, court intrigues, economic exploitation, and popular rebellions weakened the empire, but the dynasty held on for over a century more until northern invaders toppled it in 907 CE.

Organizing an Empire

The Tang Empire, a worthy successor to the Han, ranks as one of China's great dynastic polities. Although its rulers emulated

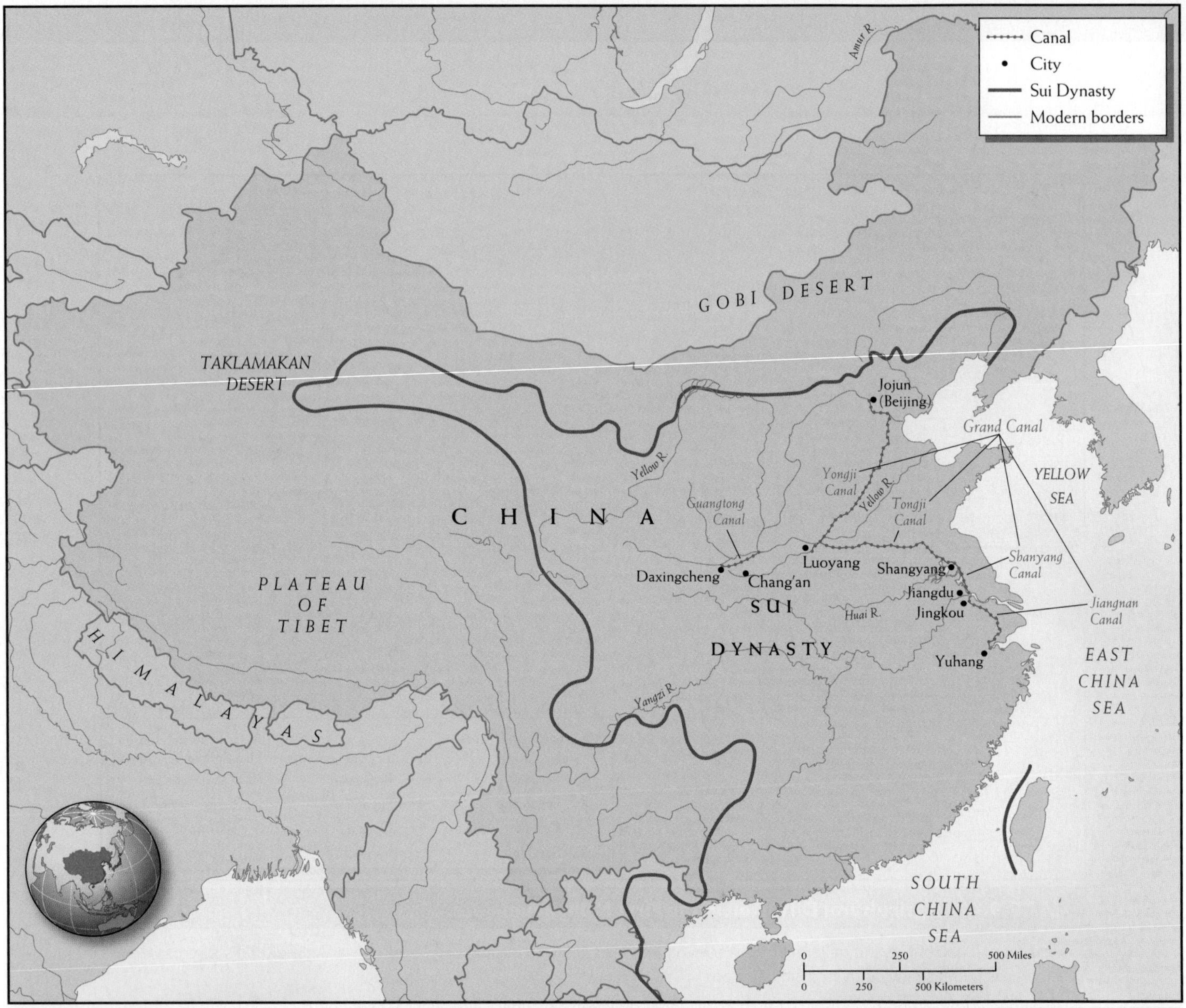

MAP 9.5 | The Sui Dynasty Canals

China, like the Islamic world, experienced a population explosion during this period.

- Where are the Sui dynasty canals on the map and the two areas showing population concentration?
- Why do you think the population concentrations are located along the canals?
- What other roles might the canals have played in addition to fostering population growth in this period within China?

the Han in many ways (for example, by compiling a legal code based on the Han's), they also introduced new institutions.

The heart of the Tang state was the magnificent capital city of Chang'an, the population of which reached 1 million, half of whom lived within its impressive city walls and half on the outside. The outer walls enclosed an immense area, 6 miles along an east-west axis and 5 miles from north to south. Internal security arrangements made it one of the safest urban locales for its age. Its more than 100 quarters were separated from each other by interior walls with gates that were closed at night, after which no one was permitted on the streets, patrolled by horsemen, until the gates reopened in the morning. As befitted a city that was in the western region of China and in close contact with central Asia, Chang'an had a large foreign population, estimated

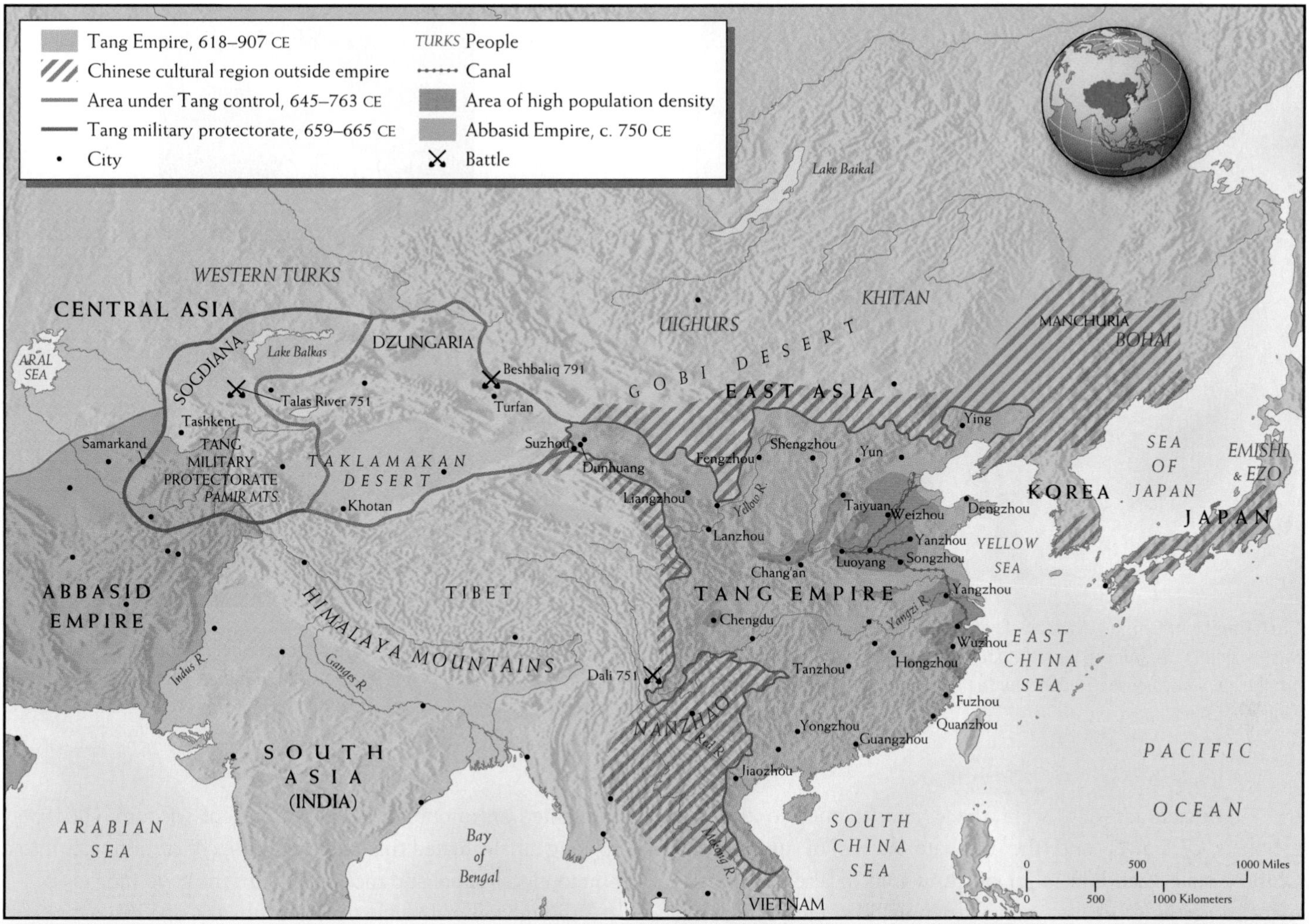

MAP 9.6 | The Tang State in East Asia, 750 CE

The Tang dynasty, at its territorial peak in 750, controlled a state that extended from central Asia to the East China Sea.

- What foreign areas are under Tang control? What areas were heavily influenced by Tang government and culture?
- How can we tell from the map that China was undergoing an economic revolution during the Tang period?
- How did the Tang maintain order and stability in such a large, dynamic realm?

at one-third of its total, and a diverse religious life. Zoroastrian fires burned as worshippers sacrificed animals and chanted temple hymns. Nestorian Christians from Syria found a welcoming community, and not to be outdone, the Buddhists boasted that they had ninety-one of their own temples in Chang'an in 722 CE.

CONFUCIAN ADMINISTRATORS Despite the Tang's reliance on military force, the day-to-day control of the empire required an efficient and loyal civil service. Whereas a shared spiritual commitment to Islam held together the multilingual, multiethnic, and even multireligious Islamic empire, the Tang found other ways to integrate remote territories and diverse groups. Their efforts, building on past practice, produced an empire-wide political culture based on Confucian teachings and classically educated elites.

Chinese integration began at the top. Entry into the ruling group required knowledge of Confucian ideas and all of the commentaries on the Confucian classics. It also required skill in the intricate classical Chinese language, in which this literature was written. A deep familiarity with these texts was as crucial in forging a Chinese cultural and political solidarity as understanding the Quran and the *sharia* were for the Abbasid state or the New Testament for Christian Europe and the Byzantine Empire.

Most important in reinforcing the Tang state were the world's first fully written **civil service examinations**. These examinations, which tested sophisticated literary skills and

Christianity in China. *As subjects of the largest Christian church of the 9th century, Nestorian priests made lasting impressions on the Tang Empire, one of which is this mural of their Palm Sunday procession in Xinjiang, China.*

Tang Official. *Tang officials were selected through competitive civil examinations in order to limit the power of Buddhist and Daoist clerics. This painted clay figure of a Tang official c. 717 was excavated in 1972.*

the Confucian classics, were the primary route to the top echelons of power and the ultimate means of uniting the Chinese state. Candidates for office, whom local elites recommended, gathered in the capital triennially to take qualifying exams. They had been trained since the age of three in the Classics and Histories, either by their families or in Buddhist temple schools. Most failed the grueling competition, but those who were successful underwent further trials to evaluate their character and determine the level of their appointments. New officials were selected from the pool of graduates on the basis of social conduct, eloquence, skill in calligraphy and mathematics, and legal knowledge. (See Primary Source: The Pressures of Maintaining Empire by Examination.) When Emperor Li Shimin observed the new officials obediently parading out of the examination hall, he slyly noted, "The heroes of the empire are all in my pocket!" (Miyazaki, *China's Examination Hell,* 13). Overall, the civil service system gave rise in China to the perennial belief in the value of a classically trained **meritocracy** (rule by persons of talent), which has lasted into modern times.

Having assumed the mandate of heaven (see Chapter 4), the Tang rulers and their supporters sought to establish a code of moral values for the whole empire. Building on Han dynasty models, they expanded the state school in the capital into an empire-wide series of select schools that accepted only fully literate candidates for the civil examinations. They also allowed the use of Daoist classics as texts for the exams, believing that the early Daoists also represented an important stream of ancient wisdom. Ultimately the Tang amalgamated this range of texts, codes, and tests into a common intellectual and moral credo for the governing classes.

Although official careers were in theory open to anyone of proven talent, in practice they were closed to certain groups. Despite Empress Wu's prominence (see below), women were not permitted to serve, nor were sons of merchants, nor those who could not afford a classical education. Over time, Tang civil examinations forced aristocrats to compete with commoner southern families, whose growing wealth gave them access to educational resources that made them the equals of the old elites. Through examinations, this new elite eventually outdistanced the sons of the northern aristocracy in the Tang government by out-studying them.

The system also brought a few benefits to the poor by underscoring education as the primary avenue for success. Even impoverished families sought the best classical education they could afford for their sons. Although few succeeded in the civil examinations, many boys and even some girls learned the fundamentals of reading and writing. In fact, the Buddhists played a crucial role in extending education across society: as part of their charitable mission, their temple schools introduced many children to primers based on classical texts. Buddhist monks would never admit that many in their own ranks had initially hoped to become Confucian officials, but in reality quite a few entered the clergy only after not qualifying for or failing the civil examinations.

PRIMARY SOURCE

The Pressures of Maintaining Empire by Examination

Young and old competed equally in the Tang examination halls. The rituals of success were alluring to youths, while the tortures of failure weighed heavily on older competitors still seeking an elusive degree. For all, the tensions of seeing the posted list of successful candidates—following years of preparation for young boys, and even more years of defeat for old men—were intensely personal responses to success or failure. The few who passed would look back on that day with relief and pride.

In the Southern Court they posted the list. (The Southern Court was where the Board of Rites ran the administration and accepted documents. All prescribed forms together with the stipulations for each [degree] category were usually publicized here.) The wall for hanging the list was by the eastern wall of the Southern Court. In a separate building a screen was erected which stood over ten feet tall, and it was surrounded with a fence. Before dawn they took the list from the Northern Court to the Southern Court where it was hung for display.

In the sixth year of Yuanhe [AD 811] a student at the University, Guo Dongli, broke through the thorn hedge. (The thorn hedge was below the fence. There was another outside the main gate of the Southern Court.) He then ripped up the ornamental list [*wenbang*]. It was because of this that afterwards they often came out of the gateway of the Department [of State Affairs] with a mock list. The real list was displayed a little later.

QUESTIONS FOR ANALYSIS

- Why were the stakes so high in the civil examinations? What happened to those who failed?
- Was the Tang civil examination system an open system that tested talent—that is, a meritocracy?
- Can you relate to the candidates' anxiety in terms of your own experiences—for example, waiting for college acceptance letters or your year-end grade point average?

Source: Wang Dingbao (870–940), quoted in Oliver J. Moore, Rituals of Recruitment in Tang China *(Leiden: Brill, 2004), p. 175.*

CHINA'S FEMALE EMPEROR Not all Tang power brokers were men. The wives and mothers of emperors also wielded influence in the court—usually behind the scenes, but sometimes publicly. Consider Empress Wu, who dominated the court in the late seventh and early eighth centuries. She deftly exploited the examination system to check the power of aristocratic families and consolidated courtly authority by creating groups of loyal bureaucrats, who in turn preserved loyalty to the dynasty at the local level.

Born into a noble family, Wu Zhao played music and mastered the Chinese classics as a young girl. By age thirteen, because she was witty, intelligent, and beautiful, she was recruited to Li Shimin's court and became his favorite concubine. She also fell in love with his son. When Li Shimin died, his son assumed power and became the Emperor Gaozong. Wu became the new emperor's favorite concubine and gave birth to the sons he required to succeed him. As the mother of the future emperor, Wu enjoyed heightened political power. Subsequently, she took the place of Gaozong's Empress Wang by accusing her of killing Wu's newborn daughter. Gaozong believed Wu and married her.

After Gaozong suffered a stroke, Wu became administrator of the court, a position equal to the emperor's. She created a secret police force to spy on her opposition, and she jailed or killed

Empress Wu. *When she seized power in her own right as Empress Wu, Wu Zhao became the first and only female ruler in Chinese history.*

those who stood in her way. Soon after her husband's death Wu seized power in her own right and made herself Empress Wu (r. 684–705 CE), becoming the only female ruler in Chinese history. She expanded the military and recruited her administrators from the civil examination candidates to oppose her enemies at court. Challenging Confucian beliefs that subordinated women, Wu elevated their position. She ordered scholars to write biographies of famous women, and she empowered her mother's clan by assigning high political posts to her relatives. Later, she moved her court from Chang'an to Luoyang, where she tried to establish a new "Zhou dynasty," seeking to imitate the widely admired era of Confucius.

Despite Wu's single-minded climb to power, her rule was relatively benign and competent. She elevated Buddhism over Daoism as the favored state religion, invited the most gifted Buddhist scholars to her capital at Luoyang, built Buddhist temples, and subsidized spectacular cave sculptures. In fact, Chinese Buddhism achieved its highest officially sponsored development in this period.

EUNUCHS Tang rulers protected themselves, their possessions, and especially their women, with loyal and well-compensated men, many of whom were **eunuchs** (surgically castrated as youths and thus sexually impotent). By the late eighth century, more than 4,500 eunuchs were fully entrenched in the Tang Empire's institutions, wielding significant power not only within the imperial household but at the court and beyond.

The Chief Eunuch controlled the military. Through him, the military power of court eunuchs extended to every province and garrison station in the empire, forming an all-encompassing network. In effect, the eunuch bureaucracy mediated between the emperor and the provincial governments.

Under Emperor Xianzong (r. 806–820 CE), eunuchs acted as a third pillar of the government, working alongside the official bureaucracy and the imperial court. By establishing clear career patterns for eunuchs that paralleled those in the civil service, Xianzong sparked a striking rise in their levels of literacy and their cultural attainments. And yet, they remained the rivals of most officials. By 838 CE, the delicate balance of power among throne, eunuchs, and civil officials had evaporated. Eunuchs became an unruly political force in late Tang politics, and their competition for influence produced political instability.

An Economic Revolution

In both the Abbasid caliphate and Tang China, political stability fueled remarkable economic achievements. Highlighting China's success were rising agricultural production based on an egalitarian land allotment system, an increasingly fine handicrafts industry, a diverse commodity market, and a dynamic urban life.

The Tang Court. *This tenth-century painting of elegant ladies of the Tang imperial court enjoying a feast and music* (left) *tells us a great deal about the aesthetic tastes of elite women in this era. It also shows the secluded "inner quarters," where court ladies passed their daily lives far from the hurly-burly of imperial politics. Castrated males, known as eunuchs* (right), *guarded the harem and protected the royal family of Tang emperors. By the late eighth century, eunuchs were fully integrated into the government and wielded a great deal of military and political power.*

An earlier short-lived dynasty, the Sui, had started this economic progress by reunifying China and building canals, especially the Grand Canal linking the north and south (see again Map 9.5). The Tang continued by centering their efforts on the Grand Canal and the Yangzi River, which flows from west to east. These waterways aided communication and transport throughout the empire and helped raise living standards. The south grew richer, largely through the backbreaking labor of immigrants from the north. Fertile land along the Yangzi became China's new granary, and areas south of the Yangzi became its demographic center.

Chinese merchants took full advantage of the Silk Road to trade with India and the Islamic world; but when rebellions in northwest China and the rise of Islam in central Asia jeopardized the land route, the "silk road by sea" became the avenue of choice. From all over Asia and Africa, merchant ships arrived in South China ports bearing intoxicating cargoes of spices, medicines, and jewelry in exchange for Chinese silks and porcelain (see again Map 9.6). Chang'an became the richest city in the world, with its million or so residents including foreigners of every description.

In the large cities of the Yangzi delta—in some ways a nascent industrial heartland—workshops proliferated. Their reputations spread far and wide for the elegance of their wares, which included rich brocades (silk fabrics), fine paper, intricately printed woodblocks, unique iron casts, and exquisite porcelains. Art collectors all across Afro-Eurasia especially valued Tang "tricolor pottery," fired up to 900 degrees Celsius and decorated with brilliant hues of yellow, green, white, brown, and blue. Meanwhile, Chinese artisans transformed locally grown cotton into highest-quality clothing. The textile industry prospered as painting and dyeing technology improved and superb silk products generated significant tax revenue. Such Chinese luxuries dominated the trading networks that reached Southwest Asia, Europe, and Africa via the Silk Road and the Indian Ocean.

Accommodating World Religions

The early Tang emperors tolerated remarkable religious diversity. Nestorian Christianity, Zoroastrianism, and Manichaeanism (a radical Christian sect) had entered China from Persia during the time of the Sasanian Empire. Islam came later. These spiritual impulses—together with Buddhism and the indigenous teachings of Daoism and Confucianism—spread throughout the Tang Empire and at first were widely used to enhance state power.

THE GROWTH OF BUDDHISM Buddhism, in particular, thrived under Tang rule. Initially, Emperor Li Shimin distrusted Buddhist monks because they avoided serving the government and paying taxes. Yet after Buddhism gained acceptance as one of the "three ways" of learning—joining Daoism and Confucianism—Li endowed huge monasteries, sent emissaries to India to collect texts and relics, and commissioned Buddhist paintings and statuary. Caves along the Silk Road, such as those at Dunhuang, provided ideal venues for monks to paint the inside walls where religious rites and meditation took place. Soon the caves boasted

One of the Four Sacred Mountains. *This monastery on Mount Song is famous because in 527 an Indian priest, Bodhidharma, arrived there to initiate the Zen school of Buddhism in China.*

ANALYZING GLOBAL DEVELOPMENTS

Islam and the Silk Trade: Adapting Religion to Opulence

Although the Silk Road emerged from the industries and commercial networks of the Han, Kushan, Parthian, and Roman Empires in the first century BCE, it was not until centuries later, after the collapse of these states, that the golden age of Eurasian trade arose with new, powerful players. Tang China inherited the Han monopoly on silk production, while the Byzantine empire utilized its Roman resources to develop its own silk weaving industry. Yet, a major threat to these monopolies appeared in the seventh century, when the first Islamic empire, the Umayyad Caliphate (661–750), built a vast, state-run textile industry to exert influence over its newly conquered cities. Not only did the establishment of textile factories throughout the empire keep the working classes in line, but the luxury textiles produced were incentives for the elite of newly conquered territories (many of which were wealthy and were more sophisticated than the Arab tent culture of early Islamic caliphs) to submit to Muslim rule.

Tensions arose between this opulent lifestyle and the Muslim way of life, which forbade its adherents from wearing silk. The political, social, and religious authority that the Islamic silk trade lent the caliphate, however, was crucial to its unity and longevity. What's more, the Islamic silk industry was rapidly expanding, with no limits in sight, unlike Byzantine and Tang silk, which were restricted by their respective emperors. And so this textile-centered culture proliferated in an unbridled fashion, eventually infiltrating even religious rituals. The Abbasid Caliphate (749–1258) became one of the wealthiest medieval states, and its capitol, Baghdad, the most cosmopolitan. To illustrate the sheer extent of the impact that the Islamic silk trade had upon the values of its people, the following table is a record of the goods that caliph Harun al-Rashid, upon whom several *Arabian Nights* stories are based, left behind upon his death in 809.

Source: Xinru Liu, The Silk Road in World History *(New York: Oxford University Press, 2010).*

QUESTIONS FOR ANALYSIS

- Looking back at Map 6.3 and assuming that the exports of each region remained relatively constant throughout the history of the Silk Road, with which cities and empires did the Abbasid Empire conduct most of its trade? The least? What might account for these differences?
- What can this list tell us about the values and activities of a caliph ca. 800 CE? What, if anything, does the inventory reveal about the values and activities of the non-elite or working classes?
- What kind of evidence from contemporary Tang China or Western Christendom would allow you to draw comparable conclusions to arguments that can be constructed from al-Rashid's inventory?

Textiles: Silk Items	
4,000	silk cloaks, lined with sable and mink
1,500	silk carpets
100	silk rugs
1,000	silk cushions and pillows
1,000	cushions with silk brocade
1,000	inscribed silk cushions
1,000	silk curtains
300	silk brocade curtains
Everyday Textile Items	
4,000	small tents with their accessories
150	marquees (large tents)

"bright" color paintings and massive statues of the Buddha and the bodhisattvas.

ANTI-BUDDHIST CAMPAIGNS By the mid-ninth century, the proliferation and growing influence of hundreds of thousands of Buddhist monks and nuns threatened China's Confucian and Daoist leaders. So they attacked Buddhism, arguing that its values conflicted with native traditions.

One of the boldest attacks came from the Confucian-trained scholar-official Han Yu, who represented the rising literati from the south. His memorial of 819 CE protested the emperor's plan to bring a relic of the Buddha to the capital for exhibition. Striking a note that would have been inconceivable under the early Tang's cosmopolitanism, Han Yu attacked Buddhism as a foreign doctrine of barbarian peoples who were different in language, culture, and knowledge. These objections earned him exile to the southern province of Guangdong.

Yet, two decades later the state began suppressing Buddhist monasteries and confiscating their wealth, fearing that religious loyalties would undermine political ones. Increasingly intolerant Confucian scholar-administrators argued that the Buddhist monastic establishment threatened the imperial order. They

Luxury Textile Items	
4,000	embroidered robes
500	pieces of velvet
1,000	Armenian carpets
300	carpets from Maysan (present-day east Iraq)
1,000	carpets from Darabjird (present-day Darab, Iran)
500	carpets from Tabaristan (southern coast of the Caspian sea)
1,000	cushions from Tabaristan
Fine Cotton Items and Garments	
2,000	drawers of various kinds
4,000	turbans
1,000	hoods
1,000	capes of various kinds
5,000	kerchiefs of different kinds
10,000	caftans (long robes)
4,000	curtains
4,000	pairs of socks
Fur and Leather Items	
4,000	boots lined with sable and mink
4,000	special saddles
30,000	common saddles
1,000	belts

Metal Goods	
500,000	dinars (cash)
2,000	brass objects of various kinds
10,000	decorated swords
50,000	swords for the guards and pages (ghulam)
150,000	lances
100,000	bows
1,000	special suits of armor
10,000	helmets
20,000	breast plates
150,000	shields
300	stoves
Aromatics and Drugs	
100,000	mithqals of musk (1 mithqual = 4.25 grams)
100,000	mithqals of ambergris (musky perfume ingredient)
	many kinds of perfume
1,000	baskets of India aloes
Jewelry and Cut Gems	
	Jewels valued by jewelers at 4 million dinars
1,000	jeweled rings
Fine Stone and Metal Vessels	
1,000	precious china vessels
1,000	ewers

claimed that members of the clergy were conspiring to destroy the state, the family, and the body.

Piecemeal measures against the monastic orders gave way in the 840s CE to open persecution. Emperor Wuzong, for instance, closed more than 4,600 monasteries and destroyed 40,000 temples and shrines. More than 260,000 Buddhist monks and nuns endured a forced return to secular life, after which the state parceled out monastery lands to taxpaying landlords and peasant farmers. To expunge the cultural impact of Buddhism, classically trained literati revived ancient prose styles and the teachings of Confucius and his followers. Linking classical scholarship, ancient literature, and Confucian morality, they constructed a cultural fortress that reversed the early Buddhist successes in China.

Ultimately, the Tang era represented the triumph of homegrown ideologies (Confucianism and Daoism) over a foreign universalizing religion (Buddhism). In addition, by permanently breaking apart huge monastic holdings, the Tang made sure that no religion would rival its power, and successor dynasties continued to keep religious establishments weak and fragmented, although Confucianism maintained a more prominent role within society as the basis of the ruling classes' ideology and as a quasi-religious belief system for a wider portion of the population. The result within China was persistent religious pluralism, including Buddhism, which continued to remain important even in the face of dynastic persecution.

The Fall of Tang China

China's deteriorating economic conditions in the ninth century led to peasant uprisings, some even led by unsuccessful examination candidates. These revolts eventually brought down the dynasty. In the tenth century, China fragmented into regional states and entered a new but much shorter era of decentralization. The Song dynasty that emerged in 960 CE could not unify the Tang territories, and even the Mongols, invading steppe peoples, were able to restore the glory of the Han and Tang empires only for a century.

EARLY KOREA AND JAPAN

While China was opening up to the cultures of its western regions, its own culture was reaching out to the east—to Korea and, eventually, to Japan (see Map 9.7). Being colored by Buddhism, these influences were somewhat flexible and less distinctly Chinese, although Confucianism in Japan, Korea, and Vietnam was tailored to each country's scale and needs.

Early Korea

By the fourth century CE, three independent states had emerged on the Korean peninsula, and Chinese influences were beginning to penetrate the peninsula and would become a decisive element in Korean history from at least the third century BCE onwards. Korea remained divided into the "Three Kingdoms" until 668 CE, when one of these states, Silla, leading a movement to prevent Chinese domination, gained control over the entire peninsula and unified it.

UNIFICATION UNDER THE SILLA Unification enabled the Koreans to establish an autonomous government, but their opposition to the Chinese did not deter them from modeling their government on the Tang imperial state. Silla dispatched annual emissaries bearing tribute payments to the Chinese capital and regularly sent students and monks. As a result, literary Chinese became the written language of Korean elites—not their vernacular (as Latin did among diverse populations in medieval Europe). Koreans much later in the fifteenth century devised a phonetic system for writing their own language based on simplified Chinese characters, but most official writing continued in the literary Chinese form. Chinese influence extended to the way in which the Silla state organized its court and the bureaucracy and to the construction of its capital city of Kumsong, which imitated the Tang capital of Chang'an.

In spite of Chinese influences the loyalty of most non-Chinese Koreans was to their kinship groups. These early Koreans believed that birth, not displays of learned achievement, should be the source of influence in religious and political life. Korean holy men and women (known today as shamans), interceded with gods, demons, and ancestral spirits and remained prominent in local village life.

Silla's fortunes became entwined with the Tang's to such an extent that once the Tang declined, Silla also began to fragment. Moreover, it had never established a full-blown Tang-style government.

THE KORYO DYNASTY In 936 CE, Wang Kon, a rebel leader, absorbed Silla into the northern-based Koryo kingdom, an act that tenuously reunified the country. The Koryo dynasty (from which the country's modern name derives) began to construct a new cultural identity by enacting a bureaucratic system, which replaced the archaic tribal system that the Silla had maintained. The Koryo went beyond earlier Silla reforms and fully established Tang-style civil service examinations to select officials who would govern at court and in the provinces. Wang Kon's heirs consolidated control over the peninsula and strengthened its political and economic foundations by following the Tang's bureaucratic and land allotment systems.

During this period Korea, like Tang China itself, suffered continual harassment from northern tribes such as the Khitan. This particular group exploited the fall of the Tang dynasty to control northern Chinese lands after 907 CE, establishing themselves in what is modern-day Manchuria. Reflecting the repercussions of this troubled period, Korean artisans anxiously carved wooden printing blocks for 81,258 scriptures from the Buddhist canon as an offering to the Buddha to protect them from invading enemies—but in vain. The Korean royal family at the time was under siege, and they hoped that the woodblocks would elicit a change in fortune. The scriptures were hidden away in a single temple, and when rediscovered they represented the most comprehensive and intact version of the Buddhist canon written in the Chinese script. The Korya dynasty lasted until 1392.

Early Japan

Like Korea, Japan also felt influences emanating from China, and it responded by thwarting and accommodating them at the same time. But Japan enjoyed added autonomy: it was an archipelago of islands, separated from the mainland although internally fragmented. In the mid-third century, a warlike group arrived by sea from Korea and imposed military and social power on southern Japan. These conquerors—known as the

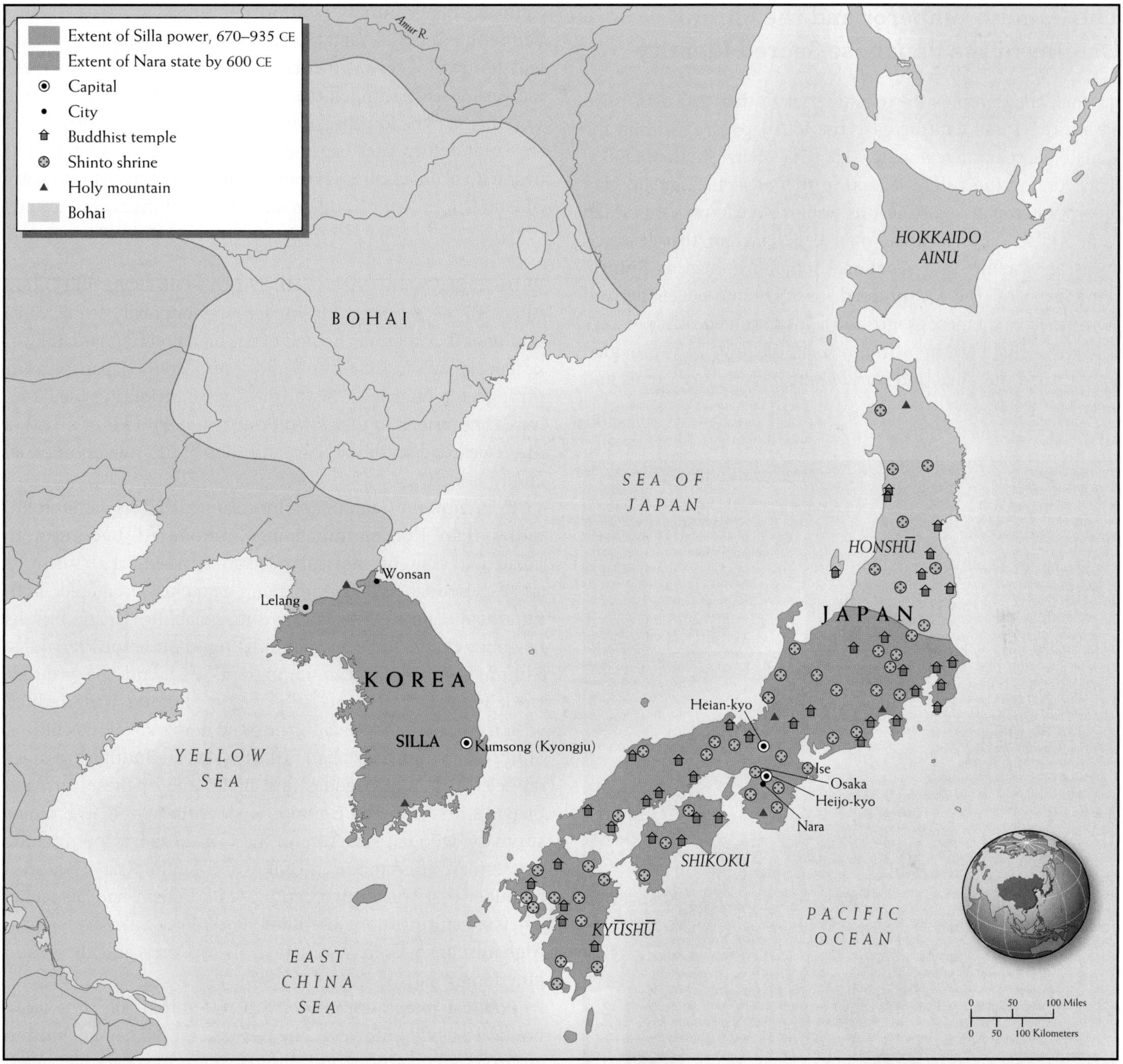

MAP 9.7 | Borderlands: Korea and Japan, 600–1000 CE

The Tang dynasty held great power over emerging Korean and Japanese states, although it never directly ruled either region.

- Based on the map, what connections do you see between Korea and Japan and the Tang Empire?
- To what extent did Korea and Japan adopt Tang customs during this period?

"Tomb Culture" because of their elevated burial sites—unified Japan by extolling their imperial ancestors and maintaining their social hierarchy. They also introduced a belief in the power of female shamans, who married into the imperial clans and became rulers of early Japanese kinship groups.

Chinese dynastic records describe the early Japanese, with whom imperial China had contact in this period, as a "dwarf" people who maintained a rice and fishing economy. The Japanese farmers also mastered Chinese-style sericulture: the production of raw silk by raising silkworms.

The Yamato Emperor and the Shinto Origins of the Japanese Sacred Identity

In time, the complex aristocratic society that had developed within the Tomb Culture gave rise to a Japanese state on the Yamato plain in the region now known as Nara, south of Osaka. In becoming the ruling faction in this area, the Yamato clan incorporated native Japanese as well as Korean migrants. Clan leaders also elevated their own belief system that featured ancestor worship into a national religion known as **Shinto**. (Shinto means "the way of the deities.") Shinto beliefs derived from the early Japanese groups and held that after death a person's soul (or spirit) became a Shinto *kami*, or local deity, provided that it was nourished and purified through proper rituals and festivals. (This burial tradition continues in Japan today.) Before the imperial Yamato clan became dominant, each clan had its own ancestral deities; but after 500 CE all Japanese increasingly worshipped the Yamato ancestors, whose origins went back to the fourth-century Tomb Culture. Other regional ancestral deities later became subordinate to the Yamato deities, who claimed direct lineage from the primary Shinto deity Amaterasu, the Sun Goddess and creator of the sacred islands of Japan.

Creation Myth. *Tsukioka Yoshitoshi (1839–1892) depicted Japan's creation myth in* Amaterasu Appearing from the Cave. *To lure Amaterasu, the goddess of the sun, out so that light would return to the world, the other gods performed a ribald dance.*

PRINCE SHOTOKU AND THE TAIKA POLITICAL REFORMS After 587 CE the Soga kinship group—originally from Korea but by 500 CE a minor branch of the Yamato imperial family—became Japan's leading family and controlled the Japanese court through intermarriage. Soon, they were attributing their cultural innovations to their own Prince Shotoku (574–622 CE), a direct descendant of the Soga and thus of the Yamato imperial family as well.

Contemporary Japanese scribes claimed that Prince Shotoku, rather than Korean immigrants, introduced Buddhism to Japan and that his illustrious reign sparked Japan's rise as an exceptional island kingdom. Shotoku promoted both Buddhism and Confucianism, thus enabling Japan, like its neighbor China, to be accommodating to numerous religions. Although earlier Korean immigrants had laid the groundwork for the growth of these views, Shotoku was credited with introducing these faiths into the native religious culture, Shinto. The prince also had ties with several Buddhist temples modeled on Tang pagodas and halls; one of these, in Nara (Japan's first imperial capital), is Horyuji Temple, the oldest surviving wooden structure in the world. Its frescoes include figures derived from the art of Iran and central Asia. They are a reminder that within two centuries Buddhism had dispersed its visual culture along the full length of the Silk Road—from Afghanistan to China, and then on to Korea and the island kingdom of Japan.

Political integration under Prince Shotoku did not mean political stability, however. In 645 CE, the Nakatomi kinship group seized the throne and eliminated the Soga and their allies. Via intermarriage with the imperial clan, the Nakatomi became the new spokesmen for the Yamato tradition. Thereafter Nakatomi no Kamatari (614–669 CE) enacted a series of reforms, known as the Taika Reform, which reflected Confucian principles of government allegedly enunciated by Shotoku. These reforms enhanced the power of the ruler, no longer portrayed simply as an ancestral kinship group leader but now depicted as an exalted "emperor" (*tenno*) who ruled by the mandate of heaven, as in China, and exercised absolute authority.

MAHAYANA BUDDHISM AND THE SANCTITY OF THE JAPANESE STATE Religious influences continued to flow

Prince Shotoku Taishi. *Shotoku was instrumental in the establishment of Buddhism in Japan, although his actual historical role was overstated. In this hanging scroll painting from the early fourteenth century* (left)*, he is idealized as a sixteen-year-old son, holding an incense censer and praying for the recovery of his sick father, the Emperor Yomei (r. 585–587 CE). The main hall of the Horyuji Temple in Nara, Japan* (right)*.*

into Japan, contributing to spiritual pluralism while bolstering the Yamato rulers. Although Prince Shotoku and later Japanese emperors turned to Confucian models for government, they also dabbled in occult arts and Daoist purification rituals. In addition, the Taika edicts promoted Buddhism as the state religion of Japan. Although the imperial family continued to support native Shinto traditions, association with Buddhism gave the Japanese state extra status by lending it the prestige of a universal religion whose appeal stretched to Korea, China, and India.

State-sponsored spiritual diversity led native Shinto cults to formalize a creed of their own. Indeed, the introduction of Confucianism and Buddhism motivated Shinto adherents to assemble their diverse religious practices into a well-organized belief system. Shinto priests now collected ancient liturgies, and Shinto rituals (such as purification rites to ward off demons and impurities) gained recognition in the official Department of Religion.

Although the Japanese welcomed elements of the Buddhist faith, they did not fully accept the traditional Buddhist view that the state was merely a vehicle to propagate moral and social justice for the ruler and his subjects. Instead, the Japanese saw their emperor (the embodiment of the state) as an object of worship, a sacred ruler, one in a line of luminous Shinto gods, a supreme *kami*—a divine force in his own right. Thus, Buddhism as imported from China and Korea changed in Japan to serve the interests of the state (much as Christianity served the interests of European monarchs, and Islam served the Islamic dynasties).

THE CHRISTIAN WEST

Seen from the Mediterranean and the Islamic worlds, Europe by now seemed little more than a warrior-dominated realm. In the fifth century, the mighty Roman military machine gave way to a multitude of warrior leaders whose principal allegiances were local affiliations. Yet major innovations were under way. The leading force was Christianity, and its universalizing agents were missionaries and monks. The political ideal of the Roman Empire cast a vast shadow over the western Europeans, but the inheritor of the mantle of Rome was a spiritual institution—the Roman Catholic Church—whose powerful head, the pope, was based in Rome (see Map 9.8.)

Charlemagne's Fledgling Empire

In 802 CE, Harun al-Rashid, the ruler of Baghdad, sent the gift of an elephant to Charlemagne, the king of the Franks, in northern Europe. The elephant caused a sensation among the Franks, who saw the gift as an acknowledgment of Charlemagne's power. In fact, Harun often sent rare beasts to distant rulers as a gracious reminder of his own formidable power. In his eyes, Charlemagne's "empire" was a minor principality.

This was an empire that Charlemagne ruled for over forty years, often traveling 2,000 miles a year on campaigns of plunder and conquest. He ultimately controlled much of western Europe, which was a significant accomplishment; yet compared with the Islamic world's rulers, he was a political lightweight.

MAP 9.8 | Christendom, 600–1000 CE

The end of the first millennium saw much of Europe divided between two versions of Christianity, each with different traditions. Locate Rome and Constantinople on the map, the two seats of power in Christianity.

- According to the map, what were the two major regions where Christianity held sway?
- In what directions did Latin Christianity and Orthodox Christianity spread?
- Why do you suppose the Catholic Church, based in Rome, was successful in expanding to the west, but not to the east?
- Why do you suppose Orthodox Christianity, based in Constantinople, expanded into eastern Europe, but not into the west?

His empire had a population of less than 15 million; he rarely commanded armies larger than 5,000; and he had a rudimentary tax system. At a time when the palace quarters of the caliph at Baghdad covered nearly 250 acres, Charlemagne's palace at Aachen was merely 330 by 655 feet. Baghdad itself was almost 40 square miles in area, whereas there was no "town" outside the palace at Aachen. It was little more than a large country house set in open countryside, close to the Ardennes woods, where Charlemagne and his Franks loved to hunt wild boar on horseback.

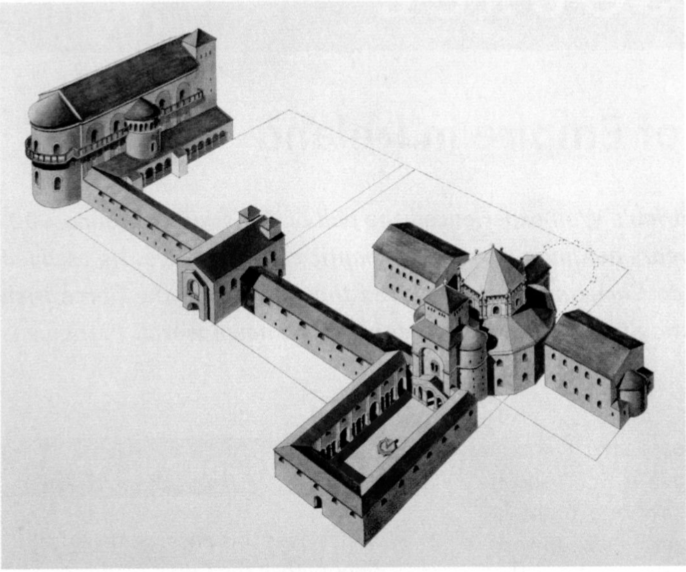

Charlemagne's Palace and Chapel. *Though not large by Byzantine or Islamic standards, Charlemagne's palace and chapel were heavy with symbolic meaning. A royal hall for banqueting in Frankish, "barbarian" style was linked by a covered walkway to the imperial domed chapel, which was meant to look like a miniature version of the Hagia Sophia of Constantinople. Outside the chapel was a courtyard, like that outside the shrine of Saint Peter at Rome.*

He and his men were representatives of the warrior class that dominated post-Roman western Europe. For a time, Roman rule had imposed an alien way of life in this rough world. After that empire faded, however, war became once again the duty and joy of the aristocrat. Buoyed up by their chieftains' mead—a heavy beer made with honey, "yellow, sweet and ensnaring"—young men eagerly followed their lords into battle "among the war horses and the blood-stained armor" (Aneirin, *Y Gododdin*, ll. 102, 840).

And although the Franks vigorously engaged in trade, that trade was based on war. In fact, Europe's principal export at this time was Europeans, and the massive sale of prisoners of war financed the Frankish empire. From Venice, which grew rich from its role as middleman, captives were sent as slaves across the sea to Alexandria, Tunis, and southern Spain. The main victims of this trade were Slavic-speaking peoples, tribal hunters and cultivators from eastern Europe. It is this trade that gave us our modern term "slave" (from *Slav*) for persons bought and sold as items of merchandise.

Yet this seemingly uncivilized and inhospitable zone offered fertile ground for Christianity to sink down roots. Although its worldwide expansion did not occur for centuries, its spiritual conquest of European peoples established institutions and fired enthusiasms that would later drive believers to carry its message to faraway lands.

A Christianity of the North

Charlemagne's empire was unquestionably primitive when compared with the Islamic empire or the Tang Empire of China. What made it significant was its location. Far removed from the old centers of high culture, it was a polity of the borderlands. It featured an expansionist Christianity that drew energy from its rough frontier mentality. Indeed, Christianity now entered a world profoundly different from the Mediterranean cities in which it had taken form.

AUGUSTINE AND THE UNIVERSAL CATHOLIC CHURCH

Christians of the west felt that theirs was the one truly universal religion. (See Primary Source: Christendom on the Edge: A View of Empire in Ireland.) Their goal was to bring rival groups into a single "catholic" church that was replacing a political unity lost in western Europe when the Roman Empire fell.

As far back as 410 CE, reacting to the Goths' sack of Rome, the Christian bishop Augustine of Hippo (a seaport in modern Algeria) had laid down the outlines of this belief. His book *The City of God* assured contemporary Christians that the barbarian takeover happening around them was not the end of the world. The "city of God" would take earthly shape in the form of the Catholic Church, and the Catholic Church was not just for Romans—it was for all times and for all peoples, "in a wide world which has always been inhabited by many differing peoples, that have so many different customs and languages, so many different forms of organization and so many languages, and who have had so many different religions" (Augustine, *City of God,* 14.1). Only one organization would bring them all to paradise: the Catholic Church.

Several developments gave rise to this attitude. First, the arrival of Christianity in northern Europe had provoked a cultural revolution. Preliterate societies now encountered a sacred text—the Bible—in a language that seemed utterly strange. Latin had become a sacred language, and books themselves were vehicles of the holy. The bound codex (see Chapter 8), which had replaced the clumsy scroll, was still a messy object. It had no divisions between words, no punctuation, no paragraphs, no chapter headings. Readers who knew Latin as a spoken language could understand the script. But Irishmen, Saxons, and Franks could not, for they had never spoken Latin; hence the care lavished in the newly Christian north on the Latin scriptures. The few parchment texts that circulated there were carefully prepared with words separated, sentences correctly punctuated and introduced by uppercase letters, and chapter headings provided. They were far more like this textbook than anything available to Romans at the height of the empire.

Second, those who produced the Bibles were starkly different from ordinary men and women. They were monks and nuns. **Monasticism** had originated in Egypt, but it suited the

PRIMARY SOURCE

Christendom on the Edge: A View of Empire in Ireland

A young Christian Briton of Roman citizenship who lived near Hadrian's Wall experienced the pull of Christianity around 400. Captured by Irish slave raiders as a teenager, Patricius spent six years herding pigs on the Atlantic coast of Mayo. He escaped but years later returned in order to convert his former captors to Christianity. He believed that in making the fierce Irish Christians, he also made them "Romans." He thus brought Christianity to the Atlantic edge of the known world. Patricius is remembered today as Saint Patrick.

16 But after I reached Ireland, well, I pastured the flocks every day. . . . I would even stay in the forests and on the mountain and would wake to pray before dawn in all weathers, snow, frost, rain. . . .

17 And it was in fact there that one night while asleep I heard a voice saying to me: 'You do well to fast, since you will soon be going to your home country;' and again, very shortly after, I heard this prophecy: 'See, your ship is ready.' And it was not near at hand but was perhaps two hundred miles away, and I had never been there and did not know a living soul there. And then I soon ran away and abandoned the man with whom I had been for six years . . . till I reached the ship.

23 And again a few years later I was in Britain with my kinsfolk. . . . And it was there that I saw one night in a vision a man coming as it were from Ireland . . . with countless letters, and he gave me one of them, and I read the heading of the letter, 'The Voice of the Irish,' and as I read these opening words aloud, I imagined at that very instant that I heard the voice of those who were beside the forest of Foclut which is near the western sea; and thus they cried, as though with one voice: 'We beg you, holy boy, to come and walk again among us.'

QUESTIONS FOR ANALYSIS

- What does this passage reveal about life in the Celtic worlds?
- How many voices or visions does Patricius experience in this passage? What other religious figure in this chapter also had a vision or a revelation?
- Based on your reading, how do St. Patrick's spiritual experiences compare to those of rulers and priests in the older Christian communities of Rome and Constantinople?

Source: St. Patrick: His Writings and Muirchu's Life, *edited and translated by A. B. E. Hood (London: Phillimore, 1978), pp. 41, 44–46, 50.*

missionary tendencies of Christianity in northern Europe particularly well. (The root of "monastic" and "monk" is the Greek *monos,* "alone": a man or a woman who chose to live alone, without the support of marriage or family.) Monasticism placed small groups of men and women in the middle of societies with which they had nothing in common. It appealed to a deep sense that the very men and women who had little in common with "normal" people were best suited to mediate between believers and God. Laypersons (common believers, not clergy) gave gifts to the monasteries and offered them protection. In return, they gained the prayers of monks and nuns and the reassurance that although they themselves were warriors and men of blood, the monks' and nuns' intercessions would keep them from going to hell.

MONKS, NUNS, AND POPES With the spread of monasticism, the Christianity of the north took a decisive turn. In Muslim (as in Jewish) societies, religious leaders emphasized what they had in common with those around them: many Islamic scholars, theologians, and mystics were married men just like the public, even merchants and courtiers. In the Christian West, the opposite was true: warrior societies honored small groups of men and women (the monks and nuns) who were utterly unlike themselves: unmarried, unfit for warfare, and intensely literate in an incomprehensible tongue. Even their hair looked different. Unlike warriors, these men were close-shaven; by contrast, the Orthodox clergy of the eastern Roman empire grew long, silvery beards (signifying wisdom and maturity; not, as in the west, the warrior's masculine strength). Catholic monks and priests shaved their heads as well.

The Catholic Church of northern Europe owed its missionary zeal to the same principles that explained the spread of Buddhism: it was a religion of monks, whose communities represented an otherworldly alternative to the warrior societies of

Celtic Bible. *Unlike the simple codex of early Christian times, the Bible came to be presented in Ireland and elsewhere in the northern world as a magical book. Its pages were filled with mysterious, intricate patterns, which imitated on parchment the jewelry and treasure for which early medieval warlords yearned.*

the time. By 800 CE, most regions of northern Europe held great monasteries, many of which were far larger than the local villages. Supported by thousands of serfs donated by kings and local warlords, the monasteries became powerhouses of prayer that kept the regions safe. Northern Christianity also gained new ties to an old center: the city of Rome. The Christian bishop of Rome had always enjoyed much prestige. But being only one bishop among many, he often took second place to his peers in Carthage, Alexandria, Antioch, and Constantinople. Though people spoke of him with respect as *papa* ("the grand old man"), many others shared that title.

By 800 CE, this picture had changed. As believers looked down from the distant north, they saw only one *papa* left in western Europe: Rome's pope. The papacy as we know it arose because of the fervor with which the Catholic Church of western Europe united behind one symbolic center, represented by the popes at Rome and the desire of new Christians in northern borderlands to find a religious leader for their hopes.

Charlemagne recognized this desire very well. In 800 CE, he went out of his way to celebrate Christmas Day by visiting the shrine of Saint Peter at Rome. There, Pope Leo III acclaimed him as the new "emperor" of the west. The ceremony ratified the aspirations of an age. A "modern" Rome—inhabited by popes, famous for shrines of the martyrs, and protected by a "modern" Christian monarch from the north—was what his subjects wanted.

The Age of the Vikings

Harun's elephant died in 813 CE, one year before Charlemagne himself. The elephant's death was noteworthy because the Franks viewed it as an omen of coming disasters. The great

The Coronation of Charlemagne. *This is how the coronation of Charlemagne at Rome in 800 CE was remembered in medieval western Europe. This painting stresses the fact that it was the pope who placed the crown on Charlemagne's head, thereby claiming him as a ruler set up by the Catholic Church for the Catholic Church. But in 800 contemporaries saw the pope as recognizing the fact that Charlemagne had already deserved to be emperor. The rise of the papacy to greater prominence and power in later medieval Europe caused this significant "re-remembering" of the event.*

Monasticism. *The great monasteries of the age of Charlemagne, such as the St. Gallen Monastery (left), were like Roman legionary settlements. Placed on the frontiers of Germany, they were vast, stone buildings, around which entire towns would gather. Their libraries, the largest in Europe, were filled with parchment volumes, carefully written out and often lavishly decorated in a "northern," Celtic style. Monasticism was also about the lonely search for God at the very end of the world, which took place in these Irish monasteries (right) on the Atlantic coast. The cells, made of loose stones piled in round domes, are called "beehives."*

beast keeled over when his handlers marched him out to confront a Viking army from Denmark. In the next half-century, the Vikings from Scandinavia exposed the weakness of Charlemagne's self-confident regime. His empire of borderland peoples met its match on the widest border of all: that between the European landmass and the mighty Atlantic (see Map 9.9).

The Vikings' motives were announced in their name, which derives from the Old Norse *vik*, "to be on the warpath." The **Vikings** sought to loot the now-wealthy Franks and replace them as the dominant warrior class of northern Europe. It was their turn to extract plunder and to sell droves of slaves across the water. They succeeded because of a deadly technological advantage: ships of unparalleled sophistication, developed by Scandinavian sailors in the Baltic Sea and the long fjords of Norway. Light and agile, with a shallow draft, they could penetrate far up the rivers of northern Europe and even be carried overland from one river system to another. Under sail, the same boats could tackle open water and cross the unexplored wastes of the North Atlantic.

In the ninth century, the Vikings set their ships on both courses. They emptied northern Europe of its treasure, sacking the great monasteries along the coasts of Ireland and Britain and overlooking the Rhine and the Seine—rivers that led into the heart of Charlemagne's empire. At the same time, Norwegian adventurers colonized the uninhabited island of Iceland, and then Greenland. By 982 CE, they had even reached the New World and established a settlement at L'Anse aux Meadows on the Labrador coast. Viking goods have been found as far west as the Inuit settlements of Baffin Island to the north of Hudson Bay, carried there along trading routes by Native Americans.

The consequences of this spectacular reach across the ocean to America were short-lived, but the penetration of eastern Europe had lasting effects. Supremely well equipped to traverse long river systems, the Vikings sailed east along the Baltic and then turned south, edging up the rivers that crossed the watershed of central Russia. Here the Dnieper, the Don, and the Volga begin to flow south into the Black Sea and the Caspian. By opening this link between the Baltic and what is now Kiev in modern Ukraine, the Vikings created an avenue of commerce that linked Scandinavia and the Baltic directly to Constantinople and Baghdad. And they added yet more slaves: Muslim geographers bluntly called this route "The Highway of the Slaves."

The Survival of the Christian Empire of the East

On reaching the Black Sea, the Vikings made straight for Constantinople. In 860 CE, more than 200 Viking long ships gathered ominously in the straits of the Bosporus, beneath the walls of Constantinople. What they found was not Charlemagne's rustic

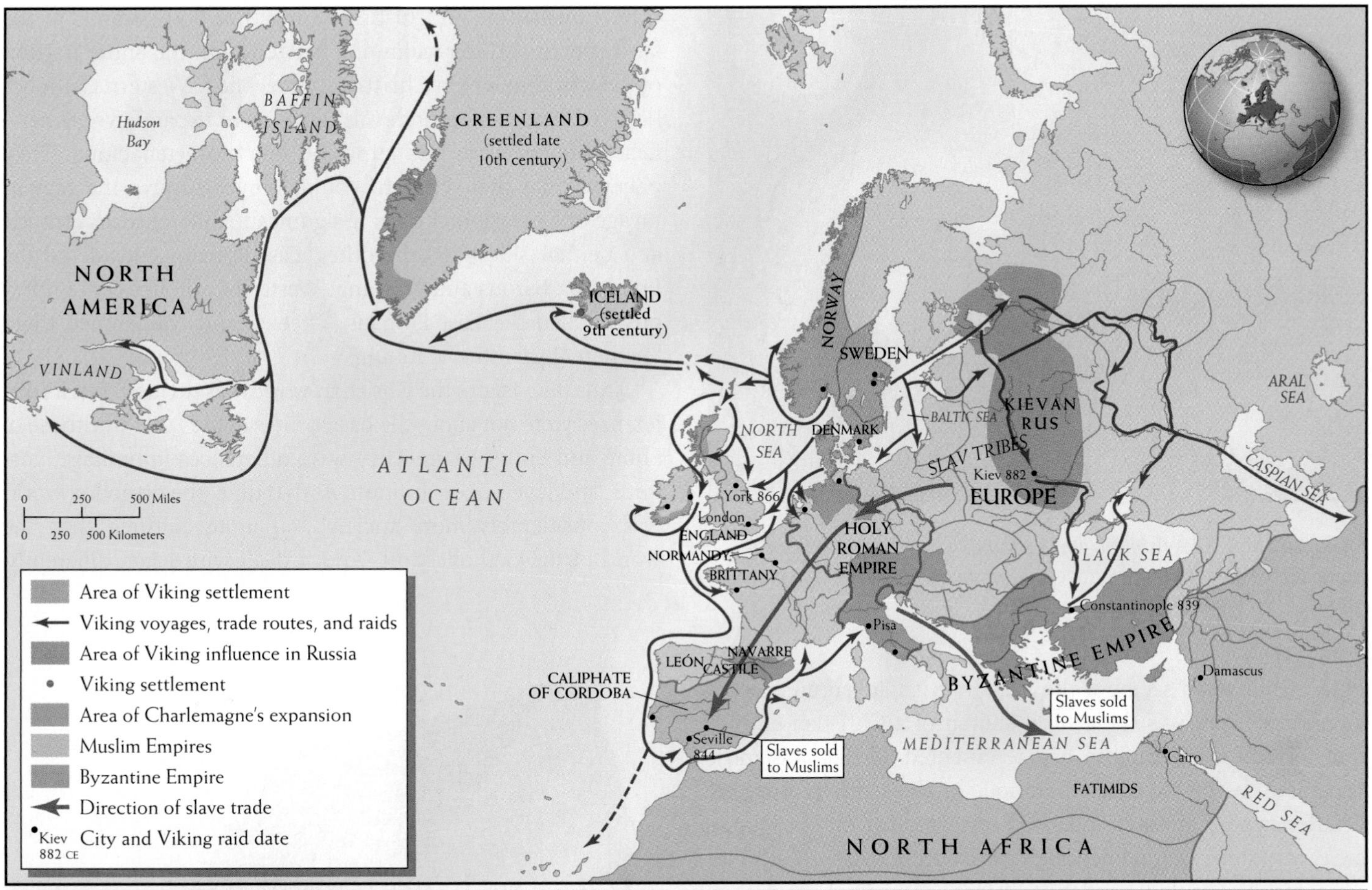

MAP 9.9 | The Age of Vikings and the Slave Trade, 800–1000 CE

Vikings from Scandinavia dramatically altered the history of Christendom.

- In what directions did the Vikings carry out their voyages, trade routes, and raids?
- What were the geographic limits of the Viking explorations in each direction?
- In what direction did the slave trade move, and what role did the Vikings and the Holy Roman emperors play in expanding the slave trade?

Aachen, but a proud city with a population exceeding 100,000 surrounded by well-engineered late Roman walls.

The Vikings had come up against a state hardened by battle. For two centuries the empire of "East Rome," centered on Constantinople, had held Islamic armies at bay. From 640 to 840 CE they faced almost yearly campaigns launched by the Islamic empire of Damascus and Baghdad, powerhouses that grew to be ten times greater than their own. For years on end, Muslim armies and navies came within striking distance of Constantinople. Each time they failed, outmaneuvered by highly professional generals and blocked by a skillfully constructed line of fortresses that controlled the roads across Anatolia. The Christian empire of East Rome fought the caliphs of Baghdad to a draw. The Viking fleet was even less well suited to assault Constantinople, as the empire of "East Rome" had a deadly technological advantage in naval warfare: Greek fire, a combination of petroleum and potassium that, when sprayed from siphons, would explode in a great sheet of flame on the water. A previous emperor had used it to destroy the Muslim fleet as it lay at anchor within sight of Constantinople. Now, a century and a half later, the experience and weaponry of East Rome were too much for the Vikings, and their raid was a spectacular failure.

GREEK ORTHODOX CHRISTIANITY In the long run, the sense of having outlasted so many military emergencies bolstered the morale of East Roman Christianity and led to its unexpected flowering. Not just Constantinople but Justinian's glorious church, the Hagia Sophia—its heart—had survived. That great building and the solemn Greek liturgy that reverberated within its domed spaces might not impress Catholic

Oseberg Ship. *The Viking ship was a triumph of design. It could be rowed up the great rivers of Europe, and, at the same time, its sail could take it across the Atlantic.*

Franks, but upon seeing it the Scandinavian adventurers were awestruck. Here was the central church of a Christian empire that for half a millennium had represented all that was most venerable in the Christian tradition. In the tenth century, as Charlemagne's empire collapsed in western Europe, large areas of eastern Europe became Greek Orthodox, not Catholic. As a result, Greek Christianity gained a spiritual empire in Southwest Asia.

The conversion of Russian peoples and Balkan Slavs to Greek Orthodox Christianity was a complex process. It reflected a deep admiration for Constantinople on the part of Russians, Bulgarians, and other Slav princes. It was an admiration as intense as that of any Western Catholic for the Roman popes. This admiration amounted to awe, as shown by the famous story of the conversion to Greek Christianity of the rulers of Kiev (descendants of Vikings):

> *The envoys reported[,]. . . "We went among the Germans [the Catholic Franks] and we saw them performing many ceremonies in their churches; but we beheld no glory there. Then we went to Greece [in fact, to Constantinople and Hagia Sophia], and the Greeks led us to the edifices where they worship their God, and we knew not whether we were in heaven or on earth. For on earth there is no such splendor or such beauty, and we are at a loss to describe it. . . . [W]e can not forget that beauty. (Cross and Sherbowitz-Westor,* The Russian Primary Chronicle, *111)*

By the year 1000, there were two Christianities: the new and confident "borderland" **Roman Catholicism** of western Europe, and an ancient **Greek Orthodoxy**, protected against extinction by the iron framework of a "Roman" state inherited from Constantine and Justinian. Together both strands of the faith constituted the realm of **Christendom**: the entire portion of the world in which Christianity prevailed. Western Catholics believed that their church was destined to expand everywhere. East Romans were less euphoric but more tenacious. They believed that their church would forever survive the regular ravages of invasion. It was a significant difference in attitude and neither side liked the other. East Romans considered the Franks barbarous and grasping; Western Catholics contemptuously called the East Romans "Greeks" and condemned them for their "Byzantine" cunning.

Thus, like Islam, the Christian world was divided. But its differences were not about the basic tenets of the faith, like those of Shiite and Sunni Islam. They were differences in heritage, customs, and levels of civilization. At that time, the orthodox world was considerably more ancient and more cultured than the world of the Catholic west. And it dealt with Islam differently.

Jelling Stone. *Carved on the side of this great stone, Christ appears to be almost swallowed up in an intricate pattern of lines. For the Vikings, complicated interweaving like serpents or twisted gold jewelry was a sign of majesty: hence, in this, the first Christian monument in Denmark, Christ is part of an ancient pattern of carving, which brought good luck and victory to the king.*

At Constantinople, eastern Christianity held off Muslim forces that constantly threatened the integrity of the great city and its Christian hinterlands. In the west, by contrast, Muslim expansionism reached all the way to the Iberian Peninsula. Western Christendom, led by the Roman papacy, did not feel the same intimidation from Islam. It set about spreading Christianity to pagan tribes in the north, and it began to contemplate retaking lands from the Muslims.

The period 600–1000 CE saw heightened movement across cultural boundaries as well as an insistence on the distinctiveness of individual societies. Commodities, technological innovations, ideas, merchants, adventurers, and scholars traveled from one end of Afro-Eurasia to the other, and up and down coastal Africa. Spreading religion into new frontiers accompanied this mercantile activity. The proximity of the period's two powerhouses—Abbasid Islam and Tang China—facilitated the dynamic movement.

CONCLUSION

Despite the intermixing, new political and cultural boundaries were developing that would split this landmass in ways it could never have imagined. The most important dividing force was Islam, which challenged and slowed the spread of Christianity. As a consequence, Afro-Eurasia's major cultural zones began to compete in terms of religious and cultural doctrines. The Islamic Abbasid Empire pushed back the borders of the Tang Empire. But the conflict grew particularly intense between the Islamic and Christian worlds, where the clash involved faith as well as frontiers.

The Tang Empire revived Confucianism, insisting on its political and moral primacy as the foundation of a new imperial order, and it embraced the classical written language as another unifying element. By doing so the Tang counteracted universalizing foreign religions—notably Buddhism but also Islam—spreading into the Chinese state. The same adaptive strategies influenced new systems on the Korean peninsula and in Japan.

In some circumstances, faith followed empire and relied on rulers' support or tolerance to spread the word. This was the case especially in East Asia. At the opposite extreme, empire followed faith—as in the case of Islam, whose believers endeavored to spread their empire in every conceivable direction. The Islamic empire and its successors represented a new force: expanding political power backed by one God whose instructions were to spread his message. In the worlds of Christianity, a common faith absorbed elements of a common culture (shared books, a language for learned classes). But in the west, political rulers never overcame inhabitants' intense allegiance to local authority.

While universalizing religions expanded and common cultures grew, debate raged within each religion over foundational principles. In spite of the diffusion of basic texts in "official" languages, variations of Christianity, Islam, and Buddhism proliferated as each belief system spread. The period demonstrated that religion, reinforced by prosperity and imperial resources, could bring peoples together in unprecedented ways. But it could also, as the next chapter will illustrate, drive them apart in bloodcurdling confrontations.

AFTER YOU READ THIS CHAPTER

Review and research on **STUDYSPACE:** wwnorton.com/studyspace

TRACING THE GLOBAL STORYLINES

FOCUS ON: *Faith and Empire*

The Islamic Empire

- Warriors from the Arabian Peninsula defeat Byzantine and Sasanian armies and establish an Islamic empire stretching from Morocco to South Asia.
- The Abbasid state takes over from the Umayyads, crystallizes the main Islamic institutions of the caliphate and Islamic law, and promotes cultural achievements in religion, philosophy, and science.
- Disputes over Muhammad's succession lead to a deep and enduring split between Sunnis and Shiites.

Tang China

- The Tang dynasty dominates East Asia, including Japan and Korea.
- Tang dynasts balance Confucian ideals with Buddhist thought and practice.
- A common written language and shared philosophy, rather than a universalizing religion, integrate the Chinese state.

Christian Europe

- Monks, nuns, and Rome-based popes spread Christianity throughout western Europe.
- Constantinople-based Eastern Orthodoxy survives the spread of Islam.

CHRONOLOGY

The Islamic World

Life of Muhammad **570–632**

Umayyad caliphate **661–750**

East Asia

Prince Shotuko initiates Taika reforms in Japan **574–622**

Europe

Arab armies conquer much of Byzantine Empire but the empire survives **632–661**

600 CE **700 CE**

KEY TERMS

caliphate p. 324

Christendom p. 354

civil service examinations p. 337

eunuchs p. 340

Greek Orthodoxy p. 354

Islam p. 321

jihad p. 322

meritocracy p. 338

monasticism p. 349

Muhammad p. 321

Quran p. 321

Roman Catholicism p. 354

sharia p. 326

Shiites p. 330

Shinto p. 346

Sunnis p. 330

Tang dynasty p. 333

ulama p. 324

Vikings p. 352

STUDY QUESTIONS

1. **Analyze** the impact of the spread of Islam on Afro-Asian societies. How did the large Islamic empire shape the movement of peoples, ideas, innovations, and commodities across the vast landmass?
2. **Describe** the process through which an expanding Islam fostered an agricultural revolution. What crops and cultivation techniques were involved?
3. **Compare and contrast** the spread of Islam, Christianity, and Buddhism between 600 and 1000 CE. What was the geographic range of each religious community? Through which methods did each religion gain new converts?
4. **Explain** the origins and basic concepts of Islam. How similar to and different from other religions that began in Southwest Asia—such as Judaism, Christianity, and Zoroastrianism—was this new religious outlook?
5. **Analyze** the successes and failures of Islamic leaders in creating one large empire to govern Islamic communities. What opponents challenged this goal?
6. **Describe** the Tang dynasty's attempts to restore political unity to East Asia. How did Tang leaders react to the growth of universal religions within their realm?
7. **Describe** the state structure that emerged in Korea and Japan during this era. How did other developments in Afro-Eurasia, such as the spread of universal religions, shape these new states?
8. **Compare and contrast** Christian communities in western Europe to those in eastern Europe and the Byzantine Empire. What factors contributed to each region's distinctiveness?
9. **Analyze** the Vikings' impact on world history during this era. How did they shape developments in the Christian world especially?

Abbasid caliphate **750–1250**

Fatimid Shiite regime founded in Egypt **969**

Tang dynasty in China **618–906**

Koryo state assumes control over much of Korea **918**

Catholic Church based in Rome begins converting much of northern Europe into Christian communities **8th century**

Charlemagne unites much of western Europe into a short-lived Christian kingdom **768–814**

Vikings raid much of Europe and establish strong commercial links across eastern Europe **9th and 10th centuries**

800 CE | **900 CE** | **1000 CE**

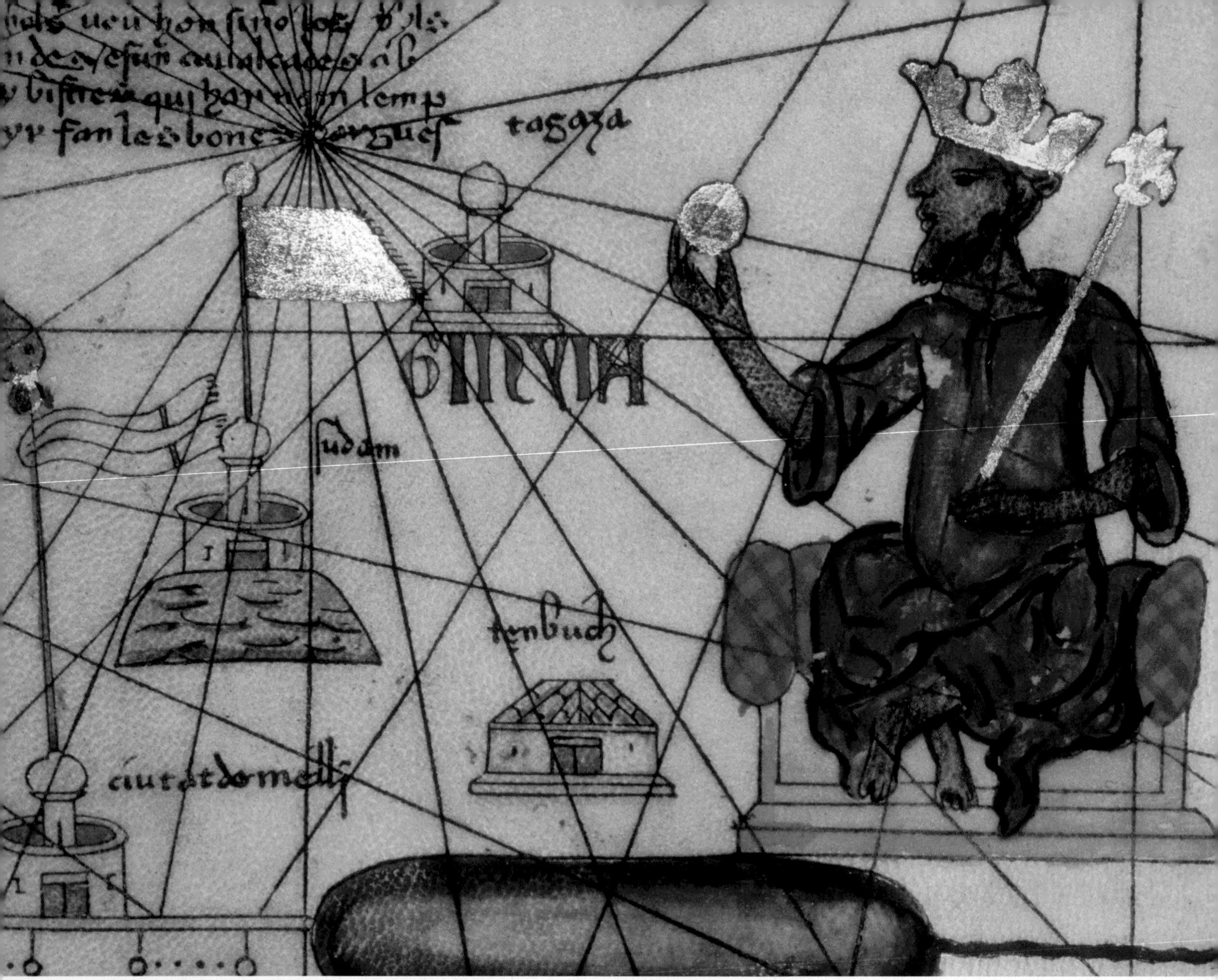

BEFORE YOU READ THIS CHAPTER

GLOBAL STORYLINES

- Trade routes shift from land to sea, transforming coastal cities into global trading hubs and elevating Afro-Eurasian trade to unprecedented levels.
- Intensified trade, linguistic, and religious integration generate the foundational cultural spheres that we recognize today: China, India, Islam, and Europe.
- The rise of the Mongol Empire integrates the world's foundational cultural spheres.

CHAPTER OUTLINE

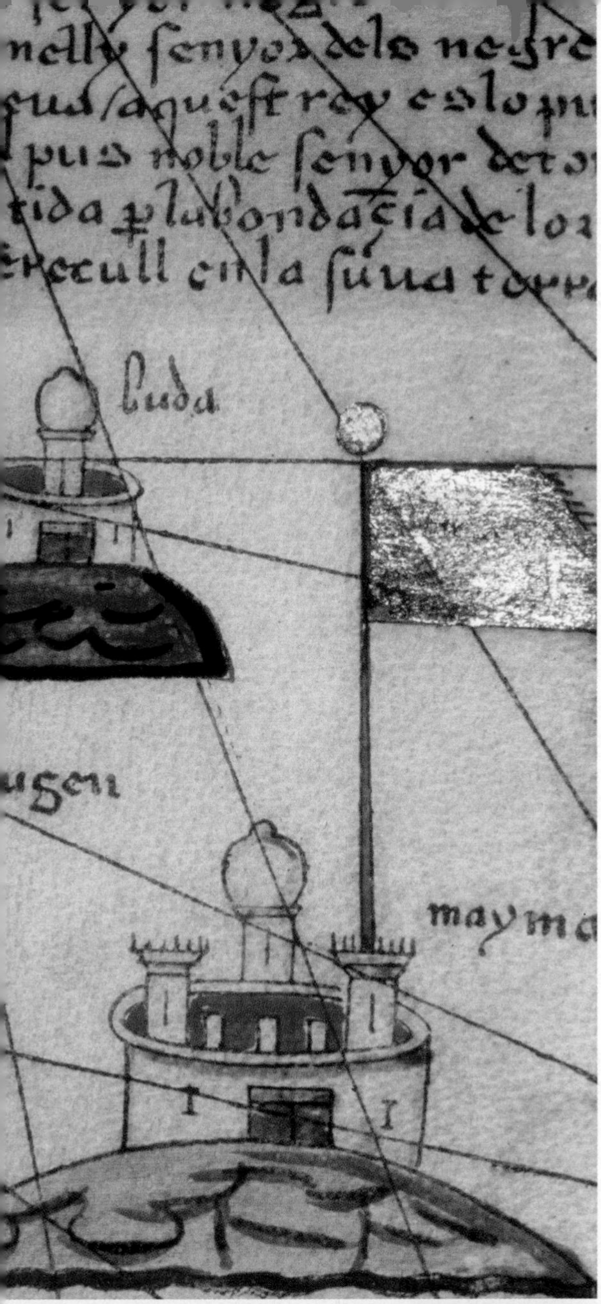

10

Becoming "The World," 1000–1300 CE

FOCUS QUESTIONS

- What factors led to the explosion of global trade between 1000 and 1300?
- What institutions and beliefs linked the peoples of the world's four major cultural spheres?
- To what extent do political, economic, and cultural integration occur in the America and sub-Saharan Africa during this era?
- How did Mongol conquest reshape Afro-Eurasian landscapes?

In the late 1270s two Christian monks, Bar Sāwmā and Markōs, voyaged into the heart of Islam. They were not Europeans. They were Uighurs, a Turkish people of central Asia, many of whom had converted to Christianity centuries earlier. Sent by the mighty Mongol ruler Kubilai Khan as he prepared to become the first emperor of China's Yuan dynasty, the monks were supposed to worship at the temple in Jerusalem. But the Great Khan also had political ambitions. He was eager to conquer Jerusalem, held by the Muslims. Accordingly, he dispatched the monks as agents to make alliances with Christian kings in the area and to gather intelligence about his potential enemy in Palestine.

By 1280, conflict and conquest had transformed many parts of the world. But friction was simply one manifestation of cultures brushing up against one another. More important was trade. Indeed, Bar Sāwmā and Markōs lingered at the magnificent trading hub of Kashgar in what is now western China, where caravan routes converged in a market for jade, exotic spices, and precious silks. Later, at Baghdad, the monks parted ways. Bar Sāwmā visited Constantinople (where the king gave him gold and silver), Rome (where he met with the pope at the shrine of Saint Peter), and

Paris (where he saw that city's vibrant university) before deciding to return to China, where the Christians of the east awaited his reports. In the end, neither monk ever returned. Yet their voyages exemplified the crisscrossing of people, money, and goods along the trade routes and sea-lanes that connected the world's regions. For just as religious conflict was a hallmark of this age, so was a surge in trade, migration, and global exchange.

The period brought to a climax many centuries of human development, and it ushered in a new, very long cycle of cultural interaction from which emerge three interrelated themes. First, trade was shifting from land-based routes to sea-based routes. Coastal trading cities began to dramatically expand. Second, intensified trade and linguistic and religious integration generated the world's four major cultural "spheres," whose inhabitants were linked by shared institutions and beliefs: China, India, Islam, and Europe. Not all cultures turned into "spheres," though. In the Americas and sub-Saharan Africa there was not the same impulse to integrate regions, which remained more fragmented but thrived nonetheless. Third, the rise of the Mongol Empire represented the peak in the long history of ties and tensions between settled and mobile peoples. From China to Persia and as far as eastern Europe, the Mongols ruled over much land in the world's major cultural spheres.

COMMERCIAL CONNECTIONS

Revolutions at Sea

By the tenth century, sea routes were eclipsing land networks for long-distance trade. Improved navigational aids, refinements in shipbuilding, better mapmaking, and new legal arrangements and accounting practices made shipping easier and slashed the costs of seaborne trade. The numbers testify to the power of the maritime revolution: while a porter could carry about 10 pounds over long distances, and animal-drawn wagons could move 100 pounds of goods over small distances, the Arab dhows plying the Indian Ocean were capable of transporting up to 5 tons of cargo. (**Dhows** are ships with triangle-shaped sails, called lateens, that allow best use of the monsoon trade winds on the Arabian Sea and the Indian Ocean.) As a result some coastal ports, like Mogadishu in eastern Africa, became vast transshipment centers for a thriving trade across the Indian Ocean.

A new navigational instrument spurred this boom: the needle **compass**. This Chinese invention initially identified promising locations for houses and tombs, but eleventh-century sailors from Guangzhou (anglicized as Canton) used it to find their way on the high seas. The device spread rapidly. Not only did it allow sailing under cloudy skies, but it also improved mapmaking. And it made all the oceans, including the Atlantic, easier to navigate.

Now shipping became less dangerous. Navigators relied on lateen-rigged dhows between the Indian Ocean and the Red Sea, heavy junks in the South China seas, and Atlantic "cogs," which linked Genoa to locations as distant as the Azores and Iceland. They also enjoyed the protection of political authorities, such as the Song dynasts in China, in guiding the trading fleets in and out of harbors. The Fatimid caliphate in Egypt, for instance, profited from maritime trade and defended merchant fleets from pirates. Armed convoys of ships escorted commercial fleets and regularized the ocean traffic. The system soon spread

Dhow. *This modern dhow in the harbor of Zanzibar displays the characteristic triangle sail. The triangle sail can make good use of the trade monsoon and thus has guided dhows on the Arabian Sea since ancient times.*

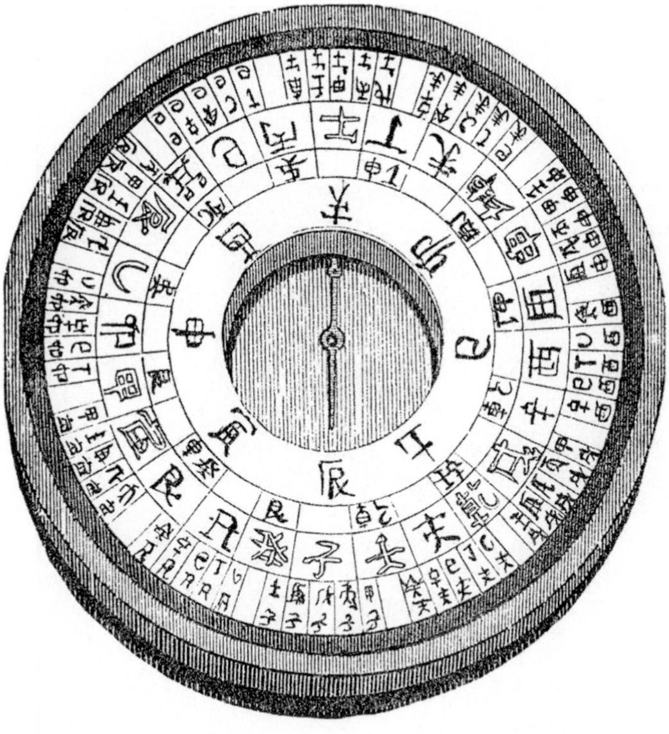

Antique Chinese Compass. *Chinese sailors from Canton started to use needle compasses in the eleventh century. By the thirteenth century, needle compasses were widely used on ships in the Indian Ocean and were starting to appear in the Mediterranean.*

to North Africa and southern Spain. Most of these shipping firms were family-based, and they sent young men of the family, sometimes servants or slaves, to work in India. Wives in Cairo could expect gifts from their husbands to arrive with the fleet.

Changes in navigation ushered in the demise of overland routes. Silk Road merchants eventually gave up using camel trains, caravansaries (inns for travelers), and oasis hubs as they switched to the sea-lanes. The shift took centuries, but overland routes and camels were no match for multiple-masted cargo ships.

Commercial Contacts

The opening of the sea-lanes also tapped into changes in world agriculture (see Map 10.1). By 1000 CE, major innovations in irrigation techniques, carried out over many centuries and in numerous locations, yielded enormous returns. New strains of cereals—and in the Americas, the refinement of maize—led to grain cultivation in vast areas that had been too cold or arid to sustain it previously. Clover, alfalfa, and other newly domesticated grasses became fodder for healthier, stronger, and fatter animals. Agriculture pushed into new regions, buoying population growth and surpluses that now could be shipped over great distances.

Global Commercial Hubs

Long-distance trade spawned the growth of commercial cities. These urban hubs became cosmopolitan nerve centers of an increasingly integrated world. Beginning in the late tenth century, regional centers became major anchorages of the maritime trade: in the west, the Egyptian port cities of Alexandria and Cairo; in the east, the Chinese city of Quanzhou; in the Malaysian Archipelago, the city of Melaka; and near the tip of the Indian peninsula, the port of Kollan (often anglicized as Quilon). These hubs thrived under the political stability of powerful dynasts who recognized that the free-for-all of trade and market life would generate wealth for them. Yemeni rulers, for instance, offered shelter to fleets in return for taxes collected on cargoes; so did Egyptian rulers for fleets moving through the Red Sea.

THE EGYPTIAN ANCHORAGE Cairo and Alexandria were the Mediterranean's main maritime commercial centers. Cairo was home to numerous Muslim and Jewish trading firms, and Alexandria was their lookout post on the Mediterranean.

Silk yarn and textiles were the most popular commodities in the global trade involving Egypt. It was through Alexandria that Europeans acquired silks from China, especially the coveted *zaytuni* (satin) fabric from Quanzhou. Spanish silks also passed through Alexandria, heading to eastern Mediterranean markets. But the new commercial hubs handled much more. Goods from the Mediterranean included olive oil, glassware, flax, corals, and metals. Gemstones and aromatic perfumes poured in from India. Also changing hands were minerals and chemicals for dyeing or tanning, and raw materials such as timber and bamboo. The real novelties were paper and books. Hand-copied Bibles, Talmuds, Qurans, legal and moral works, grammars in various languages, and Arabic books became the first best sellers of the Mediterranean.

Fleets in the Mediterranean and Red Sea were so effective, in part based on armed convoys provided by the caliphs, that ships arrived on schedule and were relied on for postal service. When an Egyptian trader in Kollam, India, around 1100, was delayed on his journey home, he was able to send a consoling message to his wife in Cairo. He apologized for his absence but promised gifts including pearl bracelets, red silk garments, a bronze basin, a ewer, and a slave girl: "I shall send them, if God wills it, with somebody who is traveling home" (Goitein, "New Light," 179).

The Islamic legal system also promoted a favorable business environment. Consider how legal specialists got around the rule that might have brought commerce to a halt—the *sharia*'s (see Chapter 9) prohibition against earning interest on loans. With the clerics' blessing, Muslim traders formed partnerships between those who had capital to lend and those who needed

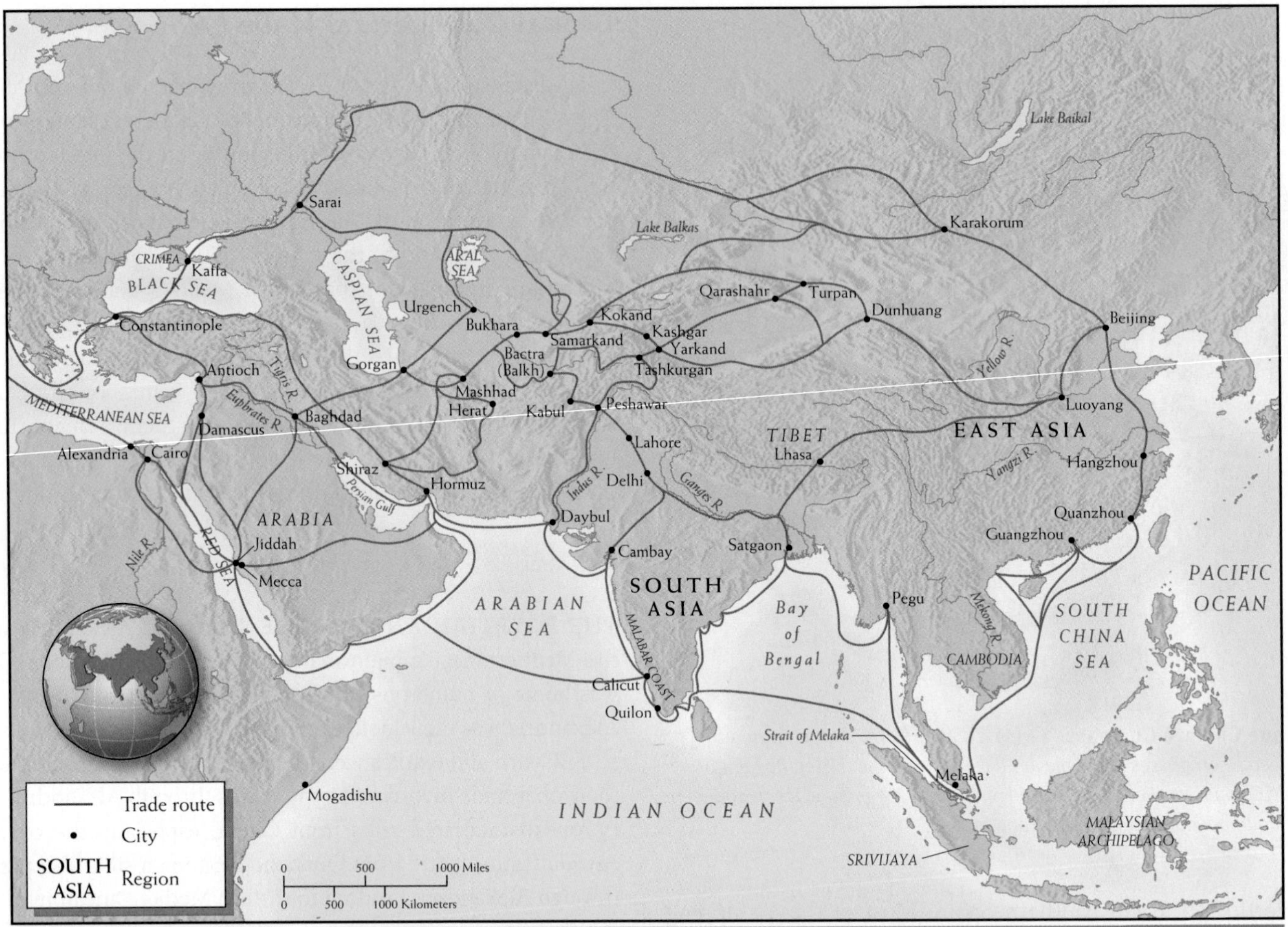

MAP 10.1 | Afro-Eurasian Trade, 1000–1300

During the early second millennium, Afro-Eurasian merchants increasingly turned to the Indian Ocean to transport their goods. Locate the global hubs of Kollam, Alexandria, Cairo, Melaka, and Quanzhou on this map.

- What regions do each of these global hubs represent?
- Based on the map, why would sea travel have been preferable to overland travel?
- According to the text, what revolutions in maritime travel facilitated this development?

money to expand their businesses. These partnerships enabled owners of capital to entrust their money or commodities to agents who, after completing their work, returned the investment and a share of the profits to the owners—and kept the rest as their reward. The English word "risk" derives from the Arabic *rizq*, the extra allowance paid to merchants in lieu of interest.

THE ANCHORAGE OF QUANZHOU In China, Quanzhou was as busy as Cairo and Alexandria. The Song government set up offices of Seafaring Affairs in its three major ports: Canton, Quanzhou, and an area near present-day Shanghai in the Yangzi delta. In return for a portion of the taxes, these offices registered cargoes, sailors, and traders, while guards kept a keen eye on the traffic.

All foreign traders were guests of the governor, who doubled as the Chief of Seafaring Affairs. Part of his mandate was to summon favorable winds for shipping. Every year, the governor took his place on a high perch facing the harbor, in front of a rock cliff filled with inscriptions that recorded the wind-calling rituals. Traders of every origin witnessed the rite, then joined the dignitaries for a sumptuous banquet.

Ships departing from Quanzhou and other Chinese ports were junks—large, flat-bottomed ships with internal sealed bulkheads and stern-mounted rudders. Their multiple watertight compartments increased stability; the largest ones boasted four decks, six masts, and a dozen sails and could carry 500 men. Those departing Quanzhou headed for Srivijaya (Java) in the Malay Archipelago, navigating through the Strait of Melaka, a choke

Mazu. *Many Quanzhou sailors sought protection at the shrine of the goddess Mazu. According to legend, before assuming godhood Mazu had performed many miracles. Her temple became prominent after 1123, when Quanzhou's governor survived a storm at sea while returning from Korea. After that, sailors and their families burned incense for the goddess and prayed for her aid in keeping them safe at sea.*

point between the South China Sea and the Indian Ocean. The final destination was Kollam on the coast of southwest India. Traders heading farther west in Arab-dominated seas unloaded their cargo and boarded small Arabian dhows.

Arabs, Persians, Jews, and Indians, as well as Chinese, traded at Quanzhou, and some stayed on to manage their businesses. Perhaps as many as 100,000 Muslims lived there during the Song dynasty. And traders could become power brokers in their own right. Although most foreign merchants did not reside apart from the rest of the city, they had their own buildings for religious worship. A mosque from this period is still standing on a busy street. Hindu traders living in Quanzhou worshipped in a Buddhist shrine where statues of Hindu deities stood alongside those of Buddhist gods.

THE CROSSROADS OF AFRO-EURASIA: MELAKA Because of its strategic location and proximity to Malayan tropical produce, Melaka became a key cosmopolitan city. Indian, Javanese, and Chinese merchants and sailors spent months in such ports selling their goods, purchasing return cargo, and waiting for the winds to change so they could reach their next destination. During peak season, Southeast Asian ports teemed with colorfully dressed foreign sailors, local Javanese artisans who produced finely textured batik handicrafts, and money-grubbing traders. The latter converged from all over Asia to flood the markets with their merchandise and to search for pungent herbs, aromatic spices, and agrarian staples such as quick-ripening strains of rice to ship out.

THE TIP OF INDIA In the tenth century, the Chola dynasty in south India supported a nerve center of maritime trade between China and the Red Sea and the Mediterranean. Although the Chola golden age lasted only about two generations, trade continued to flourish. Many Muslim traders settled in Malabar, on the southwest coast of the Indian peninsula, and Kollam became a major cosmopolitan hub. Dhows arrived, laden not only with goods from the Red Sea and Africa but also with traders, sojourners, and fugitives. Chinese junks unloaded silks and porcelain, and picked up passengers and commodities for East Asian markets. Sailors and traders strictly observed the customs of this trading port, for it was good business to respect others' norms and values while doing business with them.

Muslims, the largest foreign community, lived in their own neighborhoods. They shipped horses from Arab countries to India and the southeast islands, where kings viewed them as symbols of royalty. Because the animals could not survive well in those climates, the demand was constant. There was even trade in elephants and cattle from tropical countries, though most goods were spices, perfumes, and textiles. Traders knew each other well, and personal relationships were key. When striking a deal with a local merchant, a Chinese trader would mention his Indian neighbor in Quanzhou and that family's residence in Quilon. Global commercial hubs relied on friendship and family to keep their businesses thriving across religious and regional divides.

SUB-SAHARAN AFRICA COMES TOGETHER

During this period sub-Saharan Africa's relationship to the rest of the world changed dramatically. Before 1000 CE sub-Saharan Africa had never been a world entirely apart, but now its integration became much stronger. Africans and outsiders were determined to overcome the sea, river, and desert barriers that had blocked sub-Saharan peoples from participating in long-distance trade and intellectual exchanges (see Map 10.2). Increasingly, interior hinterlands found themselves touched by the commercial and migratory impulses emanating from the Indian Ocean and Arabian Sea transformations.

West Africa and the Mande-Speaking Peoples

Once the camel bridged the Sahara Desert (see Chapter 9), the flow of commodities and ideas linked sub-Saharan Africa to North Africa and Southwest Asia. As the savanna region became increasingly connected to developments in Afro-Eurasia, Mande-speaking peoples emerged as the primary agents for integration within and beyond West Africa. Exploiting their expertise in commerce and political organization, the Mande edged out rivals.

The Mande, or Mandinka, homeland was a vast area, 1,000 miles wide, between the bend in the Senegal River to the west and the bend of the Niger River to the east, stretching more than 2,000 miles from the Senegal River in the north to the Bandama River in the south. This was where the kingdom of Ghana had arisen (see Chapter 9) and where Ghana's successor state—the Mandinka state of Mali, discussed below—emerged around 1100.

The Mande-speaking peoples were constantly on the go and marvelously adaptable. By the eleventh century they were spreading their cultural, commercial, and political hegemony from the high savanna grasslands southward into the woodlands and tropical rain forests stretching to the Atlantic Ocean. Those dwelling in the rain forests organized small-scale societies led by local councils, while those in the savanna lands developed centralized forms of government under sacred kingships. These peoples believed that their kings had descended from the gods and that they enjoyed the gods' blessing.

As the Mande broadened their territory to the Atlantic coast, they gained access to tradable items that residents of the interior were eager to have—notably kola nuts and malaguetta peppers, for which the Mande exchanged iron products and textile manufactures. By 1300 the Mandinka merchants had followed the Senegal River to its outlet on the coast and then pushed their commercial frontiers farther inland and down the coast. Thus, even before European explorers and traders arrived in the mid-fifteenth century, West African peoples had created dynamic networks linking the hinterlands with coastal trading hubs.

From the eleventh century to the late fifteenth century, the most vigorous businesses were those that spanned the Sahara Desert. The Mande-speaking peoples, with their far-flung commercial networks and highly dispersed populations, dominated this trade as well. Here one of the most prized commodities was salt, mined in the northern Sahel around the city of Taghaza; it was in demand on both sides of the Sahara. Another valuable commodity was gold, mined within the Mande homeland and borne by camel caravans to the far northern side of the Sahara, where traders exchanged it for various manufactures. Equally important in West African commerce were slaves, who were shipped to the settled Muslim communities of North Africa and Egypt.

The Empire of Mali

As booming trade spawned new political organizations, the empire of Mali became the Mande successor state to the kingdom of Ghana. Founded in the twelfth century, it exercised political sway over a vast area for three centuries.

The Mali Empire represented the triumph of horse warriors, and its origins are enshrined in an epic, *The Epic of Sundiata,* involving the dynasty's founder, the legendary Sundiata. Sundiata might well have actually existed. Arab historian Ibn Khaldun referred to him by name and reported that he was "their [Mali's] greatest king" (Levtzion and Pouwels, p. 64). His triumph, which occurred in the thirteenth century, marked the victory of new cavalry forces over traditional foot soldiers. Horses—which had always existed in some parts of Africa—now became prestige objects of the savanna peoples, symbols of state power. (See Primary Source: An African Epic.)

Under the Mali Empire, commerce was in full swing. With Mande trade routes extending to the Atlantic Ocean and spanning the Sahara Desert, West Africa was no longer an isolated periphery of the central Muslim lands. Mali's most famous sovereign, Mansa Musa (r. 1312–1332), made a celebrated hajj, or pilgrimage to Mecca, in 1325–1326, traveling through Cairo and impressing crowds with the size of his retinue and his displays of wealth, especially many dazzling items made of gold.

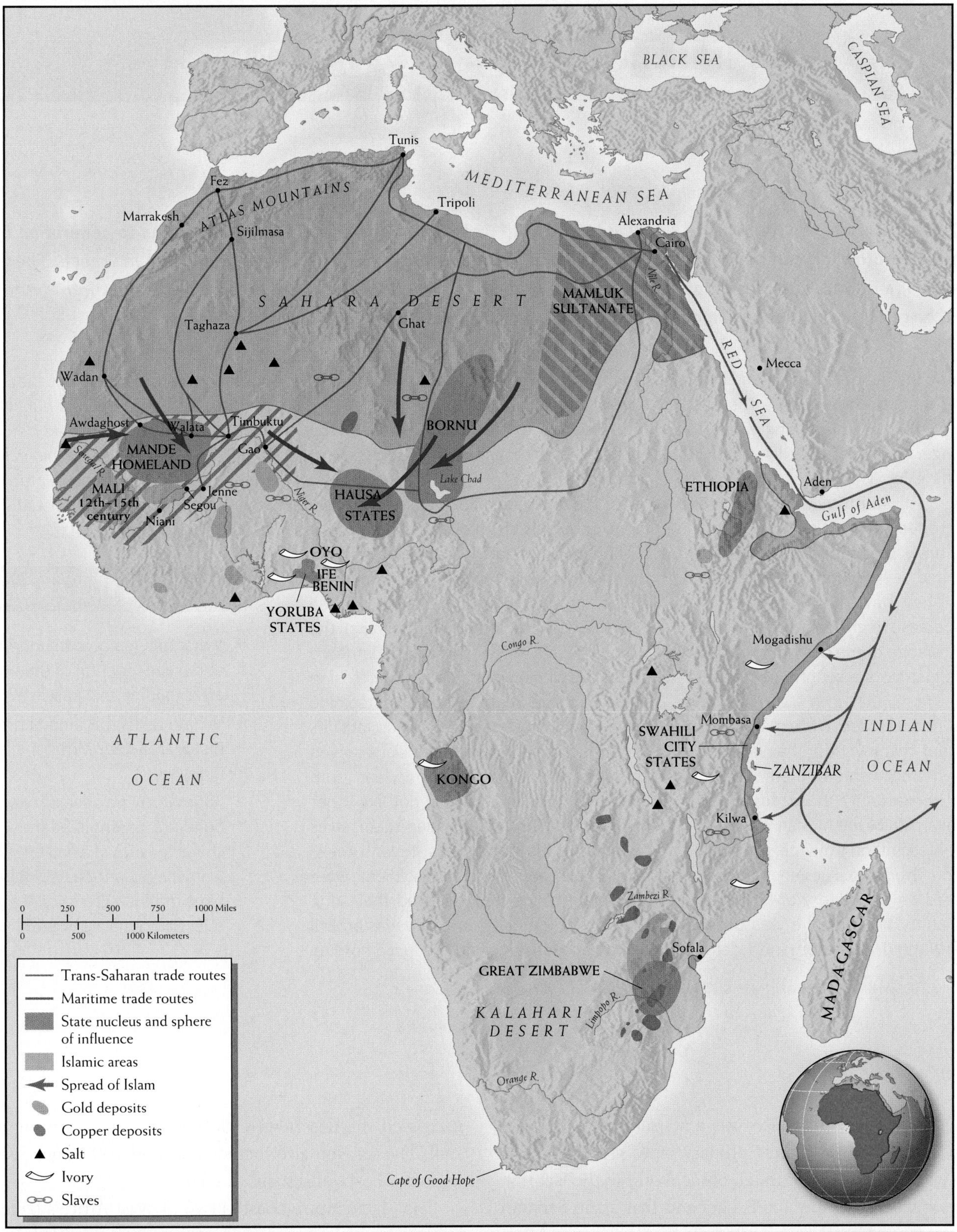

MAP 10.2 | Sub-Saharan Africa, 1300

Increased commercial contacts influenced the religious and political dimensions of sub-Saharan Africa at this time. Compare this map to Map 9.3 (p. 331).

- Where had strong Islamic communities emerged by 1300?
- According to this map, what types of activity were affecting the Mande homeland?
- To what extent had sub-Saharan Africa "come together"?

PRIMARY SOURCE

An African Epic

The traditional story of the founding of the kingdom of Mali was passed down orally from generation to generation by griots, counselors, and other official historians to the royal family. Only in 1960 was it finally written down in French. The narrative recounts the life of Sundiata, the heroic founder of the Mali state. The following passage provides insight into the role of the narrator (the griot) in the Malian kingdom, as well as some of the qualities of good and bad rulers.

Griots know the history of kings and kingdoms and that is why they are the best counsellors of kings. Every king wants to have a singer to perpetuate his memory, for it is the griot who rescues the memories of kings from oblivion, as men have short memories.

Kings have prescribed destinies just like men, and seers who probe the future know it. They have knowledge of the future, whereas we griots are depositories of the knowledge of the past. But whoever knows the history of a country can read its future.

Other peoples use writing to record the past, but this invention has killed the faculty of memory among them. They do not feel the past any more, for writing lacks the warmth of the human voice. . . .

I, Djeli Mamoudou Kouyaté, am the result of a long tradition. For generations we have passed on the history of kings from father to son. The narrative was passed on to me without alteration and I deliver it without alteration, for I received it free from all untruth.

Listen now to the story of Sundiata, the Na'Kamma, the man who had a mission to accomplish.

At the time when Sundiata was preparing to assert his claim over the kingdom of his fathers, Soumaoro was the king of kings, the most powerful king in all the lands of the setting sun. The fortified town of Sosso was the bulwark of fetishism against the word of Allah. For a long time Soumaoro defied the whole world. Since his accession to the throne of Sosso he had defeated nine kings whose heads served him as fetishes in his macabre chamber. Their skins served as seats and he cut his footwear from human skin. Soumaoro was not like other men, for the jinn had revealed themselves to him and his power was beyond measure. So his countless sofas [soldiers] were very brave since they believed their king to be invincible. But Soumaoro was an evil demon and his reign had produced nothing but bloodshed. Nothing was taboo for him. His greatest pleasure was publicly to flog venerable old men. He had defiled every family and everywhere in his vast empire there were villages populated by girls whom he had forcibly abducted from their families without marrying them.

QUESTIONS FOR ANALYSIS

- What are you able to understand about the function of the griot after reading this passage?
- What makes this kind of oral history reliable? What makes it unreliable?
- Soumaoro, the adversary of Sundiata, exemplified the characteristics of a bad ruler. What were they? Can you tell, indirectly, what the characteristics of a good ruler (like Sundiata) were?

Source: Sundiata: An Epic of Old Mali, *compiled by D. T. Niane (Harlow, UK: Longman Group, 1965), pp. 40–41.*

Mansa Musa's visit to Cairo was a sensation in its time. The stopover in one of Islam's primary cities astonished the Egyptian elite and awakened much of the world to the fact that Islam had spread far below the Sahara and that a sub-Saharan state could mount such an ostentatious display. Mansa Musa spared no expense to impress his hosts. He sent ahead an enormous gift of 50,000 dinars (a unit of money widely used in the Islamic world at this time), and his entourage included soldiers, wives, consorts, and as many as 12,000 slaves, many wearing rich brocades woven of Persian silks. And there was gold—a lot of it. He brought immense quantities and distributed it lavishly during his three-month stay. Preceding his retinue as it crossed the desert were 500 slaves, each carrying a golden staff. The caravan also included around 100 camels, each bearing two 300-pound sacks of gold.

The Mali Empire boasted two of West Africa's largest cities. Jenne, an ancient entrepôt, was a vital assembly point for caravans laden with salt, gold, and slaves preparing for journeys west to the Atlantic coast and north over the Sahara. The city had originated as an urban settlement around 200 BCE; by 1000 CE most substantial structures were made of brick. Around the city ran an impressive wall over eleven feet thick at its base and extending over a mile in length. More spectacular was the city of Timbuktu; founded around 1100 as a seasonal

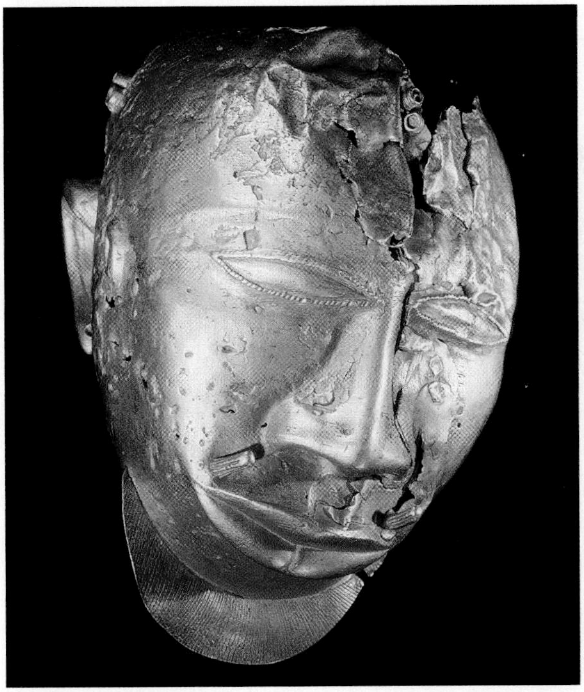

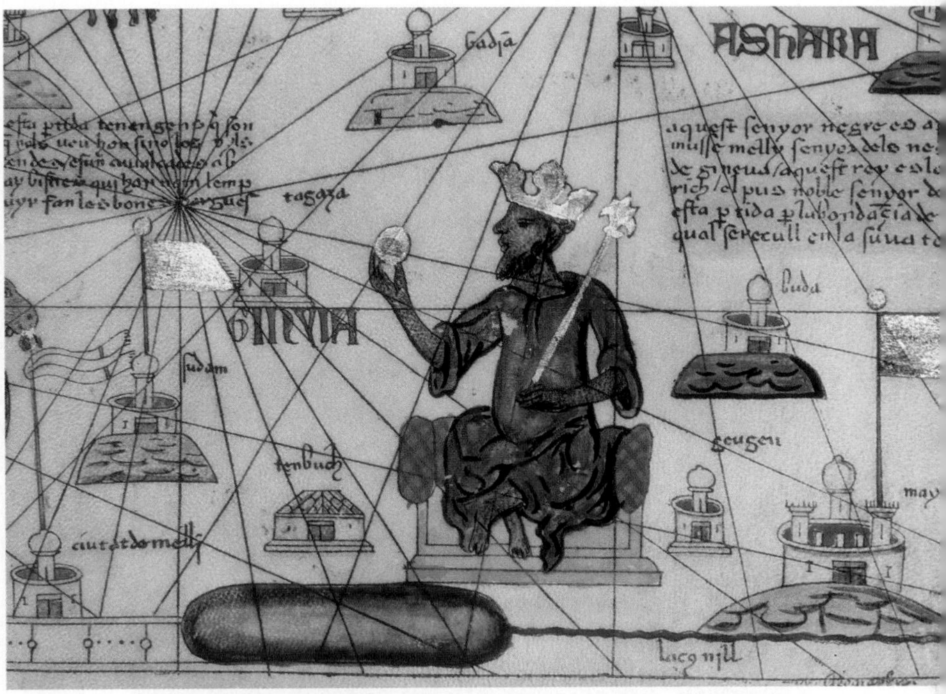

West African Asante Gold. *Although this gold head from the kingdom of Asante (*left*) was made in the eighteenth century, it shows the artistic abilities of the West African peoples. The head probably belonged to the Asante ruler, known as the Asantehene, and symbolized his power and wealth. This 1375 picture (*right*) shows the king of Mali on his throne, surrounded by images of gold.*

camp for nomads, it grew in size and importance under the patronage of various Malian kings. By the fourteenth century it was a thriving commercial and religious center famed for its two large mosques, which are still standing. Timbuktu was also renowned for its intellectual vitality. Here, West African Muslim scholars congregated to debate the tenets of Islam and to ensure that the faithful, even when distant from the Muslim heartland, practiced their religion with no taint of pagan observances. These clerics acquired treatises on Islam from all over the world for their personal libraries, remnants of which remain to this day.

East Africa and the Indian Ocean

Africa's eastern and southern regions were also integrated into long-distance trading systems. Because of monsoon winds, East Africa was a logical end point for much of the Indian Ocean trade. Swahili peoples living along that coast became brokers for trade from the Arabian Peninsula, the Persian Gulf territories, and the western coast of India. Merchants in the city of Kilwa on the coast of present-day Tanzania brought ivory, slaves, gold, and other items from the interior and shipped them to destinations around the Indian Ocean.

The most valued commodity in the trade was gold. Shona-speaking peoples grew rich by mining the ore in the highlands between the Limpopo and Zambezi rivers. By the year 1000, the Shona had founded up to fifty small religious and political centers, each one erected from stone to display its power over the peasant villages surrounding it. Around 1100 one of these centers, Great Zimbabwe, stood supreme among the Shona. Built on the fortunes made from gold, its most impressive landmark was a massive elliptical building made of stone fitted so expertly that it needed no grouting. The buildings of Great Zimbabwe probably housed the king and may also have contained smelters for melting down gold.

The Trans-Saharan and Indian Ocean Slave Trade

African slaves were as valuable as African gold in shipments to the Mediterranean and Indian Ocean markets. There had been a lively trade in African slaves (mainly from Nubia) into pharaonic Egypt well before the Common Era. After Islam spread into Africa and sailing techniques improved, the slave trade across the Sahara Desert and Indian Ocean boomed.

Although the Quran attempted to mitigate the severity of slavery, requiring Muslim slave owners to treat their slaves kindly

Great Zimbabwe. *These walls surrounded the city of Great Zimbabwe, which was a center of the gold trade between the East African coastal peoples and traders sailing on the Indian Ocean. Great Zimbabwe flourished during the thirteenth, fourteenth, and fifteenth centuries.*

and praising manumission as an act of piety, nonetheless the African slave trade flourished under Islam.

Africans became slaves during this period much as they had before: some were prisoners of war; others were considered criminals and sold into slavery as punishment. Their duties were varied. Some slaves were pressed into military service, rising in a few instances to positions of high authority. Others with seafaring skills worked as crewmen on dhows or as dockworkers. Still others, mainly women, were domestic servants, and many became concubines of Muslim political figures and businessmen. Slaves also did forced labor on plantations, the most oppressive being the agricultural estates of lower Iraq. There, slaves endured fearsome discipline and revolted in the ninth century in one of the great slave wars documented in world history. Yet in this era plantation-slave labor like that which later became prominent in the Americas was the exception, not the rule. Slaves were more prized as additions to family labor or as status symbols for their owners.

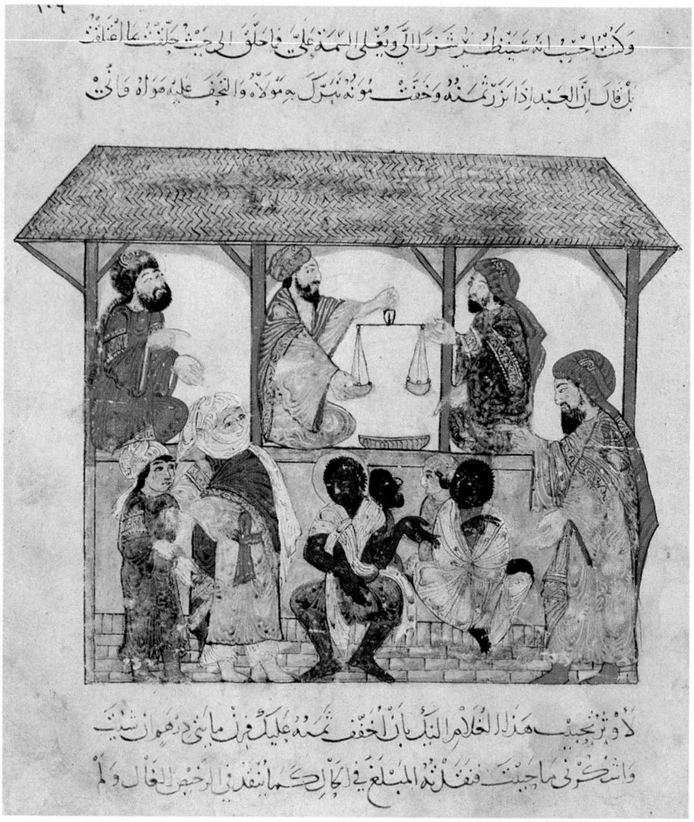

Slave Market. *Slaves were a common commodity in the marketplaces of the Islamic world. Turkish conquests during the years from 1000 to 1300 put many prisoners on the slave market.*

ISLAM IN A TIME OF POLITICAL FRAGMENTATION

Islam underwent the same burst of expansion, prosperity, and cultural diversification that swept through the rest of Afro-Eurasia (see Map 10.3 and Map 10.4). Whereas prosperity fostered greater integration in other regions, the peoples of Islam remained politically fractured. As in China, efforts to unite under a common rulership failed, giving way to defeats by marauding outsiders. The attempt to uphold centralized rule ended cataclysmically in 1258 with the Mongol sacking of Baghdad. Unlike China, Muslim leaders were unable to reunite after their collapse.

Becoming the "Middle East"

Islam responded to political fragmentation by undergoing major changes, many prompted by contacts and conflicts with neighbors. Commercial networks, sustained by Muslim merchants, carried the word of the Quran far and wide. As Islam spread, it attracted more converts.

Decisive in the spread of Islam was a popular form of the religion, highly mystical and communal, called **Sufism**. The

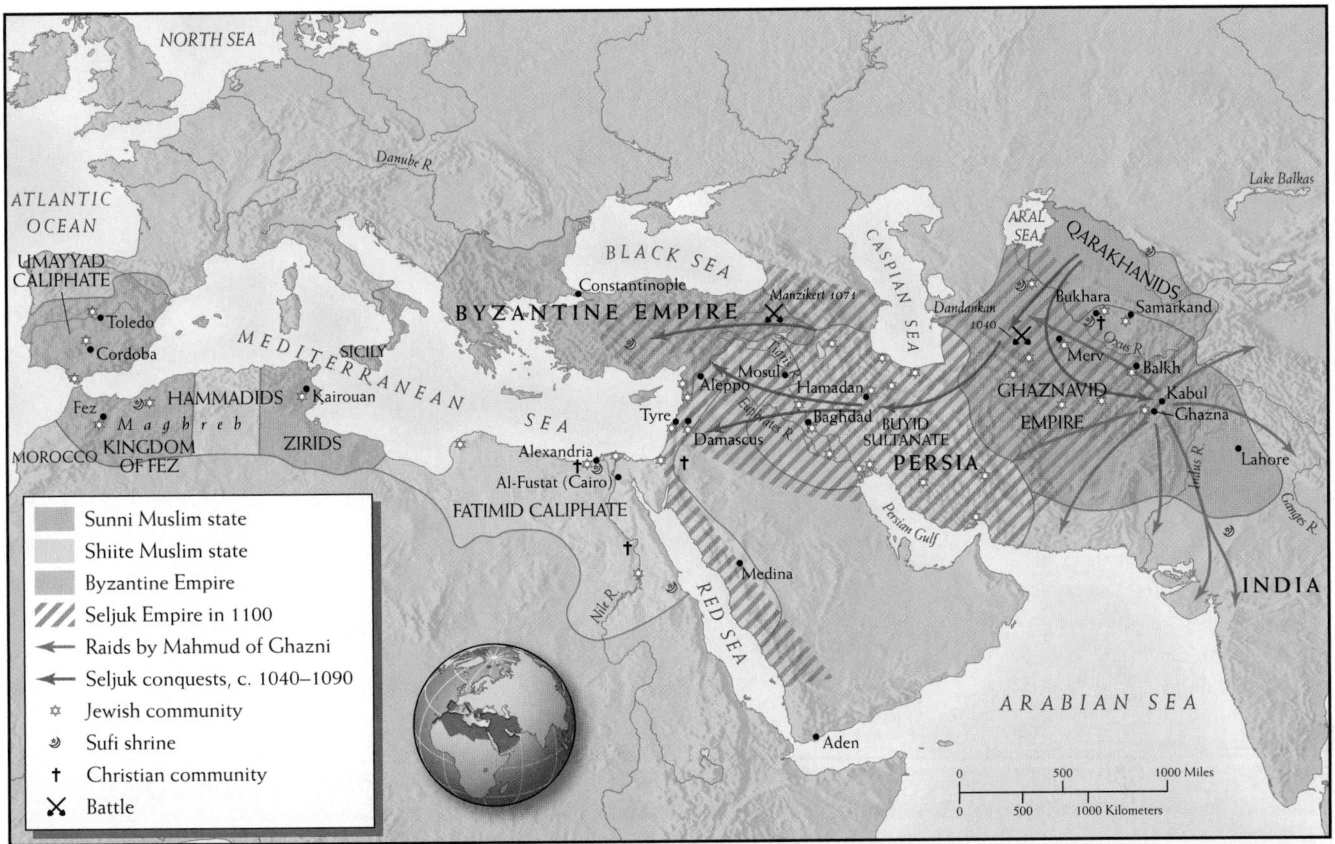

MAP 10.3 | Islam between 900 and 1200

The Muslim world experienced political disintegration in the first centuries of the second millennium.

- According to the map key, what were the two major types of Muslim states in this period and what were the two major empires?
- What were the sources of instability in this period according to the map?
- As Islam continued to expand in this period, what challenges did it face?

term *Sufi* comes from the Arabic word for wool (*suf*), which many of the early mystics wrapped themselves in to mark their penitence. Seeking closer union with God, they also performed ecstatic rituals such as repeating over and over again the name of God. In time, groups of devotees gathered to read aloud the Quran and other religious tracts. Although many clerics despised the Sufis and loathed their seeming lack of theological rigor, the movement spread with astonishing speed. Sufism's emotional content and strong social bonds, sustained in Sufi brotherhoods, made its appeal to common people irresistible. Sufi missionaries carried the universalizing faith to India, across the Sahara Desert, and to many other distant locations. It was from within these brotherhoods that Islam became truly a religion for the people.

Sufism had an intellectual and artistic dynamism that complemented its missionizing zeal. This was especially true of poetry, where the mystics' desire to experience God's love found ready expression. Most admired of Islam's mystical love poets

Dervishes. *Today, the whirling dance of dervishes is a tourist attraction, as shown in this picture from the Jerash Cultural Festival in Jordan. Though Sufis in the early second millennium* CE *were not this neatly dressed, the whirling dance was an important means of reaching union with God.*

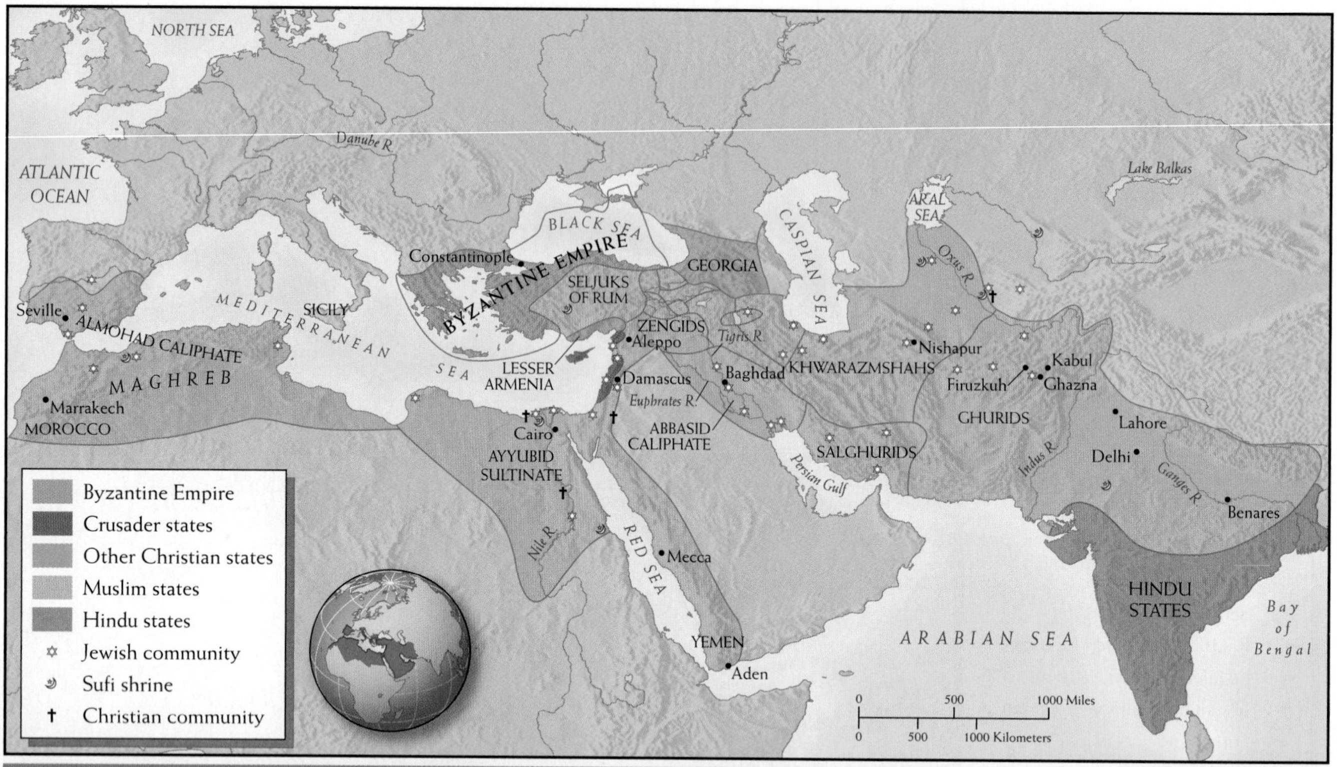

MAP 10.4 | Islamic and Hindu States and the Byzantine Empire between 1200 and 1300

Islam continued to expand after the thirteenth century.

- Where were its largest and most important gains according to the map?
- How did other religions fare under Islamic rule in this period?
- How was Islam able to continue to expand in this period?

was Jalal al-Din Rumi, spiritual founder of the Medlevi Sufi order that became famous for the ceremonial dancing of its whirling devotees, known as dervishes. Rumi, who wrote in Persian, celebrated all forms of love, spiritual and sexual, and preached a universalistic religious message:

> What is to be done of Muslims? For I do not recognize myself.
>
> I am neither Christian, nor Jew, nor Gabr (Zoroastrian), nor Muslim.

Another Sufi mystic and advocate of the universality of religions, the Spanish Muslim poet Ibn Arabi, wrote in Arabic:

> My heart has been of every form; it is a pasture for gazelles and a convent for Christian monks.
>
> And a temple for idols and the pilgrim's kaaba, and the tables of the Torah and the book of the Quran.

As trade increased and more converts appeared in the Islamic lands, urban and peasant populations came to understand the faith practiced by the political, commercial, and scholarly upper classes even while they remained attached to their Sufi brotherhood ways. Islam became even more accommodating, embracing Persian literature, Turkish ruling skills, and Arabic-language contributions in law, religion, literature, and science. In this way the world acquired a "core" region centered in what we now call the Middle East united by a shared faith and pulsating with religious and commercial energies.

Afro-Eurasian Merchants

By the thirteenth century, as the old Islamic heartland became the crossroads for commercial networks, Muslim merchants were the world's premier traders. A universal religion, an imagined political unity projected by the Abbasid caliphate, the spread of the Arabic language, and Islamic law allowed entrepreneurs of varied backgrounds to flourish. Muslim traders were joined by Armenian, Indian, and Jewish merchants, building on family connections all across Afro-Eurasia. (See Primary Source: The Merchants of Egypt.)

PRIMARY SOURCE

The Merchants of Egypt

The most comprehensive collection of eleventh- and twelfth-century commercial materials from the Islamic world comes from a repository connected to the Jewish synagogue in Cairo. (It was the custom of the Jewish community to preserve, in a special storeroom, all texts that mention God.) These papers, a rich source of information about the Jewish community in Egypt at that time, touch on all manner of activities: cultural, religious, judicial, political, and commercial. The following letter is addressed to Joseph ibn 'Awkal, one of Egypt's leading merchants in the eleventh century.

Dear and beloved elder and leader, may God prolong your life, never take away your rank, and increase his favors and benefactions to you.

I inform you, my elder, that I have arrived safely. I have written you a letter before, but have seen no answer. Happy preoccupations—I hope. In that letter I provided you with all the necessary information.

I loaded nine pieces of antimony (kohl), five in baskets and four in complete pieces, on the boat of Ibn Jubār—may God keep it; these are for you personally, sent by Mūsā Ibn al-Majjānī. On this boat, I have in partnership with you—may God keep you—a load of cast copper, a basket with (copper) fragments, and two pieces of antimony. I hope God will grant their safe arrival. Kindly take delivery of everything, my lord.

I have also sent with Banāna a camel load for you from Ibn al-Majjānī and a camel load for me in partnership with you—may God keep you. He also carries another partnership of mine, namely, with 'Ammā r Ibn Yijū, four small jugs (of oil).

With Abū Zayd I have a shipload of tin in partnership with Salāma al-Mahdawī. Your share in this partnership with him is fifty pounds. I also have seventeen small jugs of s[oap]. I hope they arrive safely. They belong to a man [called . . .] r b. Salmūn, who entrusted them to me at his own risk. Also a bundle of hammered copper, belonging to [a Muslim] man from the Maghreb, called Abū Bakr Ibn Rizq Allah. Two other bundles, on one is written Abraham, on the other M[. . .]. I agreed with the shipowner that he would transport the goods to their destination. I wish my brother Abū Nasr—may God preserve him—to take care of all the goods and carry them to his place until I shall arrive, if God wills.

Please sell the tin for me at whatever price God may grant and leave its "purse" (the money received for it) until my arrival. I am ready to travel, but must stay until I can unload the tar and oil from the ships.

Please take care of this matter and take from him the price of five skins (filled with oil). The account is with Salāma.

Al-Sabbāgh of Tripoli has bribed Bu 'l-'Alā the agent, and I shall unload my goods soon.

Kindest regards to your noble self and to my master [. . . and] Abu 'l-Fadl, may God keep them.

QUESTIONS FOR ANALYSIS

- List all the different kinds of commodities that the letter talks about.
- How many different people are named as owners, partners, dealers, and agents?
- What does the letter reveal about the ties among merchants and about how they conducted their business?

Source: Letters of Medieval Jewish Traders, *translated with introductions and notes by S. D. Goitein (Princeton, NJ: Princeton University Press, 1973), pp. 85–87.*

Diversity and Uniformity in Islam

Not until the ninth and tenth centuries did Muslims become a majority within their own Abbasid Empire (see Chapter 9). From the outset, Muslim rulers and clerics had to deal with large non-Muslim populations, even as these groups were converting to Islam. Rulers through the ***dhimma* system** accorded non-Muslims religious toleration as long as the non-Muslims accepted Islam's political dominion. Jewish, Christian, and Zoroastrian communities were free to choose their own religious leaders and to settle internal disputes in their own religious courts. They did, however, have to pay a special tax, the *jizya*, and be deferential to their rulers. The dhimma system spared the Islamic world some of the religious conflict that afflicted other areas, and it made Islamic cities hospitable environments for traders from around the world.

While tolerant, Islam was an expansionist, universalizing faith. Intense proselytizing carried the sacred word to new frontiers and, in the process, reinforced the spread of Islamic institutions that supported commercial exchange. There were also moments of intense religious passion within Islam's frontiers, especially when Muslim rulers feared that Christian minorities would align with the Europeans pressing on their borders. Ugly incidents left some Christian churches in flames. Pressures to convert to Islam were unremitting at this time. After a surge of conversions to Islam from the ninth century onward, the Christian Copts of Egypt shrank to a small community and never recovered their numbers.

Political Integration and Disintegration

Just as the Islamic faith was increasing its reach from Africa to India and ultimately to Southeast Asia, its political institutions began to fragment. From 950 to 1050, it appeared that Shiism would be the vehicle for uniting the Islamic world. The Fatimid Shiites had established their authority over Egypt and much of North Africa (see Chapter 9), and the Abbasid state in Baghdad fell under the sway of a Shiite family. Each group created universities, in Cairo and Baghdad, respectively, ensuring that leading centers of higher learning were Shiite. But divisions also sapped Shiism, as Sunni Muslims began to challenge Shiite power and establish their own strongholds. The last of the Shiite Fatimid rulers gave way to a new Sunni regime in Egypt. In Baghdad, the Shiite Buyid family surrendered to a group of Sunni strongmen.

The new strongmen were mainly Turks. Their people had been migrating into the Islamic heartland from the Asian steppes since the eighth century, bringing superior military skills and an intense devotion to Sunni Islam. Once established in Baghdad, they founded outposts in Syria and Palestine, and then moved into Anatolia after defeating Byzantine forces in 1071. But this Turkish state also crumbled, as tribesmen quarreled for preeminence. By the thirteenth century the Islamic heartland had fractured into three regions. In the east (central Asia, Iran, and eastern Iraq), the remnants of the old Abbasid state persevered. Caliphs succeeded one another, still claiming to speak for all of Islam yet deferring to their Turkish military commanders. Even in the core of the Islamic world—Egypt, Syria, and the Arabian Peninsula—where Arabic was the primary tongue, military men of non-Arab origin held the reins of power. Farther west in North Africa, Arab rulers prevailed, but the influence of Berbers, some from the northern Sahara, was extensive. Islam was a vibrant faith, but its polities were splintered.

What Was Islam?

Buoyed by Arab dhows on the high seas and carried on the backs of camels, following commercial networks, Islam had been transformed from Muhammad's original goal of creating a religion for Arab peoples. By 1300, its influence spanned Afro-Eurasia and enjoyed multitudes of non-Arabic converts. It attracted urbanites and rural peasants alike, as well as its original audience of desert nomads. Its extraordinary universal appeal generated an intense Islamic cultural flowering around 1000 CE.

Some people worried about the preservation of Islam's true nature as, for example, Arabic ceased to be the language of many Islamic believers. True, the devout read and recited the Quran in its original tongue, as the religion mandated. But Persian was now the language of Muslim philosophy and art, and Turkish was the language of law and administration. Moreover, Jerusalem and Baghdad no longer stood alone as Islamic cultural capitals. Other cities, housing universities and other centers of learning, promoted alternative, vernacular versions of Islam. In fact, some of the most dynamic thought came from Islam's fringes.

At the same time, diversity fostered cultural blossoming in all fields of high learning. Indicative of the prominence of the Islamic faith and the Arabic language in thought was the legendary Ibn Rushd (1126–1198). Known as Averroës in the western world, where scholars pored over his writings, he wrestled with the same theological issues that troubled western scholars. Steeped in the writings of Aristotle, Ibn Rushd became Islam's most thoroughgoing advocate for the use of reason in understanding the universe. His knowledge of Aristotle was so great that it influenced the thinking of the Christian world's leading philosopher and theologian, Thomas Aquinas (1225–1274). Above all, Ibn Rushd believed that faith and reason could be compatible. He also argued for a social hierarchy in which learned men would command influence akin to Confucian scholars in China or Greek philosophers in Athens. Ibn Rushd believed that the proper forms of reasoning had to be entrusted to the educated class—in the case of Islam, the *ulama*—which would serve the common people.

Equally powerful works appeared in Persian, which by now was expressing the most sophisticated ideas of culture and religion. Best representing the new Persian ethnic pride was Abu al-Qasim Firdawsi (920–1020), a devout Muslim who believed in the importance of pre-Islamic Sasanian traditions. In the epic poem *Shah Namah,* or *Book of Kings,* he celebrated the origins of Persian culture and narrated the history of the Iranian highland peoples from the dawn of time to the Muslim conquest. As part of his effort to extol a pure Persian culture, Firdawsi attempted to compose his entire poem in Persian unblemished by other languages, even avoiding Arabic words.

By the fourteenth century, Islam had achieved what early converts would have considered unthinkable. No longer a religion of a minority of peoples living among Christian, Zoroastrian, and Jewish communities, it had become the people's faith. The agents of conversion were mainly Sufi saints and Sufi

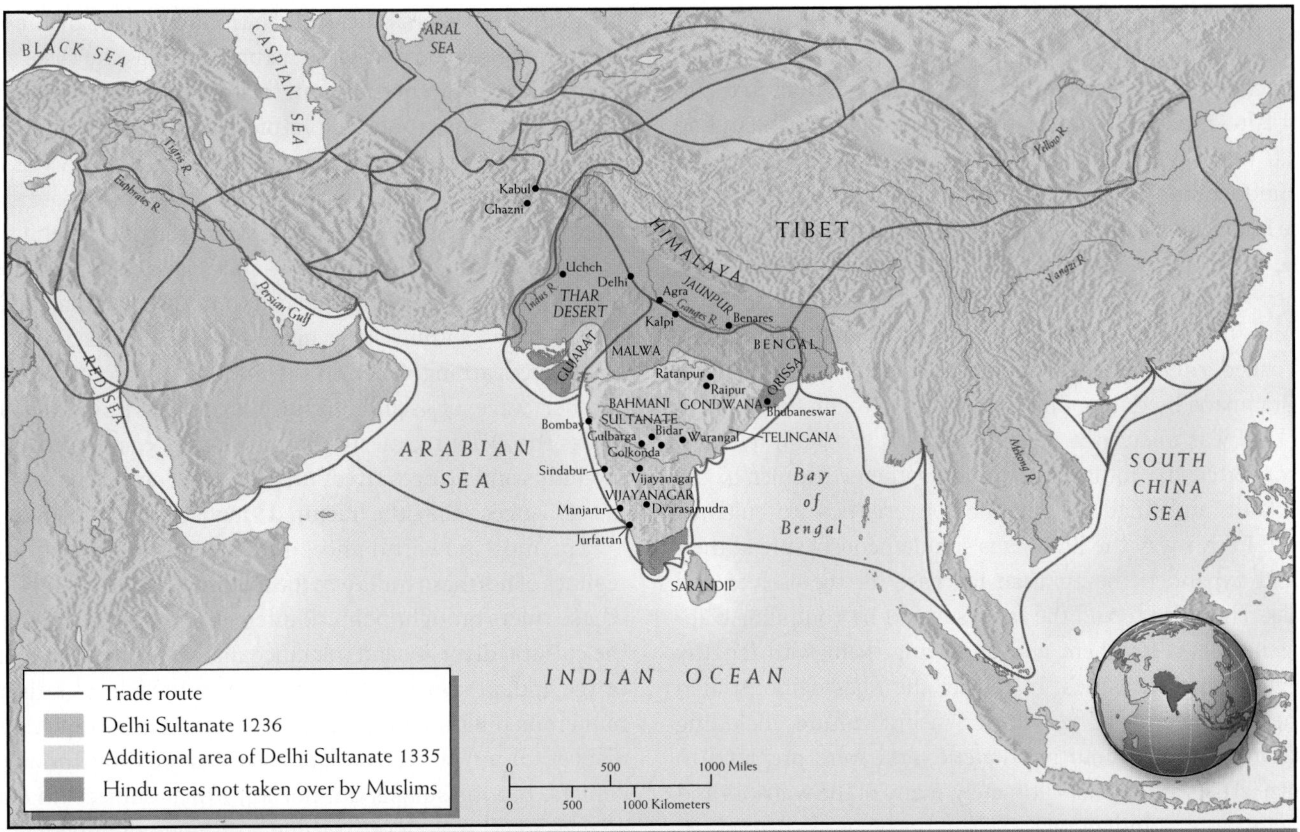

MAP 10.5 | South Asia in 1300

As the fourteenth century began, India was a blend of many cultures. Politically, the Turkish Muslim regime of the Delhi Sultanate dominated the region. Use the map key to identify the areas dominated by the Delhi Sultanate.

- How do you suppose the trade routes helped to spread the Muslims' influence in India?
- Now use the key to find the Hindu areas. Based on your reading, what factors accounted for Hinduism's continued appeal despite the Muslims' political power?

brotherhoods—not the *ulama,* whose exhortations had little impact on common people. The Sufis had carried their faith far and wide to North African Berbers, to Anatolian villagers, and to West African animists who believed that things in nature have souls. Ibn Rushd worried about the growing appeal of what he considered an "irrational" piety. But his message failed, because he did not appreciate that Islam's expansionist powers rested on its appeal to common folk. While the *sharia* was the core of Islam for the educated and scholarly classes, Sufism spoke to ordinary men and women.

During this period, Islam became one of the four cultural spheres that would play a major role in world history, laying the foundation for what would become known as the Middle East up through the middle of the twentieth century. Islam became the majority religion of most of the inhabitants of Southwest Asia and North Africa, Arabic became the everyday language for most people, and the Turks began to establish themselves as the dominant rulership force, ultimately creating the Ottoman empire, which would last into the twentieth century. The region became integral in transregional trade and the creation and maintenance of knowledge.

INDIA AS A CULTURAL MOSAIC

Trade and migration affected India, just as it did the rest of Asia and Africa. As in the case of Islam, India's growing cultural interconnections and increasing prosperity produced little political integration. Under the canopy of Hinduism it remained a cultural mosaic; Islamic faith now joined others to make the region even more diverse (see Map 10.5). India illustrates how cross-cultural integration can just as easily preserve diversity as promote internal unity.

Rajas and Sultans

India became an intersection for the trade, migration, and culture of Afro-Eurasian peoples. With 80 million inhabitants in 1000 CE, it had the second-largest population in the region, not far behind China's 120 million. Turks spilled into India as they had the Islamic heartlands, bringing their newfound Islamic beliefs. But the newcomers encountered an ethnic and religious mix that they would add to without upsetting the balance.

Before the Turks arrived, India was splintered among rival chiefs called ***rajas***. These leaders gained support from high-caste Brahmans by doling out land grants to them. Since much of the land was uncultivated, the Brahmans first built temples, then converted the indigenous hunter-gatherer peoples to the Hindu faith, and finally taught the converts how to cultivate the land. In this way the Brahmans simultaneously spread their faith and expanded the agrarian tax base for themselves and the rajas. They also repaid the rajas' support by compiling elaborate genealogies for them and endowing them with lengthy and legitimizing ancestries. In return, the rajas demonstrated that they, too, were well versed in Sanskrit culture, including equestrian skills and courtly etiquette, and were prepared to patronize artists and poets. Ultimately, many of the warriors and their heirs became Indian rajas.

Invasions and Consolidations

When the Turkish warlords began entering India, the rajas had neither the will nor resources to resist them after centuries of fighting off invaders. The Turks introduced their own customs while accepting local social structures, such as the caste system. Concerned to promote Islamic culture, the Turks constructed grandiose mosques and built impressive libraries where scholars could toil and share their wisdom with the court. Previous invaders from central Asia had reinforced the rajas' power base through intermarriage. But the Turks upset the balance of the raja kingdoms. Mahmud of Ghazna (971–1030) launched many expeditions from the Afghan heartland into northern India and, eager to win status within Islam, made his capital, Ghazni, a center of Islamic learning. Later, in the 1180s, Muhammad Ghuri led another wave of Islamic Turkish invasions from Afghanistan across the Delhi region in northern India. Wars raged between the Indus and Ganges rivers until one by one, all the way to the lower Ganges valley, the fractured kingdoms of the rajas toppled.

The most powerful and enduring of the Turkish Muslim regimes of northern India was the **Delhi Sultanate** (1206–1526), whose rulers brought political integration but also strengthened the cultural diversity and tolerance that were already a hallmark of the Indian social order. Sultans recruited local artisans for numerous building projects, and palaces and mosques became displays of Indian architectural tastes adopted by Turkish newcomers. But the sultans did not force their subjects to convert, so that South Asia never became an Islamic-dominant country. Nor did they display much interest in the flourishing commercial life along the Indian coast, permitting these areas to develop on their own and allowing Persian Zoroastrian traders to settle on the coast around modern-day Mumbai (Bombay). Farther south, the Malabar coast became the preserve of Arab traders.

Lodi Gardens. *The Lodi dynasty was the last Delhi sultanate. Lodi Gardens, the cemetery of Lodi sultans, placed central Asian Islamic architecture in an Indian landscape, thereby creating a scene of "heaven on the earth."*

Hindu Temple. *When Buddhism started to decline in India, Hinduism was on the rise. Numerous Hindu temples were built, many of them adorned with ornate carvings like this small tenth-century temple in Bhubaneshwar, east India.*

What Was India?

During the eleventh, twelfth, and thirteenth centuries India became the most diverse and, in some respects, most tolerant region in Afro-Eurasia. It is from this era that India arises as an impressive but fragile mosaic of cultures, religions, and ethnicities.

When the Turks arrived, the local Hindu population, having had much experience with foreign invaders and immigrants, assimilated these intruders as they had done earlier peoples. Before long, the newcomers thought of themselves as Indians who, however, retained their Islamic beliefs and steppe ways. They continued to wear their distinctive trousers and robes and flaunted their horse-riding skills. At the same time, the local population embraced some of their conquerors' ways, donning the tunics and trousers that characterized Central Asian peoples.

Diversity and cultural mixing became most visible in the multiple languages that flourished in India. Although the sultans spoke Turkish languages, they regarded Persian literature as a high cultural achievement and made Persian their courtly and administrative language. Meanwhile, most of their Hindu subjects spoke local languages, followed their caste regulations, and practiced diverse forms of Hindu worship. The rulers did what Muslim rulers did with Christian and Jewish communities living in their midst: they collected the *jizya* tax and permitted communities to worship as they saw fit and to administer their own communal law. Ultimately, Islam proved in India that it did not have to be a conquering religion to prosper. As rulers, sultans granted lands to *ulama* (Islamic scholars) and Sufi saints, much as Hindu rajas had earlier granted lands to Brahmans. These scholars and saints in turn attracted followers, who enjoyed the benefits of membership in a community of believers.

Although the newcomers and the locals remained loyal to their own religious traditions, nonetheless their customs began to merge. Sultans maintained their steppe lifestyle and equestrian culture and took delight in the fact that their subjects adopted central Asian–style clothing. Within only a few decades, once the subject peoples realized that sultans and Islam were there to stay, they embraced the fashions of the court. In turn, their Muslim rulers understood that ruling effectively meant mastering the local language. Before long, court scholars and Sufi holy men were writing and teaching proficiently in local dialects. In time, these dialects, mixed with Persian and Arabic words, gave rise to a common language, Hindavi, or Hindustani, the root of Urdu and Hindi.

This exchange of skills among diverse communities was not confined to governance and religion. It spilled over into the economic arena as well. The foreign artisans who had arrived with their rulers brought silk textiles, rugs, and appliances to irrigate gardens that the leading families of Delhi cherished. Soon the artisans' talents were influencing local manufacturing techniques. Native-born Indians learned from Muslims how to extract long filaments from silk cocoons and were themselves weaving fine silk textiles.

Although Buddhism had been in decline in India for centuries, it, too, became part of the cultural intermixing of these centuries. As Vedic Brahmanism evolved into Hinduism (see Chapter 8), it absorbed many Buddhist doctrines and practices, such as *ahimsa* (non-killing) and vegetarianism. The two religions became so similar that Hindus simply considered the Buddha to be one of their deities—an incarnation of the great god Vishnu. Many Buddhist moral teachings mixed with and became Hindu stories. Artistic motifs reflected a similar process of adoption and adaptation. Goddesses, some beautiful and others fierce, appeared alongside Buddhas, Vishnus, and Sivas as their consorts. The Turkish invaders' destruction of major monasteries in the thirteenth century deprived Buddhism of local spiritual leaders. Lacking dynastic support, Buddhists in India were more easily assimilated into the Hindu population or converted to Islam.

Once the initial disruptive effects of the Turkish invasions were absorbed, India remained a highly diverse and tolerant region during this period. Most importantly, it also emerged as one of the four major cultural spheres, enjoying a tremendous level of integration as Turkish-Muslim rulership and their traditions and practices were successfully intermixed into the native Hindu society, leading to a more integrated and peaceful India.

Vishnu. *In addition to the Buddha, the four-armed Vishnu has nine other avatars, some of whom are portrayed at his feet in this tenth-century sandstone sculpture.*

SONG CHINA: INSIDERS VERSUS OUTSIDERS

The preeminent world power in 1000 CE was still China, despite its recent turmoil. Once dampened, the turbulence yielded to a long era of stability and splendor, a combination that made China a regional engine of Afro-Eurasian prosperity.

In 907 CE the Tang dynasty splintered into regional kingdoms, mostly led by military generals. In 960 CE one of these generals, Zhao Kuangyin, ended the fragmentation, reunified China, and assumed the mandate of heaven for the Song dynasty (960–1279).

The following three centuries witnessed many economic and political successes, but northern nomadic tribes kept the Song from completely securing their reign (see Map 10.6 and Map 10.7). Their efforts to deter these warriors were ultimately unsuccessful, and in 1127 the Song lost control of northern China to the Jurchen (ancestors of the Manchu, who would rule China from the seventeenth until the twentieth century). After reconstituting their dynasty in southern China, their empire's most economically robust region, the Song enjoyed another century and a half of rule before falling to the Mongols.

China's Economic Progress

China, like India and the Islamic world, participated in Afro-Eurasia's powerful long-distance trade. Chinese merchants were as energetic as their Muslim and Indian counterparts. Yet China's commercial successes could not have occurred without the country's strong agrarian base—especially its vast wheat, millet, and rice fields, which fed a population that reached 120 million. Agriculture benefited from breakthroughs in metalworking that produced stronger iron plows, which the Song harnessed to sturdy water buffalo to extend the farming frontier. In 1078, for example, total Song iron production reached between 75,000 and 150,000 tons, roughly the equivalent of European iron production in the early eighteenth century. The Chinese piston-driven bellows used to provide forced air for furnaces were a marvel, and of a size unsurpassed until the nineteenth century.

Manufacturing also flourished. In the early tenth century, Chinese alchemists mixed saltpeter with sulfur and charcoal to produce a product that would burn and could be deployed on the battlefield: gunpowder. Song entrepreneurs were soon inventing a remarkable array of incendiary devices that flowed from their mastery of techniques for controlling explosions and high heat. Moreover, artisans produced increasingly light,

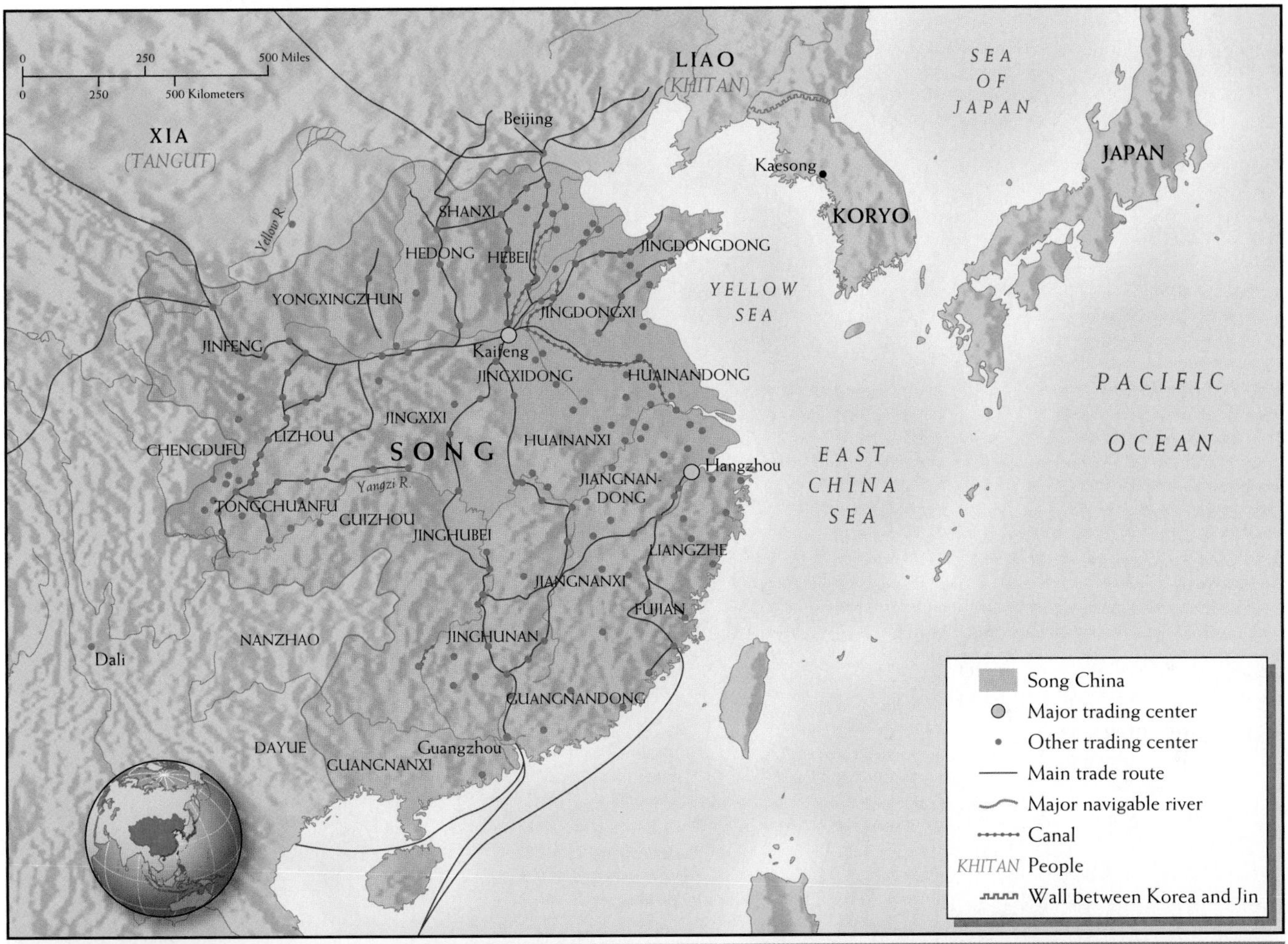

MAP 10.6 | East Asia in 1000

Several states emerged in East Asia between 1000 and 1300, but none were as strong as the Song dynasty in China. Using the key to the map, try to identify the factors that contributed to the Song state's economic dynamism.

- What external factors kept the Song dynasty from completely securing their reign?
- What factors drove the Chinese commercial revolution in this period?

durable, and exquisitely beautiful porcelains. Before long, their porcelain (now called "china") was the envy of all Afro-Eurasia. Also flowing from the artisans' skillful hands were vast amounts of clothing and handicrafts, made from the fibers grown by Song farmers. In effect, the Song Chinese oversaw the world's first manufacturing revolution, producing finished goods on a large scale for consumption far and wide.

Money and Inflation

Expanding commerce transformed the role of money and its wide circulation. By now the Song government was annually minting nearly two million strings of currency, each containing 1,000 copper coins. In fact, as the economy grew, the supply of metal currency could not match the demand. One result was East Asia's thirst for gold from East Africa. At the same time, merchant guilds in northwestern Shanxi developed the first letters of exchange, called "flying cash." These letters linked northern traders with their colleagues in the south. Before long, printed money had eclipsed coins. Even the government collected more than half its tax revenues in cash rather than grain and cloth. The government also issued more notes to pay its bills—a practice that ultimately contributed to the world's first case of runaway inflation.

New Elites

Song emperors ushered in a period of social and cultural vitality. They built on Tang institutions by expanding a central bureaucracy

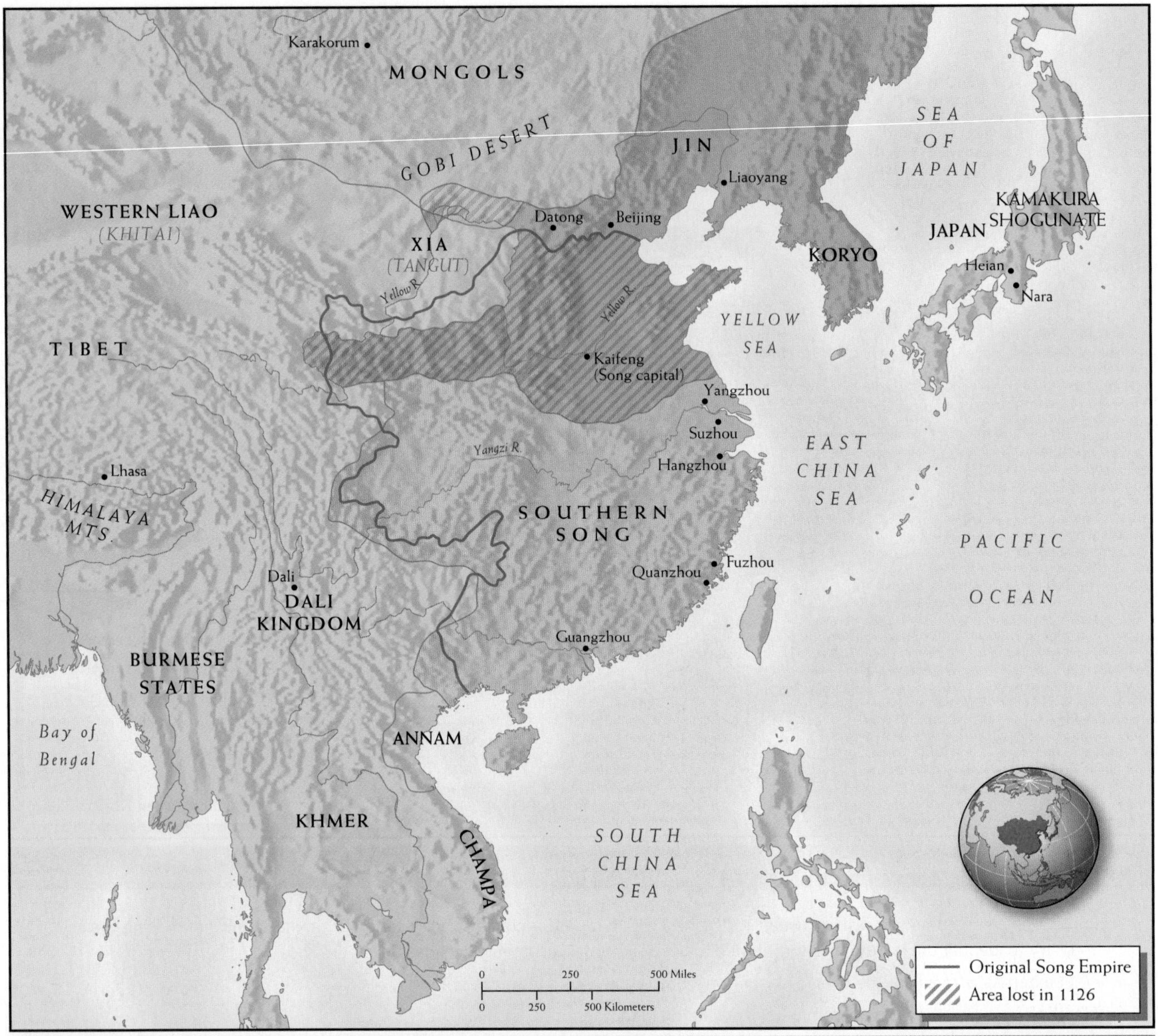

MAP 10.7 | East Asia in 1200

- The Song dynasty regularly dealt with "barbarian" neighbors. What were the major "barbarian" tribes during this period?
- Approximately what percentage of Song China was lost to the Jin in 1126?
- How did the "barbarian" tribes affect the Han Chinese identity in this period?

of scholar-officials chosen even more extensively through competitive civil service examinations. Zhao Kuangyin, or Emperor Taizu (r. 960–976 CE), himself administered the final test for all who had passed the highest-level palace examination. In subsequent dynasties, the emperor was the nation's premier examiner, symbolically demanding oaths of allegiance from successful candidates. By 1100 these ranks of learned men had accumulated sufficient power to become China's new ruling elite.

The expansion of the civil service examination system was crucial to a shift in power from the still powerful hereditary aristocracy to a less wealthy but more highly schooled class of scholar officials. Consider the career of the Northern Song reformer Wang Anshi (1021–1086), who ascended to power from a commoner family outside of Hangzhou in the south. He owed his success to gaining high marks in Song state examinations—a not insignificant achievement, for in nearby Fujian province

Wang Anshi. *He owed his rise from a commoner family to a powerful position as a reformer to the Song state examinations.*

alone, of the roughly 18,000 candidates who gathered triennially to take the provincial examination, over 90 percent failed! After gaining the emperor's ear, Wang eventually challenged the political and cultural influence of the old Tang dynasty elites from the northwest.

Negotiating with Neighbors

As the Song flourished, nomads on the outskirts eyed the Chinese successes closely. To the north, Khitan, Tungusic, Tangut, and Jurchen nomadic societies formed their own dynasties and adopted Chinese institutions. Located within the "greater China," as defined by the Han and Tang dynasties, these non-Chinese nomads saw China proper as an object both of conquest and emulation.

In military power the Song dynasts were relatively weak. Despite their sophisticated weapons, they could not match their enemies on the steppe when the latter united against them. Steel tips improved the arrows that their soldiers shot from their crossbows, and flame throwers and "crouching tiger catapults" sent incendiary bombs streaking into their enemies' ranks. But none of these breakthroughs was secret. Warrior neighbors on the steppe mastered the new arts of war more fully than did the Song dynasts themselves.

China's strength as a manufacturing powerhouse made economic diplomacy an option, so the Song relied on "gifts" and generous trade agreements with the borderlanders. For example, after losing North China to the Khitan Liao dynasty, the Song agreed to make annual payments of 100,000 ounces of silver and 200,000 bolts of silk. The treaty allowed them to live in relative peace for more than a century. Securing peace meant emptying the state coffers and then printing more paper money. The resulting inflation added economic instability to military weakness, making the Song an easy target when Jurchen invaders made their final assault.

What Was China?

Paradoxically, the increasing exchange between outsiders and insiders within China hardened the lines that divided them and gave residents of China's interior a highly developed sense of themselves as a distinctive people possessing a superior culture. Exchanges with outsiders nurtured a "Chinese" identity among those who considered themselves true insiders and referred to themselves as Han. Driven south from their ancient homeland in the eleventh century, they grew increasingly suspicious and resentful toward the outsiders living in their midst. They called these outsiders "barbarians" and treated them accordingly.

Vital in crystallizing this sense of a distinct Chinese identity was print culture. Of all Afro-Eurasian societies in 1300, the Chinese were the most advanced in their use of printing and book publishing and circulation. Moreover, their books established classical Chinese as the lingua franca of educated classes in East Asia. The Song government used its plentiful supply of

Chinese and Barbarian. *After losing the north, the Han Chinese grew resentful of outsiders. They drew a dividing line between their own agrarian society and the nomadic warriors, calling them "barbarians." Such identities were not fixed, however. Chinese and so-called barbarians were mutually dependent.*

paper to print books, especially medical texts, and to distribute calendars. The private publishing industry also expanded. Printing houses throughout the country produced Confucian classics, works on history, philosophical treatises, and literature—all of which figured in the civil examinations. Buddhist publications, too, were available everywhere.

China's resources, its huge population base coupled with a strong agrarian economy, and its strong foreign trade and diplomatic relations made it the most wealthy among the four major cultural spheres; its common language and its transfer of power to nonhereditary Confucian scholars made it the most unified.

CHINA'S NEIGHBORS ADAPT TO CHANGE

Feeling the pull of China's economic and political gravity, cultures around China consolidated their own internal political authority and defined their own identities in order to keep from being swallowed up, while increasing their commercial transactions.

The Rise of Warriors in Japan

Japan, like China, laid many political and cultural foundations for its later development in the three centuries between 1000 and 1300. Not only did its leaders distance themselves from Chinese influences during this period, but they also developed a strong sense of their islands' distinctive identity. Even so, the long-standing dominance of Chinese ways remained apparent at virtually every level of Japanese society, and was most pronounced at the imperial court in the capital city of Heian, present-day Kyoto. The city itself, founded in 795 CE, was modeled after the Chinese capital city of Chang'an. Three and a half miles from north to south and three miles from east to west, Heian-kyo, meaning the place of peace and tranquility, was surrounded by a moat and divided into squares by broad intersecting city-long roads, with the imperial court located in the north central part of the city. Although the city itself was not of imposing grandeur, those who resided in it admired its attractive gates, recessed courtyards, well-maintained and reposeful gardens, and its bustling streets and shops. To serve at the imperial court entailed a demanding knowledge of correct etiquette and ethics, based mostly on Chinese practices. Courtiers were obligated to wear the right colored robes, to carry swords of the correct length, and to know the proper salutations for greeting other members of the imperial bureaucracy.

The Tale of Genji best captures life at the Heian court. Written by Lady Murasaki Shikibu (c. 976–c. 1031), it is possibly the worlds' first novel, certainly the first novel to be written by a woman. *The Tale of Genji* reveals the imperial court's outward dedication to official rituals and values, as well as its rivalries, infighting, and sordid affairs—the stuff of court politics seemingly everywhere in the world, Yet, even this work, so preoccupied with the imperial center where Chinese institutions and values were dominant, reveals Japan's quest to create its own identity, for the work was written in the native Japanese script. (See Primary Source: The Tale of Genji.)

Outside Kyoto, however, a less China-centered way of life existed and began to impose itself on the center. Here, local notables, mainly military leaders and large landowners, began to challenge the imperial court for dominance. In 1185 one such rising clan leader, Minamoto-no-Yoritomo, supported by a large group of loyal followers in the eastern part of Japan, 300 miles away from Kyoto, consolidated his own administration there and soon extended his control over the entire country. Yoritomo was the first of many such military men who would dominate Japanese politics. As he and his successors elected to keep the Japanese emperors and their court at Kyoto in office even while stripping them of real power, Japan continued to have an emperor residing at the imperial city of Kyoto right down to 1868 when the Meiji restoration took place (see Chapter 17).

The emergence of Yoritomo marked the arrival of an important new social group in Japanese society—the warriors, or samurai. Heian aristocrats, disdaining the military and even abolishing the conscription system used to raise imperial armies, had thus allowed trained warriors, affiliated with kinship groups, to gather strength in the provinces. In lightweight leather armor, these expert horsemen defended their private estates with remarkable long-range bowmanship and superbly crafted single-edged long steel swords, lethal for close combat in warfare. The warriors also brought with them an idealization of their martial ethics, with an emphasis on loyalty, self-discipline, and a simple life tied to the land, which helped to shape Japanese society until recent times.

By the beginning of the fourteenth century, Japan had multiple sources of political and cultural power: an endangered and declining aristocracy; an imperial family with prestige but little authority; powerful landowning notables based in the provinces; and a rising and increasingly ambitious class of samurai. There was, in short, a combustible mix of refined high culture in the capital versus a warrior ethos in the provinces. Such a mix produced social intrigue in politics and led different provincial factions to vie with one another for preeminence.

Southeast Asia: A Maritime Mosaic

Southeast Asia, like India, now became a crossroads of Afro-Eurasian influences. Its sparse population of probably around 10 million in 1000 CE—tiny compared with that of China and

PRIMARY SOURCE

The Tale of Genji

Lacking a written language of their own, Heian aristocrats adopted classical Chinese as the official written language while continuing to speak Japanese. Men at the court took great pains to master the Chinese literary forms, but Japanese court ladies were not expected to do so. Lady Murasaki Shikibu, the author of* The Tale of Genji*, hid her knowledge of Chinese, fearing that she would be criticized. In the meantime, the Japanese developed a native syllabary (a table of syllables) based on Chinese written graphs. Using this syllabary, Murasaki kept a diary in Japanese that gave vivid accounts of Heian court life. Her story—possibly the world's first novel—relates the adventures of a dashing young courtier named Genji. In the passage below, Genji evidently speaks for Murasaki in explaining why fiction can be as truthful as a work of history in capturing human life and its historical significance.

Genji . . . smiled, and went on: "But I have a theory of my own about what this art of the novel is, and how it came into being. To begin with, it does not simply consist in the author's telling a story about the adventures of some other person. On the contrary, it happens because the storyteller's own experience of men and things, whether for good or ill—not only what he has passed through himself, but even events which he has only witnessed or been told of—has moved him to an emotion so passionate that he can no longer keep it shut up in his heart. Again and again something in his own life or in that around him will seem to the writer so important that he cannot bear to let it pass into oblivion. There must never come a time, he feels, when men do not know about it. That is my view of how this art arose.

"Clearly then, it is no part of the storyteller's craft to describe only what is good or beautiful. Sometimes, of course, virtue will be his theme, and he may then make such play with it as he will. But he is just as likely to have been struck by numerous examples of vice and folly in the world around him, and about them he has exactly the same feelings as about the pre-eminently good deeds which he encounters: they are more important and must all be garnered in. Thus anything whatsoever may become the subject of a novel, provided only that it happens in this mundane life and not in some fairyland beyond our human ken.

"The outward forms of this art will not of course be everywhere the same. At the court of China and in other foreign lands both the genius of the writers and their actual methods of composition are necessarily very different from ours; and even here in Japan the art of storytelling has in course of time undergone great changes. There will, too, always be a distinction between the lighter and the more serious forms of fiction. . . . So too, I think, may it be said that the art of fiction must not lose our allegiance because, in the pursuit of the main purpose to which I have alluded above, it sets virtue by the side of vice, or mingles wisdom with folly. Viewed in this light the novel is seen to be not, as is usually supposed, a mixture of useful truth with idle invention, but something which at every stage and in every part has a definite and serious purpose."

QUESTIONS FOR ANALYSIS

- According to this passage, what motivates an author to write a story (i.e., fiction)?
- Genji feels it is appropriate for a writer to address not only "what is good or beautiful" but also "vice and folly." What explanation does he give? Do you agree?

Source: Sources of Japanese Tradition, *compiled by Ryūsaku Tsunoda, Wm. Theodore de Bary, and Donald Keene (New York: Columbia University Press, 1964), vol. 1, pp. 177–79.*

India—was not immune to the foreign influences riding the sea-lanes into the archipelago. The Malay Peninsula became home to many trading ports and stopovers for traders shuttling between India and China, because it connected the Bay of Bengal and the Indian Ocean with the South China Sea (see Map 10.8).

"INDO-CHINESE" INFLUENCES Indian influence had been prominent both on the Asian mainland and in island portions of Southeast Asia since 800 CE, but Islamic expansion into the islands after 1200 gradually superseded these influences. Only Bali and a few other islands far to the east of Malaya preserved their Brahmanic-Vedic religious origins. Elsewhere in Java and Sumatra, Islam became the dominant religion. In Vietnam and northern portions of mainland Southeast Asia, Chinese cultural influences and northern schools of Mahayana Buddhism were especially prominent.

Heiji Rebellion. *This illustration from the Kamakura period depicts a battle during the Heiji Rebellion, which was fought between rival subjects of the cloistered emperor Go-Shirakawa in 1159. Riding in full armor on horseback, the fighters on both sides are armed with devastating long bows.*

MAINLAND BUFFER KINGDOMS During this period Cambodian, Burmese, and Thai peoples founded powerful mixed polities along the Mekong, Salween, Chao Phraya, and Irriwaddy river basins of the Asian mainland. Important Vedic and Buddhist kingdoms emerged here as political buffers between the strong states in China and India and brought stability and further commercial prosperity to the region.

Consider the kingdom that ruled Angkor in present-day Cambodia. With their capital in Angkor, the Khmers (889–1431) created the most powerful and wealthy empire in Southeast Asia. Countless water reservoirs enabled them to flourish on the great plain to the west of the Mekong River after the loss of eastern territories. Public works and magnificent temples dedicated to the revived Vedic gods from India went hand in hand with the earlier influence of Indian Buddhism. Eventually the Khmer kings united adjacent kingdoms and extended Khmer influence to the Thai and Burmese states along the Chaophraya and Irriwaddy rivers.

One of the greatest temple complexes in Angkor exemplified the Khmers' heavy borrowing from Vedic Indian architecture. Angkor aspired to represent the universe in the magnificence of its buildings. As signs of the ruler's power, the pagodas, pyramids, and terra-cotta friezes (ornamented walls) presented the life of the gods on earth. The crowning structure of the royal

Angkor Wat. *Mistaken by later European explorers as a remnant of Alexander the Great's conquests, the enormous temple complexes built by the Khmer people in Angkor borrowed their intricate layout and stupa (a moundlike structure containing religious relics) architecture from the Brahmanist Indian temples of the time. As the capital, Angkor was a microcosm of the world for the Khmer, who aspired to represent the macrocosm of the universe in the magnificence of Angkor's buildings and their geometric layout.*

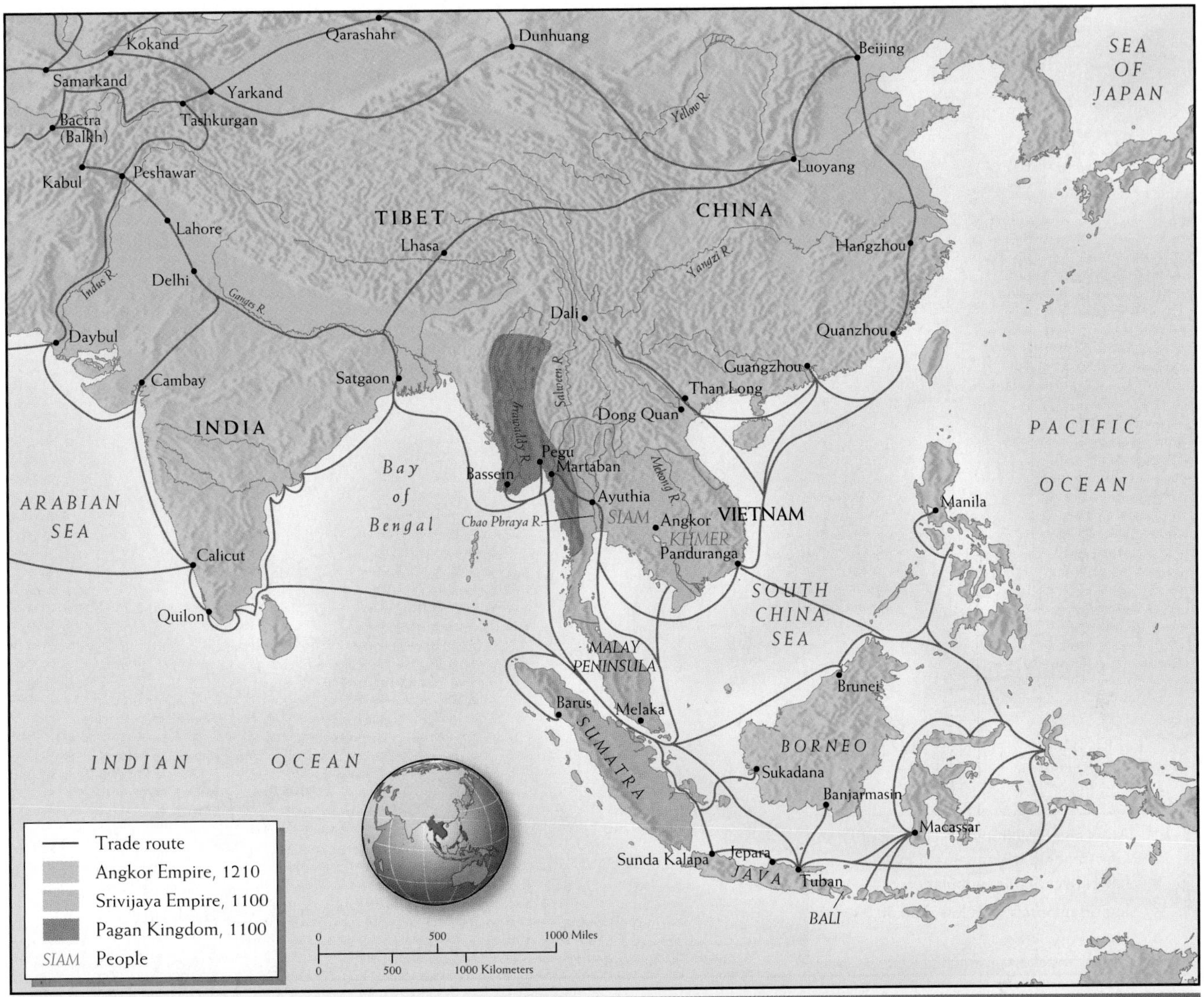

MAP 10.8 | Southeast Asia, 1000–1300

Cross-cultural influences affected Southeast Asian societies during this period.

- What makes Southeast Asia unique geographically compared to other regions of the world?
- Based on the map, why were the kingdoms of Southeast Asia exposed to so many cross-cultural influences?
- In this chapter, the term "mosaic" describes both South and Southeast Asia. Compare Map 10.5 with this map, and explain how the mosaic of Southeast Asia differed from the mosaic of India.

palace was the magnificent temple of **Angkor Wat**, possibly the largest religious structure ever built. In ornate detail and with great artistry, its buildings and statues represented the revival of the Hindu pantheon within the Khmer royal state.

CHRISTIAN EUROPE

In the far western corner of Afro-Eurasia, people were building a culture revealingly different. Although their numbers were small compared with the rest of Afro-Eurasia in 1000 CE (36 million in Europe, compared to 80 million in India and 120 million in China), their population would soar to 80 million before the arrival of the Black Death in the fourteenth century.

This was a region of strong contrasts. On the one hand, the period 1000–1300 witnessed an intense localization of politics because there was no successor to the Roman Empire or Charlemagne's (see Chapter 9). On the other hand, the territory united under a shared sense of its place in the world. Some inhabitants even began to believe in the existence of something

MAP 10.9 | Latin Christendom in 1300

Catholic Europe expanded geographically and integrated culturally during this era.

- According to this map, into what areas did western Christendom successfully expand?
- What factors contributed to the growth of a widespread common culture and shared ideas?
- How did long-distance trade shape the history of the region during this time?

called "Europe" and increasingly referred to themselves as "Europeans" (see Map 10.9).

Western and Northern Europe

The collapse of Charlemagne's empire had exposed much of northern Europe to invasion, principally from the Vikings, and left the peasantry with no central authority to protect them from local warlords. Armed with deadly weapons, these strongmen collected taxes, imposed forced labor, and became the unchallenged rulers of society. Within this growing warrior aristocracy, northern France led the way. The Franks (later called Frenchmen) were the trendsetters of eleventh- and twelfth-century western Europe.

The most important change was the peasantry's subjugation to the knightly class. Previously, well-to-do peasants had carried arms as "free" men. The moment the farmers lost the right to carry arms, they were no longer free. They slipped back to being mere agricultural laborers. Each peasant toiled under the authority of a lord, who controlled every detail of his or her life. This was the basis of a system known as **feudalism**.

The Bayeux Tapestry. *This tapestry was prepared by a queen and her ladies to celebrate the victories of William, known as the Conqueror because of his successful invasion of England in 1066. It shows the fascination of the entire "feudal" class, even women, with war, on which they depended—great horses, tightly meshed chain mail, long shields, and the stirrups that made such cavalry warfare possible.*

Assured of control of the peasantry, feudal lords watched over an agrarian breakthrough—which fueled a commercial transformation that drew Europe into the rest of the global trading networks. Lordly protection and more advanced metal tools like axes and plows, combined with heavier livestock to pull plows through the root-infested sods of northern Europe, led to massive deforestation. Above this clearing activity stood the castle. Its threatening presence ensured that the peasantry stayed within range of the collector of rents for the lords and of tithes (shares of crops, earmarked as "donations") for the church. In this blunt way, feudalism harnessed agrarian energy to its own needs. The population of western Europe as a whole leaped forward, most spectacularly in the north. As a result, northern Europe, from England to Poland, ceased to be an underdeveloped "barbarian" appendage of the Mediterranean.

Olavinilinna Castle. *This castle in Finland was the easternmost extension of a "western" feudal style of rule through great castles. It was built at the very end of the Baltic, to keep away the Russians of Novgorod.*

Eastern Europe

Nowhere did pioneering peasants develop more land than in the wide-open spaces of eastern Europe, the region's land of opportunity. Between 1100 and 1200, some 200,000 farmers emigrated from Flanders (in modern Belgium), Holland, and northern Germany to eastern frontiers. Well-watered landscapes, covered with vast forests, filled up what are now Poland, the Czech Republic, Hungary, and the Baltic states. "Little Europes," whose castles, churches, and towns echoed the landscape of France, now replaced economies that had been based on gathering honey, hunting, and the slave trade. For a thousand miles along the Baltic Sea, forest clearings dotted with new farmsteads and small towns edged inward from the coast up the river valleys.

The social structure here was a marriage of convenience between migrating peasants and local elites. The area offered the promise of freedom from the feudal lords' arbitrary justice and imposition of forced labor. Even the harsh landscape of the eastern Baltic (where the sea froze every year and impenetrable forests blocked settlers from the coast) was preferable to life in the feudal west. For their part, the elites of eastern Europe—the nobility of Poland, Bohemia, and Hungary and the princes of the Baltic—wished to live well, in the "French" style. But they could do so only if they attracted manpower to their lands by offering newcomers a liberty that they had no hope of enjoying in the west.

The Russian Lands

In Russian lands, western settlers and knights met an eastern brand of Christian devotion. This world looked toward Byzantium, not Rome. Russia was a giant borderland between the steppes of Eurasia and the booming feudalisms of Europe. Its cities lay at the crossroads of overland trade and migration, and Kiev became one of the region's greatest cities. Standing on a bluff above the Dnieper River, it straddled newly opened trade routes. With a population exceeding 20,000, including merchants from eastern and western Europe and the Middle East, Kiev was larger than Paris—larger even than the much-diminished city of Rome.

Kiev looked south to the Black Sea and to Constantinople. Under Iaroslav the Wise (1016–1054), it became a small-scale Constantinople on the Dnieper. A stone church called St. Sophia stood (as in Constantinople) beside the imperial palace. With its distinctive "Byzantine" domes, it was a miniature Hagia Sophia (see Chapter 8). Its highest dome towered a hundred feet above the floor, and its splendid mosaics depicting Byzantine saints echoed the religious art of Constantinople. But the message was political as well, for the ruler of Kiev was cast in the mold of the emperor of Constantinople. He now took the title *tsar* from the ancient Roman name given to the emperor, Caesar. From this time onward, *tsar* was the title of rulers in Russia.

The Russian form of Christianity replicated the Byzantine style of churches all along the great rivers leading to the trading cities of the north and northeast. These were not agrarian centers, but hubs of expanding long-distance trade. (See Primary Source: The Birch Bark Letters of Novgorod.) Each city became a small-scale Kiev, and a smaller-scale echo of Constantinople. The Orthodox religion looked to Byzantium's Hagia Sophia rather than the Catholic faith associated with the popes in Rome. Russian Christianity remained the Christianity of a borderland—vivid oases of high culture set against the backdrop of vast forests and widely scattered settlements.

What Was Christian Europe?

Catholicism became a universalizing faith that transformed the region becoming known as "Europe." The Christianity of post-Roman Europe had been a religion of monks, and its most dynamic centers were great monasteries. Members of the laity were expected to revere and support their monks, nuns, and clergy, but not to imitate them. By 1200, all this had changed. The internal colonization of western Europe—the clearing of woods and founding of villages—ensured that parish churches arose in all but the wildest landscapes. Their spires were visible and their bells were audible from one valley to the next. Church graveyards were the only places where good Christians could be buried; criminals' and outlaws' bodies piled up in "heathen" graves outside the cemetery walls.

Now the clergy reached more deeply into the private lives of the laity. Marriage and divorce, previously considered family matters, became a full-time preoccupation of the church. And sin was no longer an offense that just "happened"; it was a matter that every person could do something about. Regular confession to a priest became obligatory for all Catholic, western Christians. The followers of Francis of Assisi (1182–1226) emerged as an order of preachers who brought a message of repentance. They did not tell their audiences to enter the monastery. Instead, their listeners were to weep, confess their sins to local priests, and strive to be better Christians. Franciscans instilled in the hearts of all believers a Europe-wide Catholicism based on daily remorse and daily contemplation of the sufferings of Christ and his mother, Mary. From Ireland

Saint Sophia Cathedral, Novgorod. *The cathedral of Novgorod (like that of Kiev) was called Hagia Sophia. It was a deliberate imitation of the Hagia Sophia of Constantinople, showing Russia's roots in a glorious Roman/Byzantine past that had nothing to do with western Europe.*

PRIMARY SOURCE

The Birch Bark Letters of Novgorod

The city of Novgorod was a vibrant trading center with a diverse population. From 1951 onward, Russian archaeologists in Novgorod have excavated almost a thousand letters and accounts scratched on birch bark and preserved in the sodden, frequently frozen ground. Reading them, we realize how timeless people's basic concerns can be.

First, we meet the merchants. Many letters are notes by creditors of the debts owed to them by trading partners. The sums are often expressed in precious animal furs. They contain advice to relatives or to partners in other cities:

> Giorgii sends his respects to his father and mother: Sell the house and come here to Smolensk or to Kiev: for the bread is cheap there.

Then we meet neighborhood disputes:

> From Anna to Klemiata: Help me, my lord brother, in my matter with Konstantin. . . . [For I asked him,] "Why have you been so angry with my sister and her daughter. You called her a cow and her daughter a whore. And now Fedor has thrown them both out of the house."

There are even glimpses of real love. A secret marriage is planned:

> Mikiti to Ulianitza: Come to me. I love you, and you me. Ignato will act as witness.

And a poignant note from a woman was discovered in 1993:

> I have written to you three times. What is it that you hold against me, that you did not come to see me this Sunday? I regarded you as I would my own brother. Did I really offend you by that which I sent to you? If you had been pleased you would have torn yourself away from company and come to me. Write to me. If in my clumsiness I have offended you and you should spurn me, then let God be my judge. I love you.

QUESTIONS FOR ANALYSIS

- What does the range of people writing on birch bark tell us about these people?
- Think of the messages you send to friends and relatives today. Even if texting and e-mailing seem centuries distant from writing on birch bark, can you relate in any way to these ancient letter-writers?

Source: A. V. Artsikhovskii and V. I. Borkovski, Novgorodskie Gramoty na Bereste, *11 vols. (Moscow: Izd-vo Akademii nauk SSSR, 1951–2004), document nos. 424, 531, 377, and 752.*

to Riga and Budapest, Catholic Christians came to share a common piety.

UNIVERSITIES AND INTELLECTUALS Vital to the creation of Europe's Christian identity was the emergence of universities, for it was during this era that Europe acquired its first class of intellectuals. Since the late twelfth century, scholars had gathered in Paris, where they formed a *universitas*—a term borrowed from merchant communities, where it denoted a type of union. Those who belonged to the *universitas* enjoyed protection by their fellows and freedom to continue their trade. Similarly protected by their own "union," the scholars of Paris began wrestling with the new learning from Arab lands. When the bishop of Paris forbade this undertaking, they simply moved to the Left Bank of the Seine, so as to place the river between themselves and the bishop's officials, who lived around the cathedral of Notre Dame.

The scholars' ability to organize themselves gave them an advantage that their Arab contemporaries lacked. For all his genius, Ibn Rushd had to spend his life courting the favor of individual monarchs to protect him from conservative fellow Muslims, who frequently burned his books. Ironically, European scholars congregating in Paris could quietly absorb the most persuasive elements of Arabic thought, like Ibn Rushd's. Yet they endeavored to prove that Christianity was the only religion that fully met the aspirations of all rational human beings. Such was the message of the great intellectual Thomas Aquinas, who wrote *Summa contra Gentiles* (Summary of Christian Belief against Non-Christians) in 1264.

The Europe of 1300 was more culturally unified than in previous centuries. It was permeated by Catholicism, and its leading intellectuals extolled the virtues of Christian learning. Such a confident region was not, however, a tolerant place for heretics, Jews, or Muslims.

Christian Europe on the Move: The Crusades and Iberia

By the tenth and eleventh centuries, western Christianity was on the move, spreading into Scandinavia, southern Italy, the Baltic, and eastern Europe. Its ambitions to reconquer Spain and Portugal (which had been under Islamic control since the eighth century CE) demonstrated one of the effects of feudal power: the lords' self-confidence, their belief in their military capability, and their pious sense of destiny were all inflated. Besides, the wealth of the east was irresistible to those whose piety entwined with an appetite for plunder. Yet the two Christendoms formed an uneasy alliance to roll back the expanding frontiers of Islam. Europeans zealously took war outside their own borders.

CRUSADES In the late eleventh century, western Europeans launched a wave of attacks known as the **Crusades**. The First Crusade began in 1095, when Pope Urban II appealed to the warrior nobility of France to put their violence to good use: they should combine their role as pilgrims to Jerusalem with that of soldiers, and free Jerusalem from Muslim rule. What the clergy proposed was a novel kind of war. Whereas previously war had been a dirty business and a source of sin, now the clergy told the knights that good and just wars were possible. Such wars could cancel out the sins of those who waged them.

Starting in 1097, an armed host of around 60,000 men moved all the way from northwestern Europe to Jerusalem. This was a huge crowd. But it was divided. Knights in heavy armor led, as they did in Europe. But in the eastern Mediterranean they depended on poor masses who joined the movement to help besiege cities and construct a network of castles as the Christian knights drove their frontier forward. Later Crusaders brought their wives, especially those from the upper class. As in many colonial societies away from the homeland, these women felt freer. Eleanor of Aquitaine, for example, led her own army. Also, queens were crucial in opening up to the local populations. Consider the Armenian queen, Melisende (r. 1131–1152): regarded as wise and experienced in affairs of the state, she was popular with local Christians. As a result, the society of the Crusader states remained more open to women and the lower classes than in Europe. Above all, the Crusades could not have happened without the sailors and merchants of Italy. It was the fleets of Venice, Genoa, and Pisa that transported the later Crusaders and supplied their kingdom.

There were five Crusades in all, spread out over two centuries. None of the coalitions, in the end, created permanent Christian kingdoms in the lands they "reconquered." Only a small proportion of Crusaders remained in Southwest Asia, and those who did met their match in Muslim armies. (See Current Trends in World History: The Crusades from Dual Perspectives.)

Crusader. *Kneeling, this Crusader promises to serve God (as he would serve a feudal lord) by going to fight on a Crusade (as he would fight for any lord to whom he had sworn loyalty). The two kinds of loyalty—to God and to one's lord—were deliberately confused in Crusader ideas. Both were about war. But fighting for God was unambiguously good, while fighting for a lord was not always so clear-cut.*

Part of the problem was that few Crusaders had any intention of becoming colonists. Only a small proportion remained to defend the Kingdom of Jerusalem after the First Crusade. Most knights returned home, their epic pilgrimage completed. The remaining fragile network of Crusader lordships could barely threaten the Islamic heartlands.

Muslim leaders, however, did not see the Frankish knights as a threat. For them, the Crusades were irrelevant. And as far as the average Muslim of the region was concerned, the Crusaders hardly mattered at all. Jerusalem and Palestine had always been fringe areas in the Middle East. Real prosperity and the capital cities of Muslim kingdoms lay inland, away from the coast—at Cairo, Damascus, and Baghdad. The assaults' long-term effect was to harden Muslim feelings against the Franks and the millions of non-western Christians who had previously lived peacefully in Egypt and Syria. Muslims viewed the Crusaders as brave but uncivilized warriors. A neighboring Muslim wrote: "The Franks possess none of the virtues of men except courage. . . . Nobody counts for them except knights." Their lack of medical knowledge shocked this observer. He noted that they would rather chop off a man's leg than administer ointments, as Muslim doctors would have advised.

Other campaigns of Christian expansion, like the Iberian efforts to drive out the Muslims, were more successful. Beginning with the capture of Toledo in 1061, the Christian kings of northern Spain slowly pushed back the Muslims. Eventually they reached the heart of Andalusia in southern Iberia and conquered Seville, adding more than 100,000 square miles of territory to Christian Europe. Another force from northern France crossed Italy to conquer Muslim-held Sicily, ensuring Christian rule in the strategically located mid-Mediterranean island. Unlike the Crusaders' fragile foothold at the edge of the Middle East, these two conquests turned the tide in relations between Christian and Muslim power.

Christianity—in particular the rise of the Roman Catholic Church, the spread of universities, and the fight against the Muslims in their native and spiritual homelands—would be the force that would create the fourth cultural sphere known as Europe, whose peoples would become known as European, at the western end of the Afro-Eurasian landmass.

THE AMERICAS

During this period, the Americas were untouched by the connections reverberating across Afro-Eurasia. After all, navigators still could not cross the large oceans that separated the Americas from other lands. Yet, here, too, commercial and expansionist impulses fostered closer contact among peoples who lived there.

Andean States

Growth and prosperity in the Andean region gave rise to South America's first empire. Known as the Chimú Empire, it developed early in the second millennium in the fertile Moche Valley bordering the Pacific Ocean (see Map 10.10). Ultimately the Moche people expanded their influence across numerous valleys and ecological zones, from pastoral highlands to rich valley floodplains to the fecund fishing grounds of the Pacific Coast. As their geographical reach grew, so did their wealth.

Andean States. *The image to the left shows what remains of Chan Chan. The city covered fifteen square miles and was divided into neighborhoods for nobles, artisans, and commoners, with the elites living closest to the hub of governmental and spiritual power. The buildings of Tiahuanaco (below) were made of giant, hand-hewn stones assembled without mortar. Engineers had not discovered the principle of curved arches and keystones and instead relied on massive slabs atop gateways. Gateways were important symbolic features, for they were places where people acknowledged the importance of sun and moon gods.*

CURRENT TRENDS IN WORLD HISTORY

The Crusades from Dual Perspectives

World history promotes comparative historical study, and when two cultures come together, as they did in the European crusades, their meeting offers unique opportunities to see how different societies view one another, and it provides a clear sense for their own self-identity. Such a confrontation took place during the crusades between European Christians and Muslims between 1095-1272.

In 1095, Pope Urban II called for the First Crusade in the following words:

> Oh, race of Franks, race from across the mountains, race chosen and beloved by God, as shines forth in very many of your works, set apart from all nations by the situation of your country, as well as by your Catholic faith and the honor of the Holy Church! To you our discourse is addressed, and for you our exhortation is intended. We wish you to know what a grievous cause has led us to your country, what peril, threatening you and all the faithful, has brought us.

The "grievous cause" was the occupation of the Holy City of Jerusalem by the Islamic empire. Formed within the complex relationship between the Byzantine Empire and the western Christian papacy and kingdoms of Europe, the religious motivation behind the Crusades became the subject of many literary renditions of the tumultuous events. It also generated emotionally stirring and polemical (argumentative) writing, depicting either a Muslim or Christian enemy (depending on the work's author).

Polemics are often passionate, harsh, and emotional. They also inspire and reinforce the conviction of fellow believers, with little concern for accuracy. Thus authors of polemic in the time of the Crusades were usually too biased or too misinformed to present accurate portraits of their enemies. But occasionally, first-hand accounts in the form of chronicles and histories offer us unique glimpses into Christian-Muslim relations in the age of the Crusades.

Consider Usāmah ibn Munqidh (1095–1188), the learned ruler of the city of Shaizar in western Syria. Skirmishes, truces, and the ransoming of prisoners were part of his daily life, and Usāmah socialized with his Frankish neighbors as much as he fought with them. He offers a dismissive opinion of his enemies. Basically, they struck him as "animals possessing the virtues of courage and fighting, but nothing else." In particular, their medical practice appalled him. More strange, the Franks allowed their wives to walk about freely and to talk to strangers unaccompanied by male guardians. How could men be at once so brave and yet so lacking in a proper, Arab sense of honor, which would lead a man to protect his women? Unlike other Muslim authors of his time, however, Usāmah does not refer to the Franks in derogatory terms such as "infidels" or "devils." In fact, he occasionally refers to some of them as his companions and writes of a Frank who called him "my brother" (*An Arab-Syrian Gentleman and Warrior in the Time of the Crusades,* 16).

Christian authors had similar interests in documenting the customs of their enemies in battle. Jean de Joinville

The Chimú regime lasted until Incan armies invaded in the 1460s and incorporated the Pacific state into their own immense empire.

A THRIVING LOWLAND ECONOMY The Chimú economy was successful because it was highly commercialized. Agriculture was its base, and complex irrigation systems turned the arid coast into a string of fertile oases capable of feeding an increasingly dispersed population. Cotton became a lucrative export to distant markets along the Andes. Parades of llamas and porters lugged these commodities up and down the steep mountain chains that are the spine of South America. As in China, a well-trained bureaucracy oversaw the construction and maintenance of canals, with a hierarchy of provincial administrators watching over commercial hinterlands.

Between 850 and 900 CE, the Moche peoples founded their biggest city, Chan Chan, with a core population of 30,000 inhabitants. A sprawling walled metropolis, covering nearly ten square miles with extensive roads circulating through neighborhoods, it boasted ten huge palaces at its center. Protected by thick walls thirty feet high, these opulent residence halls bespoke the rulers' power. Within the compound, emperors erected mortuary monuments for storing their accumulated riches: fine cloth, gold and silver objects, splendid *Spondylus* shells, and other luxury goods. Around the compound spread neighborhoods for nobles and artisans; farther out stood rows of commoners' houses.

AN INVENTIVE HIGHLAND STATE The Andes also saw its first highland empires during this period. On the shores

(1224/1225–1317) was a chronicler of medieval France. During one crusade, while in the service of the king, Joinville had occasion to note the Muslims' social behavior:

> Whenever the Sultan was in the camp, the men of the personal Guard were quartered all round his lodging, and appointed to guard his person. At the door of the Sultan's lodging there was a little tent for the Sultan's door-keepers, and for his musicians, who had Arabian horns and drums and kettledrums; and they used to make such a din at daybreak and at nightfall that people near them could not hear one another speak, and that they could be heard plainly all through the camp. The musicians never dared sound their instruments in the daytime unless by the order of the Chief of the Guard. Thus it was, that whenever the Sultan had a proclamation to make he used to send for the Chief of the Guard, and give him the order; and then the Chief would cause all the Sultan's instruments to be sounded; and thereupon all the host would come to hear the Sultan's commands.

Jeane de Joinville. *Joinville dictating his memoir of St. Louis, in which he described the Seventh Crusade.*

Although scholars regard such literary renditions with caution, they are useful for gleaning personal details that other types of works omit. The colorful accounts by authors such as Usāmah ibn Munqidh and Joinville are invaluable resources for the social history of the Crusaders.

QUESTIONS FOR ANALYSIS

- What customs or practices of their opponents did the Muslim and the Christian writers select to write about? Why?
- What aspects of the other side's customs does the writer seem to see as good or praiseworthy? What does that tell us about their perceptions of the strangers they encountered?
- If a historian is to use polemical written sources like this to analyze societies in the past, what can he or she say is trustworthy about them?

Explore Further

Hodgson, Natasha, *Women, Crusading and the Holy Land in Historical Narrative* (2007).

Maalouf, Amin, *The Crusades Through Arab Eyes*, trans. Jon Rothschild (1984).

Peters, Edward (ed.), *The First Crusade: The Chronicle of Fulcher of Chartres and Other Source Materials* (1971).

of the plateau lake Titicaca, the people of Tiahuanaco forged a high-altitude state. Though neither as large nor as wealthy as the Chimú Empire, its residents converted the inhospitable highlands into an environment where farmers and herders thrived. There is evidence of long-distance trade with neighbors in semitropical valleys, and even signs of highlanders migrating to the lowlands to produce agrarian staples for their kin in the mountains. Dried fish and cotton came from the coast; fruits and vegetables came from lowland valleys. Trade sustained an enormous urban population of up to 115,000 people. Looming over the skyline of Tiahuanaco was an imposing pyramid of massive sandstone blocks. Its advanced engineering system conveyed water to the summit, from which an imitation rainfall coursed down the carefully carved sides—an awesome spectacle of engineering prowess in such an arid region.

Connections to the North

Additional hubs of regional trade developed farther north, showing once again that even in areas of relative geographic isolation, cultures could flourish and interact within expanding regional spheres. The Toltecs and the Cahokians are superb examples.

THE TOLTECS IN MESOAMERICA By 1000 CE, Mesoamerica had seen the rise and fall of several complex societies. Caravans of porters worked the intricate roads that connected the coast of the Gulf of Mexico to the Pacific, and the southern lowlands of Central America to the arid regions of modern Texas (see Map 10.11). The region's heartland was the rich valley of central Mexico. Here the Toltecs filled the political

MAP 10.10 | Andean States

Although the Andes region of South America was isolated from Afro-Eurasian developments before 1500, it was not stagnant. Indeed, political and cultural integration brought the peoples of this region closer together.

- Where are the areas of the Chimú Empire and Tiahuanaco influence on the map?
- What kinds of ecological niches did they govern?
- According to your reading, how did each polity encourage greater cultural and economic integration?

vacuum left by the decline of Teotihuacán (see Chapter 8) and tapped into the commercial network radiating from the valley.

The Toltecs were a combination of migrant groups, refugees from the south, and farmers from the north. They settled northwest of Teotihuacán as the city waned, making their capital at Tula. They relied on a maize-based economy supplemented by beans, squash, and dog, deer, and rabbit meat. Their rulers made sure that enterprising merchants provided them with status goods such as ornamental pottery, rare shells and stones, and precious skins and feathers.

Tula was a commercial hub, a political capital, and a ceremonial center. While its layout differed from Teotihuacán's, many features revealed borrowings from other Mesoamerican peoples. Temples consisted of giant pyramids topped by colossal stone soldiers, and ball courts where subjects and conquered peoples alike played their ritual sport were found everywhere. The architecture and monumental art reflected the mixed and migratory origins of the Toltecs: a combination of Mayan and Teotihuacáno influences. At its height, the Toltec capital teemed with 60,000 people, a huge metropolis by contemporary European standards.

THE CAHOKIANS IN NORTH AMERICA Cities took shape at the hubs of trading networks all across North America. The largest was **Cahokia**, along the Mississippi River near modern-day East St. Louis. A city of about 15,000, it approximated the size of London at the time. Farmers and hunters settled in the region around 600 CE, attracted by its rich soil, its woodlands for fuel and game, and its access to the trading artery of the Mississippi. Eventually, fields of maize and other crops fanned out toward the horizon. The hoe replaced the trusty digging stick, and satellite towns erected granaries to hold the increased yields.

Now Cahokia became a commercial center for regional and long-distance trade. The hinterlands produced staples for Cahokia's urban consumers, and in return its crafts rode inland on the backs of porters and to distant markets in canoes. The city's woven fabrics and ceramics were especially desirable. In exchange, traders brought mica from the Appalachian Mountains, seashells and sharks' teeth from the Gulf of Mexico, and copper from the upper Great Lakes. Cahokia became more than an importer and

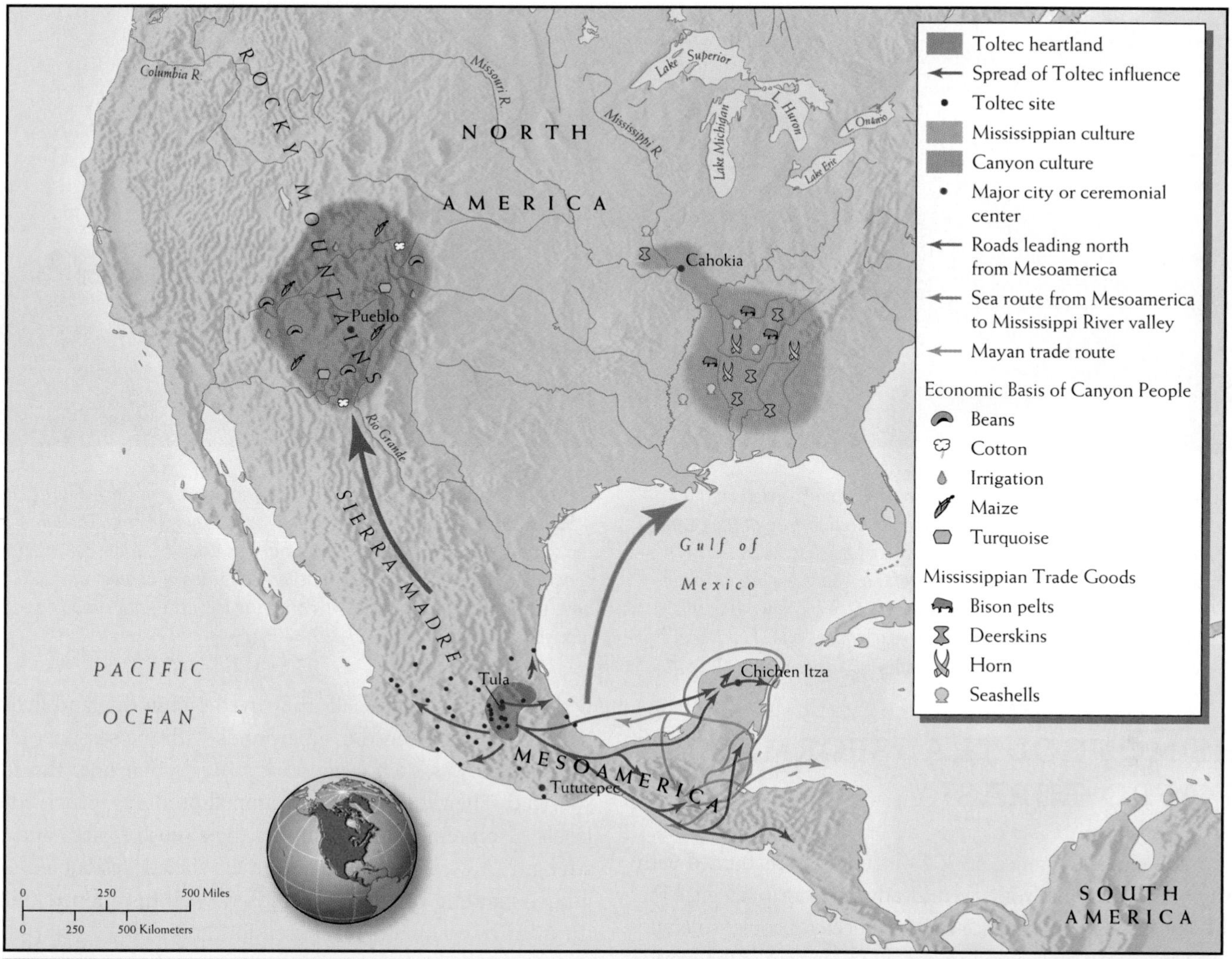

MAP 10.11 | Commercial Hubs in Mesoamerica and North America, 1000

Both Cahokia and Tula were commercial hubs of vibrant regional trade networks.

- Where are Cahokia and Tula on the map?
- According to the map, what kinds of goods circulated through these cities?
- How much political influence on the surrounding region do you think each city had?

exporter: it was the exchange hub for an entire regional network trading in salt, tools, pottery, woven stuffs, jewelry, and ceremonial goods.

Dominating Cahokia's urban landscape were enormous mounds (hence their nickname, "mound people"). These earthen monuments reveal a sophisticated design and careful maintenance: their builders applied layers of sand and clay to prevent the foundations from drying and cracking. It was from these artificial hills that the people paid homage to spiritual forces. Building this kind of infrastructure without draft animals, hydraulic tools, or even wheels was labor-intensive, so the Cahokians recruited neighboring people to help. A palisade around the city protected the metropolis from marauders.

Ultimately the city outgrew its environment, and its success bred its downfall. As woodlands fell to the axe and arable soil lost nutrients, timber and food became scarce. Because the city lacked a means to ship bulky items over long distances—in contrast to the sturdy dhows of the Arabian Sea and the bulky junks of the China Sea—its river canoes could carry only limited cargoes. Cahokia's commercial networks met their limits. When the creeks that fed its water system could not keep up with demand, engineers changed their course, but to no avail. By 1350 the city was practically empty. Nevertheless, Cahokia was a remarkable center of exchange while it lasted. It represented the growing networks of trade and migration, and the ability of North Americans to organize vibrant commercial societies.

Toltec Temple. *Tula, the capital of the Toltec Empire, carried on the Mesoamerican tradition of locating ceremonial architecture at the center of the city. The Pyramid of the Morning Star cast its shadow over all other buildings. And above them stood columns of the Atlantes, carved Toltec god-warriors, the figurative pillars of the empire itself. The walls of this pyramid were likely embellished with images of snakes and skulls. The north face of the pyramid has the image of a snake devouring a human.*

Cahokia Mounds. *This is all that is left of what was once a large city organized around temple mounds in what today is Illinois. The largest of the temples, known as Monks' Mound, was likely a burial site, with four separate terraces for crowds to gather. Centuries of neglect and erosion have taken their toll on what was once the largest human-made earthen mound in North America.*

THE MONGOL TRANSFORMATION OF AFRO-EURASIA

The world's sea-lanes grew crowded with ships; ports buzzed with activity. Commercial networks were clearly one way to integrate the world. But just as long-distance trade connected people, so could conquerors—as we have seen throughout the history of the world. Transformative conquerors now came from the Inner Eurasian steppes, the same place that centuries earlier had unleashed horse-riding warriors such as the Xiongnu (see Chapters 6 and 7).

Like the Xiongnu and the Kushans before them, the Mongols not only conquered but intensified trade and cultural exchange. By consolidating a latticework of states across northern and central Asia, they created an empire that straddled east and west (see Map 10.12). It was unstable and not as durable as other dynasties. It did not even have a shared faith; the mother of the conquering emperors, Hulagu and Kubilai Khan, was a devout Christian, reflecting Nestorian missionaries' centuries-long efforts to convert the nomads. Many Europeans prayed that the entire empire would convert. But it did not; the Mongols were a religious patchwork of Afro-Eurasian belief systems. Yet they brought far-flung parts of the world together as they conquered territories much larger than their own.

Who Were the Mongols?

The **Mongols** were a combination of forest and prairie peoples. Residing in circular, felt-covered tents, which they shared with some of their animals, they lived by hunting and livestock herding. They changed campgrounds with the seasons. Life on the steppes was such a constant struggle that only the strong survived. Their food, primarily animal products, provided high levels of protein, which built up their muscle mass and their strength. Always on the march, their society resembled a perpetual standing army with bands of well-disciplined military units led by commanders chosen for their skill.

MILITARY SKILLS Mongol archers were uniquely skilled. Wielding heavy recurved compound bows made of sinew, wood, and horns, they were deadly accurate at over 200 yards—even at full gallop. Their small but sturdy horses, capable of withstanding extreme cold, bore saddles with high supports in front and back, enabling the warriors to maneuver at high speeds. With their feet secure in iron stirrups, the archers could rise in their saddles to aim their arrows without stopping. These expert horsemen often remained in the saddle all day and night, even sleeping while their horses continued on. Each warrior kept many horses, replacing tired mounts with fresh ones so that the armies could cover up to seventy miles per day.

KINSHIP NETWORKS AND SOCIAL ROLES Mongol tribes solidified their conquests by extending kinship networks, building an empire out of an expanding confederation of familial tribes. The tents or households were interrelated mostly by marriage: they were alliances sealed by the exchange of daughters. Conquering men married conquered women, and conquered men were selected to marry the conquerors' women. Chinggis Khan may have had more than 500 wives, most of them daughters of tribes that he conquered or that allied with him.

Mongol Warriors. *This miniature painting is one of the illustrations for* History *by Rashid al Din, the most outstanding scholar under the Mongol regimes. Note the relatively small horses and strong bows used by the Mongol soldiers.*

Women in Mongol society were responsible for child-rearing, shearing and milking livestock, and processing pelts for clothing. But they also took part in battles. Kubilai Khan's niece Khutulun became famous for besting men in wrestling matches and claiming their horses as spoils. Although women were often bought and sold, Mongol wives had the right to own property and to divorce. Elite women even played important political roles. Consider Sorghaghtani Beki, Kubilai Khan's mother, who helped to engineer her sons' rule. Illiterate herself, she made sure that each son acquired a second language to aid in administering conquered lands. She gathered Confucian scholars to prepare Kubilai Khan to rule China. Chabi, Kubilai's senior wife, followed a similar pattern, offering patronage to Tibetan monks who set about converting the Mongol elite in China to Tibetan Buddhism.

Conquest and Empire

The nomads' need for grazing lands contributed to their desire to conquer the splendors of distant fertile belts and rich cities. As they acquired new lands, they increasingly craved control of richer agricultural and urban areas nearby to increase their wealth and power through tribute. The Mongols depended on settled peoples for grain and manufactured goods—including iron for tools, wagons, weapons, bridles, and stirrups—and their first expansionist forays followed caravan routes.

The expansionist thrust began in 1206 under a united cluster of tribes. A gathering of clan heads acclaimed one of those present as Chinggis (Genghis) Khan, or Supreme Ruler. Chinggis (c. 1155–1227) launched a series of conquests southward across the Great Wall of China, and westward to Afghanistan and Persia. The Mongols also invaded Korea in 1231. The armies of Chinggis's son reached both the Pacific Ocean and the Adriatic Sea. His grandsons founded dynasties in China, in Persia, and on the southern Eurasian steppes. One of them, Kubilai Khan, enlisted thousands of Koryo men and ships for ill-fated invasions of Japan. Thus, a realm took shape that touched all four of Afro-Eurasia's main worlds.

Mongol raiders ultimately built a permanent empire by incorporating conquered peoples and some of their ways. Their feat of unification was far more surprising and sudden than the ties developed incrementally by traders and travelers on ships. Now, Afro-Eurasian regions were connected by land and by sea, in historically unparalleled ways.

Mongols in China

Mongol forces under Chinggis Khan entered northern China at the beginning of the thirteenth century, defeating the Jin army, which was no match for the Mongols' superior cavalry on the North China plain. But below the Yangzi River, where the climate and weather changed, the Mongol horsemen fell ill from diseases such as malaria, and their horses perished from the heat. To conquer the semitropical south, the Mongols took to boats and fought along rivers and canals. **Kubilai Khan** (1215–1294) seized the grandest prize of all—southern China—after 1260. His cavalry penetrated the higher plateaus of southwest China and then attacked South China's economic heartland from the west. The Southern Song army fell before his warriors brandishing the latest gunpowder-based weapons (which the Mongols had borrowed from Chinese inventors only to be used against them).

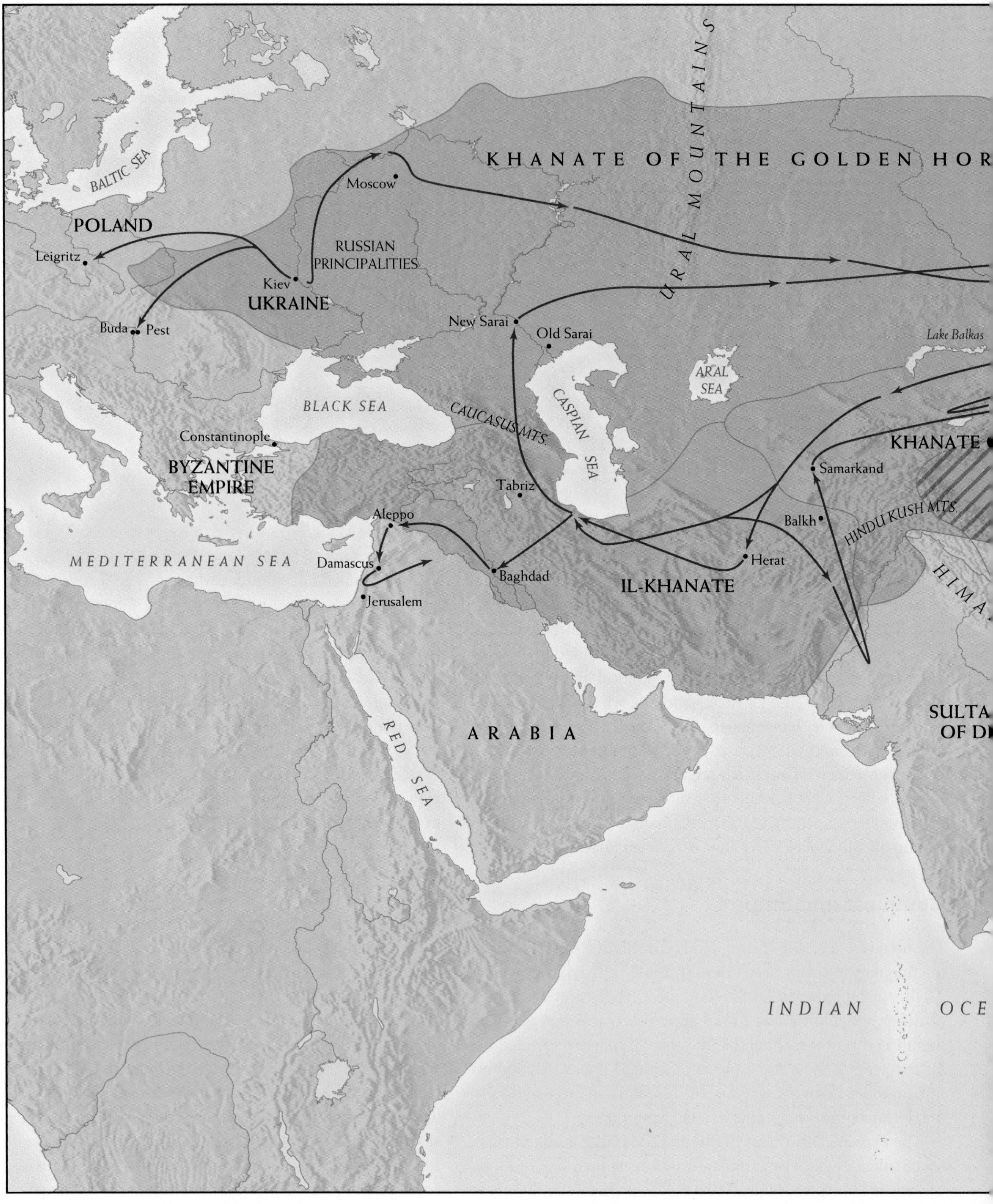
KHANATE OF THE GOLDEN HOR
URAL MOUNTAINS
BALTIC SEA
Moscow
POLAND
Leigritz
RUSSIAN PRINCIPALITIES
Kiev
UKRAINE
Buda
Pest
New Sarai
Old Sarai
Lake Balkas
ARAL SEA
BLACK SEA
CAUCASUS MTS.
CASPIAN SEA
Constantinople
BYZANTINE EMPIRE
KHANATE
Samarkand
Tabriz
Aleppo
Balkh
HINDU KUSH MTS.
MEDITERRANEAN SEA
Damascus
Baghdad
Herat
IL-KHANATE
Jerusalem
HIMA
ARABIA
RED SEA
SULTA
OF D
INDIAN
OCE

MAP 10.12 | Mongol Campaigns and Conquests, 1200–1300

Mongol campaigns and conquests brought Afro-Eurasian worlds together as never before. Trace the outline of the entire area of Mongol influence shaded on this map.

- What cultural groups did the Mongol armies conquer, partially conquer, or invade?
- How many different Khanates did the Mongols establish across Eurasia, and what were they?
- What role did geography play in limiting the spread of their influence?

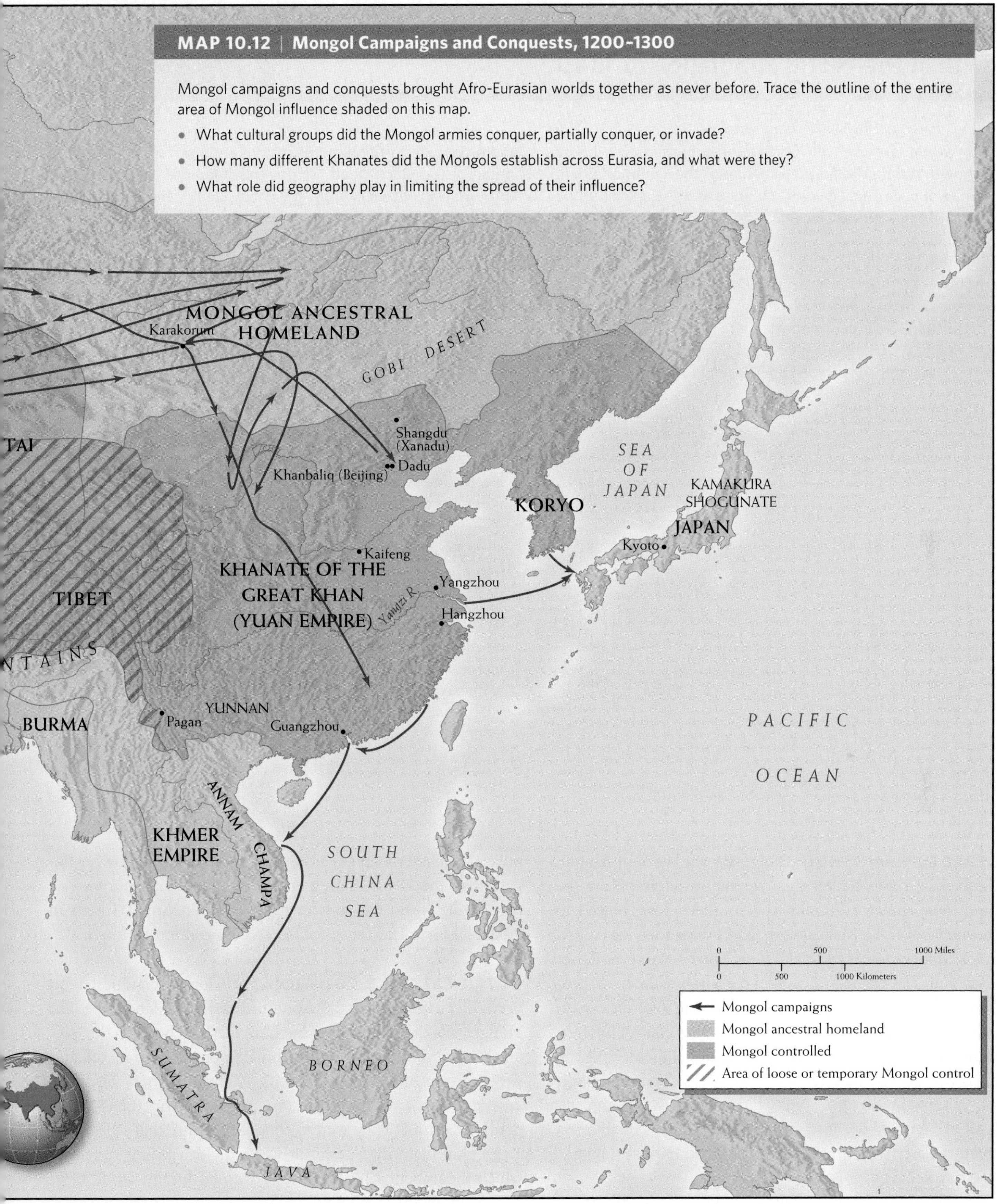

ANALYZING GLOBAL DEVELOPMENTS

Growth in the World Population to 1340

The world experienced considerable human population growth during the first millennium of the Common Era in spite of occasional downturns, such as in Asia and Europe between 200 CE and 600 CE that were the result of climate change, movement of peoples, and the decline of the Roman and Han Empires. Overall, however, an upward trajectory occurred though it averaged out to a mere .06 percent per year. For the period from 1750 to 1950 that percentage has increased to a little more than .5 percent per year, and since 1950 the number has risen to 1.75 percent per year. Even so, as we will see in the next chapter, the major populations in the Afro-Eurasian landmass were terrified by the loss of life that accompanied the spread of the Black Death across this immense area. Since the Afro-Eurasian recovery from the Black Death, the world's population has been on a steady increase, spectacularly so in the twentieth century, the result of more abundant food supplies, more accurate knowledge of the spread of diseases and a resulting control of epidemic diseases, and a general rise in the standards of living.

Regional Human Population (in millions)						
Year	**Asia**	**Europe**	**Africa**	**Americas**	**Oceania**	**World**
400 BCE	97	30	17	8	1	**153**
1 CE	172	41	26	12	1	**252**
200	160	55	30	11	1	**257**
600	136	31	24	16	1	**208**
1000	154	41	39	18	1	**253**
1200	260	64	48	26	2	**400**
1340	240	88	80	32	2	**442**

Source: Massimo Livi-Bacci, A Concise History of World Population *(Malden, MA: Wiley-Blackwell, 2012), p. 25.*

QUESTIONS FOR ANALYSIS

- Why was the rate of population growth so limited in premodern times?
- Comparing the population size of the regions in 1340, what do the numbers tell us about where the largest share of wealth and power resided? How does this compare to earlier moments in the chart?
- Why was the population of the Americas in 1340 so small considering its large territorial size?
- Why were the peoples living in the Afro-Eurasian landmass so vulnerable to epidemic diseases in the fourteenth century?
- How do changes in global population relate to the developments tracked in this chapter: a maritime revolution, a more integrally connected Africa; a thriving Abbasid caliphate; and an expanding Mongol Empire?

THE FALL OF HANGZHOU Hangzhou, the last Song capital, succumbed in 1276. Rather than see the invaders pillage the city and their emperors' tombs, the Southern Song bowed to the inevitable. Kubilai Khan's most able commander, Bayan, led his crack Mongol forces in seizing town after town, ever closer to the capital. The Empress Dowager tried to buy them off, proposing substantial tribute payments, but Bayan kept his eye on the prize: Hangzhou, which fell under Mongol control but survived reasonably intact. Bayan escorted the emperor and the Empress Dowager to Beijing, where Kubilai treated them with honor. Within three years, Song China's defeat was complete. With all of South China in their grip, the Mongols established the Yuan dynasty with a new capital at Dadu ("Great Capital," present-day Beijing).

Although it fell to Mongol control, Hangzhou was still one of the greatest cities in the world when it was visited by the Venetian traveler Marco Polo in the 1280s and by the Muslim traveler Ibn Battuta in the 1340s. Both men agreed that neither Europe nor the Islamic world had anything like it. (See Current Trends in World History: The Travels of Marco Polo and Ibn Battuta.)

OUTSIDERS TAKE CONTROL The Mongol conquest both north and south changed the political and social landscape. But Mongol rule did not impose rough steppe-land ways on the "civilized" urbanite Chinese. Non-Chinese outsiders—a mixed and varied group of Mongols, Tanguts, Khitan, Jurchen, Muslims, Tibetans, Persians, Turks, Nestorians, Jews, Armenians—took political control. They were a conquering elite that ruled over a vast Han majority. The result was a divided ruling system in which incumbent Chinese elites governed locally, while newcomers managed the central dynastic polity and collected taxes for the Mongols.

Mongols on Horseback. *Even after the Mongols became the rulers of China, the emperors remembered their steppe origin and maintained the skills of horse-riding nomads. This detail from a thirteenth/fourteenth-century silk painting shows Kubilai Khan hunting.*

Mongol Reverberations in Southeast Asia

Southeast Asia also felt the whiplash of conquest. Circling Song defenses in southern China, the Mongols galloped southwest and conquered states in Yunnan and in Burma. From there, in the 1270s, the armies headed directly back east into the soft underbelly of the Song state. In this sweep, portions of mainland Southeast Asia became annexed to China for the first time. Even the distant Khmer regime felt repercussions when the Mongol fleet, which grew out of the conquered Song navy, passed by on its way to attack Java (unsuccessfully) in 1293. Kubilai Khan used the conquered Chinese fleets to push his expansionism onto the high seas—meeting with failure during the unsuccessful 1274 and 1281 invasions of Japan from Korea. The ill-fated Javanese expedition was his last.

The Fall of Baghdad

In the thirteenth century, Mongol tribesmen streamed out of the steppes, crossing the whole of Asia and entering the eastern parts of Europe. Mongke Khan, a grandson of Chinggis, made clear the Mongol aspiration for world domination: he appointed his brother Kubilai to rule over China, Tibet, and the northern parts of India; and he commanded another brother, Hulagu, to conquer Iran, Syria, Egypt, Byzantium, and Armenia.

When Hulagu reached Baghdad in 1258, he encountered a feeble foe and a city that was a shadow of its former glorious self. Merely 10,000 horsemen faced his army of 200,000 soldiers, who were eager to acquire the booty of a wealthy city. Even before the battle had taken place, Baghdadi poets were composing elegies for their dead and mourning the defeat of Islam.

The slaughter was vast. Hulagu himself boasted of taking the lives of at least 200,000 people. The Mongols pursued their adversaries everywhere. They hunted them in wells, latrines, and sewers and followed them into the upper floors of buildings, killing them on rooftops until, as an Iraqi Arab historian observed, "blood poured from the gutters into the streets. . . . The same happened in the mosques" (Lewis, pp. 82–83). In a few weeks of sheer terror, the venerable Abbasid caliphate was demolished. Hulagu's forces showed no mercy to the caliph himself, who was rolled up in a carpet and trampled to death by horses, his blood soaked up by the rug so it would leave no mark on the ground. With Baghdad crushed, the Mongol armies pushed on to Syria, slaughtering Muslims along the way.

In the end, the Egyptian Mamluks stemmed the advancing Mongol armies and prevented Egypt from falling into their hands. The Mongol Empire had reached its outer limits. Better at conquering than governing, the Mongols struggled to rule their vast possessions in makeshift states. Bit by bit, they yielded control to local administrators and dynasts who governed as their surrogates. There was also chronic feuding among the Mongol dynasts themselves. In China and in Persia, Mongol rule collapsed in the fourteenth century.

Mongol conquest reshaped Afro-Eurasia's social landscape. Islam would never again have a unifying authority like the caliphate or a powerful center like Baghdad. China, too, was divided and changed, but in other ways. The Mongols introduced Persian, Islamic, and Byzantine influences on China's architecture, art, science, and medicine. The Yuan policy of benign tolerance also brought elements from Christianity, Judaism, Zoroastrianism, and Islam into the Chinese mix. The Mongol thrust led to a great opening, as fine goods, traders, and technology flowed from China to the rest of the world in ensuing centuries. Finally, the Mongol conquests, somewhat like those of Alexander the Great in an earlier age (see Chapter 5), encouraged an Afro-Eurasian interconnectedness, but on a scale that the huge landmass had not known before and would not experience again for hundreds of years. Out of conquest and warfare would come centuries of trade, migration, and increasing contacts among Africa, Europe, and Asia.

CURRENT TRENDS IN WORLD HISTORY

The Travels of Marco Polo and Ibn Battuta

Travelers are one of the most important resources for world historians because they create firsthand accounts of foreign rulers, their societies, and their cultures through their diaries, letters, and books. Recall from the start of the chapter our two Turkish-Christian monks, Bar Sāwmā and Markōs, whom Kubilai Khan sent to learn more about the Muslims and Europeans prior to the Mongol invasions across the Afro-Eurasian landmass. At nearly the same time they were setting out on their travels, Marco Polo, one of the most famous European travelers, was setting out to visit China and the Mongol emperor, creating one of the most widely read travel narratives in world history. It also helped motivate the search for the most direct route to China and Southeast Asia. Only fifty years later, Ibn Battuta would travel most of the known Islamic world, leaving an invaluable portrait of much of North Africa, Southwest Asia, and South Asia.

Polo and Battuta encountered a world linked by trade routes that often had as their ultimate destination the imperial court of the Great Khan in China. These two men, and less celebrated travelers, observed worlds that were highly localized and yet culturally unified.

In 1271, Marco Polo (1254–1324), the son of an enterprising Venetian merchant, set out with his father and uncle on a journey to East Asia. Making their way along the fabled Silk Road across central Asia, after a three-and-a-half-year journey the Polos arrived in Xanadu, the summer capital of the Mongol Empire. There they remained for more than two decades. When they returned to Venice in 1295, fellow townsmen greeted them with astonishment, believing that the Polos had perished years before. So, too, Marco Polo's published account of his travels generated an incredulous reaction. Some of his European readers considered his tales of eastern wonders to be mere fantasy, yet others found their appetites for Asian splendor whetted by his descriptions.

A half-century after Polo began his travels, the Moroccan-born scholar Muhammad ibn Abdullah ibn Battuta (1304–1369) embarked on a journey of his own. Then just twenty-one, he vowed to visit the whole of the Islamic world without traveling the same road twice. It was an ambitious goal, for Islam's domain extended from one end of the Afro-Eurasian landmass to the other and far into Africa as well. On his journey, Ibn Battuta eventually covered some 75,000 miles. Along his way, he claimed to have met at least sixty rulers, and in his book he recorded the names of more than 2,000 persons whom he knew personally.

The writings of Marco Polo and Ibn Battuta provide a wealth of information on the well-traversed lands of Africa, Europe, and Asia. What they and other travelers observed was the extreme diversity of Afro-Eurasian peoples, reflecting numerous ethnicities, political formations, and religious faiths. In addition, they observed that the vast majority of people lived deeply localized lives, primarily seeking to obtain the basic necessities of everyday life. Yet, they were also aware the same societies welcomed trade and cultural exchange. In fact, they wrote most eloquently about how each of the four major cultural systems of the landmass—Christian, Muslim, Indian, and Chinese—struggled

CONCLUSION

Between 1000 and 1300, Afro-Eurasia was forming large cultural spheres. As trade and migration spanned longer distances, these spheres prospered and became more integrated. In central Afro-Eurasia, Islam was firmly established, its merchants, scholars, and travelers acting as commercial and cultural intermediaries joining the landmass together, as they spread their universalizing faith. As seaborne trade expanded, India, too, became a commercial crossroads. Merchants in its port cities welcomed traders arriving from Arab lands to the west, from China, and from Southeast Asia. China also boomed, pouring its manufactures into trading networks that reached throughout Afro-Eurasia and even into Africa. Christian Europe had two centers, both of which were at war with Islam. In the east, Byzantium was a formidable empire with a resplendent and unconquerable capital city, Constantinople, in many ways the pride of Christianity. In the west, the Catholic papacy had risen from the ashes of the Roman Empire and sought to extend its ecclesiastical authority over Rome's territories in western Europe.

Trade helped outline the parts of the world. The prosperity it brought also supported new classes of people—thinkers, writers, and naturalists—who clarified what it meant to belong to the regions of Afro-Eurasia. By 1300, learned priests and writers had begun to reimagine these regions as more than just territories: they were maturing into cultures with definable geographic boundaries. Increasingly these intellectuals delivered their messages to commoners as well as to rulers.

Neither the Americas nor sub-Saharan Africa saw the same degree of integration, but trade and migration in these areas had profound effects. Certain African cultures flourished as they encountered the commercial energy of trade on the Indian

to define itself. Interestingly, if Ibn Battuta and Marco Polo had been able to travel in the "unknown" worlds—the African hinterlands, the Americas, and Oceania—they would have witnessed to varying degrees similar phenomena and challenges.

QUESTIONS FOR ANALYSIS

- To what extent were travelers like Marco Polo and Ibn Battuta connecting new worlds as opposed to following routes that had already been established by others?
- What were the different incentives that impelled Marco Polo and Ibn Battuta to undertake their journeys of exploration? And what might that tell us about how and why greatly divergent worlds contact each other?
- Why were the Polos and Ibn Battuta able to undertake very long-range journeys? What enables travelers like these to function and to strengthen connections across the globe?

Marco Polo. *This medieval painting shows the caravan of Marco Polo's father and uncle crossing Asia.*

Explore Further

Ibn Battuta, *The Travels of Ibn Battuta,* translated by H. A. R. Bigg (2002).

Polo, Marco, *The Travels of Marco Polo,* edited by Manuel Komroff, translated by William Marsden (1926).

Ocean. Africans' trade with one another linked coastal and interior regions in an ever more integrated world. American peoples also built cities that dominated cultural areas and thrived through trade. American cultures shared significant features: reliance on trade, maize, and the exchange of goods such as shells and precious feathers. And larger areas honored the same spiritual centers.

By 1300, trade, migration, and conflict were connecting Afro-Eurasian worlds in unprecedented ways. When Mongol armies swept into China, into Southeast Asia, and into the heart of Islam, they applied a thin, surface-like coating of political integration to these widespread regions and built on existing trade links. At the same time, most people's lives remained quite local, driven by the need for subsistence and governed by spiritual and governmental representatives acting at the behest of distant authorities. Still, locals noticed the evidence of cross-cultural exchanges everywhere—in the clothing styles of provincial elites, such as Chinese silks in Paris or Quetzal plumes in northern Mexico; in enticements to move (and forced removals) to new frontiers; in the news of faraway conquests or advancing armies. Worlds were coming together within themselves and across territorial boundaries, while remaining apart as they sought to maintain their own identity and traditions. In Afro-Eurasia especially, as the movement of goods and peoples shifted from ancient land routes to sea-lanes, these contacts were more frequent and far-reaching. Never before had the world seen so much activity connecting its parts. Nor within them had there been so much shared cultural similarity—linguistic, religious, legal, and military. By the time the Mongol Empire arose, the regions composing the globe were those that we now recognize as the cultural spheres of today's world.

AFTER YOU READ THIS CHAPTER

Review and research on **STUDYSPACE:** wwnorton.com/studyspace

TRACING THE GLOBAL STORYLINES

FOCUS ON: *Foundational Cultural Spheres*

The Islamic World

- Islam undergoes a burst of expansion, prosperity, and cultural diversification but remains politically fractured.
- Arab merchants and Sufi mystics spread Islam over great distances and make it more appealing to other cultures, helping to transform Islam into a foundational world.
- Islam travels across the Sahara Desert; the powerful gold- and slave-supplying empire of Mali arises in West Africa.

China

- The Song dynasty reunites China after three centuries of fragmented rulership, reaching into the past to reestablish a sense of a "true" Chinese identity as the Han, through a widespread print culture and denigration of outsiders.
- Breakthroughs in iron metallurgy allow agricultural expansion to support 120 million people and undergird Han commercial success.
- China undergoes the world's first manufacturing revolution: gunpowder, porcelain, and handicrafts are produced on a large scale for widespread consumption.

India

- India remains a mosaic under the canopy of Hinduism despite cultural interconnections and increasing prosperity.
- The invasion of Turkish Muslims leads to the Delhi Sultanate, which rules over India for three centuries, strengthening cultural diversity and tolerance.

Christian Europe

- Catholicism becomes a "mass" faith and helps to create a common European cultural identity.
- An emphasis on religious education spawns numerous universities and a new intellectual elite.
- Feudalism causes a fundamental reordering of the elite-peasant relationship, leading to agricultural and commercial expansion.
- Europe's growing confidence is manifest in the Crusades and Reconquista, an effort to drive Islam out of Christian lands.

CHRONOLOGY

Sub-Saharan Africa

Kingdom of Mali emerges (King Mansa Musa 1312–1332) **1100**

Great Zimbabwe flourishes **1100**

The Americas

Cahokia flourishes as a commercial hub in North America **1000**

Moche people found city of Chan Chan in South America **900**

Toltecs dominate valley of Mexico **900–1100**

Chimú Empire in South America **1000–1460**

The Islamic World

Turkish migrants and armies spread into Islamic world's heartland **1000**

South Asia

Central Asian invasions begin **1000**

East Asia

Southeast Asia

Europe

Reconquista of the Iberian Peninsula **1061–1492**

Crusades **1095–1272**

1000 1100

KEY TERMS

Angkor Wat p. 383

Cahokia p. 392

compass p. 360

Crusades p. 388

Delhi Sultanate p. 374

dhimma system p. 371

dhows p. 360

feudalism p. 384

Kubilai Khan p. 395

Mongols p. 394

rajas p. 374

Sufism p. 368

STUDY QUESTIONS

1. **List** the four major cultural regions in Afro-Eurasia, and briefly explain the defining characteristics of each. What did the various people and groups in these geographic areas all have in common that distinguished them from others?
2. **Explain** the role of global commercial hubs in India, China, and Egypt in fostering commercial contacts across Afro-Eurasia. How did they reflect revolutions in maritime transportation?
3. **Which areas** of sub-Saharan Africa were parts of the larger Afro-Eurasian world by 1300? How did contact with other regions shape political and cultural developments in sub-Saharan Africa?
4. **Describe** the cultural diversity within the Islamic world during this era. How did diverse Islamic communities achieve a uniform regional identity?
5. **Analyze** the impact of Muslim Turkish invaders on India. To what extent did India remain distinct from the Islamic world in this era?
6. **Describe** how the Song dynasty reacted to the military strength of its nomadic pastoral neighbors. How did these relationships foster a distinct Chinese identity?
7. **Compare and contrast** cultural and political developments in Korea, Japan, and Southeast Asia during this era. How did other regional cultures influence these societies?
8. **Describe** how Christianity expanded its geographic reach during this era. How did this expansion affect Latin Christianity in western Europe and Orthodox Christianity in eastern Europe?
9. **Analyze** the extent to which peoples in the Americas established closer contact with each other. How extensive were these contacts compared with those in the Afro-Eurasian world?
10. **Describe** the empire that the Mongols created in the thirteenth century. How did their policies promote greater contact among the various regions of Afro-Eurasia?

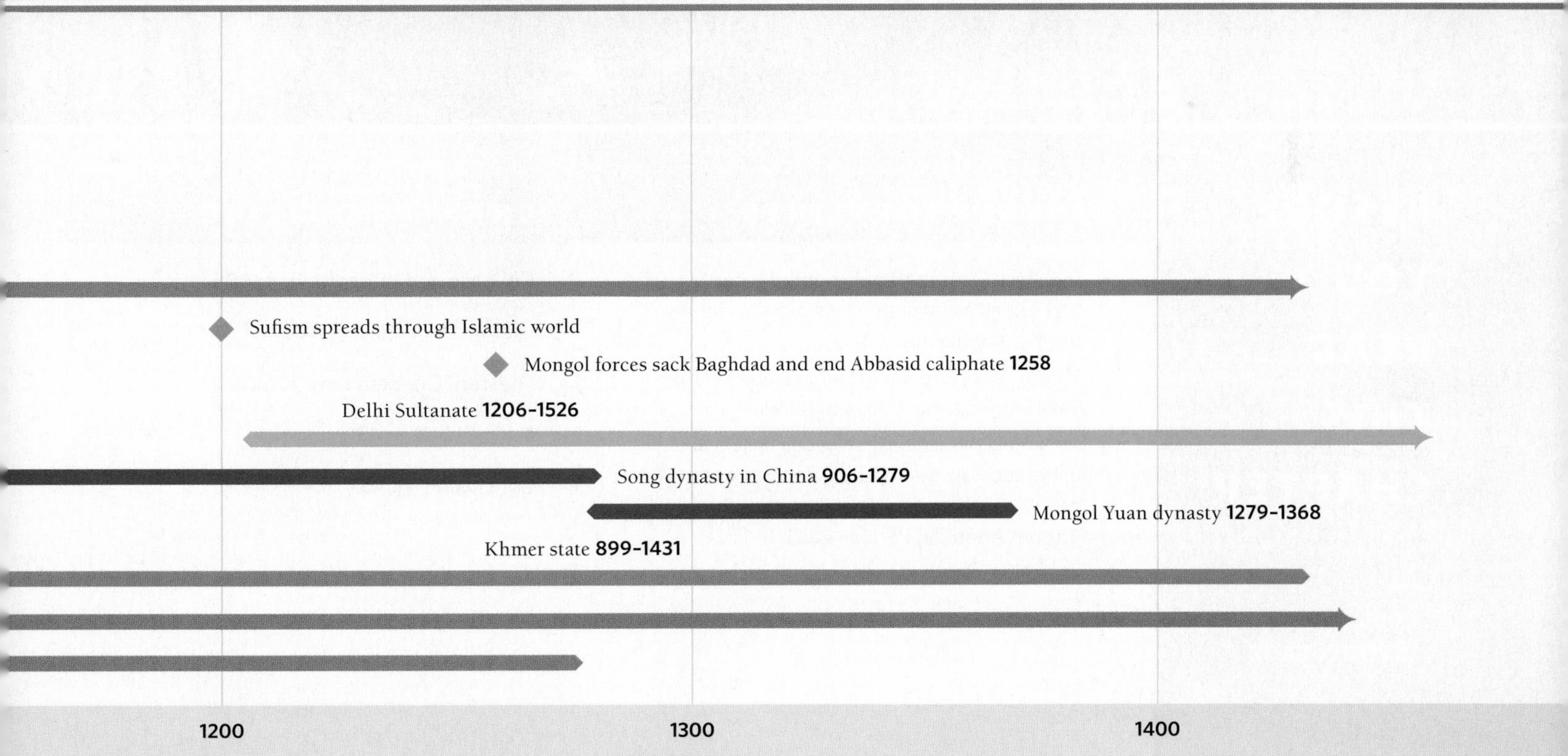

BEFORE YOU READ THIS CHAPTER

wwnorton.com/
STUDYSPACE

GLOBAL STORYLINES

- The Black Death spreading out of Inner Asia brings a staggering loss of life, claiming one-third of the population.
- Afro-Eurasians remake their societies in the wake of the plague's devastation.
- Something old remains: religious beliefs and institutions. And something new appears: radically different imperial dynasties in Europe, Anatolia, Persia (Iran), India, and China.

CHAPTER OUTLINE

11

Crises and Recovery in Afro-Eurasia, 1300–1500

FOCUS QUESTIONS

- How did Afro-Eurasian societies cope with the long-term repercussions from Mongol invasions and the Black Death?
- How were Afro-Eurasian states after the Black Death similar to and different from their predecessors?
- To what extent did the major cultural regions of Afro-Eurasia sustain their traditions and institutions under new political dynasties?
- How did state decisions regarding trade and expansion in Europe and China during this era shape world history?

When Mongol armies besieged the Genoese trading outpost of Caffa on the Black Sea in 1346, they not only damaged trading links between East Asia and the Mediterranean but also unleashed a devastating disease: the bubonic plague. Defeated Genoese merchants and soldiers withdrew, inadvertently taking the germs with them aboard their ships. By the time they arrived in Messina, Sicily, half the passengers were dead. The rest were dying. People waiting on shore for the ships' trade goods were horrified at the sight and turned the ships away. Desperately, the captains went to the next port, only to face the same fate. Despite these efforts at isolation, Europeans could not keep the plague (called the Black Death) from reaching their shores. As it spread from port to port it eventually contaminated all of Europe, killing nearly two-thirds of the population.

This story illustrates the disruptive effects of the Mongol invasions on Afro-Eurasian societies. Although the invasions ushered in an age of intensified cultural and political contact, the channels of exchange—the land trails and sea-lanes of human voyagers—became accidental conduits for deadly microbes. These germs devastated societies far more decisively than did Mongol warfare. They were the real "murderous hordes" of world history, infecting people from every community, class, and culture. So staggering was the Black Death's toll that population densities did not recover for 200 years. Most severely affected were regions that the Mongols had brought together: settlements and commercial hubs along the old Silk Road and around the Mediterranean Sea and the South China Sea. While segments of the Indian Ocean trading world experienced death and disruption, South Asian societies, which had escaped the Mongol conquest, also escaped the dying and political disruptions associated with the Black Death.

During the fourteenth and fifteenth centuries—following population loss, political crises, and social disorders—peoples struggled to remake their societies. This chapter explores the ways in which Afro-Eurasian peoples restored what they thought was valuable from the old while discarding what they felt had failed them, in favor of radically new institutions and ideas. Considering how grievously people suffered and how many had died, it is surprising that so much of the old (particularly religious beliefs and institutions) survived, though in modified forms. What was truly new and would prove enduring was a group of imperial dynasties that emerged all across Afro-Eurasia: national monarchies in Europe, Ottoman sultans in Anatolia, Safavids in Persia, Mughals in India, and Ming dynasts in China. The aftermath of Mongol rule and of the Black Death witnessed the transformation of the political setting in Afro-Eurasia. Focusing on the formation of new states with highly centralized forms of rulership, this chapter explores how societies coped with the long-term impact of the Mongol invasions and the Black Death.

Plague Victim. *The plague was highly contagious and after a series of grotesque symptoms, quickly resulted in death. Here the physician and his helper (left) cover their noses, most likely in attempt to block out the unbearable stench emanating from the patient's boils.*

COLLAPSE AND INTEGRATION

Although the Mongol invasions overturned political systems, the plague devastated society itself. Rulers could explain to their people the assaults of "barbarians," but it was much harder to make sense of an invisible enemy. Many concluded that mass death was God's wish. However, the upheaval gave ruling groups the opportunity to consolidate power by making dynastic matches through marriage, establishing new armies and taxes, and creating new systems to administer their states.

The Black Death

The spread of the Black Death out of inner Asia was the fourteenth century's most significant historical development (see Map 11.1). The disease stemmed from a combination of bubonic, pneumonic, and septicemic plague strains, and it caused a staggering loss of life. Among infected populations, death rates ranged from 25 to 65 percent.

How did the **Black Death** spread so far? One explanation may lie in climatic changes. A drying up of the central Asian steppe borderlands, where bubonic plague had existed for centuries, may have forced rodents out of their usual dwelling places and pressed pastoral peoples, who carried the strains, to move closer to settled agricultural communities. So, it is thought, began the migration of microbes. But what spread the germs across Afro-Eurasia was the Mongols' trading network. The first outbreak in a heavily populated region occurred in the 1320s in southwestern China. From there, the disease spread through China and then took its death march along the major trade routes. The main avenue of transmission was across central Asia to the Crimea and the Black Sea, and from there by ship to the Mediterranean Sea and the Italian city-states.

Secondary routes were by sea: one from China to the Red Sea, and another across the Indian Ocean, through the Persian Gulf, and into the Fertile Crescent and Iraq. All routes terminated at the Italian port cities, where ships with dead and dying men aboard arrived in 1347. From there, what Europeans called the Pestilence or the Great Mortality engulfed the western end of the landmass.

The Black Death struck an expanding Afro-Eurasian population, made vulnerable because its members had no immunities to the disease and because its major realms were thoroughly connected through trading networks. Rodents, mainly rats, carried the plague bacilli that caused the disease. Fleas transmitted the bacilli from rodent to rodent, as well as to humans. The epidemic was terrifying, for its causes were unknown at the time. Infected victims died quickly—sometimes overnight—and in great agony, coughing up blood and oozing pus and blood from ugly black sores the size of eggs. Some European sages attributed the ravaging of their societies to an unusual alignment of Saturn, Jupiter, and Mars. Many believed that God was angry with mankind. One Florentine historian compared the plague to the biblical Flood and believed that the end of mankind was imminent.

The Black Death wrought devastation throughout much of the landmass. The Chinese population plunged from around 120 million to 80 million over the course of a century. Europe saw its numbers shrink by two-thirds. When farmers were afflicted, food production collapsed. Famine then followed and killed off the weak survivors. Cities were the hardest hit. The population of London before the Black Death arrived was 100,000. Its numbers were reduced to 37,500 between 1346 and 1353. Refugees from the cities fled their homes, seeking security and food in the countryside. The shortage of food and other necessities led to rapidly rising prices, work stoppages, and unrest. Political leaders added to their unpopularity by repressing the unrest. The great Arab historian Ibn Khaldun (1332–1406), who lost his mother and father and a number of his teachers to the Black Death in Tunis, underscored the sense of desolation: "Cities and buildings were laid waste, roads and way signs were obliterated, settlements and mansions became empty, dynasties and tribes grew weak," he wrote. "The entire world changed."

Rebuilding States

Starting in the late fourteenth century, Afro-Eurasians began the task of reconstructing both their political order and their trading networks. (By then the plague had died down, though it continued to afflict peoples for centuries.) However, the rebuilding of military and civil administrations—no easy task—also required political legitimacy. Rulers needed to revive confidence in themselves and their polities, which they did by fostering beliefs and rituals that confirmed their legitimacy and by increasing their control over subjects.

The basis for power was the **dynasty**—the hereditary ruling family that passed control from one generation to the next. Dynasties sought to establish their legitimacy in three ways. First, ruling families insisted that their power derived from a divine calling: Ming emperors in China claimed for themselves what previous dynasts had asserted—the "mandate of heaven"—while European monarchs claimed to rule by "divine right." Either way, ruling households asserted that they were closer to the gods than to commoners. Second, leaders squelched squabbling among potential heirs by establishing clear rules about succession to the throne. Many European countries tried to standardize succession by passing titles to the eldest male heir, but in practice there were countless complications and quarrels. In the Islamic world, successors could be designated by the incumbent or elected by the community; here, too, struggles over succession were frequent. Third, ruling families elevated their power through conquest or alliance—by ordering armies to forcibly extend their domains, or by marrying their royal offspring to rulers of other states or members of other elite households. Once it established legitimacy, the typical royal family would consolidate power by enacting coercive laws and punishments and sending emissaries to govern far-flung territories. It would also establish standing armies and new administrative structures to collect taxes and to oversee building projects that proclaimed royal power.

The innovative state-building that occurred in the wake of the plague's devastation would not have been as successful had it not drawn on older traditions. In China, the Ming renounced the Mongol legacy by emphasizing their role in restoring Han rulership and by rejecting the Mongol eagerness to expand. In Europe, a cultural flourishing based largely on ancient Greek and Roman models gave rise to thinkers who proposed novel views of governance. The peoples of the Islamic world held fiercely to their religion as two successor states—the Ottoman Empire and the Safavid state—absorbed numerous Turkish-speaking groups. A third Islamic state—the Mughal Empire—drew on local traditions of religious and cultural tolerance as it built a new regime on the foundations of the weakened Delhi Sultanate (see Chapter 10). Many of these regimes lasted for centuries, promoting political institutions and cultural values that became deeply embedded in the fabric of their societies.

ISLAMIC DYNASTIES

The devastation of the Black Death following hard on the heels of the Mongol destruction of Islam's most important city and capital of the Abbasid Empire, Baghdad (see Chapter 10), eliminated

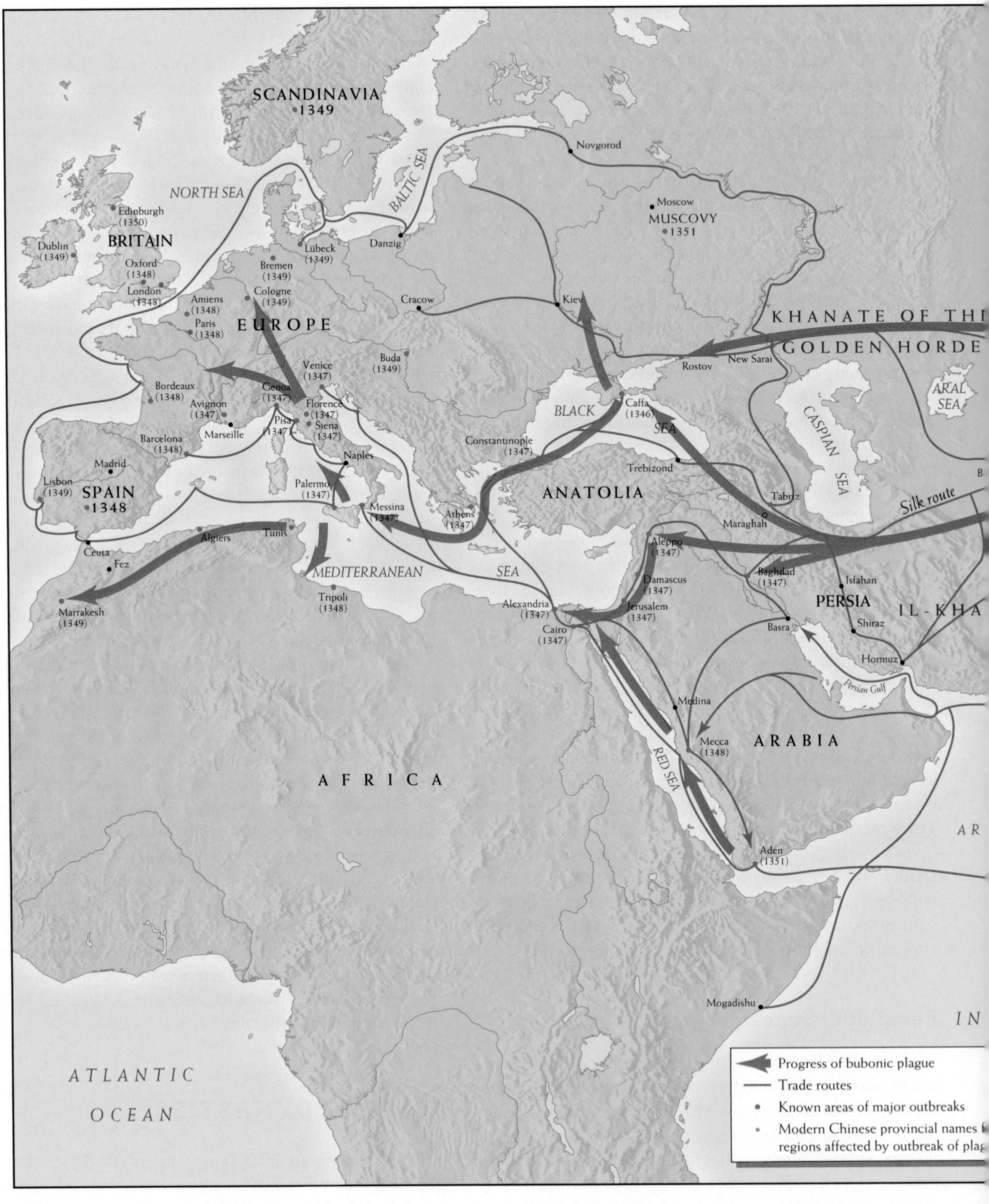
SCANDINAVIA
1349
NORTH SEA
BALTIC SEA
Novgorod
Moscow
MUSCOVY
1351
Edinburgh
(1350)
BRITAIN
Dublin
(1349)
Oxford
(1348)
London
(1348)
Lübeck
(1349)
Danzig
Bremen
(1349)
Cologne
(1349)
Amiens
(1348)
Paris
(1348)
EUROPE
Cracow
Kiev
KHANATE OF THE
GOLDEN HORDE
Rostov
New Sarai
ARAL SEA
CASPIAN SEA
Venice
(1347)
Buda
(1349)
Bordeaux
(1348)
Genoa
(1347)
Avignon
(1347)
Marseille
Florence
(1347)
Pisa
(1347)
Siena
(1347)
Barcelona
(1348)
BLACK SEA
Caffa
(1346)
Constantinople
(1347)
Trebizond
Madrid
Lisbon
(1349)
SPAIN
1348
Naples
Palermo
(1347)
Messina
(1347)
Athens
(1347)
ANATOLIA
Tabriz
Silk route
Maraghah
Ceuta
Algiers
Tunis
Fez
Aleppo
(1347)
Baghdad
(1347)
Isfahan
MEDITERRANEAN SEA
Damascus
(1347)
Tripoli
(1348)
Marrakesh
(1349)
Alexandria
(1347)
Jerusalem
(1347)
Cairo
(1347)
PERSIA
IL-KHA
Shiraz
Basra
Hormuz
Persian Gulf
Medina
Mecca
(1348)
ARABIA
RED SEA
AFRICA
Aden
(1351)
Mogadishu
ATLANTIC OCEAN
Progress of bubonic plague
Trade routes
Known areas of major outbreaks
Modern Chinese provincial names
regions affected by outbreak of plag

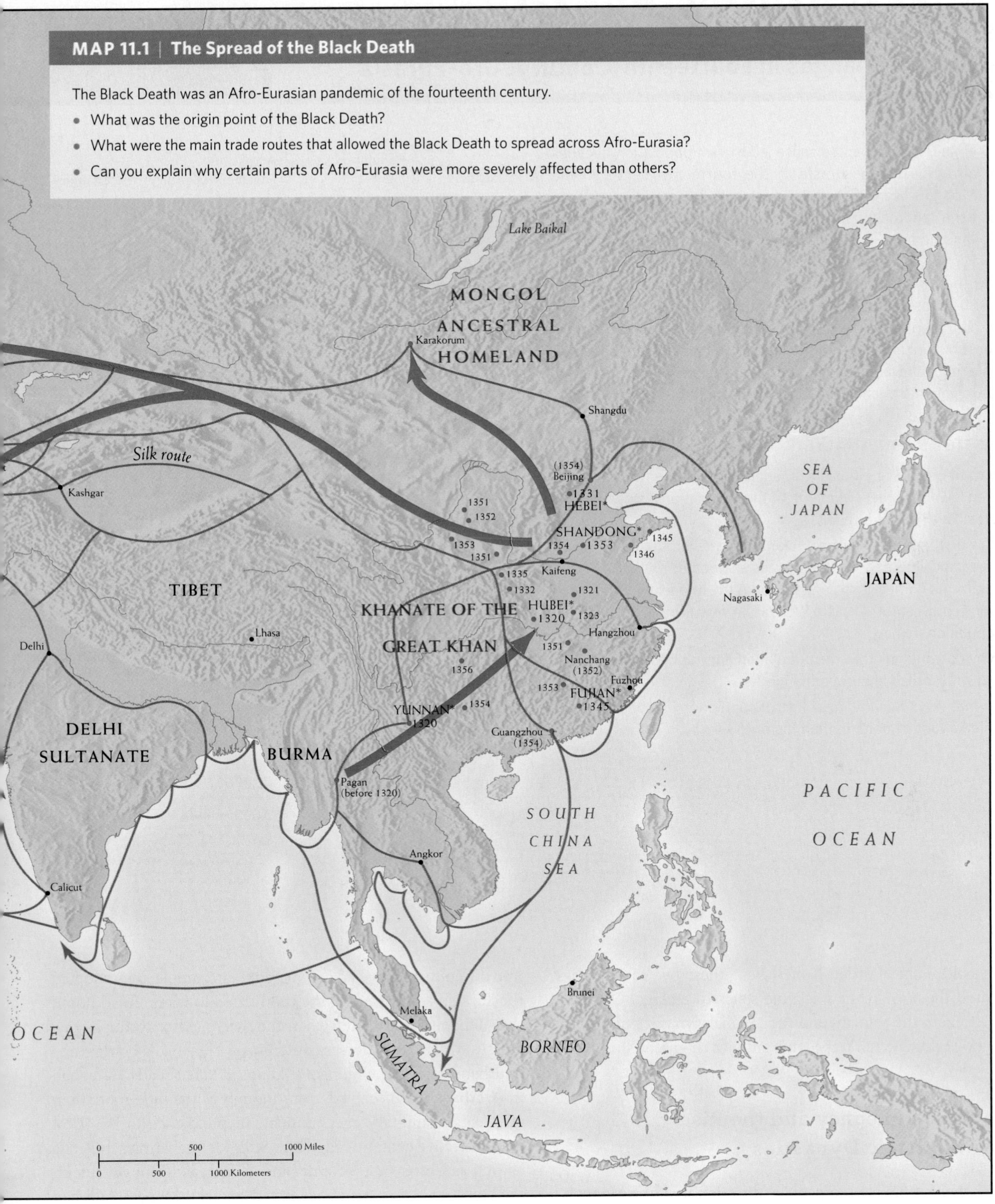

MAP 11.1 | The Spread of the Black Death

The Black Death was an Afro-Eurasian pandemic of the fourteenth century.

- What was the origin point of the Black Death?
- What were the main trade routes that allowed the Black Death to spread across Afro-Eurasia?
- Can you explain why certain parts of Afro-Eurasia were more severely affected than others?

ANALYZING GLOBAL DEVELOPMENTS

Population Changes in Fourteenth-Century Afro-Eurasia

Famine, warfare, and disease led to vast population declines all across Afro-Eurasia in the fourteenth century. The Mongols were instrumental players in spreading disease across the landmass, starting in China and moving westward along land and sea-based trading routes toward the Mediterranean World, and ultimately northern Europe (see Map 11-1). While the effects of these destructive forces were felt across the Afro-Eurasian landmass, some states and regions were less affected than others. The population data in the table come from the best historical studies of the last forty years and are based on painstaking archival research. They serve as one of the best ways for us to gain historical insight into this tumultuous century.

QUESTIONS FOR ANALYSIS

- In what regions or cities does population loss seem to have been lower? Higher? Why might those variations in death rates have been the case?
- How do the losses in urban areas compare with the losses in the region where those urban areas are located? What might that comparison suggest about the impact of fourteenth-century disasters on urban versus other populations?
- Why do you think that the population decline was more severe and widespread in Europe than in Asia?
- In what ways was the great loss of population in Europe and China a turning point in their histories?

Location	Population Figures	Across the Fourteenth Century	% Change
By Regions			
Europe	80 m in 1346	30 m in 1353	−60%
Asia	230 m in 1300	235 m in 1400	+2%
Islam	(regional data are not available)		
By Countries			
Spain	6 m in 1346	2.5 m in 1353	−60%
Italy	10 m in 1346	4.5 m in 1363	−55%
France	18 m in 1346	7.2 m in 1353	−60%
England	6 m in 1346	2.25 m in 1353	−62.5%
China	115 m in 1200	75 m in 1400	−35%
Japan	9.75 m in 1300	12.5 m in 1400	+28%
Korea	3 m in 1300	3.5 m in 1400	+17%
India	91 m in 1300	97 m in 1400	+6.5%
By Cities			
London	100,000 in 1346	37,000 in 1353	−62.5%
Florence	92,000 in 1346	37,250 in 1353	−59.5%
Siena	50,000 in 1346	20,000 in 1353	−60%
Bologna	50,000 in 1346	27,500 in 1353	−45%
Cairo	500,000 in 1300	300,000 in 1400	−40%
Damascus	80,000 in 1300	50,000 in 1400	−37%

Sources: Ole J. Benedictow, The Black Death, 1346–1353: The Complete History *(2004); Michael Dols,* The Black Death in the Middle East *(1974); Colin McEvedy and Richard Jones,* Atlas of World Population History *(1978). Ping-ti Ho,* Studies on the Population of China, 1368–1953 *(1959).*

Islam's old political order. Nonetheless, these two catastrophes prepared the way for new Islamic states to emerge. Of these, the Ottoman, the Safavid, and the Mughal dynasties ultimately grew powerful enough to become empires themselves.

The Mongol Legacy and the Rise of New Islamic Dynasties

Rather than assimilate the peoples they defeated, the Mongols, whose numbers were always small, often assimilated themselves into the cultures they had conquered. For example, they adopted the Turkish language, and they converted to Islam. In addition, the Mongols fared better when they were closer to the steppe grasses, where their horses could graze. They had a harder time in urban centers. The Mongol Il-khans in Persia made Maraghah in Azerbaijan their capital, even though it was little more than an enlarged military encampment, in preference to the great administrative center of Baghdad. Still, Mongol armies in Persia as well as China suffered a decline in prowess (Mongol rule in the southern Russian steppes lasted longer). Mongol rule had always had two components. One was an ability to terrorize opponents into voluntarily submitting by such tactics as parading the heads of resisters on pikes. But this strategy began to lose effectiveness and sometimes even backfired. The other Mongol tactic had involved borrowing skills from across the empire and promoting the exchange of technologies and knowledge. But new groups aspiring to rule could do this, too.

Muslim peoples had no respite following the Mongol conquests. The Black Death reached Baghdad by 1347, perhaps carried there by an Azerbaijani army that besieged the city. By the next year, the plague had overtaken Egypt, Syria, and Cyprus; one report from Tunis records the deaths of more than 1,000 people a day in that North African city. Animals, too, were afflicted. One Egyptian writer commented: "The country was not far from being ruined. . . . One found in the desert the bodies of savage animals with the bubos under their arms. It was the same with horses, camels, asses, and all the beasts in general, including birds, even the ostriches." In the eastern Mediterranean, the plague left much of the Islamic world in a state of near political and economic collapse.

As new polities emerged from this economic and demographic crisis, they had to build from the ground floor. Warrior chiefs and religious leaders vied to fill the political vacuum. After Mongol power waned, the new rulers—notably the Ottomans in Anatolia and the Safavids in western Persia—operated out of strategic locations in the Islamic heartland and gradually rebuilt state institutions.

Through migration, warfare, and the eventual consolidation of post-Mongol states, Islam's domain expanded. Prior to the Mongol invasions, the political, economic, and cultural centers of the Islamic world were in Egypt, Syria, and Iraq. Most of these territories' inhabitants spoke Arabic, the language of the Prophet Muhammad—hence the language of Islamic devotion and theology. These areas, along with the Arabian Peninsula, contained Islam's most holy cities: Mecca, Medina, Jerusalem, Damascus, Cairo, Baghdad, and various other cities in Iraq. Even before the Mongol invasions, Turks had migrated into these regions and Persian had become a rival language of Islamic poetry and philosophy. Yet it was the Mongol invasions, which brought devastation to Persia and Iraq and an influx of nomadic peoples, that enabled a new Islamic world to appear. (See Primary Source: Qalandar Dervishes in the Islamic World.)

THREE ISLAMIC EMPIRES This new Islamic world, now including large numbers of Turkish- and Persian-speaking populations, occupied a vast geographical triangle. It stretched from Anatolia in the west to Khurasan in the east and to the southern apex at Baghdad. Of course, the old Arabic-speaking Islamic world remained vital, still at the heart of Islam geographically, but it now had to cede authority to the new rulers and religious men.

The Ottomans, the Safavids, and the Mughals emerged as the dominant states in the old Islamic world in the early sixteenth century. They exploited the rich agrarian resources of the Indian Ocean regions and the Mediterranean Sea basin, and they benefited from a brisk seaborne and overland trade. By the mid-sixteenth century the Mughals controlled the northern Indus River valley; the Safavids occupied Persia; and the Ottomans ruled Anatolia, the Arab world, and much of southern and eastern Europe.

Despite sharing core Islamic beliefs, each empire had unique political features. The most powerful, the **Ottoman Empire**, occupied the pivotal area between Europe and Asia. The Ottomans embraced a Sunni view of Islam, while adopting traditional Byzantine ways of governance and trying new ways of integrating the diverse peoples of their expanding territories. The Safavids, though adherents of the Shiite vision of Islam, were at the same time ardently devoted to the pre-Islamic traditions of Persia (present-day Iran). An internally cohesive people, their rulers were not so effective at expanding beyond their Persian base. The Mughals ruled over the wealthy but divided realm that is much of today's India, Pakistan, and Bangladesh; here they carried even further the region's religious and political traditions of assimilating Islamic and pre-Islamic Indian ways. Their wealth and the decentralization of their domain made the Mughals constant targets for internal dissent and eventually for external aggression.

The Rise of the Ottoman Empire

Although the Mongols considered Anatolia to be a borderland region of little economic importance, their military forays against the Anatolian Seljuk Turkish state in the late thirteenth century opened up the region to new political forces. The ultimate victors here were the Ottoman Turks. They transformed themselves from warrior bands roaming the borderlands between Islamic and Christian worlds into rulers of a settled state and, finally, into sovereigns of a far-flung, highly bureaucratic empire (see Map 11.2).

Under their chief, Osman (r. 1299–1326), the Turkish Ottomans formalized a stern and disciplined warrior ethos, and they triumphed over many rivals by assimilating the techniques of settled administration from their neighbors. Other warrior bands, which lived off the land and fought for booty under charismatic military leaders, had little regard for artisans, merchants, bureaucrats, and clerics. By contrast, the Ottomans realized that the consolidation of power depended on attracting just these groups. In time, not only did the Ottoman state (based in Bursa in western Anatolia) win the favor of Islamic clerics, but it also became the champion of Sunni Islam throughout the Islamic world.

By the mid-fourteenth century, the Ottomans had expanded into the Balkans, becoming the most powerful force in the

PRIMARY SOURCE

Qalandar Dervishes in the Islamic World

The Qalandar dervish order sprang up in Damascus, Syria, and Egypt in the thirteenth century and spread rapidly throughout the Islamic world. In reaction to the period's widespread unrest, its members renounced the world and engaged in highly individualistic practices as they moved from place to place. The educated elite, however, criticized them as ignorant hypocrites living on alms obtained from gullible common folk. One of their practices was chiromancy, or palm-reading. In this excerpt Giovan Antonio Manavino, a European observer of Ottoman society, gives an obviously biased account of the Qalandars, whom he called the torlaks.

Dressed in sheepskins, the *torlaks* [Qalandars] are otherwise naked, with no headgear. Their scalps are always clean-shaven and well rubbed with oil as a precaution against the cold. They burn their temples with an old rag so that their faces will not be damaged by sweat. Illiterate and unable to do anything manly, they live like beasts, surviving on alms only. For this reason, they are to be found around taverns and public kitchens in cities. If, while roaming the countryside, they come across a well-dressed person, they try to make him one of their own, stripping him naked. Like Gypsies in Europe, they practice chiromancy, especially for women who then provide them with bread, eggs, cheese, and other foods in return for their services.

Amongst them there is usually an old man whom they revere and worship like God. When they enter a town, they gather around the best house of the town and listen in great humility to the words of this old man, who, after a spell of ecstasy, foretells the descent of a great evil upon the town. His disciples then implore him to fend off the disaster through his good services. The old man accepts the plea of his followers, though not without an initial show of reluctance, and prays to God, asking him to spare the town the imminent danger awaiting it. This time-honored trick earns them considerable sums of alms from ignorant and credulous people.

QUESTIONS FOR ANALYSIS

- Describe the way the Qalandar dervishes dressed, where they congregated, and how they obtained food. How did their lifestyle reflect the turmoil of the times?
- Why do you think the Qalandars chose individualistic practices rather than communal living?
- Why do you think Manavino is so critical of the Qalandars?

Source: Ahmet T. Karamustafa, "Dervish Groups in the Ottoman Empire, 1450–1550" from God's Unruly Friends: Dervish Groups in the Islamic Later Middle Period, 1200–1550, *pp. 6–7. Oneworld Publications, Oxford, 2006. Reprinted with the permission of Oneworld Publications.*

eastern Mediterranean and western Asia. The state controlled a vast territory, stretching in the west to the Moroccan border, in the north to Hungary and Moldavia, in the south through the Arabian Peninsula, and in the east to the Iraqi-Persian border. At the top of the Ottomans' elaborate hierarchy stood the sultan. Below him was a military and civilian bureaucracy, whose task was to demand obedience and revenue from subjects. The bureaucracy's vigilance enabled the sultan to expand his realm, which in turn forced him to invest in an even larger bureaucracy.

THE CONQUEST OF CONSTANTINOPLE The empire's spectacular expansion was primarily a military affair. To recruit followers, the Ottomans promised wealth and glory to new subjects. This was an expensive undertaking, but territorial expansion generated vast financial and administrative rewards. Moreover, by spreading the spoils of conquest and lucrative administrative positions, rulers bought off potentially discontented subordinates. Still, without military might, the Ottomans would not have enjoyed the successes associated with the brilliant reigns of Murad II (r. 1421–1451) and his aptly named successor, Mehmed the Conqueror (r. 1451–1481).

Mehmed's most spectacular triumph was the conquest of Constantinople, an ambition for Muslim rulers ever since the birth of Islam. Mehmed left no doubt that this was his primary goal: shortly after his coronation he vowed to capture the capital of the Byzantine Empire, a city of immense strategic and commercial importance. He knew this feat would require a large

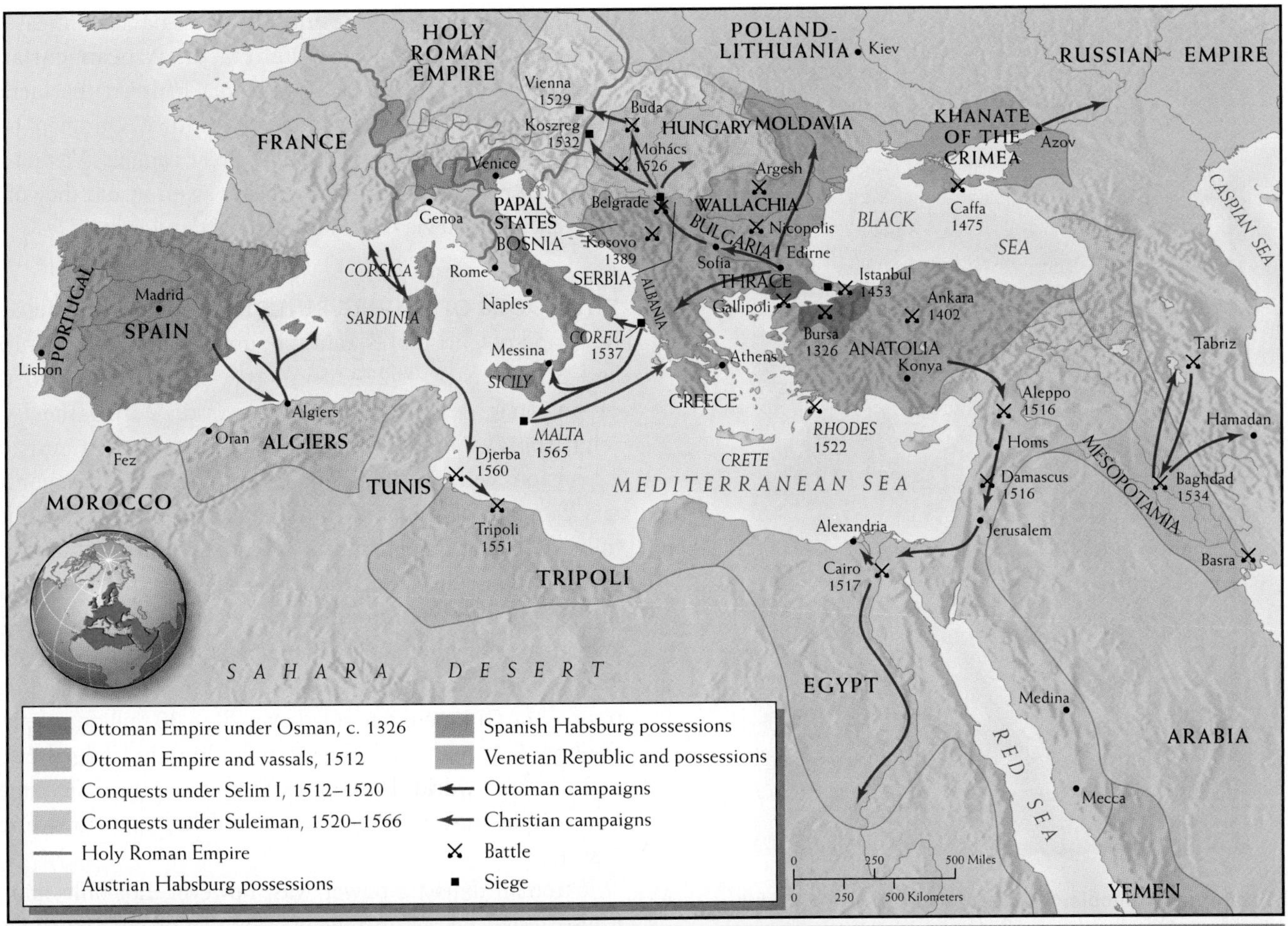

MAP 11.2 | The Ottoman Empire, 1300-1566

This map charts the expansion of the Ottoman state from the time of its founder, Osman, through the reign of Suleiman, the empire's most illustrious ruler.

- Identify the earliest part of the empire under Osman. Then identify all the areas of conquest under Suleiman. Against whom did the Ottomans fight between the years 1326 and 1566?
- What were the geographic limits of the empire?
- According to your reading, how did Ottoman rulers promote unity among such a diverse population?

and well-armed fighting force, for the heavily fortified city had kept Muslims at bay for almost a century. First he built a fortress of his own, on the European bank of the Bosporus strait, to prevent European vessels from reaching the capital. Then, by promising his soldiers free access to booty and portraying the city's conquest as a holy cause, he amassed a huge army that outnumbered the defending force of 7,000 by more than tenfold. For forty days his troops bombarded Constantinople's massive walls with artillery that included enormous cannons built by Hungarian and Italian engineers. On May 29, 1453, Ottoman troops overwhelmed the surviving soldiers and took the ancient Roman and Christian capital of Byzantium—which Mehmed promptly renamed Istanbul.

Although Christians generally portrayed the "fall" of Constantinople as an insult and a disaster, in fact the Muslim conquest had cultural benefits for western Europe. Many Christian survivors fled to ports in the west, bringing with them classical and Arabic manuscripts previously unknown in Europe. The well-educated, Greek-speaking émigrés generally became teachers and translators, thereby helping to revive Europeans' interest in classical antiquity and spreading knowledge of ancient Greek (which had virtually died out in medieval times).

The Fall of Constantinople. *The use of heavy artillery in the fifty-three-day siege of Constantinople was instrumental to the Ottoman victory. At the center of this Turkish miniature is one such cannon, possibly of Hungarian origin, which required hundreds of men and oxen to transport and secure outside the city walls.*

These manuscripts and teachers would play a vital role in Europe's Renaissance.

The Ottomans followed their capture of Constantinople with other military successes that put many of Christian Europe's great cities in peril. Their forces sacked Athens in 1458, then took Bosnia in 1463. In 1480 the Ottomans launched an invasion of Italy. They captured one port city; but Mehmed II's death, and fights between his sons for control of the empire, prevented further conquests in Italy. The Ottomans then turned to the Balkans and central Europe, invading Hungary in 1492 and Croatia in 1493. Their inroads so frightened the French king that he decided to invade Italy himself in order to lead his own crusade against the Ottomans.

Meanwhile, Mehmed made Istanbul the Ottoman capital, adopting Byzantine administrative practices to unify his enlarged state and incorporating many of Byzantium's powerful families into it. From Istanbul, Mehmed and his successors would continue their expansion, eventually seizing all of Greece and the Balkan region. As a result, Ottoman navies increasingly controlled sea-lanes in the eastern Mediterranean, curtailing European access to the rich ports that handled the lucrative caravan trade. By the late fifteenth century, Ottoman forces menaced another of Christendom's great capitals, Vienna, and European merchants feared that never again would they obtain the riches of Asia via the traditional overland route.

THE TOOLS OF EMPIRE BUILDING Having penetrated the heartland of Christian Byzantium, under Selim (r. 1512–1520) and Suleiman (r. 1520–1566), the Ottomans turned their expansionist designs to the Arab world. During the latter's reign the Ottomans reached the height of their territorial expansion, with Suleiman himself leading thirteen major military campaigns and many minor engagements. An exceptional military leader, Suleiman was an equally gifted administrator. His subjects called him "the Lawgiver" and "the Magnificent" in recognition of his attention to civil bureaucratic efficiency and justice for his people. His fame spread to Europe, where he was known as "the Great Turk." Under Suleiman's administration, the Ottoman state ruled over 20 to 30 million people. By the time Suleiman died, the Ottoman Empire bridged Europe and the Arab world. Istanbul by then was a dynamic imperial hub, dispatching bureaucrats and military men to oversee a vast domain.

Ottoman dynastic power was, however, not only military; it also rested on a firm religious foundation. At the center of this empire were the sultans, who combined a warrior ethos with an unwavering devotion to Islam. Describing themselves as the "shadow of God" on earth, they claimed to be caretakers for the welfare of the Islamic faith. Throughout the empire, the sultans devoted substantial resources to the construction of elaborate mosques and to the support of Islamic schools. As self-appointed defenders of the faithful, the sultans assumed the role of protectors of the holy cities on the Arabian Peninsula and of Jerusalem, defending the realm's internal cohesion and constantly striving to extend the borders of Islam. Thus the Islamic faith helped to unite a diverse and sprawling imperial populace, with the sultan's power fusing the sacred and the secular.

ISTANBUL AND THE TOPKAPI PALACE Istanbul reflected the splendor of this awesome empire. After the Ottoman conquest, the sultans' engineers rebuilt the city's crumbling walls, while their architects redesigned homes, public buildings, baths, inns, and marketplaces to display the majesty of Islam's new imperial center. To crown his achievements, Suleiman ordered the construction of the Suleymaniye Mosque, which sat opposite the Hagia Sophia. That domed Byzantine cathedral was formerly the most sacred of Christian cathedrals, the largest house of worship in all of Christendom, but

The Suleymaniye Mosque. *Built by Sultan Suleiman to crown his achievements, the Suleymaniye Mosque was designed by the architect Sinan to dominate the city and to have four tall minarets from which the faithful were called to prayer.*

Suleiman had it turned into a mosque. Moreover, the Ottoman dynasts welcomed (indeed, forcibly transported) thousands of Muslims and non-Muslims to the city and revived Istanbul as a major trading center. Within twenty-five years of its conquest, its population more than tripled; by the end of the sixteenth century, 400,000 people regularly swarmed through its streets and knelt in its mosques, making it the world's largest city outside China.

Istanbul's **Topkapi Palace** reflected the Ottomans' view of governance, the sultans' emphasis on religion, and the continuing influence of Ottoman familial traditions—even in the administration of a far-flung empire. Laid out by Mehmed II, the palace complex reflected a vision of Istanbul as the center of the world. As a way to exalt the sultan's magnificent power, architects designed the complex so that the buildings containing the imperial household nestled behind layers of outer courtyards, in a mosaic of mosques, courts, and special dwellings for the sultan's harem.

The growing importance of Topkapi Palace as the command post of empire represented a crucial transition in the history of Ottoman rulers. Not only was the palace the place where future bureaucrats received their training; it was also the place where the chief bureaucrat, the grand vizier, carried out the day-to-day running of the empire. Whereas the early sultans had led their soldiers into battle personally and had met face-to-face with their kinsmen, the later rulers withdrew into the sanctity of the palace, venturing out only occasionally for grand ceremonies. Still, every Friday, subjects queued up outside the palace to introduce their petitions, ask for favors, and seek justice. If they were lucky, the sultans would be there to greet them—but they did so behind grated glass, issuing their decisions by tapping on the window. The palace thus projected a sense of majestic, distant wonder, a home fit for commanders of the faithful.

And Topkapi was indeed a home—for the increasingly sedentary sultan and his harem. Among his most cherished quarters were those set aside for women. At first, women's influence

The Topkapi Palace. *A view of the inner courtyard of the seraglio, where the sultan and his harem lived.*

in the Ottoman polity was slight. But as the realm consolidated, women became a powerful political force. The harem, like the rest of Ottoman society, had its own hierarchy of rank and prestige. At the bottom were slave women; at the top were the sultan's mother and his favorite consorts. As many as 10,000 to 12,000 women inhabited the palace, often in cramped quarters. Those who had the ruler's ear conspired to have him favor their own children, which made for widespread intrigue. When a sultan died, the entire retinue of women would be sent to a distant palace poignantly called the Palace of Tears, because the women who occupied it wept at the loss of the sultan and their own banishment from power.

DIVERSITY AND CONTROL The fact that the Ottoman Empire endured into the twentieth century owed much to the ruling elite's ability to win the favor of exceedingly diverse populations. After all, neither conquest nor conversion eliminated cultural differences in the empire's distant provinces. Thus, for example, the Ottomans' language policy was one of flexibility and tolerance. Although Ottoman Turkish was the official language of administration, Arabic was the primary language of the Arab provinces, the common tongue of street life. Within the empire's European corner, the sounds and cadences of various languages continued to prevail. From the fifteenth century onward, the Ottoman Empire was more multilingual than any of its rivals.

In politics, as in language, the Ottomans showed flexibility and tolerance. The imperial bureaucracy permitted extensive regional and religious autonomy. In fact, Ottoman military cadres perfected a technique for absorbing newly conquered territories into the empire by parceling them out as revenue-producing units among loyal followers and kin. Regional appointees could collect local taxes, part of which they earmarked for Istanbul and part of which they pocketed for themselves. (This was a common administrative device for many world dynasties ruling extensive domains.)

Like other empires, the Ottoman state was always in danger of losing control over its provincial rulers. Local rulers—the group that the imperial center allowed to rule locally—found that great distances enabled them to operate independently from central authority. These local authorities kept larger amounts of tax revenues than Istanbul deemed proper. So, to clip local autonomy, the Ottomans established a corps of infantry soldiers and bureaucrats (called janissaries) who owed direct allegiance to the sultan. The system at its high point involved a conscription of Christian youths from the empire's European lands. This conscription, called the *devshirme,* required each village to hand over a certain number of males between the ages of eight and eighteen. Uprooted from their families and villages, selected for their fine physiques and good looks, these young men were converted to Islam and sent to farms to build up their bodies and learn Turkish. A select few were moved on to Topkapi Palace to learn Ottoman military, religious, and administrative techniques. Some of these men—such as the architect Sinan, who designed the Suleymaniye Mosque—later enjoyed exceptional careers in the arts and sciences. Recipients of the best education available in the Islamic world, trained in Ottoman ways, instructed in the use of modern weaponry, and shorn of all family connections, the *devshirme* recruits were prepared to serve the sultan (and the empire as a whole) rather than the interests of any particular locality or ethnic group.

The *Devshirme*. *A miniature painting from 1558 depicts the* devshirme *system of taking non-Muslim children from their families in the Balkan Peninsula as a human tribute in place of cash taxes, which the poor region could not pay. The children were educated in Ottoman Muslim ways and prepared for service in the sultan's civil and military bureaucracy.*

The Ottomans thus artfully balanced the decentralizing tendencies of the outlying regions with the centralizing forces of the imperial capital. Relying on a careful mixture of faith, patronage, and tolerance, the sultans curried loyalty and secured political stability. Indeed, so strong and stable was the polity that the Ottoman Empire dominated the coveted and highly contested crossroads between Europe and Asia for many centuries.

The Safavid Empire in Iran

The Ottoman dynasts were not the only rulers to extend Islam's political domain. In Persia, too, a new empire arose in the aftermath of the Mongols. The legitimacy of the Safavid Empire, like that of the Ottoman, rested on an Islamic foundation. But the Shiism espoused by Safavid rulers was quite different from the Sunni faith of the Ottomans, and these contrasting religious visions shaped distinct political systems.

More so than in Anatolia, the Mongol conquest and decline brought terrible destruction and political instability to Persia. Initially, Mongol conquerors refused to embrace the majority population's Islamic faith. Instead, for over seven decades the Mongol rulers practiced a form of religious toleration. Various Mongol autocrats permitted Jews to serve the state as viziers (administrators) and employed Christians as auxiliary soldiers. But in 1295, the khan of the Persian state adopted Islam as the state religion. (A **khan** is a ruler who was acclaimed at an assembly of elites and supposedly descended from Chinggis Khan [see Chapter 10] on the male line; those not descended from Chinggis continually faced challenges to their legitimacy.) When the Mongol order slipped into decline soon after, no power arose to dominate the area. The region between Konya in eastern Anatolia and Tabriz in Persia and including Iraq fell into disorder, with warrior chieftains squabbling for preeminence. Adding to the volatility were various populist Islamic movements, some of which urged followers to withdraw from society or to parade around without clothing. Among the more prominent movements was a Sufi brotherhood led by Safi al-Din (1252–1334), which gained the backing of religious adherents and Turkish-speaking warrior bands. However, his successors, known as Safaviyeh or Safavids, embraced Shiism.

The Safavid aspirants to power rallied support from tribal groups in badly devastated parts of Persia by promising to restore good governance. They also steeped themselves in the separatist sacred tradition of Shiism. As a result, of the three great Islamic empires, the Safavid state became the most single-mindedly religious, persecuting those who did not follow its Shiite form of Islam. When the most dynamic of Safi al-Din's successors, Ismail (r. 1501–1524), took power in Tabriz, he required that the call to prayer announce that "there is no God but Allah, that Muhammad is His prophet, and that Ali is the successor of Muhammad." Rejecting his advisers' counsel to tolerate the Sunni creed of the vast majority of the city's population, Ismail made Shiism the official state religion. He offered the people a choice between conversion to Shiism or death, exclaiming at the moment of conquest that "with God's help, if the people utter one word of protest, I will draw the sword and leave not one of them alive." In 1502, Ismail proclaimed himself the first shah of the Safavid Empire. (**Shah** is the Persian word for king or leader, a title that many other cultures adopted as well.) Under Ismail and his successors, the Safavid shahs restored Persian sovereignty over the entire region traditionally regarded as the homeland of Persian speakers (see Map 11.3).

In the hands of the Safavids, Islam assumed an extreme and often militant form. The Safavids revived the traditional Persian idea that rulers were ordained by God, believing the shahs to

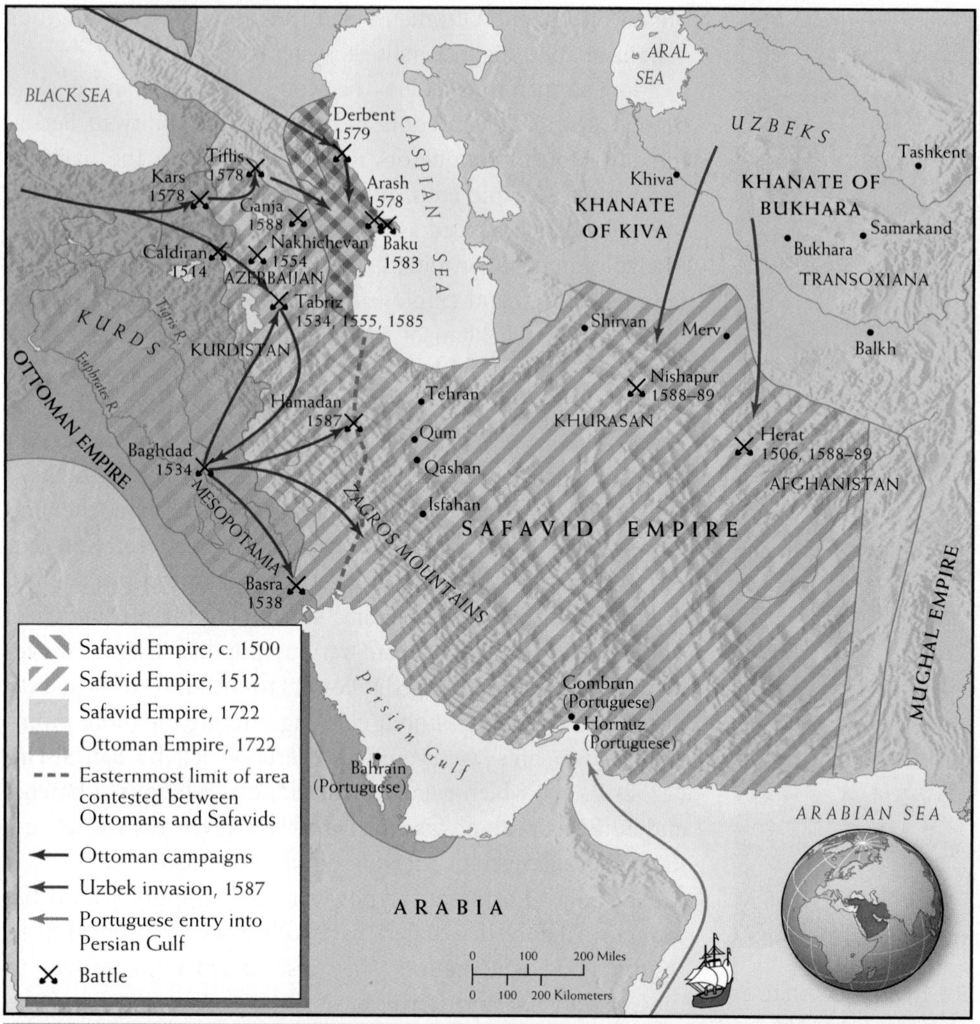

MAP 11.3 | The Safavid Empire, 1500–1722

The Safavid Empire rose to prominence alongside the Ottoman state.

- Locate the area where it originated. With which empire did the Safavids fight the most battles?
- Why were most of the battles limited to the regions of Azerbaijan, Kurdistan, and Mesopotamia?
- What were the geographical and political limits on the growth of the Safavid Empire?

be divinely chosen. Some Shiites even went so far as to affirm that there was no God but the shah. Moreover, Persian Shiism fostered an activist clergy who (in contrast to Sunni clerics) saw themselves as political and religious enforcers against any heretical authority. They compelled Safavid leaders to rule with a sacred purpose. Because the Safavids did not tolerate diversity, unlike the Ottomans, they never had as expansive an empire. Whatever territories they conquered, the Safavids ruled much more directly, based on central—and theocratic—authority. They also succeeded in transforming Iran, once a Sunni area, into a Shiite stronghold, a change that has endured down to the present.

The Delhi Sultanate and the Early Mughal Empire

A quarter century after the Safavids seized power in Persia, another Islamic dynasty, the Mughals, emerged in South Asia. Like the Ottomans and Safavids, the Mughals created a regime destined to last for many centuries. But unlike those other empires, the Mughals did not replace a Mongol regime. Instead, they erected their state on the foundations of the old Delhi Sultanate, which had come into existence in 1206. Although spared the devastating effects of the Mongols and the Black Death, nonetheless the peoples of India had to deal with an invading nomadic force every bit as destructive as the Mongols: the warriors of Tamerlane. His military forays crushed the Delhi Sultanate and opened the way for a new, even more powerful regime.

THE DECLINING DELHI SULTANATE In 1303, when Mongol forces had moved toward South Asia, the Delhi Sultanate was at its height. Its formidable military force extended imperial authority to most of the northern Indus River valley and cast a shadow over the political map of the south. The reigning sultan raised a sufficiently powerful army to drive the Mongols back toward Afghanistan. They never again disturbed the tranquility of the sultanate.

Although military strength was the foundation of the sultanate's power, it was also, ironically, a vulnerable institution. Toward the late fourteenth century, a decline in government revenues and a rise in expenditures combined to reduce resources for the military. Quarreling among nobles further weakened the sultanate and left it vulnerable to a Turkish, rather than Mongol, invader. This was a force led by Timur (Tamerlane), a Turkish warrior from central Asia. Sweeping down from the northwest, Timur's army sacked Delhi and pillaged and annexed the Punjab, an area around the headwaters of the Indus River. Thereafter death and destruction engulfed the city and much of the northern Indus River valley. Thousands were taken prisoner and carried off as

Raid on Delhi. *Timur's swift raid on Delhi in 1398 was notable for the death and destruction it caused. This sixteenth-century miniature captures the plunder and violence.*

slaves. Artisans and stonemasons who had constructed Delhi's beautiful buildings were carted away to work similar magic on the conqueror's city of Samarkand (in present-day Uzbekistan). Yet, with the approach of summer, a time when semiarid Delhi chokes with dust and the temperature hovers between 100 and 110 degrees Fahrenheit, Timur abandoned the scorching plains of northern India and returned home. Still, his conquest accelerated the fragmentation of the Delhi Sultanate.

RIVALRIES, RELIGIOUS REVIVAL, AND THE FIRST MUGHAL EMPEROR A wave of religious revival followed in the wake Timur's conquests. Bengal broke away from Delhi and soon embraced a Sufi form of mystical Islam, emphasizing personal union with God. Here, too, a special form of Hinduism, called Bhakti Hinduism, put down deep roots. Its devotees preached the doctrine of divine love. In the Punjab, previously a core area of the Delhi Sultanate, a new religion known as Sikhism came into being. **Sikhism** largely followed the teachings of Nanak (1469–1539). Although born a Hindu, he was inspired by Islamic ideals and called on his followers to renounce the caste system and to treat all believers as equal before God. (See Primary Source: Nanak's Teachings in India.)

Following Timur's attack, rival kingdoms and sultanates asserted their independence, leaving the Delhi Sultanate a mere shadow of its former self. It became just one of several competing powers in northern India, ruled first by the Sayyids and then by the Afghan dynasty of the Lodis. Surrounded by resurgent Hindu and Islamic polities, the weakened sultanate experienced something of a revival in the Lodi era. But the attempt by the last Lodi sultan to consolidate power by clipping the wings of the Afghan nobility provoked the governor of the Punjab to invite the Turkish prince Babur (the "Tiger") to India in 1526. A great-grandson of Timur, Babur traced his lineage to both the Turks and the Mongols (he was said to be a descendant of Chinggis Khan). For years, Babur had longed to conquer India. Massing an army of Turks and Afghans armed with matchlock cannons, he easily breached the wall of elephants put together by defenders of the sultan. Delhi fell, and the sultanate came to an end. Babur proclaimed himself emperor and spent the next few years snuffing out the remaining resistance to his rule (see Map 11.4). Thus he laid the foundation of the Mughal Empire, the third great Islamic dynasty (discussed in detail in Chapter 12).

By the sixteenth century, then, the Islamic heartland had seen the emergence of three new empires. Their differences were obvious, especially in the religious sphere. The Ottomans were Sunni Islam's most fervent champions, determined to eradicate the Shiite heresy on their border, where an equally determined Persian Safavid dynasty sought to expand the realm of Shiism. In contrast to these dynasties' sectarian religious commitments, the Mughals of India, drawing on well-established Indian traditions of religious and cultural tolerance, were open-minded toward non-Muslim believers and sectarian groups within the Muslim community. Yet, the political similarities of these imperial dynasties were equally clear-cut. Although these states did not hesitate to go to war against each other, they shared similar styles of rule. All established their legitimacy via military prowess, religious backing, and a loyal bureaucracy. This combination of spiritual and military weaponry enabled emperors, espousing Muhammad's preachings, to claim vast domains. Islam also bound together rulers and those whom they ruled. Moreover, their religious differences did not prevent the movement of goods, ideas, merchants, and scholars across

PRIMARY SOURCE

Nanak's Teachings in India

Nanak (1469–1539), generally recognized as the founder of Sikhism, lived in northern India and participated in the religious discussions that were prominent at the time. As in western Europe and Islamic Southwest Asia, this was a period of political turmoil and intense personal introspection. The following excerpts demonstrate Nanak's views on the failings of the age and his use of Islamic and Hindu ideas to elaborate a unique spiritual perspective. Nanak stressed the unity of God, an emphasis that reflected Islamic influences. Nonetheless, his insistence on the comparative unimportance of prophets ran counter to Islam, and his belief in rebirth was strictly Hindu.

There is but one God, whose name is true, the Creator, devoid of fear and enmity, immortal, unborn, self-existent; God the great and bountiful. Repeat His Name.

Numberless are the fools appallingly blind;
Numberless are the thieves and devourers of others' property;
Numberless are those who establish their sovereignty by force;
Numberless the cutthroats and murderers;
Numberless the liars who roam about lying;
Numberless the filthy who enjoy filthy gain;
Numberless the slandered who carry loads of calumny on their heads;
Nanak thus described the degraded.
So lowly am I, I cannot even once be a sacrifice unto Thee. Whatever pleaseth Thee is good.
O Formless One, Thou art ever secure.

The Hindus have forgotten God, and are going the wrong way.
They worship according to the instruction of Narad.
They are blind and dumb, the blindest of the blind.
The ignorant fools take stones and worship them.
O Hindus, how shall the stone which itself sinketh carry you across?

What power hath caste? It is the reality that is tested.
Poison may be held in the hand, but man dieth if he eat it.
The sovereignty of the True One is known in every age. He who obeyeth God's order shall become a noble in His court.

Those who have meditated on God as the truest of the true have done real worship and are contented;
They have refrained from evil, done good deeds, and practiced honesty;
They have lived on a little corn and water, and burst the entanglements of the world.
Thou art the great Bestower; ever Thou givest gifts which increase a quarterfold.
Those who have magnified the great God have found Him.

QUESTIONS FOR ANALYSIS

- Identify all the "numberless" groups that Nanak lists. What range of social classes do they represent? How does this enumeration reflect the tumultuous times?
- What criticisms of Hindu worship does Nanak raise?
- What lines reveal his belief in rebirth?
- How does Nanak expect true believers to behave?

political and religious boundaries—even across the most divisive boundary of all, that between Sunni Iraq and Shiite Persia.

WESTERN CHRISTENDOM

In western Afro-Eurasia, the period 1100–1300 was one of prosperity, population growth, and cultural flowering. Known as the High Middle Ages, this era saw spectacular advances in the arts, technology, learning, architecture, and banking. Expanding populations freed up laborers to move from the countryside to the cities. London, with a population of 100,000, was only one city to experience a housing crunch; in some of its poorer sections, up to twelve people slept in a single room. Though excluded from many crafts and professions, women made gains in retail trades, weaving, and food production. Wives often supervised shops or took goods to local fairs, where producers met to exchange their wares.

During the High Middle Ages, Europe's 80 million inhabitants remained largely rooted to their local communities, but

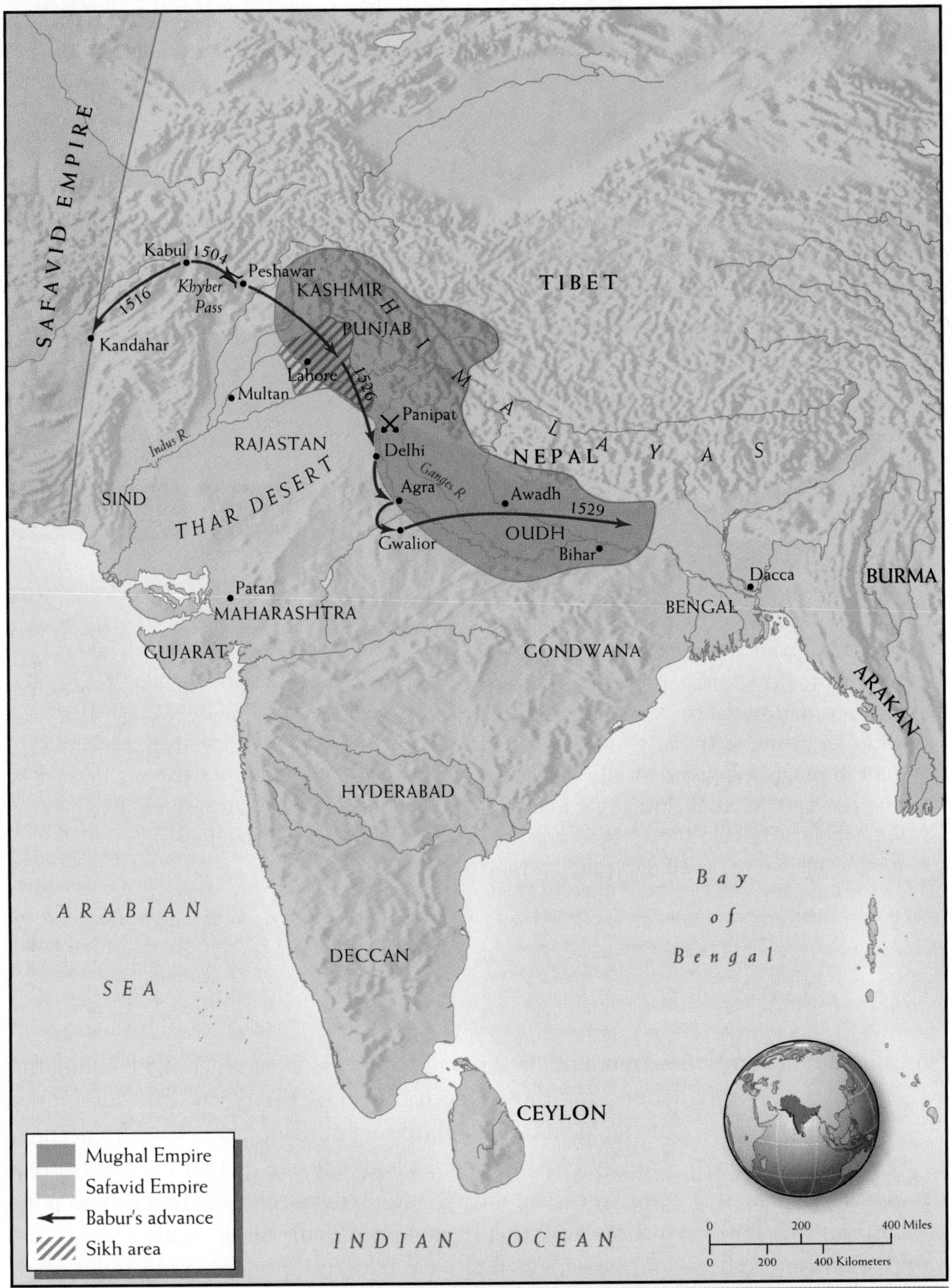

MAP 11.4 | The Mughal Empire, 1530

Compare the Mughal state with the other major Asian empires of this period, notably the Ottoman, Safavid, and Ming states (see Maps 11.2, 11.3, and 11.6).

- What geographic characteristic distinguished the Mughal state at this time from the others?
- Where in the landmass did the new state arise, and what effect do you think its place of origin had on the nature of Mughal rule?
- Based on their geographic location, to what religious traditions did the Mughals need to be sensitive?

growing wealth allowed some to widen their horizons. Bologna, Paris, Oxford, and Cambridge had universities (with medical, law, and theology faculties), and a few scholars had begun to appreciate the learning of Arabs and earlier Greeks and Romans. Thomas Aquinas (1225–1274), a leading philosopher and theologian, had laid out the main tenets of western Christianity and resolved questions of faith and reason to the satisfaction of clerical and secular intellectuals. Florentine bankers opened establishments in commercial port cities, and Greek shipbuilders expanded their trade. New devices like mechanical clocks and the compass improved the accuracy of measurements on sea and on land, while spinning wheels increased the pace of cloth production. But all of this prosperity, population growth, and innovation would be halted by the tragedies of the fourteenth century.

Reactions, Revolts, and Religion

Disastrous climatic changes struck first. Beginning around 1310, extremely harsh winters and rainy summers shortened the growing seasons and played havoc with harvests. Exhausted soils no longer supplied the resources to feed and clothe the growing urban and rural populations. Nobles squeezed the peasantry hard in an effort to maintain their luxurious lifestyle. States raised taxes to balance their growing expenditures. In this context, Europe endured the first of several disasters: famine. It appeared in 1315 and did not let up for seven cruel years, by which time millions had died of starvation or of diseases against which the malnourished population had little resistance. But this was merely the prelude to a

PRIMARY SOURCE

Flagellants in England

Like the Qalandar dervishes in the Islamic realm (see p. 369), European Flagellants renounced the world and engaged in public self-punishment in reaction to the warfare, famines, and plagues of the fourteenth century. The Flagellants carried whips (flagella) with metal pieces run through knotted thongs, which they used to beat and whip themselves until they were bruised, swollen, and bloody. Robert of Avesbury here describes the actions of Flagellants in England during the reign of King Edward III.

In that same year of 1349, about Michaelmas [29 September], more than 120 men, for the most part from Zeeland or Holland, arrived in London from Flanders. These went barefoot in procession twice a day in the sight of the people, sometimes in St Paul's church and sometimes elsewhere in the city, their bodies naked except for a linen cloth from loins to ankle. Each wore a hood painted with a red cross at front and back and carried in his right hand a whip with three thongs. Each thong had a knot in it, with something sharp, like a needle, stuck through the middle of the knot so that it stuck out on each side, and as they walked one after the other they struck themselves with these whips on their naked, bloody bodies; four of them singing in their own tongue and the rest answering in the manner of the Christian litany. Three times in each procession they would all prostrate themselves on the ground, with their arms outstretched in the shape of a cross. Still singing, and beginning with the man at the end, each in turn would step over the others, lashing the man beneath him once with his whip, until all of those lying down had gone through the same ritual. Then each one put on his usual clothes and, always with their hoods on their heads and carrying their whips, they departed to their lodgings. It was said that they performed a similar penance every night.

QUESTIONS FOR ANALYSIS

- Describe how the Flagellants dressed, and identify the languages they spoke. What elements of Christianity did these characteristics display?
- Why do you think the Flagellants whipped themselves?
- How did the Flagellants differ from the Qalanders?

Source: Robertus de Avesbury, "Flagellants in England" from The Black Death, *Rosemary Horrox, trans./ed., pp. 153–54.*

century and more of warfare, epidemic disease, famine, and social unrest.

THE PLAGUE IN EUROPE In the wake of famine came the Black Death, starting around 1346 and ravaging the Italian Peninsula; then it seized France, the Low Countries (present-day Netherlands, Belgium, and Luxembourg), Germany, and England in its deathly grip. The overcrowded and unsanitary cities were particularly vulnerable. Bremen lost at least 8,000 souls, perhaps two-thirds of its population; Hamburg, another port city, at least as many. The poor, sleeping in crowded quarters, were especially at risk. But master bakers, bankers, and aristocrats died too, unless they were able to flee to the relatively safer countryside in time to escape infection. No one had seen dying on such a scale. Nearly two-thirds of Europe's total population perished between 1346 and 1353.

After 1353, the epidemic died down, having killed all those with no natural immunities and most of the original carriers of the disease, the European black rat. But the plague would return every seven years or so for the rest of the century, as well as sporadically through the entire fifteenth century, killing the young and those who had managed to escape exposure in the first epidemic. The European population continued to decline, until by 1450 many areas had only one-quarter the number of a century earlier. Indeed, it took three centuries to return to population levels that existed prior to the Black Death.

Disaster on this scale had enduring psychological, social, economic, and political effects. Many individuals turned to pleasure, even debauchery, determined to enjoy themselves before it came their turn to die. Others retreated into a personal spirituality, convinced that they needed to put their lives in order before passing on to the next life. Occasionally, eccentric groups took shape. The Beghards, or Brethren of the Free Speech, claimed to be in a state of grace that allowed them to do as they pleased—including adultery, free love, nudity, and murder. By contrast, the Flagellants were so sure that man had incurred God's wrath that they whipped themselves to atone for human sin. They also bullied communities that they visited, demanding to be housed, clothed, and fed. (See Primary Source: Flagellants in England.)

For many who survived the plague, Thomas Aquinas's rational Christianity no longer appealed, and disappointment with the clergy smoldered. Famished peasants resented priests and monks for living lives of luxury in violation of church tenets. In addition, they despaired at the absence of clergy when they were so greatly needed. In fact, many clerics had perished while attending to their parishioners. Others had fled to rural retreats far from the ravages of the Black Death, leaving their followers to fend for themselves.

THE CHURCH'S RESPONSE In the aftermath of famine and plague, religious authorities struggled to reclaim their power. The late medieval western church found itself divided at the top (at one point there were three popes) and challenged from below, both by individuals pursuing alternative kinds of spirituality and by increasing demands on the clergy and church administration. Facing challenges to its right to define religious doctrine and practices, the church identified all that was suspect and demanded strict obedience to the true faith. This entailed the persecution of heretics, Jews, Muslims, homosexuals, prostitutes, and "witches." But during this period the church also expanded its charitable and bureaucratic functions, providing alms to the urban poor and registering births, deaths, and economic transactions.

Persecution and administration cost money. Indeed, the needs as well as the extravagances of the clergy spurred certain questionable money-making tactics. One was the selling of indulgences (certificates that reduced one's time in purgatory, where souls continued the repentance that would eventually make them fit for heaven). This sort of unconventional fund raising, and the growing gap between the church's promises and its ability to bring Christianity into people's everyday lives, more than the persecutions, eventually sparked the Protestant Reformation (see Chapter 12).

A WEAKENING FEUDAL ORDER Just as the mayhem of the fourteenth and fifteenth centuries unleashed hostility toward the church, it also undermined the feudal order. Since the Roman era, peasant uprisings had occasionally erupted. But now they escalated into large-scale insurrections. In France and England, massive revolts signaled the peasants' resentment against lords who failed to protect them from marauding military bands, as well as their exasperation with feudal restrictions that now seemed—for the few survivors of plague and famine—too much to bear. In 1358 the French revolt, or **Jacquerie**, broke out (the term derived from "Jacques Bonhomme," a name that contemptuous masters used for all peasants). Armed with only knives and staves, the peasantry went on a rampage, killing hated nobles and clergy and burning and looting all the property they could get their hands on. At issue was the peasants' insistence that they should no longer be tied to their land or have to pay for the tools they used in farming.

Peasant Revolts. *Long before the French Revolution, European peasants vented their anger against their noble masters. Lacking armaments and supplies, they usually lost—as this image of the brutal suppression of the French Jacquerie of 1358 depicts.*

A better-organized uprising took place in England in 1381. Although the **English Peasants' Revolt** began as a protest against a tax levied to raise money for a war on France, it was also fueled by post-plague labor shortages: serfs demanded the freedom to move about, and free farm workers called for higher wages and lower rents. When landlords balked at these demands, aggrieved peasants assembled at the gates of London. The protesters demanded abolition of the feudal order, but the king ruthlessly suppressed them. Nonetheless, in both France and England a free peasantry gradually emerged as labor shortages made it impossible to keep peasants bound to the soil.

State Building and Economic Recovery

In the wake of famine, plague, and peasant uprisings, Europe's rulers tried to rebuild their polities and consolidate their power. Although their efforts at state building pale in comparison with those of the empires rising in Asia, one family, the Habsburgs, established a powerful and long-lasting dynasty. They provided emperors for the Holy Roman Empire from 1440 to 1806. Yet the Habsburg monarchs never succeeded in restoring an integrated empire to western Europe (as Chinese dynasts had done by claiming the mandate of heaven).

Moreover, language did not unite Europeans. While the written literary Chinese script remained a key administrative tool for China's dynasts, and in the Islamic world Arabic was the common language of faith, Persian the language of poetry,

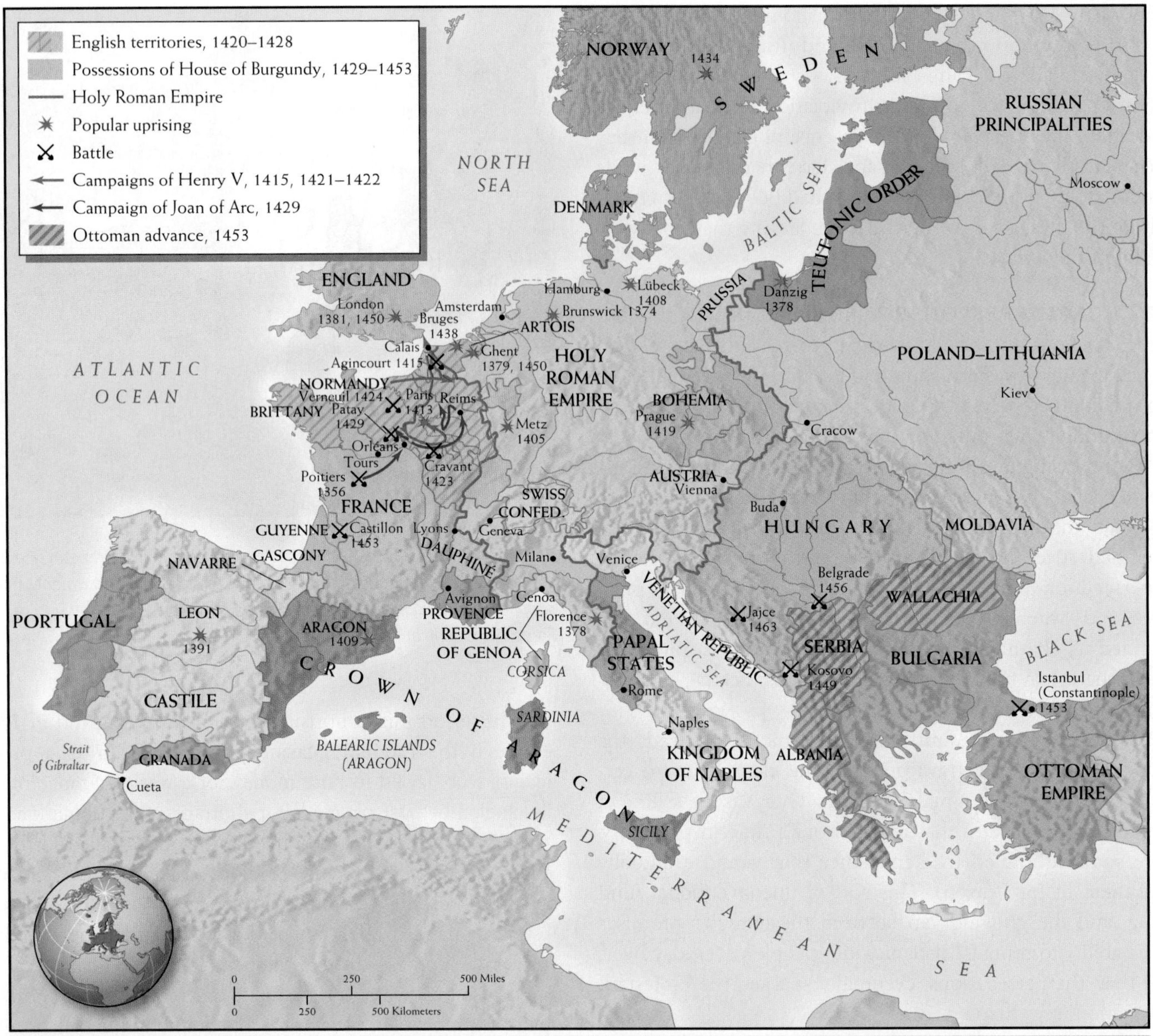

MAP 11.5 | Europe, 1400–1500

Europe was a region divided by dynastic rivalries during the fifteenth century.

- Locate the most powerful regional dynasties on the map: Portugal, Castile, Aragon, France, England, and the Holy Roman Empire. In what country did the heaviest fighting occur?
- Why do you think one state was the scene for so many battles?
- On the basis of this map, predict which European territories and polities would become powerful in subsequent centuries, and which would not.

and Turkish the language of administration, in Europe Latin lost ground as rulers chose various regional dialects to be their official state language. In 1450 Europe had no central government, no official tongue, and only a few successful commercial centers, mostly in the Mediterranean basin (see Map 11.5). Feudalism had left a legacy of political fragmentation and enshrined privileges, which made the consolidation of a unified Christian Europe even more difficult to achieve.

Those who sought to rule the emerging states faced numerous obstacles. For example, rival claimants to the throne financed threatening private armies. Also, the clergy demanded and received privileges and often meddled in politics themselves.

The church's huge landholdings and exemptions from taxation made it, too, a formidable economic powerhouse. And once the printing press became available in the 1460s, printers circulated anonymous pamphlets criticizing the court and the clergy. Some states had consultative bodies—such as the Estates General in France, the Cortes in Spain, or Parliament in England—in which princes formally asked representatives of their people for advice and, in the case of the English Parliament, for consent to new forms of taxation. Such bodies gave no voice to most nonaristocratic men and no representation to women. But they did allow the collective expression of grievances against high-handed policies.

Out of the chaos of famine, disease, and warfare, the diverse peoples of Europe found a political way forward. This path involved the formation of centralized monarchies, much as the Ottomans, Safavids, Mughals, and Ming were accomplishing in Asia. (A **monarchy** is a political system in which one individual holds supreme power and passes that power on to his or her next of kin.) Often in competition with the new monarchies a sprinkling of city-states survived, in which a handful of wealthy and influential voters selected their leaders. Consolidation of these polities occurred sometimes through strategic marriages but more often through warfare, both between local princely families and with outsiders. Political stabilization was swiftest in southern Europe, where economies rebounded through trade with Southwest Asia. The stabilization of Italian city-states such as Venice and Florence, and of monarchical rule in Portugal and Spain, led to an economic and cultural flowering known as the Renaissance (see below).

Political Consolidation and Trade in Portugal

Portugal's fortunes demonstrate how political stabilization and the revival of trade entwined. After the chaos of the fourteenth century, Spain, England, and France followed the Portuguese example and established national monarchies. In Spain and Portugal, warfare against Muslims would help unite Christian territories, and Mediterranean trade would add valuable income to state coffers. In northern Europe, by contrast, lack of access to lucrative trade routes, in addition to internal feuding, regional warfare, and (after 1517) religious fragmentation, would delay recovery for decades.

Through the fourteenth century, Portuguese Christians devoted themselves to fighting the **Moors**, who were Muslim occupants of North Africa, the western Sahara, and the Iberian Peninsula. Decisive in this struggle was the Portuguese decision to cross the Strait of Gibraltar and seize the Moorish Moroccan fortresses at Ceuta in North Africa: their ships could now sail between the Mediterranean and the Atlantic without Muslim interference. With that threat diminished, the Portuguese perceived their neighbor, Castile (part of what is now Spain), as their chief foe. Under João I (r. 1385–1433) the Castilians were defeated, and the monarchy could seek new territories and trading opportunities in the North Atlantic and along the West African coasts. João's son Prince Henrique, known later as Henry the Navigator, further expanded the family's domain by supporting expeditions down the coast of Africa and offshore to the Atlantic islands of the Madeiras and the Azores. The west and central coasts of Africa and the islands of the North and South Atlantic, including the Cape Verde Islands, São Tomé, Principe, and Fernando Po, soon became Portuguese ports of call.

The Portuguese monarchs granted the Atlantic islands to nobles as hereditary possessions on condition that the grantees colonize them, and soon the colonizers were establishing lucrative sugar plantations. In gratitude, noble families and merchants threw their political weight behind the king. Subsequent monarchs continued to reduce local elites' authority and to ensure smooth succession for members of the royal family. This political consolidation enabled Portugal to thrive in the wake of the Black Death.

Dynasty Building and Reconquest in Spain

The road to dynasty in Spain was arduous. Medieval Spain comprised rival kingdoms that quarreled ceaselessly. Also, Spain lacked religious uniformity: Muslims, Jews, and Christians lived side by side in relative harmony, and Muslim armies still occupied strategic posts in the south. Over time, however, marriages and the formation of kinship ties among nobles and between royal lineages yielded a new political order. One by one, the major houses of the Spanish kingdoms intermarried, culminating in the fateful wedding of Isabella of Castile and Ferdinand of Aragon. Thus, Spain's two most important provinces were joined, and Spain became a state to be reckoned with.

THE UNION OF CASTILE AND ARAGON By the time Isabella and Ferdinand married in 1469, Spain was recovering from the miseries of the fourteenth century. This was more than a marriage of convenience. Castile was wealthy and populous; Aragon enjoyed an extended trading network in the Mediterranean. Together, the monarchs brought unruly nobles and distant towns under their domain. They topped off their achievements by marrying their children into other European royal families—especially the Habsburgs, central Europe's most powerful dynasty.

The new rulers also sent Christian armies south to push Muslim forces out of the Iberian Peninsula. By the mid-fifteenth century only Granada, a strategic lynchpin overlooking the straits between the Mediterranean and the Atlantic, remained in Muslim hands. After a long and costly siege, Christian forces captured the fortress there. This was a victory of enormous symbolic importance, as joyous as the fall of Constantinople was depressing. Many people in Spain thumped their chests in pride, unaware or unconcerned that at the same time Ottoman armies were conquering large sections of southeastern Europe.

THE INQUISITION AND WESTWARD EXPLORATION Just as the Safavid rulers had tried to stamp out all non-Shiite forms of Islam within their domains, so Isabella and Ferdinand sought to drive all non-Catholics out of Spain. Terrified by Ottoman incursions into Europe, in 1481 they launched the **Inquisition**, taking aim especially against *conversos*—converted Jews and Muslims, whom they suspected were Christians only in name. When Granada fell, the crown ordered the expulsion of all Jews from Spain; after 1499, a more tolerant attempt to convert the Moors by persuasion gave way to forced conversion—or emigration. All told, almost half a million people were forced to flee the Spanish kingdoms.

So strong was the tide of Spanish fervor by late 1491 that the monarchs listened now to a Genoese navigator whose pleas for patronage they had previously rejected. Christopher Columbus promised them unimaginable riches that could finance their military campaigns and bankroll a crusade to liberate Jerusalem from Muslim hands. Off he sailed with a royal patent that guaranteed the monarchs a share of all he discovered. Soon the Spanish economy was reorienting itself toward the Atlantic, and Spain's merchants, missionaries, and soldiers were preparing for conquest and profiteering in what had been, just a few years before, a blank space on the map.

The Struggles of France and England, and the Success of Small States

Warfare and strategic marriages allowed the Portuguese and Spanish monarchies to consolidate state power and to lay the foundations for revived commerce. But by no means were all states immediately successful. In France and England, the great age of European monarchy had yet to dawn.

When French forces finally pushed the English back across the English Channel in the Hundred Years' War (1337–1453), the French House of Valois began a slow process of consolidating royal power. Although diplomatic marriages helped the French crown expand its domain, two more centuries of royal initiatives and civil war were required to tame the powerful nobility. In England, even thirty years of civil war between the houses of Lancaster and York did not settle which one would take the throne. Both families in this War of the Roses ultimately lost out to the Tudors, who seized the throne in 1485. (See Current Trends in World History: Joan of Arc: A Charismatic Leader in a Time of Social Turmoil.)

Even where stable states did arise, they were fairly small compared to the Ottoman and Ming empires. In the mid-sixteenth century, Portugal and Spain, Europe's two most expansionist states, had populations of 1 million and 9 million, respectively. England, excluding Wales, was a mere 3 million in 1550. Only France, with 17 million, had a population close to the Ottoman Empire's 25 million. And these numbers paled in comparison with Ming China's population of nearly 200 million in 1550 and Mughal India's 110 million in 1600.

But in Europe, small was advantageous. Portugal's relatively small population meant that the crown had fewer groups to instill with loyalty. Also, in the world of finance, the most successful merchants were those inhabiting the smaller Italian city-states and, a bit later, the cities of the northern Netherlands. The Florentines developed sophisticated banking techniques, created extensive networks of agents throughout Europe and the Mediterranean, and served as bankers to the popes. Venetian merchants enjoyed a unique role in the exchange of silks and spices from the eastern Mediterranean. It was in these prosperous city-states that the Renaissance began.

European Identity and the Renaissance

Europe's political and economic revival included a powerful outpouring of cultural achievements, led by Italian scholars and artists and financed by bankers, churchmen, and nobles. Much later, scholars coined the word **Renaissance** ("rebirth") to characterize the expanded cultural production of the Italian city-states, France, the Low Countries, England, and the Holy Roman Empire in the period 1430–1550. What was being "reborn" were ancient Greek and Roman art and learning—knowledge that could illuminate a world of expanding horizons and support the rights of secular individuals to exert power in it. Although the Renaissance was largely funded by popes and Christian kings, it broke the medieval church's monopoly on answers to the big questions and opened the way for secular forms of learning and a more human-centered understanding of the cosmos.

THE ITALIAN RENAISSANCE The Renaissance, ironically, was all about the new: new exposure, that is, to the old—to classical texts and ancient art and architectural forms. Although some Greek and Roman texts were known in Europe and the Islamic world, the fall of Constantinople and the invention of the printing press made others accessible to western scholars for the first time. Scholars now realized that the pre-Christian Greeks and Romans had known more: about how to represent and care for the human body; about geography, astronomy, and architecture; about how to properly govern states and armies. It was no longer enough to understand Christian doctrine and to trust medieval authorities; one had to accurately retranslate the original sources, which required the learning of languages and of history. This dive backward into ancient Greece and Rome became known as **humanism**, which sums up the aspiration to know more about the human experience beyond what the Christian scriptures offered.

Wealthy families, powerful rulers, and the Catholic Church were the sponsors of Renaissance achievement. For example, by the 1480s the di Medici family had been patronizing art based on ancient models for three generations. The Medici were bankers, but also influential political players in Florence and Rome. The family contributed greatly to making Florence one of the showplaces of Renaissance art and architecture, as well as the center stage for early Renaissance philosophy. Cosimo di Medici (1389–1464) funded the completion of the sumptuous Duomo, or cathedral of Florence, topped by the architect Brunelleschi's masterful dome, the largest built since antiquity. Cosimo's grandson, Lorenzo the Magnificent, supported many of the great Renaissance artists, including Leonardo da Vinci, Sandro Botticelli, and Michelangelo Buonarotti.

The artists who flourished in Florence, Rome, and Venice embraced their own form of humanism. In their case, the return to ancient sources meant reviving the principles of the Roman architect Vitruvius and the imitation of nude classical sculpture. Their masterpieces, like Leonardo's *Last Supper* or Michelangelo's *David*, used the technique of perspective and classical treatments of the body to give vivacity and three-dimensionality to paintings and sculptures—even religious ones. Raphael's madonnas portrayed the Virgin Mary as a beautiful individual and not just as a symbol of chastity; similarly, Michelangelo's Sistine Chapel ceiling gave Adam the beautiful body of a Greek god so that viewers could appreciate the glory of the Creation. Of course, these artists also hoped to draw attention to their own achievements, and they were not disappointed. For soon northern European princes, too, sought out artists and humanists who could bring this inspiring new style to their courts.

THE RENAISSANCE SPREADS By the sixteenth century, increasing economic prosperity, the circulation of books and images, and interstate competition were spreading Renaissance culture throughout Europe. Philip II of Spain, for example, purchased more than 1,000 paintings during his reign; Henry IV of France and his queen, Marie de Medici, invested a fortune in renovating the Louvre, building a new royal residence at Fontainebleau, and hiring Peter Paul Rubens to paint grand canvases. Courtiers built up-to-date palaces and invited scholars to live on their estates; Dutch, German, and French merchants also patronized the arts. All wanted their sons to be educated in the humanistic manner. Some families and religious institutions offered women access to the new learning, and some men encouraged their sisters, daughters, and wives to expand their horizons. The well-educated nun Caritas Pirckheimer (1467–1532), for example, exchanged learned letters and books with male humanists in the German states. Studying Greek, Latin, and ancient rhetoric did not make the commercial elite

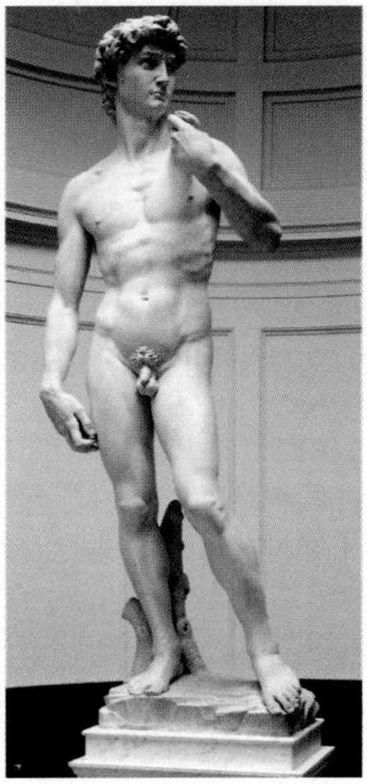

Renaissance Masterpieces. *Leonardo da Vinci's* The Last Supper (above) *depicts Christ's disciples reacting to his announcement that one of them will betray him. Michelangelo's* David (right) *stands over thirteen feet high and was conceived as an expression of Florentine civic ideals.*

CURRENT TRENDS IN WORLD HISTORY

Joan of Arc: A Charismatic Leader in a Time of Social Turmoil

The immense historical impact of a French peasant girl, Joan of Arc, demonstrates the importance of charismatic individuals—even women in male-dominated societies—during periods of social turmoil. As Europe endured plagues, famines, and war, its people sought help through the special talents of women, even in areas like warfare. Indeed, if not for Joan of Arc, the country we know today as France might not exist.

Gender is also a useful approach to study the relations between men and women in a society. World historians use it as a comparative theme across cultures and time, which makes it an even more useful lens for historical analysis.

Appearing on the scene in 1429, as the English seemed to be winning the Hundred Years' War, she rallied the French against the English occupiers and turned the tide of the war. By giving religious sanction, as well as military succor, to the Valois monarch Charles VII, she made possible the consolidation of France and left Europe an inspiring image of the female warrior-saint.

The world of Joan's childhood was a chaotic one, in which English lords were laying claim to various French-speaking principalities. By 1420, Valois authority had been greatly eroded, and English armies were conquering more and more French towns. In 1428, the English laid siege to Orléans, a large town in north-central France. To contemporaries, it seemed a symbolic battle: as Orléans went, they thought, so the war would go—and so would God wish it to go.

This is the point at which the paths of a seventeen-year-old peasant girl and the monarch of France crossed. Beginning at about age thirteen, the shy girl had received visions of saints who instructed her to rescue Orléans and bring France's ruler to be crowned king at Reims Cathedral. (He had not been crowned there, in the tradition of all French kings, because the English armies controlled Reims, Paris, and northern France.) For five years Joan resisted, but at last she obeyed her celestial advisers. Granted an audience with Charles VII in 1429, Joan impressed him with her piety and her passionate devotion to the Valois crown. He concluded that God really had sent her to serve France's cause—and his own. Joan won command of 7,000 to 8,000 men; then, wearing a suit of armor and brandishing a sword, she marched to relieve Orléans. Joan directed the assault with brilliance and inspired the French forces; her charisma came not only from a tradition of female Christian "seers," but also from the peculiarity of her appearance (a young woman in male attire) and her appeal to French speakers who resented rule by English "outsiders." After driving the English from Orléans, she then pressed on to Reims; here, thanks to her military victories, Charles VII was crowned, fulfilling her visions. He was now king of France—and though the war continued, the tide now turned in favor of the French.

The tide for Joan, however, turned for the worse. Although she continued to direct the troops with remarkable savvy, she failed to force open the gates of Paris, and jealous courtiers around Charles began to question her divine authority. She was wounded, then taken prisoner. After a year in English captivity she faced the Inquisition and was found guilty of heresy, on the grounds that her visions were false and misleading. On May 30, 1431, she was burned at the stake

equal to the aristocrats, or women equal to men, but this sort of education did enable some non-nobles to obtain social influence and to criticize the ruling elites.

THE REPUBLIC OF LETTERS Since political and religious powers were not united in Europe (as they were in China and the Islamic world), scholars and artists could play one side against the other, or, alternatively, could suffer both clerical and political persecution. Michelangelo completed commissions for the Medici, for the Florentine Wool Guild, and for Pope Julius II. Peter Paul Rubens painted for the courts of France, Spain, England, and the Netherlands, as well as selling paintings on the open market. These two painters, renowned for showing a great deal of flesh, frequently offended conservative church officials, but their secular patrons kept them in oils. The Dutch scholar Desiderius Erasmus was able to ridicule the church because he had the patronage of English, Dutch, and French supporters. Fleeing persecution in Rome, the philosopher Giordano Bruno found a warm welcome in England—but made the mistake of thinking he was forgiven, and returned to Rome only to be burned at the stake.

The search for patrons and the flight from persecution, especially after the Reformation, made Europe's educated elite increasingly cosmopolitan (as it had in China and the Islamic empires). Scholars met one another in royal palaces and cultural centers such as Florence, Antwerp, and Amsterdam. Seeking specialized information or rare books, they formed what was known as "the republic of letters"—a network of correspondents who were more interested in individual knowledge or talent than in noble titles or clerical rank.

in the marketplace in the town of Rouen. Since that time she has stood as a heroic and charismatic martyr, and the French have often invoked her name to awaken patriotism against foreign threats.

The fact that this young, illiterate woman played such an important role in the history of European warfare and state formation testifies to the fact that male aristocrats, intellectuals, and clerics were not the only important actors. At the right place, at the right time, a woman could use courage, faith, and intelligence to make her visions prevail.

QUESTIONS FOR ANALYSIS

- What other heroic figures (male/female) does Joan of Arc remind you of and why?
- Why do you think Charles VII failed to rescue Joan of Arc from her English prison?

Explore Further

Pernoud, Régine and Marie-Véronique Clin, *Joan of Arc: Her Story*, trans. Jeremy Adams (1999).

COMPETING IDEAS OF GOVERNANCE Gradually, a network of educated men and women took shape that was not wholly dependent on either the church or the state. Thus these individuals acquired the means to challenge political, clerical, and aesthetic authority. Of course, they could also use their learning to defend the older elites: for example, numerous lawyers and scholars continued to work for the popes in defending the papacy. At the same time, in contrast, men like Erasmus and Martin Luther (the leading figure of the Reformation) looked to secular princes to support their critical scholarship.

Neither in Florence nor elsewhere did the Renaissance produce a consensus about who should rule. The Florentines pioneered a form of civic humanism under which all citizens were to devote themselves to defending the state against tyrants and foreign invaders; according to this view, the state would reward their civic virtue by ensuring their liberty. Yet it was also a Florentine, Niccolò Machiavelli, who wrote the most famous treatise on authoritarian power, *The Prince* (1513). Machiavelli argued that political leadership was not about obeying God's rules but about mastering the amoral means of modern statecraft. Holding and exercising power were ends in themselves, he claimed; civic virtue was merely a pretense on the part of those (like the Medici family he knew so well) who simply wanted to keep the upper hand.

The Renaissance produced a culture of critics who went back to classical ideas in order to go forward, to address the challenges and opportunities of an expanding world. This was not a movement that trickled down much to the common people, although they, too, surely were moved by the sight of the Duomo in Florence, or indirectly touched by the spread of printed books. The Renaissance transformed the European elite, however, making it more cosmopolitan and knitting together the artists and scholars who constituted "the republic of letters." By orienting the elite toward ancient models (for poetry, rhetoric, statecraft, geography, medicine, and architecture) instead of medieval ones, the Renaissance revolutionized European culture—even if it could not unify the states and peoples who cultivated it.

MING CHINA

Like the Europeans, the Chinese saw their stable worldview and political order crumble under the cataclysms of human and bacterial invasions. Moreover, like the Europeans, people in China had long regarded outsiders as "barbarians." Together, the Mongols and the Black Death upended the political and intellectual foundations of what had appeared to be the world's most integrated society. The Mongols brought the Yuan dynasty to power; then the plague devastated China and prepared the way for the emergence of the Ming dynasty.

Chaos and Recovery

China had been ripe for the plague's pandemic. Its population had increased significantly under the Song dynasty (960–1279) and subsequent Mongol rule. But by 1300, hunger and scarcity began to spread as resources stretched thin. A weakened population was especially vulnerable to plague. For seventy years, the Black Death ravaged China and shattered the Mongols' claim to a mandate from heaven. In 1331, plague may have killed 90 percent of the population in Bei Zhili (modern Hebei) province. From there it spread throughout other provinces, reaching Fujian and the coast at Shandong. By the 1350s, most of China's large cities suffered severe outbreaks.

The reign of the last Yuan Mongol rulers was a time of utter chaos. Even as the Black Death was engulfing large parts of China, bandit groups and dissident religious sects were undercutting the state's power. As in other realms devastated by the plague, popular religious movements foretold impending doom. Most prominent was the **Red Turban Movement**, which took its name from its soldiers' red headbands. This movement blended China's diverse cultural and religious traditions, including Buddhism, Daoism, and other faiths. Its leaders emphasized strict dietary restrictions, penance, and ceremonial rituals in which the sexes freely mixed, and made proclamations that the world was drawing to an end.

In these chaotic times, only a strong military movement capable of overpowering other groups could restore order. That intervention began at the hands of a poor young man who had trained in the Red Turban Movement: Zhu Yuanzhang. He was an orphan from a peasant household in an area devastated by disease and famine, and a former novice at a Buddhist monastery. At age twenty-four Zhu joined the Red Turbans, after which he rose quickly to become a distinguished commander. Eventually, his forces defeated the Yuan and drove the Mongols from China.

The Forbidden City. *The Yongle Emperor relocated the capital to Beijing, where he began the construction of the Forbidden City, or imperial palace. The palace was designed to inspire awe in all who saw it.*

It soon became clear that Zhu had a much grander design for all of China than the ambitions of most warlords. When he took the important city of Nanjing in 1356, he renamed it Yingtian ("In response to Heaven"). Buoyed by subsequent successful military campaigns, twelve years later Zhu (r. 1368–1398) proclaimed the founding of the Ming ("brilliant") dynasty. Soon thereafter, his troops met little resistance when they seized the Yuan capital of Beijing, causing the Mongol emperor to flee to his homeland in the steppe. It would, however, take Zhu almost another twenty years to reunify the entire country.

Centralization under the Ming

Zhu and successive Ming emperors had to rebuild a devastated society from the ground up. Although in the past China had experienced natural catastrophes, wars, and social dislocation, the plague's legacy was devastation on an unprecedented scale. It left the new rulers with the formidable challenge of rebuilding the great cities, restoring respect for ruling elites, and reconstructing the bureaucracy.

IMPERIAL GRANDEUR AND KINSHIP The rebuilding began under Zhu, the Hongwu ("expansive and martial") Emperor, whose extravagant capital at Nanjing reflected imperial grandeur. When the dynasty's third emperor, the Yongle ("perpetual happiness") Emperor, relocated the capital to Beijing, he flaunted an even more grandiose style. Construction here mobilized around 100,000 artisans and 1 million laborers. The city had three separate walled enclosures. Inside the outer city walls sprawled the imperial city; within its walls lay the palace city, the Forbidden City. Traffic within the walled sections navigated through boulevards leading to the different gates, above which imposing towers soared. The palace compound, where the imperial family resided, had more than 9,000 rooms. Anyone standing in the front courts, which measured more than 400 yards on a side and boasted marble terraces and carved railings, would gasp at the sense of awesome power. That was precisely the effect the Ming emperors wanted (just as the Ottoman sultans did in building Topkapi Palace).

Marriage and kinship buttressed the power of the Ming imperial household. The dynasty's founder married the adopted daughter of a leading Red Turban rebel (her father, according to legend, was a convicted murderer), thereby consolidating his power and eliminating a threat. Empress Ma, as she was known, became Hongwu's principal wife and was praised for her compassion. Emerging as the kinder face of the regime, she tempered the harsh and sometimes cruel disposition of her spouse. He had numerous other consorts as well, including Korean and Mongol women, who bore him twenty-six sons and sixteen daughters.

BUILDING A BUREAUCRACY Faced with the challenge of reestablishing order out of turmoil, Hongwu initially sought to

Chinese Irrigation. *Farmers in imperial China used sophisticated devices to extract water for irrigation, as depicted in this illustration from the Yuan Mongol period.*

rule through his many kinsmen—by giving imperial princes generous stipends, command of large garrisons, and significant autonomy in running their domains. However, when the princes' power began to threaten the court, Hongwu slashed their stipends, reduced their privileges, and took control of their garrisons. No longer dependent on these men, he established an imperial bureaucracy beholden only to him and to his successors. These officials won appointments through their outstanding performance on a reinstated civil service examination.

In addition, Hongwu took other steps to install a centralized system of rule. He assigned bureaucrats to oversee the manufacture of porcelain, cotton, and silk products, as well as tax collection. He reestablished the Confucian school system as a means of selecting a cadre of loyal officials (not unlike the Ottoman janissaries and administrators). He also set up local networks of villages to rebuild irrigation systems and to supervise reforestation projects to prevent flooding—with the astonishing result that the amount of land reclaimed nearly tripled within eight years. Historians estimate that Hongwu's reign oversaw the planting of about 1 billion trees, including 50 million sterculia, palm, and varnish trees around Nanjing. Their products served in building a maritime expedition fleet in the early fifteenth century. For water control, 40,987 reservoirs underwent repairs or new construction.

Now the imperial palace not only projected the image of a power center, it *was* the center of power. Every official received his appointment by the emperor through the Ministry of Personnel. Hongwu also eliminated the post of prime minister (he executed the man who held the post) and henceforth ruled directly. Ming bureaucrats literally lost their seats and had to kneel before the emperor. In one eight-day period, Hongwu reputedly reviewed over 1,600 petitions dealing with 3,392 separate matters. The drawback, of course, was that he had to keep tabs on this immense system, and his bureaucrats were not always up to the task. Indeed, Hongwu constantly juggled personal and impersonal forms of authority, sometimes fortifying the administration, sometimes undermining it lest it become too autonomous. In due course, he nurtured a bureaucracy far more extensive than those of the Islamic empires. The Ming thus established the most highly centralized system of government of all the monarchies of this period. (See Primary Source: The Hongwu Emperor's Proclamation.)

Religion under the Ming

The Ming's zeal extended to the religious pantheon as well. Citing the mandate of heaven, the emperor revised and strengthened the elaborate protocol of rites and ceremonies that had undergirded dynastic power for centuries. As well as underscoring the emperor's centrality, official rituals (such as those related to the gods of soil and grain) reinforced political and social hierarchies.

Under the guise of "community" gatherings, rites and sacrifices solidified the Ming order by portraying the rulers as the moral and spiritual benefactors of their subjects. On at least ninety occasions each year, the emperor engaged in sacrificial rites, providing symbolic communion between the human and the spiritual worlds. These lavish festivities reinforced the ruler's image as mediator between otherworldly affairs of the gods and worldly concerns of the empire's subjects. The message was clear: the gods were on the side of the Ming household.

Ming Deities. *A pantheon of deities worshipped during the Ming, demonstrating the rich religious culture of the period.*

PRIMARY SOURCE

The Hongwu Emperor's Proclamation

This proclamation by the founder of the Ming dynasty, the Hongwu Emperor (r. 1368–1398), reveals how he envisioned reconstructing the devastated country as his own personal project. He sought a return to austerity by denouncing the morally corrosive effect of money and material possessions, and he especially distrusted his officials. Although frustrated in his efforts, Hongwu nonetheless set the tone for the centralization of power in the person of the emperor.

To all civil and military officials:

I have told you to refrain from evil. Doing so would enable you to bring glory to your ancestors, your wives and children, and yourselves. With your virtue, you then could assist me in my endeavors to bring good fortune and prosperity to the people. You would establish names for yourselves in Heaven and on earth, and for thousands and thousands of years, you would be praised as worthy men.

However, after assuming your posts, how many of you really followed my instructions? Those of you in charge of money and grain have stolen them yourselves; those of you in charge of criminal laws and punishments have neglected the regulations. In this way grievances are not redressed and false charges are ignored. Those with genuine grievances have nowhere to turn; even when they merely wish to state their complaints, their words never reach the higher officials. Occasionally these unjust matters come to my attention. After I discover the truth, I capture and imprison the corrupt, villainous, and oppressive officials involved. I punish them with the death penalty or forced labor or have them flogged with bamboo sticks in order to make manifest the consequences of good or evil actions. . . .

Alas, how easily money and profit can bewitch a person! With the exception of the righteous person, the true gentleman, and the sage, no one is able to avoid the temptation of money. But is it really so difficult to reject the temptation of profit? The truth is people have not really tried.

Previously, during the final years of the Yuan dynasty, there were many ambitious men competing for power who did not treasure their sons and daughters but prized jade and silk, coveted fine horses and beautiful clothes, relished drunken singing and unrestrained pleasure, and enjoyed separating people from their parents, wives, and children. I also lived in that chaotic period. How did I avoid such snares? I was able to do so because I valued my reputation and wanted to preserve my life. Therefore I did not dare to do these evil things. . . .

In order to protect my reputation and to preserve my life, I have done away with music, beautiful girls, and valuable objects. Those who love such things are usually "a success in the morning, a failure in the evening." Being aware of the fallacy of such behavior, I will not indulge such foolish fancies. It is not really that hard to do away with these tempting things.

QUESTIONS FOR ANALYSIS

- What criticisms does Hongwu level against the Mongol Yuan, whose rule he overthrew?
- What crimes does he accuse his own officials of committing, and what punishments does he carry out?
- Why would this Chinese emperor issue a decree that focuses on defining moral behavior?

Source: Lily Hwa, "Proclamations of the Hongwu Emperor." Reprinted with the permission of The Free Press, a division of Simon & Schuster, Inc., from Chinese Civilization: A Sourcebook, *Second Edition, Revised and Expanded by Patricia Buckley Ebrey.*

As an example of religious rituals reinforcing hierarchies, the emperor sanctioned official cults that were either civil or military—and further distinguished as great, middle, or minor, as well as celestial, terrestrial, or human categories. Official cults, however, often conflicted with local faiths. In this regard, they revealed the limits of Ming centralism. Consider Dongyang, a hilly interior region. As was common in Ming China, the people of Dongyang supported Buddhist institutions. Guan Yu, a legendary martial hero killed centuries earlier, was enshrined in a local Buddhist monastery there. But he was also worshipped as part of a state cult. Herein lay the problem: the state cult and the Buddhist monastery were separate entities, and imperial law held that the demands of the state cult prevailed over those of the local monastery. So the state-appointed magistrates in Dongyang kept a watchful eye on local religious leaders, although the magistrates refrained from tampering directly in the monastery's affairs. Although the imperial government insisted that people honor their contributions to the state, Dongyang's residents delivered most of their funds to the Buddhist monks. So strong were local sentiments and contributions that even the officials siphoned revenues to the monastery.

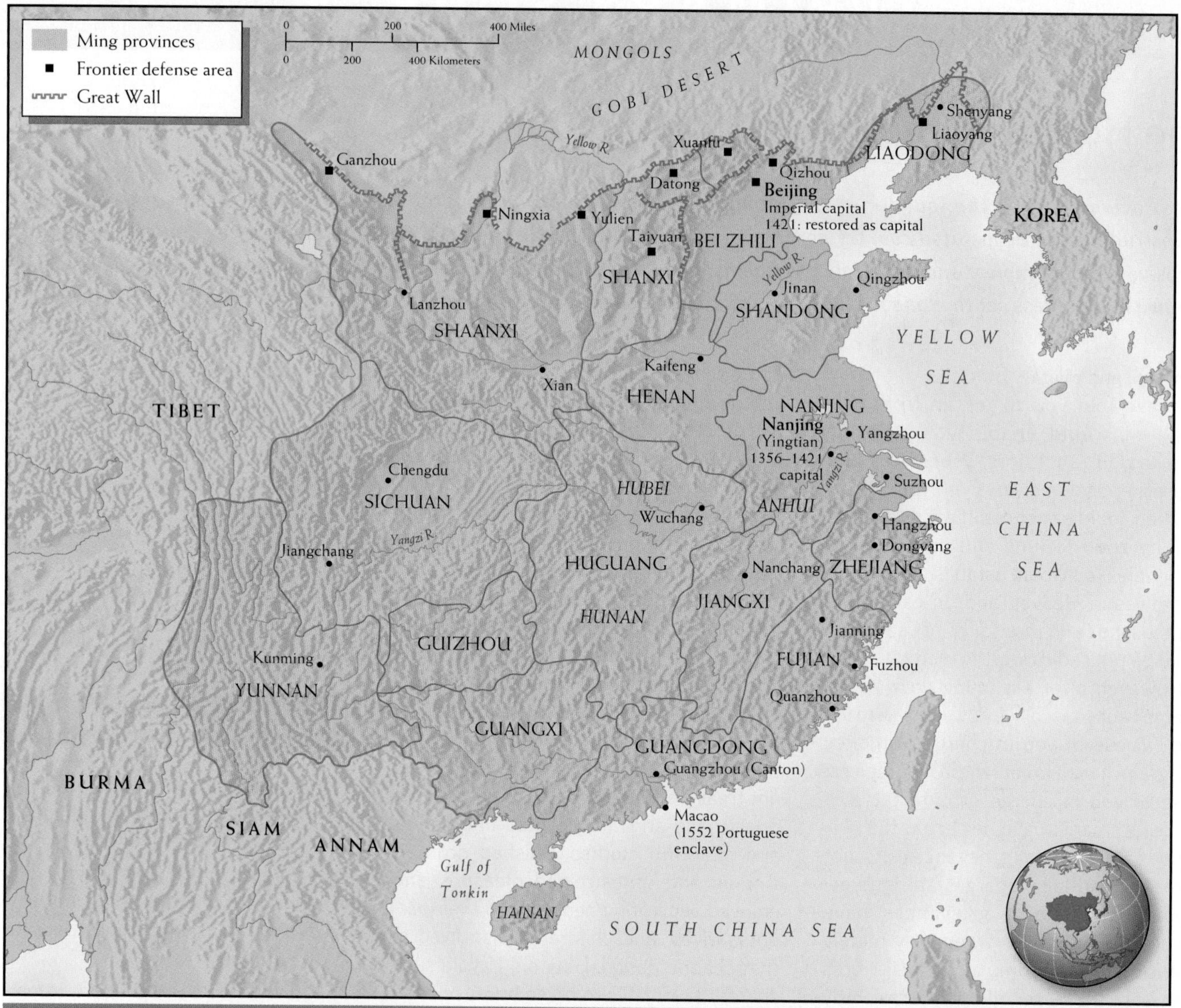

MAP 11.6 | Ming China, 1500s

The Ming state was one of the largest empires at this time—and the most populous. It had a long seacoast and even longer internal borders.

- What were the two Ming capitals, and what were the three main seaport trading cities?
- According to the map, where did the Ming rulers expect the greatest threat to their security?
- How did the Ming rulers view foreign contact and exchange during this period?

Ming Rulership

Religious sources of political power were less essential for the Ming dynasty than for the Islamic dynasties. Conquest and defense helped establish the realm, and bureaucracy kept it functioning. The empire's large scale (see Map 11.6) required a remarkably complex administration. To many outsiders (especially Europeans, whose region was in a state of constant war), Ming stability and centralization appeared to be political wizardry.

In terms of the structures underlying Ming power, the usual dynastic dilemmas were present. The emperor wished to be seen as the special guardian of his subjects. He wanted their allegiance as well as their taxes and labor. But during hard times, poor farmers were reluctant to provide resources—taxes or services—to distant officials. For these reasons alone, Hongwu preferred to entrust management of the rural world to local leaders, whom he appointed as village chiefs, village elders, or tax captains. (In fact, a popular Chinese proverb was: "The mountain is high and the emperor is far away.") Within these communities, the dynasty created a social hierarchy based on age, sex, and kinship. While women's labor remained critical for the village economy, the government reinforced a gender hierarchy by promoting women's chastity and constructing commemorative arches for widows who refrained from remarrying. The Ming thus produced a more elaborate system for classifying and controlling its subjects than did the other Afro-Eurasian dynasties.

The Ming Empire, like the European and Islamic states, also faced periodic unrest and rebellion. Rebels often proclaimed their own brand of religious beliefs, just as local elites resented central authority. Outright terror helped stymie threats to central authority. In a massive wave of carnage, Hongwu slaughtered anyone who posed a threat to his authority, from the highest of ministers to the lowliest of scribes. From 1376 to 1393, four of his purges condemned close to 100,000 subjects to execution.

Yet, despite the emperor's immense power, the Ming Empire remained under-governed. Indeed, as the population multiplied, there were too few loyal officials to handle local affairs. By the sixteenth and early seventeenth centuries, for example, some 10,000 to 15,000 officials shouldered the responsibility of managing a population exceeding 200 million people. Nonetheless, Hongwu bequeathed to his descendants a set of tools for ruling that drew on subjects' direct loyalty to the emperor and on the intricate workings of an extensive bureaucracy. His legacy enabled his successors to balance local sources of power with centralizing ambitions.

Trade under the Ming

In the fourteenth century, China began its economic recovery from the devastation of disease and political turmoil. Gradually, political stability allowed trade to revive. Now the new dynasty's merchants reestablished China's preeminence in long-distance commercial exchange. Chinese silk and cotton textiles, as well as fine porcelains, ranked among the world's most coveted luxuries. Wealthy families from Lisbon to Kalabar loved to wash their hands in delicate Chinese bowls and to flaunt fine wardrobes made from bolts of Chinese dyed linens and smoothly spun silk. When a Chinese merchant ship sailed into port, trading partners and onlookers crowded the docks to watch the unloading of precious cargoes.

OVERSEAS TRADE: SUCCESS AND SUSPICION During the Ming period, Chinese traders based in ports such as Hangzhou, Quanzhou, and Guangzhou (Canton) were as energetic as their Muslim counterparts in the Indian Ocean. These ports were home to prosperous merchants and the point of convergence for vast sea-lanes. Leaving the mainland ports, Chinese vessels carried precious wares to offshore islands, the Pescadores, and Taiwan. From there, they sailed on to the ports of Kyūshū, the Ryūkyūs, Luzon, and maritime Southeast Asia. As entrepôts for global goods, East Asian ports flourished. Former fishing villages developed into major urban centers.

The Ming dynasty viewed overseas expansion with suspicion, however. Hongwu feared that too much contact with the outside world would cause instability and undermine his rule.

Zheng He's Ship. *A testament to centuries of experience in shipbuilding and maritime activities, the largest ship in Zheng He's armada in the early fifteenth century was about five times the length of Columbus's* Santa Maria *(pictured next to Zheng's ship) and had nine times the capacity in terms of tonnage. It had nine staggered masts and twelve silk sails, all designed to demonstrate the grandeur of the Ming Empire.*

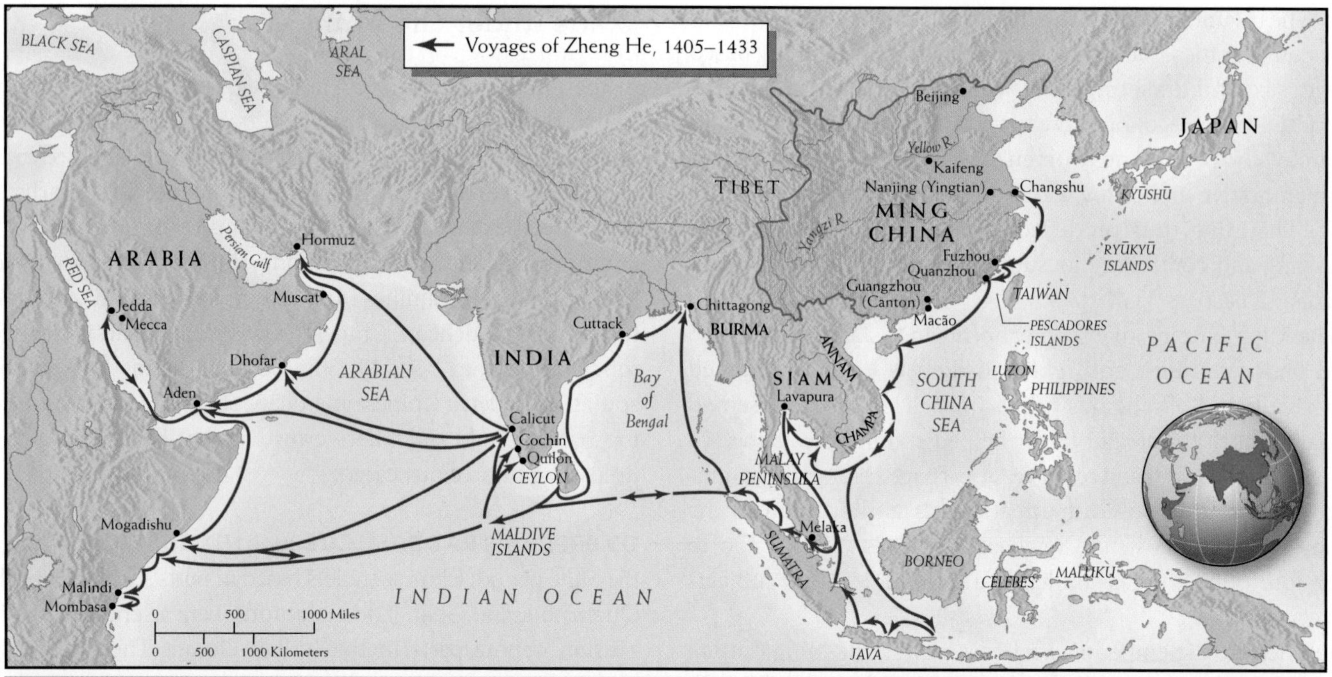

MAP 11.7 | Voyages of Zheng He, 1405-1433

Zheng He's voyages are some of the most famous in world history. Many have speculated about how history might be different if the Chinese emperors had allowed the voyages to continue.

- For how many years did Zheng's voyages go on?
- How far did Zheng go?
- Why did Chinese expeditions not have the same impact as European voyages of exploration toward the end of the fifteenth century?

In fact, he banned private maritime commerce in 1371. But enforcement was lax, and by the late fifteenth century maritime trade once again surged. Because much of the thriving business took place in defiance of official edicts, it led to constant friction between government officials and maritime traders. Although the Ming government ultimately agreed to issue licenses for overseas trade in the mid-sixteenth century, its policies continued to vacillate. To Ming officials, the sea represented problems of order and control rather than opportunities.

MARITIME EXPLORATION AND AFTERMATH One spectacular exception to the Ming's attitude toward maritime trade was a series of officially sponsored expeditions in the early fifteenth century. It was the ambitious Yongle Emperor who took the initiative. One of his loyal followers was a Muslim whom the Ming army had captured as a boy. The youth was castrated and sent to serve at the court (as a eunuch, he could not continue his family line and so theoretically owed sole allegiance to the emperor). Given the name **Zheng He** (1371–1433), he grew up to be an important military leader. The emperor entrusted him with venturing out to trade, collect tribute, and display China's power to the world.

From 1405 to 1433, Zheng He commanded the world's greatest armada and led seven naval expeditions. His larger ships stretched 400 feet in length (Columbus's *Santa Maria* was 85 feet), carried hundreds of sailors on four tiers of decks, and maneuvered with sophisticated rudders, nine masts, and watertight compartments. The first expedition set sail with a flotilla of 62 large ships and over 200 lesser ones. All 28,000 men aboard pledged to promote Ming glory.

Zheng He and his entourage aimed to establish tributary relations with far-flung territories—from Southeast Asia to the Indian Ocean ports, to the Persian Gulf, and to the east coast of Africa (see Map 11.7). These expeditions did not seek territorial expansion, but rather control of trade and tribute. Zheng traded for ivory, spices, ointments, exotic woods, and even some wildlife, including giraffes, zebras, and ostriches. He also used his considerable force to intervene in local affairs, exhibiting China's might in the process. If a community refused to pay tribute, Zheng's fleet would attack it. He encouraged rulers or envoys from Southeast Asia, India, Southwest Asia, and Africa to visit his homeland. When local rulers were uncooperative, Zheng might seize them and drag them all the way to China to face the emperor, as he did the rulers of Sumatra and Ceylon.

As spectacular as they were, Zheng's accomplishments could not survive the changing tides of events at home. Although many items gathered on his voyages delighted the court, most were not the stuff of everyday commerce. The expeditions were glamorous but expensive, and they came to an abrupt halt in 1433. Never again did the Ming undertake such large-scale maritime ventures. In fact, as early as 1424, when the Yongle Emperor died, the expeditions had already lost their most enthusiastic patron. Moreover, by the mid-fifteenth century, there was a revival of military threats from the north. At that time the Ming court was shocked to discover that during a tour of the frontiers, the emperor had been captured and held hostage by the Mongols. Recalling how the maritime-oriented Song dynasty had been overrun by invaders from the north (see Chapter 10), Ming officials withdrew imperial support for seagoing ventures and instead devoted their energies to overland ventures and defense.

Even though maritime commerce continued without official patronage, the abrupt withdrawal of imperial support led to the decline of Chinese naval power and opened the way for newcomers and rivals. Southeast Asians took advantage by constructing large oceangoing vessels, known as *jong*, which plied the regional trade routes from the fifteenth century to the early sixteenth century. These ships weighed an average of 350 to 500 tons (the largest weighed 1,000 tons) and carried 1,000 men on board. They transported cargoes and passengers not only to southern China, but also to the Indian Ocean as far west as Calicut and the Red Sea. Muslims also occupied the vacuum left by the Chinese, sailing west from ports such as Calicut across the Indian Ocean to Mombasa and Mogadishu, and east to Melaka (Malacca). In addition, Japanese pirates commandeered some of the trade. The Chinese decision to focus on internal trade and defending northern borders just at the time others began to look outward and overseas was, in a way, as monumental as that of Mehmed to take Constantinople, or that of Columbus to attempt a perilous westward voyage across "the Ocean Sea."

CONCLUSION

How could all the dying and devastation that came with the Black Death not have transformed the peoples of Afro-Eurasia? Much did change, but certain underlying ideals and institutions endured. What changed were mainly the political regimes, which took the blame for the catastrophes. The Delhi Sultanate, the Abbasid Empire, and the Yuan dynasty collapsed. In contrast, universal religions and wide-ranging cultural systems persisted even though they underwent vast transformations. The Ming dynasts in China set the stage for a long tenure by claiming as had previous rulers the mandate of heaven and stressing China's place at the center of their universe. A strict Shiite version of Islam emerged in Iran, while a fervent form of Sunni Islam found its champion in the Ottoman Empire. In Europe, national monarchies appeared in Spain, Portugal, France, and England. Yet Christianity, whose clerics had so often failed the dying and the disabled, swept back with renewed vigor.

The new states and empires had notable differences. These were evident in the ambition of a Ming warlord who established a new dynasty, the military expansionism of Turkish households bordering the Byzantine Empire, the unifying vision of Mughal rulers in northern India, and the desire of various European rulers to consolidate power. But interactions among peoples also mattered: an eagerness to reestablish and expand trade networks, and a desire to convert unbelievers to "the true faith"—be it a form of Islam, a variant of Hinduism, an exclusive Christianity, or a local type of Buddhism.

The dynasties all faced similar problems. They had to establish legitimacy, ensure smooth succession, deal with religious groups, and forge working relationships with nobles, townspeople, merchants, and peasants. Yet each state developed distinctive traits as a result of political innovation, traditional ways of ruling, and borrowing from neighbors. European monarchies achieved significant internal unity, often through warfare and in the context of a cultural Renaissance. Ottoman rulers perfected techniques for ruling an ethnically and religiously diverse empire: they moved military forces swiftly, allowed local communities a degree of political and religious autonomy, and trained a bureaucracy dedicated to the Ottoman and Sunni Islamic way of life. The Ming fashioned an imperial system based on a Confucian-trained bureaucracy and intense subordination to the emperor so that it could manage a mammoth population. The rising monarchies of Europe, the Shiite regime of the Safavids in Persia, and the Ottoman state all blazed with religious fervor and sought to eradicate or subordinate the beliefs of other groups.

The new states displayed unprecedented political and economic powers. All demonstrated military prowess, a desire for stable hierarchies and secure borders, and a drive to expand. Each legitimized its rule via dynastic marriage and succession, state-sanctioned religion, and administrative bureaucracies. Each supported vigorous commercial activity. The Islamic regimes, especially, engaged in long-distance commerce and, by conquest and conversion, extended their holdings.

For Europeans, the Ottoman conquests were decisive. They provoked Europeans to establish commercial connections to the east, south, and west. The consequences of their new toeholds would be momentous—just as the Chinese decision to turn *away* from overseas exploration and commerce marked a turning point in world history. Both decisions were instrumental in determining which worlds would come together and which would remain apart.

AFTER YOU READ THIS CHAPTER

Review and research on **STUDYSPACE:** wwnorton.com/studyspace

TRACING THE GLOBAL STORYLINES

FOCUS ON: *Rebuilding States*

Islamic Dynasties

- Ottoman, Safavid, and Mughal empires replace the Mongols.
- Ottomans overrun Constantinople and become the primary Sunni regime in the Islamic world.
- Safavids come to power in Iran as a Shiite state less tolerant of diversity than the Ottomans.
- Mughals replace the Delhi Sultanate in South Asia and continue to accommodate diverse religious beliefs.

China

- The Ming dynasty replaces the Mongol Yuan dynasty and rebuilds a strong state from the ground up.
- An elaborate, centralized bureaucracy oversees the revival of infrastructure and long-distance trade.

Western Christendom

- Devastation from the Black Death provokes revolt and extremist religious movements.
- New national monarchies appear in Portugal, Spain, France, and England.
- A rebirth of classical learning (the Renaissance) originates in Italian city-states and spreads throughout western Europe.

CHRONOLOGY

Islamic World
- Osman begins Ottoman Empire **1299**

South Asia

Europe
- Black Death reaches Italian port cities **1347**
- Peasant revolts in England and France **1358–1381**

East Asia
- Black Death begins in China **1320**
- Hongwu founds Ming dynasty **1368**

1300 | 1350

KEY TERMS

Black Death *p. 406*

dynasty *p. 407*

English Peasants' Revolt *p. 423*

humanism *p. 427*

Inquisition *p. 426*

Jacquerie *p. 423*

khan *p. 417*

monarchy *p. 425*

Moors *p. 425*

Ottoman Empire *p. 411*

Red Turban Movement *p. 430*

Renaissance *p. 426*

shah *p. 417*

Sikhism *p. 419*

Topkapi Palace *p. 415*

Zheng He *p. 436*

STUDY QUESTIONS

1. **Explain** how the Black Death, or bubonic plague, spread throughout Afro-Eurasia. What human activity facilitated its diffusion?
2. **Describe** the long-term consequences of bubonic plague for the Afro-Eurasian world. What were the plague's social, political, and economic ramifications in various parts of the landmass?
3. **Identify** the three main Islamic dynasties that emerged after the bubonic plague. How were they similar, and how were they different?
4. **Describe** how the Ming dynasty centralized its power in China in the fourteenth and fifteenth centuries. What political innovations did it pursue, and what traditions did it sustain?
5. **Describe** the goals of the Ming dynasty's maritime exhibitions. Why did the government later abandon them?
6. **Explain** why the bubonic plague undermined the feudal order of the Catholic Church. How did regional monarchs in Europe capitalize on this development?
7. **What were the key features** of the Renaissance in Europe? How did it spread and change?

Ottoman armies conquer Constantinople **1453**

Suleiman expands and consolidates Ottoman Empire **1520–1566**

Shah Ismail expands and consolidates Safavid Empire **1501–1524**

Timur sacks Delhi **1398**

Babur founds Mughal dynasty **1526**

Castile and Aragon unite to form Spain **1469**

Spain conquers Grenada **1492**

Tudor dynasty begins in England **1485**

Zheng He's voyages **1405–1433**

1400 1450 1500

BEFORE YOU READ THIS CHAPTER

wwnorton.com/
STUDYSPACE

GLOBAL STORYLINES

- European voyagers and colonizers "discover" the Americas (the so-called New World) and connect Afro-Eurasia with the Americas for the first time since the Ice Age.
- Not only do peoples move back and forth between Afro-Eurasia and the Americas; so do plants, animals, cultural products, and diseases—the Columbian exchange.
- Europeans create empires at great distances from their homelands, fail to enslave Native Americans, and bring in African captives as slave laborers, creating the Atlantic system.

CHAPTER OUTLINE

12

Contact, Commerce, and Colonization, 1450–1600

FOCUS QUESTIONS

- What was old and what was new in sixteenth-century world trade?
- How did the Portuguese attitude toward trade enable the Portuguese to exploit and dominate their trading partners?
- What did European conquerors adopt and change from the New World traditions they encountered?
- What military and maritime technologies advanced Portuguese exploration?
- What caused the political rivalries and religious rifts that divided Europe in the fifteenth and sixteenth centuries?
- Why did trade expand and wealth increase in sixteenth-century Asia?

In 1519, five ships under the command of Ferdinand Magellan set out from the Spanish mainland. Nearly three years later a single vessel returned, having successfully circumnavigated the globe. This achievement came at a high cost: four ships had been lost, and only 18 men out of 265 had staved off scurvy, starvation, and stormy seas to complete the journey. Magellan himself had died. But the survivors had become the first true world travelers. Unlike earlier adventurers who penetrated Eurasia and Africa, Magellan's transoceanic passage connected these worlds with others that, from an Afro-Eurasian viewpoint, had been apart—the Americas.

The voyages of Magellan and other European mariners intensified westerners' contact with Asia's vibrant commercial networks and gave Europeans access to a region they called the New World. Although Christopher Columbus did not intend to "discover" America when he went looking for Asia, his voyages convinced Europeans that there were still new territories to exploit and people to convert to Christianity. Moreover, in colonizing the Americas, Europeans drew on connections with West Africa. Indeed, African laborers became vital to agriculture and mining in the American colonies. Soon the New World's riches were prominent participants in the commercial circuits of Afro-Eurasia.

This chapter introduces the initial European conquest and colonization of the Americas. In the narrative of world history, few events surpass Columbus's voyages of discovery, which opened up worlds about which Afro-Eurasians had no previous knowledge. For the first time since the Ice Age migrations, peoples again moved from Afro-Eurasian landmasses to the Americas. So did animals, plants, commercial products, and—most momentous—deadly germs.

It was enormously significant that Europeans, rather than Asians or Africans, first stumbled upon the Americas and then exploited their resources. For Europeans, too, now became empire builders—but of a different nature. Their empires were overseas, far from the homeland. While the new colonies generated vast riches, they also brought unsettling changes to those who sought to make and maintain empires.

Despite the significance of Europeans' activity in the Americas, most Africans and Asians were barely aware of its importance to them. As the chapter demonstrates, Asian empires in Ottoman-controlled lands and in India and China continued to flourish after recovering from the Black Death. Nor was Europe's attention exclusively on the Americas, for its national monarchies competed for sway at home. Religious revolt in the form of the Protestant Reformation intensified these rivalries. In the wake of Columbus, the drive to build and protect empires across oceans—as well as religious conflicts abroad and at home—scattered peoples, shattered worlds, and created new cultural syntheses.

THE OLD TRADE AND THE NEW

Well before the products of the Americas entered the circuits of Afro-Eurasian trade, commerce had recovered from the destruction wrought by the Black Death. Just as political leaders had rebuilt states by mixing traditional and innovative ideas, merchant elites revived old trade patterns while establishing new networks. Increasingly, traffic across seas supplemented, if not supplanted, the overland transportation of goods. The Indian Ocean and China seas emerged as the focal points of Afro-Eurasia's maritime commerce. Across these waters moved an assortment of goods, coordinated by Arab, Persian, Indian, and Chinese merchants, who often settled in foreign lands. There they facilitated trade and mixed with locals.

European mariners and traders, searching for new routes to South and East Asia, began exploring the Atlantic coast of Africa. Lured by spices, silks, and slaves, and aided by new maritime technology, Portuguese expeditions made their way around Africa and onward to India. Meanwhile, Spanish monarchs sponsored Columbus's bid to reach Asia by sailing west across the Atlantic. Portuguese and Spanish ventures alike sought to convert "heathen" peoples to Christianity and to reap the riches abounding in Asian ports. Although Europeans still had little to offer would-be trading partners in Asia, their developing capability in overseas trade would lay the foundations for a new kind of global commerce.

The Revival of the Chinese Economy

China's economic dynamism was the crucial ingredient to Afro-Eurasia's global economic revival following the devastation wrought by the Black Death. Under the Ming dynasty, commerce rebounded and the Chinese achieved impressive economic expansion.

China's vast internal economy, not external trade, was the mainspring of the country's progress. After the Ming dynasty relocated its capital from Nanjing in the prosperous south to the northern city of Beijing, Chinese merchants, artisans, and farmers exploited the surging domestic market. Reconstruction of the Grand Canal now opened a major artery that allowed food and riches from the economically vibrant lower Yangzi area to reach the capital region of Beijing. Urban centers, such as Nanjing with a population approaching a million and Beijing at half a million, became massive and lucrative markets.

Along China's elaborate internal trading networks flowed silk and cotton textiles, rice, porcelain ceramics, paper, and many other products. The Ming's concern about the potentially disruptive effects of trade did not dampen this activity, and efforts to curb overseas commerce (following Zheng He's

Chinese Porcelain Box. *The shape, coloring, and texture of this Chinese porcelain writing box are a tribute to the exquisite craftsmanship that went into its production. This box was also a symbol of flourishing world trade and a typical example of what the French called "chinoiserie," the possession of which was a hallmark of taste and cultivation among the rich and the status-conscious in Europe.*

voyages; see Chapter 11) were largely unsuccessful. Merchants not only were tolerated but often thrived. And despite strictures on overseas trade, coastal cities remained active harbors.

Although the Chinese kept the best products for themselves, their silks and porcelain were esteemed across Afro-Eurasia. But what did foreign buyers have to trade with the Chinese? The answer was silver, which became essential to the Ming monetary system. Whereas their predecessors had used paper money, Ming consumers and traders mistrusted anything other than silver or gold for commercial dealings. Once the rulers adopted silver as a means of tax payment in the 1430s, it became the predominant medium for larger transactions.

However, China did not produce sufficient silver for its growing needs—a situation that foreigners learned to exploit. Indeed, silver and other precious metals were about the only commodities for which the Chinese would trade their precious manufactures. Through most of the sixteenth century, China's main source of silver was Japan, which one Florentine merchant called the "silver islands." Chinese and European merchants alike plied the routes from Japanese ports to the Chinese mainland.

After the 1570s, however, the Philippines, now under the control of the Spanish, became a gateway for silver coming from the New World. The Ming had developed a commercial fleet, which enabled their merchants to ship goods to Manila in exchange for silver (as well as firearms, sugar, potatoes, and tobacco). Despite official attempts to control trade, China became the final repository for much of the world's silver for roughly two hundred years. According to one estimate, one-third of all silver mined in the Americas wound up in Chinese hands. This influx fueled China's phenomenal economic expansion. New World silver also bought Europeans greater access to China's coveted goods.

The Revival of Indian Ocean Trade

China's economic expansion occurred within the revival of Indian Ocean trade. In fact, many of the same merchants seeking trade with China developed a brisk commerce that tied the whole of the Indian Ocean together. As a result, ports in East Africa and the Red Sea again enjoyed links with coastal cities of India, South Asia, and the Malay Peninsula. Muslims dominated this trade.

India was the geographic and economic center of these trade routes. With a population expanding as rapidly as China's, its large cities (such as Agra, Delhi, and Lahore) each boasted nearly half a million residents. India's manufacturing center, Bengal, exported silk and cotton textiles and rice throughout South and Southeast Asia. Like China, India had a favorable trade balance (meaning they were exporting more than they were importing) with Europe and West Asia, exporting textiles and pepper (a spice that Europeans prized) in exchange for silver.

In dealing with China, Indian merchants faced the same problem as Europeans and West Asians: they had to pay with silver. So they became as dependent on gaining access to silver as others who were courting Chinese commerce. But unlike Chinese merchants, Indian and Islamic traders in the region's commercial hubs did not obey one overarching political authority. This gave them considerable autonomy from political affairs and allowed them to occupy strategic positions in long-distance trade. Meanwhile, rulers all along the Indian Ocean enriched themselves with customs duties while flaunting their status with exotic goods. For glorifying sovereigns and worshipping deities, luxuries such as silks, porcelains, ivory, gold, silver, diamonds, spices, frankincense, myrrh, and incense were in high demand. Thus the Indian Ocean trade connected a vast array of consumers and producers long before Europeans arrived on the scene.

Of the many port cities supporting Indian Ocean commerce, none was more important than Melaka, located at a choke point between the Indian Ocean and the South China Sea. Melaka had no hinterland of farmers to support it, so it thrived exclusively as an entrepôt (a commercial hub for long-distance trade) for world traders, thousands of whom resided in the city or passed through it. Indeed, Melaka's merchants were a microcosm of the region's diverse commercial community. Arabs, Indians, Armenians, Jews, East Africans, Persians, and eventually western Europeans established themselves there to profit from the commerce that flowed in and out of the port.

Overland Commerce and Ottoman Expansion

In the fifteenth and sixteenth centuries, seaborne commerce eclipsed but did not eliminate overland caravan trading. In fact, along some routes, overland commerce thrived anew. One well-trafficked route linked the Baltic Sea, Muscovy, the Caspian Sea, the central Asian oases, and China. Other land routes carried goods to the ports of China and the Indian Ocean; from there, they crossed to the Ottoman Empire's heartland and went by land farther into Europe.

Of the many entrepôts that sprang up along caravan routes, none enjoyed more spectacular success than Aleppo in Syria. Thanks to its prime location at the end of caravan routes from India and Baghdad, Aleppo came to overshadow its Syrian rivals, Damascus and Homs. A vital supply point for Anatolia and the Mediterranean cities, Aleppo by the late sixteenth century was the most important commercial center in southwest Asia.

The Aleppans, like others within the Ottoman Empire, revered successful merchants. In popular stories such as *The Thousand and One Nights,* they celebrated these wealthy traders as shrewd men who amassed enormous wealth by mastering the intricacies of the caravan trade. Those close to the trade recognized how difficult the merchant's task was. The caravans gathered

Caravanserai. *As trade routes throughout the Ottoman Empire bustled with lucrative deals, roadside inns called caravanserais offered shrewd merchants and their helpers rest and refreshment. This illustration of a caravanserai comes from the 1581 travel journal of Venetian envoy Jacopo Soranzo.*

on the city's edge, where animals were hired, tents sewn, and saddles and packs arranged. Large caravans involved 600 to 1,000 camels and up to 400 men; smaller parties required no more than a dozen animals. Whatever the size, a good leader was essential. Only someone who knew the difficult desert routes and enjoyed the confidence of nomadic Bedouin tribes (which provided safe passage for a fee) could hope to make the journey profitable.

Ottoman authorities took a keen interest in the caravan trade, since the state gained considerable tax revenue from it. To facilitate the caravans' movement, the government maintained refreshment and military stations along the route. The largest had individual rooms to accommodate the chief merchants and could provide lodging for up to 800 travelers, as well as care for all their animals. But gathering so many traders, animals, and cargoes could also attract marauders, especially desert tribesmen. To stop the raids, authorities and merchants offered cash payments to tribal chieftains as "protection money." This was a small price to pay in order to protect the caravan trade, whose revenues ultimately supported imperial expansion.

EUROPEAN EXPLORATION AND EXPANSION

The Muslim conquest of Constantinople, Europe's gateway to the east (see Chapter 11), sent shock waves through Christendom and prompted Europeans to probe unexplored links to the east. That entailed looking south and west—and venturing across the seas. (See Map 12.1.) Taking the lead were the Portuguese, whose search for new routes to Asia led them first to Africa.

The Portuguese in Africa and Asia

Europeans had long believed that Africa was a storehouse of precious metals. In fact, a fourteenth-century map, the Catalan Atlas, depicted a single black ruler controlling a vast quantity of gold in the interior of Africa. Thus, as the price of gold skyrocketed during and after the Black Death, ambitious men decided to venture southward in search of this commodity and its twin, silver. These intrepid adventurers did not allow their fears of the world they anticipated encountering to overcome their ambitions. The first Portuguese sailors expected to find giants and Amazons, seas of darkness, and distant lands of savages and cannibals. After all, stories and myths had shaped their views of the places and peoples they would encounter.

NAVIGATION AND MILITARY ADVANCES Innovations in maritime technology and information from other mariners helped Portuguese sailors navigate the treacherous waters along the African coast. In the former category were new vessels. The carrack worked well on bodies of water like the Mediterranean; the caravel could nose in and out of estuaries and navigate unpredictable currents and winds. By using highly maneuverable caravels and perfecting the technique of tacking (sailing into the wind rather than before it), the Portuguese advanced far along the West African coast. In addition, newfound expertise with the compass and the astrolabe helped them determine latitude.

The Catalan Atlas. *This 1375 map shows the world as it was then known. Not only does it depict the location of continents and islands, but it also includes information on ancient and medieval tales, regional politics, astronomy, and astrology.*

The Portuguese also applied knowledge absorbed from ancient Greeks and Arabs and had assistance from Muslim mariners who shared their wide experience of Africa and the Indian Ocean.

The Portuguese success in the Indian Ocean was also partly the result of a revolution in military technology that owed much to borrowings from Asia. It began with the adaptation of a Chinese technology: gunpowder. The Ottomans used it to conquer Constantinople in 1453 with enormous cannons and 800-pound cannonballs. In 1492, Christians used cannons to breach the walls of Granada. Europeans also used smaller cannons, which were more mobile and propelled iron balls in relatively flat trajectories, to destroy old fortifications. When mounted against warships' gunwales, such cannons could bombard ports and rival navies—or merchant vessels—to shift the nature of ocean commerce toward military ends.

Within Europe the main beneficiaries of this revolution in warfare were the dynastic rulers, who could afford to equip large fighting forces with new armaments. Whereas in 1415 the English king had won the Battle of Agincourt against the French with fewer than 10,000 men, by 1492 the Spanish crown amassed a huge force of 60,000 Christian soldiers to drive the Moors out of Granada. Tactics shifted, too. In medieval Europe, a day of combat or a short siege of castles often settled matters. But by the mid-sixteenth century, battles often involved lengthy and inconclusive struggles. This way of war, more costly in money and manpower, gave an advantage to larger, centralized states.

SUGAR AND SLAVES Africa and the islands along its coast soon proved to be far more than a stop-off en route to India or a source of precious metals. Africa became a valued trading area, and its islands were prime locations for growing sugarcane—a crop that had exhausted the soils of Mediterranean islands, where it had been cultivated since the twelfth century. Along what they called the Gold Coast, the Portuguese established many fortresses and ports of call.

After seizing islands along the West African coast, the Portuguese introduced sugarcane cultivation on large plantations and exploited slave labor from the African mainland. The Madeira, Canary, and Cape Verde archipelagos in particular became laboratories for plantation agriculture, for their rainfall and fertile soils made them ideally suited for growing sugarcane. And because it took droves of workers to cultivate, harvest, and process sugarcane, a ready supply of slave labor enabled Portugal and Spain to build sizeable plantations in their first formal **colonies** (regions under the political control of another country). In the 1400s, these islands saw the beginnings of a system of plantation agriculture built on slavery that would travel across the Atlantic in the following century.

Caravel. *Caravels became the classic vessel for European exploration. They had many decks and plenty of portholes for cannons, could house a large crew, and had lots of storage for provisions, cargo, and booty.*

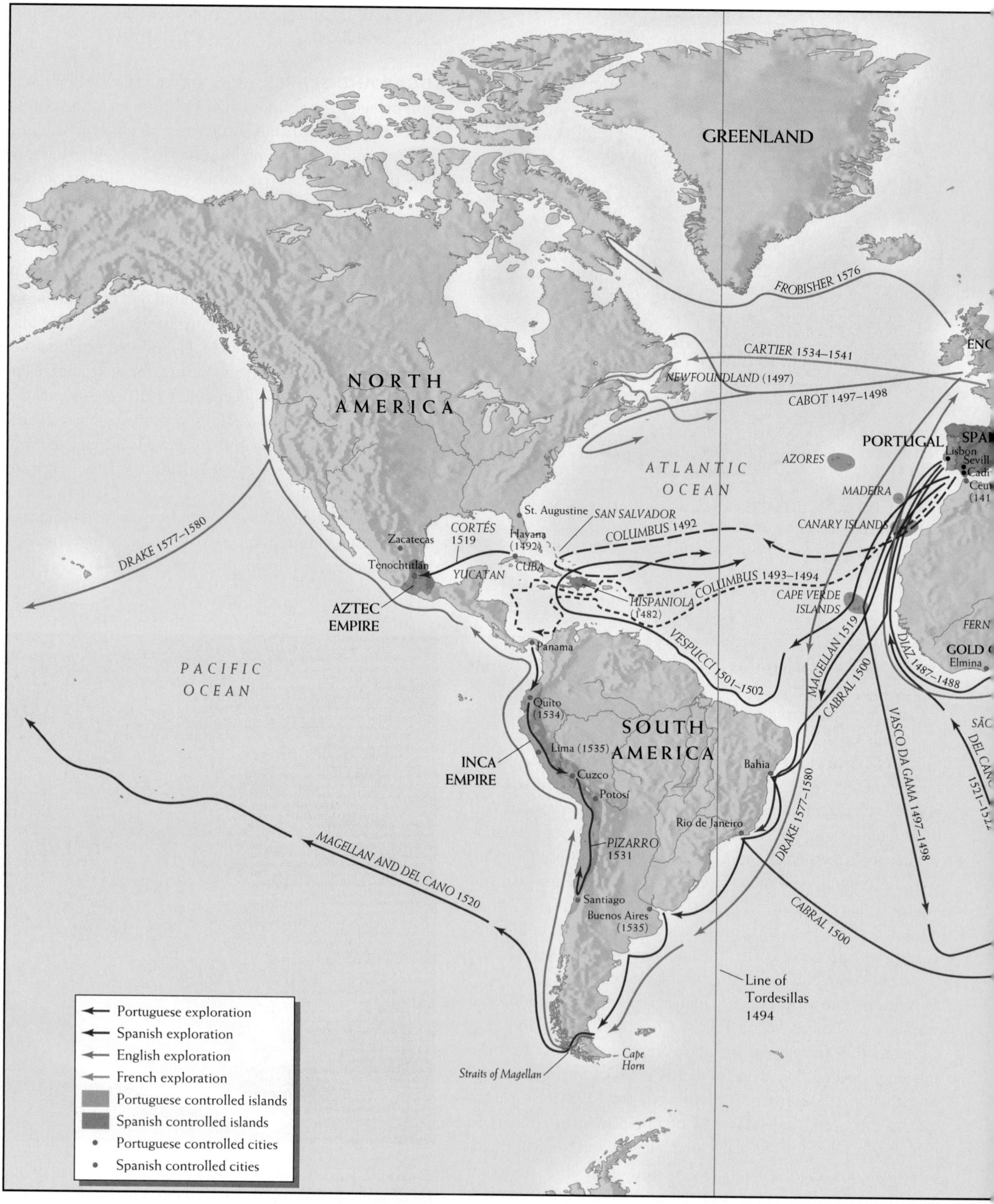
GREENLAND
FROBISHER 1576
CARTIER 1534–1541
NEWFOUNDLAND (1497)
CABOT 1497–1498
NORTH AMERICA
ATLANTIC OCEAN
PORTUGAL
Lisbon
AZORES
MADEIRA
CANARY ISLANDS
St. Augustine
SAN SALVADOR
COLUMBUS 1492
CORTÉS 1519
Zacatecas
Havana (1492)
Tenochtitlán
YUCATAN
CUBA
DRAKE 1577–1580
COLUMBUS 1493–1494
HISPANIOLA (1482)
CAPE VERDE ISLANDS
AZTEC EMPIRE
VESPUCCI 1501–1502
MAGELLAN 1519
CABRAL 1500
Panama
PACIFIC OCEAN
Quito (1534)
SOUTH AMERICA
Lima (1535)
INCA EMPIRE
Cuzco
Potosí
Bahia
Rio de Janeiro
DRAKE 1577–1580
VASCO DA GAMA 1497–1498
PIZARRO 1531
MAGELLAN AND DEL CANO 1520
Santiago
Buenos Aires (1535)
CABRAL 1500
Line of Tordesillas 1494
Cape Horn
Straits of Magellan
Elmina
Portuguese exploration
Spanish exploration
English exploration
French exploration
Portuguese controlled islands
Spanish controlled islands
Portuguese controlled cities
Spanish controlled cities

MAP 12.1 | European Exploration, 1420–1580

In the fifteenth and sixteenth centuries, sailors from Portugal, Spain, England, and France explored and mapped the coastline of most of the world.

- What empire to the east prevented Europeans from expanding trade routes by land?
- Trace the voyages that started from Portugal, and then trace the voyages that started from Spain.
- Why did Portuguese explorers concentrate on Africa and the Indian Ocean, whereas their Spanish counterparts focused on the Americas?
- What does the map tell us about the different patterns of exploration in the New World versus those in the Indian Ocean and the South China Sea?

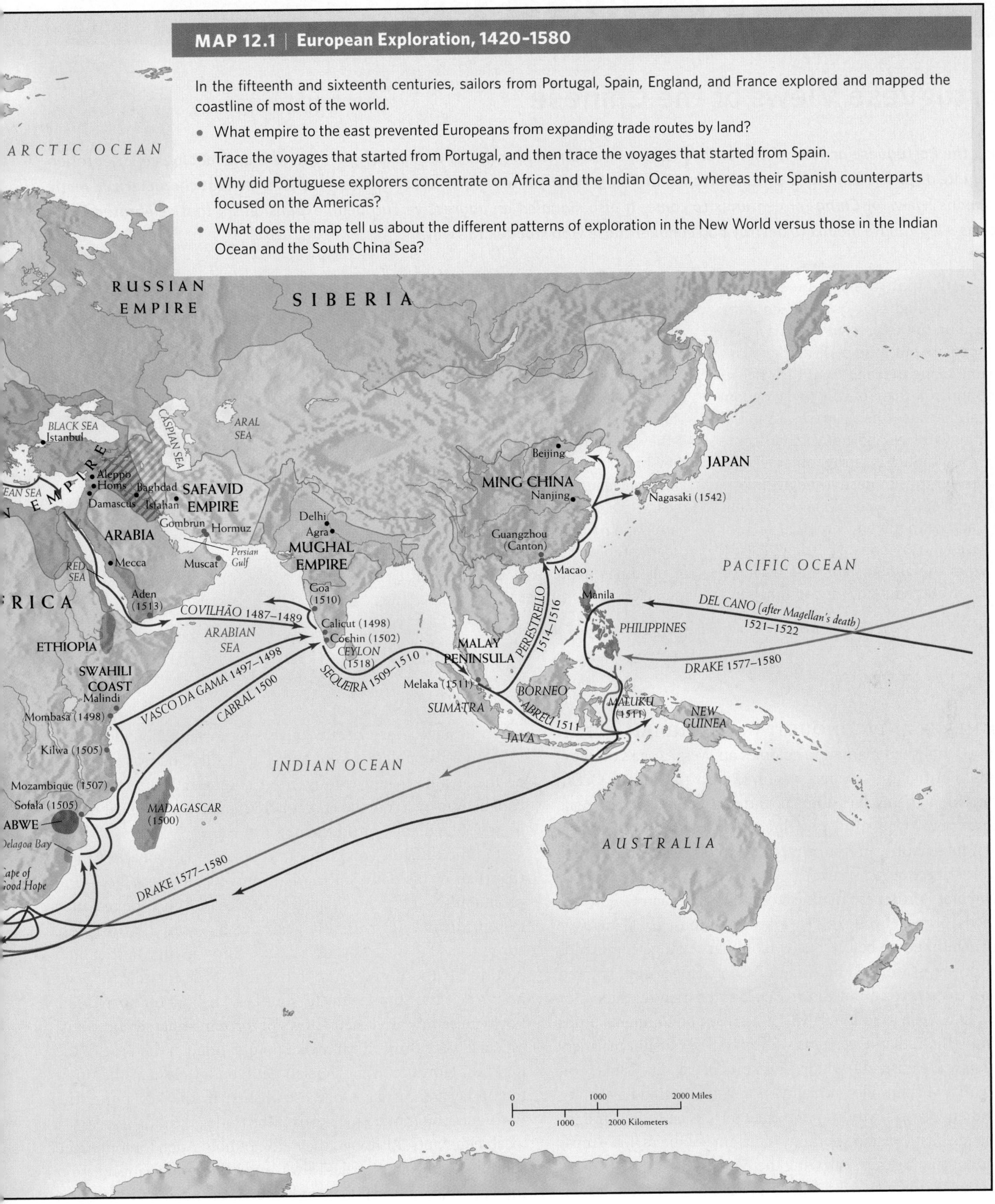

PRIMARY SOURCE

Portuguese Views of the Chinese

When the Portuguese arrived in China, they encountered an empire whose organizational structure and ideological orientation were quite different from their own. Written in 1517, this Portuguese report reflects misrepresentations that characterized many Europeans' views of China for centuries to come. It also signaled an aggressive European expansionism that celebrated brute force as a legitimate means to destroy and conquer those who stood in the way.

God grant that these Chinese may be fools enough to lose the country; because up to the present they have had no dominion, but little by little they have gone on taking the land from their neighbors; and for this reason the kingdom is great, because the Chinese are full of much cowardice, and hence they come to be presumptuous, arrogant, cruel; and because up to the present, being a cowardly people, they have managed without arms and without any practice of war, and have always gone on getting the land from their neighbors, and not by force but by stratagems and deceptions; and they imagine that no one can do them harm. They call every foreigner a savage; and their country they call the kingdom of God.

Whoever shall come now, let it be a captain with a fleet of ten or fifteen sail. The first thing will be to destroy the fleet if they should have one, which I believe they have not; let it be by fire and blood and cruel fear for this day, without sparing the life of a single person, every junk being burnt, and no one being taken prisoner, in order not to waste the provisions, because at all times a hundred Chinese will be found for one Portuguese.

QUESTIONS FOR ANALYSIS

- What do you think was the main purpose of this report?
- How could this observer's views be so inaccurate?
- What is the irony in the comment, "They call every foreigner a savage," followed by instructions to destroy, burn, and not spare "the life of a single person"?

Source: Letters from Canton, translated and edited by D. Ferguson, The Indian Antiquary *31 (January 1902), in J. H. Parry,* European Reconnaissance: Selected Documents *(New York: Walker, 1968), p. 140.*

COMMERCE AND CONQUEST IN THE INDIAN OCEAN

Having established plantation colonies on West Africa's outlying islands, Portuguese seafarers ventured into the Indian Ocean and inserted themselves into its thriving commerce. In Asia, Portugal never wanted to rule directly or to establish colonies. Rather, its seaborne empire aimed to exploit Asian commercial networks and trading systems.

The first Portuguese mariner to reach the Indian Ocean was Vasco da Gama (1469–1524). Like Columbus, da Gama was relatively unknown before his extraordinary voyage commanding four ships around the Cape of Good Hope. He explored Africa's eastern coast but did not encounter friendly traders or great riches. What he found was a network of commercial ties spanning the Indian Ocean, as well as skilled Muslim mariners who knew the currents, winds, and ports of call. Da Gama took on board a Muslim pilot at Malindi for instruction in navigating the Indian Ocean's winds and currents. He then sailed straight for the Malabar coast in southern India, one of the region's most important trading areas, arriving there in 1498.

To the Portuguese, who traded in the name of their crown, commercial access was worth fighting for. Da Gama was briefly taken hostage near Calicut, and though eventually allowed to take on a valuable cargo of spices and silks, he was incensed at the insult. While exiting from southern India, da Gama roughed up everyone he encountered, making sure local fishermen watched and spread the news.

On the difficult voyage back to Lisbon, da Gama lost more than half of his crew, but he had proved the feasibility—and profitability—of trade via the Indian Ocean. When he returned to Calicut in 1502 with a larger crew, he asserted Portuguese supremacy by boarding all twenty ships in the harbor and cutting off the noses, ears, and hands of their sailors. Then he burned the ships with the mutilated sailors on board. The Portuguese repeated their shows of force in strategic locations, especially the three naval choke points: Aden at the base of the Red Sea, Hormuz in the Persian Gulf, and Melaka at the tip of the Malay Peninsula. Once established in the key ports, the Portuguese attempted to take over the trade or, failing this, to tax local merchants. Although they did not hold Aden for long, they solidified control in Sofala, Kilwa, and other important ports on the East African coast, Goa and Calicut in India, and Macao in southern China. From these strongholds, the Portuguese soon commanded the most active sea-lanes of the Indian Ocean. (See Primary Source: Portuguese Views of the Chinese.)

To assert their domain over Indian Ocean trade (west of the Melaka Strait), the Portuguese introduced a pass system that required ships to pay for *cartazes*—documents identifying the ship's captain, size of the ship and crew, and its cargo. Indian Ocean rulers and merchants got cartazes for free, showing the limits of Portuguese control. Others calculated it was cheaper to pay than risk losses at sea from the Portuguese fleet. What made the Portuguese presence in the Indian Ocean world distinctive was that it did not interrupt the flow of luxuries among Asian and African elites; rather, the Portuguese naval captains simply kept a portion of the profits for themselves.

Over time, as Indian Ocean commodities made their way back to Lisbon, that city eclipsed Italian ports (such as Venice) that had previously been prime entrepôts for Asian goods. Even so, spices were less important in Europe than *within* the Indian Ocean world, where the Portuguese became an important player. Only with the discovery of the Americas and the conquest of Brazil did Portugal become an empire with large overseas colonies. For this to transpire, mariners would have to traverse the Atlantic Ocean itself.

THE ATLANTIC WORLD

Western European Christendom, in opening new sea-lanes in the Atlantic, set the stage for an epochal transformation in world history. New technologies aided European expansion, but diseases made the difference. In their encounters with the peoples of the Americas, Europeans introduced more than new cultures to this isolated world; they also brought devastating diseases such as smallpox, typhus, and cholera, for which Amerindian populations had no immunity. In the first years after Amerindians made contact with Europeans, their populations suffered a catastrophic decline. This decimation enabled Europeans to conquer and colonize the Americas as they could not do in Asia or Africa, where long-standing patterns of trade had resulted in the development of shared immunities.

The devastation of the Amerindian population also resulted in severe labor shortages. Thus began the large-scale introduction of slave laborers imported from Africa. After 1500, most of the people who made the Atlantic voyage were not Europeans but Africans. As a supplier of slave labor, Africa became the third corner in a triangular world order. Born of the links among the peoples and resources of Europe, Africa, and the Americas, this emerging "Atlantic system" enriched the Europeans. Through their access to the precious metals of the Americas, they now had something to offer their trading partners in Asia.

Crossing the Atlantic was a feat of monumental importance in world history. It did not occur, however, with an aim to discover new lands. Columbus had wanted to voyage into the "Ocean Sea" so as to open a more direct—and more lucrative—route to Japan and China. Fired by their victory at Granada, Ferdinand and Isabella had agreed to finance his trip, hoping for riches to bankroll a crusade to liberate Jerusalem from Muslim hands. Just as Columbus had no idea he would find a "New World," Spain's monarchs (not to mention its merchants, missionaries, and soldiers) never dreamed that soon they would be preparing for conquest and profiteering in what had been, just a few years before, a blank space on the map. (Thus the term **New World**, as applied to the Americas, reflects the Europeans' view that anything previously unknown to them was "new," even if it had existed and supported societies long before European explorers arrived on its shores.)

Although discovering the Americas was not Columbus's goal, it took scarcely a generation for Europeans to realize the significance of their accidental find. As news of Columbus's voyage spread through Europe, ambitious mariners prepared to sail west. By 1550, all of Europe's powers were scrambling, not just for a share of Indian Ocean action but also for spoils from the Atlantic. In the process, they began destroying the societies and dynasties of the New World. The devastation of its peoples coincided with a sharpening of European rivalries.

Westward Voyages of Columbus

Few figures in history embody their age more than Christopher Columbus. His three ships set sail from Spain in early 1492, stopped in the Canary Islands for supplies and repairs, and cast off into the unknown. When he stepped onto the beach of San Salvador (in the Bahamas) on October 12, 1492, Columbus ushered in a new era in world history. He did not, however, return with the precious Asian commodities he had sought. Columbus would search in vain over three subsequent voyages for the valuable products of the South China Sea and the Indian Ocean.

It is important to see Columbus as a man of his time. Like other expansion-minded Europeans, he aimed to Christianize the world while enriching himself and his backers. These goals—to save souls and to make money—drove the European colonization of the Americas and the formation of an Atlantic system. Still, it is noteworthy that Columbus's voyages aimed not to create something new but to generate revenues to cover the conquest of Granada and the reconquest of the Holy Land.

First Encounters

When Columbus made landfall in the Caribbean Sea, he unfurled the royal standard of Ferdinand and Isabella and claimed the "many islands filled with people innumerable" for Spain. It is

Columbus. *As Columbus made landfall and encountered Indians, he planted a cross to indicate the spiritual purpose of the voyage and read aloud a document proclaiming the sovereign authority of the king and queen of Spain. Quickly, he learned there was barter for precious stones and metals.*

fitting that the first encounter with Caribbean inhabitants, in this case the Tainos, drew blood. Columbus noted, "I showed them swords and they took them by the edge and through ignorance cut themselves." The Tainos had their own weapons but did not forge steel—and thus had no knowledge of such sharp edges.

For Columbus, the Tainos' naiveté in grabbing his sword symbolized the child-like primitivism of these people, whom he would mislabel "Indians" because he thought he had arrived off the coast of Asia. In Columbus's view the Tainos had no religion, but they did have at least some gold (found initially hanging as pendants from their noses). Likewise, Pedro Alvares Cabral, a Portuguese mariner whose trip down the coast of Africa in 1500 was blown off course across the Atlantic, wrote that the people of Brazil had all "the innocence of Adam." He also noted that they were ripe for conversion and that the soils "if rightly cultivated would yield everything." But, as with Africans and Asians, Europeans also developed a contradictory view of the peoples of the Americas. From the Tainos, Columbus learned of another people, the Caribs, who (according to his informants) were savage, warlike cannibals. For centuries, these contrasting images—innocents and savages—structured European (mis) understandings of the native peoples of the Americas.

We know less about what the Indians thought of Columbus or other Europeans on their first encounters. Certainly the Europeans' appearance and technologies inspired awe. The Tainos fled into the forest at the approach of European ships, which they thought were giant monsters; others thought they were floating islands. European metal goods, in particular weaponry, struck them as otherworldly. The strangely dressed white men seemed godlike to some, although many Indians soon abandoned this view. The natives found the newcomers different not for their skin color (only Europeans drew the distinction based on skin pigmentation), but for their hairiness. Indeed, the Europeans' beards, breath, and bad manners repulsed their Indian hosts. The newcomers' inability to live off the land also stood out.

In due course, the Indians realized that the strange, hairy people bearing metal weapons meant to stay and force the native population to labor for them. But by then, it was too late. The explorers had become **conquistadors** (conquerors).

First Conquests

After his first voyage, Columbus claimed that on Hispaniola (present-day Haiti and the Dominican Republic) "he had found what he was looking for"—gold. That was sufficient to persuade the Spanish crown to invest in larger expeditions, and to seek to conquer this promising new territory. Whereas Columbus first sailed with three small ships and 87 men, ten years later the Spanish outfitted an expedition with 2,500 men. Exploration now gave way to warfare, and to exploitation.

Between 1492 and 1519, the Spanish experimented with institutions of colonial rule over local populations on the Caribbean island that they renamed Hispaniola. Ultimately they created a model that the rest of the New World colonies would adapt. But the Spaniards faced problems that would recur. The first was Indian resistance. As early as 1494, starving Spaniards raided and pillaged Indian villages. When the Indians revolted, Spanish soldiers replied with punitive expeditions and began enslaving them to work in mines extracting gold. As the crown systematized grants (*encomiendas*) to the conquistadors for control over Indian labor, a rich class of *encomenderos* arose who enjoyed the fruits of the system. Although the placer gold mines soon ran dry, the model of granting favored settlers the right to coerce Indian labor endured. In return, those who received the labor rights paid special taxes on the precious metals that were extracted. Thus, both the crown and the *encomenderos* benefited from the extractive economy. The same cannot be said of the Indians, who perished in great numbers from disease, dislocation, malnutrition, and overwork.

It is no surprise that quarrels over spoils followed the conquests. The family of Columbus, in particular, had been granted a commercial monopoly on his discoveries, but some of the settlers challenged Columbus's authority. To prevent insurrection, the crown granted more *encomiendas* to other Spanish claimants. As special grants became a common feature of Spanish colonialism, less favored settlers grew disenchanted. When the Indians and the gold supplies began to disappear, many settlers pulled up their stakes and returned to Spain. Others looked for untapped territories that might yield precious metals.

Not all joined the rush for riches or celebrated the conquistadors and *encomenderos*. Dominican friars protested the abuse of the Indians, seeing them as potential converts who were equal to the Spaniards in the eyes of God. In 1511, Father Antonio Montesinos accused the settlers of barbarity: "By what right do you wage such detestable wars on these people who lived idly and peacefully in their own lands, where you have consumed infinite numbers of them with unheard-of murders and desolations?" Dissent and debate would be a permanent feature of Spanish colonialism in the New World.

The Aztec Empire and the Spanish Conquest

As Spanish colonists saw the bounty of Hispaniola dry up, they set out to discover and conquer new territories. Finding their way to the mainlands of the American landmasses, they encountered larger, more complex, and more militarized societies than those they had overrun in the Caribbean.

On the mainland, great civilizations had arisen centuries before, boasting large cities, monumental buildings, and riches based on wealthy agrarian societies. In both Mesoamerica, starting with the Olmecs (see Chapter 5), and the Andes, with the Chimú (see Chapter 10), large polities had laid the foundations for subsequent Aztec and Incan empires. The latter states were powerful. But they also represented the evolution of states and commercial systems untouched by Afro-Eurasian developments; as worlds apart, they were unprepared for the kind of assaults that European invaders had honed. In pre-Columbian Mesoamerica and then the Andes, warfare was more ceremonial, less inclined to wipe out enemies than to make them tributary subjects. As a result, the wealth of these empires made them irresistible to outside conquerors they never knew, and their habits of war made them vulnerable to conquests they could never foresee.

AZTEC SOCIETY In Mesoamerica, the ascendant Mexicas had created an empire known to us as "Aztec." Around Lake Texcoco, Mexica cities grew and formed a three-city league in 1430, which then expanded through the Central Valley of Mexico to incorporate neighboring peoples. Gradually the **Aztec Empire** united numerous small, independent states under a single monarch who ruled with the help of counselors, military leaders, and priests. By the late fifteenth century, the Aztec realm may have embraced 25 million people. Tenochtitlán, the primary city, situated on an immense island in Lake Texcoco, ranked among the world's largest.

Tenochtitlán spread in concentric circles, with the main religious and political buildings in the center and residences radiating outward. The city's outskirts connected a mosaic of floating gardens producing food for urban markets. Canals irrigated the land, waste served as fertilizer, and high-yielding produce found easy transport to markets. Entire households worked: men, women, and children all had roles in Aztec agriculture.

Extended kinship provided the scaffolding for Aztec statehood. Marriage of men and women from different villages solidified alliances and created clan-like networks. In Tenochtitlán, powerful families married their children to each other or found nuptial partners among the prominent families of other important cities. (Certain ruling houses in Europe were solidifying alliances in much the same way at this time; see Chapter 11.) Not only did this practice concentrate power in the great city, but it also ensured a pool of potential successors to the throne. Soon a lineage emerged to create a corps of "natural" rulers. Priests legitimized the new emperor in rituals to convey the image of a ruler close to the gods and to distinguish the elite from the lower orders.

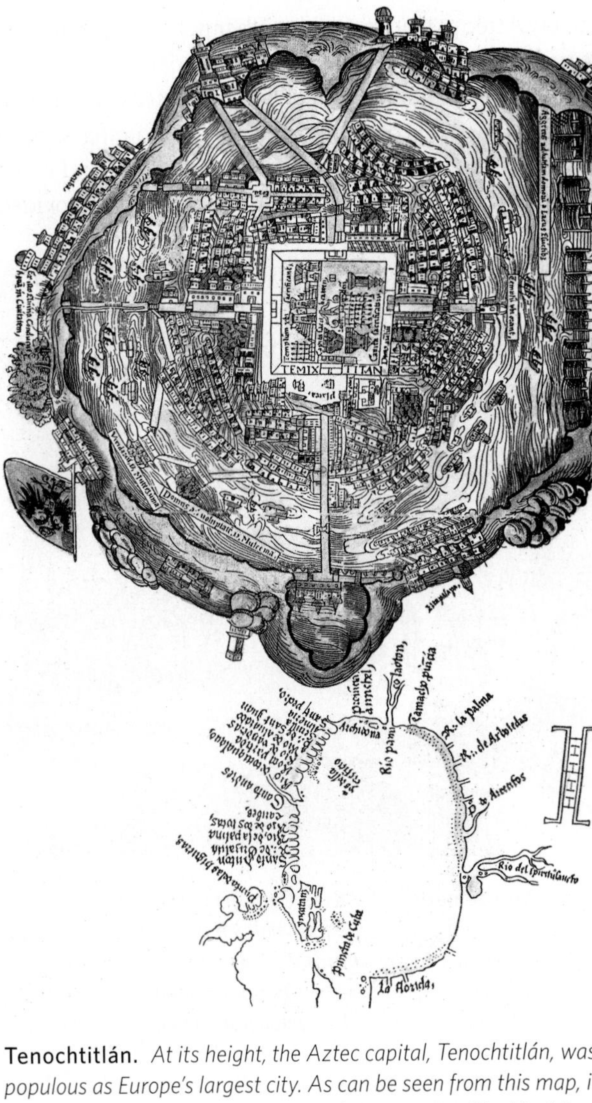

Tenochtitlán. *At its height, the Aztec capital, Tenochtitlán, was as populous as Europe's largest city. As can be seen from this map, it spread in concentric circles, with the main religious and political buildings in the center and residences radiating outward.*

A hierarchy at the village level provided the bedrock for layers of increasingly centralized political authority. Local elders developed representative councils, which selected delegates to a committee that elected the dominant civil authority, the chief speaker. As Aztec power spread, the chief speaker became a full-blown emperor. He was, however, not supreme; instead, he jockeyed with rival religious and military power-wielders. Thus at the top of the Aztec social pyramid stood a small but antagonistic nobility. This hierarchically organized society held itself together through a shared understanding of the cosmos. The Aztecs believed that the universe was prone to unceasing cycles of disaster that would eventually end in apocalypse. Such an unstable cosmos exposed mortals to repeated creations and destructions of their world. The priesthood governed relationships between people and their deities. Their challenge was to balance a belief that history was destined to run in cycles with a faith that mortals could influence the gods, and their own fate, through religious rituals.

Ultimately Aztec power spread though much of Mesoamerica, but the empire's constant wars and conquests deprived it of stability. In successive military campaigns, the Aztecs subjugated their neighbors, feeding off plunder and then forcing subject peoples to pay tribute of crops, gold, silver, textiles, and other goods that financed Aztec grandeur. Such conquests also provided a constant supply of humans for sacrifice, because the Aztecs believed that the great god of the sun required human hearts to keep on burning and blood to replace that given by the gods to moisten the earth through rain. Priests escorted captured warriors up the temple steps and tore out their hearts, offering their lives and blood as a sacrifice to the sun god. Allegedly, between 20,000 and 80,000 men, women, and children were slaughtered in a single ceremony in 1487, with the four-person-wide line of victims stretching for over two miles. In this marathon of bloodletting, knife-wielding priests collapsed from exhaustion and surrendered their places to fresh executioners.

Those whom the Aztecs sought to dominate did not submit peacefully. From 1440, the empire faced constant turmoil as subject peoples rebelled against their oppressive overlords. Tlaxcalans and Tarascans along the Gulf of Mexico waged a relentless war for freedom, pinning down entire divisions of Aztec armies. To pacify the realm, the empire diverted more and more men and money into a mushrooming military. By the time the electoral committee chose Moctezuma II as emperor in 1502, divisions among elites and pressures from the periphery placed the Aztec Empire under extreme stress.

CORTÉS AND CONQUEST Not long after Moctezuma became emperor, news arrived from the coast of strange sightings of

Cortés Meets Mesoamerican Rulers. (Left) *This colonial image depicts the meeting of Cortés (second from right) and Moctezuma (seated on the left), with Doña Marina serving as an interpreter and informer for the Spanish conquistador. Notice at the bottom what are likely Aztec offerings for the newcomer.* (Right) *This detail from a twentieth-century Mexican mural depicts the meeting of Cortés and the king of Tlaxcala (enemy of the Aztecs). As Mexicans began to celebrate their mixed-blood heritage, Doña Marina (in the middle) became the symbolic mother of the first mestizos.*

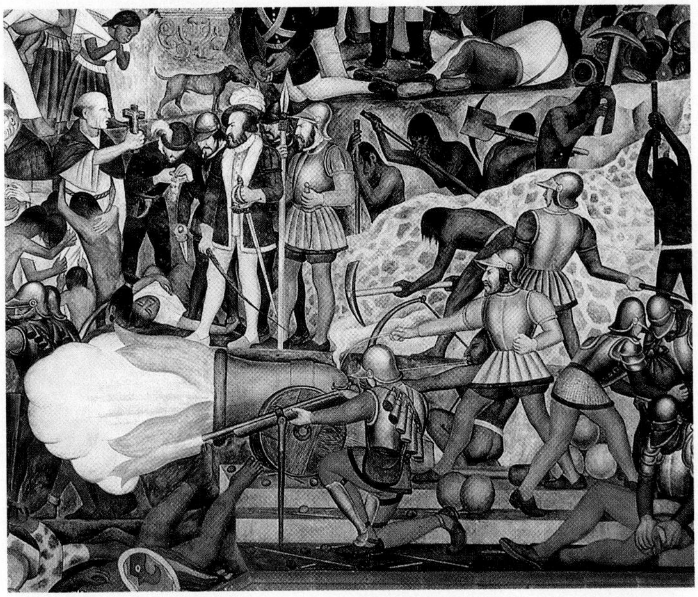

The Conquest of the Aztecs. *Diego Rivera's twentieth-century representation of the fall of Tenochtitlan (left) emphasizes the helplessness of the Aztecs to the ruthless and technologically superior Spanish soldiers. Though the Aztecs outnumber the Spanish in this portrayal, their faces are obscured in postures of grief and suffering, unlike their counterparts in the sixteenth-century illustration of the same event (right). Painted by a converted Indian and based on indigenous oral histories, it shows the Aztec warriors in a glory of their own, as well as the cruel fact that they were force to fight other Indians who had sided with the Spanish.*

floating mountains (ships) bearing pale, bearded men and monsters (horses and dogs). Moctezuma consulted with his ministers and soothsayers, wondering if these men were the god Quetzalcoátl and his entourage. The people of Tenochtitlán saw omens of impending disaster. Moctezuma sank into despair, hesitating over what to do. He sent emissaries bearing jewels and prized feathers; later he sent sorcerers to confuse and bewitch the newcomers. But he did not prepare for any military engagement. After all, Mesoamericans had no idea of the interlopers' destructive potential in weaponry and germs.

Aboard one of the ships was Hernán Cortés (1485–1547), a former law student from one of the Spanish provinces. He would become the model conquistador, just as Columbus was the model explorer. For a brief time, Cortés was an *encomendero* in Hispaniola; but when news arrived of a potentially wealthier land to the west, he set sail with over 500 men, eleven ships, sixteen horses, and artillery.

When the expedition arrived near present-day Veracruz, Cortés acquired two translators, including the daughter of a local Indian noble family. The daughter, who became known as Doña Marina, was a "gift" to the triumphant Spaniards from the ruler of the Tabasco region (a rival to the Aztecs). Fluent in several languages, Doña Marina displayed such linguistic skills and personal charms that she soon came to Cortés's attention. She became his lover and ultimately revealed several Aztec plots against the tiny Spanish force. Doña Marina subsequently bore Cortés a son, who is considered one of the first mixed-blooded Mexicans (**mestizos**).

With the assistance of Doña Marina and other native allies, Cortés marched his troops to Tenochtitlán. Upon entering, he gasped in wonder that "this city is so big and so remarkable" that it was "almost unbelievable." One of his soldiers wrote, "It was all so wonderful that I do not know how to describe this first glimpse of things never heard of, seen or dreamed of before."

How was this tiny force to overcome an empire of many millions with an elaborate warring tradition? Crucial to Spanish conquest was their alliance, negotiated through translators, with Moctezuma's enemies—especially the Tlaxcalans. After decades of yearning for release from the Aztec yoke, the Tlaxcalans and other Mesoamerican peoples embraced Cortés's promise of help. The Spaniards' second advantage was their method of warfare. The Aztecs were seasoned fighters, but they fought to capture, not to kill. Nor were they familiar with gunpowder or sharp steel swords. Although outnumbered, the Spaniards killed their foe with abandon, using superior weaponry, horses, and war dogs. The Aztecs, still unsure who these strange men were, allowed Cortés to enter their city. With the aid of the Tlaxcalans and a handful of his own men, in 1519 Cortés captured Moctezuma, who became a puppet of the Spanish conqueror. (See Primary Source: Cortés Approaches Tenochtitlán.)

Within two years, the Aztecs realized that the newcomers were not gods and that Aztec warriors, too, could fight to kill.

PRIMARY SOURCE

Cortés Approaches Tenochtitlán

When the Spanish conquered the Aztec Empire, they defeated a mighty power. The capital, Tenochtitlán, was probably the same size as Europe's biggest city. Glimpsing Tenochtitlán in 1521, Hernán Cortés marveled at its magnificence. But to justify his acts, he claimed to be bringing civilization and Christianity to the Aztecs. Note the contrast between Cortés's admiration for Tenochtitlán and his condemnation of Indian beliefs and practices—as well as his claim that he abolished cannibalism, something the Aztecs did not practice (although they did sacrifice humans).

This great city of Tenochtitlán is built on the salt lake. . . . It has four approaches by means of artificial causeways. . . . The city is as large as Seville or Cordoba. Its streets . . . are very broad and straight, some of these, and all the others, are one half land, and the other half water on which they go about in canoes. . . . There are bridges, very large, strong, and well constructed, so that, over many, ten horsemen can ride abreast. . . . The city has many squares where markets are held. . . . There is one square, twice as large as that of Salamanca, all surrounded by arcades, where there are daily more than sixty thousand souls, buying and selling. . . . [I]n the service and manners of its people, their fashion of living was almost the same as in Spain, with just as much harmony and order; and considering that these people were barbarous, so cut off from the knowledge of God and other civilized peoples, it is admirable to see to what they attained in every respect. . . .

It happened . . . that a Spaniard saw an Indian . . . eating a piece of flesh taken from the body of an Indian who had been killed. . . . I had the culprit burned, explaining that the cause was his having killed that Indian and eaten him, which was prohibited by Your Majesty, and by me in Your Royal name. I further made the chief understand that all the people . . . must abstain from this custom. . . . I came . . . to protect their lives as well as their property, and to teach them that they were to adore but one God . . . that they must turn from their idols, and the rites they had practised until then, for these were lies and deceptions which the devil . . . had invented. . . . I, likewise, had come to teach them that Your Majesty, by the will of Divine Providence, rules the universe, and that they also must submit themselves to the imperial yoke, and do all that we who are Your Majesty's ministers here might order them. . . .

QUESTIONS FOR ANALYSIS

- What does Cortés's report tell us about the city of Tenochtitlán?
- Why does Cortés justify his actions to the degree he does?
- Cortés writes, "I came . . . to protect their lives as well as their property." Based on your reading of the chapter text, would you say he accomplished these objectives?

Source: Letters of Cortés, *translated by Francis A. MacNutt (New York: G. P. Putnam, 1908), pp. 244, 256–57.*

When Spanish troops massacred an unarmed crowd in Tenochtitlán's central square while Cortés was away, they provoked a massive uprising. The Spaniards led Moctezuma to one of the palace walls to plead with his people for a truce, but the Aztecs kept up their barrage of stones, spears, and arrows—striking and killing Moctezuma. Cortés returned to reassert control; but realizing this was impossible, he gathered his loot and escaped. Left behind were hundreds of Spaniards, many of whom were dragged up the temple steps and sacrificed by Aztec priests.

With the Tlaxcalans' help, Cortés regrouped. This time he chose to defeat the Aztecs completely. He ordered the building of boats to sail across Lake Texcoco to bombard the capital with artillery. Even more devastating was the spread of smallpox, brought by the Spanish, which ran through the soldiers and commoners like wildfire. Still, led by a new ruler, Cuauhtémoc, the Aztecs rallied and nearly drove the Spaniards from Tenochtitlán. In the end starvation, disease, and lack of artillery vanquished the Aztec forces. More died from disease than from fighting—the total number of Aztec casualties may have reached 240,000. As Spanish troops retook the capital, they found it in ruins, with a population too weak to resist. Cuauhtémoc himself faced execution, thereby ending the royal Mexica lineage. The Aztecs lamented their defeat in verse: "We have pounded our hands in despair against the adobe walls, for our inheritance, our city, is lost and dead." Cortés became governor of the new Spanish colony, renamed "New Spain." He promptly allocated *encomiendas* to his loyal followers and dispatched expeditions to conquer the more distant Mesoamerican provinces.

The Mexica experience taught the Spanish an important lesson: an effective conquest had to be swift—and it had to remove completely the symbols of legitimate authority. Their winning advantage, however, was disease. The Spaniards unintentionally introduced germs that made their subsequent efforts at military conquest much easier.

The Incas

The other great Spanish conquest occurred in the Andes, where Quechua-speaking rulers, called Incas, had established an impressive polity. From its base in the valley of Cuzco, the **Inca Empire** encompassed a population of 4 to 6 million. But the Incas were internally split. Lacking a clear inheritance system, the empire suffered repeated convulsions.

In the early sixteenth century, the struggle over who would succeed Huayna Capac, the Inca ruler, was especially fierce. Huascar, his "official" son, took Cuzco (the capital), while Atahualpa, his favored son, governed the province of present-day Ecuador. Open conflict might have been averted were it not for Huayna's premature death. His killer was probably smallpox, which swept down the trade routes from Mesoamerica into the Andes (much as the bubonic plague had earlier spread through Afro-Eurasian trade routes; see Chapter 11). With the father gone, Atahualpa declared war on his brother, crushed him, forced him to witness the execution of all his supporters, and then killed him and used his skull as a vessel for maize-beer.

When the Spaniards arrived in 1532 they found an internally divided empire, a situation they quickly learned to exploit. Francisco Pizarro, who led the Spanish campaign, had been inspired by Cortés's victory and yearned for his own glory. Commanding a force of about 600 men, he invited Atahualpa to confer at the town of Cajamarca. There he laid a trap. As columns of Inca warriors and servants covered with colorful plumage and plates of silver and gold entered the main square, the Spanish soldiers were awed. One recalled, "many of us urinated without noticing it, out of sheer terror." But Pizarro's plan worked. His guns and horses shocked the Inca forces. Atahualpa himself fell into Spanish hands, later to be decapitated. Pizarro's conquistadors overran Cuzco in 1533 and then vanquished the rest of the Inca forces, a process that took decades in some areas.

Meanwhile, Spaniards began arriving in droves at the new capital of Lima. They staked their own claims for *encomiendas*, outdoing each other with greed, and soon were at war with one another. In 1541, one faction assassinated Pizarro himself. Rival factions kept up a brutal war until the Spanish king issued new laws to prevent *encomiendas* from being heritable. This act sought to block the establishment of a powerful aristocracy, to deter uncontrollable civil war, and to reinforce loyalty to Madrid (since once an *encomendero* died, his title reverted to the crown).

The defeat of the New World's two great empires had enormous repercussions for world history. First, it meant that Europeans had their way with the human and material wealth of the Americas. Second, it gave Europeans a market for their own products—goods that found little favor in Afro-Eurasia. Finally, it opened a new frontier that the Europeans could colonize as staple-producing provinces. Now, following the Portuguese push into Africa and Asia (as well as a Russian push into northern Asia; see Chapter 13), the New World conquest introduced Europeans to a new scale of imperial expansion. The outcome, however, would destabilize Europe itself.

Pizarro and the Incas. *This illustration is by the Andean native Guaman Poma, whose c. 1587 epic of the conquest of Peru depicted many of the barbarities of the Spanish. Here we see the conquistador Pizarro and a Catholic priest appealing to Atahualpa—before betraying and then killing him.*

Environmental Consequences of the Conquest

The Spanish came to the Americas for gold and silver, but in the course of conquest and settlement they also learned about crops such as potatoes and corn that would fuel a population explosion across Afro-Eurasia. They brought with them first of all devastating diseases, but also horses, wheat, grapevines, and sugarcane. Historians call this hemispheric transfer of previously unknown plants, pathogens, people, and products in the wake of Columbus's voyages the **Columbian exchange**. Over

ANALYZING GLOBAL DEVELOPMENTS

The European Conquest of the Americas and Amerindian Mortality

If the fourteenth century was an age of dying across Afro-Eurasia, the sixteenth century saw even higher mortality rates in the Americas. As a result of European conquest, the exposure to virulent diseases, and the hyperexploitation of their labor under miserable conditions, the Native American populations saw their numbers reduced by 85 percent. The numbers themselves, however, are highly controversial and have sparked intense debates. Some scholars believe that no reliable numbers can be found for the population of the Americas when Europeans first arrived. Others have used a range of methods and data sources to establish population figures, including European firsthand accounts from that period, archaeological and anthropological evidence, estimates of the maximum population size of people the land can contain indefinitely (carrying capacity), and projections built backward from more recent censuses. These estimates vary widely from as little as 8 million to as high as more than 100 million.

Area	Population in 1492	Later Populations	Mortality Rates
The Americas	53.9 m	8 m in 1650	85%
The Caribbean			
Hispaniola	1.0 m	extinct by 1600	100%
The other islands	2.0 m	extinct by 1600	100%
Mexico	17.2 m	3.5 m in 1600	80%
The Andes	15.0 m	3.0 m in 1650	80%
Central America	5.63 m	1.12 m in 1700	80%
North America	3.79 m	1.5 m in 1700	60%
		250,000 in 1900	84%

QUESTIONS FOR ANALYSIS

- Imagine yourself a historical demographer. How would you attempt to estimate the population of the Americas in 1492?
- What effect did European conquest and Amerindian dying have on the polities and religious beliefs of the Native Americans?
- Why do you think Native American population growth never recovered from the initial encounter with Europeans as Afro-Eurasian population growth eventually recovered from the Black Death?

Sources: Suzanne Austin Alchon, A Pest in the Land: New World Epidemics in a Global Perspective *(2003); David Noble Cook,* Born to Die: Disease and New World Conquest, 1492 to 1650 *(1998); William M. Denevan,* The Native Populations of the Americas in 1492 *(1992); David Henige,* Numbers from Nowhere: The Amerindian Contact Population Debate *(1998); "La catastrophe demographique,"* L'histoire, *July–August, 2007, no. 322, p. 17; Thornton, Russell,* American Indian Holocaust: A Population History since 1492 *(1987), p. xvii.*

time, this exchange would transform the environments, economies, and diets of both the new and the old worlds.

The first and most profound effect of the Columbian exchange was a destructive one: the decimation of the Amerindian population by European diseases (see Analyzing Global Developments: The European Conquest of the Americas and Amerindian Mortality). For millennia, the isolated populations of the Americas had been cut off from Afro-Eurasian microbe migrations; in this sense, in contrast, the Amerindians were indeed "worlds apart."

Sickness spread from almost the moment the Spaniards arrived. One Spanish soldier noted, upon entering the conquered Aztec capital, "the streets were so filled with dead and sick people that our men walked over nothing but bodies." Native American accounts of the fall of Tenochtitlán recalled the smallpox epidemic more vividly than the fighting. Even worse, no sooner had smallpox done its work than Indians faced a second pandemic: measles. Then came pneumonic plague and influenza. As each wave retreated, it left a population more emaciated than before, even less prepared for the next wave. The scale of death remains unprecedented: imported pathogens wiped out up to 90 percent of the Indian population. A century after smallpox arrived on Hispaniola in 1519, no more than 5 to 10 percent of the island's population was left alive. Diminished and weakened by disease, Amerindians could not resist European settlement and colonization of the Americas. Thus were Europeans the unintended beneficiaries of a horrifying catastrophe.

As time passed, all sides adopted new forms of agriculture from one-another. Indians taught Europeans how to grow potatoes and corn, crops that would become staples all across Afro-Eurasia. The Chinese found that they could grow corn in areas too dry for rice and too wet for wheat, while corn replaced, at first by fits and starts, Africa's major food grains, sorghum, millet, and rice, to become the continent's principal food crop by the twentieth century. (See Current Trends in World History:

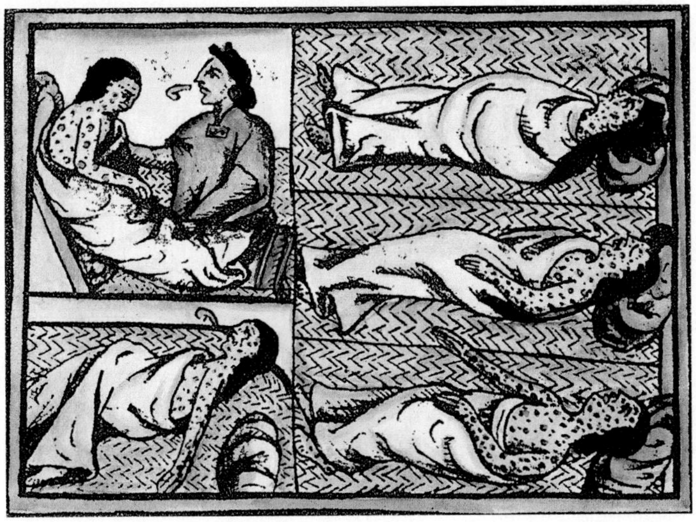

Disease and Decimation of Indians. *The real conqueror of Native Americans was not so much guns as germs. Even before Spanish soldiers seized the Aztec capital, germs had begun decimating the population. The first big killer was smallpox, recorded here by an Indian artist, covering the bodies of victims.*

Corn and the Rise of Slave-Supplying Kingdoms in West Africa.) Europeans also took away tomatoes, beans, cacao, peanuts, tobacco, and squash, while importing livestock such as cattle, swine, and horses to the New World. The environmental effects of the introduction of livestock to the Americas were manifold. In the highland regions north of the valley of central Mexico (where Native Americans had once maintained irrigated, highly productive agricultural estates), Spanish settlers opened up large herding ranches. An area that had once produced corn and squash now supported herds of sheep and cattle. Without natural predators, these animals reproduced with lightning speed, destroying entire landscapes with their hooves and their foraging.

As Europeans cleared trees and other vegetation for ranches, mines, or plantations, they undermined the habitats of many indigenous mammals and birds. On the islands of the West Indies, described by Columbus as "roses of the sea," the Spanish chopped down lush tropical and semitropical forests to make way for sugar plantations. Before long, nearly all of the islands' tall trees as well as many shrubs and ground plants were gone, and residents lamented the absence of birdsong. Over ensuing centuries, the flora and fauna of the Americas took on an increasingly European appearance—a process that the historian Alfred Crosby has called ecological imperialism.

Spain's Tributary Empire

Like the Europeans who sailed into the Indian Ocean to join existing commercial systems, the Spaniards sought to exploit the wealth of indigenous empires without fully dismantling them. Those Native Americans who survived the original encounters could be harnessed as a means to siphon tribute payments to the new masters. Spain could thereby extract wealth without extensive settlement. In Mexico and Peru, where the Inca Empire suffered the same fate as the Aztecs, conquistadors decapitated native communities but left much of their social and economic structure intact—including networks of tribute. But unlike the European penetration of the Indian Ocean, the occupation of the New World went beyond the control of commercial outposts. Instead, European colonialism in the Americas involved controlling large amounts of territory—and ultimately the entire landmass (see Map 12.2).

By fusing traditional tribute-taking with their own innovations, Spanish masters made villagers across their new American empire deliver goods and services. But because the Spanish authorities also bestowed *encomiendas*, those favored individuals could demand labor from their lands' Indian inhabitants—for mines, estates, and public works. Whereas Aztec and Inca rulers had used conscripted labor to build up their public wealth, the Spaniards did so for private gain.

Most Spanish migrants were men; only a few were women. One, Inés Suárez, reached the Indies only to find her husband, who had arrived earlier, dead. She then became mistress of the conquistador Pedro de Valdivia, and the pair worked as a conquering team. Initially, she joined an expedition to conquer Chile as Valdivia's domestic servant, but she soon became much more—nurse, caretaker, advisor, and guard, having uncovered several plots to assassinate her lover. Suárez even served as a diplomat between warring Indians and Spaniards in an effort to secure the conquest. Later, she helped to rule Chile as the wife of Rodrigo de Quiroga, governor of the province. Admittedly, hers

Silver. *Silver was an important discovery for Spanish conquerors in Mesoamerica and the Andes. Conquerors expanded the customs of Inca and Aztec labor drafts to force the natives to work in mines, often in brutal conditions.*

CURRENT TRENDS IN WORLD HISTORY

Corn and the Rise of Slave-Supplying Kingdoms in West Africa

New World varieties of corn spread rapidly throughout the Afro-Eurasian landmass soon after the arrival of Columbus in the Americas. Its hardiness and fast ripening qualities made it more desirable than many of the Old World grain products. In communities that consumed large quantities of meat, it became the main product fed to livestock.

Corn's impact on Africa was as substantial as it was in the rest of Eurasia. Seeds made their way to western regions more quickly than to the south of the Sahara along two routes. One was via European merchants calling into ports along the coast; the second was West African Muslims returning across the Sahara after participating in the pilgrimage. The first evidence of corn cultivation in sub-Saharan Africa comes from a Portuguese navigator who identified the crop being grown on the island of Cape Verde in 1540. By the early seventeenth century, corn was replacing millet and sorghum as the main grain being grown in many West African regions and was destined to transform the work routines and diets of the peoples living in the region's tropical rain forests all the way from present-day Sierra Leone in the east to Nigeria in the west. In many ways this area, which saw the rise of a group of powerful slave-supplying kingdoms in the eighteenth century, notably Asante, Dahomey, Oyo, and Benin, owed its prosperity to the cultivation of this New World crop. (See Chapter 14 for a fuller discussion of these states.)

The tropical rain forests of West and central Africa were thick with trees and ground cover in 1500. Clearing them so that they could support intensive agriculture was exhausting work, requiring enormous outlays of human energy and man-hours. Corn, a crop first domesticated in central Mexico 7,000 years ago, made this task possible. It added much-needed carbohydrates to the carbon-deficient diets of rain-forest dwellers. In addition, as a crop that matured more quickly than those that were indigenous to the region (millet, sorghum, and rice) and required less labor, it yielded two harvests in a single year. Farmers also cultivated cassava, another New World native, which in turn provided households with more carbohydrate calories. Yet corn did more than produce more food per unit of land and labor. Households put every part of the plant to use—grain, leaves, stalks, tassels, and roots were made to serve useful purposes.

Thus, at the very time that West African groups were moving southward into the rain forests, European navigators were arriving along the coast with new crops. Corn gave communities of cultivators the caloric energy to change their forest landscapes, expanding the arable areas. In a select few of these regions, enterprising clans emerged to dominate the political scene, creating centralized

was an exceptional story. More typical were women who foraged for food, tended wounded soldiers, and set up European-style settlements.

However, there were too few Spanish women to go around, so Spanish men consorted with local women. Although the crown did not approve the taking of concubines, the practice was widespread. From the onset of colonization, Spaniards also married into Indian families. After conquering the Incas, Pizarro himself wedded an Inca princess, thereby (or so he hoped) inheriting the mantle of local dynastic rule. As a result of intermarriages, mestizos became the fastest-growing segment of the population of Spanish America.

Spanish migrants and their progeny preferred towns to the countryside. Ports excepted, the major cities of Spanish America were the former centers of Indian empires. Mexico City took shape on the ruins of Tenochtitlán; Cuzco arose from the razed Inca capital. In their architecture, economy, and most intimate aspects, the Spanish colonies adopted as much as they transformed the worlds they encountered.

Silver

For the first Europeans in the Americas, the foremost measure of success was the gold and silver that they could hoard for themselves and their monarchs. But in plundering massive amounts of silver, the conquistadors introduced it to the world's commercial systems, an act that electrified them. In the twenty years after the fall of Tenochtitlán, conquistadors took more precious metals from Mexico and the Andes than all the gold accumulated by Europeans over the previous centuries.

Having looted Indian coffers, the Spanish entered the business of mining directly, opening the Andean Potosí mines in 1545. Between 1560 and 1685, Spanish America sent 25,000 to 35,000 tons of silver annually to Spain. From 1685 to 1810, this sum doubled. The two mother lodes were Potosí in present-day Bolivia and Zacatecas in northern Mexico. Silver brought bounty not only to the crown but also to a privileged group of families based in Spain's colonial capitals; thus private wealth funded the formation of local aristocracies.

Corn Plantation. *This nineteenth-century engraving by famed Italian explorer Savorgnan de Brazza shows women of the West African tribe Bateke working in corn plantations. De Brazza would later serve as the governor general of the French colony in the Congo.*

kingdoms like Asante in present-day Ghana, Dahomey in present-day Benin, and Oyo and Benin in present-day Nigeria. These elites transformed what had once been thinly settled environments into densely populated states, with elaborate bureaucracies, big cities, and large and powerful standing armies.

There was much irony in the rise of these states, which owed so much of their strength to the linking of the Americas with Afro-Eurasia. The armies that they created and the increased populations that the new crops allowed were part and parcel of the Atlantic slave trade. That which the Americas gave with one hand (new crops), it took back with the other (warfare, captives, and New World slavery).

QUESTIONS FOR ANALYSIS

- What were the major effects of growing corn in West Africa?
- How did the growing of corn reshape the history of the Atlantic world during this period?

Explore Further

McCann, James, *Maize and Grace: Africa's Encounter with a New World Crop, 1500–2000* (2005).

Colonial mines epitomized the Atlantic world's new economy. They relied on an extensive network of Indian labor, at first enslaved, subsequently drafted. Here again, the Spanish adopted Inca and Aztec practices of requiring labor from subjugated villages. Each year, under the traditional system, village elders selected a stipulated number of men to toil in the shafts, refineries, and smelters. Under the Spanish, the digging, hauling, and smelting taxed human limits to their capacity—and beyond. Those unfortunate enough to be sent underground pounded the rock walls with chisels and hammers, releasing silicon dust. Miners could not help but breathe in the toxic dust, which created lesions, and made simply inhaling seem like swallowing broken glass. (See Primary Source: Silver, the Devil, and Coca Leaf in the Andes.) But the miners' sufferings reaped huge profits, and significant consequences for the Europeans. The Spanish pumped so much New World silver into global commercial networks that they caused painful price inflation in Europe, and transformed Europe's relationship to all its trading partners, especially those in China and India.

PORTUGAL'S NEW WORLD COLONY

No sooner did Europeans—starting with the Portuguese and Spanish—venture into the seas than they carved them up to prevent a free-for-all. The Treaty of Tordesillas of 1494, drawn up by the pope, had foreseen that the non-European world—the Americas, Africa, and Asia—would be divided into spheres of interest between Spain and Portugal. Yet the treaty was unenforceable. No less interested in immediate riches than the Spanish, the Portuguese were disappointed by the absence of tributary populations and precious metals in the areas set aside for them. What they did find in Brazil, however, was abundant, fertile land on which favored persons received massive royal grants. These estate owners governed their plantations like feudal lords (see Chapter 10).

Coastal Enclaves

Hemmed in along the coast, the Portuguese created enclaves. Unlike the Spanish, they rarely intermarried with Indians, most

MAP 12.2 | The Spanish and Portuguese Empires in the Americas, 1492–1750

This map examines the growth of the Spanish and Portuguese empires in the Americas over two and a half centuries. Identify the natural resources that led the Spaniards and Portuguese to focus their empire-building where they did.

- What were the major export commodities from these colonized areas?
- Looking back to Map 12.1, why do you think Spanish settlement covered so much more area than Portuguese settlement?
- According to your reading, how did the production and export of silver and sugar shape the labor systems that evolved in both empires?

PRIMARY SOURCE

Silver, the Devil, and Coca Leaf in the Andes

When Spanish colonists forced thousands of Andean Indians to work in the silver mines of Potosí, they permitted the chewing of coca leaves (which are now used to extract cocaine). Chewing the leaves gave Indians a mild "high," alleviated their hunger, and blunted the pain of hard work and deteriorating lungs. The habit also spread to some Spaniards. In this document, Bartolomé Arzáns de Orsúa y Vela, a Spaniard born in Potosí in 1676, expresses how important coca was to Indian miners and how harmful it was for Spaniards who fell under its spell. By the time the author wrote his observations in the late seventeenth century, the use of the coca leaf had become widespread.

I wish to declare the unhappiness and great evil that, among so many felicities, this kingdom of Peru experiences in possessing the coca herb. . . . No Indian will go into the mines or to any other labor, be it building houses or working in the fields, without taking it in his mouth, even if his life depends on it. . . .

Among the Indians (and even the Spaniards by now) the custom of not entering the mines without placing this herb in the mouth is so well established that there is a superstition that the richness of the metal will be lost if they do not do so. . . .

The Indians being accustomed to taking this herb into their mouths, there is no doubt that as long as they have it there they lose all desire to sleep, and since it is extremely warming, they say that when the weather is cold they do not feel it if they have the herb in their mouths. In addition, they also say that it increases their strength and that they feel neither hunger nor thirst; hence these Indians cannot work without it.

When the herb is ground and placed in boiling water and if a person then takes a few swallows, it opens the pores, warms the body, and shortens labor in women; and this coca herb has many other virtues besides. But human perversity has caused it to become a vice, so that the devil (that inventor of vices) has made a notable harvest of souls with it, for there are many women who have taken it—and still take it—for the sin of witchcraft, invoking the devil and using it to summon him for their evil deeds. . . .

With such ferocity has the devil seized on this coca herb that—there is no doubt about it—when it becomes an addiction it impairs or destroys the judgment of its users just as if they had drunk wine to excess and makes them see terrible visions; demons appear before their eyes in frightful forms. In this city of Potosí it is sold publicly by the Indians who work in the mines, and so the harm arising from its continued abundance cannot be corrected; but neither is that harm remediable in other large cities of this realm, where the use and sale of coca have been banned under penalties as severe as that of excommunication and yet it is secretly bought and sold and used for casting spells and other like evils.

Would that our lord the king had ordered this noxious herb pulled up by the roots wherever it is found. . . . Great good would follow were it to be extirpated from this realm: the devil would be bereft of the great harvest of souls he reaps, God would be done a great service, and vast numbers of men and women would not perish (I refer to Spaniards, for no harm comes to the Indians from it).

QUESTIONS FOR ANALYSIS

- Why would the Spaniards ban the sale of the coca herb everywhere except Potosí?
- Why would Bartolomé believe that no harm would come to the Indians for taking the coca herb?
- How does this document reveal the central role of the Catholic Church in Spanish colonial thinking? Find several words and phrases that express this outlook.

Source: R. C. Padden, ed., "Claudia the Witch," pp. 117–21, from Tales of Potosí. *Copyright © 1975 by Brown University Press. Reprinted by permission of University Press of New England, Lebanon, NH, and the author.*

of whom had fled or had died from imported diseases. Failing to find established cities, the colonists remained in more dispersed settlements. By the late seventeenth century, Brazil's white population was 300,000.

The problem was where to find labor to work the rich lands. Because there was no centralized government to deal with the labor shortage, initially the Portuguese settlers tried to enlist the dispersed native population; but when recruitment became increasingly coercive, Indians turned on the settlers, whom they perceived to be interlopers. Some fought. Others fled to the vast interior. Reluctant to pursue the Indians inland, the Portuguese hugged their beachheads, extracting brazilwood (the source of a beautiful red dye) and sugar from their coastal enclaves.

Mission São Miguel. *The Jesuits were avid missionaries in the Spanish and Portuguese empires and often tried to shelter native peoples from conquistadors and labor recruiters. Missions, like this one, in the borderlands between Brazil and Spanish colonies were targets of attack from both sides.*

African slaves became the solution to this labor problem. What had worked for the Portuguese on sugarcane plantations in the Azores and other Atlantic islands now found application on their Brazilian plantations. Especially in the northeast, in the Bay of All Saints, the Atlantic world's first vast sugar-producing commercial center appeared.

Sugar Plantations

Along with silver, sugar emerged as the most valuable export from the Americas. It also was decisive in rearranging relations between peoples around the Atlantic. Cultivation of sugarcane had originated in India, spread to the Mediterranean region, and then reached the coastal islands of West Africa. The Portuguese transported the West African model to Brazil, and other Europeans took it to the Caribbean. By the early seventeenth century, sugar had become a major export from the New World. By the eighteenth century, its production required continuous and enormous transfers of labor from Africa, and its value surpassed that of silver as an export from the Americas to Europe.

Most Brazilian sugar plantations were fairly small, employing between 60 and 100 slaves. But they were efficient enough to create an alternative model of empire, one that resulted in full-scale colonization and dislocation of the existing population. The slaves lived in wretched conditions: their barracks were miserable, and their diets were insufficient to keep them alive under backbreaking work routines. Moreover, these slaves were disproportionately men. As they rapidly died off, the only way to ensure replenishment was to import more Africans. This model of settlement relied on the transatlantic flow of slaves.

Beginnings of the Transatlantic Slave Trade

Although African slaves were imported into the Americas starting in the fifteenth century, the first direct voyage carrying them from Africa to the Americas occurred in 1525. The transatlantic slave trade began modestly in support of one commodity, sugar. As European demand for sugar increased, the slave trade expanded. From the time of Columbus until 1820, more than five times as many Africans as Europeans moved to the Americas: approximately 2 million Europeans (voluntarily) and 12 million Africans (involuntarily) crossed the Atlantic—though the especially high mortality rate for Africans meant that only 10 million survived to reach New World shores.

First to master long-distance seafaring, the Portuguese also led the way in human cargo. Trade in slaves grew steadily throughout the sixteenth century, then surged in the seventeenth and eighteenth centuries (see Chapter 13). Initially, all European powers participated—Portuguese, Spanish, Dutch, English, and French. Eventually, New World merchants in both North and South America also established direct trade links with Africa.

Well before European merchants arrived off its western coast, Africa had known long-distance slave trading. In fact, the overall number of Africans sold into captivity in the Muslim world exceeded that of the Atlantic slave trade. Moreover, Africans maintained slaves themselves. African slavery, like its American counterpart, was a response to labor scarcities. In many parts of Africa, however, slaves did not face permanent servitude. Instead, they were assimilated into families, gradually losing their servile status and swelling the size and power of their adopted lineage-based groups.

With the additional European demand for slaves to work New World plantations alongside the ongoing Muslim slave trade, pressure on the supply of African slaves intensified. Only a narrow band stretching down the spine of the African landmass, from present-day Uganda and the highlands of Kenya to Zambia and Zimbabwe, escaped the impact of Asian and European slave traders.

Within Africa, the social and political consequences were not fully evident until the great age of the slave trade in the eighteenth century, but already some economic consequences were clear. The overwhelming trend was to further limit Africa's population. Indeed, African laborers fetched high enough prices to more than cover the costs of their capture and transportation across the Atlantic.

By the late sixteenth century, important pieces had fallen into place to create a new Atlantic world, one that could not have been imagined a century earlier. This was the three-cornered **Atlantic system**, with Africa supplying labor, the Americas land and minerals, and Europeans the technology and military power to hold the system together. In time, the wealth flows to Europe and the slave-based development of the Americas would alter the world balance of power.

THE TRANSFORMATION OF EUROPE

Instead of uniting Europeans, the Atlantic system deepened the region's internal divides. In particular, the growing wealth of the Spanish Empire added to the Habsburg dynasty's power and attracted the attention of jealous competitors. On top of the transformations wrought by transatlantic opportunities and rivalries, a split within the Roman Catholic Church (the Reformation, discussed below) led to profound religious rifts among states and brought additional divisions to the continent.

The Habsburgs and the Quest for Universal Empire in Europe

The European dream of a continent-wide empire, which had persisted since the fall of ancient Rome, found expression under the Habsburg dynasts. They were heirs to the eastern half of Charlemagne's empire. Here a loose confederation of principalities, the **Holy Roman Empire,** continued to obey an emperor elected by elite lower-level sovereigns (dukes, archbishops, and kings of individual states like Bavaria). After 1273, the emperor usually came from the Austrian house of Habsburg. The Holy Roman Empire included territory incorporated into the Netherlands, Germany, Austria, Belgium, Croatia, and parts of present-day Italy, Poland, and Switzerland. Although the realm was enormous, it never enjoyed effectively centralized power.

In 1519, the Habsburg prince Charles V was elected Holy Roman Emperor, and for a few decades he controlled a transatlantic empire larger than any before or since. As grandson of Spanish monarchs Isabella and Ferdinand and of Holy Roman Emperor Maximilian I, Charles inherited both Spain and its territories in the Americas, as well as the Habsburgs' traditional central European holdings. Overstretched by trying to keep such an ambitious empire intact, and unable to prevent some central European princes from embracing the new Protestant faith, Charles abdicated in 1556 and divided the realm between his younger brother Ferdinand and his son Philip. Ferdinand (r. 1556–1564) took the Austrian, German, and central European territories that straddled the Danube and became Holy Roman Emperor in 1556, enabling the Austrian Habsburgs to maintain dominance over central Europe.

Philip II (r. Spain 1556–1598) received Spain, Belgium, the Netherlands, southern Italy, and the New World possessions. Moreover, he inherited the Portuguese throne (from his mother), adding Portugal and its colonial possessions to his empire. This gave him a monopoly on Atlantic commerce. Yet the Spanish Habsburgs had to defend their empire against Dutch revolts, as well as confront Ottoman harassment on land and at sea. The size and wealth of Habsburg Spain continued to provoke enormous tension within Europe.

Conflict in Europe and the Demise of Universal Empire

As the situation on the European mainland grew tense, French, English, and Dutch elites envied the riches of Portuguese and Spanish colonial possessions. These rivals yearned for their own profitable colonies. But in their New World explorations, the French, English, and Dutch had not yet found gold and silver, nor had they discovered an easier route to Asia. Still, they managed to claim a share of the wealth of the Americas by stealing it on the high seas. Some of the plunderers were pirates who raided for their own benefit; others were privateers who stole with official sanction and shared the profits with their monarchs. Often the distinction between pirate and privateer was blurred.

The most famous raider was Sir Francis Drake, whom the English crown commissioned to plunder Spanish possessions. Circling the globe between 1577 and 1580, Drake plundered one Spanish port after another. His favorite hunting ground was the Caribbean, where Mesoamerican and Andean silver, loaded onto Spanish galleons (heavy, square-rigged ships used for war or commerce), made lucrative targets. Besides, the many islands provided natural shelter. Although Drake undertook his exploits for personal gain, Queen Elizabeth approved of his assaults on the Spanish Empire and rewarded him with a knighthood.

To retaliate against English plundering and to prevent Elizabeth from supporting the Dutch revolt, the Spanish sailed a mighty armada of 130 ships and almost 20,000 men into the English Channel. But England amassed even more vessels from its Royal Navy and private merchant fleet. The subsequent defeat of the Spanish Armada saw the burning and destruction of many prized battleships. Thereafter the conflict between a rising England and Spain continued in other seas, and Drake returned to privateering. When news of Drake's death in the Caribbean (from yellow fever) arrived in Madrid, the Spanish court erupted in jubilation. However, two months later an English fleet sailed into Spain's premier port of Cádiz, occupied the city for two weeks, burned 200 Spanish ships, and seized massive treasure from the Indies. Spain, the powerhouse of the Atlantic world, had been severely humbled. Two years later a despondent King Philip died. The dream of universal empire within Europe had failed, largely because Christendom continued to be at war with itself.

The Reformation

Like the Renaissance, the **Protestant Reformation** in Europe began as a movement devoted to returning to ancient sources—in this case, to biblical scriptures. Long before Martin Luther came on the scene, some scholars and believers had despaired of the Catholic Church's ability to satisfy their longings for deeper, more individualized religious experience. But interpreting Christian doctrine for oneself was still very dangerous in the fourteenth and fifteenth centuries, for the church feared that heresies and challenges to its authority would arise if laypersons were allowed to read the scriptures as they pleased. The church was right: for when Luther and his followers seized the right to read and interpret the Bible in a new way, they paved the way for a "Protestant" Reformation that split Christendom for good.

MARTIN LUTHER CHALLENGES THE CHURCH The opening challenge to the authority of the pope and the Catholic Church originated in Germany. Here a monk and a professor of theology, Martin Luther (1483–1546), used his knowledge of the Bible to criticize the church's ideas and practices. He sought no revolution but hoped to persuade church leaders to make reforms.

Beginning his career as a pious Catholic believer, Luther nonetheless believed that mortals were so given to sin that none would ever be worthy of salvation. In 1516, Luther found an answer to his quest for salvation in reading Paul's Letters to the Romans: since no human acts could be sufficient to earn admittance to heaven, individuals could only be saved by their faith in God's grace. God's free gift of forgiveness, Luther believed, did not depend on taking sacraments or performing good deeds. This faith, moreover, was something Christians could obtain just from reading the Bible—rather than by having a priest tell them what to believe. Finally, Luther concluded that Christians did not need specially appointed mediators to speak to God for them; all were, in his eyes, priests, equally bound by God's laws and obliged to minister to one another's spiritual needs.

These became the three main principles that launched Luther's reforming efforts: (1) belief that faith alone saves, (2) belief that the scriptures alone hold the key to Christian truth, and (3) belief in the priesthood of all believers. But other things motivated Luther as well: corrupt practices in the church, such as the keeping of mistresses by monks, priests, and even popes; and the selling of indulgences, certificates that would supposedly shorten the buyer's time in Purgatory. In the 1510s, clerics were hawking indulgences across Europe in an effort to raise money for the sumptuous new Saint Peter's basilica in Rome.

In 1517, Luther formulated ninety-five statements, or theses, and posted them on the doors to the Wittenberg cathedral, hoping to stir up his colleagues in debate. Before long his theses made him famous—and bolder in his criticisms. In a widely circulated pamphlet called *On the Freedom of the Christian Man* (1520), he upbraided "the Roman Church, which in past ages was the holiest of all" for having "become a den of murderers beyond

Protestant Reformation. *Following Luther's lead, many Reformers created inexpensive pamphlets to increase the circulation of their message. Pictured here is a woodcut from one such pamphlet, which shows Luther and his followers fending off the corrupt Pope Leo X.*

all other dens of murderers, a thieves' castle beyond all other thieves' castles, the head and empire of every sin, as well as of death and damnation." As Luther's ideas spread, a highly important "colleague" entered the debate: Pope Leo X.

The church and the Habsburg emperor, Charles V, demanded that Luther take back his criticisms and theological claims. When he refused, he was declared a heretic and narrowly avoided being burned at the stake. Luther wrote many more pamphlets attacking the church and the pope, whom he now described as the anti-Christ. In 1525, he attacked another aspect of Catholic doctrine by marrying a former nun, Katharina von Bora. In Luther's view, God approved of human sexuality within the bonds of marriage, and encouraging marriage for both the clergy and the laity was the only way to prevent illicit forms of sexual behavior. Luther also translated the New Testament from Latin into German so that laypersons could have direct access, without the clergy, to the word of God. This act spurred many other daring scholars across Europe to undertake translations of their own, and it encouraged the Protestant clergy to teach children (and adults) to read their national languages.

OTHER "PROTESTANT" REFORMERS Spread by printed books and ardent preachers in all the common languages of Europe, Luther's doctrines won widespread support. In fact, many German princes embraced the reformed faith to assert their independence from the Holy Roman Emperor. Those who followed the new faith identified themselves as "Protestants," and they promised that their reformed version of Christianity provided both an answer to individual spiritual needs and a new moral foundation for community life. The renewed Christian creed appealed to commoners as well as elites, especially in communities that resented rule by Catholic "outsiders" (like the Dutch, who resented being ruled by Philip II, a Habsburg prince who lived in Spain). Thus the reformed ideas took particularly firm hold in the German states, France, Switzerland, Scandinavia, the Low Countries, and England.

Some zealous reformers, like Jean Calvin (1509–1564) in France, modified Luther's ideas. To Luther's emphasis on the individual's relationship to God, Calvin added a focus on moral regeneration through church discipline and the autonomy of religious communities. He laid out the doctrine of predestination—the notion that each person is "predestined" for damnation or salvation even before birth. The "elect," he thought, should also be free to govern themselves, a doctrine that upheld radical political dissent (as in the case of Puritans in England) and the rule of the clergy (as in the Swiss city-state of Geneva). Calvinism proved especially popular in Switzerland, the Netherlands, northeastern France, and Scotland (where it was called Presbyterianism). In contrast, those who remained loyal to the original Protestant cause now described themselves as Lutherans.

In England, Henry VIII (r. 1509–1547) and his daughter Elizabeth (r. 1558–1603) crafted a moderate reformed religion—a "middle way"—called Anglicanism, which retained many Catholic practices and a hierarchy topped by bishops. (American followers would later call themselves Episcopalians, from the Latin word for bishop, *episcopus*). Although Anglican rule was imposed on Ireland, most nonelite Irishmen remained Catholic. The Scots maintained a fierce devotion to their Presbyterian Church, ensuring a measure of religious diversity within the British Isles. In England, as with the rest of Europe, more radical Protestant sects like Anabaptists and Quakers also developed. While all Protestants were opposed to Catholicism and distrustful of the papal hierarchy, these different communities sometimes developed animosities toward one another as well (see Map 12.3).

COUNTER-REFORMATION AND PERSECUTION The Catholic Church responded to Luther and Calvin by embarking on its own renovation, which became known as the **Counter-Reformation**. At the Council of Trent, whose twenty-five sessions stretched from 1545 to 1563, Catholic leaders reaffirmed numerous things: the church's doctrines, sacraments, acts of charity, papal supremacy, the clergy's distinctive role, and the insistence that priests, monks, and nuns remain celibate. But the council also enacted reforms to answer the Protestants' assaults on clerical corruption. In contrast to many of their predecessors, the popes who headed the Catholic Church late in the sixteenth century became renowned for their piety and asceticism. They also installed bishops and abbots who generally steered clear of unscrupulous practices. Taking on the Protestant theological challenge, Catholicism gave greater emphasis to individual spirituality. Like the Protestants, the reformed Catholics carried their message overseas—especially through an order established by Ignatius Loyola (1491–1556). Loyola founded a brotherhood of priests, the Society of Jesus, or **Jesuits**, dedicated to the revival of the Catholic Church. From bases in Lisbon, Rome, Paris, and elsewhere in Europe, the Jesuits opened missions as far as South and North America, India, Japan, and China.

Yet the Vatican continued to use repression and persecution to combat what it regarded as heretical beliefs. Priests in Augsburg performed public exorcisms, seeking to free Protestant parishioners from possession by "demons." The Index of Prohibited Books (a list of books and theological treatises banned by the Catholic Church) and the medieval Inquisition (from 1184) were weapons against those deemed to be the church's enemies. But the proliferation of printing presses and the spread of Protestantism made it impossible for the Catholic Counter-Reformation to turn back the tide leading toward increased autonomy from the papacy.

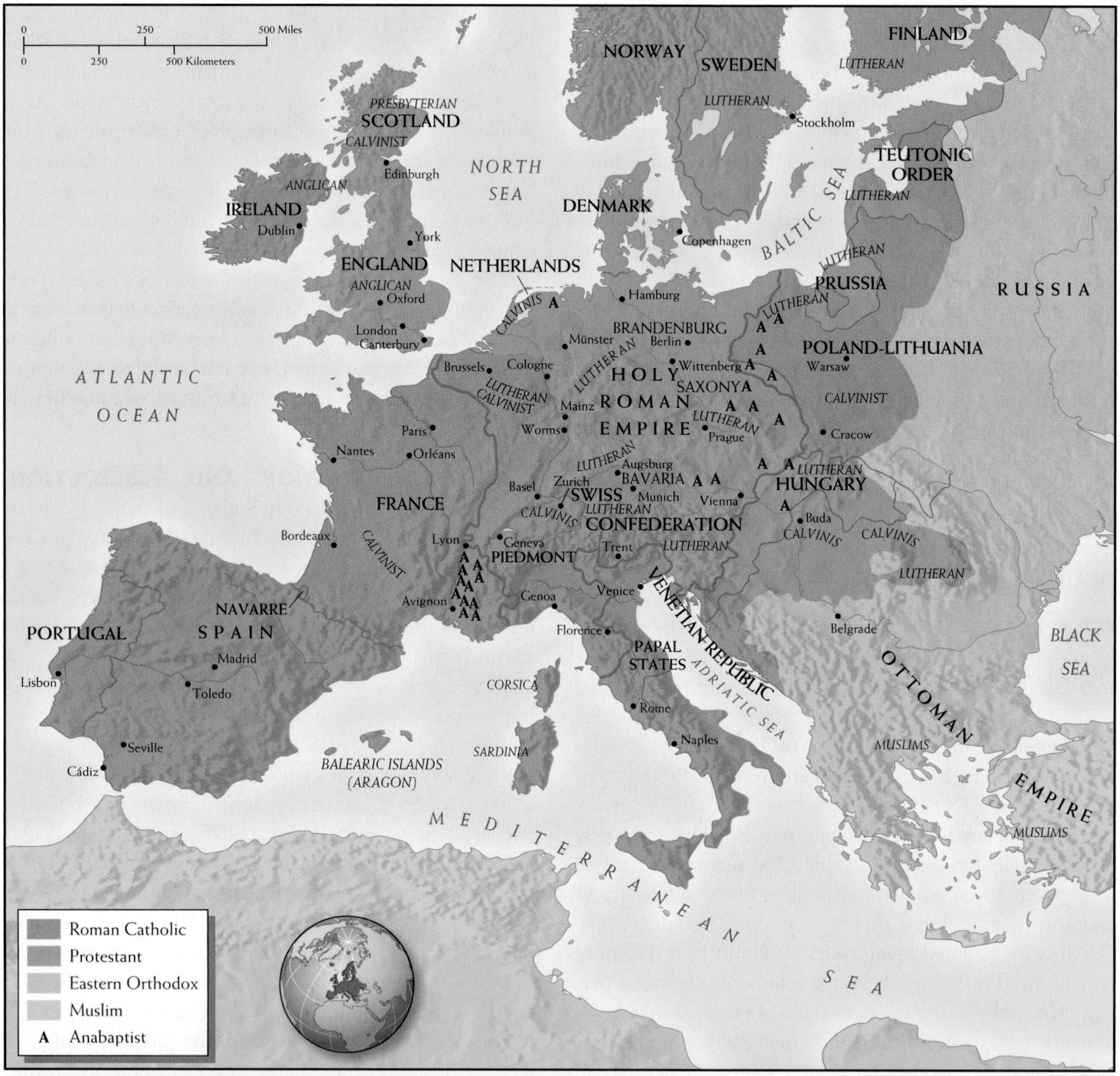

MAP 12.3 | Religious Divisions in Europe after the Reformation, 1590

The Protestant Reformation divided Europe religiously and politically.

- Within the formerly all-Catholic Holy Roman Empire, what Protestant groups took hold?
- Looking at the map, can you identify any geographic patterns in the distribution of Protestant communities?
- In what regions would you expect Protestant-Catholic tensions to be the most intense?

Both Catholics and Protestants persecuted witches. Between about 1500 and 1700, up to 100,000 people, mostly women, were accused of being witches. Many were tried, tortured, burned at the stake, or hanged. Older women, widows, and nurses were especially vulnerable to charges of cursing or poisoning babies. Other charges included killing livestock, causing hailstorms, and scotching marriage arrangements. People also believed that weak and susceptible women might have sex with the devil or be tempted to do his bidding. Clearly, by no means did the Reformation—or the Catholic response to it—make Europe a more tolerant society.

Religious Warfare in Europe

The religious revival led Europe into another round of ferocious wars. Their ultimate effect was to weaken the Holy Roman Empire and strengthen the English, French, and Dutch. Already in the 1520s, the circulation of books presenting Luther's ideas sparked peasant revolts across central Europe. Some peasants, hoping that Luther's assault on the church's authority would help liberate them, rose up against repressive feudal landlords. In contrast to earlier wars, in which one noble's retinue fought a rival's, the defense of the Catholic mass and the Protestant Bible brought crowds of simple folk to arms. Now wars between and within central European states raged for nearly forty years. In 1555, the exhausted Holy Roman Emperor Charles V was compelled to allow the German princes the right to choose Lutheranism or Catholicism as the official religion within their domains (Calvinism was still outlawed). However, this concession did not end Europe's religious wars.

Religious conflicts both weakened European dynasties and whetted their appetite for conquest abroad. Spain, with its massive empire and its silver mines in the New World, spent much of its new fortune waging war in Europe. Most debilitating was its costly effort to subdue recently acquired Dutch territories. After a series of wars spanning nearly a hundred years, Catholic Spain finally conceded the Protestant Netherlands its independence.

Wars took their toll on the Spanish Empire, which was soon wallowing in debts; not even the riches of its American silver mines could bail out the court. In the late 1550s, Philip II could not meet his obligations to creditors. Within two decades, Spain was declared bankrupt three times. Its decline opened the way for the Dutch and the English to extend their trading networks into Asia and the New World. Competition between the latter two bred trade wars, indicating that religious differences were not the only sources of inter-European strife.

Religious conflicts also sparked civil wars. In France, the divide between Catholics and Protestants exploded in the St. Bartholomew's Day Massacre of 1572. Catholic crowds rampaged through the streets of Paris murdering Huguenot (Protestant) men, women, and children and dumping their bodies into the Seine River; parades of rioters displayed Protestants' severed heads on pikes. The number of dead reached 3,000 in Paris and 10,000 in provincial towns. Slaughter on this scale did not break the Huguenots' spirit, but it did bring more disrepute to the monarchy for failing to ensure peace. This was the beginning of the end of the Valois dynasty. Another round of warfare exhausted the French and brought Henry of Navarre, a Protestant prince, to the throne. To become king, Henry IV converted to Catholicism. Shortly thereafter he issued the Edict of Nantes, a proclamation that declared France a Catholic country but also tolerated some Protestant worship.

St. Bartholomew's Day Massacre. *An important wedding between French Catholic and Huguenot families in Paris was scheduled for August 24, 1572, St. Bartholomew's Day; but instead of reconciliation, that day saw a massacre, as Catholics tried to stamp out Protestantism in France's capital city.*

As princes sought to resolve religious questions within their domains, states increasingly became identified with one or another form of Christian faith—and, for Protestants, with a national language. In this way, religious strife propelled forward the process of state building and the forming of national identities. At the same time, religious conflict fueled rivalries for wealth and territory overseas. Thus, Europe entered its age of overseas exploration as a collection of increasingly powerful yet irreconcilably competitive rival states, whose differences stemmed not just from language but from the ways they worshipped the Christian God.

Akbar Hears a Petition. *In keeping with the multiethnic and multireligious character of Akbar's empire, the image reflects the diversity of peoples seeking to have their petitions heard by the Mughal emperor.*

PROSPERITY IN ASIA

While Europe was experiencing religious warfare, Asian empires were expanding and consolidating their power, and trade was flourishing. If anything, the arrival of European sailors and traders in the Indian Ocean strengthened trading ties across the region and enhanced the political power and expansionist interests of Asia's imperial regimes. These regimes have left their mark on world history. The Ming dynasty's elegant manufactures enjoyed worldwide renown, and its ability to govern vast numbers of highly diverse peoples led outsiders to consider China the model imperial state. The Mughal ruler, Akbar, and the Ottoman sultan, Suleiman the Magnificent (see Chapter 11), were equally effective and esteemed rulers.

Mughal India and Commerce

The **Mughal Empire** became one of the world's wealthiest just when Europeans were establishing sustained connections with India. These connections, however, only touched the outer layer of Mughal India, one of Islam's greatest regimes. Established in 1526, it was a vigorous, centralized state whose political authority encompassed most of modern-day India. During the sixteenth century, it had a population of between 100 and 150 million.

The Mughals' strength rested on their military power (see Chapter 11). The dynasty's founder, Babur, had introduced horsemanship, artillery, and field cannons from central Asia, and gunpowder had secured his swift military victories over northern India. Under his grandson, Akbar (r. 1556–1605), the empire enjoyed expansion and consolidation that continued (under his own grandson, Aurangzeb) until it covered almost all of India (see Map 12.4). Known as the "Great Mughal," Akbar was skilled not only in military tactics but also in the art of alliance making. Deals with Hindu chieftains through favors and intermarriage also undergirded his empire.

Akbar's court benefited from commercial expansion in the Indian Ocean. Although the Mughals possessed no ocean navy, merchants from Mughal lands used overland routes and rivers to exchange Indian cottons, tobacco, saffron, betel leaf, sugar, and indigo for Iranian melons, dried fruits, nuts, silks, carpets, and precious metals, or for Russian pelts, leathers, walrus tusks, saddles, and chain-mail armor. Every year, Akbar ordered 1,000 new suits stitched of the most exquisite material. His harem preened in fine silks dripping with gold, brocades, and pearls. Carpets, mirrors, and precious metals adorned nobles' households and camps, while perfume and wine flowed freely. Soldiers, servants, and even horses and elephants sported elaborate attire.

During the sixteenth century, expanded trade with Europe brought more wealth to the Mughal polity, while the empire's

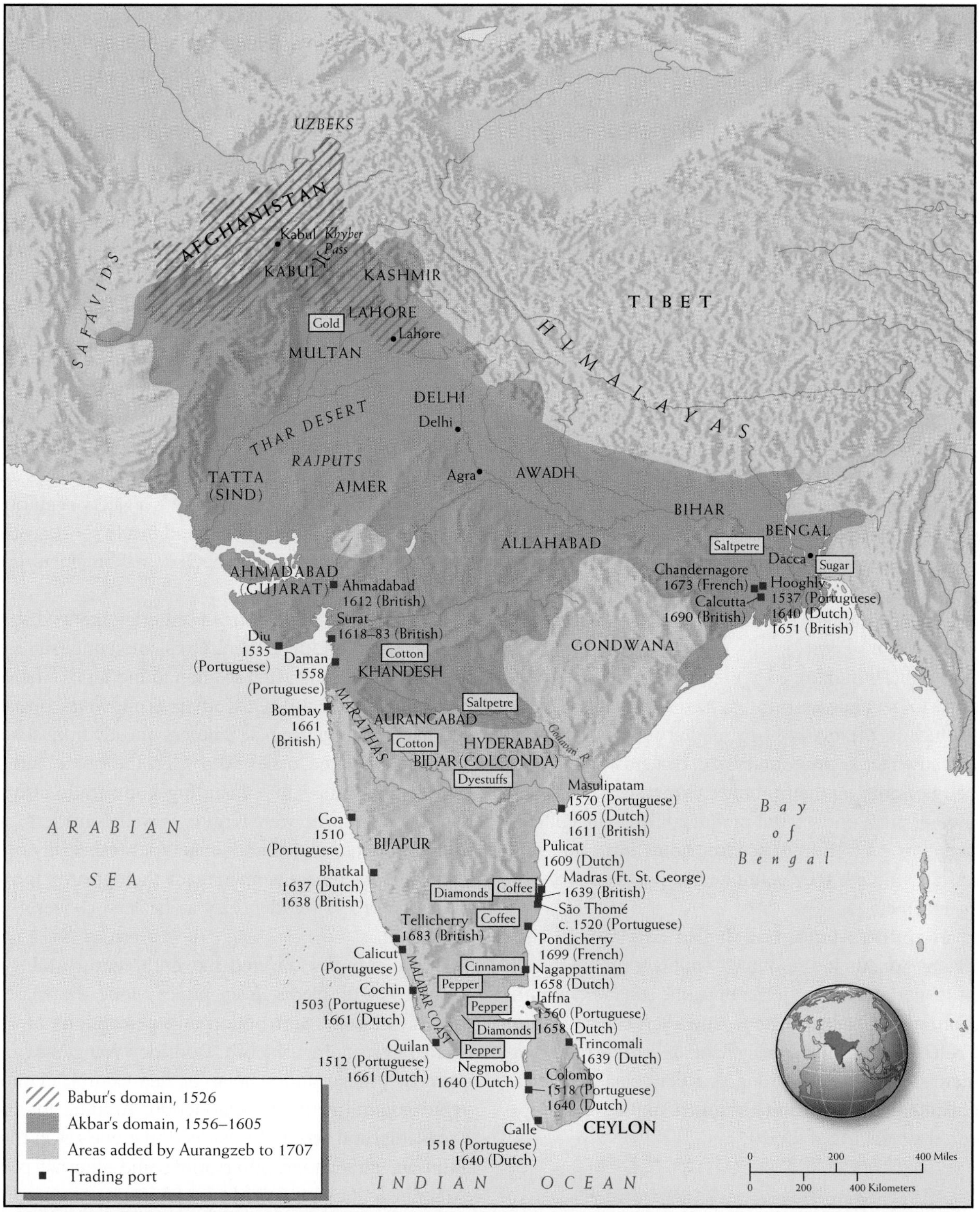

MAP 12.4 | Expansion of the Mughal Empire, 1556–1707

Under Akbar and Aurangzeb, the Mughal Empire expanded and dominated much of South Asia. Yet, by looking at the trading ports along the Indian coast, one can see the growing influence of Portuguese, Dutch, French, and English interests.

- Look at the dates for each port, and identify which traders came first and which came last.
- Compare this map with Map 12.1 (showing the earlier period 1420–1580): to what extent do the trading posts shown here reflect increased European influence in the region?
- How would these European outposts have affected Mughal policies?

strength limited European incursions. Although the Portuguese occupied Goa and Bombay on the Indian coast, they had little presence elsewhere and dared not antagonize the Mughal emperor. In 1578, Akbar recognized the credentials of a Portuguese ambassador and allowed a Jesuit missionary to enter his court. Thereafter, commercial ties between Mughals and Portuguese intensified, but the merchants were still restricted to a handful of ports. In the 1580s and 1590s, the Mughals ended the Portuguese monopoly on trade with Europe by allowing Dutch and English merchantmen to dock in Indian ports.

Akbar used the commercial boom to overhaul his revenue system. Until the 1560s, the Mughal state relied on a network of decentralized tribute collectors called *zamindars*. These collectors possessed rights to claim a share of the harvest while earmarking part of their earnings for the emperor. But the Mughals did not always receive their agreed share and the peasants resented the high levies, so local populations resisted. As flourishing trade bolstered the money supply, Akbar's officials monetized the tax assessment system and curbed the *zamindars'* power. After other centralizing reforms, increased imperial revenues helped finance military expeditions and the extravagant beautification of Akbar's court.

Such fiscal policies reinforced the empire's growing commercialization. To generate cash to pay taxes, peasants had to sell their produce in the market—so market towns and ports flourished. Meanwhile, in the countryside, dealers in grain and money helped peasants get their produce to market. Up to one-third the value of burgeoning rural produce filled state coffers. Now the *zamindars* evolved from private tribute lords into servants of the state, though they continued to pocket a share of the peasants' income.

Centered in northern India, the Mughal Empire used surrounding regions' wealth and resources—military, architectural, and artistic—to glorify the court. Over time, the enhanced wealth caused friction among Indian regions, and even between merchants and rulers. Yet as long as merchants relied on rulers for their commercial gains, and as long as rulers balanced local and imperial interests, the realm remained unified and kept Europeans on the outskirts of society.

Prosperity in Ming China

In the late sixteenth century, China also prospered from increased commerce. Like the Mughals, the Ming seemed unconcerned with the increasing appearance of foreigners, including Europeans bearing silver. As in India, the Ming confined European traders to port cities. Silver from the Americas did, however, circulate widely in China. It allowed employers to pay their workers with money rather than with produce or goods. It also contributed to soaring production in agriculture and handicrafts. Through the sixteenth century, rural industries in China flourished. A cotton boom, for example, made spinning and weaving China's largest industry.

One measure of greater prosperity under the Ming was its population surge. By the mid-seventeenth century, China's population probably accounted for more than one-third of the total world population. Although 90 percent of Chinese people lived in the countryside, large numbers filled the cities. Beijing, the Ming capital, grew to over 1 million; Nanjing, the secondary capital, nearly matched that number. Cities offered diversions ranging from literary and theatrical societies to schools of learning, religious societies, urban associations, and manufactures from all over the empire. The elegance and material prosperity of Chinese cities dazzled European visitors. One Jesuit missionary described Nanjing as surpassing all other cities "in beauty and grandeur. . . . It is literally filled with palaces and temples and towers and bridges. . . . There is a gaiety of spirit among the people who are well mannered and nicely spoken." (In contrast, see Primary Source: Commentary on Foreigners from a Ming Official.)

Urban prosperity fostered entertainment districts where people could indulge themselves anonymously and in relative freedom. Some Ming women found a place here as refined entertainers and courtesans, others as midwives, poets, sorcerers, and matchmakers. Female painters, mostly from scholar-official families, emulated males who used the home and garden for creative pursuits. The expanding book trade also accommodated women, who were writers as well as readers, not to mention literary characters and archetypes (especially of Confucian virtues). But Chinese women made their greatest fortunes inside the emperor's Forbidden City as healers, consorts, and power brokers.

To be sure, by the mid-sixteenth century Ming rule faced a variety of problems, from piracy along the coasts to ineptness in the state. Corruption and perceptions of social decay elicited even more criticism. Consider Wang Yangming, a government official and scholar of neo-Confucian thought who urged commitment to social action. Arguing for the unity of knowledge and action, he claimed that one's own thoughts and intuition, rather than observations and external principles (as earlier neo-Confucian thinkers had emphasized), could provide the answers to problems. His more radical followers suggested, against traditional belief, that women were equal to men intellectually and should receive full educations—a position that earned these radicals banishment from the elite establishment. But even as such new ideas and the state's weaknesses created discord, Ming society remained commercially vibrant. This vitality survived the dynasty's fall in 1644, laying the foundation for increased population growth and territorial expansion in subsequent centuries.

PRIMARY SOURCE

Commentary on Foreigners from a Ming Official

Although China had a long history of trade with the outside world, Ming officials were often hostile toward contact with foreigners. The bureaucrat He Ao (Ho Ao) wrote this commentary around 1520, portraying the Europeans (whom he called Feringis) as unruly, untrustworthy, and a threat to the country's security. Such sentiments were also common among officials in subsequent centuries, even as China thrived in the commercial exchanges of an increasingly connected world.

The Feringis are most cruel and crafty. Their arms are superior to those of other foreigners. Some years ago they came suddenly to the city of Canton, and the noise of their cannon shook the earth [these were cannon shots fired as a salute by the fleet of Fernão Peres]. Those who remained at the post-station [places where foreigners were lodged] disobeyed the law and had intercourse with others. Those who came to the Capital were proud and struggled [among themselves?] to become head. Now if we allow them to come and go and to carry on their trade, it will inevitably lead to fighting and bloodshed, and the misfortune of our South may be boundless.

In the time of our ancestors, foreigners came to bring tribute only at fixed periods, and the law provided for precautionary measures, therefore the foreigners who could come were not many. But some time ago the Provincial Treasurer, Wu T'ing-chü, saying that he needed spice to be sent to the Court, took some of their goods no matter when they came. It was due to what he did that foreigner ships have never ceased visiting our shores and that barbarians have lived scattered in our departmental cities. Prohibition and precaution having been neglected, the Feringis became more and more familiar with our fair ways. And thus availing themselves of the situation the Feringis came into our port.

I pray that all the foreign junks in our bay and the foreigners who secretly live (in our territory) be driven away, that private intercourse be prohibited and that our strategical defence be close, so that that part of our country will have peace.

QUESTIONS FOR ANALYSIS

- According to this document, what was the Chinese view of foreigners?
- How does this document compare to the earlier report from the European trader? (See Primary Source reading on p. 448.)
- In this translation, *intercourse* means "commerce" or "business." Find the two places where this term occurs. Does the context indicate a difference of opinion between officials and merchants in Ming China?

Source: T'ien-Tse Chang, Sino-Portuguese Trade from 1514 to 1644: A Synthesis of Portuguese and Chinese Sources *(Leyden: E. J. Brill, 1934), pp. 51–52. Reprinted by permission of Koninklijke Brill NV.*

Asian Relations with Europe

Europeans' overseas expansion had originally looked toward Asia, and now the products from their New World colonies enabled them to realize some of those dreams. The Portuguese led the way, being the first Europeans to join the overseas trading networks bridging East Africa and China. Before long, they became either important commercial intermediaries or collectors of customs duties from Asian traders. In 1557, the Portuguese arrival at Macao, a port along the southern coast of China, enabled them to penetrate China's expanding import-export trade. Within five years the number of Portuguese in Macao neared 1,000 (see Map 12.5).

True, Macao hosted many more Melakans, Indians, and Africans, who all enlivened the port. Moreover, although Ming authorities permitted a Portuguese presence there, the court refused to establish an official relationship with European traders. Like the Mughals, the Ming confined the merchants to a coastal enclave. In fact, in 1574 the Chinese built a wall at the isthmus connecting Macao with the mainland; this barrier, and the soldiers who guarded it, restricted Portuguese access to inland trade. Nonetheless the Portuguese became important shippers of China's prized porcelains and silks throughout Asia and beyond to Europe. They also dominated the silver trade from Japan.

Seeing how much the Portuguese were earning on Asian trade, the Spanish, English, and Dutch also ventured into Asian waters. With its monopoly on American silver, Spain enjoyed a competitive advantage. In 1565, the first Spanish trading galleon reached the Philippines; in 1571, after capturing Manila and making it a colonial capital, the Spanish established a brisk trade with China. Each year, ships from Spain's colonies in the Americas crossed the Pacific to Manila, bearing cargoes of silver. They returned carrying porcelain and silks for well-to-do

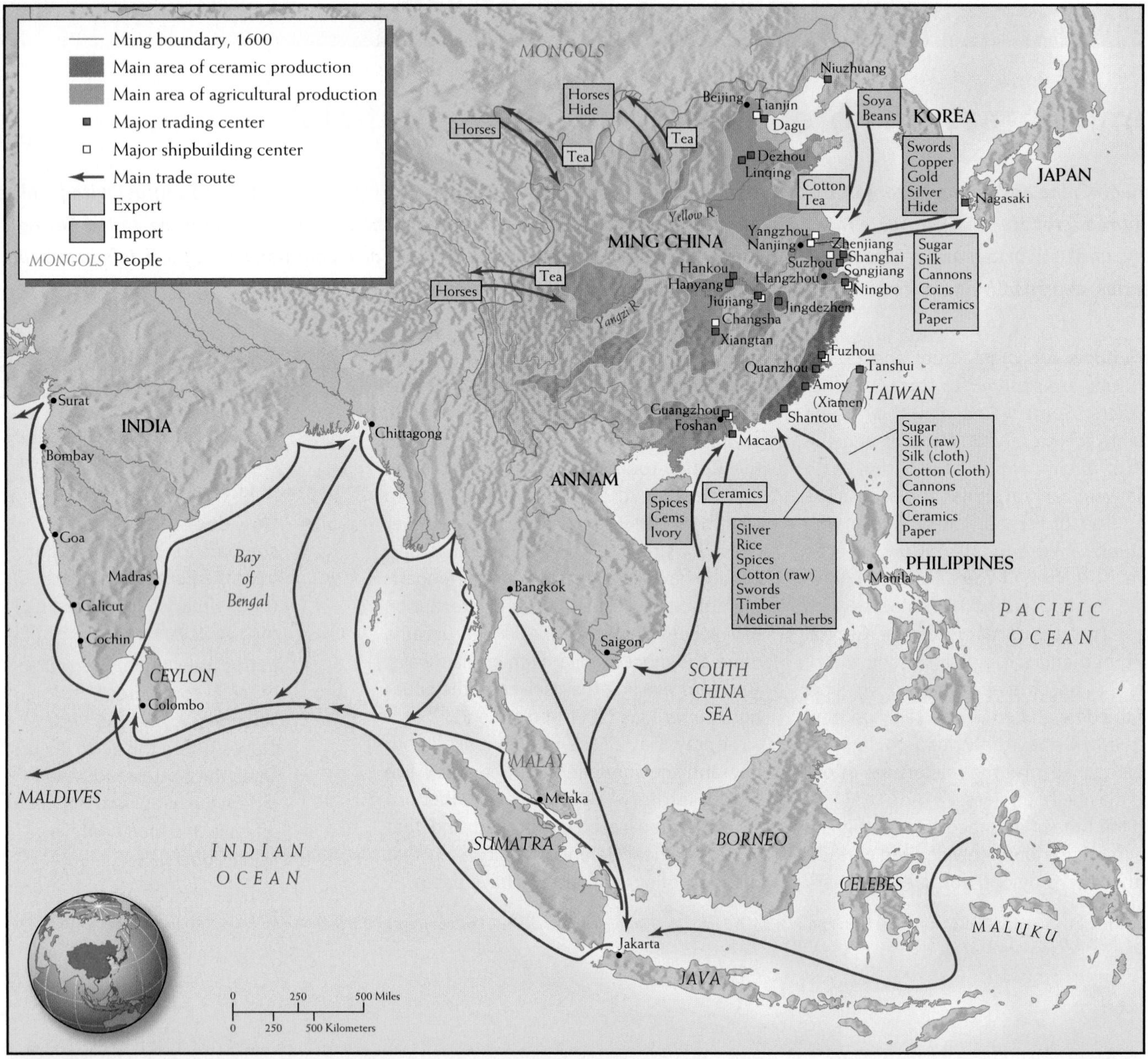

MAP 12.5 | Trade and Production in Ming China

The Ming Empire in the early seventeenth century was the world's most populous state and arguably its wealthiest.

- According to this map, what were the main items involved in China's export-import trade, and what were some of the regions that purchased its exports?
- In what way does the activity represented on this map indicate why China was the world's leading importer of silver at this time?
- Locate the major trading and shipbuilding centers, and then explain how important the export trade was to the Ming Empire's prosperity.

European consumers. Merchants in Manila also procured silks, tapestries, and feathers from the China seas for shipment to the Americas, where the mining elite eagerly awaited these imports.

The year 1571 was decisive in the history of the modern world, for in that year Spain inaugurated a trade circuit that made good on Magellan's earlier achievement. As Spanish ships circled the globe from the New World to China and from China back to Europe, the world became commercially interconnected. Silver solidified the linkage, being the only foreign commodity for which the Chinese had an insatiable demand. From the mother lodes of the Andes and Mesoamerica, silver made the commerce of the world go round.

Macao. *This Chinese painting depicts the Portuguese enclave of Macao on the southern border of China around 1800.*

Other Europeans, too, wanted their share of Asia's wealth. The English and the Dutch reached the South China Sea late in the sixteenth century. Captain James Lancaster made the first English voyage to the East Indies between 1591 and 1594. Five years later, 101 English subscribers pooled their funds and formed a joint-stock company (an association in which each member owned shares of capital). This English East India Company soon won a royal charter granting it exclusive rights to import East Indian goods. Soon the company displaced the Portuguese in the Arabian Sea and the Persian Gulf. Doing a brisk trade in indigo, saltpeter, pepper, and cotton textiles, the English East India Company eventually acquired control of ports on both coasts of India—Fort St. George (Madras; 1639), Bombay (1661), and Calcutta (1690).

It is tempting to see the Europeans' arrival in the South China Sea and the Indian Ocean as the beginning of the end of Asian autonomy. This was hardly the case, however. Through the sixteenth century, Europeans forged very weak connections to Asian societies. For the moment, the Europeans' increased presence enhanced the wealth and might of Asian dynasties.

CONCLUSION

In this multicentered world of the fifteenth century, Europe was a poor cousin. However, a new spirit of adventure and achievement animated its peoples, stirred up by the rediscovery of antiquity (the Renaissance), an ambitious mercantile elite, and the spiritual fervor of the Reformation and Counter-Reformation. Learning from Arab seamen, European sailors perfected techniques for sailing into dangerous waters. Desiring Asian luxury goods, European merchants and mariners were eager to exploit trade routes leading eastward. More important, Europe's location promoted expansion across the largely unknown Atlantic Ocean. With the Ottomans controlling Constantinople and the eastern Mediterranean, Atlantic sea-lanes offered an alternative route to Asia. As Europeans searched for routes around Islamic territory, they first sailed down the coast of Africa and then across the Atlantic.

Encountering the "New World" was an accident of monumental significance. In the Americas, Europeans found riches. Mountains of silver and rivers of gold gave them the currency they needed for dealing with Asian traders. Europeans also found opportunities for exchange, conquest, and colonization. Yet, establishing these transatlantic empires heightened tensions within Europe, as rivals fought over the spoils and a religious schism turned into a divisive political and spiritual struggle.

Thus two conquests characterize this age of increasing world interconnections. The Islamic conquest of Constantinople drove Europeans to find new links to Asia, thereby demonstrating Islam's pivotal role in shaping modern world history. In turn, the Spanish conquest of the Aztecs and the Incas gave Europeans access to silver, which bought them an increased presence in Asian trading networks.

American Indians also played an important role, as Europeans sought to conquer their lands, exploit their labor, and confiscate their gold and silver. Sometimes Indians worked with Europeans, sometimes under Europeans, sometimes against Europeans—and sometimes none were left to work at all. Then Europeans brought in African laborers, compounding the calamity of the encounter with the tragedy of slavery. Out of the catastrophe of contact, a new oceanic system arose to link Africa, America, and Europe. This was the Atlantic system. Unlike the tributary and trading orders of the Indian Ocean and China seas, the Atlantic Ocean supported a system of formal imperial control and settlement of distant colonies, and profoundly transformed the economies, agricultural practices, and environments across the globe. These catastrophes and exchanges would be foundational for the ways in which worlds connected and collided in the following centuries.

AFTER YOU READ THIS CHAPTER

Review and research materials on **StudySpace:** wwnorton.com/studyspace

TRACING THE GLOBAL STORYLINES

FOCUS ON: ***Regional Impacts of European Colonization and Trade***

Europe

- Portugal creates a trading empire in the Indian Ocean and the South China Sea.
- Spain and Portugal establish colonies in the Americas, discover silver, and establish export-oriented plantation economies.
- As the balance of power in Europe shifts, the Protestant Reformation breaks out in northern and western Europe, splitting the Catholic Church.

The Americas

- Native Americans, lacking immunity to European diseases, perish everywhere.
- Spanish conquest and disease destroy the two great Native American empires in Mexico (the Aztecs) and Peru (the Incas).

Africa

- Trade in African captives fuels the Atlantic slave trade, which furnishes labor for European plantations in the Americas.

Asia

- Asian empires—the Mughals in India, the Ming in China, the Safavids in Iran, and the Ottomans in western Asia and the eastern Mediterranean—barely notice the Americas but profit economically from enhanced global trade.

CHRONOLOGY

Europe

- Luther begins Protestant Reformation **1517**

The Americas

- Columbus discovers the New World **1492**
- Cortés conquers Aztec Empire **1522**
- Pizarro conquers Inca Empire **1533**

South Asia

- Da Gama sails to India **1498**
- Portuguese establish bases around Indian Ocean **1508–1511**

East Asia

1500 | 1510 | 1520 | 1530 | 1540

KEY TERMS

Atlantic system p. 462

Aztec Empire p. 451

colonies p. 445

Columbian exchange p. 455

conquistadors p. 450

Counter-Reformation p. 465

Holy Roman Empire p. 463

Inca Empire p. 455

Jesuits p. 465

mestizos p. 453

Mughal Empire p. 468

New World p. 449

Protestant Reformation p. 464

STUDY QUESTIONS

1. **Describe** the new trade patterns in the Afro-Eurasian world during the fifteenth century. How similar and different were they from trade patterns during the Mongol period?
2. **Describe** how Spain created a vast empire in the Americas. How did the spread of lethal disease influence this outcome?
3. **Explain** the environmental consequences of the first contacts between Europeans and Amerindians. What consequences did the Columbian exchange have on regions both beyond the Atlantic world and within it?
4. **Compare and contrast** Spain's "tributary empire" in the Americas with Portugal's "seaborne empire" in the Indian ocean. Why did these empires pursue such different strategies?
5. **Explain** what conditions promoted the strengthening of regional dynasties in Europe in the sixteenth century as opposed to the growth of one large European empire.
6. **Explain** the transformation of the African slave trade during this period. What role did the growth of sugar plantations play?
7. **Compare and contrast** political and commercial developments in the Mughal and Ming dynasties during the sixteenth century. How did the expansion of global commerce affect each region?
8. **Evaluate** to what extent an increased European presence altered the political balance of power in Asia at this time. How did Asian dynasties react to increased European contacts?
9. **Explain** the role of silver in transforming global trade patterns during the sixteenth century. Which regions and dynasties benefited from the increased use of silver for monetary transactions?

Religious and dynastic wars **1520s–1570s**

Expansion and consolidation of Mughal dynasty **1556–1605**

Portuguese establish trading port in Macao **1557**

Spanish establish the port of Manila **1571**

1550 | 1560 | 1570 | 1580 | 1590 | 1600

BEFORE YOU READ THIS CHAPTER

wwnorton.com/
StudySpace

GLOBAL STORYLINES

- Increased global trade brings the regions of the world more closely together, enriching some, destabilizing others, and provoking bitter rivalries.
- Silver and sugar are the major commodities of world trade.
- Western European states and Tsarist Russia expand their empires while the Ottoman, Safavid, Mughal, and Ming dynasties are shaken.

CHAPTER OUTLINE

13

Worlds Entangled, 1600–1750

FOCUS QUESTIONS

- How did global economic integration affect economic and political systems?
- How did European mercantilism and colonialism transform the Americas?
- How did the slave trade affect African societies?
- How did global trade affect the Asian dynasties?
- Why did Europe's economic and political centers shift northward?

In 1720, a financial panic engulfed Europe, making rich men into paupers and ruining many political careers. The panic arose from a speculative mania over anticipated profits from trade with the Americas. A group of British merchants established the South Sea Trading Company to compete with French firms and obtained privileged trading rights with all of Spanish America. Most coveted was the exclusive right to sell African slaves to Spanish colonies. As enthusiasm for such companies soared, eager investors sent share prices skyrocketing. But rumors of fantastic spoils gave way to word that the original investors were dumping their shares and that the companies were worthless. Then the speculative bubble burst. Share prices plummeted, nearly all the new companies went bankrupt, and many older firms collapsed. The so-called South Sea Bubble reflected the euphoria—and the perils—of global trade and investment.

From 1600 to 1750, global trading networks propelled commerce across the world's oceans. Sugar flowed from Brazil and the Caribbean, spices from Southeast Asia, cotton textiles from India, silks from China, and, increasingly, silver from Mesoamerica and the Andes. New World

CURRENT TRENDS IN WORLD HISTORY

Stimulants, Sociability, and Coffeehouses

While armies, travelers, missionaries, and diseases have breached the world's main political and cultural barriers, commodities have been the least respectful of the lines that separate communities. It has been difficult for ruling elites to curtail the desire of their populations to dress themselves in fine garments, to possess jewelry, and to consume satisfying food and drink no matter where these products may originate. The history of commodities, thus, is a core area for world historical research, for products span cultural barriers and connect peoples over long distances. As the world's trading networks expanded in the seventeenth and eighteenth centuries, merchants in Europe, Asia, Africa, and the Americas distributed many new commodities. By far the most popular were a group of stimulants—coffee, cocoa, sugar, tobacco, and tea—all of which (except for sugar) were addictive and also produced a sense of well-being. Previously, many of these products had been grown in isolated parts of the world: the coffee bean in Yemen, tobacco and cocoa in the New World, and sugar in Bengal. Yet, by the seventeenth century, in nearly every corner of the world, the well-to-do began to congregate in coffeehouses, consuming these new products and engaging in sociable activities.

Coffeehouses everywhere served as locations for social exchange, political discussions, and business activities. Yet they also varied from cultural area to cultural area, reflecting the values of the societies in which they arose.

The coffeehouse first appeared in Islamic lands late in the fifteenth century. As coffee consumption caught on among the wealthy and leisured classes in

Coffee. *Coffee drinkers at an Ottoman banquet (above) and in an English coffeehouse (left).*

silver was especially crucial to these networks: it gave Europeans a commodity to exchange with Asians, and it tilted the balance of wealth and power in a westerly direction across Afro-Eurasia.

Imperial expansion and transoceanic trade now brought the world together as never before. Europeans conquered and colonized more of the Americas, the demand for African slaves to work New World plantations leaped upward, and global trade intensified. Conquest, colonization, and commerce created riches for some but also provoked bitter rivalries. In the Americas, Spain and Portugal faced new competitors—primarily England and France. With religious tensions added to the mix, the stage was set for decades of bloody warfare in Europe and the Americas. At the same time, rulers in India, China, and Japan enlarged their empires, while Russia's tsars incorporated Siberian territories into their domain. Meanwhile, the Ottoman, Safavid, and Mughal dynasties, though resisting most European intrusions, found their stability profoundly shaken by the forces that entangled the world.

ECONOMIC AND POLITICAL EFFECTS OF GLOBAL COMMERCE

Global trade affected not only merchant groups and their sponsoring nations but also individual rulers and common people. Increasing economic ties brought new places and products into world markets: furs from French North America, sugar from the Caribbean, tobacco from British colonies on the American mainland, and coffee from Southeast Asia and the Middle East. (See Current Trends in World History: Stimulants, Sociability, and Coffeehouses.) Such products became so important that interruptions in availability sometimes destabilized economic and political systems. For example, gold and silver from the Americas were vital to the global networks (see Map 13.1). The supply of precious metals might fall when political disturbances caused work stoppages, or surge when new mines opened. Commodity prices could soar or drop, bringing prosperity to some and bankruptcy to others.

the Arabian Peninsula and the Ottoman Empire, local growers protected their advantage by monopolizing its cultivation and sale and refusing to allow any seeds or cuttings from the coffee tree to be taken abroad.

Despite some religious opposition, coffee spread into Egypt and throughout the Ottoman Empire in the sixteenth century. Ottoman bureaucrats, merchants, and artists assembled in coffeehouses to trade stories, read, listen to poetry, and play chess and backgammon. Indeed, so deeply connected were coffeehouses with literary and artistic pursuits that people referred to them as schools of knowledge.

From the Ottoman territories, the culture of coffee drinking spread to western Europe. The first coffeehouse in London opened in 1652, and within sixty years the city claimed no fewer than 500 such establishments. In fact, the Fleet Street area of London had so many that the English essayist Charles Lamb commented, "[T]he man must have a rare recipe for melancholy who can be dull in Fleet Street." Although coffeehouses attracted people from all levels of society, they especially appealed to the new mercantile and professional classes as locations where stimulating beverages like coffee, cocoa, and tea promoted lively conversations. Here, too, opponents claimed that excessive coffee drinking destabilized the thinking processes and even caused conversions to Islam. But against such opposition, the pleasures of coffee, tea, and cocoa prevailed. These bitter beverages in turn required liberal doses of the sweetener sugar. A smoke of tobacco topped off the experience. In this environment of pleasure, patrons of the coffeehouses indulged their addictions, engaged in gossip, conducted business, and talked politics.

QUESTIONS FOR ANALYSIS

- What factors drove the consumption of stimulants like coffee on a global scale?
- What other commodities from earlier in world history played a similar role? Were there differences in the underlying factors such as scale of consumption between the different periods?

Explore Further

Hattox, Ralph S., *Coffee and Coffeehouses: The Origins of a Social Beverage in the Medieval Near East* (1985).

Closer economic contact enhanced the power of certain states and destabilized others. It bolstered the legitimacy of England and France, and it prompted strong local support of new rulers in Japan and parts of sub-Saharan Africa. But also in England, France, Japan, Russia, and Africa, linkages led to civil wars and social unrest. In the Ottoman state, outlying provinces slipped from central control; the Safavid regime foundered and then ended; the Ming dynasty gave way to the Qing. In India, rivalries among princes and merchants eroded the Mughals' authority, compounding the instability caused by peasant uprisings.

Extracting Wealth: Mercantilism

Transformations in global relations began in the Atlantic, where the extraction and shipment of gold and silver siphoned wealth from the New World (the Americas) to the Old World (Afro-Eurasia). Mined by Indian and African workers and delivered into the hands of merchants and monarchs, silver from the Andes and Mesoamerica boosted the world's supply. In addition, a boom in gold production made Brazil the world's largest producer of that metal at this time.

American mining was so lucrative for Spain and Portugal that other European powers wanted a share in the bounty, so they, too, launched colonizing ventures in the New World. Although these latecomers found few precious minerals, they devised other ways to extract wealth, for the Americas had fertile lands on which to cultivate sugarcane, cotton, tobacco, indigo, and rice. The New World also had fur-bearing wildlife, whose pelts were prized in Europe. Better still from the colonizers' perspective, it was easy and inexpensive to produce and transport the New World crops and skins.

If silver quickened the pace of global trade, sugar transformed the European diet. First domesticated in Polynesia, sugar was not central to European diets before the New World plantations started exporting it. Previously, Europeans had used honey for sweetener, but they soon became insatiable consumers of sugar.

GREENLAND
ALASKA
ICELAND
NETHERLANDS
RUPERT'S LAND
Québec
NEWFOUND-LAND
NOVA SCOTIA
NEW FRANCE
LOUISIANA
Boston
New York
Philadelphia
THIRTEEN COLONIES
New Orleans
VICEROYALTY OF NEW SPAIN
Zacatecas
MEXICO
Mexico City
Veracruz
Acapulco
Silk
Spices
Tobacco
Rice
Furs
Indigo
Meat
Timber
Grain
Taxes
From North America and Carribean
Sugar
Gold
Hides
Coffee
Diamonds
Calico
Taxes
PORTUGAL
Lisbon
Cadiz
From South America
Manufactures
Sugar
Coffee
Indigo
Cotton
Sugar
Indigo
Hides
Taxes
ATLANTIC OCEAN
CURAÇAO
Slaves
Cartagena
Panama
SURINAM
VICEROYALTY OF GRANADA
Quito
Timbuktu
Iron
Copper
Textiles
Cutlery
Firearms
Accra
DUTCH BRAZIL
Recife
Bahia
Lima
VICEROYALTY OF BRAZIL
PACIFIC OCEAN
VICEROYALTY OF PERU
Potosí
Slaves
Tobacco
Sugar
Rio de Janeiro
Buenos Aires
Spices
Silk
Calico
China
Silk
Calico
Coffee
Pepper
Indigo
Drugs
India
Line of Tordesillas 1494

MAP 13.1 | Trade in Silver and Other Commodities, 1650–1750

The seventeenth and eighteenth centuries were the first centuries of true global commerce. Silver was the one item that was traded all over the world.

- Can you trace the flows of silver from the Americas around the globe (by following the thick red arrows) and identify the commodities that silver was exchanged for in different parts of the world?
- Does the map provide enough information for you to conclude which of these global empires was the wealthiest and most powerful?
- According to this map, how did increased trade shape European states' territorial ambitions?

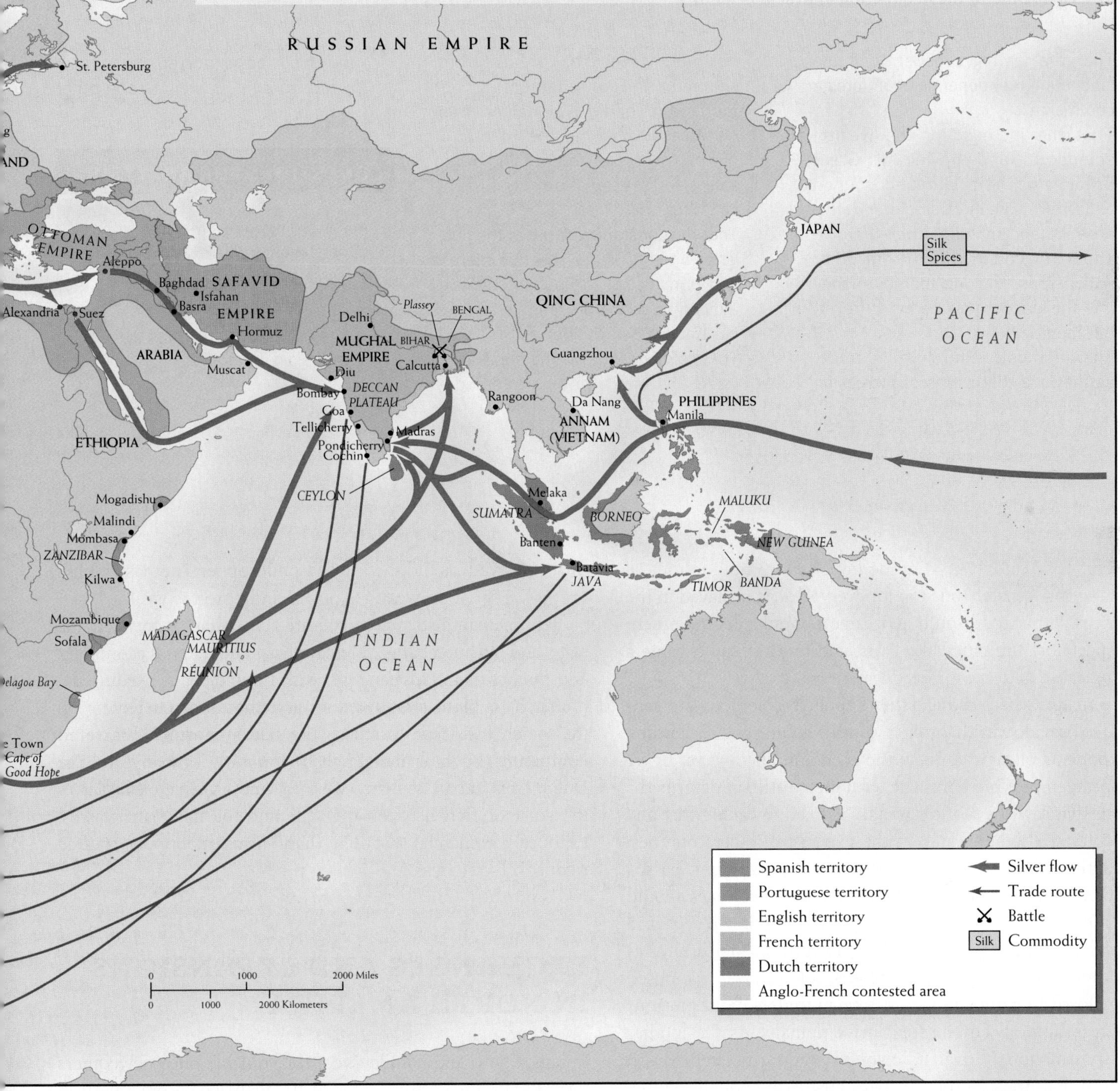

PRIMARY SOURCE

The Principles of Mercantilism

In 1757, a British commercial expert by the name of Malachy Postlewayt published a commercial dictionary,* The Universal Dictionary of Trade and Commerce. *Under the entry "trade," he set forth "some maxims relating to trade that should seem to be confirmed in the course of this work." The first five convey the economic philosophy of mercantilism and the importance that countries attached to the acquisition of precious metals.

I. That the lasting prosperity of the landed interest depends upon foreign commerce.

II. That the increase of the wealth, splendour, and power of Great Britain and Ireland depends upon exporting more in value of our native produce and manufactures than we import of commodities from other nations and bringing thereby money into the kingdom by means of freight by shipping.

III. That domestic and foreign trade, as they are the means of increasing national treasure, of breeding seamen, and of augmenting our mercantile and royal navies they necessarily become the means of our permanent prosperity and of the safety and preservation of our happy constitution.

IV. That the constant security of the public credit and the payment of interest and principal of the public creditors depend upon the prosperous state of our trade and navigation.

V. That gold and silver is the measure of trade, and that silver is a commodity and may be exported, especially in foreign coin as well as any other commodity.

Source: Malachy Postlewayt, The Universal Dictionary of Trade and Commerce, *vol. 2, p. 792.*

QUESTIONS FOR ANALYSIS

- According to this reading, whom does mercantilism serve?
- What are the key tenets of mercantilism?
- Why is silver more important than gold in trade?

Between 1690 and 1790, Europe imported 12 million tons of sugar—approximately one ton for every African enslaved in the Americas. Public tooth-pulling became a popular entertainment (for spectators!) in cities like Paris, and tooth decay became a leading cause of death for Europeans.

No matter what products they supplied, colonies were supposed to provide wealth for their "mother countries"—according to exponents of mercantilism, the economic theory that drove European empire-builders. The term **mercantilism** described a system that saw the world's wealth as fixed, meaning that any one country's wealth came at the expense of other countries. Mercantilism further assumed that overseas possessions existed solely to enrich European motherlands. Thus, colonies should ship more "value" to the mother country than they received in return. (See Primary Source: The Principles of Mercantilism.) In addition to creating trade surpluses, colonies were supposed to be closed to competitors, lest foreign traders drain precious resources from an empire's exclusive domain. As the mother country's monopoly over its colonies' trade generated wealth for royal treasuries, European states grew rich enough to wage almost unceasing wars against one another. Ultimately, mercantilists believed, as did the English philosopher Thomas Hobbes (1588–1679), that "wealth is power and power is wealth."

The mercantilist system required an alliance between the state and its merchants. Mercantilists understood economics and politics as interdependent, with the merchant needing the monarch to protect his interests and the monarch relying on the merchant's trade to enrich the state's treasury. **Chartered companies**, such as the (English) Virginia Company and the Dutch East India Company, were the most visible examples of the collaboration between the state and the merchant classes. European monarchs awarded these firms monopoly trading rights over vast areas.

EXCHANGES AND EXPANSIONS IN NORTH AMERICA

Entanglement and conflict were unavoidable once newcomers joined Spain and Portugal in the rush to reap riches from American colonies and to take a greater share of global commerce. As rulers in England, France, and Holland granted monopolies to merchant companies, they began to dominate the settlement and trade of new colonies in the Americas (see Map 13.2). Although the search for precious metals or water routes to Asia had initially spurred many of these enterprises, the new colonizers learned that only by exploiting other resources could their claims in the Americas generate profits. Also, differences among New World societies required rethinking the character of colonial regimes.

In their colonies along the Atlantic seaboard, the English established one model for new colonies in the Americas. Although these territories failed to yield precious metals or a waterway across the continent, they did boast land suitable for growing a variety of crops. Within the English domain, different climates and soils made for very different agricultural possibilities, but all the English colonies shared a common feature: population growth fed greater hunger for farmlands, which put pressure on Indian holdings. The result: a souring of relations between Amerindians and colonists, often ferocious wars between natives and newcomers, and, over the course of the seventeenth and eighteenth centuries, the dispossession of Indians from lands between the Atlantic Ocean and the Appalachian Mountains.

By contrast, Dutch and French colonies rested not on the expulsion of natives, but on dependence on them. Holland's North American venture, however, proved short-lived, as the English took over New Netherland and renamed it New York in 1664. French claims were more enduring and extended across a vast swath of the continent, encompassing eastern Canada, the Great Lakes, and the Mississippi Valley. But in much of this territory, the French presence remained limited to small numbers of missionaries and traders. The latter were especially dependent on Amerindians, though fragile ecological foundations did shift the balance of trade and power over time. Still, well into the eighteenth century, Amerindians in the middle of North America continued to control where Europeans lived and what they did.

Crucial to the trade between Europeans and Amerindians in the northern parts of North America was the beaver, an animal for which Indian peoples previously had little use. In response to the Europeans' interest, one local hunter proclaimed, "The beaver does everything perfectly well; it makes kettles, hatchets, swords, knives, bread; in short it makes everything." As long as there were beavers to be trapped, trade between the French and their Indian partners flourished.

The distinctive aspect of the fur trade was the Europeans' utter dependence on Indian know-how. After all, trapping required familiarity with the beaver's habits and habitats, which Europeans lacked. This reliance forced the French to adapt to Indian ways, which is evident in their pattern of exchange. Although the French wanted to export furs purely

Woodlands Indians. *This late-sixteenth-century drawing by John White, a pioneer settler on Roanoke Island off the coast of North Carolina, depicts the Indian village of Secoton in eastern Virginia. In contrast to the great empires that the Spanish conquered in the valley of Mexico and in the Andes, the Indians whom English, French, and Dutch colonizers encountered in the woodlands of eastern North America generally lived in villages that were politically autonomous entities.*

as a commercial venture, they were willing to permit exchanges with their Indian partners to go beyond material concerns. Responding to Indian desires to use trade as an instrument to cement familial bonds, the French gave gifts, participated in Indian diplomatic rituals, and even married into Indian families. As a result, *métis* (French-Indian offspring) played an important role in New France as interpreters, traders, and guides. Thus, the French colonization of the Americas—owing to their reliance on Indians as trading partners, military allies,

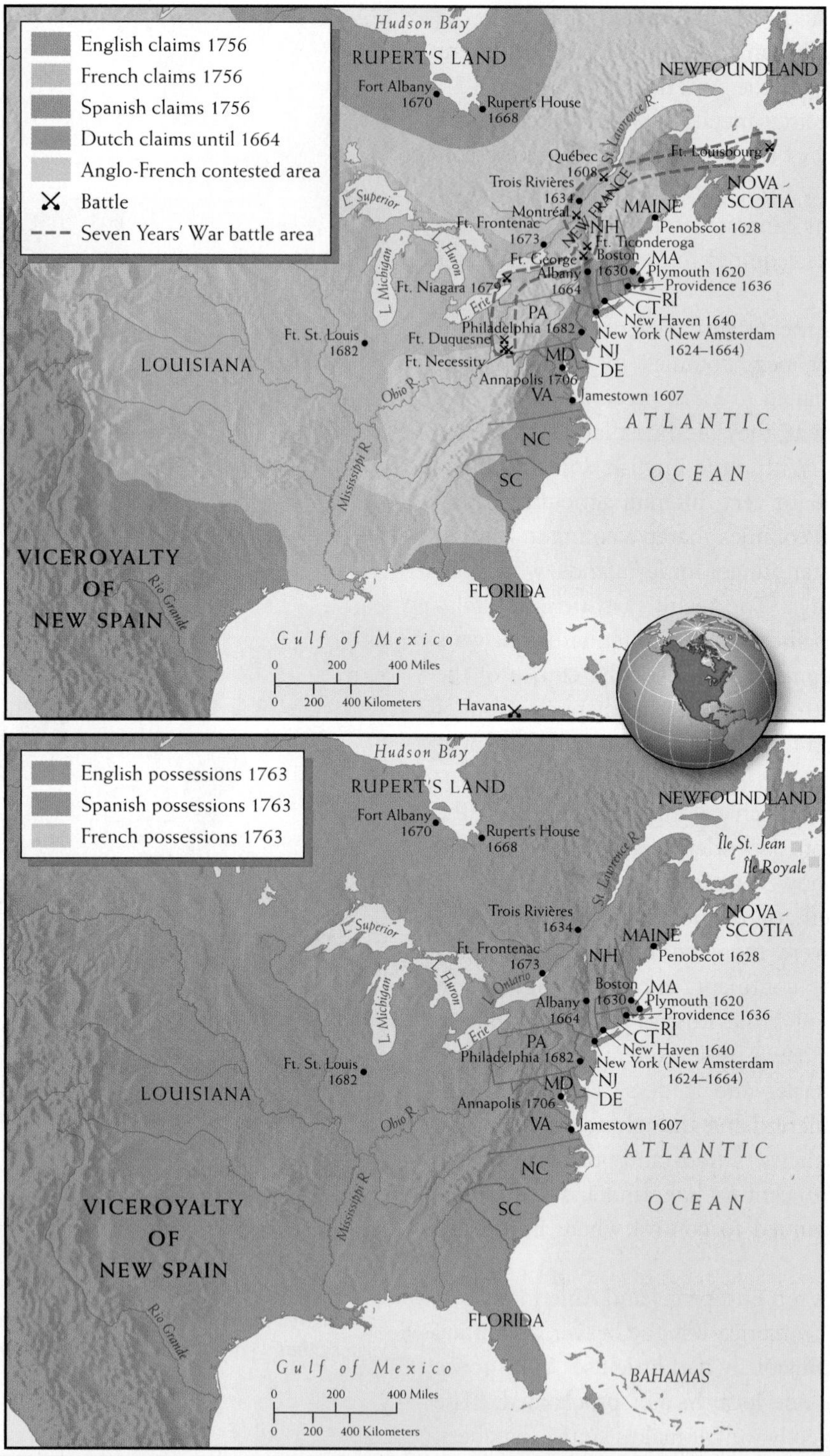

MAP 13.2 | Colonies in North America, 1607–1763

France, England, and Spain laid claim to much of North America at this time.

- Where was each of these colonial powers strongest before the outbreak of the Seven Years' War in 1756? (See p. 514 for a discussion of the Seven Years' War.)
- Which empire gained the most North American territory, and who lost the most at the end of the war in 1763?
- How do you think Native American peoples reacted to the territorial arrangements agreed to by Spain, France, and England at the Peace of Paris, which ended the war?

and mates—rested more on cooperation than conquest, especially compared to the empires built by their Spanish and English rivals.

The beaver could do "everything perfectly well" as long as there were lots of beavers and the Indians' demand for European things was limited (as it generally was) to metal tools. But as French (as well as English) traders introduced guns into the exchange networks, they initiated an arms race among Indians. To get more guns, Indians had to collect more skins, which resulted in the depletion of beavers in heavily trapped areas. That, in turn, pushed Indians to expand their hunting/trapping zones, which heightened conflicts between groups now increasingly competing for hunting territories. Alcohol, too, became a potent weapon for Europeans. It gave them a commodity that Indians wanted badly enough to undermine long-standing understandings of the relationship between humans and animals and to overwhelm strictures against overhunting.

The advantages that Europeans gained from their guns, alcohol, germs, and other "weapons" of "ecological imperialism" were becoming more apparent in eastern North America over the course of the seventeenth and eighteenth centuries. But in the middle of the continent and to the west of French outposts, a different dynamic was playing out. On the Great Plains, some Indian peoples were also losing ground to newcomers, but here the winners were other Indian groups. On the northern plains, the Lakotas, who had migrated westward onto the grasslands, emerged as the most successful expansionists. Coming eastward, the Comanches reigned across a vast swath of the southern plains. These and other invaders displaced existing indigenous societies from some lands, added to their ranks by capturing and often enslaving large numbers of people (especially females), and enriched themselves by their raiding and through their control over trading. The effective realm of "Comancheria" included territory that the Spanish mapped as theirs and extended not only over other Indians in the area, but also over Spaniards.

There was considerable irony in the fact that Spanish colonizers had empowered the Plains Amerindians. The Spanish, after all, had brought horses to the Americas, and it was the acquisition of these animals that revolutionized Indian life and enabled the expansions that took place on the Great Plains. Recognizing the role that horses played in their conquests, the Spanish had tried to keep them out of Indian hands. They failed. Raiders targeted horses. Once introduced into Indian circuits, the animals dispersed and flourished on the grasses of the Plains. So did the Indians who had greatest access to horses and who most decisively adapted to equestrianism. On horseback, Indians could kill bison much more effectively, which encouraged some groups to forsake farming for hunting, and other groups, like the Lakotas and Comanches, to move on to the Plains and move around them in pursuit of buffalo. Astride horses, Indians also gained military superiority over more sedentary peoples, whose villages and cornfields were vulnerable to mobile forces.

Not all prospered, however, and certainly not all equally. The gains of nomadic equestrians often came at the expense

The Fur Trade. *For Europeans in northern North America, no commodity was as important as beaver skins. For the French especially, the fur trade determined the character of their colonial regime in North America. For Indians, it offered access to European goods, but overhunting depleted resources and provoked intertribal conflicts.*

Tobacco. *The cultivation of tobacco saved the Virginia colony from ruin and brought prosperity to increasing numbers of planters. The spread of tobacco plantations also pushed Indians off their lands and led planters to turn to Africa for a labor force.*

of those who remained wedded to a mixture of horticulture and hunting. Within horse cultures, new inequalities materialized. More successful raiders and hunters earned not only greater honor, but also acquired more horses—and with more horses usually came higher status and more wives. At the same time, the status of women generally declined in the transition from horticultural to hunting societies. Their burdens, however, did not, as there were now more buffalo waiting to be turned by women into the products that sustained Plains Indian life.

The Plantation Complex in the Caribbean

As late as 1670, the most populous English colony was not on the North American mainland, but on the Caribbean island of Barbados. Because sugar was so desirable, from the mid-seventeenth century onward the English- and French-controlled islands of the Caribbean replicated the Portuguese sugarcane plantations of Brazil. All was not sweet here, however. Because no colonial power held a monopoly, competition to control the region—and sugar production—was fierce. The resulting turbulence did not simply reflect imperial rivalry; it also reflected labor arrangements in the colonies. Because the native populations had been wiped out in Columbus's wake (see Chapter 12), owners of Caribbean estates looked to Africa to obtain workers for their plantations.

Sugar was a killing crop. So deadly was the hot, humid environment in which sugarcane flourished (as fertile for disease as for sugarcane), many sugar barons spent little time on their plantations. Management fell to overseers, who worked their slaves to death. Despite having immunities to yellow fever and malaria from their homeland's similar environment, Africans could not withstand the regimen. Inadequate food, atrocious living conditions, and filthy sanitation added to their miseries. Moreover, plantation managers treated their slaves as nonhumans: for example, on the first day all new slaves suffered branding with the planter's seal. One English gentleman commented that slaves were like cows, "as near as beasts may be, setting their souls aside."

More than disease and inadequate rations, the work itself decimated the enslaved. Average life expectancy was three years. Six days a week slaves rose before dawn, labored until noon, ate a short lunch, and then worked until dusk. At harvest time, sixteen-hour days saw hundreds of men, women, and children doubled over to cut the sugarcane and transport it to refineries,

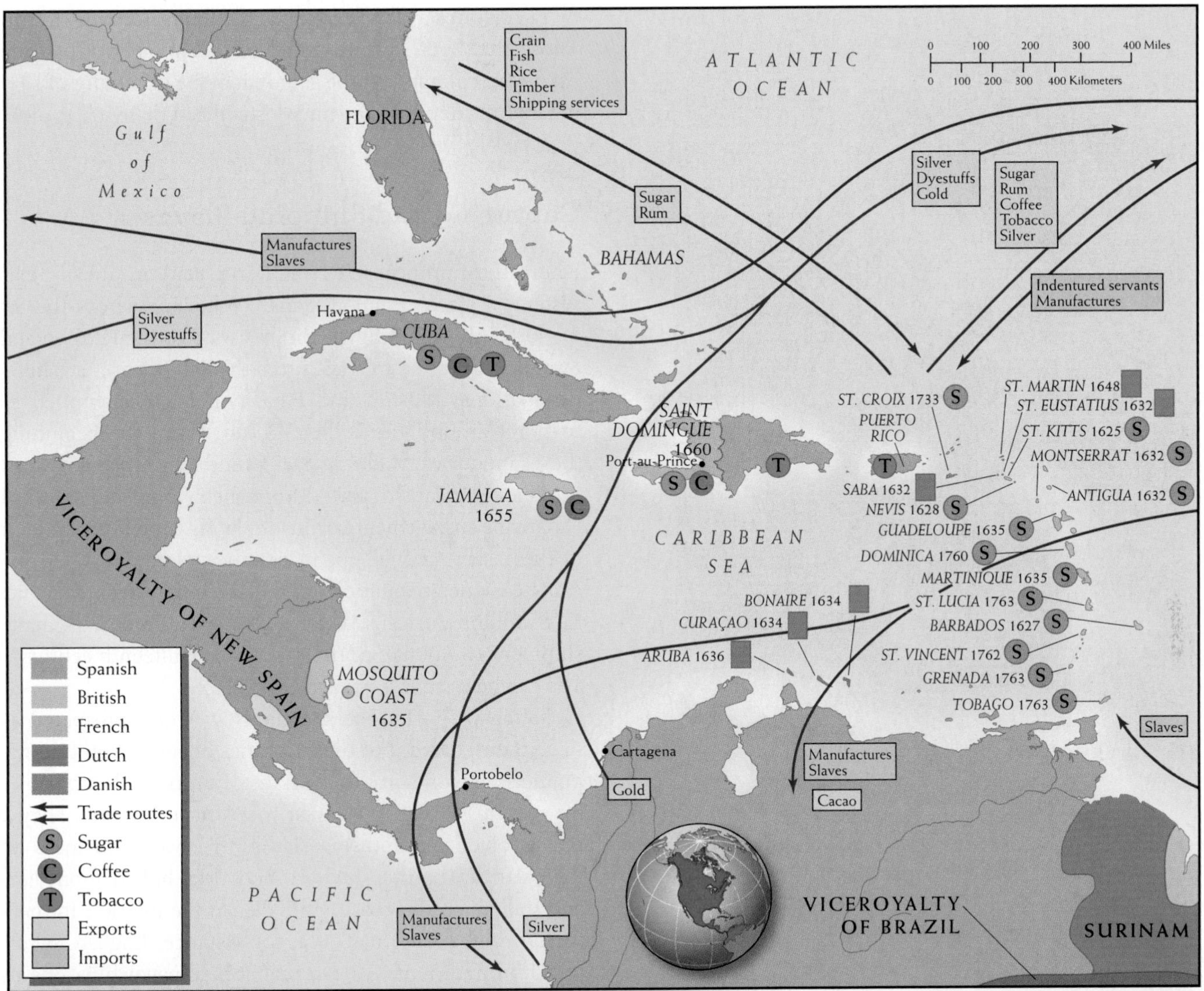

MAP 13.3 | Caribbean Colonies, 1625–1763

The Caribbean was a region of expanding trade in the seventeenth and eighteenth centuries.

- What were its major exports and imports?
- Who were its main colonizers and trading partners?
- According to your reading, how did the transformation of this region shape other societies in the Atlantic world?

sometimes seven days per week. Under this brutal schedule, slaves occasionally dropped dead from exhaustion.

Amid disease and toil, the enslaved resisted as they could. The most dramatic expression of resistance was violent revolt. In the early sixteenth century, in fact, slave revolts were so frequent in Panama that the crown banned all slave trade to the region. In the early seventeenth century, in parts of coastal Mexico, the viceroy negotiated an armistice with slaves to pacify the region. A more common form of resistance was flight. Seeking refuge from overseers, thousands of slaves took to the hills—for example, to the remote highlands of Caribbean islands or to Brazil's vast interior. Those who remained on the plantations resisted via foot dragging, pilfering, and sabotage.

Caribbean settlements and slaveholdings were not restricted to any single European power. But it was the latecomers—the Dutch, the English, and especially the French—who concentrated on the Antilles. The English took Jamaica from the Spanish and made it the premier site of Caribbean sugar by the 1740s. When the French seized half of Santo Domingo in the 1660s (renaming it Saint-Domingue, which is present-day

Slaves Cutting Cane. *Sugar was the preeminent agricultural export from the New World for centuries. Owners of sugarcane plantations relied almost exclusively on African slaves to produce the sweetener. Labor in the fields was especially harsh, as slaves worked in the blistering sun from dawn until dusk. This image shows how women and men toiled side by side.*

Haiti), they created one of the wealthiest societies based on slavery of all time. This French colony's exports eclipsed those of all the Spanish and English Antilles combined. The capital, Port-au-Prince, was one of the richest cities in the Atlantic world. The colony's merchants and planters built immense mansions worthy of the highest European nobles. Thus the Atlantic system benefited elite Europeans, who amassed new fortunes by exploiting the colonies' natural resources and the African slaves' labor.

THE SLAVE TRADE AND AFRICA

Although the slave trade began in the mid-fifteenth century, only in the seventeenth and eighteenth centuries did the numbers of human exports from Africa begin to soar (see Map 13.4). By 1820, four slaves had crossed the Atlantic for every European. Those numbers were essential to the prosperity of Europe's American colonies. At the same time, the departure of so many inhabitants depopulated and destabilized many parts of Africa.

Capturing and Shipping Slaves

Before the Europeans' arrival, Africa had an already existing system of slave commerce, mainly flowing across the Sahara to North Africa and Egypt and eastward to the Red Sea and the Swahili coast of East Africa. From the Red Sea and Swahili coast destinations, Muslim and Hindu merchants shipped slaves to ports around the Indian Ocean. From the beginnings of the Islamic slave trade, in the seventh century, no fewer than 9 million Africans departed from their homeland south of the Sahara for enslavement in Muslim lands. However, the number of these slaves could not match the volume destined for the Americas once plantation agriculture began to spread. Indeed, 12.8 million Africans departed for forcible enslavement and shipment to Atlantic ports from the late fifteenth century until 1867, when the last voyage took place.

Merchants in Europe and the New World prospered as the slave trade soared, but their fortunes depended on trading and political networks in Africa. In fact, European slavers took little interest in the happenings in the African interior. They were not involved in capturing slaves; this was a business left to their African partners, whose networks linked moneylenders and traders on the coast with allies in the interior. In the West African Bight (bay) of Biafra, for instance, English merchants relied on traditional African practices of pawnship—the use of human "pawns" to secure European commodities in advance of the delivery of slaves. According to custom, a secret male society called Ekpe enforced payments of promised slave deliveries. If a trader failed to deliver on his promise, his pawns (often members of his own kin group) were sold instead. By the mid-eighteenth century, Ekpe had powerful networks stretching deep into African hinterlands and supplying the slave trade in the port of Old Calabar.

Now the slave ports along the African coast became gruesome entrepôts. Indeed, high death rates occurred on the African side of the shipping; many slaves who perished did so before losing sight of Africa. Stuck in vast holding camps where disease and hunger were rampant, the slaves were then forced aboard vessels in cramped and wretched conditions. These ships waited for weeks to fill their holds while their human cargoes wasted away below deck. Crew members tossed dead Africans overboard as they loaded on other Africans from the shore. When the cargo was complete, the ships set sail. In their wake, crews continued to dump bodies. Most died of gastrointestinal diseases leading to dehydration. Smallpox and dysentery were also scourges.

PRIMARY SOURCE

Olaudah Equiano on the Atlantic Crossing

The most compelling description of the horrifying conditions that captives endured on the African coast as they awaited the arrival of slaving ships and the perils of the Atlantic crossing came from the pen of a former slave, Olaudah Equiano (c. 1745–1797). After purchasing his freedom and becoming a skilled writer, Equiano published **The Interesting Narrative of the Life of Olaudah Equiano, or Gustavus Vassa, the African. Written by Himself** ***(1789). An instantaneous best seller, within ten years the book saw nine English editions and appeared in American, Dutch, German, Russian, and French editions. Although some critics have questioned the authenticity of Equiano's birth and early life in Africa, the scholarly consensus remains that he was indeed born in Igboland (in the eastern part of present-day Nigeria) and made the voyage across the Atlantic after his capture at age nine.***

The first object which saluted my eyes when I arrived on the coast was the sea, and a slave ship, which was then riding at anchor, and waiting for its cargo. These filled me with astonishment, which was soon converted into terror when I was carried on board. I was immediately handled and tossed up to see if I were sound by some of the crew; and I was now persuaded that I had gotten into a world of bad spirits, and that they were going to kill me. Their complexions too differing so much from ours, their long hair, and the language they spoke, (which was very different from any I had ever heard) united to confirm me in this belief. Indeed such were the horrors of my views and fears at the moment, that, if ten thousand worlds had been my own, I would have freely parted with them all to have exchanged my condition with that of the meanest slave in my own country. When I looked round the ship too and saw a large furnace or copper boiling, and a multitude of black people of every description chained together, every one of their countenances expressing dejection and sorrow, I no longer doubted of my fate; and, quite overpowered with horror and anguish, I fell motionless on the deck and fainted. When I recovered a little I found some black people about me, who I believed were some of those who brought me on board, and had been receiving their pay; they talked to me in order to cheer me, but all in vain. I asked them if we were not to be eaten by those white men with horrible looks, red faces, and loose hair. They told me I was not . . .

In a little time after, amongst the poor chained men, I found some of my own nation, which in a small degree gave ease to my mind. I inquired of these what was to be done with us; they gave me to understand we were to be carried to these white people's country to work for them. I then was a little revived, and thought, if it were no worse than working, my situation was not so desperate: but still I feared I should be put to death, the white people looked and acted, as I thought, in so savage a manner; for I had never seen among any people such instances of brutal cruelty; and this not only shewn towards us blacks, but also to some of the whites themselves. . . .

At last, when the ship we were in had got in all her cargo, they made ready with many fearful noises, and we were all put under deck, so that we could not see how they managed the vessel. But this disappointment was the least of my sorrow. The stench of the hold while we were on the coast was so intolerably loathsome, that it was dangerous to remain there for any time, and some of us had been permitted to stay on the deck for the fresh air; but now that the whole ship's cargo were confined together, it became absolutely pestilential. The closeness of the place, and the heat of the climate, added to the number in the ship, which was so crowded that each had scarcely room to turn himself, almost suffocated us. This produced copious perspirations, so that the air soon became unfit for respiration, from a variety of loathsome smells, and brought on a sickness among the slaves, of which many died, thus falling victims to the improvident avarice, as I may call it, of their purchasers. This wretched situation was again aggravated by the galling of the chains, now become insupportable; and the filth of the necessary tubs [latrines], into which the children often fell, and were almost suffocated. The shrieks of the women, and the groans of the dying, rendered the whole a scene of horror almost inconceivable.

QUESTIONS FOR ANALYSIS

- The slave trade involved capturing Africans from various parts of the interior of the continent. Which lines in the reading give evidence of this?
- Equiano's book came out in 1789 in the midst of a campaign to abolish the slave trade. Considering the formality of his language, what type of audience do you suppose he was seeking to reach?
- Why would this book describing the horrors of the slave trade have appeared only in the late 1700s, even though such brutal conditions had been existing for more than two centuries?

Source: Werner Sollors, ed., The Interesting Narrative of the Life of Olaudah Equiano, or Gustavus Vassa, the African, Written by Himself, *A Norton Critical Edition (New York: Norton, 2001), pp. 38–41.*

MAP 13.4 | The African Slave Trade , 1501–1867

The Atlantic slave trade flourished from the sixteenth to the nineteenth centuries, linking many parts of Africa with the Americas through enslavement and human trafficking on a massive scale. This map reflects recent estimates of the number of slaves transported during this period.

- What were the main areas of Africa from which the slaves were taken? What were the main areas that they were taken to in the Americas?
- What was the relationship between sugar cultivation in the Americas and the demand for African slave labor?
- How and where did the slave trade reshape African societies?

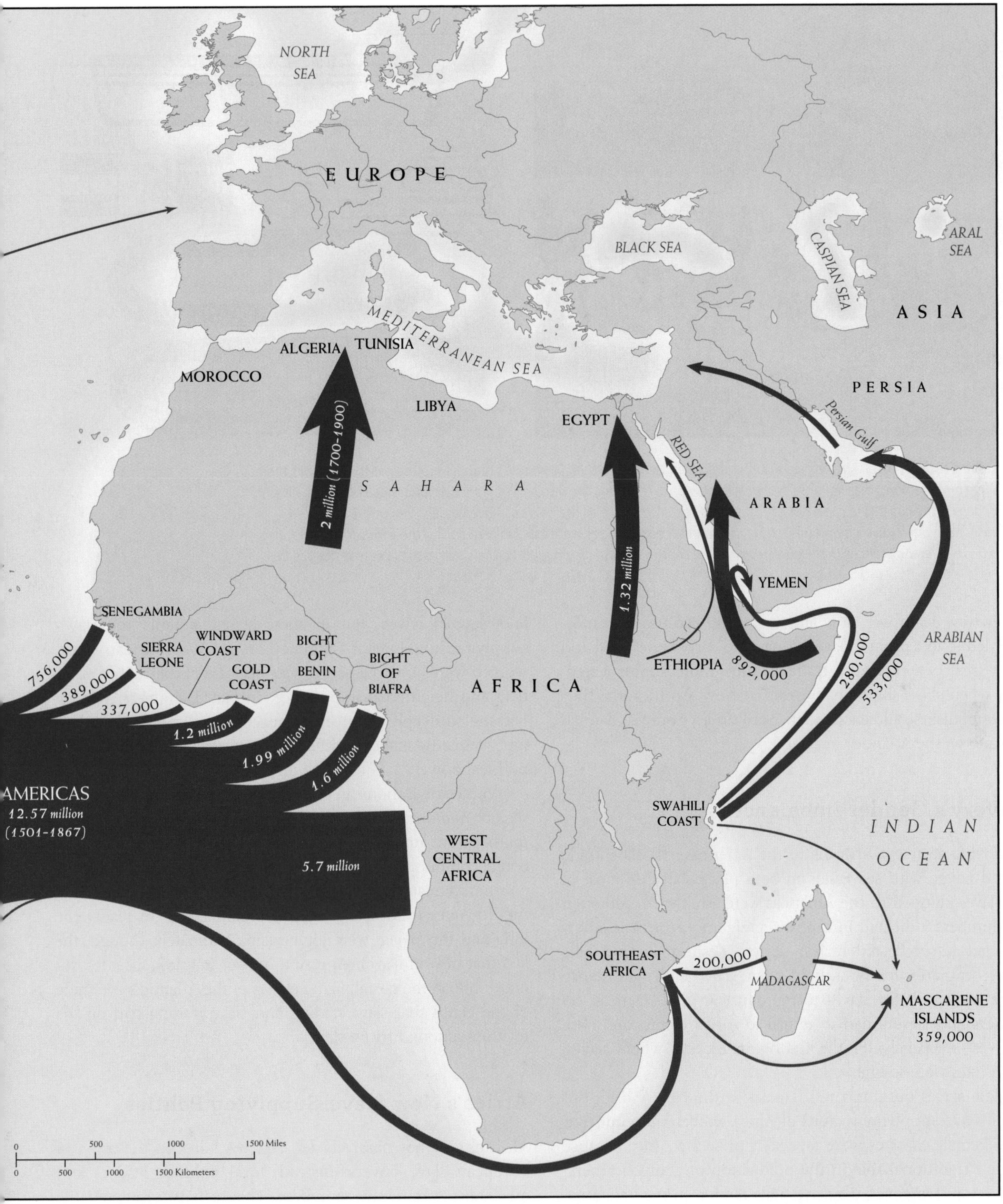

NORTH SEA
EUROPE
BLACK SEA
CASPIAN SEA
ARAL SEA
ASIA
MEDITERRANEAN SEA
ALGERIA
TUNISIA
MOROCCO
LIBYA
EGYPT
PERSIA
Persian Gulf
RED SEA
2 million (1700–1900)
SAHARA
1.32 million
ARABIA
YEMEN
SENEGAMBIA
SIERRA LEONE
WINDWARD COAST
GOLD COAST
BIGHT OF BENIN
BIGHT OF BIAFRA
ETHIOPIA
892,000
AFRICA
280,000
533,000
ARABIAN SEA
756,000
389,000
337,000
1.2 million
1.99 million
1.6 million
AMERICAS
12.57 million
(1501–1867)
5.7 million
WEST CENTRAL AFRICA
SWAHILI COAST
INDIAN OCEAN
SOUTHEAST AFRICA
200,000
MADAGASCAR
MASCARENE ISLANDS
359,000
0
500
1000
1500 Miles
0
500
1000
1500 Kilometers

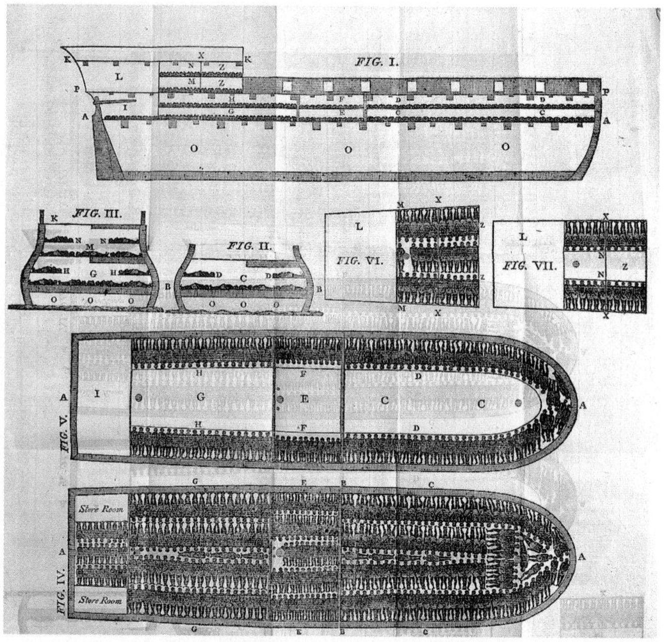

The Slave Trade. (Left) *Africans were captured in the interior and then bound and marched to the coast. Note that there is only one woman among the men (and a couple of children), reflecting the gender imbalance among those captured.* (Right) *After reaching the coast, the captured Africans would be crammed into the holds of slave vessels, where they suffered grievously from overcrowding and unsanitary conditions. Long voyages were especially deadly. If the winds failed or ships had to travel longer distances than usual, many of the captives would die en route to the slave markets across the ocean.*

Either way, death was slow and agonizing. Because high mortality led to lost profits, slavers learned to carry better food and more fresh water as the trade became more sophisticated. Still, when slave ships finally reached New World ports, they reeked of disease and excrement. (See Primary Source: Olaudah Equiano on the Atlantic Crossing.)

Slavery's Gender Imbalance

In moving so many Africans to the Americas, the slave trade played havoc with sex ratios in both places because most of the slaves shipped to the Americas were adult men. Although the numbers indicated Europeans' preferences for male laborers, they also reflected African slavers' desire to keep female slaves, primarily for household work. The gender imbalance made it difficult for slaves to reproduce in the Americas. So planters and slavers had to return to Africa to procure more captives—especially for the Caribbean islands, where slaves' death rates were so high.

Male slaves outnumbered females in the New World, but in the slave-supplying regions of Africa women outnumbered men. Female captives were especially prized in Africa because of their traditional role in the production of grains, leathers, and cotton. Moreover, the slave trade reinforced the traditional practice of polygyny—allowing relatively scarce men to take several wives. But in some states, notably the slave-supplying kingdom of Dahomey on the West African coast, women were able to assert power because of their large numbers and heightened importance. In fact, Dahomean women became so deeply involved in succession disputes that their intrigues could make the difference between winning and losing political power.

Within the Dahomean court the most powerful woman was the queen mother, the *kpojito*. Each new ruler selected his queen mother from among his predecessors' wives. Believing that she could communicate with the supernatural, the king and his courtiers consulted her before making important decisions. Indeed, queen mothers were so influential that in reality the king and the *kpojito* were joint rulers. Ultimately, though, the fact that powerful women rose to power in a few societies did not diminish the destabilizing effects of the Atlantic slave trade or the chaos that slave raiding and slave trading had on the relations among African states.

Africa's New Slave-Supplying Polities

Africans did not passively let captives fall into the arms of European slave buyers; instead, local political leaders and merchants were active suppliers. This activity promoted the growth of centralized polities, particularly in West African rain

ANALYZING GLOBAL DEVELOPMENTS

The Atlantic Trade in Slaves from Africa (1501–1900)

The world's leading slave traders were also the world's most important maritime powers during the period from 1501 to 1900. The following two tables focus on which countries transported these slaves and where they ended up. The Spanish and Portuguese established the first European empires in the Americas and created the model for the early slave trade. But northern European powers like Great Britain and France, reflecting their growing strength in maritime commerce, dominated the Atlantic slave trade between 1642 and 1808. In the final phase of the Atlantic slave trade, 1808–1867, the northern European powers and the United States disengaged from the trade, allowing the Portuguese and the Spanish once again to dominate the trade now centered largely on Cuba and Brazil.

In recent decades, scholars of the Atlantic slave trade have created the Trans-Atlantic Slave Trade Database, which can be accessed at the Voyages Web site (www.slavevoyages.org). Constructed from nearly 35,000 documented voyages during this period, this database incorporates roughly 80 percent of the slave ventures that set out for Africa to obtain slaves from all around the Atlantic world during this era. Through painstaking research, historians have been able to reconstruct the Atlantic world slave trade and offer a clear insight into the experiences of all those involved and the impact of this trade on the global economy during four centuries.

QUESTIONS FOR ANALYSIS

- Which countries were the most heavily invested in the Atlantic slave trade based on the data in the first table? How do you know?
- What was the relationship between the slave-trading countries and the colonies in the New World based on the entries in both tables?
- Why is the total number of slaves traded different from the number of slaves that disembarked? Did you expect the differences between these two numbers to be greater than they are? If so, why?

Number of Slaves Taken from Africa to Americas by Nationality of Vessels That Carried Them (1501–1867)

Vessel Nationality	Number of Slaves
Portugal/Brazil	5,849,300
Great Britain	3,259,900
France	1,380,970
Spain/Uruguay	1,060,900
Netherlands	555,300
United States	305,800
Baltic States	110,400
Total Atlantic World	**12,522,570**

Disembarkation of Slaves from Africa to the Americas (1501–1900)

Disembarking Country/Colony	Number of Slaves
Brazil (Portugal)	4.72 m
Smaller Caribbean Islands (mix)	1.75 m
Jamaica (Spain then Great Britain)	1.00 m
Saint-Domingue (Spain then France)	792,000
Cuba (Spain)	779,000
Spanish Caribbean Mainland	390,000
United States	389,000
Dutch Guiana	294,000
Amazonia	142,000
Total	**10,703,000**

Source: David Eltis and David Richardson, Atlas of the Transatlantic Slave Trade *(2010).*

forest areas. The trade also shifted control of wealth away from households owning large herds or lands to those who profited from the capture and exchange of slaves—urban merchants and warrior elites.

THE KONGO KINGDOM In some parts of Africa, the booming slave trade wreaked havoc as local leaders feuded over control of the traffic. In the Kongo kingdom, civil wars raged for over a century after 1665, and captured warriors were sold as slaves. As members of the royal family clashed, entire provinces saw their populations vanish. Most important to the conduct of war and the control of trade were firearms and gunpowder, which made the capturing of slaves highly efficient. Moreover, kidnapping became so prevalent

The Port of Loango. *Partly as a result of the profits of the slave trade, African rulers and merchants were able to create large and prosperous port cities such as Loango (pictured here), which was on the west coast of south-central Africa.*

that cultivators worked their fields bearing weapons, leaving their children behind in guarded stockades.

Some leaders of the Kongo kingdom fought back. Consider Queen Nzinga (1583–1663), a masterful diplomat and a shrewd military planner. Having converted to Christianity, she managed to keep the Portuguese slavers at bay during her long reign. Even after Portuguese forces defeated her troops in open battle, she conducted effective guerrilla warfare into her sixties.

Consider also the Christian visionary Dona Beatriz Kimpa Vita. Born in the Kongo in 1684 and baptized as a Christian, at age twenty she claimed to have received visions from St. Anthony of Padua. She believed that she died every Friday and was transported to heaven to converse with God, returning to earth on Monday to broadcast God's commands to believers. Her message aimed to end the Kongo civil wars and re-create a unified kingdom. Although she gained a large following, she failed to win the support of leading political figures. In 1706 she was captured and burned at the stake.

OYO, ASANTE, AND OTHER GROUPS As some African merchants and warlords sold other Africans, their commercial success enabled them to consolidate political power and grow wealthy. Their wealth financed additional weapons, with which they subdued neighbors and extended political control. Among the most durable new polities was the Asante state, which arose in the West African tropical rain forest in 1701 and expanded through 1750. This state benefited from its access to gold, which it used to acquire firearms (from European traders) to raid nearby communities for servile workers. From its capital city at Kumasi, the state eventually encompassed almost all of present-day Ghana. Main roads spread out from the capital like spokes of a wheel, each approximately twenty days' travel from the center. Through the Asante trading networks African traders bought, bartered, and sold slaves, who wound up in the hands of European merchants waiting in ports with vessels carrying manufactures and weaponry.

Also active in the slave trade—and enriched by it—was the Oyo Empire. This territory, which straddled the main trade routes, linked tropical rain forests with interior markets of the northern savannah areas. The empire's strength rested on its impressive army brandishing weapons secured from trade with Europeans. Deploying cavalry units in the savannah and infantry units in the rain forest, the Oyo's military campaigns became annual events, only suspended so that warriors could return home for their agricultural duties. Every dry season, Oyo armies marched on their neighbors to capture entire villages.

Slavery and the emergence of new political organizations enriched and empowered some Africans, but they cost Africa dearly. For the princes, warriors, and merchants who organized the slave trade, their business (like that of Amerindian fur suppliers) enabled them to obtain European goods—especially alcohol, tobacco, textiles, and guns. The Atlantic system also tilted wealth away from rural dwellers and village elders and increasingly toward port cities. Across the landmass, the slave trade thinned the population. True, Africa was spared a demographic catastrophe equal to the devastation of American Indians. The introduction of American food crops—notably maize and cassava, producing many more calories per acre than the old staples of millet and sorghum—blunted the trade's depopulating aspects. Yet some areas suffered grievously from three centuries of heavy involvement in the slave trade. The Atlantic trade enhanced the warrior class, who carried out raids for captives; the dislocations, internal power struggles, and economic hardships that followed precipitated the rise and fall of West African kingdoms.

ASIA IN THE SEVENTEENTH AND EIGHTEENTH CENTURIES

Global trading networks blossomed as vigorously in Asia as they did in the Americas. In Asia, however, the Europeans were less dominant. Although they could penetrate Asian markets with American silver, they could not conquer Asian empires or colonize vast portions of the region. Nor were they able to enslave Asian peoples as they had Africans. The Mughal Empire continued to grow, and the Qing dynasty, which had wrested control from the Ming, significantly expanded China's borders. China remained the richest state in the world, but in some places the balance of power was tilting in Europe's direction. Not only did the Ottomans' borders contract, but by the late eighteenth century Europeans had established economic and military dominance in parts of India and much of Southeast Asia.

The Dutch in Southeast Asia

In Southeast Asia the Dutch already enjoyed a dominant position by the seventeenth century. Although the Portuguese had seized the vibrant port city of Melaka in 1511 and the Spaniards had taken Manila in 1571, neither was able to monopolize the lucrative spice trade. To challenge them, the Dutch government persuaded its merchants to charter the Dutch East India Company (abbreviated as VOC) in 1602. Benefiting from Amsterdam's position as the most efficient money market with the lowest interest rates in the world, the VOC raised ten times the capital of its English counterpart—the royal chartered English East India Company. The advantages of chartered companies were evident in the VOC's scale of operation: at its peak the company had 257 ships and employed 12,000 persons. Throughout two centuries it sent ships manned by a total of one million men to Asia.

The VOC's main impact was in Southeast Asia, where spices, coffee, tea, and teak wood were key exports (see again Map 13.1). The company's objective was to secure a trade monopoly wherever it could, fix prices, and replace the native population with Dutch planters. In 1619, under the leadership of Jan Pieterszoon Coen (who once said that trade could not be conducted without war nor war without trade), the Dutch swept into the Javanese port of Jakarta (renamed Batavia by the Dutch). In defiance of local rulers and English rivals, the Dutch burned all the houses, drove out the population, and constructed a fortress from which to control the Southeast Asian trade. Two years later, Coen's forces took over a cluster of nutmeg-producing islands known as Banda. The traditional chiefs and almost the entire population were killed outright, left to starve, or taken into slavery. Dutch planters and their slaves replaced the decimated local population and sent their produce to the VOC. The motive for such rapacious action was the huge profit to be made by buying nutmeg at a low price in the Bandanese Islands and selling it at many times that price in Europe.

With their monopoly of nutmeg secured, the Dutch went after the market in cloves. Their strategy was to control production in one region and then destroy the rest, which entailed, once again, wars against producers and traders in other areas. Portuguese Melaka soon fell to the Dutch and became a VOC outpost. Although this aggressive expansion met widespread resistance from the local population and other merchants involved in the region's trade, by 1670 the Dutch controlled all of the lucrative spice trade from the Maluku islands.

Next, the VOC set its sights on pepper. In this gambit, it gained control of Bantam (present-day Banten), the largest pepper-exporting port. However, the Dutch had to share this commerce with Chinese and English competitors. Moreover, since there was no demand for European products in Asia, the Dutch had to participate more in inter-Asian trade as a way to reduce their need to make payments in precious metals. So they purchased, for example, calicoes (plain white cotton cloths) in India or copper in Japan for resale in Melaka and Java. They also diversified into trading silk, cotton, tea, and coffee, in addition to spices.

As a result of the Dutch enterprise, European outposts such as Dutch Batavia and Spanish Manila soon eclipsed old cosmopolitan cities such as Bantam. Indeed, as Europeans competed for supremacy in the borderlands of Southeast Asia, they made local societies serve their own ambitions and began replacing traditional networks with trade routes that primarily served European interests.

Transformations in Islam

Compared with Southeast Asia, the Islamic empires did not feel such direct effects of European intrusion. They did, however, face internal difficulties. While the Ottoman and Mughal empires remained resilient, the Safavid Empire fell into chaos.

Attack on Bantam. *This engraving depicts a Dutch attack on Bantam in the late seventeenth century as part of the VOC's effort to expand its empire in Southeast Asia.*

THE SAFAVID EMPIRE From its inception, the Safavid Empire had always required a powerful, religiously inspired ruler to enforce Shiite religious orthodoxy and to hold together the realm's tribal, pastoral, mercantile, and agricultural factions. The founding figure and his strongest successor had succeeded at this challenge. But when such a figure was not present, the state foundered. By 1722, after a series of weak rulers, it was under assault from within and without.

Internal turmoil was partly the result of a change in trade routes away from Persia and partly the result of tribal incursions against the central government. Such incursions were always a threat to political stability, but especially so when weak rulers sat on the throne. Meanwhile, neighboring Afghan clansmen invaded Safavid territory, overran the inept and divided armies, and besieged the capital at Isfahan (see Map 13.1). As the city's inhabitants perished from hunger and disease, some desperate survivors ate the corpses of the deceased. After the shah abdicated, the invaders executed thousands of officials and members of the royal household. The empire limped along until 1773, when a revolt toppled the last ruler from the throne.

THE OTTOMAN EMPIRE Having attained a high point under Suleiman (see Chapter 11), the Ottoman Empire, too, entered a period of territorial losses and a sense of decline. After Suleiman's reign, Ottoman armies and navies tried unsuccessfully to expand the empire's borders—losing, for example, on the western flank to the European Habsburgs. As military campaigns and a growing population strained the realm's limited resources, Ottoman intellectuals worried that the empire's glory was ebbing.

Even as the empire's strength waned, by the seventeenth century its sultans faced a commercially more connected world. Once New World silver entered Ottoman networks of commerce and money lending, its presence eventually destabilized the empire. Although early Ottoman rulers had avoided trade with the outside world, the lure of silver broke through state regulations. Now Ottoman merchants established black markets for commodities that eager European buyers paid for in silver—especially wheat, copper, and wool. Because these exports were illegal, their sale did not generate tax revenues to support the state's civilian and military administration. So Ottoman rulers had to rely on loans of silver from the merchants. Such financial dependence meant that rulers could ill afford to impose official rules on those who bankrolled them.

More silver and budget deficits were a recipe for inflation. Indeed, prices doubled and then tripled between 1550 and 1650. Runaway inflation caused hard-hit peasants in Anatolia, suffering from high food prices, shortages, and increasing taxes (used to pay off dynastic debts), to join together in uprisings that threatened the state's stability. By the time of Sultan Ibrahim's reign (1640–1648), the cycle of spending, taxing, borrowing, and inflation was so severe that his own officials murdered him. Moreover, disorder at the center of the empire was accompanied by difficulties in the provinces, where breakaway regimes appeared.

THE MAMLUKS IN OTTOMAN EGYPT The most threatening of the breakaway pressures occurred in Egypt beginning in the seventeenth century. In 1517, Egypt had become the Ottoman Empire's greatest conquest. As the wealthiest Ottoman territory, it was an important source of revenue, and its people shouldered heavy tax burdens.

The group that asserted Egypt's political and commercial autonomy from Istanbul were military men, known as **Mamluks** (Arabic for "owned" or "possessed"), who had ruled Egypt as an independent regime until the Ottoman conquest of the country (see Chapter 10). Although the Ottoman army had routed Mamluk forces on the battlefield in 1517, Ottoman governors in Egypt allowed the Mamluks to reform themselves. By the seventeenth century, these military men were nearly as powerful as their ancestors had been in the fifteenth century when they ruled Egypt independently. Turning the Ottoman administrator of Egypt into a mere figurehead, this new provincial elite kept much of the area's fiscal resources for themselves at the expense not only of the imperial coffers but also of the local peasantry. Mamluk households also enhanced their power by aligning with Egyptian merchants and catering to the Egyptian *ulama*.

THE OTTOMANS' KOPRULU REFORMS The Ottoman system also had elements of resilience—especially at the center, where decaying leadership provoked demands for reform from administrative elites. Late in the seventeenth century, the Koprulu family controlled the office of grand vizier and spearheaded changes to revitalize the empire. Mehmed Koprulu, the first to assume office, had been born into an obscure Albanian family. Taken as a slave in the *devshirme* (see Chapter 11), he slowly ascended the bureaucratic ladder and became grand vizier at age eighty. Pragmatic and incorruptible, Mehmed not only rooted out his corrupt peers but also balanced the budget and reversed the Ottoman armies' misfortunes. His death in 1661 did not halt the reforms, for he had groomed his son, Fazil Ahmed Koprulu, to continue them. The young grand vizier continued to trim the administration and strengthen the armies for another fifteen years.

Known as the Koprulu reforms, the changes in administration gave the state a new burst of energy and enabled the military to reacquire some of its lost possessions. Revenues again increased, and inflation decreased. Fired by revived expansionist ambitions, Istanbul decided to renew its assault on Christianity (see Chapter 11)—beginning with rekindled plans to seize Vienna under the leadership of Fazil Ahmed's brother-in-law, Kara Mustafa Pasha. Although the Ottomans gathered an enormous force outside the Habsburg capital in 1683, both sides suffered heavy losses and the Ottoman forces ultimately retreated. They planned to renew the assault months later, but the sultan, fearing disgrace, had Kara Mustafa strangled. Thereafter, the Ottomans halted their military advances. Worse still, under the treaty that ended the Austro-Ottoman

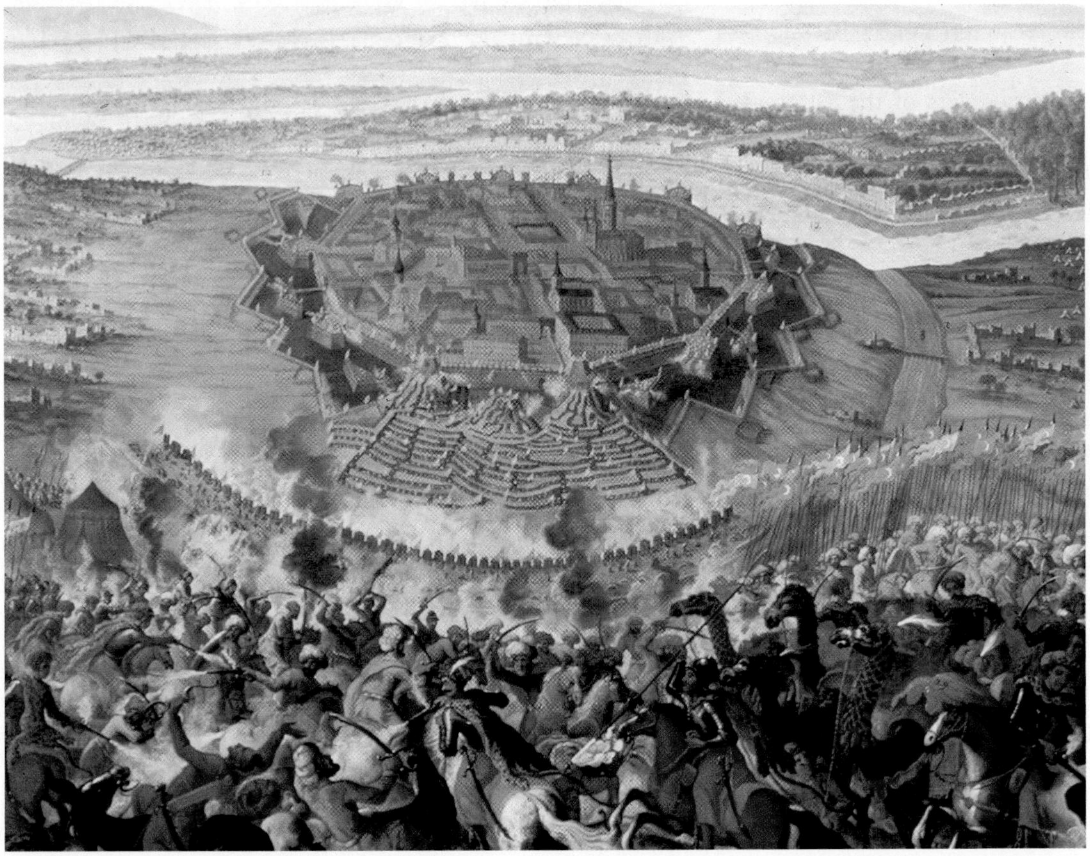

Siege of Vienna. *This seventeenth-century painting depicts the Ottoman siege of Vienna, which began on July 14, 1683, and ended on September 12. The city might have fallen if the Polish king, John III, had not answered the pope's plea to defend Christendom and sent an army to assist German and Austrian troops in defeating the Ottomans.*

Indian Cotton. *European traders were drawn to India by its famed cotton textiles. This image from c. 1800 shows a woman separating the cotton from the seeds; it captures the preindustrial technology of cotton production in India.*

war, the Ottomans lost major European territorial possessions, including Hungary.

Whereas in the sixteenth century rulers of the Ottoman Empire had wanted to create a self-contained and self-sufficient imperial economy, silver undermined this vision as it had elsewhere in the global economy. Indeed, the influx of silver opened Ottoman-controlled lands to trade with the rest of the world, producing intellectual ferment, breakaway regimes, widespread inflation, and social discontent.

THE MUGHAL EMPIRE In contrast to the Ottomans' setbacks, the Mughal Empire reached its height in the 1600s. The period saw Mughal rulers extend their domain over almost all of India and enjoy increased domestic and international trade. But they eventually had problems governing dispersed and resistant provinces, where many villages retained traditional religions and cultures.

Before the Mughals, India had never had a single political authority. Akbar and his successors had conquered territory in the north (see Chapter 12, Map 12.4), so now the Mughals turned to the south and gained control over most of that region by 1689. As the new provinces provided an additional source of resources, local lords, and warriors, the Mughal bureaucracy grew better at extracting services and taxes.

Imperial stability and prosperity did not depend entirely on the Indian Ocean trading system. Indeed, although the Mughals profited from seaborne trade, they never undertook overseas expansion. The main source of their wealth was land rents, which increased via incentives to bring new land into cultivation. Here peasants planted, in part, New World crops like maize and tobacco. But the imperial economy also benefited from Europeans' increased demand for Indian goods and services—such as a sixfold rise in the English East India Company's textile purchases within twenty years. Dutch trade with India saw similar trends. As precious metals flowed in from Japan and the New World to finance this booming trade, the imperial mint struck increasing numbers of silver coins, which fueled a cycle of greater trade and the use of **specie** (money in coin) for exchange.

Aurangzeb. *The last powerful Mughal emperor, Aurangzeb continued the conquest of the Indian subcontinent. Pictured in his old age, he is shown here with his courtiers.*

LOCAL AUTONOMY IN MUGHAL INDIA Mughals were victims of their own success. More than a century of imperial expansion, commercial prosperity, and agricultural development placed substantial resources in the hands of local and regional authorities. As a result, local warrior elites became more autonomous. By the late seventeenth century, many regional leaders were well positioned to resist Mughal authority.

As in the Ottoman Empire, then, distant provinces began to challenge central rulers. Under Aurangzeb (r. 1658–1707), as the Mughals pushed their frontier deep into southern India, they encountered fierce opposition from the Marathas in the northwestern Deccan plateau (see Map 13.1). To finance this expansion, Aurangzeb raised taxes on the peasants. Then resentment spread, and even the elite grew restive at the drain on imperial finances. Seeking support from the orthodox *ulama,* the monarch abandoned the toleration of heterodoxy and of non-Muslims that his predecessors had allowed. Ultimately, only the strong hand of Aurangzeb kept order in the empire.

When Aurangzeb died in 1707, a war of succession broke out. The revenue system eroded as local tax collectors pocketed more of the returns. Prosperous local elites rallied military forces of their own, annexing neighboring lands and chipping away at imperial authority. All this turmoil set the stage for successful peasant revolts.

Now the Indian peasants (like their counterparts in Ming China, Safavid Persia, and the Ottoman Empire) capitalized on weakening central authority to assert their independence. Many rose in rebellions; others took up banditry. Consider the revolt of the Jat peasant caste in northern India in the late seventeenth century: refusing to pay taxes, the Jat people killed a Mughal official and then seized lands and plundered the region. A half-century later, peasant cultivators of the Punjab turned their own closely knit community into a military power that stymied the Mughal forces. Peasants were also critical in the rise of the Marathas of western India, whose charismatic leader harnessed hatred of imperial oppression to fiercely resist Mughal control.

At this point the Mughal emperors had to accept diminished power over a loose unity of provincial "successor states." Most of these areas accepted Mughal control in name only, administering semiautonomous regimes through access to local resources. Yet India still flourished, and landed elites brought new territories into agrarian production. Cotton, for instance, supported a thriving textile industry as peasant households focused on weaving and cloth production. Much of their production was destined for export as the region deepened its integration into world trading systems.

PRIVATE COMMERCIAL ENTERPRISE The Mughals themselves paid scant attention to commercial matters, but local rulers welcomed Europeans into Indian ports. As more European ships arrived, these authorities struck deals with merchants from Portugal and, increasingly, from England and Holland. Some Indian merchants formed trading companies of their own to control the sale of regional produce to competing Europeans; others established intricate trading networks that reached as far north as Russia.

One of these companies built a trading and banking empire that demonstrated how local prosperity could undercut imperial power. This was the house of Jagat Seths, which at first specialized in shipping Bengal cloth through Asian and European merchants. Increasingly, however, most of their business in the provinces of Bengal and Bihar was tax-farming, whereby they collected taxes for the imperial coffers. (See Map 13.1.) The Jagat Seths maintained their own retinue of agents to gather levies from farmers while pocketing substantial profits for themselves. In this way, they and other mercantile houses grew richer and gained greater political influence over financially strapped emperors. Thus, even as global commercial entanglements enriched some in India, the effects undercut the Mughal dynasty.

From Ming to Qing in China

Like India, China prospered in the seventeenth and eighteenth centuries; but here, too, sizeable wealth undermined central control and contributed to the fall of a long-lasting dynasty. As in Mughal India, local power holders in China increasingly defied the Ming government. Moreover, because Ming sovereigns discouraged overseas commerce and forbade travel abroad, they did not reap the rewards of long-distance exchange. Rather, such profits went to traders and adventurers who evaded imperial edicts. Together, the persistence of local autonomy and the accelerating economic and social changes brought unprecedented challenges until finally, in 1644, the Ming dynasty collapsed.

ADMINISTRATIVE PROBLEMS How did a dynasty that in the early seventeenth century governed the world's most economically advanced society (and perhaps a third of the world's population) fall from power? As in the Ottoman Empire, responsibility often lay with the rulers. Consider the disastrous reign of Zhu Yijun, the Wanli Emperor (r. 1573–1620). This precocious youth ascended to the throne at age nine and, like his predecessors, grew up within the confines of the Forbidden City (see Chapter 11). The emperor was secluded despite being surrounded by a staff of 20,000 eunuchs and 3,000 women. The "Son of Heaven" rarely ventured outside the palace compound, and when he moved within it a large retinue accompanied him, led by eunuchs clearing his path with whips. His day was filled with state functions, for which he had to change clothes to suit each occasion—including formal headgear with curtain-like beads that forced him to move solemnly and deliberately.

Ming emperors like Wanli quickly discovered that despite the elaborate arrangements and ritual performances affirming their position as the Son of Heaven, they had scant control over the vast bureaucracy. An emperor frustrated with his officials could do little more than punish them or refuse to cooperate. Unable to change this system, Wanli avoided any involvement with managing the realm; he even refused to meet with officials or preside over state rituals. A mountain of reports and petitions piled up in his study unattended, while some of his bureaucrats exploited his neglect to accumulate wealth for themselves. During his long reign, Wanli's inaction as a ruler was in clear contrast to the ideal image of a wise and caring emperor.

ECONOMIC PROBLEMS The timing of administrative breakdown in the Ming government was unfortunate, because expanding opportunities for trade led many individuals to circumvent official rules. From the mid-sixteenth century, bands of supposedly Japanese pirates ravaged the Chinese coast. Indeed, the Ming government had difficulties regulating trade with Japan. Japanese missions, often armed and several hundred people strong, looted Chinese coastal villages. Yet, while Ming officials labeled all pirates as Japanese, many of the marauders were in fact Chinese.

Silver. *This seventeenth-century helmet from the Ming (1368–1633) or the Qing dynasties (1644–1911) features steel, gold, silver, and textiles, all of which were vital to the Chinese economy during this century. Silver was especially important, for its large influx from Japan and the Americas led to severe economic problems, political unrest, and the overthrow of Ming dynasty.*

Operating out of the empire's coastal towns, as well as from ports in Japan and Southeast Asia, these maritime adventurers deeply disturbed the Ming authorities. In tough times, the roving gangs terrorized sea-lanes and harbors. In better times, some functioned like mercantile groups: their leaders mingled with elites, foreign trade representatives, and imperial officials. What made these predators so resilient—and their business so lucrative—was their ability to move among the mosaic of East Asian cultures.

Just like in the Islamic empires, the influx of silver from the New World and Japan, while at first stimulating the Chinese economy, led to severe economic (and, eventually, political) dislocations. As noted in Chapter 12, Europeans used New World silver to pay for their purchases of Chinese goods. As a result, by the early seventeenth century silver imports exceeded domestic **bullion** production (uncoined gold or silver) by some twentyfold. Increasing **monetization** of the economy, which entailed silver becoming the primary medium of exchange, bolstered market activity and state revenues at the same time.

Yet the primacy of silver pressured peasants, who now needed that metal to pay their taxes and purchase goods. (See Primary Source: Huang Liuhong on Eliminating Authorized Silversmiths.) When silver supplies were abundant, the peasants faced inflationary prices. When supplies were scant, the peasants could not meet their obligations to state officials and merchants. The frustrated masses thus often seethed with resentment, which quickly turned to rebellion.

Market fluctuations abroad also affected the Chinese economy, introducing new sources of instability. After 1610, Dutch and English assaults on Spanish ships heading to Asia cut down on silver flows into China. Then, in 1639, Japanese authorities clamped down on foreign traders, a move that curbed the outflow of Japanese specie to China. All these blows to the Asian trading system destabilized China's money supply and weakened its economy.

THE COLLAPSE OF MING AUTHORITY By the seventeenth century, the Ming's administrative and economic difficulties were affecting their subjects' daily lives. This was particularly evident when the regime failed to cope with devastation caused by natural disasters, as in the northwestern province of Shaanxi. As the price of grain soared there, the poor and the hungry fanned out to find food by whatever means they could muster. To deal with the crisis, the government imposed heavier taxes and cut the military budget. Bands of dispossessed Chinese peasants and mutinous soldiers then vented their anger at local tax collectors and officials.

Now the cycle of rebellion and weakened central authority that played out in so many other places took its predictable toll. Outlaw armies grew large under charismatic leaders. Numerous

PRIMARY SOURCE

Huang Liuhong on Eliminating Authorized Silversmiths

The influx of silver into China had profound effects on its economy and government. For instance, silver became the medium for assessing taxes. In his magistrate's manual from around 1694, Huang Liuhong (Huang Liu-hung) indicated the problems that arose from involving authorized silversmiths in the payment process. The situation demonstrates how silver had become an integral part of the lives of the Chinese people.

The purpose of using an authorized silversmith in the collection of tax money is twofold. First, the quality of the silver delivered by the taxpayers must be up to standard. The authorized silversmith is expected to reject any substandard silver. Second, when the silver is delivered to the provincial treasury, it should be melted and cast into ingots to avoid theft while in transit. But, to get his commission, the authorized silversmith has to pay a fee and arrange for a guarantor. In addition, he has to pay bribes to the clerks of the revenue section and to absorb the operating expenses of his shop—rent, food, coal, wages for his employees, and so on. If he does not impose a surcharge on the taxpayers, how can he maintain his business?

There are many ways for an authorized silversmith to defraud the taxpayers. First, he can declare that the quality of the silver is not up to standard and a larger amount is required. Second, he can insist that all small pieces of silver have to be melted and cast into ingots; hence there will be wastage in the process of melting. Third, he may demand that all ingots, no matter how small they are, be stamped with his seal, and of course charge a stamping fee. Fourth, he may require a fee for each melting as a legitimate charge for the service. Fifth, he can procrastinate until the taxpayer becomes impatient and is willing to double the melting fee. Last, if the taxpayer seems naive or simple minded, the smith can purposely upset the melting container and put the blame on the taxpayer. All these tricks are prevalent, and little can be done to thwart them.

When the silver ingots are delivered to the provincial treasury, few of them are up to standard. The authorized silversmith often blames the taxpayers for bringing in silver of inferior quality although it would be easy for him to reject them at the time of melting. Powerful official families and audacious licentiates often put poor quality silver in sealed envelopes, which the authorized silversmith is not empowered to examine. Therefore, the use of an authorized silversmith contributes very little to the business of tax collection; it only increases the burden of small taxpayers. . . .

QUESTIONS FOR ANALYSIS

- What are the six ways that an authorized silversmith can defraud taxpayers?
- Why does the author suggest that the use of authorized silversmiths increases the burden of small taxpayers?
- What reasons would the Chinese state have for maintaining such a "flawed" system?

Source: Huang Liu-hung, "Elimination of Authorized Silversmiths" from A Complete Book Concerning Happiness and Benevolence: A Manual for Local Magistrates in Seventeenth Century China, *translated and edited by Djang Chu, pp. 190–91.*

mobile armies—the so-called roving bandits—took shape. The most famous rebel leader, the "dashing prince" Li Zicheng, arrived at the outskirts of Beijing in 1644. Only a few companies of soldiers and a few thousand eunuchs were there to defend the capital's twenty-one miles of walls, so Li Zicheng seized Beijing easily. Two days later, the emperor hanged himself. On the following day, the triumphant "dashing prince" rode into the capital and claimed the throne.

News of the fall of the Ming capital sent shock waves around the empire. One hundred and seventy miles to the northeast, where China meets Manchuria, the army's commander received the news within a matter of days. His task in the area was to defend the Ming against their menacing neighbor, a group that had begun to identify itself as Manchu. Immediately the commander's position became precarious. Caught between an advancing rebel army on the one side and the Manchus on the other, he made a fateful decision: he appealed for the Manchus' cooperation to fight the "dashing prince," promising his new allies that "gold and treasure" awaited them in the capital. Thus, without shedding a drop of blood, the Manchus joined the Ming forces. After years of coveting the Ming Empire, the Manchus were finally on their way to Beijing (see Map 13.5).

THE QING DYNASTY ASSERTS CONTROL Despite their small numbers, the Manchus overcame early resistance to their rule and oversaw an impressive expansion of their realm. The

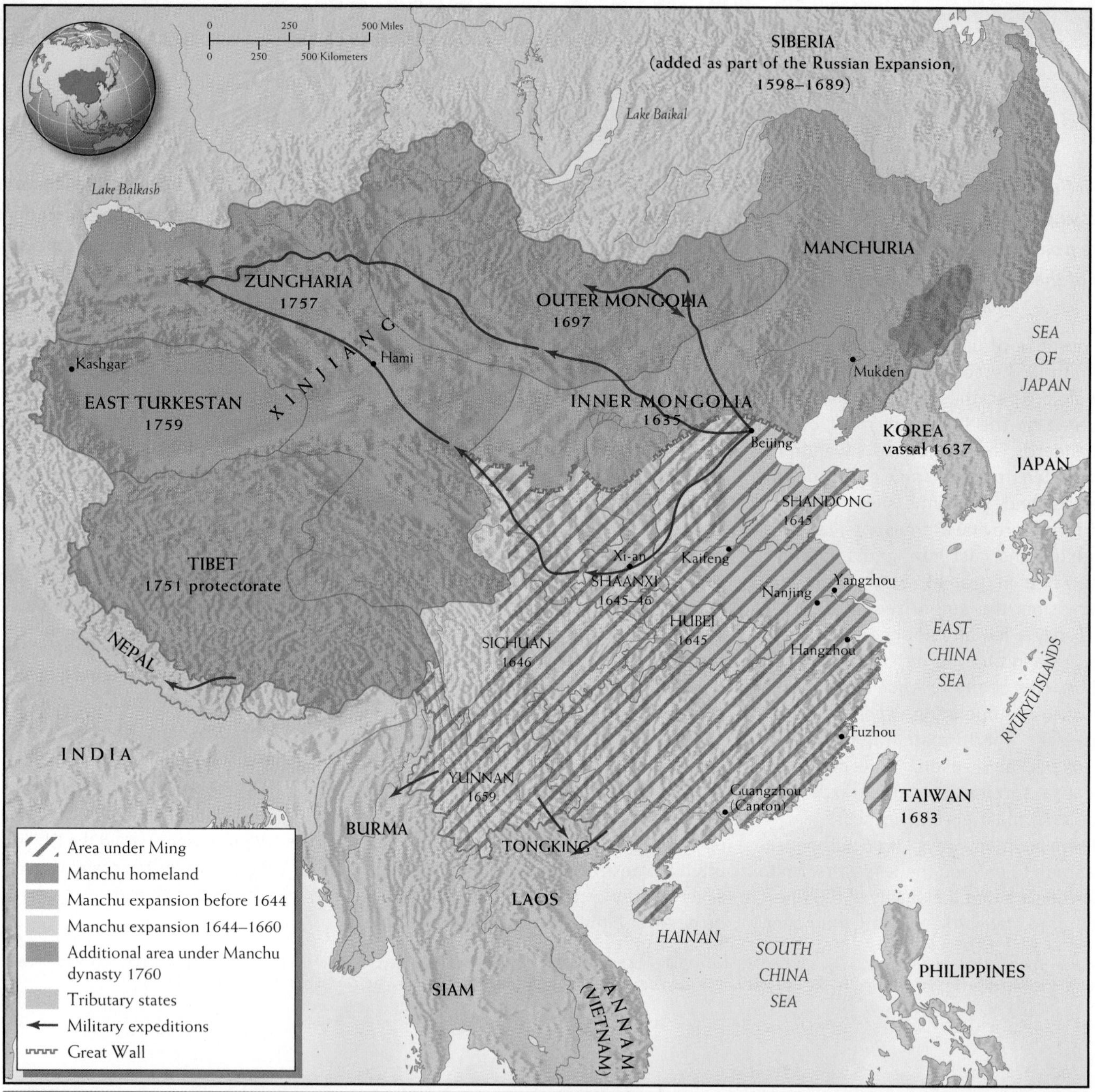

MAP 13.5 | From Ming to Qing China, 1644–1760

Qing China under the Manchus expanded its territory significantly during this period. Find the Manchu homeland and then the area of Manchu expansion after 1644, when the Manchus established the Qing dynasty.

- Where did the Qing dynasty expand?
- Based on the map, why do you think the Qing dynasty expanded so aggressively during this period?
- What does the location of Manchuria tell you about the historical origins of the Qing?

Manchus—the name was first used in 1635—were descendants of the Jurchens (see Chapter 10). They emerged as a force early in the seventeenth century, when their leader claimed the title of khan after securing the allegiance of various Mongol groups in northeastern Asia, paving the way for their eventual conquest of China.

When the Manchus defeated Li Zicheng and seized power in Beijing, they numbered around 1 million. Assuming control of a domain that included perhaps 250 million people, they were keenly aware of their minority status. Taking power was one thing; keeping it was another. But keep it they did. In fact, during the eighteenth century, the Manchu **Qing** ("pure") **dynasty** (1644–1911) incorporated new territories, experienced substantial population growth, and sustained significant economic growth. All this occurred without the kind of economic and political turmoil that rocked the societies of the Atlantic world.

The key to China's relatively stable economic and geographic expansion lay in its rulers' shrewd and flexible policies. The early Manchu emperors were able and diligent administrators. They also knew that to govern a diverse population they had to adapt to local ways. To promote continuity with previous practices, they respected Confucian codes and ethics and kept the classic texts as the basis of the prestigious civil service examinations (see Chapter 9). Social hierarchies of age, gender, and kin—indeed, the entire image of the family as the bedrock of social organization—endured. In some areas, like Taiwan, the Manchus added new territories to existing provinces. Elsewhere, they gave newly acquired territories, like Mongolia, Tibet, and Xinjiang, their own form of local administration. Imperial envoys in these regions administered through staffs of locals and relied on native institutions. Until the late nineteenth century, the Qing dynasty showed little interest in integrating those regions into "China proper."

At the same time, Qing rulers were determined to convey a clear sense of their own majesty and legitimacy. Rulers relentlessly promoted patriarchal values. Widows who remained "chaste" enjoyed public praise, and women in general were urged to lead a "virtuous" life serving male kin and family. To the majority Han population, the Manchu emperor represented himself as the worthy upholder of familial values and classical Chinese civilization; to the Tibetan Buddhists, the Manchu state offered imperial patronage. So, too, with Islamic subjects. Although the Islamic Uighurs, as well as other Muslim subjects, might have disliked the Manchus' easygoing religious attitude, they accepted the emperor's favors and generally endorsed his claim to rule.

However, insinuating themselves into an existing order and appeasing subject peoples did not satisfy the Manchu yearning to leave their imprint. They also introduced measures that emphasized their authority, their distinctiveness, and the submission of their mostly Han Chinese subjects. For example, Qing officials composed or translated important documents into Manchu and banned intermarriage between Manchu and Han (although this was difficult to enforce). Other edicts imposed Manchu ways. For example, the day after the Manchus entered Beijing, a decree required all Han males to follow the Manchu practice of shaving their foreheads and braiding their hair at the back in a queue. Although strong protests led to temporary shelving of the policy, a year later the Manchus reissued the order and gave their subjects the stark choice of shaving their hair or losing their heads. This time, the policy stood firm. In a similar vein, the Qing decreed that Han males adopt Manchu garb: instead of loose Ming-style robes, they had to wear high collars and tight jackets.

Qing Theater with Female Impersonators. *The Qing court banned women from performing in theaters, which led to the practice of using young boys in female roles.*

Nothing earned the regime's disapproval more than the urban elites' conspicuous consumption and indulgence in sensual pleasure. The Qing court regarded the "decadence" of the late Ming, symbolized by its famous actresses, as one of the Ming's principal failings. In 1723 the Qing banned female performers from the court, after which the practice spread to commercial theaters, with young boys taking female roles on stage. The Qing also tried to further regulate commercial theater by excluding women from the audience. The popularity of female impersonators on stage, however, brought a new cachet to homosexual relationships. A gulf began to open between the government's aspirations and its ability to police society. For example, the urban public continued to flock to performances by female impersonators in defiance of the Qing's bans.

Manchu impositions fell mostly on the peasantry, for the Qing financed their administrative structure through taxes on peasant households. In response the peasants sought new lands to cultivate in border areas, often planting New World crops that grew well in difficult soils. This move introduced an important change in Chinese diets: while rice remained the staple diet of the wealthy, peasants increasingly subsisted on corn and sweet potatoes.

EXPANSION AND TRADE UNDER THE QING Despite public disregard for certain imperial edicts, the Qing dynasty enjoyed a heyday during the eighteenth century. It forged tributary relations with Korea, Vietnam, Burma, and Nepal, and its territorial expansion reached far into central Asia, Tibet, and Mongolia. In particular, the Manchus confronted the Junghars of western Mongolia, who controlled much of central Asia in the mid-seventeenth century and whose predecessors had once captured an early Ming emperor. Wary of a potential alliance between the Junghars and an emerging Russia on its northern frontiers, the Qing dynasty launched successive campaigns and dealt a decisive blow to the Junghars by the mid-eighteenth century.

While officials redoubled their reliance on an agrarian base, trade and commerce flourished. Chinese merchants continued to ply the waters stretching from Southeast Asia to Japan, exchanging textiles, ceramics, and medicine for spices and rice. Although the Qing state vacillated about permitting maritime trade with foreigners in its early years, it sought to regulate external commerce more formally as it consolidated its rule. In 1720, in Canton, a group of merchants formed a monopolistic guild to trade with Europeans seeking coveted Chinese goods and peddling their own wares. Although the guild disbanded in the face of opposition from other merchants, it revived after the Qing restricted European trade to Canton. The **Canton system**, officially established by imperial decree in 1759, required European traders to have guild merchants act as guarantors for their good behavior and payment of fees.

Canton. *Not only were foreigners not allowed to trade with the Chinese outside of Canton, but they were also required to have Chinese guild members act as guarantors of their good behavior and payment of fees.*

China, in sum, negotiated a century of upheaval without dismantling established ways in politics and economics. The peasantry continued to practice popular faiths, cultivate crops, and stay close to fields and villages. Trade with the outside world was marginal to overall commercial life; like the Ming, the Qing cared more about the agrarian than the commercial health of the empire, believing the former to be the foundation of prosperity and tranquility. As long as China's peasantry could keep the dynasty's coffers full, the government was content to squeeze the merchants when it needed funds. Some historians view this practice as a failure to adapt to a changing world order, as it ultimately left China vulnerable to outsiders—especially Europeans. But this view puts the historical cart before the horse. By the mid-eighteenth century, Europe still needed China more than the other way around. For the majority of Chinese, no superior model of belief, politics, or economics was conceivable. Indeed, although the Qing had taken over a crumbling empire in 1644, a century later China was enjoying a new level of prosperity.

Tokugawa Japan

Integration with the Asian trading system exposed Japan to new external pressures, even as the islands grappled with internal turmoil. But the Japanese dealt with these pressures more successfully than the mainland Asian empires (Ottoman, Safavid, Mughal, and Ming), which saw political fragmentation and even the overthrow of ruling dynasties. In Japan, a single ruling family emerged. This dynastic state, the **Tokugawa shogunate**, accomplished something that most of the world's other regimes did not: it regulated foreign intrusion. While Japan played a modest role in the expanding global trade, it remained free of outside exploitation.

UNIFICATION OF JAPAN During the sixteenth century, Japan had suffered from political instability as banditry and civil strife disrupted the countryside. Regional ruling families, called *daimyos,* had commanded private armies of warriors known as samurai. The daimyos sometimes brought order to their domains, but no one family could establish preeminence over others. Although Japan had an emperor, his authority did not extend beyond the court in Kyoto.

Ultimately, several military leaders attempted to unify Japan. One general, who became the supreme minister, arranged marriages among the children of local authorities to solidify political bonds. Also, to coax cooperation from the daimyos, he ordered that their wives and children be kept as semihostages in the residences they were required to maintain in Edo. After the general died, one of the daimyos, Tokugawa Ieyasu, took power for himself. This was a decisive moment. In 1603, Ieyasu assumed the title of shogun (military ruler). He also solved the problem of succession, declaring that rulership would be hereditary and that his family would be the ruling household. This hereditary Tokugawa shogunate lasted until 1867.

Now administrative authority shifted from Kyoto to the site of Ieyasu's domain headquarters: the castle town called Edo (later renamed Tokyo; see Map 13.6). The Tokugawa built Edo out of a small earthen fortification clinging to a coastal bluff. Behind Edo lay a village in a swampy plain. In a monumental work of engineering, the rulers ordered the swamp drained, the forest cleared, many of the hills leveled, canals dredged, bridges built, the seashore extended by landfill, and a new stone castle completed. By the time Ieyasu died, Edo had a population of 150,000.

The Tokugawa shoguns ensured a flow of resources from the working population to the rulers and from the provinces to the capital. Villages paid taxes to the daimyos, who transferred resources to the seat of shogunate authority. No longer engaged in constant warfare, the samurai became administrators. Peace brought prosperity. Agriculture thrived. Improved farming techniques and land reclamation projects enabled the country's population to grow from 10 million in 1550 to 16 million in 1600 and 30 million in 1700.

FOREIGN AFFAIRS AND FOREIGNERS Internal peace and prosperity did not insulate Japan from external challenges. When Japanese rulers tackled foreign affairs, their most pressing concern was the intrusion of Christian missionaries and European traders. Initially, Japanese officials welcomed these foreigners out of an eagerness to acquire muskets, gunpowder, and other new technology. But once the ranks of Christian converts swelled, Japanese authorities realized that Christians were intolerant of other faiths, believed Christ to be superior to any authority, and fought among themselves. Trying to stem the tide, the shoguns prohibited conversion to Christianity and attempted to ban its practice. After a rebellion in which converted peasants rose up in protest against high rents and taxes,

Edo in the Rain. *This facsimile of an* ukiyo-e *("floating world") print by Hiroshige (1797–1858) depicts one of several bridges in the bustling city of Edo (later Tokyo), with Mount Fuji in the background.*

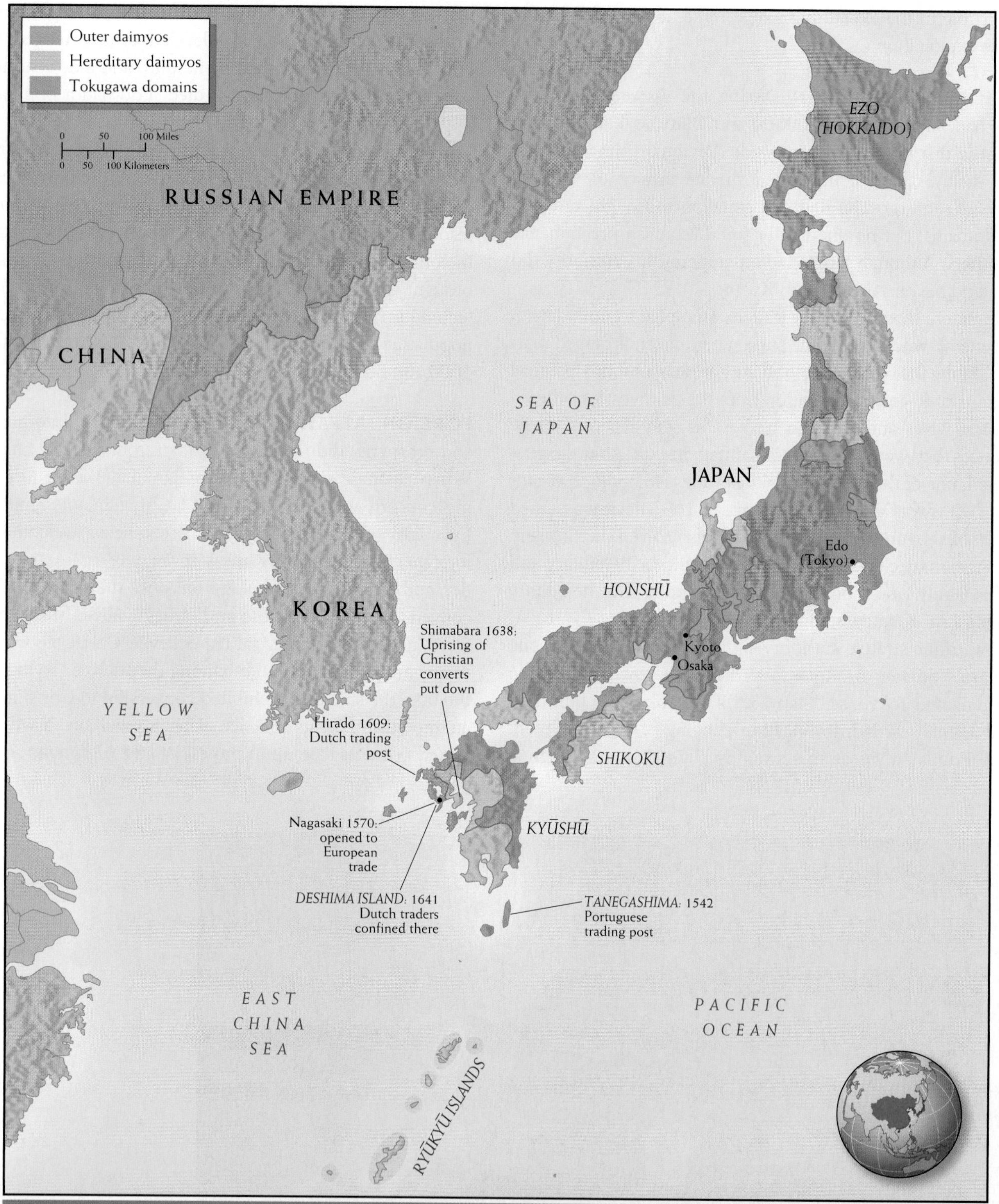

MAP 13.6 | Tokugawa Japan, 1603-1867

The Tokugawa shoguns created a strong central state in Japan at this time.

- According to this map, how extensive was their control?
- What foreign states were interested in trade with Japan?
- How did Tokugawa leaders attempt to control relations with foreign states and other entities?

Portuguese Arriving in Japan. *In the 1540s, the Portuguese arrival on the islands of Japan sparked a fascination with the strange costumes and the great ships of these "southern barbarians" (so called because they had approached Japan from the south). Silk-screen paintings depicted Portuguese prowess in exaggerated form, such as in the impossible height of the fore and aft of the vessel pictured here.*

the government suppressed Christianity and drove European missionaries from the country.

Even more troublesome was the lure of trade with Europeans. The Tokugawa knew that trading at various Japanese ports would pull the commercial regions in various directions, away from the capital. When it became clear that European traders preferred the ports of Kyūshū (the southernmost island), the shogunate restricted Europeans to trade only in ports under Edo's direct rule in Honshū. Then, Japanese authorities expelled all European competitors. Only the Protestant (and nonmissionizing) Dutch won permission to remain in Japan, confined to an island near Nagasaki. The Dutch were allowed to unload just one ship each year, under strict supervision by Japanese authorities.

These measures did not close Tokugawa Japan to the outside world, however. Trade with China and Korea flourished, and the shogun received missions from Korea and the Ryūkyū islands. Edo also gathered information about the outside world from the resident Dutch and Chinese (who included monks, physicians, and painters). A few Japanese were permitted to learn Dutch and to study European technology, shipbuilding, and medicine (see Chapter 14). By limiting such encounters, the authorities ensured that foreigners would not threaten Japan's security.

Ruling over three islands, Tokugawa Japan was surrounded by "vassals" that were neither part of the realm nor entirely independent. Most important were the Ryūkyūs in the south and the island of Ezo to the north, which the Japanese maintained as buffers. Such areas helped define a distinct Japanese identity for all peoples living "on the inside." When, beginning in 1697, the Russians approached Japan to open relations, the Japanese instead sought to deal with them through the northern buffer zone. As the Russians tried harder to open Japan to trade, the Japanese annexed and began to colonize Ezo (what would eventually be called Hokkaidō), the country's fourth main island and a strong barrier to foreign penetration. In regulating outside contacts, Japanese rulers suppressed potential sources of upheaval and consolidated a dynasty that lasted well into the nineteenth century.

The rulers of Japan invented an approach to relations with the outside world on Japanese terms. They permitted trade and diplomatic relations with the Dutch, Chinese, and Koreans, but in a controlled fashion, and they generally did not permit such relations with the Russians or Christian missionaries. In this, the Japanese were aided by their island status, which had also protected them from the Mongols.

TRANSFORMATIONS IN EUROPE

Between 1600 and 1750, religious conflict, commercial expansion, and the consolidation of dynastic power transformed Europe. Commercial centers shifted northward, and Spain and Portugal lost ground to England and France. Even farther to the north, the state of Muscovy expanded dramatically to become the sprawling Russian Empire.

Expansion and Dynastic Change in Russia

During this period the Russian Empire expanded to become the world's largest-ever state. It gained positions on the Baltic Sea and the Pacific Ocean, and it established political borders with both the Qing Empire and Japan. These momentous shifts involved the elimination of steppe nomads as an independent force. Culturally, Europeans as well as Russians debated whether Russia belonged more to Europe or to Asia. The answer was both.

MAP 13.7 | Russian Expansion, 1462-1795

The state of Muscovy incorporated vast territories through overland expansion as it grew and became the Russian Empire. It did so in part because of its geographical position and its strategic needs.

- Using the map key, identify how many different expansions the Russian Empire underwent between 1462 and 1795 and in what directions generally.
- With what countries and cultures did the Russian Empire come into contact?
- What drove such dramatic expansion?

MUSCOVY BECOMES THE RUSSIAN EMPIRE The principality of Moscow, or Muscovy, like Japan and China, used territorial expansion and commercial networks to consolidate a powerful state. This was the Russian Empire, the name given to Muscovy by Tsar Peter the Great around 1700. Originally a mixture of Slavs, Finnish tribes, Turkic speakers, and many others, **Muscovy** expanded to become a huge empire that spanned parts of Europe, much of northern Asia, numerous North Pacific islands, and even—for a time—a corner of North America (Alaska).

Like Japan, Russia emerged out of turmoil. Three factors inspired the regime to seize territory: security concerns; the ambitions of private individuals; and religious conviction. Security concerns were foremost, as expansion was inseparable from security. Because the steppe, which stretches deep into Asia, remained a highway for nomadic peoples (especially descendants of the powerful Mongols), Muscovy sought to dominate the areas south and east of Moscow. By marrying the niece of the last Byzantine emperor, the Muscovite grand prince Ivan III (r. 1462–1505) added a religious dimension to his expansionist claims: he could assert that Moscow was the center of the Byzantine faith and heir to the conquered city of Constantinople. Later expansion secured Muscovy's eastern borders by reaching into Siberia. Beginning in the 1590s, Russian authorities built forts and trading posts along Siberian rivers at the same time that privateers, enticed by the fur trade, pushed even farther east. By 1639 the state's borders had reached the Pacific. Thus in just over a century, Muscovy had claimed an empire straddling Eurasia and incorporating peoples of many languages and religions (see Map 13.7).

Much of this expansion occurred despite dynastic chaos that followed the death of Ivan IV in 1584. Ultimately a group of prominent families reestablished central authority and threw their weight behind a new family of rulers. These were the Romanovs, court barons who set about reviving the Kremlin's fortunes. (The Kremlin was a medieval walled fortress where the Muscovite grand princes—later, tsars—resided.) Like the Ottoman and Qing dynasts, Romanov tsars and their aristocratic supporters would retain power into the twentieth century.

Catherine the Great. *Catherine the Great styled herself an enlightened despot of the baroque epoch, furthering the Russian Empire's adaptation of European high culture.*

ABSOLUTIST GOVERNMENT AND SERFDOM In the seventeenth and eighteenth centuries, the Romanovs created an absolutist system of government. Only the tsar and his retinue had the right to make war, tax, judge, and coin money. The Romanovs also made the nobles serve as state officials. Now Russia became a despotic state that had no political assemblies for nobles or other groups, other than mere consultative bodies like the imperial senate. Indeed, away from Moscow, local aristocrats enjoyed nearly unlimited authority in exchange for loyalty and tribute to the tsar.

During this period, Russia's peasantry bore the burden of maintaining the wealth of the small nobility and the monarchy. Most peasant families gathered into communes, isolated rural worlds where people helped one another deal with the harsh climate, severe landlords, and occasional poor harvests. Communes functioned like extended kin networks in that members reciprocated favors and chores. The typical peasant hut was a single chamber heated by a wood-burning stove with no chimney. Livestock and humans often shared the same quarters. In 1649, peasants were legally bound as serfs to the nobles and the tsar, meaning they had to perform obligatory services and deliver part of their produce to their lords. In fact, the lords essentially controlled all aspects of their serfs' lives.

Nenets Hunters. *Hunters of the Nenets tribe in far North Asia's treeless tundra, show off their warm animal-skin clothing and self-fashioned weapons, as depicted in a 1620 engraving by Theodore de Bry, one of the first Europeans to come into contact with them.*

IMPERIAL EXPANSION AND MIGRATION Three factors were key to Russia's becoming an empire: (1) the conquest of Siberia, which brought vast territory and riches in furs; (2) incorporation of the fertile southern steppes, known as Ukraine; and (3) victory in a prolonged war with Sweden. Peter the Great (r. 1682–1725) accomplished the victory in Sweden, after which he founded a new capital at St. Petersburg. Yet even as he triumphed over Sweden he sought to imitate a Swedish-style bureaucracy in Russia. Thereafter Russia developed a formidable military-fiscal state bureaucracy, but the aristocracy, not the civil service, remained predominant.

Under Peter's successors, including the hard-nosed Catherine the Great, Russia added even more territory. Catherine placed her former lover on the Polish throne and subsequently, together with the Austrians and Prussians, carved up the medieval state of Poland. Her victories against the Ottomans allowed Russia to annex Ukraine, the grain-growing "breadbasket" of eastern Europe. By the late eighteenth century, Russia's grasp extended from the Baltic Sea through the heart of Europe, Ukraine, and the Crimea on the Black Sea and into the ancient lands of Armenia and Georgia in the Caucasus Mountains.

The Russian Empire was a harsh but colossal space that induced the movement of peoples within it. Many people migrated eastward, into Siberia. Some were fleeing serfdom; others were being deported for having rejected changes in the state's official Eastern Orthodox religious services. Battling astoundingly harsh temperatures (falling to –40 degrees Centigrade/Fahrenheit) and frigid Arctic winds, these individuals traveled on horseback and trudged on foot to resettle in the east. But the difficulties of clearing forested lands or planting crops in boggy Siberian soils, combined with extraordinarily harsh winters, meant that many settlers died or tried to return. Isolation was a problem, too. There was no established land route back to Moscow until the 1770s, when exiles completed the Great Siberian Post Road through the swamps and peat bogs of western Siberia. The writer Anton Chekhov later called it "the longest and ugliest road in the whole world."

Whereas initially over 90 percent of Siberia's inhabitants were natives, by 1750 the number of immigrants almost matched the native population and soon surpassed it. Although many of the immigrants were runaway serfs, others who were religious or political outcasts would later make Siberia infamous as a land for prisoners instead of a destination of freedom. "The road to Siberia is wide," went the saying, "the way back, narrow."

Economic and Political Fluctuations in Western Europe

During this period European economies became more commercialized, especially after recovering from the Thirty Years' War. As in Asia, developments in distant parts of the world shaped the region's economic upturns and downturns. Compounding these pressures was the continuation of dynastic rivalries and religious conflicts.

THE THIRTY YEARS' WAR For a century after Martin Luther broke with the Catholic Church (see Chapter 12), religious warfare raged in Europe. So did contests over territory, power, and trade. The **Thirty Years' War** (1618–1648) was all three of these—a war between Protestant princes and the Catholic emperor for religious predominance in central Europe; a struggle for regional control among Catholic powers (the Spanish and Austrian Habsburgs and the French); and a bid for independence (from Spain) by the Dutch, who wanted to trade and worship as they liked.

The brutal conflict began as a struggle between Protestants and Catholics within the Habsburg Empire, but it soon became a war for preeminence in Europe. It took the lives of civilians as well as soldiers. Just when it seemed as if Protestantism would vanish from central Europe, the Swedish king made a timely intervention, reenergizing the Protestant cause. In the course of a war fought heavily by ill-paid and poorly fed mercenaries, both sides committed many atrocities against civilians. Most famously, in 1631, Catholic forces besieged and then destroyed the beautiful German town of Magdeburg, killing three-quarters of the civilian inhabitants. In total, fighting, disease, and famine wiped out a third of the German states' urban population and two-fifths of their rural population. The war also depopulated Sweden and Poland. Ultimately the Treaty of Westphalia (1648) stated, in essence, that as there was a rough balance of power between Protestant and Catholic states, they would simply have to put up with each other. The Dutch won their independence, but the war's enormous costs provoked severe discontent in Spain, France, and England. Central Europe was so devastated that it did

The Thirty Years' War. *The mercenary armies of the Thirty Years' War were renowned for pillaging and tormenting the civilians of central Europe. Here, the townsfolk exact revenge on some of these soldiers, hanging, as the engraving's caption claims, "damned and infamous thieves, like bad fruit, from this tree."*

Amsterdam Stock Exchange. *The high concentration of deeply religious merchants in Amsterdam naturally gave way to the world's first stock exchange in the seventeenth century. This diverse gathering of men trading stocks and preparing to participate in auctions, as depicted by renowned painter Emanuel de Witte, was a common sight throughout the Dutch Golden Age.*

not recover in economic or demographic terms for more than a century.

The Thirty Years' War transformed war making. Whereas most medieval struggles had been sieges between nobles leading small armies, centralized states fielding standing armies now waged decisive, grand-scale campaigns. The war also changed the ranks of soldiers: as the conflict ground on, local enlisted men defending their king, country, and faith gave way to hired mercenaries or criminals doing forced service. Even officers, who previously obtained their stripes by purchase or royal decree, now had to earn them. Gunpowder, cannons, and handguns became standardized. By the eighteenth century, Europe's wars featured huge standing armies boasting a professional officer corps, deadly artillery, and long supply lines bringing food and ammunition to the front. The costs—material and human—of war began to soar.

WESTERN EUROPEAN ECONOMIES In spite of the toll that warfare took on economic activity, the European states enjoyed significant commercial expansion. Northern Europe gained more than did the south, however. Spain, for example, started losing ground to its rivals as the costs of defending its empire soared and merchants from northern Europe cut in on its trading networks. The weighty costs of its involvement in the Thirty Years' War dealt the Spanish economy a final, disastrous blow. Other previously robust economies also suffered under the pressures of greater economic connection and competition. Venice, for example, which before the era of transoceanic shipping had been Europe's chief gateway to Asia, saw its economy decline.

As European commercial dynamism shifted northward, the Dutch led the way with innovative commercial practices and a new mercantile elite. They specialized in shipping and in financing regional and long-distance trade. Their famous *fluitschips* carried heavy, bulky cargoes (like Baltic wood) with relatively small crews. Now shipping costs throughout the Atlantic world dropped as Dutch ships transported their own and other countries' goods. Amsterdam's merchants founded an exchange bank, established a rudimentary stock exchange, and pioneered systems of underwriting and insuring cargoes. As Europe's other mercantile centers followed suit, the Dutch share of commercial activity eventually shrank. But their pioneering ways set an early example for trading and financing practices that further integrated the Atlantic economies.

England and France also became commercial powerhouses, establishing aggressive policies to promote national business and drive out competitors. Consider the English Navigation Act of 1651. By stipulating that only English ships could carry goods between the mother country and its colonies, it protected English shippers and merchants—especially from the Dutch. The English

Versailles. *Louis XIV's Versailles, just southwest of Paris, was a hunting lodge that was converted at colossal cost in the 1670s–1680s into a grand royal chateau with expansive grounds. Much envied and imitated across Europe, the palace became the epicenter of a luxurious court life that included entertainment such as plays and musical offerings, state receptions, royal hunts, boating, and gambling. Thousands of nobles at Versailles vied with each other for closer proximity to the king in the performance of court rituals.*

subsequently launched several effective trade wars against Holland. The French, too, followed aggressive mercantilist policies and ultimately joined forces with England to invade Holland.

Economic development was not limited to port towns: the countryside, too, enjoyed breakthroughs in production. Most important was expansion in the production of food. In northwestern Europe investments in water drainage, larger livestock herds, and improved cultivation practices generated much greater yields. Also, a four-field crop rotation involving wheat, clover, barley, and turnips kept nutrients in the soil and provided year-round fodder for livestock. As a result (and as we have seen many times throughout history), increased output supported a growing urban population. By contrast, in Spain and Italy, agricultural change and population growth came more slowly.

Production rose most where the organization of rural property changed. Consider again the transformation that occurred in England. Here, in a movement known as **enclosure**, landowners took control of lands that traditionally had been common property serving local needs. Claiming exclusive rights to these lands, the landowners planted new crops or pastured sheep with the aim of selling the products in distant markets—especially cities. The largest landowners put their farms in the hands of tenants, who hired wage laborers to till, plant, and harvest. Thus, in England, peasant agriculture gave way to farms run by wealthy families who exploited the marketplace to buy what they needed (including labor) and to sell what they produced. In this regard, England led the way in a Europe-wide process of commercializing the countryside.

DYNASTIC MONARCHIES: FRANCE AND ENGLAND

European monarchs had varying success with centralizing state power. In France, Louis XIII (r. 1610–1643) and especially his

Queen Elizabeth of England. *This portrait (c. 1600) depicts an idealized Queen Elizabeth near the end of her long reign. The queen is pictured riding in a procession in the midst of an admiring crowd composed of the most important nobles of the realm.*

chief minister, Cardinal Richelieu, concentrated power in the hands of the king. Under his successor, the Bourbon family established a monarchy in which succession passed to the oldest male in the male line. After 1614, kings refused to convene the Estates-General, a medieval advisory body. Composed of representatives of three groups—the clergy (the First Estate, those who pray), the nobility (the Second Estate, those who fight), and the unprivileged remainder of the population (the Third Estate, those who work)—the Estates-General was an obstacle to the king's full empowerment. Instead of sharing power, the king and his counselors wanted him to rule free of external checks, to create in the words of the age an **absolute monarchy.** The ruler was not to be a tyrant, but his authority was to be complete and thorough, and his state free of bloody disorders. The king's rule would be lawful; but he, not his jurists, would dictate the last legal word. If the king made a mistake, only God could call him to account. Thus the Europeans believed in the "divine right of kings," a political belief not greatly different from imperial China where the emperor was thought to rule with the mandate of heaven.

In absolutist France, privileges and state offices flowed from the king's grace. All patronage networks ultimately linked to the king. The great palace Louis XIV built at Versailles teemed with nobles from all over France seeking favor, dressing according to the king's expensive fashion code, and attending the latest tragedies, comedies, and concerts. Just as the Japanese shogun monitored the daimyos by keeping their families in Edo, Louis XIV kept a watchful eye on the French nobility at Versailles.

The French dynastic monarchy provided a model of absolute rule for other European dynasts, like the Habsburgs of the Holy Roman Empire, the Hohenzollerns of Prussia, and the Romanovs of Muscovy. The king and his ministers controlled all public power, while other social groups, from the nobility to the peasantry, had no formal body to represent their interests. Nonetheless, French absolutist government was not as absolute as the king would have wished. Pockets of stalwart Protestants practiced their religion secretly in the plateau villages of central France. Peasant disturbances continued. Criticism of court life, wars, and religious policies filled anonymous pamphlets, jurists' notebooks, and courtiers' private journals. Members of the nobility also grumbled about their political misfortunes, but since the king would not call the Estates-General, they had no formal way to express their concerns.

England might also have evolved into an absolutist regime, but there were important differences between England and France. Queen Elizabeth (r. 1558–1603) and her successors used many policies similar to those of the French monarchy, such as control of patronage (to grant privileges) and elaborate court festivities. Also, refusing to share her power with a man, the "Virgin Queen" never married and exerted sole control over the church, military, and aristocracy. However, not only did the English system of succession allow women to rule as queens in their own right, but the English Parliament remained an important force. Whereas the French kings did not need the consent of the Estates-General to enact taxes, the English monarchs had to convene Parliament to raise money.

Under Elizabeth's successors, fierce quarrels broke out over taxation, religion, and royal efforts to rule without parliamentary consent. Tensions ran high between Puritans (who preferred a simpler form of worship and more egalitarian church government) and Anglicans (who supported the state-sponsored, hierarchically organized Church of England headed by the king). Social and economic grievances led to civil war in the 1640s and an ultimate victory for the parliamentary army (largely Puritan)—and the beheading of King Charles I. Twelve years of government as a commonwealth without a king followed. During that time the middle and lower classes enjoyed political and religious power, but the commonwealth became a military dictatorship.

In 1660 the monarchy was restored, but without resolving issues of religious tolerance and the king's relation to Parliament. Charles II and his successor, James II, aroused opposition by their autocracy and secret efforts to bring England back into the Catholic fold. The conflict between an aspiring absolutist throne and Parliament's insistence on shared sovereignty and Protestant succession culminated in the Glorious Revolution of 1688–1689. In a bloodless upheaval, James II fled to France and Parliament offered the crown to William of Orange and his wife, Mary (a Protestant). The outcome of the conflict established the principle that English monarchs must rule in conjunction with Parliament. Although the Church of England was reaffirmed as the official state church, Presbyterians and Jews were allowed to practice their religions. Catholic worship, still officially forbidden, was tolerated as long as the Catholics kept quiet. By 1700, then, England's nobility and merchant classes had a guaranteed say in public affairs and assurance that state activity would privilege the propertied classes as well as the ruler.

Events in France and England stimulated much political writing. In England, Thomas Hobbes published *Leviathan* (1651), a defense of the state's absolute power over all competing forces. John Locke published *Two Treatises of Civil Government* (1689), which argued not only for the natural rights to liberty and property but also for the rights of peoples to form a government and then to disband and reform it when it did not live up to its contract. French theorists also proposed new ways of conducting politics and making law. As writers discussed the costs of unchecked state power, they differed over the extent to which elites could check the king. As the eighteenth century unfolded, the question of where sovereignty lay grew more pressing.

MERCANTILIST WARS The rise of new powers in Europe, especially France and England, intensified rivalries for control of the Atlantic system. As conflicts over colonies and sea-lanes replaced earlier religious and territorial struggles, commercial struggles became worldwide wars. Across the globe, European empires constantly skirmished over control of trade and territory. English and Dutch trading companies took aim at Portuguese outposts in Asia and the Americas, and then at each other. Ports in India suffered repeated assaults and counterassaults. In response, European powers built huge navies to protect their colonies and trade routes and to attack their rivals.

Smuggling became rampant. English and French traders, sometimes backed by political authorities, violated the sovereign claims of rival colonies. Curaçao, for instance, became an entrepôt for traders from England and the Low Countries selling illegal goods in South America (see Map 13.1). French and English traders set up shop in southern Brazil to smuggle goods in return for Andean silver. All around the Gulf of Mexico and the Caribbean, merchants sneaked their goods into enemies' colonies.

After 1715, mercantilist wars occurred mainly outside Europe, as empires feuded over colonial possessions. These conflicts were especially bitter in border areas, particularly in the Caribbean and North America. Each round of warfare ratcheted up the scale and cost of fighting.

The **Seven Years' War** (known as the French and Indian War in the United States) marked the culmination of this rivalry among European empires around the globe. Fought from 1756 to 1763, it saw Native Americans, African slaves, Bengali princes, Filipino militiamen, and European foot soldiers dragged into a contest over imperial possessions and control of the seas. Some fleets, like the French at the Battle of Quiberon Bay, were dispatched to the bottom of the ocean. Some fortresses, like Spain's Havana, and Quebec City fell to invaders. The battles in Europe were relatively indecisive (despite being large), except in the hinterlands. After all, what sparked the war was a skirmish of British colonial troops (featuring a lieutenant colonel named George Washington) allied with Seneca warriors against French soldiers in the Ohio Valley (see Map 13.2 for North American references). In India, the war had a decisive outcome, for here the East India Company trader Robert Clive rallied 850 European officers and 2,100 Indian recruits to defeat the French (there were but 40 French artillerymen) and their 50,000 Maratha allies at Plassey. The British seized the upper hand—over everyone—in India. Not only did the British drive off the French from the rich Bengali interior, but they also crippled Indian rulers' resistance against European intruders (see Map 12.4 for India references).

The Seven Years' War changed the balance of power around the world. Britain emerged as the foremost colonial empire. Its rivals, especially France and Spain, took a pounding; France lost its North American colonies, and Spain lost Florida (though it gained the Louisiana Territory west of the Mississippi in a secret deal with France). In India, as well, the French were losers and had to acknowledge British supremacy in the wealthy provinces of Bihar and Bengal. But overwhelmingly, the biggest losers were indigenous peoples everywhere. With the rise of one empire over all others, it was harder for Native Americans to play the Europeans off against each other. Maratha princes faced the same problem. Clearly, as worlds became more entangled, the gaps between winners and losers grew more pronounced.

CONCLUSION

In the 1750s, the world's regions were more economically connected than they had been a century and a half earlier. The process of integrating the resources of previous worlds apart that had begun with Christopher Columbus's voyages intensified during this period. Traders shipped a wider variety of commodities—from Baltic wood to Indian cotton, from New World silver and sugar to Chinese silks and porcelain—over longer distances. People increasingly wore clothes manufactured elsewhere, consumed beverages made from products cultivated in far-off locations, and used imported guns to settle local conflicts.

Everywhere, this integration and the consumer opportunities that it made possible came at a heavy price. Nowhere was it more costly than in the Americas, where colonization and exploitation led to the expulsion of Indians from their lands and the decimation of their numbers. The cost was also very high for the millions of Africans forced across the Atlantic to work New World plantations and for the millions more who did not survive the journey.

Along with sugar, silver was the product from the Americas that most transformed global trading networks and that showed how greater entanglements could both enrich and destabilize. Although Spanish colonizers mined New World silver and shipped it to western Europe and Asia, it was Spain's main competitors in Europe that gained the upper hand in the seventeenth and eighteenth centuries. Nearly one-third of the silver from the New World ended up in China as payment for products like porcelains and silks that consumers still regarded as the world's finest manufactures. But if China's economy remained vibrant, silver did play a part in the fall of one dynasty and the rise of another. For the Ottoman, Mughal, and Safavid empires, the influx of silver created rampant inflation and undermined their previous economic autonomy.

Certain societies coped with increased commercial exchange more successfully than others. The Safavid and Ming dynasties could not withstand the pressures; both collapsed. The Spanish, Ottoman, and Mughal dynasties managed to survive but faced increasing pressure from aggressive rivals. For newcomers to the integrating world, the opportunity to trade helped support new dynasties. Japan, Russia, and England emerged on the world stage. But even in these newer regimes, commerce and competition did not erase conflict. To the contrary, while the world was more together economically than ever before, greater prosperity for some hardly translated into peace for most.

TRACING THE GLOBAL STORYLINES

AFTER YOU READ THIS CHAPTER

FOCUS ON: *The Regional Impact of World Trade*

The Americas

- England, France, and Holland join Spain and Portugal as colonial powers in the Americas.
- The English and French colonies in the Caribbean become the world's major exporters of sugar.

Africa

- The Atlantic slave trade increases to record proportions, creating gender imbalances, impoverishing some regions, and elevating the power of slave-supplying states.

Southeast Asia

- The Dutch East India Company takes over the major islands of Southeast Asia.

Islam

- World trade destabilizes the economies of the Safavid, Ottoman, and Mughal empires.

East Asia

- The Ming dynasty in China loses the mandate of heaven and is replaced by the Qing.
- The Tokugawa shogunate unifies Japan and limits the influence of Europeans in the country.

Europe

- Tsarist Russia expands toward the Baltic Sea and the Pacific Ocean and becomes the largest state in the world.
- Europe recovers from thirty years of political and religious warfare (1618–1648), with Holland, England, and France emerging as economic powerhouses.

Review and research materials on STUDYSPACE: wwnorton.com/studyspace

CHRONOLOGY

The Americas

Africa — Massive expansion of Atlantic slave trade

South Asia — Aurangzeb's expansion weakens the Mughal dynasty **1658–1707**

East Asia — Tokugawa shogunate formed in Japan **1603**; Ming dynasty falls, Qing dynasty founded **1644**

Europe — Thirty Years' War **1618–1648**; England, France, Netherlands pursue mercantilist expansion abroad

The Islamic World

Russia — Romanov dynasty founded **1613**

1600 — 1650

KEY TERMS

absolute monarchy p. 513
bullion p. 500
Canton system p. 504
chartered companies p. 482
enclosure p. 512
Mamluks p. 497
Manchus p. 502
mercantilism p. 482
monetization p. 500
Muscovy p. 508
Qing dynasty p. 503
Seven Years' War p. 514
specie p. 498
Thirty Years' War p. 510
Tokugawa shogunate p. 504

STUDY QUESTIONS

1. **Define** mercantilism, and analyze how mercantilist practices affected all regions of the Atlantic world between 1600 and 1750.
2. **Describe** the plantation complex in the Caribbean. Why was it so valued by Europeans relative to other regions of the Americas?
3. **Analyze** how the Atlantic slave trade reshaped sub-Saharan African societies. Which regions and groups benefited from Africa's growing entanglements in global commerce?
4. **Analyze** how global trade affected the Ottoman and Mughal empires during this era. How did each regime respond to these growing entanglements?
5. **List and describe** major factors that caused the end of the Ming dynasty and the rise of the Qing dynasty in China. How did global trade affect this outcome? How did Qing rulers react to global commerce?
6. **Analyze** to what extent the Tokugawa shogunate succeeded in creating a strong central government in Japan. How did it avoid the problems associated with expanding trade that many other dynasties faced at this time?
7. **Compare and contrast** the expansionist policies of the Russian state with those pursued by the British and French regimes during this period. How were they similar and how were they different?
8. **Analyze** how increased global trade shaped the history of Europe during this period. Why did England tend to be the largest beneficiary of these trends in terms of regional dynastic rivalries? What other social and political groups were strongly affected by Europe's increased global entanglements?
9. **Compare and contrast** the impact of global commerce on European and Asian dynasties. Did any dynasty hold an advantage over others in controlling commercial networks and using them to enrich their societies?

Sugar complex emerges in the Caribbean region **17th century**
French and Dutch merchants establish fur trade in North America **17th century**
British defeat French forces in North America during the Seven Years' War **1754–1761**

Asante state founded **1701**
Expansion of Oyo state **17th century**

British assume control of French interests in South Asia during Seven Years' War **1756–1763**

Seven Years' War **1756–1763**

Koprulu reforms stabilize Ottoman Empire **mid-17th century**
Safavid dynasty collapses **1773**

Expansion into Siberia **17th century**
Peter the Great reigns **1682–1725**

1700 **1750**

BEFORE YOU READ THIS CHAPTER

wwnorton.com/
STUDYSPACE

GLOBAL STORYLINES

- Growing global commerce enriches and shapes cultures worldwide.
- The major regions demonstrate pride in their traditions and celebrate political, economic, and cultural achievements.
- Europeans and peoples of European descent in the Americas argue that their races and cultures are superior to all others.

CHAPTER OUTLINE

14

Cultures of Splendor and Power, 1500–1780

FOCUS QUESTIONS

- How did increased wealth and new patterns of exchange affect cultures around the world between 1600 and 1750?
- Which groups of people tended to benefit from the global cultural renaissance of this age and which did not?
- To what extent were Islamic, South Asian, and East Asian leaders open to outside cultural influence?
- How did aboriginal peoples in the Americas and Oceania respond to European cultural imperialism?
- How did the cultural developments affect women in this era?

In 1664, a sixteen-year-old girl from the provinces of New Spain asked her parents for permission to attend the university in the capital. Although she had mastered Greek logic, taught Latin, and become a proficient mathematician, she had two strikes against her: she was a woman, and her thinking ran against the grain of the Catholic Church. So keen was she to pursue her studies that she proposed to disguise herself as a man. But her parents denied her requests, and instead of attending the university she entered a convent in Mexico City, where she would spend the rest of her life. Fortunately, the convent turned out to be a sanctuary for her. There she studied science and mathematics and composed remarkable poetry. Sor (Sister) Juana Inés de la Cruz was her name, and she was the bard of a new world where people mixed in faraway places, where new wealth created new customs, and where new ideas began to take hold. One of her poems, called "You Men," began: "Silly, you men—so very adept / at wrongly faulting womankind, not seeing you're alone to blame / for faults you plant in woman's mind." Her poetry is an example of how new discoveries and new knowledge challenged old ways. But her life story also reminds us of the fierce resistance to new ways. Sor Juana's poetry enraged church authorities, who forced her to recant her words and who burned her books. Only the intervention of the viceroy's wife prevented officials from torching the nun's complete works before she died of a plague in 1695.

Sor Juana's story attests to the conflicts between new ideas and old orders that occurred once the entanglements of commerce and the consolidation of empires fostered knowledge of foreign ways. On the one hand, global commerce created riches that supported arts, architecture, and scientific ventures. On the other, experimentations in new ways caused discomfort among defenders of the old order and provoked attempts to subdue and silence purveyors of innovation.

This chapter explores how global commerce enriched and reshaped cultures in the centuries after the Americas ceased to be worlds apart from Afro-Eurasia. Profiting from trade in New World commodities, many rulers and merchants displayed their power by commissioning fabulous works of art and majestic palaces and sprawling plazas. These cultural splendors were meant to impress, which they surely did. These efforts also demonstrated the growing connections between distant societies, reflecting how exotic, borrowed influences could blend with domestic traditions. Book production and consumption soared with some publications finding their way around the world. The spread of books and ideas and increasing cultural contact led to experiments in religious toleration and helped foster cultural diversity. Yet even as Europeans, who were the greatest beneficiaries of New World riches, claimed to advance new universal truths, cultural productions around the globe still showed the resilience of local traditions.

TRADE AND CULTURE

It is not surprising that in 1500 the world's most dynamic cultures were in Asia, in areas profiting from the Indian Ocean and China Sea trades. It was in China and the Islamic world that the spice and luxury trades first flourished; here, too, rulers had successfully established political stability and centralized control of taxation, law making, and military force. This often involved recruiting people from diverse backgrounds and promoting new kinds of secular (nonreligious) education. Although older ways did not die out, both trade and empire building contributed to the spread of knowledge about distant people and foreign cultures.

Of course, some rulers and polities were more eager for change than others. Moreover, certain societies—in the Americas and the South Pacific, for example—found that contact, conquest, and commerce undermined indigenous cultural life. Although Europeans and native peoples often exchanged ideas and practices, these transfers were not equal. Native Americans, for example, adapted to European missionizing by creating mixed forms of religious worship—but only because they were under pressure to do so. And as the Europeans swallowed up new territories, it was *their* culture that spread and diversified. Indeed, the Europeans absorbed much from Native Americans and African slaves but offered them little share of sovereignty or wealth in return.

For many groups, the global cultural flourishing of this period owed much to the benefits of burgeoning world trade, which allowed some rulers to consolidate wealth, administration, and military power. These rulers were eager to patronize the arts as a way to legitimize their power and reflect their cultural sophistication. In Europe, monarchs known as **enlightened absolutists** restricted the clergy and nobility and hired loyal bureaucrats who championed the knowledge of the new age. British monarchs, though they were not absolutists (because they shared power with Parliament), followed suit. Mughal emperors, Safavid shahs, and Ottoman sultans glorified their regimes by bringing artists and artisans from all over the world to give an Islamic flavor to their major cities and buildings. Rulers in China and Japan also looked to artists to extol their achievements. And in Africa, the wealth garnered from slave trading underwrote cultural productions of extraordinary merit.

Despite the unifying aspects of world trade, each society retained core aspects of its individuality. Ruling classes disseminated values based on cherished classical texts and long-established moral and religious principles. They used space in new ways to establish and project their power. (See Current Trends in World History: The Political Uses of Space.) They mapped their geographies and wrote their histories according to their traditional visions of the universe. Even as global trade drew their attention outward and in some cases introduced foreign influences, societies celebrated their achievements in politics, economics, and culture with pride in their own heritages.

CULTURE IN THE ISLAMIC WORLD

For centuries, Muslim elites had generously funded cultural development. As the Ottoman, Safavid, and Mughal empires gained greater expanses of territory, they acquired new resources to fund more such pursuits. Rulers supported new schools and building projects, and the elite produced books, artworks, and luxury goods. Cultural life was connected to the politics of empire building, as emperors and elites sought greater prestige by patronizing intellectuals and artists.

Forged under contrasting imperial auspices, Islamic cultural and intellectual life now reflected three distinct worlds. In place of an earlier Islamic cosmopolitanism, unique cultural patterns prevailed within each empire. Although the Ottomans, the Safavids, and the Mughals shared a common faith, each developed a relatively autonomous form of Muslim culture.

The Ottoman Cultural Synthesis

By the sixteenth century, the Ottoman Empire was enjoying a remarkably rich culture that reflected a variety of mixing influences. Its blend of ethnic, religious, and linguistic elements exceeded those of previous Islamic empires. The Ottomans' cultural synthesis accommodated both Sufis (mystics who stressed contemplation and ecstasy through poetry, music, and dance) and ultraorthodox *ulama* (Islamic jurists who stressed tradition and religious law). It also balanced the interests of military men and administrators with those of clerics. Finally, it allowed autonomy to the minority faiths of Christianity and Judaism.

RELIGION AND LAW The Ottoman world achieved cultural unity, above all, by an outstanding intellectual achievement—its system of administrative law. As the empire absorbed diverse cultures and territories, the sultans realized that the *sharia* (Islamic holy law) would not suffice because it was silent on many secular matters. Moreover, the Ottoman state needed comprehensive laws to bridge differences among the many social and legal systems under its rule. Mehmed II, conqueror of Constantinople, began the reform. By recruiting young boys, rather than noblemen, for training as bureaucrats or military men and making them accountable directly to the sultan, he fashioned a professional bureaucracy with unswerving loyalty to the ruler. Mehmed's successor, Suleiman the Magnificent and the Lawgiver, continued this work by compiling a comprehensive legal code. The code addressed subjects' rights and duties, proper clothing, and how Muslims were to relate to non-Muslims. The code also reconciled many differences between administrative and religious law.

EDUCATION A sophisticated educational system was crucial for the empire's religious and intellectual integration and for its cultural achievements. Here, too, the Ottomans tolerated difference. They encouraged three educational systems that produced three streams of talent—civil and military bureaucrats, *ulama*, and Sufi masters. The administrative elite attended hierarchically organized schools that culminated in the palace schools at Topkapi (see Chapter 11). Graduates from these institutions staffed the civil and military bureaucracy all across the empire. In the religious sphere, an equally elaborate system took students from elementary schools (where they learned reading, writing, and numbers) on to higher schools, or *madrasas* (where they learned law, religious sciences, the Quran, and the regular

Islamic Scientists. *This fifteenth-century Persian miniature shows Islamic scholars working with sophisticated navigational and astronomical instruments and reflects the importance that the educated classes in the Islamic world attached to observing and recording the regularities in the natural world. Indeed, many of Europe's advances in sailing drew upon knowledge from the Muslim world.*

sciences). These graduates became *ulama* who served as judges, experts in religious law, or teachers. Yet another set of schools, *tekkes*, taught the devotional strategies and religious knowledge for students to enter Sufi orders.

Each set of schools created lasting linkages between the ruling elite and the orthodox religious elite. The *tekkes*, especially, promoted social and religious solidarity and helped integrate Muslim peoples living under Ottoman rule. The value that the Ottomans placed on education and scholarship was evident in the saying that "an hour of learning was worth more than a year of prayer." It was also evident in the important advances that those schooled in Ottoman institutions made in astronomy and physics, as well as in history, geography, and politics.

SCIENCE AND THE ARTS Under the patronage of a reformist-minded grand vizier, Ottoman intellectuals also took an interest in works of European science. Some of these appeared in Turkish translation for the first time in the eighteenth century. The Ottomans' most impressive effort to spread European knowledge occurred when a Hungarian convert to Islam, Ibrahim Muteferrika, set up a printing press in Istanbul in 1729.

Muteferrika published works on science, history, and geography. One included sections on geometry; the works of Copernicus, Galileo, and Descartes; and a plea to the Ottoman elite to learn from Europe. When his patron was killed, however, the *ulama* promptly closed off this promising avenue of contact with western learning.

The Ottomans combined inherited traditions with new elements in art as well. For example, portraiture became popular after the Italian painter Gentile Bellini visited Istanbul and composed a portrait of Mehmed II. In other areas, though, the Ottomans kept their own styles. Consider the magnificent architectural monuments of the sixteenth through eighteenth centuries, including mosques, gardens, tombs, forts, and palaces: these showed scant western influence. Nor were the Ottomans interested in western literature or music. For the most part, they believed that God had given the Islamic world a monopoly on truth and enlightenment and that their military successes proved his favor.

Ottoman Court Women. *This eighteenth-century watercolor found in Topkapi Palace in Istanbul shows various musical instruments being played by court women, who were often called upon to provide entertainment.*

The Ottomans' capacity to celebrate their well-being and prosperity was most elegantly displayed during the so-called Tulip Period, which occurred in the first half of the eighteenth century. The elite had long admired the tulip's bold colors and graceful blooms, and for centuries the flower served as the sultans' symbol. In fact, both Mehmed the Conqueror and Suleiman the Magnificent grew tulips in the most secluded and prestigious courtyards at Topkapi Palace in Istanbul. And many Ottoman warriors heading into battle wore undergarments embroidered with tulips to ensure victory. By the early eighteenth century, estate owners had begun to specialize in growing the bulb; tulip designs appeared on tiles, fabrics, and public buildings, and authorities sponsored elaborate tulip festivals.

Fascination with the tulip represented a widespread delight in worldly things, which Grand Vizier Damat Ibrahim (r. 1718–1730) encouraged. As well as restoring order to the empire, Ibrahim loosened the *ulama*'s controls over social activities and sanctioned the elite's consumption of luxury goods. Commoners, too, now celebrated life's pleasures—in coffeehouses and taverns. Indeed, Ottoman demand for luxury goods grew so extensive (seeking lemons, soap, pepper, metal tools, coffee, and wine) that a well-traveled diplomat looked askance at the supposed wealth of Europe. He wrote, "In most of the provinces [of Europe], poverty is widespread, as a punishment for being infidels. Anyone who travels in these areas must confess that goodness and abundance are reserved for the Ottoman realms." Thus, despite challenges from western Europe and foreboding that their best days were behind them, the Ottomans took some foreign elements into their culture while preserving inherited ways.

Safavid Culture

The Safavid Empire in Persia (modern-day Iran) was not as long-lived as the Ottoman Empire, but it was significant for giving Shiism a home base and a location for displaying Shiite culture. There had been Shiite governments before, such as the Fatimid state in Egypt (see Chapter 9). But once the Mamluks overthrew the Fatimids in the thirteenth century, Shiism became overwhelmingly a religion of opposition to established rulers.

THE SHIITE EMPHASIS The Safavids faced a critical dilemma when they seized power. They had owed their rise to the support of Turkish-speaking tribesmen who followed a populist form of Islam. But in order to hold on to power, the Safavid

The Ottomans and the Tulip. *From the earliest times, the Ottomans admired the beauty of the tulip.* (Left) *Sultan Mehmed II smelling a tulip, symbol of the Ottoman sultans.* (Right) *The Ottomans used tulip motifs to decorate tiles in homes and mosques and pottery wares, as on the plate shown here.*

shahs needed to cultivate powerful and conservative elements of Iranian society: Persian-speaking landowners and orthodox *ulama*. Thus they turned away from the more popular Turkish-speaking Islamic brotherhoods with their mystical and Sufi qualities and, instead, built a mixed political and religious system that extolled a Shiite vision of law and society and drew on older Persian imperial traditions. The brilliant culture that emerged during the Safavid period provided a unique blend of Shiism and Persia's distinctive historical identity. It found its highest expression in the city of Isfahan, capital of the Safavid state from its creation in 1598 until the empire's end in 1722.

Just as the Ottomans' great achievement was in blending Sufism and clerical orthodoxy, so the Safavids' triumph was in creating a mixed political and religious system based on Shiism and loyalty to the royal family. Also like the Ottomans, the Safavids used established institutions like the *madrasas*, brotherhood lodges, and the *ulama* to promote Shiite orthodoxy and a Shiite-dominated culture. Even after the Safavids lost power in the eighteenth century, Shiism remained the fundamental religion of the Iranian people.

The most effective architect of a cultural life based on Shiite religious principles and Persian royal absolutism was Shah Abbas I (r. 1587–1629). The location that he chose to display the wealth and royal power of his state, its Persian and Shiite heritages, and its artistic sensibility was the new capital city of Isfahan. For this purpose the shah hired skilled artists and architects to design a city that would dwarf even Delhi and Istanbul, the other showplaces of the Islamic world. The architectural goal was to create an earthly representation of heavenly paradise.

ARCHITECTURE AND OTHER CULTURAL PRODUCTIONS The Safavid shahs were unique among Afro-Eurasian rulers of this era, for they sought to project both absolute authority and accessibility. For example, their dwellings were unlike those of other rulers—such as Topkapi Palace in Istanbul, the Citadel in Cairo, and the Red Forts of the Mughals. Those were enclosed and fortified buildings, designed to enhance rulers' power by concealing them from their subjects. In contrast, the buildings of Isfahan were open to the outside, demonstrating the Safavid rulers' desire to connect with their people.

Isfahan's centerpiece was the great plaza next to the royal palace and the royal mosque at the heart of the capital. The plaza, surrounded by elaborate public and religious buildings, measured 83,000 square meters—only slightly less than Tiananmen Square in Beijing, and seven times bigger than the plaza of San Marco in Venice. A seventeenth-century English visitor was suitably impressed, noting that the plaza was 1,000 paces from north to south and 200 from east to west and far larger than the largest urban squares in London and Paris. He added that it "is without doubt as spacious, as pleasant, and aromatic a market as any in the universe."

Other aspects of intellectual life also reflected the elites' aspirations, wealth, and commitment to Shiite principles. Safavid artists perfected the illustrated book, the outstanding example being *The King's Book of Kings,* which contained 250 miniature illustrations. Here, artists demonstrated their mastery of three-dimensional representation and their ability to harmonize different colors. In areas other than painting, proficient weavers produced highly ornate and beautiful silks and carpets for trade throughout the world; artisans painted tiles in vibrant colors and created mosaics that adorned mosques and other buildings. Moreover, the Safavids developed an elaborate calligraphy that was the envy of artists throughout the Islamic world. (See Primary Source: Islamic Views of the World.) In all these ways—but especially in Shah Abbas's pride and joy, the city

PRIMARY SOURCE

Islamic Views of the World

Although maps give the impression of objectivity and geographic precision, they actually reveal the mapmakers' views of the world (via the way they arrange the world, names of locations, areas placed in the center or at the peripheries, and accompanying text). In most cultures, official maps located their own major administrative and religious sites at the center of the universe and reflected local elites' ideas about how the world was organized.

The two maps shown here are from the Islamic world. The map of al-Idrisi, dating from the twelfth century, was a standard one of the period. Showing the world as Afro-Eurasian peoples knew it at that time, the map features only three landmasses: Africa, Asia, and Europe. The second map, made in Iran around 1700, was unabashedly Islamic: it offers a grid that measures the distances from any location in the Islamic world to the holy city of Mecca.

QUESTIONS FOR ANALYSIS

- What does each map reveal about the worldview of these Islamic societies?
- What do you think each map was used for?

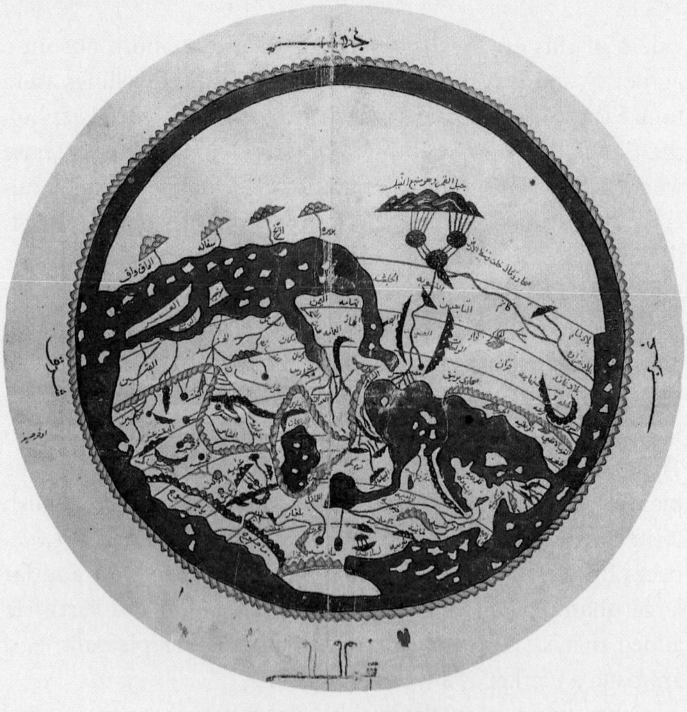

Al-Idrisi map, twelfth century

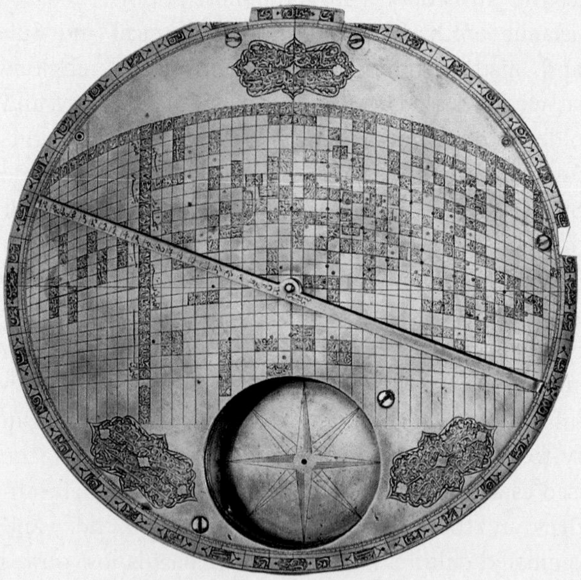

Iranian map, seventeenth century

Sources: (left) Giraudon/Art Resource, NY; (right) Private Collection, courtesy of the owner and D. A. King, contributor; photo by Christie's of London.

of Isfahan—the Safavids gave a Persian and Shiite emphasis to their stunning cultural flourishing.

Power and Culture under the Mughals

Like the Safavids and the Ottomans, the Mughals fostered a courtly high culture. Because they ruled over a large non-Muslim population, the culture that they developed in South Asia was broad and open. So highly did it value art and learning that it welcomed non-Muslims into its circle. Thus, while Islamic traditions dominated the empire's political and judicial systems, Hindus shared with Muslims the flourishing of learning, music, painting, and architecture. In this arena, aesthetic refinement and philosophical sophistication could bridge religious differences.

RELIGION Mughal rulers were flexible toward their realm's diverse peoples, especially in spiritual affairs. Though its primary

Akbar Leading Religious Discussion. *This miniature painting from 1604 shows Akbar receiving Muslim theologians and Jesuits. The Jesuits (in the black robes on the left) hold a page relating, in Persian, the birth of Christ. A lively debate will follow the Jesuits' claims on behalf of Christianity.*

commitment to Islam stood firm, the imperial court also patronized other beliefs, displaying a tolerance that earned it widespread legitimacy. The contrast with Europe, where religious differences drove deep fractures within and between states, was stark.

The promise of an open Islamic high culture found its greatest fulfillment under the emperor Akbar (r. 1556–1605). This skillful military leader was also a popular ruler who allowed common people as well as nobles from all ethnic groups to converse with him at court. Unlike European monarchs, who tried to enforce religious uniformity, Akbar studied comparative religion and hosted regular debates among Hindu, Muslim, Jain, Parsi, and Christian theologians. His quest for universal truths outside the strict *sharia* led him to develop a religion of his own, which incorporated many aspects of Hindu belief and ritual practice (see Chapter 12). Ultimately he introduced at his court a "Divine Faith" (Dīn-i Ilāhī) that was a mix of Quranic, Catholic, and other influences; it emphasized virtues such as piety, prudence, gentleness, liberality, and a yearning for God.

Dīn-i Ilāhī reflected Akbar's desire to strengthen his position against the *ulama* and his interest in philosophical skepticism. Akbar had both a Hindu and a Christian wife (besides a Muslim wife, as well as concubines of many nationalities and religions), and his palace boasted temples to each faith. His tolerance kept a multifaceted spiritual kingdom under one political roof. Akbar's trusted advisor Abulfazl encouraged his cultural pursuits and composed a tribute to the ruler and his predecessors, the *Akbarnamah* (the Book of Akbar). It describes Akbar as receiving kingship as a gift from God because he was a true philosopher and had been born a perfect person in the Sufi sense. The *Akbarnamah* remains one of the major sources of early Mughal history.

ARCHITECTURE AND THE ARTS In architecture, too, the Mughals produced masterpieces that blended styles. This was already evident as builders combined Persian, Indian, and Ottoman elements in tombs and mosques built by Akbar's predecessors. But Akbar enhanced this mixture in the elaborate city he built at Fatehpur Sikri, beginning in 1571. The buildings included residences for nobles (whose loyalty Akbar wanted), gardens, a drinking and gambling zone, and even an experimental school devoted to studying language acquisition in children. Building the huge complex took a decade, much less time than it took for construction of Louis XIV's comparable royal residence—a century later—at Versailles.

Akbar's descendant Shah Jahan was also a lavish patron of architecture and the arts. In 1630, Shah Jahan ordered the building in Agra of a magnificent white marble tomb for his beloved wife, Mumtaz Mahal. Like many other women in the Mughal court, she had been an important political counselor. Designed by an Indian architect of Persian origin, this structure, the **Taj Mahal**, took twenty years and 20,000 workers to build. The 42-acre complex included a main gateway, a garden, minarets, and a mosque. The translucent marble mausoleum lay squarely in the middle of the structure, enclosed by four identical facades and crowned by a majestic central dome rising to 240 feet. The stone inlays of different types and hues, organized in geometrical and floral patterns, and featuring Quranic verses inscribed in Arabic calligraphy gave the surface an appearance of delicacy and lightness. Blending Persian and Islamic design with Indian materials and motifs, this poetry in stone represented the most splendid example of Mughal high culture and the combining of cultural traditions. Like Shah Abbas's great plaza, the Taj Mahal gave a sense of refined grandeur to this empire's power and splendor. (See Current Trends in World History: The Political Uses of Space.)

FOREIGN INFLUENCES VERSUS ISLAMIC CULTURE Under later emperors, Mughal culture remained vibrant although not quite so brilliant. François Bernier, a seventeenth-century

The Taj Mahal. *A symbol of Mughal splendor, the Taj Mahal was a mausoleum that was built of white marble. Often described as poetry in stone, it was constructed under Shah Jahan as an homage to his deceased wife, Mumtaz Mahal* (right).

French traveler, wrote admiringly of the broad philosophical interests of Danishmand Khan, whom the emperor Aurangzeb had appointed as governor of Delhi. According to Bernier, Khan avidly read the works of the French philosophers Gassendi and Descartes and studied Sanskrit treatises to understand different philosophical traditions. But Aurangzeb, a pious Muslim, favored Islamic arts and sciences. He dismissed many of the court's painters and musicians, and in 1669 ordered that all recently built non-Islamic places of worship be torn down. In his court, intellectuals debated whether metaphysics, astronomy, medicine, mathematics, and ethics were of use in the practice of Islam. Women, at least at court, apparently were allowed to pursue the arts, for two of Aurangzeb's daughters were accomplished poets.

Well into the eighteenth century, the Mughal nobility exuded confidence and lived in unrivaled luxury. The presence of foreign scholars and artists enhanced the courtly culture, and the elite eagerly consumed exotic goods from China and Europe. Foreign trade also brought in more silver, advancing the money economy and supporting the nobles' sumptuous lifestyles. In addition, the Mughals assimilated European military technology: they hired Europeans as gunners and military engineers in their armies, employed them to forge guns, and bought guns and cannons from them. However, Mughal appreciation for other European knowledge and technology was limited. Thus, when a representative of the English East India Company presented an edition of Mercator's *Maps of the World* to the emperor in 1617, the emperor returned it a fortnight later with the remark that no one could read or understand it. The Mughals, like the Ottomans, remained supremely confident of their own cultural world.

The Islamic world drew on intellectual currents that spanned the Eurasian–North African landmass, for its centers were in Istanbul, Cairo, Isfahan, and Delhi. From Islam's founding, Muslims had looked to India and China, not to Europe, for inspiration. True, the Crusades had proved that Europeans could be worthy military rivals (see Chapter 10), and the increasing wealth and power of Christian kingdoms enriched by New World colonies made those cultures more imposing. Yet even as Muslims brought a few new European elements into their cultural mix, most still regarded Europeans as rude barbarians. More impressive in the eyes of elites in Persia, India, and the Ottoman Empire were the cultural splendors to be found to the east, not the west.

CULTURE AND POLITICS IN EAST ASIA

Like the Ottomans, Safavids, and Mughals, the Chinese did not need to prove the richness of their scholarly and artistic traditions. China had long been a renowned center of learning, with its emperors and elites supporting artists, poets, musicians, scientists, and teachers. But in late Ming and early Qing China, cultural flourishing owed less to imperial patronage than to a booming internal market. Indeed, a growing population and extensive commercial networks propelled the circulation of ideas as well as goods. As a result, China's cultural sphere expanded and diversified well before similar changes occurred elsewhere.

In Japan, too, prosperity promoted cultural dynamism. Because of its giant neighbor across the sea, the Japanese people had always been aware of outside influences. Like the Chinese government, the Tokugawa shogunate tried to promote Confucian notions of a social hierarchy organized on the basis of social position, age, gender, and kin. It also tried to shield the country from highly egalitarian ideas that would threaten the strict social hierarchy. But the forces that undermined governmental control of knowledge in China proved even stronger in Japan. Here, a decentralized political system enabled different cultural influences to spread, including European ideas and practices. By the eighteenth century, in struggling to define its own identity through these contending currents, the cultural scene in Japan was more lively, open, and varied than its counterpart in China.

China: The Challenge of Expansion and Diversity

While China had become increasingly connected with the outside world in the sixteenth and seventeenth centuries, the sources for its cultural flourishing during the period came primarily from within. Although new opportunities for cultural exchange with foreigners left their mark, it was internal social changes that propelled the circulation of books and ideas.

PUBLISHING AND THE TRANSMISSION OF IDEAS Broader circulation of ideas had more to do with the decentralization of book production than with technological innovations. After all, woodblock and moveable type printing had been present in China for centuries. Although initially the state had spurred book production by printing Confucian texts, before long the economy's increasing commercialization weakened government controls over what got printed. Even as officials clamped down on unorthodox texts, there was no centralized system of censorship, and unauthorized opinions circulated freely.

By the late Ming era, a burgeoning publishing sector catered to the diverse social, cultural, and religious needs of educated elites and urban populations. European visitors admired the vast collections of printed materials housed in Chinese libraries, describing them as "magnificently built" and "finely adorn'd." In fact, the late Ming was an age of collections of other sorts as well. Members of the increasingly affluent elite acquired objects for display (such as paintings, ceramics, and calligraphy) as a sign of their status and refinement. Connoisseurship of all the arts reached unprecedented levels. Consumers could build collections by purchasing artworks from multiple sources—from roadside peddlers to monks to gentlemen dealers, whose proclaimed love of art masked the commercial orientation of their passions.

Chinese Civil Service Exam. *Lining the sides of this Chinese examination compound were cells in which candidates sat for the examination. Other than three long boards—the highest served as a shelf, the middle one as a desk, and the lowest as a seat—the cell had neither furniture nor a door. Indeed, the cells were little more than spaces partitioned on three sides by brick walls and covered by a roof; the floors were packed dirt. Generations of candidates spent three days and two nights in succession in these cells as they strove to enter officialdom.*

CURRENT TRENDS IN WORLD HISTORY

The Political Uses of Space

The use of space for political purposes is a theme we can trace across world history. It has also allowed us to look at political history in new and different ways through a cultural lens by considering the ways rulers used symbols and space to convey this sense of power. In the early modern period, many kings and emperors opted to build grand palaces to create lavish power centers, from which they could project their influence over their kingdoms; petitioners and potential rivals would have to come to *them* to ask for favors or to complete their business. Monarchs sculpted these environments, creating a series of spaces, each of them open to a smaller and smaller number of the king's favorites. Both palaces and their surrounding grounds were ornate and splendid, were expensive to construct, and involved the best craftsmen and artists available, which often meant borrowing ideas and designs from neighboring cultures. Palace complexes of this type, built in Beijing, in Istanbul, and just outside of Paris, used space to project the rulers' power and to show who was boss.

The **Forbidden City of Beijing** was the earliest of these impressive sites of royal power. (See illustration on p. 430.) Its construction took about four years—from 1416 to 1420—although the actual name "Forbidden City" did not appear until 1576. The entrance of the city was straddled by the Meridian Gate, the tallest structure of the entire complex, which towered over all other buildings at more than 35 meters above the ground. It was from this lofty position that the emperor extended his gaze toward his empire as he oversaw various court ceremonies, including the important annual proclamation of the calendar that governed the entire country's agricultural and ritual activities. Foreign emissaries received by the court were also often allowed to use one of the passageways through the gate, where they were expected to be duly awed. As for the officials' daily audience with the emperor, they had to line up outside the Meridian Gate around 3 A.M. before proceeding to the Hall of Supreme Harmony. It was typical of the entire construction project that this impressive hall with vermilion walls and golden tiles was built at considerable cost. For the columns of the hall, fragrant hardwood had to be found in the tiger-ridden forests of the remote southwest, while the mountain forests of the south and southwest were searched for other timbers that eventually made their way to the capital through the Grand Canal.

The **Topkapi Palace** in Istanbul, capital of the Ottoman Empire, began to take shape in 1458 under Mehmed II and underwent steady expansion over the years. (See illustration on p. 000.) Topkapi projected royal authority in much the same way as the Forbidden City emphasized Chinese emperors' power: governing officials worked enclosed within massive walls, and monarchs rarely went outside their inner domain.

More than two centuries later, in the 1670s and 1680s, the French monarch Louis XIV built the **Palace of Versailles** on the site of a royal hunting lodge eleven miles from Paris, the French capital. (See illustration on p. 512.) This enormously costly complex was built to house Louis's leading clergymen and nobles, who were obliged to visit at least twice a year. Louis hoped that by taking wealthy and powerful men and women away from their local power bases, and by diverting them with entertainments, he could keep them from plotting new forms of religious schism or challenging his right to rule. Going to Versailles also allowed him to escape the pressures and demands of the population of Paris. Many European monarchs—including Russia's Peter the Great—would build palace complexes modeled on Versailles.

If in China, the Ottoman Empire, and France emperors built what were essentially private spaces in which to conduct and dominate state business, Shah Abbas (r. 1587–1629) of the Safavid Empire chose to create a great new public space instead. In the early seventeenth century, Shah

Perhaps more important, books and other luxury goods were now more affordable. For example, a low-quality commentary on the Confucian classics published in 1615 cost only half a tael of silver (a measurement based on the silver's weight). Even a low-level private tutor could earn more than forty taels a year, making it possible to gradually develop a small personal library. Increasingly, publishers offered a mix of wares: guidebooks for patrons of the arts, travelers, or merchants; handbooks for performing rituals, choosing dates for ceremonies, or writing proper letters; almanacs and encyclopedias; morality books; medical manuals.

Especially popular were study aids for the civil service examination. In fact, after the late fifteenth century, when examinees had to submit a highly structured eight-part essay, model essays flooded the market. In 1595, Beijing reeled with scandal over news that the second-place graduate had reproduced verbatim several model essays published by commercial printers. Just over twenty years later, the top graduate plagiarized a winning essay submitted years earlier. Ironically, then, the increased circulation of knowledge led critics to bemoan a decline in real learning; instead of mastering the classics, they charged, examination candidates were simply memorizing the work of others.

Abbas oversaw the construction of the **great plaza at Isfahan**, a structure which reflected his desire to bring trade, government, and religion together under the authority of the supreme political leader. An enormous public mosque, the Shah Abbas Mosque, dominated one end of the plaza, which measured 1,667 feet by 517 feet. At the other end were trading stalls and markets. Along one side sat government offices; the other side offered the exquisite Mosque of Shaykh Lutfollah. If the other rulers of this era devoted their (considerable) income to creating rich *private* spaces, Shah Abbas used the vast open space of the plaza to open up his city to all comers, keeping only the Mosque of Shaykh Lutfollah for his personal use.

The royal use of space says a great deal about how monarchs in this era wished to be seen and remembered, and about how they wanted to rule. While some wanted to retreat from the rest of society, Shah Abbas wanted to create an open space for trade and the exchanging of ideas. World history is full of palaces and plazas (the Piazza San Marco in Venice might be compared to the royal plaza at Isfahan); we can still visit and admire them. But when we do, we should also remember that space, and the architecture that either opens up to the public or sets aside privileged spaces, has always had political as well as cultural functions.

Isfahan. *On the great plaza at Isfahan, markets and government offices operated in close proximity to the public Shah Abbas Mosque, shown here, and the shah's private mosque. This structure represented Shah Abbas's desire to unite control of trade, government, and religion under one leader.*

QUESTIONS FOR ANALYSIS

- Choose one of the places discussed in this feature. How did the architectural layout shape the political power exercised by that space?
- How did private spaces, like the palace at Versailles, differ from public spaces, like the great plaza at Isfahan? What political goals could be accomplished by each?

Explore Further

Babaie, Sussan, *Isfahan and its Palaces: Statecraft, Shi'ism and the Architecture of Conviviality in Early Modern Iran* (2008).

Necipoğlu, Gülru, *Architecture, Ceremonial, and Power: The Topkapi Palace in the Fifteenth and Sixteenth Centuries* (1991).

Examination hopefuls were not the only beneficiaries of the book trade, for elite women also joined China's literary culture. As readers, writers, and editors, these women now began to penetrate what used to be an exclusively male domain. Anthologies of women's poetry were especially popular, not only in the market but when issued in limited circulation to celebrate the refinement of the writer's family. Men of letters soon recognized the market potential of women's writings; some also saw women's less regularized style (usually acquired through family channels rather than state-sponsored schools) as a means to challenge stifling stylistic conformity. On rare occasions, women even served as publishers themselves.

Although elite women enjoyed success in the world of culture, the period brought increasing restrictions on their lives. Remarriage of widows and premarital sex might have met with disapproval in earlier times, but now they were utterly unthinkable for women from "good" families. Ironically, the thriving publishing sector indirectly promoted the stricter morality by printing plays and novels that echoed the government's conservative attitudes. Meanwhile, the practice of footbinding (which elite women first adopted around

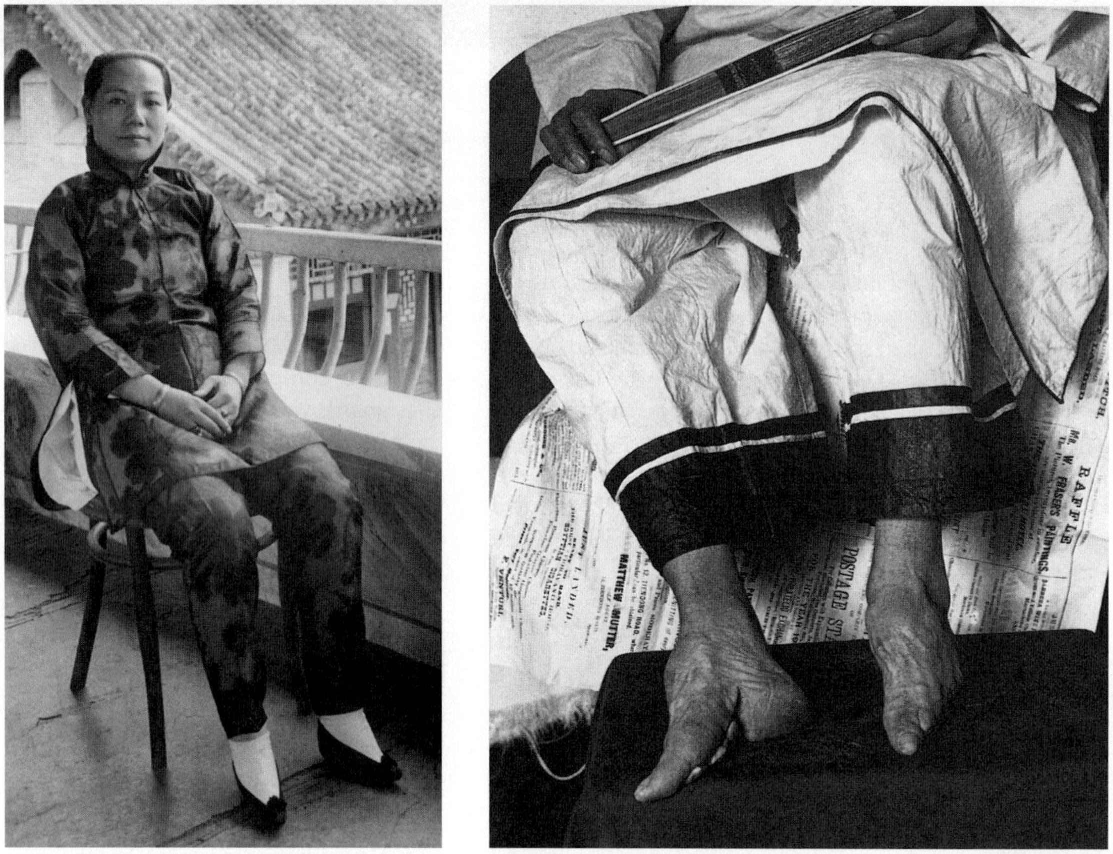

Footbinding. *Two images of bound feet: (left) as an emblem of feminine respectability when wrapped and concealed, as on this well-to-do Chinese woman; (right) as an object of curiosity and condemnation when exposed for the world to see.*

the late Tang-Song period) continued to spread among common people, as small, delicate feet came to signify femininity and respectability.

POPULAR CULTURE AND RELIGION Important as the book trade was, it had only an indirect impact on most men and women in late Ming China. Those who could not read well or at all absorbed cultural values through oral communication, ritual performance, and daily practices. The Ming government tried to control these channels, too. It appointed village elders as guardians of local society, and it instituted "village compacts" to ensure shared responsibility for proper conduct and observation of the laws.

Still, the everyday life of rural and small-town dwellers went on outside these official networks. Apart from toiling in the field, villagers participated in various religious and cultural practices, such as honoring local guardian spirits, patronizing Buddhist and Daoist temples, or watching performances by touring theater groups. Furthermore, villagers often took group pilgrimages to religious sites and attended markets in nearby towns, which drew them in with restaurants, brothels, and other types of entertainment. At the marketplaces the visitors would gather news and gossip in the teahouses or listen to the tales of itinerant storytellers and traveling monks. The open-ended nature of such cultural activities meant that village audiences had opportunities to reinterpret official norms to serve their own purposes and to contest the government's rules. For example, the common people could take officially approved morality tales celebrating the deeds of just and impartial officials and use them to challenge the real-life behavior of government bureaucrats.

Another manifestation of late-Ming cultural flourishing was the fervor associated with popular religions that mingled various cultural traditions. Here, at the grassroots level, there was little distinction among Buddhist, Daoist, and local cults. After all, the Chinese believed in cosmic unity; and although they venerated spiritual forces, they did not consider any of them to be a Supreme Being who favored one sect over another. They believed it was the emperor, rather than any religious group, who held the mandate of heaven. To the Chinese, the enforcement of orthodox values was more a matter of political than of religious control. Unless sects posed an obvious threat, the emperor had no reason to regulate their spiritual practices. This situation promoted religious tolerance and avoided the sectarian warfare that plagued post-Reformation Europe.

TECHNOLOGY AND CARTOGRAPHY Belief in cosmic unity did not prevent the Chinese from devising technologies to master nature's operations in this world. For example, the magnetic compass, gunpowder, and the printing press were all Chinese inventions. Moreover, Chinese technicians had mastered iron casting and produced mechanical clocks centuries before Europeans did.

PRIMARY SOURCE

Chinese Views of the World

The Chinese developed cartographical skills early in their history. A third-century map, no longer in existence, was designed to enable the emperors to "comprehend the four corners of the world without ever having to leave their imperial quarters." The *Huayi tu* (Map of Chinese and Foreign Lands) from 1136 depicted the whole world on stone stele, including 500 place names and textual information on foreign lands. Chinese maps typically devoted more attention to textual explanations with moral and political messages than to locating places accurately. One such map, the Chinese wheel map from the 1760s, is full of textual explanations.

QUESTIONS FOR ANALYSIS

- Why do you think Chinese maps included messages that focused on moral and political themes?
- How are these maps similar to and different from the Islamic maps shown on p. 524?

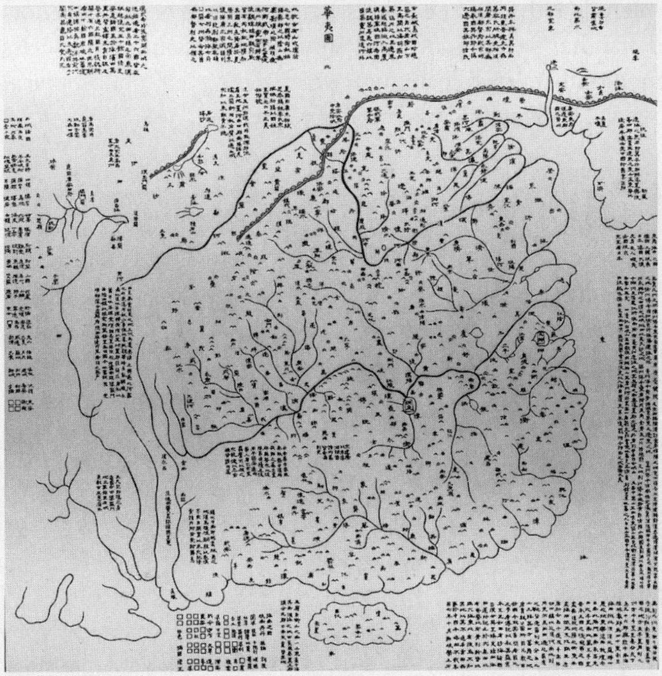

The Huayi tu *map, 1136*

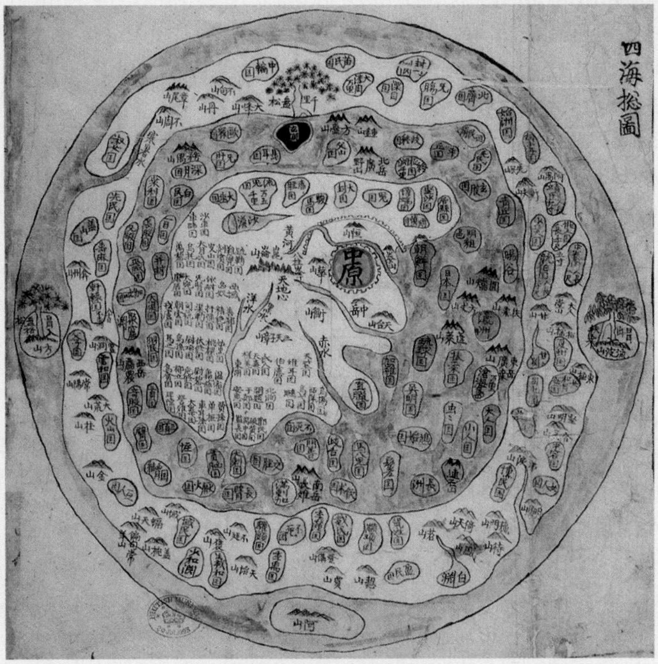

Chinese wheel map, 1760s

Sources: (left) The Needham Research Institute; (right) The British Library, London.

Chinese astronomers also compiled accurate records of eclipses, comets, novae, and meteors. In part, the emperor's needs drove their interest in astronomy and calendrical science. After all, it was his job as the Son of Heaven, and thus mediator between heaven and earth, to determine the best dates for planting, holding festivities, scheduling mourning periods, and convening judicial court sessions. The Chinese believed that the empire's stability depended on correct calculation of these dates.

European missionaries and traders arriving in China were awed by Chinese technological expertise, eloquence, and artistic refinement. Nonetheless, convinced that their sciences were superior, Christian missionaries tried to promote their own knowledge in areas such as astronomy and **cartography** (mapmaking). Possessing sophisticated sciences of their own, the Chinese were selective in appropriating these novel European practices. To be sure, members of the Jesuit order served in the imperial astronomy bureau and, in the early eighteenth century, undertook monumental surveys for the Qing emperor. However, the Europeans' overall cultural impact in China during this period was limited.

In the realm of cartography, the Chinese demonstrated most clearly their understanding of the world. Their maps encompassed elements of history, literature, and art—not just technical detail. It was not that "scientific" techniques were lacking; a map made as early as 1136 reveals that Chinese cartographers could readily draw to scale. Yet, valuing written text over visual and other forms of representation, Chinese elites did not always treat geometric and mathematical precision as the main objective of cartography. Reflecting the elites' worldview, most maps placed the realm of the Chinese emperor, as the ruler of "All under Heaven," at the center, surrounded by foreign countries. Thus the physical scale of China and distances to other lands were distorted. Still, some of the maps cover a vast expanse: one includes an area stretching from Japan to the Atlantic, encompassing Europe and Africa. (See Primary Source: Chinese Views of the World.)

Europeans did not know what to make of the Chinese resistance to their science. In 1583, the Jesuit missionary Matteo Ricci brought European maps to China, hoping to impress the elite with European learning. Challenging their belief that the world was flat, his maps demonstrated that the earth was spherical—and that China was just one country among many others. Yet Chinese critics complained that Ricci treated the Ming Empire as "a small unimportant country." As a concession, he placed China closer to the center of the maps and provided additional textual information. Still, his maps had a negligible impact, as neither the earth's shape nor precise scale was particularly important to most Chinese geographers.

Before the nineteenth century, the Chinese had fairly incomplete knowledge about foreign lands despite a long history of contact. The empire saw itself as superior to all others (a common feature of many cultures). Chinese writers, for example, often identified groups of other people through distinctive and, to them, odd physical features. A Ming geographical publication portrayed the Portuguese as "seven feet tall, having eyes like a cat, a mouth like an oriole, an ash-white face, thick and curly beards like black gauze, and almost red hair." Chinese elites glorified their "white" complexions against the peasants' dark skin; against the black, wavy-haired "devils" of Southeast Asia; and against the Europeans' "ash-white" pallor. Qing authors in the eighteenth century confused France with the Portugal known during Ming times, and they characterized England and Sweden as dependencies of Holland. During this period of cultural flourishing, in short, most Chinese did not feel compelled to revise their view of the world.

Cultural Identity and Tokugawa Japan

Chinese cultural influence had long crossed the Sea of Japan, but under the Tokugawa shogunate there was also interest in European culture. This interest grew via the Dutch presence in Japan and via limited contacts with Russians. At the same time, there was a surge in the study of Japanese traditions and culture. Thus, Tokugawa Japan engaged in a three-cornered conversation among time-honored Chinese ways (transmitted via Korea), European teachings, and distinctly Japanese traditions.

NATIVE ARTS AND POPULAR CULTURE Until the sixteenth and seventeenth centuries, the main patrons of Japanese culture were the imperial court in Kyoto, the hereditary shogunate, religious institutions, and a small upper class. These groups developed an elite culture of theater and stylized painting. Samurai (former warriors turned bureaucrats) and daimyo (regional lords) favored a masked theater, called Nō, and an elegant ritual for making tea and engaging in contemplation. In their gardens, the lords built teahouses with stages for Nō drama. These gave rise to hereditary schools of actors, tea masters, and flower arrangers. The elites also hired commoner-painters to decorate tea utensils and other fine articles and to paint the brilliant interiors and standing screens in grand stone castles. Some upper-class men did their own painting, which conveyed philosophical thoughts. Calligraphy was proof of refinement.

Artist and Geisha at Tea. *The erotic, luxuriant atmosphere of Japan's urban pleasure quarters was captured in a new art form, the* ukiyo-e, *or "pictures from a floating world." In this image set in Tokyo's celebrated Yoshiwara district, several geisha flutter about a male artist.*

Kabuki Theater. *Kabuki originated among dance troupes in the environs of temples and shrines in Kyoto in the late sixteenth and early seventeenth centuries. As kabuki spread to the urban centers of Japan, the theater designs enabled the actors to enter and exit from many directions and to step out into the audience, lending the skillful, raucous shows great intimacy.*

Alongside the elite culture arose a rougher urban one that artisans and merchants patronized. Urban dwellers could purchase, for example, works of fiction and colorful prints (often risqué) made from carved wood blocks, and they could enjoy the company of female entertainers known as geisha. These women were skilled (*gei*) in playing the three-stringed instrument (*shamisen*), storytelling, and performing; some were also prostitutes. Geisha worked in the cities' pleasure quarters, which were famous for their geisha houses, public baths, brothels, and theaters. Kabuki—a type of theater that combined song, dance, and skillful staging to dramatize conflicts between duty and passion—became wildly popular. This art form featured dazzling acting, brilliant makeup, and sumptuous costumes. In 1629 the shogunate, concerned for public order, banned female actors; thereafter men played women's roles. These male actors sometimes maintained their impersonations offstage, inspiring fashion trends for urban women.

Much popular entertainment chronicled the world of the common people rather than politics or high society. The urbanites' pleasure-oriented culture was known as "the floating world" (*ukiyo*), and the woodblock prints depicting it as *ukiyo-e* (*e* meaning "picture"). Here, the social order was temporarily turned upside down. Those who were usually considered inferior—actors, musicians, courtesans, and others seen as possessing low morals—became idols. Even some upper-class samurai partook of this "lower" culture. But to enter the pleasure quarters they had to leave behind their swords, a mark of rank, since commoners were not allowed to carry such weapons.

Literacy in Japan now surged, especially among men. The most popular novels sold 10,000 to 12,000 copies. In the late eighteenth century, Edo had some sixty booksellers and hundreds of book lenders. In fact, the presence of so many lenders allowed books to spread to a wider public that previously could not afford to buy them. By the late eighteenth century, as more books circulated and some of them criticized the government, officials tried to censor certain publications.

THE INFLUENCE OF CHINA In the realm of higher culture, China loomed large in the Tokugawa world. Japanese scholars wrote imperial histories of Japan in the Chinese style, and Chinese law codes and other books attracted a significant readership. Some Japanese traveled south to Nagasaki to meet Zen Buddhist masters and Chinese residents there. A few Chinese monks even won permission to found monasteries outside Nagasaki and to give lectures and construct temples in Kyoto and Edo.

Although Buddhist temples grew in number, they did not displace the native Japanese practice of venerating ancestors and worshipping gods in nature. Later called Shintō ("the way of the gods"), this practice boasted a network of shrines throughout the country. Shintō developed from time-honored beliefs in spirits, or *kami*, who were associated with places (mountains, rivers, waterfalls, rocks, the moon) and activities (harvest, fertility). Seeking healing or other assistance, adherents appealed to these spirits in nature and daily life through incantations and offerings. Some women under Shintō served as *mikos*, a kind of shaman with special divinatory powers.

Shintō rituals competed with a powerful strain of neo-Confucianism that issued moral and behavioral guidelines. For example, in 1762 "Greater Learning for Females" appeared—an influential text that made Confucian teachings understandable for nonscholars. In particular, it outlined social roles that stressed hierarchy based on age and gender as a way to ensure order. At the same time, merit became important in determining one's place in the social hierarchy. Doing the right thing (propriety) and being virtuous were key.

By the early eighteenth century, neo-Confucian teachings of filial piety and loyalty to superiors had become the official state

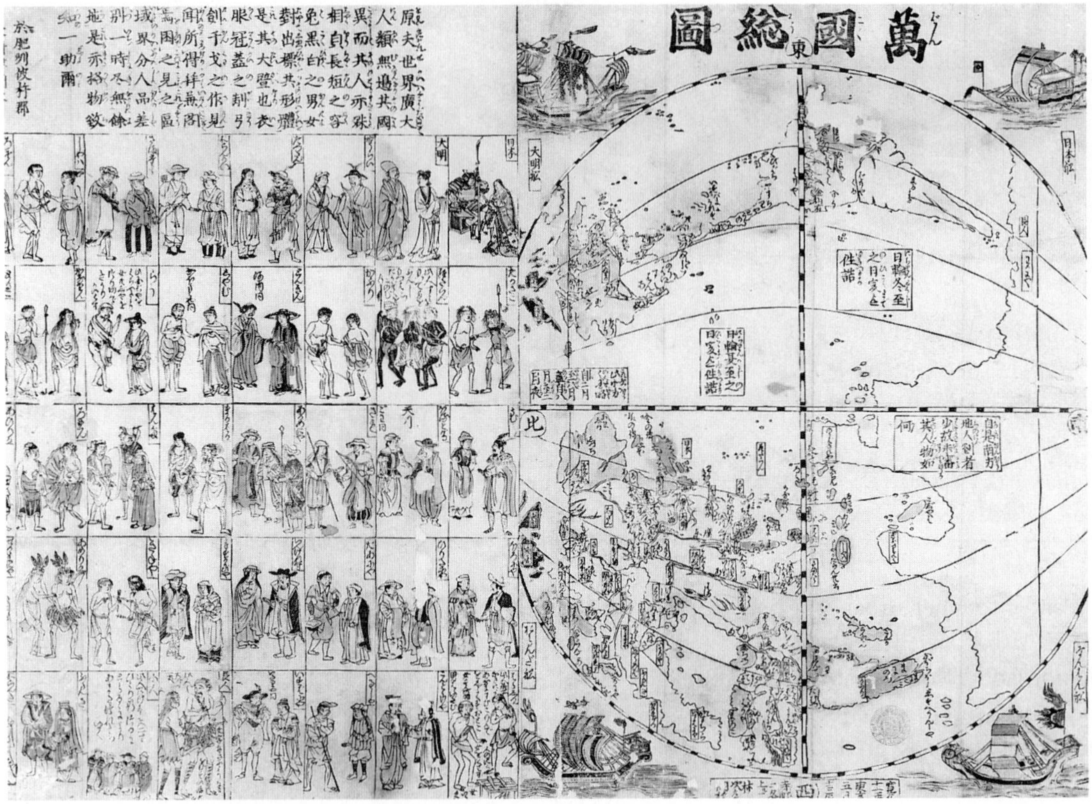

Japanese Map of the World. *Japanese maps underwent a shift in connection with encounters with the Dutch. Here, in a map dated 1671, much information is incorporated about distant lands, both cartographically on the globe and pictorially, to the left, in two-person images representing various peoples of the world in their purported typical costumes.*

creed. This philosophy legitimated the social hierarchy and the absolutism of political authorities, but it also instructed the shogun and the upper class to provide "benevolent administration" for the people's benefit. That meant taking into account petitioners' complaints and requests, whether for improved irrigation and roads or for punishment of unfair officials.

Reacting to a creed adapted from non-native traditions, and desiring to honor their own country's greatness, some thinkers promoted intellectual traditions from Japan's past. These efforts stressed "native learning," Japanese texts, and Japanese uniqueness. In so doing, they formalized a Japanese religious and cultural tradition, and they denounced Confucianism and Buddhism as foreign contaminants. A few thinkers also looked to the uninterrupted imperial line in Kyoto (which did not govern) for validation of Japan's intellectual lineage and cultural superiority. Some who called for restored rule by the emperor faced arrest by the shogun's military men, but others went on to develop Japanese poetry. This art form, which expressed a yearning for a glorious lost age, became popular with both upper and lower classes.

EUROPEAN INFLUENCES Not only did Chinese intellectual influences compete with revived native learning, but by the late seventeenth century Japan was also tapping other sources of knowledge. At this time Portuguese was the common language in East Asia, and even the Dutch used it in communicating with the Japanese. By 1670, however, a guild of Japanese interpreters in Nagasaki who could speak and read Dutch accompanied Dutch merchants on trips to Edo. As European knowledge spread to high circles in Edo, in 1720 the shogunate lifted its ban on foreign books. Thereafter European ideas, called "Dutch learning," circulated more openly. Scientific, geographical, and medical texts appeared in Japanese translations and in some cases displaced Chinese texts. A Japanese-Dutch dictionary appeared in 1745, and the first official school of Dutch learning followed. Students of Dutch or European teachings remained a limited segment of Japanese society, but the demand for translations intensified.

Japan's internal debates about what to borrow from the Europeans and the Chinese illustrate the changes that the world had undergone in recent centuries. A few hundred years earlier, products and ideas generally did not travel beyond coastal regions and had only a limited effect (especially inland) on local cultural practices. By the eighteenth century, though, expanded networks of exchange and new prosperity made the integration of foreign ideas feasible and, sometimes, desirable. The Japanese were especially eager to transform useful new ideas and practices. They did not consider the embracing of outside influences as a mark of inferiority or subordination, particularly when they could put those influences to good use. This was not the case for the great Asian land-based empires, which were eager lenders but hesitant borrowers.

THE ENLIGHTENMENT IN EUROPE

An extraordinary cultural flowering also blossomed in Europe during the seventeenth and eighteenth centuries. Often the **Enlightenment** is defined purely in intellectual terms as the spreading of faith in reason and in universal rights and laws, but this era encompassed broader developments, such as the expansion of literacy, the spread of critical thinking, and the decline of religious persecution. Part of what gave Enlightenment thinkers such influence in Europe and beyond was that they wanted not just to convey new ideas to the elite but also to spread them widely. They hoped to change their contemporaries' worldviews and to transform political and social institutions.

Crucial for the success of this endeavor were widening patronage networks. Previously such networks had involved religious and monarchical supporters of arts and sciences, but they now extended to the lower aristocracy and bureaucratic and commercial elites as well. Equally important were cafés and intellectual salons, public theaters, exchanges of correspondence, and newspaper and book publishing. The male and female thinkers of this period disagreed about many things, but they shared a desire to "spread light" and to speak their minds about how to improve their societies, something that often made them troublesome to religious and political authorities.

Abandoning Christian belief in God's mysterious tampering with natural forces and human events, Enlightenment thinkers wanted to know the world in new ways. They sought universal and objective knowledge that would not reflect any particular religion, political view, class, or gender. Recognizing no territorial boundaries, these scholars struggled to formulate natural laws that would, they presumed, apply everywhere and to all peoples. Most of these thinkers were unaware of the extent to which European, upper-class male perspectives colored their "objective" knowledge.

Origins of the Enlightenment

While the sixteenth century brought new prosperity, the seventeenth century produced civil and religious wars, dynastic conflicts, and famine. These crises devastated central Europe. They bankrupted the Spanish, caused chaos in France, led to the execution of the English king, and saw the Dutch break free from Spanish control. They also contributed to the spread of Protestantism in Europe. At the same time, the crises made some intellectuals wish to turn their backs on religious strife, and to develop useful ways for understanding and improving *this* world. By 1750, too, in some western countries, a larger share of the population was eager to join in these discussions. As literate, middle-class men and women gained confidence in being able to reason for themselves, to understand the world without calling on traditional authorities, and to publicly criticize what they found distasteful or wrong, contemporaries recognized that they were living in an increasingly "enlightened" age.

It helps to pause and consider the development of this confidence, and of Enlightenment knowledge as a whole. First, the Reformation and Counter-Reformation (see Chapter 12) were significant in increasing literacy and diffusing the new science and its premises. Second, greater contacts between Europeans and the wider world after the fourteenth century were key. After all, Europeans had become eager consumers of other peoples' cultural goods. From Native American trapping methods to African slaves' crop cultivation techniques, from Chinese porcelain to New World tobacco and chocolate, contact with others influenced Europe in the seventeenth and eighteenth centuries. Yet the more they learned, the more European intellectuals became critical of other cultures—and more confident that their own culture was unique, superior, and the standard against which to judge all others. (See Primary Source: European Views of the World.)

The New Science

The search for new, testable knowledge began centuries before the Enlightenment, in the efforts of Nicolaus Copernicus (1473–1542) and Galileo Galilei (1564–1642) to understand the behavior of the heavens. These men were both astronomers and mathematicians. Making their own mathematical calculations and observations of the stars and planets, these scholars came to conclusions that contradicted age-old assumptions. By no means was trusting one's own work rather than the accepted authorities easy, or without risk: when Galileo confirmed Copernicus's claims that the earth revolved around the sun, he was put on trial for heresy.

In the seventeenth century, a small but influential group of scholars committed themselves, similarly, to experimentation, calculation, and observation. They adopted a method for "scientific" inquiry laid out by the philosopher Sir Francis Bacon (1561–1626), who claimed that real science entailed the formulation of hypotheses that could be tested in carefully controlled experiments. Bacon believed that traditional authorities could never be trusted; only by conducting experiments could humans begin to comprehend the workings of nature. Bacon was chiefly wary of classical and medieval authorities, but his principle also applied to traditional knowledge that European scientists were encountering in the rest of the world. Confident of their calculations performed according to the new **scientific method**, scientists like Isaac Newton (1642–1727) defined what

PRIMARY SOURCE

European Views of the World

As Europeans became world travelers and traders, they needed accurate information on places and distances so they could get home as well as return to the sites they had visited. Europe's first printed map of the New World, the Waldseemüller map (produced in 1507), portrayed the Americas as a long and narrow strip of land. Asia and Africa dwarf its unexplored landmass. By the mid-seventeenth century, European maps were seemingly more objective, yet they still grouped the rest of the world around the European countries. Moreover, the effort to make world maps that served navigational purposes led to distortions (like the stretching of polar zones in the 1569 Mercator projection) that made Europe seem disproportionately large and central.

QUESTIONS FOR ANALYSIS

- What are the most striking differences between the two maps?
- How are these European maps similar to and different from the Islamic and Chinese ones shown on pp. 524 and 531?

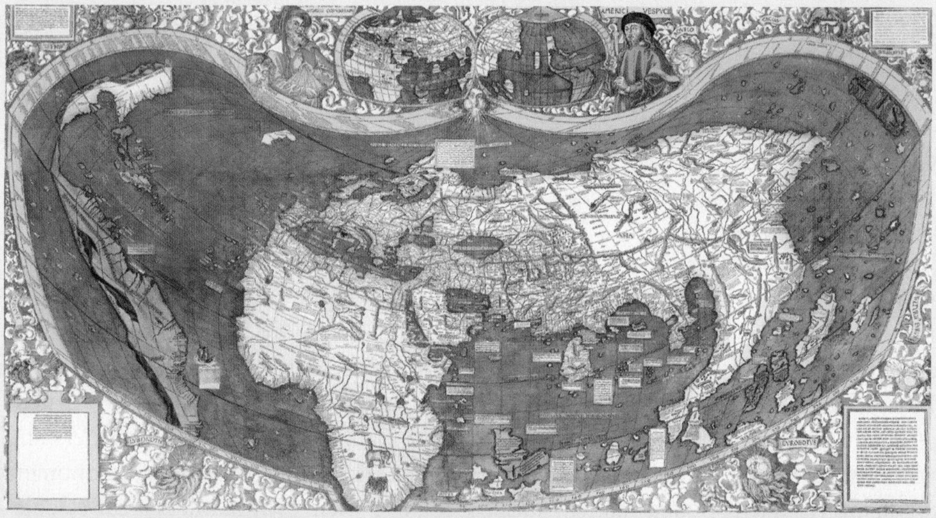

Waldseemüller map, 1507

Mercator projection, 1569

Sources: (top) Courtesy Wychwood Editions; (bottom) Rare Books Division, The News York Public Library, Astor, Lenox and Tilden Foundations.

Galileo. *Worried that the new science would undermine the Christian faith, the Catholic Church put Italian scientist Galileo on trial in 1633 for espousing heretical beliefs and condemned him to house arrest until his death in 1642.*

they believed were universal laws that applied to all matter and motion; they criticized older conceptions of nature (from Aristotelian ideas to folkloric and foreign ones) as absurd and obsolete. Thus, in his *Principia Mathematica* Newton set forth the laws of motion—including the famous law of gravitation, which simultaneously explained falling bodies on earth and planetary motion.

It is no longer fashionable to call these changes a scientific revolution, for European thinking did not change overnight. Only gradually did thinkers come to see the natural world as operating according to inviolable laws that experimenters could figure out. But by the late seventeenth century many rulers had developed a new interest in science's discoveries, and they established royal academies of science to encourage local endeavors. This patronage, of course, had a political function. By incorporating the British Royal Society in 1662, for example, Charles II hoped to show not only that the crown backed scientific progress but also that England's great minds backed the crown. Similar reasoning lay behind Louis XIV's founding of the French Royal Academy of Sciences and building of the fabulously expensive palace complex at Versailles. Like other monarchs, Louis also did his best to subordinate the clergy to the crown. All of France, he meant to say, needed to look to him for cultural, religious, and political guidance.

Gradually, the new science expanded beyond the court to gain popularity among elite circles. Marquise de Chatelet-Lomont built a scientific laboratory in her home and translated Newton's *Principia* into French. Well-to-do landowners formed societies to discuss the latest methods of animal breeding. Military schools increasingly stressed engineering methods and produced graduates with sophisticated technical skills. By about 1750, even artisans and journalists were applying Newtonian mechanics to their practical problems and inventions. In Italy, numerous female natural philosophers emerged, and the genre of scientific literature for "ladies" took hold. In 1763, the mathematician Diamante Medaglia Faini delivered an oration recommending that all women increase their knowledge of science. A consensus emerged among proponents of the new science that useful knowledge came from collecting data and organizing them into universally valid systems, rather than from studying revered classical texts.

By no means, however, did the scientific worldview dominate European thinking. Most people still understood their relationships with God, nature, and fellow humans via Christian doctrines and local customs. Although literacy was increasing, it was far from universal; schools remained church-governed or elite, male institutions. All governments employed censors and punished radical thinkers, peasants still suffered under arbitrary systems of taxation, and judicial regimes were as harsh as during medieval times. Science and rationality certainly did not pervade all spheres of European life by 1700. If that had been so, there would have been no need for the movement we now call the Enlightenment.

Marquise de Chatelet-Lomont. *The Marquise de Chatelet-Lomont (1706–1749) was one of the few in her day to understand Newtonian physics. Her French translation of Newton's* Principia Mathematica *included extensive explanations of the science that informed Newton's thinking. Her lover and admirer Voltaire wrote of her, "She was a great man whose only fault was in being a woman."*

Enlightenment Thinkers

Enlightenment thinkers believed in the power of human reason and the perfectibility of humankind; they rejected the medieval belief in man's sinful nature and helplessness in the face of earthly evils. Such thinkers included the French writers Voltaire (1694–1778) and Denis Diderot (1713–1784) and the Scottish economist Adam Smith (1723–1790). But these writers also called attention to the evils and flaws of human society: Voltaire criticized the torture of criminals, Diderot denounced the despotic tendencies of the French kings Louis XIV and Louis XV, and Smith exposed the inefficiencies of mercantilism.

In general, Enlightenment thinkers trusted nature and individual human reason and distrusted institutions and traditions. "Man is born good," wrote Jean-Jacques Rousseau (1712–1778); "it is society that corrupts him." Rousseau also followed the Englishman John Locke (1632–1704) in insisting on the sovereignty of the people; since all political institutions derived from the original "social contract" made between a people and its ruler, Locke and Rousseau argued, when a government became tyrannical, it violated that contract. In such a case, the people had the right to rebel and create a new contract. If these thinkers showed how traditional political authorities could be challenged, Voltaire repeatedly ridiculed the nobility and clergy for its stupidity, greed, and injustice. Other Enlightenment thinkers, similarly, saw the need for great improvements in human society. They mainly criticized contemporary European conditions, and they often suffered imprisonment or exile for writing about what they considered to be superstitious beliefs and corrupt political structures.

The Enlightenment touched all of Europe, but the extent of its reach varied. In France and Britain, enlightened learning spread widely; in Spain, Poland, and Scandinavia, enlightened circles were small and had little influence on rulers or the general population. Enlightened thought flourished in commercial centers like Amsterdam and Edinburgh and in colonial ports like Philadelphia and Boston. As education and literacy levels rose in these cities, book sales and newspaper circulation surged. By 1770, approximately 3,500 different books and pamphlets were appearing each year in France alone, compared to 1,000 fifty years earlier. By 1776, about 12 million copies of newspapers were circulating in Britain.

POPULAR CULTURE In the emerging marketplace for new books and new ideas, some of the most popular works were not from high intellectuals. They came from the pens of more sensationalist essayists. Pamphlets charging widespread corruption, fraudulent stock speculation, and insider trading circulated widely. Sex, too, sold well. Works like *Venus in the Cloister or the Nun in a Nightgown* racked up as many sales as the now-classic works of the Enlightenment. Bawdy and irreligious, these vulgar best-sellers exploited consumer demand—but they also seized the opportunity to mock authority figures, such as nuns and priests. Some even dared to go after the royal family, portraying Marie Antoinette as having sex with her court confessor. In these cases, pornography—some of it even philosophical—spilled into the literary marketplace for political satire. Such works displayed the seamier side of the Enlightenment, but they also revealed a willingness (on the part of high and low intellectuals alike) to explore modes of thought that defied established beliefs and institutions.

The reading public itself helped generate new cultural institutions and practices. In Britain and Germany, book clubs and coffeehouses sprang up to cater to sober men of business and learning; here, aristocrats and well-to-do commoners could read news sheets or discuss stock prices, political affairs, and technological novelties. The same sort of noncourtly socializing occurred in Parisian salons, where aristocratic women presided. Speaking their minds more openly in these private settings than at court or at public assemblies, women here freely exchanged ideas with men. The number of female readers, and writers, soared, and the relatively new genre of the novel, as well as

Salon of Madame Geoffrin *Much of the important work—and wit—of the Enlightenment was the product of private gatherings known as salons. Often hosted, like the one depicted here, by aristocratic women, these salons also welcomed down-at-the-heels writers and artists, offering everyone, at least in theory, the opportunity to discuss the sciences, the arts, politics, and the idiocies of their fellow humans on an equal basis.*

specialized women's journals, appealed especially to them. It is important to note, however, that most funding for intellectuals still came from aristocrats, royal families, and the church. For example, in the German states, Enlightenment thinkers were chiefly university professors, bureaucrats, and pastors. Art collecting boomed—primarily because it gave aristocrats a way to display their good taste, wealth, and distance from the common people. The cultural life of the European Enlightenment was one that remained heavily dominated by the elite.

CHALLENGES TO AUTHORITY AND TRADITION Even though they took the aristocracy's money, many Enlightenment thinkers tried overturn the status distinctions that characterized European society. They emphasized merit rather than birth as the basis for status. In his *Treatise on Human Understanding* (1690), John Locke claimed that man was born with a mind that was a clean slate (*tabula rasa*) and acquired all his ideas through experience. Locke stressed that cultural differences were not the result of unequal natural abilities, but of unequal opportunities to develop one's abilities. Similarly, in *The Wealth of Nations,* Adam Smith remarked that there was little difference (other than education) between a philosopher and a street porter: both were born, he claimed, with the ability to reason, and both were (or should be) free to rise in society according to their talents. Yet, Locke and Smith still believed that a mixed set of social and political institutions was necessary to regulate relationships among ever-imperfect humans. Moreover, they did not believe that women could act as independent, rational individuals in the same way that all men, presumably, could. Although educated women like Mary Wollstonecraft and Olympe de Gouges took up the pen to protest these inequities (see Chapter 15 for further discussion), the Enlightenment did little to change the subordinate status of women in European society.

SEEKING UNIVERSAL LAWS Inspired by the new science, many thinkers sought to discover the "laws" of human behavior, an endeavor linked with criticism of existing governments. Explaining the laws of economic relations was chiefly the work of Adam Smith, whose book *The Wealth of Nations* described universal economic laws. It became one of the most influential and long-lived of enlightened works. Smith claimed that unregulated markets in a laissez-faire economy best suited mankind because they allowed man's "trucking and bartering" nature to express itself fully. (**Laissez-faire** expresses the concept that the economy works best when it is left alone—that is, when the state does not regulate or interfere with the workings of the market.) In Smith's view, the "invisible hand" of the market, rather than government regulations, would lead to prosperity and social peace. Smith was conscious of growing economic gaps between "civilized and thriving" nations and "savage" ones; the latter were so miserably poor that, Smith claimed, they were reduced to infanticide, starvation, and euthanasia. Yet, he believed that until these nations learned to play by what he called nature's laws, they could not expect a happy fate. Smith was just one of many writers who felt that non-Europeans had no other choice but to follow the Enlightenment's "universal" laws.

One of the most controversial areas for applying universal laws was religion. Although few Enlightenment thinkers were

ANALYZING GLOBAL DEVELOPMENTS

How Can We Measure the Impact of an Idea?

The single most important work of the European Enlightenment, which set out to provide an objective compendium of all human knowledge, Denis Diderot's *Encyclopédie* was very French. Of its more than 130 authors, only sixteen were foreign, and, of those sixteen, seven came from the French-speaking city of Geneva, just across the border. All of them were men. Within France, the authors came primarily from the north, especially from Paris. Noble and clerical authors weighed more heavily on the list of authors than in society at large (this had to do with literacy rates, which were much higher among the elite); most of Diderot's authors came from the Third Estate. None of those bourgeois authors had much to do with capitalism, nor did the aristocratic authors have much to do with feudalism. There were large contingents of doctors, lawyers, government officials, and skilled artisans.

We know very little about the production and diffusion of the first edition of the *Encyclopédie*, produced from 1751–1772 under Diderot's direction. The first four editions, in fact, were expensive luxury items, relatively unimportant in terms of diffusion. The great mass of *Encyclopédie*s that circulated in prerevolutionary Europe came from cut-rate quarto and octavo editions published between 1777 and 1782, when the final, revised version, the *Encyclopédie méthodique*, began to appear. For these later editions, thorough records have survived, raising far-reaching questions about how ideas circulated and where during the Enlightenment, at least within Europe. (We know very little about the circulation of the *Encyclopédie* beyond Europe.) Where did the writers come from, where did their ideas go, and how, if at all, did their origins influence the content and ultimate significance of their project? We include a table of key words and their classification in thematic categories from the original edition, to give a sense of its contents and priorities.

Terms	Word Count	Principal Categories
Commerce	5713	Commerce, Geography
Science	2095	[Multiple Categories]
Christ	1821	Theology, Holy Scripture
African	1772	Geography, History, Natural History, Botany
Slavery	238	Natural Law, Ethics, Religion, Ancient History
African slavery (*La traite des nègres*)	15	Commerce
Negro	536	Natural History, Commerce
Saint-Domingue	96	Geography, Botany
China	957	Agriculture, Chemistry, History, Natural History, Geography, Metaphysics, Tapestry
Turk or Turkey	701	Geography, History
Muhammad	356	Theology, History, Philosophy

QUESTIONS FOR ANALYSIS

- What does the diffusion of the *Encyclopédie* within France and across Europe tell us about its influence? How should we evaluate the influence of a book?
- Do you think the *Encyclopédie*'s local origins compromise its universal ambitions?
- How do you think the social origins of the contributors shaped the kinds of topics covered by the *Encyclopédie*?

Source: Darnton, Robert, The Business of Enlightenment: Publishing History of the Encyclopedie, 1775–1800 *(1979).*

atheists (people who do not believe in any god), most of them called for religious toleration. They insisted that the use of reason, not force, was the best way to create a community of believers and morally good people. Their critiques of church authorities and practices were highly controversial. Governments often reacted by censoring books or exiling writers, but the arguments managed to persuade some rulers. Thus, in the late eighteenth century, governments from Denmark to Austria passed acts offering religious minorities some freedom of worship. However, toleration did not mean full civil rights—especially for Catholics in England or Jews anywhere in Europe. Toleration simply meant a loosening of religious uniformity, and the population as a whole often resented even this.

SEEKING UNIVERSAL KNOWLEDGE The Enlightenment produced numerous works that attempted to encompass universal knowledge. Most important was the French *Encyclopedia*, which ultimately comprised twenty-eight volumes containing essays by nearly 200 intellectuals. It was extremely popular among the elite despite its political, religious, and intellectual

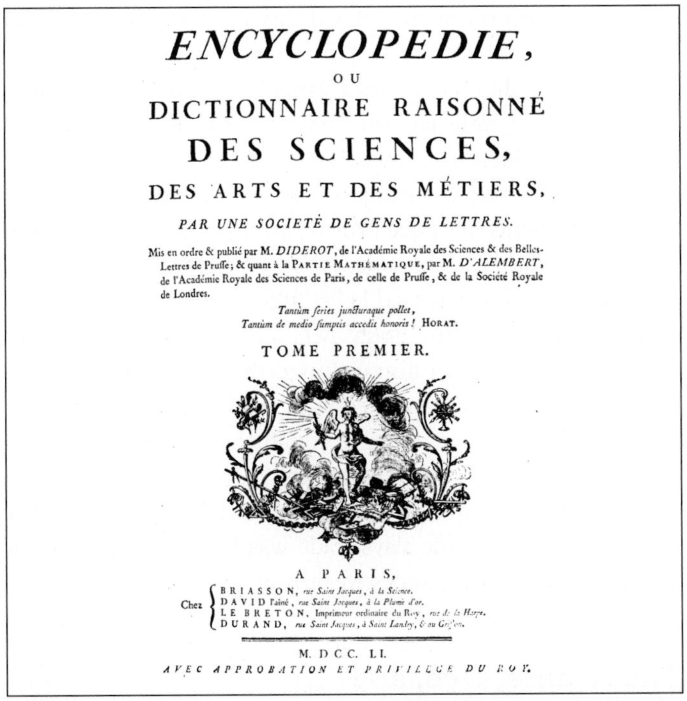
ENCYCLOPEDIE,
OU
DICTIONNAIRE RAISONNÉ
DES SCIENCES,
DES ARTS ET DES MÉTIERS,
PAR UNE SOCIETÉ DE GENS DE LETTRES.
Mis en ordre & publié par M. DIDEROT, de l'Académie Royale des Sciences & des Belles-Lettres de Prusse; & quant à la PARTIE MATHÉMATIQUE, par M. D'ALEMBERT, de l'Académie Royale des Sciences de Paris, de celle de Prusse, & de la Société Royale de Londres.
Tantùm series juncturaque pollet,
Tantùm de medio sumptis accedit honoris! HORAT.
TOME PREMIER.
A PARIS,
Chez BRIASSON, rue Saint Jacques, à la Science.
DAVID l'aîné, rue Saint Jacques, à la Plume d'or.
LE BRETON, Imprimeur ordinaire du Roy, rue de la Harpe.
DURAND, rue Saint Jacques, à Saint Landry, & au Griffon.
M. DCC. LI.
AVEC APPROBATION ET PRIVILEGE DU ROY.

The *Encyclopédie.* *Originally published in 1751, the* Encyclopédie *was the most comprehensive work of learning of the French Enlightenment. The title page (left) features an image of light and reason being dispersed throughout the land. The title itself identifies the work as a dictionary, based on reason, that deals not just with the sciences but also with the arts and occupations. It identifies two of the leading men of letters (gens de lettres), Denis Diderot and Jean le Rond d'Alembert, as the primary authors of the work. Contributors to the* Encyclopedia *included craftsmen as well as intellectuals. The detailed illustrations of a pin factory and the processes and machinery employed in pin making shown below are from a plate in the fourth volume of the* Encyclopedia *and demonstrate its emphasis on practical information.*

radicalism. Its purpose was "to collect all the knowledge scattered over the face of the earth" and to make it useful to men and women in the present and future. Indeed, the *Encyclopedia* offered a wealth of information about the rest of the world, including more than 2,300 articles on Islam. Here, quite typically, the authors praised Arab culture for preserving and extending Greek and Roman science—and in doing so, preparing the way for scientific advances in Europe. But at the same time the authors portrayed Islam with the same ill will that they applied to other organized religions, condemning Muhammad for promoting a bloodthirsty religion and Muslim culture in general for not rejecting superstition.

Enlightenment thinkers valued commerce and rationality, so they placed all regions that supposedly lacked these ingredients at the bottom of the world's cultures. While praising some cultures like the Chinese for having achieved much in these areas, Enlightenment thinkers were confident that Europe was advancing over the rest of the world in its acquisition of goods and universal knowledge.

Absolutist governments did not entirely reject enlightened ideas. After all, they recognized the virtues of universality (as in a universally applicable system of taxation) and precision (as in a well-drilled army). Also, social mobility allowed more skilled bureaucrats to rise through the ranks, while commerce provided the state with new riches. The idea of collecting knowledge, too, appealed to states that wanted greater control over their subjects. Consider Louis XIV, who was persuaded to establish a census (though he never carried it out) so that he could "know with certitude in what consists his grandeur, his wealth, and his strength." Some enlightened princes—in Prussia and Austria, for example—even made impressive legal reforms and supported innovations in the arts and agriculture. Indeed, the Enlightenment spread the idea of liberty far and wide, even to women, lower-class men, and enslaved peoples whom European elites felt might not deserve it. In fact, many other eighteenth-century male thinkers, like their absolutist rulers, were uncomfortable with the idea of offering liberty and equality (not to mention sovereignty) to *all* the people.

AFRICAN CULTURAL FLOURISHING

The wealth that spurred artistic achievement and displays of power in Europe, Asia, and the Americas did not overlook African states. Proceeds from the slave trade enabled African upper classes to fund cultural activities and invigorate strong artisanal and artistic traditions that dated back many centuries. As in East Asia, African artisans maintained local forms of cultural production, such as wood carving, weaving, and metal working.

Cultural traditions in Africa varied from kingdom to kingdom, but there were patterns among them. For example, all West African elites encouraged craftsmen to produce carvings, statues, masks, and other objects that would glorify the power and achievements of rulers. (Royal patrons in Europe, Asia, and the Islamic world did the same with architecture and painting). There was also a widespread belief that rulers and their families had the blessing of the gods. Arts and crafts not only celebrated royal power but also captured the energy of a universe that people believed was filled with spiritual beings. Starting in the 1500s and continuing through the eighteenth century when the slave trade reached its peak, African rulers had even more reason—and means—to support cultural pursuits. After all, as destructive as the slave trade was for African peoples, it made the slave-trading states wealthy and powerful.

The Asante, Oyo, and Benin Cultural Traditions

The kingdom of Asante, which the charismatic leader and first king (Asantehene) of the large Akan-speaking region in what is present-day Ghana, Osei Tutu (d. 1717) unified, led the way in cultural attainments. The kingdom's access to gold and the revenues that it derived from selling captives undergirded its prosperity, making it the richest state in West Africa, perhaps even in the whole of sub-Saharan Africa. So deeply imbued with a desire to achieve economic success were the citizens of Asante that they accorded the highest respect to entrepreneurs who made money and were able to surround themselves with retainers and slaves. The adages of the age were inevitably about becoming rich: "money is king" or "nothing is as important as money" or "money is what it is all about." Households that had wealth displayed it ostentatiously, beginning to wear special garments that told others that they were persons of wealth

Brass Oba Head. *The brass head of an Oba, or king, of Benin. The kingdom's brass and bronze work was among the finest in all of Africa.*

and power. Those who could command the services of at least 1,000 subjects were entitled to wear a special cloth and to have a horsetail switch carried in front of them. Even more coveted was the right to carry the elephant-tail whip, which carried with it an esteemed title.

Artisans celebrated these traditions through the crafting of magnificent seats or stools coated with gold as symbols of authority; the most ornate were reserved for the head of the Asante federation, the Asantehene, who ruled this far-flung empire from the capital city of Kumasi. By the eighteenth century, these monarchs ventured out from the secluded royal palace only on ceremonial and feast days, when they wore sumptuous silk garments featuring many dazzling colors and geometric patterns, all joined together in interwoven strips. Known as Kente cloth, this fabric could be worn only by the rulers. Kings also had a golden elephant tail carried in front of them, the symbol of the highest level of wealth. Held aloft on these celebratory occasions were maces, spears, staffs, and other symbols of power fashioned from the kingdom's abundant gold supplies. These reminded the common people of the Asantehene's connection to the gods.

Equally resplendent were rulers of the Oyo Empire and Benin, located in the territory that now constitutes Nigeria. Elegant, refined metalwork in the form of West African bronzes reflects these rulers' awesome power and their peoples' highest esteem. The bronze heads of Ife, capital city of the Yoruba Oyo Empire, are among the world's most sophisticated pieces of art. According to one commentator, "little that Italy or Greece or Egypt ever produced could be finer, and the appeal of their beauty is immediate and universal." The Ife heads mark the high point of Yoruba craft and artistic tradition that dates back to the first millennium CE. Artisans fashioned the best known of these works in the thirteenth century (before the slave trade era), but the tradition continued and became more elaborate in the seventeenth and eighteenth centuries.

Bronzes from Benin, too, displayed exquisite craftsmanship. Although historical records have portrayed Benin as one of Africa's most brutal slave-trading regimes, it also produced art of the highest order. Whether Benin's reputation for brutality was deserved or simply part of Europeans' later desire to label African rulers as "savage" in order to justify their conquest of the landmass, it cannot detract from the splendor of its artisans' creations.

HYBRID CULTURES IN THE AMERICAS

In the Americas, mingling between European colonizers and native peoples (as well as African slaves) produced hybrid cultures. But the mixing of cultures grew increasingly unbalanced as Europeans imposed authority over more of the Americas. For Native Americans, the pressure to adapt their cultures to those of the colonists began from the start. Over time, Indians faced mounting pressure as Europeans insisted that their conquests were not simply military endeavors but also spiritual errands. In addition to guns and germs, all of Europe's colonizers brought Bibles, prayer books, and crucifixes. With these, they set out to Christianize and "civilize" Indian and African populations in the Americas. Yet missionary efforts produced uneven and often unpredictable outcomes. Even as Indians and African slaves adopted Christian beliefs and practices, they often retained older religious practices too.

European colonists likewise borrowed from the peoples they subjugated and enslaved. This was especially true in the sixteenth and seventeenth centuries, when the colonists' survival in the New World often depended on adapting. Before long, however, many American settlements had become stable and prosperous, to the extent that colonists preferred not to admit their past dependence on others. New sorts of hierarchies emerged, and elites in Latin America and North America increasingly followed the tastes and fashions of European aristocrats. Yet, even as they imitated Old World ways, these colonials forged identities that separated them from Europe.

Spiritual Encounters

Settlers in the New World had the military and economic power to impose their culture—especially their religion—on indigenous peoples. Although the Jesuits had little impact in China and the Islamic world, Christian missionaries in the Americas had armies and officials to back up their insistence that Native Americans and African slaves abandon their own deities and spirits for Christ.

FORCING CONVERSIONS European missionaries, especially Catholics, used numerous techniques to bring Indians within the Christian fold. Smashing idols, razing temples, and whipping backsliders all belonged to the missionaries' arsenal. Catholic orders (principally Dominicans, Jesuits, and Franciscans) also learned what they could about Indian beliefs and rituals—and then exploited that knowledge to make conversions to Christianity. For example, many missionaries found it useful to demonize local gods, subvert indigenous spiritual leaders, and transform Indian iconography into Christian symbols. But at the same time, the missionaries preserved much linguistic and ethnographic information about Native American communities. In sixteenth-century Mexico, the Dominican friar Bernardino de Sahagún compiled an immense ethnography of Mexican ways and beliefs. In seventeenth-century Canada, French Jesuits

Indians Becoming Christians. *This image is from a colonial chronicle, illustrated and narrated by indigenous scribes who had converted to Christianity. The picture of Indians before the conquest entering a house of prayer is intended to represent the Indians as proto-Christians.*

prepared dictionaries and grammars of the Iroquoian and Algonquian languages and translated Christian hymns into Amerindian tongues.

Neither gentle persuasion nor violent coercion produced the results that missionaries desired. When conversions did occur, the Christian practices that resulted were usually hybrid forms in which indigenous deities and rituals merged with Christian ones. Among Andean mountain people, for example, priestesses of local cults took the Christian name Maria to mask their secret worship of traditional deities. In other cases, indigenous communities turned their backs on Christianity and accused missionaries of bringing disease and death. Those who did convert saw Christian spiritual power as an addition to, not a replacement for, their own religions.

MIXING CULTURES More distressing to missionaries than the blending of beliefs or outright defiance were the Indians' successes in converting captured colonists. Many Indian groups had a tradition of adopting their captives as a way to replace lost kin. It deeply troubled the missionaries that quite a few captured colonists adjusted to their situation, accepted their adoptions, and refused to return to colonial society when given the chance. Moreover, some other Europeans voluntarily chose to live among the Indians. Comparing the records of cultural conversion, one eighteenth-century colonist suggested that "thousands of Europeans are Indians," yet "we have no examples of even one of those Aborigines having from choice become European." (Aborigines are original, native inhabitants of a region, as opposed to invaders, colonizers, or later peoples of mixed ancestry.) While this calculation may be exaggerated, it reflects the fact that Europeans who adopted Indian culture, like Christianized Indians, lived in a mixed cultural world. In fact, their familiarity with both Indian and European ways made them ideal intermediaries for diplomatic arrangements and economic exchanges.

Beyond the attractions of Indian cultures, Europeans mixed with Indians because there were many more men than women among the colonists. Almost all the early European traders, missionaries, and settlers were men (although the British North American settlements saw more women arrive relatively early on). In response to the scarcity of women and as a way to help Amerindians accept the newcomers' culture, the Portuguese crown authorized intermarriage between Portuguese men and local women. These relations often amounted to little more than rape, but longer-lasting relationships developed in places where Indians kept their independence—as among French fur traders and Indian women in Canada, the Great Lakes region, and the Mississippi Valley. Whether by coercion or consent, sexual relations between European men and Indian women resulted in offspring of mixed ancestry. In fact, the mestizos of Spanish colonies and the métis of French outposts soon outnumbered settlers of wholly European descent.

The increasing numbers of African slaves in the Americas complicated the mix of New World cultures even further. Unlike marriages between fur traders and Indian women, in which the women held considerable power because of their connections to Indian trading partners, sexual intercourse between European men and enslaved African women was almost always forced. Children born from such unions swelled the ranks of mixed-ancestry people in the colonial population. Europeans attempted to Christianize slaves, though many slave owners doubted the wisdom of converting persons they regarded as mere property. Protestants had more difficulty than Catholics in accepting that Africans could be both slaves and Christians, and their missionary efforts were less aggressive than the Catholics'.

Sent forth with the pope's blessing, Catholic priests targeted slave populations in the American colonies of Portugal, Spain, and France. Applying many of the same techniques that missionaries used with Indian "heathens," these priests produced similarly mixed results. Often converts blended Islamic or traditional African religions with Catholicism. Converted slaves wove remembered practices and beliefs from their homeland into their American Christianity, transforming both along the way. In northeastern Brazil, for example, slaves combined the Yoruba faiths of their ancestors with Catholic beliefs, and they

Racial Mixing. (Left) *This image shows racial mixing in colonial Mexico—the father is Spanish, the mother Indian, and the child a mestizo. This is a well-to-do family, illustrating how Europeans married into the native aristocracy.* (Right) *Here too we see a racially mixed family. The father is Spanish, the mother black or African, and the child a mulatto. Observe, however, the less aristocratic and markedly less peaceful nature of this family.*

frequently attributed powers of African deities to Christian saints. Sometimes Christian and African faiths were practiced side by side. In Saint-Domingue, slaves and free blacks practiced *vodun* ("spirit" in the Dahomey tongue); in Cuba, *santería* ("cult of saints" in Spanish), a faith of similar origins.

Just as slaveholders feared, Christianity—especially in its hybrid forms—could inspire resistance, even revolt, among slaves. Indeed, a major runaway slave leader in mid-eighteenth-century Surinam was a Christian. Those held in bondage in the English colonies drew inspiration from Christian hymns that promised deliverance, and they embraced as their own the Old Testament story of Moses leading the Israelites out of Egypt. By the late eighteenth century, freed slaves like the Methodist Olaudah Equiano (see Chapter 13) were saying in their own voices that slavery was unjust and incompatible with Christian brotherhood.

Making Americans

The colonization of the Americas brought Europeans, Africans, and Indians into sustained contact, though the nature of the colonies and the character of the contact varied considerably. Where their dominance was most certain, European colonists imposed their ways on subjugated populations and imported what they took to be the chief attributes of the countries and cultures they had left behind. Yet Europeans were not immune to cultural influences from the groups they dispossessed and enslaved, and over time the colonists developed a sense of their own distinctive "American" identities. The cultures and identities of Indians and African slaves also underwent significant transformations, though often what Europeans imposed was only partially and selectively adapted.

THE CREOLE IDENTITY In Spanish America, ethnic and cultural mixing produced a powerful new class, the **creoles**—persons of European descent who were born in the Americas. By the late eighteenth century, creoles increasingly resented the control that **peninsulars**—men and women born in Spain or Portugal but living in the Americas—had over colonial society. Creoles especially chafed under the exclusive privileges given to peninsular rulers, like those that forbade creoles from trading with other colonial ports. Also, they disliked the fact that royal ministers gave most official posts to peninsulars. While the Spanish and Portuguese rulers did occasionally soften their discrimination for fear of angering the creoles, their reforms usually aggravated tensions with peninsulars.

The growing creole identity gained strength from new ideas spreading in the colonies, especially those circulating under the umbrella of the Enlightenment. The French writer Abbé Raynal's *History of the Settlements and Trade of the Europeans in the East and West Indies* (1770), for example, was a favorite text among colonial reading circles in Buenos Aires and Rio de Janeiro. As a history of colonization in the New World, it was unkind to Iberian (Spanish and Portuguese) emperors and conquerors—and often helped creoles justify their dissatisfaction. Other French works were also popular, especially those of Rousseau. So were some English texts, like Adam Smith's *The Wealth of Nations*. Smith's reformist spirit contributed to creole impressions that mercantilist Iberian authorities lagged behind them in political and economic matters.

In many cities of the Spanish and Portuguese empires, reading clubs and salons hosted energetic discussions of fresh ideas. In one university in Peru, Catholic scholars taught their students that Spanish labor drafts and taxes on Andean natives not only violated divine justice but also offended the natural rights of free men. The Spanish crown, recognizing the role of printing presses in spreading troublesome ideas, strictly controlled the number and location of printers in the colonies. In Brazil, royal authorities banned them altogether. Nonetheless books, pamphlets, and simple gossip allowed new notions of science, history, and politics to circulate among literate creoles.

ANGLICIZATION In one important sense, wealthy colonists in British America were similar to the creole elites in Spanish and Portuguese America: they too copied European ways. For example, they constructed "big houses" (in Virginia) modeled on the country estates of English gentlemen, imported opulent furnishings and fashions from the finest British stores, and exercised more control over colonial assemblies. Imitating the English also involved tightening patriarchal authority. In seventeenth-century Virginia, men had vastly outnumbered women, which gave women some power (widows in particular gained greater control over property and more choices when they remarried). During the eighteenth century, however, sex ratios became more equal, and women's property rights diminished as English customs took precedence. Overall, patriarchal authority was evident in family portraits, where husband-patriarchs sat or stood in front of their wives and children.

Intellectually, too, British Americans were linked to Europe. Importing enormous numbers of books and journals, these Americans played a significant role in the Enlightenment as producers and consumers of political pamphlets, scientific treatises, and social critiques. Indeed, drawing on the words of numerous Enlightenment thinkers, American intellectuals created the most famous of enlightened documents: the Declaration of Independence. It announced that all men were endowed with equal rights and were created to pursue worldly happiness. In this way Anglicized Americans showed themselves, like the creole elites of Latin America, to be products of both European and New World encounters.

Chronometer. *In the 1760s, the English clockmaker John Harrison perfected the chronometer, a timepiece mariners could use to reckon longitude while at sea. Although the Royal Scientific Society initially refused to believe that Harrison had solved this long-standing problem, Harrison's instrument made navigation so much safer and more predictable that it became standard equipment on European ships.*

THE MAKING OF A NEO-EUROPEAN CULTURE IN OCEANIA

Not only in Europe and the Americas but also in the South Pacific, an "enlightened" form of cultural expansionism took shape in the eighteenth century. Though in centuries past Hindu, Buddhist, Islamic, and Chinese missionaries and traders had traveled to Malaysia and nearby islands, they had not ventured beyond Timor (see Map 14.1). Europeans began to do so in the years after 1770, turning their sights on **Oceania** (Australia, New Zealand, and the islands of the southwest Pacific). Using their new wealth to fund voyages with scientific and political objectives, Europeans invaded these remaining unexplored areas. The results were mixed: while some islands maintained their autonomy, the biggest prize, Australia, underwent thorough Anglicization.

Until Europeans colonized it in the late eighteenth century, Australia was, like the Americas before Columbus, truly a world apart. Separated by water and sheer distance from other regions, Australia's main features were harsh natural conditions and a sparse population. At the time of the European colonization, the island was home to around 300,000 people, mostly hunter-gatherers. While seafarers from Java, Timor, and particularly the port of Makassar may have ventured into the area in the past, there was little evidence that either Chinese or Muslim merchants had ever strayed that far south.

Europeans had visited Oceania before the eighteenth century. Spices had drawn the Portuguese and Dutch into the South Pacific (see Chapter 13), and the Spanish had plied Pacific waters while traveling between Manila and Acapulco, but they had stopped only in Guam and the Mariana Islands. In the 1670s and 1680s they attempted to conquer these islands, and despite considerable resistance they succeeded by 1700. The Dutch visited Easter Island in 1722, and the French arrived in Tahiti in 1767. Both the Portuguese and the Dutch had seen the northern and western coasts of Australia, but they had found only sand, flies, and Aborigines. Not until the late eighteenth century did

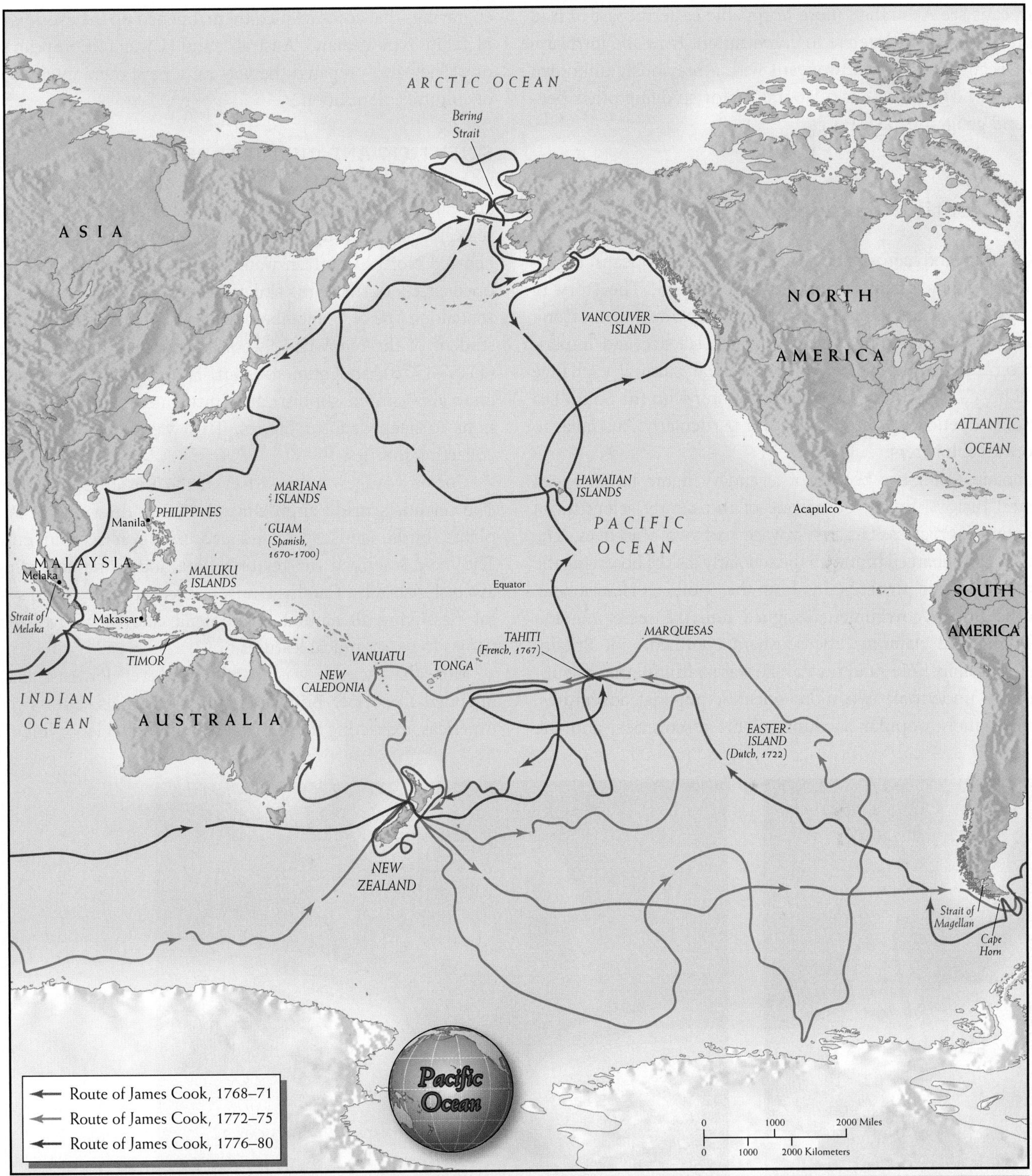

MAP 14.1 | Southeast Asia

Captain Cook's voyages throughout the Pacific Ocean symbolized a new era in European exploration of other societies.

- According to this map, how many voyages did Cook take?
- Where did Cook explore, and what peoples did he encounter?
- According to your reading, how did Cook's endeavors symbolize "scientific" imperialism?

Europeans see Australia's more hospitable eastern coast or find grounds for serious interest in colonization. Now the intrusion into Oceania presented Europeans with a previously unknown region that could serve as a laboratory for studying other peoples and geographical settings.

The Scientific Voyages of Captain Cook

In Oceania and across the South Pacific, Europeans experimented with a scientific form of imperialism. The story of the region's most famous explorer, Captain James Cook (1728–1779), shows how closely related science and imperialist ventures could be, and how unequal cultural exchange could be. Cook's voyages and his encounter with the South Sea Islanders opened up the Pacific, and particularly Australia, to European colonizers.

Captain Cook has become a legendary figure in European cultural history, portrayed as one of the saintly scientists of enlightened progress. His first voyage had two objectives. The Royal Society charged him with the scholarly task of observing the movement of the planet Venus from the Southern Hemisphere, and the British government assigned him the secret mission of finding and claiming "the southern continent" for Britain. Cook set sail in 1768, and his voyage was so fruitful that he subsequently undertook two more scientific-imperial adventures. The extremely popular accounts of his discoveries, and the engravings that accompanied them, opened up the exotic worlds of Tahiti, New Zealand, Australia, and Hawaii to European scrutiny. They also prepared the way for a new, more intensive sort of cultural colonization.

SCIENTIFIC AND CULTURAL ASPECTS Cook was chosen to head the first expedition because of his scientific interests and skills. Although he had little schooling, he had gone to sea early and, through long experience in navigating the uncharted North American waters of Newfoundland, had developed excellent surveying skills. Besides Cook, the Royal Society sent along one of its members who was a botanist; a doctor and student of the renowned Swedish naturalist Carolus Linnaeus (1707–1778); and numerous artists and other scientists. The crew also carried sophisticated instruments and had instructions to keep detailed diaries. This was to be a grand data-collecting journey.

Cook's voyages surpassed even the Royal Society's hopes. The scientists made approximately 3,000 drawings of Pacific plants, birds, landscapes, and peoples never seen in Europe. The men described the region's flora and fauna according to Swedish naturalist Carolus Linnaeus's recently developed system for classifying all natural phenomena, and they gave English names to geographical features.

More than science was at stake, however, for Australia was intended to supply Britain with raw materials. But as in the Americas, extracting those materials required a labor force, and

The Voyages of Captain James Cook. *During his celebrated voyages to the South Pacific, Cook (left) kept meticulous maps and diaries. Although he had little formal education, he became one of the great exemplars of enlightened learning through experience and experiment. (Right) Kangaroos were unknown in the West until Cook and his colleagues encountered (and ate) them on their first visit to Australia. This engraving of the animal (which unlike most animals, plants, and geographical features actually kept the name the Aborigines had given it) from Cook's 1773 travelogue,* A Voyage Round the World in the Years 1768–1771, *lovingly depicts the kangaroo's environs and even emotions.*

the Aborigines of Australia, like the Indians of the Americas, perished in great numbers from imported diseases. Those who survived generally fled to escape control by British masters. Thus, to secure a labor force, plans arose for grand-scale conquest and resettlement by British colonists. On his third voyage, Cook took along an astonishing array of animals and plants with which to turn the South Pacific into a European-style garden. His lieutenant later brought apples, quinces, strawberries, and rosemary to Australia; the seventy sheep imported in 1788 laid the foundations for the region's wool-growing economy. In fact, the domestication of Australia arose from the Europeans' certainty about their superior know-how and a desire to make the entire landmass serve British interests.

In 1788, a British military expedition took official possession of the eastern half of Australia. The intent was, in part, to establish a prison colony far from home. This plan belonged as well to the realm of "enlightened" dreams: that of ridding "civilized" society of all evils by resettling lawbreakers among the "uncivilized." The intent was also to exploit Australia for its timber and flax and to use it as a strategic base against Dutch and French expansion. In the next decades, immigration—free and forced—increased the Anglo-Australian population from an original 1,000 to about 1.2 million by 1860. Importing their customs and their capital, British settlers turned Australia into a frontier version of home, just as they had done in British America. Yet, such large-scale immigration had disastrous consequences for the surviving Aborigines. Like the Native Americans, the original inhabitants of Australia were decimated by diseases and increasingly forced westward by European settlement.

Omai. *Omai, the South Sea Islander brought to England by Captain Cook, was the object of much curiosity in London in the 1780s.*

STUDYING FOREIGNERS In one important way, Cook continued practices of the past. Earlier travelers had developed an efficient way to study foreign peoples and their languages: by taking some of them to Europe, through kidnapping if necessary. On Columbus's first voyage to the New World, he had captured six Amerindians and taken them back to Spain—to show them off as exotic people, and to enable them to learn Spanish so they could serve as intermediaries between the two cultures. Other explorers did the same, seizing local people, taking them to Europe, and putting them on display.

This was not the way that Europeans learned about peoples whom they considered to be civilized—for example, the Chinese and the Arabs. For such "civilized" peoples, texts stood in for living bodies. But exhibiting live individuals continued to be a crude means for studying those whom the Europeans considered uncivilized. Cook himself captured and transported to England a highly skilled Polynesian navigator, Omai. Omai quickly became the talk of London society and symbolized for some people the innocence and beauty that were vanishing as Europe developed complicated machines and stock exchanges. Cook's return of Omai to his home on his third voyage was a sensation of equal proportions, seen as a colossally generous act by the revered British explorer.

The Enlightenment and the Origins of Racial Thought

Cook's description of the South Sea Islanders underscores the place that "race" had come to occupy in Europeans' views of themselves and others. Previously, the word *race* referred to a swift current in a stream or a test of speed, and sometimes it meant a lineage (mainly that of a royal or noble family). By the late seventeenth century, a few writers were expanding the definition to designate a European ethnic lineage, identifying, for example, the indomitable spirit and freedom-loving ethos of the Anglo-Saxon race.

The Frenchman François Bernier, who had traveled in Asia, may have been the first European to attempt to classify the peoples of the world. He used a variety of criteria, including those that were to become standard from the late eighteenth century down to the present, such as skin color, facial features, and hair texture. Bernier published this work in his *New Division of the Earth by the Different Groups or Races Who Inhabit It* (1684). In addition to the Swedish naturalist Carolus Linnaeus, the French scholar Georges Louis LeClerc, the comte de Buffon (1707–1788), and the German anatomist Johann Friedrich Blumenbach (1752–1840) were the first to use racial principles to classify humankind.

CATEGORIZING HUMAN GROUPS In his *Systema Naturae* (1735), Europe's most accomplished naturalist, Carolus Linnaeus, sought to classify all the world's plants and animals by giving each a binomial, or two-worded, name. In subsequent editions of his *Systema* Linnaeus perfected his system, identifying five subspecies of the mammal he called *Homo sapiens*, or "wise man." Linnaeus gave each of the continents a subspecies: there was *Homo europaeus, Homo americanus, Homo afer*, and *Homo asiaticus*. He added a fifth category, *Homo monstrosus*, for "wild" men and "monstrous" types.

Linnaeus's classifications were based on a combination of physical characteristics that included skin color and social qualities. He characterized Europeans as light-skinned and governed by laws; Asians as "sooty" and governed by opinion; indigenous American peoples as copper-skinned and governed by custom; and Africans (whom he consigned to the lowest rung of the human ladder) as ruled by personal whim. Later eighteenth-century natural historians dismissed Linnaeus's fifth category, which contained mythical monstrous races and people with mental and physical disabilities, but the habit of ranking "races" and lumping together physical and cultural characteristics persisted.

THE EUROPEAN BIAS In inventorying the world's peoples and assigning each group a place on the ladder of human achievement, Europeans applied their reverence for classical sculpture. Those who most resembled Greek nudes were considered the most beautiful, as well as the most civilized and suited for world power. In his *Natural History* (1750), the comte de Buffon insisted that classical sculptures had established the proper proportion for the human form. Having divided humans into distinct "races," he determined that white peoples were the most admirable, and Africans the most contemptible.

In these emerging racial hierarchies, South Sea Islanders fell somewhere between Caucasians and Ethiopians. To some, their isolation from European and Asian cultures and their residence in a tropical "paradise" made them seem like direct descendants of Adam and Eve—a virtuous, uncorrupted people who fit the description of the "noble savage" popularized by Jean-Jacques Rousseau. But in succeeding decades Europeans would come to emphasize not the nobility but the savagery of the South Sea Islanders. Declining appreciation for their innocence and simplicity may have begun with the final act in the Cook legend: his killing by the Hawaiians in 1779. The news scandalized Cook's homeland; the king himself, it is said, shed tears. Thereafter Europeans began to write about a "darker side" of South Pacific cultures.

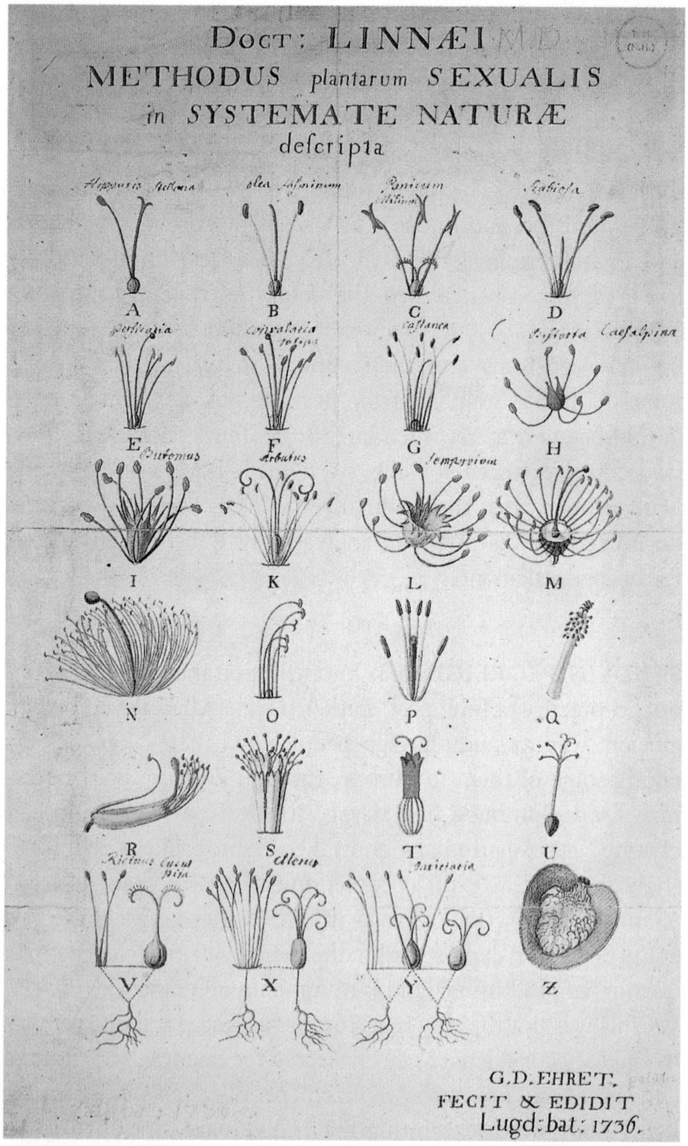

Linnaeus and Classification. *Linnaeus's famous system of plant and animal classifications, which depended on sexual forms (such as the stamen and pistil in plants), was in wide use by the end of the eighteenth century.*

CONCLUSION

New wealth produced by commerce and state building created the conditions for a global cultural renaissance in the sixteenth, seventeenth, and eighteenth centuries. It began in the Chinese and Islamic empires and then stretched into Europe, Africa, and previous worlds apart in the Americas and Oceania. Experiments in religious toleration encouraged cultural exchange; book production and consumption soared; grand new monuments took shape; luxury goods became available for wider enjoyment.

A striking aspect of this cultural renaissance was its unevenness. While elites and sometimes the middle classes benefited, the poor did not. They remained illiterate, undernourished, and often subjected to brutal treatment by rulers and landowners. Elite women in Europe and China increasingly joined literate society, but they gained no new rights. Urban areas also profited more from the new wealth than rural ones, so people seeking refinement flocked to the cities. Some former cultural centers, like the Italian peninsula, lost their luster as new, more commercially and culturally dynamic centers took their place.

Among states, too, cultural inequalities were glaring. Although the Islamic and Chinese worlds confidently retained their own systems of knowing, believing, and representing, the Americas and Oceania increasingly faced European cultural pressures. Here, while hybrid practices became widespread by the late eighteenth century, European beliefs and habits took over as the standards for judging degrees of "civilization." African cultures largely escaped this influence, though their homelands felt the impact of European expansionism because of the slave trade.

From a commercial standpoint, the world was more integrated than ever before. But the exposure and cultural borrowing that global trade promoted largely reconfirmed established ways. The Chinese, for instance, still believed in the superiority of their traditional knowledge and customs. Muslim rulers, confident of the primacy of Islam, allowed others to form subordinate cultural communities within their realm and adopted the Europeans' knowledge only when it served their own imperial purposes.

Only the Europeans were constructing knowledge that they believed was both universal and objective, enabling mortals to master the world of nature and all its inhabitants. This view would prove consequential, as well as controversial, in the centuries to come.

AFTER YOU READ THIS CHAPTER

Review and research on **STUDYSPACE:** wwnorton.com/studyspace

TRACING THE GLOBAL STORYLINES

FOCUS ON: *The Flourishing of Regional Cultures*

The Islamic World

- The Ottomans' unique cultural synthesis accommodates not only mystical Sufis and ultraorthodox *ulama* but also military men, administrators, and clerics.
- The Safavid state proclaims the triumph of Shiism and Persian influences in the sumptuous new capital, Isfahan.
- Mughal courtly culture values art and learning and welcomes non-Muslim contributions.

East Asia

- China's cultural flourishing, coming from within, is evident in the broad circulation of traditional ideas, publishing, and mapmaking.
- Japan's imperial court at Kyoto develops an elite culture of theater, stylized painting, tea ceremonies, and flower arranging.

Europe

- Cultural flourishing known as the Enlightenment yields a faith in reason and a belief in humans' ability to fathom the laws of nature and human behavior.
- European thinkers articulate a belief in unending human progress.
- Europeans expand into Australia and the South Pacific.

Africa

- Slave-trading states such as Asante, Oyo, and Benin celebrate royal power and wealth through art.

The Americas

- Even as Euro-Americans participate in the Enlightenment, their culture reflects Native American and African influences.

CHRONOLOGY

The Islamic World

- Shah Abbas builds Isfahan **1587–1629**
- Taj Mahal built in Mughal dynasty **1630–1650**

Europe

East Asia

- Growing circulation of books and ideas in China **1600s**
- "Floating worlds" appear in Japanese cities **1600s**

Africa

- Oyo and Asante kingdoms produce vibrant artistic works **1600s**

The Americas

- Hybrid cultures appear **1600s**

1600 1650

KEY TERMS

cartography *p. 531*

creoles *p. 545*

enlightened absolutists *p. 520*

Enlightenment *p. 535*

Forbidden City of Beijing *p. 528*

great plaza at Isfahan *p. 529*

laissez-faire *p. 539*

Oceania *p. 546*

Palace of Versailles *p. 528*

peninsulars *p. 545*

scientific method *p. 535*

Taj Mahal *p. 525*

Topkapi Palace *p. 528*

STUDY QUESTIONS

1. **Explain** the processes that brought forth cultural syntheses in the three Islamic dynasties during this era. To what extent did European culture influence each empire?
2. **Describe** Chinese and Japanese cultural achievements during this period. How did foreign influences affect each dynasty?
3. **Define** the term *Enlightenment* as it pertained to Europe. How did Enlightenment ideas shape European attitudes toward other cultures?
4. **Explain** the various factors that contributed to the growth of hybrid cultures in the Americas during this era. How similar and different were these new societies across the Americas?
5. **Analyze** the impact of Enlightenment ideas in the Americas. Did the spread of this philosophy bring communities across the Atlantic together, or did it drive them apart?
6. **Compare and contrast** European exploration of Oceania in the eighteenth century to European exploration of the Americas in the sixteenth century (see Chapter 12). How did European exploration of Oceania transform European attitudes toward non-European groups around the world?
7. **Explain** how global trade changed world cultures at this time.
8. **Analyze** the extent to which dynastic rulers around the world were able to control cultural developments during this period. How did new cultural productions potentially undermine local governments?

Tulip Period in Ottoman Empire **1720s**

Isaac Newton publishes *Principia Mathematica* **1687**

Enlightenment philosophy spreads among educated elites **1700s**

Adam Smith publishes *The Wealth of Nations* **1776**

Voyages of Captain Cook **1768–1779**

Enlightenment philosophy spreads among colonial elites **1700s**

1700 | 1750 | 1800

BEFORE YOU READ THIS CHAPTER

wwnorton.com/
STUDYSPACE

GLOBAL STORYLINES

- A new era based on radically new ideas of freedom and the nation-state emerges in Europe and the Americas.
- The watchwords of the age are free inquiry, free markets, free labor, and governments freely chosen by free individuals.
- The worldwide balance of power changes.

CHAPTER OUTLINE

FOCUS QUESTIONS

- What were the new languages of freedom and how did they alter social, economic, and political relations in the Atlantic world?
- How did the concept of the nation-state challenge traditional political and social arrangements?
- What were the industrious and industrial revolutions and how did they transform the global economy?
- How did transformations in the Atlantic world alter the economic, political, and military balance in the world?

15

Reordering the World, 1750–1850

In 1798, the French commander Napoleon Bonaparte invaded Egypt. At the time, Europeans regarded this territory as the cradle of a once-great culture, a land bridge to the Red Sea and trade with Asia, and an outpost of the Ottoman Empire. Occupying the country would allow Napoleon to introduce some of the principles of the French Revolution and to seize control of trade routes to Asia. Napoleon also hoped that by defeating the Ottomans, who ruled over Egypt, he would augment his and France's historic greatness. But events did not go as Napoleon planned, for his troops faced a resentful Egyptian population.

Although Napoleon soon returned to France and his dream of a French Egypt was short-lived, his invasion challenged Ottoman rule and threatened the balance of power in Europe. Indeed, Napoleon's actions in Africa, the Americas, and Europe, combined with the principles of the French Revolution, laid the foundations for a new era—one based on a radically new idea—freedom—which first rang out across western Europe and the Americas. Freedom was expected to manifest itself in personal relationships, economic exchanges, and political action. In Europe and the Americas, though not elsewhere, the era also witnessed the emergence of the nation-state. This new form of political organization derived legitimacy from its inhabitants, often referred to as citizens, who in theory, if not always in practice, shared a common culture, ethnicity, and language.

The demand for freedom had its roots in the Atlantic world, where it destroyed the American colonial domains of Spain, Portugal, Britain, and France and brought new nations to the stage. The impulse for change was a belief that new, unfettered institutions would benefit all. The watchwords of the age were free inquiry, free markets, free labor, and governments freely chosen by free individuals. Yet, freedom in some corners of the globe set the stage for unfreedoms elsewhere and led inexorably to changes in the worldwide balance of power. Even as western European countries lost their New World colonies, they gained economic and military strength, which further challenged Asian and African governments. In China, the ruling Manchus faced European pressure to permit expanded trade. In Egypt and the Ottoman Empire, reform-minded leaders tried to modernize. When the rise of Egypt threatened Europe's strategic interests in the eastern Mediterranean, the European states intervened to rein in that country's ambitions. Underlying much of these political and social upheavals were major changes in the world economy, in which countries began to produce goods less for their own population and more for people living in other places and countries around the globe, intensifying the trend for worlds coming together.

REVOLUTIONARY TRANSFORMATIONS AND NEW LANGUAGES OF FREEDOM

In the eighteenth century, the circulation of goods, people, and ideas created pressures for reform around the Atlantic world. As economies expanded, many people felt that the restrictive mercantilist system prevented them from sharing in the new wealth and power. Similarly, an increasingly literate public called for their states to adopt just practices, including the abolition of torture and the accountability of rulers. Although elites resisted the demands for more freedom to trade and more influence in government, power holders could not stamp out these demands before they became—in several places—full-scale revolutions.

Reformers wanted to establish **popular sovereignty** (power residing in the people themselves) and argued that unregulated economies would produce faster economic growth. In fact, they argued that three important aspects of such economies would yield more just and more efficient societies, ultimately benefiting everyone everywhere in the world. These three aspects were **free trade**, that is, domestic and international trade unencumbered by tariff barriers, quotas, and fees; **free markets**, which would be unregulated; and **free labor**, which meant wage-paying rather than slave labor.

The struggle to create new political and economic relationships gave people the chance to think differently. Two new ideas were especially appealing: **nationalism** (the idea that members of a shared community called a "nation" should have sovereignty within the borders of their state) and **democracy** (the idea that these people, through membership in a nation, should choose their own representatives and be governed by them). The first expression of this new thinking occurred in thirteen of Britain's North American colonies and in France. In both places, the "nation" and the "people" toppled their former rulers.

As democratic and nationalist ideas emerged in the American and French revolutions, questions arose as to how far freedom should be extended. Should women, Native Americans, and slaves be given the rights of citizens? Should people without property be given the vote? Should freedom be extended to non-Europeans? For the most part, European and Euro-American elites answered no. The same elites who wanted a freer world often exploited slaves, denied women equal treatment, restricted colonial economies, and tried to forcibly open Asia's and Africa's markets to European trade and investment. In Africa, another corner of the Atlantic world, idealistic upheavals did not lead to free and sovereign peoples, but to greater enslavement.

POLITICAL REORDERINGS

Late in the eighteenth century, revolutionary ideas spread across the Atlantic world (see Map 15.1) following the trail of Enlightenment ideas about freedom and reason. As more newspapers, pamphlets, and books circulated in European countries and American colonies, readers began to discuss their societies' problems and to believe they had the right to participate in governance.

The slogans of independence, freedom, liberty, and equality seemed to promise an end to oppression, hardship, and inequities. In the North American colonies and in France, revolutions ultimately brought down monarchies and blossomed in republics. The examples of the United States and France soon encouraged others in the Caribbean and Central and South America to reject the rule of monarchs. In all of these revolutionary environments, new institutions—such as written constitutions and permanent parliaments—claimed to represent the people. The claims of popular sovereignty also became rooted in the idea of the nation (people of a common language, common culture, and common history), giving rise to the notion of the **nation-state**.

The North American War of Independence, 1776–1783

By the mid-eighteenth century, Britain's colonies in North America swelled with people and prosperity. Bustling port cities like Charleston, Philadelphia, New York, and Boston saw inflows of African slaves, European migrants, and manufactured goods, while agricultural staples flowed out. A "genteel" class of merchants and landowning planters dominated colonial affairs.

But with settlers arriving from Europe and slaves from Africa, land was a constant source of dispute. Planters struggled with independent farmers (yeomen). Sons and daughters of farmers, often unable to inherit or acquire land near their parents, moved westward, where they came into conflict with Amerindian peoples. To defend their lands, many Indians allied with Britain's rival, France. After losing the Seven Years' War (see Chapter 13), however, France ceded its Canadian colony to Britain. This left many Indians no choice but to turn to Britain to help them resist the aggressive advances of land-hungry colonists. British officials did make some concessions to Indian interests, most visibly by issuing the Proclamation of 1763, which drew a line at the crest of the Appalachians beyond which Indian lands were to be protected from colonial settlement. Still, Britain did not have the troops to police the line, so while the proclamation antagonized some colonists, it did not really secure Indian lands.

ASSERTING INDEPENDENCE FROM BRITAIN Even as tensions simmered and sometimes boiled over into bloodshed on the western frontier of British North America, the situation of the British in North America still looked very strong in the mid-1760s. At that point, Britain stood supreme in the Atlantic world, with its greatest foes defeated and its empire expanding. Political revolution seemed unimaginable. And yet, a decade later, that is what occurred.

The spark came from King George III, who insisted that colonists help pay for Britain's war with France and for the benefits of being subjects of the British Empire. It seemed only reasonable to King George and his ministers, faced with staggering war debts, that colonists contribute to the crown that protected them. Accordingly, the king's officials imposed taxes on a variety of commodities and tried to end the lucrative smuggling by which colonists had been evading the restrictions that mercantilism was supposed to impose on colonial trade. To the king's surprise and dismay, colonists raised vigorous objections to the new measures and protested having to pay taxes when they lacked political representation in the British Parliament. (See Primary Source: The Other Revolution of 1776.)

In 1775, resistance in the form of petitions and boycotts turned into open warfare between a colonial militia and British

The Boston Massacre. *Paul Revere's idealized view of the Boston Massacre of March 5, 1770. In the years after the Seven Years' War, Bostonians grew increasingly disenchanted with British efforts to enforce imperial regulations. When British troops fired on and killed several members of an angry mob in what came to be called the "Boston Massacre," the resulting frenzy stirred revolutionary sentiments among the populace.*

troops in Massachusetts. Once blood was spilled, more radical voices came to the fore. Previously, leaders of the resistance to taxation without representation had claimed to revere the British Empire while fearing its corruptions. Now calls for severing the ties to Britain became more prominent. Thomas Paine, a recent immigrant from England, captured the new mood in a pamphlet he published in 1776, arguing that it was "common sense" for people to govern themselves. Later that year, the Continental Congress (in which representatives from thirteen colonies gathered) adapted part of Payne's popular pamphlet for the Declaration of Independence.

Drawing on Enlightenment themes (see Chapter 14), the declaration written by Thomas Jefferson stated the people's natural rights to govern themselves. It also drew inspiration from the writings of the British philosopher John Locke, notably the idea that governments should be based on a **social contract** in which the law binds both ruler and people. Locke had even written that the people had the right to rebel against their government if it broke the contract and infringed on their rights.

With the Declaration of Independence, the rebels announced their right to rid themselves of the English king and form their own government. But neither the Declaration of Independence nor Locke's writings explained how these colonists (now calling themselves Americans) should organize a nonmonarchical

Hudson Bay
RUSSIA
BRITISH NORTH AMERICA
OREGON (Claimed by Spain, Russia and Britain)
Quebec
Boston
New York
Philadelphia
Washington, D.C.
LOUISIANA
UNITED STATES
1776 (independence recognized by Great Britain 1783)
Santa Fe
Charleston
MEXICO 1821
FLORIDA
ATLANTIC OCEAN
Gulf of Mexico
CUBA
PUERTO RICO
Mexico City
BELIZE
JAMAICA
REPUBLIC OF HAITI 1804
GUADELOUPE (Fr.)
MARTINIQUE (Fr.)
UNITED PROVINCES OF CENTRAL AMERICA 1823
Cartagena
Caracas
TRINIDAD (Br.)
PACIFIC OCEAN
REPUBLIC OF COLOMBIA 1819
GUIANA
Quito
PERU 1821
Lima
BRAZIL 1822
BOLIVIA 1825
PARAGUAY 1811
Rio de Janeiro
CHILE 1818
PROVINCES OF LA PLATA 1816
URUGUAY 1828
Buenos Aires
Montevideo
British possessions
Spanish possessions
French possessions
Portuguese possessions
Dutch possessions
Ottoman possessions
Russian Empire
1776 Date of political independence from European (or Ottoman) colonial rule
0 1000 2000 Miles
0 1000 2000 Kilometers

MAP 15.1 | Revolutions of National Independence in the Atlantic World, 1776–1829

Influenced by Enlightenment thinkers and the French Revolution, colonies gained independence from European powers (and in the case of Greece, from the Ottoman Empire) in the late eighteenth and early nineteenth centuries.

- Which European powers granted independence to their colonial possessions in the Americas during this period? What were the first two colonial territories to become independent in the Americas?
- Given that the second American republic arose from a violent slave revolt, why do you suppose the United States was reluctant to recognize its political independence?
- According to your reading, why did colonies in Spanish and Portuguese America obtain political independence decades after the United States won its independence?

PRIMARY SOURCE

The Other Revolution of 1776

The year 1776 is mainly known as the year American colonists declared their independence from the British Empire. But it also marked the publication of Adam Smith's* An Inquiry into the Nature and Causes of the Wealth of Nations, *the most important book in the history of economic thought. Smith, a Scottish philosopher, felt that constraints on trade (by governments or private monopolies) prevented people from achieving their full potential and thereby impoverished nations. Although he was not opposed to colonies per se, in this selection Smith warns British authorities that mercantilist controls on their colonies are not only unjust but counterproductive. Thus, "free trade" is tied to the fate of Europe's colonies.

The exclusive trade of the mother countries tends to diminish, or, at least, to keep down below what they would otherwise rise to, both the enjoyments and industry of all those nations in general, and of the American colonies in particular. . . . By rendering the colony produce dearer in all other countries, it lessens its consumption, and thereby cramps the industry of the colonies, and both the enjoyments and the industry of all other countries, which both enjoy less when they pay more for what they enjoy, and produce less when they get less for what they produce.

By rendering the produce of all other countries dearer in the colonies, it cramps, in the same manner, the industry of all other countries, and both the enjoyments and the industry of the colonies. It is a clog which, for the supposed benefit of some particular countries, embarrasses the pleasures, and encumbers the industry of all other countries; but of the colonies more than of any other.

It not only excludes, as much as possible, all other countries from one particular market; but it confines, as much as possible, the colonies to one particular market: and the difference is very great between being excluded from one particular market, when all others are open, and being confined to one particular market, when all others are shut up. The surplus produce of the colonies, however, is the original source of all that increase of enjoyments and industry which Europe derives from the discovery and colonization of America; and the exclusive trade of the mother countries tends to render this source much less abundant than it otherwise would be.

QUESTIONS FOR ANALYSIS

- In terms of the American colonies, who is "the mother country"?
- According to Smith, how does exclusive trade between the mother country and the colonists diminish the colonies' development?

Source: Adam Smith, An Inquiry into the Nature and Causes of the Wealth of Nations, *Book 4, edited by Edwin Cannan (Chicago: University of Chicago Press, 1776/1977), pp. 105–106.*

government—or how thirteen weakly connected colonies (now calling themselves states) might prevail against the world's most powerful empire. Nonetheless, the colonies soon became embroiled in a revolution that would turn the world upside down.

During their War of Independence, Americans designed new political arrangements. First, individual states elected delegates to constitutional conventions, where they drafted written constitutions to govern the workings of each state. Second, by eliminating royal authority, the state constitutions gave extensive powers to legislative bodies, whose members "the people" would elect. But who constituted the people? That is, who had voting rights? Not women. Not slaves. Not Indians. Not even adult white men who owned no property.

Despite the limited extent of voting rights, the notion that all men were created equal overturned former social hierarchies. Thus common men no longer automatically deferred to gentlemen of higher rank. Many women claimed that their contributions to the Revolution's cause (by managing farms and shops in their husbands' absence) earned them greater equality in marriage, including property rights. In letters to her husband, John Adams, who was a representative in the Continental Congress and a champion of American independence, Abigail Adams stopped referring to the family farm as "yours" and instead called it "ours." Most revolutionary of all, many slaves sided against the Revolution, for it was the British who offered them freedom—most directly in exchange for military service.

Alas, their hopes for freedom were thwarted when Britain conceded the loss of its rebellious American colonies. That improbable outcome owed to a war in which British armies won most of the major battles but could not finish off the Continental Army under the command of General George Washington. Washington

Abigail Adams. *Abigail Adams was the wife of John Adams, a leader in the movement for American independence and later the second president of the United States. Abigail's letters to her husband testified to the ways in which revolutionary enthusiasm for liberty and equality began to reach into women's minds. In the spring of 1776, Abigail wrote to implore that the men in the Continental Congress "remember the ladies, and be more generous and favorable to them than your ancestors. . . . If particular care and attention is not paid to the Ladies we are determined to foment a Rebellion, and will not hold ourselves bound by any Laws in which we have no voice, or Representation."*

hung on and held his troops together long enough to convince the French that the American cause was not hopeless and that supporting it might be a way to settle a score against the British. This they did, and with the Treaty of Paris (1783) the United States gained its independence.

BUILDING A REPUBLICAN GOVERNMENT With independence, the former colonists had to build a new government. They generally agreed that theirs was not to be a monarchy. But what it *was* to be remained through the 1780s a source of much debate, involving heated words and sometimes heated action.

Amid the political revolution against monarchy, the prospect of a social revolution of women, slaves, and artisans generated a reaction against what American elites called the "excesses of democracy." Their fears increased after farmers in Massachusetts, led by Daniel Shays, interrupted court proceedings in which the state tried to foreclose on their properties for nonpayment of taxes. The farmers who joined in Shays's rebellion in 1786 also denounced illegitimate taxation—this time, by their state's government. Acting in the interests of the fledgling government, Massachusetts militiamen defeated the rebel army. But to save the young nation from falling into "anarchy," propertied men convened the Constitutional Convention in Philadelphia a year later.

This gathering aimed to forge a document that would create a more powerful national government and a more unified nation. After fierce debate, the convention drafted a charter for a **republican government** in which power and rulership would rest with representatives of the people—not a king. When it went before the states for approval, the Constitution was controversial. Its critics, known as Anti-Federalists, feared the growth of a potentially tyrannical national government and insisted on including a Bill of Rights to protect individual liberties from abusive government intrusions. Ultimately the Constitution won ratification, and it was soon amended by the Bill of Rights.

Ratification of the Constitution and the addition of the Bill of Rights did not end arguments about the scope and power of the national government of the United States, although they did quiet the most heated controversies. In an uneasy truce, political leaders agreed not to let the debate over whether to abolish slavery escalate into a cause for disunion. As the frontier pushed westward, however, the question of which new states would or would not allow slavery sparked debates again. Initially, the existence of ample land postponed a confrontation. In 1800, Thomas Jefferson's election as the third president of the United States marked the triumph of a model of sending pioneers out to new lands in order to reduce conflict on old lands. In the same year, however, a Virginia slave named Gabriel Prosser raised an army of slaves to seize the state capital at Richmond and won support from white artisans and laborers for a more inclusive republic. His dream of an egalitarian revolution fell victim to white terror and black betrayal, though: twenty-seven slaves, including Prosser, went to the gallows. With them, for the moment, died the dream of a multiracial republic in which all men were truly created equal.

But the issue of slavery did not go away. Indeed, with ideas of the dignity and rights of free labor gaining popularity in the northern states, the truce by which political leaders tried to keep debates over slavery from escalating into a cause for disunion became even more uneasy.

In a larger Atlantic world context, the American Revolution ushered in a new age based on ideas of freedom. The successful defiance of Europe's most powerful empire and the establishment of a nonmonarchical, republican form of government sent shock waves through the Americas and Europe and even into distant corners of Asia and Africa.

The French Revolution, 1789–1799

Partly inspired by the American Revolution, French men and women soon began to call for liberty too—and the result profoundly shook Europe's dynasties and social hierarchies. Its impact, though, reached well beyond Europe, for the French Revolution, even more than the American, inspired rebels and terrified rulers around the globe.

ORIGINS AND OUTBREAK For decades, enlightened thinkers had attacked France's old regime—the court, the aristocracy, and the church—at the risk of imprisonment or exile. But by the mid-eighteenth century, discontent had spread beyond the educated few. In the countryside, peasants grumbled about having to pay taxes and tithes to the church, whereas nobles and clergy paid almost no taxes. Also, despite improved health and nutrition, peasants still suffered occasional deprivation. A combination of these pressures, as well as a fiscal crisis, unleashed the French Revolution of 1789.

Ironically, the king himself opened the door to revolution. Eager to weaken his rival, England, Louis XVI spent huge sums in support of the American rebels—and thereby overloaded the state's debt. It was not the size of the debt but the French king's inability to raise funds that put him in a bind. To restore his credit, Louis needed to raise taxes on the privileged classes, but to do so he was forced to convene the Estates-General, a medieval advisory body that had not met for over a century. Like the American colonists, French nobles argued that taxation gave them the right of representation. When the king reluctantly agreed to summon the Estates-General in 1788, he still thought he would prevail. After all, the delegates of the clergy (the First Estate) and the aristocracy (the Second Estate) could overrule the delegates representing everyone else (the Third Estate), because each estate voted as one body. This meant that it was possible to outvote the Third Estate.

However, when the delegates assembled, the Third Estate refused to be outvoted. It insisted that those who worked and paid taxes *were* the nation, and it demanded that all delegates sit together in one chamber and vote as individuals. The privileged few, critics claimed, were parasites. As arguments raged, peasants began to attack castles in another indication that "the people" were throwing off old inequalities. Soon delegates of the Third Estate declared themselves to be the "National Assembly," the body that should determine France's future.

On July 14, 1789, a Parisian crowd attacked a medieval armory in search of weapons. Not only did this armory—the Bastille—hold gunpowder, but it was also an infamous prison for political prisoners. The crowd stormed the prison and murdered the commanding officer, then cut off his head and paraded it through the streets of Paris. On this day (Bastille Day), the king made the fateful decision not to call out the army, and the capital city belonged to the crowd. As news spread to the countryside, peasants torched manor houses and destroyed municipal archives containing records of the hated feudal dues. Barely three weeks later, the French National Assembly abolished the feudal privileges of the nobility and the clergy. It also declared a new era of liberty, equality, and fraternity.

REVOLUTIONARY TRANSFORMATIONS The "Declaration of the Rights of Man and Citizen" followed a few weeks later. It echoed the Americans' Declaration of Independence, but in more radical terms. It guaranteed all citizens of the French nation inviolable liberties and gave all men equality under the law. It also proclaimed that "the principle of all sovereignty rests essentially in the nation." Thus, the French Revolution connected more closely the concept of a people with a nation. Both the rhetorical and the real war against feudal privileges threatened to end dynastic and aristocratic rule in Europe.

The "Tennis Court Oath." *Locked out of the chambers of the Estates-General, the deputies of the Third Estate reconvened at a nearby indoor tennis court in June 1789; there they swore an oath not to disband until the king recognized the sovereignty of a national assembly.*

Women March on Versailles. *On October 5, 1789, a group of market women, many of them fishwives (traditionally regarded as leaders of the poor), marched on the Paris city hall to demand bread. Quickly, their numbers grew, and they redirected their march to Versailles, some twelve miles away and the symbol of the entire political order. In response to the women, the king finally appeared on the balcony and agreed to sign the revolutionary decree and return with the women to Paris.*

Relations in social hierarchies changed too, as women felt that the new principles of citizenship should include women's rights. In 1791, a group of women demanded the right to bear arms to defend the revolution, but they stopped short of claiming equal rights for both sexes. In their view, women would become citizens by being good revolutionary wives and mothers, not because of any natural rights. In the same year, Olympe de Gouges composed the "Declaration of the Rights of Woman and Citizen," proposing rights to divorce, hold property in marriage, be educated, and have public careers. The all-male assembly did not take up these issues, believing that a "fraternity" of free *men* composed the nation. (For a statement claiming similar rights for women in Britain, see Primary Source: Mary Wollstonecraft on the Rights of Women.)

As the revolution gained momentum, more nobles and clergy fled the country. In late 1790, all clergy had to take an oath of loyalty to the new state—an action that enraged Catholics. Meanwhile, the revolutionary ranks began to splinter, as men and women argued over the revolution's proper goals. Soon a new National Convention was elected by universal manhood suffrage, meaning that all adult males could vote—the first such election in Europe. In 1792, the first French Republic was proclaimed. But radicalization continued, and by early 1793 Louis XVI had lost his head to the guillotine, and France was at war with many of its neighbors.

THE TERROR After the king's execution, radicals known as Jacobins, who wanted to extend the revolution beyond France's borders, launched the Reign of Terror to purge the nation of its internal enemies. Jacobin leaders, including the lawyer Maximilien Robespierre, oversaw the execution of as many as 40,000 so-called enemies of the people—mostly peasants and laborers.

To spread revolution to other parts of Europe, the radicals instituted the first national draft. By 1794 France's army numbered some 800,000 soldiers, making it the world's largest. Most French officers now came from the middle classes, some even from the lower class. Foot soldiers identified with the French fatherland and demonstrated their solidarity by singing songs like "The Marseillaise."

The revolutionaries understood that to change society they would have to eliminate all symbols of the old regime. So they changed street names to honor revolutionary heroes, destroyed monuments to the royal family, adopted a new flag, eliminated titles, and insisted that everyone be addressed as "Citizen." They were so exhilarated by the new world they were creating that they changed time itself. Now they reckoned time not from the birth of Christ but from the moment the French Republic was proclaimed. Thus September 22, 1792, became day 1 of year 1 of the new age. The radicals also unsuccessfully attempted to replace the Catholic faith, which they accused of corruption and inequality, with a religion of reason.

By mid-1794, enthusiasm for Robespierre's measures had lost popular support, and Robespierre himself went to the guillotine on 9 Thermidor (July 28, 1794). His execution marked the end of the Terror. Several years later, following more political turmoil, a coup d'état brought to power a thirty-year-old general from the recently annexed Mediterranean island of Corsica.

The general, **Napoleon Bonaparte** (1769–1821), put security and order ahead of social reform. True, his regime retained many of the revolutionary changes, especially those associated with more efficient state government, but retreating from the Jacobins' anti-Catholicism, he allowed religion to be freely practiced again in France. Determined not only to reform France but also to prevail over its enemies, he retreated from republican principles. Napoleon first was a member of a three-man consulate;

PRIMARY SOURCE

Mary Wollstonecraft on the Rights of Women

As revolutionaries stressed the rights of "man" across the Atlantic world, Mary Wollstonecraft (1759–1797), an English writer, teacher, editor, and proponent of spreading education, resented her male colleagues' celebration of their newfound liberties. In* A Vindication of the Rights of Woman *(1792), one of the founding works of modern feminism, she argued that the superiority of men was as arbitrary as the divine right of kings. For this, male progressives denounced her. The author is a "hyena in petticoats," noted one critic. In fact, she was arguing that women had the same rights to be reasonable creatures as men and that education should be available equally to both sexes.

I love man as my fellow; but his sceptre, real or usurped, extends not to me, unless the reason of an individual demands my homage; and even then the submission is to reason, and not to man. In fact, the conduct of an accountable being must be regulated by the operations of its own reason; or on what foundation rests the throne of God?

It appears to me necessary to dwell on these obvious truths, because females have been insulated, as it were; and while they have been stripped of the virtues that should clothe humanity, they have been decked with artificial graces that enable them to exercise a short-lived tyranny. Love, in their bosoms, taking the place of every nobler passion, their sole ambition is to be fair, to raise emotion instead of inspiring respect; and this ignoble desire, like the servility in absolute monarchies, destroys all strength of character. Liberty is the mother of virtue, and if women be, by their very constitution, slaves, and not allowed to breathe the sharp invigorating air of freedom, they must ever languish like exotics, and be reckoned beautiful flaws in nature. Let it also be remembered, that they are the only flaw.

As to the argument respecting the subjection in which the sex has ever been held, it retorts on man. The many have always been enthralled by the few; and monsters, who scarcely have shown any discernment of human excellence, have tyrannized over thousands of their fellow-creatures. Why have men of superior endowments submitted to such degradation? For, is it not universally acknowledged that kings, viewed collectively, have ever been inferior, in abilities and virtue, to the same number of men taken from the common mass of mankind—yet have they not, and are they not still treated with a degree of reverence that is an insult to reason? China is not the only country where a living man has been made a God. *Men* have submitted to superior strength to enjoy with impunity the pleasure of the moment; *women* have only done the same, and therefore till it is proved that the courtier, who servilely resigns the birthright of a man, is not a moral agent, it cannot be demonstrated that woman is essentially inferior to man because she has always been subjugated.

QUESTIONS FOR ANALYSIS

- Wollstonecraft compares men to kings and women to slaves. What are her criticisms of kings, and why does she call them "monsters"?
- In what ways are Wollstonecraft's ideas an outgrowth of Enlightenment thinking?
- Do you find Wollstonecraft's arguments compelling? Explain why or why not.

Source: Mary Wollstonecraft, A Vindication of the Rights of Woman, *edited by Miriam Brody (New York: Penguin Books, 1792/1993), pp. 122–23.*

then he became first consul; finally, he proclaimed himself emperor. But he took the title Emperor of the French, not Emperor of France, and prepared a constitution subject to a vote of approval. He also centralized government administration and created a system of rational tax collection. Most important, he created a civil legal code—the "Code Napoleon"—that applied throughout all of France (and the French colonies, including the Louisiana Territory). By designing a law code applicable to the nation as a whole, Napoleon created a model that would be widely imitated by emerging nation-states in Europe and the Americas in the century to come.

Napoleon's Empire, 1799–1815

Determined to extend the reach of French influence, Napoleon had his armies trumpet the principles of liberty, equality, and fraternity wherever they went. Many local populations actually embraced the French, regarding them as liberators from the old order. Although Napoleon thought the entire world would take up his cause, this was not always the case, as he learned in Egypt. After defeating Mamluk troops there in 1798, Napoleon soon faced a rebellious local Egyptian population.

Battle of the Pyramids. *The French army invaded Egypt with grand ambitions and high hopes. Napoleon brought a large cadre of scholars along with his 36,000-man army, intending to win Egyptians to the cause of the French Revolution and to establish a French imperial presence on the banks of the Nile. This idealized portrait of the famous* Battle of the Pyramids, *fought on July 21, 1798, shows Napoleon and his forces crushing the Mamluk military forces.*

In Portugal, Spain, and Russia, French troops also faced fierce popular resistance. Portuguese and Spanish soldiers and peasants formed bands of resisters called guerrillas, and British troops joined them to fight the French in the Peninsular War (1808–1813). In Germany and Italy, as local inhabitants grew tired of hearing that the French occupiers' ways were superior, many looked to their past for inspiration to oppose the French. Now they discovered something they had barely recognized before: *national* traditions and borders. In fact, one of the ironies of Napoleon's attempt to bring all of Europe under French rule was that instead of creating a unified continent, it laid the foundations for nationalist strife.

In Europe, Napoleon extended his empire from the Iberian Peninsula to the Austrian and Prussian borders (see Map 15.2). By 1812, when he invaded Russia, however, his forces were too overstretched and undersupplied to survive the harsh winter. Until this point, divisions among his enemies had aided Napoleon's progress. But after his failed attack on Russia, all the major European powers united against him. Forced to retreat, Napoleon and his army were vanquished in Paris. Subsequently Napoleon escaped exile to lead his troops one last time; but at the Battle of Waterloo in Belgium in 1815, armies from Prussia, Austria, Russia, and Britain crushed his troops as they made their last stand.

In 1815, delegates from the victorious states met at the Congress of Vienna. They agreed to respect one another's borders and to cooperate in preventing future revolutions and war. They restored thrones to monarchs deposed by the French under Napoleon, and they returned France itself to the care of a new Bourbon king. Great Britain and Russia—one a constitutional monarchy (ruled by a prime minister and legislative body, with oversight by a king), the other an autocracy (in which the ruler did not share power with anyone)—cooperated to prevent any future attempts to dominate the continent.

The impact of the French Revolution and Napoleon's conquests, however, was far-reaching. In numerous German states, the changes introduced under French revolutionary occupation remained in place. Napoleon's occupation of the Italian peninsula also sparked underground movements for liberty and for Italian unification, much to the chagrin of Austrian and French monarchs. These upheavals even affected Spain and Portugal's links to their colonies in the Americas. The stage was now set for a century-long struggle between those who wanted to restore society as it was before the French Revolution and those who wanted to guarantee a more liberal order based on individual rights, limited government, and free trade.

Revolutions in the Caribbean and Iberian America

REVOLUTION IN SAINT DOMINGUE (HAITI) The thirteen colonies were not the only ones to secede from European masters. France also saw colonies break away in this age of new freedoms. This was the case in Saint Domingue. Unlike most of British North America, here the revolution came from the

MAP 15.2 | Napoleon's Empire, 1812

Early in the first decade of the nineteenth century, Napoleon controlled almost all of Europe.

- What major states were under French control? What countries were allied to France?
- Compare this map with the European part of Map 15.1, and explain how Napoleon redrew the map of Europe. What major country was not under French control?
- How was Napoleon able to control and build alliances with so many states and kingdoms?

bottom rungs of the social ladder: slaves. In this Caribbean colony, freedom therefore meant not just liberation from Europe, but emancipation from white planters. Saint Domingue therefore added a second, global dimension to the nineteenth-century struggle over personal liberties. It also posed very dramatically the question: how universal were these new rights?

The French Revolution sent shock waves through this highly prized French colony. At the time, the island's black slave population numbered 500,000, compared with 40,000 white French settlers and about 30,000 free "people of color" (individuals of mixed black and white ancestry, as well as freed black slaves). Almost two-thirds of the slaves were relatively recent arrivals, brought to the colony to toil on its renowned sugar plantations. The slave population was an angry majority producing wealth for a rich minority of a different race.

After the events of 1789 in France, white settlers in Saint Domingue sought self-government, while slaves borrowed the revolutionary language to denounce their masters. As civil war erupted, Dominican slaves fought French forces that had arrived to restore order. Finally, in 1793, the National Convention in France abolished slavery. In part, the motive was to declare the universality of liberty, equality, and fraternity within the French nation, which included colonies. In part, it was to restore order to the colony.

Once liberated, the former slaves took control of the island, but their struggles were not over. First they had to fight British and Spanish forces on the island. Then Napoleon took power in France, restored slavery, and sent an army to suppress forces led by Toussaint L'Ouverture, a former slave. But before long a combination of guerrilla fighters and yellow fever decimated the French army. In 1804, General Jean-Jacques Dessalines declared "Haiti" independent (see Current Trends in World History: Two Case Studies of Greed and Environmental Degradation as Evidence that History Matters).

The specter of a free country ruled by former slaves sent shudders across the Western Hemisphere. What if the revolt went viral? All around the Caribbean, news circulated about slave conspiracies. In Florida, fugitive slaves banded together with Seminole Indians to drive European settlers into the sea. The Haitian government contributed money and some troops to insurrectionists in South America. Charleston, South Carolina, went into a panic in 1793 when Dominican slaves were freed. As far away as Albany, New York, slaves were executed for arson. Jamaican rulers went on high alert. A version of martial law was declared in Venezuela. Even Thomas Jefferson, author of the Declaration of Independence and U.S. president at the time, refused to recognize Haiti. Like other American slave owners, he worried that the example of a successful slave uprising might inspire similar revolts in the United States.

Revolution in Saint Domingue. *In 1791, slaves and people of color rose up against white planters. This engraving was based on a German report on the uprising and depicts white fears of slave rebellion as much as the actual events themselves.*

The revolution in Saint Domingue therefore tilted the scales of campaigns for liberty far beyond the island. Fear of the contagion of slave revolt forced some governments to rethink the commitment to slavery altogether. The British government curtailed the expansion of plantation agriculture in Trinidad. One by one, European and American governments began to question the wisdom of importing more African slaves lest they lose control of their colonies. It was not just exalted ideals of liberty that fueled the abolitionist movement, but also the fear of what would happen if slaves rose up violently to claim rights given to other humans. Conservative thinkers like Edmund Burke took note; when he heard that 10,000 British soldiers died fighting Haitian slaves, he declared that fighting against such revolutionaries was like trying to conquer a cemetery! One of the greatest German philosophers of all time, Georg Wilhelm Friedrich Hegel, was an avid reader of the influential political journal *Minerva*. Hegel pored over the news of events in Saint Domingue and the freedom struggle of blacks as he was writing his famous treatise, *The Phenomenology of Mind*. That book would present a powerful image that would guide thinkers for the nineteenth and twentieth centuries: the image of slaves and masters locked in a struggle for mutual recognition and rights. Among those most charged by this image was Karl Marx.

From North America and France, revolutionary enthusiasm spread through Spanish and Portuguese America. But unlike the colonists' war of independence that produced the United States, political upheaval in the rest of the Americas began first of all from subordinated people of color. Then it was fueled by Napoleon's wider, global ambitions (see Map 15.3).

Even before the French Revolution, Andean Indians rebelled against Spanish colonial authority. In a spectacular uprising in the 1780s, they demanded freedom from forced labor and compulsory consumption of Spanish wares. After an army of 40,000 to 60,000 Andean Indians besieged the ancient capital of Cuzco and nearly vanquished Spanish armies, it took Spanish forces many years to eliminate the insurgents.

After this uprising, Iberian-American elites who feared their Indian or slave majorities renewed their loyalty to the Spanish or Portuguese crown. They hesitated to imitate the independence-seeking Anglo-American colonists, lest they unleash a social revolution. Ultimately, however, the French Revolution and Napoleonic wars shattered the ties between Spain and Portugal and their American colonies. Nonetheless, elites limited local power by interpreting "liberty" to apply just to property-owning classes.

CURRENT TRENDS IN WORLD HISTORY

Two Case Studies in Greed and Environmental Degradation

The Caribbean has four large islands, known as the Greater Antilles, each of which has a distinctive history—Cuba, Jamaica, Puerto Rico, and Hispaniola. Our discussion here is about the island of Hispaniola, which Columbus discovered in 1492 and which briefly became the center of Spain's New World empire. Later, in the seventeenth century, the French took over the smaller, western part of the island, and when political independence came to the Caribbean the island evolved into the two present-day states of Haiti and the Dominican Republic. Although both are relatively poor countries, their present economic and social differences are markedly and surprisingly different, especially considering that they share a relatively small island.

Haiti is the poorest country in the Americas. It is 99 percent deforested, suffers from massive soil erosion, and has a government unable to provide even the most basic services of water, electricity, and education to its people. Right next door, the Dominican Republic, with a population roughly the same size as Haiti's, has five times as many cars and trucks, six times as many paved roads, seven times as many college and university graduates, and eight times as many physicians. Its citizens enjoy significantly longer life expectancy and lower infant mortality than their Haitian neighbors. The differences cry out for an explanation, and one can be found only by examining the radically different histories of the two lands.

Two hundred and fifty years ago, Haiti, which was under French colonial rule at that time and known as Saint Domingue, was the richest colony in the Americas, perhaps even the richest colony in the world, accounting for two-thirds of France's worldwide investment. In contrast, Spanish-ruled Santo Domingo, which had ceased to be of interest to the Spanish colonial elites, who had turned their attention to the more populous and resource-rich territories of Mexico and Peru, was a backwater colonial territory. Saint Domingue's extraordinary wealth came from large, white-owned sugar plantations that used a massive and highly coerced slave population. The slaves' lives were short and brutal, lasting on average only fifteen years; hence the wealthy planter class had to replenish their labor supplies from Africa at frequent intervals.

White planters on the island were eager to amass quick fortunes so that they could sell out and return to France. Vastly outnumbered by enslaved Africans at a time when abolitionist sentiments were gaining ground in Europe and even

Toussaint L'Ouverture. *In the 1790s, Toussaint L'Ouverture led the slaves of the French colony of Saint Domingue in the world's largest and most successful slave insurrection. Toussaint embraced the principles of the French Revolution and demanded that universal rights be applied to people of African descent.*

BRAZIL AND CONSTITUTIONAL MONARCHY Brazil was a prized Portuguese colony whose path to independence saw little political turmoil and no social revolution. In 1807, French troops stormed Lisbon, the capital of Portugal, but not before the royals and their associates fled to Rio de Janeiro, then the capital of Brazil. There they made reforms in administration, agriculture, and manufacturing, and they established schools, hospitals, and a library. In fact, the royals' migration prevented the need for colonial claims for autonomy, because with their presence Brazil was now the center of the Portuguese empire. Furthermore, the royal family willingly shared power with the local planter aristocracy, so the economy prospered and slavery expanded.

In 1821, the exiled Portuguese king returned to Lisbon, instructing his son Pedro to preserve the family lineage in Rio de Janeiro. Soon, however, Brazilian elites rejected Portugal altogether. Fearing that colonists might topple the dynasty in Rio de Janeiro and spark regional disputes, in 1822 Pedro declared Brazil an independent empire. Shortly thereafter he established a constitutional monarchy, which would last until the late nineteenth century.

Now Brazilian business elites and bureaucrats cooperated to minimize conflicts, lest a slave revolt erupt. They crushed circulating among slaves in the Americas, the planters' families knew that their prosperity was unlikely to last. They gave little thought to sustainable growth and were not troubled that they were destroying their environment.

Yet, the planters greeted the onset of the French Revolution in 1789 with enthusiasm. They saw an opportunity to assert their independence from France, to engage in wider trading contacts with North America and the rest of the world, and thus to become even richer. They ignored the possibility that the ideals of the French Revolution—especially its slogan of liberty, equality, and fraternity—could inspire the island's free blacks, free mulattoes, and slaves. Indeed, no sooner had the white planters thrown in their lot with the Third Estate in France than a slave rebellion broke out in Saint Domingue. From its beginnings in 1791, it led, after great loss of life to African slaves and French soldiers, to the proclamation of an independent state in Haiti in 1804, ruled by African Americans. Haiti became the Americas' second independent republican government.

Although the revolt brought political independence to its black population, it only intensified the land's environmental deterioration. Not only did sugarcane fields become scorched battlefields, but freed slaves rushed to stake out independent plots on the old plantations and in wooded areas. In both places, the new peasant class energetically cleared the land. The small country became even more deforested, and intensive cultivation increased erosion and soil depletion. Haiti fell into a more vicious cycle of environmental degradation and poverty.

The second case study of greed leading to the destruction of the environment comes from the independent Brazilian state where the ruling elite, having achieved autonomy from Portugal, expanded the agrarian frontier. Landowners oversaw the clearing of ancient hardwood forests so that slaves and squatters could plant coffee trees. The clearing process had begun with sugarcane in the coastal regions, but it accelerated with coffee plantings in the hilly regions of São Paulo. In fact, coffee was a worse threat to Brazil's forests than any other invader in the previous 300 years. Consider that coffee trees thrive on soils that are neither soggy nor overly dry. Therefore planters razed the "virgin" forest, which contained a balanced variety of trees and undergrowth, and Brazil's once-fertile soil suffered rapid depletion by a single-crop industry. Within one generation the clear-cutting led to infertile soils and extensive erosion, which drove planters farther into the frontier to destroy even more forest and plant more coffee groves. The environmental impact was monumental: between 1788 and 1888, when slavery was abolished, Brazil produced about 10 million tons of coffee at the expense of 300 million tons of ancient forest biomass (the accumulated biological material from living organisms).

QUESTIONS FOR ANALYSIS

- Who intensified the deforestation and degradation in each story, and why did they do it?
- Why do you think deforestation increased in intensity after Haitians and Brazilians gained their autonomy/independence?

Explore Further

David Geggus (ed.), *The Impact of the Haitian Revolution in the Atlantic World* (2001).

Diamond, Jared, and James A. Robinson (eds.), *Natural Experiments of History* (2010).

regional uprisings, like the fledgling Republic of the Equator, and a campaign seeking a decentralized federation of southern provinces free from the Rio de Janeiro rulers. Even the largest urban slave revolt in the Americas, led by African Muslims in the state of Bahia, was quashed in a matter of days. By the 1840s, Brazil had achieved a political stability unmatched in the Americas. Its socially controlled transition from colony to nation was unique in Latin America.

MEXICO'S INDEPENDENCE When Napoleon occupied Spain, he sparked a crisis in the Spanish empire. Because the ruling Spanish Bourbons fell captive to Napoleon in 1807, colonial elites in Buenos Aires (Argentina), Caracas (Venezuela), and Mexico City (Mexico) enjoyed self-rule without an emperor. Once the Bourbons returned to power in 1814 after Napoleon was crushed, creoles (American-born Spaniards) resented it when Spain reinstated peninsulars (colonial officials born in Spain) and wanted to free themselves of these officials.

In Mexico, the royal army prevailed as long as there was any hope that the emperor in Madrid could maintain political authority. But from 1810 to 1813 two rural priests, Father Miguel Hidalgo and Father José María Morelos, galvanized

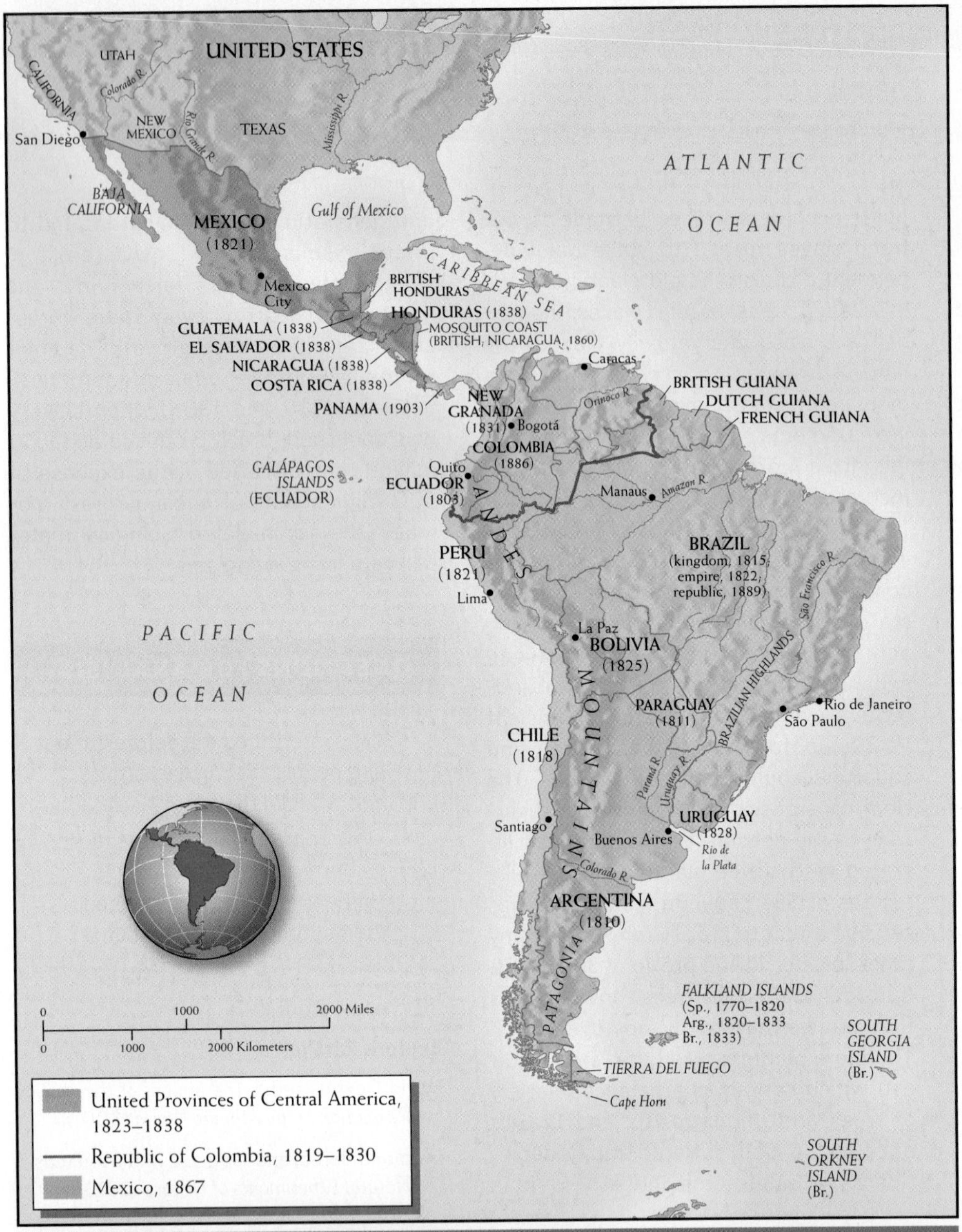

MAP 15.3 | Latin American Nation Building

Creating strong, unified nation-states proved difficult in Latin America. The map highlights this experience in Mexico, the United Provinces of Central America, and the Republic of Colombia. In each case, the governments' territorial and nation-building ambitions failed to some degree.

- During what period did a majority of the colonies in Latin America gain independence?
- Which European countries lost the most in Latin America during this period?
- Why did all these colonies gain their independence during this time?

an insurrection of peasants, Indians, and artisans. They sought an end to abuses by the elite, denounced bad government, and called for redistribution of wealth, return of land to the Indians, and respect for the Virgin of Guadalupe (who later became Mexico's patron saint). The rebellion nearly choked off Mexico City, the colony's capital, which horrified peninsulars and creoles alike and led them to support royal armies that eventually crushed the uprising.

Despite the military victory, Spain's hold on its colony weakened. Like the creoles of South America, those of Mexico identified themselves more as Mexicans and less as Spanish Americans. So when the Spanish king appeared unable to govern effectively abroad and even within Spain, the colonists considered home rule. A critical factor was the army, which remained faithful to the crown. However, when anarchy seemed to spread through Spain in 1820, Mexican generals (with support of the creoles) proclaimed Mexican independence in 1821. Unlike in Brazil, Mexican secession did not lead to stability.

OTHER SOUTH AMERICAN REVOLUTIONS The loosening of Spain's grip on its colonies was more prolonged and militarized than Britain's separation from its American colonies. Venezuela's **Simón Bolívar** (1783–1830), the son of a merchant-planter family who was educated on Enlightenment texts, dreamed of a land governed by reason. He revered Napoleonic France as a model state built on military heroism and constitutional proclamations. So did the Argentine leader General José de San Martín (1778–1850). Men like Bolívar, San Martín, and their many generals waged extended wars of independence against Spanish armies and their allies between 1810 and 1824. In some areas, like present-day Uruguay and Venezuela, the wars left entire provinces depopulated.

What started in South America as a political revolution against Spanish colonial authority escalated into a social struggle among Indians, mestizos, slaves, and whites. The militarized populace threatened the planters and merchants; rural folk battled against aristocratic creoles; Andean Indians fled the mines and occupied great estates. Provinces fought

Latin American Revolutionaries. (Left) *At the center of this Juan O'Gorman mural is the Mexican priest and revolutionary Miguel Hidalgo y Costilla, who led—as O'Gorman portrays—a multiclass and multiethnic movement.* (Right) *Simón Bolívar fought Spanish armies from Venezuela to Bolivia, securing the independence of five countries with the greater goal of transforming the former colonies into modern republics. Among his favorite models were George Washington and Napoleon Bonaparte, whose iconic portrait by Jacques-Louis David inspired this painting of Bolívar.*

their neighbors. Popular armies, having defeated Spanish forces by the 1820s, fought civil wars over the new postcolonial order.

New states and collective identities of nationhood now emerged. However, a narrow elite led these political communities, and their guiding principles were contradictory. Simón Bolívar, for instance, urged his followers to become "American," to overcome their local identities. He wanted the liberated countries to form a Latin American confederation, urging Peru and Bolivia to join Venezuela, Ecuador, and Colombia in the "Gran Colombia." But local identities prevailed, giving way to unstable national republics. Bolívar died surrounded by enemies; San Martín died in exile. The real heirs to independence were local military chieftains, who often forged alliances with landowners. Thus the legacy of the Spanish American revolutions was contradictory: the triumph of wealthy elites under a banner of liberty, yet often at the expense of poorer, ethnic, and mixed populations.

CHANGE AND TRADE IN AFRICA

Africa also was swept up in revolutionary tides, as increased domestic and world trade—including the selling of African slaves—shifted the terms of state building across the continent. The main catalyst for Africa's political shake-up was the rapid growth and then the demise of the Atlantic slave trade.

Abolition of the Slave Trade

Even as it enriched and empowered some Africans and many Europeans, the slave trade became a subject of fierce debate in the late eighteenth century. Some European and American revolutionaries argued that slave labor was inherently less productive than free wage labor and ought to be abolished. At the same time, another group favoring abolition of the slave trade insisted that traffic in slaves was immoral. In London they created committees, often led by Quakers, to lobby Parliament for an end to the slave trade. Quakers in Philadelphia did likewise. Pamphlets, reports, and personal narratives denounced the traffic in people. (See Primary Source: Frederick Douglass Asks, "What to the Slave Is the Fourth of July?")

In response to abolitionist efforts, North Atlantic powers moved to prohibit the slave trade. Denmark acted first in 1803, Great Britain followed in 1807, and the United States joined the campaign in 1808. Over time, the British persuaded the French and other European governments to do likewise. To enforce the ban, Britain posted a naval squadron off the coast of West Africa to prevent any slave trade above the equator and compelled Brazil's emperor to end slave imports. After 1850, Atlantic slave-shipping dropped sharply.

But until the 1860s, slavers continued to buy and ship captives illegally. British squadrons that stopped these smugglers

PRIMARY SOURCE

Frederick Douglass Asks, "What to the Slave Is the Fourth of July?"

Frederick Douglass spent the first twenty years of his life as a slave. After running away in 1838, he toured the northern United States delivering speeches that attacked the institution of slavery. The publication of his autobiography in 1845 cemented his standing as a leading abolitionist. In the excerpt below, taken from an address delivered on July 5, 1852, Douglass contrasts the freedom and natural rights extolled in the Declaration of Independence and celebrated on the Fourth of July with the dehumanizing condition—and lack of freedom—of African American slaves.

Fellow-Citizens—pardon me, and allow me to ask, why am I called upon to speak here to-day? What have I, or those I represent, to do with your national independence? Are the great principles of political freedom and of natural justice, embodied in that Declaration of Independence, extended to us? and am I, therefore, called upon to bring our humble offering to the national altar, and to confess the benefits, and express devout gratitude for the blessings, resulting from your independence to us?. . .

But, such is not the state of the case. I say it with a sad sense of the disparity between us. I am not included within the pale of this glorious anniversary! Your high independence only reveals the immeasurable distance between us. The blessings in which you this day rejoice, are not enjoyed in common. The rich inheritance of justice, liberty, prosperity, and independence, bequeathed by your fathers, is shared by you, not by me. The sunlight that brought life and healing to you, has brought stripes and death to me. This Fourth of July is *yours,* not *mine. You* may rejoice, *I* must mourn. . . .

Must I undertake to prove that the slave is a man? That point is conceded already. Nobody doubts it. The slaveholders themselves acknowledge it in the enactment of laws for their government. They acknowledge it when they punish disobedience on the part of the slave. There are seventy-two crimes in the state of Virginia, which, if committed by a black man (no matter how ignorant he be) subject him to the punishment of death; while only two of these same crimes will subject a white man to the like punishment. What is this but the acknowledgment that the slave is a moral, intellectual, and responsible being. The manhood of the slave is conceded. It is admitted in the fact that southern statute books are covered with enactments forbidding, under severe fines and penalties, the teaching of the slave to read or write. When you can point to any such laws, in reference to the beasts of the field, then I may consent to argue the manhood of the slave. When the dogs in your streets, when the fowls of the air, when the cattle on your hills, when the fish of the sea, and the reptiles that crawl, shall be unable to distinguish the slave from a brute, then will I argue with you that the slave is a man!

QUESTIONS FOR ANALYSIS

- What examples does Douglass give of the disparity between slaves and free white Americans?
- How does Douglass suggest that slaves are human beings?
- What is the significance of the last sentence of the speech?

Source: David W. Blight (ed.), Narrative of the Life of Frederick Douglass: An American Slave, Written by Himself *(Boston: Bedford Books, 1993), pp. 141–45.*

took the freed captives to the British base at Sierra Leone and resettled them there. Liberia, too, became a refuge for freed captives and for former slaves returning from the Americas.

New Trade with Africa

Even as the Atlantic slave trade died down, Europeans promoted commerce with Africa. Now they wanted Africans to export raw materials and to purchase European manufactures. What Europeans liked to call "legitimate" trade aimed to raise the Africans' standards of living by substituting trade in produce for trade in slaves. West Africans responded by exporting palm kernels and peanuts. The real bonanza was in vegetable oils to lubricate machinery and make candles and in palm oil to produce soap. Africa's palm and peanut plantations were less devastating to the environment than their predecessors in the West Indies had been. There, planters had felled forests to establish sugar estates (see Chapter 12). In West Africa, where palm products became crucial exports, the palm tree had always grown

Chasing Slave Dhows. *From being the major proponents of the Atlantic slave trade the British became its chief opponents, using their naval forces to suppress those European and African slave traders who attempted to subvert the injunction against slave trading. Here a British vessel chases an East African slaving dhow trying to run slaves from the island of Zanzibar.*

wild. Although intensive cultivation caused some deforestation, the results were not as extreme as in the Caribbean. Regardless of the environmental impact, European merchants argued that by becoming vibrant export societies, Africans would earn the wealth to profitably import European wares.

SUCCESS IN THE AGE OF LEGITIMATE COMMERCE Arising in the age of legitimate commerce, the new trade gave rise to a generation of successful West African merchants. There were many rags-to-riches stories, like that of King Jaja of Opobo (1821–1891). Kidnapped and sold into slavery as a youngster, he started out paddling canoes carrying palm oil to coastal ports. Ultimately becoming the head of a coastal canoe house, as a merchant-prince and chief he founded the port of Opobo and could summon a flotilla of war canoes on command. Another freed slave, a Yoruba, William Lewis, made his way back to Africa and settled in Sierra Leone in 1828. Starting with a few utensils and a small plot of land, he became a successful merchant who sent his son Samuel to England for his education. Samuel eventually became an important political leader in Sierra Leone.

EFFECTS IN AFRICA Just as the slave trade shaped African political communities, its demise brought sharp adjustments. For some, it was a welcome end to the constant drainage of people. For others, it was a disaster because it cut off income necessary to buy European arms and luxury goods. Many West African regimes, like the Yoruba kingdom, collapsed once chieftains could no longer use the slave trade to finance their retinues and armies.

The rise of free labor in the Atlantic world and the dwindling foreign slave trade had an unanticipated and perverse effect in Africa. It strengthened slavery. In some areas, by the mid-nineteenth century, slaves accounted for more than half the population. No longer did they comfortably serve in domestic employment; instead, they toiled on palm oil plantations or, in East Africa, on clove plantations. They also served in the military forces, bore palm oil and ivory to markets as porters, or paddled cargo-carrying canoes along rivers leading to the coast. In 1850, northern Nigeria's ruling class had more slaves than independent Brazil, and almost as many as the United States. No longer the world's supplier of slaves, Africa itself had become the world's largest slaveholding region.

ECONOMIC REORDERING

Behind the political and social upheavals, profound changes were occurring in the world economy. Until the middle of the eighteenth century, global trade touched only the edges of societies, most of which produced for their own subsistence. Surpluses of special goods, from porcelains to silks, entered trade arteries but did not change the cultures that produced them. An exception was the Americas, where especially in the slave societies of the Caribbean, Brazil, and the southern United States, plantations produced goods for export. Yet, this commercial specialization anticipated developments to come, in which communities would be transformed to produce for other societies and less and less for themselves. This gradual, halting, but ineluctable process would gather speed in the eighteenth century and bring the world together in ways that were unimaginable during the age of older European empires.

An Industrious Revolution

Many of these developments took place first in northwestern Europe and British North America. Here, as elsewhere in the world, households had always produced mainly for themselves and made available for marketplaces only meager surpluses of goods and services. But dramatic changes occurred when family members, including wives and children, decided to work harder and longer in order to produce more for the market and purchase more in the market. In these locations, households devoted less time to leisure activities and more time to working, using the additional income from hard work to improve their standards of living. Scholars recently have come to call this change an **industrious revolution**. Beginning in the second half of the seventeenth century, it gained speed in the eighteenth century and laid the foundations for the industrial revolution of the late eighteenth and early nineteenth centuries.

The willingness on the part of families to work more and an eagerness to eat more diverse foods, to wear better clothes, and to consume products that had once been available as luxuries only to the wealthy classes led in turn to a large expansion in trade—both regionally and globally. By the eighteenth century, separate trading spheres described in earlier chapters were merging increasingly into integrated circuits. Sugar and silver were the pioneering products. But by the eighteenth century, other staples joined the long-distance trading business. Tea, for instance, became a beverage of world trade. Its leaves came from China, the sugar to cut its bitterness from the Caribbean, the slaves to harvest the sweetener from Africa, and the ceramics from which to drink a proper cup from the English Midlands.

The significance of growing cross-cultural trade and specialization, and the shift away from a few precious cargoes to basic staples, can be seen in the story of a single commodity: soap. By the 1840s, the American entrepreneur William Colgate was importing palm oil from West Africa, coconut oil from Malabar and Ceylon, and poppy seed oil from South Asia, all to make aromatic bars of soap. A London barber called Andrew Pears added glycerine to his product to give it a clean, transparent look, and his grandson-in-law, Thomas Barratt, launched an aggressive marketing campaign—in 1886 buying a painting from the *Illustrated London News* called "Bubbles" to enhance the image of his family's soap. Colgate and his Atlantic rivals in the toiletry trade like Pears advertised their products as necessities for the prim and proper home. Pears promised African and Indian buyers that his product would actually whiten their skin.

Global trading trickled its way down from elites to ordinary folk. Even ordinary people could purchase imported goods with their earnings. Thus, the poor began to enjoy—some would say became addicted to—coffee, tea, and sugar, and eventually

New Farming Technologies. *Although new technologies only gradually transformed agriculture, the spread of more intensive cultivation led to increased yields.*

even felt the need to use soap. European artisans and farmers purchased tools, furnishings, and home decorations. Slaves and colonial laborers also used their meager earnings to buy imported cotton cloth made in Europe from the raw cotton they themselves had picked several seasons earlier.

The expansion of global trade had important social and political consequences. In many dynastic societies, merchants had long stood high in the social hierarchy, but few extended their business beyond provincial confines. As new goods flowed from ever more distant corners of the globe, immense fortunes grew. To support their enterprise, traders needed new services, in insurance, bookkeeping, and the recording of legal documents. Trade helped nurture the emergence of new classes of professionals—accountants and lawyers. The new cities of the commercial revolution, hubs like Bristol, Bombay, and Buenos Aires, provided the homes and flourishing neighborhoods for a class of men and women known as the **bourgeoisie**.

As Europe moved to the center of this new economic order, one class in particular moved to the top: the trader-financiers. Like the merchandiser, the financier did not have to emerge from the high and mighty of Eurasia's dynasties. Consider Mayer Amschel Rothschild (1744–1812): born the son of a money changer in the Jewish ghetto of Frankfurt, Rothschild progressed from coin dealing to money changing, then from trading textiles to lending funds to kings and governments. By the time of his death he owned the world's biggest banking operation and his five sons were running powerful branches in London, Paris, Vienna, Naples, and Frankfurt.

By extending credit, families like the Rothschilds also enabled traders to ship goods across long distances without having to worry about immediate payment. All these financial changes implied world integration through the flow of goods as well as the flow of money. In the 1820s, sizeable funds amassed in London flowed to Egypt, Mexico, and New York to support trade, public investment, and, of course, speculation.

The Industrial Revolution

Trade and finance repositioned western Europe's relationship with the rest of the world. So did the emergence of manufacturing—a big leap, as in agriculture, in the output, in this case of industrial commodities. The heart of this process was a gradual accumulation and diffusion of technical knowledge. Lots of little inventions, their applications, and their diffusion across the Atlantic world gradually built up a stock of technical knowledge and practice. Historians have traditionally called these changes the **industrial revolution**, a term first used by the British economic historian Arnold Toynbee in the late nineteenth century. Although the term suggests radical and rapid economic change, the reality was much more gradual and less dramatic than originally believed. Yet, the term still has great validity, for the major economic changes that occurred in Britain, northwestern Europe, and North America catapulted these countries ahead of the rest of the world in industrial and agricultural output and standards of living.

Nowhere was this industrial revolution more evident than in Britain. Britain had a few advantages, like large supplies of coal and iron—key materials used in manufactured products. It also had a political and social environment that allowed merchants and industrialists to invest heavily while also expanding their internal and international markets. Among their investments was the application of steam power to textile production—which enabled Britain's manufacturers to produce cheaper goods in larger quantities. Finally, Britain had access to New World lands as sources of financial investment, raw materials, and markets for manufactured goods. These factors' convergence in Britain promoted self-sustaining economic growth.

An example of the new alliance of the inventor and the investor that fueled the industrial revolution was the advent of the steam engine. Such engines burned coal to boil water, and the resulting steam drove mechanized devices. There were several tinkerers working on the device. But the most famous was James Watt (1736–1819) of Scotland, who managed to separate steam condensers from piston cylinders so that pistons could stay hot and run constantly, and who also joined forces with the industrialist Matthew Boulton, who marketed the steam engine and set up a laboratory where Watt could refine his device. The steam engine catalyzed a revolution in transportation. Steam-powered engines also improved sugar refining, pottery making, and other industrial processes, generating more products at lower cost than when workers had made them by hand.

Technical changes made possible the consolidation of textile manufacturing within a single factory. With new machinery, a single textile operator handled many looms and spindles at once and produced bolts of cloth with stunning efficiency. Gone were the hand tools, the family traditions, and the loosely organized and dispersed systems of households putting out cloth for local merchants to carry to markets. The material was also stronger, finer, and more uniform. All the while, the price of cotton cloth almost halved between 1780 and 1850. As England became the world's largest cloth producer, it imported cotton from Brazil, Egypt, India, and the United States.

Most raw cotton for the British cloth industry had come from colonial India until 1793, when the American inventor Eli Whitney (1765–1825) patented a "cotton gin" that separated cotton seeds from fiber. After that, cotton farming spread so quickly in the southern United States that by the 1850s it was producing more than 80 percent of the world's cotton supply. In turn, every black slave in the Americas and many Indians in British India were consumers of cheap, British-produced cotton shirts.

A Cotton Textile Mill in the 1830s. *The region of Lancashire became one of the major industrial hubs for textile production in the world. By the 1830s, mills had made the shift from artisanal work to highly mechanical mass production. Among the great breakthroughs was the discovery that cloth could be printed with designs, such as paisley or calico (as in this image), and marketed to middle-class consumers.*

It is important to note that the industrial revolution did not imply the creation of large-scale industries. The large factory was rare in manufacturing. Indeed, the largest employers at the time were the slave plantations of the Americas that produced the staples for industrial consumption. Small-scale production remained the norm, mass production the exception. Small-scale production simply became more efficient through innovations in techniques and machinery. The silks of Lyon, cutlery of Solingen, calicoes of Alsace, and cottons of Pawtucket, Rhode Island, were all products of small firms in heavily industrialized belts.

Wherever the industrial revolution took hold, it allowed societies to outdistance rivals in manufacturing and elevated them to a new place in the emerging global economic order (see Map 15.4). But why did this revolution cluster mainly in the Atlantic world? This is an important question, because the unequal distribution of global wealth, the gap between the haves and have-nots, really took off in this era of revolutions. In much of Asia and Africa, technical change altered modes of production and business practices, but it was not followed by a continuous cascade of changes. The great mystery was China, the home of astronomical water clocks and gunpowder. Why did China not become the epicenter of the industrial revolution?

There are two reasons. China did not foster experimental science of the kind that allowed Watt to stumble onto the possibility of steam, or Procter and Gamble to invent floating soap. Experimentation, testing, and the links between thinkers and investors were a distinctly Atlantic phenomenon. The Qing, like the Mughal and Ottoman dynasties, swept the great minds into the bureaucracy and reinforced the old agrarian system based on peasant exploitation and tribute. Second, Chinese rulers did not support overseas expansion and trade that helped create the commercial revolution in the Atlantic world. The agrarian dynasties of China and India neither showered favors on local merchants nor effectively shut out interlopers. This made them vulnerable to cheap manufactured imports from European traders backed by their governments extolling the virtues of free trade.

The effects were profound. Historically, Europe had a trade imbalance with partners to the east—furs from Russia, and spices and silks from Asia. It made up for this with silver from the Americas. But the new economic order meant that by the nineteenth century, western Europe not only had manufactures like soap to export to Asia, it also had capital. One of Europe's biggest debtors was none other than the sultan of the Ottoman Empire, whose tax system could not keep up with spending necessary to keep the realm together. More and more, Asian, African, and American governments found themselves borrowing from Europe's financiers just as their people were buying industrial products from Europe and selling their primary products to European consumers and producers.

Working and Living

The industrial revolution brought more demanding work routines—not only in the manufacturing economies of western Europe and North America but also on the farms and plantations of Asia and Africa. Although the European side of the story is better known, cultivators toiled harder and for longer hours throughout the rest of the world.

MAP 15.4 | Industrial Europe around 1850

By 1850 much of western Europe was industrial and urban, with major cities linked to one another through a network of railroads.

- According to this map, what natural resources contributed to the growth of the industrial revolution? What effects did it have on urban population densities?
- Explain how the presence of an extensive railroad system helped to accelerate industrialization.
- According to your reading, why were the effects of the industrial revolution more rapidly apparent in Great Britain and in north-central Europe?

URBAN LIFE AND WORK ROUTINES Increasingly, Europe's workers made their livings in cities. London, Europe's largest city in 1700, saw its population nearly double over the next century to almost 1 million. By the 1820s, population growth was even greater in the industrial hubs of Leeds, Glasgow, Birmingham, Liverpool, and Manchester. By contrast, in the Low Countries (Belgium and the Netherlands) and France, where small-scale, rural-based manufacturing flourished, the shift to cities was less extreme.

For most urban dwellers, cities were not healthy places. Water that powered the mills, along with chemicals used in dyeing, went directly back into waterways that provided drinking water. Overcrowded tenements shared just a few outhouses. Most European cities as late as 1850 had no running water, no garbage pickup, no underground sewer system. The result was widespread disease. (In fact, no European city at this time had as clean a water supply as the largest towns of the ancient Roman Empire once had.)

As families found jobs in factories, their wages bolstered family revenues. Children, wives, and husbands increasingly worked outside the home for cash, though some still made handicrafts inside the home as well. Urban employers experimented with paying according to the tasks performed or the number of goods produced per day. To earn subsistence wages, men, women, and children frequently stayed on the job for twelve or more hours at a time.

Changes in work affected the understanding of time. Whereas most farmers' workloads had followed seasonal rhythms, after 1800 industrial settings imposed a rigid concept of work discipline. To keep the machinery operating, factory and mill owners installed huge clocks and used bells or horns to signify the workday's beginning and end. Employers also measured output per hour and compared workers' performance. Josiah Wedgwood, a maker of teacups and other porcelain, installed a Boulton & Watt steam engine in his manufacturing plant and made his workers use it efficiently. He rang a bell at 5:45 in the morning so employees could start work as day broke. At 8:30 the bell rang for breakfast, at 9:00 to call them back, and at 12:00 for a half-hour lunch; it last tolled when darkness put an end to the workday. Sometimes, though, factory clocks were turned back in the morning and forward at night, falsely extending the exhausted laborers' workday.

Despite higher production, industrialization imposed numbing work routines and paltry wages. Worse, however, was having no work at all. As families abandoned their farmland and depended on wages, being idle meant having no income. Periodic downturns in the economy put wage workers at risk, and many responded by organizing protests. In 1834, the British Parliament centralized the administration of all poor relief and deprived able-bodied workers of any relief unless they joined a workhouse, where working conditions resembled those of a prison.

SOCIAL PROTEST AND EMIGRATION While entrepreneurs accumulated private wealth, the effects of the industrial revolution on working-class families raised widespread concern. In the 1810s in England, groups of jobless craftsmen, called Luddites, smashed the machines that had left them

A Model Textile Mill. *Distressed by the terrible working conditions of nineteenth-century textile mills, Welsh industrialist and reformer Robert Owen sought to create humane factories. From maintaining the orderliness of the factory floor to posting work rules on the walls, Owen's reforms saw significant improvements in the health and morale of his workers. Nonetheless, he would continue to employ children in his factories, like most of his contemporaries.*

ANALYZING GLOBAL DEVELOPMENTS

Town and Countryside, Core and Periphery in the Nineteenth Century

The textile industry was by far the most dynamic sector of the world economy in the nineteenth century. It was dependent on cotton, whose production was labor intensive but required relatively little capital investment and benefited little from economies of scale. In the first half of the century, cotton was primarily produced by slaves in the southern United States. By the late 1850s, the United States accounted for 77 percent of the cotton consumed in Britain, for 90 percent in France, and for about 92 percent in Russia. After the U.S. Civil War and subsequent slave emancipations, sharecroppers continued to produce the crop, though cotton production began to flourish in Brazil, Egypt, West Africa, and India.

Wheat, on the other hand, was the basic staple of European and Mediterranean diets well into the nineteenth century, and it remains vitally important. Before the advent of railroads, most wheat was consumed locally. In the second half of the century, however, vast quantities of wheat came onto world markets as railroads spread through the Midwest of the United States and the plains of Central and Eastern Europe. Grown on large, capital-intensive farms, that wheat—as well as rye, corn, millet, and other grains—fed radically expanding European and American industrial cities and factory towns, linking them to rich agricultural hinterlands and contributing unwittingly to the economic volatility of the nineteenth century. Here we chart the fortunes of two of the most important commodities of the nineteenth-century world—cotton and wheat—against the growth of cities and railroads.

QUESTIONS FOR ANALYSIS

- Which countries appear to be the most dynamic? Pay attention to relative change over time—not only in the biggest cities and most extensive rail networks but also in those growing the fastest.
- How do the growth of railroads and cities vary by country? What does this tell us about the relationship between economic core regions and their peripheries, and about patterns of inequality more generally?
- How did the extension of railroads, and the economic integration they fostered, influence patterns of inequality worldwide?

Population of Major Cities (in thousands)

	1800	1830	1850	1880	1900
Alexandria	15		60	231	320
Delhi		150	152	173	209
Rio de Janeiro	43	125	166	360	523
London	1,117		2,685	4,770	6,586
Paris	576		1,053	2,269	2,714
Moscow	250		365	748	989
New York City	60	161	340	847	1,478
Tokyo	457			824	1,819

Population Estimates (in thousands)

	1800	1825	1850	1875	1900
Egypt	3,854	4,541	4,752	6,961	10,186
India	255,000	257,000	285,000	306,000	
Brazil			7,678	9,930	17,438
England	8,893	12,000	17,928	22,712	32,528
France	27,349	30,462	35,783	36,906	38,451
Russia	35,500	52,300	68,500	90,200	132,900
America	5,297	11,252	23,261	45,073	76,094
Japan	25,622	26,602	27,201	25,037	44,359

Output of Cotton (in thousand metric tons)

	1800	1825	1850	1875	1900
Egypt				132	293
India			12	533	536
America	17	121	484	1,050	2,120

Wheat Production (in thousand metric tons)

	1825	1850	1875	1900
France	4,580	6,600	7,550	8,860
Russia			53	136
America		2,722	8,546	16,302

Length of Open Railway Lines (in kilometers)

	1825	1850	1875	1900
Egypt		1,184	1,410	2,237
India		32	10,527	39,834
Brazil		14	1,801	15,316
England	43	9,797	23,365	30,079
France	17	2,915	19,351	38,109
Russia	27	501	19,029	53,234
America	37	14,518	119,246	311,160
Japan		29	62	6,300

Source: Beckert, S., "Emancipation and Empire: Reconstructing the Worldwide Web of Cotton Production in the Age of the American Civil War," The American Historical Review *109, no. 5 (December 2004): 1405–1438; Mitchell, B.R.,* International Historical Statistics: Africa, Asia, and Oceania, 1750–2005, International Historical Statistics: The Americas, 1750–2005, *and* International Historical Statistics: Europe, 1750–2005 *(London : Palgrave Macmillan, 2007).*

unemployed. In 1849, the English novelist Charlotte Brontë published a novel, *Shirley,* depicting the misfortunes caused by the power loom. Charles Dickens described a mythic Coketown to evoke pity for the working class in his 1854 classic, *Hard Times*. Both Elizabeth Gaskell, in England, and Émile Zola, in France, described the hardships of women whose malnourished children were pressed into the workforce too early. Gaskell and Zola also highlighted the hunger, loneliness, and illness that prostitutes and widows endured. These social advocates sought protective legislation for workers, including curbing child labor, limiting the workday, and, in some countries, legalizing prostitution for the sake of monitoring the prostitutes' health.

Some people, however, could not wait for legislative reform. Thus, the period saw unprecedented emigration, as unemployed workers or peasants abandoned their homes to seek their fortunes in America, Canada, and Australia. During the Irish Potato Famine of 1845–1849, at least 1 million Irish citizens left their country (and a further million or so died) when fungi attacked their subsistence crop. Desperate to escape starvation, they booked cheap passage to North America on ships so notorious for disease and malnutrition that they earned the name "Coffin Ships." Those who did survive faced discrimination in their new land, for many Americans feared the immigrants would drive down wages or create social unrest.

PERSISTENCE AND CHANGE IN AFRO-EURASIA

Western Europe's military might, its technological achievements, and its economic strength represented a threat to the remaining Afro-Eurasian empires. Across the continent, western European merchants and industrialists sought closer economic and (in some cases) political ties. They did so in the name of gaining "free" access to Asian markets and products. In response, Russian and Ottoman rulers modernized their military organizations and hoped to achieve similar economic strides while distancing themselves from the democratic principles of the French Revolution. The remote Chinese empire was largely unaffected by the upheavals in Europe and America—until the first Opium War of the early 1840s forced the Chinese to acknowledge their military weaknesses. Thus, changes in the Atlantic world unleashed new pressures around the globe, though with varying degrees of intensity.

Revamping the Russian Monarchy

Some eastern European dynasties responded to the pressures by strengthening their traditional rulers, through modest reforms and the suppression of domestic opposition. This was how Russian rulers reacted. Tsar Alexander I (r. 1801–1825) was fortunate that Napoleon committed several blunders and lost his formidable army in the Russian snows. Yet the French Revolution and its massive, patriotic armies struck at the heart of Russian political institutions, which rested upon a huge peasant population laboring as serfs.

The tsars could no longer easily justify their absolutism by claiming that enlightened despotism was the most advanced form of government, since a new model, rooted in popular sovereignty and the concept of the nation, had arisen. In December 1825, when Alexander died unexpectedly and childless, there was a question over succession. Some Russian officers launched a patriotic revolt, hoping to convince Alexander's brother Constantine to take the throne (and to guarantee a constitution) in place of a more conservative brother, Nicholas. The Decembrists, as they were called, came primarily from elite families and were familiar with western European life and institutions. A few Decembrists called for a constitutional monarchy to replace Russia's despotism; others favored a tsar-less republic and the abolition of serfdom. But the officers' conspiracy failed to win over conservatives or the peasantry, who still believed in the tsar's divine right to rule. Constantine supported Nicholas's claim to power, so Nicholas (r. 1825–1855) became tsar and brutally suppressed the insurrectionists. For the time being, the influence of the French Revolution was quashed.

Still, Alexander's successors faced a world in which powerful European states had constitutions and national armies of citizens, not subjects. In trying to maintain absolutist rule, Russian tsars portrayed the monarch's family as the ideal historical embodiment of the nation with direct ties to the people. Nicholas himself prevented rebellion by expanding the secret police, enforcing censorship, conducting impressive military exercises, and maintaining serfdom. And in the 1830s he introduced a conservative ideology that stressed religious faith, hierarchy, and obedience. Even some officials and members of society who supported the monarchy wondered whether this would be enough to enable Russia to remain a competitive great power.

Reforming Egypt and the Ottoman Empire

Unlike in Russia, where Napoleon's army had reached Moscow, the Ottoman capital in Istanbul never faced a threat by French troops. Still, Napoleon's invasion of Egypt shook the Ottoman Empire. Even before this trauma, imperial authorities faced the challenge posed by increased trade with Europe—and the greater presence of European merchants and missionaries. In addition, many non-Muslim religious communities in the sultan's empire wanted the European powers to advance their interests. In the

Decembrists in St. Petersburg. *Russians energetically participated in the coalition that defeated Napoleon, but the ideas of the French Revolution greatly appealed to the educated upper classes, including aristocrats of the officer corps. In December 1825, at the death of Tsar Alexander I, some regimental officers staged an uprising of about 3,000 men, demanding a constitution and the end of serfdom. But Nicholas I, the new tsar, called in loyal troops and brutally dispersed the "Decembrists," executing or exiling their leaders.*

wake of Napoleon, who had promised to remake Egyptian society, reformist energies swept from Egypt to the center of the Ottoman domain. (See Primary Source: An Egyptian Intellectual's Reaction to the French Occupation of Egypt.)

REFORMS IN EGYPT In Egypt, far-reaching changes came with **Muhammad Ali**, a skillful, modernizing ruler. After the French withdrawal in 1801, Muhammad Ali (r. 1805–1848) won a chaotic struggle for supreme power in Egypt and aligned himself with influential Egyptian families. Yet he looked to revolutionary France for a model of modern state building. As with Napoleon (and with Simón Bolívar in Latin America), the key to his hold on power was the army. With the help of French advisors, the modernized Egyptian army became the most powerful fighting force in the Middle East.

Muhammad Ali also reformed education and agriculture. He established a school of engineering and opened the first modern medical school in Cairo under the supervision of a French military doctor. And his efforts in the countryside made Egypt one of the world's leading cotton exporters. A summer crop, cotton required steady watering when the Nile's irrigation waters were in short supply. So Muhammad Ali's public works department, advised by European engineers, deepened the irrigation canals and constructed a series of dams across the Nile. These efforts transformed Egypt, making it the most powerful state in the eastern Mediterranean and alarming the Ottoman state and the great powers in Europe.

Muhammad Ali's modernizing reforms, however, disrupted the habits of the peasantry. After all, incorporation into the industrial world economy involved harder work (as English wage workers had discovered), often with little additional pay. Because irrigation improvements permitted year-round cultivation, Egyptian peasants now had to plant and harvest three crops instead of one or two. Moreover, the state controlled the prices of cultivated products, so peasants saw little profit from their extra efforts. Young men also faced conscription into the state's enlarged army, while whole families had to toil, unpaid, on public works projects. In addition, a state-sponsored program of industrialization aimed to put Egypt on a par with Europe: before long, textile and munitions factories employed 200,000 workers. But Egypt had few skilled laborers or cheap sources of energy, so by the time of Muhammad Ali's death in 1849 few of the factories survived.

External forces also limited Muhammad Ali's ambitious plans. At first, his new army enjoyed spectacular success. But Muhammad Ali overplayed his hand when he sent forces into Syria in the 1830s and later when he threatened Anatolia, the heart of the Ottoman state. Fearing that an Egyptian ruler might attempt to overthrow the Ottoman sultan and threaten the balance of power in the eastern Mediterranean region, the European powers compelled Egypt to withdraw from Anatolia and reduce its army.

OTTOMAN REFORMS Under political and economic pressures like those facing Muhammad Ali in Egypt, Ottoman rulers also made reforms. Indeed, military defeats and humiliating treaties with Europe were painful reminders of the sultans' vulnerability. In 1805 Sultan Selim III tried to create a new infantry, trained by western European officers. But before he could bring this force up to fighting strength, the janissaries

PRIMARY SOURCE

An Egyptian Intellectual's Reaction to the French Occupation of Egypt

In the 1798 invasion of Egypt, Napoleon Bonaparte attempted to win rank-and-file Egyptian support against the country's Mamluks, who were the most powerful group in Egypt at the time though the country was still under the authority of the Ottoman sultan. Bonaparte portrayed himself as a liberator and invoked the ideals of the French Revolution, as he had done with great success all over Europe. His Egyptian campaign did not succeed, however, and local opposition was bitter. The chronicler Abd al-Rahman al-Jabarti has left one of the most perceptive accounts of these years.

On Monday news arrived that the French had reached Damanhur and Rosetta [in the Nile Delta]. . . . They printed a large proclamation in Arabic, calling on the people to obey them. . . . In this proclamation were inducements, warnings, all manner of wiliness and stipulations. Some copies were sent from the provinces to Cairo and its text is:

In the name of God, the Merciful, the Compassionate. There is no God but God. He has no son nor has He an associate in His Dominion.

On behalf of the French Republic which is based upon the foundation of liberty and equality, General Bonaparte, Commander-in-Chief of the French armies makes known to all the Egyptian people that for a long time the Sanjaqs [its Mamluk rulers] who lorded it over Egypt have treated the French community basely and contemptuously and have persecuted its merchants with all manner of extortion and violence. Therefore the hour of punishment has now come.

Unfortunately, this group of Mamluks . . . have acted corruptly for ages in the fairest land that is to be found upon the face of the globe. However, the Lord of the Universe, the Almighty, has decreed the end of their power.

O ye Egyptians . . . I have not come to you except for the purpose of restoring your rights from the hands of the oppressors and that I more than the Mamluks serve God. . . .

And tell them also that all people are equal in the eyes of God and the only circumstances which distinguish one from the other are reason, virtue, and knowledge. . . . Formerly, in the lands of Egypt there were great cities, and wide canals and extensive commerce and nothing ruined all this but the avarice and the tyranny of the Mamluks.

[Jabarti then challenged the arguments in the French proclamation and portrayed the French as godless invaders, inspired by false ideals.] They follow this rule: great and small, high and low, male and female are all equal. Sometimes they break this rule according to their whims and inclinations or reasoning. Their women do not veil themselves and have no modesty. . . . Whenever a Frenchman has to perform an act of nature he does so where he happens to be, even in full view of people, and he goes away as he is, without washing his private parts after defecation. . . .

His saying "[all people] are equal in the eyes of God" the Almighty is a lie and stupidity. How can this be when God has made some superior to others as is testified by the dwellers in the Heavens and on Earth?. . .

So those people are opposed to both Christians and Muslims, and do not hold fast to any religion. You see that they are materialists, who deny all God's attributes. . . . May God hurry misfortune and punishment upon them, may He strike their tongues with dumbness, may He scatter their hosts, and disperse them.

QUESTIONS FOR ANALYSIS

- When the proclamation speaks of "the fairest land that is to be found upon the face of the globe," what land is it referring to?
- Why do you think Napoleon's appeals to the ideals of the French Revolution failed with Egyptians?
- Why does al-Jabarti claim that the invaders are godless even though the proclamation clearly suggests otherwise?

Source: Abd al-Rahman al-Jabarti, Napoleon in Egypt: Al-Jabarti's Chronicle of the French Occupation, 1798, *translated by Shmuel Moreh (Princeton, NJ: Markus Wiener Publishing, 1993), pp. 24–29.*

stormed the palace, killed its officers, and deposed Selim in 1807. Over the next few decades, janissary military men and clerical scholars (*ulama*) cobbled together an alliance that continuously thwarted reformers.

Why did reform falter in the Ottoman state before it could be implemented? After all, in France and Spain the old regimes were also inefficient and burdened with debts and military losses. But reform was possible only if the forces of restraint—especially

Muhammad Ali. *The Middle Eastern ruler who most successfully assimilated the educational, technological, and economic advances of nineteenth-century Europe was Muhammad Ali, ruler of Egypt from 1805 until 1848.*

in the military—were weak and the reformers strong. In the Ottoman Empire, the janissary class had grown powerful, providing the main resistance to change. Ottoman authority depended on clerical support, and the Muslim clergy also resisted change. Blocked at the top, Ottoman rulers were hesitant to appeal for popular support in a struggle against anti-reformers. Such an appeal, in the new age of popular sovereignty and national feeling, would be dangerous for an unelected dynast in a multiethnic and multireligious realm.

Mahmud II (r. 1808–1839), who acknowledged Europe's rising power, broke the political deadlock. He shrewdly manipulated his conservative opponents. Convincing some clerics that the janissaries neglected traditions of discipline and piety, and promising that a new corps would pray fervently, the sultan won the *ulama*'s support and in 1826 established a European-style army corps. When the janissaries plotted their inevitable mutiny, Mahmud rallied clerics, students, and subjects. The schemers retreated to their barracks, only to be shelled by the sultan's artillery and then destroyed in flames. Thousands of other janissaries were rounded up and executed.

The sultan could now pursue reform within an autocratic framework. Like Muhammad Ali in Egypt, Mahmud brought in European officers to advise his forces. Here, too, military reform spilled over into nonmilitary areas. The Ottoman modernizers created a medical college, then a school of military sciences. To understand Europe better and to create a first-rate diplomatic corps, the Ottomans schooled their officials in European languages and had European classics translated into Turkish. As Mahmud's successors extended reforms into civilian life, this era—known as the Tanzimat, or Reorganization period—saw legislation that guaranteed equality for all Ottoman subjects, regardless of religion.

The reforms, however, stopped well short of revolutionary change. For one thing, reform relied too much on the personal whim of rulers. Also, the bureaucratic and religious infrastructure remained committed to old ways. Moreover, any effort to reform the rural sector met resistance by the landed interests. Finally, the merchant classes profited from business with a debt-ridden sultan. By preventing the empire's fiscal collapse through financial support to the state, bankers lessened the pressure for reform and removed the spark that had fired the revolutions in Europe. Together, these factors impeded reform in the Ottoman Empire.

Colonial Reordering in India

Europe's most important colonial possession in Asia between 1750 and 1850 was British India. Unlike in North America, the changes that the British fostered in Asia did not lead to political independence. Instead, India was increasingly dominated by the **East India Company**, which the crown had chartered in 1600. The company's control over India's imports and exports in the eighteenth and nineteenth centuries, however, contradicted British claims about their allegiance to a world economic system based on "free trade."

THE EAST INDIA COMPANY'S MONOPOLY Initially the British, through the East India Company, tried to control India's commerce by establishing trading posts along the coast but without taking complete political control. After conquering the state of Bengal in 1757, the company began to fill its coffers and its officials began to amass personal fortunes. Even the British governor of Bengal pocketed a portion of the tax revenues. Such unbridled abuse of power caused the Bengal army, along with forces of the Mughal emperor and of the ruler of Awadh, to revolt. Although the rebels were unsuccessful, British officials left the emperor and most provincial leaders in place—as nominal rulers. Nonetheless, the British secured the right for the East India Company to collect tax revenues in

Indian Resistance to Company Rule. *Tipu Sultan, the Mysore ruler, put up a determined resistance against the British. This painting by Robert Home shows Cornwallis, the East India Company's governor, receiving Tipu's two sons as hostages after defeating him in the 1792 war. The boys remained in British custody for two years. Tipu returned to fighting the British and was killed in the war of 1799.*

Bengal, Bihar, and Orissa and to trade free of duties throughout Mughal territory. In return, the emperor would receive a hefty annual pension. The company went on to annex other territories, bringing much of South Asia under its rule by the early 1800s (see Map 15.5).

To carry out its responsibilities, the East India Company needed to establish a civil administration. Rather than place Britons in these positions, the company enlisted Hindu kings and Muslim princes; they retained royal privileges while losing their autonomy. The emperor himself was now permanently under the thumb of the company's administrators. Yet the company did not depend entirely on local leaders, for it also maintained a large standing army and a centralized bureaucracy. Together, the military force, the bureaucracy, and an array of local leaders enabled the company state to guarantee security and the smooth collection of revenues.

To rule with minimal interference, however, required knowing the conquered society. This led to Orientalist scholarship: English scholar-officials wrote the first modern histories of South Asia, translated Sanskrit and Persian texts, identified philosophical writings, and compiled Hindu and Muslim law books. Through their efforts, the company state presented itself as a force for revitalizing authentic Hinduism and recovering India's literary and cultural treasures. Although the Orientalist scholars admired Sanskrit language and literature, they still supported English colonial rule and did not necessarily agree with local beliefs.

EFFECTS IN INDIA Maintaining a sizeable military and civilian bureaucracy also required taxation. Indeed, taxes on land were the East India Company's largest source of revenue. From 1793 onward, land policies required large and small landowners alike to pay taxes to the company. As a result, large estate owners gained more power and joined with the company in determining who could own property. Whenever smaller proprietors defaulted on their taxes, the company put their properties up for auction, with the firm's own employees and large estate owners often obtaining title.

Company rule and booming trade altered India's urban geography as well. By the early nineteenth century, colonial cities like Calcutta, Madras, and Bombay became the new centers at the expense of older Mughal cities like Agra, Delhi, Murshidabad, and Hyderabad. As the colonial cities attracted British merchants and Indian clerks, artisans, and laborers, their populations surged. Calcutta's reached 350,000 in 1820; Bombay's jumped to 200,000 by 1825. In these cities, Europeans lived close to the company's fort and trading stations, while migrants from the countryside clustered in crowded quarters called "black towns."

Back in Britain, the debts of rural Indians and the conditions of black towns generated little concern. Instead, calls for reform

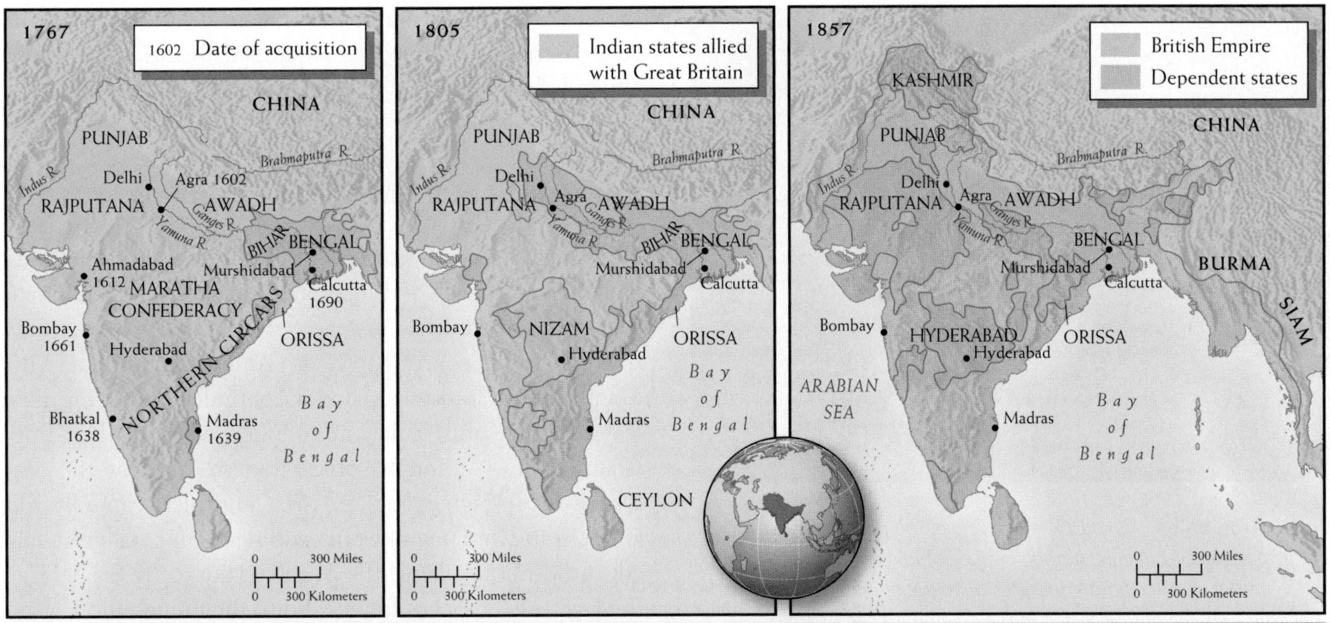

MAP 15.5 | The British in India, 1767–1857

Starting from locations in eastern and northeastern India, the British East India Company extended its authority over much of South Asia prior to the outbreak of the Indian Rebellion of 1857.

- What type of location did the British first acquire in India? How did the company expand into the interior of India and administer these possessions?
- Why did Britain choose a strategy of direct and indirect rule over different areas within the larger region?

focused on the East India Company's monopoly: its sole access to Indian wealth, and its protection of company shareholders and investors. In 1813 the British Parliament, responding to merchants' and traders' demands to participate in the Indian economy, abolished the company's monopoly over trade with India.

India now had to serve the interests of an industrializing Britain, so it became an importer of British textiles and an exporter of raw cotton—a reversal of its traditional pattern of trade. In the past, India had been an important textile manufacturer, exporting fine cotton goods throughout the Indian Ocean and to Europe. But its elites could not resist the appeal of cheap British textiles. As a result, India's own process of industrialization slowed down. In addition, the import of British manufactures caused unfavorable trade balances that changed India from a net importer of gold and silver to an exporter of these precious metals.

Calcutta. *Designated the capital of British India in 1772, Calcutta became vital to the British East India Company's activities as a main exporter of goods as cotton and opium. The wealthy British merchants and Anglo-Indians that Calcutta attracted utterly transformed its landscape, as shown in this 1910 photograph of the Great Eastern Hotel, which was commonly hailed the "Jewel of the East." This street scene of wide paved roads, carriages, and Victorian architecture would be difficult to distinguish from one of turn-of-the-century London, were it not for the Indian figures in traditional dress.*

Packing Cotton Bales. *This 1864 engraving of the packing of cotton bales registers the shift in cotton trade between India and Britain: from being an exporter of cotton manufactures up to the eighteenth century, India became a source of raw cotton in the nineteenth century.*

PROMOTING CULTURAL CHANGE The British did more than alter the Indian economy; they also advocated far-reaching changes in Indian culture so that its people would value British goods and culture. In 1817, James Mill, a philosopher and an employee of the East India Company, condemned what he saw as backward social practices and cultural traditions. He and his son, John Stuart Mill, argued that only dictatorial rule could bring good government and economic progress to India, whose people they considered unfit for self-rule or liberalism. (See Primary Source: James Mill on Indian Tradition.)

Evangelicals and liberal reformers also tried to change Hindu and Muslim social practices, through legislation and European-style education. For example, they sought to stop the practice of *sati,* by which women burned to death on the funeral pyres of their dead husbands. Now the mood swung away from the Orientalists' respect for India's classical languages, philosophies, cultures, and texts. In 1835, when the British poet, historian, and Liberal politician Lord Macaulay was making recommendations on educational policies, he urged that English replace Persian as the language of administration and that European education replace Oriental learning. The result, reformers hoped, would be a class that was Indian in blood and color but English in tastes and culture.

This was a new colonial order, but it was not stable. Most wealthy landowners resented the loss of their land and authority. Peasants, thrown to the mercy of the market, moneylenders, and landlords, were in turmoil. Dispossessed artisans stirred up towns and cities. And merchants and industrialists chafed under the British-dominated economy. Even though India was part of a more interconnected world and thereby supported Europe's industrialization, it was doing so as a colony. As freedom expanded in Europe, exploitation expanded in India.

Persistence of the Qing Empire

The Qing dynasty, which had taken power in 1644, was still enjoying prosperity and territorial expansion as the nineteenth century dawned. The Chinese were largely unaware of revolutionary events occurring in North America, France, and Britain. Their sense of imperial splendor continued to rest on the political structure and social order inherited from the Ming (see Chapter 11). Although some Chinese felt that the Manchu Qing were foreign occupiers, the Qing rulers carefully adapted Chinese institutions and philosophies. Thus, Chinese elites at court did not challenge the dynasty's authority (as delegates to the Estates-General in France did to the French monarchy).

EXPANSION OF THE EMPIRE The Qing had a talent for extending the empire's boundaries and settling frontier lands. Before 1750, they conquered Taiwan (the stronghold of remaining Ming forces), pushed westward into central Asia, and annexed Tibet. Qing troops then eliminated the threat of the powerful Junghars in western Mongolia and halted Russian efforts to take southern Siberia in the 1750s. To secure these territorial gains, the Qing encouraged settlement of frontier lands like Xinjiang. New crops from the Americas aided this process—especially corn and sweet potatoes, which grow well in less fertile soils.

Through rising agricultural productivity and population growth, rural life became commercialized and state revenues surged. Furthermore, despite the Chinese ideal for women to stay home while men worked the land, in reality most rural women had toiled at fieldwork for centuries—and now their labor became even more important. In the eighteenth century, rural markets participated in more interregional trade in grain, cotton, tea, and silk. As rural industries proliferated, peasant households became the backbone of early manufactures (as in Europe), especially in textiles.

Like their European counterparts, Chinese peasants were on the move. But migration occurred in Qing China for different reasons. The state-sponsored westward movement into Xinjiang, for example, aimed to secure a recently pacified frontier region through military colonization, after which civilians would follow. So peasants received promises of land, tools, seed, and the loan of silver and a horse—all with the dual objectives of producing enough food grain to supply the troops and relieve pressure on the poor and arid northwestern part of the country. These efforts brought so much land under cultivation by 1840 that the region's ecological and social landscape completely changed.

PRIMARY SOURCE

James Mill on Indian Tradition

James Mill was a Scottish political economist and philosopher who believed that according to the principles of utilitarianism, law and government were essential for maximizing a people's usefulness and happiness. Thus his* History of British India *(1818) criticized India's Hindu and Muslim cultures and attributed their so-called backwardness to the absence of a systematic form of law. Mill's critique was also an attack on earlier British Orientalists, whose close engagement with Indian culture and Indian texts led them to oppose interfering in traditional practices. A year after the book's publication, the East India Company appointed him as an official.

The condition of the women is one of the most remarkable circumstances in the manners of nations. Among rude people, the women are generally degraded; among civilized people they are exalted.

▪ ▪ ▪

Nothing can exceed the habitual contempt which the Hindus entertain for their women. Hardly are they ever mentioned in their laws, or other books, but as wretches of the most base and vicious inclinations, on whose natures no virtuous or useful qualities can be engrafted. "Their husbands," says the sacred code, "should be diligently careful in guarding them: though they well know the disposition with which the lord of creation formed them; Manu allotted to such women a love of their bed, of their seat, and of ornament, impure appetites, wrath, weak flexibility, desire of mischief, and bad conduct."

▪ ▪ ▪

They are held, accordingly, in extreme degradation. They are not accounted worthy to partake of religious rites but in conjunction with their husbands. They are entirely excluded from the sacred books. . . .

▪ ▪ ▪

They [the Hindus] are remarkably prone to flattery; the most prevailing mode of address from the weak to the strong, while men are still ignorant and unreflecting. The Hindus are full of dissimulation and falsehood, the universal concomitants of oppression. The vices of falsehood, indeed, they carry to a height almost unexampled among other races of men. Judicial perjury is more than common; it is almost universal.

▪ ▪ ▪

This religion has produced a practice, which has strongly engaged the curiosity of Europeans; a superstitious care of the life of the inferior animals. A Hindu lives in perpetual terror of killing even an insect; and hardly any crime can equal that of being unintentionally the cause of death to any animal of the more sacred species. This feeble circumstance, however, is counteracted by so many gloomy and malignant principles, that their religion, instead of humanizing the character, must have had no inconsiderable effect in fostering that disposition to revenge, that insensibility to the sufferings of others, and often that active cruelty, which lurks under the smiling exterior of the Hindu.

▪ ▪ ▪

Few nations are surpassed by the Hindus, in the total want of physical purity, in their streets, houses, and persons. Mr. Forster, whose long residence in India, and knowledge of the country, render him an excellent witness, says of the narrow streets of Benares: "In addition to the pernicious effect which must proceed from a confined atmosphere, there is, in the hot season, an intolerable stench arising from the many pieces of stagnated water dispersed in different quarters of the town. The filth also which is indiscriminately thrown into the streets, and there left exposed, (for the Hindus possess but a small portion of general cleanliness) add to the compound of ill smells so offensive to the European inhabitants of this city."

▪ ▪ ▪

The attachment with which the Hindus, in common with all ignorant nations, bear to astrology, is a part of their manners exerting a strong influence upon the train of their actions. "The Hindus of the present age," says a partial observer, "do not undertake any affair of consequence without consulting their astrologers, who are always Brahmans." The belief of witchcraft and sorcery continues universally prevalent.

QUESTIONS FOR ANALYSIS

- What did James Mill hold to be the chief indicator of a civilization's accomplishment?
- In what ways do Mill's views on India reflect a deep disagreement with British Orientalists?

Source: James Mill, The History of British India *(New Delhi: Atlantic Publishers & Distributors, 1990), pp. 279, 281–82, 286–87, 288, 289, 297, 299.*

Rice cultivation. *From hand-sowing seedlings to harvesting the grains in leech-infested waters, the process of rice cultivation was so labor-intensive that multi-generational households cropped up throughout imperial China to yield the necessary manpower.*

Other migrants were on the move by their own initiative. The ever-growing competition for land even drove them into areas where the Qing regime had tried to restrict migration (because of excessive administrative costs), such as Manchuria and Taiwan. As the migrants introduced their own agricultural techniques, they reshaped the environment through land reclamation and irrigation projects and sparked large population increases.

PROBLEMS OF THE EMPIRE Despite their success in expanding the empire, the Qing faced nagging problems. As a ruling minority, they took a conservative approach to innovation. And only late in the eighteenth century did they deal with rapid population growth. On the one hand, the tripling of China's population since 1300 demonstrated the realm's prosperity; on the other, a population of over 300 million severely strained resources—especially soil for growing crops and wood for fuel.

Bureaucrats were understaffed. And as local authorities introduced many new taxes, the common people regarded them as corrupt. In the late eighteenth and early nineteenth centuries, uprisings inspired by mystical beliefs in folk Buddhism, and at times by the idea of restoring the Ming, engulfed northern China.

In spite of the difficulties that beset the Qing, European rulers and upper classes remained eager consumers of Chinese silks, teas, carved jade, tableware, jewelry, paper for covering walls, and ceramics. The Chinese, for their part, had little interest in most European manufactures. In 1793, Emperor Qianlong wrote in response to a request for trade by Britain's king that "as your ambassador can see for himself, we possess all things," adding, "I have no use for your country's manufactures."

By the mid-nineteenth century, however, extraordinary changes had made western European powers stronger than ever before, and the Qing could no longer dismiss their demands. The first clear evidence of an altered balance of power was a British-Chinese war over a narcotic. Indeed, the **Opium War** exposed China's vulnerability in a new era of European ascendancy.

THE OPIUM WAR AND THE "OPENING" OF CHINA Europeans had been selling staples and intoxicants in China for a long time. For example, tobacco, a New World crop, had become widely popular in China by the seventeenth century. Initially, few people would have predicted that tobacco smoking would lead to the widespread use of opium, previously used as a medicine or an aphrodisiac. But before long people in Southeast Asia, Taiwan, and China were smoking crude opium mixed with tobacco. By the late eighteenth century, opium smokers with their long-stemmed pipes were conspicuous at every level of Chinese society.

Although the Qing banned opium imports in 1729, the Chinese continued to smoke the drug and import it illegally. Sensing its economic potential, the East India Company created an opium monopoly in India in 1773. The reason was a rapid growth in the company's purchase of tea. Because the Chinese showed little taste for British goods, the British had been financing their tea imports with exports of silver to China. But by the late eighteenth century, the company's tea purchases had become too large to finance with silver. Fortunately for the company, the Chinese were eager for Indian cotton and opium, and then mostly just opium. Thus the British exported essentially no silver after 1804. Given the drug's importance, the company expanded its cultivation by offering loans to Indian peasants: they agreed to grow opium and sell it to the company's agents at a predetermined price.

The illegal opium traffic could not have flourished without the involvement of corrupt Chinese bureaucrats and a network of local brokers and distributors. Although another official ban in 1799 slowed the flow of opium into China for a while, the volume increased eightfold by 1839. The dramatic increase reflected an influx of private British merchants after the British government revoked the East India Company's monopoly over trade with China.

Opium. (Left) *A common sight in late Qing China were establishments catering specifically to opium smoking. Taken from a volume condemning the practice, this picture shows opium smokers idling their day away.* (Right) *Having established a monopoly in the 1770s over opium cultivation in India, the British greatly expanded their manufacture and export of opium to China to balance their rapidly growing import of Chinese tea and silk. This picture from the 1880s shows an opium warehouse in India where the commodity was stored before being transported to China.*

Opium's impact on the empire's balance of trade was devastating. In a reversal from earlier trends, silver began to flow out of instead of into China. Once silver shortages occurred, the peasants' tax burden grew heavier because they had to pay in silver (see Chapter 13). Consequently, long-simmering unrest in the countryside gained momentum. At the Qing court, some officials wanted to legalize the opium trade so as to eliminate corruption and boost revenues. (After all, as long as opium was an illegal substance, the government could not tax its traffic). Others wanted stiffer prohibitions. In 1838 the emperor sent a special commissioner to Canton, the main center of the trade, to eradicate the influx of opium. In a letter to Queen Victoria of Britain, the commissioner, Lin Zexu, claimed that China exported tea and silk for no other reason than "to share the benefit with the people of the whole world." He asked, therefore, why the British inflicted harm on the Chinese people through opium imports.

Lin demanded that foreigners hand over their opium stocks to the Chinese government (for destruction) and stop the trade. When British merchants in Canton resisted, Lin ordered the arrest of the president of the British Chamber of Commerce. After this man refused to comply, 350 foreigners were blockaded inside their own quarters. Lin ultimately convinced the foreign community to surrender 20,283 chests of opium with an estimated value of $9 million—an enormous sum in those days. But merchants had overstocked in anticipation of the trade's legalization, and the British government representative in Canton promised to compensate them for their losses. For Lin, the surrendering of the opium (which the Chinese flushed out to sea) was proof that the foreigners accepted submission. The Chinese victory, however, was short-lived. War soon broke out.

Though determined, the Chinese were no match for Britain's modern military technology. After a British fleet—including four steam-powered battleships—entered Chinese waters in June 1840, the warships bombarded coastal regions near Canton and sailed upriver for a short way (see Map 15.6). On land, Qing soldiers used spears, clubs, and a few imported matchlock muskets against the modern artillery of British troops, many of whom were Indians supplied with percussion cap rifles. Along the Yangzi River, outgunned Qing forces fought fiercely, as soldiers killed their own wives and children before committing suicide themselves.

FORCING MORE TRADE The Qing ruling elite capitulated, and with the 1842 Treaty of Nanjing, the British acquired the island of Hong Kong and the right to trade in five treaty ports. They also forced the Chinese to repay their costs for the war—and the value of the opium Lin had destroyed. British traders now won the right to trade directly with the Chinese and to live in the treaty ports.

Subsequent treaties guaranteed that the British and other foreign nationals would be tried in their own courts for crimes, rather than in Chinese courts, and would be exempt from Chinese law. Moreover, the British insisted that any privileges granted through treaties with other parties would also apply to them. Other

MAP 15.6 | The Qing Empire and the Opium War

- How many treaty ports were there after the opium war? What was their significance?
- How did the opium war change relations between China and the western powers?

Western nations followed the British example in demanding the same right, and the arrangement thus guaranteed all Europeans and North Americans a privileged position in China.

Still, China did not become a formal colony. To the contrary, in the mid-nineteenth century Europeans and North Americans were trading only on its outskirts. Most Chinese did not encounter the Europeans. Daily life for most people went on as it had before the Opium War. Only the political leaders and urban dwellers were beginning to feel the foreign presence and wondering what steps China might take to acquire European technologies, goods, and learning.

CONCLUSION

During the period 1750–1850, changes in politics, commerce, industry, and technology reverberated throughout the Atlantic world and, to varying degrees, elsewhere around the globe. By 1850, the world was more integrated economically, with Europe increasingly at the center.

In the Americas, colonial ties broke apart. In France, the people toppled the monarchy. Dissidents threatened the same in Russia. Such upheavals introduced a new public vocabulary—the language of the nation—and made the idea of revolution empowering. In the Americas and parts of Europe, nation-states took shape around redefined hierarchies of class, gender, and color. Britain and France emerged from the political crises of the late eighteenth century determined to expand their borders. Their drive forced older empires such as Russia and the Ottoman state to make reforms.

As commerce and industrialization transformed economic and political power, European governments compelled others (including Egypt, India, and China) to expand their trade with European merchants. Ultimately, such countries had to participate in a European-centered economy as exporters of raw materials and importers of European manufactures.

By the 1850s, many of the world's peoples became more industrious, producing less for themselves and more for distant

Trade in Canton. *In this painting, we can see the hongs, the buildings that made up the factories, or establishments, where foreign merchants conducted their business in Canton. From the mid-eighteenth century to 1842, Canton was the only Chinese port open to European trade.*

markets. Through changes in manufacturing, some areas of the world also made more goods than ever before. With its emphasis on free trade, Europe began to force open new markets—even to the point of colonizing them. Gold and silver now flowed out of China and India to pay for European-dominated products like opium and textiles.

However, global reordering did not mean that Europe's rulers had uncontested control over other people, or that the institutions and cultures of Asia and Africa ceased to be dynamic. Some countries became dependent on Europe commercially; others became colonies. China escaped colonial rule but was forced into unfavorable trade relations with the Europeans. In sum, dramatic changes combined to unsettle systems of rulership and to alter the economic and military balance between western Europe and the rest of the world.

AFTER YOU READ THIS CHAPTER

Review and research on STUDYSPACE wwnorton.com/studyspace

TRACING THE GLOBAL STORYLINES

FOCUS ON: The Global Effects of the "New Ideas"

The Atlantic World

- North American colonists revolt against British rule and establish a nonmonarchical, republican form of government.
- Inspired by the American Revolution, the French citizenry abolishes feudalism; proclaims a new era of liberty, equality, and fraternity; and executes opponents of their revolution, notably the king and queen of France.
- Napoleon's French empire extends many principles of the French Revolution throughout Europe.
- Drawing on the ideals of the French Revolution, Haitian slaves throw off French rule, abolish slavery, and create an independent state.
- Napoleon's invasion of Iberia frees Portuguese and Spanish America from colonial rule.
- The British lead a successful campaign to abolish the Atlantic slave trade and promote new sources of trade with Africa.
- An industrial revolution spreads outward from Britain to the rest of the world.
- The Russian monarchy strengthens its power through modest reforms and suppression of rebellion.

Africa, India, and Asia

- In Egypt, a military adventurer, Muhammad Ali, modernizes the country and threatens the political integrity of the Ottoman Empire.
- The British East India Company increasingly dominates the Indian subcontinent.
- The Qing Empire persists despite major European encroachments on its sovereignty.

CHRONOLOGY

The Americas	The American Revolution **1776–1783**; The Haitian Revolution **1791–1804**
Europe	James Watt invents the steam engine **1769**; The French Revolution **1789–1799**
East Asia	
South Asia	British East India Company rules India **1757–1858**
Africa	
Ottoman Empire	

1750 · 1775

KEY TERMS

Simón Bolívar p. 570

Napoleon Bonaparte p. 563

bourgeoisie p. 575

democracy p. 556

East India Company p. 583

free labor p. 556

free markets p. 556

free trade p. 556

industrial revolution p. 575

industrious revolution p. 574

Muhammad Ali p. 581

nationalism p. 556

nation-state p. 556

Opium War p. 588

popular sovereignty p. 556

republican government p. 561

social contract p. 557

STUDY QUESTIONS

1. **Describe** the political and social revolutions that occurred in the Atlantic world between 1750 and 1850. What ideas inspired these changes? How far did revolutionaries extend these changes?

2. **Compare and contrast** the way Latin American peoples achieved independence to the similar process in the United States. How similar were their goals? How well did they achieve these goals?

3. **Explain** Napoleon's role in spreading the ideas of political and social revolution. How did his armies spread the concept of nationalism? How did Napoleon's military pursuits affect political and social ferment in the Americas?

4. **Explain** how the Atlantic world's political and social revolution led to the end of the Atlantic slave trade. What economic, social, and political consequences did this development have on sub-Saharan Africa?

5. **Explain** the relationship between industrialization and the "industrious revolution." Where did the industrial revolution begin? What other parts of the Atlantic world did it spread to during this time?

6. **Explore** how industrialization altered the societies that began to industrialize during this time. What impact did this process have on the environment? How were gender roles and familial relationships altered?

7. **Analyze** how the two intertwined Atlantic revolutions (political and industrial) altered the global balance of power. How did the Russian, Mughal, Ottoman, and Qing dynasties respond to this change?

8. **To what extent** did Great Britain emerge as the leading global power between 1750 and 1850? How did the British state shape political and economic developments around the world during this time?

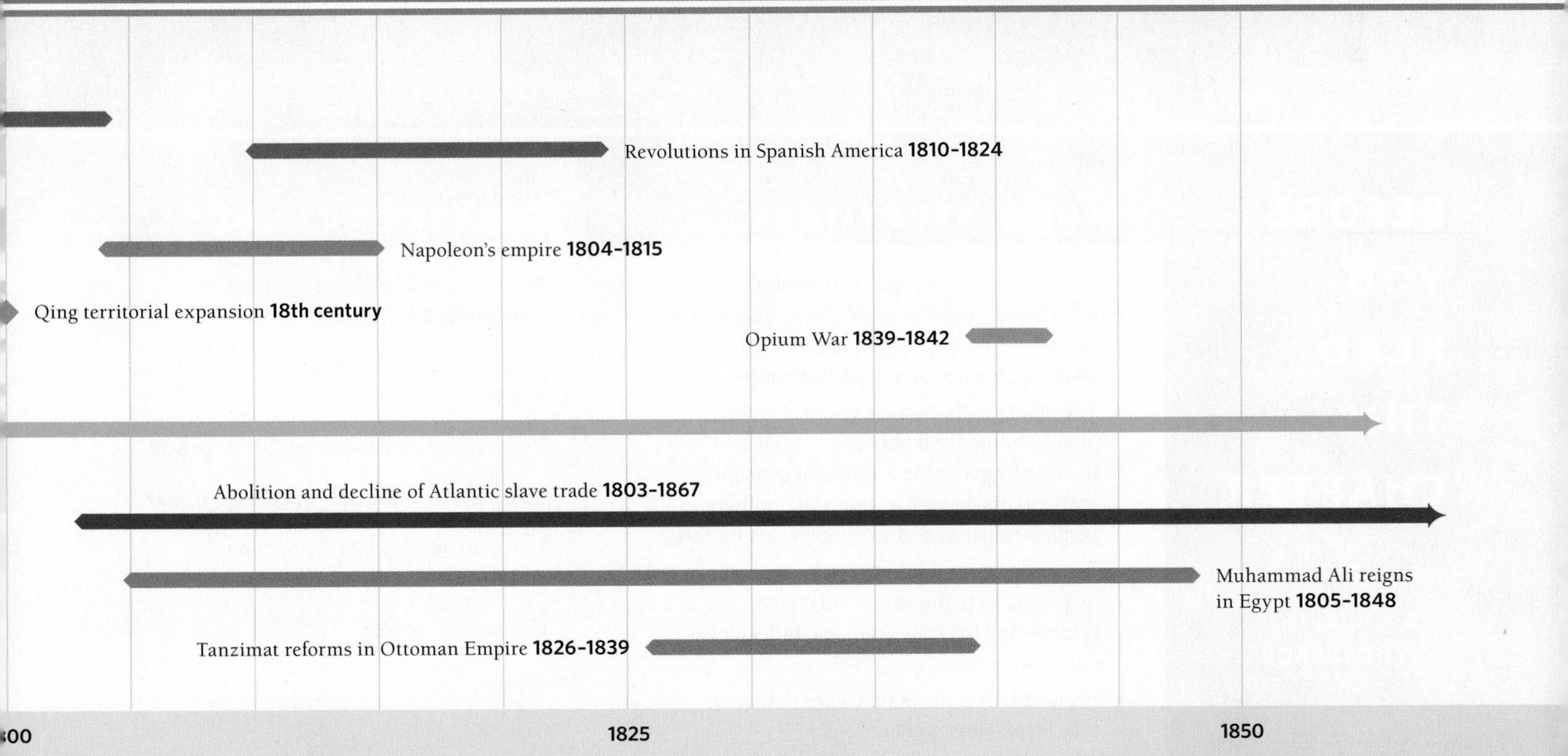

BEFORE YOU READ THIS CHAPTER

wwnorton.com/
StudySpace

GLOBAL STORYLINES

- Protest movements based on ideals of the French and American revolutions, laissez-faire capitalism, the nation-state, and industrialization challenge the nineteenth-century order.
- The movements express visions of ideal, utopian futures and offer opportunities to hear the usually overlooked voices of peasants and workers, as well as those of prophets, political radicals, and anticolonial insurgents.
- The movements differ markedly depending on proximity to the centers of change (Europe and the Americas) and reflect local circumstances.
- Although most movements are defeated, they inspire later generations.

CHAPTER OUTLINE

FOCUS QUESTIONS

- Why did alternative visions to capitalism, colonialism, and nation-states emerge in the nineteenth century?
- What traits and goals did these movements share?
- What factors accounted for the differences among them?
- What groups supported these alternative movements?
- What were the legacies of these disparate movements?

16

Alternative Visions of the Nineteenth Century

By the late nineteenth century, territorial expansion in the United States confined almost all Indians to reservations. Across the American West, many Indians fell into despair. One was a Paiute Indian named Wovoka. But in 1889, he had a vision of a much brighter future. In his dream, the "Supreme Being" told Wovoka that if Indians lived harmoniously, shunned white ways (especially alcohol), and performed the cleansing Ghost Dance, then the buffalo would return and Indians, including the dead, would be reborn to live in eternal happiness.

As word spread of Wovoka's vision, Indians from hundreds of miles around made pilgrimages to the lodge of this new prophet. Many proclaimed him the Indians' messiah or the "Red Man's Christ," an impression fostered by scars on his hands. Especially among the Shoshone, Arapaho, Cheyenne, and Sioux peoples of the northern Plains, Wovoka's message inspired new hope. Soon increasing numbers joined in the ritual Ghost Dance, hoping it would restore the good life that colonialism had extinguished. Among the hopefuls was Sitting Bull, a revered Sioux chief who was himself famous for his visions. Yet, less than two years after

Wovoka's vision, Sitting Bull died at the hands of police forces on a Sioux reservation. A few days later, on December 29, 1890, Sioux Ghost Dancers were massacred at a South Dakota creek called Wounded Knee.

Though it failed, this movement was one of many prophetic crusades that challenged an emerging nineteenth-century order. The ideals of the French and American revolutions, laissez-faire capitalism, the nation-state organization, new technologies, and industrial organizations now provided the dominant answers to age-old questions of who should govern and what beliefs should prevail. But these answers did not stamp out other views. A diverse assortment of political radicals, charismatic prophets, peasant rebels, and anticolonial insurgents put forward striking counterproposals to those that capitalists, colonial modernizers, and nation-state builders had developed. The people making these counterproposals were motivated by the impending loss of their existing worlds and were energized by visions of ideal, utopian futures.

This chapter attends to the voices and visions of those who opposed a nineteenth-century world in which capitalism, colonialism, and nation-states held sway. It puts the spotlight on challengers who shared a dislike of global capitalism and European (and North American) colonialism. Beyond that similarity they differed in significant ways, for the alternatives they proposed reflected the local circumstances in which each of them developed. Although many of the leaders and movements they inspired suffered devastating defeats, like the Ghost Dancers at Wounded Knee, the dreams that aroused their fervor did not always die with them. Some of these alternative visions of the nineteenth century endured to propel the great transformations of the twentieth.

REACTIONS TO SOCIAL AND POLITICAL CHANGE

The transformations of the late eighteenth and early nineteenth centuries had upset polities and economies around the globe. In Europe, the old order had been either swept aside or severely battered by the tide of political and economic revolutions. In North America, the newly independent United States began an expansion westward. Territorial growth led to the dispossession of hundreds of Indian tribes and the acquisition of nearly half of Mexico by conquest. In Latin America, fledgling nation-states that now replaced the Spanish Empire struggled to control their subject populations. And in Asia and Africa, rulers and common people alike confronted the growing might of western military and industrial power. At stake were issues of how to define and rule territories, and what social and cultural visions they would embody.

The alternatives to the dominant trends varied considerably. Some rebels and dissidents called for the revitalization of traditional religions; others wanted to strengthen village and communal bonds; still others imagined a society where there was no private property and where people shared goods equally. The actions of these dissenters depended on their local traditions and the degree of contact they had with the effects of industrial capitalism, European colonialism, and centralizing nation-states.

This era of rapid social change, when differing visions of power and justice vied with one another, offers unique opportunities to hear the voices of the lower orders—the peasants and workers, whose perspectives the elites often ignored or suppressed. While there are few written records that capture the views of the illiterate and the marginalized, we do have traditions of folklore, dreams, rumors, and prophecies. Handed down orally from generation to generation, these resources illuminate the visions of common folk.

The alternative visions that challenged the dominance of colonialism, capitalism, and nation-states differed markedly. In Europe and the Americas, the heartlands of industrial capitalism and the nation-state, radical thinkers dreamed of far-reaching changes. They sought nothing less than an end to private property and a socialist alternative to capitalism. In Africa, the Middle East, and China, regions not yet colonized by Europeans, dynamic religious prophets and charismatic military leaders emerged. Here, men (and sometimes women) revitalized traditional ways, rejuvenated destabilized communities, and reorganized societies in hopes of preventing the spread of unwelcome foreign ideas and institutions. Finally, in South Asia and the Americas, where indigenous groups had come under the domination of Europeans and peoples of European descent, rebellions targeted the authority of the state. Just as Wovoka inspired a revolt against the U.S. government, the Mayans similarly fought to defend their cultural and political autonomy against the power of the Mexican state. So, too, did Indian peasants and old elites join forces in a fierce revolt against their colonial masters in British India.

PROPHECY AND REVITALIZATION IN THE ISLAMIC WORLD AND AFRICA

By the end of the eighteenth century, the Islamic world and non-Islamic Africa had reached a crossroads. The Ottomans, Safavids, and Mughals had extended Muslim trading zones, facilitated cross-cultural communication, and promoted common knowledge over vast territories—but now their era of flowering had ended, and political and military declines had begun.

Although much of this territory had not been colonized and was only partially involved with European-dominated trading networks, a sense of alarm intensified as Christian Europe's power spread. (See Current Trends in World History: Islam: An Enduring Alternative.) In Egypt and the Ottoman Empire, leaders responded by attempting to modernize their states along European lines (see Chapter 15). Farther away from the main trade routes and political centers, however, this sense of alarm also bred religious revitalization movements that sought to recapture the glories of past traditions. Led by prophets who feared that Islam was in trouble, these movements spoke the language of revival and restoration as they sought to replace Muslim monarchs they regarded as corrupt and insufficiently faithful with new theocratic governments.

Prophecy also exerted a strong influence in non-Islamic Africa, where long-distance trade and population growth were upending the social order. Just as Muslim clerics and political leaders sought solutions to unsettling changes by rereading Islamic classics, African communities looked to charismatic leaders who drew strength from their peoples' spiritual and magical traditions. Often uniting disparate groups behind their dynamic visions, prophetic leaders and other "big men" gained power because they were able to resolve local crises—mostly caused by drought, a shortage of arable land, or some other issue related to the harsh environment.

Islamic Revitalization

Movements to revitalize Islam took place on the peripheries—in areas that seemed immune from the potentially threatening repercussions of the world economy. Here, religious leaders rejected westernizing influences (see Map 16.1). Instead, revitalization movements looked back to Islamic traditions and modeled their revolts on the life of Muhammad. But even as they looked to the past, they attempted to establish something new: full-scale theocratic polities. These reformers conceived of the state as the primary instrument of God's will and as the vehicle for purifying Islamic culture.

WAHHABISM One of the most powerful reformist movements arose on the Arabian Peninsula, the birthplace of the Muslim faith. In the Najd region, an area surrounded by mountains and deserts, a religious cleric named Muhammad Ibn abd al-Wahhab (1703–1792) galvanized the population by attacking what he regarded as lax religious practices. His message found a ready response among local inhabitants, who felt threatened by the new commercial activities and fresh intellectual currents swirling around them. Abd al-Wahhab demanded a return to the pure Islam of Muhammad and the early caliphs.

Although Najd was far removed from the currents of the expanding world economy, Abd al-Wahhab himself was not. Having been educated in Iraq, Iran, and the Hijaz (a region on the western end of modern Saudi Arabia, on the Red Sea), he believed that Islam had fallen into a degraded state, particularly in its birthplace. He railed against the polytheistic beliefs that had taken hold of the people, complaining that in defiance of Muhammad's tenets men and women were worshipping trees, stones, and tombs and making sacrifices to false images. Abd al-Wahhab's movement stressed the absolute oneness of Allah (hence his followers were called *Muwahhidin*, or Unitarians) and severely criticized Sufi sects for extolling the lives of saints over the worship of God.

As **Wahhabism** swept across the Arabian Peninsula, the movement posed less of a threat to European power than it did to the Ottomans' hold on the region. Wahhabism gained a powerful political ally in the Najdian House of Saud, whose followers, inspired by the Wahhabis' religious zeal, undertook a militant religious campaign. They sacked the Shiite shrines of Karbala in southern Iraq, and in 1803 they overran the holy cities of Mecca and Medina, damaging the tombs of the saints. Their assault on the Shiite sites reflected their commitment to Sunni Islam, while their destruction of the tombs of Sufi saints stemmed from a belief that monuments to individuals whose beliefs were distant from the mainstream beliefs of Islam desecrated Islam's two holiest cities. Frightened by the Wahhabi challenge, the Ottoman sultan persuaded the provincial ruler of Egypt to send troops to the Arabian Peninsula to suppress the movement. The Egyptians defeated the Saudis, but Wahhabism and the House of Saud continued to represent a pure Islamic faith that attracted clerics and common folk throughout the Muslim world.

USMAN DAN FODIO AND THE FULANI In West Africa, Muslim revolts erupted from Senegal to Nigeria, responding in part to increased trade with the outside world and the circulation of religious ideas from across the Sahara Desert. In this region, the Fulani people were decisive in religious uprisings that sought, like the Wahhabi movement, to re-create a supposedly purer Islamic past. Although the Fulani had originated in the eastern part of present-day Senegal (and retain a powerful presence there today), they moved eastward to escape drought and, over time, set down roots across the savannah lands of West Africa. The majority were cattle-keepers, practicing a pastoral and nomadic way of life. But some were sedentary, and people in this group converted to Islam, read the Islamic classics, and communicated with holy men of North Africa, Egypt, and the Arabian Peninsula. They concluded that West African peoples were violating Islamic beliefs and engaging in irreligious practices.

CURRENT TRENDS IN WORLD HISTORY

Islam: An Enduring Alternative

Many of the alternative movements featured in this chapter derived their impetus from deeply held religious beliefs. Religion played a role in the Indian mutiny and in the visions that spurred the Taiping rebels. In Muslim locations far from the main currents of Western influence, like the Arabian Peninsula and northern Nigeria, it generated revivalist movements. But elsewhere it became a political force, and one that developed a palpably anti-European nature as well as the power to endure long beyond the victory of European invaders. World historians like to study political and social movements like these because they bring into relief the relationship between the colonizer and the colonized and, in the case of these alternative movements, the relationship between peoples living on the peripheries of empires and those living in the center who are part of the ruling elite, including indigenous elites.

This was the case in particular along the old Ottoman periphery, one of the major targets for European colonization. Strikingly, in the first decades of the nineteenth century, in the Ottomans' Balkan domains of Serbia and Greece, Christianity had linked together opponents against the empire. In the decades to follow, as Ottoman power receded, it left behind it Islamic groups who also used religion as the glue that bound together otherwise diverse peoples. The example below highlights the importance of Islam in galvanizing resistance to French imperialism in Algeria. But it would also be possible to cite examples from the Caucasus Mountains, another Ottoman periphery, where Islam linked together Chechen and other groups in opposition to Russian colonization in the 1840s and 1850s; in the early twentieth century, Libyans attempted to oppose Italian colonization by rallying behind the green flag of the prophet. Unquestionably, the more Europeans sought to dominate lands inhabited by Muslims, the more they called forth in reaction Islamic alternatives and politicized forms of Islamic resistance.

In 1830, through a series of mishaps and miscalculations, the French found themselves in possession of the Regency of Algiers, a territory of 60,000 square miles where previously 10,000 Ottoman Turks had ruled over 3 million Arab and Berber tribesmen. The French invasion had been an ill-considered adventure, designed to divert attention from the fact that the backward-looking French king, Charles X, had lost his legitimacy at home. In 1830, Charles was toppled by the so-called July Revolution, but his successor, King Louis Philippe (r. 1830–1848), decided to pursue France's adventure abroad. This was a risky and in the long run costly plan, however, as the French controlled only a few coastal enclaves and the capital city of Algiers; in 1831, the European civilian population was a mere 3,228. Moreover, although the French had driven out the Turks, they had emboldened Arab tribes in the western part of the land to found their own independent state.

In seeking a leader to unite them, the Arab tribes turned to Abd al-Qadir (1807–1883), a charismatic and domineering personality although he was only twenty-five years old. His father, head of the most important Sufi Brotherhood in Algeria, had groomed his son to be a leader, and taught him to despise the Ottoman overlords. Abd al-Qadir and his followers had already committed themselves to overthrowing the Ottomans; but once the French arrived, they were even more determined to rid the area of invaders they regarded as infidels who were intent on seizing their lands and imposing their way

The most powerful of these reform movements flourished in what is today northern Nigeria. Its leader was a Fulani Muslim cleric, **Usman dan Fodio** (1754–1817), who ultimately created a vast Islamic empire. Dan Fodio's movement had all the trappings of the Islamic revolts of this period. It sought inspiration in the life of Muhammad and demanded a return to early Islamic practices. It attacked false belief and heathenism and urged followers to wage holy war (*jihad*) against unbelievers. Usman dan Fodio's adversaries were the old Hausa rulers (city-states that emerged between 1000 and1200), who, in his view, were not sufficiently faithful to Islamic beliefs and practices. So dan Fodio withdrew from his original habitation in Konni and established a new community of believers at Gudu, citing the ancient precedent of Muhammad's withdrawal from Mecca to establish a community of true believers at Medina (see Chapter 9). The practice of withdrawal, called *hijra* in Muhammad's time, was yet another of the prophet's inspirations that religious reformers invoked at this time.

Dan Fodio was a member of the Qadiriyya, one of many Sufi brotherhoods that had helped spread Islam into West Africa. Sufism, the mystical and popular form of Islam, sought an emotional connection with God through a strict regimen of

Abd al-Qadir. *Polish artist Stanislaw Chlebowski painted Abd al-Qadir in 1866 during his exile in Constantinople.*

of life on them. In organizing resistance to the French, it mattered greatly that Abd al-Qadir was also known as a holy man and a scholar, rather than as merely the head of one of the tribes. In preparation for battle he called on his soldiers to follow him in a holy war (*jihad*) against Christian invaders, promising those who joined him in battle that "anyone of you who dies, will die a martyr; those of you who survive will gain glory and live happily." Tribes that might not have fought together, or fought together so long, did so because they were united by their loyalty to a religious as well as a political leader. Abd al-Qadir succeeded in part because he was a forceful personality, but in part, too, because he stood for Islam, a powerful faith that the native Algerians shared, whatever their kinship ties or their loyalties to local leaders.

For fifteen years, Abd al-Qadir's forces held out, only surrendering to a massive French force of 108,000 men in 1847. Although often defeated in pitched battles, Abd al-Qadir used his superior knowledge of the terrain and his ability to wait in ambush for French column to frustrate the French. The French government was finally compelled to send its most accomplished military man, Thomas-Robert Bugeaud, marshal of France, and to provide him with one-third of its entire military force, to finish the job of "pacifying" Algeria.

France's conquest of Algeria marks one of the bloodiest episodes in the history of those two lands. No fewer than 300,000 Algerians perished during these years. Although the French portrayed Abd al-Qadir as a Muslim fanatic, determined to take his people back to a dark age, their message fell on deaf ears. The Algerians extolled him for resisting the French and later made him an iconic figure of the nationalist movement. One of the first acts carried out by the independent Algerian government in 1962 was to tear down the statue of Marshal Bugeaud and replace it with one of Abd al-Qadir. The religiously motivated resistance leader had prevailed over the secular political conquerors after all.

QUESTIONS FOR ANALYSIS

- What impact did Algeria's geographic location have in determining its role in these revolutionary events?
- How did the native Algerians view their former Ottoman rulers compared to the French Europeans? What was the Algerians' ultimate goal?

Explore Further

Clancy-Smith, Julia, *Rebel and Saint: Muslim Notables, Populist Protest, Colonial Encounter (Algeria and Tunisia, 1800–1904)* (1994).

Danziger, Raphael, *Abd al-Qadir: Resistance to the French and Internal Consolidation* (1977).

Ruedy, John, *Modern Algeria: The Origins and Development of a Nation* (2005).

prayers, fasting, and religious exercises to obtain mystical states. Like Wovoka and Sitting Bull in North America, dan Fodio had visions that led him to challenge the West African ruling classes. In one vision, the founder of the Qadiriyya order instructed him to unsheathe the sword of truth against the enemies of Islam.

Dan Fodio won the support of devout Muslims in the area, who agreed that the people were not properly practicing Islam. He also gained the backing of his Fulani tribes and many of the Hausa peasantry, who had suffered under the rule of the Hausa landlord class. The revolt, initiated in 1804, resulted in the overthrow of the Hausa rulers and the creation of a confederation of Islamic emirates, almost all of which were in the hands of the Fulani allies of dan Fodio.

Fulani women of northern Nigeria made critical contributions to the success of the religious revolt. Although dan Fodio and other male leaders of the purification movement expected women to obey the *sharia* (Islamic law), being modest in their dress and their association with men outside the family, they also expected women to support the community's military and religious endeavors. In this effort, they cited women's important role in the first days of Islam. The best known of the Muslim women leaders was Nana Asma'u, daughter of dan

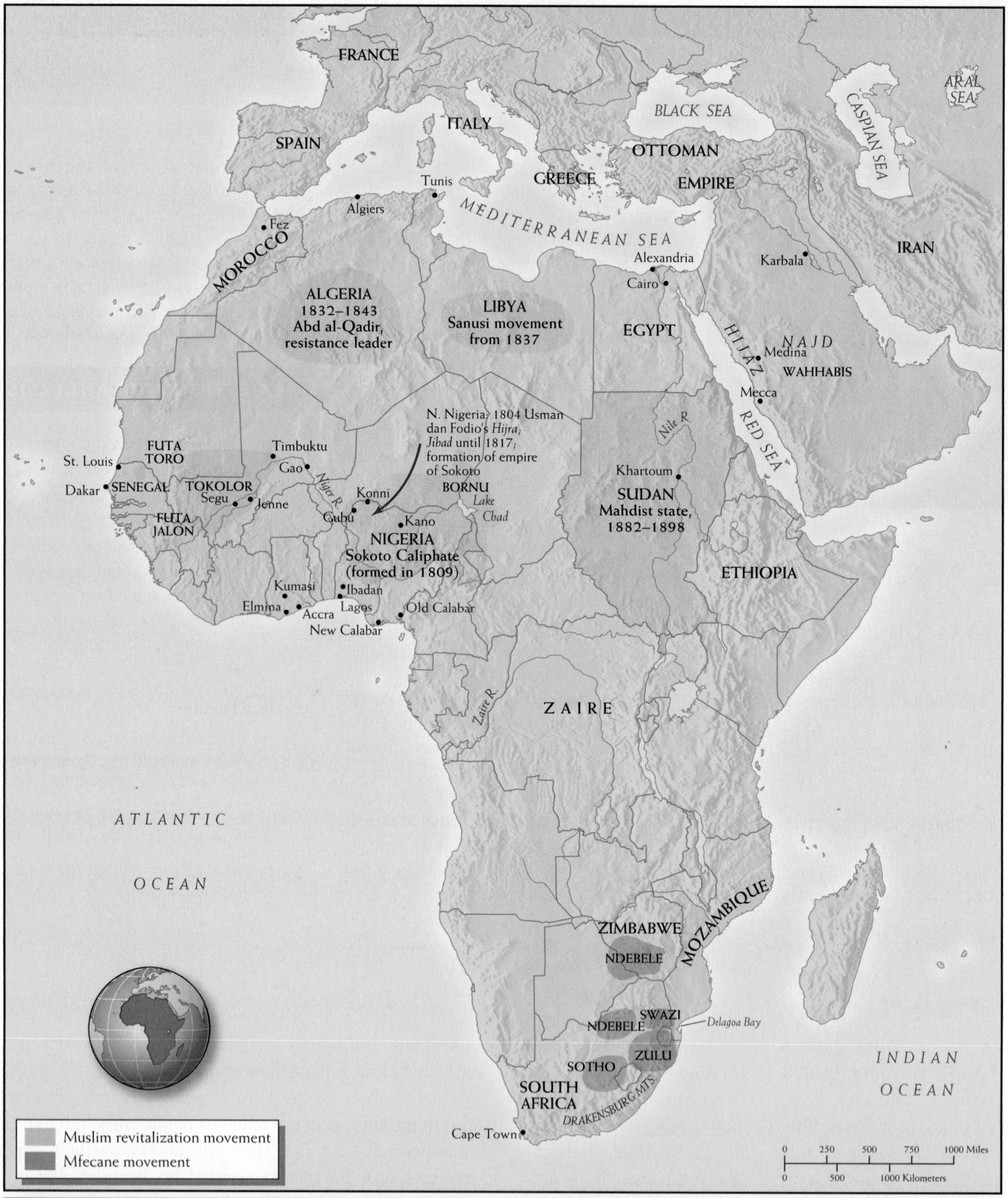

MAP 16.1 | Muslim Revitalization Movements in the Middle East and Africa, and the *Mfecane* Movement in Southern Africa

During the nineteenth century, a series of Muslim revitalization movements took place throughout the Middle East and North Africa.

- According to this map, in how many different areas did the revitalization movements occur?
- Based on their geographic location within their larger regions, did these movements occur in central or peripheral areas?
- Were any of the same factors that led to Islamic revitalization involved in the *Mfecane* developments in southern Africa?

Fodio. Fulani women of the upper ranks acquired an Islamic education, and Asma'u was as astute a reader of Islamic texts as any of the learned men in her society. Like other Muslim Fulani devotees, she accompanied the warriors on their campaigns, encamped with them, prepared food for them, bound up their wounds, and provided daily encouragement. According to many accounts, Asma'u inspired the warriors at their most crucial battle, hurling a burning spear into the midst of the enemy army. Her poem "Song of the Circular Journey" celebrates the triumphs of military forces that trekked thousands of miles to bring a reformed Islam to the area. (For another poem by Asma'u, see Primary Source: A Female Muslim Voice in Africa.)

Usman dan Fodio considered himself a cleric first and a political and military man second. Although his political leadership was decisive in the revolt's success, thereafter he retired to a life of scholarship and writing. He delegated the political and administrative functions of the new empire to his brother and his son. An enduring decentralized state structure, which became known as the Sokoto caliphate in 1809, developed into a stable empire that helped spread Islam through the region. A century later, the faith of a small minority of people living in northern Nigeria had become the religion of the vast majority.

Charismatic Military Men in Non-Islamic Africa

Non-Islamic Africa saw revolts, new states, and prophetic movements arise from the same combination of factors that influenced the rest of the world—particularly long-distance trade and population increase. Local communities here also looked to religious traditions and, as was so often the case in African history, expected "big men" to provide political leadership.

In southern Africa, early in the nineteenth century, a group of political revolts reordered the political map. Collectively known as the ***Mfecane* movement** ("the crushing" in Zulu), its epicenter was a large tract of land lying east of the Drakensberg Mountains, an area where growing populations and land resources existed in a precarious balance (see again Map 16.1). Compounding this pressure, trade with the Portuguese in Mozambique and with other Europeans at Delagoa Bay had disrupted the traditional social order. This set the stage for a political crisis for the northern Nguni (Bantu-speaking) peoples.

Many branches of Bantu-speaking peoples had inhabited the southern part of the African landmass for centuries. At the end of the eighteenth century, however, their political organizations

Shaka and His Zulu Regiments. *Though he is renowned for his reforms and infamous for his brutality, the only existing image of Shaka is this engraving (left) by English trader Henry Francis Fynn, the first white settler in Natal, a British colony near the Zulu kingdom. Nonetheless, Shaka's awesome presence and strength is as obvious to modern viewers as it would have been to his young warriors, who were deeply loyal to him and superbly trained. At right is a Zulu regimental camp; warrior huts were arranged in a circular pattern to surround a courtyard, where the warriors did their drills and practiced close combat.*

PRIMARY SOURCE

A Female Muslim Voice in Africa

The Islamic scholar, writer, and poet Nana Asma'u was the daughter of Usman dan Fodio, the leader of the Fulani revolt in northern Nigeria at the turn of the nineteenth century. Many of her poems conveyed religious inspiration and sought to demonstrate how much her father's revolt was inspired by the life and message of the Prophet Muhammad. She was also deeply attached to her brother, Muhammad Bello, who succeeded their father as head of the Sokoto caliphate. Muhammad Bello looked to his sister to promote traditional Muslim values among the female population in his empire, and she worked to extend education to rural women. Following is an elegy, written in poetic form, that Nana Asma'u composed in praise of her brother, underlining his commitment to an Islamic way of life.

I give thanks to the King of Heaven, the One God. I invoke blessings on the Prophet and set down my poem.

The Lord made Heaven and earth and created all things, sent prophets to enlighten mankind.

Believe in them for your own sake, learn from them and be saved, believe in and act upon their sayings.

I invoke blessings on the Prophet who brought the Book, the Qur'an: he brought the *hadith* to complete the enlightenment.

Muslim scholars have explained knowledge and used it, following in the footsteps of the Prophet.

It is my intention to set down Bello's characteristics and explain his ways.

For I wish to assuage my loneliness, requite my love, find peace of mind through my religion.

These are his characteristics: he was learned in all branches of knowledge and feared God in public and in private.

He obeyed religious injunctions and distanced himself from forbidden things: this is what is known about him.

He concentrated on understanding what is right to know about the Oneness of God.

He preached to people and instructed them about God: he caused them to long for Paradise.

He set an example in his focus on eternal values: he strove to end oppression and sin.

He upheld the *shari'a,* honored it, implemented it aright, that was his way, everyone knows.

And he made his views known to those who visited him: he said to them "Follow the *shari'a,* which is sacred."

He eschewed worldly things and discriminated against anything of ill repute; he was modest and a repository of useful knowledge.

He was exceedingly level-headed and generous, he enjoyed periods of quietude: but was energetic when he put his hand to things.

He was thoughtful, calm, a confident statesman, and quick-witted.

He honored people's status: he could sort out difficulties and advise those who sought his help.

still operated on a small scale, revolving around families and clans and modest chieftaincies. These tiny polities could not cope with the overpopulation and competition for land that now dominated southern Africa. A branch of the Nguni, the Zulus, produced a fierce war leader, Shaka (1787–1828), who created a ruthless warrior state. It drove other populations out of the region and forced a shift from small clan communities to large, centralized monarchies throughout southern and central Africa.

Shaka was the son of a minor chief who emerged victorious in the struggle for cattle-grazing and farming lands that arose during a severe drought. A muscular and physically imposing figure, Shaka was also a violent man who used terror to intimidate his subjects and to overawe his adversaries. His enemies knew that the price of opposition would be a massacre, even of women and children. Nor was he much kinder to his own people. Following the death of his beloved mother, for example, Shaka executed those who were not properly contrite and did not weep profusely. Reportedly, it took 7,000 lives to assuage his grief.

Shaka built a new state around his own military and organizational skills and the fear that his personal ferocity produced. He drilled his men relentlessly in the use of short stabbing spears and in discipline under pressure. Like the Mongols, he had a remarkable ability to incorporate defeated communities into the state and to absorb young men into his ultra-dedicated warrior forces. His army of 40,000 men comprised regiments that lived, studied, and fought together. Forbidden from marrying until they were discharged from the army, Shaka's warriors developed an intense esprit de corps and regarded no sacrifice as too great in the service of the state. So overpowering were these forces that other peoples of the region fled from

He had nothing to do with worldly concerns, but tried to restore to a healthy state things which he could. These were his characteristics.

He never broke promises, but faithfully kept them: he sought out righteous things. Ask and you will hear.

He divorced himself entirely from bribery and was totally scrupulous: He flung back at the givers money offered for titles.

One day Garange [chief of Mafora] sent him a splendid gift, but Bello told the messenger Zitaro to take it back.

He said to the envoy who had brought the bribe, "Have nothing to do with forbidden things."

And furthermore he said, "Tell him that the gift was sent for unlawful purposes; it is wrong to respond to evil intent."

He was able to expedite matters: he facilitated learning, commerce, and defense, and encouraged everything good.

He propagated good relationships between different tribes and between kinsmen. He afforded protection; everyone knows this.

When strangers came he met them, and taught about religious matters, explaining things: he tried to enlighten them.

He lived in a state of preparedness, he had his affairs in order and had an excellent intelligence service.

He had nothing to do with double agents and said it was better to ignore them, for they pervert Islamic principles.

He was a very pleasant companion to friends and acquaintances: he was intelligent, with a lively mind.

He fulfilled promises and took care of affairs, but he did not act hastily.

He shouldered responsibilities and patiently endured adversities.

He was watchful and capable of restoring to good order matters which had gone wrong.

He was resourceful and could undo mischief, no matter how serious, because he was a man of ideas.

He was gracious to important people and was hospitable to all visitors, including non-Muslims.

He drew good people close to him and distanced himself from people of ill repute.

Those are his characteristics. I have recounted a few examples that are sufficient to provide a model for emulation and benefit.

May God forgive him and have mercy on him: May we be united with him in Paradise, the place we aspire to.

For the sake of the Prophet, the Compassionate, who was sent with mercy to mankind.

May God pour blessings on the Prophet and his kinsmen and all other followers.

May God accept this poem. I have concluded it in the year 1254 AH [after *hijra*, the Muslim dating system].

QUESTIONS FOR ANALYSIS

- In what ways does this description convey a sense of proper Muslim values?
- Identify at least ten ways in which Bello was exemplary, according to this poem.
- Why would Nana Asma'u feel compelled to write a poem in praise of her brother?

Source: "Gikku Bello" from One Woman's Jihad: Nana Asma'u, Scholar and Scribe *by Beverly B. Mack and Jean Boyd. Copyright © 2000 by Beverly B. Mack and Jean Boyd. Reprinted by permission of Indiana University Press.*

their home areas, and Shaka claimed their estates for himself and his followers.

Thus did the Zulus under Shaka create a ruthless warrior state that conquered much territory in southern and central Africa, assimilating some peoples and forcing others to fashion their own similarly centralized polities. Shaka's defeated foes adopted many of the Zulu state's military innovations. They did so first to defend themselves and then to take over new land as they fled their old areas. The new states of the Ndebele in what later became Zimbabwe and of the Sotho of South Africa came into existence in the mid-nineteenth century in this way and proved long-lasting.

In turning southern Africa from a region of smaller polities into an area with larger and more powerful ones, Shaka seemed very much a man of the modern, nineteenth-century world. Yet he was, in his own unique way, a familiar kind of African leader. He shared a charismatic and prophetic style with others who emerged during periods of acute social change. He was, in this sense, one of many big men to seek dominance.

PROPHECY AND REBELLION IN CHINA

In the mid-nineteenth century China witnessed an explosive popular rebellion that incorporated Christian beliefs into its long tradition of peasant revolts. Just as European influence began to creep into Africa and the Islamic world, China too was no longer isolated. Even before 1842, European opium traders had conducted a brisk trade with the Chinese through Canton, the only port open to western commerce. After the Opium

War, however, westerners forced Qing rulers to open up a number of other ports to trade. To be sure, the dynasty retained authority over almost the whole realm, and western influence remained confined to a small minority of merchants and missionaries. Nevertheless, foreign gunboats and extraterritorial rights reminded the Chinese of the looming power of the West.

As in the Islamic world and other parts of sub-Saharan Africa, population increases in China—from 250 million in 1644 to around 450 million by the 1850s—were putting considerable pressure on land and other resources. Moreover, the rising consumption of opium, grown in India and brought to China by English traders, was producing further social instability and financial crisis. As banditry and rebellions spread, the Qing dynasts turned to the gentry to maintain order in the countryside. But as the gentry raised its militia to suppress these troublemakers, it whittled away at the authority of the Qing Manchu rulers. Faced with these changes, the Qing dynasty, already weakened by the humiliating Treaty of Nanjing following the Opium War, struggled to maintain control and legitimacy. Searching for an alternative present and future, beginning in 1850 hundreds of thousands of disillusioned peasants joined what became known as the Taiping Rebellion.

MAP 16.2 | The Taiping Rebellion in China, 1851–1864

Note that the Taiping Rebellion started in the southwestern part of the country. The rebels, however, went on to control much of the lower Yangzi region and part of the coastal area.

- What cities did the rebels' march start and end in?
- Why do you think the Taiping rebels were so successful in southern China and not in northern regions?
- How did western powers react to the Taiping Rebellion?
- Would they have been as concerned if the rebellion took place farther to the north or west?

The uprising drew on China's long history of peasant revolts. Traditionally, these rebellions ignited within popular religious sects whose visions were egalitarian or **millenarian** (convinced of the imminent coming of a just and ideal society). Moreover, in contrast to orthodox institutions, here women played important roles. Inspired by Daoists, who revered a past golden age before the world was corrupted by human conventions, or by Buddhist sources, these sects threatened the established order. In times of political breakdown, millenarian sects could transform local revolts into large-scale rebellions. Thus did the Taiping Rebellion, which began as a local movement in southern China, tap into the millenarian tradition and spread rapidly.

The Dream

The story of the rebellion begins with a complex dream that inspired its founding prophet, Hong Xiuquan (1813–1864). A native of Guangdong province in the southernmost part of the country (see Map 16.2), Hong first encountered Christian missionaries in the 1830s. He was then trying, unsuccessfully, to pass the civil service examination, which would have won him entry into the elite and a potential career in the Qing bureaucracy. Disappointed by his poor showing, Hong began to have visions, including a dream in 1837 that led him to form the Society of God Worshippers and the Taiping Heavenly Kingdom (see below).

In this dream, a ceremonial retinue of heavenly guards escorted Hong to heaven. The group included a cock-like figure that he later identified as Leigong, the Duke of Thunder, a familiar figure in Chinese mythology. When Hong reached heaven, his belly was slit open and his internal organs were replaced with new ones. As the operation for his renewal was completed, heavenly texts were unrolled for him to read. The "Heavenly Mother" then met and thoroughly cleansed him. She addressed him as "Son" before bringing him in front of the "Old Father." Although not part of the heavenly bureaucracy, Confucius and women generals from the Song dynasty were also present. Upon meeting Hong, the "Old Father" complained that human beings had been led astray by demons, as demonstrated by the vanity of their shaven heads (a practice the Manchu Qing regime imposed), their consumption of opium, and other forms of debauchery. The "Old Father" even denounced Confucius, who, after being flogged and begging for mercy before Hong's heavenly "Elder Brother," was allowed to stay in heaven but forbidden to teach again. Still, the world was not yet free of demons. So the "Old Father" instructed Hong to leave his heavenly family behind and return to earth to rescue human beings from demons.

How much of this account has been embellished with hindsight scholars will probably never know. What we do know is that Hong, after failing the civil service exam for the third time, suffered a strange "illness" in which he had visions of combating demons. He also began proclaiming himself the Heavenly King. Relatives and neighbors thought he might have gone mad, but Hong gradually returned to his normal state. In 1843, after failing the exam for the fourth time, Hong immersed himself in a Christian tract entitled *Good Words for Exhorting the Age*. Reportedly, reading this tract enabled Hong to realize the full significance of his earlier dream. All the pieces suddenly fell into place. The "Old Father," he concluded, was the Lord Ye-huo-hua (a Chinese rendering of "Jehovah"), the creator of heaven and earth. Accordingly, the cleansing ritual foretold Hong's baptism. The "Elder Brother" was Jesus the Savior, the son of God. He, Hong Xiuquan, was the younger brother of Jesus—God's other son. Just as God had previously sent Jesus to save mankind, Hong thought that God was now sending *him* to rid the world of evil. What was once a dream was now a prophetic vision.

The Rebellion

Unlike earlier sectarian leaders whose plots for rebellion were secret before exploding onto the public arena, Hong chose a more audacious path. Once convinced of his vision, he began to preach his doctrines openly, baptizing converts and destroying Confucian idols and ancestral shrines. Such assaults on the establishment testified to his conviction that he was carrying out God's will. Hong's message of revitalization of a troubled land and restoration of the "heavenly kingdom," imagined as a just and egalitarian order, appealed to the subordinate classes caught in the flux of social change. Drawing on a largely rural social base and asserting allegiance to Christianity, the **Taiping** ("Great Peace") **Rebellion** claimed to herald a new era of economic and social justice.

Taiping Rebellion. *The tens of thousands who had joined the "Heavenly King" became such a formidable force that they swiftly conquered and settled in many of the cities they encountered. Depicted in this mid-nineteenth-century painting are Imperial Chinese troops driving the Taiping rebels from their stronghold in Tientsin.*

Many early followers came from the margins of local society—those whose anger at social and economic dislocations caused by the Opium War was directed not at the Europeans, but at the Qing government. The Taiping identified the ruling Manchus as the "demons" and as the chief obstacle to realizing God's kingdom on earth. Taiping policies were strict: they prohibited the consumption of alcohol, the smoking of opium, or any indulgence in sensual pleasure. Men and women were segregated for administrative and residential purposes.

PRIMARY SOURCE

The Taiping on the Principles of the Heavenly Nature

In this excerpt from 1854, the Taiping leaders envision a radically new community based on values that challenge those of conventional Chinese society. Inspired by their understanding of Christianity, the Taiping leadership confronted the central role of the family and ancestral worship in Chinese society by urging all its followers to regard themselves as belonging to a single family. It also advocated the segregation of the sexes, despite striving to improve women's lives in some of its other policy proclamations.

We brothers and sisters, enjoying today the greatest mercy of our Heavenly Father, have become as one family and are able to enjoy true blessings; each of us must always be thankful. Speaking in terms of our ordinary human feelings, it is true that each has his own parents and there must be a distinction in family names; it is also true that as each has his own household, there must be a distinction between this boundary and that boundary.

Yet we must know that the ten thousand names derive from the one name, and the one name from one ancestor. Thus our origins are not different. Since our Heavenly Father gave us birth and nourishment, we are of one form though of separate bodies, and we breathe the same air though in different places. This is why we say, "All are brothers within the four seas." Now, basking in the profound mercy of Heaven, we are of one family. . . .

We brothers, our minds having been awakened by our Heavenly Father, joined the camp in the earlier days to support our Sovereign, many bringing parents, wives, uncles, brothers, and whole families. It is a matter of course that we should attend to our parents and look after our wives and children, but when one first creates a new rule, the state must come first and the family last, public interests first and private interests last.

Moreover, as it is advisable to avoid suspicion [of improper conduct] between the inner [female] and the outer [male] and to distinguish between male and female, so men must have male quarters and women must have female quarters; only thus can we be dignified and avoid confusion. There must be no common mixing of the male and female groups, which would cause debauchery and violation of Heaven's commandments. Although to pay respects to parents and to visit wives and children occasionally are in keeping with human nature and not prohibited, yet it is only proper to converse before the door, stand a few steps apart and speak in a loud voice; one must not enter the sisters' camp or permit the mixing of men and women. Only thus, by complying with rules and commands, can we become sons and daughters of Heaven.

QUESTIONS FOR ANALYSIS

- What reasons do the Taiping leaders give for telling their followers "we are of one family"?
- Why do they insist that men and women have separate quarters?

Source: The Principles of the Heavenly Nature, *in* Sources of Chinese Tradition, *2nd ed., Vol. 2, compiled by W. Theodore de Bary and Richard Lufrano (New York: Columbia University Press, 2000), pp. 229–30.*

(See Primary Source: The Taiping on the Principles of the Heavenly Nature.) At the same time, in a drastic departure from dynastic practice, women joined the army in segregated units. These female military units mostly comprised Hakka women. Hakka is an ethnic subgroup within the Han (to which Hong Xiuquan, the founder of the Taiping, belonged) with a distinct identity. An important part of their culture was that Hakka women did not bind their feet.

There were further challenges to established social and cultural norms. For example, women could serve in the Taiping bureaucracy. Also, examinations now focused on a translated version of the Bible and assorted religious and literary compositions by Hong. Finally, all land was to be divided among the families according to family size, with men and women receiving equal shares. Once each family met its own needs for sustenance, the communities would share the remaining surplus. These were all radical departures from Chinese traditions. But the Taiping opposition to the Manchus did not involve the formation of a modern nation-state. The rebellion remained caught between the modern and the traditional.

By 1850, Hong's movement had amassed a following of over 20,000, giving Qing rulers cause for concern. When they sent troops to arrest Hong and other rebel leaders, Taiping forces repelled them and then took their turmoil beyond the southwestern part of the country. In 1851, Hong declared himself Heavenly King of the "Taiping Heavenly Kingdom" (or "Heavenly Kingdom of Great Peace"). By 1853, the rebels had captured major cities. Upon capturing Nanjing, the Taiping cleansed the city of "demons" by systematically killing all the Manchus they could find—men, women, and children. Then they established their own "heavenly" capital in the city.

But the rebels could not sustain their vision. Several factors contributed to the fall of the Heavenly Kingdom: struggles within the leadership, excessively rigid codes of conduct, and the rallying of Manchu and Han elites around the embattled dynasty. Disturbed by the Taiping's repudiation of Confucianism and wanting to protect their property, landowning gentry led militias against the Taiping. Moreover, western governments also opposed the rebellion, claiming that its doctrines represented a perversion of Christianity. Thus did a mercenary army led by foreign officers take part in suppressing the rebellion. Hong himself perished as his heavenly capital fell in 1864. With the Qing victory imminent, few of the perhaps 100,000 rebels in Nanjing surrendered. Their slaughter prepared the stage for a determined attempt by imperial bureaucrats and elite intellectuals to rejuvenate the Qing state. Although the Taiping's millenarian vision vanished, the desire to reconstitute Chinese society and government did not. The rebellion, in that sense, continued to inspire reformers as well as future peasant uprisings.

Like their counterparts in the Islamic world and Africa, the Taiping rebels promised to restore lost harmony. Despite all the differences of cultural and historical background, what Abd al-Wahhab, dan Fodio, Shaka, and Hong had in common was the perception that the present world was unjust. Thus, they sought to reorganize their communities—an endeavor that involved confronting established authorities. In this regard, the language of revitalization used by prophets in Islamic areas and China was crucial, for it provided an alternative vocabulary of political and spiritual legitimacy. Although in non-Islamic Africa the impulse was not religious revitalization, it still was an appeal to tradition—to communal solidarity and to the familiar role of "big men" in stateless societies. By mobilizing masses eager to return to an imagined golden age, these prophets and charismatic leaders gave voice to those dispossessed by global change, while producing new, alternative ways of organizing society and politics.

SOCIALISTS AND RADICALS IN EUROPE

Europe and North America were the core areas of capitalist activity, nation-state building, and colonialism. But there, too, the main currents of thought and activity faced challenges. Prophets of all stripes—political, social, cultural, and religious—voiced antiestablishment values and dreamed of alternative arrangements. Radicals, liberals, utopian socialists, nationalists, abolitionists, and religious mavericks made plans for better worlds to come. They did so in the face of a new era dominated by conservative monarchies. This conservatism was pervasive in central Europe, where reestablished kings and aristocrats revived most of their former power and privileges (see Map 16.3). Restoration of the old regimes had occurred at the Congress of Vienna in 1815, at the end of the French Revolution and Napoleon's conquests (see Chapter 15). However, opposition to this arrangement was widespread, and radical voices confidently predicted the coming of a new day.

Congress of Vienna. *At the Congress of Vienna in 1815, the Austrian prime minister Clemens von Metternich took the lead in drafting a peace settlement that would balance power among the states of Europe.*

Restoration and Resistance

The social and political ferment of the **Restoration period** (1815–1848) owed a great deal to the ambiguous legacies of the French Revolution and the Napoleonic wars. Kings had been toppled and replaced by republics, and then by Napoleon and his relatives; these experiments gave Restoration-era states and radicals many political options to choose from. The revolutionaries' attempt to replace Christianity with reason resulted in the clergy's loss of power and property, but very few Europeans actually gave up their religious beliefs. In the 1820s, the reactionary powers tried to reinstitute religious orthodoxy and clerical power, hoping to use the churches to suppress radical ideas. But in the religious sphere as in the political one, ideas and forces had been unleashed that would be impossible to tame.

Europeans in the Restoration era could draw not only on revolutionary ideas, but also on longer traditions of religious radicalism and reformist thought. Like purification movements in the Islamic world and religious sects in China, fundamentalist beliefs fueled social and political rebellions in Europe.

MAP 16.3 | Civil Unrest and Revolutions in Europe, 1819–1848

Civil unrest and revolutions swept Europe after the Congress of Vienna established a peace settlement at the end of the French Revolution and Napoleon's conquests. Conservative governments had to fight off liberal rebellions and demands for change.

- How many sites of revolutionary activity can you locate on this map?
- What parts of Europe appear to have been politically stable, and what parts rebellious?
- Can you explain the stability of some parts of Europe and the instability of others?

For example, the sixteenth- and seventeenth-century English Puritans and German Anabaptists had sought to remake communities from the ground up. In predicting an apocalyptic end for those who lived under sinful and oppressive rulers, these radical dissenters had established principles of both violent and passive resistance that now found application again.

Radicals could also invoke the early egalitarian image of "Pansophia," an ideal republic of inquisitive Christians united in the search for knowledge of nature as a means of loving God. This idea was promoted by the Czech Protestant John Amos Comenius, who championed education for all as early as the 1620s—at a time, that is, when most believed that learning was a privilege reserved for the elite. Forced into exile by Catholic victories during the Thirty Years' War, Comenius traveled widely in Protestant Europe, inspiring egalitarian movements in many countries. Alternatively, the Europeans could refer to certain Enlightenment thinkers who were confident that mankind was already well on its way to scientific, political, and even biological perfection. Critics of the old regime in the Restoration period appeared in many stripes, but all of them reflected, in one way or another, a combination of recent experience and older traditions.

Self-conscious "reactionaries" also emerged at this time. Their crusade was not just to restore privileges to kings and nobles but also to reverse the religious and democratizing concessions that sovereigns had made during the revolutionary and Napoleonic periods. In Russia, for example, the Slavophiles touted what they regarded as "native" traditions and institutions against the excessively "westernizing" reforms introduced by Peter the Great and continued by his self-styled "enlightened despot" successors. Many Slavophiles were ardent monarchists. Their desire for a strong yet "traditional" Russia brought them into conflict with the conservative, but modernizing, tsarist state.

The liberals, in contrast, wanted their states to carry through the legal and political reforms envisioned in 1789—but not to attempt economic leveling in the manner of the radical Jacobins (see Chapter 15). Liberals were eager to curb the states' restrictions on trade, destroy the churches' stranglehold on education, and give more people the right to vote—all the while preserving the free market, the Christian churches, and the rule of law. Proponents of **liberalism** insisted on the individual's right to think, speak, act, and vote as he or she pleased, so long as no harm came to people or property. Liberals feared that powerful states would become corrupt or tyrannical and held that the proper role of government was to foster civil liberties and promote legal equality.

In sum, the reactionaries wanted a return to the traditionally ordered societies that existed prior to the French Revolution; the liberals wanted reforms that would limit the power of government and the church and promote the rights of individuals and free trade. For the most part, the reactionaries got their way in eastern, central, and southern Europe; in Britain, France, and the Low Countries, liberals had greater sway. But neither group dominated fully, and the rivalry between these two groups continued to define the political landscape until at least the 1840s.

Radical Visions

If reactionaries and liberals offered contrasting solutions to social and political questions, they also had to contend with alternative groups even more determined to effect grand-scale change, the radicals. The term *radicals* refers to those who favored the total reconfiguration of the old regime's state system: going to the root of the problem and continuing the revolution, not reversing it or stopping reform. In general, radicals shared a bitter hatred for the status quo and an insistence on popular sovereignty, but beyond this consensus there was much dissension in their ranks. If some radicals demanded the equalization or abolition of private property, others (like Serbian, Greek, Polish, and Italian nationalists) were primarily interested in throwing off the oppressive overlordship of the Ottoman, Russian, and Austrian empires and creating their own nation-states. It was the radicals' threat of a return to revolutions that ultimately reconciled both liberals and reactionaries to preserving the status quo.

NATIONALISTS In the period before 1848, nationalism was a cause dear to liberals and radicals, and threatening to the conservative balance of power introduced into Europe at the Congress of Vienna in 1815. The age of revolutions had spread the idea of popular sovereignty, but the question remained: who exactly were "the people"? For radicals who longed for liberation from the multiethnic empires, "the people" encompassed all those who shared a common language and what was thought to be a common history, and each "people" deserved its own state.

Each fledgling nationalist movement—whether Polish, Czech, Greek, Italian, or German—had different contours, but they all drew backers from the liberal aristocracy and the well-educated and commercially active middle classes. University students were especially active in these movements. Most nationalist movements were, at first, weak and easily crushed, such as attempted Polish uprisings inside tsarist Russia in 1830–1831 and 1863–1864. The movements' leaders instead pursued educational and cultural programs to arouse and unite their nation for eventual statehood. By contrast, the Greeks, inspired by religious revivalism and enlightened ideas, managed to wrest independence from the Ottoman Turks after nearly a decade of small-scale, yet brutal, warfare.

Invoking both the classical tradition and their membership in the community of Christians, Greek patriots won support among Europeans in their fight against the Muslim Ottoman Empire. However, most of this support had to come in the form of private donations or volunteer soldiers, for European rulers feared that any sympathy they might show for the oppressed Greeks would fan the flames of revolution or separatism at home. Still, the Europeans sent their ships to the Mediterranean and defeated the Ottomans at Navarino in 1827. The Ottomans finally recognized Greek independence in 1829.

In the new state, the Greeks could not resolve differences between those who wanted a small, essentially secular republic and those who wanted to reclaim Istanbul (Constantinople) for Greek Orthodoxy. So they ended up inviting Otto, a Bavarian prince, to be king of Greece. The new Greek state had won its independence from the Ottomans, but it was neither the resurrected Athens nor the revived Byzantium that the revolutionaries had envisioned.

Other nationalist movements were suppressed or at least slowed down with little bloodshed. In places like the German principalities, the Italian states, and the Hungarian parts of the Habsburg Empire, secret societies of young men—students and intellectuals—gathered to plan bright, republican futures. Regrettably for these patriots, however, organizations like Young Italy, founded in 1832 to promote national unification and renewal, had little popular or foreign support. Censorship and a few strategic executions suppressed them. Yet many of these movements would ultimately succeed in the century's second half, when conservatives and liberals alike in western Europe employed nationalist fervor to advance their own great power ambitions. However, in central Europe, nationalism pitted many claimants for the same territories against one another, like the Czechs, Serbs, Slovaks, Poles, and Ruthenians (Ukrainians). They did not understand why they could not have a nation-state too.

SOCIALISTS AND COMMUNISTS Much more threatening to the ruling elite were the radicals who believed that the French Revolution had not gone far enough. They longed for a grander revolution that would sweep away the Restoration's political *and* economic order. Early socialists and communists (the terms were more or less interchangeable at the time) insisted that political reforms offered no effective answer to the more pressing "social question": what was to be done about the inequalities that industrial capitalism was introducing? The socialists worried in particular about two things. One was the growing gap between impoverished workers and newly wealthy employers. The other concern was that the division of labor—that is, the dividing up and simplifying of tasks so that each worker performs most efficiently—might make people into soulless, brainless machines. The socialists believed that the whole free market economy, not just the state, had to be transformed to save the human race from self-destruction. Liberty and equality, they insisted, could not be separated; aristocratic privilege along with capitalism belonged on history's ash heap.

No more than a handful of radical prophets hatched revolutionary plans in the years after 1815, but ordinary workers, artisans, domestic servants, and women employed in textile manufacturing joined them in staging strikes, riots, peasant uprisings, and protest meetings. A few socialists and feminists campaigned for social and political equality of the sexes. In Britain in 1819, Manchester workers at St. Peter's Field demonstrated peacefully for increased representation in Parliament, but panicking guardsmen fired on the crowd, leaving 11 dead and 460 injured in an incident later dubbed the Peterloo Massacre. In 1839 and 1842, nearly half the adult population of Britain signed the People's Charter, which called for universal suffrage for all adult males, the secret ballot, equal electoral districts, and annual parliamentary elections. This mass movement, known as **Chartism**, like most such endeavors, ended in defeat. Parliament rejected the charter in 1839, 1842, and 1848.

FOURIER AND UTOPIAN SOCIALISM Despite their many defeats, the radicals kept trying. Some sense of this age of revolutionary aspirations reveals itself in one European visionary who had big grievances and even bigger plans: Charles Fourier (1772–1837). Fourier's **utopian socialism** was perhaps the most visionary and influential of all Restoration-era alternative movements. He introduced planning, whereas the revolutionaries invoked violence, and he generally rejected the equalizing of conditions, fearing the suppression of diversity. Still, he and like-minded socialists dreamed of transforming states, workplaces, and human relations in a much more thorough way than their religious or political predecessors.

Fired by the egalitarian hopes and the cataclysmic failings of the French Revolution, Fourier believed himself to be the scientific prophet of the new world to come. He was a highly imaginative, self-taught man who earned his keep in the cloth trade,

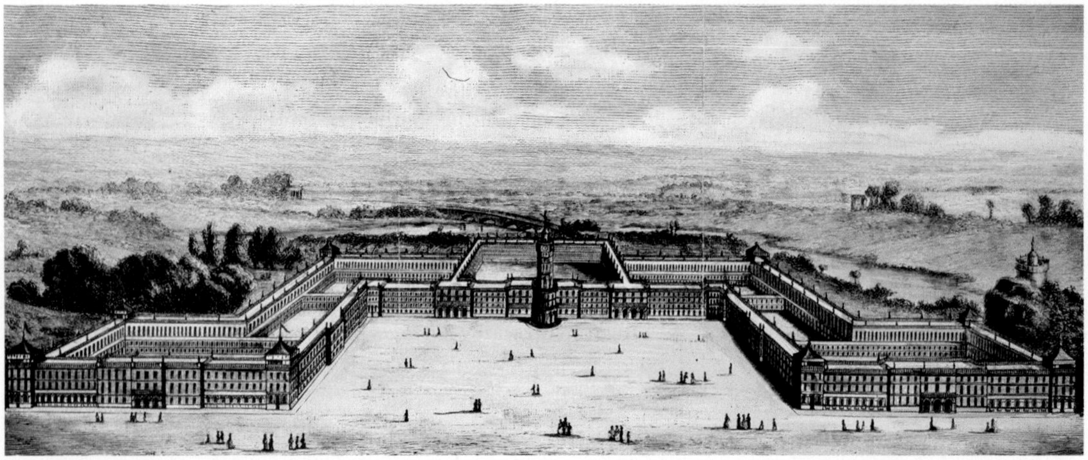

The Phalanx. *The Phalanx, as one of Fourier's German followers envisioned it. In this rendering, the idealized home for the residents of the cooperative social system is represented as a building architecturally similar to the home of the French kings, the Louvre.*

an occupation that gave him an intense hatred for merchants and middlemen. Convinced that the division of labor and repressive moral conventions were destroying mankind's natural talents and passions, Fourier concluded that a revolution grander than that of 1789 was needed. But this utopian transformation of economic, social, and political conditions, he thought, could occur through organization, not through bloodshed. Indeed, by 1808 Fourier believed that the thoroughly corrupt world was on the brink of giving way to a new and harmonious age, of which he was the oracle.

First formulated in 1808, his "system" envisioned the reorganization of human communities into what he called phalanxes. In these harmonious collectives of 1,500 to 1,600 people and 810 personality types, diversity would be preserved, but efficiency maintained; best of all, work would become enjoyable. All members of the phalanx, rich and poor, would work, though not necessarily at the same tasks. All would work in short spurts of no more than two hours, so as to make labor more interesting and sleep, idleness, and overindulgence less attractive. A typical rich man's day would begin at 3:30 A.M. for eating breakfast, reviewing the previous day, and participating in an industrial parade. At 5:30 he would hunt; at 7:00 he would turn to fishing. At 8:00 he would have lunch and read the newspapers (though what news there might be in this world is hard to fathom). At 9:00 he would meet with horticulturists, and at 10:00 he would go to mass. At 10:30 he would meet with a pheasant breeder; later he would tend exotic plants, herd sheep, and attend a concert. Each man would cultivate what he wanted to eat and learn about what he wanted to know. As for unpleasant tasks, they would become less so because they would now occur in more comfortable settings, such as warmed barns and spotless factories. Truly undesirable jobs, like sweeping out stables or cleaning latrines, would fall to young adolescents, who, Fourier argued, actually liked mucking about in filth.

Fourier's phalanxes by no means constituted an Eden in which humankind lived without knowing what it was like to sweat; rather, it was a workers' paradise in which comforts and rewards made working enjoyable. However, this system of production and distribution would run without merchants. Fourier intentionally excluded middlemen like himself from his plan for paradise. He believed that they corrupted civilization and introduced unnaturalness into the division of labor.

Fourier's writings gained popularity in the 1830s, appealing to radicals who supported a variety of causes. In France, women were particularly active in spreading his ideas. Longing for social and moral reforms that would address problems such as prostitution, poverty, illegitimacy, and the exploitation of workers (including women and children), some women saw in **Fourierism** a higher form of Christian communalism. By reshaping the phalanx to accommodate monogamous families and Christian values, women helped to make his work more respectable to middle-class readers. In Russia, Fourier's works fired the imaginations of the young writer Fyodor Dostoevsky. He and fourteen others in the radical circle to which he belonged were sentenced to death for their views (though their executions were called off at the last minute). In 1835–1836, both the young Italian nationalist Giuseppe Mazzini and the Spanish republican Joaquin Abreu published important articles on Fourier's thought. Karl Marx read Fourier with great care, and there are many remnants of utopian thought in his work. In *The German Ideology* Marx describes life in an ideal communist society; in a postrevolutionary world, he predicts that "nobody has one exclusive sphere of activity but each can become accomplished in any branch he wishes, society regulates the general production and thus makes it possible for me to do one thing today and another tomorrow, to hunt in the morning, fish in the afternoon, rear cattle in the evening, [and] criticize after dinner."

MARXISM Karl Marx proved to be the most important Restoration-era radical. University-educated and philosophically radical, Marx (1818–1883) took up a career in journalism. Required to cover legislative debates over property rights and taxation, he was forced to deal with economics. His understanding of *capitalism*, a term he was instrumental in popularizing, deepened through his collaboration with Friedrich Engels (1820–1895). Engels was a German-born radical who, after observing conditions in the factories owned by his wealthy father in Manchester, England, published a hair-raising indictment of industrial wage-labor entitled *The Condition of the Working Class in England*.

Together, Marx and Engels developed what they called "scientific socialism," which they contrasted with the "utopian socialism" of others like Fourier. Scientific socialism was rooted, they argued, in a materialist theory of history: what mattered in history were the production of material goods and the ways in which society was organized into classes of producers and

Karl Marx. *The author (with Friedrich Engels) of* The Communist Manifesto, *Karl Marx argued that the exploitation of wage laborers would trigger a proletarian revolution and would lead to socialism supplanting capitalism.*

PRIMARY SOURCE

"Bourgeoisie and Proletariat": From *The Communist Manifesto*

In January 1848, Karl Marx and Friedrich Engels prepared a party program for the Communist League, a German workingman's association. Published in French as* The Communist Manifesto*, the document foretold the inevitable overthrow of bourgeois-dominated capitalism by the working classes and the transition to socialism and ultimately to communism. The following excerpt demonstrates their certainty that history, driven by economic factors and class conflict, was moving unavoidably toward the revolution of the proletariat. Marx and Engels defined the bourgeoisie as capitalists, owners of the means of production and employers of wage laborers. They defined the proletariat as wage laborers who had to sell their labor to live.

A spectre is haunting Europe—the spectre of Communism. . . .

The history of all hitherto existing society is the history of class struggles. . . .

The modern bourgeois society that has sprouted from the ruins of feudal society has not done away with class antagonisms. It has but established new classes, new conditions of oppression, new forms of struggle in place of the old ones.

Our epoch, the epoch of the bourgeoisie, possesses, however, this distinctive feature: it has simplified the class antagonisms: Society as a whole is more and more splitting up into two great hostile camps, into two great classes directly facing each other: Bourgeoisie and Proletariat. . . .

The bourgeoisie . . . has put an end to all feudal, patriarchal, idyllic relations. It has pitilessly torn asunder the motley feudal ties that bound man to his "natural superiors," and has left remaining no other nexus between man and man than naked self-interest, than callous "cash payment.". . .

The need of a constantly expanding market for its products chases the bourgeoisie over the whole surface of the globe. It must nestle everywhere, settle everywhere, establish connexions everywhere. . . .

The bourgeoisie, by the rapid improvement of all instruments of production, by the immensely facilitated means of communication, draws all, even the most barbarian, nations into civilisation. The cheap prices of its commodities are the heavy artillery with which it batters down all Chinese walls, with which it forces the barbarians' intensely obstinate hatred of foreigners to capitulate. . . .

The weapons with which the bourgeoisie felled feudalism to the ground are now turned against the bourgeoisie itself.

But not only has the bourgeoisie forged the weapons that bring death to itself; it has also called into existence the men who are to wield those weapons—the modern working class—the proletarians. . . . These labourers, who must sell themselves piece-meal, are a commodity, like every other article of commerce, and are consequently exposed to all the vicissitudes of competition, to all the fluctuations of the market. . . .

But with the development of industry the proletariat not only increases in number; it becomes concentrated in greater masses, its strength grows, and it feels that strength more. . . . Thereupon the workers begin to form combinations (Trades Unions) against the bourgeois; they club together in order to keep up the rate of wages; they found permanent associations in order to make provision beforehand for these occasional revolts. Here and there the contest breaks out into riots.

Now and then the workers are victorious, but only for a time. The real fruit of their battles lies, not in the immediate result, but in the ever-expanding union of the workers. . . .

What the bourgeoisie, therefore, produces, above all, is its own grave-diggers. Its fall and the victory of the proletariat are equally inevitable.

QUESTIONS FOR ANALYSIS

- According to Marx and Engels, how does the bourgeoisie draw "all, even the most barbarian, nations into civilization"?
- How does the bourgeoisie contribute to its own downfall?
- Is the new social system supposed to arise automatically, or is human action required to bring it about?

Source: Karl Marx and Friedrich Engels, The Communist Manifesto, *in* The Marx-Engels Reader, *2nd ed., edited by Robert C. Tucker (New York: Norton, 1978), pp. 473–83, 490–91, 500.*

exploiters. History, they claimed, consisted of successive forms of exploitative production and rebellions against them. Capitalist exploitation of the wage worker was only the latest, and worst, version of class conflict, Marx and Engels contended. In industrialized societies, capitalists owned the means of production (the factories and machinery) and exploited the wage workers. Marx and Engels were confident that the clashes between industrial wage workers—or **proletarians**—and capitalists would end in a colossal transformation of human society and would usher in a new world of true liberty, equality, and fraternity. These beliefs constituted the fundamentals of **Marxism**. For Marx and Engels, history moved through stages: feudalism to capitalism, to socialism, and eventually to communism.

From these fundamentals, Marx and Engels issued a comprehensive critique of post-1815 Europe. They identified a whole class of the exploited—the working class. They believed that more and more people would fall into this class as industrialization proceeded and that the masses would not share in the rising prosperity that capitalists monopolized. Marx and Engels predicted that there would be overproduction and underconsumption, which would lead to lower profits for capitalists and, consequently, to lower wages or unemployment for workers—which would ultimately spark a proletarian revolution. This revolution would result in a "dictatorship of the proletariat" and the end of private property. With the destruction of capitalism, the men claimed, exploitation would cease and the state would wither away.

In 1848, revolutionary fervor ignited uprisings in France, Austria, Russia, Italy, Hungary, and the German states. After hearing that revolution had broken out in France, Marx and Engels published *The Communist Manifesto,* calling on the workers of all nations to unite in overthrowing capitalism. (See Primary Source: "Bourgeoisie and Proletariat": From *The Communist Manifesto*.) But the men were sorely disappointed (not to mention exiled) by the reactionary crackdowns that followed the 1848 revolutions. After 1850, Marx and Engels took up permanent residence in England, where they tried to organize an international workers' movement. In the doldrums of midcentury they turned to science, but they never abandoned the dream of total social reconfiguration. Nor would their many admirers and heirs. The failure of the 1848 revolutions did not doom prophecy itself or diminish commitment to alternative social landscapes.

INSURGENCIES AGAINST COLONIZING AND CENTRALIZING STATES

Outside Europe, for Native Americans and for Britain's colonial subjects in India, the greatest threat to traditional worlds was the colonizing process itself, not industrial capitalism and centralizing states. While European radicals looked back to revolutionary legacies in imagining a transformed society, Native American insurgents and rebels in British India drew on their traditional cultural and political resources to imagine local alternatives to foreign impositions. Like the peoples of China, Africa, and the Middle East, native groups in the Americas and India met the period's challenges with prophecy, charismatic leadership, and rebellion. Everywhere the insurgents spoke in languages of the past, but the new worlds they envisioned bore unmistakable marks of the present as well.

Alternative to the Expanding United States: Native American Prophets

Like other native peoples threatened by imperial expansion, the Indians of North America's Ohio Valley dreamed of a world in which intrusive colonizers disappeared. Taking such dreams as prophecies, in 1805 many Indians flocked to hear the revelations of a Shawnee Indian named Tenskwatawa. Facing a dark present and a darker future, they enthusiastically embraced the Shawnee Prophet's visions, which (like that of the Paiute prophet Wovoka nearly a century later) foretold how invaders would vanish if Indians returned to their customary ways and traditional rites.

EARLY CALLS FOR RESISTANCE AND A RETURN TO TRADITION Tenskwatawa's visions—and the anticolonial uprising they inspired—drew on a long tradition of visionary leaders. From the first encounters with Europeans, Indian seers had periodically encouraged native peoples to purge their worlds of colonial influences and to revitalize indigenous traditions. Often these prophets had aroused their followers not only to engage in cleansing ceremonies but also to cooperate in violent, anticolonial uprisings. In 1680, for example, previously divided Pueblo villagers in New Mexico had united behind the prophet Popé to chase Spanish missionaries, soldiers, and settlers out of that colony. After their victory, Popé's followers destroyed all things European: they torched wheat fields and fruit orchards, slaughtered livestock, and ransacked Catholic churches. For a dozen years the Indians of New Mexico reclaimed control over their lands, but soon divisions within native ranks prepared the way for Spanish reconquest in 1692.

Seventy years later and half a landmass away, the charismatic oratory of the Delaware shaman Neolin encouraged Indians of the Ohio Valley and Great Lakes to take up arms against the British, leading to the capture of several British military posts. Although the British put down the uprising, imperial officials learned a lesson from the conflict: they assumed a less arrogant posture toward Ohio Valley and Great Lakes Indians, and to preserve peace they forbade colonists from trespassing on lands west of the Appalachian Mountains. The British, however, were incapable of restraining the flow of settlers across the mountains, and the problem became much worse for the Indians once the American Revolution ended. With the Ohio Valley transferred to the new United States, American settlers crossed the Appalachians and flooded into Kentucky and Tennessee.

MAP 16.4 | Native American Revolts in the United States and Mexico

The new world order of expanding nation-states and industrial markets strongly affected indigenous peoples in North America.

- According to this map, where did the fiercest resistance to centralizing states and global market pressures occur?
- What regions of the United States were Indians forced to leave?
- According to your reading, to what extent, if any, did the natives' alternative visions create or preserve an alternative to the new emerging order?

Despite the settlers' considerable migration, much of the territory between the Appalachian Mountains and the Mississippi River, which Americans referred to as the "western country," remained an Indian country. North and south of Kentucky and Tennessee, Indian warriors more than held their own against American forces. As in previous anticolonial campaigns, the visions of various prophets bolstered the confidence and unity of Indian warriors, who twice joined together to rout invading American armies. But their confederation failed in a third encounter, in 1794, and their leaders had to surrender lands in what is now the state of Ohio to the United States (see Map 16.4).

TENSKWATAWA: THE SHAWNEE PROPHET The Shawnees, who lost most of their holdings, were among the most bitter—and bitterly divided—of Indian peoples living in the Ohio Valley. Some Shawnee leaders concluded that their people's survival now required that they cooperate with American officials and Christian missionaries. This strategy, they realized, entailed wrenching changes in Shawnee culture. European reformers, after all, insisted that Indian men give up hunting and take up farming, an occupation that the Shawnees and their neighbors had always considered "women's work." Moreover, the Shawnees were pushed to abandon communal traditions in favor of private property rights. Of course, missionaries prodded Indians to quit their "heathen" beliefs and practices and become faithful, "civilized" Christians. For many Shawnees, these demands went too far; worse, they promised no immediate relief from the dispossession and impoverishment that now

PRIMARY SOURCE

Tenskwatawa's Vision

In the first decade of the nineteenth century, the Shawnee Indian leader Tenskwatawa recalled an earlier, happier time for the Indian peoples of the Great Lakes and Ohio Valley. It was a time before the coming of the Europeans. In this oration, Tenskwatawa recounts how contact with the "white men's goods" contaminated and corrupted the Indians. He urges them to spurn the ways of white Americans and return to the pure ways of a precolonial past.

Our Creator put us on this wide, rich land, and told us we were free to go where the game was, where the soil was good for planting. That was our state of true happiness. We did not have to beg for anything. Our Creator had taught us how to find and make everything we needed, from trees and plants and animals and stone. We lived in bark, and we wore only the skins of animals.

Thus were we created. Thus we lived for a long time, proud and happy. We had never eaten pig meat, nor tasted the poison called whiskey, nor worn wool from sheep, nor struck fire or dug earth with steel, nor cooked in iron, nor hunted and fought with loud guns, nor ever had diseases which soured our blood or rotted our organs. We were pure, so we were strong and happy.

For many years we traded furs to the English or the French, for wool blankets and guns and iron things, for steel awls and needles and axes, for mirrors, for pretty things made of beads and silver. And for liquor. This was foolish, but we did not know it. We shut our ears to the Great Good Spirit. We did not want to hear that we were being foolish.

But now those things of the white men have corrupted us, and made us weak and needful. Our men forgot how to hunt without noisy guns. Our women don't want to make fire without steel, or cook without iron, or sew without metal awls and needles, or fish without steel hooks. Some look in those mirrors all the time, and no longer teach their daughters to make leather or render bear oil. We learned to need the white men's goods, and so now a People who never had to beg for anything must beg for everything! . . .

And that is why Our Creator purified me and sent me down to you full of the shining power, to make you what you were before!

No red man must ever drink liquor, or he will go and have the hot lead poured in his mouth! . . .

Do not eat any food that is raised or cooked by a white person. It is not good for us. Eat not their bread made of wheat, for Our Creator gave us corn for our bread. . . .

The Great Good Spirit wants our men to hunt and kill game as in the ancient days, with the silent arrow and the lance and the snare, and no longer with guns.

If we hunt in the old ways, we will not have to depend upon white men, for new guns and powder and lead, or go to them to have broken guns repaired. Remember it is the wish of the Great Good Spirit that we have no more commerce with white men! . . .

. . . Our Creator told me that all red men who refuse to obey these laws are bad people, or witches, and must be put to death. . . .

The Great Good Spirit will appoint a place to be our holy town, and at that place I will call all red men to come and share this shining power. For the People in all tribes are corrupt and miserable! In that holy town we will pray every morning and every night for the earth to be fruitful, and the game and fish to be plentiful again.

QUESTIONS FOR ANALYSIS

- Tenskwatawa mentions many commodities and habits that the Indians had been adopting from white men. Identify at least ten.
- According to Tenskwatawa, how has this dependency reduced a proud people to begging?
- What rules did "Our Creator" give Tenskwatawa to help him make his people "what you were before"?

Source: Words of Tenskwatawa, in Messages and Letters of William Henry Harrison, *edited by Logan Esarey (Indianapolis: Indiana Historical Commission, 1922). Retrieved from http://history.missouristate.edu/FTMiller/EarlyRepublic/tecandtensk.htm*

marked the natives' daily lives. Young men especially grew angry and frustrated.

Among the demoralized was **Tenskwatawa** (1775–1836), whose story of overcoming personal failures through religious visions and embracing a strict moral code has uncanny parallels with that of Hong Xiuquan, the Taiping leader. In his first thirty years, Tenskwatawa could claim few accomplishments. He had failed as a hunter and as a medicine man, had blinded himself in one eye, and had earned a reputation as an obnoxious braggart. All this changed in the spring of 1805, however, after he fell into a trance and experienced a vision, which he vividly recounted to one and all. In this dream, Tenskwatawa encountered a heaven where the virtuous enjoyed the traditional Shawnee way of life and a hell where evildoers suffered punishments. Additional revelations followed, and Tenskwatawa soon stitched these together into a new social gospel that urged disciples to abstain from alcohol and return to traditional customs.

Like other prophets, Tenskwatawa exhorted Indians to reduce their dependence on European trade goods and to sever their connections to Christian missionaries. Thus he urged his audiences to replace imported cloth and metal tools with animal skins and implements fashioned from wood, stone, and bone. Livestock, too, was to be banished, as Indian men again gathered meat by hunting wild animals with bows and arrows, instead of guns and powder. If Indians obeyed these dictates, Tenskwatawa promised, the deer, which "were half a tree's length under the ground," would come back in abundant numbers to the earth's surface. Likewise, he claimed, Indians killed in conflict with colonial intruders would be resurrected, while evil Americans would depart from the country west of the Appalachians. (See Primary Source: Tenskwatawa's Vision.)

Like the Qing's response to Hong's visions, American officials initially dismissed Tenskwatawa as deluded but harmless; their concerns grew, however, as the Shawnee Prophet gathered more followers. These converts came not only from among the Shawnees but also from Delaware, Ottawa, Wyandot, Kickapoo, and Seneca villages. The spread of Tenskwatawa's message raised anew the specter of a pan-Indian confederacy. Hoping to undermine the Shawnee Prophet's claims to supernatural power, territorial governor William Henry Harrison challenged Tenskwatawa to make the sun stand still. But Tenskwatawa one-upped Harrison. Having learned of an impending eclipse from white astronomers, Tenskwatawa assembled his followers on June 16, 1806. Right on schedule, and as if on command, the sky darkened. Claiming credit for the eclipse, Tenskwatawa saw his standing soar, as did the ranks of his disciples. Now aware of the growing threat, American officials tried to bribe Tenskwatawa, hoping that cash payments might dim his vision and quiet his voice. Failing that, they wondered if one of the prophet's Indian adversaries might be encouraged to assassinate him.

In fact, Tenskwatawa had made plenty of enemies among his fellow Indians. His visions, after all, consigned drinkers to hell (where they would be forced to swallow molten metal) and singled out those who cooperated with colonial authorities for punishment in this world and the next. Indeed, Tenskwatawa condemned as witches those Indians who rejected his preaching in favor of the teachings of Christian missionaries and American authorities. (To be sure, Tenskwatawa's damnation of Christianized Indians was somewhat paradoxical, for missionary doctrines obviously influenced his vision of a burning hell for sinners and his crusade against alcohol.)

TECUMSEH AND THE WISH FOR INDIAN UNITY Although Tenskwatawa's accusations alienated some Indians, his prophecies gave heart to many more. This was particularly the case once his brother, **Tecumseh** (1768–1813), helped circulate the message of Indian renaissance among Indian villages from the Great Lakes to the Gulf Coast. On his journeys after 1805, Tecumseh did more than spread his brother's visions; he also wed them to the idea of a renewed and enlarged Indian confederation. Moving around the Great Lakes and traveling across the southern half of the western country, Tecumseh preached the need for Indian unity. He repeatedly urged Indians to resist any American attempts to get them to sell more land. In response, thousands of followers renounced their ties to colonial ways and prepared to combat the expansion of the United States.

By 1810, Tecumseh had emerged, at least in the eyes of American officials, as even more dangerous than his brother. Impressed by Tecumseh's charismatic organizational talents, William Harrison warned that this new "Indian menace" was forming "an Empire that would rival in glory" that of the Aztecs and the Incas. In 1811, while Tecumseh was traveling among southern tribes, Harrison had his troops attack Tenskwatawa's village, Prophet's Town, on the Tippecanoe River in what is now the state of Indiana. The resulting battle was evenly fought, but the Indians eventually gave ground and American forces burned Prophet's Town. That defeat discredited Tenskwatawa, who had promised his followers protection from destruction at American hands. Spurned by his former disciples, including his brother, Tenskwatawa fled to Canada.

Tecumseh soldiered on. Although he mistrusted the British, he recognized that only a British victory over the Americans in the War of 1812 could check further American expansion. So he aligned himself with the British. Commissioned as a brigadier general in the British army, Tecumseh recruited many Indians to the British cause, though his real aim remained the building of a pan-Indian union. But in 1813, with the war's outcome in doubt and the pan-Indian confederacy still fragile, Tecumseh perished at the Battle of the Thames, north of Lake Erie.

INDIAN REMOVALS The discrediting of Tenskwatawa and the death of Tecumseh damaged the cause of Indian unity; then British betrayal dealt it a fatal blow. Following the war's end in 1814, the British withdrew their support and left the Indians south of the Great Lakes to fend for themselves against land-hungry American settlers and the armies of the United States. By 1815, American citizens outnumbered Indians in the western country by a seven-to-one margin, and this gap dramatically widened in the next few years. Recognizing the hopelessness of military resistance, Indians south of the Great Lakes resigned themselves to relocation. During the 1820s, most of the peoples north of the Ohio River were removed to lands

Visions of American Indian Unification. (Left) *A portrait of Tenskwatawa, the "Shawnee Prophet," whose visions stirred thousands of Indians in the Ohio Valley and Great Lakes to renounce dependence on colonial imports and resist the expansion of the United States.* (Right) *A portrait of his brother, Tecumseh, who succeeded in building a significant pan-Indian confederation, although it unraveled following his death at the Battle of Thames in 1813.*

west of the Mississippi River. During the 1830s, the southern tribes were cleared out, completing what amounted to an ethnic cleansing of Indian peoples from the region between the Appalachians and the Mississippi.

In the midst of these final removals, Tenskwatawa died, though his dream of an alternative to American expansion had faded for his people years earlier. Through the rest of the nineteenth century, however, other Indian prophets emerged, and their visions continued to inspire followers with the hope of an alternative to life under the colonial rule of the United States. But like Wovoka and the Ghost Dancers in 1890, these dreams failed to halt the expansion of the United States and the contraction of Indian lands.

Alternative to the Central State: The Caste War of the Yucatan

As in North America, the Spanish establishment of an expansionist nation-state in Mexico sparked widespread revolts by indigenous peoples. The most protracted was the Mayan revolt in the Yucatan. The revolt started in 1847, and its flames were not finally doused until the full occupation of the Yucatan by Mexican national troops in 1901.

EARLY MAYAN AUTONOMY The strength and endurance of the Mayan revolt stemmed in large measure from the unusual features of the Spanish conquest in southern Mesoamerica. Because this area was not a repository of precious metals or fertile lands, Spain and its rivals focused their efforts elsewhere—on central and northern Mexico and the Caribbean islands. As a result, the Mayan Indians escaped forced recruitment for silver mines or sugar plantations. This does not mean, however, that global processes sidestepped the Mayan Indians. In fact, the production of dyes and foodstuffs for shipment to other regions drew the Yucatan into long-distance trading networks. Nonetheless, cultivation and commerce were much less disruptive to indigenous lives in the Yucatan than elsewhere in the New World.

The dismantling of the Spanish Empire early in the nineteenth century gave way to almost a century of political turmoil in Latin America. In the Yucatan, civil strife brought the region autonomy by default, allowing Mayan ways to survive without much upheaval. Their villages still constituted the chief political domain, ruled by elders; ownership of their land was collective, the property of families and not individuals. Corn, a mere staple to white consumers, continued to enjoy sacred status in Mayan culture.

GROWING PRESSURES FROM THE SUGAR TRADE Local developments, however, encroached on the Mayan world. First, regional elites—mainly white, but often with the support of mestizo populations—bickered for supremacy so long as the central authority of Mexico City remained weak. Weaponry flowed freely through the peninsula, and some belligerents even appealed for Mayan support. At the same time, regional and international trade spurred the spread of sugar estates, which threatened traditional corn cultivation. Over the decades, plantations encroached on Mayan properties. Planters used several devices to lure independent Mayans to work, especially in the harvest. The most important device, debt peonage, involved giving small cash advances to Indian families, which obligated fathers and sons to work for meager wages to pay off the debts. In addition, Mexico's costly wars, culminating in a showdown with the United States in 1846, drove tax collectors and army recruiters into villages in search of revenues and soldiers.

The combination of spiritual, material, and physical threats was explosive. When a small band of Mayans, fed up with rising taxes and ebbing autonomy, used firearms to drive back white intruders in 1847, they sparked a war that took a half-century to complete. The rebels were primarily free Mayans who had not yet been absorbed into the sugar economy. They wanted to dismantle old definitions of Indians as a caste—a status that deprived the Indians of rights to defend their sovereignty on equal legal footing with whites and that also subjected the Indians to special taxes. Thus, local Mayan leaders, like Jacinto Pat and Cecilio Chi, upheld a republican model in the name of formal equality of all political subjects and devotion to a spiritual order that did not distinguish between Christians and non-Christians. "If the Indians revolt," one Mayan rebel explained, "it is because the whites gave them reason; because the whites say they do not believe in Jesus Christ, because they have burned the cornfield."

Caste War of the Yucatan. *The ruthless slaughter of Mayan farmers by Mexican troops is captured in this 1850 painting. The intimacy of the bloodstained straw hats strewn on the road suggests this work was an eyewitness account.*

THE CASTE WAR Horrified, the local white elites reacted to the uprising with vicious repression and dubbed the ensuing conflict a **Caste War**. In their view, the bloody conflict was a struggle between forward-looking liberals and backward-looking Indians. At first, whites and mestizos were no match for the determined Mayans, whose forces seized town after town, demolishing as they did so the whipping posts where Indians had endured public humiliation and punishment. By 1848, Indian armies controlled three-quarters of the peninsula and were poised to take the Yucatan's largest city, Mérida. Fear seized the embattled whites, who appealed for U.S. and British help, offering the peninsula for foreign annexation in return for military rescue from the Mayans.

In the end, fortune, not political savvy, saved the Yucatan's whites. The Mayan farmers, who had taken up arms to defend their world, returned to their farms when planting season came, declaring that "the time has come for us to make our planting, for if we do not we shall have no Grace of God to fill the bellies of our children." Like many ordinary people, the farmers were unaware of international changes that had an impact on their situation. In 1848, the Mexican-American War ended with Washington paying the Mexican government $15 million for giving up its northern provinces. Thereafter, Mexico could spend freely to build up its southern armies. The Mexican government soon fielded a force of 17,000 soldiers and waged a scorched-earth campaign to drive back the depleted Mayan forces.

By 1849, the confrontation had entered a new phase in which Mexican troops engaged in mass repression of the Mayans. Mexican armies set Indian fields and villages ablaze. Slaughtering Indians became a blood sport of barbaric proportions. Between 30 and 40 percent of the Mayan population perished in the war and its repressive aftermath. The white governor even sold captured Indians into slavery to Cuban sugar planters. Indeed, the white formulation of the caste nature of the war eventually became a self-fulfilling prophecy. Entire Mayan cities pulled up stakes and withdrew to isolated districts protected by fortified villages. War between armies degenerated into guerrilla warfare between an occupying Mexican army and mobile bands of Mayan squadrons, inflicting a gruesome toll on the invaders. As years passed, the war ground to a stalemate, especially once the U.S. funds ran out and Mexican soldiers began deserting in droves.

RECLAIMING A MAYAN IDENTITY Warfare prompted a spiritual transformation that reinforced a purely Mayan identity against the invaders' "national" project. Thus, a struggle that began with demands for legal equality and relative cultural autonomy became a crusade for spiritual salvation and the complete cultural separation of the Mayan Indians. A particularly influential group under José María Barrera retreated to a hamlet called Chan Santa Cruz. There, at the site where he found a cross shape carved into a mahogany tree, Barrera had a vision of a divine encounter. Thereafter a swath of Yucatan villages refashioned themselves as moral communities orbiting around Chan Santa Cruz. Leaders created a polity, with soldiers, priests, and tax collectors pledging loyalty to the Speaking Cross. As with the followers of Hong in China's Taiping Rebellion, Indian rebels forged an alternative religion: it blended Christian rituals, faiths, and icons with Mayan legends and beliefs. At the center was a stone temple, Balam Na ("House of God"), 100 feet long and 60 feet wide. Through pious pilgrimages to Balam Na and the secular justice of Indian judges, the Mayans soon governed their autonomous domain in the Yucatan, almost completely cut off from the rest of Mexico.

This alternative to Latin American state formation, however, faced formidable hurdles. For example, disease ravaged the people of the Speaking Cross. Once counting 40,000 inhabitants, the villages dwindled to 10,000 by 1900. Also a new crop, henequen, used to bind bales for North American farms and to stuff the seats of automobiles, began to spread across the Yucatan. In place of the peninsula's mixed agrarian societies, it now became a desiccated region producing a single crop, driving the people to seek refuge farther into the interior. As profits from henequen production rose, white landowners began turning the Yucatan into a giant plantation. But Mayan villagers refused to give up their autonomy and rejected labor recruiters.

Finally, the Mexican oligarchy, having resolved its internal disputes, threw its weight behind the strong-arm ruler General Porfirio Díaz (r. 1876–1911). The general sent one of his veteran commanders, Ignacio Bravo, to do what no other Mexican could accomplish: vanquish Chan Santa Cruz and drive Mayans into the henequen cash economy. When General Bravo finally entered the town, he found the once-imposing temple Balam Na covered in vegetation. Nature was reclaiming the territories of the Speaking Cross. Hunger and arms finally drove the Mayans to work on white Mexican plantations; the alternative vision was vanquished.

The Rebellion of 1857 in India

Like Native Americans, the peoples of nineteenth-century India had a long history of opposition to colonial domination. Armed revolts had occurred since the onset of rule by the English East India Company (see Chapter 15). Nonetheless, the uprising of 1857 was unprecedented in its scale, and it posed a greater threat than had any previous rebellion. Marx, with the hope for revolution dashed in Europe, cast his eyes on the revolt in British India, eagerly following the events and commenting on them in daily columns for the New York *Daily Tribune*. Though led primarily by the old nobility and petty landlords, it was a popular uprising with strong support from the lower orders of Indian society. The rebels appealed to bonds of local and communal solidarity, invoked religious sentiments, and reimagined traditional hierarchies in egalitarian terms. They did this to pose alternatives to British rule and the deepening involvement of India in a network of capitalist relationships.

INDIA UNDER COMPANY RULE When the revolt broke out in 1857, the East India Company's rule in India was a century old. During that time, the company had become an increasingly autocratic power whose reach encompassed the whole region. Mughal rule still existed in name, but the emperor lived in Delhi, all but forgotten and without any effective power. For a while, the existence of several princely states with which the British had entered into alliances prevented the British from

Rebellion of 1857. *Russian painter Vasili Vereshchagin depicts the cruel and unusual method in which British officers executed the Indian rebels—by strapping them to the mouths of cannons. The inhumanity of this practice was not soon forgotten by Europeans; this particular reproduction of the painting comes from* Raubstaat England *("Robber State England"), an anti-British pamphlet published by the Nazis during World War II.*

exercising complete control over all of India. These princely domains enjoyed a measure of fiscal and judicial authority within the British Empire. They also contained landed aristocrats who held the right to shares in the produce and maintained their own militias.

Believing that the princely powers and landed aristocracies were out of date, the company instituted far-reaching changes in administration in the 1840s. These infuriated local peoples and laid the foundations for one of the world's most violent and concerted movements of protest against colonial authority. Lord Dalhousie, upon his appointment as governor-general in 1848, immediately began annexing what had been independent princely domains and stripping native aristocrats of their privileges. Swallowing one princely state after another, the British removed their former allies. The government also decided to collect taxes directly from peasants, displacing the landed nobles as intermediaries. In disarming the landed nobility, the British threw the retainers and militia of the notables into unemployment. Moreover, the company's new systems of land settlement eroded peasant rights and enhanced the power of moneylenders. Meanwhile, the company transferred judicial authority to an administration that was insulated from the Indian social hierarchy.

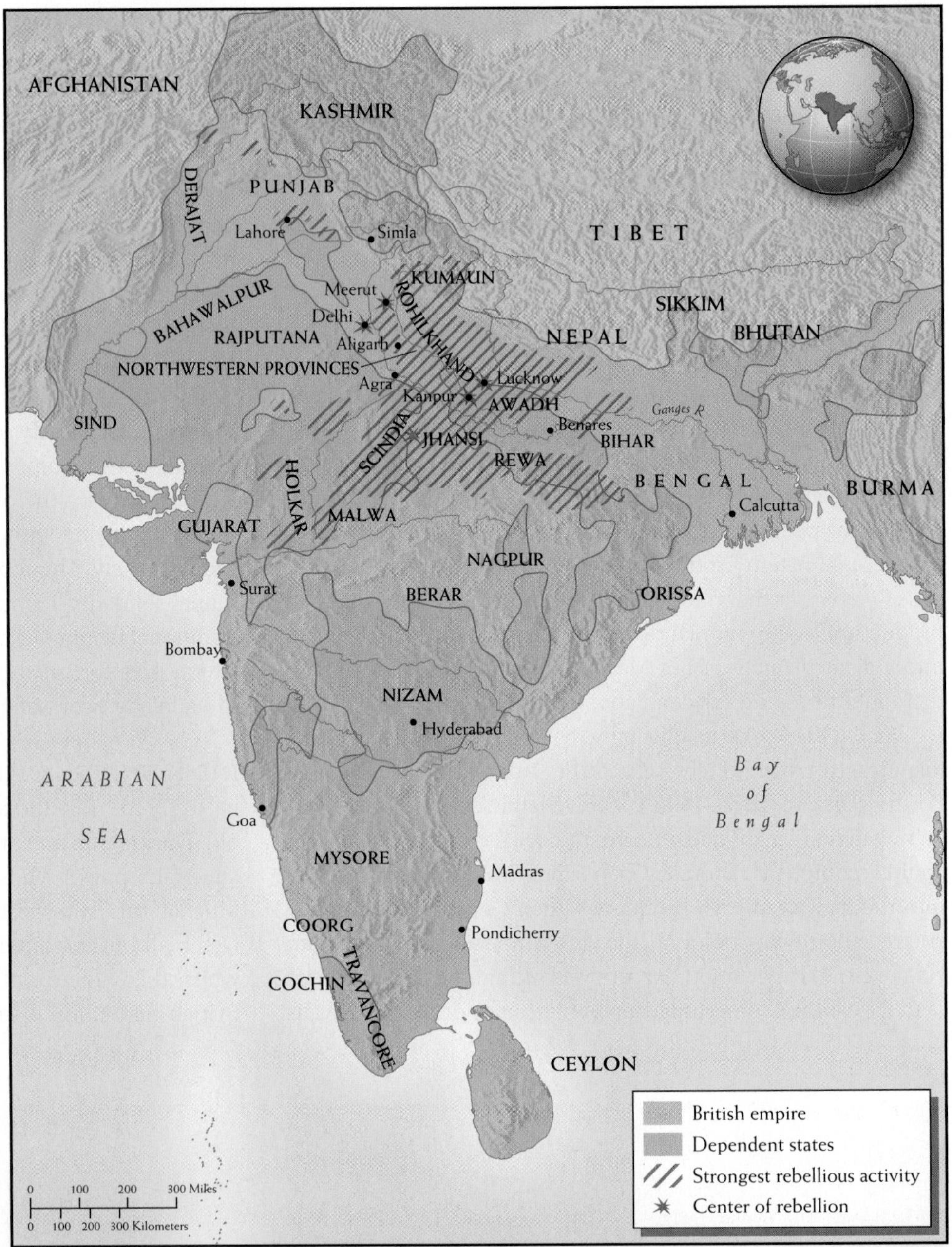

MAP 16.5 | Indian Rebellion of 1857

The Indian Rebellion of 1857 broke out first among the Indian soldiers of the British army. Other groups soon joined the struggle.

- According to this map, how many centers of rebellion were located in British territory, and how many in dependent states?
- Can you speculate on why the rebellion occurred in the interior of the subcontinent rather than along the coasts?
- In what way was the company's expansion into formerly autonomous areas during the first half of the nineteenth century a factor in the rebellion?

The most prized object for annexation was the kingdom of Awadh in northern India (see Map 16.5). Founded in 1722 by an Iranian adventurer, it was one of the first successor states to have gained a measure of independence from the Mughal ruler in Delhi. With access to the fertile resources of the Ganges Plain, its opulent court in Lucknow was one place where Mughal splendor still survived. In 1765, the company imposed a treaty on Awadh under which the ruler paid an annual tribute for British troops stationed in his territory to "protect" his kingdom from internal and external enemies. The British constantly ratcheted up their demands for tribute and abused their position to monopolize the lucrative trade in cotton,

The Indian Sepoys. *Pictured here are Indian soldiers, or sepoys, who were armed, drilled, and commanded by British officers. The sepoys were drawn from indigenous groups that the British considered to be "martial races." This photograph shows the Sikhs, designated as one such "race."*

indigo, textiles, and other commodities. But the more successful they were in exploiting Awadh, the more they longed to annex it completely. Thus, Dalhousie declared in 1851 that Awadh was "a cherry which will drop into our mouths some day."

TREATY VIOLATIONS AND ANNEXATION In 1856, citing misgovernment and deterioration in law and order, the East India Company violated its treaty obligations and sent its troops to Lucknow to take control of the province. Nawab Wajid Ali Shah, the poet-king of Awadh, whom the British saw as effete and debauched, refused to sign the treaty of abdication. Instead, he came dressed in his mourning robes to meet with the British official charged to take over the province. After pleading unsuccessfully for his legal rights under the treaty, he handed over his turban to the official and then left for Calcutta to argue his case before Dalhousie. There was widespread distress at the treatment he received. Dirges were recited, and religious men rushed to Lucknow to denounce the annexation.

In fact, the annexation of princely domains and the abolition of feudal privileges formed part of the developing practices of European imperialism. To the policy of annexation, Dalhousie added an ambitious program of building railroads, telegraph lines, and a postal network to unify the disjointed territory into a single "network of iron sinew" under British control. Dalhousie saw these infrastructures as key to developing India into a productive colony—a supplier of raw materials for British industry, and a market for its manufactures.

A year after Dalhousie's departure in 1856, India went up in flames. The spark that ignited the simmering discontent into a furious rebellion—the **Rebellion of 1857 (Great Rebellion)**—was the "greased cartridge" controversy. At the end of 1856, the British army, which consisted of hundreds of thousands of Hindu and Muslim recruits (sepoys) commanded by British officers, introduced the new Enfield rifle to replace the old-style musket. To load the rifle, soldiers had to bite the cartridge open. Although manufacturing instructions stated that linseed oil and beeswax be used to grease the cartridge, a rumor circulated that cow and pig fat had been used. But biting into cartridges greased with animal fat meant violating the Hindu and Muslim sepoys' religious traditions. The sepoys became convinced that there was a plot afoot to defile them and to compel their conversion to Christianity. So a wave of rebellion spread among the 270,000 Indian soldiers, who greatly outnumbered the 40,000 British soldiers employed to rule over 200 million Indians.

REBELLION BREAKS OUT The mutiny broke out on May 10, 1857, at the military barracks in Meerut. The previous day, the native soldiers had witnessed eighty-five of their comrades being manacled and shackled in irons and marched off to the prison for refusing to load their rifles. The next day, all three regiments at Meerut mutinied, killed their British officers, and marched thirty miles south to Delhi, where their comrades in regiments there welcomed them joyfully. Together, they "restored" the aging Bahadur Shah as the Mughal emperor, which lent legitimacy to the uprising.

The revolt soon turned from a limited military mutiny into a widespread civil rebellion that involved peasants, artisans, day laborers, and religious leaders. While the insurgents did not eliminate the power of the East India Company, which managed to retain the loyalty of princes and landed aristocrats in some places, they did throw the company into a crisis. Before

PRIMARY SOURCE

The Azamgarh Proclamation

The Indian leaders of the Rebellion of 1857 issued numerous proclamations. The Azamgarh Proclamation, excerpted below, is representative of these petitions. The emperor, Bahadur Shah, issued it in August 1857 on behalf of the mutineers who had seized the garrison town of Azamgarh, sixty miles north of Benares. Like other proclamations, it attacks the British for subverting Indian traditions and calls on its followers to restore the pre-British order—in this case, the Mughal Empire.

It is well known to all, that in this age the people of Hindoostan, both Hindoos and Mohammedans, are being ruined under the tyranny and oppression of the infidel and treacherous English. It is therefore the bounden duty of all the wealthy people of India, especially of those who have any sort of connection with any of the Mohammedan royal families, and are considered the pastors and masters of their people, to stake their lives and property for the well being of the public. . . .

Several of the Hindoo and Mussalman chiefs, who have long since quitted their homes for the preservation of their religion, and have been trying their best to root out the English in India, have presented themselves to me, and taken part in the reigning Indian crusade. . . . Parties anxious to participate in the common cause, but having no means to provide for themselves, shall receive their daily subsistence from me; and be it known to all, that the ancient works, both of the Hindoos and the Mohammedans, the writings of the miracle-workers and the calculations of the astrologers, pundits, and rammals, all agree in asserting that the English will no longer have any footing in India or elsewhere. . . .

Section I—Regarding Zemindars [large landholders, responsible for collecting land taxes for the government]. It is evident, that the British Government in making zemindary settlements have imposed exorbitant *Jumas* [revenue assessments], and have disgraced and ruined several zemindars. . . . Such extortions will have no manner of existence in the Badshahi Government; but on the contrary, the *Jumas* will be light, the dignity and honour of the zemindars safe, and every zemindar will have absolute rule in his own zemindary. . . .

Section II—Regarding Merchants. It is plain that the infidel and treacherous British Government have monopolized the trade of all the fine and valuable merchandise, such as indigo, cloth, and other articles of shipping, leaving only the trade of trifles to the people, and even in this they are not without their share of the profits, which they secure by means of customs and stamp fees, &c. in money suits, so that the people have merely a trade in name. . . . When the Badshahi Government is established, all these aforesaid fraudulent practices shall be dispensed with, and the trade of every article, without exception, both by land and water, shall be open to the native merchants of India. . . .

Section IV—Regarding Artisans. It is evident that the Europeans, by the introduction of English articles into India, have thrown the weavers, the cotton dressers, the carpenters, the blacksmiths, and the shoemakers, &c., out of employ, and have engrossed their occupations, so that every description of native artisan has been reduced to beggary. But under the Badshahi Government the native artisan will exclusively be employed in the services of the kings, the rajahs, and the rich. . . .

Section V—Regarding Pundits, Fakirs and other learned persons. The pundits and fakirs being the guardians of the Hindoo and Mohammedan religions respectively, and the Europeans being the enemies of both the religions, and as at present a war is raging against the English on account of religion, the pundits and fakirs are bound to present themselves to me, and take their share in the holy war.

QUESTIONS FOR ANALYSIS

- What are the main grievances against the English in India?
- How will the emperor's Badshahi Government alleviate these grievous conditions?
- What was the role of religion in the 1857 rebellion?

Source: "Proclamation of Emperor Bahadur Shah," in India in 1857: The Revolt against Foreign Rule, *edited by Ainslie T. Embree (Delhi: Chanakya Publications, 1987), pp. 3–6.*

long, the mutineers in Delhi issued a proclamation declaring that because the British were determined to destroy the religion of both Hindus and Muslims, it was the duty of the wealthy and the privileged to support the rebellion. (See Primary Source: The Azamgarh Proclamation.) To promote Hindu-Muslim unity, rebel leaders asked Muslims to refrain from killing cows in deference to Hindu sentiments.

Triumphant in Delhi, the rebellion spread to other parts of India. In Awadh, proclamations in Hindi, Urdu, and Persian called on Hindus and Muslims to revolt. Troops at the garrison in Lucknow, Awadh's capital, did just that. Seizing control of the town, the rebels urged all classes to unite in expelling the British and succeeded in compelling the colonial forces to retreat.

Although the dispossessed aristocracy and petty landholders led the rebellion, leaders also appeared from the lower classes. Bakht Khan, who had been a junior noncommissioned officer in the British army, became commander-in-chief of the rebel forces in Delhi, replacing one of the Mughal emperor's sons. And Devi Singh, a wealthy peasant, set himself up as a peasant king. Dressed in yellow, the insignia of Hindu royalty, he constituted a government of his own, modeling it on the British administration. While his imitation of company rule showed his respect for the British bureaucracy, he defied British authority by leading an armed peasantry against the hated local moneylenders. The call to popular forces also marked the rebel career of Maulavi Ahmadullah Shah, a Muslim theologian. He stood at the head of the rebel forces in Lucknow, leading an army composed primarily of ordinary soldiers and people from the lower orders. Claiming to be an "Incarnation of the Deity," and thus inspired by divine will, he emerged as a prophetic leader of the common people. He voiced his undying hatred of the British in religious terms, calling on Hindus and Muslims to destroy British rule and warning his followers against betrayal by landed authorities.

PARTICIPATION BY THE PEASANTRY The presence of popular leadership points to the role of lower classes as historical actors. Although feudal chieftains often brought them into the rebellion, the peasantry made it their own. The organizing principle of their uprising was the common experience of oppression. Thus, they destroyed anything that represented the authority of the company: prisons, factories, police posts, railway stations, European bungalows, and law courts. Equally significant, the peasantry attacked native moneylenders and local power-holders who had purchased land at government auctions and were seen as benefiting from company rule.

Vigorous and militant as the popular rebellion was, it was limited in its territorial and ideological horizons. To begin with, the uprisings were local in scale and vision. Peasant rebels attacked the closest seats of administration and sought to settle scores with their most immediate and visible oppressors. They did not carry their action beyond the village or collection of villages. Their loyalties remained intensely local, based on village attachments and religious, caste, and clan ties. Nor did popular militants seek to undo traditional hierarchies of caste and religion.

COUNTERINSURGENCY AND PACIFICATION Convinced that the rebellion was the result of plotting by a few troublemakers, the British carried out their counterinsurgency with brutal vengeance. Villages were torched, and rebels were tied to cannons and blown to bits to teach Indians a lesson in power. Delhi fell in September 1857; Lucknow in March 1858. The British exiled the unfortunate Mughal emperor to Burma, where he died, and murdered his sons. Most of the other rebel leaders were either killed in battle or captured and executed. When, at the same time, the British also moved to annex the state of Jhansi in northern India, its female leader, Lakshmi Bai, mounted a counterattack. After a two-week siege, Jhansi fell to the British, but Lakshmi Bai escaped on horseback, only to die in the fighting for control of a nearby fortress. Her intelligence, bravery, and youth (she was twenty-eight) made her the subject of many popular Indian ballads in the decades to follow.

The Rani of Jhansi. *The Rani of Jhansi, who was deposed by the British, rose up during the revolt of 1857. In subsequent nationalist iconography, as this twentieth-century watercolor illustrates, she is remembered as a heroic rebel, all the more so because of her gender.*

ANALYZING GLOBAL DEVELOPMENTS

Alternative Movements in Asia and Africa

During the nineteenth century, five uprisings of global significance occurred in Africa and Asia. Two of these were carried out on a massive scale (the Taiping Rebellion and the Great Rebellion); the other three involved much smaller numbers. The two large-scale uprisings did not last as long as the three movements in sub-Saharan Africa and the Arabian Peninsula and were put down with great loss of life. In contrast, the political and cultural successes of the Wahhabi revolt in the Arabian Peninsula, Shaka's Zulu state in southern Africa, and the Fulani revolt in northern Nigeria can be seen clearly even to this day.

QUESTIONS FOR ANALYSIS

- Why were Europeans involved in suppressing the larger-scale uprisings in China and India but not the smaller-scale ones in Africa and the Arabian Peninsula?
- Although all five movements suffered stinging military defeats (the Fulani at the hands of the British in 1900, the Zulu state at the hands of the British in 1878, the Wahhabis at the hands of Egyptian troops at the beginning of the nineteenth century, the Taiping rebels at the hands of the Qing rulers, and the Indian rebels by British soldiers), were their long-term consequences markedly different?
- What holds these diverse movements together and allows us to represent them as alternatives to the main developments under way in western Europe and North America, the regions that had become dynamic centers of historical change?

Movement/Leader	Short-Term Consequences	Long-Term Consequences
Smaller-Scale Uprisings		
Fulani Revolt Northern Nigeria (1804–1817)	• Created largest state in sub-Saharan Africa • Occupied two-thirds of present day Nigeria	• Gained independence in 1960 • Fulani elite families who worked with British now rule over present-day Nigeria
Usman dan Fodio (1754–1817)	• British conquered it in early twentieth century	
Shaka's Zulu State	• Created an army of 40,000 warriors	• British conquered Zulu in 1878
Shaka (1787–1828)	• Created Zulu State covering 11,500 sq. miles in South Africa	• Zulu maintained their identity through apartheid • Population of 11 million today
Wahhabi Rebellion Arabian Peninsula (1744–1818)	• Ruled over much of the Arabian Peninsula	• Created the House of Saud, which rules over Saudi Arabia today
Ibn Abd al-Wahhab (1703–1792)	• Defeated by Egyptian army in 1812	• Retains commitment Wahhab principles today
Larger-Scale Uprisings		
Taiping Rebellion (1851–1864)	• Accrued half a million members	• Rebellion caused 20 million deaths by 1853
Hong Xiuquan (1813–1864)	• Leader Hong and rebels ruled over central and southern China from Nanjing for eleven years	• Nearly toppled Qing Dynasty; Mao Zedong viewed it as precursor to peasant-led Communist movement; now viewed as threat to social order due to large-scale violence
Great Rebellion (1857–1858)	• Indian sepoys of East India Company started revolt	• British crown ended company rule after suppressing rebellion brutally
Geographic Leaders, no monolithic figure	• Sepoys pledged support to Mughal emperor • Revolt included sepoys, peasants, small landholders, and religious leaders across north India	• Laid the foundation for later Indian populist and nationalist resistance

Sources: Dalrymple, William, The Last Mughal: The Fall of a Dynasty: Delhi, 1857 *(2007); Hamilton, Carolyn (ed.),* The Mfecane Aftermath: Reconstructive Debates in Southern African History *(1995); Hiskett, Mervyn,* The Sword of Truth: The Life and Times of the Shehu Usman dan Fodio *(1994); Spence, Jonathan,* God's Chinese Son: The Taiping Heavenly Kingdom of Hong Xiuquan *(1996).*

By July 1858, the vicious pacification campaign had achieved its goal. Yet, in August, the British Parliament abolished company rule and the company itself, and transferred responsibility for the governing of India to the crown. In November, Queen Victoria issued a proclamation guaranteeing religious toleration, promising improvements, and allowing Indians to serve in the government. She promised to honor the treaties and agreements with princes and chiefs and to refrain from interfering in religious matters. The insurgents had risen up not as a nation, but as a multitude of communities acting independently, and their determination to find a new order shocked the British and threw them into a panic. Having crushed the uprising, the British resumed the work of transforming India into a modern colonial state and economy. But the desire for radical alternatives and traditions of popular insurgency, though vanquished, did not vanish.

CONCLUSION

The nineteenth century was a time of turmoil and transformation. While powerful forces reconfigured the world as a place for capitalism, colonialism, and nation-states, so too did prophets, charismatic leaders, radicals, peasant rebels, and anticolonial insurgents arise to offer alternatives. Reflecting local circumstances and traditions, the struggles of these men and women for a different future opened up spaces for the ideas and activities of subordinate classes.

Conventional historical accounts either neglect these struggles or fail to view them as a whole. These individuals were not just romantic, last-ditch resisters, as some scholars have argued. Even after defeat, their messages remained alive within their communities. Nor were their actions isolated and atypical events, for when viewed on a global scale they bring to light a world that looks very different from the one that became dominant. To see the Wahhabi movement in the Arabian Peninsula together with the Shawnee Prophet in North America, the utopians and radicals in Europe with the peasant insurgents in British India, and the Taiping rebels with the Mayans in the Yucatan is to glimpse a world of marginalized regions and groups. It was a world that more powerful groups endeavored to suppress but could not erase.

In this world, prophets and rebel leaders usually cultivated power and prestige locally; the emergence of an alternative polity in one region did not impinge on communities and political organizations in others. As much as these individuals had in common, they envisioned widely different kinds of futures. Even Marx, who called the workers of the world to unite, was acutely aware that the call for a proletarian revolution applied only to the industrialized countries of Europe. Other dissenters had even more localized horizons. A world fashioned by movements for alternatives meant a world with multiple centers and different historical paths.

What gave force to a different mapping of the world was the fact that common people were at the center of these alternative visions, and their voices, however muted, gained a place on the historical stage. Egalitarianism in different forms defined efforts to reconstitute alternative worlds. In Islamic regions, the egalitarianism practiced by revitalization movements was evident in their mobilization of all Muslims, not just the elites. Even charismatic military leaders in Africa, for all their use of raw power, used the framework of community to build new polities. The Taiping Rebellion distinguished itself by seeking to establish an equal society of men and women in service of the Heavenly Kingdom. Operating under very different conditions, the European radicals imagined a society free from aristocratic privileges and bourgeois property. Anticolonial rebels and insurgents depended on local solidarities and proposed alternative moral communities. In so doing, these movements compelled ruling elites to adjust the way they governed. The next chapter explores this challenge.

AFTER YOU READ THIS CHAPTER

Review and research on STUDYSPACE: wwnorton.com/studyspace

TRACING THE GLOBAL STORYLINES

FOCUS ON: *Regional Variations in Alternative Visions*

Europe and the Americas—The Heartland of Modernizing Change

- European socialists and radicals envision a world free of exploitation and inequalities, while nationalists work to create new independent nation-states.
- Native American prophets in the United States imagine a world restored to its customary ways and traditional rites.
- Mayans in the Yucatan defy the central Mexican government in a rebellion known as the Caste War.

The Islamic World and Africa

- Revivalist movements in the Arabian Peninsula and West Africa demand a return to traditional Islam.
- A charismatic warrior, Shaka, creates a powerful state in southern Africa.

Semi-colonial China

- An inspired prophetic figure, Hong Xiuquan, leads the Taiping Rebellion against the Qing dynasty and European encroachment on China.

Colonial India

- Indian troops mutiny against the British and attempt to restore Mughal rule.

CHRONOLOGY

The Americas

Tecumseh's Rebellion (North America) **1810–1813**

South Asia

East Asia

Europe

Greek independence **1829**

Fourier's utopian socialism gains popularity **1830s**

Africa and the Middle East

Dan Fodio's movement in West Africa **1804–1809**

Wahhabis wage militant religious campaign in Arabian Peninsula **1813–1815**

Shaka creates Zulu Empire in South Africa **1818–1828**

1800 **1820**

KEY TERMS

Caste War *p. 618*

Chartism *p. 610*

Usman dan Fodio *p. 598*

Fourierism *p. 611*

liberalism *p. 609*

Marxism *p. 613*

Mfecane movement *p. 601*

millenarian *p. 604*

proletarians *p. 612*

Rebellion of 1857 (Great Rebellion) *p. 621*

Restoration period *p. 607*

Taiping Rebellion *p. 605*

Tecumseh *p. 616*

Tenskwatawa *p. 615*

utopian socialism *p. 610*

Wahhabism *p. 597*

STUDY QUESTIONS

1. **Define** the global order emerging in the nineteenth century in light of the revolutions in the Atlantic world studied in Chapter 15. How did it challenge social relations within societies?

2. **Explain** the goals of Islamic revitalization movements such as Wahhabism in the Arabian Peninsula and dan Fodio's movement in West Africa. How were these regions affected by the new world order? What alternative did Islamic revitalization propose?

3. **Describe** Hong Xiuquan's vision for China during the Taiping Rebellion. How did he propose reordering Chinese society?

4. **Describe** the various alternative visions to the status quo that European radicals proposed in the nineteenth century. What traditions and beliefs did they reflect?

5. **Compare and contrast** the Shawnee rebellion in the United States and the Caste War in Mexico. How did they reflect tensions between Native Americans and European Americans?

6. **Analyze** to what extent the Indian Rebellion of 1857 encouraged a new identity among its followers. What goals did participants in the rebellion share?

7. **Explore** the role of women in promoting alternative visions around the world in the nineteenth century. Which alternative vision movements proposed new roles for women in society?

8. **List** major similarities among the alternative visions explored in this chapter. Why did they all fail to achieve their objectives? Did they have any important legacies?

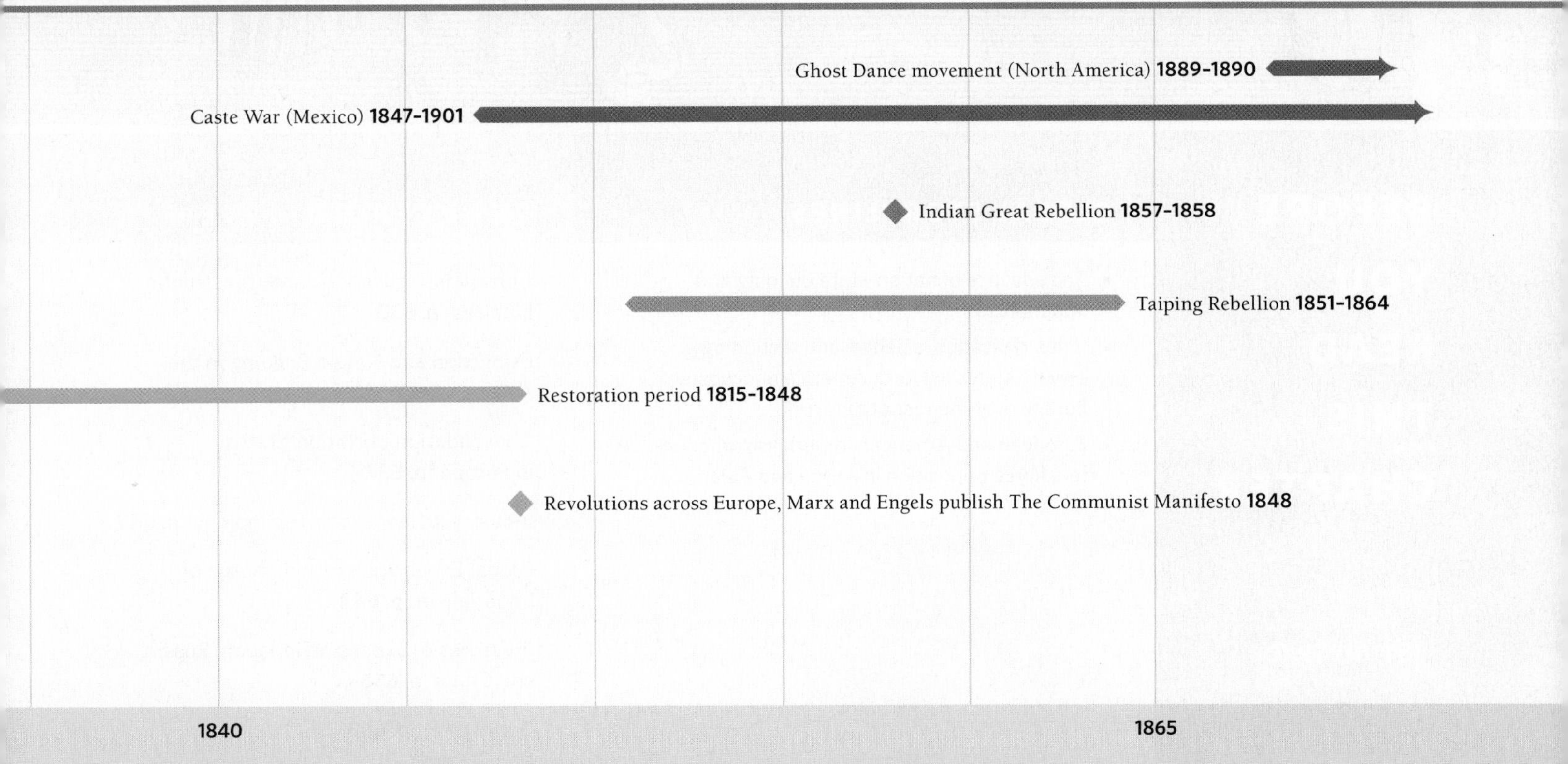

BEFORE YOU READ THIS CHAPTER

wwnorton.com/
StudySpace

GLOBAL STORYLINES

- The advance of nation-state building and imperialism.
- Industrialization, science, and technology elevate states in North America and western Europe over the rest of the world.
- European and American imperialism encounters fierce opposition in Africa and Asia.

CHAPTER OUTLINE

17

Nations and Empires, 1850–1914

FOCUS QUESTIONS

- How were nations conceptualized and how were nation-states built?
- Why did nationalism often lead to colonization and/or territorial expansion?
- How did colonization and territorial expansion shape the lives of indigenous people?
- How did new developments in industry, science, and technology reorder the relationships among different parts of the world?
- How did developments in technology, finance, and business reshuffle people and resources?

In 1895, the Cuban patriot José Martí launched a rebellion against the last Spanish holdings in the Americas. The anti-Spanish struggle continued until 1898, when Spain withdrew from Cuba and Puerto Rico. Martí hoped to bring freedom to a new Cuban nation and equality to all Cubans. But even as he helped secure freedom from the declining Spanish empire, he could not prevent Cuba's military occupation and political domination by the world's newest imperial power, the United States.

Martí's hopes and frustrations found parallels around the world. After 1850, the building of nation-states and the expansion of their empires changed the map of the world, exhilarating some peoples and frustrating others. The communities that benefited most were Europeans and peoples of European descent. During these decades the nation-states of Europe, now locked in intense political and economic rivalry, projected their power across the entire world. Much of the rivalry among European states intensified through disruptions in the European balance of power, caused by the unification of two new states (Italy and Germany). Across the Atlantic, the United States forsook its anticolonial origins and annexed overseas possessions. Yet, imperial expansion did not go unchallenged. It encountered fierce resistance from communities being incorporated into the new empires. In Asia and Africa resisters struggled to repel their invaders, often demanding the right to govern themselves.

The second half of the nineteenth century, as this chapter details, witnessed the simultaneous—and entwined—advance of nationalism and imperialism. These decades also saw the further expansion of the industrial revolution. Taken together, the era's political and economic developments allowed western Europe and the United States to attain greater primacy in world affairs. But tensions inside these nations and their empires, as well as within other states, made the new world order anything but stable.

CONSOLIDATING NATIONS AND CONSTRUCTING EMPIRES

During the second half of the nineteenth century, the idea of building nation-states engulfed the globe. In the previous century a series of wars, ending with the Napoleonic Wars, had made Europeans increasingly conscious of political and cultural borders—and of the power of new bureaucracies. Enlightenment thinkers had emphasized the importance of nations, defined as peoples who shared a common past, territory, culture, and traditions. To many people it seemed natural that once absolutist rulers had fallen, the state should draw its power and legitimacy from those who lived within its borders and that the body of institutions governing each territory should be uniquely concerned with promoting the welfare of that particular people. This seemed such a natural process that little thought was given to how nation-states arose; they were simply supposed to well up from the people's longing for liberty and togetherness.

Building Nationalism

In practice, nations did not usually well up from people's longings for liberty and togetherness. More often than not, ruling elites themselves created nations. They did so by compelling diverse groups of people and regions to accept a unified network of laws, a central administration, time zones, national markets, and a single regional dialect as the "national" language. To overcome strong regional identities, state administrators broadened public education in the national language and imposed universal military service to build a national army. These efforts nurtured the notion of a one-to-one correspondence between a "people" and a nation-state, and they radiated the values and institutions of dominant elites outward to regions throughout each nation-state and beyond their national borders.

The world's major nation-states of the late nineteenth century were not all alike, however. They took many forms. Some had been in existence for years, such as Japan, England, France, Spain, Portugal, and the United States; here, citizens widely embraced their national identities. Two nation-states (Germany and Italy) were entirely new, forged through strategic military conquests. Elsewhere, plans for nation-states like those in central Europe, the Balkans, Poland, and the Ukraine were chiefly the inventions of local elites; their plans displeased Russian, Austrian, and Ottoman monarchs and were of little interest to the multilingual, multiethnic peasantry in these areas. In many parts of the world, intellectuals were the primary agents agitating for new nation-states, often urging new states to break away from existing empires. That secessionist impulse posed a particularly thorny challenge to the rulers of multinational empires like Russia and Austria.

Expanding the Empires

In countries that became nation-states, the processes of nation building and the acquisition of new territories, often called **imperialism**, went hand in hand. Their rulers measured national strength not only by their people's unity and the possession of the most modern means of production but also by the conquest of new territories. Thus Germany, France, the United States, Russia, and Japan rivaled Britain by expanding and modernizing their industries and seizing nearby or far-off territories. By the century's end, gaining new territory had become so important that these states scrambled to colonize peoples from Africa to the Amazon, from California to Korea.

Never before had there been such a rapid reshuffling of peoples and resources. As transportation costs declined, workers left their homelands in search of better opportunities. Japanese moved to Brazil, Indians to South Africa and the Caribbean, Chinese to California, and Italians to New York and Buenos Aires. At the same time, American capitalists invested outside the United States, and British investors financed the construction of railroads in China and India. Raw materials from Africa and Southeast Asia flowed to the manufacturing nations of Europe and the Americas.

Imperial rule facilitated a widespread movement of labor, capital, commodities, and information. As scholars studied previously unknown tribes and races, new schools taught colonized peoples the languages, religions, scientific practices, and cultural traditions of their colonizers. Publications and products from the "mother country" circulated widely among indigenous elites. Yet empire builders did not extend to nonwhite inhabitants of their colonies the same rights as they gave to inhabitants of their own nations; here, nation and empire were incompatible. Not only were colonial subjects prohibited from participating in government, but they were also not considered members of the nation at all. As a result, imperialism produced diametrically opposed reactions: exultation among the colonizers, and bitterness among the colonized.

EXPANSION AND NATION BUILDING IN THE AMERICAS

Once freed from European control, the elites of the Americas set about creating political communities of their own. By the 1850s, they shared a desire both to create widespread loyalty to their political institutions and to expand territorial domains. This required refining the tools of government to include national laws and court systems, standardized money, and national political parties. It also meant finding ways to settle hinterlands that previously belonged to indigenous populations. Having once been European colonies, New World territories became vibrant nation-states based on growing prosperity and industrialization.

Although nation-states took shape throughout the world, the Americas saw the most complete assimilation of new possessions. Instead of treating outlying areas as colonial outposts, American nation-state builders turned them into new provinces. With the help of rifles, railroads, schools, and land surveys, frontiers became staging areas for the expanding populations of North and South American societies. For indigenous peoples, however, such national expansion meant the loss of traditional lands on a vast scale.

Not all national consolidations in the Americas were the same. The United States, Canada, and Brazil, for example, experienced different processes of nation building, territorial expansion, and economic development. Each one incorporated frontier regions into national polities and economies, although they used different techniques for subjugating indigenous peoples and administering their new holdings.

The United States

Military might, fortuitous diplomacy, and the power of numbers enabled the United States to claim territory that spanned the North American continent (see Map 17.1). At its independence, the nation had been a barely united confederation of states. Indian resistance and Spanish and British rivalry hemmed in the "Americans" (as they came to call themselves). At the same time, the disunited states threatened to fracture into northern and southern polities, for questions of slavery versus free labor intruded into national politics. Yet, rallying to the rhetoric of **Manifest Destiny**, which maintained that it was God's will for the United States to "overspread" North America, Americans pushed their boundaries westward. They acquired territories via purchase agreements and treaties with France, Spain, and Britain and via warfare and treaties with diverse Indian nations and Mexico. (See Primary Source: Manifest Destiny.)

As part of the territories taken from Mexico after the Mexican-American War (1846–1848), the United States gained California, where the discovery of gold brought migration on an unprecedented scale. As news of the find spread, hopeful prospectors raced to stake their claims. In the next few years, over 100,000 Americans took to the overland trails and to the seas in quest of California's riches.

The California gold rush, however, was not only a great American migration; it also inspired tens of thousands of individuals from Latin America, Australia, Asia, and Europe to pour into California. What had just a few years earlier been a sparsely populated corner of northwestern Mexico was transformed almost overnight into the most cosmopolitan place on earth. In the 1850s, California was truly where worlds came together.

CIVIL WAR AND STATES' RIGHTS Ironically, California and the territories that the United States took from Mexico also spurred the coming apart of the American nation. The deeply divisive issue was whether these lands would be open to slavery or restricted to free labor. Following the 1860 election of Abraham Lincoln, who pledged to halt the expansion of slavery, the United States divided between North and South and plunged into a gruesome Civil War (1861–1865).

The bloody conflict led to the abolition of slavery, and the struggle to extend voting and citizenship rights to freed slaves qualified the Civil War as a second American Revolution. It gave the nation a new generation of heroes and martyrs such as the assassinated president, Abraham Lincoln. He had promised a new model of freedom for a nation reborn out of bloodshed. Its cornerstone would be the incorporation of freed slaves as citizens of the United States. Alas, the experiments in biracial democracy during the Reconstruction period (1867–1877) were short-lived. In the decades after the Civil War, counterrevolutionary pressure led to the denial of voting rights to African Americans and the restoration of (white) planter rule in the southern states. This pressure was spearheaded by the terrorism of the Ku Klux Klan, a group of former Confederates that sought to reverse freedmen's legal and political gains and to restore planters to power in the South.

Nonetheless, the war brought enduring changes across the United States. The defeat of the South established the preeminence of the national government. After the Civil War, Americans learned to speak of their nation in the singular ("the United States is" in contrast to "the United States are"). With an invigorated nationalism came an enlarged national government.

Even more dizzying were social and economic changes. Within ten years of the war's end, the industrial output of the United States had climbed by 75 percent. Symbolizing

MAP 17.1 | U.S. and Canadian Westward Expansion, 1803–1912

Americans and Canadians expanded westward in the second half of the nineteenth century, aided greatly by railways.

- How many railroad lines ultimately reached the western borders of Canada and the United States?
- By what years were the territorial expansions of Canada and the United States complete? How did territorial expansion strengthen Canadian and American nationalism?
- What were the major events that led to the annexation of the western half of the United States?

PRIMARY SOURCE

Manifest Destiny

In July 1845, the New York newspaper editor John L. O'Sullivan coined the phrase* Manifest Destiny *to explain how the "manifest design of Providence" supported the territorial expansion of the United States. In this excerpt, O'Sullivan outlines the reasons why the United States was justified in annexing Texas and why it must soon do the same in replacing Mexican rule in California. Claims of Manifest Destiny often accompanied American conquest and colonization of new territories.

. . . Texas has been absorbed into the Union in the inevitable fulfilment of the general law which is rolling our population westward; the connexion of which with that ratio of growth in population which is destined within a hundred years to swell our numbers to the enormous population of *two hundred and fifty millions* (if not more), is too evident to leave us in doubt of the manifest design of Providence in regard to the occupation of this continent. It was disintegrated from Mexico in the natural course of events, by a process perfectly legitimate on its own part, blameless on ours; and in which all the censures due to wrong, perfidy and folly, rest on Mexico alone. And possessed as it was by a population which was in truth but a colonial detachment from our own, and which was still bound by myriad ties of the very heart strings to its old relations, domestic and political, their incorporation into the Union was not only inevitable, but the most natural, right and proper thing in the world. . . .

California will, probably, next fall away from the loose adhesion which, in such a country as Mexico, holds a remote province in a slight equivocal kind of dependence on the metropolis. Imbecile and distracted, Mexico never can exert any real governmental authority over such a country. The impotence of the one and the distance of the other, must make the relation one of virtual independence. . . . The Anglo-Saxon foot is already on its borders. Already the advance guard of the irresistible army of Anglo-Saxon emigration has begun to pour down upon it, armed with the plough and the rifle, and marking its trail with schools and colleges, courts and representative halls, mills and meeting-houses. A population will soon be in actual occupation of California, over which it will be idle for Mexico to dream of dominion. They will necessarily become independent.

QUESTIONS FOR ANALYSIS

- What is the main reason O'Sullivan gives for why the United States must expand westward?
- How does O'Sullivan justify the annexation of Texas by the United States?
- In terms of California, in what ways is "the Anglo-Saxon foot already on its borders"?
- Why does O'Sullivan think that the people of Texas and California will want to join the United States?

Source: John L. O'Sullivan, "Manifest Destiny," Democratic Review *(July 1845), pp. 7–10, in Clark C. Spence, ed.,* The American West: A Source Book *(New York: Thomas Y. Crowell Company, 1966), pp. 108–9.*

this growth was the expansion of railroad lines. In 1865, the United States boasted 35,000 miles of track. By 1900, nearly 200,000 miles of track connected the Atlantic to the Pacific and crisscrossed the American territory in between. Increasingly, steam-powered machines replaced human muscle as the engine of production, bringing dramatic improvements in output. Before the Civil War, it took sixty-one hours of labor to produce an acre of wheat; by 1900, new machinery cut the time to a little over three hours. Mechanization boosted production on farms and in factories, and rapid railroad transportation permitted the shipment of more goods at lower prices across greater distances.

ECONOMIC AND INDUSTRIAL DEVELOPMENT Americans made such impressive industrial gains that the United States soon joined Britain and Germany atop the list of economic giants. (The gains were in technical education, inventions, factory routines, marketing, and the mobilization of capital.) A potent instrument of capital accumulation appeared at this time—the **limited-liability joint-stock company**. Firms such as Standard Oil and U.S. Steel mobilized capital from shareholders, who left the running of these enterprises to paid managers. Intermediaries, like J. Pierpont Morgan, the New York financial giant who became the world's wealthiest man, loaned money and brokered big deals on the New York Stock Exchange. So great were the fortunes amassed by leading financiers and industrialists that by 1890 the richest 1 percent of Americans owned nearly 90 percent of the nation's wealth.

African American Gains and Losses. *In the immediate aftermath of the American Civil War, "Radical Republicans" asserted political control by passing laws and constitutional amendments ending slavery, guaranteeing equal rights, and enfranchising freedmen. One result was the election of African Americans* (above) *to the U.S. Congress. During the 1870s, however, white leaders retreated from the commitment to black rights, allowing ex-Confederates to re-assert control over southern politics.* (Right) *The Ku Klux Klan terrorized African Americans in the post-Civil War South. Klan violence reversed many of the legal and political gains made by freedmen and helped restore planters to power in the South.*

As mechanized production churned out ever more goods, farms and factories produced more than Americans needed or could afford to purchase. In the 1890s, overproduction plunged the American economy into a harsh depression. Millions of urban workers lost their jobs; others suffered sharp cuts in wages. Soon radical labor leaders called for the dismantling of the industrial capitalist state, and strikes proliferated. In the countryside, declining prices and excessive railroad freight charges pushed countless farmers toward bankruptcy.

Meanwhile, Americans were continuing their migrations west. Joined by throngs of immigrants from Europe, they were attracted by homestead acts promising nearly free acreage to settlers and by the railroad's real estate promoters. (Railroad corporations had been given enormous land grants as a subsidy for building transcontinental lines.) The migrations sparked another round of wars with Indians, which resulted in their dispossession and concentration on reservations.

By now the United States had become a major world power. It boasted an economy that despite its troubles in the 1890s had expanded rapidly over the last decades of the nineteenth century. It also was a more integrated nation after the Civil War, with an amended constitution that claimed to uphold the equality of all members of the American nation. But there was no agreement on what that equality should involve or how the country would adjust to a new century in which the nation's "destiny" had already been fulfilled.

Canada

Canadians also built a new nation, enjoyed economic success, and followed an expansionist course. Like the United States, Canada had access to a vast frontier prairie for growing agricultural exports. And as in the United States, these lands became the homes and farms of more European immigrants. However, whereas the United States had waged a war to gain independence, Canada's separation from Britain was peaceful. From the 1830s to the 1860s, Britain gradually passed authority to the colony, leaving Canadians to grapple with the task of creating a shared national community.

BUILDING A NATION Sharp internal divisions made that task especially difficult. For one thing, there was a well-established French population. It had remained after the British took control of France's northernmost North American colony in 1763. Wanting to keep their villages, their culture, their religion, and their language intact, these French Canadians did not feel integrated into the emerging Canadian national community. Nor were they eager to join the English-speaking population in settling new areas, lest such migration dilute their French-Canadian presence.

The English-speakers were equally unenthusiastic about creating an independent nation. Fear of being absorbed into the American republic reinforced these Canadians' loyalty to

Oklahoma Land Rush. *This photograph captures the rush of homesteaders to claim lands on the "Cherokee Strip" on September 16, 1893. The opening of land that had previously been restricted to Indians set off several similar rushes in the Oklahoma Territory.*

the British crown and made them content with colonial status. Indeed, when Canada finally gained its independence in 1867, it was by an Act of Parliament in London and not by revolution. But even with nationhood granted, Canadians promised to remain loyal to the British crown and declared themselves a "dominion" within the British Commonwealth.

TERRITORIAL EXPANSION Lacking cultural and linguistic unity, not to mention an imperial overlord, Canadians used territorial expansion to build an integrated state. But their process differed from that of their neighbor to the south. In response to the U.S. purchase of Alaska from Russia and the movement of settlers onto the American plains, Canadian leaders realized that they had to incorporate their own western territories, lest these, too, fall into American hands. Pioneers seemed unwilling to venture to these prairies—it was far, it was cold, and the growing season was cruelly short. So the state lured emigrant farmers from Europe and the United States with subsidized railway rates and the promise of fortunes to be made. It also offered attractive terms to railway companies to connect agrarian hinterlands with Montreal and Toronto (see again Map 17.1), and *not* with commercial cities in the United States.

The Canadian state also faced friction with Indians. Frontier warfare threatened to drive away investors and settlers, who could always find property south of the border instead. To prevent the kind of bloodletting that characterized the United States' westward expansion, the Canadian government signed treaties with Indians to ensure strict separation between natives and newcomers. It also created a special police force, the Royal Canadian Mounted Police, to patrol the territories.

Canadian expansion was hardly bloodless, however. Many Indians and mixed-blood peoples (*métis*) resented the treaties. Moreover, the Canadian government was often less than honest in its dealings. As in the United States, the government's Indian policy in Canada sought to turn Indians into farmers and then incorporate them into Canadian society—regardless of whether they wanted to become farmers or join the nation.

The need to accommodate resident French speakers, defensive expansionism, and a degree of legality in dealing with Indians gave the Canadian government a strong foundation. Indeed, it acquired significant powers to intervene, regulate, and mediate social conflict and relations. (These powers, in fact, were fuller than those of the U.S. government.) But even though the state was relatively strong, the sense of a national identity was comparatively weak. Expansionism helped Canada remain an autonomous state, but it did not solve the question of what it meant to belong to a Canadian nation.

Latin America

Latin American elites also engaged in nation-state building and expanded their territorial borders. But unlike in the United States and Canada, expansion did not always create homesteader frontiers that could help expand democracy and forge national identities. Instead, civil conflict fractured certain countries in the region (see Chapters 15 and 16), although one—Brazil—remained united.

Much of Latin America shared a common social history. Far more than in North America, the richest lands in Latin America went not to small farmers, but to large estate holders producing

Opera House in Manaus. *The turn-of-the-century rubber boom brought immense wealth to the Amazon jungle. As in many boom-and-bust cycles in Latin America, the proceeds flowed to a small elite and diminished when the rubber supply outstripped the demand. But the wealth produced was sufficient to prompt the local elite to build temples of modernity in the midst of the jungle. Pictured here is the Opera House in the rubber capital of Manaus. Like other works built by Latin American elites of the period, this one emulated the original in Paris.*

exports such as sugar, coffee, or beef. The result: privileged elites monopolized power more than in North America's young democracies. Even though territorial expansion and strong economic growth were Latin American hallmarks, these processes sidelined the poor, the Indians, and the blacks.

CONSOLIDATION VERSUS FRAGMENTATION Indian and peasant uprisings were a major worry in new Latin American republics. Fearing insurrections, elites devised governing systems that protected private property and investments while limiting the political rights of the poor and the propertyless. Likewise, the specter of slave revolts, driven home not just by earlier, brutal events in Haiti (see Chapter 15) but also by daily rumors of rebellions, kept elites in a state of alarm. One Argentine writer echoed the concern about giving too much power to the masses, and he described the challenge of nation-state building in Latin America as a struggle between elitist "civilization" and popular "barbarism." Creating strong nations, it seemed to many Latin American elites, required excluding large groups of people from power.

BRAZIL: AN "EXCLUSIVE" NATION-STATE Brazil illustrates the process by which Latin American rulers built nation-states that excluded much of the population from both the "nation" and the "state." Through the nineteenth century, rulers in Rio de Janeiro defused political conflict by allowing planters to retain the reins of power. Moreover, although the Brazilian government officially abolished the slave trade in 1830, it allowed illegal slave imports to continue for another two decades (until British pressure compelled Brazil to enforce the ban).

The end of the slave trade, coupled with slave resistance, began to choke the planters' system by driving up the price of slaves within the region. Sensing that the system of forced labor was unraveling, slaves began to flee the sugar and coffee plantations, and army personnel refused to hunt them down. In the 1880s, even while laws still upheld slave labor, country roads in the state of São Paulo were filled with fugitive slaves looking for relatives or access to land. Finally, in 1888, the Brazilian emperor abolished slavery.

Thereafter, as in the United States, Brazilian elites followed two strategies in creating a new labor force for their estates. They retained some former slaves as gang-workers or sharecroppers, and they also imported new workers—especially from Italy, Spain, and Portugal. These laborers often came as seasonal migrant workers or indentured tenant farmers. Indeed, European and even Japanese migration to Brazil helped planters preserve their holdings in the post-slavery era. In all, 2 million Europeans and some 70,000 Japanese moved to Brazil.

The Brazilian state was deliberately exclusive. The constitution of 1891, which established a federal system and proclaimed Brazil a republic, separated those who could be trusted with power from the rest. After all, with the abolition of slavery, the sudden enfranchisement of millions of freedmen would have threatened to flood the electoral lists with propertyless, potentially uncontrollable voters. As in the United States, politicians responded by slapping severe restrictions on suffrage and by rigging rules to reduce political competition. However, given the greater share of the black population in Brazil, restrictions there excluded a larger share of the potential electorate than in the United States.

BRAZIL: EXPANSION AND ECONOMIC DEVELOPMENT Like Canada and the United States, the Brazilian state extended its reach to distant areas and incorporated them as provinces. The largest land-grab occurred in the Amazon River basin, the world's largest drainage watershed and tropical forest. It had built up over millennia around the meandering tributaries that convey runoffs from the eastern slopes of the Andean mountains all the way to the Atlantic Ocean. It was a massive yet delicate habitat of balanced biomass suspended by towering trees with a canopy of leaves and vines that kept the basin ecologically diverse. Here, the Brazilian state gave giant concessions to local capitalists to extract rubber latex. When combined with sulfur, rubber was a key raw material for tire manufacturing in European and North American bicycle and automobile industries.

Rubber Plantation Workers. *A worker harvests latex, a milky fluid that is secreted from a rubber tree via taps in its trunk (left). The worker must work quickly to collect (right) and process it into dry rubber before it coagulates.*

As Brazil became the world's exclusive exporter of rubber, its planters, merchants, and workers prospered. Rich merchants became lenders and financiers, not only to workers but also to landowners themselves. The mercantile elite of Manaus, the capital of the Amazon region, designed and decorated their city to reflect their new fortunes. Although the streets were still paved with mud, the town's elite built a replica of the Paris Opera House, and Manaus became a regular stopover for European opera singers on the circuit between Buenos Aires and New York. Rubber workers also benefited from the boom. Mostly either Indians or mixed-blood people, they sent their wages home to families elsewhere in the Amazon jungle or on the northeastern coast of Brazil.

But the Brazilian rubber boom soon went bust. One problem was the ecosystem: such a diversified biomass could not tolerate a regimented form of production that emphasized the cultivation of rubber trees at the expense of other vegetation and made the forest vulnerable to nonhuman predators. Leaf blight and ferocious ants destroyed all experiments at creating more sustainable rubber plantations. Moreover, it was expensive to haul the rubber latex out of the jungle all the way to the coast along the slow-moving Amazon River. Another problem was that Brazilian rubber faced severe competition after a British scientist smuggled rubber plant seeds out of Brazil in 1876. Following years of experimentation, British patrons transplanted a blight-resistant hybrid to the British colony of Ceylon (present-day Sri Lanka). As competition led to increased supplies and reduced prices, Brazilian producers went bankrupt. Merchants called in their loans, landowners forfeited their titles, and rubber workers returned to their subsistence economies. Tropical vines crept over the Manaus Opera House, and it gradually fell into disrepair.

Throughout the Americas, nineteenth-century societies worked to adapt obsolete elite models of politics and to satisfy popular demands for inclusion. While the ideal was to construct nation-states that could reconcile differences among their citizens and pave the way for economic prosperity, in fact political autonomy did not bring prosperity, or even the right to vote, to all. As each nation-state expanded its territorial boundaries, many new inhabitants were left out of the political realm.

CONSOLIDATION OF NATION-STATES IN EUROPE

In Europe, no "frontier" existed into which new nations could expand. Instead, nation-states took shape out of older monarchies, and their borders were determined by diplomats or by battles between rival claimants. In the wake of the French Revolution, the idea caught on that "the people" should form the basis for the nation and that nations should be culturally homogenous—but no one could agree on who "the people" should be. Yet, over the course of the nineteenth century, as literacy, the cities, industrial production, and the number and prosperity of property owners expanded, ruling elites had no choice but to share power with a wider group of citizens. These citizens, in turn, increasingly defined themselves as, say, Frenchmen or Germans, rather than as residents of Marseilles or subjects of the King of Bavaria.

Defining "The Nation"

For a very long time, in most places, "the nation" was understood to comprise kings, clergymen, nobles—and occasionally rich merchants or lawyers—and no one else. Although some peoples, such as the English and the Spanish, were already self-conscious about their unique histories, only in the late eighteenth century were the crucial building blocks of European nationalism put in place.

To begin with, intellectuals laid the ideological foundations of the nation. In 1776, Adam Smith had described the wealth of each nation as equivalent to the combined output of all its producers, not the sum in the king's treasury. Then, in 1789, the left-leaning French clergyman Emmanuel Joseph Sieyès had published a widely circulated pamphlet arguing that the nation consisted of all of those who worked to enrich it, and that those who were "parasites" (Sieyès meant the clergy and the aristocracy) did not belong. Sieyès's revolutionary Declaration of the Rights of Man and the Citizen, inspired by the American Declaration of Independence, declared that all men were equal under the law and insisted that "the principle of all sovereignty lies essentially in the nation."

Material and social conditions also prepared the way for nation-states. During the nineteenth century, a huge expansion of literacy and the periodical press made it possible for people all across Europe to read books and newspapers in their own languages. At the same time, the emerging industrial economy brought people into closer contact and made merchants anxious to standardize laws, taxation policies, and weights and measures. States invested huge sums in building roads and then railroads—and these linked provincial towns and bigger cities, laying the foundations for a closer political integration.

But who were the people, and what constituted a viable nation-state? Neither Smith's treatise nor Sieyès's pamphlet could clarify which people belonged inside which nation-state, for belonging to a nation had long been associated with the sharing of cultural or religious traditions. For some people, the nation was a collection of all those who spoke one language; for others, it was all those who lived in the domains of one prince, or who shared a religious heritage. This was a particularly acute problem in multiethnic central and southeastern Europe, where even peasants were often multilingual. But some who shared the same language objected to being lumped into one nation-state. The Irish, for example, spoke English but were predominately Catholics and wanted to be free from Anglican rule.

The Europe-wide revolutions of 1848 (see Chapters 15 and 16) sought to put "the people" in power; in many cases, too, rebels sought to create unified nation-states, each of which would serve one particular cultural and linguistic group. (Examples include the Czechs and Italians, both of whom wanted states independent from the Habsburg Empire.) But the revolutions ran into difficulties defining who "the people" were and how to fashion new nations out of Europe's multiethnic empires. Deep divisions opened among ethnic groups and between middle-class liberals and radicals, some of whom wanted to share out the nation's wealth. Monarchs took advantage of the chaos and restored their regimes. The troubling questions continued to agitate Europe for many years to come. (See Primary Source: What Is a Nation?)

Unification in Germany and Italy

Two of Europe's fledgling nation-states came into being when the dynastic states of Prussia and Piedmont-Sardinia swallowed their smaller, linguistically related neighbors, creating the German and Italian nation-states (see Map 17.2). In both regions, conservative prime ministers—Count Otto von Bismarck of Prussia and Count Camillo di Cavour of Piedmont—exploited radical, and especially liberal, nationalist sentiment to rearrange the map of Europe.

BUILDING UNIFIED STATES The unification of Germany and Italy posed all the familiar problems of who the people were and who should be included in the new nation-states. To begin with, German-speakers were spread all across central and eastern Europe, a result of more than a millennium of eastward colonization. For centuries, they had lived in many different states. Similarly, Italian-speakers had lived separately in city-states and small kingdoms on the Italian peninsula. The historical experiences and economic developments had made Bavarian Germans (Catholic) quite different from Prussian Germans (Protestant); likewise, the Milanese (who lived in a wealthy urban industrial center) shared little with the typical Sardinian peasant. But liberal nationalists had made the case that a shared language and literature overrode all these differences, and emotional appeals by poets, composers, and orators convinced many people that this was indeed the case.

Ultimately, two conservative leaders, Bismarck and Cavour, merged nationalist rhetoric with clever diplomacy to forge united German and Italian polities. Nor did they ignore military might. In a famous address in 1862, Bismarck bellowed: "Not through speeches and majority decisions are the great questions of the day decided—that was the great mistake of 1848 and 1849—but through blood and iron." True to his word, Bismarck accomplished the unification of northern German states by war: with Denmark in 1864, Austria in 1866, and France (over the western provinces of Alsace and Lorraine) in 1870–1871. Italy also was united through a series of small conflicts, many of them engineered to prevent the establishment of more radical republics.

STATES' INTERNAL CONFLICTS These "unified" states rejected democracy. In the new Italy, which was a constitutional monarchy, not a republic, less than 5 percent of the 25 million people could vote. The new German empire (the Reich) did have an assembly elected by all adult males (the Reichstag), but

PRIMARY SOURCE

What Is a Nation?

The French linguist and historian of religion Ernest Renan explored the concept of nationhood in an 1882 essay entitled "What Is a Nation?" Arguing with racial, religious, and language-based interpretations of nationhood, Renan offers an explicitly republican model.

. . . The principle of nations is our principle. But what, then, is a nation? . . . Why is Switzerland, with its three languages, its two religions, and three or four races, a nation, when Tuscany, for example, which is so homogeneous, is not? Why is Austria a state and not a nation? In what does the principle of nations differ from that of races? . . .

Ethnographic considerations have . . . played no part in the formation of modern nations. France is Celtic, Iberic, and Germanic. Germany is Germanic, Celtic, and Slav. Italy is the country in which ethnography finds its greatest difficulties. Here Gauls, Etruscans, Pelasgians, and Greeks are crossed in an unintelligible medley. The British Isles, taken as a whole, exhibit a mixture of Celtic and Germanic blood, the proportions of which are particularly difficult to define.

The truth is that no race is pure, and that to base politics on ethnographic analysis is tantamount to basing it on a chimera. . . .

What we have said about race, applies also to language. Language invites union, without, however, compelling it. The United States and England, as also Spanish America and Spain, speak the same language without forming a single nation. Switzerland, on the contrary, whose foundations are solid because they are based on the assent of the various parties, contains three or four languages. There exists in man a something which is above language: and that is his will. The will of Switzerland to be united, in spite of the variety of these forms of speech, is a much more important fact than a similarity of language, often attained by vexatious measures. . . .

Nor can religion provide a satisfactory basis for a modern nationality. . . . Nowadays . . . everyone believes and practices religion in his own way according to his capacities and wishes. State religion has ceased to exist; and a man can be a Frenchman, an Englishman, or a German, and at the same time a Catholic, a Protestant, or a Jew, or practice no form of worship at all.

A nation is a soul, a spiritual principle. Two things, which are really only one, go to make up this soul or spiritual principle. One of these things lies in the past, the other in the present. The one is the possession in common of a rich heritage of memories; and the other is actual agreement, the desire to live together, and the will to continue to make the most of the joint inheritance. . . . The nation, like the individual, is the fruit of a long past spent in toil, sacrifice, and devotion. . . . To share the glories of the past, and a common will in the present; to have done great deeds together, and to desire to do more— . . . These are things which are understood, in spite of differences in race and language.

. . . The existence of a nation is . . . a daily plebiscite. . . . A province means to us its inhabitants; and if anyone has a right to be consulted in the matter, it is the inhabitant. It is never to the true interest of a nation to annex or keep a country against its will. The people's wish is after all the only justifiable criterion, to which we must always come back.

QUESTIONS FOR ANALYSIS

- According to Renan, what are the two key ingredients needed to create a nation-state?
- What arguments does Renan offer against basing nationhood on a common race, religion, or language?

Source: Ernest Renan, "What Is a Nation?" in The Nationalism Reader, *edited by Omar Dahbour and Micheline R. Ishay (Atlantic Highlands, NJ: Humanities Press, 1995), pp. 143–55.*

it was ruled by a combination of aristocrats and bureaucrats under a monarch. Liberals dominated in many localities, but only the emperor (the kaiser) could depose the prime minister. In fact, Bismarck continued to dominate Prussian politics for twenty-eight years, until fired in 1890 by Kaiser Wilhelm II, who was even more authoritarian and bellicose.

The new states were not internally cohesive. In Italy, Piedmontese liberals in the north hoped that centralized rule would transform southern Italy into a prosperous, commercial, and industrial region like their own. But southern notables, who owned large agricultural estates, had little interest in northern customs. While the northern provinces industrialized and developed commercial links with Switzerland and France, the southern ones remained agrarian and largely isolated from modernizing processes. In Germany, many non-Germans—Poles in Silesia, French in Alsace and Lorraine, Danes in the provinces of

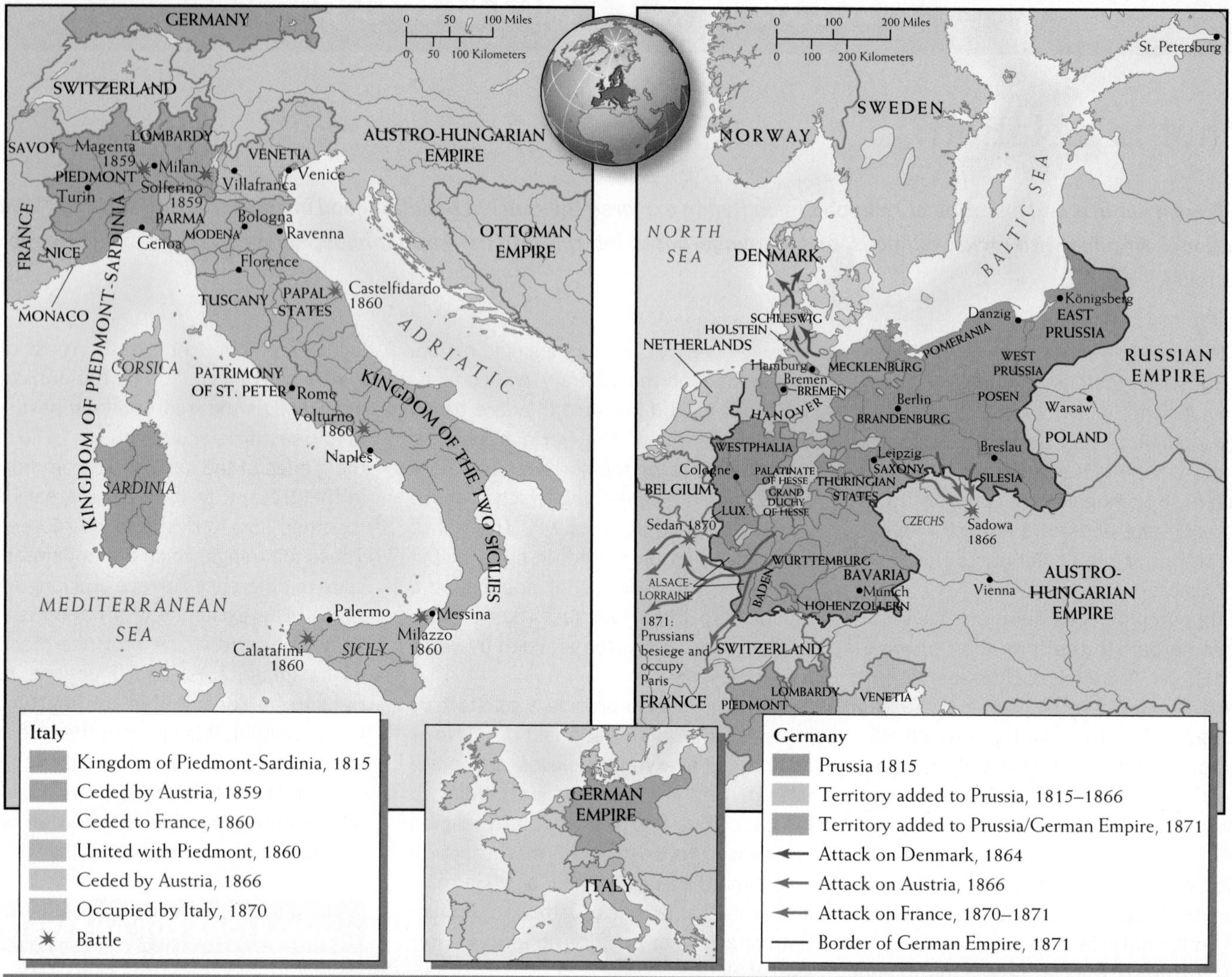

MAP 17.2 | Italian Unification and German Unification, 1815–1871

Italian unification and German unification altered the political map of Europe.

- What were the names of the two original states that grew to become Italy and Germany? Who were the big losers in these territorial transfers?
- According to your reading, what problems did the new Italian and German states face in creating strong national communities?

Schleswig-Holstein—became "national minorities" whose rights remained in question. In the 1870s, Bismarck branded both Catholics and socialists as traitors to the new state; both retaliated by forming powerful political movements. By the 1890s, unification had yielded brisk economic growth, especially for the Germans, but conflict between regions and political groups continued.

Berlin, the capital of Prussia, now became the capital of the German Reich. Although Kaiser Wilhelm II remarked in 1892 that "the glory of Paris robs Berliners of their sleep," Berlin was on the rise. Its population of 1 million people in 1875 had doubled by 1910. The overall German population boomed as well, and the French, whose birthrates were dropping, worried about swelling battalions of well-drilled German soldiers.

Nation Building and Ethnic Conflict in the Austro-Hungarian Empire

Bismarck's wars of unification came at the expense of Habsburg supremacy in central Europe and of French territory and influence in the west. Following Germany's swift victory over the Austrian army in 1866, the Hungarian nobles who controlled the eastern Habsburg Empire forced the weakened dynasts to grant them home rule. In the Compromise of 1867, the Habsburgs agreed that their state would officially be known as the Austro-Hungarian Empire. But this move did not solve Austria-Hungary's nationality problems. In both the Hungarian and the Austrian halves of the dual state, Czechs, Poles, and other Slavs now began to clamor for their own power-sharing "compromise" or autonomous national homelands.

In 1871, the Habsburg emperor seemed prepared to accommodate the Czechs and put them politically on a par with the Hungarians. But the emperor's Hungarian partners scuttled the deal. After this point, interethnic conflict increased over divisive issues such as whether the Czech (or Italian, Serbo-Croatian, Polish, Ukrainian, etc.) language could be used instead of German in regional administrative and educational settings and whether bureaucrats should have to be able to speak more than one language. Moreover, by the 1880s, a wave of impoverished eastern European Jews and non-Jewish Slavs migrating from the countryside entered Austria-Hungary's larger cities, stimulating anti-Semitic feeling and racist political pressure groups. Still, loyalty to the emperor was widespread and multinationalism flourished in the imperial bureaucracy, in the army officers' corps (whose members had to speak both German and the languages of the soldiers under their command), in the upper administration of the Catholic Church, and in the highly cosmopolitan cities.

Domestic Discontents in France and Britain

Although already unified as nation-states, Britain and France, too, faced major difficulties. For the French, dealing with military defeat at the hands of the Germans was the primary national concern in the decades leading up to World War I. For the British, issues of Irish separatism, the rise of the working class, and feminists' demands troubled the political arena.

DESTABILIZATION IN FRANCE Bismarck launched the Franco-Prussian War of 1870–1871 in order to complete the unification of Germany; he did not intend to destabilize France. But the sound drubbing the French troops received, and the capture of Napoleon III early in the conflict, proved embarrassing and upsetting. Even more catastrophic for France was the German siege of Paris, which lasted for more than three months. Unprepared, Parisians had no food stocks and were compelled to eat all sorts of things, including two zoo elephants. Under terrible conditions and without effective leadership, the French capital resisted until January 1871, when the government signed a humiliating peace treaty—in the Hall of Mirrors at Versailles, formerly the residence of France's powerful "Sun King." The Germans left in place a weak provisional French government. Furious Parisians vented their rage and established a socialist commune proclaiming the city a utopia for workers. The leftist commune lasted until the provisional government's predominantly peasant army stormed Paris a few months later. At least 25,000 Parisians died in the bloody mop-up that followed.

A "Third Republic" took the place of Napoleon III's empire, but its conservative leaders were wary of the socialists and workers. They also were determined to revenge themselves for their humiliation in 1871. For the French, the years to follow would bring two unsettling developments: increasingly sharp conflict between classes over the shape of the republic, and rising anti-German nationalism. Some of this antagonism also radiated outward to target French colonial subjects, who now experienced more virulent forms of racism.

IRISH NATIONALISM IN GREAT BRITAIN Although the English had long thought of themselves as a nation, the idea that all Britons belonged in the same state was much more problematic. Great Britain—composed of England, Wales, Scotland, and Ireland—was home to people whose historical experiences, religious backgrounds, and economic opportunities were very different. In the nineteenth century, British leaders wrestled in particular with lower-class agitation and demands for independence from Irish nationalists. England responded to these pressures by extending political rights to all men but not women. Thereafter, free trade and progress became the priorities of a middle class flush with new wealth generated by industry and empire. The long reign of Queen Victoria (r. 1837–1901), as well as England's prosperity, overseas conquests, and world power, increasingly bound both workers and owners to the nation.

Yet Ireland remained England's Achilles' heel. Although in 1836 Irish Catholics finally became equal to Protestants before the law, the two communities' political and economic conditions remained very uneven. The English were widely condemned for their failure to relieve Irish suffering during the potato famine of 1846–1849 (see Chapter 15); even though millions of poor Irish and Scottish workers made their way to England, seeking either passage to North America or work in the English mill towns, they did not assimilate easily and often got the lowliest jobs. All of this, on top of 300 years of repressive English domination, spawned a mass movement for Irish home rule.

Born in opposition to the old monarchical regimes, European nationalism by the end of the nineteenth century had become a means used by liberal and conservative leaders alike to unite "the people" behind them. In most places, aside from Russia, "the people" essentially meant all adult males—and that group had won the right to vote in national elections (though most states still had monarchs as well). The new nation-states had been shaped by increasing literacy and urbanization, but also by warfare.

INDUSTRY, SCIENCE, AND TECHNOLOGY

A powerful combination of industry, science, and technology shaped the emerging nation-states in North America and western Europe. It also reordered the relationships among different parts of the world. One critical factor was that after 1850 western Europe and North America experienced a new phase of industrial development—essentially a second industrial revolution. Japan, too, joined the ranks of industrializing nations as its state-led program of industrial development started to pay dividends. These changes transformed the global economy and intensified rivalries among industrial societies. For example, Britain now had to contend with competition from the United States and Germany.

New Materials, Technologies, and Business Practices

New materials and new technologies were vital in late-nineteenth-century economic development. For example, **steel**, which was more malleable and stronger than iron, became essential for industries like shipbuilding and railways. The world output of steel shot up from half a million tons in 1870 to 28 million tons in 1900. The miracle of steel was celebrated through the construction of the Eiffel Tower (completed in 1889) in Paris, an aggressively modern monument that loomed over the picturesque cityscape and was double the height of any other building in the world at the time. Steel was part of a bundle of innovations that included chemicals, oil, pharmaceuticals, and mass transportation vehicles like trolleys and automobiles.

The late nineteenth century witnessed major technological changes with the arrival of new organic sources of power (like oil) and new ways to get old organic sources (like coal) to processing plants. These changes freed manufacturers from having to locate their plants close to their fuel sources. Not only did the most important new source of energy—electricity—permit factories to arise in areas with plenty of skilled workers, but it also slashed production costs. Scientific research, too, boosted industrial development. German companies led the way in creating laboratories where university-trained chemists and physicists conducted research to serve industrial production. The United States likewise wedded scientific research with capitalist enterprise: universities and corporate laboratories produced swelling ranks of engineers and scientists, as well as patents.

The breakthroughs of the second industrial revolution ushered in new business practices, especially mass production and the giant integrated firm. No longer would modest investments suffice, as they had in Britain a century earlier. Now large banks were the major providers of funds. In Europe, limited-liability joint-stock companies were as wildly successful in raising capital on stock markets as they were in the United States. Companies like Standard Oil, U.S. Steel, and Siemens mobilized capital from a large number of investors, called shareholders. The scale of these firms was awesome. U.S. Steel alone produced over half the world's steel ingots, castings, rails, and heavy structural shapes—and nearly half of all its steel plates and sheets, which were vital in the construction of buildings, railroads, ships, and the like.

Eiffel Tower. *This 1890 photograph of an illuminated Eiffel Tower encapsulates the fact and spirit of early twentieth-century technological innovation, from the architectural breakthrough of the tower itself to the harnessing of electricity to truly render Paris its namesake—The City of Light.*

Integration of the World Economy

Not only did industrial change concentrate power in North Atlantic societies, but it also reinforced their power on the world economic stage. Of course, Europe and the United States increased their exports in new products; but at the same time, they grew eager to control the importation of tropical commodities such as cocoa and coffee. While the North Atlantic societies were still largely self-sufficient in coal, iron, cotton, wool, and wheat (the major commodities of the first industrial revolution), the second industrial revolution bred a need for rubber, copper,

Railroad Workers. *The construction of railroad lines across the United States was dangerous work, much of it done by immigrant laborers, including large numbers of Chinese, such as those in this photograph taken in 1886.*

oil, and bauxite (an ore used to make aluminum), which were not available domestically. Equally important, large pools of money became available for investing overseas. London may have lost its industrial leadership, but it retained dominance over the world's financial operations. By 1913, the British had the huge sum of £4 billion invested overseas—funds that generated an annual income of £200 million, or one-tenth of Britain's national income.

MOVEMENTS OF LABOR AND TECHNOLOGY Because the more integrated world economy needed workers for fields, factories, and mines, vast movements of the laboring population took place. Indians moved thousands of miles to work on sugar plantations in the Caribbean, Mauritius, and Fiji, and to build railroads in East Africa. Chinese workers constructed railroads in the western United States and toiled on sugar plantations in Cuba. The Irish, Poles, Jews, Italians, and Greeks flocked to North America to fill its burgeoning factories. Italians also moved to Argentina to harvest wheat and corn.

New technologies of warfare, transportation, and communication eased global economic integration—and strengthened European domination. With steam-powered gunboats and breech-loading rifles, Europeans opened new territories for trade and conquest. At home and in their colonial possessions, imperial powers constructed networks of railroads that carried people and goods from hinterlands to the coasts. From there, steamships bore them across the seas. Completion of the Suez Canal in 1869 shortened ship voyages between Europe and Asia and lowered the costs of interregional trade. Information moved even faster than cargoes, thanks to the laying of telegraph cables under the oceans, supplemented by overland telegraph lines.

CHARLES DARWIN AND NATURAL SELECTION Although machines were the most visible evidence that humans could master the universe, perhaps the most momentous shift in the conception of nature derived from the travels of one British scientist: **Charles Darwin** (1809–1882). Longing to see exotic fauna, in 1831 he signed on for a four-year voyage on a surveying vessel bound for Latin America and the South Seas. As the ship's naturalist, Darwin collected large quantities of specimens and recorded observations daily. After returning to England, he became convinced that the species of organic life had evolved under the uniform pressure of natural laws, not by means of a special, one-time creation as described in the Bible.

Suez Canal. *The Suez Canal opened to world shipping in 1869 and reduced the time it took to sail between Europe and Asian ports. Although the French and the Egyptians supplied most of the money and the construction plans and Egyptians were the main workforce, British shipping dominated canal traffic from the outset.*

Charles Darwin. *Darwin testing the speed of a tortoise in the Galapagos Islands. It was during his visit to these islands that Darwin developed many of the ideas that he would put forth in his 1859* Origin of Species.

Darwin's theory, articulated in his *Origin of Species* (1859), laid out the principles of **natural selection**. Inevitably, he claimed, populations grew faster than the food supply; this condition created a "struggle for existence" among species. In later work he showed how the passing on of individual traits was also determined by what he called sexual selection—according to which the "best" mates are chosen for their strength, beauty, or talents. The outcome: the "fittest" survived to reproduce, while the less adaptable did not. The "economy of nature" was, Darwin confessed, a painful reality: people would rather behold "nature's face bright with gladness" than recognize that some animals must be others' prey and that shortages are, ultimately, part of nature's "miraculous efficiency." Although Darwin's book dealt exclusively with animals (and mostly with birds), his readers immediately wondered what his theory implied for humans. (See Primary Source: *The Origin of Species*.)

A passionate debate began among scientists and laymen, clerics and anthropologists. Some read Darwin's doctrine of the "survival of the fittest" to mean that it was natural for the strong nations to dominate the weak, or justifiable to allow disabled persons to die—something Darwin explicitly refuted. As more groups (mis)interpreted Darwin's theory to suit their own objectives, a set of beliefs known as Social Darwinism legitimated the suffering of the underclasses in industrial society: it was unnatural, Social Darwinists claimed, to tamper with natural selection. In subsequent years Europeans would repeatedly suggest that they had evolved more than Africans and Asians. Extending Darwinian ideas far beyond the scientist's intent, some Europeans came to believe that therefore nature itself gave them the right to rule others.

GLOBAL EXPANSIONISM AND AN AGE OF IMPERIALISM

Increasing rivalries among nations and social tensions within them produced an expansionist wave late in the nineteenth century. Although Africa became the primary focus of interest, a frenzy of territorial conquest overtook Asia as well. The period witnessed the French occupation of Vietnam, Cambodia, and Laos, and the British expansion in Malaya (present-day Malaysia). In China's territories, competition by foreign powers to establish spheres of influence heated up in the 1890s. And in India, imperial ambitions provoked the British to conquer Burma (present-day Myanmar). Moreover, Britain and Russia competed for preeminence from their respective outposts in Afghanistan and central Asia. In the Americas, expansion usually involved the incorporation of new territories as provinces, making them integral parts of the nation.

In Asia and Africa, however, European imperialism turned far-flung territories into colonial possessions. Here, inhabitants were usually designated as subjects of the empire without the rights and privileges of citizens. Britain's imperial regime in India provided lessons to a generation of European colonial officials in Africa and other parts of Asia on how to build this kind of empire.

PRIMARY SOURCE

The Origin of Species

Charles Darwin's* Origin of Species *(1859) was the product of his many years of studying animals and plants. In addressing the question "How and why are new species created?" the book described the process of natural selection, according to which nature creates overabundance so that the "fittest" species survive and adapt themselves to their environments. Although Darwin's book said nothing about human beings, his contemporaries speculated on his theory's implications for the evolution of human beings.

Again, it may be asked, how is it that varieties, which I have called incipient species, become ultimately converted into good and distinct species, which in most cases obviously differ from each other far more than do the varieties of the same species? How do those groups of species, which constitute what are called distinct genera, and which differ from each other more than do the species of the same genus, arise? All these results . . . follow inevitably from the struggle for life. Owing to this struggle for life, any variation, however slight and from whatever cause proceeding, if it be in any degree profitable to an individual of any species, in its infinitely complex relations to other organic beings and to external nature, will tend to the preservation of that individual, and will generally be inherited by its offspring. The offspring, also, will thus have a better chance of surviving, for, of the many individuals of any species which are periodically born, but a small number can survive. I have called this principle, by which each slight variation, if useful, is preserved, by the term of Natural Selection, in order to mark its relation to man's power of selection. We have seen that man by selection can certainly produce great results, and can adapt organic beings to his own uses, through the accumulation of slight but useful variations, given to him by the hand of Nature. But Natural Selection, as we shall hereafter see, is a power incessantly ready for action, and is as immeasurably superior to man's feeble efforts, as the works of Nature are to those of Art.

We will now discuss in a little more detail the struggle for existence. . . . I should premise that I use the term Struggle for Existence in a large and metaphorical sense, including dependence of one being on another, and including (which is more important) not only the life of the individual, but success in leaving progeny. Two canine animals in a time of dearth, may be truly said to struggle with each other which shall get food and live. But a plant on the edge of a desert is said to struggle for life against the drought, though more properly it should be said to be dependent on the moisture. . . .

A struggle for existence inevitably follows from the high rate at which all organic beings tend to increase. Every being, which during its natural lifetime produces several eggs or seeds, must suffer destruction during some period of its life, and during some season or occasional year, otherwise, on the principle of geometrical increase, its numbers would quickly become so inordinately great that no country could support the product. Hence, as more individuals are produced than can possibly survive, there must in every case be a struggle for existence, either one individual with another of the same species, or with the individuals of distinct species, or with the physical conditions of life. . . . Although some species may be now increasing, more or less rapidly, in numbers, all cannot do so, for the world would not hold them.

It may be said that natural selection is daily and hourly scrutinising, throughout the world, every variation, even the slightest; rejecting that which is bad, preserving and adding up all that is good; silently and insensibly working, whenever and wherever opportunity offers, at the improvement of each organic being in relation to its organic and inorganic conditions of life. We see nothing of these slow changes in progress, until the hand of time has marked the long lapses of ages, and then so imperfect is our view into long past geological ages, that we only see that the forms of life are now different from what they formerly were.

Source: Charles Darwin, The Origin of Species, *Chapters 3 and 4.*

QUESTIONS FOR ANALYSIS

- How does Darwin explain the divergence of species?
- Why does Darwin think struggle is inevitable for all living beings?

India and the Imperial Model

Britain's successful colonial rule in India provided a model for others, but its methods of rule also were responses to popular discontent. Having suppressed the Indian Rebellion of 1857 (see Chapter 16), authorities revamped the colonial administration. Indians were not to be appeased—and certainly not brought into British public life. But they did have to be governed, and the economy had to be revived. So, after replacing East India Company rule by crown government in 1858, the British set out

Sinews of the Raj. (Top) *During the second half of the nineteenth century, the British built an extensive system of railroads to develop India as a profitable colony and to maintain military security. This engraving shows the East India Railway around 1863.* (Bottom) *The British allowed several native princes to remain in power as long as they accepted imperial paramountcy. This photograph shows a road-building project in one such princely state. Officials of the Muslim princely ruler and British advisers supervise the workers.*

to make India into a more secure and productive colony. This period of British sovereignty was known as the **Raj** ("rule").

The most urgent tasks facing the British in India were those of modernizing its transportation and communication systems and transforming the country into an integrated colonial state. These changes had begun under the governor-general of the East India Company, Lord Dalhousie, who oversaw the development of India's modern infrastructure. When he left office in 1856, he boasted that he had harnessed India to the "great engines of social improvement—I mean Railways, uniform Postage, and the Electric Telegraph." A year later, northern India exploded in the 1857 rebellion. But the rebellion also demonstrated the military value of railroads and telegraphs, for these modern systems were useful tools for rushing British troops to severely affected regions. After the British suppressed the revolt, they took up the construction of public works with renewed vigor. Railways were a key element in this project, attracting approximately £150 million of British capital. (Though it came from British investors, Indian taxpayers paid off the debt through their taxes.) The first railway line opened in 1853, and by 1910 India had 30,627 miles of track in operation—the fourth largest railway system in the world.

Construction of other public works followed. Engineers built dams across rivers to tame their force and to irrigate lands; workers installed a grid of telegraph lines that opened communication between distant parts of the region. These public works served imperial and economic purposes: India was to become a consumer of British manufactures and a supplier of primary staples such as cotton, tea, wheat, vegetable oil seeds, and jute (used for making rope or burlap sacking). The control of India's massive rivers allowed farmers to cultivate the rich floodplains, transforming them into lucrative cotton-producing provinces.

On the hillsides of the island of Ceylon and the northeastern plains of India, the British established vast plantations to grow tea—which was then marketed in England as a healthier alternative to Chinese green tea. India also became an important consumer of British manufactures, especially textiles, in an ironic turnaround to its centuries-old tradition of exporting its own cotton and silk textiles.

India recorded a consistent surplus in its foreign trade through the export of agricultural goods and raw materials. But what India gained from its trade to the world it lost to Britain, its colonial master, because it had to pay for interest on railroad loans, salaries to colonial officers (even when they went on furlough in Britain), and the maintenance of imperial troops outside India. In reality, India ended up balancing Britain's huge trade deficits with the rest of the world, especially the Americas.

Nonetheless, administrative programs made India into a unified territory and enabled its inhabitants to regard themselves as "Indians." These were the first steps to becoming a "nation"—like Italy and the United States. But there were profound differences. Indians lacked a single national language, and they were not citizens of their political community who enjoyed sovereignty. Rather, they were colonial subjects ruled by outsiders.

Dutch Colonial Rule in Indonesia

The Dutch, like the British, joined the parade of governments trying to modernize and integrate their colonies economically without welcoming colonial peoples into the life of the nation at home. Decades before the British government took control of India away from the East India Company, Holland had terminated the rule of the Dutch East India Company over Indonesia. Beginning in the 1830s, the Dutch government took administrative responsibility over Indonesian affairs. Holland's new colonial officials envisioned a more regulated colonial economy than that of their British counterparts in India. For example, they ordered Indonesian villagers to allocate one-third of their land for cultivating coffee beans, an important export. In return, the colonial government paid a set price (well below world market prices) and placed a ceiling on rents owed to landowners.

These policies had dreadful local consequences. For example, increased production of the export crops of coffee beans, sugar, and tobacco meant reduced food production for the local population. By the 1840s and 1850s, famine spread across Java; over 300,000 Indonesians perished from starvation. Surviving villagers voiced growing discontent, prompting harsh crackdowns by colonial forces. Back in Holland, the embarrassing spectacle of colonial oppression prompted calls for reform. Thus in the 1860s the Dutch government introduced what it called an ethical policy for governing Asian colonies: it reduced governmental exploitation and encouraged Dutch settlement of the islands and more private enterprise. For Indonesians, however, the replacement of government agents with private merchants made little difference. In some areas, islanders put up fierce resistance. On the sprawling island of Sumatra, for instance, armed villagers fought off Dutch invaders. After decades of warfare, Sumatra was finally subdued in 1904. The shipping of Indonesian staples continued to enrich the Dutch.

Colonizing Africa

No region felt the impact of European colonialism more powerfully than Africa. In 1880, the only two large European colonial possessions there were French Algeria and two British-ruled South African states, the Cape Colony and Natal. But within a mere thirty years, seven European states had carved almost all of Africa into colonial possessions (see Map 17.4).

A major moment in initiating the European scramble for African colonies occurred in 1882 when the British invaded and occupied Egypt. This action provoked the French, who had regarded Egypt as their special sphere of influence ever since Napoleon's 1798 invasion. Indeed, Britain's move not only intensified the two powers' rivalry to seize additional territories in Africa, but it also alarmed the other European states, fearful that they might be left behind. As these powers joined the

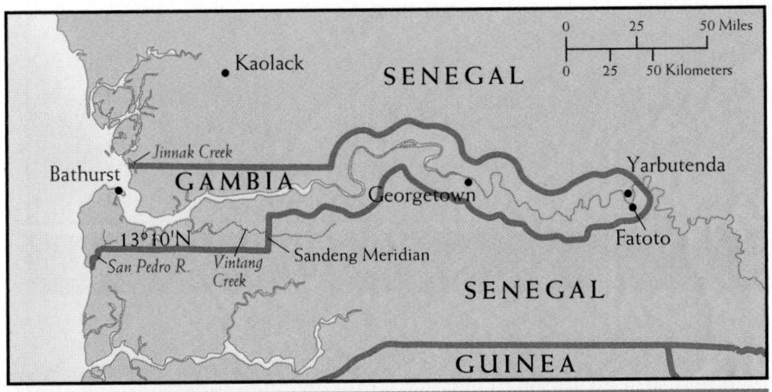

MAP 17.3A | Senegal and Gambia

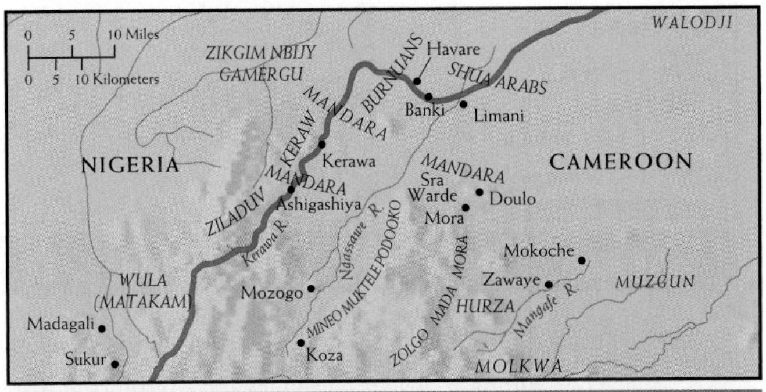

MAP 17.3B | Mandara Peoples

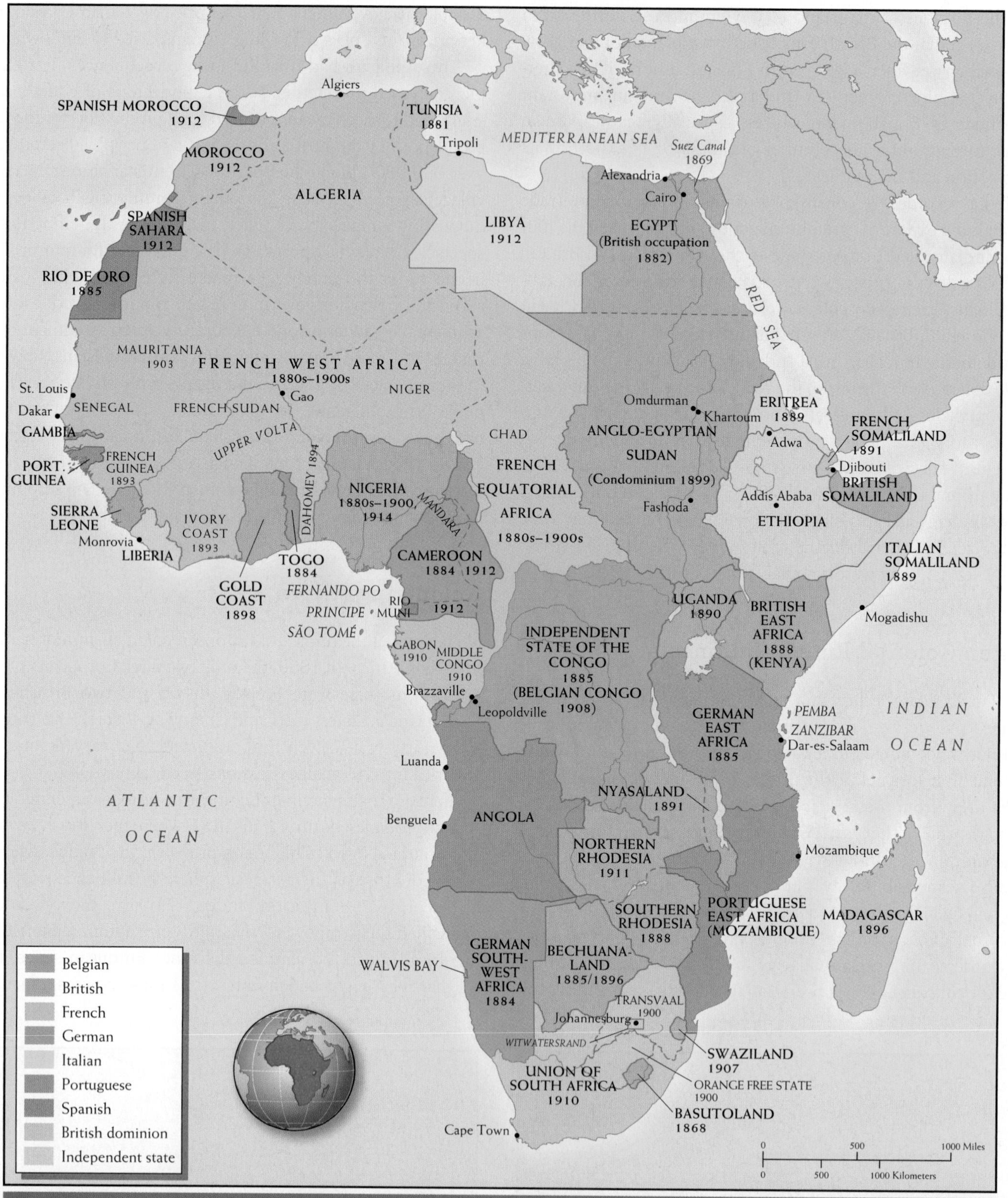

MAP 17.4 | Partition of Africa, 1880–1914

The partition of Africa took place between the early 1880s and the outbreak of World War I.

- Which two European powers gained the most territory in Africa? Which two African states managed to remain independent?
- What kind of economic and political gain did European powers realize through the colonization of Africa? Did any of the European states fully realize their ambitions in Africa?

scramble, Portugal called for an international conference to discuss claims to Africa. Meeting in Berlin between 1884 and 1885, delegates from Germany, Portugal, Britain, France, Belgium, Spain, Italy, the United States, and the Ottoman Empire agreed to carve up Africa and to recognize the acquisitions of any European power that had achieved occupation on the ground.

PARTITIONING THE AFRICAN LANDMASS The consequences for Africa were devastating. Nearly 70 percent of the newly drawn borders failed to correspond to older demarcations of ethnicity, language, culture, and commerce—for Europeans knew little of the landmass beyond its coast and rivers. They based their new colonial boundaries on European trading centers rather than on the location of African population groups. In West Africa, for example, the Yoruba were split between the French in Dahomey and the British in southwestern Nigeria. In fact, Nigeria became an administrative nightmare, as the British attempted to integrate the politically centralized Muslim populations of the north with the city-state Yoruba dwellers and small tribes of the Ibos of the south.

Several motives led the European powers into their frenzied partition of Africa. Although European businesses were primarily interested in Egypt and South Africa, where their investments were lucrative, small-scale traders and investors harbored fantasies of great treasures locked in the vast uncharted interior. Politicians, publicists, and the reading public also took an interest. The writings of explorers like David Livingstone (1813–1873), a Scottish doctor and missionary, and Henry Morton Stanley (1841–1904), an adventurer in the pay of the *New York Herald*, excited readers with accounts of Africa as a continent of unlimited economic potential.

There was also the lure of building personal fortunes and reputations. In eastern Africa, Carl Peters (1856–1918) aspired to found a vast German colony, and he brought German East Africa into existence, although his ruthlessness eventually caused the German Parliament to force him to give up control of "his" state.

Europeans in Africa. (Left) *Henry Morton Stanley was one of the most famous of the nineteenth-century explorers in Africa. He first made his reputation when he located the British missionary-explorer David Livingstone, feared dead, in the interior of Africa, uttering the famous words, "Dr. Livingstone, I presume." Stanley worked on behalf of King Leopold, establishing the Belgian king's claims to territories in the Congo and often using superior weaponry to cow African opponents.* (Right) *The ardent British imperialist Cecil Rhodes endeavored to bring as much of Africa as he could under British colonial rule. He had an ambition to create a swath of British-controlled territory that would stretch from the Cape in South Africa to Cairo in Egypt, as this cartoon shows.*

CURRENT TRENDS IN WORLD HISTORY

Africa's Newest Hunters and Gatherers: Greed, Environmental Degradation, and Resistance

As we have noted, Africa was the birthplace of hunting and gathering (see Chapter 1). Ironically, although the European colonizers justified their partition of Africa on the grounds of bringing civilization to a benighted people, in fact, in their quest to enrich themselves, the first generation of colonizers despoiled the continent, enslaved and killed huge numbers of people, and returned parts of the continent to a hunting and gathering mode of production. The most driven and greediest of these figures was Leopold II, king of the Belgians, who was determined, in spite of sweet-sounding rhetoric, to do whatever it took to line his pockets and make himself a formidable figure in European politics. King Leopold's story—and others like it—fascinates world historians because it conveys in the starkest detail the nature of the relationship between the rulers and the ruled. It also provides a strong point of comparison for the different models of ruling that each European power instituted in their colonies.

Even before ascending the throne in 1865, Leopold cast about for ways to become more than the constitutional monarch of a small, recently established, and neutral state. A voracious reader on colonialism, he was struck forcibly by one book: *How the Dutch Ruled Java*, published in 1861. By demonstrating how the Dutch colonial state had expropriated money from the East Indies (called Indonesia today) to spend on projects at home, the book fired his imagination. Could he not do the same? Could he not stake out a colony, take money from it to swell his own exchequer, and use some of it on public works at home—to beautify the cities of Belgium the way Paris had been beautified in the 1850s and 1860s?

Fixing his gaze on central Africa, in the 1880s Leopold manipulated the other European states into recognizing him as the sovereign head of a "Congo Free State," in which he lead a European effort to "civilize" (and especially to exploit) the Congo River basin. Leopold hired the world-famous explorer Henry Stanley to "pacify" the country and ready it for economic development.

King Leopold. *Despite the inhumane ways in which he funded his vast array of public buildings, Leopold is sometimes called, not unaffectionately, the "Builder King" by Belgians today.*

But how to make these lands pay off? They were almost entirely unexplored and unsurveyed, and though in time they would yield some of the richest mineral deposits in the world, these prospects were unknown to Leopold and his administrators at first. What the rain forests of Africa had was wild products, especially rubber and ivory. But how to get Africans, who at that point hardly participated in

---

The most determined of the African empire builders was Leopold II (r. 1865–1909), king of the Belgians. (See Current Trends in World History: Africa's Newest Hunters and Gatherers: Greed, Environmental Degradation, and Resistance.) In southern Africa, the British champion of imperialism Cecil Rhodes (1853–1902) brought the Rhodesias, Nyasaland, Bechuanaland, the Transvaal, and the Orange Free State into the British Empire. He was delighted that the Rhodesias bore his name.

Other Europeans saw Africa as a grand opportunity for converting souls to Christianity. In fact, Europe's civilizing mission was an important motive in the scramble for African territory. In Uganda, northern Nigeria, and central Africa, missionaries went ahead of European armies, begging the European statesmen to follow their lead.

AFRICAN RESISTANCE Contrary to European assumptions, Africans did not welcome European "civilization." Resistance, however, was largely futile. Africans faced two unappealing options: they could capitulate to the Europeans and negotiate to limit the loss of their autonomy, or they could fight to preserve their sovereignty. Only a few chose the course of moderation. Lat Dior, a Muslim warlord in Senegal, refused to let the French build a railway through his kingdom. "As long as I live, be well assured," he wrote the French commandant, "I shall oppose with all my might the construction of this railway. I will always answer no, no, and I will never make you any other reply. Even were I to go to rest, my horse, *Malay*, would give you the same answer." Conflict was inevitable, and Lat Dior lost his life in a battle with the French in 1886.

world trade, to tap wild rubber vines and hunt elephants? The solution here and elsewhere in similar African environments was to create large standing armies (known in Leopold's state as the Force Publique), fix quotas for districts to procure, and compel villagers to bring in baskets of rubber and elephant tusks.

For Leopold the results were little short of astonishing. He extracted vast sums from the Congo, spending lavishly on himself and on Belgium. He sank millions of francs into making the seaside city of Ostend one of the finest resorts in the world. At Tervuren, while a choir sang the new Congo anthem, Leopold laid the foundation stone of a world college for overseas colonial administration. In Brussels he spent over $5 million renovating royal palaces and constructing parks, avenues, casinos, and racecourses.

For the Congolese, Leopold's state was nothing more than a reign of terror. Forced to roam farther and farther from their home villages in search of rubber and elephants to keep pace with ever-escalating quotas, villagers suffered an immense loss of life. Perhaps as many as 10 million Africans perished in a population that had been roughly 20 million before Leopold's agents arrived.

Henry Stanley in the Congo. *Stanley was given the nickname "Bula Matari," meaning "Breaker of Stones," by the native Congolese.*

Leopold's brutality did not go unobserved, however. Already in 1899, the writer Joseph Conrad took the Congo as his model of rapacious European imperialism in his novella *Heart of Darkness*. African villagers rebelled, though unsuccessfully, and, by the first decade of the twentieth century, rumors and then detailed reports painted a stark picture of terror and environment degradation. In 1908, just a year before his death, Leopold was compelled, against his wishes, to turn the administration of the Congo over to the Belgian parliament.

QUESTIONS FOR ANALYSIS

- Why do you think King Leopold was able to rule over the Congo for as many years as he did unchecked by his own government? By the other governments in Europe?
- While the Congo story is arguably the most brutal of all stories of colonial exploitation and resistance, which other episodes in world history does it remind you of and why?

Explore Further

Herbst, Jeffrey, *States and Power in Africa: Comparative Lessons in Authority and Control* (2000).

Hochschild, Adam, *King Leopold's Ghost* (New York, 1998).

Only Menelik II of Ethiopia repulsed the Europeans, for he knew how to play rivals off one another. By doing so, he procured weapons from the French, British, Russians, and Italians. He also had a united, loyal, and well-equipped army. In 1896, his troops routed Italian forces at the Battle of Adwa, after which Adwa became a celebrated moment in African history. Its memory inspired many of Africa's later nationalist leaders.

Most resisters were ignorant of the disparity in military technology between Africans and Europeans—especially the killing power of European breech-loading weapons and the Maxim machine gun. In addition, the European armies had better tactics and a more sustained appetite for battle. Africa's armies fought during the nonagricultural season, engaging in open battles so as to achieve quick and decisive results and then returning to their farms. Such military traditions were effective in fighting neighbors, but not well-equipped invaders.

Some African forces did adapt their military techniques to the European challenge. For example, Samori Touré (1830–1900) proved a stubborn foe for the French, employing guerrilla warfare and avoiding full-scale battles in the savannah lands of West Africa. From 1882 until 1898, Touré eluded the French. Dividing his 35,000-man army, Touré had one part take over territories not yet conquered by the French and there reestablish a fully autonomous domain. A smaller contingent conducted a scorched-earth campaign in the regions from which it was retreating, leaving the French with parched and wasted new possessions. But these tactics only delayed the inevitable. The French finally defeated and captured Touré and sent him into exile in Gabon, where he died in 1900.

Battle of Adwa. *Portrait of King Menelik, who defeated the Italian forces at the battle of Adwa in 1896, thus saving his country from European colonization.*

COLONIAL ADMINISTRATIONS IN AFRICA Once the euphoria of partition and conquest had worn off, power fell to "men on the spot"—military adventurers, settlers, and entrepreneurs whose main goal was to get rich quick. As these individuals established near-fiefdoms in some areas, Africans (like Native Americans on the other side of the Atlantic) found themselves confined to territories where they could barely provide for themselves. To uphold such an invasive system at minimal expense, Europeans created permanent standing armies by equipping their African supporters, whom they either bribed or compelled to join their side. Such armies bullied local communities into doing the colonial authorities' bidding.

Eventually, these rough-and-ready systems led to violent revolts from aggrieved Africans, and in their aftermath the colonial rulers had to create more efficient and rational administrations. As in India, colonial powers in Africa laid the foundations for future nation-state organizations. Once information trickling out of Africa revealed that the imperial governments were not realizing their goal of bringing "civilization" to the "uncivilized," each European power implemented a new form of colonial rule, stripping the strongman conquerors of their absolute powers.

However much the colonial systems of the European states differed, all had three similar goals. First, the colony was to pay for its own administration. Second, administrators on the spot had to preserve the peace; nothing brought swifter criticism from the mother country than a colonial rebellion. Third, colonial rule was to attract other European groups, such as missionaries, settlers, and merchants. Missionaries came to convert "heathens" to Christianity, convinced that they were battling with Islam for the soul of the continent. Settlers went only to those parts of Africa that had climatic conditions similar to those in Europe. They poured into Algeria and South Africa but only trickled into Kenya, Southern Rhodesia, Angola, and Mozambique, attracted by advertising at home that stressed comfortable living conditions and promised that these areas would someday become white man's territories. Moreover, colonial governments' promises to construct railroads, roads, and deep-water facilities persuaded European merchants and investors to take out bigger commercial stakes in Africa.

Eventually, stabilized colonies began to deliver on their economic promise. Whereas early imperialism in Africa had relied on the export of ivory and wild rubber, after these resources became depleted the colonies pursued other exports. From the rain forests came cocoa, coffee, palm oil, and palm kernels. From the highlands of East Africa came tea, coffee, sisal (used in cord and twine), and pyrethrum (a flower used to make insecticide). Another important commodity was long-staple, high-quality cotton, grown in Egypt and the Anglo-Egyptian Sudan. Indeed, tropical commodities from all across Africa (as from India and Latin America) flowed to industrializing societies.

Thus, European colonial administrators saw Africa as fitting into the world economy in the same way that British administrators viewed India—as an exporter of raw materials and an importer of manufactures. They expected Africa to profit from this role. But, in truth, African workers gained little from participating in colonial commerce, while the price they paid in disruption to traditional social and economic patterns was substantial.

Such disruptions were particularly acute in southern Africa, where mining operations lured African men thousands of miles from their homes. Meanwhile, women had to take care of subsistence and cash crop production in the home villages. By the turn of the century the gold mines of Witwatersrand in South Africa required a workforce of 100,000, drawing miners from as far away as Mozambique, the Rhodesias, and Nyasaland, as well as from South Africa itself. Because work below ground was hazardous and health services were inadequate, workers often tried to flee. But armed guards and barbed-wired compounds kept them in the mines. Companies made enormous profits for their European shareholders, while the workers toiled in dangerous conditions and barely eked out a living wage.

To observers, the European empires in Africa seemed solid and durable, but in fact, European colonial rule there was fragile. For all of British Africa, the only all-British force was 5,000 men garrisoned in Egypt. Elsewhere, European officers depended on

ANALYZING GLOBAL DEVELOPMENTS

Imperialism and the African Trade Revolution

The colonial period initiated a trade revolution in Africa, which, as we have seen, had been a supplier of human labor to the Americas from the fifteenth century until the middle of the nineteenth century (see Chapter 13). Even as the Europeans endeavored to eradicate the African institution of slavery and slave trading within the continent, they also promoted the reintegration of African economies into the world economy through the export of important, often new cash crops like cocoa from West Africa, significant minerals like gold and diamonds from South Africa, and the import of European manufactures. To this end, the colonial powers financed railways and deepened harbors. Already by the outbreak of World War I, West Africa had become the leading exporter of cocoa, South Africa the leading exporter of diamonds and gold, and Egypt, along with the United States, the leading exporter of high-quality cotton.

QUESTIONS FOR ANALYSIS

- Is there a correlation between the increase in the number of railroads built and the amount of natural resources taken out of Africa? If so, how can you tell?
- During what period were the largest increases in the construction of the railroads and the exportation of cocoa and gold?
- Do you think the general trend towards increasing production continued well into the twentieth century, or do you think this was the high point? Please explain your answer.

Length of Railway Line Opened (in kilometers)

Year	Africa
1880	4,579
1885	6,813
1890	9,202
1895	11,962
1900	16,319
1905	25,574
1910	37,768
1915	47,624

Cocoa Exports from the Gold Coast and Nigeria (in tons)

Year	Gold Coast	Nigeria
1900	536	202
1905	5,090	470
1910	22,600	2,932
1915	77,300	9,105
1920	125,000	17,155

Union of South Africa Gold Mines (in ounces)

Year	Total Output	Estimated % of World Output
1897	2,744	24%
1907	6,451	32.4%
1913	8,799	39.3%
1916	9,297	42.3%
1921	8,129	50.9%

Sources: Mitchell, B. R., International Historical Statistics: Africa, Asia, and Oceania, 1750–2005 (2007); *Hill, Polly,* The Gold Coast Cocoa Farmer: A Preliminary Survey (1965); *Berry, Sara,* Cocoa, Custom and Socio-Economic Change in Western Nigeria (1975); *Frankel, S. Herbert,* Capital Investment in Africa: Its Course and Effects (1938).

African military and police forces. And prior to 1914, the number of British administrative officers available for the whole of northern Nigeria was less than 500. These were hardly strong foundations for statehood. It would not take much to destabilize the European order in Africa.

The American Empire

The United States, like Europe, was drawn into the mania of overseas expansion and empire building. Echoing the rhetoric of Manifest Destiny from the 1840s, the expansionists of the 1890s claimed that Americans still had a divine mission to spread their superior civilization and their Christian faith around the globe. However, America's new imperialists followed the European model of colonialism from Asia and Africa: colonies were to provide harbors for American vessels, supply raw materials to American industries, and purchase the surplus production of American farms and factories. These new territorial acquisitions were not intended for American settlement or statehood. Nor were their inhabitants to become American citizens, for nonwhite foreigners were considered unfit for incorporation into the American nation.

The pressure to expand came to a head in the late 1890s, when the United States declared war on Spain and invaded the Philippines, Puerto Rico, and Cuba. From 1895, Cuban patriots had been slowly pushing back Spanish troops and occupying

Diamond Mine. *The discovery of diamonds and gold in South Africa in the late nineteenth century led to the investment of large amounts of overseas capital, the mobilization of severely exploited African mine workers, and the Boer War of 1899 to 1902, which resulted in the incorporation of the Afrikaner states of the Transvaal and the Orange Free State into the Union of South Africa.*

sugar plantations—some of which belonged to American planters. Fearing social revolution off the shores of Florida, the American expansionists presented themselves as the saviors of Spanish colonials yearning for freedom, while at the same time safeguarding property for foreign interests in the Spanish-American War (1898). After defeating Spanish regulars in Cuba, American forces began disarming Cuban rebels and returning lands to their owners.

Although the Americans claimed that they were intervening to promote freedom in Spain's colonies, they quickly forgot their promises. The United States annexed Puerto Rico after minimal protest, but Cubans and Filipinos resisted becoming colonial subjects. Bitterness ran particularly high among Filipinos, to whom American leaders had promised independence if they joined in the war against Spain. Betrayed, Filipino rebels launched a war for independence in the name of a Filipino nation. In two years of fighting, over 5,000 Americans and perhaps 200,000 Filipinos perished. The outcome: the Philippines became a colony of the United States.

Colonies in the Philippines and Cuba laid the foundations for a revised model of U.S. expansionism. The earlier pattern had been to turn Indian lands into privately owned farmsteads and to extend the Atlantic market across the continent. But now, in this new era, the nation's largest corporations (with government support) aggressively intervened in the affairs of neighbors near and far. Following the Spanish-American War,

"That wicked man is going to gobble you up, my child!"

Uncle Sam Leading Cuba. *In the years before the Spanish-American War, cartoonists who wished to see the United States intervene on behalf of Cuba in the islanders' struggle for independence from Spain typically depicted Cuba as a white woman in distress. By contrast, in this and other cartoons following the Spanish-American War, Cubans were drawn as black, and usually as infants or boys unable to care for themselves and in need of the benevolent paternal rule of the United States.*

The Women of Algiers in Their Apartment. *An oil painting by Eugène Delacroix (1798–1863) of Algerian women being attended by a black servant. European painters in the nineteenth century often used images of women to portray Arab Muslim society.*

the United States repeatedly sent troops to many Caribbean and Central American countries. The Americans preferred to turn these regimes into dependent client states, rather than making them part of the United States itself (as with Alaska and Hawaii) or converting them into formal colonies (as the Europeans had done in Africa and Asia). The entire world was an object for the powerful states to shape to their needs.

Imperialism and Culture

At least since the Crusades, Europeans had regularly written and thought about others. These images and ideas had grown more numerous and varied as commerce and colonialism in Asia and the Atlantic world increased; they served various purposes, including those of informing, entertaining, flattering, and criticizing European culture. As Europeans began to exert more control over various parts of the world, they found it easier to force open closed cultures and to carry away treasures. As Europeans and Americans grew more and more confident that they were the knowers and the collectors, they became convinced that their arts and sciences were superior—and curiosity often turned to disdain. Exerting full imperial control then gave new legitimacy to ideas of European and American cultural superiority, and such ideas made imperialism seem natural and just. In time, Europeans presumed that the only true modern civilization was their own; other peoples might have reigned over great empires in antiquity, but had since fallen into decadence and decline. In literature and painting, for example, a new genre known as **Orientalism** portrayed nonwestern peoples as exotic, sensuous, and economically backward. Rather than depicting Egyptian dock workers or middle-class Algerian women, these paintings featured snake charmers and inhabitants of the harem, thereby suggesting that the whole region was inhabited by people of these types, in contrast to a uniformly progressive Europe, inhabited by industrial workers and men of science.

Darwinism, and even Darwin himself, in his 1873 *The Descent of Man*, ratified this view of "lower" and "higher" races, the former stuck in the past and the latter anointed by God (or in Darwin's case, by Nature itself) to define and dictate civilization's future. Europeans' relationship to others might now be one of condescending sympathy or of ruthless exploitation, but the bottom line was that it was up to white Europeans and Americans to create modern culture; the darker people, the cultural Darwinians argued, were not nearly as fully "evolved" as the Europeans, and could not hope to catch up (or to offer a viable alternative model for poetry or painting, for example). At best, they could be taught European languages, sciences, and religions, and perhaps be made to evolve more quickly. It is telling that French colonial subjects who did well at French schools were known as "evolués," "the evolved ones."

The Civilizing Mission. *This advertisement for Pears' Soap shamelessly tapped into the idea of Europeans bringing civilization to the people of their colonies. It said that use of Pears' Soap would teach the virtues of cleanliness to the "natives" and implied that it would even lighten their skin.*

CELEBRATING IMPERIALISM Especially in middle- and upper-class circles, Europeans celebrated their imperial triumphs. After the invention of photographic film and the Eastman Kodak camera in 1888, imperial images surfaced in popular forms such as postcards and advertisements. Imperial themes also decorated packaging materials; tins of coffee, tea, tobacco, and chocolates featured pictures highlighting the commodities' colonial origins. Cigarettes often had names like "Admiral," "Royal Navy," "Fighter," and "Grand Fleet." Some of this served as propaganda, produced by investors in imperial commodities or by colonial pressure groups.

Propaganda promoted imperialism abroad but also inspired changes at home. For example, champions of empire argued that if the British population did not grow fast enough to fill the world's sparsely settled regions, then the population of other nations would. Population was power, and the number of healthy children provided an accurate measure of global influence. "Empire cannot be built on rickety and flat-chested citizens," warned a British member of Parliament in 1905. In addition, writers for young audiences often invoked colonial settings and themes. Whereas girls' literature stressed domestic service, child rearing, and nurturing, boys' readings depicted exotic locales, devious Orientals and savage Africans, and daring colonial exploits.

It should be noted, however, that empire, and imperial culture, did not affect, or interest, all Europeans equally. In general, the extension and upkeep of colonies directly involved only a small minority of Europeans, and those who saw "orientalist" paintings saw many other types of paintings too, including those of scantily clad Greeks and Romans. Nor were all students of Asian languages complicit in imperialist exploitation; some were truly curious about other peoples' histories and cultures, and laid the foundations for studies of world history today. But even they were beneficiaries of imperialism, which made the world's cultures newly accessible to Europeans, for the purposes of both exploiting others and learning more about them.

PRESSURES OF EXPANSION IN JAPAN, RUSSIA, AND CHINA

The challenge of integrating political communities and extending territorial borders was a problem not just for western Europe and the United States. Other societies also aimed to overcome domestic

Perry Arrives in Japan. *A Japanese woodblock print portraying the uninvited arrival into Edo (Tokyo) Bay on August 7, 1853, of a tall American ship, which was commanded by Matthew Perry. This arrival marked the end of Japan's ability to fully control the terms of its interactions with foreigners.*

Economic Transformation of Japan. *During the Meiji period, the government transformed the economy by building railroads, laying telegraph lines, founding a postal system, and encouraging the formation of giant firms known as* zaibatsu, *which were family organizations consisting of factories, import-export businesses, and banks. Here we see a raw-silk-reeling factory that was run by one of the* zaibatsu.

dissent and establish larger domains. Japan, Russia, and China provide three contrasting models; their differing forms of expansion eventually led them to fight over possessions in East Asia.

Japan's Transformation and Expansion

Starting in the 1860s, Japanese rulers tried to recast their country less as an old dynasty and more like a modern nation-state. Since the early seventeenth century, the Tokugawa Shogunate had kept outsiders within strict limits and thwarted internal unrest. But after an American naval officer, Commodore Matthew Perry, entered Edo Bay in 1853 with a fleet of steam-powered ships, other Americans, Russians, Dutch, and British followed in his wake. These outsiders forced the Tokugawa rulers to sign humiliating treaties that opened Japanese ports, slapped limits on Japanese tariffs, and exempted foreigners from Japanese laws. Younger Japanese, especially among the military (samurai) elites, felt that Japan should respond by adopting, not rejecting, western practices. They respected the power demonstrated by the intruding ships and weaponry; yet in adapting Western technology, they expected to remain true to their own culture.

In 1868, a group of reformers toppled the Tokugawa Shogunate and promised to return Japan to its mythic greatness. Then Emperor Mutsuhito—the Meiji ("Enlightened Rule") Emperor—became the symbol of a new Japan. His reign (1868–1912) was called the **Meiji Restoration**. By founding schools, initiating a propaganda campaign, and revamping the army to create a single "national" fighting force, the Meiji government promoted a political community that stressed linguistic and ethnic homogeneity, as well as superiority compared to others. In this way the Meiji leaders overcame age-old regional divisions, subdued local political authorities, and mobilized the country to face the threat from powerful Europeans.

ECONOMIC DEVELOPMENT One of the Meiji period's remarkable achievements was the nation's economic transformation. After 1871, when the government banned the feudal system and allowed peasants to become small landowners, farmers improved their agrarian techniques and saw their standard of living rise. Some business practices that underlay the economic transformation had taken shape under the Tokugawa Shogunate, but the Meiji government was far more activist in terms of internal modernization. For example, stressing the slogan "rich country, strong army," the energetic new government unified the currency around the yen, created a postal system, introduced tax reforms, laid telegraph lines, formed compulsory foreign trade associations, launched savings and export campaigns, established an advanced civil service system, began to build railroads, and hired thousands of foreign consultants. In 1889, the Meiji government introduced a constitution (based largely on the German model). The following year, 450,000 people—about 1 percent of the population—elected Japan's first parliament, the Imperial Diet.

As the government sold valuable enterprises to the people it knew best, it created private economic dynasties. The new large companies (such as Sumitomo, Yasuda, Mitsubishi, and Mitsui) were family organizations. Fathers, sons, cousins, and uncles

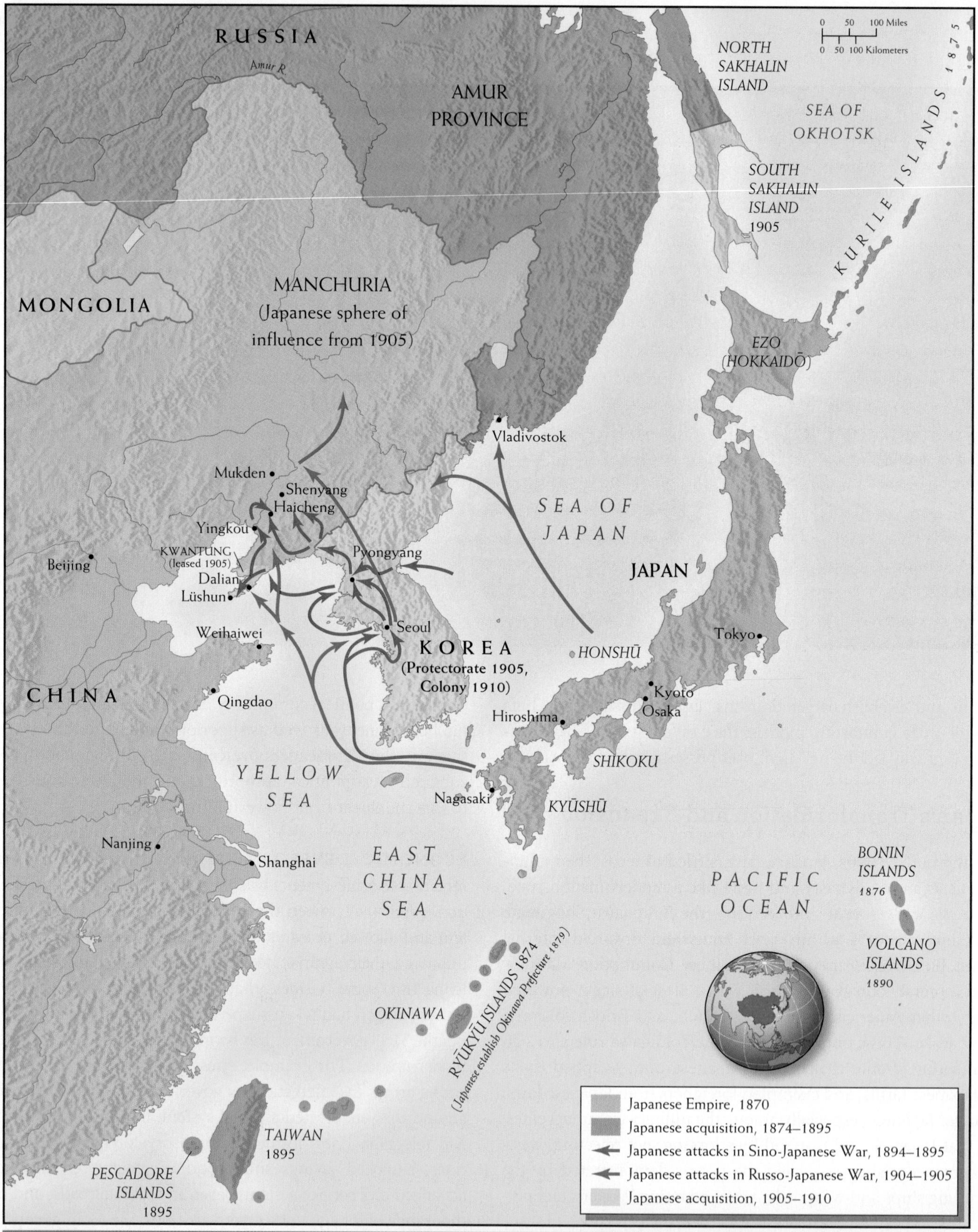

Map 17.5 | Japanese Expansion, 1870–1910

Under the Meiji Restoration, the Japanese state built a strong national identity and competed with foreign powers for imperial advantage in East Asia.

- According to the map, what were the first areas that the Japanese Empire acquired as it started to expand?
- What two empires' spheres of influence were affected by Japan's aggressive attempts at expansion?
- What were the new Japanese state's objectives? How were they similar to or different from European expansionism of the same period?

ran different parts of large integrated corporations—some in charge of banks, some running the trade wing, some overseeing factories. Women played a crucial role, not just as custodians of the home but also as cultivators of important family alliances, especially among potential marriage partners. In contrast to American limited-liability firms, which issued shares on stock markets to anonymous buyers, Japan's version of large-scale managerial capitalism was a personal affair.

EXPANSIONISM AND CONFLICT WITH NEIGHBORS As in many other emerging nation-states, expansion in Japan was a tempting prospect. It offered the promise of more markets for selling goods and obtaining staples, and it was a way to burnish the image of national superiority and greatness. Japanese ventures abroad were initially spectacularly successful. The Meiji moved first to take over the kingdom of the Ryūkyūs, southwest of Japan (see Map 17.5). A small show of force, only 160 Japanese soldiers, was enough to establish the new Okinawa Prefecture there in 1879. The Japanese regarded the people of the Ryūkyūs as an ethnic minority and refused to incorporate them into the nation-state on equal terms. In contrast with the British in India or the Americans in Puerto Rico, the Japanese conquerors refused to train a native Ryūkyūs governing class. Meiji intellectuals insisted that the "backward" Okinawans were unfit for local self-rule and representation.

In 1876, the Japanese fixed upon Korea, which put their plans on a collision course with China's sphere of influence. In a formal treaty, the Japanese recognized Korea as an independent state, opened Korea to trade, and won extraterritorial rights. As a result, the Chinese worried that soon the Japanese would try to take over Korea. These fears were well founded, for Japanese designs on Korea eventually sparked the Sino-Japanese War of 1894–1895, in which the Chinese suffered a humiliating defeat.

The Sino-Japanese War accelerated Japan's rapid transformation to a nation-state and a colonial power with no peer in Asia. Having lost the war, China ceded the province of Taiwan to the Japanese. Japan also annexed Korea in 1910 and converted Taiwan and Korea into the twin jewels of its young empire. The colonial administration built transportation networks and established educational and health institutions—while keeping the colonized people out of top managerial and technical positions. Like the British in India, the Japanese regarded their colonial subjects as racially inferior and unworthy of the privileges of citizenship. And like other imperial powers, the Japanese expected their possessions to serve the metropolitan center. Densely populated and short of land, Japan wanted these colonies to become granaries, sending rice to the mother country. Moreover, the Meiji regime exploited Taiwanese sugar exports to relieve a Japanese economy heavily dependent on imports. Indeed, by serving as staple-exporting regions, Korea and Taiwan were a source of foreign exchange that helped defray Japan's trade deficits. They had grown huge as a result of massive imports to build up new industries.

Russian Transformation and Expansion

Russia expanded out of a sense of mission and a need to defend against other countries expanding along its immense border. Facing an emerging Germany, a British presence in the Middle East and Persia, a consolidating China, and an ascendant Japan, Russia knew it would have to enlarge its territorial domain. So it established a number of expansionist fronts simultaneously: southwest to the Black Sea, south into the Caucasus and Turkestan, and east into Manchuria (see Map 17.6). Success depended on annexing territories and establishing protectorates over vulnerable conquered peoples.

Looking west and south, Russia invaded the Ottoman territories of Moldavia (present-day Moldova) and Walachia (present-day Romania) in 1853. The invasion provoked opposition from Britain and France, who joined with the Ottomans to defeat Russia in the Crimean War (1853–1856). By exposing Russia's lack of modern weapons and its problems in supplying troops without a railway system, the defeat spurred a course of aggressive modernization and expansion.

MODERNIZATION AND INTERNAL REFORM In the 1860s, Tsar Alexander II launched a wave of "Great Reforms" to make Russia more competitive. Autocratic rule continued, but officials reintegrated the society. In 1861, for example, a decree emancipated peasants from serfdom. Other changes included a sharp reduction in the duration of military service, a program of education for the conscripts, and the beginnings of a mass school system to teach children reading, writing, and Russian culture. Starting in the 1890s, as railroads and factories expanded, so did the steel, coal, and petroleum industries. But while the reforms strengthened the state, they did not enhance the lives of common people. Workers in Russia were brutally exploited, even by the standards of the industrial revolution. Also, large landowners had kept most of the empire's fertile land, and the peasants had to pay substantial redemption fees for the poorer-quality plots they received.

The reforms revealed a fundamental problem: the rulers were eager to reform society, but not the basis of government (autocracy). This caused liberals, conservatives, and malcontents alike to question the state-led modernizing mission. Before long, in the press, courtrooms, and streets, men and women denounced the regime. Revolutionaries engaged in terror and assassination. In 1881, a terrorist bomb blew the tsar to pieces. In the 1890s, following another famine, the radical doctrines of Marxism (see Chapter 16) gained popularity in Russia. Even aristocratic intellectuals, such as the author of *War and Peace,* Count Leo Tolstoy, lamented their despotic government.

TERRITORIAL EXPANSION Yet the critics of internal reform did not hold back the Russian expansionists, who believed they had to take over certain lands to keep them out of rivals' hands.

Map 17.6 | Russian Expansion, 1801–1914

The Russian state continued to expand in the nineteenth century.

- According to this map, what lands did Russia acquire during the period 1796–1855? What lands did it acquire next?
- Compare this map on Russian expansion with Map 13.7 (p. 508). How did the direction of Russia's expansion change in the nineteenth century? Which states did the expanding Russian Empire more resemble in this era, western Europe (such as Great Britain) or American states (such as the United States)?

So they conquered the highland people of the Caucasus Mountains to prevent Ottomans and Persians from encroaching on Russia's southern flank. And they battled the British over areas between Turkestan and British India, such as Persia (Iran) and Afghanistan. Although some Russians moved to these lands, they never became a majority there. The new provinces were multiethnic, multireligious communities that were only partially integrated into the Russian state. (See Primary Source: Two Faces of Empire.)

Perhaps the most impressive Russian expansion occurred in East Asia, where the underpopulated Amur River basin boasted rich lands, mineral deposits, and access to the Pacific Ocean. The Chinese also wanted to colonize this area, which lay just north of Manchuria. After twenty years of struggle, Russia claimed the land north and south of the Amur River and in 1860 founded Vladivostok, a port on the Pacific Ocean whose name signified "Rule the East." Deciding to focus on these areas in Asia, the Russian government sold its one territory in North America (Alaska) to the United States. Then, to link the capital (Moscow) and the western part of the country to its East Asian spoils, the government began construction of the Trans-Siberian Railroad. When it was completed in 1903, the new railroad bridged the east and the west. Russia then began to eye the Korean peninsula, on which Japan, too, had set its sights.

GOVERNING A DIVERSE NATION Russia was a huge empire whose rulers were only partially effective at integrating its diverse parts into a political community. In 1897, during the first complete population census, ethnographers struggled over what to call all the empire's peoples: nations or tribes. In the end, authorities chose the term *nationalities,* recognizing 104

PRIMARY SOURCE

Two Faces of Empire

Russification (forced assimilation) was one of the Russian Empire's responses to the challenge of the nation-state idea. In 1863 the tsar prohibited publication of the Bible in the Little Russian (Ukrainian) language, alienating many otherwise loyal Slavic subjects. By contrast, most non-Christians, such as the Muslims of newly annexed Turkestan (central Asia), were exempted from Russification because they were considered "aliens" who should be ruled separately. The excerpts below present an 1876 edict prohibiting the use of Ukrainian, and a celebration of colonialism by a member of the Russian governor-general's office in Turkestan.

RUSSIFICATION IN UKRAINE

In order to halt what is, from the state's point of view, the dangerous activity of the Ukrainophiles, it is appropriate to take the following measures immediately: 1. To prohibit the import into the empire of any books published abroad in the Little Russian dialect [Ukrainian], without the special permission of the Chief Press Administration. 2. To prohibit the printing inside of the empire of any original works or translations in this dialect, with the exception of historical documents.... 3. Equally to prohibit any dramatic productions, musical lyrics and public lectures (which at present have the charter of Ukrainophile demonstrations) in this dialect.... 6. To strengthen supervision by the local educational administration so as not to allow any subjects in primary schools be taught in the Little Russian dialect. . . . 7. To clear the libraries of all primary and secondary schools in the Little Russian provinces of books and pamphlets prohibited by paragraph 2. . . . 8. . . . To demand from the heads of these districts a list of teachers with a note as to their reliability in relation to Ukrainophile tendencies. Those noted as unreliable or doubtful should be transferred to Great Russian provinces.

COLONIALISM IN TURKESTAN

Our battalion arrived in Tashkent four years after Turkestan had been annexed to the empire. Tashkent at that time looked more like a military settlement than the chief city of the region, that is the capital of Russian Central Asia. The majority of the inhabitants were soldiers, either resting after some campaign or else about to go out on a new expedition. Civilians and women were a rarity. Now, thirty-six years later, looking proudly at the path we have followed, I can see the colossal results achieved by the Russian government, always humane to the vanquished, but insistently pursuing its civilising mission. Of course, there have been many mistakes, there have been abuses, but this has not halted the rational and expedient intentions of the government. We went into a region which had a population alien to us.... They had for many centuries been accustomed to submitting humbly to the barbaric and cruel despotism of their rulers, but they nevertheless came to terms with their position because their rulers were of their own faith. . . . The fanatical mullahs began rumours amongst the mass of the population that, instead of true believer khans, they were to be ruled by heathens who would convert them to Christianity, put crosses around their necks, send them to be soldiers, introduce their own laws, revoke the Sharia [the fundamental law of Islam] and make their wives and daughters uncover their faces.

... Frequent outbursts, uprisings and disorders took place and repression followed. But at the same time the natives saw that the very first steps of the first Governor-General proved the complete falseness of the mullahs. . . . It was announced solemnly everywhere to the local population, that as subjects of the Russian monarch, the population would keep its faith, its national customs, its courts and its judges, that all taxes demanded by the previous collectors were illegal and burdensome in the extreme and would be revoked, and that instead just taxes would be imposed, and that the position of women would remain inviolable. All this of course soon calmed the population and an industrious people settled down to a peaceful life.

QUESTIONS FOR ANALYSIS

- Based on the "Russification in Ukraine" document, explain how important the arts and education can be in maintaining a people's identity—and in subverting a foreign power's authority.
- According to the "Colonialism in Turkestan" document, what steps did the Russians take to calm the Muslims' fears of colonial domination?

Source: Martin McCauley and Peter Waldron, The Emergence of the Modern Russian State, 1855–1881 *(Totowa, NJ: Barnes and Noble Books, 1988), pp. 209, 211–12.*

of them, speaking 146 languages and dialects. Ethnic Russians accounted for slightly more than half the population.

Counting and categorizing peoples formed part of the state's attempts to figure out how to govern this diverse realm. As the United States did, Russia made conquered regions into full parts of the empire. But unlike the United States, Russia was suspicious of decentralized federalism, fearing it would lead groups to demand secession. Moreover, the tsars were terrified

The Trans-Siberian Railroad. *Russia's decision to build a railway across Siberia to the Pacific Ocean derived from a desire to expand the empire's power in East Asia and to forestall British advances in Asia. The colossal undertaking, which claimed the lives of thousands of workers, reached completion just as Russia clashed militarily with Japan. The new railroad ferried Russian troops over long distances to battles, such as the one at Mukden, in Manchuria, which was then the largest land battle in the history of warfare.*

by the idea of popular sovereignty. Preferring the tried-and-true method of centralized autocracy, they divided most of the empire into governorships ruled by appointed civilian or military governors who were supposed to function like local tsars or autocrats.

Unlike the United States, which displaced or slaughtered native populations during its expansion across an entire continent, Russia mostly assimilated the new peoples. In this daunting task, the state's approach ranged from outright repression (of Poles and Jews) to favoritism (toward Baltic Germans and Finns), although the beneficiaries of favoritism often later lost favor if they became too strong. Further, unlike the United States, which managed to pacify borders with its weaker neighbors, Russia faced the constant suspicions of Persians and Ottomans and the menace of British troops in Afghanistan. (The troops were there to prevent Russia from cutting off the overland route to India.) In East Asia, a clash with expansionist Japan loomed on the horizon.

Such expansionism was a constant fiscal drain and a heavy burden on the population. To promote the image of a great Russian Empire, rulers leaned more heavily on the rural poor and pursued intensive modernization, but that generated instability. For the time being, Moscow's main threat did not come from within Russia's borders. It came from the outside.

China under Pressure

While the Russians and Japanese scrambled to copy European models of industrialism and imperialism, the Qing were slower to mobilize against threats from the west. Even as the European powers were dividing up China into spheres of influence, Qing officials were much more worried about internal revolts and threats from their northern borders. Into the 1850s and 1860s, many Qing officials still regarded the increasing European incursions and demands as a lesser danger by comparison.

ADOPTING WESTERN LEARNING AND SKILLS A growing number of Chinese officials, however, recognized the superior armaments and technology of rival powers and were deeply troubled by the threat posed by European military might. Starting in the 1860s, reformist bureaucrats sought to adopt elements of western learning and technological skills—but with the intention of keeping the core Chinese culture intact.

This so-called **Self-Strengthening movement** included a variety of new ventures: arsenals, shipyards, coal mines, a steamship company to contest the foreign domination of coastal shipping, and schools for learning foreign ways and languages. Most interesting was the dispatch abroad of about 120 schoolboys under the charge of Yung Wing. The first Chinese graduate of an American college (Yale University, 1854), Yung believed that western education would greatly benefit Chinese students, so he took his charges to Connecticut in the 1870s to attend school and live with American families. Conservatives at the Qing court were soon dismayed by reports of the students' interest in Christianity and aptitude for baseball. In 1881, after the U.S. government refused to admit the boys into military academies, they summoned the students home.

Yung Wing's abortive educational mission was not the only setback for the Self-Strengthening movement, for skepticism about western technology was rife among conservative officials. Some insisted that the introduction of machinery would lead to unemployment; others worried that railways would facilitate western military maneuvers and lead to an invasion; still others complained that the crisscrossing tracks disturbed the harmony between humans and nature. The first short railway track ever laid in China was torn up in 1877 shortly after being built, and the country had only 288 kilometers of track prior to 1895.

Although they did not acknowledge the railroad's usefulness, the Chinese did adopt other new technologies to access a wider range of information. For example, by the early 1890s there were about a dozen Chinese-language newspapers (as distinct from the foreign-language press) published in major cities, with the largest ones having a circulation of 10,000 to 15,000. To avoid government intervention, these papers sidestepped political controversy; instead, they featured commercial news and literary contributions. In 1882, the newspaper ***Shenbao*** made use of a new telegraph line to publish dispatches within China.

INTERNAL REFORM EFFORTS China's defeat by Japan in the Sino-Japanese War (1894–1895), sparked by quarrels over Korea, prompted the first serious attempt at reform by the Qing. Known as the Hundred Days' Reform, the episode lasted only from June to September 1898. The force behind it was a thirty-seven-year-old scholar named Kang Youwei and his twenty-two-year-old student Liang Qichao. Citing rulers such as Peter the Great of Russia and the Meiji Emperor of Japan as their inspiration, the reformers urged Chinese leaders to develop a railway network, a state banking system, a modern postal service, and institutions to foster the development of agriculture, industry, and commerce.

The reformers' opportunity to accelerate change came in the summer of 1898 when the twenty-seven-year-old Guangxu emperor decided to implement many of their ideas, including changes in the venerable civil service examination system. But the effort was short-lived, for conservative officials rallied behind Guangxu's aunt, the Empress Dowager Cixi, who emerged from retirement to overturn the reforms. The young emperor was put under house arrest. Kang and Liang fled for their lives and went into exile. It would take still more military defeats to finally jolt the Qing court into action, but by then it was too late to save the regime.

The reforms of the Self-Strengthening movement were too modest and poorly implemented. Very few Chinese acquired new skills. Despite talk of modernizing, the civil service examination remained based on Confucian classics and still opened the only doors to government service. Governing elites were not yet ready to reinvent the principles of their political community, and they adhered instead to the traditional dynastic structure.

By the late nineteenth century, the success of the Qing regime in expanding its territories a century earlier seemed like a distant memory, as various powers repeatedly forced it to make economic and territorial concessions. Unlike Japan or Russia, however, the Qing government resisted any comprehensive social reforms (until after the turn of the twentieth century), and its policies left the country vulnerable to both external aggression and internal instability.

CONCLUSION

Between 1850 and 1914, most of the world's people lived not in nation-states but in landed empires or in the colonies of nation-states. But as reformers sought a new political framework in response to popular upheavals and economic changes, the nation-state became a desirable form of governance.

Although the ideal of "a people" united by territory, history, and culture grew increasingly popular worldwide, it was not easy to make it a reality. Official histories, national heroes, novels, poetry, and music helped, but central to the process of nation formation were the actions of bureaucrats. Asserting sovereignty over what it claimed as national territory, the state "nationalized" diverse populations by creating a unified system of law, education, military service, and government.

Colonization beyond borders was another part of nation building in many societies. In these efforts, territorial conquests took place under the banner of nationalist endeavors. In Europe, the Americas, Japan, and to some extent Russia, the intertwined processes of nation building and territorial expansion were most effective. The Amazon River basin, Okinawa, and especially the North American West became important provinces of integrated nation-states, populated with settlers who produced for national and international markets.

However, the integrating impulses of emerging nations did not wipe out local differences, mute class antagonisms, or eliminate gender inequalities. Even as Europeans and Americans came to see themselves as chosen—by God or by natural selection—to rule the rest, they suffered deep divisions. Not everyone identified with the nation-state or the empire, or agreed on what it meant to belong or to conquer. But by the century's end, racist advocates and colonial lobbyists seem to have convinced many that their interests and destinies were bound up with their nations' unity, prosperity, and global clout.

Ironically, nation building had an unintended consequence, for self-determination could also apply to racial or ethnic minorities at home and in the colonies. Armed with the rhetoric of progress and uplift, colonial authorities tried to subjugate distant people, but colonial subjects themselves often asserted the language of "nation" and accused imperial overlords of betraying their own lofty principles. As the twentieth century opened, Filipino and Cuban rebels used Thomas Jefferson's Declaration of Independence to oppose American invaders, Koreans defined themselves as a nation crushed under Japanese heels, and Indian nationalists made colonial governors feel shame for violating English standards of "fair play."

AFTER YOU READ THIS CHAPTER

Review and research on **STUDYSPACE** wwnorton.com/StudySpace

TRACING THE GLOBAL STORYLINES

FOCUS ON: *Nationalism, Imperialism, and Scientific/Technological Innovations*

The Americas and Europe: Consolidating Nations

- Residents of the United States claim territory across the North American continent after fighting a bloody civil war to preserve the union and abolish slavery.
- Canadians also build a new nation and expand across the continent.
- Brazilians create a prosperous nation-state that excludes much of the population from the privileges of belonging to the "nation" and the "state."
- The dynastic states of Prussia and Sardinia-Piedmont create German and Italian nation-states at the expense of France and the Austrian Empire.

Industry, Science, and Technology on a Global Scale

- Continued industrialization, coupled with scientific research, transforms the global economy.
- New technologies of warfare, transportation, and communication ease global economic integration.
- Charles Darwin's *Origin of Species* overturns previous conceptions of nature, arguing that present-day life forms evolved from simpler ones over long periods.

Empires

- After suppressing the Indian Mutiny, the British reorganize their rule in India.
- The Dutch take over administrative responsibilities in Indonesia from the Dutch East India Company.
- Seven European powers partition the entire African continent (except for Ethiopia and Liberia) despite intense African resistance.
- Americans win the Spanish-American War, annex Puerto Rico, and establish colonial rule over the Philippines.
- The expansionist aims of Japan, Russia, and China lead to clashes over possessions in East Asia, with Russia gaining much territory and Japan defeating the Chinese.
- Colonial rule spurs nationalist sentiments among the colonized.

CHRONOLOGY

The Americas
U.S. Civil War **1861–1865**
Canada gains self-rule **1867**

Europe
Origin of Species published **1859**
Unifications of Germany and Italy **1870–71**

East and Southeast Asia
Commodore Perry "opens" Japan **1853**
French and British expansion in Southeast Asia **1860s–1890s**

Africa and the Middle East
European expansion in sub-Saharan Africa **1870s–1890s**

South Asia

Russia
Crimean War **1853–1856**
Great Reforms to modernize Russia **1860s**

1850

KEY TERMS

Charles Darwin p. 643

imperialism p. 630

limited-liability joint-stock company p. 633

Manifest Destiny p. 631

Meiji Restoration p. 657

natural selection p. 644

Orientalism p. 655

Raj p. 646

Self-Strengthening movement p. 662

steel p. 642

STUDY QUESTIONS

1. **Explain** the process of nation building that occurred in the nineteenth century. What polities initiated these efforts, and what different strategies were involved?
2. **Identify** where strong nation-states emerged during this period. How did the nation-state idea challenge certain polities and other organized groups?
3. **Define** imperialism. Why did state-directed efforts at nation building often lead to imperialist efforts and other forms of territorial expansion?
4. **List and explain** several major sources of the new wave of imperialism that occurred in the second half of the nineteenth century. To what extent did these ideas find support among the populations of imperialist states?
5. **Analyze** to what extent different colonized societies resisted imperialist efforts. How successful were their actions?
6. **Describe** the policies that imperial powers used to govern their overseas colonies. What were the goals of imperial administrations, and how successful were they in achieving them?
7. **Analyze** the cultural impact of imperialist ambitions on imperialist nations themselves. How did colonization and territorial expansion shape notions of race and ethnicity there?
8. **Analyze** how the spread of nationalism and imperialism shaped state behavior in China, Russia, and Japan. To what extent did each state adapt to these new patterns?
9. **Explain** how nation-state building, territorial expansion, and imperialism reshaped the global economy. How would you describe the relationship between industrial regions and the rest of the world's societies?

Brazil abolishes slavery **1888**

Spanish-American War **1898**

Meiji Era in Japan **1868–1912**

Sino-Japanese War **1894–1895**

British occupation of Egypt **1882**

British Raj **1858–1947**

Construction of Trans-Siberian Railroad **1890s**

1900

BEFORE YOU READ THIS CHAPTER

wwnorton.com/
StudySpace

GLOBAL STORYLINES

- Numerous factors lead to global anxieties: vast population movements, deep-seated poverty, failure of nation-states to achieve important goals, and hatred of colonial domination.
- The tumult challenges Europeans' faith in "progress."
- Turmoil promotes new scientific thinking and artistic expression, known as cultural modernism.

CHAPTER OUTLINE

18

An Unsettled World, 1890–1914

FOCUS QUESTIONS

- What developments produced global anxieties and insecurities at the beginning of the twentieth century?
- What was modernism and how did it challenge traditional ways of thinking across the globe?
- How did states respond to growing economic and political inequities?
- How did new conceptions of race, nation, and class challenge the political status quo during this era?
- How did shifting economic and political structures affect women?

In 1905 a young African man, Kinjikitile Ngwale, began to move among various ethnic groups in German East Africa, spreading a message of opposition to German colonial authorities. In the tradition of visionary prophets (see Chapter 16), Kinjikitile claimed that by anointing his followers with blessed water (*maji* in Swahili), he could protect them from European bullets and drive the Germans from East Africa. Kinjikitile's reputation spread rapidly, drawing followers from across 100,000 square miles of territory. Although German officials soon executed Kinjikitile, they could not prevent a broad uprising, called the Maji-Maji Revolt. The Germans brutally suppressed the revolt, killing between 200,000 and 300,000 Africans.

At the very moment when the movement of goods, ideas, and armies was linking together the world's peoples in unprecedented—and for groups like the Maji-Maji, disastrous—ways, events like the one described above revealed that many of the world's citizens were deeply dissatisfied with global inequalities in wealth and power. In Asia, Africa, and Latin America, anticolonial critics and exploited classes protested European domination and organized increasingly powerful and violent forms of opposition. But dissatisfaction was not restricted to the non-European world. At home in Europe and America, faith in capitalism, industrialization, and the idea of progress endured, but was challenged by internal critics, especially women, wage workers, and frustrated nationalists, who felt deprived of the full benefits of industrializing nation-states. Strikes, political assassination, and the rise of increasingly powerful popular political movements threatened the status quo; competition between empires increasingly touched off armed conflicts. The rising intensity of these conflicts unsettled the world, even as new forms of communication, investment, and transportation linked it, increasingly, together.

This chapter tackles the anxieties and insecurities that unsettled the world around the turn of the twentieth century. It ties them in particular to several key factors: (1) the uprooting of millions of people from countryside to city and from one continent to another, (2) discontent with the poverty that many suffered even as economic production leaped upward, (3) frustration with the incomplete expansion of rights within nation-states and the incomplete realization of national aspirations, and, (4) in Asia and Africa, resentment of and resistance to European domination. Around the globe, this tumult caused a questioning of old ideas that led to a flowering of new thinking and fresh artistic expression under the label of "modernism." Championed by some and despised by others, modernism *meant* to be unsettling—to represent the world in shocking new ways—and thus tells us a great deal, then, about the conflicts and crises that defined this era.

PROGRESS, UPHEAVAL, AND MOVEMENT

The decades leading up to 1914 were a time of unprecedented possibility for some, and social disruption and economic frustration for others. They were also years of anxiety worldwide. Rapid economic progress brought challenges to the established order and the people in power. In Europe and the United States, radicals and middle-class reformers agitated for political and social change. In areas colonized by European countries and the United States, resentment focused on either colonial rulers or indigenous elites. Even in nations such as China, which had not been formally colonized but which faced repeated intrusions, popular discontent targeted domination by Europeans. In China, Mexico, and Russia, angry peasants and workers allied with frustrated reformers to topple autocratic regimes.

In the late nineteenth century, whole new industries fueled economic growth, especially in the industrial countries and in territories that exported vital raw materials to Europe and the United States. But industrial capitalism also spurred inequalities within industrial countries and, especially, between the world's industrial and nonindustrial regions. It also brought unwelcome changes in how and where people worked and lived. Rural folk flocked into the cities, hoping to escape the poverty that encumbered most people in the countryside. In the cities, even though public building projects produced sewer systems, museums, parks, and libraries, the poor had little access to them. Anxieties intensified when economic downturns left thousands out of work. This led, in some cases, to organized opposition to authoritarian regimes or to the free market system.

In Europe and North America, as industrialization expanded, a generation of younger artists, writers, and scientists known as **modernists** broke with older conventions and sought new ways of seeing and describing the world. In Asia, Africa, and South America as well, many modernists were energized by the idea of moving beyond traditional forms of art, literature, music, and science. But the modernist generation's exuberance worried those who were not ready to give up their cultural traditions and institutions. In the colonized world, and in areas threatened by colonial domination, "modernism" seemed to some to mean full-on "westernization" and with it, the loss of cultural autonomy. The acceleration of cultural change, like that of economic advances, sparked new conflicts and new anxieties both within states and across the globe.

Peoples in Motion

If the world was being *unsettled* by political, economic, and cultural changes, it was also being *resettled* by mass emigration (see Map 18.1). Consider what historian Alfred Crosby called the "Caucasian tsunami": the emigration of throngs of Europeans to North America, Australia, Argentina, Africa, and Cuba. The "tsunami" began after the Napoleonic wars and gathered momentum in the 1840s, when the Irish fled their starving communities to seek better lives in North America. After 1870, the flow of Europeans became a torrent. The United States was the favored destination, with European migrants exceeding by sixfold the number of Europeans who migrated to Argentina (the second-place receiving country) between 1871 and 1920. The high point occurred between 1901 and 1910, when over 6 million Europeans entered the United States. This was nothing less than a demographic revolution.

EMIGRATION, IMMIGRATION, INTERNAL MIGRATION

Europeans were not the only peoples on the move. Between the 1840s and the 1940s, 29 million South Asians migrated into the Malay Peninsula and Burma (British colonies), the Dutch

Indies (Indonesia), East Africa, and the Caribbean. Most were recruited to labor on plantations, railways, and mines in British-controlled territories. Merchants followed laborers, making the South Asian migrant populations more diverse. Meanwhile, the Chinese, too, emigrated in significant numbers. Between 1845 and 1900, forces such as population pressure, a shortage of cultivable land, and social turmoil drove 800,000 Chinese to seek new homes in North and South America, New Zealand, Hawaii, and the West Indies. Close to four times as many settled in Southeast Asia.

At the same time, industrial changes caused millions to migrate *within* their own countries or to neighboring ones, seeking employment in the burgeoning cities or other opportunities in frontier regions. In North America, hundreds of thousands headed west, while millions relocated from the countryside to the cities. In Asia, about 10 million Russians went east to Siberia and central Asia, and 2 million Koreans moved northwest to Manchuria. In Africa, small numbers of South Africans moved north into Northern and Southern Rhodesia in search of arable land and precious metals. Across the world, gold rushes, silver rushes, copper rushes, and a diamond rush took people across landmasses and across oceans. Mostly men, these emigrants were hell-bent on profit and often willing to destroy the land in order to extract precious commodities as quickly as possible.

People traveled with varying credentials and goals. Some went as colonial officials or soldiers; some as missionaries or big-game hunters—most of these folks did not plan to stay. Merchants and traders were more likely to settle in for the long term. Several million East Asians (mostly Chinese) went to the Philippines and South Africa, California and Cuba, British Columbia and Singapore, Guyana and Trinidad, replacing freed slaves on plantations or doing construction. Japanese laborers migrated to Peru to mine guano for fertilizer and to Hawaii to harvest sugar.

Migrants took big risks. Travel was often hazardous, and leaving behind native cultures and kin groups was painful. Many experienced conflicts with resident populations, as did Chinese migrants who ventured into Taiwan and other frontier regions. In the cities, tensions mounted as migrant workers faced low wages, poor working and living conditions, and barriers to higher-paying positions. In China, women without male relatives to protect them sometimes suffered abuse or exploitation. And yet, the economic rewards were substantial enough that the risks of sending the men abroad seemed worth taking.

Until 1914, governments imposed almost no controls on immigration or emigration. The Qing government tried to restrict emigration into the Manchus' northeastern homelands, but it failed. The United States allowed entry to anyone who was not a prostitute, a convict, or a "lunatic"; but in 1882, racist reactions spurred legislation that barred entry to almost all Chinese. Travel within Europe required no passports or work permits; foreign-born criminals were subject to deportation, but that was the extent of immigration policy. In fact, there generally was no reason to have an immigration policy, because immigration seemed doubly good: emigrants allowed large productivity gains in the countries they *left* (because low-productivity populations departed), and immigrants fueled economic growth in the countries they *entered*. This was especially true in North America, where funds were flowing for building railroads and other infrastructure, and where a growing population meant growing consumer markets. Overall, immigration to the New World prompted enormous leaps in productivity.

URBAN LIFE AND CHANGING IDENTITIES Cities boomed, with both positive and negative repercussions. Tokyo's population climbed from 500,000 in 1863 to 1,750,000 in 1908, and London's passed 6.5 million. Major cities faced housing shortages, despite governments' massive rebuilding and beautification projects. This was the era in which city planning came into its own—to widen and regularize thoroughfares for train and streetcar traffic, and to make crowded city life attractive to new inhabitants. City governments in Paris, New York, Cairo, Buenos Aires, and Brussels spent lavishly on opera houses, libraries, sewers, and parks, hoping to ward off disease and crime and to impress others with their modernity. Still, modern amenities did not yet make much difference for the vast majority of city dwellers, who labored long (if they could find steady work) for low wages and lived in overcrowded and unsanitary conditions.

Life in the metropolis at the turn of the century was different from city life in the mid-1800s. Workplaces were farther away from residences, and different social classes lived in separate districts. The lives of western women in particular were transformed. They had long worked as domestic servants, textile workers, or agricultural laborers, but now some took positions as shop girls, secretaries, or—thanks to educational opportunities—teachers; a few became doctors, although their practices were largely limited to treating other women. Increasing female literacy and the falling price of books and magazines gave western women access to new models of acceptable behavior. In cities it became respectable, even fashionable, for women to be seen on the boulevards. The availability in some places of ready-made clothes and packaged goods offered relief from household drudgery (provided one could afford them). Yet, for most women, leisure time and luxury consumption were still dreams more than realities.

Personal and national identities now came under scrutiny, not just in cities but in entire nations. In response to political

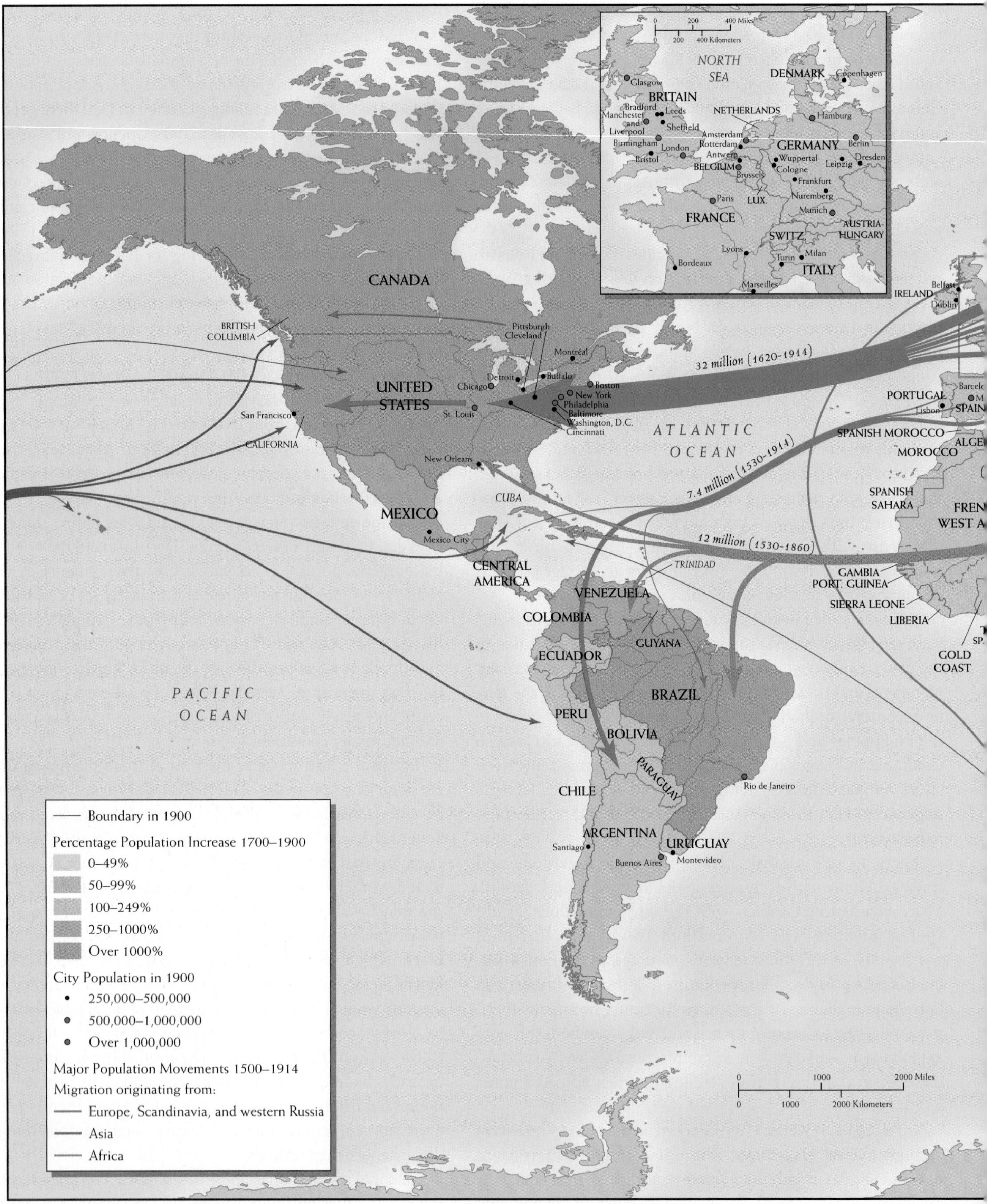
0 200 400 Miles
0 200 400 Kilometers
NORTH SEA
DENMARK
Copenhagen
Glasgow
BRITAIN
Bradford
Leeds
Manchester and Liverpool
Sheffield
Birmingham
London
Bristol
NETHERLANDS
Amsterdam
Rotterdam
Antwerp
BELGIUM
Brussels
Hamburg
GERMANY
Berlin
Wuppertal
Cologne
Leipzig
Dresden
Frankfurt
Nuremberg
Munich
Paris
LUX.
FRANCE
AUSTRIA-HUNGARY
SWITZ.
Lyons
Turin
Milan
Bordeaux
ITALY
Marseilles
IRELAND
Belfast
Dublin
CANADA
BRITISH COLUMBIA
Pittsburgh
Cleveland
Montréal
Detroit
Buffalo
Boston
New York
Philadelphia
Baltimore
Washington, D.C.
Cincinnati
Chicago
St. Louis
UNITED STATES
San Francisco
CALIFORNIA
New Orleans
32 million (1620–1914)
PORTUGAL
Lisbon
SPAIN
Barcelo
SPANISH MOROCCO
MOROCCO
ALGE
ATLANTIC OCEAN
7.4 million (1530–1914)
12 million (1530–1860)
CUBA
MEXICO
Mexico City
CENTRAL AMERICA
TRINIDAD
SPANISH SAHARA
FREN WEST A
GAMBIA
PORT. GUINEA
SIERRA LEONE
LIBERIA
GOLD COAST
SP.
VENEZUELA
COLOMBIA
GUYANA
ECUADOR
BRAZIL
PERU
BOLIVIA
PARAGUAY
Rio de Janeiro
CHILE
ARGENTINA
URUGUAY
Santiago
Buenos Aires
Montevideo
PACIFIC OCEAN
Boundary in 1900
Percentage Population Increase 1700–1900
0–49%
50–99%
100–249%
250–1000%
Over 1000%
City Population in 1900
250,000–500,000
500,000–1,000,000
Over 1,000,000
Major Population Movements 1500–1914
Migration originating from:
Europe, Scandinavia, and western Russia
Asia
Africa
0 1000 2000 Miles
0 1000 2000 Kilometers

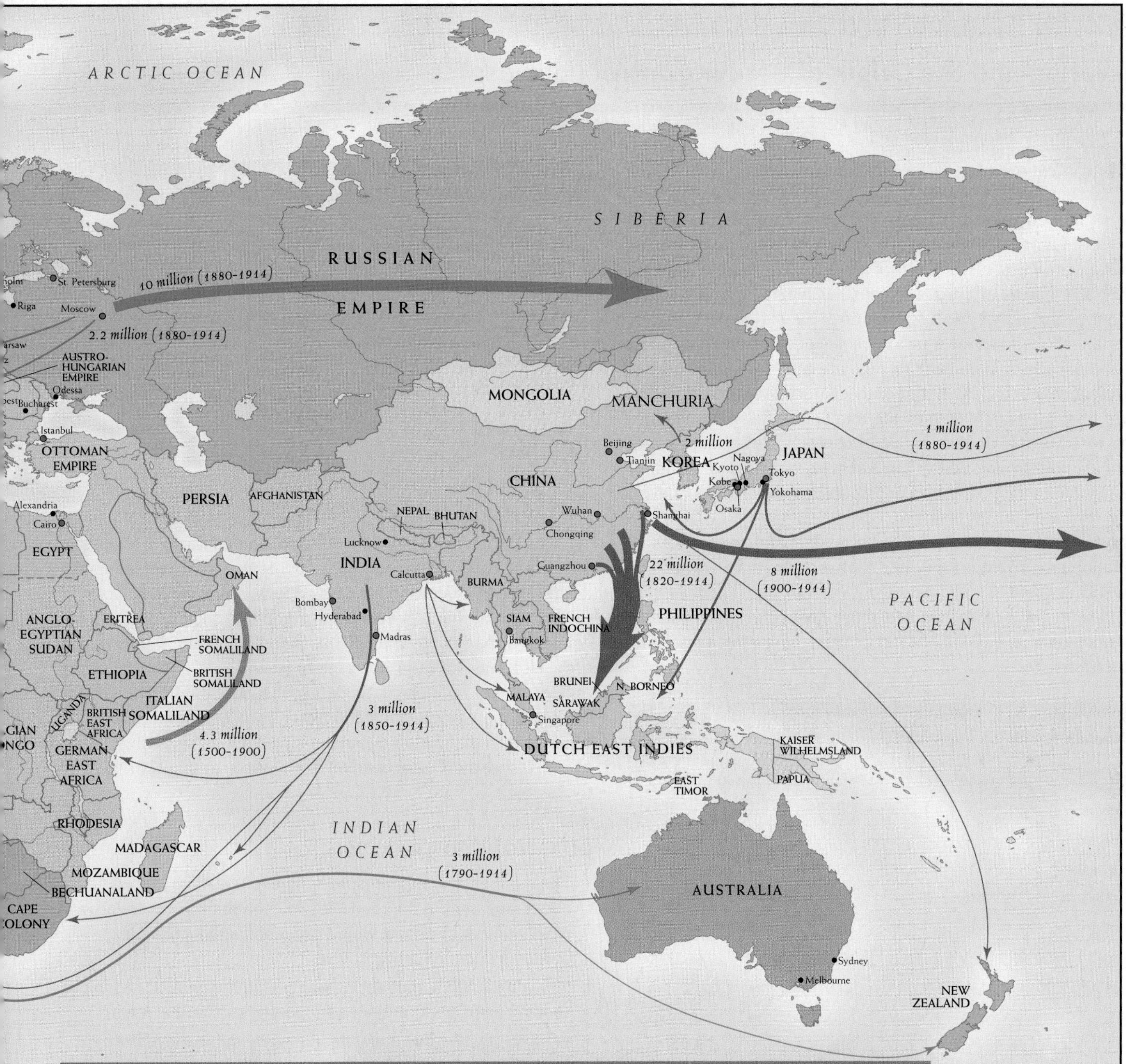

MAP 18.1 | Nineteenth-Century Migration

The nineteenth century witnessed a demographic revolution in terms of migration, urbanization patterns, and population growth. The world's population also rose from roughly 625 million in 1700 to 1.65 billion in 1900 (a two-and-a-half-fold increase).

- To what areas did most of the migrants from Europe go? What about the migrants from China, India, and Africa?
- What four areas saw the greatest population increase by 1900?
- How were migration flows and urbanization connected?
- What factor most accounted for this demographic trend, internal growth or external migration?

ANALYZING GLOBAL DEVELOPMENTS

Migration and the Origin of Border Control Policies

The movement of large numbers of people within and across regions—namely, the spread of the Mongols, the Atlantic world slave trade, and nineteenth-century migrations from Europe and Asia to the Americas—is not a new phenomenon in world history. What is relatively more recent to world history is the effort over the last 150 years to increase border control and identity documentation of people(s) on the move. Historian Adam McKeown in a recent work has demonstrated that the origins of the effort to regulate and document border control go back to late-nineteenth-century America and the efforts to substantially restrict the number of Asian immigrants trying to enter the United States. In contrast, earlier arguments held that modern day border control grew out of long-standing sovereignty practices of states and countries dating back to even earlier centuries.

In the first table below, we see a comparison of the rates of population growth from 1850–1950 between the major regions of the world.

In the second table, we see more concretely the number of people on the move in terms of their points of origin and destinations.

World Population Growth, 1850–1950 (in millions)

	1850 Population	1950 Population	Average Annual Growth (%)
Receiving			
Americas	59	325	1.72
North Asia	22	104	1.57
Southeast Asia	42	177	1.45
Sending			
Europe	265	515	0.67
South Asia	230	445	0.66
China	420	520	0.21
Africa	81	205	0.93
World	1,200	2,500	0.74

Global Long-Distance Migration, 1840–1940

Destination	Origins	Migrants (millions)	Auxiliary Origins
Americas	Europe	55–58	2.5 million from India, China, Japan, Africa
Southeast Asia, Indian Ocean Rim, Australasia	India South China	48–52	5 million from Africa, Europe, Northeast Asia, Middle East
Manchuria, Siberia, Central Asia, Japan	Northeast Asia Russia	46–51	

This data was compiled from port and customs statistics at significant entry points to major countries. What we see in the data is that the receiving nation's populations grew by a factor of 4.0-5.5 during this 100-year period, and that their overall growth was more than twice that of the "sending" regions during this time. Not only was the population growth rate of the receiving nations much more dramatic during this period, but the redistribution of the world's population was equally dramatic. In 1850, 10 percent of the world's population lived in the "receiving" areas; by 1950, nearly 25 percent of the world's population lived in those areas.

QUESTIONS FOR ANALYSIS

- The number of immigrants from Asia to the Americas was only about 3 percent of the total. Why do you think such a relatively small number of people would cause a dramatic change in border and identification control?
- Why do you think that during this period the populations in the sending areas also continued to grow at substantial rates?
- Why do you think so many people were on the move from South China and India to other parts of the Indian Ocean world? From northeast Asia to East Asia and Inner Asia?

Sources: Colin McEvedy and Richard Jones, Atlas of World Population History *(1978); Adam McKeown, "Global Migration, 1846–1940,"* Journal of World History *15 (2004); McKeown,* Melancholy Order: Asian Migration and the Globalization of Borders *(2008).*

and economic upheaval, social disruption, massive migration, and modern thinking, western notions of race became key in defining identities and justifying inequalities. Seeking to unify nations internally, many writers, artists, and political leaders created mythic histories that aimed to give diverse groups a common story of nationhood. Such inventions were crucial in nation building, but they also fueled conflict among nations that in 1914 erupted in the Great War—an event that would generate another huge wave of emigration, much of it involuntary.

Urban Transportation. (Left) *Streetcars in Tokyo, Japan's capital, are watched over by sword-bearing patrolmen in 1905, during the Russo-Japanese War. The first electric streetcar began running in Japan in 1895. Note the elevated electricity lines, which dated to the 1880s.* (Right) *Heavy traffic in London, in about 1910, points to an urban population on the move. Note the many kinds of transportation—motor buses as well as horse-drawn wagons; the railings in the foreground mark the entrance to the Underground, or subway.*

DISCONTENT WITH IMPERIALISM

In the decades before the Great War, opposition to European domination in Asia and Africa gathered strength. During the nineteenth century, as Europeans touted imperialism as a "civilizing mission," local prophets had voiced alternative visions contesting European supremacy (see Chapter 16). Although these movements were quashed, opposition did not stop. While imperialists consolidated their hold, suppression of unrest in the colonies required ever more force and bloodshed. As the cycle of resistance and repression escalated, many Europeans back home questioned the harsh means of controlling their colonies. By 1914, these questions were intensifying as colonial subjects across Asia and Africa challenged imperial domination. In China, too, where Europeans were scrambling for trading opportunities without actually establishing formal colonial power, local populations were resisting foreign influences.

Unrest in Africa

Africa witnessed many anticolonial uprisings in the first decades of colonial rule (see Map 18.2). Violent conflicts embroiled not only the Belgians and the Germans, who ruled autocratically, but also the British, whose colonial system left traditional African rulers in place. These uprisings made Europeans uneasy: why were Africans resisting regimes that had huge advantages in firepower and transport and that were bringing medical skills, literacy, and other fruits of European civilization? Some Europeans concluded that Africans were too stubborn or unsophisticated to appreciate Europe's generosity. Others, shocked by colonial cruelty, called for reform. A few radicals even demanded an end to imperialism.

African opposition was too spirited to ignore. Across the continent, organized armies and unorganized villagers rose up to challenge the European conquest. The resistance of villagers in the central highlands of British East Africa (Kenya) was so intense that the British mounted savage punitive expeditions to bring the area back under their control. Nonetheless, Africans continued to revolt against imperial authority—especially in areas where colonial rulers imposed forced labor, increased taxes, and appropriated land.

THE ANGLO-BOER WAR The continent's most devastating anticolonial uprising occurred in South Africa. This unique struggle pitted two white communities against each other: the British in the Cape Colony and Natal against the Afrikaners,

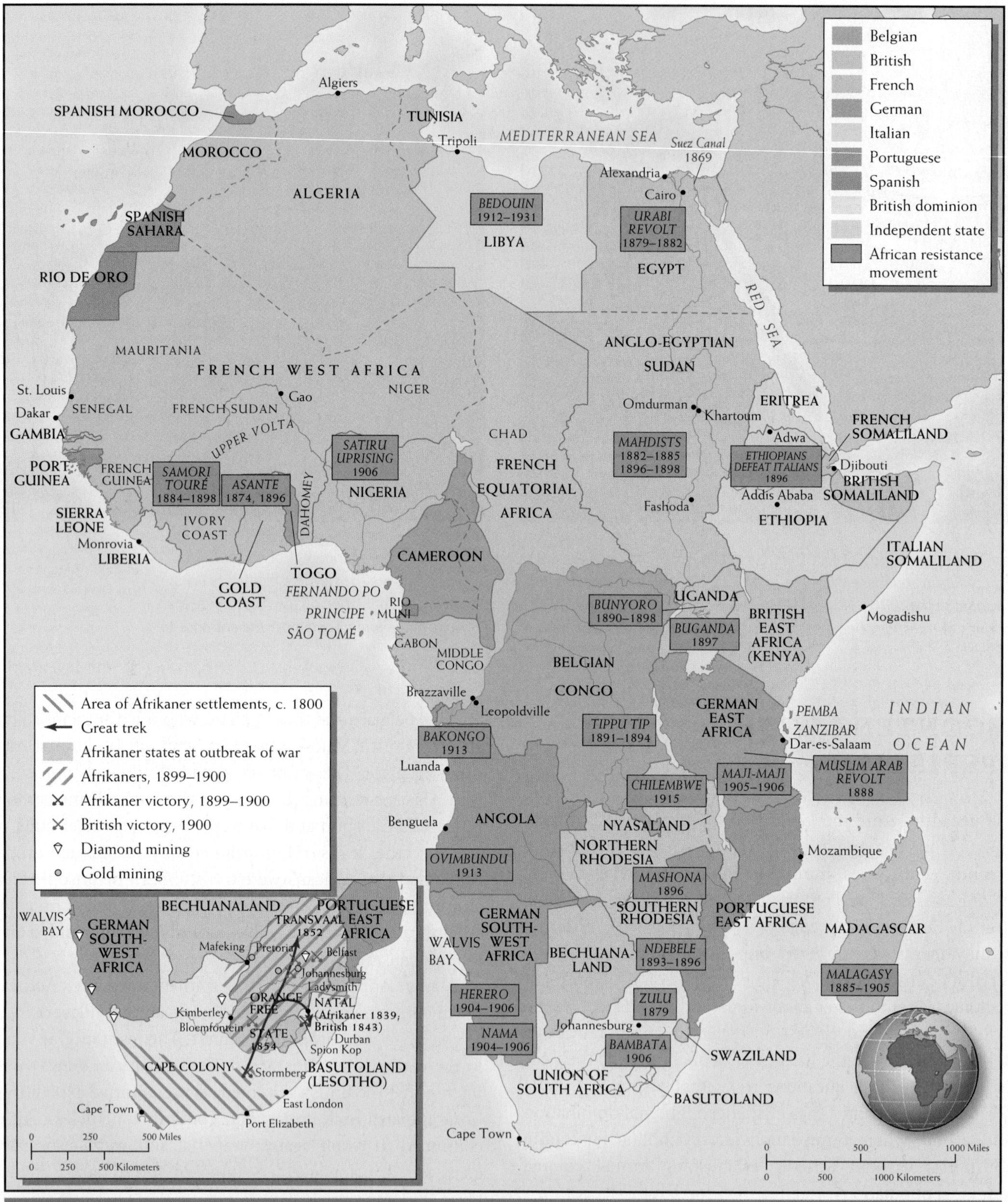

MAP 18.2 | Uprisings and Wars in Africa

The European partition and conquest of Africa were violent affairs.

• How many separate African resistance movements can you count on this map? • Where was resistance the most prolonged? • According to your reading, why were Ethiopians, who sustained their autonomy, able to do what other African opponents of European armies were not?

descendants of original Dutch settlers who lived in the Transvaal and the Orange Free State (see Map 18.2 inset). Although two white regimes were the main adversaries, the **Anglo-Boer War** (1899–1902) involved the area's 4 million black inhabitants as fully as its 1 million whites. Its horrors also traumatized the British at home, who regarded themselves as Europe's most enlightened and efficient colonial rulers.

The war's origins lay in the discovery of gold in the Transvaal in the mid-1880s. As the area rapidly became Africa's richest state, the prospect that Afrikaner republics might become the powerhouse in southern Africa was more than British imperialists could accept. Joseph Chamberlain, colonial secretary in London, and Cecil Rhodes, the leading politician in the Cape Colony, found allies in the British population living in the Afrikaner republics. Lacking voting rights and experiencing other forms of discrimination, these outsiders protested the Afrikaner governments' policies and pressed the British government to intervene. For their part, Afrikaner leaders emphasized the rights of a free people to resist.

Fearing that war was inevitable, the president of the Transvaal launched a preemptive strike against the British. In late 1899, Afrikaner forces crossed into South Africa. Fighting a relentless guerrilla campaign, Afrikaners waged a war that would last three years and cost Britain 20,000 soldiers and £200 million. Britain's frustrated attempts to respond to the Afrikaner insurgency and to cut its soldiers off from the local civilian population led the British to institute a terrifying innovation: the concentration camp. At one moment in the war, at least 155,000 captured men, women, and children were held in camps surrounded by barbed wire. Nor were the camps restricted to Afrikaners. The British also rounded up Africans whom they feared would side with the "anticolonial" Dutch descendants. The suffering and loss in these camps were appalling; by the war's end, 28,000 Afrikaner women and children, as well as 14,000 black Africans, had perished there. Thanks to a new sort of international actor, the war correspondent, newspaper reports and photographs brought the misery of the Anglo-Boer War, including reports of its atrocities, back to Europe. The British were scandalized by how long it had taken for the "empire on which the sun never sets" to subdue such a ragtag opponent, but they did, eventually, win the war, bringing the Transvaal and the Orange Free State—with their vast gold reserves—under their control.

OTHER STRUGGLES IN COLONIZED AFRICA The revulsion that the Anglo-Boer War sent through western public opinion deepened after Germany's activities in Africa also went

The Anglo-Boer War. *The British sent a large contingent of troops to South Africa to deal with the resistance of the two Boer republics—the Orange Free State and the Transvaal. The loss of life and the cruelties inflicted on soldiers and civilians alike during the war, which lasted from 1899 to 1902, did much to undermine the British people's views of their imperial mission. Transvaal and the Orange Free State fought valiantly to keep from becoming part of the British Empire. In the end, they lost.*

Extermination of the Herero. *The Germans carried out a campaign of near-extermination against the Herero population in German Southwest Africa in 1904–5. Nearly 90 percent of the Herero were killed. In this 1906 photograph, a German soldier stands guard over Herero women and children in a prison camp.*

brutally wrong. Germany had established colonies in Southwest Africa (present-day Namibia), Cameroon, and Togo in 1884 and in East Africa in 1885. In German Southwest Africa, the Herero and San people resisted German settlers' attempts to seize their native pasture lands, and in German East Africa (modern-day Tanzania), the Muslim Arab peoples rebelled. Between 1904 and 1906, fighting in German Southwest Africa escalated to such an extent that the German commander issued a genocidal extermination order against the Herero population. Equally troubling was the Maji-Maji Revolt in German East Africa of 1905–1906, described at the beginning of this chapter.

Apologists for imperial violence tried to dampen public outcries. Journalists portrayed the Maji-Maji rebels as fanatics in the thrall of a demonic African witch doctor, Kinjikitile Ngwale, and the Afrikaners as uncouth ruffians who deserved what they got. According to defenders, the unjustifiable horrors of Leopold's Belgian Congo (see Chapter 17) were an exception, created by a dissolute and reckless monarch who had no scruples when it came to enhancing his own wealth and political power. Apologists from all the European powers argued that these incidents did not represent the reality of empire—at least not *their* nation's empire. Thus, the British denounced the Belgians to highlight their own benevolence, while the French spread gory images of German repression to underscore their own success at uplifting Africans. Portraying Africans as either accepting subjects or childlike primitives, the European powers sought to redouble their coercive efforts and, in many cases, the number of officials and soldiers stationed in the colonies.

The Boxer Uprising in China

At the turn of the century, forces from within and without also unsettled China. Although China's turmoil differed from Africa's, it, too, arose from concern about European intrusions. As the population swelled to over half a billion and outstripped the country's resources, problems of landlessness, poverty, and peasant discontent (constants in China's modern history) led many to mourn the decay of political authority. In response, in 1898 the Qing emperor tried to modernize industry, agriculture, commerce, education, and the military. But opponents blocked the emperor's designs. Before long the emperor faced house arrest in the palace, while the Empress Dowager Cixi, whom conservatives supported, actually ruled.

EXTERNAL FACTORS The breakdown of dynastic authority originated largely with foreign pressure. For one thing, China's defeat in the Sino-Japanese War of 1894–1895 (see Chapter 17) was deeply humiliating. Although Japan, which acquired Taiwan as its first major colony, was the immediate beneficiary of the war, Britain, France, Germany, and Russia quickly scrambled for additional concessions from China. They demanded that the Qing government grant them specific areas within China as their respective "spheres of influence" (see Map 18.3). The United States argued instead for maintaining an "open door" policy that would keep access available to all traders. But the Americans also wanted the Qing to accept western norms of political and economic exchange and to acknowledge the superiority

Cixi's Allies. *The Empress Dowager Cixi emerged as the most powerful figure in the Qing court in the last decades of the dynasty, from the 1860s until her death in 1908. Highly able, she approved many of the early reforms of the Self-Strengthening movement, but her commitment to the preservation of the Manchu Qing dynasty made her suspicious of more fundamental and wide-ranging changes. Here she is shown surrounded by court eunuchs; Cixi relied upon them, especially as her relationships with orthodox officials were often ambivalent.*

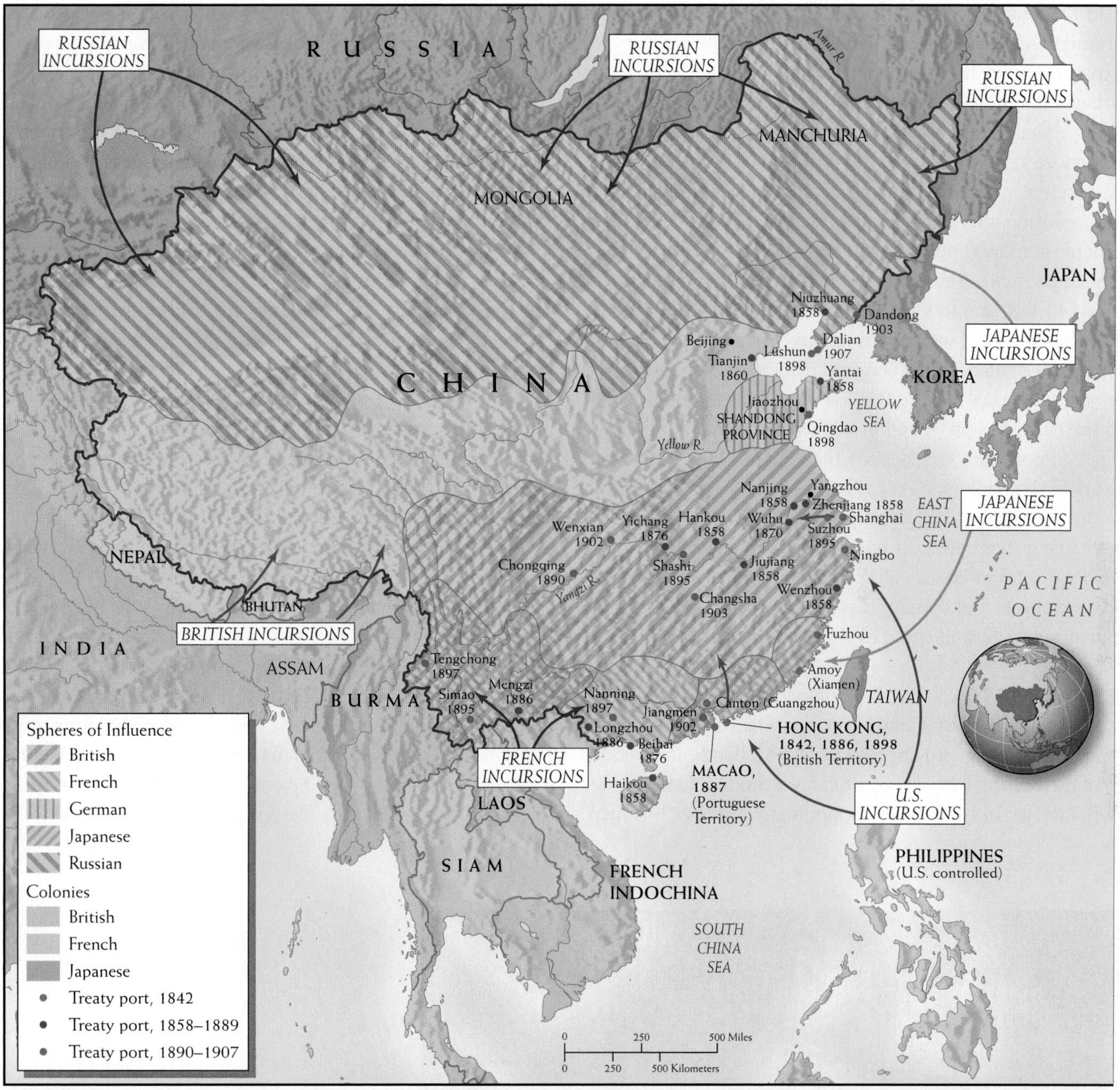

MAP 18.3 | Foreign Spheres of Influence in China, 1842–1907

While technically independent, the Qing dynasty could not prevent foreign penetration and domination of its economy during the nineteenth century.

• Which five powers established spheres of influence in China? • At what time was the greatest number of treaty ports established? According to your reading, what did the foreign powers hope to achieve within their spheres of influence? • What kinds of local opposition did the foreign influence inspire?

of Christian civilization. In response, some Chinese elites developed an anti-European stance while advocating the use of European ideas and technology to strengthen China itself.

The most explosive reaction to these pressures, the **Boxer Uprising**, started within the peasantry. Like colonized peoples in Africa, the Boxers violently resisted European meddling in their communities. And like the Taiping Rebellion decades earlier (see Chapter 16), the story of the Boxers was tied to missionary activities. Whereas in earlier centuries Jesuit missionaries had sought to convert the court and the elites, by the mid-nineteenth century the missionary goal was to convert commoners. After the Taiping Rebellion, Christian missionaries had streamed into China, impatient to make new converts in the hinterlands and confident of their governments' backing. With the Qing dynasty in a weakened state, Christian missionaries became more aggressive.

An incident in 1897, in which Chinese residents killed two German missionaries in the northern province of Shandong, brought tensions to a boil. In retribution, the German government demanded the right to construct three cathedrals, to remove hostile local officials, and to seize the northeastern port of Jiaozhou. As tensions mounted, martial arts groups in the region began to attack the missionaries and converts, calling for an end to the Christians' privileges. In early 1899, several of these groups united under the name Boxers United in Righteousness and adopted the slogan, "Support the Qing, destroy the foreign." Like the African followers of Kinjikitile, the Boxers believed that divine protection made them immune to all earthly weapons: "We requested the gods to attach themselves to our bodies. When they had done so, we became Spirit Boxers, after which we were invulnerable to swords and spears, our courage was enhanced, and in fighting we were unafraid to die and dared to charge straight ahead."

INTERNAL FACTORS The Boxer movement flourished especially where natural disasters and harsh economic conditions spread hardships. Shandong province had suffered floods throughout much of the decade, followed by prolonged drought in the winter of 1898. Idle, restless, and often hungry, many peasants, boatmen, and peddlers turned to the Boxers for support. They also liked the Boxers' message that the gods were angry over the foreign presence in general and Christian activities in particular.

As these activists, many of them young men, swelled the Boxers' ranks, women also found a place in the movement. The so-called Red Lanterns were mostly teenage girls and unmarried women who announced their loyalty by wearing red garments. Although the Red Lanterns were segregated from the male Boxers—they worshipped at their own altars and practiced martial arts at separate boxing grounds—they were important to the movement in counteracting the influence of Christian women. Indeed, one of the Boxers' greatest fears was that cunning Christian women would use their guile to weaken the Boxers' spirits. The rebels believed that their invulnerability came from spirit possession and that the inherent polluting power of women threatened their "magic." However, they claimed that the "purity" of the Red Lanterns could counter this threat. The Red Lanterns were supposedly capable of incredible feats: they could walk on water or fly through the air. Belief in their magical powers provided critical assistance for the uprising.

As the movement gained momentum, the Qing vacillated between viewing the Boxers as a threat to order and embracing them as a force to check foreign intrusion. Early in 1900, Qing troops clashed with the Boxers in an escalating cycle of violence. By spring, however, the Qing could no longer control the tens of thousands of Boxers roaming the vicinities of Beijing and Tianjin. Embracing the Boxers' cause, the empress dowager declared war against the foreign powers in June 1900.

The Boxer Uprising in China. *The Boxer Uprising was eventually suppressed by a foreign army made up of Japanese, European, and American troops that arrived in Beijing in August 1900. The picture here shows fighting between the foreign troops and the combined forces of Qing soldiers and the Boxers. After a period of vacillation, the Qing court, against the advice of some of its officials, finally threw its support behind the quixotic struggle of the Boxers against the foreign presence, laying the ground for the military intervention of the imperialist powers.*

FOREIGN INVOLVEMENT AND AFTERMATH Acting without any discernible plan or leadership, the Boxers went after Christian and foreign symbols and persons. They harassed and sometimes killed Chinese Christians in parts of northern China, destroyed railroad tracks and telegraph lines, and attacked owners of foreign objects such as lamps and clocks. In Beijing, the Boxers besieged foreign embassy compounds where diplomats and their families cowered in fear. The Boxers also reduced the Southern Cathedral to ruins and then besieged the Northern Cathedral, where more than 3,000 Catholics and 40 French and Italian marines had sought refuge. Those inside were rescued only with the arrival of a foreign expeditionary force.

In August 1900, a foreign army of 20,000 troops crushed the Boxers. About half came from Japan; the rest came primarily from Russia, Britain, Germany, France, and the United States. Thereafter, the victors forced the Chinese to sign the punitive Boxer Protocol. Among other punishments, it required the regime to pay an exorbitant compensation in gold (about twice the empire's annual income) for damages to foreign life and property. The protocol also authorized western powers to station troops in Beijing. Furthermore, although the defeat prompted the Qing to make a last-ditch effort at reform, it dealt another blow to the dynasty's standing both internally and externally.

Even in defeat, the Boxers' anti-western uprising showed how much had changed in China since the Taiping Rebellion. Although the Boxers were primarily peasants, even they had felt the unsettledness generated by European inroads into China. Indeed, the Europeans' commercial and spiritual reach, once confined to elites and port cities, had extended across much of China. Whereas the Taiping Rebellion had mobilized millions against the Qing, the Boxers remained loyal to the dynasty and focused their wrath on foreigners and Chinese Christians. The Boxer Rebellion, like the Maji-Maji Revolt in East Africa, revealed the widespread political opposition to westernization and the willingness of local disaffected populations to resist western programs.

WORLDWIDE INSECURITIES

Protests against European intrusion in Africa and China were distant movements that most Europeans could disregard. News of unrest in the colonies and in China generally did not lead them to question their ways. Instead, it reinforced their belief in the inferiority of other cultures. In Africa, for example, unrest in a rival's empire was taken as a sign of poor management. Anxiety here reflected the difficulty of the "civilizing mission," although a few did begin to question imperial ethics. At the same time, however, conflicts closer to home tore at European and North American confidence. These included rivalries among western powers, the booms and busts of expanding industrial economies, new types of class conflict, challenges about the proper roles of women, and problems of uncontrolled urbanization (see again Map 18.1).

Imperial Rivalries at Home

The rise of a European-centered world deepened rivalries within Europe and promoted instability there. Numerous factors fostered conflict, including France's smoldering resentment at its defeat in the Franco-Prussian War (see Chapter 17), but tension increased as the European states competed for raw materials and colonial footholds. Even as these powers built up their supply of weapons, as well as ships and railroads to transport troops, not everyone supported the buildup. Many Europeans, for example, disapproved of spending on massive steam-powered warships. Others warned that the arms race would end in a devastating war.

Intra-European rivalry had powerful effects on Germany and Russia. In fact, the unifications of Germany and Italy at the expense of France and the Austrian Empire had smashed the old balance of power in Europe. New alliances began to crystallize after 1890, as German–French hostility persisted and German–Russian friendship broke down. This left Germany surrounded by foes: Britain and France to the west, Russia to the east. As ethnic nationalism spread among the Arabs, Turks, Czechs, and southern Slavs, the multinational Ottoman and Habsburg empires began to fragment; the Balkans in particular became a hotbed of interethnic violence. Roiled by internal conflicts, the two venerable empires looked likely to collapse, leaving power vacuums in central and southeastern Europe. Sensing conflict on the horizon, Britain, Germany, France, and Russia entered into a massive arms race.

FINANCIAL, INDUSTRIAL, AND TECHNOLOGICAL INSECURITIES Economic developments helped make powers "great," but they could also unsettle societies. Indeed, pride about wealth and growth coincided with laments about changes in national and international economies. To begin with, Americans and Europeans recognized that the small-scale, laissez-faire capitalism championed by Adam Smith (see Chapter 14) was giving way to an economic order dominated by huge, heavily capitalized firms. Gone, it seemed, was Smith's vision of many small producers in vigorous competition with one another, all benefiting from efficient—but not exploitative—divisions of labor.

Instead of smooth progress, the economy of the West in the nineteenth century bounced between booms and busts: long-term business cycles of rapid growth followed by counter-cycles of stagnation. Late in the century, the pace of economic change accelerated. Large-scale steel production, railroad building, and textile manufacturing expanded at breakneck speed, while

Labor Disputes. *The late nineteenth century witnessed a surge in industrial strife, worker strikes, and violent suppression of labor movements.* (Left) *One of the deadliest confrontations in the United States occurred in May 1892, when a strike against the Carnegie Steel Company escalated into a gunfight, which left ten dead and many more wounded. Here, a group of striking workers keeps watch over the steel mill in Homestead, Pennsylvania.* (Right) *Striking dock workers rally in London's Trafalgar Square, 1911. By this time, residents of European cities were used to seeing crowds of protesters pressing for improved working conditions or political reform.*

waves of bank closures, bankruptcies, and agricultural crises ruined many small property owners, including farmers. By the century's end, European and North American economies were dominated as never before by a few large-scale firms.

GLOBAL FINANCIAL AND INDUSTRIAL INTEGRATION

These were years of heady international financial integration. More and more countries joined the world system of borrowing and lending; more and more countries were linked financially because their national currencies were all backed by gold. At the hub of this world system were the banks of London, which since the Napoleonic wars had been a major source of capital for international borrowers.

The rise of giant banks and huge industrial corporations caused alarm, for it seemed to signal an end to free markets and competitive capitalism. In the United States, an entire generation of journalists cut their teeth exposing the skullduggery (shady dealings) of financial and industrial giants. These "muckrakers" portrayed the captains of finance like J. P. Morgan and John D. Rockefeller as bent on amassing private power at the expense of working families and public authorities. In Europe, too, critics lamented a similar trend in which lack of competition created greater disparities of wealth between the owners of firms and the workforce.

Rather than longing for the return of truly free markets, many critics sought reforms that would protect people from economic instability. Indeed, starting in the 1890s, the reaction against economic competition gathered steam. Producers, big and small, grew unhappy with supply and demand mechanisms. To cope with an unruly market, farmers created cooperatives. For their part, big industrialists fashioned monopolies, or cartels, in the name of improving efficiency, correcting failures in the market, and heightening profits. At the same time, government officials and academic specialists worried that modern economies were inherently unstable, prone to overproduce, and vulnerable to bankruptcy and crisis. The solution, many economists thought, was for the state to manage the market's inefficiencies.

FINANCIAL CRISES Banking especially seemed in need of closer government supervision. Many industrial societies already had central banks, and London's Bank of England had long since overseen local and international money markets. But public institutions did not yet have the resources to protect all investments during times of economic crisis. Between 1890 and 1893, fully 550 American banks collapsed, and only the intervention of J. P. Morgan prevented the depletion of the nation's gold reserves.

The road to regulation, however, was hardly smooth. In 1907, a more serious crisis threatened, caused by a panic on Wall Street that led to a run on the banks. Once again, it fell to J. P. Morgan to rescue the American dollar from financial panic—by compelling financier after financier to commit unprecedented funds (eventually $35 million) to protect banks and trusts against depositors' panic. Morgan himself lost $21 million and emerged from the bank panic convinced that some sort of public oversight was needed. By 1913, the U.S. Congress ratified the Federal Reserve Act, creating boards to monitor the supply and demand of the nation's money.

The crisis of 1907 showed how national financial matters could quickly become international affairs. The sell-off of the shares of banks and trusts in the United States also led American investors to withdraw their funds from other countries that relied on American capital. As a result, Canada, for instance, suffered a bank crisis of its own. Countries like Egypt and Mexico, far apart geographically yet linked through international capital, also suffered either withdrawal of investors' funds or a suspension of new investments and a string of bankruptcies. Although the head of Mexico's government, General Porfirio Díaz, tried to regain investors' confidence and their funds, Mexico fell into a severe recession as U.S. capital dried up. In turn, Mexicans lost faith in their own economic—and political—system. Unemployed and suffering new hardships, many Mexicans flocked to Díaz's political opponents, who eventually raised the flag of rebellion in 1910. A year later, the entire regime collapsed in revolution (see below).

INDUSTRIALIZATION AND THE MODERN ECONOMY Just as financial circuits linked nations as never before, so did industrialization. Backed by big banks, industrialists could afford to extend their enterprises physically and geographically. So heavy industries now came to new places. In Russia, for example, industrial activity quickened. With loans from European (especially French, Belgian, and British) investors, Russia built railways, telegraph lines, and factories and developed coal, iron, steel, and petroleum industries. By 1900, Russia was producing half of the world's oil and a considerable amount of steel. Yet industrial development remained uneven: southern Europe and the American South continued to lag behind northern regions. The gap was even more pronounced in colonial territories, which contained few industrial enterprises aside from railroad building and mining.

By 1914, the factory and the railroad had become global symbols of the modern economy—and of its positive and negative effects. Everywhere, the coming of the railroad to one's town or village was a big event: for some, it represented an exhilarating leap into the modern world; for others, a terrifying abandonment of the past. Ocean liners, automobiles, and airplanes, likewise, could be both dazzling and disorienting. The older conservative elite found technological development more worrisome than did urban liberals, who increasingly set state policies.

For ordinary people, the new economy brought benefits and drawbacks. Factories produced cheaper goods, but they belched clouds of black smoke. Railways offered faster transport, but they ruined small towns unlucky enough to be left off the branch line. Machines (when operating properly) were more efficient than human and animal labor, but workers who used them felt reduced to machines themselves. Indeed, the American Frederick Winslow Taylor proposed a system of "scientific management" to make human bodies perform more like machines, maximizing the efficiency of workers' movements. But workers did not want to be managed or to cede control of the pace of production to employers. Labor's resistance to "Taylorization" led to numerous strikes. For strikers, as for conservatives, the course of progress had taken an unsettling turn.

The "Woman Question"

Complicating the situation was turmoil about the politics of domesticity, or the "woman question." In the West, female activists demanded that women be given more rights as citizens, and more radical voices called for fundamental changes to the family and the larger society. At the same time, imperial architects claimed that colonial rule was bringing great improvements to women in Asia and Africa. But the "woman question" was no more easily settled there than elsewhere.

WOMEN'S ISSUES IN THE WEST In western countries, for most of the nineteenth century, a belief in "separate spheres" had supposedly confined women to domestic matters, while leaving men in charge of public life and economic undertakings. (In practice, only women from middle- and upper-class families avoided working outside the home for wages.) Men did not mind having women work for their charities or churches, or educate their daughters at home. But most men as well as most women continued to think that higher education and public activism were not suitable for "ladies"—and, if possible, these "ladies" too should not have to labor outside the home or acquire a profession. But as economic developments created new jobs for women and greater access to education, women who craved new opportunities increasingly did find work as teachers, secretaries, typists, department store clerks, social workers, and telephone operators. These jobs offered greater economic and social independence, at least for a few.

Changes in women's social status did not, however, translate into electoral reform at the national level. By midcentury, several women's suffrage movements had appeared, but these campaigns bore little immediate fruit. In 1868, women received the right to vote in local elections in Britain. Within a few years, Finland, Sweden, and some American states allowed single, property-owning women the right to cast ballots—again, only

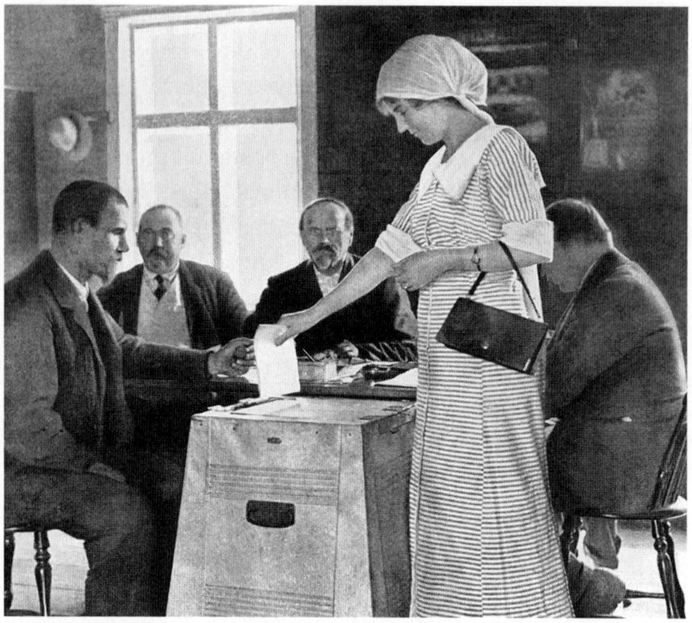

Woman Suffrage in Finland. *The British and then the French introduced the concept of citizenship with universal rhetoric, but in practice the category of citizen was generally restricted to property-holding males. Finland granted its women the right to vote in 1906, earlier than most countries. In this photograph, a Finnish woman casts her ballot in the election of 1906.*

in local elections. Women obtained the right to vote in national elections in New Zealand in 1893, in Australia in 1902, in Finland in 1906, and in Norway in 1913. Despite these gains, male alarmists portrayed women's suffrage and women's rights as the beginning of civilization's end.

Quietly, and without conferring with one another, many women began to take charge of their lives in another way, and that was to assert control over reproduction. Although in numerous countries the use of contraceptive devices was illegal, women still found ways to limit the number of children they bore. The French birthrate fell so precipitously in the second half of the nineteenth century that commentators began to worry about France's "degeneration." Early in the twentieth century, the birthrate in America was half of what it had been a century before. As women well knew, having fewer children was one way to raise the class status of the rest of the household, and to leave more income for the smaller family's education, housing, and leisure activities.

VARYING VIEWS ON FEMINISM Most middle-class women in Europe and the Americas were not seeking to make women equal to men. Indeed, many bourgeois women recoiled from the close relationships between socialism and feminism, and feared that too much equality would make women abominably "mannish." But there were radical women in Europe and America, as well as elsewhere, some of whom, like the Polish-German communist Rosa Luxemburg, became powerful philosophers and political organizers in their own right.

Radical women met stiff repression wherever they challenged the established order. This was especially true outside Europe and the Americas, where the feminist movement was not strong and where women's education and entry into the professions lagged far behind those of men. In 1903, China's Qiu Jin (1875–1907) left her husband and headed to Japan to study. There she befriended other radicals and made a name for herself by dressing in men's clothing, carrying a sword, and trying her hand at bomb making. Returning to China in 1906, she founded the *Chinese Women's Journal* (*Zhongguo nübao*) and wrote articles urging women to fight for their rights and to leave home if necessary. (See Primary Source: A Chinese Feminist Condemns Injustices to Women.) Qing authorities executed Qiu Jin after she participated in a failed attempt to topple the dynasty.

WOMEN'S STATUS IN COLONIES In the colonial world, the woman question was a contentious issue—but it was mainly argued among men. European authorities liked to boast that colonial rule improved women's status. Citing examples of traditional societies' subordination of women, they criticized as barbaric the veiling of women in Islamic societies, the binding of women's feet in China, widow burning (*sati*) in India, and female genital mutilation in Africa. Europeans believed that prohibiting such acts was a justification for colonial intervention.

And yet, for women in Africa, the Middle East, and India, colonialism added to their burdens. As male workers headed into the export economy, formerly shared agricultural work fell exclusively on women's shoulders. In Africa, for example, the opening of vast gold and diamond mines drew thousands of men away to work in the mines, leaving women to fend for themselves. Similarly, the rise of European-owned agricultural estates in Kenya and Southern Rhodesia depleted surrounding villages of male family members, who went to work on the estates. In these circumstances, women kept the local, food-producing economy afloat.

Nor did colonial "civilizing" rhetoric improve women's political or cultural circumstances. In fact, European missionaries preached a message of domesticity to Asian and African families, emphasizing that women's place was in the home raising children and that women's education should be different from men's. Thus males overwhelmingly dominated the new schools that Europeans built. Moreover, customary law in colonial Africa, as interpreted by chiefs who collaborated with colonial officials, favored men. As a result, African women often lost landholding and other rights that they had enjoyed before the Europeans' arrival. (See Primary Source: Industrialization and Women's Freedom in Egypt.)

PRIMARY SOURCE

A Chinese Feminist Condemns Injustices to Women

Although a small minority, Chinese feminists of the early twentieth century were vocal in condemning the injustices inflicted on women in China. In this essay from 1904, directed to her countrywomen, Qiu Jin compares the treatment of Chinese women to slavery. She also displays a strong nationalistic streak as she ties the future of Chinese women to the fate of the Chinese nation.

Alas! The greatest injustice in this world must be the injustice suffered by our female population of two hundred million. If a girl is lucky enough to have a good father, then her childhood is at least tolerable. But if by chance her father is an ill-tempered and unreasonable man, he may curse her birth: "What rotten luck: another useless thing." Some men go as far as killing baby girls while most hold the opinion that "girls are eventually someone else's property" and treat them with coldness and disdain. In a few years, without thinking about whether it is right or wrong, he forcibly binds his daughter's soft, white feet with white cloth so that even in her sleep she cannot find comfort and relief until the flesh becomes rotten and the bones broken. What is all this misery for? Is it just so that on the girl's wedding day friends and neighbors will compliment him, saying, "Your daughter's feet are really small"? Is that what the pain is for?

But that is not the worst of it. When the time for marriage comes, a girl's future life is placed in the hands of a couple of shameless matchmakers and a family seeking rich and powerful in-laws. A match can be made without anyone ever inquiring whether the prospective bridegroom is honest, kind, or educated. On the day of the marriage the girl is forced into a red and green bridal sedan chair, and all this time she is not allowed to breathe one word about her future. . . .

When Heaven created people it never intended such injustice because if the world is without women, how can men be born? Why is there no justice for women? We constantly hear men say, "The human mind is just and we must treat people with fairness and equality." Then why do they greet women like black slaves from Africa?

How did inequality and injustice reach this state? . . .

I hope that we all shall put aside the past and work hard for the future. Let us all put aside our former selves and be resurrected as complete human beings. Those of you who are old, do not call yourselves old and useless. If your husbands want to open schools, don't stop them; if your good sons want to study abroad, don't hold them back. Those among us who are middle-aged, don't hold back your husbands lest they lose their ambition and spirit and fail in their work. After your sons are born, send them to schools. You must do the same for your daughters and, whatever you do, don't bind their feet. As for you young girls among us, go to school if you can. If not, read and study at home. Those of you who are rich, persuade your husbands to open schools, build factories, and contribute to charitable organizations. Those of you who are poor, work hard and help your husbands. Don't be lazy, don't eat idle rice. These are what I hope for you. You must know that when a country is near destruction, women cannot rely on the men any more because they aren't even able to protect themselves. If we don't take heart now and shape up, it will be too late when China is destroyed.

Sisters, we must follow through on these ideas!

QUESTIONS FOR ANALYSIS

- Identify at least three ways in which Chinese women suffer injustice, according to Qiu Jin.
- In what way does the Qiu Jin's comparison of Chinese women to "black slaves from Africa" reveal a growing global awareness within the Chinese population?
- Why is nationalism an important part of Qiu Jin's message?

Source: Qiu Jin, "An Address to Two Hundred Million Fellow Countrywomen." Reprinted with the permission of The Free Press, a division of Simon & Schuster, Inc., from Chinese Civilization: A Sourcebook, *Second Edition, revised and expanded by Patricia Buckley Ebrey.*

Class Conflict in a New Key

Capitalism's volatility shook confidence in free market economies and sharpened conflicts between classes; the tone of political debates was transformed as new, more strident voices called for radical change. Although living conditions for European and North American workers improved over time, widening inequalities in income and the slow pace of reform led to frustration. Most workers remained committed to peaceful agitation, but some radicals turned to violence. Often, especially in eastern Europe and Russia, the closed character of political systems fueled frustration—and radicalism. This was also the case in

PRIMARY SOURCE

Industrialization and Women's Freedom in Egypt

In this selection, taken from a 1909 lecture in Cairo open only to women, an educated upper-class Egyptian woman insists that female confinement is unnatural and absurd. She demands a place for women in the workplace. The writer, Bahithat al-Badiya, criticizes the effect of traditional religious practices on women's freedom and blames men for not allowing women to enter the professions and enjoy the freedoms that men take for granted.

Men say when we become educated we shall push them out of work and abandon the role for which God created us. But isn't it rather men who have pushed women out of work? Before, women used to spin and to weave cloth for clothes for themselves and their children, but men invented machines for spinning and weaving and put women out of work. . . . Since male inventors and workers have taken away a lot of our work should we waste our time in idleness or seek other work to occupy us? Of course, we should do the latter. . . . Obviously, I am not urging women to neglect their home and children to go out and become lawyers or judges or railway engineers. But if any of us wish to work in such professions our personal freedom should not be infringed. . . .

Men say to us categorically, "You women have been created for the house and we have been created to be bread-winners." Is this a God-given dictate? How are we to know this since no holy book has spelled it out? Political economy calls for a division of labor but if women enter the learned professions it does not upset the system. The division of labor is merely a human creation. . . . If men say to us that we have been created weak we say to them, "No it is you who made us weak through the path you made us follow." After long centuries of enslavement by men, our minds rusted and our bodies weakened. . . .

Men criticize the way we dress in the street. They have a point because we have exceeded the bounds of custom and propriety. . . . [But] veiling should not prevent us from breathing fresh air or going out to buy what we need if no one can buy it for us. It must not prevent us from gaining an education nor cause our health to deteriorate. When we have finished our work and feel restless and if our house does not have a spacious garden why shouldn't we go to the outskirts of the city and take the fresh air that God has created for everyone and not just put in boxes exclusively for men.

QUESTIONS FOR ANALYSIS

- How has al-Badiya's Muslim faith influenced her views on the role of women in society? Find two places in the reading where these influences are apparent.
- How have western influences affected her views on the role of women in society? Find at least two places in the reading where these influences are evident.

Source: Bahithat al-Badiya, "A Public Lecture for Women Only in the Club of the Umma Party," from "Industrialization and Women's Freedom in Egypt," in Opening the Gates: A Century of Arab Feminist Writing*, edited by Margot Badran and Miriam Cooke. Copyright © 1990. Reprinted with permission of Indiana University Press.*

Latin America, where even the middle classes were largely shut out of politics until new parties offered fresh opportunities for political expression. In Argentina, for example, urban workers found outlets for protest within movements known as **syndicalism** (the organization of workplace associations that included unskilled laborers), socialism, and **anarchism** (the belief that society should be a free association of members, not subject to government, laws, or police).

STRIKES AND REVOLTS In the Americas and in Europe, radicals adopted numerous tactics for asserting the interests of the working class. In Europe, the franchise was gradually expanded in hopes that the lower classes would prefer voting to revolution—and indeed, most of the new political parties that catered to workers had no desire to overthrow the state. But conservatives feared them anyway, especially as they gained electoral clout. The Labour Party, founded in Britain in 1900, quickly boasted a large share of the vote. By 1912, the German Social Democratic Party was the largest party in the Reichstag. But it was not the legally sanctioned parties that sparked violent street protests and strikes in the century's last decades. A whole array of syndicalists, anarchists, radical royalists, and revolutionary socialists sprang up in this period, making work stoppages everyday affairs.

Although the United States did not have similarly radical factions or successful labor parties, American workers were also organizing. The labor movement's power burst forth dramatically in 1894 when the American Railway Union launched a strike that spread across the nation. Spawned by wage cuts and firings following an economic downturn, the Pullman Strike (directed against the maker of railway sleeping cars, George Pullman) involved approximately 3 million workers. The strike's conclusion, however, revealed the enduring power of the status quo. After hiring replacement workers to break the strike, Pullman requested federal troops to protect his operation. When the troops arrived, infuriated strikers reacted with violence—which led to a further crackdown by the government against the union. After its leaders were jailed, the strike collapsed.

A few upheavals from below did succeed, at least briefly. In 1905, in the wake of the Russo-Japanese War (in which the Russians lost to the Japanese), revolt briefly shook the tsarist state and yielded a fledgling form of representative government. The revolutionaries tried some new forms, most notably workers' soviets, which were groups of delegates representing particular industries. Ultimately, however, the army put down both urban and rural unrest. Autocracy was reestablished. Both liberals and radicals were excluded from power.

REVOLUTION IN MEXICO Perhaps the most successful turn-of-the-century revolution occurred in Mexico. A peasant uprising, it thoroughly transformed the country. Fueled by the unequal distribution of land and by disgruntled workers, the **Mexican Revolution** erupted in 1910 when political elites split over the succession of General Porfirio Díaz after decades of his strong-arm rule. Dissidents balked when Díaz refused to step down, and peasants and workers rallied to the call to arms.

What destroyed the Díaz regime and its powerful army was the swelling flood of peasants, farmers, cattlemen, and rural workers who were desperate for a change in the social order. From the north (led by the charismatic Pancho Villa) to the south (under the legendary Emiliano Zapata), rural folk helped topple the Díaz regime. In the name of providing land for farmers and ending oligarchic rule, peasant armies defeated Díaz's troops and then proceeded to destroy many large estates. The fighting lasted for ten brutal years, during which almost 10 percent of the country's population perished.

Thereafter, political leaders had to accept popular demands for democracy, respect for the sovereignty of peasant communities, and land reform. As a result the Constitution of 1917 incorporated widespread reform, and by 1920 an emerging generation of politicians recognized the power of a militarized peasantry and initiated deep-seated changes in Mexico's social structure. These leaders also realized that their new regime had to appeal ideologically to common folk. Revolutionaries gave trade unions sweeping rights to organize, paving the way for nationalizing the country's mines and oil industries. But perhaps the radicals' most lasting legacy was the creation of rural

The Mexican Revolution. (Left) *By 1915, Mexican peasants, workers, and farmers had destroyed much of the old elitist system. This was the first popular, peasant revolution of the twentieth century. Among the most famous leaders were Pancho Villa and Emiliano Zapata. They are pictured here in the presidential office in the capital. Villa took the president's chair jokingly. Zapata, carrying the broad hat typical of his people, refused to wear military gear and glowered at the camera suspiciously.* (Right) *By the 1920s, Mexican artists and writers were putting recent events into images and words. Pictured here is one of the muralist Diego Rivera's paintings of the Mexican Revolution. Notice the nationalist interpretation: Porfirio Díaz's troops defend foreign oil companies and white aristocrats against middle-class and peasant (and darker-skinned) reformers who call for a "social revolution." Observe also the absence of women in this epic mural.*

CURRENT TRENDS IN WORLD HISTORY

Industrialization and Its Antidotes: Conservation and Regulation

As the impact of industrialization spread during the late nineteenth century, a few individuals, including those who championed rapid economic development, recognized that this progress brought unwanted consequences. A new awareness dawned—that while industrialization allowed production to increase dramatically, it also resulted in the depletion of natural resources and the degradation of the quality of life for humans. Awakened to the ecological costs of economic progress, these environmentalist pioneers tried to reverse a trend of humankind's growing tendency to pollute the environment, overgraze marginal areas, and exploit resources to their exhaustion.

One of the first world leaders to take seriously industrialization's threats to the environment—and to national character—was President Theodore Roosevelt. A man who delighted in hunting, riding, and testing himself against the elements, Roosevelt worried that as the United States became an increasingly industrialized and urbanized society, the American people would lose the courage, fitness, and "rugged individualism" that the taming of wildernesses had supposedly imbued in them. He was especially struck by George Perkins Marsh's 1864 *Man and Nature*, which explored the ways in which the depletion of forests and other natural resources had determined the rise and fall of civilizations around the ancient Mediterranean. If the United States failed to curb its destruction of woodlands, Marsh suggested, it faced a collapse similar to that of Greece and Rome. Although several "national" parks and forests had been founded before Roosevelt became U.S. president in 1901, he was extremely active in pushing forward legislation to conserve more land, especially in the West. By offering visitors the opportunity to experience wilderness conditions, the national parks were to provide a partial antidote to what Roosevelt saw as the effeminizing tendencies of modern society.

But Roosevelt had other objects in view, too, in pressing the state to take a more activist role in the economy. Noting that on the European continent, "progressives" and urban-based reformers were augmenting the reach and power of the state to combat economic inequalities and to build infrastructures that benefited all, Roosevelt pushed for a departure from the laissez-faire principles that had dominated American political-economic discourse in the last decades of the nineteenth century. With European state-funded projects like the straightening of the Rhine River in mind, Roosevelt argued that the state should itself tackle projects that were too large to be built by private enterprises.

In yet another area, Roosevelt created a national regulatory solution to a problem that the market could not solve by itself. In the decade or so before he came into office, newspaper reporters had exposed hundreds of schemes by sellers of home remedies such as Mrs. Winslow's Soothing Syrup to get rich by promising consumers that their "patent" medicines would cure any disease. In truth, many of these "medicines" contained alcohol, cocaine, or just cod-liver oil; some were harmful, others were simply useless. Other investigators, such as the novelist Upton Sinclair, exposed horrors in the meatpacking industry. Sinclair's realist novel *The Jungle* (1906), for example, contained

communes for Mexico's peasantry, especially for indigenous people or villagers who had taken on collective ways. These communal village holdings, called *ejidos*, sought to re-enliven a precolonial way of life. The revolution thus spawned a set of new national myths, based on the heroism of rural peoples, Mexican nationalism, and a celebration of the Aztec past.

PRESERVING ESTABLISHED ORDERS Although the Mexican Revolution succeeded in toppling the old elite, elsewhere in Latin America the ruling establishment remained united against assaults from below. Already in 1897, the Brazilian army had mercilessly suppressed a peasant movement in the northeastern part of the country. Moreover, in Cuba, the Spanish and then the American armies crushed tenant farmers' efforts to reclaim land from sugar estates. In Guatemala, Mayan Indians lost land to coffee barons.

Much the same occurred in Europe and the United States, where the preservation of established orders did not rest on repression alone. Here, too, elites grudgingly agreed to gradual change. Indeed, by the century's end, left-wing agitators, muckraking reporters, and middle-class reformers began to win meaningful social improvements. Unable to suppress the socialist movement, Otto von Bismarck, the German chancellor, defused the appeal of socialism by enacting social welfare measures in 1883–1884 (as did France in 1904 and England in 1906). He enacted legislation insuring workers against illness, accidents, and old age and establishing maximum working hours. In the United States, it took lurid journalistic accounts reports of extremely unsanitary workplace conditions and of workers falling into fat-rendering machines and being canned along with the beef. In the same year that Sinclair's hugely influential novel appeared, Roosevelt oversaw the creation of the Food and Drug Administration and the passage of the Pure Food and Drug Act. The FDA's charge was to implement this act and to look after public health—something that did not concern profit-hungry corporations—by regulating food and medicines against contamination. In the wake of the banking panic of 1907 too, Americans came to accept that they needed banking regulations as well, and in 1913 Congress enacted the Federal Reserve Act.

Americans were not alone in beginning to temper capitalism with regulation and industrialization with conservation. Europeans at last began to enact legislation to protect workers from dangerous workplaces, and to create large green spaces in cities so that the industrialized world might have "lungs" with which to breathe. In Argentina, many were drawn to mountainous regions to escape becoming too "soft" in urban surroundings, and a conservation movement began that would hit its stride in the 1930s. Although such developments only slightly moderated the industrialized world's contributions to environmental degradation and the exploitation of mass consumers, they did signal the reality that some, at least, had begun to recognize that progress, too, had its price.

Patent Medicines. *Like Mrs. Winslow's Soothing Syrup, Hamlin's Wizard Oil claimed to cure anything from headaches to cancer, in humans and animals alike.*

QUESTIONS FOR ANALYSIS

- Who benefited from Roosevelt's national parks and the Pure Food and Drug Act? Who may have suffered from these regulations?
- Roosevelt considered courage, fitness, and "rugged individualism" vital to the American identity. Why did he choose these traits specifically, and are these traits as vital today? Explain.

Explore Further

Brinkley, Douglas, *Wilderness Warrior: Theodore Roosevelt and the Crusade to Save America* (2010).

Morris, Edmund, *Theodore Rex* (2002).

of unsanitary practices in Chicago slaughterhouses, a series of bank failures (see above, under Financial Crises), and anxieties about the ill effects of the "closing of the frontier" in the American West to spur the federal government into action. (See Current Trends in World History: Industrialization's Antidotes: Conservation and Regulation.) In 1906, President Theodore Roosevelt signed a Meat Inspection Act that provided for government supervision of meatpacking operations. In other cases (banking, steel production, railroads), the federal government's enhanced supervisory authority served corporate interests as well.

These consumer and family protection measures reflected a broader reform movement, one dedicated to creating a more efficient society and correcting the undesirable consequences of urbanization and industrialization. At local and state levels, **progressive reformers** attacked corrupt city governments that had allegedly fallen into the hands of immigrant-dominated "political machines." The progressives also attacked other vices, such as gambling, drinking, and prostitution—all associated with industrialized, urban settings. The creation of city parks preoccupied urban planners, who hoped parks' green spaces would offer healthier forms of entertainment than houses of prostitution, gambling dens, and bars. In Europe and the United States, thousands of associations took shape against capitalism's excesses. From Scandinavia to California, the proponents of old-age pensions and public ownership of utilities put pressure on lawmakers, and they occasionally succeeded in changing state policies. Intervening in the market and supporting the poor, the aged, the unemployed, and the sick in ways never dreamed of in classical liberal philosophy, progressive reform movements laid the foundations for the modern welfare state.

CULTURAL MODERNISM

The intellectuals, artists, and scientists of the fin de siècle wrestled with uncertainty, increasing social tensions, and the acceleration of the pace of change just as did revolutionaries and reformers. What we call modernism—the sense of having broken with tradition—came to prominence in many fields, from physics to architecture, from painting to the social sciences. The movement largely originated from the experimental thinking shaped by turn-of-the-century anxieties and opportunities. Emblematic of the new ideas was the work of Pablo Picasso (1881–1973), a Spanish painter who spent much of his life in Paris: inspired by seeing African masks in Paris's ethnographic museum, Picasso broke with the Renaissance style of representation in producing his *Les Demoiselles d'Avignon* (1907). Shocking in its form, this painting also depicted a series of nude prostitutes, who confront the viewer and seem to say, "Go ahead and look at me and here see what really lies beneath your civilized exterior." No wonder modernism remained, throughout its existence, controversial: it meant to break the rules, and sometimes to terrorize the rule makers.

Pablo Picasso. *The Franco-Spanish artist Pablo Picasso was one of the first to incorporate "primitive" artistic forms into his work, as displayed in his breakthrough canvas,* Les Demoiselles d'Avignon *(The Courtesans of Avignon, 1907), which was inspired by the artist's study of African sculpture and masks.*

Modernist movements were notably international, but sometimes also elitist. Egyptian social scientists read the works of European thinkers, while French and German painters flocked to museums to inspect artifacts from Africa and Oceania. But increasingly it took expertise to understand or appreciate modern art, like that of Picasso, or modern music, which abandoned the comfort of harmonic and diatonic sound (the eight-tone scale standard in classical western music at the time). Many artists demonstrated their cutting-edge originality by spurning sales figures for loftier ambitions. "Art for art's sake" became their motto; their aim was to speak to posterity. Modern science grew to depend more and more on laboratory work, or on high-level mathematical training—though it proved possible for a patent-office clerk, Albert Einstein (1879–1955), to publish papers on special relativity (showing that measurements are not absolute, but depend on the position of the measurer) in the first years of the twentieth century; there were at the time only a small handful of readers able to read and understand Einstein's physics, and even fewer able to appreciate the transformative potential of his ideas.

If modernism in arts and sciences did not appeal to all, it did, gradually, transform cultural production across the globe, and as it did so, it replaced the certainties of the Renaissance and the Enlightenment with the unsettledness of the new age. It is telling that Picasso broke with Renaissance conventions of representation at just about the same time that Einstein introduced special relativity to physics. No longer confident about European "laws," and increasingly critical of urban and industrial "progress," artists and scientists struggled to make sense of a world in which older beliefs and traditional faiths had given way. What would come next, however, no one could say.

Popular Culture Comes of Age

Changes in elite culture were crucial, but by the fin de siècle, too, the world of popular culture had expanded enormously. The change derived mainly from new urban settings, technological innovations, and increased leisure time. As education (especially in America and Europe) became nearly universal, there were many more readers and museumgoers. At the same time, cultural works now found their way down to nonelite members of society. Middle-class art lovers who could not afford original paintings eagerly purchased lithographs and mass-produced engravings; millions who could not attend operas and formal dress balls attended dance halls and vaudeville shows (entertainment by singers, dancers, and comedians). People flocked to hear lectures given by travelers, often accompanied by slide shows. For the first time, sports attracted mass followings. Soccer in Europe, baseball in the United States, and cricket in India had wildly devoted middle- and working-class fans. Thus did a truly **popular culture** emerge, delivering affordable and accessible forms of art and entertainment to "the masses."

By the century's close, the press constituted a major form of popular entertainment and information. This was partly because publishers were offering different wares to different classes of readers and partly because many more people could read, especially in Europe and the Americas. The "yellow press" was full of stories of murder and sensationalism that appealed to the urban masses. By now, the English *Daily Mail* and the French *Petit Parisien* boasted circulations of over 1 million. In the United States, urban dwellers, many of whom were immigrants, avidly read newspapers—some in English, others in their native languages. Here, too, banner headlines, sensational stories, and simple language drew in readers with little education or poor English skills. Books, too, proliferated and fell in price; penny novels about cowboys, murder, and romance became the rage.

By now the kind of culture one consumed had become a reflection of one's real (or desired) status in society, a central part of one's identity. For many Latin American workers, for example, reading one's own newspaper or comic strip was part of the business of being a worker. Argentina's socialist newspaper, *La Vanguardia*, was one of Buenos Aires's most prominent periodicals, read and debated at work and in the cafés of working-class neighborhoods. Anyone seen reading the bourgeois paper, *La Prensa*, faced heckling and ridicule by proletarian peers.

As the community of cultural consumers broadened, and as ideas from across the globe flooded in, writers, artists, and scholars struggled to adapt. Their attempts to confront the brave new world in the making resulted in the remarkable innovations that characterize modernism—the breaking with tradition.

Díaz and the Liberal Party. *In this 1910 print, the Mexican satirist José Guadalupe Posada portrays the leaders of the popular Liberal Party as being literally under the feet of the elitist followers of General Porfirio Díaz.*

Modernism in European Culture

In intellectual and artistic terms, Europe at the turn of the twentieth century experienced perhaps its richest age since the Renaissance. A desire to understand social and imperial maladies laid the foundations for the twentieth century's social sciences. The French scholar Emile Durkheim (1858–1917), for example, pioneered the field of sociology by studying a characteristic affliction of his age—suicide. In 1895, the French social psychologist Gustave Le Bon (1841–1931) wrote a treatise on crowd behavior that became a classic in Europe and beyond; he equated the unconscious volatility of crowds with the irrationality of women and "primitives." Le Bon's work became wildly popular, appealing even to Benito Mussolini in Italy and Vladimir Lenin in Russia.

Artists' work reflected their ambivalence about the modern, as represented by the railroad, the big city, and the factory. While the impressionists and realists of the mid-nineteenth century had largely celebrated progress, the painters and novelists of the century's end took a darker view. They turned away from enlightened clarity and descriptive prose, searching for more instinctual truths. Now the primitive came to symbolize both Europe's lost innocence and the forces that reason could not control, such as sexual drives, religious fervor, or brute strength. The painter who led the way in incorporating these themes into modern art was Paul Gauguin (1848–1903), who left Europe for Tahiti in 1891, and there found new forms

Impressionism. *These two paintings, Claude Monet's* The Gare Saint-Lazare (left) *and Camille Pissarro's* Sunset over the Boieldieu Bridge at Rouen (right), *exemplify the impressionists' celebration of nineteenth-century progress.*

of contentment and new ways of representing the world that he believed were less artificial than those practiced in Europe. In paintings such as *Where Do We Come From? What Are We? Where Are We Going?* (1897), Gauguin posed humankind's great questions, and intimated that the Polynesians—despite European contempt for their religious rituals and lack of "progress"—might have more answers than did his "civilized" compatriots back home.

However, the arts alone did not undermine older views of the world. Even science, in which the Enlightenment had placed so much faith, worked a disenchanting magic on the midcentury bourgeois worldview. After the century's turn, pioneering physicists and mathematicians like Einstein took apart the Enlightenment's conviction that man could achieve full knowledge of, and control over, nature. In his later work, Einstein drew on the previously ridiculed work of the Indian physicist Satyendra Nath Bose (1894–1974), who understood light to be a gas composed of particles. These particles were too tiny to be distinguished by any microscope, but their existence could be hypothesized through the application of statistics. The work of Einstein, Bose, and other scholars of their generation laid the foundations for today's quantum physics.

Paul Gauguin, *Where Do We Come From? What Are We? Where Are We Going?* *In this large-scale painting, Gauguin used Tahitian rather than European biblical figures to pose some of humanity's deepest questions about the meaning of life, the relationship between humans and gods, and our destinies after death.*

Sigmund Freud, at Work in His Study in Vienna. *Freud surrounded himself not only with books but also with Egyptian figurines and African masks, expressions of universal artistic prowess—and irrational psychological drives.*

In this modernist form of science, probabilities took the place of certainties. Although most scientists continued to collect data feeling certain that they could plumb nature's depths, some of their colleagues began to question the arrogance of this view.

From the time of the Enlightenment, Europeans had prided themselves on their "reason." To be rational was to be civilized; respectable, middle-class nineteenth-century men were thought to embody these virtues. But in the late nineteenth century, faith in rationality began to falter. Perhaps reason was *not* man's highest attainment, said some; perhaps reason was too hard for man to sustain, said others. Friedrich Nietzsche (1844–1900) claimed that conventional European attempts to assert The Truth—including science and Judeo-Christian moral codes—were nothing more than life-destroying quests for power; individuals would do better to dispense with the old forms and invent new forms of truth to live by. Sigmund Freud (1856–1939) began to excavate layers of the human subconscious, where irrational desires and fears lay buried. For Freud, human nature was not as simple as it had seemed to Enlightenment thinkers. Instead, he asserted, humans were driven by sexual longings and childhood traumas, some revealed only as neuroses, in dreams, or during extensive psychoanalysis. Neither Nietzsche nor Freud was well loved among liberal elites. But in the new century, Nietzsche would become the prophet for many antiliberal, antirational causes, from nudism to Nazism; and Freud's dark vision would become central to the twentieth century's understanding of the self.

Cultural Modernism in China

As in Europe, Chinese artists and scientists at the turn of the century were active experimenters and innovators, reflecting critically upon their own traditions as well as selectively importing western ideas. As in the West, Chinese writers and artists now had wider audiences for their work; by the late nineteenth century, more than 170 presses in China were serving a potential readership of 2 to 4 million concentrated mostly in the urban areas. These cities were more economically vibrant and culturally fluid than the hinterlands. Not only was there an expanding body of readers, but newly rich beneficiaries of the treaty-port economy now patronized the arts. These new opportunities made for increased cultural diversity. Indeed, some scholars have described the late Qing period as a time of competing cultural *modernities,* in contrast to the post-Qing era, which pursued a single, western-oriented *modernity*.

In art as in literature, late Qing intellectuals integrated indigenous and foreign styles into their explorations of topics such as the self, sexuality, and China's future. In the late nineteenth century, for example, painters from the lower Yangzi region congregated in Shanghai. Collectively known as the **Shanghai School**, these classically trained painters appropriated western technical novelties into their artistic practice. Consider the self-portrait of the artist Ren Xiong (1820–1857): bareheaded and legs apart, he

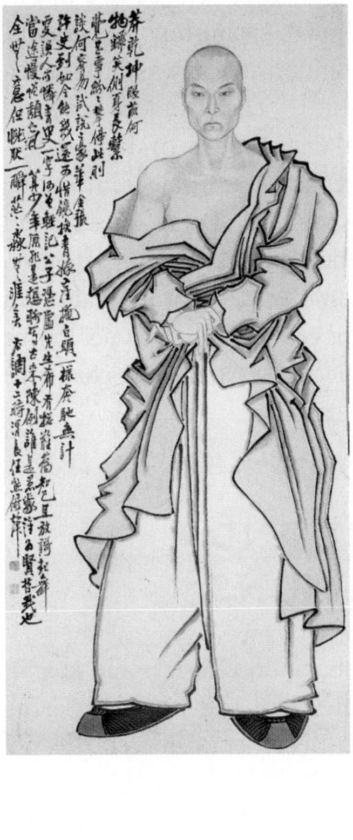

Ren Xiong, Self-Portrait. *This famous self-portrait of Ren Xiong was most likely produced in the 1850s. Ren Xiong was probably familiar with the new practice of portrait photography in the treaty ports. Although his self-portrait reproduced some old conventions of Chinese scholarly art, such as the unity of the visual image with a lengthy self-composed inscription, it is also clear that, through its rather unconventional pose and image, Ren Xiong had pointed to the establishment of a new kind of subject position characteristic of the trend of cultural modernism in China during this period.*

stands upright and stares straight at the viewer. Ren Xiong's work reflected the influence of photography, a new visual medium. Similarly, experimental writers drew on modern science, sometimes in order to explore the question of China's future relations with the West. The novel *New Era* (1908), for example, put its opening scenes in the year 1999, by which time, as the story envisioned, China would be a supreme world power and a constitutional monarchy. Depicting China at war with western powers, *New Era* celebrated military strength but also introduced inventions such as electricity-repellent clothing and bulletproof satin. More visionary still was the *The Stone of Goddess Nüwa* (1905), whose male author imagined a technologically advanced feminist utopia. Its female residents studied subjects ranging from the arts to physics, drove electric cars, and ate purified liquid food extracts. Their mission was to save China by eliminating corrupt male officials. Such works, combining the fanciful with the critical, offered a new and provocative vision of China.

Yet the integration of western science into Chinese culture was an intellectual challenge. Did being modern mean giving up China's scholarly traditions and values? The nineteenth century had seen Christian missionaries use their scientific knowledge to attract followers. For example, John Fryer, an English missionary and translator, founded *The Science Journal* (*Gezhi huibian*) in 1876. Other publications in the same period included *The Universal Gazette* (*Wanguo gongbao*). Recognizing the usefulness of western science, many Chinese scholars helped missionaries promote it—although they considered it mostly as a way to acquire national wealth and power, rather than as a way of understanding the world.

It is not surprising that the Chinese scholars took this stance, for western visitors to China also presented science as a means to material betterment. Thus, although steamships, telegraphs, and railroads captured public attention, there was little interest in changing fundamental Chinese beliefs. Indeed, even as Chinese intellectuals recognized new modes of knowledge, many of the elite insisted that Chinese learning remain the principal source of all knowledge. What kind of balance should exist between western thought and Chinese learning, or even whether the ancient classics should keep their fundamental role, was an issue that would haunt generations to come. In this respect, the Chinese dilemma reflected a worldwide challenge to accepting the impulses of modernism.

RETHINKING RACE AND REIMAGINING NATIONS

Ironically, at this time of huge population transfers and shared technological modernization, individuals and nations became passionate defenders of the idea that identities were deeply rooted and unchangeable. Although physical characteristics had always played *some* role in identifying persons, by the late nineteenth century the Linnaean classifications (see Chapter 14) had become the means for ranking the worth of whole nations.

Race now defined who could belong to the nation and enjoy its rights and privileges; by the century's close, racial roots had also become a crucial part of cultural identity. This was the era of ethnographic museums, folkloric collectors, national essence movements, and racial genealogies. People wanted to know who they (and their neighbors) were—especially in terms of *biological* ancestry. Now the idea of inheritance took on new weight, in both cultural and biological forms. Doctors, officials, and novelists described the genetic inheritance of madness, alcoholism, criminality, and even homosexuality; nationalists spoke of the uniqueness of the Slavic soul, the German mind, and the Hispanic race. They spoke of Hindu spirituality and of Islamic principles, as if there were no variations or conflicts within these categories. The preoccupation with race reflected a worldwide longing for fixed roots in an age that seemed to be burning all its bridges to the past.

Nationalist and racial ideas were different in different parts of the world. In Europe and America, debates about race and national purity reflected several concerns: fear of losing individuality in a technological world, rising tensions among states, and fear of being overrun by the brown, black, and yellow peoples beyond the borders of "civilization." By contrast, in India these ideas were part of the anticolonial debate, and they helped to mobilize people politically. This was also the case in China, Latin America, and the Islamic world, where discussions of identity went hand in hand with opposition to western domination and corrupt indigenous elites. Especially in the colonial world, racial identity was primarily a question about the community's coherence and endurance, not about the races of humankind in general.

These new impulses produced a variety of national movements, from China's anti-Qing campaign to India's Swadeshi movement (see below). At the same time, pan-ethnic movements looked beyond the nation-state, envisioning communities based on ethnicity. Behind these movements was the notion that political communities should be built on racial purity or unsullied indigenous traditions. These views indicated just how unsettled the world was by the century's end and how urgent the questions of identity and belonging had become.

Nation and Race in North America and Europe

In the United States, the changing mood was striking. Americans greeted the end of the century with a combination of chest-beating pride and shoulder-slumping pessimism. In the early 1890s, for example, Americans flocked to extravagant commemorations of the four hundredth anniversary of Christopher Columbus's discovery. The largest was the Columbian Exposition in Chicago. Such events displayed the most modern machinery and celebrated the nation's marvelous destiny. Yet, at the same time, Americans feared for their future. They especially worried that America had exhausted its supposedly infinite supply of new land and resources—as evidenced by the disappearance of the buffalo, the erosion of soils, and the depletion of timber stands by aggressive logging companies. Conservationists' alarm grew more intense with the Census Bureau's 1890 announcement that the American frontier had "closed."

RESTRICTING IMMIGRATION Some white Americans may have worried that the closing of the "frontier" spelled the end of American pioneer individualism. But most did not agonize about what the African American intellectual W. E. B. Du Bois (1868–1963) predicted would be "the problem of the twentieth century"—that is, "the problem of the color line." Rather, white Americans were busily drawing new color lines, initiating new forms of racial discrimination where old forms (like slavery) had broken down. In the American West, animosity toward Chinese workers led to the 1882 Exclusion Act, which prohibited almost all immigration from China. In the American South, where most of the nation's 7 million African Americans resided, a system of "Jim Crow" laws upheld racial segregation and inequality.

The Columbian Exposition. *More than 27 million people attended the Columbian Exposition in Chicago in 1893. Like many of the era's world's fairs, this one celebrated technological progress, including the spread of electricity, as evidenced by the General Electric Tower of Light.*

White Americans grew even more anxious as throngs of "swarthy" immigrants entered the United States. These people came primarily from southern and eastern Europe, but to the champions of "Anglo-Saxonism" they were not "white." Even more threatening were darker peoples who were colonial subjects in the Philippines, Puerto Rico, and Cuba. Talk of the end of white America fueled support for more restrictive immigration policies.

Across the North Atlantic, European elites engaged in similar discussions. For them, the final divvying up of Africa was in many respects equivalent to the closing of the American frontier. The Germans and Italians, in particular, complained about the lack of new territories on which to plant their flags. The French and British began to worry about how to preserve their empires, especially in light of the anticolonial sentiments seething in their colonies.

FACING NEW SOCIAL ISSUES Like Americans, Europeans also expressed concerns about trends at home. For example, intellectuals suggested that mechanization deprived men of their vitality. At the same time, Darwinist theory provoked new anxieties about inherited diseases, racial mixing, and the dying out of white "civilizers." Sexual relations between European colonizers and indigenous women—and their mixed offspring—had almost always been a part of European expansionism, but as racial identities hardened, such relations now seemed to threaten the moral fiber of the whole nation. Talk of virility arose, partly provoked by doctors' and scientists' involvement in treating social problems. Before long, English and American schoolboys were encouraged to play sports, to avoid becoming too weak to defend the nation. In addition, medical attention focused on homosexuality, regarding it as a disease and a threat to Anglo-Saxon civilization. In France, the falling birthrate seemed to signal a period of decadence characterized by weak, sickly men and irrational women.

Some people tied decadence to debates about whether Jews—defined by religious practice or, increasingly, by ethnicity—could be fully assimilated into European society. Even though Jews had gained rights as citizens in most European nations by the late nineteenth century, powerful prejudices persisted. In the 1880s and 1890s, violent pogroms, often involving police complicity, targeted the large Jewish populations in the Russian Empire's western territories and pushed the persecuted farther westward. These emigrants' presence, in turn, stirred up fear and resentment, especially in Austria, Germany, and France. Reactionaries began to talk about the "pollution" of the European races by mixing with Semites and to circulate rumors about Jewish bankers' conspiratorial powers. Perhaps because nothing else seemed stable and enduring, wealthy white male Europeans (like their American counterparts) promoted programs of racial purity to shore up the civilizations they saw coming apart at the seams.

Race-Mixing and the Problem of Nationhood in Latin America

In Latin America, debates about identity chiefly addressed ethnic intermixing and the legacy of a system of government that, unlike much of the North Atlantic world, excluded rather than included the populace. After all, social hierarchies reaching back to the sixteenth century ranked white Iberians at the top, creole elites in the middle, and indigenous and African populations at the bottom. Thus, the higher on the social ladder, the more likely the people were to be white.

CONTESTED MIXTURES It is important to note that "mixing" did not lead to a shared heritage. Nor did it necessarily lead to homogeneity. In fact, the "racial" order did not stick, since some Iberians occupied the lower ranks, while a few people of color did manage to ascend the social ladder. Moreover, starting in the 1880s, the racial hierarchy saw further disruption by the deluge of poor European immigrants; they were flooding into prospering Latin American countrysides or into booming cities like Buenos Aires in Argentina and São Paulo in Brazil. Latin American societies, then, did not easily become homogeneous "nations." Indeed, many Latin American observers wondered whether national identities could survive these transformations at all.

In an age of acute nationalism, the mixed racial composition of Latin Americans generated special anxieties. In the 1870s in Mexico, it was common to view Indians as obstacles to change. One demographer, Antonio García Cubas, considered indigenous people "decadent and degenerate." According to him, their presence deprived the republic of the right kind of citizens. In Cuba and Brazil, observers made the same claims about blacks. According to many modernizers, Latin America's own people were holding it back. The solution, argued some writers, was to attract white immigrants and to establish educational programs that would uplift Indians, blacks, and people of mixed descent. Thus, many intellectuals joined the crusade to modernize and westernize their populations. In the effort to "whiten" their republics, many Latin American governments made especially strong pitches for northern European migrants, despite the mounting evidence that they often made lousy farmers and did not work well with others. So, even by 1900, some of the shine of "pure" white races was rubbing off, not least because European migrants did not live up to the propagandists' expectations.

Diego Rivera's *History of Mexico*. *This is one of the most famous works of Mexican art, a portrait of the history of Mexico by the radical nationalist painter Diego Rivera. In this chapter, and in previous chapters, we have shown parts of this mural. In stepping back to view the whole work, which is in the National Palace in Mexico City, we can see how Rivera envisioned the history of his people generally. Completed in 1935, this work seeks to show a people fighting constantly against outside aggressors, from their glorious preconquest days (lower center), winding like a grand epic through the conquest, colonial exploitation, the revolution for independence, nineteenth-century invasions from France and the United States, to the popular 1910 Revolution. It culminates in an image of Karl Marx, framed by a "scientific sun"—pointing to a future of progress and prosperity for all, as if restoring a modern Tenochtitlán of the Aztecs. This work captured many Mexicans' efforts to return to the indigenous roots of the nation and to fuse them with modern scientific ideas.*

PROMOTING NATIONHOOD BY CELEBRATING THE PAST For their part, Latin American leaders began to exalt bygone glories as a way to promote national selfhood. Inventing successful myths could make a government seem more legitimate—as the heir to a rightful struggle of the past. Thus in Mexico, General Díaz placed the bell that Father Hidalgo had tolled on September 16, 1810, to mark the beginning of the war against Spain (see Chapter 15), in the National Palace in Mexico City. In the month of that centennial in 1910, grand processions wound through the capital. Many of the parades celebrated Aztec grandeur, thereby creating a mythic arc from the greatness of the Aztec past to the triumphal story of Mexican independence—and to the benevolence and progress of the Díaz regime. As the government glorified the Aztecs with pageants, statues, and pavilions, however, it continued to ignore modern Aztec descendants, who lived in squalor.

Some thinkers now began to celebrate ancient heritages as a basis for modern national identities. For example, in Mexico and eventually in the Andes, the pre-Spanish past became a crucial foundation stone of the nation-state. The young Mexican writer José Vasconcelos (1882–1959) grew disenchanted with the brutal rule of Díaz and his westernizing ambitions. Nonetheless, he endorsed Díaz's celebration of the Indian past, for he believed that Mexicans were capable of a superior form of civilization. He insisted that if they had fewer material concerns, their combined Aztec and Spanish Catholic origins could create a spiritual realm of even higher achievement. In Vasconcelos's view, Mexico's greatness flowed not in spite of, but because of, its mixed nature.

Sun Yat-sen and the Making of a Chinese Nation

Just as Latin American thought celebrated an authentic past, so did Chinese writers emphasize the power and depth of Chinese culture—in contrast to the Qing Empire's failing political and social strength. Here, writers used race to emphasize the superiority of the Han Chinese. Here, too, the pace of change generated a desire to trace one's roots back to secure foundations. Moreover, traditions were reinvented in the hope of saving the Chinese soul threatened by modernity.

In China, as elsewhere, scholars and political mobilizers took up the challenge of redefining identities. By the century's end, prominent members of both groups had abandoned their commitment to preserving the old order but were not ready to fully adopt western practices. Their attempts at combining traditions and values from home and abroad gave rise to the modern Chinese intelligentsia and modern Chinese nationalism.

PROMOTING HAN NATIONALISM Symbolizing the challenge of nation building were the endeavors of **Sun Yat-sen** (1866–1925), who was part of an emerging generation of critics of the old regime. Like his European counterparts, Sun dreamed of a political community reshaped along national lines. Born into a modest rural household in southern China, he studied medicine in the British colony of Hong Kong and then turned to politics during the Sino-Japanese War. When the Qing government rejected his offer of service to the Chinese cause, he became convinced that China's rulers were out of touch with the times. Subsequently he established an organization based in Hawaii to advocate the Qing downfall and the cause of republicanism. The cornerstone of his message was Chinese—specifically, Han—nationalism.

Sun blasted the feeble rule by outsiders, the Manchus, and trumpeted a sovereign political community of "true" Chinese. No ruler, he argued, could enjoy legitimacy without the nation's consent. He envisioned a new China free of Manchu rule, building a democratic form of government and an economic system based on equalized land rights. In this fashion, Sun claimed, China would join the world of nation-states and have the power to defend its borders.

Sun's nationalism did not catch on immediately in China itself, partly because the Qing regime persecuted all dissenters. His ideas fared better among the hundreds of thousands of Chinese who had emigrated in the second half of the nineteenth century. Often facing discrimination in their adopted homelands, these overseas communities applauded Sun's racial nationalism and democratic ideas. In addition, Chinese students studying abroad found inspiration in his message.

REPLACING THE QING AND RECONSTITUTING A NATION Sun's nationalist and republican call resonated more powerfully as the Qing Empire grew weaker early in the twentieth century. Military defeat at the hands of the Japanese was especially humiliating, coming from those whom the Chinese had historically considered a "lowly" folk. Realizing that reforms were necessary, the Manchu court began overhauling the administrative system and the military in the aftermath of the Boxer Uprising. Yet these changes came too late. The old elites grumbled, and the new class of urban merchants, entrepreneurs, and professionals (who often benefited from business with westerners) regarded the government as outmoded. Peasants and laborers resented the high cost of the reforms, which seemed to help only the rulers.

A mutiny, sparked in part by the government's nationalization of railroads and its low compensation to native Chinese investors, broke out in the city of Wuchang in central China in 1911. As it spread to other parts of the country, Sun Yat-sen hurried home from traveling in the United States. Few people rallied to the emperor's cause, and the Qing dynasty collapsed—an abrupt end to a dynastic tradition of more than 2,000 years. In the provinces, coalitions of gentry, merchants, and military leaders ran the government.

Sun Yat-sen. *Through the medium of clothing, these two images of Sun Yat-sen, the man generally known as the "father of the Chinese nation," epitomize the evolving cultural ambiguities of China in the late nineteenth and early twentieth centuries.* (Left) *As a young man studying medicine in the British colony of Hong Kong in the late 1880s, Sun and his friends dressed in the conventional Qing garb of Chinese gentlemen.* (Right) *Two decades later, in early 1912, Sun and the officials of the new republic appeared in public in full western-style jackets and ties. Clothing, like so many parts of the cultural arena in China during this period, had become a contested ground in the battle to forge a new nation's identity.*

China would soon be reconstituted, and Sun's ideas, especially those regarding race, would play a central role. The original flag of the republic, for example, consisted of five colors representing the citizenry's major racial groups: red for the Han, yellow for the Manchus, blue for the Mongols, white for the Tibetans, and black for the Muslims. But Sun had reservations about this multiracial flag, believing there should be only one Chinese race. The existence of different groups in China, he argued, was the result of incomplete assimilation—a problem that the modern nation now had to confront.

Nationalism and Invented Traditions in India

British imperial rule persisted in India, but the turn of the century saw cracks in its stranglehold. Four strands had woven the territory together: the consolidation of colonial administration, the establishment of railways and telegraphs, the growth of western education and ideas, and the development of colonial capitalism. Now it was possible to speak of India as a single unit. And it was also possible for anticolonial thinkers to imagine seizing and ruling India by themselves. Thus a new form of resistance emerged, different from peasant rebellions of the past. Now, dissenters talked of Indians as "a people" who had both a national past and national traditions.

A MODERNIZING ELITE Leaders of the nationalist opposition were western-educated intellectuals from colonial cities and towns. Although a tiny minority of the Indian population, they gained influence through their access to the official world and their familiarity with European knowledge and history. This elite group used their knowledge to develop modern cultural forms. For example, they turned colloquial languages (such as Hindi, Urdu, Bengali, Tamil, and Malayalam) into standardized, literary forms for writing novels and dramas. Now the publication of journals, magazines, newspapers, pamphlets, novels, and dramas surged, facilitating communication throughout British India.

Along with print culture came a growing public sphere where intellectuals debated social and political matters. By 1885, voluntary associations in big cities had united to establish a political party, the Indian National Congress. Lawyers, prominent merchants, and local notables dominated its early leadership. The congress demanded greater representation of Indians in administrative and legislative bodies, criticized the government's economic policies, and encouraged India's industrialization.

Underlying this political nationalism, embodied by the Indian National Congress, was cultural nationalism. The nationalists claimed that Indians might not be a single race but were at least a unified people, because of their unique culture and common colonial history. Indeed, nationalism in India (unlike in Europe) developed with an acute awareness of Indians as colonial subjects. The critical question was: could India be a modern nation *and* hold on to its Indian identity?

BUILDING A MODERN IDENTITY ON REWRITTEN TRADITIONS The recovery of traditions became a way to establish a modern Indian identity without acknowledging the recent subjugation by British colonizers. So Indian intellectuals (like those in Latin America) turned to the past and rewrote the histories of ancient empires and kingdoms. In this way, Indian intellectuals promoted the idea of the nation-state even though the region had no integrated, national history prior to colonization.

To portray Indians as a people with a unifying religious creed, intellectuals reconfigured Hinduism so that it resembled western religion. This was no easy task, for traditional Hinduism did not have a supreme textual authority, a monotheistic God, an organized church, or an established creed. Nonetheless, nationalist Hindu intellectuals combined various philosophical texts, cultural beliefs, social practices, and Hindu traditions into a mix that they labeled the authentic Hindu religion. Other Indian revivalists, too, explored the roots of a national culture. Some researched ancient Indian contributions to astronomy, mathematics, algebra, chemistry, and medicine and called for a national science. In the fine arts, intellectuals constructed an imaginary line of continuity to the glorious past to promote a specifically Indian art and aesthetics (sense of beauty).

Modern Indian Art. *Painter Abanindranath Tagore's 1902* The Passing of Shah Jahan *incorporates elements typical to Western art, like perspective and foreshortening, while it retains the palette, patterns, and figures of prominence that reach back to India's glorious past.*

While fashioning hybrid forms, revivalists also narrowed the definition of Indian traditions. As Hindu intellectuals looked back, they identified Hindu traditions and the pre-Islamic past as the only sources of India's culture. Other contributors to the region's mosaic past were forgotten; the Muslim past, in particular, had no prominent role. However, the Muslims and other religious, ethnic, and linguistic groups also attempted to mobilize their communities for modern, secular purposes. The Indian National Muslim League, for example, which formed in 1906, advanced the ***political*** interests of Muslims, not the Islamic religion.

HINDU REVIVALISM Hindu revivalism became a powerful political force in the late nineteenth century, when the nationalist challenge to the colonial regime took a militant turn. New leaders rejected constitutionalism and called for militant agitation. The British decision to partition Bengal in 1905 into two provinces—one predominantly Muslim, the other Hindu—drew militants into the streets to urge the boycott of British goods. Rabindranath Tagore, a famous Bengali poet and future Nobel laureate, composed stirring nationalist poetry. Activists formed voluntary organizations, called Swadeshi ("one's own country") Samities ("societies"), that championed indigenous enterprises for manufacturing soap, cloth, medicine, iron, and paper, as well as schools for imparting nationalist education. Although few of these ventures succeeded, the efforts reflected the nationalist desire to assert Indians' autonomy as a people.

Rabindranath Tagore. *The Bengali writer, philosopher, and teacher Rabindranath Tagore became the poet laureate of the Swadeshi Movement in Bengal in 1903–1908. The first Asian Nobel laureate, he became disenchanted with nationalism, viewing it as narrow and not universalistic. The photo shows Tagore reading to a group of his students in 1929.*

The Swadeshi movement swept aside the moderate leadership of the Indian National Congress and installed a radical leadership that broadened the nationalist agitation. Although the people did not topple the colonial regime, Indian mass mobilization was enough to alarm the British rulers, who turned to force to keep the colony intact. When the movement slipped into a campaign of terrorism in 1908, the government responded by imprisoning militant leaders. However, the colonial administrators also annulled their partition of Bengal in 1911.

Late-nineteenth-century Indian nationalism posed a different kind of challenge to the British than the suppressed 1857 rebellion. Back then, insurgents had wanted to preserve local identities against the encroaching modern state and colonial economy. Now, in contrast, nationalist leaders imagined a modern national community. Invoking religious and ethnic symbols, they formed modern political associations to operate in a national public arena. Unlike the insurgents of 1857, they did not seek a radical alternative to the colonial order; instead, they fought for the political rights of Indians as a secular, national community. In these new nationalists, British rulers discovered an enemy not so different from themselves.

The Birth of the Turkish Nation. *Sultan Abdul Hamid II bestows a constitution on the Turkish people.*

The Pan Movements

India and China were not the only places where activists dreamed of founding new states. Across the globe, groups had begun to imagine new communities based on ethnicity or, in some cases, religion. **Pan movements** (from the Greek *pan,* "all") sought to link people across state boundaries. The grand aspiration of all these movements—which included pan-Asianism, pan-Islamism, pan-Africanism, pan-Slavism, pan-Turkism, pan-Arabism, pan-Germanism, and Zionism—was the rearrangement of borders in order to unite dispersed communities. But such remappings posed a threat to rulers of the Russian, Austrian, and Ottoman empires, as well as to overseers of the British and the French colonial empires.

PAN-ISLAMISM Within the Muslim world, intellectuals and political leaders begged their coreligionists to put aside sectarian and political differences so that they could unite under the banner of Islam in opposition to European incursions. The leading spokesman for pan-Islamism was the well-traveled Jamal al-Din al-Afghani (1839–1897). Born in Iran and given a Shiite upbringing, he nonetheless called on Muslims worldwide to overcome their Sunni and Shiite differences so that they could work together against the West. During a sojourn in Egypt, he joined with a young Egyptian reformer, Muhammad Abduh (1849–1905), to inspire an Islamic protest against Europe. Later, Afghani and Abduh (then living in Paris) published a pan-Islamic newspaper. Afghani subsequently made his way to Istanbul, where he supported the pan-Islamic ambitions of Sultan Abdul Hamid II, who promoted the defense of Islam as a way to thwart European schemes to divide up the Ottoman Empire.

The pan-Islamic appeal only added to Muslims' confusion as they confronted the West. Indeed, Arab Muslims living as Ottoman subjects had many calls on their loyalties. Should they support the Ottoman Empire to resist European encroachments? Or should they embrace the Islamism of Afghani? Most decided to work within the fledgling nation-states of the Islamic world, looking to a Syrian or Lebanese identity as the way to deal with the West and gain autonomy. But Afghani and his disciples had struck a chord in Muslim culture, and their Islamic message has long retained a powerful appeal. (See Primary Source: A Muslim Philosopher Describes Why Islam Has Become Weak.)

PAN-GERMANISM AND PAN-SLAVISM Pan-Germanism found followers across central Europe, where it often competed with a pan-Slavic movement that sought to unite all Slavs against their Austrian, German, and Ottoman overlords. This area had traditionally been ruled by German-speaking elites, who owned the land farmed by Poles, Czechs, Russians, and other Slavs. German elites began to feel increasingly uneasy as

PRIMARY SOURCE

A Muslim Philosopher Describes Why Islam has become Weak

Jamal al-Din al-Afghani is one of the most perplexing and mysterious figures in modern Islamic history. Born in Iran and raised in its Shiite tradition, he claimed Afghani birth and traveled widely in the Sunni world. His early sojourn in India, almost immediately after the Rebellion of 1857, left him with an undying hatred of the British and a conviction to unite the Islamic world. Although he believed that Islam was capable of reform, he devoted most of his energies to convincing the intellectual and political leaders in Arab and Ottoman-ruled lands to put aside their many differences and draw on their shared commitment to Islam in order to ward off Europe's ambitions in their region.

At the height of his influence in Egypt between 1871 and 1879, he gathered around him young men of leadership potential, though he would soon be exiled for his radical ideas and watch Egypt fall under British colonial power.

The undated document below was probably written toward the end of Afghani's career, which he spent in the court of Abdul Hamid II, sultan of the Ottoman Empire (r. 1876–1909), who also shared Afghani's vision of Islamic unity. It contrasts past Muslim greatness with present-day decline, and encourages united resistance to western dominance; these are themes that have reverberated throughout the Islamic world ever since.

"God changes not what is in a people, until they change what is in themselves." (13:11)

"That is because God would never change His favour that He conferred on a people until they change what was within themselves." (8:55)

These are verses of the Honourable Qur'an, the Admonitory Book which leads to the Right Path, and which calls [men] to the true religion. . . The Qur'an is the Book of God which He has sent down for the guidance [of mankind] and what is necessary for his life in this world and the world to come. It is a cure for the disease of straying [from the right path] and a remedy for the disease of ignorance. . . .

God roused the Islamic *umma* with a small number of people and gave them the highest rank to the point that the Muslims trod upon the lofty mountains and shook them with awe. . . . Their astonishing advent frightened every soul and their extraordinary progress amazed every intellect. The inhabitants of the world bit their fingers in astonishment at the unbelievable progress which these people achieved in a short period of time. They wondered . . . how the brave nations of the world had fallen helpless in facing them; and how the powerful states had been worn out under the hoofs of their horses. . . .

Let us now take a look at the present situation of the Muslims and compare it with their past and clarify their progress vis à vis their decline. The Muslim population in the world today is more than . . . two thousand times as large as the Muslim population at the time of their conquest of the territories of the world. The Islamic state extended from the shore of the Atlantic Ocean in West Africa to the heart of China. All these areas were independent and prosperous lands located in the best regions of the earth. . . .

In spite of this, the Islamic states today are unfortunately pillaged and their property stolen; their territory is occupied by foreigners and their wealth in the possession of others. There is no day in which foreigners do not grab a part of the Islamic lands, and there is no night in which foreigners do not make a group of Muslims obey their rule. They disgrace the Muslims and dissipate their pride. . . . Sometimes they call them savages and sometimes regard them as hard-hearted and cruel and finally consider them insane animals. What a disaster! What an affliction! . . .

What should be done then? Where can we find the cause? Where can we look for the reason and whom should we ask? [There is no answer to these questions] except to say that: "God changes not what is in a people, until they change what is in themselves."(13:11)

QUESTIONS FOR ANALYSIS

- What is Afghani suggesting about the quality of his fellow Muslims when he points to the origins of the Islamic *umma*?
- Explain why Afghani uses the land mass of the Islamic state as a measure of the devoutness of the Muslims within it.
- Following the fall of Egypt to British rule, Afghani argued that *jihad* obligated every individual to defend the remaining Muslim land from European domination. What is *jihad*? Do you think the introspective self-reform that Afghani calls for is at odds with *jihad*?

Source: Sayid Jamāl al-Dīn al Afghānī and Abdul-Hādī Hā'irī, "Afghānī on the Decline of Islam," in Die Welt des Islams, *New Series, vol. 13, no. 1/2 (1971): 121–125.*

PRIMARY SOURCE

A Pan-German Leader Rails against the Rising Power of the Slavs and the Jews in the Austro-Hungarian Empire

Georg von Schönerer was a right-wing radical and member of the Austrian House of Deputies. A German of Austrian descent, he was one of the first to object vehemently to the rising aspirations of the Slavic peoples of the Austro-Hungarian Empire for rights equal to those of the German population. For Schönerer, any sharing of cultural or political power with the Slavs or Jews was a threat to the dominance of ethnic Germans in the Empire. Claiming (falsely) that Jews were taking all of the good jobs in the empire, controlling the press, and manipulating financial markets, he aimed not just at keeping them out of the economy, but, as he states below, at eliminating Jewish influence "in all areas of the administration, law making, and public life as a whole."

Schönerer delivered the following speech on April 28, 1887, before the Austrian House of Deputies. His attempt to push through anti-Semitic legislation a month later was unsuccessful, but he continued to campaign for such pan-German causes for the rest of his life. Although they never met in person, Schönerer would become a hero to another Austrian pan-German and anti-Semite, Adolf Hitler.

This I must say in advance: we can only lament, that some Germans have set out on a false path and most sincerely believe that if the foreigner, whether he be a Jew, or a Negro, or a Chinese, or a Singhalese, learns to speak German and declares himself without a religion, or allows himself to be baptized Christian, then he can be welcomed with friendship as a German brother. . . . Today I have . . . set myself the task . . . of discussing the social question together first of all with respect to the Jewish nation. Now as a few days ago the highest imperial court has supported the community's right to free expression of its opinion, I must also hope that that I, as a representative of the people in the Parliament also will not have this right taken away from me today (bravo, bravo, on the far left). . . I must also today most decidedly take the opportunity to announce, from our German-national standpoint, the division of Bohemia that has been advocated and perhaps even planned by various parties. Such a division must, in our view, necessarily lead to the division of other territories, such as Carinthia or Steiermark or other partially linguistically-mixed regions, and materially damage not only the solidarity of all the Germans in Austria, but also the united character of the formerly German federal states of Austria. Thus together with my party members in the German national party and in agreement with those who are most closely sympathetic with our views outside this House, I have requested again to present our program publicly, and particularly to today present important parts of it which bear on the so vital reforms in the social and economic sector.

This proposed, and we believe, authentic, racially organic reform legislation, is also . . . of great significance for our national struggles. The foundations, however, of this social political reformist measures especially lie, in our view, *first in protections to be created against the falsification of public opinion by the press; and secondly, in the pushing out of Jewish influence in all areas of the administration, law making, and public life as a whole.*

Above all, I must, in the name of the German Nationals, stress the fact that we are proud to be members of a great people (*Volk*) and that as such we feel a holy duty to stand up for the welfare and the power, for the securing of national identity and for the protection of the national life of the German community in Austria at all times and incessantly. We Germans in Austria are certainly obliged to maintain ourselves in between the expanded power-positions of the Slavs, remembering that our German brothers in the Empire have repeatedly fought and bled for our nation against the enemy [the French] in the West. . . . We will also never forget, especially in the light of the unremitting, threatening influx of Slavdom into ancient German-language territory, that the German lands of Austria have for a long time formed part of Germany, and we see it as our national duty, to enduringly strengthen the existing alliances between Germany and Austria with legal and economic laws, in order that the existing union organically and permanently grows together.

QUESTIONS FOR ANALYSIS

- According to Schönerer, what characteristics must a person possess in order to be properly deemed a German?
- Why does Schönerer consider this pan-German cause a "holy duty"? What other "holy duties" have you encountered in this book that ultimately resulted in violent conflict?
- Outline the political, economic, and cultural changes that Schönerer proposes in this speech.

Source: *Fünf Reden der Reichsratabgeordneten Georg Ritter von Schönerer* (Horn: Ferdinand Berger, 1891), pp. 89–90. Translated by Suzanne Marchand.

Slavic nationalisms (spurred by the midcentury revivals of traditional Czech, Polish, Serbian, and Ukrainian languages and cultures) became more popular. Even more threatening was the fact that the Slavic populations were growing faster than the German. As pogroms in the Russian Empire's borderlands in the 1880s, as well as economic opportunities, drove crowds of eastern European Jews westward, German resentment toward these newcomers also increased.

What made pan-Germanism a movement, however, was the intervention of a former liberal, Georg von Schönerer (1842–1921). In 1882, Schönerer, outraged by the Habsburg Empire's failure to favor Germans, founded the League of German Nationalists. It comprised students, artisans, teachers, and small businessmen in the interests of uniting German Austrians with the Germans in Bismarck's Empire. Schönerer detested the Jews, defining them by their "racial characteristics" rather than by their religious practices. After his election to the Austrian upper house, he attempted to pass anti-Jewish legislation modeled on the American Chinese Exclusion Act of 1882. Although Schönerer's plans were too radical for most German Austrians, his anti-Semitism found echoes in a milder form by Viennese mayor Karl Lueger in the late 1890s and in a stronger form by Adolf Hitler after 1933. (See Primary Source: A Pan-German Leader Rails against the Rising Power of the Slavs and the Jews in the Austro-Hungarian Empire.)

The rhetoric of pan-Germanism motivated central Europeans to think of themselves as members of a German *race,* their identities determined by blood rather than defined by state boundaries. This, too, was the lesson of pan-Slavism. Both movements led fanatics to take actions that were dangerous to existing states. The organization of networks of radical southern Slavs, for example, unsettled Serbia and Herzegovina (annexed by the Austrians in 1908). Indeed, it was a Serbian proponent of plans to carve an independent Slav state out of Austrian territory in the Balkans who assassinated the heir to the Habsburg throne in June 1914. By August, the whole of Europe had descended into mass warfare, bringing much of the rest of the world directly or indirectly into the conflict as well. Eventually, the war would fulfill the pan-Slav, pan-German, and anti-Ottoman Muslim nationalist longing to tear down the Ottoman and Habsburg empires.

CONCLUSION

Ever since the Enlightenment, Europeans had put their faith in "progress." Through the nineteenth century, educated elites took pride in their booming industries, bustling cities, and burgeoning colonial empires. Yet by the century's end, urbanization and industrialization seemed more disrupting than uplifting, more disorienting than reassuring. Moreover, colonized people's resistance to the "civilizing mission" fueled doubts about the course of progress.

Especially unsettling to the ruling elite was the realization that "the people" not only were against them but also were developing ways to unseat them. In colonial settings, nationalists learned how to mobilize large populations. In Europe, socialist and right-wing leaders challenged liberal political power. By contrast, old elites, whose politics relied on closed-door negotiations between "rational" gentlemen, were unprepared to deal with modern ideas and identities.

Nor were the elites able to control the scope of change, for the expansion of empires had drawn ever more people into an unbalanced global economy. Everywhere, disparities in wealth appeared—especially in Africa, Asia, and Latin America. Moreover, the size and power of industrial operations threatened small firms and made individuals seem insignificant. Even some cities seemed too big and too dangerous. All these social and economic challenges stretched the capacities of gentlemanly politics.

Yet anxieties stimulated creative energy. Western artists borrowed nonwestern images and vocabularies; nonwestern intellectuals looked to the West for inspiration, even as they formulated anti-western ideas. The upheavals of modern experience propelled scholars to study the past and to fabricate utopian visions of the future.

Revivals and dislocations, as well as cultural and political movements, influenced the reformulating of identities. However, this was an incomplete process. For even as these changes unsettled the European-centered world, they intensified rivalries among Europe's powers themselves. Thus, this order was unstable at its center—Europe itself. And in the massive conflict that destroyed this era's faith in progress, Europe would ravage itself. The Great War would yield an age of even more rapid change—and even more violent consequences.

AFTER YOU READ THIS CHAPTER

Review and research **STUDYSPACE:** wwnorton.com/studyspace

TRACING THE GLOBAL STORYLINES

FOCUS ON: ***Sources of Global Anxieties and Expressions of Cultural Modernism***

Global Trends

- Mass migrations and unprecedented urban expansion challenge national identities.

Africa and China: Anti-Colonialism

- The Anglo-Boer War and violent uprisings against colonial rule in Africa call Europe's imperializing mission into question.
- The Chinese rise up against European encroachments in the Boxer Rebellion.

Europe and North America: Mounting Tensions

- Intense political rivalries, financial insecurities and crises, rapid industrialization, feminism, and class conflict roil Europe and spread to the rest of the world.

Mexico: Resentment toward Elites

- The most widespread revolution from below takes place in Mexico.

Cultural Modernism

- Popular culture comes of age.
- Elite culture explores new forms in painting, architecture, music, literature, and science in order to break with the past and differentiate itself more dramatically from popular culture.
- New ideas of race emerge, as does a renewed emphasis on the nation-state and nationalism.

CHRONOLOGY

	1870	1880	1890
The Americas		Jim Crow laws (United States) **1890s**	
Europe			
South Asia		Indian National Congress founded **1885**	
East Asia			
Russia			
Africa			

KEY TERMS

anarchism p. 684
Anglo-Boer War p. 675
Boxer Uprising p. 677
Mexican Revolution p. 685
modernists p. 668
pan movements p. 698
popular culture p. 689
progressive reformers p. 687
Shanghai School p. 691
Sun Yat-sen p. 695
syndicalism p. 684

STUDY QUESTIONS

1. **Explain** why westerners used the term *progress* to describe the world at the end of the nineteenth and beginning of the twentieth centuries. What did they believe were the sources of this progress?
2. **List and explain** various examples of worldwide anxieties that challenged the idea of progress during this time. Which groups protested the status quo?
3. **Describe** the armed uprisings against western imperialism in Africa and China during this era. How similar were these movements to other alternative visions to the new world order explored in Chapter 16?
4. **Compare and contrast** revolutionary and reform movements in Latin America and China during this era. How were their goals and methods similar and different?
5. **Analyze** how anxieties about progress shaped cultural developments around the world. What was cultural modernism, and how did it challenge traditional assumptions about art and science?
6. **Define** the term *popular culture*. Why did it become so powerful during this time, and how did it shape individuals' identity?
7. **Analyze** to what extent new ideas of race and nation created tension within and between states. What new forms of nationalism emerged during this time?

Labor unrest **1880s–1910s**

Progressive reforms (United States) **1900–1920**

Mexican Revolution **1910–1920**

Labor unrest **1880s–1910s**

Social welfare laws enacted in many states **1880s–1910**

Picasso unveils *Les Demoiselles d'Avignon* **1907**

Indian National Muslim League founded **1906**

Boxer Uprising **1899–1900**

Chinese Republican Revolution **1911**

Russo-Japanese War **1904–1905**

Revolts in Russian Empire **1905**

South African War **1899–1902**

Herrero Revolt **1904–1906**

Maji-Maji Revolt **1905–1906**

1900 **1910** **1920**

BEFORE YOU READ THIS CHAPTER

wwnorton.com/
STUDYSPACE

GLOBAL STORYLINES

- The Great War (World War I) engulfs the entire globe, exhausts Europe, and promotes production and consumption on a mass scale.
- The harsh terms of the peace settlement unbalance the global economy and lead directly to the Great Depression.
- Three strikingly different visions for building a better world arise: liberal democratic, authoritarian, and anticolonial.

CHAPTER OUTLINE

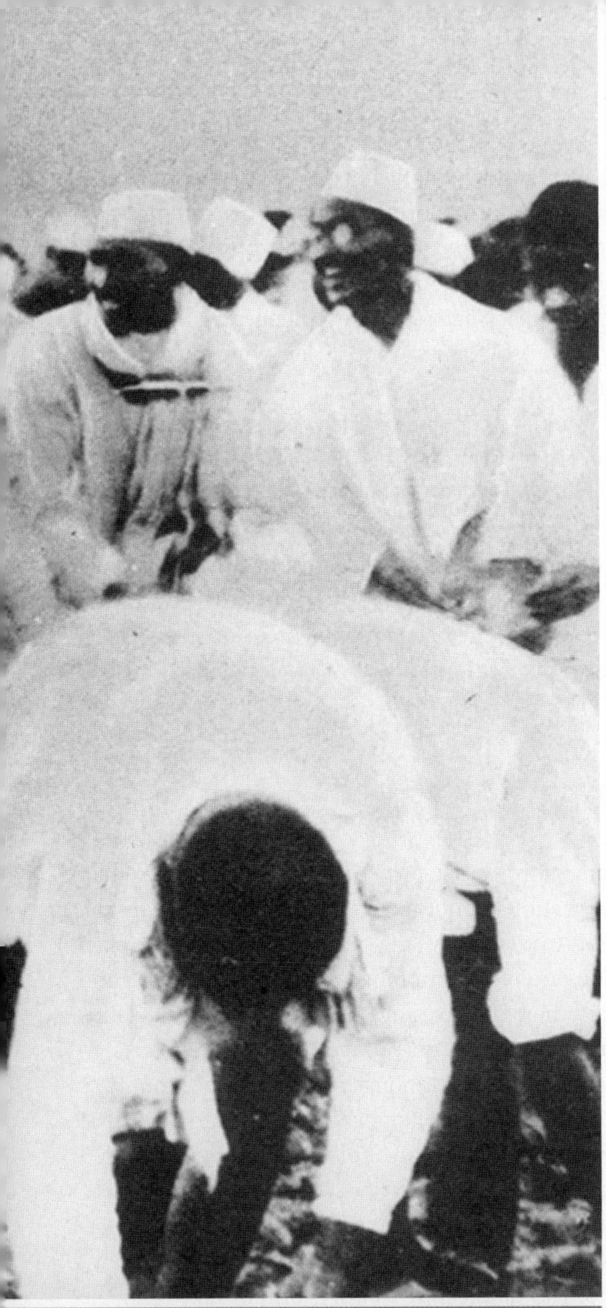

19

Of Masses and Visions of the Modern, 1910–1939

FOCUS QUESTIONS

- How did World War I disrupt societies around the world?
- How did the war usher in the age of "mass society"?
- How did authoritarian, liberal, and anticolonial visions propose to reorder their societies during the 1920s and 1930s?

The last guns of the Great War (World War I) fell silent not on the bloody battlefields of Europe, but in a remote corner of East Africa. It took a full day for news of the armistice to reach that region where African soldiers, under British and German officers, were battling for control of German East Africa. Here, 10,000 German-led African soldiers used guerrilla tactics to thwart the efforts of over 300,000 British-led African soldiers. Thousands of African troops died in these battles, beyond the spotlight of international opinion. Thus did this world conflagration come to a close outside Europe.

Raging from August 1914 to November 1918, World War I shook the foundations of the European-centered world. Although most major battles occurred on European soil, multitudes of American, African, and Asian soldiers were ferried across oceans to join the killing and maiming there. Campaigns also bloodied the soil in Turkey, Egypt, Syria, and sub-Saharan Africa. This was the first modern war involving whole societies. Its impact was thoroughly global. In addition to involving countless soldiers from Europe's colonies, its aftermath fostered notions of freedom and self-determination and a growing disillusionment with

European rule in these locations. Elsewhere, nations grappled with competing visions for building a viable, modern society.

This chapter deals with the Great War and its global impact. First, because the war was fought on a worldwide scale and to utter exhaustion in Europe, it required the resources of a large part of the world. Therefore it prompted production and consumption on a mass scale. These in turn became defining features of economic modernity. Wartime leaders used new media such as radio and film to promote national loyalties and to discredit enemies—and thereby helped to spread a mass culture. Second, the harsh terms of the peace settlement unbalanced the global economy and led directly to the Great Depression. Third, political turmoil surrounding the war inflamed disputes over how to manage mass societies and build a better world. To this end, three strikingly different visions arose: liberal democratic, authoritarian, and anticolonial. These ideologies competed for preeminence in the decades leading up to World War II.

THE QUEST FOR THE MODERN

When people spoke of "being modern" in the 1920s and 1930s, they disagreed on what it meant. Most agreed, however, that in economic terms modernity involved mass production and mass consumption. In the West, for example, the automobile, the gramophone (a record player), the cinema, and the radio reflected the benefits of economic and cultural modernism. In terms of political issues, being modern meant the involvement of the masses in politics. Everywhere people favored strong leadership to reinvigorate their societies; some wanted more democracy to replace monarchical and colonial rule. Following the Great Depression in the 1930s, even more intense debates arose. These debates led to bitter divisions on how to build modern societies.

The first political vision of modernism—the *liberal democratic* one—confronted economic failings without sacrificing market economies or parliamentary democracy. It did so through widened participation in governance but also gave greater power to state regulatory bureaucracies. However, after the Great Depression spread hard times and unemployment, this predominantly American and western European model linking capitalism and democracy no longer seemed so promising. Around the world, people considered alternatives that might better deliver the promises of modernity. Although many rejected the parliamentary or liberal perspective, the system survived in the United States, parts of western Europe, and several Latin American nations.

For many observers, liberal democracies failed to match the astonishing dynamism of a second perspective—*authoritarianism*. Authoritarian regimes rejected parliamentary rule, subordinated the individual to the state, managed and often owned most aspects of the production process, used censorship and terror to enforce loyalty, and exalted an all-powerful leader. Authoritarianism was evident in both right-wing dictatorships (Fascist Italy, Nazi Germany, dictatorial Spain and Portugal, and militaristic Japan) and a left-wing dictatorship (the Soviet Union).

The third vision—*anticolonial*—also questioned the liberal democratic order, primarily because of its connection to colonialism. However, most anticolonialists did not reject parliaments or private enterprise. Resentful of European rulers who preached democracy but practiced despotism, anticolonial leaders sought to oust their colonial rulers and then find their own path to modernity. They generally favored mixing western ideas with indigenous traditions.

THE GREAT WAR

Few events were more decisive in drawing men and women worldwide into national and international politics than the **Great War**. For over four years, millions of soldiers from Europe, as well as from its dominions and colonies, killed and mutilated one another. Such carnage damaged European claims to civilized superiority and encouraged colonial subjects to break from imperial masters. Among Europeans, too, the war's effects shook the hierarchies of prewar society. Above all, the war made clear how much the power of the state now depended on the support of the people.

The war's causes were complex. The bedrock cause was the combustible rivalry between Great Britain and Germany. Through most of the nineteenth century, Britain had been the preeminent power. By the century's end, however, German industrial output had surpassed Britain's, and Germany had begun building a navy. For the British, who controlled the world's seas, the German navy was an affront; for the Germans, it was a logical step in their expanding ambitions. This Anglo-German antagonism drew in the other powers in rival alliances. Germany joined Austria-Hungary to form the **Central Powers**; Britain affiliated itself with France and Russia in the Triple Entente (called the **Allied Powers** later, after Italy joined).

Well armed and secretly pledged to defend their partners, the rivals lacked only a spark to ignite open hostilities. That came in August 1914, when the heir to the Habsburg throne was assassinated in Sarajevo, the capital of Austrian Bosnia. The assassin hoped to trigger an independence movement that would detach South-Slav territories from the Austro-Hungarian Empire (see Chapter 18) and unite them with independent Serbia. But as the Ottoman Empire was pushed out of the Balkans, Russia and Austria-Hungary competed for influence and territory there.

Russia backed the Serbs against Austria-Hungary, and the British, French, and Germans were drawn into the conflict in support of their partners. The world war that followed dragged in Europe's colonies, too.

The Fighting

The declarations of war drew cries of jubilation from those who anticipated a short triumphal conflict for their side. Dreams of glory inspired tens of thousands of men to enlist. But the fighting did not go as expected.

BATTLE FRONTS, STALEMATE, AND CARNAGE Despite hopes for a swift resolution, the war became infamous for its duration and horrors. The initial German offensive, which intended to thrust through neutral Belgium, stalled thirty miles outside Paris at the battle of the Marne in September 1914 (see Map 19.1). A stalemate ensued. Instead of a quick war, vast land armies dug trenches along the Western Front—from the English Channel through Belgium and France to the Alps—installing barbed wire and setting up machine-gun posts. The troops became immobilized. Anything but glorious, life in the trenches mixed boredom, dampness, dirt, vermin, and disease, punctuated by the terror of being ordered to "go over the top" to attack the enemy's entrenched position. Doing so meant running across a "no man's land" in which machine guns mowed down almost all attackers.

On the other side of Europe, Russian troops advanced into East Prussia and Austria-Hungary along the Eastern Front. Although the Russians defeated Austro-Hungarian troops in Galicia (between present-day Poland and Ukraine) and scored initial victories in eastern Germany, they suffered devastating reversals in East Prussia once the Germans threw in well-trained divisions that were better armed and better provisioned than the Russian troops.

By 1915, the war had ground to a gruesome standstill. Along the Western Front, neither the Allies nor the Central Powers could advance. On the Eastern Front, the Russians had been driven back and had lost much of Poland. At Ypres in 1915, the Germans tried to break the stalemate by introducing poison gas, but a countermove of equipping soldiers with gas masks nullified that advantage. In July 1916, the British launched an offensive along the Somme River in northeastern France. By November, when the futile attack halted, approximately 600,000 British and French and 500,000 Germans had perished. Yet the battle lines had hardly budged. Attempts to win by opening other fronts—in Turkey, the Middle East, and Africa—failed and added to the war's carnage (see Map 19.2).

The death toll forced governments to call up more men than ever before. More than 70 million men worldwide fought in the war, including almost all of Europe's young adult males. From 1914 to 1918, 13 million served in the German army. In Russia, more than 15 million men took up arms. The British Empire mobilized nearly 9 million soldiers, and the British nation's 5.25 million troops constituted almost half the prewar population

Trenches in World War I. *The anticipated war of mobility turned out to be an illusion; instead, armies dug trenches and filled them with foot soldiers and machine guns. To advance entailed walking into a hail of machine-gun fire. Life in the trenches meant cold, dampness, rats, disease, and boredom.*

MAP 19.1 | World War I: The European and Middle Eastern Theaters

Most of the fighting in World War I, despite its designation as a world war, occurred in Europe. Although millions of soldiers fought on both sides, the territorial advances were relatively small.

• Look at the maps above, and identify all the countries where Allies and Central Powers made advances. Which countries had to fight a two-front war? • Did the armies of the Central Powers or the Allies gain the most territory during the war? • According to your reading, how did this factor affect the war's outcome?

of men age fifteen to forty-nine. In France, around 8 million served, nearly 80 percent of the same prewar age-group population. For those who fought, the personal outcomes were mainly unhappy. Over half of the men who were mobilized died, were wounded or taken prisoner, or were reported missing in action.

Mass mobilization also undermined traditional gender boundaries. Tens of thousands of women served at or near the front as doctors, nurses, and technicians. Even more women mobilized on the "home front," taking on previously male occupations—especially in munitions plants. But women could also turn against the state. Particularly in central Europe and Russia, the war's demands for soldiers and supplies left farms untended and caused food shortages. Bread riots and peaceful protests by women, traumatized by loss and desperate to feed their children, put states on notice that their citizens expected compensation for their sacrifices. Indeed, civilian pressure forced many states to make promises they would have to fulfill after the war, in the form of welfare provisions, expanded suffrage, and pensions for widows and the wounded.

In the four years of war, military deaths exceeded 9 million. Another 21 million soldiers were wounded. Vast numbers of survivors bore artificial limbs. Naval blockades and aerial bombardments had aggravated civilian food shortages and left people susceptible to epidemics, like influenza. As demobilizing soldiers spread disease into their communities, influenza claimed 50 million people worldwide.

Women's War Effort. *With armies conscripting nearly every able-bodied man, women filled their places in factories, especially in those that manufactured war materials, such as the French plant pictured here in 1916.*

EMPIRE AND WAR The war's horrors reached across the world's regions (see again Map 19.2). The sprawling Ottoman Empire sided with the Central Powers, battling British- and Russian-led forces in Egypt, Iraq, Anatolia, and the Caucasus. In 1915–1916, Ottoman forces massacred or deported 1.3 million Armenians, who were accused en masse of collaborating with the Russians. Many analysts regard these attacks as the world's first genocide, the intentional elimination of a whole people. To increase their forces, the British and the French conscripted colonial subjects: India provided 1 million soldiers; over 1 million Africans fought in Africa and Europe for their colonial masters, and another 3 million transported war supplies. Even the sparsely populated British dominions of Australia, New Zealand, and Canada dispatched over a million loyal young men to fight for the empire.

Despair and disillusionment at the prolonged, bloody war turned into revolt and revolution. In British-ruled Nyasaland, a mission-educated African, John Chilembwe, directed his compatriots to refuse British military demands and to stand up for "Africa for the Africans." Although the British suppressed the insurrection and executed the rebel leader, Chilembwe's death did not stop the growing desire to undo bonds to the mother country.

Controlling the mobilized masses proved even more difficult in Europe. In 1916, after the second winter of deprivation, antiwar demonstrations broke out. The next year, strikes roiled Germany, France, Britain, Italy, and Russia. Meanwhile, in trying to break the battlefield stalemate, Allied commanders introduced devastating new weapons such as the tank. Neither civilian protest nor new armaments could stop the war's devastation, though. As a result, Europe's postwar leaders reaped a bitter harvest of anger, sorrow, and despair.

THE RUSSIAN REVOLUTION The war destroyed entire empires. The first to go was Romanov Russia. In February 1917, Tsar Nicholas II stepped down under pressure from his generals. They wanted to quash the mass unrest in the capital, which, they believed, threatened the war effort along the Eastern Front. Some members of the Russian parliament formed a provisional government; at the same time, grassroots councils (soviets) sprang up in factories, garrisons, and towns. The irony of Russia's February Revolution, which brought an end to the monarchy, was that the military and civilian elites wanted to restore order, and implement a more "bourgeois" parliamentary form of government, not encourage a revolution. With the tsar removed, millions of peasants seized land, soldiers and sailors abandoned the front, and borderland nationalities declared autonomy from the crumbling Russian Empire.

In October 1917, left-wing socialists calling themselves **Bolsheviks** seized power. Led by Vladimir Lenin and Leon Trotsky, the Bolsheviks drew support among radicalized soldiers, sailors, and factory workers organized in the soviets. Arresting provisional government members and claiming power in the name

GREENLAND
CANADA
UNITED STATES
NORWAY
SWEDEN
FINLAND
DENMARK
BALTIC SEA
UNITED KINGDOM
GERMANY
POLAND
FRANCE
AUSTRIA-HUNGARY
ROMANIA
BULGARIA
BLACK S
SERBIA
ITALY
MONTENEGRO
ALBANIA
GREECE
PORTUGAL
SPAIN
OTTOMAN EMPIRE
TUNISIA
MOROCCO
ALGERIA
LIBYA
EGYPT
RIO DE ORO
ATLANTIC OCEAN
BRITISH HONDURAS
BAHAMAS
CUBA
JAMAICA
WEST INDIES
HONDURAS
NICARAGUA
COSTA RICA
PANAMA
COLOMBIA
VENEZUELA
BRITISH GUIANA
DUTCH GUIANA
FRENCH GUIANA
ECUADOR
PERU
BRAZIL
BOLIVIA
PARAGUAY
CHILE
ARGENTINA
URUGUAY
PACIFIC OCEAN
GAMBIA
GUINEA
SIERRA LEONE
GOLD COAST
TOGO
NIGERIA
CAMEROON
ANGLO-EGYPTIAN SUDAN
UGANDA
NORTHERN RHODESIA
SOUTHERN RHODESIA
GERMAN SOUTH-WEST AFRICA
SOUTH AFRICA
Allied Powers, colonies and allies
Central Powers and colonies
Neutral nations throughout the war
Troop movements
0 1000 2000 Miles
0 1000 2000 Kilometers

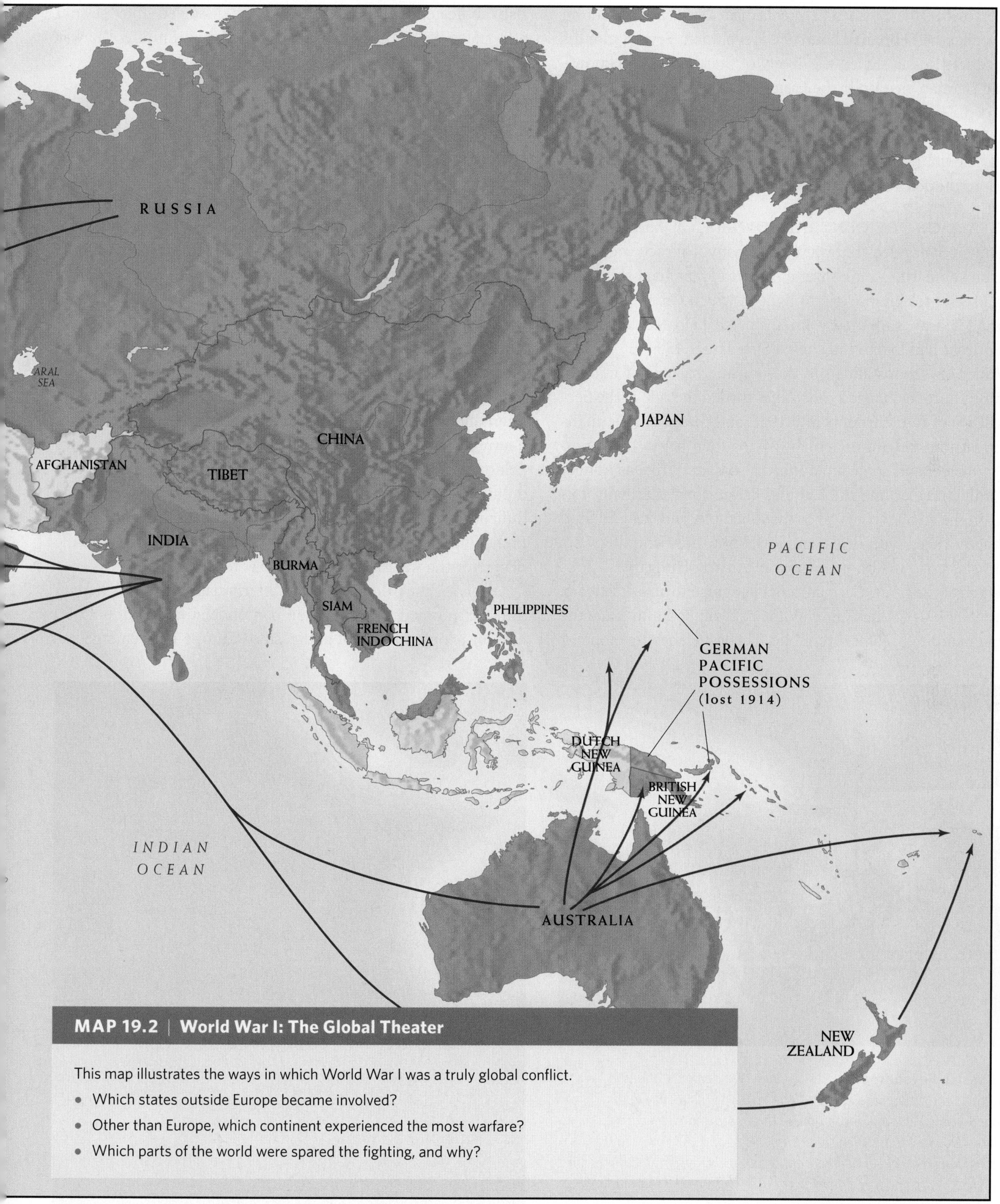

MAP 19.2 | World War I: The Global Theater

This map illustrates the ways in which World War I was a truly global conflict.

- Which states outside Europe became involved?
- Other than Europe, which continent experienced the most warfare?
- Which parts of the world were spared the fighting, and why?

of the soviets, the Bolsheviks proclaimed a socialist revolution to overtake the February "bourgeois" revolution. Several months later, Soviet Russia signed the Treaty of Brest-Litovsk, acknowledging German victory on the Eastern Front as the Russian army collapsed. For protection, the Bolshevik leadership relocated the capital to Moscow and set up a so-called dictatorship of the proletariat. Lenin insisted on accepting the peace treaty and the loss of vast territories to safeguard the socialist revolution.

THE FALL OF THE CENTRAL POWERS On April 2, 1917, the United States declared war on Germany. This occurred after German submarines sank several American merchant ships and after a secret telegram came to light in which German officials sought Mexican support by promising to help Mexico regain territories it had lost to the United States in 1848.

With U.S. troops added to the fray, the balance of military power in Europe changed. The Allies turned the tide at the Second Battle of the Marne in July 1918 and forced the Germans to retreat into Belgium. German troops then began to surrender en masse, and some announced a soldiers' strike as hunger and influenza became unbearable. Before long, Germany tottered on the edge of civil war as the Allied blockade caused food shortages. Faced with defeat and civil strife, the Central Powers fell in succession. Although most of Austria-Hungary's troops remained at the front, German generals agreed to an armistice in November 1918. After Kaiser Wilhelm II slipped into exile, the German empire became a republic. The last Habsburg emperor also abdicated, and Austria-Hungary dissolved into several new states. With the collapse of the Ottoman Empire, the war claimed a fourth dynasty among its casualties.

The Peace Settlement and the Impact of the War

To decide the fate of vanquished empires and the future of the modern world, the victors convened five peace conferences, one for each of the Central Powers. Most important was the conference to negotiate peace with Germany, held at Versailles, France, in January 1919. Delegates drew many of their ideas from American President Woodrow Wilson's "Fourteen Points," a blueprint he had devised for making peace in Europe. Wilson especially insisted that postwar borders be redrawn by following the principle of "self-determination of nations" and that an international **League of Nations** be set up to negotiate further quarrels. Such high-minded ideas were appealing, but once delegates got down to the business of carving up Europe and doling out Germany's colonies, negotiations became tense and difficult. Over the objections of the Americans and British, the French insisted on a punitive treaty that assigned Germany sole blame for the war and forced it to pay reparations.

Applying the principle of self-determination was much more difficult in practice than Wilson had understood. Suddenly, 60 million people in central and eastern Europe now emerged as

The Russian Revolution. (Left) *The July 1917 demonstrations in Petrograd were among the largest in the Russian Empire during that turbulent year of war and revolution. In this photo, marchers carry banners, "Down with the Ministers-Capitalists" and "All Power to the Soviets of Worker, Soldier and Peasant Deputies."* (Right) *Vladimir Lenin died just six years and three months after the October 1917 revolution, but he lived on in his writings and images, such as in this painting by Pavel Kuznetsov. Artists and propagandists helped make Lenin a ubiquitous icon of the new Soviet order.*

MAP 19.3 | Outcomes of World War I in Europe, North Africa, and Some of the Middle East

The political map of Europe and the Middle East changed greatly after the peace treaty of 1919.

- Comparing this map with Map 19.1, which shows the European and Middle Eastern theaters of war, identify the European countries that came into existence after the war. What happened to the Ottoman Empire, and what powers gained control over many territories of the Ottoman state?
- What states emerged from the Austro-Hungarian Empire?

inhabitants of new nation-states (see Map 19.3). The patchwork nature of the old multiethnic empires here meant that as many as 25 million now lived in states in which they were ethnic minorities and vulnerable to persecution in the tumultuous years after the armistice. The limits of self-determination were even more telling in terms of non-Europeans' rights, for the peacemakers were not prepared to extend self-determination beyond Europe.

ANALYZING GLOBAL DEVELOPMENTS

Measuring Casualties in World War I

You would think that tabulating historical data would be a fairly easy thing to do. At different points in this text, however, we have seen that it takes painstaking efforts on the part of historians and demographers to first figure out the best way to collect the data and second to then accurately categorize and count it. Figuring out the number of Africans that left on slave ships and where they embarked and disembarked during the Atlantic slave trade is a great example of this kind of work. Historian Jay Winter and others have worked tirelessly for thirty years to come up with accurate death tolls for the soldiers and civilians in World War I. In a landmark book, *The Great War and the British People*, Winter used a range of archival sources from government agencies' data and mortality rate tables from major insurance companies to estimate and calculate the number of deaths among people in Britain and Ireland. While the carnage in World War I seems beyond measure, Winter, in one paradoxical finding, demonstrated that death rates among civilians actually went down during that war in Britain and Ireland. He suggests that the best explanation for this development was the efforts of the state to mobilize the civilian population and provide health insurance, and, most important, to improve nutrition.

The table below builds on Winter's early efforts and shows the best estimates for the military death tolls across all the major participants in World War I.

QUESTIONS FOR ANALYSIS

- Based on data provided in the table, did the mobilization for the war have a greater impact on the societies of the Central Powers or the Allied Powers? Please justify your answer.
- While the number of people mobilized was a factor of 1.5 greater in the Central Powers, why do you think the dead, wounded, and missing/POW rates were nearly twice as high as those of the Allied Powers?
- The United State played a major role in World War I, but why were the number of its dead, wounded, and missing/POW so low compared to that of the other major combatants?

Military participation and military losses in World War I

Allied Powers	Mobilized	Dead	Wounded	POW/Missing	Total	% Casualties
Russia	15,798,000	1,800,000	4,950,000	2,500,000	9,250,000	59
France	7,891,000	1,375,800	4,266,000	537,000	6,178,800	78
GB, incl. empire	8,904,467	908,371	2,090,212	191,652	3,190,235	36
Italy	5,615,000	578,000	947,000	600,000	2,125,000	38
United States	4,273,000	114,000	234,000	4,526	352,526	8
Japan	800,000	300	907	3	1,210	0
Romania	1,000,000	250,706	120,000	80,000	450,706	45
Serbia	750,000	278,000	133,148	15,958	427,106	57
Belgium	365,000	38,716	44,686	34,659	118,061	32
Greece	353,000	26,000	21,000	1,000	48,000	14
Portugal	100,000	7,222	13,751	12,318	33,291	33
Montenegro	50,000	3,000	10,000	7,000	20,000	40
Total	**45,899,467**	**5,380,115**	**12,380,704**	**3,984,116**	**22,194,935**	**46**
Central Powers						
Germany	13,200,000	2,037,000	4,216,058	1,152,800	7,405,858	56
Austria-Hungary	900,000	1,100,000	3,620,000	2,200,000	6,920,000	77
Turkey	2,998,000	804,000	400,000	250,000	1,454,000	48
Bulgaria	400,000	87,500	152,390	27,029	266,919	67
Total	**25,598,000**	**4,028,500**	**8,388,448**	**3,629,829**	**16,046,777**	**63**
Grand Total	**71,497,467**	**9,408,615**	**21,219,152**	**7,613,945**	**38,241,712**	**53**

Sources: John Horne (ed.), A Companion to World War I *(2010); Tucker Spencer (ed.),* The European Powers in the First World War: An Encyclopedia *(1996); J. M. Winter,* The Great War and the British People *(1985).*

Instead of granting independence to the inhabitants of Germany's former colonies in Africa, the treaty parceled them out to the French, the British, the Belgians, and the South Africans. They were assigned as mandates under the oversight of the League of Nations. The same was true of the Arab provinces of the Ottoman Empire (Syria, Lebanon, Palestine, Jordan, and Iraq), which were turned over to the British and the French.

Whatever idealism survived the peacemaking process absorbed another blow when the U.S. Senate, reflecting a resurgence of isolationism, turned down the Treaty of Versailles and kept the United States out of the League of Nations. Russia, too, was outside the league. For Britain, France, Japan, and the United States, keeping communist "Red" Russia isolated became a postwar priority.

Demobilization hit societies hard, especially working women; when soldiers hobbled home, women faced layoffs from their wartime jobs. Still, they did not retreat entirely. Within a few years, women gained the vote in Russia, Britain, Germany, and the United States. France held out until 1944, partly because the left feared that French women were under the thumb of the conservative Catholic Church. Nonetheless, in all these nations women claimed new privileges. Young, unmarried women went out in public unescorted, dressed as they saw fit, and maintained their own apartments. Such behavior shocked cultural conservatives, but young women and men alike were determined to enjoy the new, modern world.

MASS SOCIETY: CULTURE, PRODUCTION, AND CONSUMPTION

The war also contributed to another modern phenomenon: the making of mass societies. Even before World War I mobilized entire societies to produce and to fight, parliamentary regimes had begun to democratize, in many cases granting non–property holders and women the right to vote. Authoritarian regimes, meanwhile, had begun to mobilize the people via rallies and mass organizations. And new technologies, such as radio, were helping to create mass cultures that spanned geographic and class divides.

Mass Culture

Indicative of the modern world were new forms of mass communication and entertainment. These were partially wartime products. In an effort to mobilize populations for total war, leaders had disseminated propaganda as never before—through public lectures, theatrical productions, musical compositions, and (censored) newspapers. Indeed, the war's impact had politicized cultural activities while broadening the audience for nationally oriented information and entertainment. Together with new media, the war was instrumental in fostering mass culture.

Postwar **mass culture** was distinctive. First, it differed from elite culture (opera, classical music, paintings, literature) because it reflected the tastes of the working and the middle classes, who now had more time and money to spend on entertainment. Second, mass culture relied on new technologies, especially film and radio, which could reach an entire nation's population and consolidate their sense of being a single state.

RADIO Radio entered its golden age after World War I. Invented early in the twentieth century, it made little impact until the 1920s, when powerful transmitters permitted stations to reach much larger audiences—often with nationally syndicated programs. Radio "broadcasts" gave listeners a sense of intimacy with newscasters and stars, addressing consumers as personal friends and drawing them into the lives of serial heroes. Special programs targeted children and women, making radio listening something for the whole family. Even the illiterate could enjoy the programs, such as *The Lone Ranger.* By the late 1920s, nearly two-thirds of homes in the United States had at least one radio. Britain achieved similar radio saturation a decade later.

Radio also was a way to mobilize the masses, especially in authoritarian regimes. For example, the Italian dictator Benito Mussolini pioneered the radio address to the nation. Later, Soviet and Nazi propagandists used this format with great regularity and effect. In Japan, too, radio became a tool to promote the right-wing government's goals. But even dictatorships could not exert total control over mass culture. Although the Nazis regarded jazz as racially inferior music and the Soviets regarded it as "bourgeois," neither could prevent young or old from tuning in to foreign radio broadcasts, smuggling gramophone records over the borders, or creating their own jazz bands.

FILM AND ADVERTISING Film, too, had profound effects. For traditionalists, Hollywood by the 1920s signified vulgarity and decadence because the silver screen prominently displayed modern sexual habits. And like radio, film served political purposes. Here, again, antiliberal governments took the lead. German filmmaker Leni Riefenstahl's movie of the Nazi Nuremberg rally of 1934, *Triumph of the Will,* is a key example of propagandistic cinema. Nazi-era films were comedies, musicals, melodramas, detective films, and adventure epics—sometimes framed by racial stereotypes and political goals. Soviet film studios also produced Hollywood-style musicals alongside didactic pictures about Socialist triumphs.

In market economies, radio and film grew into big businesses, and with expanded product advertising they promoted other enterprises as well. Especially in the United States, advertising became a major industry, with radio commercials shaping national consumer tastes. Increasingly, too, American-produced entertainment,

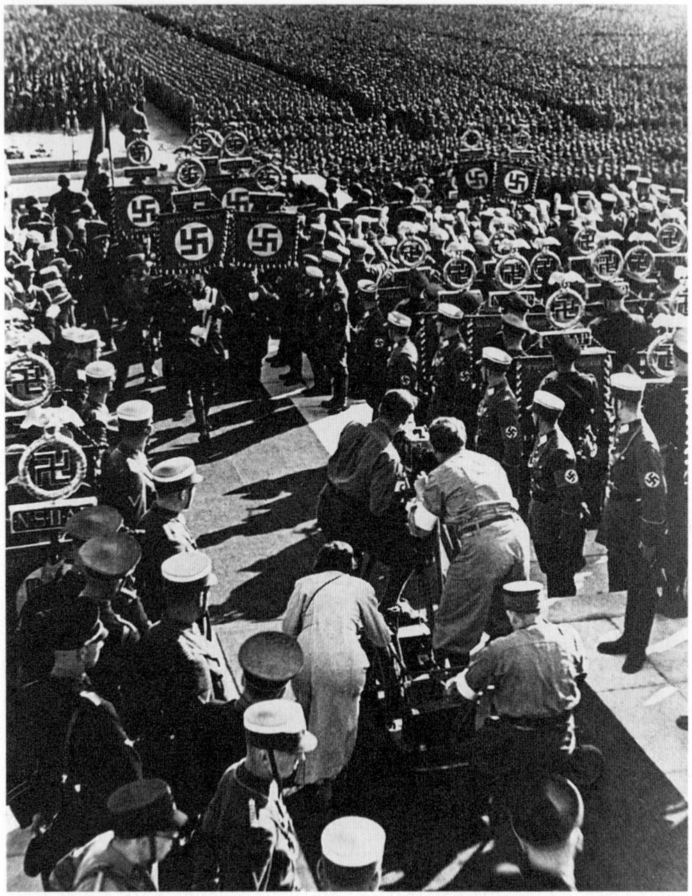

Triumph of the Will. *The shooting of* Triumph of the Will, *perhaps the greatest propaganda film ever, directed by Leni Riefenstahl. The film, later denounced, won gold medals in Venice in 1935 and at the World's Fair in 1937.*

radio programs, and cinematic epics reached an international audience. Thanks to new media, America and the world began to share mass-produced images and fantasies.

Mass Production and Mass Consumption

The same factors that promoted mass culture also enhanced production and consumption on a mass scale. In fact, World War I paid perverse tribute to the power of industry, for machine technologies produced war materials with abundant and devastating effect.

Never before had armies had so much firepower at their disposal. Whereas in 1809 Napoleon's artillery had discharged 90,000 shells over two days during the largest battle waged in Europe to that point, by 1916 German guns were firing 100,000 rounds of shells per hour over the full twelve hours of the Battle of Verdun. To sustain military production, millions of men and women worked in factories at home and in the colonies. Producing huge quantities of identical guns, gas masks, bandage rolls, and boots, these factories reflected the modern world's demands for greater volume, faster speed, reduced cost, and standardized output—key characteristics of **mass production**.

The war reshuffled the world's economic balance of power, boosting the United States as an economic powerhouse. As its share of world industrial production climbed above one-third in 1929 (roughly equal to that of Britain, Germany, and Russia combined), people around the globe regarded the United States as a "working vision of modernity" in which not only production but also consumption boomed.

THE AUTOMOBILE ASSEMBLY LINE The most outstanding example of the relationship between mass production and consumption in the United States was the motor car. It symbolized the machine age and the American road to modernization. Before World War I, the automobile had been a rich man's toy. Then came Henry Ford, who founded the Ford Motor Company in 1903. Five years later, he began production of the Model T, a car that at $850 was within the reach of middle-class consumers. Soon popular demand outstripped supply. Seeking to make more cars faster and cheaper, Ford used mechanized conveyors to send the auto frame along a track, or assembly line, where each worker performed one simplified, repetitious task. By standardizing the manufacturing process, subdividing work, and substituting machinery for manual labor, Ford's assembly line brought a new efficiency to the mass production of automobiles.

By the 1920s, a finished car rolled off Ford's assembly line every ten seconds. Although workers complained about becoming "cogs" in a depersonalized labor process, the system boosted output and reduced costs. The effects reverberated throughout the nation's economy. Ford's factory near Detroit employed 68,000 workers—the largest factory in the world. In addition, millions of cars required millions of tons of steel alloys, as well as vast amounts of glass, rubber, textiles, and petroleum. Cars also needed roads to drive on and service stations to keep them running. Altogether, nearly 4 million jobs related directly or indirectly to the automobile—an impressive total in a labor force of 45 million workers.

After World War I, automobile ownership became more common among Americans. By the 1920s, assembly-line production had dropped the Model T's price to $290. Ford further expanded the market for cars by paying his own workers $5 per day—approximately twice the average manufacturing wage in the United States. He understood that without **mass consumption**, increased purchasing power in the middle classes, and appetite for goods there could be no mass production. Whereas in 1920 Americans owned 8 million motor cars, a decade later they owned 23 million. The automobile's rapid spread seemed to demonstrate that mass production worked. (See Primary Source: Bruce Barton's Gospel of Mass Production.)

THE GREAT DEPRESSION Not all was easy listening or smooth motoring in countries where mass societies were taking root. During the 1920s, many producers of foodstuffs, coal, and ores

Car Assembly Line. *Mass production was made possible by the invention of the electric motor in the 1880s, and it enacted three principles: the standardization of core aspects of products, the subdivision of work on assembly lines, and the replacement of manual labor by machinery as well as by reorganizing flow among shops. The greatest successes occurred in the auto plants of Henry Ford, shown here in 1930. With each worker along the line assigned a single task, millions of automobiles rolled off the Ford assembly line, and millions of Americans became owners of automobiles.*

faced sagging prices because of overproduction. As staple prices declined in proportion to manufactured goods, farmers throughout the United States, Canada, Australia, and Latin America lamented their dwindling fortunes compared to those of their urban cousins.

On October 24, 1929—Black Tuesday—the American stock market collapsed, plunging not only the American economy but also international financial and trading systems into crisis. This event led the world into the **Great Depression**. Its causes went back to the Great War, which had left European nations in deep debt as they struggled to rebuild their economies and pay off war debts. To restore stability, Europeans borrowed heavily from the United States. When wobbly governments and small investors defaulted on their loans, the U.S. Federal Reserve reacted by raising interest rates. Starting in central Europe, financial institutions began to collapse. As banks fell, other lenders scrambled to call in their loans. Companies, governments, and private borrowers were soon floating in a sea of debt. The panic then spread to the world's stock markets, which led to the Wall Street crash of 1929, which spurred more bank closures.

Financial turmoil produced a major contraction of world trade. Striving to protect workers and investors from the influx of cheap foreign goods, governments raised tariff barriers against imports. After the United States enacted protective tariffs, other governments abandoned free trade in favor of protectionism.

Stock Traders after the Crash. *On October 24, 1929, the American stock market crashed. Here traders are pictured congregating in the financial district of New York City, on what came to be known as "Black Tuesday." As stock values plummeted, panic gripped Wall Street and soon spread across the nation. The market crash was followed by even more devastating bank runs as the Great Depression overtook the world.*

PRIMARY SOURCE

Bruce Barton's Gospel of Mass Production

In 1925, the journalist (and, later, advertising executive) Bruce Barton published* The Man Nobody Knows, *which became a best-seller. In the book, Barton interpreted the life and teachings of Jesus as a gospel for success in modern business. In the excerpt below, Barton uses Henry Ford, whose Model T automobile reigned as the era's marvel of mass production, to show the profitable connections between religion and commerce.

"If you're forever thinking about saving your life," Jesus said, "you'll lose it; but the man who loses his life shall find it."

Because he said it and he was a religious teacher, because it's printed in the Bible, the world has dismissed it as high minded ethics but not hard headed sense. But look again! . . .

What did Henry Ford mean, one spring morning, when he tipped a kitchen chair back against the whitewashed wall of his tractor plant and talked about his career?

"Have you ever noticed that the man who starts out in life with a determination to make money, never makes very much?" he asked. It was rather a startling question; and without waiting for my comment he went on to answer it: "He may gather together a competence, of course, a few tens of thousands or even hundreds of thousands, but he'll never amass a really great fortune. But let a man start out in life to build something better and sell it cheaper than it has ever been built or sold before—let him have *that* determination, and, give his whole self to it—and the money will roll in so fast that it will bury him if he doesn't look out.

"When we were building our original model, do you suppose that it was money we were thinking about? Of course we expected that it would be profitable, if it succeeded, but that wasn't in the front of our minds. We wanted to make a car so cheap that every family in the United States could afford to have one. So we worked morning, noon and night, until our muscles ached and our nerves were so ragged that it seemed as if we just couldn't stand it to hear anyone mention the word automobile again. One night, when we were almost at the breaking point I said to the boys, 'Well, there's one consolation,' I said, 'Nobody can take this business away from us unless he's willing to work harder than we've worked.' And so far," he concluded with a whimsical smile, "nobody has been willing to do that."

QUESTIONS FOR ANALYSIS

- What are the key ingredients to success, according to Ford?
- What was foremost on Ford's mind when he set out to build "our original model"?
- How do the lessons from the Bible and Henry Ford relate to each other? Do you think the indirect analogy is effective? Explain why or why not.

Source: Bruce Barton, The Man Nobody Knows: A Discovery of the Real Jesus, *in Loren Baritz, ed.,* The Culture of the Twenties *(Indianapolis: Bobbs-Merrill, 1925), pp. 241–42.*

Manufacturers cut back production, laid off millions of workers, and often went out of business. By 1935, world trade had shrunk to one-third of its 1929 level. Primary producers felt the harshest effects, for their international markets shut down almost completely. World prices for Argentine beef, Chilean nitrates, and Indonesian sugar all dropped sharply. The combination of shrinking markets and drastic shortages of credit forced industries and farms worldwide into bankruptcy.

The Great Depression soon spawned rethinking of the tenet that markets should govern themselves, the core of laissez-faire liberalism (see Chapter 14). By the late 1930s, the exuberant embrace of private mass production had ceded to a new conviction: state intervention to regulate the economy was critical to prevent disaster. In 1936, the British economist John Maynard Keynes published a landmark treatise, *The General Theory of Employment, Interest, and Money*. He argued that the market could not always adjust to its own failures and that sometimes the state had to stimulate it by increasing the money supply and creating jobs. Although the "Keynesian Revolution" took years to transform economic policy and to produce the welfare state, many governments were determining that capitalism had to be saved from itself. This unsettling realization called into question political liberalism.

MASS POLITICS: COMPETING VISIONS FOR BUILDING MODERN STATES

World War I heightened the prewar unsettling of class, gender, and colonial relations, further challenging the liberal vision of technological progress, free markets, and societies guided by the educated few. On battlefronts and home fronts, countless workers, peasants, women, and colonial subjects had sacrificed and now expected to share in the fruits of peace. Many, even in victorious nations, lost confidence in traditional authorities who had failed to prevent the cataclysm and allowed it to go on so long.

Politics, no longer contained in genteel chambers, shifted to the street. Everywhere except in the United States, variants of socialism gained throngs of new adherents. In the Soviet Union, the Bolsheviks began to construct a society whose rules defied capitalist principles. Elsewhere, mass movements sought to replace imperiled liberal democratic states, as in Germany, Italy, and Spain. Even liberal democratic empires such as Britain and France faced challenges to square their rule over colonial subjects with their rhetoric of freedom. And a hybrid political order, mixing democratic and authoritarian institutions, emerged in Latin America. Meanwhile, the Great Depression further undermined capitalism and parliaments. (See Current Trends in World History: Population Movements: Filling Up the Empty Spaces and Spreading Capitalism).

Authoritarian solutions to problems like mass unemployment grew increasingly popular, especially as the communist Soviet Union, Nazi Germany, fascist Italy, dictatorial Portugal and Spain, and militaristic Japan projected images of national strength and pride. Outside Europe, anticolonial movements gathered steam; here, liberal models could not cope with the scale and diversity of the new politics. Thus, by the late 1930s, the states that retained democracy and capitalism in some form appeared weak and vulnerable. Dictators seemed to be riding the wave of the future, and colonies were threatening to go their own separate ways.

Liberal Democracy under Pressure

In Europe of the 1920s, anxiety about modernization increased. Reacting to the war's carnage, elite Europeans looked longingly for supposedly pristine worlds that their own corrupting civilization had not destroyed. This trend found expression in the arts. For example, Josephine Baker, an African American dancer who performed nude, wild dances on the Parisian stage, enjoyed colossal popularity. So did Oswald Spengler's *The Decline of the West* (1919), a best-seller whose title seemed to capture the trajectory of liberal modernity.

The demands of fighting a total war had offered European states the opportunity to experiment with illiberal policies. Indeed, the war brought both the suspension of parliamentary rule and an effort by governments to manage industry and distribution. States on both sides of the conflict jailed many individuals who opposed the war. Governments regulated both production and, through rationing, consumption. Above all, the war revolutionized the size and scope of the state.

BRITISH AND FRENCH RESPONSES TO ECONOMIC CRISES At the war's end, liberal democratic elites wished to return to free-market policies, but women, veterans, and workers insisted that the states for which they had fought address their needs—for jobs, housing, and compensation for war wounds. Recurrent economic crises, especially the Great Depression, forced most liberal democrats to rethink their ideas. By 1930, even Britain had given up on free trade, and other countries were seeking economic self-sufficiency.

Britain and France retained their parliamentary systems, but even here, old-fashioned liberal democracy was on the run. Strife rippled across the British Empire, and in the home isles Britain gave independence to what became the Republic of Ireland in 1922. Britain's working-class Labour Party came to power twice between 1923 and 1931; but either alone or in coalition with Liberals and Conservatives, Labour could not lift the country

Josephine Baker. *The African-American entertainer Josephine Baker was a sensation on the stage in interwar Paris. Many of her shows exoticized or even caricatured her African descent.*

CURRENT TRENDS IN WORLD HISTORY

Population Movements: Filling Up the Empty Spaces and Spreading Capitalism

As we have seen in Chapters 12 and 13, the European discovery of the Americas resulted in a vast movement of peoples across the Atlantic Ocean from Europe and Africa into the western hemisphere. These population movements, among the largest in world history to that point, pale when measured against the long-distance migrations that occurred in the hundred years between 1840 and 1940. During these years, 150 million individuals of European and Asian descent filled up the less populated parts of the world, moving from Europe, South Asia, and China into the Americas, Southeast Asia, and northern Asia in unprecedented numbers and spreading a capitalist mode of production wherever they moved. A great many of the migrants went as laborers in the factories and on the plains of the Americas and on the rubber, sugar, tea, and coffee plantations springing up in the Dutch East Indies and East and southern Africa. They were as essential to the expansion of the capitalist system in these regions as the 12 million African captives transported to the Americas during the Atlantic slave trade were for the economic expansion of the Americas. Although the new watchword in economic relations was free labor, not all of the men and women who moved were in fact free workers. Indentured servitude—that is, agreeing to work for a certain number of years, usually between three and seven, in return for transportation to the region, food, housing, and clothing—was widely used with Chinese and Indian workers.

A good example of the movement and use of semi-coerced or indentured workers in less-developing regions comes from East Africa. There, the British and Germans were engaged in a furious political rivalry to extend their control over territories, and British officials believed that constructing a railway from the coast of East Africa at the port of Mombasa to Kisumu at Lake Victoria would enhance their territorial ambitions in East Africa. They also concluded that they would be unable to recruit a sufficient supply of African workers to accomplish the task. Not surprisingly, they looked to the government of India to assist them in providing the necessary work force.

The British government of India did more than help them. In all, it made available nearly 35,000 indentured South Asian workers on three-year contracts for the construction of what was known as the Uganda Railway, the track for which, covering a distance of 582 miles, was completed in a mere five years from 1896 to 1901. The work was arduous, the living conditions in the work camps were horrific, yet the British official overseeing the construction concluded that had it not been for this work force, it is doubtful if the project could have been completed

out of its economic crisis. In 1926, 162 million working days were lost to strikes. Still, despite hard times, the British retained their commitment to parliamentarianism and capitalism.

Disorder was even more pronounced in France, which had lost 10 percent of its young men and seen the destruction of vast territory. In 1932–1933, six government coalitions came and went over the course of just nineteen months. Against the threat of a rightist coup, a coalition of the moderate and radical left, including the French communist party, formed the Popular Front government (1936–1939). It introduced the right of collective bargaining, a forty-hour workweek, two-week paid vacations, and minimum wages.

THE AMERICAN NEW DEAL In the United States, too, markets and liberalism faced challenges. When the Great Depression shattered the nation's fortunes, pressure intensified to create a more secure political and economic system.

In contrast to postwar Europe, where labor parties and socialist movements were surging, the 1920s saw a conservative tide engulf American politics. Calling for a "return to normalcy" (a retreat from the government activism that had characterized the presidencies of Theodore Roosevelt and Woodrow Wilson), Warren Harding won the presidency in 1920 with a resounding 60 percent of the popular vote. Four years later, Calvin Coolidge scored an even greater landslide; his remark that the "business of America is business" reflected his dislike of government interference in free enterprise. With the election of Herbert Hoover in 1928, Republicans continued their string of presidential triumphs.

Largely left behind was the nation's African American population. In the rural American South, "Jim Crow" laws enforced social segregation, economic inequality, and political disenfranchisement. Like rural whites, millions of blacks quit the countryside and moved to northern cities such as New York and Chicago. Here they found some relief from the legal barriers that had limited their opportunities and rights, but discrimination continued to hold them down and to restrict their residences to urban ghettos. Still, within black neighborhoods, most famously New York City's Harlem, a vibrant cultural scene blossomed. The New Negro Movement, or Harlem Renaissance,

Ugandan Railway. *Indian workers cut rock for the Uganda Railway in this 1905 photograph, taken in British East Africa.*

QUESTIONS FOR ANALYSIS

- Why do you think that in some cases, like the building of the Uganda Railway, governments had to be involved in forcibly moving workers to where they were needed rather than letting market forces draw the workers to where work was available?
- What do you see as some of the similarities and differences between the way that the African slaves were treated versus the forced or indentured servants during this period?

in under twenty years. The building of the Uganda Railway is one of many examples where we see significant numbers of people moving to new places and regions, sometimes by their own choosing and sometimes not, to play an important role in the expansion of the capitalist system and the rivalries between colonial powers.

Explore Further

McKeown, Adam, *Melancholy Order: Asian Migration and the Globalization of Border* (2008).

showcased black novelists, poets, painters, and musicians, many of whom used their art to protest racial subordination.

With the Great Depression came deeper challenges to liberal modernity. By the end of 1930, more than 4 million American workers had lost their jobs. As President Hoover insisted that citizens' thrift and self-reliance, not government handouts, would restore prosperity, the economic situation worsened. By 1933, industrial production had dropped by a staggering 50 percent since 1929. The hard times were even worse in the countryside, where farm income plummeted by two-thirds between 1929 and 1932.

In the 1932 presidential election, a Democrat, Franklin Delano Roosevelt, won by a landslide. He promptly launched what came to be called the **New Deal**, a set of programs and regulations that dramatically expanded the scope of the American national government and its role in the nation's economic life. In his first hundred days in office, Roosevelt obtained legislation to provide relief for the jobless and to rebuild the shattered economy. Among his administration's experiments were the Federal Deposit Insurance Corporation to guarantee bank deposits up to $5,000, the Securities and Exchange Commission to monitor the stock market, and the Federal Emergency Relief Administration to help states and local governments assist the needy. Subsequently, in 1935, the Works Progress Administration put nearly 3 million people to work building roads, bridges, airports, and post offices. In addition, the Social Security Act inaugurated old-age pensions supported by the federal government.

Never before had the U.S. federal government expended so much on social welfare programs or intervened so directly in the national economy. Yet the Depression lingered, and before long unemployment again climbed—from 7 million in 1937 to 11 million in 1938.

The persistence of hard times opened the New Deal to attacks from both the left and the right. Emboldened labor leaders, resurgent radicals, and populist demagogues claimed that the New Deal was not addressing the problems of the poor and the unemployed. But Roosevelt continued on a moderate course. The New Deal did not substantially redistribute national income. Likewise, although Roosevelt's administration established public agencies to build dams and to oversee the

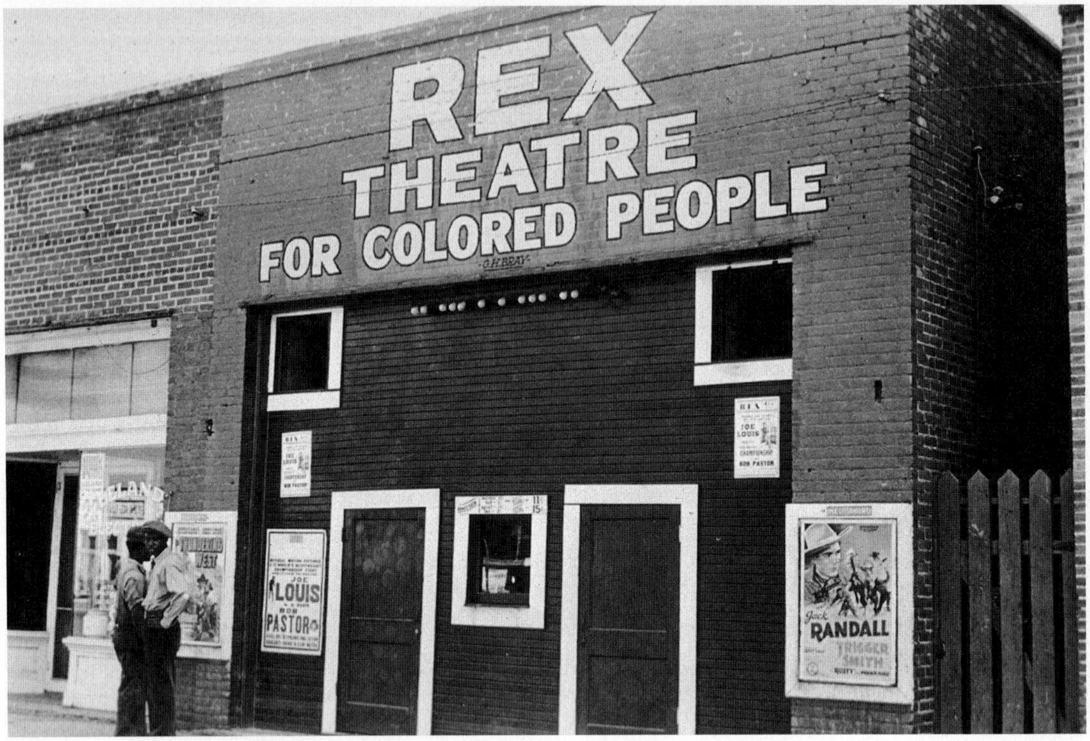

"Jim Crow." *"Jim Crow" laws mandated the segregation of races in the American South, with African Americans forced to use separate, and usually unequal, facilities, including schools, hotels, and theaters, such as this one in Mississippi.*

irrigation of arid lands and the electrification of rural districts, these were exceptions. Privately owned enterprises continued to dominate American society. Roosevelt's aim was not to destroy capitalism, but to save it. In this regard the New Deal succeeded, for it staved off authoritarian solutions to modern problems.

Authoritarianism and Mass Mobilization

Like the liberal systems they challenged, authoritarian regimes came in various stripes. On the right arose dictatorships in Italy, Germany, and Japan. Although differing in important respects, all disliked the left-wing dictatorship of the Soviet Union. The Soviets had no liking for the Fascists. Yet all the postwar dictatorships were forged principally in opposition to the liberal democracies. In place of liberal inertia, these regimes touted their success in mobilizing the masses to create dynamic yet orderly societies. They also had charismatic leaders, who personified the power and unity of the societies over which they ruled.

Although rejecting liberal democracy, post–World War I dictators insisted that they had their people's support. True, they treated their people as a mass conscript army that needed firm leadership to build new societies and guarantee well-being. But their demands, the leaders maintained, would yield robust economies, restore order, and renew pride. In addition, dictators gained support by embracing public welfare programs. They also vowed to deliver on all of modernity's promises (prosperity, national pride, technology) without having to endure any of its costs (class divisions, unemployment, urban-industrial squalor, moral breakdown). For a time, many of the globe's inhabitants believed them.

THE SOVIET UNION AND SOCIALISM The most dramatic blow against liberal capitalism occurred in Russia when the highly radical Bolshevik Party seized power. The coup aroused opposition inside and outside the country. Fearing the spread of socialist revolution, Britain, France, Japan, and the United States sent armies to Russia to contain Bolshevism. But after executing the tsar and his family, the Bolsheviks rallied support by defending the homeland against its invaders. They also mobilized people to fight (and win) a civil war (1918–1921) in the name of defending the revolution. The conflict pitted an array of disunified forces (former tsarist supporters but also some social democrats and independent peasant armies) against the Bolsheviks and their supporters (many soldiers, sailors, workers, and state functionaries).

In the all-out mobilization against those whom they labeled the Whites, or counterrevolutionaries, the Bolsheviks, calling themselves the Reds, began to rebuild state institutions. Amid this turmoil, the need to requisition grain from the peasantry as well as the extensive military operations weighed heavily on the population and interfered with the harvest. From 1921 to 1923, Russia suffered a severe famine in which some 7 to 10 million people died from hunger and disease.

To revive the economy, the Bolsheviks grudgingly legalized private trade and private property. In 1924, with the country

Stalin. *Joseph Stalin posing at the Allies' "Big Three" conference in Yalta, on Soviet soil, February 1945. Much had changed since Stalin became leader of the communist party of the Soviet Union in 1922.*

still recovering from civil war, the undisputed leader of the revolution, Lenin, died. No one had done more to shape the institutions of the revolutionary regime, including creating expectations for a single ruler. After eliminating his rivals, **Joseph Stalin** (1878–1953) emerged as the new leader of the communist party and the country, which soon became the Union of Soviet Socialist Republics (U.S.S.R.), or Soviet Union.

THE SOVIETS BUILD SOCIALISM Since socialism as a fully developed social and political order did not exist anywhere in the 1920s, no one was sure how it would actually work. Stalin resolved this dilemma by defining Soviet or revolutionary socialism in opposition to capitalism. Since capitalism had "bourgeois" parliaments serving the interests of the rich, socialism, as elaborated by Stalinist leaders, would have soviets (councils) of worker and peasant deputies. Since capitalism had unregulated markets, which led to inefficiency and unemployment, socialism would have economic planning and full employment. And since capitalism relied on the "exploitation" of private ownership, socialism would outlaw private trade and private property. In short, socialism would eradicate capitalism and then invent socialist forms in housing, culture, values, dress, and even modes of reasoning.

The efforts to build a noncapitalist society required class war, and these began in the heavily populated countryside. Peasants already lived in village communes, leasing the land together while working it individually (as households). Stalin wanted to combine the farms into larger units owned and worked collectively, and run by regime loyalists. Tens of thousands of urban activists and Red Army soldiers led a drive to establish these collective farms and to compel farmers to sell all their grain and livestock at state-run collection points for whatever price the state was willing to pay (often very little).

In protest, many peasants burned their crops, killed their livestock, and destroyed their farm machinery. The government responded by deporting these protesters, along with many bystanders, to remote areas. Villages had to fill quotas for deportation; often those selected were people who had slept with someone's wife rather than those whose cows produced the most milk. Thus, "class warfare" reflected personal animosities, greed, and ambition. Meanwhile harvests again declined, and a second famine claimed millions more lives. Grudgingly, the regime conceded household plots to the collectivized peasants. Here they could grow their own food and take some of their produce to approved markets. But few escaped the collectives, which depended on the state for seed, fertilizers, and machinery.

Collectivized Agriculture. *Soviet plans for the socialist village envisioned the formation of large collectives supplied with advanced machinery, thereby transforming peasant labor into an industrial process. The realities behind the images of smiling farmers—such as in this poster, exhorting "Give first priority to gathering the Soviet harvest!"—were low productivity, enormous waste, and often broken-down machinery.*

MAP 19.4 | The Soviet Union

The Union of Soviet Socialist Republics (U.S.S.R.) came into being after World War I.

- How did its boundaries compare with those of the older Russian Empire, as shown in Map 17.6 (p. 660)?
- What does the large number of Soviet republics suggest about the ethnic diversity within the Soviet Union?
- According to your reading, how did Soviet leaders govern non-Russian minorities within the new state?

The late 1920s saw the beginning of a frenzied Five-Year Plan to "catch and overtake" the leading capitalist countries. Now millions of enthusiasts (as well as deported peasants) set about building a socialist urban utopia founded on advanced technology, almost all of it purchased from the Depression-mired capitalist countries. More than 10 million people helped build or rebuild hundreds of factories, hospitals, and schools. Huge hydroelectric dams, automobile and tractor factories, and heavy machine-building plants symbolized the promise of Soviet-style modernity, which eliminated unemployment during the capitalist Great Depression.

Soviet authorities also started building socialism in the borderlands. In 1922, the U.S.S.R. joined the independent states of Ukraine, Belorussia (Belarus), and the Transcaucasian Federation with Soviet Russia to form a single federal state. The U.S.S.R. also soon included several new republics, such as those in central Asia; eventually there were fifteen (see Map 19.4), all of which acquired their own institutions—but under centralized rule from Moscow. In the 1930s, collectivization and mass arrests devastated the peasants and nomads as well as the officials of the republics, but industrialization and urbanization strengthened local elites.

MASS TERROR AND STALIN'S DICTATORSHIP The Soviet political system became more despotic as the state expanded. Police power grew the most, partly from forcing peasants into collectives and organizing mass deportations. As the party's ranks swelled, ongoing loyalty verifications also led to the removal of party members, even when they professed absolute loyalty. From 1936 to 1938, trials of supposedly treasonous "enemies of the people" resulted in the execution of around 750,000 people and the arrest or deportation of several million more. They were sent to forced labor camps, collectively known as the Gulag. Such purges decimated the loyal Soviet elite—party officials, state officials, intelligentsia, army officers, and even members of the police who had enforced the terror.

Behind this mass terror loomed fear, a sense of omnipresent conspiracies, and the Soviet leader's overpowering personal dictatorship. Although Stalin initiated mass terror against the elite, his motives remain unclear. Neither he nor the regime was under threat, and the leaders' loyalty was not in doubt. What is clear is that the political police, given sizeable arrest quotas, often exceeded them. In addition, millions of ordinary people helped implement the terror. Some reluctantly turned in neighbors; some did so to try to save themselves; many showed fanatical zeal in fingering "enemies." In the end, the terror manifested highly petty motives as well as a desire to participate in the violent crusade of building socialism in a hostile world, full of internal and external enemies.

ITALIAN FASCISM Long before the Soviets had created a new anticapitalist model, the political situation in capitalist societies had begun to change. Two key factors were disillusionment with the costs of the Great War and fear that a communist takeover like that in Russia could occur in western Europe. In Italy, for example, mass strikes, occupations of factories, and peasant land seizures swept the country in 1919 and 1920. Amid this disorder, rightists seized power. Their leader was **Benito Mussolini** (1883–1945), a former socialist journalist.

In 1919, Mussolini sought to organize disaffected veterans into a mass political movement called **fascism**. His early programs mixed nationalism with social radicalism and revealed a yearning to sweep away all the institutions discredited by the war. Fascist supporters demanded the annexation of "Italian" lands in the Alps and on the Dalmatian coast and called for female suffrage, an eight-hour workday, a share of factory control for workers, a tax on capital, land redistribution, and a constituent assembly—in short, a populist program.

Fascists attracted numerous followers. Their violence-prone shock troops wore black shirts and loose trousers tucked into high black leather boots and saluted with a dagger thrust into the air. In 1920, the squads received money from landowners and factory owners to beat up socialist leaders, after which Italian fascism became fully identified with the right. Still, the fascists saw themselves as champions of the little guy, of peasants and workers, as well as of war veterans, students, and white-collar types.

Mussolini. *Benito Mussolini liked to puff out his chest, particularly when appearing in public. Il Duce pioneered the leader's radio address to the people, and he encouraged fascist versions of the mass spectacles that also became common in Soviet Russia.*

In 1922, Mussolini announced a march on Rome. The march was a bluff, yet it intimidated the king, who opposed fascist ruffians but feared bloodshed. So he withheld use of the army against the lightly armed marchers. When the Italian government resigned in protest, the monarch invited Mussolini to become prime minister, despite the fact that fascists had won only a small minority of seats in the 1921 elections.

The 1924 elections, in which fascists won 65 percent of the vote, took place in an atmosphere of intimidation and fraud. Mussolini dealt with other challenges by mobilizing the squads and police for crackdowns on the liberal and socialist opposition. Soon a series of decrees transformed Italy from a constitutional monarchy into a dictatorship. Within two years, all parties except that of the fascists had been dissolved.

Mussolini's dictatorship made deals with big business and the church, thus falling short of a total social revolution. Nonetheless, it was skilled at using parades, films, radio, and visions of recapturing Roman imperial grandeur to boost support during the troubled times of the Depression. The cult of the leader, *Il Duce*, also provided cohesion. As the first antiliberal, anti-socialist alternative, Italian fascism served as a model for other countries.

GERMAN NAZISM In Germany, too, fear of Bolshevism and anger over the war's outcome propelled the right to power. Here, the dictator was **Adolf Hitler** (1889–1945). After a small nationalist workers' organization took shape in Munich, dedicated to winning workers over from socialism, the army high command ordered a young demobilized corporal to infiltrate the group. That corporal, Hitler, soon dominated the nationalist workers' movement, whose name he changed to the National Socialist German Workers' Party (*National-Sozialistische Arbeits-Partei,* or **Nazis**).

Unlike Mussolini, the young Hitler was never a socialist. The first Nazi Party platform, set forth in 1920, combined nationalism with anticapitalism and anti-Semitism. It also called for the renunciation of the Treaty of Versailles. It was an assertion of Germany's grievances against the world and of the small man's grievances against the rich. At first, Hitler and the Nazis were unsuccessful, and Hitler himself was arrested. He was sentenced to five years in prison for treason, but served less than a year. While in prison he wrote an autobiographical and fanatically anti-Semitic treatise called *Mein Kampf* (My Struggle, 1925), which subsequently became wildly popular among Nazis.

The Weimar Republic enjoyed a period of stability after hyperinflation was curtailed by the intervention of American bankers, and in the 1926 elections the Nazi Party received only 2.6 percent of the votes. It only gained popularity after the

Hitler. *Adolf Hitler and his advisors mastered the staging of mass rallies. These rallies and marches projected an image of dynamism and collective will, which Hitler claimed to embody.*

collapse of the American stock market in 1929, when short-term loans were called in. As more and more people lost their jobs, farms, and small businesses, Germans considered radical alternatives. In this atmosphere, fearing popular support of the communist and socialist parties and convinced that he could control Hitler, Germany's president appointed Hitler chancellor (prime minister) in 1933. Initially, Hitler pledged that traditional conservatives would dominate the government. Thus, like Mussolini, Hitler came to power peacefully and legally.

Hitler's first step as chancellor was to heighten fear of a communist conspiracy to take power. The burning of the Reichstag building in Berlin the following month provided the opportunity. The Nazis blamed the fire on the communists, immediately suspended civil liberties "as a defensive measure against the communists," and forced the left-wing press out of business. The latter move robbed opponents of the ability to criticize the regime publicly. Hitler then proposed legislation that would enable him to promulgate laws on his authority as chancellor without the parliament's approval.

Within a month Hitler was free from the control of parliament and the conservative elites. Soon the government seized the offices, banks, and newspapers of trade unions and arrested their leaders. The socialist and communist parties were outlawed; others were dissolved. By July 1933, the Nazis were the only legal party and Hitler was dictator of Germany. He aggressively curbed dissent and banned strikes, jailing political opponents and building the first concentration camps (initially to house political prisoners) when the jails overflowed.

He also unleashed a campaign of persecution against the Jews, believing that assimilated Jews controlled the banks and that eastern Jewish emigrants carried disease. Like many other right-wing Germans, Hitler also believed that a Jewish-socialist conspiracy had stabbed the German army in the back, causing its surrender in World War I, and that intermarriage with Jews was destroying the supposed purity of the Aryan race (which included northern, white, Europeans). Hitler and the Nazis did not believe that religious practice defined Jewishness; instead, they held, it was transmitted biologically from parents to children. Once he became dictator, Hitler instituted legal measures that excluded Jews from the civil service and the professions, forced them to sell their property, deprived them of citizenship, and forbade them to marry or have sex with Aryans. Hitler also encouraged the use of terror against Jews, destroying their businesses, homes, and marriages with non-Jews, frightening them into leaving Germany, and ultimately eliminating all traces of Jewish life and culture in Nazi-dominated central Europe.

Although some Germans opposed Hitler's illiberal activism, the Nazis won popular support for restoring order and reviving the economy. In 1935, defying the Treaty of Versailles, Hitler began a vast rearmament program that absorbed the unemployed. Now economic despair and national disgrace turned into fierce pride and impressive national power. The state also financed public works including reforestation and swamp drainage projects; organized leisure, entertainment, travel, and vacations; and built highways and public housing. Anti-Semitism

PRIMARY SOURCE

Cult of the Dynamic Leader

Nazi political theorists offered no apologies for dictatorship. On the contrary, they bragged about it as the best way of mobilizing the masses and directing the state. The Führer, or Leader, stood above the Nazi Party and all government institutions and embodied the supposed will of the German nation. He also decided who belonged, or did not belong, to the nation. The following excerpt, taken from the writings of Ernst Rudolf Huber, Germany's major constitutional expert of the 1930s, elaborated on the awesome powers being conferred on Hitler as Führer.

The office of Führer has developed out of the National Socialist movement. In its origins it is not a State office. This fact must never be forgotten if one wishes to understand the current political and legal position of the Führer. The office of Führer has grown out of the movement into the Reich, firstly through the Führer taking over the authority of the Reich Chancellor and then through his taking over the position of Head of State. Primary importance must be accorded to the position of "Führer of the movement"; it has absorbed the two highest functions of the political leadership of the Reich and thereby created the new office of "Führer of the Nation and of the Reich."...

The position of Führer combines in itself all sovereign power of the Reich; all public power in the State as in the movement is derived from the Führer power. If we wish to define political power in the Third Reich correctly, we must not speak of "State power" but of "Führer power." For it is not the State as an impersonal entity which is the source of political power but rather political power is given to the Führer as the executor of the nation's common will. Führer power is comprehensive and total; it unites within itself all means of creative political activity; it embraces all spheres of national life; it includes all national comrades who are bound to the Führer in loyalty and obedience. Führer power is not restricted by safeguards and controls, by autonomous protected spheres, and by vested individual rights, but rather it is free and independent, exclusive and unlimited.

QUESTIONS FOR ANALYSIS

- How did the office of Führer arise, according to Huber?
- What are the source and scope of "Führer power"?

Source: Ernst Rudolf Huber, "Führergewalt," from Nazism 1919–1945: A Documentary Reader; Volume 2: State, Economy, and Society, 1933–1939, *pp. 198–99, edited by J. Noakes and G. Pridham. Reprinted by permission of University of Exeter Press.*

mixed with full employment and social welfare programs that privileged racially approved groups.

Germany reemerged as a great power with expansionist aspirations. Hitler called his state the Third Reich (the first being the Holy Roman Empire, or Reich, and the second the Reich created by Bismarck in 1871). He claimed that, like the Holy Roman Empire, his empire would last 1,000 years. Hitler also harbored grand aspirations to impose racial purity and German power in Europe and perhaps beyond. (See Primary Source: Cult of the Dynamic Leader.)

DICTATORSHIPS IN SPAIN AND PORTUGAL As authoritarian regimes spread across Europe, the military took over and instituted dictatorships in Spain and Portugal. Their effort to seize power in Spain provoked a brutal civil war from 1936 to 1939, which left 250,000 dead.

The Spanish civil war was, from the start, an international war. When the Spanish republican government introduced reforms to break the hold of the church and landlords on the state, the military intervened and all of Europe's major powers got involved. The military's attack against the republic at first failed, but with the help of German and Italian weapons (above all, airplanes), Generalissimo Francisco Franco gained the upper hand. Meanwhile, Britain and France dithered and only Stalin's Russia supported the republican government, allowing Franco to establish a dictatorship.

MILITARIST JAPAN Unlike authoritarian regimes, Japan did not suffer wounded power and pride during World War I. In fact, because wartime disruptions reduced European and American competition, Japanese products found new markets in Asia. Japan expanded production, exporting munitions, textiles, and consumer goods to Asian and western markets. During the war, the Japanese gross national product (GNP) grew 40 percent, and the country built the world's third largest navy. After a devastating earthquake and fire in 1923, Tokyo was rebuilt with steel and reinforced concrete, symbolizing the new, modern Japan.

MAP 19.5 | The Japanese Empire in Asia, 1933

Hoping to become a great imperial power like the European states, Japan established numerous colonies and spheres of influence early in the twentieth century.

- What were the main territorial components of the Japanese Empire?
- How far did the Japanese succeed in extending their political influence throughout East Asia?
- According to your reading, what problems did the desire to extend Japanese influence in China present to Japanese leaders?

Hirohito. *A portrait of Crown Prince Hirohito of Japan in 1925, the year before he ascended the Japanese throne. Hirohito presided over Japan's war in Asia, beginning with the 1931 seizure of Manchuria and culminating in the 1945 surrender, but he remained emperor for another four decades. When he died in 1989, his wartime responsibility was still a difficult subject for many.*

Manchurian Incident. *Taken from among the throng of Japanese troops, this September 1931 photograph documents the Japanese invasion of Manchuria after the bombing of the South Manchurian Railroad, later known as the Manchurian Incident.*

Initially, post–World War I Japan seemed headed down the liberal democratic road. When Japan's Meiji Emperor died in 1912, his third son succeeded him and oversaw the rise of mass political parties. Suffrage expanded in 1925, increasing the electorate roughly fourfold. But along with democratization came repressive measures. Although the Meiji Constitution remained in effect, a new Peace Preservation Law specified up to ten years' hard labor for any member of an organization advocating change in the political system or abolition of private property. The law served as a club against the mass leftist parties.

Japan veered still further from the liberal democratic road after Emperor Hirohito came to power in 1926. In Japan, as in Germany, the Great Depression spurred the eventual shift to dictatorship. Japan's trade with the outside world had more than tripled between 1913 and 1929, but after 1929 China and the United States imposed barriers on Japanese exports in preference for domestic products. These measures contributed to a 50 percent decline in Japanese exports. Unemployment surged.

Such turmoil invited calls for stronger leadership, which military commanders were eager to provide. Already beyond civilian control, in 1927 and 1928 the army flexed its muscles by twice forcing prime ministers out of office. New "patriotic societies" used violence to intimidate political opponents. Violence culminated in the assassination of Japan's prime minister, accompanied by an uprising of young naval officers and army cadets. Their coup failed, but it further eclipsed the power of political parties.

It was in the Japanese Empire that militarism and expansionism received a boost. In 1931, a group of army officers arranged an explosion on the Japanese-owned South Manchurian Railroad as a pretext for taking over Manchuria. In 1932, adding Manchuria to its Korean and Taiwanese colonies (see Map 19.5), Japan oversaw the proclamation of the puppet state of Manchukuo. In 1933, the Japanese army seized the Chinese province of Jehol to use as a buffer zone between China proper and Manchukuo. Later, they annexed it to the Empire of Manchukuo. Meanwhile, at home, "patriots" continued a campaign of terror against uncooperative businessmen and critics of the military. As in Italy and Germany, the state in Japan took on a sacred aura. This occurred through the promotion of an official religion, Shinto, and of Emperor Hirohito's divinity. By 1940, the clique at the top had merged all political parties into the Imperial Rule Assistance Association, ending even the semblance of parliamentary rule.

COMMON FEATURES OF AUTHORITARIAN REGIMES

Despite important differences, the major authoritarian regimes of this period—communist Soviet Union, fascist Italy, Nazi Germany, and militarist Japan—shared many traits. All rejected parliamentary rule and sought to revive their countries' power through authoritarianism, violence, and a cult of the leader.

All claimed that modern economies required state direction. In Japan, the government fostered huge business conglomerates; in Italy, it encouraged big business to form cartels. The German state also regarded the private sector as the vehicle of economic growth, but it expected entrepreneurs to support the Nazis' racial, antidemocratic, and expansionist aims. The most thorough form of economic coordination occurred in the Soviet Union, which adopted American-style mass production while eliminating private enterprise. Instead, the Soviet state owned and managed all the country's industry. Here, as elsewhere, state-organized labor forces replaced independent labor unions.

Another common feature involved using mass organizations for state purposes. Russia, Italy, and Germany had single mass parties; Japan had various rightist groups until the 1940 merger. All promoted dynamic youth movements, such as the Hitler Youth and the Union of German Girls, the Soviet Communist Youth League, and the Italian squads marching to the anthem "Giovinezza" (Youth).

Hitler Youth. *Like the communists in the Soviet Union, the Nazis organized and indoctrinated boys and girls in the hopes of making them strong supporters of the regime. Pictured here are members of the Hitler Youth, about 1939.*

Three of the states adopted extensive social welfare policies. The Nazis emphasized full employment, built public housing, and provided assistance to needy Aryan families. The Italian National Agency for Maternity and Infancy provided services for unwed mothers and infant care. Soviet programs addressed maternity, disability, sickness, and old age. In fact, the Soviet state viewed welfare assistance as an ongoing program that distinguished socialism from capitalism. Although Japan did not enact innovative social welfare legislation, its Home Affairs Ministry enlisted helpmates among civic groups, seeking to raise savings rates and improve childrearing practices.

A fourth common feature was ambivalence about women in public roles—the Soviet Union excepted. But even that state eventually promoted higher rates of reproduction, rewarding mothers who had many children and restricting abortion. State officials were eager to honor new mothers as a way to repair the loss of so many young men during the Great War. Yet, many more women were also entering professional careers, and some were becoming their families' primary wage earners. In Italy, fascist authorities had to accept the existence of *la maschietta*—the new woman, or flapper, who wore short skirts, bobbed her hair, smoked cigarettes, and engaged in freer sex. In Japan, the *mogā* or *modan gāru* ("modern girl") phenomenon provoked considerable negative comment, but authorities could not suppress it. The Soviets demonstrated the most contradictory behavior. In 1918, they declared men and women equal, legalized (and subsidized) abortion, and eased divorce laws. However, by 1935–1936 new laws made divorce nearly impossible, drove abortion underground, and rewarded "hero mothers" of multiple children. Nonetheless, the rapidly industrializing Soviets had the highest percentage of women in the paid workforce.

Finally, all the dictatorships used violence and terror against their own citizens, colonial subjects, and "foreigners" living within their state borders. These tools served as levers for remaking the sociopolitical order. The Italians and the Japanese were not shy about arresting political opponents, particularly in their colonies. However, it was the Nazis and especially the Soviets who filled concentration and labor camps with alleged enemies of the state, whether Jews or supposed counterrevolutionaries.

Still, brutal as these regimes were, their successes in mastering the masses drew envious glances even from those trying to stay on the liberal democratic road. They also attracted imitators. British and French fascists and communists, though they never came to power, formed national parties and proclaimed support for foreign models. Certain politicians, intellectuals, and labor organizers in South and North America admired Hitler, Lenin, and Stalin. Many also hoped to use the methods of mass mobilization and mass violence for their own ends. This was particularly true of anticolonial movements.

The Hybrid Nature of Latin American Corporatism

Latin American nations felt the same pressures that produced liberal democratic and authoritarian responses in Europe,

Russia, and Japan. However, the Latin American leaders devised solutions that combined democratic and authoritarian elements.

ECONOMIC TURMOIL Latin American countries had stayed out of the fighting in World War I, but their export economies had suffered. As trade plummeted, popular confidence in oligarchic regimes fell, and radical agitation surged. During the war years, trade unionists in the port of Buenos Aires took control of the city's docks, and the women of São Paulo's needle trades inspired Brazil's first general strike. Bolivian tin miners, inspired by events in Russia, proclaimed a full-blown socialist revolution.

The Great Depression brought even sharper challenges from workers' groups. More than in any other region, the Depression battered Latin America's trading and financial systems because they were most dependent on the exports of basic staples, from sugar to wheat, and faced stiff protection or evaporating demand for their commodities. The region, in fact, suffered a double whammy because it had borrowed so much money to invest in infrastructure and expansion. When world money markets went belly-up, creditors called in their loans from Latin America. This move drove borrowers to default. In response, Latin American governments—with enthusiastic backing from the middle classes, nationalist intellectuals, and urban workers—turned to their domestic rather than foreign markets as the main engine of growth. Here, too, the state took on a more interventionist role in market activity.

After the war, Latin American elites confronted the mass age by establishing mass parties and encouraging interest groups to associate with them. Collective bodies such as chambers of commerce, trade unions, peasant associations, and organizations for minorities like blacks and Indians all operated with state sponsorship. This form of modern politics, often labeled corporatist, used social groups to bridge the gap between ruling elites and the general population.

CORPORATIST POLITICS IN BRAZIL Corporatist politics took hold especially in Brazil, where the old republic collapsed in 1930. In its place, a coalition led by the skilled politician Getúlio Vargas (1883–1954) cultivated a strong following by enacting socially popular reforms.

Dubbing himself the "father of the poor," Vargas encouraged workers to organize, erected monuments to national heroes, and supported the building of schools and the paving of roads. He made special efforts to appeal to Brazilian blacks, who had been excluded from public life since the abolition of slavery. Thus he legalized many previously forbidden Afro-Brazilian practices, such as the ritual *candomblé* dance, whose African and martial overtones seemed threatening to white elites. Vargas also supported samba schools, organizations that not only taught popular dances but also raised funds for public works. Moreover, Vargas addressed maternity and housing policies and enfranchised women (although they had to be able to read, as did male voters). Although he condemned the old elites for betraying the country to serve the interests of foreign consumers and investors, he also arranged foreign funding and technical transfers to build steel mills and factories. However, he took this step to create domestic industry so that Brazil would not be so dependent on imports.

Ruling as a patriarch enabled Vargas to squelch dissent and build new lines of loyalty. When he revamped the constitution in 1937, he banned competitive political parties and created forms of national representation along corporatist lines. Each social

Getúlio Vargas. *This cartoon of Vargas, governor of the southern state of Rio Grande do Sul, portrays him as a country bumpkin even as he leads the overthrowing of Brazil's Old Republic.*

Samba dancers. *The dance started in the shanty towns of Rio de Janeiro and eventually became popular throughout the world, thanks to films, photographs, and long-playing records that featured samba music.*

sector or class would be represented by its function in society (for example, as workers, industrialists, or educators), and each would pledge allegiance to the all-powerful state. Although his opponents complained about losing their democratic rights, Vargas also created rights for previously excluded groups like trade unions, who now could use their corporatist representatives to press for demands. To bolster the system, he employed a small army of modern propagandists using billboards, loudspeakers, and radio to broadcast the benevolence of "Father" Vargas.

Anticolonial Visions of Modern Life

Debates over liberal democratic versus authoritarian models engaged the world's colonial and semicolonial regions as well. But here there was a larger concern: what to do about colonial authority? Throughout Asia, most educated members of these communities wanted to roll back the European and American imperial presence. Some Asians even accepted Japanese imperialism as an antidote, under the slogan "Asia for the Asians." In Africa, however, where the European colonial presence was more recent, intellectuals still questioned the real meaning of colonial rule: were the British and the French sincerely committed to African improvement, or were they obstacles to African peoples' well-being?

World War I crippled Europe but gave it more colonies than ever before. Ottoman territories, in particular, wound up in Allied hands. Great Britain emerged with an empire that straddled one-quarter of the earth. Rechristened as the British Commonwealth of Nations, Britain conferred dominion status on white-settler colonies in Canada, Australia, and New Zealand. This meant independence in internal and external affairs in exchange for continuing loyalty to the crown. But no such privileges went to possessions in Africa and India, where nonwhite peoples were the vast majority. Here the British fell back on an old line: nonwhite peoples were not yet ready for self-government.

In Africa as well as Asia, then, the search for the modern encompassed demands for power sharing or full political independence. Anticolonialism was the preeminent vision. To overcome the contradictions of European democratic liberalism, educated Asians and Africans proposed various incarnations of nationalism.

Behind the Asian and African nationalist movements were profound disagreements about how best to govern nations once they gained independence and how to define citizenship. For many intellectuals, the democratic ethos of the imperial powers was appealing. Others liked the radical authoritarianism of fascism and communism, with their promises of rapid change to modernity. Whatever their political preferences, most literate colonials also regarded their own religious and cultural traditions as sources for political mobilization. Thus Muslim, Hindu, Chinese, and African values became vehicles for galvanizing the rank and file. The colonial figures involved in political and intellectual movements insisted that the societies they sought to establish were going to be modern *and* at the same time retain their indigenous characteristics.

AFRICAN STIRRINGS Africa contained the most recent territories to come under the Europeans' control, so anticolonial nationalist movements there were quite young. The region's fate remained very much in the hands of Europeans. After 1918, however, African peoples probed more deeply for the meaning of Europe's imperial presence.

In some parts of Africa, environmental degradation contributed to resentment. In the peanut belt of Senegal, for example, African cultivators pushed into more arid regions, cutting down trees and eventually exhausting the soil. Across the continent, in Kenya, where African peoples were confined to specific locations so as to make land available to European settlers, Africans began to overgraze and overcultivate their lands. A severe problem occurred among the Kamba people living near Nairobi. Their herds had become so large that the government attempted to implement a forcible campaign of culling. Refusing to cooperate, the Kamba joined the chorus of African protesters against British authority.

There was some room (but not much) for voicing African interests under colonialism. The French had long held to a vision of assimilating their colonial peoples into French culture. In France's primary West African colony, Senegal, four coastal cities had traditionally elected one delegate (of mixed African and European ancestry) to the French National Assembly. This practice lasted until 1914, when Blaise Diagne (1872–1934), an African candidate, ran for office and won, invoking his African origins and garnering the African vote. While the British allowed Africans to elect delegates to municipal bodies, they refused to permit colonial representatives to sit in Parliament.

Blaise Diagne. *Diagne was the first African elected to the French National Assembly. He won the election to the French Parliament in 1914, beating white and mixed-race candidates by appealing to the majority black African population that lived in the four communes of Senegal.*

PRIMARY SOURCE

Facing Mount Kenya

Jomo Kenyatta, one of Kenya's leading nationalists, wrote a moving account of his own Kikuyu community in* Facing Mount Kenya *(1937). The book demonstrated the cohesion and strong tribal bonds of precolonial Kikuyu society, as well as the destructive elements of the colonial assault on African traditions. The excerpt below is from the conclusion.

And it is the culture which he inherits that gives a man his human dignity as well as his material prosperity. It teaches him his mental and moral values and makes him feel it worth while to work and fight for liberty.

But a culture has no meaning apart from the social organisation of life on which it is built. When the European comes to the Gikuyu country and robs the people of their land, he is taking away not only their livelihood, but the material symbol that holds family and tribe together. In doing this he gives one blow which cuts away the foundations from the whole of Gikuyu life, social, moral, and economic. When he explains, to his own satisfaction and after the most superficial glance at the issues involved, that he is doing this for the sake of the Africans, to "civilise" them, "teach them the disciplinary value of regular work," and "give them the benefit of European progressive ideas," he is adding insult to injury, and need expect to convince no one but himself.

There certainly are some progressive ideas among the Europeans. They include the ideas of material prosperity, of medicine, and hygiene, and literacy which enables people to take part in world culture. But so far the Europeans who visit Africa have not been conspicuously zealous in imparting these parts of their inheritance to the Africans, and seem to think that the only way to do it is by police discipline and armed force. They speak as if it was somehow beneficial to an African to work for them instead of for himself, and to make sure that he will receive this benefit they do their best to take away his land and leave him with no alternative. Along with his land they rob him of his government, condemn his religious ideas, and ignore his fundamental conceptions of justice and morals, all in the name of civilisation and progress.

If Africans were left in peace on their own lands, Europeans would have to offer them the benefits of white civilisation in real earnest before they could obtain the African labour which they want so much. They would have to offer the African a way of life which was really superior to the one his fathers lived before him, and a share in the prosperity given them by their command of science. They would have to let the African choose what parts of European culture would be beneficially transplanted, and how they could be adapted. He would probably not choose the gas bomb or the armed police force, but he might ask for some other things of which he does not get so much today. As it is, by driving him off his ancestral lands, the Europeans have robbed him of the material foundations of his culture, and reduced him to a state of serfdom incompatible with human happiness. The African is conditioned, by the cultural and social institutions of centuries, to a freedom of which Europe has little conception, and it is not in his nature to accept serfdom for ever. He realises that he must fight unceasingly for his own complete emancipation; for without this he is doomed to remain the prey of rival imperialisms, which in every successive year will drive their fangs more deeply into his vitality and strength.

QUESTIONS FOR ANALYSIS

- According to Kenyatta, why is it so devastating when European imperialists rob African people of their land?
- Why do you think the Europeans were not zealous in imparting "progressive ideas" to the Africans?
- Why does Kenyatta think the Africans would not choose to adopt "the gas bomb or the armed police force" from European culture?

Source: Excerpt from Facing Mount Kenya: The Tribal Life of the Gikuyu *by Jomo Kenyatta, published by Vintage Books, a division of Random House, Inc. Used by permission of Alfred A. Knopf, a division of Random House, Inc.*

Committed to democracy at home, the European powers were steadfastly against it in their colonies.

Excluded from representative bodies, Africans experimented with various forms of protest. For example, in southeastern Nigeria in 1929, Ibo and Ibibio women responded to a new tax by breaking off contact with the local colonial chiefs. Moving beyond boycotts of local officials, women burned down chiefs' huts, as well as European and Lebanese trading establishments, to protest their exploitation.

Opposition was still not widespread in Africa, for protests ran up against not only colonial administrators but also western-educated African elites. These individuals often built western-style homes, drove automobiles, wore western clothing, and consumed western foods. Yet, even this privileged group began to reconsider its relationship to colonial authorities. In Kenya, immediately after World War I, a small contingent of mission-educated Africans called on the British to provide more and better schools and to return lands they claimed European settlers had stolen. Although they enlisted the support of liberal missionaries, their pleas fell on deaf ears and their leader was arrested. Although defeated in this instance, the young nationalists drew important lessons from their confrontation with the authorities. They now viewed colonialism in a more combative light. Their new spokesperson, Jomo Kenyatta (1898–1978), invoked their precolonial Kikuyu traditions as a basis for resisting colonialism. (See Primary Source: Facing Mount Kenya.)

IMAGINING AN INDIAN NATION As Africans explored the use of modern politics against Europeans, opposition in India took on a more advanced form. The war and its aftermath brought full-blown challenges to British rule. Indeed, the Indian nationalist challenge provided inspiration for other anticolonial movements.

For over a century, Indians had heard British authorities extol the virtues of parliamentary government, yet they were excluded from participation. In 1919, the British did slightly enlarge the franchise in India and allowed more local self-government, but these moves did not satisfy Indians' nationalist longings. During the 1920s and 1930s, the nationalists, led by **Mohandas Karamchand (Mahatma) Gandhi** (1869–1948), laid the foundations for an alternative, anticolonial movement.

GANDHI AND NONVIOLENT RESISTANCE Gandhi had studied law in England and had worked in South Africa on behalf of Indian immigrants before returning to India in 1915. Thereafter, he assumed leadership in local struggles. He also spelled out the moral and political philosophy of *satyagraha*, or **nonviolent resistance**, which he had developed while in South Africa. His message to Indians was simple: Develop your own resources and inner strength and control the instincts and activities that encourage participation in colonial economy and government, and you shall achieve *swaraj* ("self-rule"). Faced with Indian self-reliance and self-control pursued nonviolently, Gandhi claimed, the British eventually would have to leave. (See Primary Source: India and Self-Government.)

A crucial event in rising opposition to British rule was a massacre in 1919 of Indian civilians protesting British policies in the Punjab. The incident, in which a British general ordered soldiers to fire on the protesters, left 379 Indian civilians dead and more than 1,200 wounded. As news of the massacre spread, many Indians were infuriated—especially when they learned that British authorities were not punishing the general.

This and other conflicts spurred the nationalists to oppose cooperation with government officials, to boycott goods made in Britain, to refuse to send their children to British schools, and to withhold taxes. Gandhi added his voice, calling for an all-India *satyagraha*. He also formed an alliance with Muslim leaders and began turning the Indian National Congress from an elite organization of lawyers and merchants into a mass organization open to anyone who paid dues, even the illiterate and poor.

When the Depression struck India in 1930, Gandhi singled out salt as a testing ground for his ideas on civil disobedience. Every Indian used salt, whose production was a heavily taxed government monopoly. Thus, salt symbolized the Indians' subjugation to an alien government. To break the colonial government's

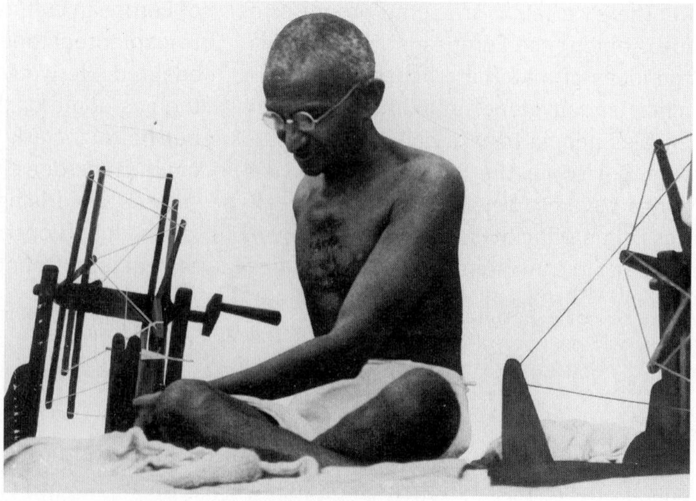

Gandhi and the Road to Independence. (Left) *Gandhi launched a civil disobedience movement in 1930 by violating the British government's tax on salt. Calling it "the most inhuman poll tax the ingenuity of man can devise," Gandhi, accompanied by his followers, set out on a month-long march on foot covering 240 miles to Dandi on the Gujarat coast. The picture shows Gandhi arriving at the sea, where he and his followers broke the law by scooping up handfuls of salt.* (Right) *Gandhi believed that India had been colonized by becoming enslaved to modern industrial civilization. Indians would achieve independence, he argued, when they became self-reliant. Thus, he made the spinning wheel a symbol of* swaraj *and handspun cloth the virtual uniform of the nation.*

PRIMARY SOURCE

India and Self-Government

The following excerpt is from Mohandas (Mahatma) Gandhi's* Hind Swaraj, *a pamphlet that he wrote in 1909 to explain why India needed self-government. Gandhi wrote it as a dialogue between a newspaper editor and a reader. Taking the role of the editor, he criticized modernity as represented by modern western civilization, which was based on industry and materialism. In contrast, Gandhi's imagined civilization of India derived from religion and harmonious village life. According to Gandhi, India demanded modern nationhood (or self-rule,* swaraj*) so that it could restore the best elements of its age-old civilization.

READER: . . . I would now like to know your views on Swaraj. . . .

EDITOR [GANDHI]: It is quite possible that we do not attach the same meaning to the term. You and I and all Indians are impatient to obtain Swaraj, but we are certainly not decided as to what it is. . . .

Why do we want to drive away the English?

READER: Because India has become impoverished by their Government. They take away our money from year to year. The most important posts are reserved for themselves. We are kept in a state of slavery. They behave insolently towards us, and disregard our feelings.

EDITOR: Supposing we get self-government similar to what the Canadians and the South Africans have, will it be good enough?

READER: . . .We must own our navy, our army, and we must have our own splendour, and then will India's voice ring through the world.

EDITOR: . . . In effect it means this: that we want English rule without the Englishman. You want the tiger's nature, but not the tiger; that is to say, you would make India English, and, when it becomes English, it will be called not Hindustan but Englistan. This is not the Swaraj that I want.

READER: Then from your statement I deduce that the Government of England is not desirable and not worth copying by us.

EDITOR: . . . If India copies England, it is my firm conviction that she will be ruined.

READER: To what do you ascribe this state of England?

EDITOR: It is not due to any peculiar fault of the English people, but the condition is due to modern civilisation. It is a civilisation only in name. Under it the nations of Europe are becoming degraded and ruined day by day.

READER: . . . I should like to know your views about the condition of our country.

EDITOR: . . . India is being ground down not under the English heel but under that of modern civilisation. It is groaning under the monster's terrible weight. . . . India is becoming irreligious. Here I am not thinking of the Hindu, the Mahomedan, or the Zoroastrian religion, but of that religion which underlies all religions. We are turning away from God.

READER: You have denounced railways, lawyers and doctors. I can see that you will discard all machinery. What, then, is civilisation?

READER: . . . The tendency of Indian civilisation is to elevate the moral being, that of the Western civilisation is to propagate immorality. The latter is godless, the former is based on a belief in God. So understanding and so believing, it behooves every lover of India to cling to the old Indian civilisation even as a child clings to its mother's breast.

READER: . . . What, then, . . . would you suggest for freeing India?

EDITOR: . . . Those alone who have been affected by Western civilisation have become enslaved. . . . If we become free, India is free. And in this thought you have a definition of Swaraj. It is Swaraj when we learn to rule ourselves.

QUESTIONS FOR ANALYSIS

- What are Gandhi's complaints about English colonial rule?
- Why does Gandhi reject modern civilization?
- According to Gandhi, what are the best aspects of "the old Indian civilisation"?

Source: M. K. Gandhi, Hind Swaraj and Other Writings, *edited by Anthony J. Parel (Cambridge: Cambridge University Press, 1997), pp. 26–91.*

monopoly, Gandhi began a 240-mile march from western India to the coast to gather sea salt for free. Accompanying him were seventy-one followers representing different regions and religions of India. News wire services and mass circulation newspapers worldwide reported on the drama of the sixty-one-year-old Gandhi, wooden staff in hand, dressed in coarse homespun garments, leading the march. Thousands of people gathering en route were moved by the sight of the frail apostle of nonviolence encouraging them to embrace independence from colonial rule. The air thickened with tension as observers speculated on the British reaction to Gandhi's arrival at the sea. After nearly three weeks of walking, Gandhi waded into the surf, picked up a lump of natural salt, held it high, confessed that he had broken the salt law, and invited every Indian to do the same.

Inspired by Gandhi's example, millions of Indians joined strikes, boycotted foreign goods, and substituted indigenous hand-woven cloth for imported textiles. Many Indian officials in the colonial administration resigned in solidarity. The colonizers were taken aback by the mass mobilization. Yet, British denunciations of Gandhi only added to his personal aura and to the anticolonial crusade. By insisting that Indians follow their conscience (always through nonviolent protest), by exciting the masses through his defiance of colonial power, and by using symbols like homespun cloth to counter foreign, machine-spun textiles, Gandhi instilled in the people a sense of pride, resourcefulness, and Indian national awareness.

A DIVIDED ANTICOLONIAL MOVEMENT Unlike the charismatic authoritarians who dominated Italy, Germany, and Russia, Gandhi did not aspire to dictatorial power. Moreover, his program met opposition from within, for many in the Indian National Congress Party did not share his vision of community as the source of public life. Cambridge-educated Jawaharlal Nehru (1889–1964), for example, believed that only by embracing science and technology could India develop as a modern nation.

Even less enamored were radical activists who wanted a revolution, not peaceful protest. In the countryside, these radicals sought to organize peasants to overthrow colonial domination. Other activists galvanized the growing industrial proletariat by organizing trade unions. Their stress on class conflict ran against Gandhi's ideals of national unity.

Religion, too, threatened to fracture Gandhi's hope for anticolonial unity. The Hindu-Muslim alliance crafted by nationalists in the early 1920s splintered over who represented them and how to ensure their political rights. The gulf widened after the Government of India Act of 1935 conceded substantial provincial autonomy and enlarged the franchise. The Muslim community found an impressive leader in Muhammad Ali Jinnah, who set about making the Muslim League the sole representative organization of the Muslim community. In 1940, the Muslim League passed a resolution demanding independent Muslim states in provinces where they constituted a majority, on the grounds that Muslims were not a religious minority of the Indian nation, but a nation themselves.

Hindus also sought a political role on the basis of religious identity. Movements to revitalize Hinduism began organizing Hindus as a religious nation. Indeed, the influence of Hindu culture on Indian nationalism was broad. Hindu symbols and a Hindu ethos colored the fabric of Indian nationalism woven by Gandhi and the Indian National Congress Party.

A further challenge came from women. Long-standing efforts to "uplift" women now escalated into a demand for women's rights, including suffrage. Following the formation of the All India Women's Conference in 1927, activists took up issues relating to women workers, health, employment, education, and literacy and demanded legislative seats for women. The Indian National Congress Party, however, elevated its nationalist agenda above women's demands, just as it had done in dealing with the lower castes and the relations between Hindus and Muslims.

In 1937, the British belatedly granted India provincial assemblies, a bicameral (having two chambers or bodies) national legislature, and a self-governing executive. By then, however, India's people were deeply politicized. The Congress Party, which inspired the masses to overthrow British rule, struggled to contain the different ideologies and new political institutions, such as labor unions, peasant associations, religious parties, and

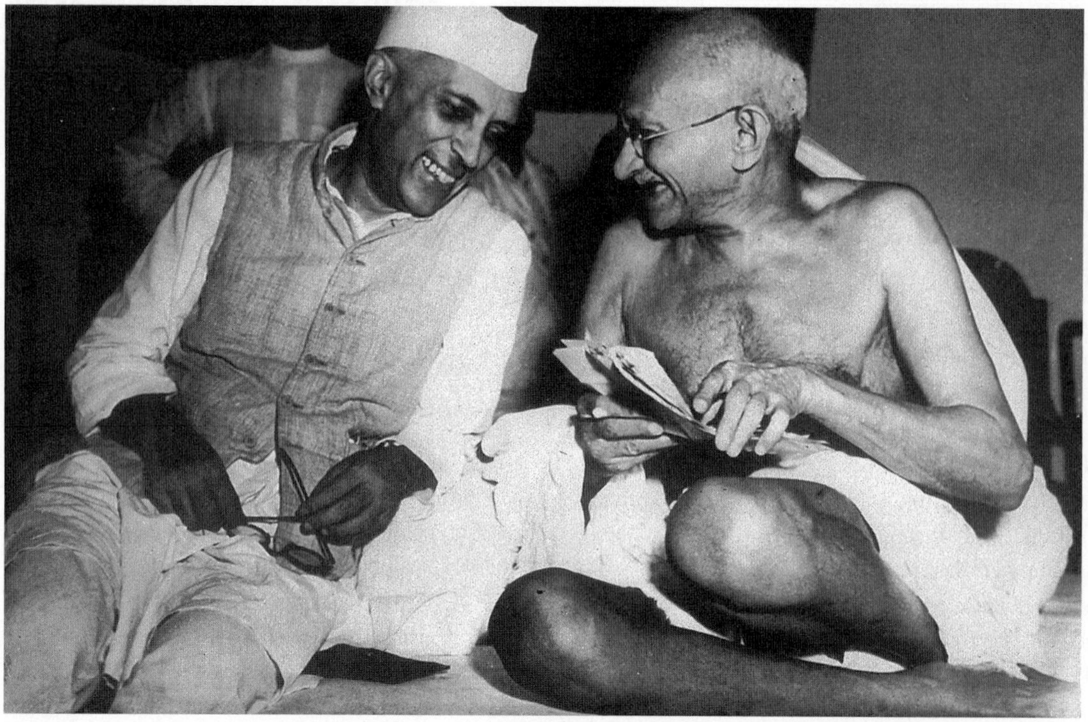

Gandhi and Nehru Sharing a Light Moment. *Despite their divergent views on modernity, Gandhi was personally close to Nehru, who was his chosen political heir.*

communal organizations. Seeking a path to economic modernization, Gandhi, on one side, envisioned independent India as an updated collection of village republics organized around the benevolent authority of male-dominated households. Nehru, on another side, hoped for a socioeconomic transformation powered by science and state-sponsored planning. Both believed that India's traditions of collective welfare and humane religious and philosophical practices set it apart from the modern West. By the outbreak of World War II, India was well on its way toward political independence, but British policies and India's divisions foretold a violent end to imperial rule (see Chapter 20).

CHINESE NATIONALISM Unlike India and Africa, China was never formally colonized. But foreign powers' "concession areas" on Chinese soil compromised its sovereignty. Indeed, foreign nationals living in China enjoyed many privileges, including immunity from Chinese law. Furthermore, unequal treaties imposed on the Qing government had robbed China of its customs and tariff autonomy. Thus, the Chinese nationalists' vision of a modern alternative echoed that of the Indian nationalists: ridding the nation of foreign domination was the initial condition of national fulfillment. For many, the 1911 Revolution (as the fall of the Qing dynasty came to be known; see Chapter 18) symbolized the first step toward transforming a crumbling agrarian empire into a modern nation.

Despite high hopes, the new republic could not establish legitimacy. For one thing, factional and regional conflicts made the government little more than a loose alliance of gentry, merchants, and military leaders. Its intellectual inspiration came from the ideas of the nationalist leader Sun Yat-sen. In 1912, after the Qing emperor stepped down, a military strongman, Yuan Shikai, forced Sun Yat-sen to concede the presidency to him. Although Sun had organized his followers into a political party, the Guomindang, Yuan dismissed all efforts to further democracy and dissolved the parliament. Only Yuan's death in 1916 ended his attempt to establish a new personal dynasty.

The republic endured another blow when the Treaty of Versailles awarded Germany's old concession rights in the Shandong peninsula to Japan. On May 4, 1919, thousands of Chinese students demonstrated in Beijing. As the protests spread to other cities, students appealed to workers and merchants to join their ranks. In what became known as the May Fourth movement, workers went on strike and merchants closed shops. Across the country, the Chinese boycotted Japanese goods.

As the Guomindang, still led by Sun Yat-sen, tried to rejuvenate itself, it looked to students and workers as well as the Russian Revolution for inspiration. In 1923, Sun reached an agreement with the Russians and admitted Chinese communists to the Guomindang as individual members. Under the banner of anti-imperialism, the reorganized party sponsored mass organizations of workers' unions, peasant leagues, and women's associations.

In 1926, amid a renewed tide of antiforeign agitation, **Chiang Kai-shek** (1887–1975) seized control of the party following Sun's death. Chiang launched a partially successful military campaign to reunify the country and established a new national government with its capital in Nanjing. However, he broke with the Soviets and the Chinese communists, whom he viewed as more threat than ally. Furthermore, instead of repudiating foreign treaty rights and concessions, Chiang's regime modified its anti-imperialism platform and sought to revise the concessions through diplomacy.

Still, Chiang acknowledged that China needed to change in order to succeed as a modern nation. He believed that the Chinese masses had to be mobilized. The New Life movement, launched with a torchlight parade in 1934 in Nanchang, exemplified his aspiration for a new Chinese national consciousness. Drawing on diverse ideas (from Confucian precepts to Social Darwinism) and fascist practices such as the militarization of everyday life in the name of sacrificing for the nation, the New Life movement aimed to instill discipline and moral purpose into a unified citizenry. It promoted dress codes for women, condemned casual sexual liaisons, and campaigned against spitting, urinating, or smoking in public.

PEASANT POPULISM IN CHINA: WHITE WOLF For many Guomindang leaders, the peasant population represented a backward class. Thus, the leadership failed to tap into the revolutionary potential of the countryside, which was alive with grassroots movements such as that of White Wolf.

From late 1913 to 1914, Chinese newspapers circulated reports about a roving band of armed men led by a mysterious figure known as White Wolf. This figure terrified members of the elite with his almost magical power. It is unlikely that the band, rumored to have close to a million followers, had more than 20,000 members even at its height. But the mythology surrounding White Wolf was so widespread that the movement's impact reverberated well beyond its physical presence.

Popular myth depicted White Wolf as a Chinese Robin Hood with the mission to restore order. The band's objective was to rid the country of the injustices of Yuan Shikai's government.

Chiang Kai-shek. *Riding the current of anti-imperialism, Chiang Kai-shek, shown here in 1924 in military dress, led the Guomindang on a military campaign in 1926–1928 and seized power, establishing a new national government based in Nanjing.*

Raiding major trade routes and market towns, White Wolf's followers gained a reputation for robbing the rich and aiding the poor. It was said that once the band captured a town, "cash and notes were flung out to the poor." Such stories won the White Wolf army many followers in rural China, where local peasants joined temporarily as fighters and then returned home when the band moved on.

Although the White Wolf army lacked the power to restore order to the countryside, its presence reflected the changes that had come to China. The army struck areas where inhabitants were feeling the effects of the new market forces. In the northwestern province of Shaanxi (Shensi), for example, where the band made its most famous march, markets that formerly flourished with trade in Chinese cotton now awaited camels carrying cotton bales shipped from Fall River, Massachusetts. The fact that the Guomindang never managed to bridge the differences between themselves and a rural-based movement such as that of White Wolf showed the limits of their nationalist vision. The challenge fell to the Chinese communists, who had fled to the countryside to escape Chiang's persecution. They learned that the rural population could indeed become a mass political force—a lesson that served them well during the subsequent war and Japanese occupation in the 1930s and 1940s.

Ataturk. *In the 1920s, Mustafa Kemal, known as Ataturk, introduced the Latin alphabet for the Turkish language as part of his campaign to modernize and secularize Turkey. He underscored his commitment to change by being photographed while giving instruction in the use of the new alphabet.*

A POST-IMPERIAL TURKISH NATION Of all the postwar anticolonial movements, none was more successful or more committed to European models than that of **Mustafa Kemal Ataturk** (1881–1938), who helped forge the modern Turkish nation-state. Until 1914, the Ottoman Empire was a colonial power in its own right. But having fought on the losing German side, it saw its realm shrink to a part of Anatolia under the Treaty of Sèvres, which ended the war between the Allies and the Ottoman Empire.

Some of its former territories, such as those in southern Europe, became independent states; others, such as those in the Middle East, came under British and French administration as mandates of the League of Nations. Fearing that the rest of the empire would be colonized, Ottoman military leaders, many of whom had resisted Turkish nationalism, now embraced the cause. What made modern Turkish nationalism so successful was its ability to convert the mainstay of the old regime, the army, to the goal of creating a Turkish nation-state. These men, in turn, mobilized the masses and launched a state-led drive for modernity.

In 1920, an Ottoman army officer and military hero named Mustafa Kemal harnessed this groundswell of Turkish nationalism into opposition to Greek troops who had been sent to enforce the peace treaty. Rallying his own troops to defend the fledgling Turkish nation, Kemal reconquered most of Anatolia and the area around Istanbul and secured international recognition for the new state in 1923 at the Treaty of Lausanne. Thereafter, a vast, forcible exchange of populations occurred. Approximately 1.2 million Greek Christians left Turkey to settle in Greece, and 400,000 Muslims relocated from Greece to Turkey.

With the Ottoman Empire gone, Kemal and his followers moved to build a state based on Turkish national consciousness. First they deposed the sultan. Then they abolished the Ottoman caliphate and proclaimed Turkey a republic, whose supreme authority would be an elected House of Assembly. Later, after Kemal insisted that the people adopt European-style surnames, the assembly conferred on Kemal the mythic name Ataturk, "father of the Turks."

In forging a Turkish nation, Kemal looked to construct a European-style secular state and to eliminate Islam's hold over civil and political affairs. The Turkish elite replaced Muslim religious law with the Swiss civil code, instituted the western (Christian) calendar, and abolished the once-powerful dervish religious orders. They also suppressed Arabic and Persian words from Turkish, substituted Roman script for Arabic letters, forbade polygamy, made wearing the fez (a brimless cap) a crime, and instructed Turks to wear European-style hats. The veil, though not outlawed, was denounced as a relic. In 1934, the government enfranchised Turkish women, granted them property rights in marriage and inheritance, and allowed them to enter the professions. Schools, too, were taken out of the hands of Muslim clerics, placed under state control, and, along with military service, became the chief instrument for making the masses conscious of belonging to a Turkish nation. Yet, many villagers did not accept

Ataturk's non-Islamic nationalism, remaining devoted to Islam and resentful of the prohibitions against dervish dancing.

In imitating Europe, Kemal borrowed many of its antidemocratic models. Inspired by the Soviets, he inaugurated a five-year plan for the economy emphasizing centralized coordination. During the 1930s, Turkish nationalists also drew on Nazi examples by advocating racial theories that posited central Asian Turks as the founders of all civilization. In another authoritarian move, Kemal occasionally rigged parliamentary elections, while using the police and judiciary to silence his critics. The Kemalist revolution in Turkey was the most far-reaching and enduring transformation that had occurred outside Europe and the Americas up to that point. It offered an important model for the founding of secular, authoritarian states in the Islamic world.

NATIONALISM AND THE RISE OF THE MUSLIM BROTHERHOOD IN EGYPT Elsewhere in the Middle East, where France and Britain expanded their holdings at the Ottomans' expense, anticolonial movements borrowed from European models while putting their own stamp on nation-making and modernization campaigns. In Egypt, British occupation predated the fall of the Ottoman Empire, but here, too, World War I energized the forces of anticolonial nationalism.

When the war ended, Sa'd Zaghlul (1857–1927), an educated Egyptian patriot, pressed for an Egyptian delegation to be invited to the peace conference at Versailles. He hoped to present Egypt's case for national independence. Instead, British officials arrested and exiled him and his most vocal supporters. When news of this action came out, the country burst into revolt. Rural rebels broke away from the central government, proclaiming local republics. Villagers tore up railway lines and telegraph wires, the symbols of British authority.

After defusing the conflict, British authorities tried to mollify Egyptian sensibilities. In 1922, Britain proclaimed Egypt independent, though it retained the right to station British troops on Egyptian soil. Ostensibly, this provision would protect traffic through the Suez Canal and foreign populations residing in Egypt, but it also enabled the British to continue to influence Egyptian politics. Two years later, elections placed Zaghlul's nationalist party, the Wafd, in office. But the British prevented the Wafd from exercising real power.

This subversion of independence and democracy provided an opening for antiliberal variants of anticolonialism. During the Depression years, a fascist group, Young Egypt, garnered wide appeal. Much more influential and destined to have an enduring influence throughout the Arab world was an Islamic group, the Muslim Brotherhood, which attacked liberal democracy as a facade for middle-class, business, and landowning interests. The Muslim Brotherhood was anticolonial and anti-British, but its members considered mere political independence insufficient. Egyptians, they argued, must also renounce the lure of the West (whether liberal capitalism or godless communism) and return to a purified form of Islam. For the Muslim Brotherhood, Islam offered a complete way of life. A "return to Islam" through the nation-state created yet another model of modernity for colonial and semicolonial peoples.

CONCLUSION

The Great War and its aftermath accelerated the trend toward mass society and the debate over how to organize it. Because mass society meant production and consumption on a staggering scale, satisfying the populace became a pressing concern for rulers worldwide. Competing programs vied for ascendancy in the new, broader, public domain.

Most programs fell into one of three categories: liberal democratic, authoritarian, or anticolonial. Liberal democracy defined the political and economic systems in western Europe and the Americas. Resting on faith in free enterprise and representative democracy (with a restricted franchise), liberal regimes had already been unsettled before the Great War. Turn-of-the-century reforms broadened electorates and brought government oversight and regulation into private economic activity. But during the Great Depression, dissatisfaction again deepened. Only far-reaching reforms, introducing greater regulation and more aggressive government intervention to provide for the citizenry's welfare, saved capitalist economies and democratic political systems from collapse.

Still, through the 1930s, liberal democracy was in retreat. Authoritarianism seemed better positioned to satisfy the masses while representing the dynamism of modernity. While authoritarians differed about the faults of capitalism, they joined in the condemnation of electoral democracy. Authoritarians mobilized the masses to put the interests of the nation above the individual. That mobilization often involved brutal repression, yet it seemed also to restore pride and purpose to the masses.

Meanwhile, the colonial and semicolonial world searched for ways to escape from European domination. In Asia and Africa, anticolonial leaders sought to eliminate foreign rule while turning colonies into nations and subjects into citizens. Some looked to the liberal democratic West for models of nation building, but others rejected liberalism because it was associated with colonial rule. Instead, socialism, fascism, and a return to religious traditions offered more promising paths.

The two decades after the end of World War I brought great political upheavals and deep economic dislocations. At times, the competition among liberal democracy, authoritarianism (both right and left), and anticolonial nationalism grew heated. Yet the traumas were tame compared to what followed with the outbreak in 1939 of World War II.

AFTER YOU READ THIS CHAPTER

TRACING THE GLOBAL STORYLINES

FOCUS ON: *World War I and Its Aftermath*

The great war

- The war destroys empires, starting with the Bolshevik Revolution against the tsarist regime in Russia, followed by the defeat and dissolution of the German, Austro-Hungarian, and Ottoman empires.
- Mass mobilization sees almost 70 million men join the fighting, undermines traditional gender boundaries, and forces states to recognize their peoples' demands for compensation afterward.
- Mass culture spreads as leaders use the new media of radio and film to promote national loyalties and discredit enemies.

The aftermath

- Liberal democracies in France, Britain, and the United States survive the Great Depression by enacting far-reaching changes in their political systems and free market economies.
- Authoritarian (communist and fascist) dictatorships with many political similarities emerge in the Soviet Union, Italy, Germany, Spain, and Portugal.
- Latin American leaders devise hybrid solutions that combine democratic and authoritarian elements.
- Peoples living under colonial rule in Asia and Africa mobilize traditional values to oppose imperial rulers.
- Key individuals emerge in the struggle to define newly independent nations: Kenyatta, Gandhi, Chiang Kai-shek, and Ataturk.

Review and research materials on STUDYSPACE: wwnorton.com/studyspace

CHRONOLOGY

The Americas
- U.S. enters World War I **1917**

Europe
- World War I **1914–1918**
- Mussolini takes over Italy **1922**

Soviet Union
- Bolshevik Revolution **1917**
- Russian civil war **1918–1921**

East Asia

South Asia

Middle East
- Mustafa Kemal creates modern Turkish nation-state **1923**

1910

KEY TERMS

Allied Powers p. 706

Mustafa Kemal Ataturk p. 738

Bolsheviks p. 709

Central Powers p. 706

Chiang Kai-shek p. 737

fascism p. 725

Mohandas Karamchand (Mahatma) Gandhi p. 734

Great Depression p. 717

Great War (World War I) p. 706

Adolf Hitler p. 725

League of Nations p. 712

mass consumption p. 716

mass culture p. 715

mass production p. 716

Benito Mussolini p. 725

Nazis p. 725

New Deal p. 721

nonviolent resistance p. 734

Joseph Stalin p. 723

STUDY QUESTIONS

1. **List and explain** the numerous ways in which World War I changed the world. How did it usher in a new age for diverse societies?
2. **Define** the terms *mass culture, mass production,* and *mass consumption.* How did World War I help to diffuse these concepts across the world's cultures?
3. **Analyze** how the Great Depression challenged political establishments after World War I. How were the two events linked? What values and assumptions did the Great Depression challenge?
4. **Explain** competing visions of modernity that emerged across the globe during the period covered in this chapter. How were they similar and how were they different?
5. **Compare and contrast** the liberal democratic and authoritarian visions of modernity as epitomized by various states in the 1930s. What features did they have in common?
6. **List and explain** various anticolonial visions of modern life that emerged in the first half of the twentieth century. To what extent did they reflect borrowed developments versus native traditions and ideas?
7. **Describe** how Latin American societies adjusted to modern ideas at this time. How did visions of modernity affect states and societies in that region of the world?

Great Depression begins **1929**

Vargas becomes leader of Brazil **1930**

New Deal reforms (United States) **1933–1941**

Hitler takes over Germany **1933**

Popular Front rules France **1936–1939**

Collectivization and Five Year Plans instituted **1929–1935**

Political purges **1936–1938**

Chiang Kai-shek becomes leader of China **1928**

Japan annexes Manchuria **1932**

Gandhi's March to the Sea **1930**

Muslim Brotherhood founded in Egypt **1928**

1940

BEFORE YOU READ THIS CHAPTER

GLOBAL STORYLINES

- World War II shatters the European-centered order and lays the groundwork for a world divided into three camps: an American-led liberal democratic order; a communist world led by the Soviet Union; and newly independent, decolonized states in Asia, Africa, and Latin America.
- War and postwar reconstruction enhance the reach and functions of the modern nation-state.
- Allies during World War II, the United States and the Soviet Union engage in an ideological cold war, each touting the superiority of its views on how best to organize societies, while decolonized states in Asia, Africa, and Latin America struggle to find a "third way" but find themselves caught between rival superpowers.

CHAPTER OUTLINE

20

The Three-World Order, 1940–1975

FOCUS QUESTIONS

- How did World War II contribute to the creation of the three-world order after 1945?
- What major similarities and differences existed between the three worlds in terms of goals and aspirations?
- How did cold war rivalries shape developments in the third world?
- What successes and failures did each world experience from 1945 to 1975?
- What major fissures developed in the three-world order by 1975?

In February 1945, the three leaders of the World War II Allies—President Franklin Delano Roosevelt of the United States, Prime Minister Winston Churchill of Great Britain, and Premier Joseph Stalin of the Soviet Union—met to prepare for the postwar world. By then, Germany, Italy, and Japan were losing the war. But the world's reordering was a source of deep contention, for the three leaders had profoundly different visions. Roosevelt, who envisioned independent nation-states kept at peace by an international body, had no interest in restoring the old European empires. Churchill, however, resisted liquidation of the British Empire. Stalin's negotiations left no doubt that he intended to secure influence in eastern Europe and Asia and to weaken Germany so that it could never again menace the Soviet Union.

When the fighting finally stopped, it was clear that the European-centered order, shocked by World War I, had been shattered by World War II. Empires either lay in ruins or faced dismantling by colonial independence movements. The nation-state had emerged as the prevailing political organization. Moreover, the state's reach had expanded as it took on new functions related to postwar reconstruction. Meanwhile, with the weakening of Great Britain, France, and Germany, a new three-world order emerged.

This chapter explores the development of the three-world order in the wake of World War II. Heading the "First World" was the United States, which with its allies championed capitalism and democracy as the best way to bring unprecedented prosperity in the decades after 1945. Leading the "Second World" was the Soviet Union, the crucial ally of the United States during World War II, which became its chief adversary in the protracted cold war that followed. As leader of the communist bloc, the Soviet Union contested capitalist societies' claims and trumpeted socialism's accomplishments. Caught in between (and sometimes literally caught in the crossfire when the cold war turned hot) were formerly colonized and semicolonized people. Lumped together as the "Third World," these nations emerged from the war eager to seek their own ways forward.

COMPETING BLOCS

The roots of the world's division into three blocs lay in the breakup of Europe's empires and the demise of European world leadership. The destruction of Europe and the defeat of Japan left a power vacuum, which the United States and the Soviet Union rushed to fill. Both believed that their respective systems—capitalism and communism—had universal application. They were now **superpowers** because of the size of their economies and arsenals, the transcontinental reach of their political influence, and the fact that each embodied a model of civilization applicable to the whole world. As their spheres of influence expanded, they engaged in a bitter ideological rivalry known as the **cold war** because no direct military conflict occurred between the superpowers, both of which after 1949 possessed the atomic bomb.

While the capitalist and communist blocs embarked on a cold war, conflicts in the Third World got very hot. In Asia and Africa, anticolonial leaders intensified their campaigns for independence. Winning popular support by mobilizing deep-seated desires for justice and autonomy, they swept away foreign rulers and asserted their claims for national independence. Latin American countries, too, sought progress and nationhood. But newfound political freedom did not easily translate into economic development or social equity. Moreover, as the two superpowers looked for allies and client states, they militarized rival states and factions within the Third World.

Each superpower also faced internal problems. Even as the United States maintained that its booming industrial economy, abundant consumer goods, liberal democracy, and vibrant popular culture were proof of capitalism's superiority, the nation also wrestled with racism and became involved in unpopular wars to stop the spread of communism—most notably in Vietnam. The Soviet Union celebrated its own economic prowess and social welfare policies, but it continued to imprison and persecute reformers and dissenters and to operate a command economy, oriented to heavy industrial products and armaments. By the 1960s, the USSR's use of military force to crush socialist reform efforts within the Soviet bloc was undermining communism's allure.

By the 1960s and the early 1970s, tensions were simmering in the three-world order. The United States and the Soviet Union faced discontent within their societies and opposition within their respective blocs. At the same time, the rising economic might of Japan and the other Pacific economies, the emerging clout of oil-rich states, and the specter of radical revolution in Africa, Asia, and Latin America suggested a shift in the balance of wealth and power away from the First and Second worlds.

WORLD WAR II AND ITS AFTERMATH

World War II grew out of unresolved problems connected to the Great War. World War I had not been, as many had prophesied, "the war to end all wars." It became instead merely the *First* World War after the *Second* World War began in 1939. Especially influential were the resentments bred by the harsh provisions and controversial state boundaries set out in the treaties signed at the war's end.

World War II also resulted from the aggressive ambitions and racial theories of Germany and Japan. Both states sought to impose racial hierarchy (master and inferior races) through conquest and coerced labor. By the late 1930s, German and Japanese ambitions to become colonial powers brought these conservative dictatorships (which along with Italy constituted the **Axis powers**) into conflict with France, Britain, the Soviet Union, and eventually the United States (the **Allied powers**).

Even more than its predecessor, World War II was truly a world conflict, and a devastatingly total one. Fighting occurred in Europe, Africa, and Asia, the Atlantic and the Pacific, and the Northern and Southern hemispheres. Warring nations mobilized millions of people, including the colonized, into armed forces and placed enormous demands on civilians. Noncombatants in places such as India and Greece, Yugoslavia and Korea, Poland and the Philippines suffered terrible hardships, including famines, reprisal killings, and deportations in the course of this war without mercy. Moreover, as aerial bombardment of cities caused colossal civilian casualties, the total war erased the old distinction between soldiers and civilians. Women—as victims and as collaborators, as volunteers and as forced laborers, as workers behind the scenes and as witnesses to the conflict—were involved as never before. They, together with children, the infirm, and the elderly, also swelled the

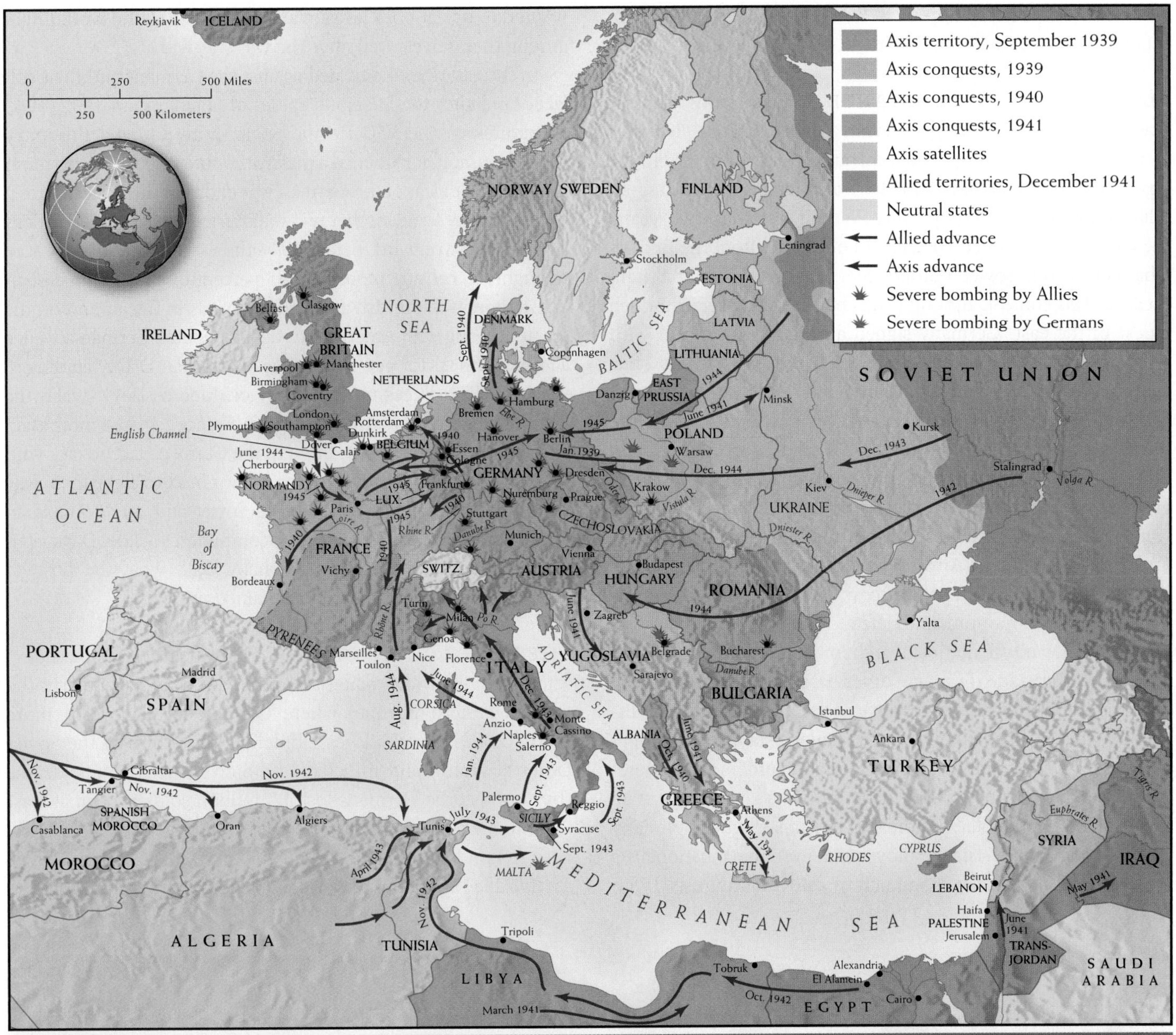

MAP 20.1 | World War II: The European Theater

The Axis armies enjoyed great success during the early stages of World War II.

- Which states were within the Axis territory when World War II began in September 1939? What were the territorial boundaries when the Axis powers reached their greatest extent?
- When did the military balance begin to turn against Germany and Italy?

enormous population of refugees seeking safety in the midst of worldwide chaos.

World War II also completed the decline of European world dominance that World War I had set in motion. The unspeakable acts of barbarism perpetrated during the Second World War, including the Nazi genocides directed against Jews and others, robbed Europe of its lingering claims as a superior civilization. In the war's wake, anticolonial movements demanded national self-determination from battered and morally bankrupted European powers.

The War in Europe

Although Hitler had annexed Austria and parts of Czechoslovakia in 1938, World War II officially began in Europe in September 1939, with Germany's invasion of Poland and the British and French decision to oppose it. Before it was all over in 1945, much of Europe, including Germany, had been leveled.

BLITZKRIEG AND RESISTANCE Hitler's early success was staggering. His troops overran Poland, France, Norway, Denmark, Luxembourg, Belgium, and Holland. In 1940 he signed the Tripartite Pact with Italy and Japan, formalizing an alliance among the Axis powers. Within less than two years, the Germans controlled virtually all of Europe from the English Channel to the Soviet border (see Map 20.1). Only Britain escaped Axis control, although Nazi bombers pulverized British cities. In the east, Germany signed a nonaggression pact with the Soviet Union in 1939, after which the two powers once again partitioned Poland, murdering and deporting thousands. But in 1941 the German army broke its pact and invaded the Soviet Union with 170 divisions, 3,000 tanks, and 3.2 million men—an invasion force of a size unmatched before or since. Here, as elsewhere, the Germans fought a *blitzkrieg* ("lightning war") of tank-led assaults followed by motorized infantrymen and then foot soldiers. Already by October 1941, the Germans had reached the outskirts of Moscow. The Soviet Union seemed on the verge of a monumental defeat.

The Nazi war was not just a grab for land and raw materials; it was also a crusade for a new order based on race. Nazi racial occupation policies created massive social, economic, and political upheavals throughout Europe. Hitler established puppet governments that complied with deportation orders against Jews and dissidents. His new order made Europe a giant police state and spawned both collaborators and resistance fighters of many types. Among the resistance movements were both nationalists (who opposed German domination) and communists (who wanted to defeat both fascism and capitalism), who would fight among themselves even after the war was won.

In the east, the tide turned against the Germans and their collaborators after the ferocious battles of Stalingrad in 1942–1943 and Kursk in 1943. Once the Soviet army blunted the initial German assault, it launched a massive counteroffensive. This move initiated the defeat of the German war effort on the Eastern Front, but full retreat took another two years as the Soviets drove Hitler's army slowly westward. Before 1944 the Soviets bore the brunt of the fighting, causing more than 85 percent of all German casualties, although the British attacked the Nazis in the air and on the sea and, along with American troops, stopped a German advance across North Africa into Egypt. The spectacular D-Day landing of western Allied forces in Normandy on June 6, 1944 (when the Germans had a mere 15 divisions in France, against more than 300 on the Eastern Front), brought the Germans face to face with American and British troops also determined to fight their way to Germany. On April 30, 1945, as Soviet and Anglo-American forces converged on Berlin, Hitler committed suicide. Days later, Germany surrendered unconditionally. Still, what the postwar European map would look like remained unclear.

THE BITTER COSTS OF WAR The war in Europe had devastating human and material costs. This was particularly the case in eastern Europe, where German forces leveled more than 70,000 Soviet villages, obliterated one-third of the Soviet Union's wealth, and inflicted 7 million Soviet military deaths (by contrast, the Germans lost 3.5 million soldiers) and at least 20 million civilian deaths. German bombing of British cities, such as London, inflicted a heavy toll on civilians and buildings, as did Allied bombing of war plants and Axis cities like Dresden

The Devastation of War. (Left) *In the Battle of Britain, Nazi warplanes strafed British cities in an effort to break British morale. But the devastating bombing raids, such as this one in Coventry in November 1940, helped rally the British, who refused to give in.* (Right) *In November 1942, Nazi troops entered Stalingrad, some 2,000 miles from Berlin. Hitler wanted to capture the city not only to exploit the surrounding wheat fields and the oil of the Caucasus but also for its very name. With handheld flamethrowers and sometimes just their fists, Soviet troops drove out the Germans in February 1943.*

MAP 20.2 | World War II: The Pacific Theater

Like Germany and Italy, Japan experienced stunning military successes in the war's early years.

- In what directions did the Japanese direct their military offensives? Analyzing this map, why do you think the Japanese were so concerned about an American presence in East Asia, when the United States was so geographically distant? According to your reading, how did the Allied strategies to defeat the Japanese Empire shape postwar relations in the region?

and Tokyo. Urban casualties were perhaps greatest in Leningrad, a city that was surrounded and besieged for nine hundred days; 900,000 people lost their lives during this struggle. By the war's end, Poland had lost 6 million people and Great Britain had lost 400,000. Tens of millions in the east and west were left homeless.

Europe's Jews paid an especially high price. Hitler had long talked of "freeing" Europe of all Jews. At the war's outset, the Nazis herded Jews into ghettos and labor camps and then seized their property. As the German army moved eastward, more and more Jews came under their control. At first the Nazi bureaucrats

ANALYZING GLOBAL DEVELOPMENTS

World War II Casualties

World War II was the most destructive armed conflict in recorded history. It mobilized more than 120 million military personnel; more than 20 million died. The death toll of civilian populations was substantially greater. Civilian deaths directly caused by the war, including genocide, bombing, starvation, and disease, were estimated to range from 30 million to 55 million. Historians now put the total at roughly 60 million dead, including the 6 million Jews killed in the Holocaust, more than double the number killed in World War I.

A total reordering of the globe was at stake from the outset of World War II. The war was a struggle not only for the control of resources and territory, as World War I had been, but it was also fought to decide which peoples would control the world's resources and which peoples would be destroyed, because the aggressors decided that they were undesirable.

QUESTIONS FOR ANALYSIS

- Compare and contrast the casualties for World Wars I and II. (See the Analyzing Global Developments feature in Chapter 19.)
- Which countries endured the greatest loss of life in World War II and why? Which of the major participants in the war endured the fewest casualties and why?
- Contrast civilian and military casualties in World War II and explain why civilian casualty rates were so much higher than military losses?
- Many historians regard World War I as a greater turning point in European and western history than World War II, with its extraordinarily high loss of life. Why do you think historians would hold to this view? What is your view of the relative global importance of the two wars?

World War II Casualties

Nation	Population in 1939	Max. No. Mobilized	Military Deaths	Missing in Action	Civilian Deaths Due to War	Estimated Total Deaths
Belgium	8,386,000	800,000	22,651	55,513	76,000	88,000
Brazil	40,289,000	200,000		4,222		1,000
British Commonwealth		4,683,000	400,000	369,267	92,673	466,000
Australia	6,968,000	680,000	37,467	39,803		24,000
Canada	11,267,000	780,000	42,666	53,174		38,000
India	311,820,000	2,150,000	48,674	64,354		1,500,000
New Zealand	1,628,500	157,000	13,081	19,314		10,000
South Africa	10,160,000	140,000	8,681	14,363		7,000
UK	47,760,000	4,683,000	403,195	369,267	92,673	357,000
China	517,568,000	5,000,000	2,220,000	14,685,593		10,000,000
Czechoslovakia	15,300,000 (1938)	180,000	10,000	8,017	215,000	225,000

World War II Casualties (*continued*)						
Nation	**Population in 1939**	**Max. No. Mobilized**	**Military Deaths**	**Missing in Action**	**Civilian Deaths Due to War**	**Estimated Total Deaths**
Denmark	3,795,000	15,000	6,400	2,000	2,000	4,000
France	40,000,000	5,000,000	245,000	390,000	350,000	563,000
Greece	7,221,900	414,000	88,300	42,290	325,000	413,000
Netherlands	8,729,000	500,000	7,900	2,860	200,000	208,000
Norway	2,944,900	25,000	3,000	364	7,000	10,000
Poland	34,775,700	1,000,000	597,320	766,606	56,75,000	5,800,000
Philippines	16,000,300	105,000	127,000		91,000	118,000
United States	131,028,000	16,353,659	292,000	671,801	6,000	298,000
USSR	108,377,000	12,500,000	8,700,000	14,685,593		27,000,000
Yugoslavia	5,510,100	500,000	305,000	425,000	1,200,000	1,505,000
Bulgaria	6,458,000	450,000	18,500	21,878	10,000	20,000
Finland	3,700,000	250,000	82,000	50,000	2,000	84,000
Germany	69,622,500	9,200,000	325,000	7,250,000	780,000	4,200,000
Hungary	9,129,000	350,000	200,000	89,313	290,000	490,000
Italy	44,394,000	4,000,000	380,000	225,000	152,941	395,000
Japan	71,380,000	6,095,000	1,740,955	326,000	672,000	2,700,000
Romania	19,933,800	600,000	300,000		200,000	500,000
Indonesia	69,435,000					4,000,000

Total WWII Deaths: 60 million (including 6 million Jews)

Sources: Alan Axelrod (ed.), Encyclopedia of World War II, *vol. 1 (2007); John Dower,* War without Mercy *(1986); Geoffrey Hosking,* Rulers and Victims: The Russians in the Soviet Union *(2006).*

contemplated deportation but then ruled out transporting "subhumans" as too costly, and so settled for starving them and crowding them together in unsanitary ghettoes. By the summer of 1941, special troops operating behind the army on the Eastern Front had begun mass shootings of communists and Jewish civilians, and by fall 1941, Hitler and the S.S. (the *Schutzstaffel*, or special security forces) were building a series of killing centers. The largest concentration camp was Auschwitz-Birkenau in Poland. Cattle cars shipped Jews from all over Europe to the extermination sites in the east, where Nazis used the latest technology to kill men, women, and children. The deliberate racial extermination of the Jews, known as the **Holocaust**, claimed around 6 million European Jews. About half of this number died in the gas chambers of concentration camps; the others perished in face-to-face executions or from starvation, disease, or exhaustion. The Nazis also turned their mass killing apparatus against gypsies, homosexuals, communists, and Slavs, with deportations to the death camps continuing to the very end of the war.

Japanese Aggression. *The brutal Battle of Shanghai (August–November 1937) marked the beginning of what turned out to be World War II in Asia. Claiming to be "protecting" China from European imperialists and expecting a relatively easy victory, the Japanese instead met with stiff resistance from the Chinese troops under Chiang Kai-shek. Here we see Japanese marines parading through the streets of the city after they finally broke through Chinese defenses. About a quarter of a million Chinese soldiers, close to 60 percent of Chiang's best troops, were killed or wounded in the campaign, a blow from which Chiang's regime never recovered. The Japanese sustained more than 40,000 casualties.*

The Pacific War

Like the war in Europe, the conflict in the Pacific transformed the military and political landscape (see Map 20.2). The war broke out when Japan's ambitions to dominate Asia targeted American interests and might.

JAPAN'S EFFORTS TO EXPAND Japan's expansionist aims became clear when its military invaded and occupied Manchuria in 1931 and then launched an offensive against the rest of China in 1937. Although the Japanese did not achieve China's complete submission, the invaders exacted a terrible toll on the population. Most infamous was the so-called rape of Nanjing, in which Japanese aggressors slaughtered at least 100,000 civilians and raped thousands of women in the Chinese city between December 1937 and February 1938.

Meanwhile, events in Europe opened opportunities for further Japanese expansion in Asia. Germany's swift occupation of western Europe left defeated nations' colonies at the mercy of Japanese forces. After concluding a pact with Germany in 1940, the Japanese occupied French Indochina in 1941 and made demands on the Dutch East Indies for oil and rubber. Now the chief obstacle to further expansion in the Pacific was the United States, which already had imperial interests in places like China and the Philippines, as well as other Pacific islands. Hoping to strike the United States before it was prepared for war, the Japanese launched a surprise air attack on the American naval base at Pearl Harbor in Hawaii on December 7, 1941. As the United States entered the war, Germany and Italy also declared war on America.

Now Japan's expansion shifted into high gear. During 1942, its military racked up victory after victory over the tottering western armies. With French Indochina already under their control, the Japanese turned against the American colony of the Philippines and against the Dutch East Indies, both of which fell in 1942. By coordinating their army, naval, and air force units and using tactical surprise, the Japanese seized a huge swath of territory that included British-ruled Hong Kong, Singapore, Malaya, and Burma, while threatening the British Empire's hold on India as well.

Japan justified its aggression on the grounds that it was anticolonial and pan-Asian; Japan promised to drive out the European imperialists and to build a new order reflecting "Asia for Asians." In practice, however, the Japanese made terrible demands on fellow Asians for resources, developed myths of Japanese racial purity and supremacy, and treated Chinese and Koreans with brutality. During the war, Japan put up to 4 million Koreans to work for its empire, forcibly imported another 700,000 Korean men as laborers, and pressed up to 200,000 young women into service as prostitutes for Japanese soldiers. (In a similar move, the Nazi war effort in Europe involved forcing 12 million foreign laborers—including 2 million prisoners of war—to settle and work in Germany.)

ALLIED ADVANCES AND THE ATOMIC BOMB Like the Germans in their war against Russia, the Japanese could not

The Aftermath of the Atomic Bomb. (Left) *A view of Nagasaki less than half a mile from "ground zero" after the atomic bomb was dropped in August 1945. A few reinforced concrete buildings still stand.* (Right) *Thousands of people were immediately crushed or burned to death in the blast. Many died later from horrendous burns and radiation poisoning.*

sustain their military successes against the United States. By mid-1943, U.S. forces had put the Japanese on the defensive. Fighting from island to island, American troops recaptured the Philippines, and a combined force of British, American, and Chinese troops returned Burma to Britain. The Allies then moved toward the Japanese mainland. By summer 1945, American bombers had all but devastated the major cities of Japan. Yet Japan did not surrender.

Anticipating that an invasion of Japan would cost hundreds of thousands of American lives, U.S. president Harry Truman unleashed the Americans' secret weapon. It was the work of a team of scientists who were predominantly European refugees. On August 6, 1945, an American plane dropped an atomic bomb on the city of Hiroshima, killing or maiming over 100,000 people, and poisoning the air, soil, and groundwater for decades to come. Three days later, the Americans dropped a second atomic bomb on Nagasaki. Within days, Emperor Hirohito announced Japan's surrender.

THE BEGINNING OF THE COLD WAR

World War II left much of Europe in ruins. Charred embers lay where great cities had once stood. Major bridges lay crumbled at the bottom of rivers; railway lines were twisted scrap; sunken ships blocked harbors. Scarcity and hunger were widespread. Millions had died; tens of millions more were wounded, displaced, widowed, and orphaned. "What is Europe now?" mused British prime minister Winston Churchill. "A rubble heap, a charnel house, a breeding ground of pestilence and hate."

Rebuilding Europe

The task of political rebuilding was daunting, for the old order had been discredited. By contrast, communism gained new appeal because its credo promised a clean slate. Many eastern

Postwar Planning at Yalta. *The "Big Three" allies confer about the end of the war at the Black Sea resort of Yalta in February 1945. On the left is British prime minister Winston Churchill; at the center is American president Franklin Roosevelt; and on the right is Soviet premier Joseph Stalin.*

Europeans, following the horrors of fascism and not knowing the extent of Stalin's crimes, looked to the Soviets for answers. Even many of those opposed to the Soviets saw some form of socialism as a way to create powerful, modern, egalitarian societies in Europe.

Europe's leftward tilt alarmed U.S. policymakers. They feared that the Soviets would use their ideological influence and the territory taken over by the Red Army to spread communism. They also worried that Stalin might seize Europe's overseas possessions and create communist regimes outside Europe. But no one wished to fight another "hot" war. As President Truman began advocating a policy of containment to prevent the further advance of communism, an American journalist popularized the term *cold war* in 1946 to describe the new struggle.

Truman's containment policy was tested when the Soviets attempted to seize control of Berlin. Like the rest of Germany, Berlin had been partitioned into British, French, American, and Soviet zones of occupation; but the city itself was an island lying within the Soviet zone. In 1948, the Soviets attempted to cut the city off from western access by blocking western routes to the capital. The Allies responded with the Berlin Airlift, which involved transporting supplies in planes to western Berlin to keep the population from capitulating to the Soviets. This crisis lasted for almost a year, until Stalin allowed trucks to roll through the eastern zone in May 1949.

In that same year, occupied Germany was split into two hostile states: the democratic Federal Republic of Germany in the west, and the communist German Democratic Republic in the east. In 1961, leaders in the German Democratic Republic built a wall around West Berlin to insulate the east from capitalist propaganda and to halt a flood of émigrés fleeing communism. The **Berlin Wall** became the great symbol of a divided Europe and of the cold war. U.S. policymakers wanted to shore up democratic governments in Europe, so Truman promised American military and economic aid. Containing the spread of communism meant securing a capitalist future for western Europe, a job that fell to Truman's secretary of state, General George C. Marshall. He launched the Marshall Plan, an ambitious program that provided over $13 billion in grants and credits to reconstruct Europe and facilitate an economic revival. U.S. policymakers hoped the aid would dim communism's appeal by fostering economic prosperity, muting class tensions, and integrating western European nations into an alliance of capitalist democracies.

Stalin saw the Marshall Plan as a threat to the Soviet Union. He felt the same about the formation in 1949 of the **North Atlantic Treaty Organization (NATO)**, a military alliance between countries in western Europe and North America. He believed that the Soviet Union, having sacrificed millions of people to the war against fascism, deserved to be dominant in eastern Europe. Soviet troops had occupied eastern European nations at the war's end, and both communists and leftist members of other parties formed Soviet-backed coalition governments there. By tricking their moderate leftist allies and repressing their critics and opponents, the communists established dictatorships in Bulgaria, Romania, Hungary, and

The Berlin Airlift. *In summer 1948, a new currency was issued for the united occupation zones of West Germany. It began to circulate in Berlin at more favorable exchange rates than the eastern zone's currency, and Berlin seemed poised to become an outpost of the West inside the Soviet occupation zone. The Soviets responded by blocking western traffic into Berlin; the West countered with an airlift, forcing the Soviets to back down in May 1949 but hastening the division of Germany into two countries.*

MAP 20.3 | NATO and Warsaw Pact Countries

The cold war divided Europe into two competing blocs: those joined with the United States in the North Atlantic Treaty Organization (NATO) and those linked to the Soviet Union under the Warsaw Pact.

- Which nations had borders with nations belonging to the opposite bloc?
- Comparing this map with Map 20.1, explain how combat patterns in World War II shaped the dividing line between the two blocs.
- According to the map, where would you expect cold war tensions to be the most intense?

Czechoslovakia in 1948. In 1955, the Soviets formally allied themselves with these communist nations in the **Warsaw Pact**, a military alliance of their own (see Map 20.3). The tense confrontations between NATO and the Warsaw Pact in Europe and in other parts of the world in the 1950s and 1960s brought the world to the brink of an atomic World War III.

War in The Nuclear Age: The Korean War

The dropping of the atomic bombs on Japan in 1945 changed military affairs forever. Spurred by the onset of the cold war, the Soviets worked hard to catch up to the Americans, and in 1949 tested their first nuclear bomb. Thereafter, each side rushed to stockpile nuclear weapons and update its military technologies. By 1960, the explosive power of these weapons had increased so greatly that nuclear war might lead to the world's destruction without a soldier firing a single shot. This sobering realization changed the rules of the game. Each side now possessed the power to inflict total destruction on the other, a circumstance that inhibited direct confrontations but sparked smaller conflicts in parts of Asia, such as Korea, where the postwar settlement was murky.

In 1950, North Korean troops backed by the Soviet Union invaded U.S.-backed South Korea, setting off the **Korean War** (see Map 20.4). Claiming this violated the Charter of the United Nations, which had been established in 1945 to safeguard world peace and protect human rights, President Truman ordered American troops to drive back the North Koreans. The U.N. Security Council, thanks to a Soviet boycott, also sent troops from fifteen nations to restore peace. Within a year, the invaders had been routed and were near collapse. When U.N. troops advanced to the Chinese border, however, Stalin maneuvered his communist Chinese allies into rescuing the communist regime in North Korea and driving the South Korean and U.N. forces back to the old boundary. Across the Korean isthmus, communist and American-led U.N. troops waged a seesaw war. The fighting continued until 1953, when an armistice divided the country at roughly the same spot as at the start of the war. Nothing had been gained. Losses, however, included 33,000 Americans, at least 250,000 Chinese, and up to 3 million Koreans.

The Korean War energized America's anticommunist commitments and spurred a rapid increase in NATO forces. U.S. policy shifted because Japan now was seen as a bulwark against communism. Although Japan renounced war in its postwar constitution, a 1951 treaty with the United States stipulated that the Japanese could rearm for self-defense and that American troops could be stationed in Japan. Moreover, the United States resolved to rebuild Japanese economic power. Like West Germany, Japan went from being the enemy in World War II to being a valued ally during the cold war.

Atom Bomb Anxiety. *Schoolchildren taking shelter under their desks during an A-bomb drill in Brooklyn, New York, 1951. The Soviets had exploded their first test bomb in 1949. Underground bomb shelters were built in many American urban areas as places in which to survive a doomsday attack.*

DECOLONIZATION

The unsettling of all empires during the war inspired colonial peoples to reconsider their political futures. Rid of the Japanese, the liberated Asian territories had no desire to restore colonial or quasi-colonial rule. Africa, too, felt increasing pressure for decolonization. A weakened Europe emboldened anticolonial leaders to dismantle the European order and create a world of their own.

The process of **decolonization** and nation building followed three patterns: civil war, negotiated independence, and incomplete decolonization. The first occurred principally in China, where the ousting of Japanese occupiers led to a civil war that ended in a communist triumph. Here, national independence was associated with a socialist revolution. The second pattern, involving negotiated independence, played out in India and much of Africa. Algeria and South Africa illustrate the third pattern, in which the presence of sizeable European settler populations complicated the path from colony to nation.

The Chinese Revolution

The communist movement in China had its origins in post–World War I hostility toward the western powers. In this period, communists had vowed to free China from colonialism,

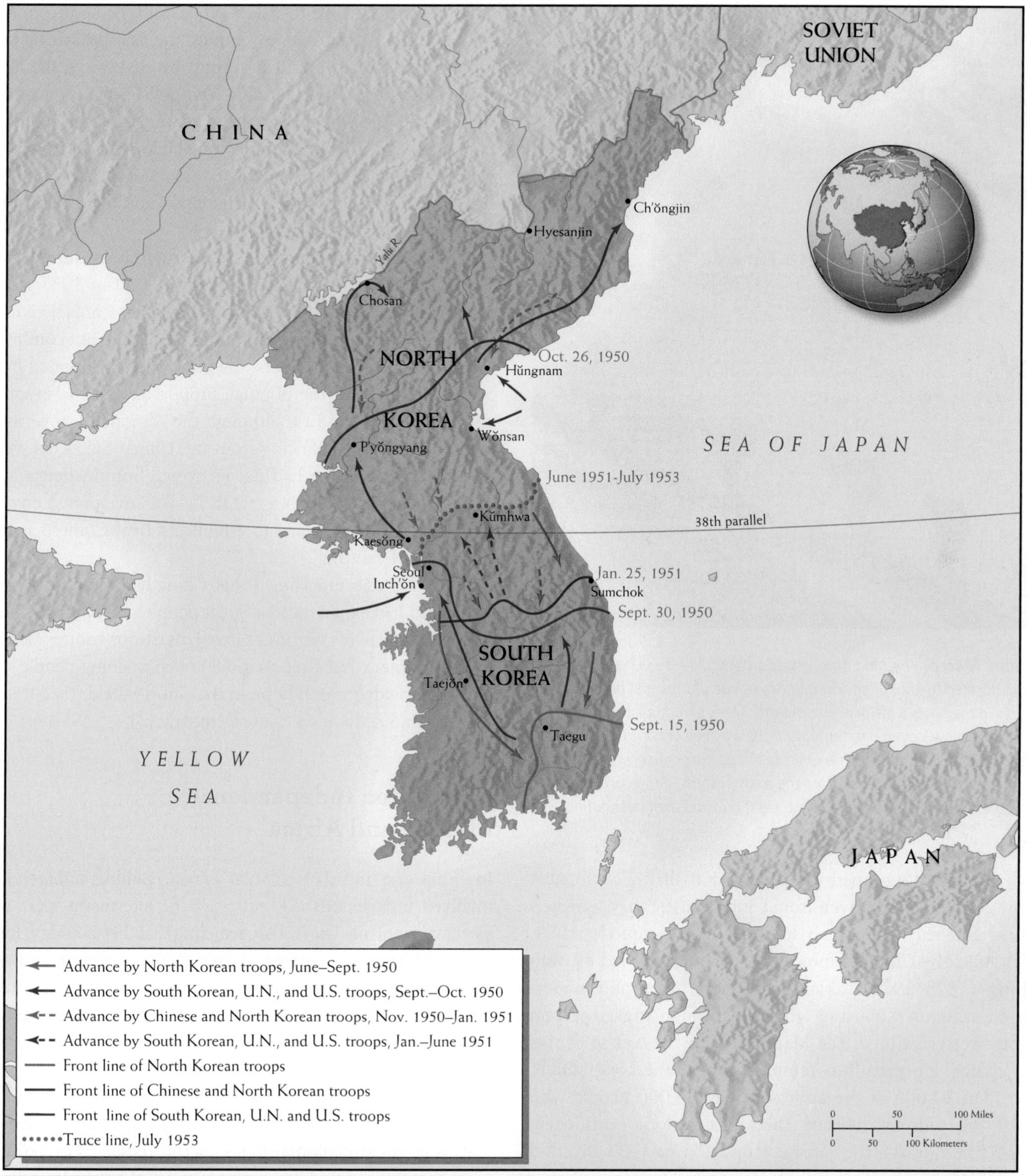

MAP 20.4 | The Korean War

The Korean War was an early confrontation between the capitalist and communist blocs during the cold war era.

- What were the dates of each side's farthest advance into the other side's territory?
- Why was this peninsula strategically important?
- According to your reading, how did the outcome of the war shape political affairs in East Asia for the next several decades?

The Long March. *In China, the Long March of 1934–1935 has been commemorated by the ruling communists as one of the most heroic episodes in the party's history. This picture shows communist partisans crossing the snow-covered mountains in the western province of Sichuan in 1935. Despite their efforts, the ranks of the party were decimated by the end of the 6,000-mile journey from the southeastern to the northwestern part of the country—fewer than one in eight reached their destination.*

but had been outgunned by Chiang Kai-shek's Nationalist regime and had been driven from China's cities; they retreated into the interior, where they founded base camps. In 1934, under attack by Chiang's forces, the communists, led by **Mao Zedong** (1893–1976), abandoned their bases and undertook an arduous 6,000-mile journey through rugged terrain of northwestern China (see Map 20.5). In the course of this great escape, glorified in communist lore as the Long March, fewer than 10,000 of the approximately 80,000 people who started the journey reached their destination. Fortunately for the communists, the Japanese invasion in 1937 diverted Nationalist troops and offered Mao and the survivors a chance to regroup.

The Japanese forces not only inflicted irreparable damage on the Nationalist military; they also further debilitated the capacity of Chiang's regime to govern areas that had not fallen to the invaders. Nationalist soldiers and citizens alike were often left to fend for themselves and became increasingly demoralized and disaffected. When the Japanese invaders seized China's major cities but were unable to control the countryside, the communists expanded their support among the vast peasantry. Mao's followers cultivated popular support by advocating the lowering of taxes, cooperative farming, and policies aimed at women, such as the outlawing of arranged marriages and the legalization of divorce. Like many anticolonial reformers, Mao regarded women's emancipation as a key component in building a new nation, since he considered their oppression to be both unjust and an obstacle to progress.

The communist expansion in the rural areas during World War II swelled its membership from 40,000 in 1937 to over a million in 1945. After Japan's surrender, China's civil war between Nationalists and communists resumed. But communist forces now had the numbers, the guns (mostly supplied by the Soviet Union), and the popular support to assault Nationalist strongholds. By contrast, although the Nationalist government had weapons and financing from the United States, as well as control of the cities, it had not recovered from its defeat at the hands of the Japanese. No match for the invigorated communists, the Nationalists fled to establish a rival Chinese state on the island of Taiwan.

In 1949, Mao proclaimed that China had "stood up" to the world and had experienced a "great people's revolution." Subsequently, many of his ventures proved disastrous failures (see later in this chapter), but China's model of an ongoing people's revolution provided much hope in the Third World. (See Primary Source: Mao Zedong on "New Democracy.")

Negotiated Independence in India and Africa

In India and most of colonial Africa, gaining independence involved little bloodshed, although the aftermaths were often extremely violent. The British, realizing that they could no longer rule India without coercion, bowed to the inevitable and withdrew. Much the same happened in Africa, even though British and French colonial officials knew that African territories were much less ready for independence than India.

INDIA Unlike China, India achieved political independence without an insurrection. But it did veer dangerously close to civil war. As anticolonial elites in the Indian National Congress Party negotiated a peaceful transfer of power from British rule, they disagreed about what kind of state an independent India should have. Should it, as Gandhi wished, be a nonmodern utopia of self-governing village communities, or should it emulate western and Soviet models with the goal of establishing a modern nation-state? Even more pressing was the question of relations between a Hindu majority and the Muslim minority.

MAP 20.5 | The Long March, 1934–1935

During the Long March, which took place during the struggle for power between the Guomindang (Nationalists) and the communists within China, communist forces traveled over 6,000 miles to save their lives and their movement.

- What route did the communist forces take?
- Why did the communists take this particular route?
- How did this movement affect the outcome of this internal struggle in the long run?

The Founding of the People's Republic of China. (Left) *Mao Zedong standing atop the reviewing stand at Tiananmen Square declares the founding of the People's Republic of China on October 1, 1949. Although most Chinese knew little about the communist party, many had high hopes for a new, independent, and liberated China.* (Right) *With flags flying, the crowd celebrates the dawn of a new era.*

For the most part, the congress leadership retained tight control over the mass movement that it had mobilized in the 1920s and 1930s. Even Gandhi hesitated to leave the initiative to the common people, believing that they had not yet assimilated the doctrine of nonviolence. Accordingly, Gandhi and the leadership worked hard to convince the British that they, the middle-class leaders, spoke for the nation. At the same time, the threat of a mass peasant uprising with radical aims (as was occurring in China) encouraged the British to transfer power quickly.

As negotiations moved forward, Hindu-Muslim unity deteriorated. Whose culture would define the new nation? The Indian nationalism that had existed in the late nineteenth century reflected the culture of the Hindu majority. Yet this movement masked the multiplicity of regional, linguistic, caste, and class differences ***within*** the Hindu community, just as Muslim movements that arose in reaction to Hindu-dominated Indian nationalism overlooked divisions within their own ranks. Now the prospect of defining "India" created a grand contest between newly self-conscious communities. Riots broke out between Hindus and Muslims in 1946, which increased the mutual distrust between congress and Muslim League leaders. The leader of the Muslim League demanded that British India be partitioned into separate Hindu and Muslim states if there were no constitutional guarantees for Muslims. The specter of civil war haunted the proceedings, as outgoing colonial rulers decided to divide the subcontinent into two states: India and Pakistan.

On August 14, 1947, Pakistan gained independence from Britain; a day later, India did the same. The euphoria of decolonization, however, drowned in a frenzy of brutality. Shortly after independence, up to 1 million Hindus and Muslims killed one another. Fearing further violence, 12 million Hindus and Muslims left their homes to relocate in the new countries

Jawaharlal Nehru. *Nehru, the leader of independent India, sought to create a "mixed economy" of private and public sectors with democracy to chart an independent path for India. The photo shows him at a public meeting in 1952.*

PRIMARY SOURCE

Mao Zedong on "New Democracy"

Many twentieth-century Chinese political and intellectual leaders, including the communists, believed that the rejuvenation of China required changing its culture. The key question was what to embrace and what to discard. Here we find Mao in 1940 explaining the New-Democratic culture—nationalistic, scientific, and mass-based—that he regarded as a transitional stage to communism. He cautions against the wholesale importation of western values and practices, including Marxism, and emphasizes instead the specific conditions of the Chinese revolution.

New-Democratic culture is national. It opposes imperialist oppression and upholds the dignity and independence of the Chinese nation. . . . China should absorb on a large scale the progressive cultures of foreign countries as an ingredient for her own culture; in the past we did not do enough work of this kind. We must absorb whatever we today find useful, not only from the present socialist or New-Democratic cultures of other nations, but also from the older cultures of foreign countries, such as those of the various capitalist countries in the age of enlightenment. However, we must treat these foreign materials as we do our food, which should be chewed in the mouth, submitted to the working of the stomach and intestines, mixed with saliva, gastric juice, and intestinal secretions, and then separated into essence to be absorbed and waste matter to be discarded—only thus can food benefit our body; we should never swallow anything raw or absorb it uncritically.

So-called wholesale Westernization is a mistaken viewpoint. China has suffered a great deal in the past from the formalist absorption of foreign things. Likewise, in applying Marxism to China, Chinese Communists must fully and properly unite the universal truth of Marxism with the specific practice of the Chinese revolution; that is to say, the truth of Marxism must be integrated with the characteristics of the nation and given a definite national form before it can be useful; it must not be applied subjectively as a mere formula. . . .

Communists may form an anti-imperialist and anti-feudal united front for political action with certain idealists and even with religious followers, but we can never approve of their idealism or religious doctrines. A splendid ancient culture was created during the long period of China's feudal society. To clarify the process of development of this ancient culture, to throw away its feudal dross, and to absorb its democratic essence is a necessary condition for the development of our new national culture and for the increase of our national self confidence; but we should never absorb anything and everything uncritically.

QUESTIONS FOR ANALYSIS

- How does Mao expect to integrate Marxism with the Chinese revolution?
- What does Mao think of China's "splendid ancient culture"? In this regard, how does he differ from previous rulers of China?

Source: Mao Zedong, Selected Works, *in* Sources of Chinese Tradition, *2nd ed., vol. 2, edited by Wm. Theodore de Bary and Richard Lufrano (New York: Columbia University Press, 2000), pp. 422–23.*

where they would be in the majority. Distraught by the rampage, Gandhi fasted, refusing sustenance until the killings stopped. The violence abated. This was perhaps Gandhi's finest hour. But animosity and fanaticism remained. Less than six months later, a Hindu zealot shot Gandhi dead as he walked to a prayer meeting.

Had Gandhi lived, he would not have approved of the direction independent India took. He had already voiced disapproval of industrialization and of equipping the Indian state with army and police forces. But India's first prime minister and leader of the Indian National Congress Party, Jawaharlal Nehru, and other leaders in the congress were committed to state-directed modernization. Inspired by Soviet-style planned development, on the one hand, and by western democratic institutions, on the other, Nehru sought a "socialistic pattern of society" based on a mixed economy of public and private sectors. Declaring that he wanted to give India the "garb of modernity," Nehru asked Indians to consider hydroelectric dams and steel plants the temples of modern India. He made his watchwords education and economic development, believing that these would loosen the hold of religion on Muslims and encourage them to join the national mainstream. He also hoped that the diminished role of religious traditions would improve women's condition. Such a vision allowed Nehru, until his death in 1964, to guide Indian modernization along a third path. (See Primary Source: Nehru on Building a Modern Nation.)

PRIMARY SOURCE

Nehru on Building a Modern Nation

The following excerpt, written by Jawaharlal Nehru in 1940, documents the centrality of planning in the desire to build a modern nation. Although the idea of planning derived from the Soviet experience, Nehru did not want India to adopt communism. He saw planned development as a scientific instrument for achieving rapid economic growth and fundamental social changes. Planning would avoid the excesses and inequalities of capitalism and provide a "third way"—equally distanced from both communism and capitalism.

The octopus of war grips and strangles the world and the energy of mankind is more and more directed to destroying what man has built up with infinite patience and labour. Yet it is clear that war by itself cannot solve any problem. It is by conscious, constructive and planned effort alone that national and international problems can be solved. In India many people thought, with reason, that it was premature to plan, so long as we did not have the power to give effect to our planning. The political and economic freedom of India was a prerequisite to any planning, and till this was achieved our national and international policy would continue to be governed, as heretofore, in the interests of the City of London and other vested interests. And yet we started, wisely I think, a National Planning Committee and we are trying, even in these days of world conflict and war, to draw up a picture of planned society in the free India of the future.

Our immediate problem is to attack the appalling poverty and unemployment of India and to raise the standards of our people. That means vastly greater production which must be allied to juster and more equitable distribution, so that the increased wealth may spread out among the people. That means a rapid growth of industry, scientific agriculture and the social services, all co-ordinated together, under more or less state control, and directed towards the betterment of the people as a whole. The resources of India are vast and if wisely used should yield rich results in the near future.

We do not believe in a rigid autarchy, but we do want to make India self-sufficient in regard to her needs as far as this is possible. We want to develop international trade, importing articles which we cannot easily produce and exporting such articles as the rest of the world wants from us. We do not propose to submit to the economic imperialism of any other country or to impose our own on others. We believe that nations of the world can co-operate together in building a world economy which is advantageous for all and in this work we shall gladly co-operate. But this economy cannot be based on the individual profit motive, nor can it subsist within the framework of an imperialist system. It means a new world order, both politically and economically, and free nations cooperating together for their own as well as the larger good.

QUESTIONS FOR ANALYSIS

- According to Nehru, what are the key problems that India faces?
- How does Nehru's vision of India compare to Gandhi's (see Chapter 19, p. 735)?

Source: Jawaharlal Nehru, "A Note to the Members of the National Planning Committee," May 1, 1940, in Jawaharlal Nehru: An Anthology, *edited by Sarvepalli Gopal (Delhi: Oxford University Press, 1980), pp. 306–7.*

AFRICA FOR AFRICANS Shortly after Indian independence, most African states also gained their sovereignty. Except for southern Africa, where minority white rule persisted, the old colonial states ceded to indigenous rulers. One reason for this rapid decolonization was the fact that nationalist movements had made gains during the interwar period. These years had taught a generation of nationalists to seek wider support for their political parties. World War II, then, swelled the ranks of anticolonial political parties, as many African soldiers expected tangible rewards for serving in imperial armies.

The postwar years also saw throngs of Africans flock to the cities in search of a better life. As expanding educational systems produced a wave of primary and secondary school graduates, these educated young people and other new urban dwellers became disgruntled when attractive employment opportunities were not forthcoming. The three groups—former servicemen, the urban unemployed or underemployed, and the educated—led the nationalist agitation that began in the late 1940s and early 1950s (see Map 20.6).

Faced with rising nationalist demands, and too much in debt themselves to invest more in pacifying the discontented, European powers agreed to decolonize. The new world powers, the Soviet Union and the United States, for their own reasons, also favored decolonization. Thus decolonization in most

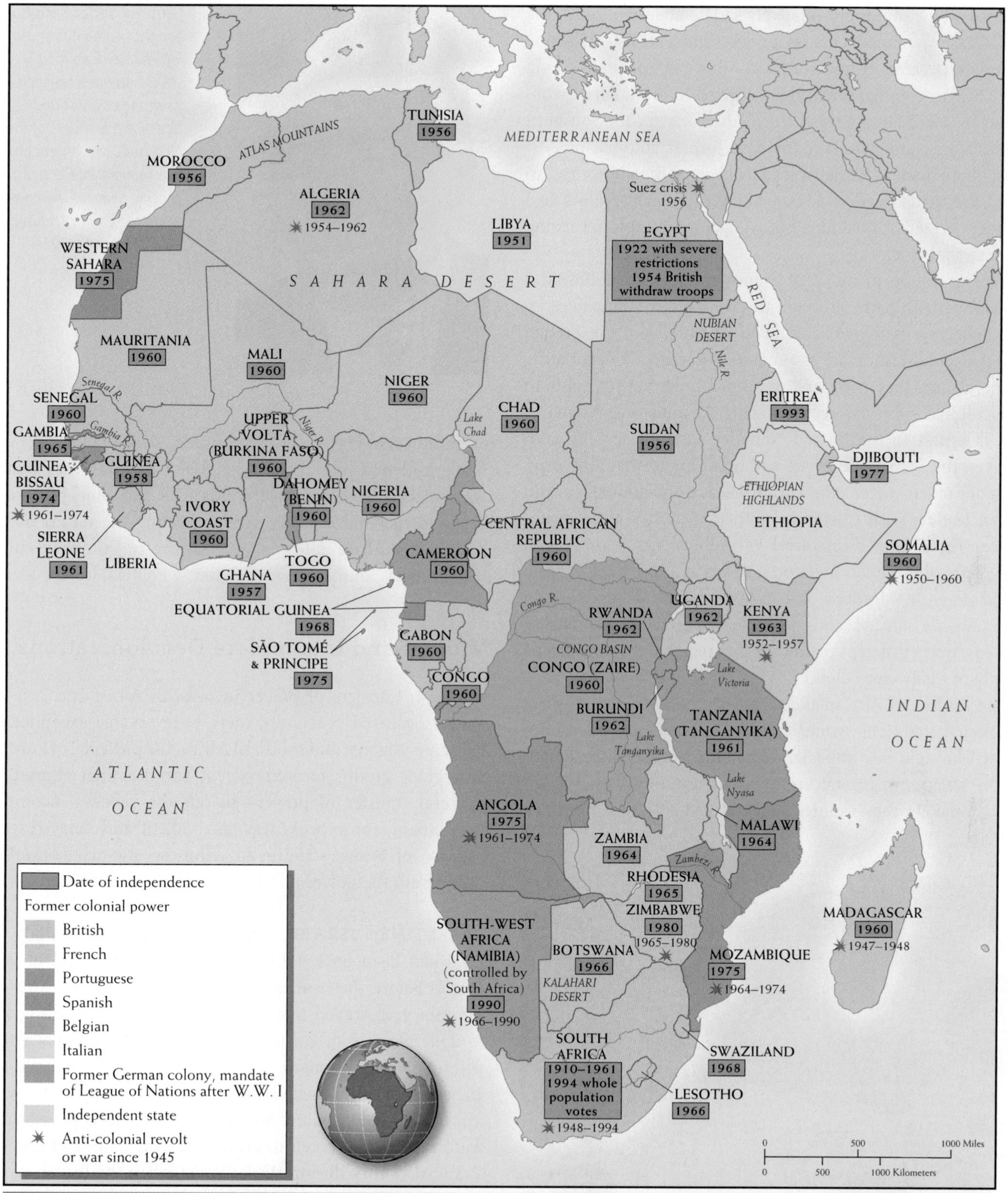

MAP 20.6 | Decolonization in Africa

African decolonization occurred after World War II, largely in the 1950s, 1960s, and 1970s.

- Find at least four areas that won independence in the 1950s, and identify which former colonial power had ruled each area.
- What areas took longer to gain independence?
- According to your reading, what problems and tensions contributed to this uneven process across Africa?

of Africa was a rapid and relatively sedate affair. In 1957, the Gold Coast (renamed Ghana) under Prime Minister Kwame Nkrumah became tropical Africa's first independent state. Other British colonial territories followed in rapid succession, so that by 1963 all of British-ruled Africa except for Southern Rhodesia was independent. In these former colonial possessions, charismatic nationalist leaders became the authorities to whom the British ceded power. Many of the new rulers had obtained western educations but were committed to returning Africa to the Africans.

Decolonization in much of French-ruled Africa followed a similarly smooth path, although the French were initially resistant. Believing their own culture to be unrivaled, the French treated decolonization as assimilation: instead of negotiating independence, they tried first to accord fuller voting rights to their colonial subjects, even allowing Africans and Asians to send delegates to the French National Assembly. In the end, however, the French electorate had no desire to share the privileges of French citizenship with overseas populations. Nor did African leaders wish to submerge their identities in a Greater France. Thus, France dissolved its political ties with French West Africa and French Equatorial Africa in 1960, having given protectorates in Morocco and Tunisia their independence in 1956. Algeria, always considered an integral part of France overseas, was a different matter. Its independence did not come quickly or easily (see below).

The leaders of African independence believed that Africa's precolonial traditions would enable the region to move from colonialism right into a special African form of socialism, escaping the ravages of capitalism. Without rejecting western culture completely, they vaunted the so-called African personality, exemplified by the idea of "Negritude" developed by Senegal's first president, Léopold Sédar Senghor. Negritude, they claimed, was steeped in communal solidarities and able to embrace social justice and equality, while rejecting the naked individualism that Africans felt lay at the core of European culture. (See Primary Source: Senghor's View of Political Independence.)

Léopold Sédar Senghor. *Senghor combined sharp intellect with political savvy. An accomplished poet and essayist and one of the founders of the Negritude movement among Francophone intellectuals, he became Senegal's first president when the country gained full independence in 1960.*

Kwame Nkrumah. *West Africa's leading nationalist Kwame Nkrumah mobilized the peoples of the Gold Coast and, through electoral successes, convinced the British to confer independence on the Gold Coast, which was renamed Ghana in 1957.*

Violent and Incomplete Decolonizations

Although transfers of power in most of Africa and Asia ultimately occurred peacefully, there were notable exceptions. In Palestine, Algeria, and southern Africa, the presence of European immigrant groups created violent conflicts that aborted any peaceful transfer of power—or left the process incomplete. In Vietnam, the process was also violent and delayed, partly because of France's desire to reimpose colonial control and partly from the power politics of cold war competition.

PALESTINE, ISRAEL, EGYPT In Palestine, Arabs and Jews had been on a collision course since the end of World War I. Before that war, a group of European Jews, known as Zionists, had argued that only an exodus from existing states to their place of origin in Palestine could lead to Jewish self-determination. **Zionism** combined a yearning to realize the ancient biblical injunction to return to the holy lands with a fear of anti-Semitism and anguish over increasing Jewish assimilation. Zionists wanted to create a Jewish state, and they won a crucial victory during World War I when the British government, under the Balfour Declaration, promised a homeland for the Jews in Palestine. But when the British awarded themselves Palestine as a mandate after 1918, they also guaranteed the rights of indigenous Palestinians, and sought to mediate between an increasing number of Zionist settlers and their Arab and Christian neighbors.

PRIMARY SOURCE

Senghor's View of Political Independence

One of the most striking visions of African independence as a "third way" came from the pen of Léopold Sédar Senghor, a Senegalese nationalist leader who became the first president of Senegal. The first excerpt, drawn from an essay published in 1959, differentiates the socialism of Africa from Marxism. The second excerpt, taken from a speech delivered in 1961, develops the idea of "Negritude," or black civilization, markedly different from but not inferior to European cultural forms.

AFRICAN SOCIALISM

In the respective programs of our former parties, all of us used to proclaim our attachment to socialism. This was a good thing, but it was not enough. Most of the time, we were satisfied with stereotyped formulas and vague aspirations, which we called scientific socialism—as if socialism did not mean a return to original sources. Above all, we need to make an effort to rethink the basic texts in the light of the Negro African realities. . . .

Can we integrate Negro African cultural values, especially religious values, into socialism? We must answer that question once and for all with an unequivocal "Yes." . . .

We are not Communists for a practical reason. The anxiety for human dignity, the need for freedom—man's freedom, the freedoms of collectivities—which animate Marx's thought and provide its revolutionary ferment—this anxiety and this need are unknown to Communism, whose major deviation is Stalinism. The "dictatorship of the proletariat," which was to be only temporary, becomes the dictatorship of the part and state by perpetuating itself. . . .

The paradox of socialistic construction in Communist countries—in the Soviet Union at least—is that it increasingly resembles capitalistic construction in the United States, the American way of life, with high salaries, refrigerators, washing machines, and television sets. And it has less art and freedom of thought. Nevertheless, we shall not be won over by a regime of liberal capitalism and free enterprise. We cannot close our eyes to segregation, although the government combats it; nor can we accept the elevation of material success to a way of life.

We stand for a middle course, for a *democratic socialism* which goes so far as to integrate spiritual values, a socialism which ties in with the old ethical current of the French socialists. . . . In so far as they are idealists, they fulfill the requirements of the Negro African soul, the requirements of men of all races and countries. . . .

A third revolution is taking place, as a reaction against capitalistic and Communistic materialism—one that will integrate moral, if not religious, values with the political and economic contributions of the two great revolutions. In this revolution, the colored peoples, including the Negro African, must play their part; they must bring their contribution to the construction of the new planetary civilization.

"WHAT IS NEGRITUDE?"

Assimilation was a failure; we could assimilate mathematics or the French language, but we could never strip off our black skins or root out black souls. And so we set out on a fervent quest for the "holy grail": our collective soul. And we came upon it. . . .

Negritude is the *whole complex of civilized values—cultural, economic, social, and political—which characterize the black peoples,* or, more precisely, the Negro-African world. All these values are essentially informed by intuitive reason, because this sentient reason, the reason which comes to grips, expresses itself emotionally, through that self-surrender, that coalescence of subject and object; through myths, by which I mean the archetypal images of the collective soul; and, above all, through primordial rhythms, synchronized with those of the cosmos. In other words, the sense of communion, the gift of mythmaking, the gift of rhythm, such are the essential elements of Negritude, which you will find indelibly stamped on all the works and activities of the black man.

QUESTIONS FOR ANALYSIS

- What is African socialism for Senghor?
- In what way, according to Senghor, does Negritude express Negro Africans' "collective soul"?

As more Jews settled in Palestine, buying up land and seeking to increase their political influence, tensions rose between Zionists and Palestinian Arabs; both grew dissatisfied with British rule. Arabs resented the presence of Jews, who did not conceal their intention to create their own independent state and continued to buy land and displace farmers who had lived on the land for generations. The Zionists became especially enraged: when Hitler began persecuting the Jews of Europe, the British, authorities, mindful of Arab opposition and the Arab states' strategic oil wealth, vacillated over supporting Zionist

The Creation of the State of Israel. *Standing beneath a portrait of Theodore Herzl, the founder of the Zionist movement, David Ben Gurion, the first Israeli prime minister, proclaimed independence for the state of Israel in May 1948.*

demands for greater immigration. After World War II, the pressure to allow more immigration increased as hundreds of thousands of concentration camp survivors clamored for entry into Palestine, and Zionist militants began using force to attempt to gain control of the state.

In 1947, after the British announced that they would leave negotiations over the area's fate to the United Nations, that body voted to partition Palestine into Arab and Jewish territories. The Arab states rejected the partition, and the Zionist Agency only reluctantly accepted it. When the British withdrew their troops in 1948, a Jewish provisional government proclaimed the establishment of the state of Israel. Although the Jews were delighted to have an independent state, they were unhappy about its small size, its indefensible borders, and the fact that it did not include all the lands that had belonged to ancient Israel. For their part, the Palestinians were shocked at the partition, and they looked to their better-armed Arab neighbors to regain the territories set aside for the new state of Israel.

The ensuing **Arab-Israeli War** of 1948–1949 shattered the legitimacy of Arab ruling elites. Arab states entered the war poorly prepared to take on the well-run and enthusiastically supported Israeli Defense Force. By the time the United Nations finally negotiated a truce, Israel had extended its boundaries and more than 1 million Palestinians had become refugees in surrounding Arab countries.

Embittered by this defeat, a group of young officers in the Egyptian army plotted to overthrow a regime that they felt had not yet shed its colonial subordination. Although Egypt had acquired legal independence from Britain in 1936, the plotters believed that incompetent leaders were squandering the nation's sovereignty. One of the officers, Gamal Abdel Nasser, became the head of a secret organization of junior military officers—the Free Officers Movement. These men had ties with communists and other dissident groups, including the Muslim Brotherhood, which favored a return to Islamic rule. They launched a successful coup in 1952, forcing the king to abdicate and leave the country. Then they enacted a land reform scheme that deprived large estate owners of lands in excess of 200 acres and redistributed these lands to the landless and smallholders, who instantly became ardent supporters of the new regime. The new regime also dissolved the parliament, banned political parties (including the communists and the Muslim Brotherhood), and stripped the old elite of its wealth.

In 1956, Nasser moved to nationalize the Suez Canal Company (an Egyptian company, mainly run by French businessmen and experts), inciting the Israelis, the British, and the French to invade Egypt and seize territory along the Suez Canal. Opposition by the United States and the Soviet Union forced them to withdraw, providing Nasser with a spectacular diplomatic triumph. As Egyptian forces reclaimed the canal, Nasser's reputation as leader of the Arab world soared. He became the chief symbol of a pan-Arab nationalism that swept across the Middle East and North Africa and especially through the camps of Palestinian refugees.

THE ALGERIAN WAR OF INDEPENDENCE The appeal of Arab nationalism was particularly strong in Algeria, where

The Anglo-Egyptian Treaty. *The photo shows Egyptian president Nasser signing the Anglo-Egyptian Treaty with the British minister of state in 1954. The agreement ended the stationing of British troops on Egyptian soil and called for the withdrawal of British troops stationed at the Suez Canal military base. But shortly after the last British soldiers left Egypt in early 1956, Britain invaded the country in a vain effort to block Nasser's nationalization of the Suez Canal Company and to remove the Egyptian leader from power.*

a sizeable French settler population (the *colons*) stood in the way of a complete and peaceful decolonization. Indeed, French leaders claimed that Algeria was an integral part of France, an overseas department that was legally no different from Brittany or Normandy. Although the *colons* were a minority, they held the best land and lived in wealthy residential quarters in the major cities. Also, although all residents of Algeria were supposedly entitled to the same rights as the French citizenry, in fact the *colons* reserved these advantages to themselves.

As elsewhere, anticolonial nationalism in Algeria gathered force after World War II. When the French military responded with harsh countermeasures, the independence movement gained strength. The Front de Libération Nationale (FLN), the leading nationalist party, used violence to provoke its opponents and to make the local population choose between supporting the nationalist cause or the *colons*. The full-fledged revolt that erupted in 1954 pitted FLN troops and guerrillas against thousands of French troops. Atrocities and terrorist acts occurred on both sides.

The war dragged on for eight years, at a cost of perhaps 300,000 lives. At home, French society was torn asunder, for many French citizens had accepted the myth that Algeria was not a colonial territory but part of France itself. The *colons* insisted that they had emigrated to Algeria in response to their government's promises and that yielding power to the nationalists would be a betrayal. After an insurrection led by *colons* and army officers brought down the French government in 1958, the new French president, Charles de Gaulle, negotiated a peace accord.

Shortly after handing over power to FLN leaders, more than 300,000 *colons* left Algeria. By late 1962, over nine-tenths of the European population had departed. At independence, then, Algeria had a population mix no different from that of the other North African countries.

EASTERN AND SOUTHERN AFRICA The bloody conflict in Algeria highlights a harsh reality of African decolonization: the presence of European settlers prevented the smooth transfer of power. Even in British-ruled Kenya, where the European settler population had never been large, a violent war of independence broke out between European settlers and African nationalists. Employing secrecy and intimidation, the Kikuyu peoples, Kenya's largest ethnic group, organized a revolt. This uprising, which began in 1952, forced the British to fly in troops to suppress it, but ultimately the British government conceded independence to Kenya in 1963. Decolonization proved even more difficult in the southern third of the continent, where Portuguese Angola, Portuguese Mozambique, and British Southern Rhodesia (present-day Zimbabwe) did not gain independence until the 1970s.

Mau Mau Rebellion. *A large segment of the Kikuyu population rose up against the British colonial occupation of Kenya. This revolt, which began in 1952, was finally suppressed by British arms and Kikuyu "loyalists." Nonetheless, the Mau Mau Revolt led to Kenya's independence from British rule.*

Women played vital roles in these decolonization struggles. In Egypt, for example, the leading nationalists were all men, but they gained crucial support from educated and modernizing women, many of whom organized impressive demonstrations on their behalf. The wife of Sa'd Zaghlul, Egypt's most dynamic nationalist figure after World War I, gained a large following and a reputation as mother of the nation. Moreover, during Kenya's battle against British colonial rule, women supplied the fighters with food, medical resources, and information about the British. Those who were caught ended up in concentration camps and suffered brutal treatment from their prison guards. Yet, once independence was achieved, most women reverted to their traditional subordinate status.

South Africa, which held the continent's largest and wealthiest settler population (a mixture of Afrikaans-and English-speaking peoples of European descent), defied black majority rule longer than other African states. After winning the elections of 1948, the Afrikaner-dominated National Party enacted an extreme form of racial segregation known as **apartheid**. Under apartheid, laws stripped Africans, Indians, and colored persons (those of mixed descent) of their few political rights. Racial mixing of any kind was forbidden, and schools were strictly segregated. The Group Areas Act, passed in 1950, divided the country into separate racial and tribal areas and required Africans to live in their own racial areas, called homelands. Pass laws prohibited Africans from traveling outside their homelands without special work or travel passes.

The ruling party tolerated no protest. Nelson Mandela, one of the leaders of the African National Congress (ANC) who campaigned for an end to discriminatory legislation, was repeatedly harassed, detained, and tried by the government, even though he urged peaceful resistance. After the Sharpeville massacre in 1960, in which police killed demonstrators who were peacefully protesting the pass laws, Mandela and the ANC decided to oppose the apartheid regime with violence. Subsequently the government announced a state of emergency, banned the ANC, and arrested those of its leaders who had not fled the country or gone underground. A South African court sentenced Mandela to life imprisonment. Other black leaders were tortured or beaten to death. Here, too, women kept resistance flames burning. The most dynamic of these individuals was Winnie Mandela, wife of the imprisoned Nelson Mandela. Unlike many of the ANC leaders, who opposed the regime from exile, she remained behind and openly and courageously spoke out against the apartheid government. Despite such human rights violations, the whites retained external support. Through the 1950s and 1960s, western powers (especially the United States) saw South Africa as a bulwark against the spread of communism in Africa.

Apartheid Protest. *In Johannesburg, South Africans march in the street to protest the new restrictions on African citizens, soon to be known worldwide as apartheid, implemented by the white minority government of Daniel Malan. During the Malan administration (1948–1954), informal discrimination was systematically made law, and all electoral, housing, civil, and employment rights of African citizens were dismantled.*

VIETNAM The same concern to contain communism also drew the United States into support for a regime in South Vietnam. Vietnam had come under French rule in the 1880s, and by the 1920s approximately 40,000 Europeans were living among and ruling over roughly 19 million Vietnamese. To promote an export economy of rice, mining, and rubber, the colonial rulers granted vast land concessions to French companies and local collaborators, while leaving large numbers of peasants landless.

The colonial system also generated a new intelligentsia. Primarily schooled in French and Franco-Vietnamese schools, educated Vietnamese worked as clerks, shopkeepers, teachers, and petty officials. Yet they had few opportunities for advancement in the French-dominated colonial system. Thus, discontented, they turned from the traditional ideology of Confucianism to modern nationalism. Vietnamese intellectuals overseas, notably Ho Chi Minh, took the lead in imagining a new Vietnamese nation-state.

Ho had left Vietnam at an early age and found his way to London and Paris. During the interwar period he read the writings of Marx, Engels, and Lenin, and he discovered not only an ideology for opposing French exploitation but also a vision for transforming the common people into a political force. He was

Ho Chi Minh. *Ho Chi Minh's formation of the League for the Independence of Vietnam, or Viet Minh, in 1941 set the stage for Ho's rise at the end of World War II. Here he attends a youth rally in October 1955, just over a year after the victory of his forces at Dien Bien Phu, which resulted in the ousting of the French from Vietnam.*

a founding member of the French communist party and subsequently founded the Indochinese communist party. After the Japanese occupied Indochina, he traveled to China, embraced the idea of an agrarian revolution, and established the Viet Minh, a liberation force, in 1941. Back in Vietnam, the communist-led Viet Minh became a powerful nationalist organization as it mobilized the peasantry.

When the French tried to restore their rule in Vietnam after Japan's defeat in 1945, Ho appealed to the United States (for whom he had been an intelligence agent during the war) for diplomatic and moral support. His appeals fell on deaf ears, but the Viet Minh declared independence anyway. War with France followed (1946–1954), featuring guerrilla tactics to undermine French positions. The Viet Minh were most successful in the north, but even in the south their campaign bled the French. Finally, in 1954, the anticolonial forces won a decisive military victory. At the Geneva Peace Conference, Vietnam (like Korea) was divided into two zones. Ho controlled the north, while a government with French and American support took charge in the south.

Although the French departed, decolonization in Vietnam was incomplete. North Vietnam supported the Viet Cong—communist guerrillas—who combined anti-imperialist nationalism with a land reform program that appealed greatly to the peasants. Determined to contain the spread of communism in Southeast Asia, the United States began smuggling arms to the regime in the south. During the early 1960s, U.S. involvement escalated. In 1965, large numbers of American troops entered the country to fight on behalf of South Vietnam, while communist North Vietnam turned to the Soviet Union for supplies. Over the next several years, the United States sent some 500,000 soldiers to fight the **Vietnam War**, but peasant support enabled the Viet Cong to continue fierce guerrilla fighting. Even the bombing of villages and the deployment of counterinsurgency forces failed to prevent the spread of communism in Southeast Asia.

Faced with antiwar opposition at home and ferocious resistance from the Vietnamese, the U.S. government adopted the policy of "Vietnamization"—that is, placing the responsibility of fighting the communists on the South Vietnamese puppet government. Vietnamization was a convenient fiction spun to enable the United States to withdraw without losing face. In 1975, just two years after the final withdrawal of American troops, the South Vietnamese government collapsed.

THREE WORLDS

World War II made the Soviet Union and the United States into superpowers. Possessing nuclear weapons, superior armies, and industrial might, they vied for global influence. As decolonization spread, the two cold war belligerents offered new leaders their models for modernization. On one side, the United States, together with its western European allies and Japan, had developed democratic forms of governance and a dynamic capitalist economy that produced immense quantities of affordable consumer goods. The Soviet Union, on the other side, trumpeted the communist party's egalitarian ideology and its rapid transition from being "backward" to highly industrialized. Both the First World and the Second World expected the decolonized Third World to adopt their models.

The decolonized, however, had their own ideas. With the communist takeover in 1949, China had shrugged off semicolonial status, but Mao soon broke from Soviet direction. Other decolonized nations in Asia and Africa had underdeveloped economies and could not leap into capitalist or communist industrial development. Moreover, in some places decolonization remained incomplete, and civilians were not allowed even a "cold" peace.

The First World

As the cold war spread in the early 1950s, western Europe and North America became known as the **First World**, or "the free world." Later on, Japan joined this group. Following the principles of liberal modernism, First World states sought to organize the world on the basis of capitalism and democracy. Yet, in struggling against communism, the free world sometimes aligned with Third World dictators, thereby sacrificing its commitment to freedom and democracy for the sake of propping up pro-western regimes.

WESTERN EUROPE The reconstruction of western Europe after World War II was a spectacular success. By the late 1950s, most nations' economies there were thriving, thanks in part to massive American economic assistance. Improvements in agriculture were particularly impressive. With increased mechanization and the use of pesticides, fewer farmers were feeding more people. In 1950, for example, each French farmer had produced enough food for seven people; by 1962, one farmer could feed forty. And as industrial production boomed and wages rose, goods that had been luxuries before the war—refrigerators, telephones, automobiles, indoor plumbing—became commonplace. Prosperity and the dismantling of national military establishments allowed governments to expand social welfare systems, such that by the late 1950s education and health care were within the reach of virtually all citizens.

Western Europe's economic recovery blunted the appeal of socialist and communist programs. Moreover, the cold war slowed down efforts to punish fascists, Nazis, and collaborators. Although war crimes trials brought the conviction of a number of prominent Nazis, the fear was that a complete de-Nazification would deprive Germany of political and economic leaders, leaving it susceptible to communist subversion.

THE UNITED STATES While Europe lay in ruins, the United States enjoyed economic expansion and a rising standard of living. Americans could afford more consumer goods than ever before—almost always U.S. manufactures. Home ownership became more common, especially in the burgeoning suburbs. Stimulating suburban development was a baby boom that reversed more than a century of declining birth rates. Indeed, in contrast to the gloomy 1930s, in the 1950s Americans enjoyed unprecedented prosperity.

Yet, even as suburbanites basked in the affluence that they credited to free enterprise, anxieties about the future of the free world abounded. Following the Soviet Union's explosion of an atomic bomb, the communist revolution in China, and the outbreak of the Korean War, fear of the communist threat prompted increasingly harsh rhetoric. In fact, anticommunist hysteria led the Republican senator from Wisconsin, Joseph McCarthy, to initiate a campaign to uncover closet communists in the State Department and in Hollywood. Televised congressional hearings broadcast his views to the entire nation. Although by late 1954 the tide had turned against him, McCarthyism persisted in American foreign policy. Now almost all elected officials, not wanting to seem "soft" on communism, voted to spend more money on American armies and armaments.

Postwar American prosperity did not benefit all citizens equally. During the prosperous 1950s, nearly a quarter of the American population lived in poverty. But many African

Levittown. *In the decades after World War II, the American population shifted from the cities to the suburbs. To satisfy the demand for single-family homes, private developers, assisted by government policies, built thousands of new communities on the outskirts of urban centers. Places like Long Island's Levittown (pictured here), made affordable by the use of standard designs and construction, enabled many middle-class Americans to own their own homes.*

Anticommunism. *As the Cold War heated up, anticommunist fervor swept the United States. Leading the charge against the "communist conspiracy" was Wisconsin senator Joseph McCarthy, pictured here with his aide, the attorney Roy Cohn.*

Civil Rights Movement. *The 1955 arrest of Rosa Parks* (left), *for refusing to relinquish her seat on a Montgomery, Alabama, bus, led to a boycott that brought Martin Luther King, Jr. to prominence and galvanized the challenge to legal racial segregation in the American South.* (Right) *Borrowing from Gandhi's tactics of nonviolent civil disobedience, protesters staged "sit-ins" across the southern United States in the 1950s and early 1960s, as in this photograph of black and white students seated together at a segregated lunch counter in Jackson, Mississippi.*

Americans, a group disproportionately trapped below the poverty line, participated in a powerful movement for equal rights and the end of racial segregation. The National Association for the Advancement of Colored People (NAACP) won court victories that mandated the desegregation of schools. Boycotts, too, became a weapon of the growing **civil rights movement**, with **Martin Luther King, Jr.** (1929–1968) leading a successful strike against injustices in the bus system of Montgomery, Alabama. Here and in subsequent campaigns against white supremacy, King borrowed his most effective weapon—the commitment to nonviolent protest and the appeal to conscience—from Gandhi. As the civil rights movement spread, the federal government gradually supported programs for racial equality.

THE JAPANESE "MIRACLE" An impressive triumph for the western liberal capitalist vision was the emergence of Japan as a postwar economic powerhouse. The war had ended with Japan's unconditional surrender in 1945, its dreams of dominating East Asia dashed, and its homeland devastated. But after 1945, in an attempt to incorporate Japan into the First World, American military protection, investment, and transfers of technology helped to rebuild Japanese society. The Japanese government guided this economic development through directed investment, partnerships with private firms, and protectionist policies. To promote an export-driven economy, the government encouraged its citizens to save, not spend. By the mid-1970s, Japan, formerly a dictatorship, was a politically stable civilian regime with a thriving economy.

The Second World

The scourge of World War II and the shadow of the cold war fell heavily on the Soviet Union, which with its satellites in eastern and central Europe as well as Mongolia and North Korea constituted the **Second World**. Having suffered more deaths and more damage than any other industrialized nation, the Soviet Union was determined to insulate itself from future aggression from the West. That meant turning eastern Europe into a bloc of communist buffer states.

THE APPEAL OF THE SOVIET MODEL The Soviet model's egalitarian ideology and success with rapid industrialization made it seem a worthy alternative to capitalism. Here, there was no private property and thus, in Marxist terms, no exploitation. Workers "owned" the factories and worked for themselves. The Soviet state promised full employment, boasting that a state-run economy would be immune from upturns and downturns in business cycles. Freedom from exploitation, combined with security, was contrasted with the capitalist model of owners hoarding profits and suddenly firing loyal workers when they were not needed.

Soviet Model. *The rapid infrastructural development under Stalin was certainly a great feat, though at the great loss of human life. Displayed in this German poster is a map of new canals constructed in this period as part of Stalin's Five Year Plan.*

The Soviet system touted protections for workers, inexpensive mass transit, paid maternity leave, free health care, and universally available education. Whereas under the tsarist regime less than one-third of the Russian Empire's population had been literate, by the 1950s the literacy rate soared above 80 percent. True, Soviet policies did not provide material abundance of the sort that First World nations were enjoying. But if consumer goods were often scarce, they were always cheap. Likewise, while it sometimes took ten years to obtain a small apartment through waiting lists at work, when one's turn finally came the apartment carried low annual rent and could be passed on to one's children.

Critical to the Soviet system's attractiveness was the fact that few among the population knew how their counterparts lived in the capitalist world. Government censors skewed news about the First World and suppressed unfavorable information about the Soviet Union and the communist bloc. Yet, even when people learned about the prosperity of western Europe and the United States (usually from western films and radio), they still contended that the Soviet Union was the more just society. Theirs, they believed, was a land with no racial or class divisions at all. If members of the Soviet elite lived in privileged circumstances, their luxurious lifestyles were well concealed. Indeed, socialism's internal critics did not typically seek to overthrow the system and restore capitalism. Rather, they wanted the Soviet regime to introduce reforms that would create "socialism with a human face."

REPRESSION OF DISSENT Few outside the Soviet sphere knew just how inhuman Soviet communism was, and few within knew the extent of the brutality. After the war, the leadership tightened its grip. Surviving soldiers who had been prisoners of war in Germany and civilians who had survived being slave laborers for the Germans were sent to special screening camps, simply because they had been abroad; many disappeared. By the time of Stalin's death in 1953, the vast gulag (labor camp complex) confined several million people, who dug for gold and uranium and survived on hunks of bread and gruel.

Stalin's successors had to face hard questions: What to do with so many prisoners? How to explain the existence of the labor camp system? This problem became acute when strikes rocked the camps. In 1956, the new party leader, Nikita Khrushchev, delivered a speech at a closed session of the Communist Party Congress in which he attempted to separate Stalin's crimes from true communism. The speech was never published in the Soviet Union, but party members distributed

The Gulag. *The Soviet labor camp system was an integral part of the Soviet economy. At any given time, around 3 million prisoners labored in camps, like this one in Perm, Siberia, felling timber, building railroads, or digging for gold. Several million more were forced into exile in isolated locales. During World War II, the gulag population fell drastically, as inmates were sent to certain death at the front or perished from starvation. Between the war's end and Khrushchev's destalinization in the 1950s, the gulag system reached its peak, with German and Japanese POWs, the deportation of entire nations, and the Soviet internment of its own returnees from German camps.*

it to party organizations abroad. The crimes that Khrushchev revealed came as a terrible shock.

Repercussions were far-reaching. Eastern European leaders interpreted Khrushchev's speech as an endorsement for political liberation and economic experimentation. Right away, Polish intellectuals began a drive to break free from the communist ideological straitjacket. Soon Polish workers organized a general strike in Poznań—first over bread and wages, then against Soviet occupation. Emboldened by these events, Hungarian intellectuals and students held demonstrations demanding an uncensored press, free elections with genuine alternative parties, and the withdrawal of Soviet troops. The Hungarian Party leader, Imre Nagy, endorsed the campaign for reform and threatened to withdraw from the Warsaw Pact.

But the seeming liberalization promised by Khrushchev's speech proved short-lived. Rather than let eastern Europeans stray, the Soviet leadership crushed dissent. In Poland, the security police massacred strikers. In Hungary, tanks from the Soviet Union and other Warsaw Pact members invaded and installed a new government that aimed to smash all "counterrevolutionary" activities; Nagy was kidnapped, then murdered. After the revolts, Hungary and Poland did win some economic and cultural autonomy; but unquestionably, the Second World remained very much the dominion of the Soviet Union.

Despite its repressive policies, the Soviet Union was undeniably a superpower. In fact, its status surged after the launching of Sputnik, the first satellite, into space in 1957. Students from Third World countries flocked to the Soviets' excellent education system for training as engineers, scientists, army commanders, and revolutionaries. The updated 1961 communist party program predicted euphorically that within twenty years the Soviet Union would surpass the United States and eclipse the First World, but reckless industrialization left terrible scars both on the population and on the landscape. (See Current Trends in World History: Soviet Ecocide.)

The Third World

In the 1950s, French intellectuals coined the term **Third World** (*tiers monde*) to describe those countries that, like the "third estate" in the 1789 French Revolution, represented the majority of the population but were oppressed. By the early 1960s, the term characterized a large bloc of countries in Asia, Africa, and Latin America. All had experienced colonial domination and now aimed to create more just societies than those of the First and Second worlds. Their leaders believed that they could build strong democratic societies, like those in the West, and promote rapid economic development, as the Soviet Union had done. All this could occur, they felt, without the empty materialism of western capitalism or the state oppression of communist regimes.

The early 1960s were years of heady optimism in the Third World. Ghanaian prime minister Kwame Nkrumah trumpeted pan-Africanism as a way to reach a par with the rest of the world. Egyptian president Gamal Abdel Nasser boasted that his

Hungarian Revolt. *Khrushchev's secret 1956 speech denouncing Stalin's crimes unintentionally destabilized the communist bloc. Tanks of the Soviet-led Warsaw Pact crossed into Hungary to put down a revolt that year, restoring the Soviet-style system but damaging Soviet prestige. Some American officials and especially American-supported radio had encouraged the Hungarians to rise up but then did nothing to support them, damaging U.S. prestige. The upshot was a turn to "national communism" in the Soviet satellites as a way to promote stability and loyalty.*

CURRENT TRENDS IN WORLD HISTORY

Soviet Ecocide

Before the twentieth century, the spread of peasant agriculture, settlement in the steppe and forest zones, and the hunting of fur-bearing forest animals brought profound changes in the Russian environment, including soil degradation, deforestation, and depopulation of species. But the environmental impact of Soviet-era industrialization was staggering. No other industrial civilization poisoned its land, air, water, and people so systematically and over so long a time. Scholars have deemed the Soviet environmental catastrophe an "ecocide."

Soviet economic planners and propagandists celebrated the plumes of purple and orange smoke in their skies as evidence of their huge quantities of industrial production. Pollution-control devices remained unheard of well after their 1950s introduction in Europe and the United States; even when installed in Soviet factories, they were rarely turned on so as not to depress output. Sulfur dioxide, hydrogen sulfide, and solid phenols in water, the food supply, and the air caused epidemic levels of respiratory and intestinal ailments, blood diseases, and birth defects. The giant steel plant at Magnitogorsk, once the pride of Stalin's industrial leap, became a zone of atmospheric and soil devastation 120 miles long and 40 miles wide; inside, chronic bronchitis, asthma, and cancers attacked the population.

In agriculture, the Soviet Union continued to use the fertilizer DDT long after its 1972 banning in the U.S. Despite the socialist country's overall development, in the 1970s Soviet life expectancy began to decline and infant mortality to rise. By 1989, Soviet men lived an average of 63.9 years from birth, down from 66.1 in 1965. Infant mortality by the late 1980s rose to 25.4 per 1,000—roughly the same as in Malaysia, a developing country, and Harlem, NY. Alcoholism also contributed mightily to adverse health trends.

The April 1986 Chernobyl nuclear disaster exposed 20 million people in Ukraine and Belarus to excess radiation. Although there was no bomb concussion, the accident spewed more radioactive material into the atmosphere than had been released in the atomic bombs over Hiroshima and Nagasaki. The Chernobyl cleanup claimed around 7,000 lives. Soviet Uzbekistan, with twice the population of Soviet Belarus, was served by only one-third the hospitals.

Few symbols of Soviet ecocide surpassed the Aral Sea. Because of dams built for wasteful power plants and excess irrigation for cotton production, the Aral's volume shrank by two-thirds and gave way to huge white, lifeless salt marshes. Soviet cosmonauts looking down from space in 1975 were astonished to see immense storms of dust and salt over Central Asia. Toxic salt rain wreaked enormous damage on human and animal lungs.

From the 1950s, Lake Baikal, the largest fresh body of water, and once among

democratic socialism was neither western nor Soviet and that Egypt would remain neutral in the cold war struggle. Indian prime minister Jawaharlal Nehru blended democratic politics and vigorous state planning to promote India's quest for political independence and economic autonomy.

LIMITS TO AUTONOMY Charting a third way proved difficult. Both the Soviets and the Americans saw the Third World as "underdeveloped," and Americans especially wanted to ensure that market structures and private property underlay modernization. The western powers looked to two new instruments of global capitalism, the World Bank and the International Monetary Fund (IMF), to provide crucial economic guidance in the Third World. The World Bank funded loans for projects to lift poor societies out of poverty (such as providing electricity in India and building roads in Indonesia), while the IMF supported the new governments' monetary systems when they experienced economic woes (as in Ghana, Nigeria, and Egypt). Yet both institutions also intruded on these states' autonomy.

Another force that threatened Third World economic autonomy was the multinational corporation. In the rush to acquire advanced technology, Africans, Asians, and Latin Americans struck deals with multinationals to import their know-how. Owned primarily by American, European, and Japanese entrepreneurs, firms such as United Fruit, Firestone, and Volkswagen expanded cash cropping and plantation activities and established manufacturing branches worldwide. But such corporations impeded the growth of indigenous firms. Although the world's nations were more economically interdependent, the West still made the decisions—and reaped most of the profits.

Whether dealing with the West or the Soviet Union, Third World leaders had limited options because neither side welcomed neutral parties. To create more client states, the Soviet Union backed communist insurgencies around the globe, while the United States supported almost all leaders who declared their anticommunism. Indeed, to contain communist expansion, the United States formed a number of military alliances. Following the 1949 creation of NATO, similar regional arrangements

Aral Sea catastrophe. *What was once one of the largest lakes in the world shrank to less than 10 percent of its original size, due to the aggressive Soviet construction of irrigation canals in the sixties to bolster cotton production. Here a shipping vessel is moored in the field of the former Aral Sea, in present-day Kazakhstan.*

the cleanest, suffered the construction of factories on its perimeter, especially a cellulose cord plant (for tires on Soviet bombers) and pulp plant (for paper). The threat to Baikal, as well as the Aral Sea catastrophe, sparked grassroots environmental groups in an otherwise tightly controlled Soviet society. Scientists led the way in breaking censorship taboos, and people from all walks of life turned up at unsanctioned meetings and signed their names to petitions to stop the damage and protect the environment.

QUESTIONS FOR ANALYSIS

- Why do you think environmental degradation was so much more severe in the Soviet Union compared to western powers?
- Why do you think environmental awareness developed much sooner in the United States than in the Soviet Union?

Explore Further

Feshbach Murray, and Alfred Friendly, Jr. *Ecocide in the USSR: Health and Nation under Siege* (1992).

Wiener, Douglas R. *A Little Corner of Freedom: Russian Nature Protection from Stalin to Gorbachev* (2002).

took shape in Southeast Asia (SEATO) and in the Middle East (the Baghdad Pact). These organizations brought many Third World nations into American-led alliances and allowed the United States to establish military bases in foreign territories. The Soviet Union countered by positioning its own forces in other Third World countries.

Nowhere was the militarization of Third World countries more threatening to economic development than in Africa. Whereas in the colonial era African states had spent little on military forces, this trend ended abruptly once the states became independent and were drawn into the cold war. Civil wars, like the one that splintered Nigeria between 1967 and 1970, were opportunities for the great powers to wield influence. When the West refused to sell weapons to the Nigerian government so it could suppress the breakaway eastern province of Biafra, the Soviets supplied MIG aircraft and other vital weapons. A similar situation occurred in Egypt, a strategic region to both superpowers. After the founding of Israel, Egypt's new military rulers insisted that their country never again be caught militarily unprepared. Aware of the West's support for Israel, the Egyptians turned to the Soviet bloc. The resulting arms race between Egypt and Israel left the region bristling with modern weaponry.

Thus, Third World nations now confronted a situation that has been called **neocolonialism**. How were they to apply liberal or socialist models to their own situations? How were they to deal with economic relations that seemed to reduce their autonomy and limit their development? And how might they escape being puppets of the West or the Soviet Union? No wonder Third World nations grew frustrated about prospects for an alternative way to modernity.

By the mid-1960s, as the euphoria of decolonization evaporated and new states became mired in debt and dependency, many Third World nations fell into dictatorship and authoritarian rule. Although some dictators still spoke about forging a third way, they did so mainly to justify their own corrupt regimes. They had forgotten the democratic commitments that were promised at independence. Most also had been drawn into the cold war, the better to extract arms and assistance from one of the superpowers.

REVOLUTIONARIES AND RADICALS Against the background of blasted expectations, Third World radicalism emerged as a powerful force. Revolutionary movements in the late 1950s and the 1960s sought to transform their societies. But while some radicals seized power, they, too, had trouble cracking the existing world order.

Third World revolutionaries drew on the pioneering writings of Frantz Fanon (1925–1961). While serving as a psychiatrist in French Algeria, Fanon (who was born in a French Caribbean colony) became aware of the psychological damage of European racism. He subsequently joined the Algerian Revolution and became a radical theorist of liberation. His 1961 book *The Wretched of the Earth* urged Third World peoples to achieve catharsis through violence against their European oppressors. The book also scathingly criticized those Third World nationalists who wished merely to replace European masters without making radical social changes.

THE MAOIST MODEL While Fanon moved people with his writings, others did so by building radical political organizations and undertaking revolutionary social experiments. One model was Mao Zedong. In 1958, Mao introduced the Great Leap Forward—an audacious attempt to unleash the people's energy. Mao's program organized China into 24,000 social and economic units, called communes. Peasants took up industrial production in their own backyards. The campaign aimed to catapult China past the developed countries, but the communes failed to feed the people and the industrial goods were inferior. Thus China took an economic leap backward. As many as 45 million people may have subsequently perished from famine and malnutrition, forcing the government to abandon the experiment. The Great Leap also exacted a devastating environmental cost from the country. The drive for a dramatic—and unrealistic—increase in steel production, for example, led to widespread deforestation, as farmers everywhere made a mad dash to cut down trees for fuel for their backyard furnaces. In some areas, up to 80 percent of forest land disappeared, leading to severe problems of soil erosion and water loss.

Fearing that China's revolution was losing spirit, in 1966 Mao launched the Great Proletarian Cultural Revolution. This time Mao turned against his associates in the communist party and appealed to China's young people. They enthusiastically responded. Organized into "Red Guards," over 10 million of them journeyed to Beijing to participate in huge rallies. Chanting, crying, screaming, and waving the little red book of Mao's quotations, they pledged to cleanse the party of its corrupt elements and to thoroughly remake Chinese society.

With help from the army, the Red Guards set out to rid society of the "four olds"—old customs, old habits, old culture,

The Cultural Revolution in China. (Left) *Young women were an important part of the Red Guards during the Cultural Revolution. Here female Red Guards, armed with their "little red books," march in the front row of a parade in the capital city of Beijing under a sign that reads "Rise."* (Right) *In their campaign to cleanse the country of undesirable elements, the Red Guards often turned to public denunciation as a way to rally the crowd. Here a senior provincial party official is made to stand on a chair wearing a dunce's cap, while the young detractors chant slogans and wave their fists in the air.*

and old ideas. They ransacked homes, libraries, museums, and temples. They destroyed classical texts, artworks, and monuments. With its rhetoric of struggle against American imperialism and Soviet revisionism, the Cultural Revolution also targeted anything foreign. Knowledge of a foreign language was enough to compromise a person's revolutionary credentials. The Red Guards attacked government officials, party cadres, or just plain strangers in an escalating cycle of violence. Even family members and friends were pressured to denounce one another; all had to prove themselves faithful followers of Chairman Mao. As chaos mounted, in late 1967 the army moved in to quell the disorder and reestablish control. To forestall further disruption, the government created an entire "lost generation" when, between 1967 and 1976, it deprived some 17 million Red Guards and students of their formal education and relocated them to the countryside "to learn from the peasants."

Given the costs of the Great Leap Forward and the Cultural Revolution, many of Mao's revolutionary policies were hard to celebrate. But radicals in much of the Third World were unaware of these costs and found the style of rapid and massive—if deeply undemocratic—uplift of the populace attractive. At least rhetorically, such policies aimed to transform poor countries within a generation.

LATIN AMERICAN REVOLUTION Most Third World radicals did not go as far as Mao, but they still dreamed of overturning the social order. In Latin America, such dreams excited those who wished to throw off the influence of U.S.-owned multinational corporations and local elites.

Reform programs in Latin America addressed numerous concerns. Economic nationalists urged greater protection for domestic industries and sought to curb the multinationals. Liberal reformers wanted to democratize political systems and redistribute land, lest discontent erupt into full-blown revolutions like China's. But when liberals and nationalists joined forces, as in Guatemala in the 1950s, their reforms met resistance from local conservatives and from the United States. In Guatemala, the banana-producing American multinational United Fruit Company (which was the largest landowner and controlled the country's railroads and its major port) opposed land reform. Still, the progressive and nationalist regime of Jacobo Arbenz persevered with plans for agrarian reform and proposed taking over uncultivated land owned by United Fruit. Despite Arbenz's intention of compensating the company for its land, the U.S. Central Intelligence Agency (CIA) plotted with sectors of the Guatemalan army to put an end to reform, culminating in a coup d'état. Through moves such as this, the United States warned other governments that Washington would not tolerate assaults on its national interests in what it deemed its backyard.

In Cuba, the failure to address political, social, and economic concerns spurred a revolution. Since the Spanish-American War of 1898, Cuba had been ruled by governments better known for their compliance with U.S. interests than with popular sentiment. In 1933, during the crisis resulting from the Great Depression, Sergeant Fulgencio Batista emerged as a strongman, and in 1952 he led a military coup that deposed a corrupt civilian government and made him dictator. Under the Batista dictatorship, sugar planters, casino operators, and North American investors prospered, but middle- and working-class Cubans did not. The latter demanded a voice in politics and a new moral bond between the people and their government. In 1953, a group composed heavily of university students launched a botched assault on a military garrison. One of the leaders, a law student named **Fidel Castro**, gave a stirring speech at the rebels' trial, which made him a national hero. After his release from prison in 1955, he fled to Mexico. Several years later, he returned and started organizing guerrilla raids.

Batista's fortunes nose-dived when the U.S. Congress suspended military supplies and aid in response to newspaper reports about his thuggery. Deprived of American support, his regime crumbled in 1958. Entire regiments of his army defected to the rebels. On New Year's Day 1959, Batista announced that he was leaving Cuba. Within days, guerrillas, including Fidel Castro, seized the capital.

Castro then set about consolidating power, elbowing aside rivals and wresting control of the economy from the wealthy

Fidel Castro and Cuba's National Liberation. *The Cuban Revolution of 1958–1959 was a powerful model for many national liberation movements elsewhere in the world. No sooner did Cuban rebels force a break with the United States in 1959 than they discovered that they needed outside support to survive. The Soviet Union, eager to lay a toehold for communism close to the United States, began to provide economic and military subsidies to their Caribbean ally. Here Castro grasps the hand of Nikita Khrushchev atop the Lenin Mausoleum for the May Day parade in 1963.*

elite, who fled to exile. As his policies grew increasingly radical, American leaders began to plot his demise. When Castro announced a massive redistribution of land and the nationalization of foreign oil refineries, the United States ended all aid and sealed off the American market to Cuban sugar. Then, in 1961, the CIA mounted an invasion by Cuban exiles, landing at the Bay of Pigs. The invasion not only failed to overthrow Castro but further radicalized his ambitions for Cuba. He now declared himself a socialist and aligned himself with the Soviet Union. It was over Cuba and its radicalizing revolution that the world came closest to nuclear Armageddon in the Cuban Missile Crisis of 1962. To deter further U.S. attacks, Castro appealed to the Soviet Union to install nuclear weapons in Cuba—a mere ninety miles off the coast of Florida. When U.S. intelligence detected the weapons, President John F. Kennedy ordered a blockade of Cuba just as weapons-bearing Soviet ships were heading toward Havana. For several weeks, the world was paralyzed with anxiety as Kennedy, Khrushchev, and Castro matched threats. In the end, Kennedy succeeded in getting the Soviets to withdraw their nuclear missiles from Cuba.

The Cuban Revolution was a turning point in the making of the Third World. By rejecting the power of capitalist industrial societies, Castro and his followers promoted revolution, not reform, as a way to achieve Third World liberation. The symbol of this new spirit was Castro's closest lieutenant, Ernesto "Che" Guevara (1928–1967). "El Che" grew up in Argentina and traveled widely around Latin America as a student. Shortly after receiving his medical degree in 1953, he arrived in Guatemala in time to witness the CIA-backed overthrow of the progressive Arbenz government. Thereafter, Guevara became increasingly bitter about American influences in Latin America. He joined Castro's forces and helped topple the pro-American regime of Fulgencio Batista in Cuba in 1958. After 1959, he held several posts in the Cuban government but grew restive for more action. Latin America, he felt, should challenge the world power of the United States. Soon his casual military uniform, his patchy beard, his cigar, and his moral energy became legendary symbols of revolt.

The idea of revolution as a way to overcome underdevelopment and to free Third World societies spread beyond Latin America. Che became Castro's envoy to world meetings and summits of Third World state leaders, where he celebrated the Cuban road to freedom. Returning to Latin America, Che set up his center of operations in highland Bolivia in 1966, among South America's most downtrodden Indians. "We have to create another Vietnam in the Americas with its center in Bolivia," he proclaimed. Guevara did not, however, know the local Indian language, and he had little logistical support. He and his two-dozen fighters launched their region-wide war in absolute isolation. Thus, it took little time for the Bolivian army and CIA operators to capture the rebels. After a brief interrogation, Bolivian officers ordered that the guerrilla commander be killed on the spot.

Che Guevara. *Ernesto "Che" Guevara, shown here addressing a conference in Uruguay in 1961 at which he denounced U.S. interventions in Latin America, was a chief lieutenant to Cuba's Fidel Castro and a fierce champion of Third World radicalism.*

If radicals could make a revolution ninety miles off the coast of the United States, what did this spell for the rest of the hemisphere? To combat the germ of revolution, the Kennedy administration sent American advisers throughout Latin America to dole out aid, explain how to reform local land systems, and demonstrate the benefits of liberal capitalism. But to most Latin American radicals, these were inadequate Band-Aids. Instead, inspired by the Cuban Revolution, peasants in Colombia and Venezuela seized estates; workers in Argentina occupied factories. And in Chile, a leftist alliance led by President Salvador Allende triumphed at the ballot box in 1970.

Reacting to revolutionary insurgency, the United States and its allies in the region bolstered their own counterinsurgency program. Working with American advisers, Latin American militaries were trained to root out radicalism. They learned that gaining the support of indigent civilians was the key to defeating the guerrillas. Even Salvador Allende's democratically elected socialist government in Chile was not spared; the CIA and U.S. policymakers aided General Augusto Pinochet's military coup against the regime in 1973 and looked the other way while political opponents were butchered. By 1975, rebel forces had been liquidated in Argentina, Uruguay, Brazil, Mexico, Bolivia, and Venezuela. Elsewhere, they hunkered down in isolated hamlets. Where civilian governments failed to keep stability, militaries took over—not just to topple weak governments, but to rule directly.

Latin American Human Rights. *By the early 1980s, human rights movements were gaining strength all over Latin America, even in Chile under the repressive General Pinochet. Here, a crowd of 400,000 demonstrates against his rule in November 1983.*

TENSIONS IN THE THREE-WORLD ORDER

Third World radicalism did not alter the balance of global wealth and power, but it exposed vulnerabilities in the three-world order. So did the continuation of the Vietnam War, which opened fissures within the First World. As antiwar and civil rights movements mushroomed, the United States experienced social unrest on a scale not seen since the Great Depression. In the Second World, too, dissent challenged the Soviet Union's hold on world communism. Satellite states in eastern Europe sought more flexible orbits, while Mao's China charted a course at odds with Soviet designs. Finally, in the 1970s, the rising fortunes of oil-producing nations and of Japan introduced new problems in the relations within and among worlds.

Tensions in the First World

Although the First World enjoyed great prosperity in the decades after World War II, a variety of issues created friction within these societies and between allies. In the United States, the problem of racial discrimination became a source of greater internal strain and international embarrassment. In western Europe, the expansion of the welfare states that preserved free enterprise while limiting the excesses of capitalism eased, though hardly eliminated, the pressure from economic inequality. In both hemispheres, the demands of women and minorities contributed to postwar tensions.

WOMEN'S ISSUES, CIVIL RIGHTS, AND ENVIRONMENTAL CONCERNS One source of dissension was the "woman question," which became more acute as women made gains after World War II. In Italy, France, and Belgium, women obtained the right to vote. Throughout Europe, as women filled new jobs in the service sector, the female workforce grew to comprise not just single servant or factory girls but mature women in offices, stores, hospitals, and schoolrooms. Although women made gains in employment outside the home, they still awaited a decrease in domestic responsibilities. This fault line would create long-lasting conflict in western societies.

There were other sources of tension. During the 1960s, students in Europe protested the deployment of nuclear weapons in their countries, as well as the rigid social and educational institutions that preserved power and high culture for the elite few. Protests reached their apex in Paris in 1968, when workers joined students in a general strike and clashed violently with police. Sons and daughters criticized their parents, and radicals attacked colonial governments for their oppressive and racist policies.

In these same years, American society lost some of the confidence and much of the contentment that had characterized the previous decade. Prosperity no longer translated into complacency. First there was the assassination of President Kennedy in 1963, and then violent race riots in major cities. In 1964, resistance to the civil rights movement turned lethal in Mississippi with the murders of three civil rights workers and the bombing and burning of two-dozen African American churches.

Under Kennedy's successor, Lyndon Johnson, the federal government promoted a bold plan to ensure civil rights and

Urban Riots. *Racial tensions boiled over in a number of American cities during the 1960s. This photograph of a man being taken into custody was snapped on July 23, 1967, the first day of what turned out to be five days of rioting in Detroit. The unrest left 43 people dead, 467 injured, and more than 2,000 buildings burned down.*

end poverty. The Civil Rights Act of 1964 banned segregation in public facilities and outlawed racial discrimination in employment, and the Voting Rights Act of 1965 gave millions of previously disenfranchised African Americans an opportunity to exercise equal political rights. The Johnson administration also supported programs targeting social security, health, education, and assistance to the poor. Aided by impressive economic growth, the War on Poverty nearly halved the U.S. poverty rate. But legacies of racism and inequality were not easy to overcome. In spite of Supreme Court decisions, most schools remained racially homogeneous not only in the South but across the United States, as "white flight" to the suburbs left inner-city neighborhoods and schools to minorities. Especially in Atlanta, Philadelphia, Detroit, Miami, and St. Louis, African Americans' frustration over discrimination and lack of jobs led to violence. Militant voices, like those of Malcolm X and the Black Panthers, became prominent. Instead of integration, these radicals advocated black separatism; instead of Americanism, they espoused pan-Africanism.

African American struggles inspired Native Americans, Mexican Americans, homosexuals, and women to initiate their own campaigns for equality and empowerment. Women now questioned a life built around taking care of home and family. In fact, the introduction of the birth control pill in 1960 and the publication of Betty Friedan's *The Feminine Mystique* in 1963 stand as watershed moments in American women's history. Because oral contraception allowed women to limit childbearing and to have sex with less fear of pregnancy, the resulting freedom helped unleash a **sexual revolution**. Moreover, Friedan blasted the myth of middle-class domestic contentment, describing the idealized 1950s suburban home as a "comfortable concentration camp" from which women must escape. Despite rising numbers of married women and college-educated women in the workforce, their compensation and opportunity for advancement lagged far behind those of men. (See Primary Source: Betty Friedan on "The Problem That Has No Name.")

Feminism. *Betty Friedan, author of* The Feminine Mystique, *leads a 1970 march in New York City on the fiftieth anniversary of the passing of the Nineteenth Amendment, which granted American women the right to vote.*

PRIMARY SOURCE

Betty Friedan on "The Problem That Has No Name"

In 1963, Betty Friedan published* The Feminine Mystique*, which challenged the idea that women found fulfillment solely by getting married, keeping house, and raising children. Friedan's book contributed to the rise of the women's movement in the United States. In this excerpt, Friedan writes about "the problem" that afflicted suburban housewives—a problem that, she suggested, was widely shared but as yet had "no name."

The problem lay buried, unspoken, for many years in the minds of American women. It was a strange stirring, a sense of dissatisfaction, a yearning that women suffered in the middle of the twentieth century in the United States. Each suburban wife struggled with it alone. As she made the beds, shopped for groceries, matched slipcover material, ate peanut butter sandwiches with her children, chauffeured Cub Scouts and Brownies, lay beside her husband at night—she was afraid to ask even of herself the silent question—"Is this all?"

For over fifteen years there was no word of this yearning in the millions of words written about women, for women, in all the columns, books, and articles by experts telling women their role was to seek fulfillment as wives and mothers. Over and over women heard in voices of tradition and of Freudian sophistication that they could desire no greater destiny than to glory in their own femininity. Experts told them how to catch a man and keep him, how to breastfeed children and handle their toilet training, how to cope with sibling rivalry and adolescent rebellion; how to buy a dishwasher, bake bread, cook gourmet snails, and build a swimming pool with their own hands; how to dress, look, and act more feminine and make marriage more exciting; how to keep their husbands from dying young and their sons from growing into delinquents. They were taught to pity the neurotic, unfeminine, unhappy women who wanted to be poets or physicists or presidents. They learned that truly feminine women do not want careers, higher education, political rights—the independence and the opportunities that the old-fashioned feminists fought for. Some women, in their forties and fifties, still remembered painfully giving up those dreams, but most of the younger women no longer even thought about them. A thousand expert voices applauded their femininity, their adjustment, their new maturity. All they had to do was devote their lives from earliest girlhood to finding a husband and bearing children.

By the end of the 1950s, the average marriage age of women in America dropped to 20, and was still dropping, into the teens. Fourteen million girls were engaged by 17. The proportion of women attending college in comparison with men dropped from 47 per cent in 1920 to 35 per cent in 1958. A century earlier, women had fought for higher education; now girls went to college to get a husband. By the mid-fifties, 60 per cent dropped out of college to marry, or because they were afraid too much education would be a marriage bar. Colleges built dormitories for "married students," but the students were almost always husbands. A new degree was instituted for the wives - "Ph.T." (Putting Husband through). . . .

The suburban housewife—she was the dream image of the young American women and the envy, it was said, of women all over the world. The American housewife—freed by science and labor-saving appliances from the drudgery, the dangers of childbirth, and the illnesses of her grandmother. She was healthy, beautiful, educated, concerned only about her husband, her children, her home. She had found true feminine fulfillment. As a housewife and mother, she was respected as a full and equal partner to man in his world. She was free to choose automobiles, clothes, appliances, supermarkets; she had everything that women ever dreamed of. . . .

If a woman had a problem in the 1950s and 1960s, she knew that something must be wrong with her marriage, or with herself. Other women were satisfied with their lives, she thought. What kind of a woman was she if she did not feel this mysterious fulfillment waxing the kitchen floor? She was so ashamed to admit her dissatisfaction that she never knew how many other women shared it. If she tried to tell her husband, he didn't understand what she was talking about. She did not really understand it herself. . . .

If I am right, the problem that has no name stirring in the minds of so many American women today is not a matter of loss of femininity or too much education, or the demands of domesticity. It is far more important than anyone recognizes. It is the key to these other new and old problems which have been torturing women and their husbands and children, and puzzling their doctors and educators for years. It may well be the key to our future as a nation and a culture. We can no longer ignore that voice within women that says, "I want something more than my husband and my children and my home."

QUESTIONS FOR ANALYSIS

- What criticisms do you think were leveled at Friedan's book when it appeared in 1963?
- What criticisms have emerged in subsequent decades?

A year before Friedan authored her challenge to the subordination of women, Rachel Carson published *The Silent Spring*, a book that was equally revolutionary in its attack against long-held practices. In particular, Carson's book took on the use of synthetic pesticides such as dichlorodiphenyltrichloroethane (DDT), which she said caused cancer, devastated wildlife, and destroyed natural ecosystems. Although chemical manufacturers responded that pesticides had vastly multiplied agricultural yields, *The Silent Spring* stirred opposition that ultimately led to the banning of DDT in the United States in 1972. More broadly, Carson's book spurred the development of an environmental movement that questioned many of the ideas about economic progress and material prosperity upon which the "American Dream" had rested.

PROTESTS AGAINST THE VIETNAM WAR The civil rights and women's movements led many white college students to question the ideals of American society, but what spurred them to massive resistance was escalation of the Vietnam War. As the United States increased troop levels there in the 1960s, it conscripted more men. Tens of thousands of young Americans fled the country to escape the draft. Upwards of 250,000 simply did not register; another 100,000 burned their draft cards. After President Richard Nixon sent American troops into Cambodia in 1970 to root out North Vietnamese soldiers, students at over 500 campuses occupied buildings and closed down universities. At Kent State University in Ohio, National Guardsmen attempting to stop the protests killed four students. The United States withdrew from Vietnam in 1973, but not before the divisions created by the war had strained the country almost to the breaking point.

Tensions in World Communism

The unity of the communist world also came under increasing pressure. As early as 1948, Yugoslavia had broken free of the Soviet yoke and embarked on its own road to building socialism. Other satellites within the Soviet bloc had more trouble freeing themselves. In 1956, Poland and Hungary were forced back in line. Twelve years later, Czechoslovakia experienced the **Prague Spring**, in which communist authorities experimented with creating a democratic and pluralist socialist world. Workers and students rallied behind the reformist government of Alexander Dubček, calling for more freedom of expression, more autonomy for workers and consumers, and more debate within the ruling party. Once again, Soviet tanks crushed what they branded a "counterrevolutionary" movement. As the tanks rolled into Prague, the Czech capital, one desperate student doused himself with gasoline and lit a match—his public suicide a gesture of defiance against communist rule.

Thereafter, the Prague Spring served as a symbol for dissenters, who were divided between those who still wanted to reform socialism and those who wanted to overturn it. Underground reading groups proliferated throughout eastern Europe, and many Russians renewed their faith in Orthodox Christianity, their prerevolutionary religion. Many dissidents were exiled from the Soviet Union. Most famous by the early 1970s was the Russian novelist Alexander Solzhenitsyn. His masterwork, *The Gulag Archipelago*, repudiated the notion that socialism could be reformed by a turn away from Stalin's policies. Yet very few people in the Soviet Union could obtain copies of Solzhenitsyn's exposé, which had been published abroad and was a best-seller in the West. In 1974 the author himself was expelled from the USSR.

Still, there were important changes within the Second World. During the 1950s and 1960s, "national communism" became the rule throughout eastern Europe, even in countries that experienced Soviet invasions. National variations also arose within the Soviet Union, where Moscow conceded some autonomy to the communist party machines of its fifteen republics—in exchange for fundamental loyalty. Dissidents were still persecuted, but by the 1970s, many fewer were murdered outright, and the population of the gulags declined. Shared antipathy for the United States created a Sino-Soviet alliance in the years just after the Chinese Revolution of 1949. By the late 1950s, the Soviet Union had contributed massive military and economic aid to China. But the Chinese increasingly sought to define their own brand of Marxism and criticized Khrushchev's efforts to reduce tensions with the United States and the West. Preferring to accentuate confrontation, the Chinese built their own nuclear weapons and began to tout themselves as a peasant-socialist alternative to the Soviet model of development, especially for Third World countries. The fissure raised China's profile throughout Asia and even in eastern Europe. Indeed, Romania achieved a measure of autonomy in foreign policy by playing off China and the Soviet Union. Albania declared its allegiance to China. African nations, interested in Soviet aid, increased their demands with subtle hints that they might consider deepening ties with China instead. Clearly, the Second World was no monolith.

Tensions in the Third World

In contrast to the First and Second worlds, the Third World was never unified by economic, military, or political alliances. Despite a common history of domination and the shared search for a "third way," the cold war polarized Third World nations. It pushed them to choose between alignment with the First World or the Second. Nonetheless, radicalism nourished new hopes for unifying and empowering the Third World.

One effort at collaboration was the formation in 1960 of a cartel of oil exporters. The Organization of Petroleum Exporting Countries (OPEC)—which included Algeria, Ecuador, Gabon, Indonesia, Iran, Iraq, Kuwait, Libya, Nigeria, Qatar, Saudi Arabia, the United Arab Emirates, and Venezuela—had little impact in raising oil revenues through the 1960s, even though several members nationalized their oil fields. But after the fourth major Arab-Israeli war broke out in 1973, OPEC's Arab members decided to pressure Israel's First World allies by halting oil exports to them. Overnight, the embargo lifted oil prices more than threefold, a bonanza that enriched all oil producers and led to an oil crisis in the West. To many, the bulging treasuries of OPEC nations seemed like the Third World's revenge. Here were Saudi Arabian princes, Venezuelan magnates, and Indonesian ministers dictating world prices to industrial consumers.

But the realignment was not thorough. Third World producers of raw materials such as coffee and rubber tried unsuccessfully to duplicate OPEC's model, and OPEC itself had trouble controlling the world's oil market. During the 1970s, discoveries in the North Sea, Mexico, and Canada reduced pressures on the large oil-consuming states to be more fuel efficient. With supply up, prices fell. To compensate for lost revenue, various OPEC states raised their own production, putting further downward pressure on prices.

Nor did oil revenues help overcome poverty and dependency in the Third World as a whole. To the contrary, most revenue surpluses from OPEC simply flowed back to First World banks or boosted real-estate holdings in Europe and the United States. Some of it was in turn reloaned to the world's poorest countries in Africa, Asia, and Latin America, at high interest rates, to pay for more expensive imports—including oil! The biggest bonanza went to multinational petroleum firms whose control over production, refining, and distribution yielded enormous profits.

For all the talk in the mid-1970s of changing the balance of international economic relations between the world's rich and poor countries, fundamental inequalities persisted. Those nations that appeared to break out of the cycle of poverty, like South Korea and Taiwan, did not achieve success through international markets. Rather, these states regulated markets, nurtured new industries, educated the populace, and required multinationals to work collaboratively with local firms. These were exceptions that proved the general rule: the international economy reinforced existing structures.

CONCLUSION

The three-world order arose on the ruins of European empires and their Japanese counterpart. First, the Soviet Union and the United States became superpowers. Second, World War II affirmed the nation-state rather than the empire as the primary form for organizing communities. Third, in spite of the rhetoric of individualism and the free market, the war and postwar reconstruction enhanced the reach and functions of the modern state. In the Third World, too, leaders of new nations saw the state as the primary instrument for promoting economic development.

The organization of the world into three blocs lasted into the mid-1970s. This arrangement fostered the economic recovery of western Europe and Japan from the wounds inflicted by war. These nations' recovery grew out of a cold war alliance with the United States, where anticommunist hysteria accompanied an economic boom. The cold war also cast a shadow over the citizens of the Soviet Union and eastern Europe. Gulags and political surveillance became widespread, while the Soviets and their satellite regimes mobilized resources for military purposes. The Third World, squeezed by its inability to reduce poverty, on the one hand, and superpower rivalry, on the other, struggled to pursue a "third way." While some states maintained democratic institutions and promoted economic development, many tumbled into dictatorships and authoritarian regimes, and often suffered irreparable environmental damage.

In this context Third World revolutionaries sought radical social and political transformation, seeking paths different from both western capitalism and Soviet communism. Though not successful, they energized considerable tensions in the three-world order. These tensions intensified in the late 1960s and early 1970s as Vietnamese communists defeated the United States, an oil crisis struck the West, and protests escalated in the First and Second worlds. Thirty years after the war's end, the world order forged after 1945 was beginning to give way.

AFTER YOU READ THIS CHAPTER

TRACING THE GLOBAL STORYLINES

FOCUS ON: *World War II and a New Global Order*

World War II

- World War II grows out of unresolved problems connected to World War I, especially the aggressive plans of Germany and Japan to expand their political and economic influence.
- The war brings unheard-of human and material costs and ushers in an age of nuclear weapons.
- At war's end, the United States, fearing the spread of communism and Soviet influence, rebuilds war-torn Europe and Japan and creates military and political alliances to contain Soviet expansionist ambitions.

A new global order

- The Soviet Union and the United States become superpowers.
- Japan emerges as an economic powerhouse and a U.S. ally.
- A weakened Europe cannot resist demands for independence from Asian and African nationalists.
- Chinese communists engineer a revolution, while Indian nationalists and many African leaders achieve independence through negotiations.
- Elsewhere, decolonization is violent (Palestine, Israel, Egypt, Algeria, and Kenya) or incomplete (southern Africa).
- Actions by Latin American reformers and revolutionary insurgents spark counterinsurgency efforts by the United States and its regional allies.
- An insecure three-world order emerges after most Asian and African states achieve independence.

Review and research materials on **STUDYSPACE:** wwnorton.com/studyspace

CHRONOLOGY

The Americas
- United States emerges as a global superpower **1945**

Europe
- World War II **1939–1945**
- NATO formed **1949**

Soviet Union
- Soviet Union emerges as a global superpower, creates client states in Eastern Europe **1945**

Africa
- Decolonization **1940s and 1950s**

Middle East
- The United Nations partitions Palestine **1948**

South Asia
- British Raj ends, India and Pakistan declare independence **1947**

East Asia
- World War II **1937–1945**
- Communist victory in Chinese civil war **1949**
- Korean War **1950–1953**
- Vietnamese fight for independence **1950–1975**

1935 | 1940 | 1945 | 1950

KEY TERMS

Allied powers p. 744
apartheid p. 766
Arab-Israeli War p. 764
Axis powers p. 744
Berlin Wall p. 752
Fidel Castro p. 775
civil rights movement p. 769
cold war p. 744
decolonization p. 754
First World p. 767
Holocaust p. 750
Martin Luther King, Jr. p. 769
Korean War p. 754
Mao Zedong p. 756
neocolonialism p. 773
North Atlantic Treaty Organization (NATO) p. 752
Prague Spring p. 780
Second World p. 769
sexual revolution p. 778
superpowers p. 744
Third World p. 771
Vietnam War p. 767
Warsaw Pact p. 754
Zionism p. 762

STUDY QUESTIONS

1. **Analyze** how World War II was a truly global war and why it led to the end of a European-dominated world. How did the war challenge the ideological justifications for imperialism?
2. **Define** the term *cold war*. How did the task of rebuilding Europe and Asia after World War II lead to this intense global rivalry between the Soviet Union and the United States?
3. **Describe** the other process that dominated world affairs during these years—decolonization. What forms did it take?
4. **Compare and contrast** the three worlds of the postwar order. What was each world attempting to achieve? How successful was each one in achieving these goals?
5. **List and explain** tensions among the three worlds of the postwar era. How did cold war rivalries affect the Third World?
6. **List and explain** various successes and failures in the three competing worlds as they struggled to create "modern societies." What problems did the Third World face?
7. **Evaluate** the impact of Third World revolutionaries and radicals in transforming their societies. How successful were Mao and Castro in challenging the international status quo?
8. **Assess** the impact of nuclear weapons on state rivalries and relations after World War II. How did the proliferation of these weapons affect Soviet-American relations?
9. What tensions emerged between 1945 and 1975 to challenge the three-world order? What challenges did they present for various states?

- U.S. civil rights movement **1950s and 1960s**
- Ascendance of Fidel Castro in Cuba **1959**
- Warsaw Pact formed **1955**
- Prague Spring **1968**
- Stalin dies **1953**
- Soviets launch Sputnik **1957**
- Decolonization **1950s–1970s**
- South African state bans the ANC **1960**
- Arab OPEC oil boycott of Israeli allies **1973**
- Mao's Great Leap Forward in China **1958–1961**
- China's Cultural Revolution **1966**
- Japanese economic "miracle" **1950s–1970s**

1955 | 1960 | 1965 | 1970 | 1975

BEFORE YOU READ THIS CHAPTER

wwnorton.com/
STUDYSPACE

GLOBAL STORYLINES

- A new architecture of power organized around electoral systems and market economies after the collapse of the three-world order creates large disparities between those who participate in the networks of globalization and those who do not.
- The United States emerges as the most influential society in the world, with its cultures and institutions spreading to most corners of the globe, while the world also comes to America and shapes its texture.
- Transnational forces like migration, investment networks, and trade begin to operate independently of the nation-state via international organizations like the United Nations and the International Monetary Fund, which erode the power of the nation-state.

CHAPTER OUTLINE

21

Globalization, 1970–2000

FOCUS QUESTIONS

- What forces drove global integration at the end of the twentieth century?
- What were the characteristics of globalization?
- What possibilities and disparities did globalization create for many?
- How did globalization shape personal identities?

Consider the following comparison. In the thirteenth century, few people could imagine moving beyond their local regions. Venetian explorer Marco Polo, who traveled through China, and Arab scholar Ibn Battuta, who traversed the Islamic world, were rare exceptions. In contrast, by the late twentieth century people traversed in a matter of hours the distances that it took Marco Polo and Ibn Battuta years to cover. Many others staying at home could "travel" the world via the Internet, books, newspapers, and televisions.

But not all travelers moved about so comfortably. Many migrants—desperate to escape political chaos, religious persecution, or poverty—slipped across borders in the dark of night, traveled as human cargo inside containers, or used their own feet to flee their homelands. Billions of others still had no access to the global age's technological wonders and economic opportunities. Thus, while **globalization** (the development of integrated worldwide cultural and economic structures) created possibilities for some, it also caused deeper disparities.

Moreover, consider two different settings: a fishing village in the Amazon River basin, and cosmopolitan Los Angeles. Picture an elderly

Amazonian fisherman trying to teach his children their parents' tongue, Cocama-Cocamilla, but to no avail. All his children speak Spanish instead. "I tried to teach them. It's like paddling against the current." Seven centuries ago, over 500 languages rang throughout the Amazon River basin. As of 2000, only 57 languages survived there. Evidently, one effect of globalization is to reduce diversity. But it can also increase local diversity. For example, Los Angeles, once the emblem of white, suburban America, became a cacophonous city with over 100 languages spoken in its public schools.

This chapter observes the impact of globalization in several ways: (1) the movement of families and groups, as well as goods and ideas, across boundaries that once divided religious, ethnic, and national communities; (2) the role of international financial organizations in addressing world financial issues; (3) the power of multinational corporations in transforming local markets into international ones; and (4) unexpected effects such as galvanizing discontent, sparking a revival of traditional religions (to counter secular and materialist influences), and driving deeper divisions among and within the world's regions—even while bringing them closer together.

GLOBAL INTEGRATION

The full impact of globalization remains unknown. Clearly, though, by the late twentieth century the forces driving global integration—and inequality—were no longer the political empires of old. By the mid-twentieth century, the European empires had lost their sway. The cold war and decolonization movements that had produced the three-world order had also lost their salience. Power structures in the First World, under such stress in the 1970s, did not crack. But those in the Second World did. Thus did the cold war end with the implosion of the Soviet bloc. The Third World also splintered, with some areas becoming highly advanced and others falling into deep poverty; the term **developing world** obscured these differences. Now a new architecture of power organized the world into a unified marketplace with unhindered flows of capital, commerce, culture, and labor. By 2000, most societies had endorsed electoral systems and adopted some form of market economy.

Because the United States promoted these changes, globalization has looked to some like Americanization. The United States unquestionably stood as the world's most influential society, with its music, food, principles of representative government, and free markets spreading worldwide. Yet the process did not run one way. The world also came to America and shaped its society: people living in the United States, their inventions, sports stars, and musical inspirations increasingly came from elsewhere.

Nor was the United States immune from transnational forces challenging the power of the nation-state itself. In the United States, as elsewhere, globalization functioned through networks of investment, trade, and migration that operated relatively independently of nation-states. In the process, globalization shook entrenched forms of political and social identification, from religious to military authority. Members of societies now often identified more with local, subnational, or international movements or cultures, rather than with nation-states. To be sure, nation-states remained essential for establishing democratic institutions and protecting human rights, but supranational institutions like the European Union and the International Monetary Fund (see later discussion) often impinged on their autonomy.

REMOVING OBSTACLES TO GLOBALIZATION

In the mid-1970s, political practices and institutions associated with the three-world order started to deteriorate. By the late 1980s, the communist Second World was disintegrating. The collapse of the Soviet Union brought the cold war to an end. At the same time, the capitalist First World gave up its last colonial possessions, and the remnants of white settler supremacy disintegrated. But as this occurred, the formerly colonized Third World's dream of a "third way" also vanished. As empires withdrew, they revealed a world integrated by ties other than forced loyalties to imperial masters.

Ending the Cold War

A world divided between two hostile factions limited the prospects for a global exchange of peoples, ideas, and resources. There was widespread exchange within the rival blocs—that is, among socialist countries and among capitalist countries—but for other countries the pressure from the Soviet Union and the United States to align with a superpower imposed limits to interaction, even with neighboring nations. A few countries, like Egypt, managed to switch sides (from the Soviets to the Americans), opening up some new global links while closing off others. Pushing against the cold war superpower framework, however, were strong nationalist aspirations and religious movements, which the cold war order tried to control, or in some cases inflame, at great cost.

MOUNTING COSTS The many regional conflicts of the cold war era (Vietnam, Afghanistan, Nicaragua) were costly for countries caught in the ideological crossfire. Vietnam became a battleground for Russian, Chinese, and American ambitions. This war spilled over into Laos and Cambodia, dragging them to ruin along with Vietnam. China attracted several client states in the competition for influence in the Third World and within the communist bloc. In Afghanistan, Moscow propped up a puppet regime, only to fall into a bloody war against Islamic and tribal guerrillas financed and armed by the United States, Saudi Arabia, and Pakistan. In Central America, U.S. president Ronald Reagan and his advisers opposed the victory of the left-leaning Nicaraguan Sandinista coalition in 1979. During the 1980s the U.S. government pumped millions of dollars to the Contras (right-wing opponents of the left-wing Sandinistas) and lent military and monetary assistance to other Central American anti-communist forces. Thus, for much of the world, the cold war was a real confrontation with tremendously high costs for local powers.

Rivalry was costly to the superpowers, too, for the 1970s and 1980s saw the largest peacetime accumulation of arms in history. Despite myriad treaties and summits, the United States and the Soviet Union stockpiled nuclear and conventional weaponry. Furthermore, in 1983 Reagan unveiled the Strategic Defense Initiative ("Star Wars"), a plan to use satellites and space missiles to insulate the United States from incoming nuclear bombs. For both sides, military spending sprees brought economic troubles. The U.S. national debt increased; Soviet life expectancy began to decline and infant mortality to rise.

Cracks on either side of the conflict appeared in the 1970s. The intelligence organizations of both the Soviet Union and the United States produced secret memos questioning whether the Soviet bloc could sustain its global position. As stalemate in Afghanistan undermined the image of the mighty Soviet armed forces, mothers of Soviet soldiers protested their government's involvements abroad. The eastern European satellites became dependent on western European loans and consumer goods. At the same time, the western alliance itself faced internal tensions. In Europe and North America, the antinuclear movement rallied millions to the streets. Western industrialists worried about competition from Japan, which had been plowing money into rapid industrialization rather than arms. Political leaders also grappled with distressingly high unemployment rates. Thus, both sides shared a common crisis: fatigue from the cold war, and an economic challenge from East Asia.

THE SOVIET BLOC COLLAPSES In the end, the Soviet bloc collapsed (see Map 21.1). Even though planned economies employed the entire Soviet population, they failed to fill stores with sufficient consumer goods. Socialist health care and benefits lagged behind those of the capitalist welfare states. Authoritarian political structures relied on deception and coercion rather than elections and civic activism. Although the communist party had promised to beat capitalism by building socialism on the way to achieving full communism, the latter paradise was nowhere on the horizon. The gap between socialism and capitalism was growing.

One catalyst in socialism's undoing was Poland. A critical event was the naming of a Polish archbishop as pope in 1978. The first non-Italian pope in 455 years, John Paul opposed the Soviet form of socialism. In 1979, he made a pilgrimage to his native Poland, holding enormous outdoor masses; in 1980, he supported mass strikes at the Gdansk shipyard, which led to the formation of the Soviet bloc's first independent trade union, Solidarity. As communist party members in Poland defected to its side, the union became a society-wide movement; it aimed not to reform socialism (as in Czechoslovakia in 1968; see Chapter 20) but to overcome it. A crackdown by the Polish military and police put most of Solidarity's leadership in prison and drove the movement underground, but Soviet intelligence officials secretly worried that Solidarity could not be easily eradicated.

The most consequential factor in the collapse of the Soviet superpower was Mikhail Gorbachev, who became general secretary of the Soviet communist party in 1985 and launched an effort to reform the Soviet system. Under this effort (*perestroika*, "reconstruction"), Gorbachev permitted contested elections for communist party posts, relaxed censorship, sanctioned civic associations, legalized small nonstate businesses, granted autonomy to state firms, and encouraged the republics to be responsible for their own affairs within the Soviet Union. These reforms were linked with dramatic arms control initiatives to

Lech Walesa. *A Polish electrician from the Lenin Shipyard in the Baltic port city of Gdansk, Walesa spearheaded the formation of Solidarity, a mass independent trade union of workers who battled the communist regime that ruled in their name. He later was elected president of post-communist Poland.*

MAP 21.1 | Collapse of the Communist Bloc in Europe

The Soviet Union's domination of eastern Europe ended precipitously in 1989. The political map of eastern and central Europe took on a different shape under European integration.

- What significant event in many communist countries signaled the collapse of communism?
- In what part of eastern and central Europe did the most political instability and conflict occur?
- According to your reading, why did the end of communist rule cause the reshuffling of political boundaries in the region?

ease the superpower burden on the Soviet Union. Gorbachev then began withdrawing troops from Afghanistan and informed eastern European leaders that they could not count on Moscow's armed intervention to prop up their regimes.

Having set out to improve socialism, however, Gorbachev instead destabilized it. Civic groups called not for reform of the system, but for its liquidation. Eastern Europe declared its intention to leave the Soviet orbit, and some of the union republics began to push for independence. In response, disgruntled factions within the communist party and the Soviet military tried to preserve the destabilized old order by staging a coup attempt in 1991. However, the former communist party boss of Moscow and elected president of the Russian republic, Boris Yeltsin, rallied the opposition and faced down the hard-liners. Under Yeltsin, Russia, like Ukraine and the other republics of the Soviet Union, became a refuge for beleaguered Soviet elites. Thereafter they abandoned the cause of the Soviet Union and socialism and divided up state property among themselves.

When communist regimes collapsed, the European and Asian political maps changed dramatically. Old states disappeared, and new ones emerged. In Asia, although the division between North and South Korea remained, Vietnam was united and, along with China, welcomed western capitalism under communist party rule. In Europe, East Germany ceased to exist; West Germany absorbed its remnants after the Berlin Wall came down in 1989. (See Primary Source: Tidal Pull of the West: East Germany Disappears.) Soon thereafter the Soviet empire dissolved into independent states (see Map 21.2). But the end of Soviet-style socialism was not entirely peaceful. The worst carnage occurred in the former Yugoslavia, which suffered wars of dissolution as leaders exploited ethnic fears. Serbs and Croats, in particular, engaged in savage struggles over territories in the Balkans.

By historical standards the cold war had been relatively brief, spanning four decades. But communism had played a major role in the military conflicts and the headlong modernization of Russia and China, and it exercised important influence on India. However, it could not keep up the cold war *and* deliver the good life to its adherents *and* survive in a more competitive world economy.

The Berlin Wall. *The breaching of the Berlin Wall in November 1989 spelled the end of the Soviet bloc. Decades of debate over whether communism could be reformed turned out to be moot. In the face of competition from the richer, consumer-oriented West, communism collapsed.*

Africa and the End of White Rule

Although the aftermath of World War II saw the dismantling of most of Europe's empires, remnants of colonial rule remained in southern Africa (see Map 20.6 on p. 759). Here, whites clung to centuries-old notions of their racial superiority over non-Europeans. Final decolonization meant that self-rule would return to all of Africa.

THE LAST HOLDOUTS The last fortresses under direct European control were the Portuguese colonies of southern and western Africa. However, by the mid-1970s efforts to suppress African nationalist movements had exhausted Portugal's resources. Demoralized Portuguese officers now pushed aside their nation's dictatorship and began the Portuguese experiment with democracy. As African nationalist demands led to a hurried Portuguese withdrawal from Guinea-Bissau, Angola, and Mozambique, formal European colonialism in Africa came to an end.

But white rule still prevailed elsewhere in Africa. In Rhodesia, a white minority resisted all international pressure to allow black rule. In the end, independent African neighbors helped support a liberation guerrilla movement under Robert Mugabe. Surrounded, Rhodesian whites finally capitulated. Mugabe swept to power with massive electoral support in 1979. The new constitutional government renamed the country Zimbabwe, erasing from Africa's map the name of the long-deceased British expansionist Cecil Rhodes (see Chapter 17).

SOUTH AFRICA AND NELSON MANDELA The final outpost of white rule was South Africa, where a European minority was larger, richer, and more entrenched than elsewhere in the region—and highly invulnerable to outside pressures. Although powerful international firms operated there, they were reluctant to risk their investments by boycotting the racist regime. In addition, the U.S. government regarded South Africa's large army as a useful tool to fight Soviet allies elsewhere in southern Africa. In any case the ruling Afrikaner-led National Party used ruthless tactics against internal critics. Yet, in the countryside and cities, defiance of white rule was growing. Africans lobbed rocks and crude bombs (Molotov cocktails) at tanks and organized mass strikes in the multinational-owned mines.

At the same time, pressures from abroad were mounting. The International Olympic Committee banned South African athletes starting in 1970. American students insisted that their universities divest themselves of companies with investments in South Africa. As international pressures grew, foreign governments—even that of the United States, once South Africa's staunchest ally—applied economic sanctions against South Africa. A swelling worldwide chorus demanded that **Nelson Mandela**, the imprisoned leader of the African National Congress (ANC), be freed. The white political elite eventually realized that it was better to negotiate new arrangements than to endure international ostracism and

PRIMARY SOURCE

Tidal Pull of the West: East Germany Disappears

After Soviet premier Mikhail Gorbachev instituted a series of reforms to save socialism, dissenters in eastern Europe saw their chance to throw off Russian dominance. The Berlin Wall (erected in 1961) was the most visible symbol of Soviet oppression. Here journalist Ann Tusa recalls the November 1989 press conference that accidentally led to the opening of the Berlin Wall. As both the wall and East Germany fell, Russia kept its nearly 400,000 troops that were on East German soil confined to their barracks.

At about 7 o'clock on the evening of November 9, 1989, some 300 journalists from all over the world are crammed into a room in East Berlin for a routine press conference. . . . For the first time since the foundation of a separate Communist East German state in 1946, the German Democratic Republic, there have been massive demonstrations against the regime. . . .

East Germans, who have not known a free election since 1933, have been voting with their feet. From January to October 1989, some 200,000 people had left their country. By early November the figure was up to 250,000—and that was out of a total population of 16.7 million. At first, many East Germans went out on "holiday visas" to Iron Curtain countries [European states under Soviet domination], then claimed asylum in West German embassies in Warsaw, Budapest or Prague. Thousands more have driven or walked round the East German frontiers looking for an undefended crossing or a guard with a blind eye, wriggled across, then headed for Austria and a refugee camp. . . .

The November 9 press conference is handled by Günter Schabowski. . . . This evening he feeds the press a startling hint that there might soon be free elections. Good story. Everyone wants to go out and file it. But then Schabowski turns up a sheet from the bottom of the pile of papers on his table. "This will be interesting for you." And in a style that suggests it is all news to him, slowly reads aloud: "Today the decision was taken to make it possible for all citizens to leave the country through the official border crossing points. All citizens of the GDR can now be issued with visas for the purposes of travel or visiting relatives in the West. This order is to take effect at once. . . ."

The news is broadcast on an East German television bulletin at 7:30 P.M. The station's switchboard is immediately jammed with callers. "Is it true? I can't believe it." They always believed West German television, though, and it is soon flashing the announcement. A few East and West Berliners go to the Wall to see what is happening. . . . Then at 10:30 a discussion program on Sender Freies Berlin, the West Berlin television station, is interrupted by a live broadcast from the Wall. No preamble, just shots of a small crowd milling round a checkpoint, then a man runs toward the camera: "They've opened the crossing at Bornholmer Strasse." After that the news spreads like wildfire, by radio, television, telephone, shouts in the street. The trickle across the Wall swells to a flood. That weekend 2 million East Germans are reckoned to have stood in West Berlin. One reaction is common to them all: "We've seen the West on TV, of course. But this is real."

. . . The fatal piece of paper had been hurriedly swept up as he left for the press conference. It had never been intended for publication. It was a draft based on a recent Politburo decision: unable to control the tide of refugees, thrashing around for ways to quiet the demonstrators on the streets, they had decided that in their own good time they would ease travel restrictions, having first made arrangements for a limited issue of visas under carefully controlled circumstances.

QUESTIONS FOR ANALYSIS

- The Berlin Wall (and other border defenses) kept East Germans and West Germans apart for twenty-eight years. How did some East Germans try to circumvent the barriers during that time?
- Why didn't the 400,000 Soviet troops in East Germany intervene during the collapse of the Berlin Wall?
- What does this piece tell us about the state of mind of the East German government at this time?

years of internal warfare against a majority population. In 1990, President F. W. de Klerk (of the National Party) released Mandela from prison and legalized the ANC and the communist party of South Africa. Ensuing negotiations produced South Africa's first free, mass elections in 1994. These brought an overwhelming victory to the ANC, with Nelson Mandela elected as president. Majority rule had finally come to South Africa, and for the first time in centuries Africans ruled over all of Africa.

In Nelson Mandela, South Africa's white rulers found a man of exceptional integrity and political savvy. He had spent more than two decades in prison, much of it at hard labor. But he looked beyond past injustices to ease the transition

MAP 21.2 | The Breakup of the Soviet Union

The Soviet Union broke apart in 1991. Compare this map with Map 17.6 (see p. 660), which illustrates Russian expansion in the nineteenth century.

- Which parts of the old Russian Empire remained under Russian rule, and which territories established their own states?
- In what areas did large migrations accompany the breakup, and for what reasons?
- According to your reading, how did the breakup of the Soviet Union change Russia's status in Europe and Asia?

to full democracy. Besides, he was aware that, with the country veering toward civil war, only a negotiated change would preserve South Africa's industries, wealth, and educational system.

Still, the leaders of independent Africa faced immense problems in building stable political communities. Although they set out to destroy the vestiges of colonial political structures and to erect African-based public institutions, local contests for

The End of Apartheid. *Nelson Mandela, running for president in 1994 as the candidate of the African National Congress, here casts a ballot in the first all-races election in South Africa. This election ended apartheid and saw the African National Congress take control of the Republic of South Africa.*

political power impeded this process. Ethnic and religious rivalries, held in check during the colonial period, now blazed forth. Civil wars erupted in many countries (most violently in Nigeria, Sudan, and Zaire), and military leaders were drawn into politics. Coups d'état were common. Nigeria, for instance, had six military coups between 1966 and 1999. The ruling elements increasingly maintained power by using the state's resources to reward their clients and to punish their enemies. By the 1990s, the continent was aflame with civil strife—armed conflicts that started with the cold war and lasted well after it ended.

UNLEASHING GLOBALIZATION

As obstacles to international integration began to dissolve, capital, commodities, people, and culture crossed borders with ever-greater freedom. Even though trade, foreign investment, migration, and cultural borrowing had long been hallmarks of modern history, the global age changed their scale. At the same time, never had there been such unequal access to the fruits of globalization. Several factors contributed to increasing integration and to new power arrangements: international banking, expanded international trade, population migrations, and technical breakthroughs in communications.

Finance and Trade

The increased international flow of goods and capital was well under way in the 1970s, but the end of the cold war removed many impediments to globalization. During the 1990s, even the strongest nation-states felt the effects of economic globalization.

GLOBAL FINANCIAL TRANSFERS AND DEREGULATED MARKETS Major transformations occurred in the world's financial system in the 1970s. America's budget and trade deficits prompted President Richard Nixon to take the dollar off the gold standard, an action that enabled the yen, the lira, the pound, the franc, and other national currencies to cut their ties to the American dollar. Now international financiers enjoyed greater freedom from national regulators and found fresh business opportunities. A new system of informal money management across borders replaced an older system of formal management within borders. Where formal management of world financial relations existed, it fell increasingly under international authorities such as the World Bank and the International Monetary Fund.

The primary agents of the heightened global financial activity were banks. Based mainly in London, New York, and Tokyo, big, highly diversified financial banks became conduits for mobile capital looking for lucrative ventures. Revenues from oil producers provided a large infusion of cash into the global economy in the 1970s. At the same time, banks joined forces to issue mammoth loans to developing nations.

International financial firms found academic allies who outlined the economic rules for a global economic environment. These intellectuals were primarily North American–trained economists whose new framework minimized the welfare concerns of the Keynesian approach (see Chapter 19). Instead, these economists emphasized unfettered markets and profit motivations as the cornerstone of capitalist economic development. Employed in banks and ministries worldwide, they argued that the old regulatory policies of nation-states prevented rather than promoted economic growth. Working as advisers in many governments (especially under Margaret Thatcher in Britain and Ronald Reagan in the United States), these economists guided public policy to deregulate market life.

No international financial organization was more influential than the **International Monetary Fund (IMF)**. During the 1980s it emerged as a central player, especially in response to the so-called debt crisis in Third World and eastern-bloc countries. Throughout the 1970s, European, Japanese, and North American banks had loaned money on very easy terms to cash-strapped Third World and eastern-bloc borrowers. But what was once good business soon turned sour. In 1982, a wave of defaults threatened to overrun Latin America in particular. Throughout the 1980s, international banks and the IMF kept heavily indebted customers solvent. The IMF offered short-term loans to governments on condition that recipients adopt new fiscal ways and compel civilian populations to tighten their belts. Latin Americans pioneered the process of merging their domestic markets with international ones. Trade barriers crumbled, state enterprises became private firms, and foreign investors called the former debtors "emerging markets." Eastern Europe and Asia followed suit in the 1990s, and emerging-market mania buoyed a boom in international finance.

EFFECTS OF INTEGRATED NETWORKS New technologies and institutions enabled many more financial investors and traders to participate in the integrated networks of world finance. The Internet and online trading accelerated the mobility—and volatility—of capital across borders. Volatility soon created problems, however. In the 1990s, currency devaluations in Mexico, in Russia, and across East Asia shocked financiers. When the Mexican economy went into paralysis in 1994, the crisis was so extreme that not even the IMF could bail it out; the U.S. Treasury had to issue the largest international loan in history to pull Mexico out of its economic tailspin. Despite acting as the lender in that instance, the United States emerged in the new financial order as the world's largest borrower. Early in the new millennium, its net foreign debt soared past $2 trillion—a 700 percent increase since the early 1990s. Much of this debt was owed to Asian, especially Chinese, bankers.

Globalization increased commercial, as well as financial, interdependence. The total value of world trade increased nearly tenfold between 1973 and 1998, and trade in Asia grew even faster. In 1960, trade accounted for 24 percent of the world gross domestic product (GDP; the total value of all goods and services produced in a country in a single year). By 1995, that share had almost doubled. Where an American would once have worn American-made clothes (Levi's), driven an American car (a Ford), and watched an American television (Zenith), such was rarely the case by century's end. Increasingly, consumers bought foreign goods and services and sold a greater share of their own output abroad. This pattern had always been true of smaller regions like Central America and southern Africa. But in the 1980s it intensified, with Hong Kong and Singapore prospering through expanding world trade.

International trade also shifted the international division of labor. After World War II, Europeans and North Americans dominated manufacturing, while Third World countries supplied raw materials. But by the 1990s this was no longer the case. Brazil became a major airplane maker, South Korea exported millions of automobiles, and China emerged as the world's largest source of textiles, footwear, and electronics.

The most remarkable global shift involved East Asian industry and commerce. Manufactured goods, including high-technology products, now issued from the eastern fringe of Afro-Eurasia as often as from its western fringe. Japan blazed the Asian trail: between 1965 and 1990, its share of world trade doubled to almost 10 percent. China, too, flexed its economic muscle. When Deng Xiaoping took power in 1978, China was already a growing economy. Under Deng, China started to become an economic powerhouse. For the next two decades, China chalked up astounding 10 percent annual growth rates, swelling its share of world GDP from 5 percent to 12 percent.

Globalization. *In the past, Americans mostly bought products, such as cars, that were manufactured domestically. Now, Americans often buy products made abroad.*

For East Asia as a whole, the share of world exports doubled in the same period, with smaller countries like Singapore, Taiwan, South Korea, and Hong Kong becoming mini-powerhouses. By the early 1990s, these countries and Japan were major investors abroad. Overall, East Asia's share of world production rose from 13.6 percent to 25.3 percent between 1965 and 1989. By contrast, over the same period, the U.S. and European shares decreased.

REGIONAL TRADE BLOCS AND GROWING DISPARITIES Industrialization of previously less developed countries, combined with lower trade barriers, increased the pressures of world competition on national economies. Some areas responded by creating regional blocs. In North America, much trade and finance flowed back and forth across the U.S.-Canadian border. By the 1980s, fearing competition from inexpensive Asian manufactures, the two countries admitted Mexico into the trading bloc to encourage plants to locate within the region. They negotiated a North American Free Trade Agreement (NAFTA) in 1992.

Meanwhile, the most complete regional integration occurred in Europe. Indeed, Europeans slashed trade barriers and harmonized their commercial policies toward the rest of the world. In 1993, the Maastricht Treaty established the **European Union (EU)** under its current name, and what had been conceived as a trading and financial bloc began to evolve into a political union as well. In hopes of establishing permanent peace and prosperity, European states agreed to give up aspects of their sovereignty and allowed European-wide legislative and judicial bodies (the European Parliament and the Court of Justice of the European Union) to make binding political and legal decisions. In 2002, a number of the European Union states deepened their economic interdependence by adopting a single currency, the euro. A few nations—most notably the United Kingdom—did not want to give up control of their own currency. By 2012, the European Union had twenty-seven members, and the Eurozone seventeen members. Trade integration and interdependence coincided with a transformation in traded commodities. Pharmaceuticals, computers, software, and services from insurance to banking became key exports and imports. High technology, in particular, now occupied an ever-greater share of the manufacturing and exports of the world's richest countries.

Competition and the shift to producing sophisticated goods affected world incomes. For "rich" countries as a whole, about half of total GDP reflected the production and distribution of such goods and services, giving those countries a competitive advantage. In general, where global incomes were lower and people were less educated, the share of knowledge as a contributor to wealth was also lower. Poor nations remained, with few exceptions, locked in the production of low-tech goods and the export of raw materials. Increasingly, technology and knowledge now divided the world into affluent, technically sophisticated countries and poor, technically underdeveloped regions.

Migration

Migration, a constant feature of world history, became more pronounced in the twentieth century (see Map 21.3). Although after 1970 fewer Europeans were on the move, many more Asians, Africans, and Latin Americans were. By 2000, there were 120 million migrants scattered across 152 countries, up from 75 million in 1965. Most left poorer countries for richer destinations.

PATTERNS OF MIGRATION Migratory flows often followed the contours of existing political relations. Where North America and Europe had had colonies or dependencies, their political withdrawal left tracks for migrants to follow. Indians and Pakistanis moved to Britain. Dominicans, Haitians, and Mexicans went to the United States. Algerians and Vietnamese moved to France. And where emerging rich societies cultivated close diplomatic ties, these relations opened migratory gates. This was true of Germany's relationship with Turkey, of Japan's with South Korea, and of Canada's with Hong Kong. In most cases, economic factors propelled migrants across national borders.

International migration was often an extension of regional and national migration from poorer, rural areas to urban centers. In Nigeria, for example, rural-urban migration intensified after 1970. In 1900, Nigeria's capital at the time, Lagos, had a population of 41,847. At the century's end, Lagos had more than 10 million people, with predictions that it would double by 2025. The key to Lagos's boom in the 1970s was the existence of large oil reserves inside the country and the high prices that oil fetched in international markets. When the Organization of Petroleum Exporting Countries (OPEC) sent oil prices soaring, money poured into Nigeria. The government kept most of it in its largest city. That, in turn, spurred people to move to Lagos. This rural-urban migration increased Lagos's population by 14 percent per year in the 1970s and 1980s. No government—least of all a new, weakly supported one like Nigeria's—could cope with such a huge influx. Electricity supplies failed regularly. There were never enough schools, teachers, or textbooks. But the city burst with the vitality of new arrivals, prompting one immigrant to exclaim: "It's a terrible place; I want to go there!"

The search for opportunities also pushed people to move from less developed to more developed nations. Although many corporations relocated their manufacturing plants in poorer countries, where unskilled labor was abundant and government regulations were few, these jobs remained less attractive than even the lowest-wage positions available in richer nations. Thus, the possibility for better wages—and the hope for better lives—inspired millions to leave their homelands.

TEMPORARY MIGRANTS Some migrants moved for temporary sojourns. At least that was the original intent. In the 1950s and 1960s, southern Europeans moved northward; but when Spain, Portugal, Greece, and Italy also became wealthy societies, not only did the exodus decline, but these countries became magnets for Middle Eastern, North African, and (more recently) eastern European migrants. However, Europeans' strong identification with their nations did not permit the easy integration of foreigners. Nor did European states support the permanent settlement of immigrants. Most migrants from Asia and Africa went initially to Europe in search of temporary jobs as guest workers. With time they settled in their host countries, often living in urban slums (for example, Pakistanis in Britain's city of Leeds, and Algerians in impoverished suburbs of Paris).

In Japan, too, immigrants were not easily incorporated. Tokyo's policy in the 1970s resembled the European guest worker program. Discouraging permanent settlement and immigration, Japan encouraged mainly itinerant workers to move to the country, yet its economy required increasing numbers of these sojourners. Indeed, Japan's deep reluctance to integrate migrants led to dire labor shortages.

Lagos, Nigeria. *During the twentieth century, Lagos was one of the fastest-growing and most crowded cities in Africa.*

After Japan, the economic tigers of Hong Kong, Taiwan, and Malaysia all became hosts for temporary migrants. So millions of guest workers moved there, but ultimately the migrants sank deeper roots, especially once their children entered schools. This presented a challenge to host societies that were accustomed to thinking of their national communities as ethnically homogeneous. At times, discrimination led to violent conflicts among recent immigrants, long-time residents, and the state's security forces. Governments also grappled with the challenge of extending citizenship rights to and culturally assimilating newcomers who wanted to dress according to religious custom, as in the case of Muslims in France (10 percent of that country's population).

DEMOGRAPHIC CHANGES IN THE UNITED STATES One society that had fewer problems integrating migrants, and that attracted the lion's share of international migrants, was the United States. Long a magnet for Europeans, the United States enacted an immigration reform in 1965 that opened its gates to the world's migrants. By 2000, 27 million immigrants lived there, accounting for almost 10 percent of the population—double the share in 1970.

The profile of migration also changed. In 1970, there were more Canadians or Germans living in the United States than Mexicans. Over the next thirty years, the Mexican influx rose tenfold and by 2000 accounted for almost one-third of immigrants in the United States. The numbers migrating from Asia also surged, accounting for over 40 percent of all immigrants to the United States in the 1990s, with the flow of legal and illegal immigrants from Mexico and Central America having an especially dramatic impact on the border states. A backlash developed against the new immigration. Opponents called for tighter policing of the border between the United States and Mexico and campaigned for laws that cut off public benefits from those who had come into the United States illegally. Several states passed "English only" statutes aimed at forcing immigrants, both legal and illegal, to "Americanize."

RESIDENT NONCITIZENS AND REFUGEES Arguments in Los Angeles over schools and health care for resident noncitizens became part of a global debate. In Argentina, up to 500,000 undocumented Peruvians, Bolivians, and Paraguayans also lived without rights as citizens. Even more staggering, between 3 and 8 million migrants moved from Mozambique, Zimbabwe, and Lesotho to South Africa. In some Middle Eastern countries, like Saudi Arabia and Kuwait, foreign-born workers constituted over 70 percent of the workforce. In general, migrants were only partially accommodated, while many were fully excluded from host societies. Thus, even though population movements flowed across political, kinship, and market networks, demographic reshuffling heightened national concerns about the ethnic makeup of political communities.

Finally, forced migrations remained a hallmark of the modern world. In contrast to earlier centuries' forced migration of slaves from Africa, recent involuntary flows involved refugees fleeing civil war and torture. Many suffered for weeks, months, or years in refugee camps on the periphery of violence. The greatest concentration of refugees occurred in the world's poorest region—Africa. Those Africans unable to reach wealthier areas were often

East Europeans 1918–1919
CANADA
East Europeans 1918–1919
Russian Jews to USA 1980s and 1990s
European Jews to USA 1930s
GREA
BRITA
FR
UNITED
STATES
SPAIN
West Indians to Britain
Jamaicans, Haitians, and Dominicans to USA 1990–
Spaniards to Mexico 1936
1950–
MOROCCO
ATLANTIC
OCEAN
ALGE
1950–
1960–
CUBA
1960–1980
MEXICO
BELIZE
HAITI
GUATEMALA
NICARAGUA
1970
COLOMBIA
IVORY
COAST
PACIFIC
OCEAN
BRAZIL
1980
ARGENTINA
Foreign-born people as percentage of total population (latest available year)
Less than 1.5%
1.5%–2.9%
3.0%–7.5%
More than 7.5%
Data not available
Migration
0
1000
2000 Miles
0
1000
2000 Kilometers

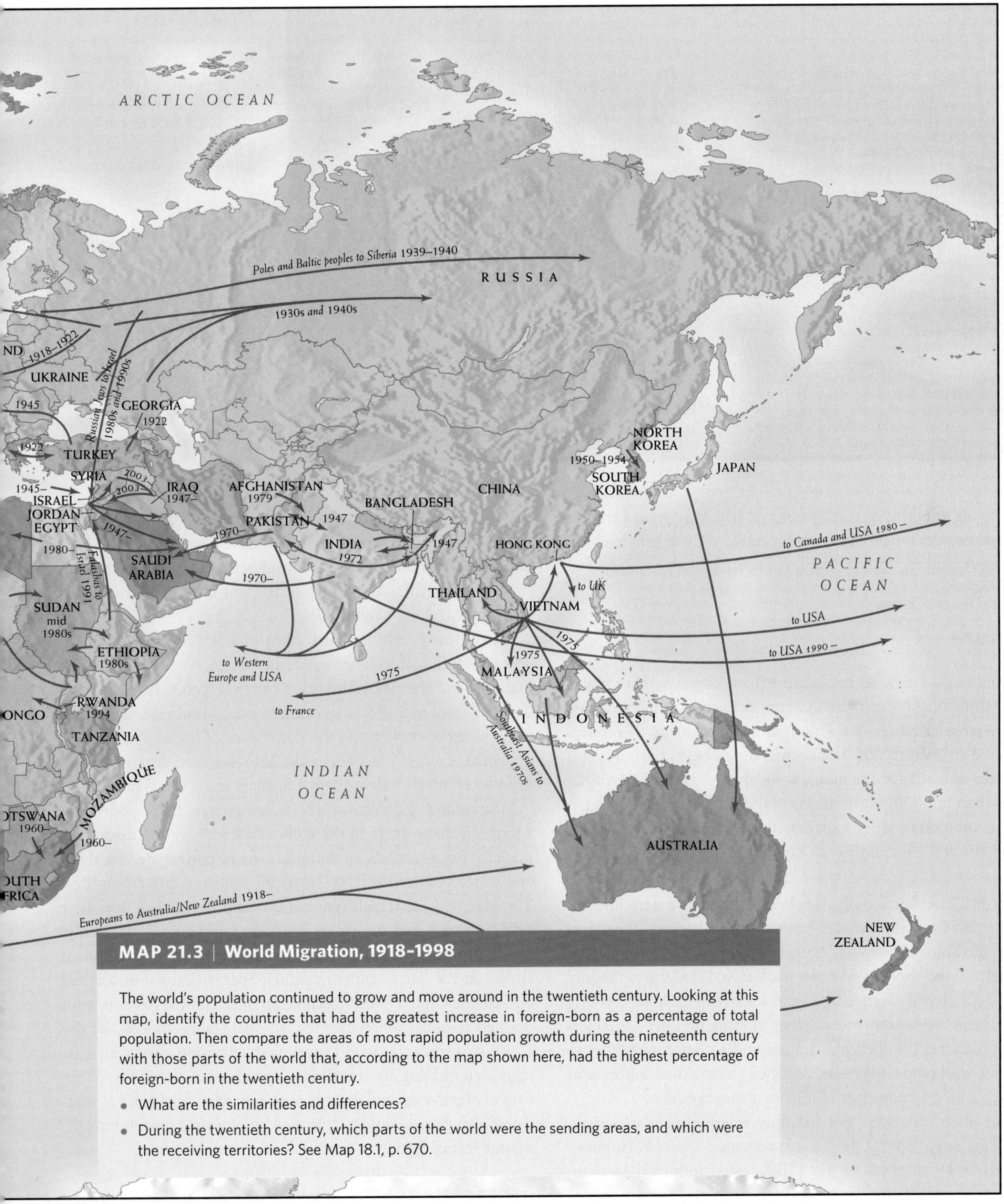

MAP 21.3 | World Migration, 1918–1998

The world's population continued to grow and move around in the twentieth century. Looking at this map, identify the countries that had the greatest increase in foreign-born as a percentage of total population. Then compare the areas of most rapid population growth during the nineteenth century with those parts of the world that, according to the map shown here, had the highest percentage of foreign-born in the twentieth century.

- What are the similarities and differences?
- During the twentieth century, which parts of the world were the sending areas, and which were the receiving territories? See Map 18.1, p. 670.

African Refugees. *During the late twentieth century, Africa became a continent of displaced persons and refugee camps. Pictured here is a camp in Chad for Sudanese driven out of the Darfur region by government-sponsored raids.*

caught up in ethnic and religious conflicts that generated vast refugee camps, where survival depended on the generosity of host governments and international contributions.

Culture

Migrations and new technologies helped create a more global entertainment culture. In this domain, globalization often equated with Americanization. Yet American entertainments themselves reflected artistic practices from across the globe, as one mass culture met another. On the global scale, there was less diversity in 2000 than in 1300; but in terms of individuals' everyday experience, the potential for experiencing cultural diversity (if one could afford the technology to do so) increased.

NEW MEDIA Technology was key in diffusing entertainment. In the 1970s, for example, cassette tapes became the dominant medium for popular music, sidelining the long-playing record and the short-lived eight-track tape. Bootleggers illegally mass-reproduced cassette tapes and sold them cheaply to young consumers. Television was another globalizing force, as American producers bundled old dramas and situation comedies to stations worldwide. Likewise, American movie distributors sent movies and videocassettes of movies across borders.

But Americans were not the only entertainment exporters. Brazilian soap operas began to penetrate Spanish-language American TV markets in the 1980s, often inducing Mexican viewers to rush home from work to catch the latest episode. Latin American television shows and music were distributed in the United States in areas with large Spanish-speaking populations. Bombay also produced its fair share of programs for viewers of British television. Movies and actors from New Zealand, Australia, France, Italy, China, India, and Iran found audiences in Europe and the United States.

In the early 1980s, a new form of television programming spread rapidly: cable. Once again, the United States pioneered the medium, but the innovation soon caught on elsewhere. Increasingly, viewers had access to dozens, even hundreds, of specialized channels, challenging the dominance of traditional national networks. Cable TV networks like MTV featured pop music and introduced music videos, both a musical and a visual product.

Television's globalizing effects were especially evident in sports. In many parts of the globe, American sports made particularly deep inroads as more foreigners participated in them and as television broadcast American games in other countries. The National Basketball Association (and the athletic footwear firm Nike) was particularly successful in international marketing; in the process, it made Michael Jordan the world's best-known athlete in the late twentieth century. Soccer (known as football outside the United States) became an international passion, with devoted national followings for national teams. Indeed, by the 1980s soccer was *the* world sport, with television ratings increasingly determining its schedule. Organizers of the 1986 World Cup in Mexico insisted that big soccer matches take place at midday so that games could be televised live at prime time in Europe, despite teams' having to play under the scorching sun.

GLOBAL CULTURE Technology was not the only driving force of world cultures, for migration and exchange were also

Bob Marley. *In the 1970s, young Europeans and North Americans began to listen to music from the Third World. Among the most popular was Jamaican-based reggae, and its most renowned artist, Bob Marley. Marley's music combined rock and roll with African rhythms and lyrics about freedom and redemption for the downtrodden of the world.*

important. For example, as people moved around they brought their own musical tastes and borrowed others. Reggae, born in the 1960s among Jamaica's Rastafarians, became a hit sensation in London and Toronto, where large West Indian communities had migrated. Reggae lyrics and realist imagery invoked a black countercultural sensibility and a redemptive call for a return to African roots. Soon, Bob Marley and the Wailers, reggae's flagship band, played to audiences worldwide. In northeast Brazil, where African culture emerged from decades of disdain, Bob Marley became a folk hero. In Soweto, South Africa, populated by black workers, he was a symbol of resistance.

Reggae propelled a shift in black American music. In broadcasting reggae, DJs merged sounds and chant lyrics over a beat, a "talkover" form that soon characterized rap music as well. This was a disruptive concept in the late 1970s, but within ten years rap had become a club favorite—and a nonconventional provocation. Rap lyrics emulated reggae realism by focusing on black problems, but they also opened a new domain of controversies involving gang worldviews. On the world stage, Latino rappers stressed multicultural themes, often in "Spanglish." Asian rap stressed the genre as a vehicle for cross-cultural sharing.

The effects of migration on global music were also evident in Latin American transformations of North American genres. Latin music came into its own thanks to Latin American migrants to the United States. In New York and New Jersey, Puerto Ricans and Dominicans popularized boogaloo, salsa, and merengue. In Los Angeles, Mexican *corridos* (ballads) became pop hits.

What reinforced cross-cultural borrowing was not just the medium of production and distribution of entertainment across borders, but also the message. Increasingly, world popular culture was youth culture—especially its message of generational opposition. Consider Egypt's popular TV serial *The School of Troublemakers*, which carried a resolutely antiestablishment message: it showed schoolboys challenging their teachers' authority and then reveling in the chaos that resulted. In Argentina, rock and roll was crucial to the counterculture during the military dictatorship of the 1970s and 1980s. Charlie García urged Buenos Aires audiences to defy authorities by daring to dream of a different order. Indeed, in countries where repressive regimes quashed public cultures, pop culture was usually counterculture.

The same globalizing effects influenced sports. Consider the staple of American identity, baseball, whose major league teams took on a more global cast. Beginning in the 1960s, the number

Baseball Goes International. *The 1980s and 1990s saw an influx of ballplayers from Latin America and quite a few from Asia as well. (Left) Boston Red Sox slugger David Ortiz hails from the Dominican Republic. (Right) New York Yankees superstar Ichiro Suzuki is from Japan.*

CURRENT TRENDS IN WORLD HISTORY

Urbanization as a Global Phenomenon: Transforming Bombay to Mumbai

The city has played a pivotal role in world history since it first emerged thousands of years ago along the Tigris and Euphrates Rivers in Mesopotamia (modern day Iraq). People have since flocked to cities for the social and economic advantages that these locations offered. By the end of the twentieth century, the proportion of people living in cities, usually defined as having populations over 5,000 or 10,000, exceeded 50 percent in the wealthiest countries and was approaching that proportion in the less developed countries as well.

Of the burgeoning cities in the Southern Hemisphere, one of the most dynamic is Mumbai in India. Acquired in the sixteenth century by the Portuguese, who then transferred its control to the British East India Company, Bombay (as it was named at that time) developed as a port city for colonial commerce. It profited from the cotton trade, developed a vibrant textile industry, attracted migrants, and acquired a cosmopolitan image. After India's independence in 1947, Bombay was renamed Mumbai in 1996, though it still epitomized the modern face of the nation, and its heterogeneous population symbolized the Indian melting pot.

Beginning in the 1980s, however, the nature of the city's relationship with the world economy started to change. The cotton textile industry, Bombay's economic backbone, went into a decline. Industrial employment fell sharply. Moreover, the share of informal household enterprises, small shops, petty subcontractors, and casual laborers rose, along with banking and insurance. Economic liberalization removed hurdles against foreign businesses and brought the city directly into the global economy.

Today Mumbai occupies a strategic place in transnational geography. This is evident in the increasing presence of financial institutions, trading organizations, insurance companies, telecommunications corporations, and information technology enterprises with worldwide operations. Even the city's vibrant film industry addresses a global, not just national, audience; rather appropriately, Bombay cinema has acquired the nickname "Bollywood."

The city, however, still attracts a large number of poor migrants who live in slums or call the pavements their home. The gap between Mumbai's rich and poor has grown alarmingly. Millions who eke out a miserable living stand in stark contrast to a tiny elite enriched by the global economy.

Globalization has also affected its residents' identity. In the 1990s, the political party in power was the Shiv Sena,

of Latin Americans playing in North American professional leagues grew steadily. Notable in the 1980s was the Mexican pitcher Fernando Valenzuela, whose exploits as a member of the Los Angeles Dodgers made him a hero to that city's Mexican population and in his native land as well. The Dodgers also took the lead in reaching for Asian talent. In the 1990s, as Los Angeles experienced a growing Asian immigrant population, the Dodgers signed the Japanese pitcher Hideo Nomo. Meanwhile, in the Dominican Republic, baseball fans were riveted by their favorite players in the big leagues: slugger Sammy Sosa and ace pitcher Pedro Martínez.

LOCAL CULTURE World cultures may have become more integrated and homogeneous, but they did not completely replace national and local cultures. Indeed, technology and migration often reinforced the appeal of "national" cultural icons, as national celebrities gained popularity among immigrant groups abroad. Inexpensive new technology introduced these stars to more and more people. In Egypt, the most popular singer of the Nasser years was Umm Kalthum, who became the favorite of the middle classes via radio. In 1975 she was given a state funeral, the likes of which had rarely been seen. Egypt's more liberal policies under Nasser's successor, President Anwar al-Sadat, created new national pop stars. Some, like Muhammad Abd al-Wahhab, blended western and eastern musical themes. Educated in Quranic schools, he fused Quranic vocals and chants with western synthesizers and beats to become a national sensation.

As the market for world cultures grew increasingly competitive, there was more room for acceptable performance. Among the breakthroughs that occurred since the 1970s was the triumph of black performers (Bob Marley, Whitney Houston), black athletes (Pelé, Michael Jordan), and black writers (Toni Morrison, Chinua Achebe). Competition also shattered some sexual biases. Female performers like Madonna became popular icons. So did gay performers, starting with the Village People, whose campy multicultural anthem "YMCA" created a place for a new generation of homosexual or bisexual artists. Of course, beyond Europe and North America, flirting with sexual conventions had its limits. In the Middle East, female video artists continued to wear veils—but they still swung their hips.

Because globalization introduced world consumers to a set of common icons—athletic, musical, and performing—it

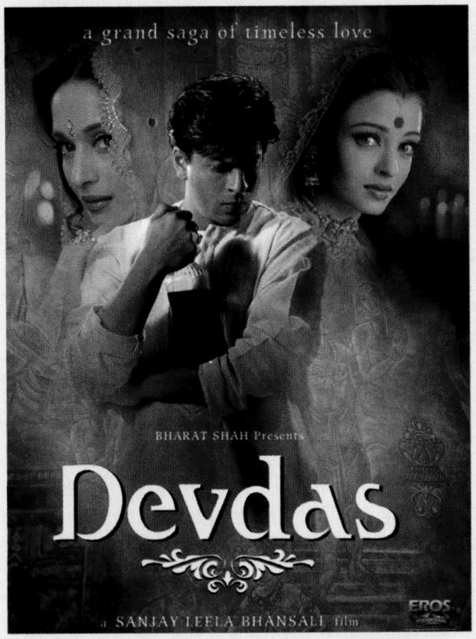

Bollywood. *Bombay cinema, or Bollywood, has an increasing global presence. This is the poster for* Devdas, *a three-hour romance that won awards in India and around the world.*

a nativist regional party named after a seventeenth-century Maratha chieftain who opposed the Mughal Empire. As the industrial economy and trade unions gave way to the service sector and unorganized labor, the Shiv Sena utilized the social and political fluidity produced by globalization to win support for its nativist ideology. Mumbai's cosmopolitan image went up in smoke in 1992–1993, when the Shiv Sena led pogroms against the city's Muslim residents. In response, a Muslim underworld don engineered a series of bomb blasts in March 1993. Since then the city has experienced episodes of violence, none more gruesome than the terrorist attacks on two luxury hotels, a crowded railway station, and a Jewish center in November 2006. Ironically, the terrorists chose to attack Mumbai for its reputation as a cosmopolitan city.

Mumbai today illustrates the uneven effects of globalization. The society is sharply divided, economic disparities are great, and the city's politics is a cauldron of conflicting identities. These are the local forms in which this vast and influential city experiences globalization.

QUESTIONS FOR ANALYSIS

- What similarities and differences emerge when you compare the vignette of Los Angeles in the chapter introduction to Mumbai here?
- How does Mumbai fit into the larger theme of worlds together and worlds apart?

Explore Further

Mehta, Suketu, *Maximum City: Bombay Lost and Found* (2005).

Prakash, Gyan, *Mumbai Fables* (2010).

promoted a more homogeneous world culture. Mass culture from the United States became an especially important purveyor of products worldwide, even as local cultures became more diverse. Relatively homogeneous national cultures, often dominated by men representing the ethnic majority, gave way to a wide variety of entertainers and artists who broke loose of confining local cultures.

Communications

Migration, markets, and mass entertainment were not the only forms that now enjoy global networks; even more important was a revolution in communications. By the 1970s, satellites relayed telecommunications into living rooms worldwide. Television brought the world home—but it was not interactive. Starting in the 1970s and early 1980s, however, engineers based primarily in California's Santa Clara Valley (so-called **Silicon Valley**) tinkered with the idea of computers for personal use. (Computers had served government and corporate needs since the 1940s.) At first these big, underpowered machines had little memory, but with the invention of the silicon chip, the computer weighed less and gained enormous memory capacity. On the heels of this hardware revolution, a software revolution enabled people to process words, run businesses, play games, and eventually communicate with one another via computer terminals.

Computer technology galvanized interactive communications. In the late 1980s, while working in Switzerland, the British physicist Tim Berners-Lee devised a means to pool data stored on various computers. Whereas previous electronic links had existed only between major universities and research stations, Berners-Lee made data more accessible by creating the World Wide Web. With each use and each connection, and as people entered more data, however, the Web grew unmanageably crowded. The early 1990s saw the first commercial browsers used in navigating the so-called Internet. Within a few years, the computer revolution had achieved a fully interactive form of communications and storage with the clarity and resolution of a television. Suddenly people were communicating across global networks more easily than with neighbors and more inexpensively than with local phone calls.

The change created a new generation of wealth. CEOs of top companies like General Motors, Royal Dutch Shell, and Merck had less net worth than Michael Dell (hardware maker), Bill Gates (software maker), and Jeff Bezos (creator of Amazon.com). Shares of Internet firms, known as dot-coms, swept the world's stock markets. Money from these companies flowed globally as they established offices worldwide. Software and Internet technologies developed enormous economies of scale and thus became prone to monopolization. Monoliths emerged by taking over small companies.

Hardware, software, and the Internet were not purely American innovations. Within a few years of their invention, personal computers were being made in Mexico and computer chips mass-produced in Taiwan. The brains behind the Internet were likely to be students from Indian institutes of technology. Originally engineering schools, these institutes trained a whole generation of pioneering computing engineers, many of whom resettled in California's Silicon Valley. By 1996, Indians held half of the 55,000 temporary work visas issued by the U.S. government for high-tech employees. Roughly half of Silicon Valley start-up companies in the late 1990s were the brainchildren of Indian entrepreneurs.

While this revolution provided new means to share and sell information, it also reinforced hierarchies between haves and have-nots. Great swathes of the world's population living outside big cities had no access to the Internet. According to World Bank calculations, in the late 1990s countries with low-income economies had, on average, 26 phone lines per 1,000 people; countries with high-income economies had 550 lines per 1,000 people. The biggest losers were the billions living in rural areas or towns neglected by state and private communications providers.

The have-nots were poor not just from lack of capital but from lack of access to knowledge and new media. The result: a widening gap between rich and poor. In 1870, the average American made nine times what the average African earned; by 1990, an American earned forty-five times the income of someone in Chad or Ethiopia. From 1990, as globalization intensified, world inequities became massive. Paradoxically, globalization both integrated the world's peoples more tightly and intensified disparities among them. (See Current Trends in World History: Urbanization as a Global Phenomenon.)

CHARACTERISTICS OF THE NEW GLOBAL ORDER

By 2000, globalization had promoted recognizable social and economic characteristics. Populations expanded dramatically, requiring greater industrial and agricultural output from all parts of the world. Families changed, and life spans increased. Decent education and good health determined one's status in society as never before. In general, while providing access to an unimaginable array of goods and services, globalization also deepened world inequalities.

The Demography of Globalization

It took 160 years (1800–1960) for the world's population to increase from 1 billion to 3 billion; over the next 40 years (1960–2000) it jumped from 3 billion to over 6 billion. Behind this steepening curve were two important developments: a decline in mortality, especially among children, and a rise in life expectancy.

Population growth was hardly equal worldwide (see Map 21.4). In Europe, population growth peaked around 1900, and it moved upward only gradually from 400 million to 730 million during the twentieth century, with little growth after the 1970s. North America's population quadrupled over the same period, mainly because of immigration. The population booms in the twentieth century occurred in Asia (400 percent), Africa (550 percent), and Latin America (700 percent). China and India each passed the billion-person mark. Increases were greatest in the cities. By the 1980s, the world's largest cities were Asian, African, and Latin American. Greater Tokyo-Yokohama had 30 million inhabitants, while Mexico City had 20 million, São Paulo, 17 million; Cairo, 16 million; Calcutta, 15 million; and Jakarta, 12 million.

Population growth slowed most dramatically in richer societies. For some, like Italy, the growth rate declined to zero. More recently enriched societies like Korea, Taiwan, and Hong Kong also had fewer births. Societies that did not see their birthrates decline by the same rate (much of Africa, southern Asia, and impoverished parts of Latin America) had difficulty raising income levels. But even among poor nations, birthrates declined after the 1970s.

The most remarkable turnaround occurred in China, where the government instituted a "one-child family" policy with rewards for compliance and penalties for transgression. Inducements included cash subsidies, preferential access to nurseries and kindergartens, priority in medical care, and the promise of favored treatment in housing, education, and employment. The policy also prompted an imbalance in sex ratio at birth. The bias in favor of sons (long a feature of China's patrilineal system, which emphasized descent through the male line), together with the availability of ultrasound scanners, promoted the widespread—albeit illegal—practice of prenatal sex selection.

In general, however, declining family size resulted from choice. In rich countries, more women deferred having children as education, career prospects, and birth control devices provided incentives and methods to postpone starting a family.

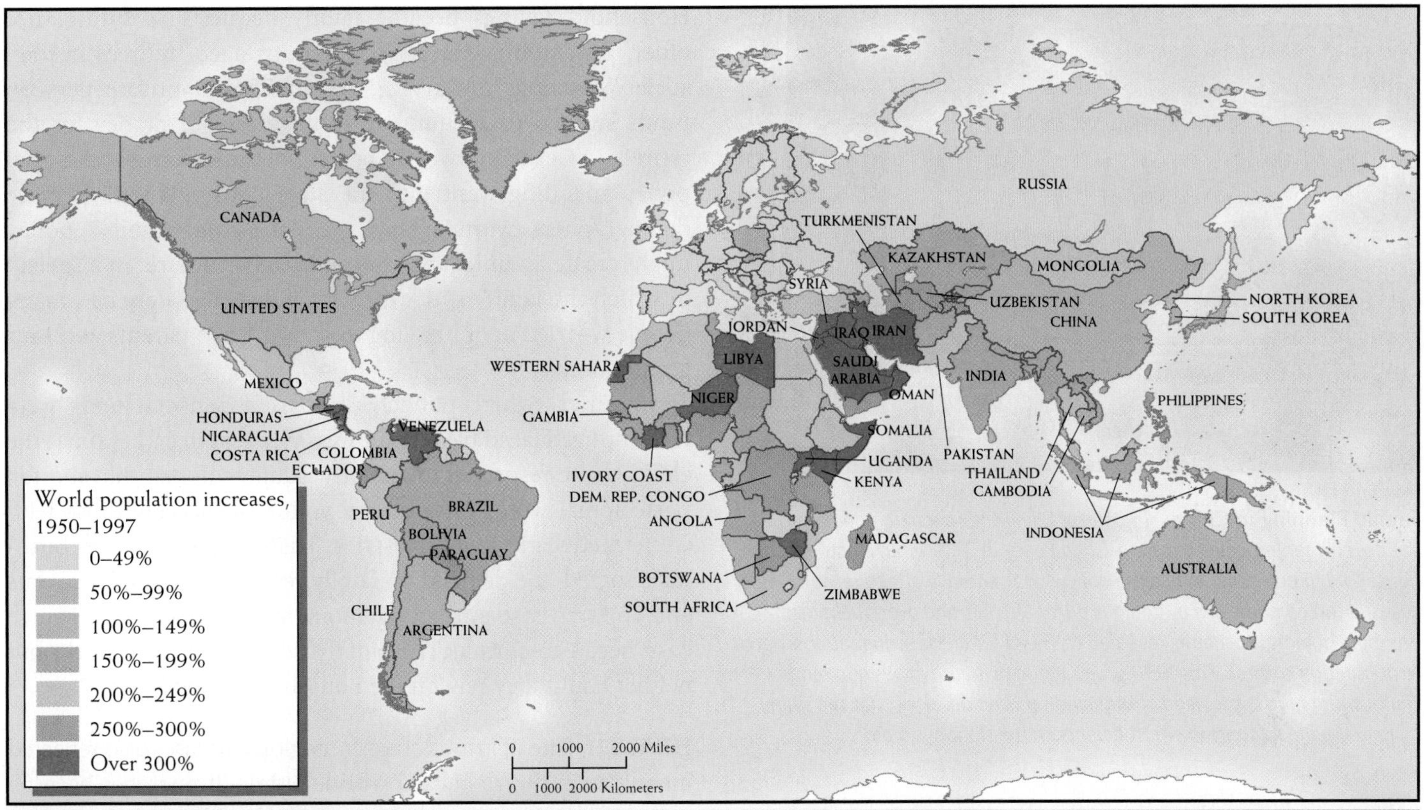

MAP 21.4 | World Population Increases, 1950–1997

The world's population more than doubled between 1950 and 1997, rising from approximately 2.5 billion to nearly 6 billion.

- Which countries had the largest population increases over these five decades? Why do you suppose these countries experienced such high population increases?
- According to your reading, why did western Europe and Russia have the lowest population increases?

In addition, love became a precondition to marriage and family formation in societies that had traditionally emphasized arranged marriages.

FAMILIES The legal definition of families became more fluid in this period. Here again, the change reflected women's choices and the relationship between love and marriage. First, couples chose to end their marriages at unprecedented rates. In the United States, for example, the divorce rate doubled between 1970 and 1998; by the century's end, one in two marriages ended in divorce. In Belgium and Britain late in the twentieth century, fewer than half of all marriages survived. China's divorce rate soared too. In Beijing, by century's end it approached 25 percent—double the 1990 rate. As of 2000, women initiated more than 70 percent of divorces.

As marriages became shorter-lived, new forms of childrearing proliferated. In the United States, out-of-wedlock childbirths constituted one-third of all births in the late 1990s, with only about half of American children living in households with both parents (compared with nearly three-quarters of children in the early 1970s). Europeans, too, including the supposedly more traditional Italians and Greeks, abandoned nuclear family conventions. In those European countries where divorce remained difficult, more couples lived together without getting married.

AGING Longer life spans also affected family fortunes, as more infants survived childhood and lived to be old. Also, along with other industrialized nations, the U.S. population "grayed" considerably. Fewer children and longer-living adults caused a marked increase in the median age of the American population: whereas in 1970 half of all Americans were twenty-eight or under, by 1990 the median age had risen to thirty-four. Likewise, the percentage of Americans over age sixty-five grew from 8 percent in 1950 to 13 percent in 1990. In western Europe and Japan, graying rates were even more marked. Japan's birthrate plummeted, and the citizenry aged at such a rate that the country began to depopulate. From a population of 127 million in 2000, estimates forecast a decline to 105 million by 2050.

Family Planning in China. *To control China's burgeoning population, the government enacted the One-Child Policy in 1979, which restricts each household to one child. While the policy was generally effective, numerous cases of forced abortions by zealous party officials and overwhelming numbers of female orphans revealed the need for a less stringent approach to population control. This 1996 propaganda billboard in Wuhan reads: "Family planning is the need of mankind." It is no accident that the single child in the ideal family illustrated beneath the slogan is a girl.*

The aging population presented new challenges for families. For centuries, being a parent meant providing for children until they could be self-sufficient. Old age, the years of relatively unproductive labor, was brief. Communities and households absorbed the cost of caring for the elderly. Household savings became family bequests to future, not older, generations. But as populations aged, retirees needed society's savings to survive. So public and private pension funds swelled to accumulate future pools of money for the retired. In Germany, over 30 percent of the government's social policy spending went into the state pension fund. Chinese demographers warned that the "one-child family" policy might create an unbalanced population structure. In a society in which the family still largely provided the safety net, many people worried about having to support two parents and four grandparents.

In Africa, where publicly supported pension funds were rare, the aged faced bleaker futures. Whereas in earlier times the elderly were respected founts of wisdom, colonial rule and the postcolonial world elevated the young—especially those with western educations and lifestyles. Then, in the 1970s, as birthrates soared, the demand on family resources to care for infants and children rose at the very moment when society's resource base began to shrink. The elderly could no longer work, but neither could they rely on the household's support.

HEALTH The distribution of contagious diseases also reflected inequities in the globalized world. Although microbes have no respect for borders, the effects of public health regulations, antibiotics, and vaccination campaigns reduced the spread of contagions. By the late twentieth century, not only did nutrition and healthy habits count (as they always had), but access to medicines did too.

Wedding Ceremonies. *(Left) The union of bride and groom is symbolized in this Northern Indian Hindu ceremony by the knot between their clothes. (Right) South Korean martial artist Kim Jong-bok holds his bride, actress Song Hee-jung, during their 2005 wedding ceremony, held on the Tokto islets off the Korean peninsula to protest Japan's claim of the territory.*

What used to be universal afflictions in previous centuries (such as the Black Death) now just affected certain peoples. Water treatment and proper sewerage, for example, had banished cholera from most urban centers by the mid-twentieth century. More recently, however, its deadly grip again reached across Asia and into the eastern Mediterranean, parts of Latin America, and much of sub-Saharan Africa. From the 1970s, Africa suffered frequent outbreaks. The crucial cause of the re-spread of cholera was urban developers' failure to keep sanitation systems growing apace with the demand for water. Thus, diseases proliferated where urban squalor was most acute—in cities with the greatest post-1970s population growth.

In the 1970s, entirely new diseases began to devastate the world's population. Consider **AIDS (Acquired Immuno Deficiency Syndrome)**, which in its first two decades killed 12 million people. Transmitted through contact with the semen or blood of an infected person, AIDS compromises the ability of the infected person's immune system to ward off disease. First detected in 1981, AIDS was initially stigmatized as a "gay cancer" (it appeared primarily in homosexual men) and received little attention. But as it spread to heterosexuals and public awareness about it increased, a new campaign urged the practice of safe sex, control of blood supplies, and restrictions on sharing hypodermic needles. In Europe and North America, where the campaigns intensified and new drugs kept the virus under control, AIDS rates stabilized.

New treatments were very expensive, however, leaving the poor and disadvantaged still vulnerable to infection. By 2000, 33 million people had AIDS (the vast majority in poor countries) and even more were infected with HIV, the human immunodeficiency virus that causes AIDS (see Map 21.5). At least two-thirds of those with AIDS lived in Africa below the Sahara. In India, 7 million carried the virus; in China, the figure topped 1 million.

Other factors behind the geographic and demographic prevalence of AIDS were schooling and literacy. Better education led to safer sexual practices. Worldwide, more educated men and women showed higher use of condoms. One Tanzanian survey showed that 20 percent of women with four to five years of education insisted that their sexual partners use condoms, whereas only 6 percent of women with no education insisted on using condoms during sex with a casual partner.

EDUCATION Access to decent education increasingly separated the haves from the have-nots. Moreover, because educational opportunities usually favored men, schooling shaped differences between males and females. In sub-Saharan Africa and in India, for example, literacy rates were, respectively, 63 and 64 percent for men and only 39 and 40 percent for women as of 2000. In the Arab world, the gap between men and women decreased somewhat by the end of the twentieth century. Yet low levels of literacy overall and the depressed levels for women continued to impede each region's efforts to combat poverty. (See Primary Source: Education and Inequality: Why Gender Matters.)

Gender bias also remained in rich societies. For decades, however, women and girls pressed for equal access, with some astounding results. In the United States, by the late 1980s, more

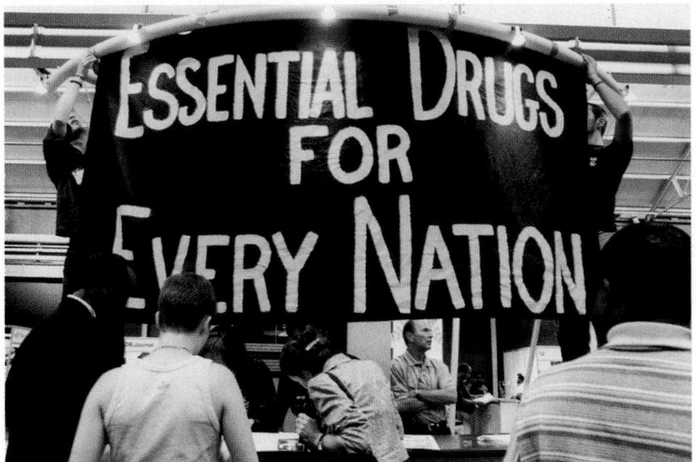

AIDS Treatment and Education. (Left) *At the Thirteenth International AIDS Conference in Durban, South Africa, in July 2000, AIDS activists express their displeasure at the high prices and unavailability of life-saving drugs for most of those in the Third World who are affected by AIDS.* (Right) *African governments did not tackle the problem of AIDS in their severely affected continent with the energy that it warrants. Pictured here, however, a doctor seeks to impress on the youth of a local community how they should conduct their social and sexual lives in light of the AIDS crisis.*

ANALYZING GLOBAL DEVELOPMENTS

Globalization: One World or Many?

People, funds, commodities and information move around the world with lightning speed. This rapid mobility has contributed to radical changes in population growth rates from one country to the next and one continent to the next, and it has led to significant changes in the rate of economic growth worldwide. But do these kinds of changes dictate a growing uniformity in the world? In other words, is globalization creating a single world community? The following two tables reveal some striking demographic differences, by continent and country, with respect to rapid or not-so-rapid population growth rates, the age distribution of populations, and the Gross National Product per person.

QUESTIONS FOR ANALYSIS

- Which of the continents is the fastest growing in terms of population and why would this be the case?
- Although this table does not provide data on the AIDS epidemic (see Map E.5 for that data), we know that Africa has been the most severely impacted continent. What impact is AIDS having on Africa population growth rates? Why do you think that its effects are so muted?
- Two of the countries in this table, Russia and Japan, have negative population growth rates. What are the reasons that would account for these differences and what sorts of problems do you think that these countries are likely to encounter?
- Japan and Germany are the only countries in this table that have a smaller percentage of the population under the age of fifteen than over the age of sixty-five. On the other hand, the countries of sub-Saharan Africa have the largest proportion of their populations under the age of fifteen. What is the cause for these developments and what problems are these countries likely to encounter as they move forward?
- Does this data suggest that the world is becoming more unified or integrated?

Table 1. Ten Most Populous Countries, 2012 and 2050

2012	Population in Millions	2050	Population in Millions
China	1,350	India	1,691
India	1,260	China	1,311
United States	314	United States	423
Indonesia	241	Nigeria	402
Brazil	194	Pakistan	314
Pakistan	180	Indonesia	309
Nigeria	170	Bangladesh	226
Bangladesh	153	Brazil	213
Russia	143	Democratic Republic of Congo	194
Japan	128	Ethiopia	166

than half of all college degrees went to women (up from 38 percent in 1960). More dramatic was the proportion of women earning postgraduate degrees (up from 3 percent to 35 percent). Chinese women made even greater strides, although roadblocks persisted. Ironically, with China's recent market reforms women's access to basic education regressed, as families, particularly in rural areas, reverted to spending their limited resources on educating sons. Thus, in 2000, up to 70 percent of China's 140 million illiterates were female.

WORK Although more women held jobs outside the home, they lacked full equity at work. Limited by job discrimination and burdens of child-rearing, women's participation in the workforce reached a fairly stable level by the 1980s. However, in Russia and Mexico, middle-class women pursuing professional careers often encountered informal obstacles and found themselves channeled into feminized professions such as nursing, teaching, and marketing. The percentage of women at the top of the corporate pyramid was considerably smaller than their

Table 2. World Population References for 2012 and Projection for 2050						
				Percent of Population		
Continents and Selected Countries	Population, 2012 (millions)	Rate of Natural Increase (%)	Projected Population, 2050 (millions)	under age 15	over age 65	GNP per capita (US $)
World	**7,058**	**+1.2**	**9,624**	**26**	**8**	**10,760**
AFRICA	1,072	+2.5	2,339	41	3	2,630
Egypt	82.3	+2.0	135.6	32	4	5,760
Nigeria	170.1	+2.6	402.4	44	3	1,910
South Africa	51.1	+0.9	57.2	31	5	2,240
Democratic Republic of Congo	69.1	+2.8	194.2	46	3	320
THE AMERICAS	948	+1.0	1,212	25	9	23,870
United States	349	+0.5	471	20	13	47,310
Brazil	194.3	+1.0	213.4	24	7	11,000
Mexico	116.1	+1.5	143.9	29	6	14,400
Haiti	10.3	+1.8	14.2	36	4	1,180
ASIA	4,260	+1.1	5,284	25	7	6,860
China	1,350.4	+0.5	1,310.7	16	9	7,640
India	1,259.7	+1.5	1,691.1	31	5	3,430
Japan	127.6	−0.2	119.8	13	24	34,610
Indonesia	241.0	+1.3	309.4	27	6	4,200
EUROPE	740	0.0	732	16	16	27,080
United Kingdom	63.2	0.4	79.6	18	17	35,840
France	63.6	0.4	78.4	19	17	34,750
Germany	81.8	−0.2	71.5	13	21	38,100
Russia	143.2	−0.1	127.8	15	13	19,240

Source: Population Reference Bureau, 2012: World Population Data Sheet, Washington D.C., pp. 2, 6, 7, 8, and 9.

proportion in the labor force or their college graduation rates. In 1995, the Chinese government claimed that Chinese women had made better advances than their U.S. counterparts: there were more Chinese women (10 percent) than American women (3 percent) in senior managerial posts. Still, Chinese women graduates complained of discrimination in the job market. In 2000, some 60 percent of China's unemployed were women, and the number was growing. Women worldwide had difficulties breaking through the "glass ceiling"—a seemingly invisible barrier to women's advancement. Consequently, while income disparities between men and women narrowed, a significant gap persisted.

Working outside the home led to problems inside the home. Who would take care of the children? Jamaican and Filipino women migrated by the thousands in the 1970s and 1980s to Canada and Australia to work as nannies to raise money to send back home, where they had often left their own children. In South Africa and Brazil, local women served as domestic

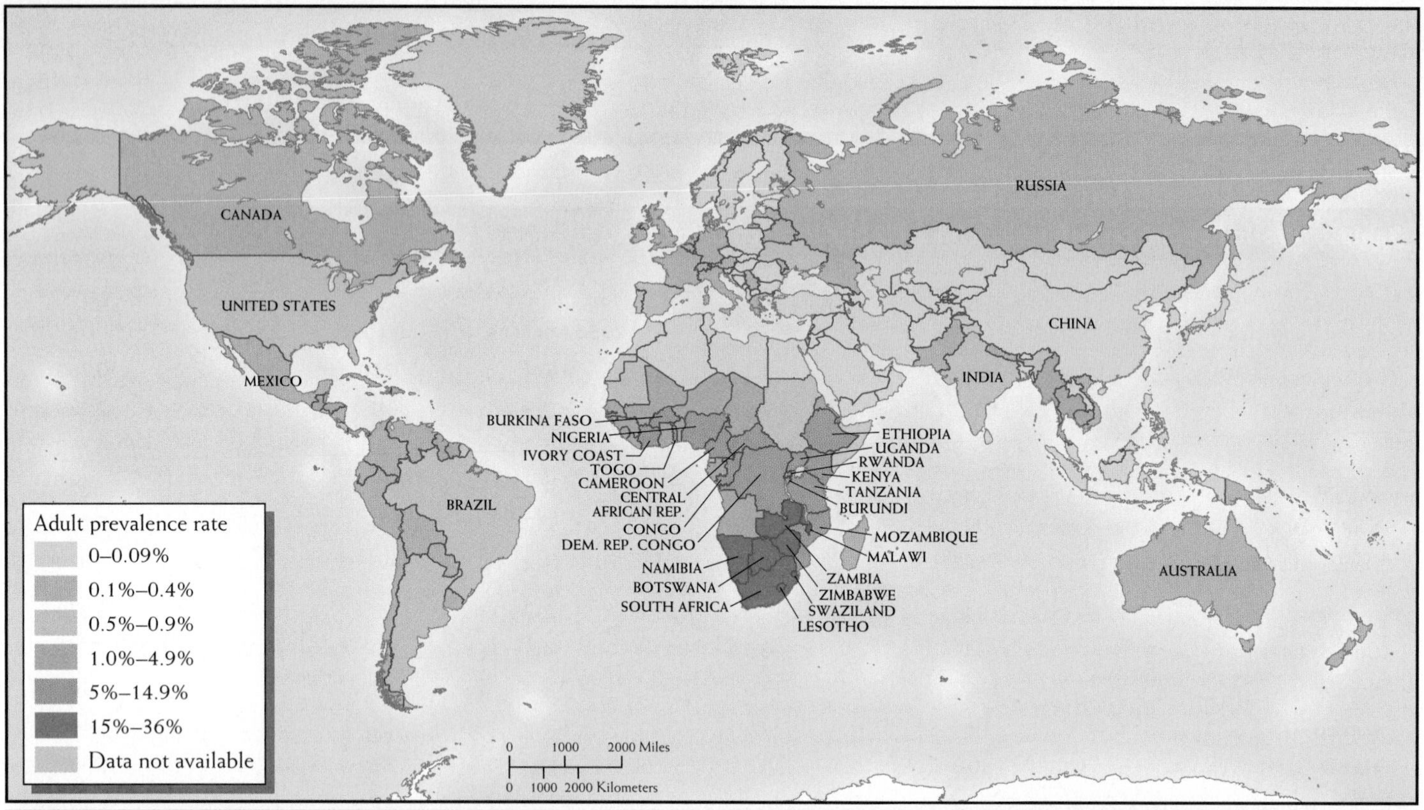

MAP 21.5 | HIV Infection across the World, 1999

HIV, which leads to AIDS, spread across the whole world, providing further evidence of global interconnectedness. The outbreak began in Africa.

- Where in Africa have the highest rates of HIV infection occurred? Which countries *outside* the African continent have had the highest rates of infection, and why is this so?
- Why have Egypt, North Africa, and much of the rest of the Islamic world, despite their close connections with Africa below the Sahara, thus far been little affected?

servants and nannies. They were doing the jobs that once belonged to middle- and upper-class homemakers, women who now wanted the same rights as men: to parent *and* to work.

FEMINISM The deeply ingrained inequality between men and women prompted calls for change. **Feminist movements** arose mainly in Europe and in North America in the 1960s and then become global in the 1970s. In 1975, the first truly international women's forum took place in Mexico City. But becoming global did not necessarily imply overturning local customs. What feminists called for was not the abolition of gender differences,

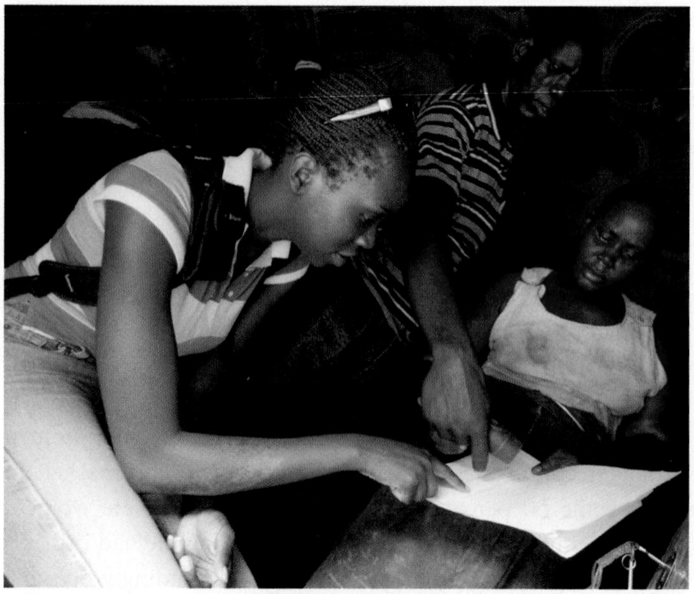

African Women and Education. *Though women's education lagged behind that of men in Africa, a number of women, like Stella Kenyi, pictured here, graduated from African high schools and attended universities at home or abroad. Kenyi taught business skills to men and women in Sudan after completing an undergraduate degree at Davidson College in North Carolina.*

PRIMARY SOURCE

Education and Inequality: Why Gender Matters

In the 1970s, aid agencies recognized that reducing world poverty means improving educational opportunities. So international organizations urged national governments to plow resources into schools. The results were stunning. But a disparity appeared: the beneficiaries were mainly boys. Thus, beginning in the 1980s, aid organizations became especially active in trying to channel educational opportunities to girls. In the World Bank study excerpted here, researchers found that development among the poor improves not just with better education, but especially with better education for girls.

Evaluations of recent initiatives that subsidize the costs of schooling indicate that demand-side interventions can increase girls' enrollments and close gender gaps in education. A school stipend program established in Bangladesh in 1982 subsidizes various school expenses for girls who enroll in secondary school. In the first program evaluation girls' enrollment rate in the pilot areas rose from 27 percent, similar to the national average, to 44 percent over five years, more than twice the national average. . . . After girls' tuition was eliminated nationwide in 1992 and the stipend program was expanded to all rural areas, girls' enrollment rate climbed to 48 percent at the national level. There have also been gains in the number of girls appearing for exams and in women's enrollments at intermediate colleges. . . . While boys' enrollment rates also rose during this period, they did not rise as quickly as girls'.

Two recent programs in Balochistan, Pakistan, illustrate the potential benefits of reducing costs and improving physical access. Before the projects there were questions about whether girls' low enrollments were due to cultural barriers that cause parents to hold their daughters out of school or to inadequate supply of appropriate schools. Program evaluations suggest that improved physical access, subsidized costs, and culturally appropriate design can sharply increase girls' enrollments.

The first program, in Quetta, the capital of Balochistan, uses a subsidy tied to girls' enrollment to support the creation of schools in poor urban neighborhoods by local NGOs. The schools admit boys as long as they make up less than half of total enrollments. In rural Balochistan the second program has been expanding the supply of local, single-sex primary schools for girls by encouraging parental involvement in establishing the schools and by subsidizing the recruitment of female teachers from the local community. The results: girls' enrollments rose 33 percent in Quetta and 22 percent in rural areas. Interestingly, both programs appear to have also expanded boys' enrollments, suggesting that increasing girls' educational opportunities may have spillover benefits for boys.

QUESTIONS FOR ANALYSIS

- What does this excerpt reveal about the ways that organizations like the World Bank promote change in developing countries?
- Why do you think there was a spillover effect for boys that coincided with these programs?

Source: Reproduced with permission of the World Bank from "Using Subsidies to Close Gender Gaps in Education," World Development Report 2000–2001, *p. 122, Box 7.2. Copyright 2000 by World Bank. Permission conveyed through Copyright Clearance Center, Inc.*

but equal treatment—equal pay and equal opportunities for obtaining jobs and advancement.

Women took increasingly active stances against discrimination in government and in the workplace. Indeed, as economic integration intensified with regional trade pacts (usually negotiated by men in the interest of male-owned and male-run firms), women struggled to ensure that globalization did not cut them out of new opportunities. For instance, after Argentina, Uruguay, Paraguay, and Brazil negotiated the Mercosur free trade pact, traffic across South American borders soared. But as trade grew, so did government efforts to monitor illegal commerce and foster approved trade along new highways and bridges. Women were responsible for one kind of illicit commerce, because for generations they had transported goods across the river separating Argentina and Paraguay. When customs officers tried to stop this practice in the mid-1990s, Argentine and Paraguayan women locked arms to occupy the new bridge that male truckers used to ship Mercosur products, protesting the restrictions on their age-old enterprise.

The rising tide of global feminism culminated in a conference in Beijing in 1995. Government delegates from more than 180 countries attended the Fourth World Conference on

Forum on Women. *Women representing different cultures of the world hold a "peace torch" during the opening ceremony of the Non-Governmental Organizations Forum for Women in Beijing in 1995.*

Women to produce "a platform for action" regarding women's rights in politics, business, education, and health. Alongside the official conference was a parallel conference for nearly 30,000 representatives at the NGO Forum for Women. These grassroots activists represented 2,000 nongovernmental organizations from every corner of the globe. Representatives planned strategies and coordinated programs on how to improve women's living and working conditions. What emerged from the conference were associations and groups that pledged to lobby for the rights of women and girls worldwide.

Production and Consumption in the Global Economy

The growing world population, the desire for more education and better health, the entry of women into paid employment, and the promise of rising standards of living spurred unprecedented production and consumption of the world's resources. The most immediate challenge was how to feed so many people while developing sustainable practices that do not use up limited natural resources.

AGRICULTURAL PRODUCTION Changing agrarian practices made a huge difference in increasing food production. Starting in the 1950s, chemistry increased outputs dramatically. The "green revolution," largely involving nonfarm inputs such as chemical fertilizers, herbicides, and pesticides, produced dramatically larger harvests. Then, in the 1970s, biologists began offering genetically engineered crops that multiplied yields at an even faster rate.

But these breakthroughs were not evenly distributed. American farmers, the biggest innovators, were the greatest beneficiaries. For example, by century's end they produced approximately one-ninth of the world's wheat and two-fifths of its corn. From this output, American exports accounted for about one-third of the world's international wheat trade and four-fifths of all corn exports. At the heart of the innovation was political power, for farmers had the clout to force officials to maintain roads, subsidize credit and prices, and mop up surplus supply. But Asian rice farmers made impressive innovations, too. In Taiwan and Korea, chemical and biological breakthroughs allowed rice yields to jump by 53 and 132 percent, respectively, between 1965 and 1985. And as Indian wheat farmers deployed chemical fertilizers, new seed varieties, and irrigation systems to double their output, the Ganges River basin supported an ever-larger urban population. The most miraculous transformation occurred in China. Beginning in the late 1970s, the Chinese government broke up some of the old collective farms and restored the individual household as the basic economic unit in rural areas. Thereafter, agricultural output surged by roughly 9 percent per year between 1978 and 1986.

Other agricultural producers also replied to world demand, but sometimes their added production was disruptive. While biology and chemistry allowed some farmers to get more out of their land, others simply opened up new lands to cultivation. Lacking access to credit, seed, and good land, small farmers had to go where land was cheap. In Java, farmers cleared sloping woodland to make way for coffee plantings. In southern Colombia, peasants moved into semitropical woodlands to cultivate coca bushes (the source of cocaine) at profits that other cultivators could never realize.

The most notorious frontier expansion occurred in the Amazon River basin. Populations flocked to the Amazon frontier, largely from impoverished areas in northeastern Brazil. They cleared (by fire) cheap land, staked their claims, and, like nineteenth-century American homesteaders, tried to climb the social ladder by cultivating crops and raising livestock. But the promise of bounty failed: the soils were poor and easily eroded, and land titles provided little security, especially once large speculators moved into the area. So the frontiersmen moved farther inland to repeat the cycle. By the 1980s, migrants to the Amazon River basin had burned away much of the jungle, contaminated the biosphere (the environment in which life exists), reduced the stock of diverse plant and animal life, and fostered social conflict in the Brazilian hinterland.

Nor were breadbaskets always able to feed exploding populations. This was especially true in Africa from the 1970s onward, when domestic food production could not keep pace with population growth (see Map 21.6). Food shortages thereafter increased in frequency and duration, wiping out

Saving the Amazon. *The rise of an international environmental movement in the 1970s led to alliances with local indigenous and environmental leaders, especially in the Amazon.* (Left) *One of the most prominent advocates of the rights of indigenous people and the need to protect imperiled jungles was the British musician Sting. Here he is pictured alongside one of the Amazon's foremost Indian leaders, Bep Koroti Paiakan.* (Right) *Farmers and ranchers cut and burned the Amazon at a ferocious rate in pursuit of frontier lands. In these remote regions, it was hard for local authorities to enforce conservation laws.*

large numbers of sub-Saharan peoples. The protruding ribs on African children became a clichéd image of the region.

What explained Africa's famines? As the Indian Nobel Prize–winning economist Amartya Sen observed, famines—and their increasing frequency—are not natural disasters; they are man-made. Food shortages in Africa stemmed largely from governments that ignored the rural sector and its politically unorganized farmers. Unable to persuade their governments to raise prices for their crops, the farmers lacked incentives to expand production. Food shortages were also by-products of global inequities. African countries, earmarking hefty chunks of their economies to agrarian exports to repay debts incurred in the 1970s, could not produce enough foodstuffs domestically and thus became food importers.

NATURAL RESOURCES While American farmers now produced a large share of the world's food, Americans also consumed a high proportion of its natural resources. By 2000, they were using water at a per-capita rate three times the world's average. Indeed, extensive irrigation was crucial to California's agricultural sector, the most productive and profitable in the world. Gathering more water also allowed a desert metropolis like Los Angeles to grow.

Energy consumption presented a similar story, although America's enormous appetite for fossil fuels generated a domestic debate about reliance on foreign sources and pollution of the environment. In the United States and Canada, attempts to curb energy consumption saw little success, and the United States grew more dependent on imported oil. In the late 1990s, North American demand for fuel-guzzling sport utility vehicles intensified oil imports. Dependence on foreign sources locked oil importers into recurring clashes with oil exporters. In the 1970s, OPEC raised the price of crude oil (see Chapter 20). The cartel weakened in the 1980s, partly because new oil fields opened elsewhere in the world and partly because internal struggles divided the exporters.

The harshest conflict over oil occurred in the mid-1980s between Iran and Iraq, followed by the 1990 Iraqi invasion of Kuwait. Iraq was poised to become dominant in the area and thus to control oil policies. The conquest of Kuwait would have given Iraq control over about 7 percent of world oil supplies and nearly 20 percent of the world's known reserves. Only Iraq's neighbors Saudi Arabia and Iran would have been larger oil exporters, and Iraq would have been in a position to menace both. As the situation threatened to unsettle the regional balance of power, the U.S. government moved to restore it. Rallying a coalition of other nations, the Americans and their allies launched a military invasion called Operation Desert Storm. The ensuing Gulf War, which ended with Iraq's expulsion from Kuwait, restored an order in which the global distribution of power favored oil consumers over producers and preserved a regional balance of power.

ENVIRONMENTAL EFFECTS The consumption of water, oil, and other natural resources became matters of international concern late in the twentieth century. So did pollution control and the disposal of waste products. Part of this internationalization reflected the recognition that individual nations could not

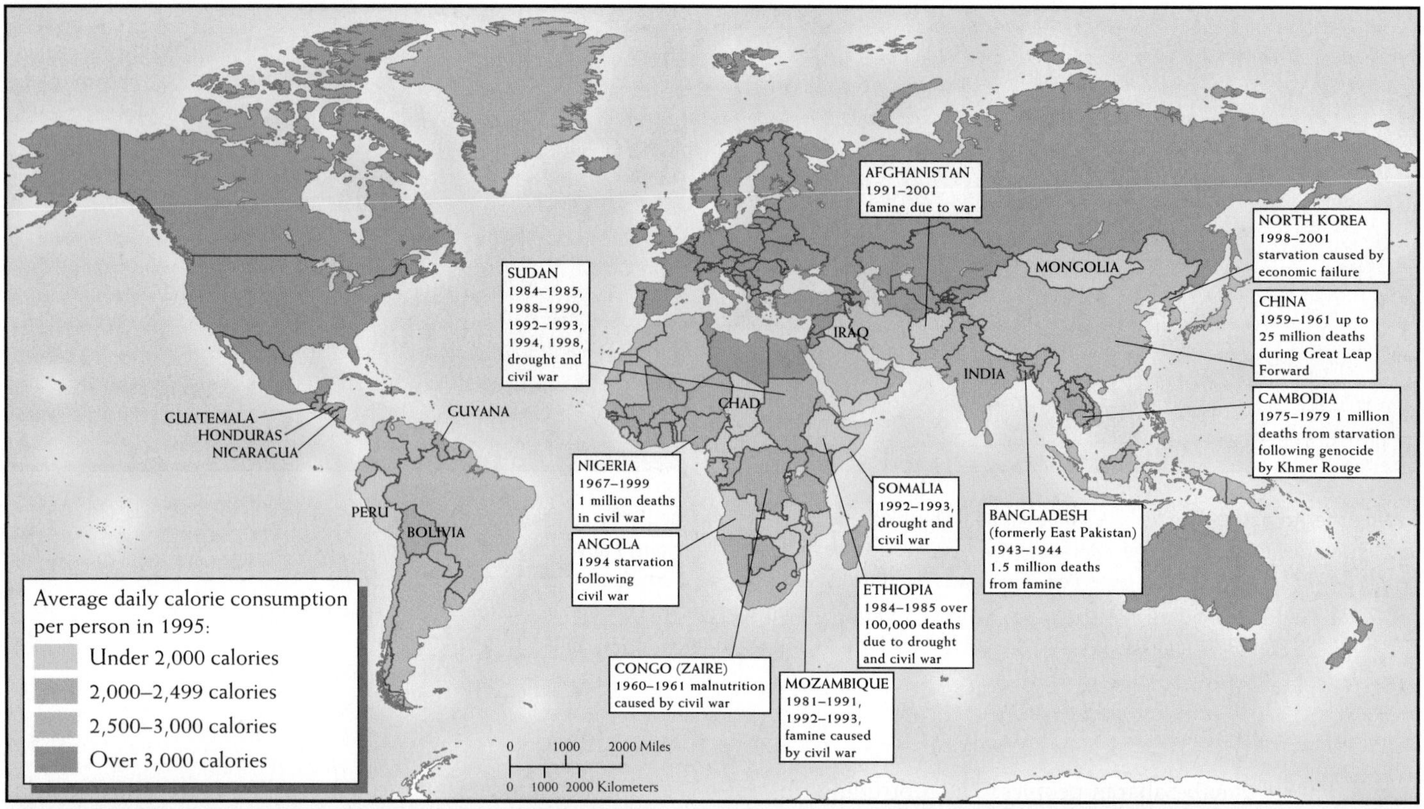

MAP 21.6 | Food Consumption and Famine since the 1940s

There is perhaps no better indicator of the division of the world into rich and poor, haves and have-nots, than this map on food consumption and famine.

- Which parts of the world have had the most difficulty in feeding their populations? What have been some of the causes of famine and malnourishment in these regions?
- How much have they been due to human agency, and how much to climate and other matters over which human beings have little control?

solve environmental issues on their own. Air and water, after all, do not stop flowing at political boundaries.

As Canadians saw their northern lakes fill up with acid rain (precipitation laced with sulfur, mainly from coal-fired plants), they urged their southern neighbor to curb emissions. Thus, reciprocal agreements between Canada and the United States took shape in the 1980s. Europeans, also beset by acidification, likewise negotiated regional environmental treaties. But some polluters simply moved overseas to poorer and less powerful nations. As the West cleaned up its environment, the rest of the world paid the price.

Other problems crossed man-made borders as well. These included the greenhouse effect and **global warming** (release into the air of human-made carbons that contribute to rising temperatures worldwide), ocean pollution, and declining biological diversity. International meetings addressed these threats inconclusively. After all, it was difficult to enforce an international solution on all national authorities when the forces of globalization compelled some of them to rely on energy-intensive industries, which generated massive emissions, in order to produce exports to pay off their debts. In 1992, the world's governments flocked to the first Earth Summit in Rio de Janeiro. But eco-friendly fanfare yielded only ineffective accords. Several years later, world leaders again met (in Kyoto, Japan) to draft a plan to enforce compliance. Even the grumblers agreed that it was necessary to reverse the emission of gases that led to global warming. However, when the administration of George W. Bush came to power in Washington in 2001, it revoked U.S. support for the Kyoto Treaty, which led others to defect as well. As a result, global climate change did not gain a global accord.

The relationship between power and resources was especially stark in dealing with contaminants. Increasing numbers of automobiles, emitting carbon fumes, caused serious air pollution in cities like Los Angeles, Tokyo, Mexico City, and Jakarta. But where environmentalists acquired political

Kyoto Protocol. *That America would no longer participate in the Kyoto Protocol was especially infuriating to the global audience, as America is the largest emitter of carbon dioxide and other major greenhouse gases. Here, Greenpeace environmental activists look on as one of their cohorts, dressed as Bush, brandishes a flaming globe in a dramatic protest outside of the US embassy in Mexico City.*

power, they forced regulators to curb emissions. Starting in the late 1960s, Japanese local governments slapped pollution controls on coal plants. Japan pioneered what one historian has called an "environmental miracle," spreading its regulations to many contaminating activities. By 1978, Japanese cars discharged only 10 percent as much pollution as in 1968. In 1987, Japan banned leaded gas altogether. But controls on fossil fuel emissions depended on power and wealth, for it was hard to impose restrictions in societies where high energy use seemed a necessity of economic life. Even the Japanese pioneers of clean fuel were polluters in other spheres. With increasing controls at home, Japanese industrialists went abroad to unload hazardous waste. U.S. industrialists did the same, sending hazardous waste to Mexico. Argentina and Canada sent their nuclear waste not abroad, but to poor provinces desperate for jobs.

Environmental problems gained new urgency after the meltdown of a Soviet nuclear reactor in Chernobyl in 1986. Initially, communist authorities tried to cover up the disaster; but when the fallout reached Sweden, they had to accept responsibility. The delayed response was disastrous for Ukraine and Belarussia (present-day Belarus). Being relatively powerless under a centralized authoritarian regime, they had no political voice to cry out for help in addressing the contamination. As Chernobyl and global warming demonstrated, environmental concerns did not observe boundary lines. Yet at the end of the twentieth century, global guidelines for regulating the impact of human activities on the environment had eluded the world's leaders.

CITIZENSHIP IN THE GLOBAL WORLD

Globalization distributed its benefits unequally. In general, people with access to better education and more opportunities profited from the border-crossing freedoms that the new order permitted. For most of the world's population, however, the new power structure was not so kind. Finding little opportunity in the globalized world, disadvantaged groups often invoked older religious and nationalist ideals. As globalization fostered human rights, environmental and labor standards, and women's rights worldwide, critics claimed that the language of international rights and standards was promoting neocolonial power in the form of a new "civilizing mission."

In particular, globalization posed massive problems for the nation-state. Since the nineteenth century, nation-states were supposed to be key in defining the rights of citizens. But now the rapid movement of ideas, goods, capital, and people across national boundaries undercut the authority of even the most powerful nations. Accordingly, other political spheres emerged to define and defend citizens. After the 1970s, people realized that international organizations often had more influence over their lives than did their own national governments. These organizations became increasingly important in shaping the meaning of citizenship. This was true especially in the Third World, where nation-states struggled hardest to accommodate globalization.

Supranational Organizations

Various organizations with international responsibilities took shape after World War II for the purpose of facilitating global activities. Although these **supranational organizations** often successfully managed crisis situations, they also impinged on the autonomy of all but the most powerful states.

The most prominent supranational organizations were the World Bank and the International Monetary Fund, which provided vital economic assistance to poorer nations. Indeed, these bodies financed and offered technical information for some of the largest development programs in the Third World. The **World Bank** made available funds for the Volta River Project in Ghana to create an electrical power grid, as well as a system of national parks in the Philippines to help indigenous people manage rain forests, coral reefs, and other threatened ecological zones. Nonetheless, the World Bank required that recipient governments implement far-reaching economic reforms, which were often unpopular. Not infrequently, World Bank– and IMF-imposed programs required local governments to abolish subsidies for essential foodstuffs, leading to riots and charges that these international groups were agents of a new kind of imperialism.

Another set of supranational bodies, **nongovernmental organizations (NGOs)**, also stepped forward late in the twentieth century. Many championed human rights or highlighted environmental problems. Others, like the International Committee of the Red Cross, once dedicated to war relief, became more active in peacetime, sheltering the homeless or providing food for famine victims. What united NGOs was not so much their goals but the way they pursued them: autonomously from state power. NGOs created a layer of international forces that rivaled the political power of nation-states.

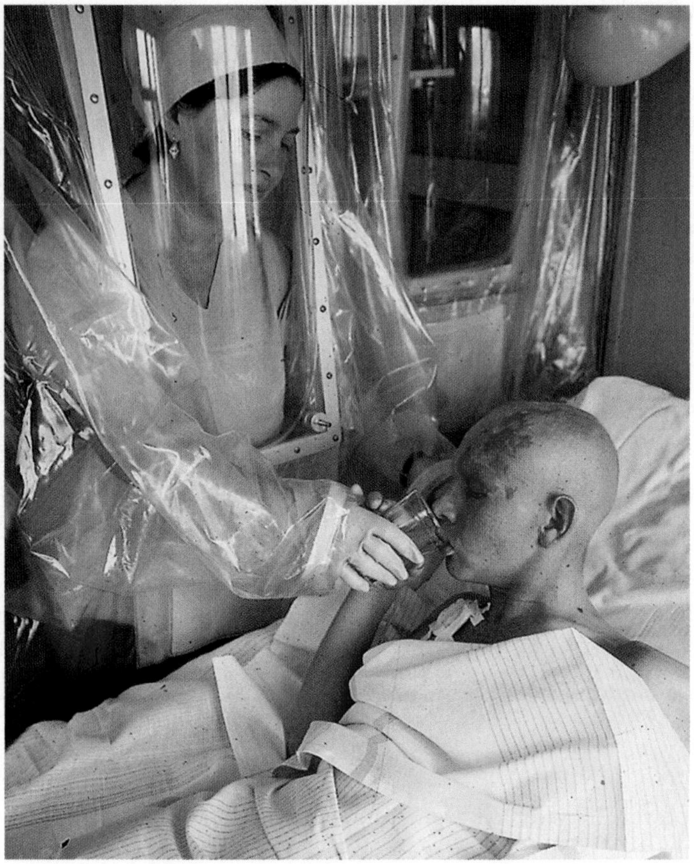

Chernobyl and Protest. *Among the victims of the 1986 explosion at the Chernobyl power plant, history's worst nuclear meltdown, were firefighters, such as the man pictured here, sent in to put out the blaze. Chernobyl turned Mikhail Gorbachev's* glasnost, *or openness, into more than a slogan, and it became a rallying cry for the populace, which hoped for political change and improvements in daily life.*

International NGOs reached a new level of influence in the 1970s because most nation-states at that time were still not democracies. Of the 121 countries in 1980, only 37 were democracies, accounting for only 35 percent of the world population. People found it difficult to rely on authoritarians to uphold their rights as citizens. Indeed, the United Nations itself was a latecomer to enforcing human rights provisions, largely because its own members were the self-same authoritarians.

NGOs, then, took the lead in trying to make the language of human rights stick. The brutality of military regimes in Latin America inspired the emerging network of international human rights organizations to take action. After the overthrow of Chile's Salvador Allende in 1973, solidarity groups proliferated to protest the military junta's harsh repression. When the Argentine military began killing tens of thousands of innocent civilians in 1976 and news of their torture techniques leaked out, human rights movements again took action. Prominent among them was Amnesty International. Formed in 1961 to defend prisoners of conscience (detained for their beliefs, color, sex, ethnic origin, language, or religion), Amnesty International catalogued human rights violations worldwide. The organization became one of the most influential human rights organizations in the world. Moreover, even American foundations recognized NGOs' importance. The biggest one, the Ford Foundation, initiated support for human rights groups and research. By 2000, an extensive network of associations was informing the public, lobbying governments, and pressuring U.N. member nations to live up to commitments to respect the rights of citizens.

Violence

International organizations and NGOs could play only a limited role in preserving peace and strengthening human rights. The end of the cold war left entire regions in such turmoil that even the most effective humanitarian agencies could not prevent mass killings.

Consider the Balkans in the 1990s. In the territorial remains of Yugoslavia, groups of Serbs, Croats, Bosnians, ethnic Albanians, and others fought for control. Former neighbors, fueled by opportunistic leaders' rhetoric, no longer saw themselves as citizens of pluralistic political communities. Instead, demagogues trumpeted the superiority of ethnically defined states. Serbians took up arms against their Croat neighbors, and vice versa. When international agencies moved in to try to bolster public authority, they failed as Yugoslavia's ethnic mosaic imploded into civil war. The Dayton Accords of 1995 ended the bloodshed by partitioning Bosnia and assigning several international organizations to maintain peace. But in 1999 Serbian president Slobodan Milosevic sent troops to suppress unrest in the province of Kosovo; only NATO air strikes on Serbia's capital, Belgrade, convinced Milosevic to back down. Subsequently Milosevic was found guilty of war crimes and crimes against humanity.

The most gruesome political violence occurred in Africa, where nation-states capable of upholding the rule of law for all citizens were weakest. Here, tension often erupted in conflict between ethnic groups. The failure of African agriculture to sustain growing populations, as well as unequal access to resources like education, made ethnic rivalries worse. Droughts, famine, and corruption ignited the rivalries into riots and killings—even into bitter civil war and the breakdown of centralized authority.

Rwanda reflected Africa's horrifying experience with political violence. Friction grew between the majority Hutus (agrarian people, often very poor) and the minority Tutsis (herders, often with better education and more wealth) after the two peoples had intermarried and lived side by side for many generations. Some resentful Hutus blamed the Tutsis for all their woes. As tensions mounted, the United Nations dispatched peacekeeping troops. Moderate Hutus urged peaceful coexistence, only to be shouted down by government forces in command of radio stations and a mass propaganda machine. Although alerted to the impending problem, U.N. forces, fearing a clash and uncertain of their mandate, failed to prevent the violence.

The failure on the part of the international community, including the United States, which did not have troops on the ground and which had no clear policy toward Rwanda, gave the Hutu government a green light to wipe out opponents. In one hundred days of carnage in 1994, Hutu militias massacred 800,000 Tutsis and moderate Hutus. This was not, as many proclaimed, the militarization of ancient ethnic rivalries, for many Hutus were butchered as they tried to defend Tutsi friends, relatives, and neighbors. Meanwhile, the ensuing refugee crisis destabilized neighboring countries. The civil war in Rwanda sent riptides across eastern and central Africa, creating a whole new generation of conflicts.

Bosnia in the Midst of War. *Despite extensive destruction and perpetual sniper fire, the multiethnic population of Sarajevo refused to abandon their city. With the help of U.N. soldiers and aid workers, they kept alive the hope for the peaceful coexistence of Muslims, Serbs, and Croats in Bosnia.*

Some societies, however, tried to put political violence behind them. In Argentina, El Salvador, Guatemala, and South Africa, the transition to democracy compelled elected rulers to establish inquiries into past rulers' human rights abuses. These **truth commissions** were vital for creating a new aura of legitimacy for democracies and for promising to uphold the rights of individuals. In South Africa, many blacks backed the new president, Nelson Mandela, but also demanded a reckoning with the punitive experience of the apartheid past. To avoid a backlash against the former white rulers, the South African leadership opted to record the past events rather than avenge them. Truth, the new leaders argued, would be powerful enough to heal old wounds. The Truth and Reconciliation Commission, chaired by Nobel Peace Prize winner and longtime opponent of apartheid Bishop Desmond Tutu, called on all who had been involved in political crimes, whites as well as blacks, to come before its

Rwandan Refugees. *Perhaps as many as 800,000 Tutsis were killed in 1994 as the Hutus turned against the local Tutsi population while Rwanda was being invaded by a Tutsi-led army from Uganda. Not surprisingly, the massacre led to an enormous refugee crisis.*

tribunal and speak the truth. Although the truth alone did not fully settle old scores, a more open discussion of basic liberties fostered new bonds between public authority and citizens.

Religious Foundations of Politics

Secular concerns for human rights and international peace were not the only foundations for politics after the cold war. In many regions, people wanted religion to define the moral fabric of political communities. Very often, religion provided a way to re-imagine the nation-state, just as globalization was undermining national autonomy.

HINDU NATIONALISM In India, Hindu nationalism offered a communal identity for a country being rapidly transformed by globalization. In the 1980s, India freed market forces, privatized state firms, and withdrew from its role as welfare provider. Economic reforms under the ruling Congress Party sparked economic growth, thereby creating Asia's largest, best-educated, and most affluent middle class. But because these changes also widened the gap between rich and poor, lower classes and castes formed political parties to challenge the traditional elites. With established hierarchies and loyalties eroding, Hindu nationalists argued that religion could now fill the role once occupied by a secular state. Claiming that the ideology of Hindutva ("Hinduness") would bring the help that secular nationalism had failed to give, Hindu militants trumpeted the idea of India as a nation of Hindus (the majority), with minorities relegated to a lesser status.

The chief beneficiary of the politics established by economic liberalization was a Hindu nationalist party, the Bhartiya Janata Party (BJP), or Indian People's Party. It was the political arm of an alliance of Hindu organizations devoted to establishing India as a Hindu state. By the late 1980s, the BJP and other like-minded parties were advancing an anti-minority (chiefly anti-Muslim) ideology. Claiming that the state had systematically appeased the minorities and trampled on the rights of the majority, they urged Hindus to overthrow "pseudo secularism." This communal ideology was a winning formula, and by 1998 a BJP coalition came to power. Hindu nationalists sought to transform the secular nation-state into a moral community, but without challenging the economic forces of globalization.

ISLAMIC CONSERVATISM In some cases, religion provided a way to resist seemingly American-dominated globalization. One of the most spirited challenges arose in the Islamic Middle East. Here, many people believed that modernizing and westernizing programs were leading their societies toward rampant materialism and unchecked individualism. Critics included traditional clerics and young western-educated elites whose job prospects seemed bleak and who felt that the promise of modernization had failed. Having criticized modernizing processes since the nineteenth century, Islamic conservatives

Ayatollah Khomeini. *After fifteen years of exile in France due to his outspoken opposition to the shah, Ayatollah Khomeini returned to Tehran in 1979 to the ardent welcome of his supporters.*

flourished once more in the 1970s, as global markets and social dislocations undermined the moral foundations of secular leadership.

The most revolutionary Islamic movement arose in Iran, where clerics forced the shah from power in 1979. The revolt pitted a cadre of religious officials possessing only pamphlets, tracts, and tapes against the military arsenal and the vast intelligence apparatus of the Iranian state. Shah Mohammad Reza Pahlavi had enjoyed U.S. technical and military support since the Americans had helped place him on the throne in 1953. His bloated army and police force, as well as his brutally effective intelligence service, had crushed all challenges to his authority. The shah also had benefited from oil revenues, which soared after 1973. Yet the uneven distribution of income, the oppressive police state, and the royal family's ostentatious lifestyle fueled widespread discontent. As discontent rose, so did repression. And as repression intensified, so did the feeling that the government had abandoned the people.

The most vociferous critique came from the mullahs (Muslim scholars or religious teachers), who found in the **Ayatollah Ruhollah Khomeini** a courageous leader. Khomeini used his traditional Islamic education and his training in Muslim ethics to accuse the shah's government of gross violations of Islamic norms. He also identified the shah's ally, America, as the great Satan. With opposition mounting, the shah fled the country in 1979. In his wake, Khomeini established a theocratic state ruled by a council of Islamic clerics. Although some Iranians grumbled about aspects of this return to Islam (women's reduced status, leaders' arbitrariness, ruptured relations with the West, and the failure to institute democratic procedures), they prided themselves on having inspired a revolution based on principles other than those drawn from the West.

RELIGIOUS CONSERVATISM IN THE UNITED STATES

The search for moral foundations of politics in the global age reached beyond nonwestern societies. Indeed, in the United States, religion became a potent force after the 1970s as the membership and activism of conservative, fundamentalist Prot-

American Hostage Crisis in Iran. *The United States was stunned in 1979 by Iran's Islamic Revolution, which overthrew the shah and brought the exiled cleric Ayatollah Ruhollah Khomeini to power. After radical students captured the U.S. embassy, as well as fifty-three hostages, an American rescue raid failed, leading to celebration by Iranians, as shown here.*

estant churches eclipsed mainline denominations. Insisting on literal interpretation of the Bible, Protestant fundamentalists railed against secularizing trends in American society. This traditionalist crusade took up a broad range of cultural and political issues. Religious conservatives (predominantly evangelical Protestants, but including some Catholics and Orthodox Jews) attacked many of the social changes that had emerged from liberation movements of the 1960s. Shifting sexual and familial relations were sore points, but the religious conservatives especially targeted public leaders who, they felt, had abandoned the moral purpose of authority by legalizing abortion and supporting secular values.

Acceptance of and Resistance to Democracy

New sources of power and new social movements drastically changed politics in the global age. Increasingly, international organizations were decisive in defining the conditions of democratic citizenship.

Perhaps most remarkable was how much democracy spread toward the end of the twentieth century. In South Africa, Russia, and Guatemala, elections now decided politicians' fate. In this sense, the world's societies embraced the idea that people have a right to choose their own representatives. Nevertheless, democracy did not triumph everywhere. An important holdout was China. Mao died in 1976, and within a few years his successor, Deng Xiaoping, opened the nation's economy to market forces. But Deng and other Chinese communist party leaders resisted multiparty competition. Instead of capitalism and western-style democracy, they maintained that China should follow its own path to modernity.

By the late 1980s, economic reforms had produced spectacular increases in production and rising standards of living for most of China's people. But the widening gap between rich and poor, together with increasing public awareness of corruption within the party and the government, triggered popular discontent. Worker strikes and slowdowns, peasant unrest, and student activism spread. On April 22, 1989, some 100,000 people gathered in **Tiananmen Square** at the heart of Beijing in silent defiance of a government ban on assembling. The following month brought a greater show of defiance when television cameras and world journalists converged on China to cover the historic visit of Soviet leader Mikhail Gorbachev. Several hundred students, flanked by thousands of supporters, began a hunger strike at the square to demand democratic reform. Tiananmen Square was now their stage and the world their audience. Within days, the strike spread to other cities. In Beijing, where well over a million people filled the city center, a carnivalesque atmosphere prevailed as the students sang and danced to rock songs and folk ballads.

The regime responded by declaring martial law. Two huge protest demonstrations followed, and residents erected barricades to defend the city against government troops. As the protest's momentum waned, a twenty-eight-foot icon, partly inspired by the Statue of Liberty, was unveiled at the square, capturing the imagination of the crowd and the attention of the cameras. But by then the government had assembled troops to crush the movement. In a night of terror that began at dusk on June 3, the People's Liberation Army turned their guns against the people. Most students in the square negotiated a

Tiananmen Square. *This white plaster and styrofoam statue, inspired in part by the Statue of Liberty and dubbed the Goddess of Democracy, was created by students in Beijing in the spring of 1989. It was brought to Tiananmen Square and unveiled at the end of May in an attempt to reinvigorate the democracy movement and the spirits of the protesters. For five days it captured worldwide attention, until it was toppled by a tank on June 4 and crushed as the Chinese People's Liberation Army cleared the square of its democracy advocates.*

safe passage; those who lost their lives—estimates vary from 2,000 to 7,000—were the nameless people who wielded Molotov cocktails, sticks, or bricks in a futile attempt to repel the troops.

The Chinese government weathered the storm. It continued to suppress unofficial social organizations; to control access to information, including that obtained over the Internet; and to crack down on dissidents. But it could not completely control the forces of globalization. Some organizations, like the quasi-religious group Falun Gong, eluded authorities and even used the Internet to enlist international support. At the dawn of the twenty-first century, signs of change were apparent. A visible urban entrepreneurial class had emerged, whose top echelon conducted its global businesses over nearly ubiquitous cellular phones. Rural dwellers paid what little they had to be smuggled abroad, at great risk and often with lethal consequences, so that they could make a better living in America or Europe. Within China, tens of millions of people lived a transient existence, with tens of thousands daily leaving the countryside for the cities. There they often suffered economic and social exploitation, as well as police and other government abuse. Existing at the margins of the new prosperity, they, too, served as reminders of the uneven effects of globalization.

In Mexico, democracy finally triumphed, as the single party that had dominated the country for seventy-one years fell after the election of Vicente Fox in 2000. Until that time, Mexican rulers had combined patronage and rigged elections to stay in office. By the 1980s, corruption and abuse permeated the system. The abuse of democratic rights fell hardest on poor communities, especially those with large numbers of indigenous people.

Consider the state of Chiapas. An impoverished area with many Mayan descendants, Chiapas had trouble coping with social and economic change in the 1980s. The president stripped Indians of their right to communal land and let the ruling party run Chiapas like a fiefdom. By the early 1990s, the province was demanding material betterment, cultural recognition of Indian rights, and local democracy. When one group of rebels, the Zapatistas, rose up in Mexico City against the government in 1994, the government prepared to crush the insurgents. (See Primary Source: Indigenous People in Mexico Speak Out.) But no one anticipated how supranational forces would play a role in helping local democracy: Cable News Network (CNN) broadcast the clash worldwide, and the rebel leader created a Web site that drew thousands of "hits." Thereafter, international news media flooded Chiapas, filming Indians waving flags and pronouncing victory. Leaders in Mexico City, deeply embarrassed, asked local church authorities to negotiate peace and spearhead a commission to hear the villagers' concerns. In 2000, national elections toppled the ruling party (including its representatives in Chiapas), and Mexico dismantled its one-party ruling system.

Mexico, South Africa, and China were powerful examples of how men and women in every corner of the earth yearned

Protests in Mexico. (Left) *After generations of oppression and exclusion, peasants of Chiapas, in southern Mexico, called for democracy and respect for their right to land. When Mexican authorities refused to bend, peasants took up arms. While they knew that they posed no military threat to the Mexican army, the Zapatista rebels used the world media and international organizations to embarrass the national political establishment into allowing reforms.* (Right) *Among the great Mexican muralists of the twentieth century, David Alfaro Siqueiros most advocated class struggle. In this 1957 mural image,* The People in Arms, *Siqueiros portrays Mexican peasants as they pick up arms in 1910 to fight for a new order. Paintings such as these provided inspiration for movements such as the Chiapas Rebellion.*

PRIMARY SOURCE

Indigenous People in Mexico Speak Out

In late 1993, peasants of Chiapas rejected the false promises of the Mexican national government. Mostly Indians living in a jungle region, they had seen their land rights taken away and had tired of living under oppressive authorities. On January 1, 1994, they took up arms against the government, calling for a restoration of the principles of the Mexican Revolution: land for the hungry, democracy, and an end to centuries of neglect and oppression of Indians across the Americas. They formed the Zapatista Army for National Liberation (EZLN), mounted a brilliant public relations campaign, and enlisted massive international support. Here is an excerpt from their declaration of war against the Mexican government.

We are a product of 500 years of struggle: first against slavery, during the War of Independence against Spain led by the insurgents; afterward to avoid being absorbed by American imperialism; then to promulgate our constitution and expel the French Empire from our soil; and later the Porfirista dictatorship denied us just application of the Reform laws, and the people rebelled, forming their own leaders; . . . we have nothing, absolutely nothing, not even a decent roof over our heads, no land, no work, no health care, no food, or education; without the right to freely and democratically elect our authorities; without independence from foreigners, without peace or justice for ourselves and our children.

But TODAY WE SAY, ENOUGH! We are the heirs of those who truly forged our nationality. We the dispossessed are millions, and we call on our brothers to join in this call as the only path in order not to die of hunger in the face of the insatiable ambition of a dictatorship for more than 70 years led by a clique of traitors who represent the most conservative and sell-out groups in the country. They are the same as those who opposed Hidalgo and Morelos, who betrayed Vicente Guerrero, the same as those who sold over half our territory to the foreign invader, the same as those who brought a European prince to rule us, the same as those who formed the dictatorship of the Porfirista "scientists," the same as those who opposed the Oil Expropriation, the same as those who massacred the railroad workers in 1958 and the students in 1968, the same as those who today take everything from us, absolutely everything.

To prevent this, and as our last hope, after having tried everything to put into practice the legality based on our Magna Carta, we resort to it, to our Constitution, to apply Constitutional Article 39, which says:

"National sovereignty resides essentially and originally in the people. All public power emanates from the people and is instituted for the people's benefit. The people have, at all times, the unalienable right to alter or modify the form of their government."

Therefore, according to our Constitution, we issue this statement to the Mexican federal army, the basic pillar of the Mexican dictatorship that we suffer . . .

In conformity with this Declaration of War, we ask the other branches of the Nation's government to meet to restore the legality and the stability of the Nation by deposing the dictator. . . .

PEOPLE OF MEXICO: We, upright and free men and women, are conscious that the war we declare is a last resort, but it is just. The dictators have been applying an undeclared genocidal war against our people for many years. Therefore we ask for your decided participation in support of this plan of the Mexican people in their struggle for work, land, housing, food, health care, education, independence, liberty, democracy, justice, and peace.

QUESTIONS FOR ANALYSIS

- In what other periods in this book have we encountered the ancestors of the Chiapas peasants?
- What does this declaration of war suggest about current and past Mexican governments?

Source: General Council of the EZLN, Declaración de la Selva Lacandona, 1993 (www.ezln.org, January 1, 1994).

to choose their own leaders. In 1994, millions of previously disenfranchised South Africans lined up for hours to cast a vote for their new black African president, Nelson Mandela. In 2000, the Mexican electorate turned out the ruling party, while in China the ruling communist party had to call in the army to prevent regime change and democratic reforms.

CONCLUSION

In the thirteenth century (as long before), a few travelers like Ibn Battuta and Marco Polo ventured over long distances to trade, to explore, and to convert souls; yet communications technology was rudimentary, making long-distance mobility and exchange expensive, rare, and perilous. The world was much more a series of communities set apart than a world bound together by culture, capital, and communication networks.

By the late twentieth century, that balance had changed. Food, entertainment, clothing, and even family life were becoming more similar worldwide. To be sure, some local differences remained. In 2000, the local lived on, and in some cases was revived, through challenges to the authority of nation-states. No longer did the nation-state or any single level of community life define collective identities. At the same time, worldwide purveyors of cultural and commercial resources offered local communities the same kinds of products, from aspirin to Nike shoes. Exchanges across local and national boundaries became easier. For the first time, many of the world's peoples felt they belonged to a global culture.

New technologies, new methods of production and investment, and the greater importance of personal health and education for human betterment created new possibilities and greater inequalities. Indeed, the disparities between haves and have-nots in 2000 were astonishing. For as humanity harnessed new technologies to accelerate exchanges across and within cultures, an ever-larger gulf separated those who participated in global networks from those who languished on the margins. This disparity produced divergent political and cultural forms, despite the collapse of the three-world order. Thus, as the world became more integrated, it also grew apart along ever-deeper lines.

AFTER YOU READ THIS CHAPTER

Review and research on **STUDYSPACE:** wwnorton.com/StudySpace

TRACING THE GLOBAL STORYLINES

FOCUS ON: *Globalization*

Removing obstacles to globalization

- Communism's fall and the end of the cold war improve prospects for global exchange of peoples, ideas, and resources.
- Final decolonization in Angola and Mozambique and the end of apartheid in South Africa return self-rule throughout Africa.

Unleashing globalization

- Financial deregulation and the end of gold and silver standards allow money to move freely across borders but lead to a Third World debt crisis.
- Widespread migrations occur as people in Africa, Asia, and Latin America move to Europe and America, following the tracks of their former colonizers.
- Revolutions in culture and communications spread American culture worldwide, but also make cultural diversity more possible for those who can afford it.

The new global order

- Globalization leads to dramatic population expansion, requiring greater agricultural and industrial output.
- Family structure changes, life spans increase, and more goods are available, yet inequalities deepen as decent education and good health determine social status as never before.
- As globalization erodes the power of the nation-state, greater violence occurs between and within states. Nongovernmental organizations (NGOs) and religion become resources for dealing with violence and inequality and for reimagining the nation-state.

CHRONOLOGY

The Americas
United States announces Strategic Defense Initiative (SDI) **1983**

Europe

Soviet Union
Gorbachev assumes power **1985**
Chernobyl nuclear accident **1986**

Africa

The Middle East
Khomeini establishes theocratic state in Iran **1979**

Asia

East Asia

1975

KEY TERMS

AIDS (Acquired Immuno Deficiency Syndrome) *p. 805*

developing world *p. 786*

European Union (EU) *p. 794*

feminist movements *p. 808*

globalization *p. 785*

global warming *p. 812*

International Monetary Fund (IMF) *p. 792*

Ayatollah Ruhollah Khomeini *p. 817*

Nelson Mandela *p. 789*

nongovernmental organizations (NGOs) *p. 814*

Silicon Valley *p. 801*

supranational organizations *p. 814*

Tiananmen Square *p. 818*

truth commissions *p. 815*

World Bank *p. 814*

STUDY QUESTIONS

1. **To what extent** did the three-world order discussed in Chapter 20 not exist by 1975? What architecture of power was replacing it?
2. **What** led to the end of the cold war? How did U.S. containment policies contribute to the Soviet Union's demise?
3. **Describe** the process through which apartheid was dismantled in South Africa. Why was the process relatively nonviolent?
4. **Analyze** how globalization transformed popular culture. To what extent does global popular culture reflect American culture?
5. **Explain** how globalization transformed world demography. What patterns emerged in terms of international migration?
6. **Discuss** how globalization affected women. How did new patterns in trade, production, and finance help or hinder opportunities for women worldwide?
7. **Explain** trends in agricultural production and natural resource consumption over the last several decades. Who produced the goods, and who consumed them?
8. **Analyze** how globalization affected the world's environment. How effectively has the global community addressed new environmental concerns?
9. **Explain** how globalization altered people's sense of identity. How did globalization challenge national identity and the idea of the nation-state?

- North American Free Trade Association approved **1992**
- Chiapas Rebellion in Mexico **1994**
- Eastern European communist regimes collapse **1989**
- Yugoslavia dissolves, ethnic cleansing ensues **1989–1995**
- European Union formed **1991**
- Soviet war in Afghanistan **1979–1989**
- Dissolution of the Soviet Union **1991**
- Mandela released from prison **1990**
- Free elections in South Africa **1994**
- Ethnic cleansing in Rwanda **1998**
- First Gulf War **1991**
- BJP Party heads government in India **1998**
- Deng Xiaoping reforms China **1978–1992**
- Chinese state cracks down on Tiananmen Square protesters **1989**

2000

THE TRUE ADMINISTRATION OF JUSTICE IS THE FIRMEST PILLAR OF
porations" PEOPLE too" ?!
JOBS, JUSTICE AND EDUCATION
99:1
JOBS NOT CUTS

Epilogue

2001–The Present

On December 31, 1999, people worldwide celebrated the beginning of a new millennium. With the cold war over, optimists hoped for an end to the history of ideological conflict that had bloodied the twentieth century. They looked forward to an era of peace and prosperity. But in the first decade of the new millennium, it became painfully clear that while the global economy and technologies had brought the world together as never before, divergent ideals could still blow things apart. People across the world grappled with common challenges while also experiencing possibilities and problems specific to their region.

GLOBAL CHALLENGES

Barely nine months into the twenty-first century, terrorist violence shattered the exuberance that had welcomed the new millennium. On September 11, 2001, nineteen hijackers commandeered four airplanes.

The hijackers slammed two of the planes into the World Trade Center in New York City and a third into the Pentagon Building (home of the U.S. Department of Defense) in Washington, D.C. The fourth hijacked plane was deterred from its intended target—the White House or the Capitol—by the courageous actions of its passengers and crashed in a field in southwestern Pennsylvania. Television captured the event live for global viewers, recording the horrifying images of the Trade Center's twin towers engulfed in flames, then crumbling into a heap of ash and twisted metal.

War on Terror

The terrorist attack of 9/11 created revulsion across the world. "We are all New Yorkers" was heard in far corners of the globe. In the United States, grief unified the nation. Anger focused on Osama bin Laden and al-Qaeda, the militant Islamist group that had organized the attack. The militants claimed that it was a response to America's imperialist policies in the Middle East and retribution for American troops' presence in Saudi Arabia (during the first Iraq War). Many Americans likened 9/11 to the Japanese bombing of Pearl Harbor sixty years earlier. George W. Bush, who had become president after a close and disputed election the year before, gained broad public support for his tough talk about bringing terrorists to justice and for his insistence that the events of September 11 had introduced a divide between the "pre-9/11 world" and the "post-9/11" one. Domestically, Bush pushed for security measures to curb future terrorist violence, protect freedom, and secure the American homeland.

Internationally, President Bush declared a "global war on terror." With the nearly unanimous backing of the American people, as well as strong support from many nations, Bush unsuccessfully sent American forces to Afghanistan to hunt down bin Laden, destroy al-Qaeda training camps, and topple the Taliban government that had provided a haven for the terrorists. Expanding the battlefront of the war on terror, in 2003 the Bush administration ordered an invasion of Iraq, falsely charging its brutal dictator, Saddam Hussein, with abetting the terrorist assault of 9/11 and producing weapons of mass destruction. As in Afghanistan, the initial offensive went well: the United States and a military coalition representing Britain, Spain, Italy, and several eastern European nations quickly overthrew Hussein's regime. But defeating the Iraqi army and finding Hussein proved easier than restoring order to the country, improving living standards, and persuading the population to rally around the American vision of a democratic polity.

Moreover, the failure to find weapons of mass destruction or to uncover indisputable links between Hussein and al-Qaeda, together with mounting American losses from an ongoing insurgency, left many U.S. citizens questioning the wisdom of this war. Although Bush won reelection in 2004, the national and global unity so evident right after September 11 seemed increasingly distant—as was the sense that the new century

9/11. (Left) *The North Tower already aflame, this photograph captures a second hijacked jet, an instant before it crashed into the South Tower of New York's World Trade Center on September 11, 2001.* (Right) *Firefighters search for survivors in the smoldering ruins.*

would be one of peace and prosperity under an American-led world order.

In Afghanistan, the situation shifted noticeably. U.S.-led coalition forces started to find themselves in a quagmire like the one that the Soviets had fallen into two decades earlier (see Chapter 21). Early successes to maintain stability became more challenging as local warlords exercised personal power toward achieving their own goals and as the revitalized Taliban received support from neighboring Pakistan.

While the campaigns in Iraq and Afghanistan faltered, the United States doubled down on its terrorist manhunts. Meanwhile, the American image internationally suffered with the exposés of its programs of extensive surveillance, including those of U.S. citizens, the use of coercive interrogation techniques, "rendition" of suspected militants to sites where they could be tortured to extract information, the inhumane treatment of Iraqi prisoners at the Abu Ghraib prison, and the harsh and indefinite detention of suspected terrorists at Guantanamo. The domestic support for the Bush administration also eroded.

Helped by the growing chorus of disapproval of the Iraq war, Barack Obama secured the presidency in 2008 and the Democratic Party took over both houses of Congress. Following his campaign promise, President Obama announced plans to end the Iraq war and refocus attention on Afghanistan. With an increased military presence, the Americans assaulted Taliban strongholds in the countryside and carried the terrorist manhunt across the border into Pakistan by sharply escalating unmanned drone strikes. On May 2, 2011, the U.S. forces carried out a daring operation in Pakistan, killing Osama bin Laden. The Democratic president ended the Iraq occupation in 2011, and announced that American troops would withdraw from Afghanistan in 2014.

Iraqi Elections. *Iraqis voted on December 15, 2005, while the country was under American and allied military occupation. Voters' fingers were stained after voting so that they could not vote twice; many walked away from the polling booths showing their stained fingers with pride.*

Islamic Militancy

In spite of the war on terror, Islamic militancy has gained a strong foothold in many parts of the world. Elections in Iraq under American occupation were won by sectarian and regionalist parties. The major Shiite religious party won heavily in Shiite areas, while the Kurdish party swept the northern, predominantly Kurdish, region of Iraq. The Sunni population, living in the center of the country, supported its own religious party. Secular parties had no success at all. Similarly, in the 2006 elections in Palestine, Hamas, the radical Islamist party and avowed foe of Israel, triumphed over Fatah, the party of the once-dominant Palestine Liberation Organization. In Afghanistan, American and NATO troops have weakened al-Qaeda, but the Taliban remains a formidable force. In Pakistan, militant groups, long supported and used by the military in its proxy wars in Kashmir and Afghanistan, have proliferated, with some even turning against the regime itself in order to impose their radical agenda.

The power of a revivified Islam reaches far beyond the Middle East and South Asia. Among the many Muslim communities of northern Nigeria, for instance, one state after another has embraced the *sharia* as its legal guide and moral compass. In 2012, militant Islamists took control of northern Mali, imposing a strict version of Islamic law. Radical Islam has found pockets of appeal even among the Muslim communities in Europe.

At the most general level, the appeal of radical Islam is connected to globalization. Confronting a world transformed and woven ever so tightly by economic, political, and cultural forces larger than the nation, the radical Islamists offer a return to the fundamental elements of the Muslim faith as a global alternative to what they consider as modern, western, and un-Islamic influences.

Local conditions have conspired to lend traction to this global vision. In the Arab world, with the exception of oil-rich Persian Gulf states, which are awash in petroleum dollars, poverty and economic insecurity are widespread. The long domination of the region by oppressive and dictatorial regimes has bred discontent that, in the absence of democratic institutions, finds an outlet in radical Islam. The continuing plight of Palestinians is a source of fury against Israel and its principal ally, the United States. Although the U.S. government claimed that the invasion of Iraq aimed to free Iraqis from the tyrannical rule of Saddam Hussein and bring democratic governance to the region, the occupation bred new resentments against the Americans. Drone attacks in Pakistan, claiming many innocent lives, serve to produce recruits for radical Islamists. Many in the Asian and African world see the recent actions of the United States and western powers through the memory of their previous colonial and imperial history. This is also true in Europe itself, where its Muslims citizens see their exclusion, discrimination, and attacks on identity as a continuation of the colonial past.

The Global Economic Crisis

If the global political environment was a specter of uncertainty, there was no uncertainty about another crisis: the nosedive of the world economy beginning in 2007. The problem began in the financial sector, the most globally interlinked of all. Investors from around the world poured their money into riskier and riskier investments—many of which were so complex that not even the regulators in charge of monitoring the financial sector could understand them.

One of the most enticing of these risky bets was real estate in the United States, whose bubble burst, leading to a plunge in property values. This meant not only that banks and financial agencies were stuck with increasingly worthless assets but also that millions of homeowners went belly-up. Massive defaults on loans ripped through the world financial system and led to a seizure of credit. By the summer of 2008, there was a worldwide panic. The elaborate banking system collapsed with a series of high-profile failures like Northern Rock (in Britain), Lehman Brothers (in the United States), and several European institutions. As credit dried up and consumers stopped spending, factories shut down and stores went bankrupt. Between 2000 and 2007, the United States had accounted for fully one-third of the world's consumption. So, when the financial crisis blew a massive hole in American wallets, it dragged much of the rest of the world down, too. Germany and Japan each saw their gross domestic product sink by 15 percent; Mexico's and Russia's dropped by almost one-quarter in the first half of 2009. Ireland, Spain, Italy, Portugal, and Greece were hit by a severe debt crisis; although these states have been helped by bailouts and loans offered by the European Union, each government has been compelled to make deep cuts in state spending in order to show that they are worthy to remain within the Eurozone. Layoffs, higher taxes, and reduced consumption have resulted in the contraction of these economies and in skyrocketing unemployment; in early 2013, overall unemployment in Greece and Spain exceeded 25 percent; for young people eighteen to twenty-five, the rates topped 55 percent. The world had not seen a contraction of production, employment, and trade of this magnitude since the 1930s (see Chapter 19). Times have changed, and lessons have been learned; in the 1930s, countries often tried to solve their economic problems through strategies that hurt their neighbors. By contrast, nowadays the degree of global interdependence is so great that governments generally avoid protectionism; there is now talk—although it is very premature—of a more coordinated global monitoring system of world finance. But states still do try to protect their own economies. The Chinese, for example, have refused to allow the appreciation of their currency; this keeps Chinese exports cheap and stems the influx of foreign goods. The United States has simply borrowed more money in order to inject "stimulus" spending into the economy. The bailouts offered by the European Union have stabilized the situation for the present but compelled debtor states such as Greece and Spain to impose austerity measures and suffer high unemployment.

Global Financial Crisis. *When the major investment firm Lehman Brothers declared bankruptcy in September 2008, the world's increasingly integrated financial system teetered on the brink of collapse. Although massive government interventions kept the system afloat, they did not prevent severe downturns and sharply rising unemployment rates.*

The financial crisis has brought signs of gathering discontent. To forestall a change in government, desperate Argentine leaders nationalized the private pension system for revenues in 2008, and in 2009 they made a grab at the Central Bank's reserves. In Europe, where, at last, economic and political integration had seemed to promise an end to conflict between states, the crisis has created new tensions. In Greece, radical new parties have arisen to protest austerity measures or to take out frustrations on immigrants, and many blame the richer nations, especially the Germans, for having profited from the creation of the Eurozone at the expense of the poorer nations. For the first time in decades, vehement nationalist slogans have come into wide circulation, and some pundits have predicted that the Eurozone—and perhaps even the European Union—in its current form will not last.

Global Stirrings

The turmoil of war, militancy, and economic crisis was part of a broader set of changes at the global level. The very same ongoing integration of the world economy that globalized the economic crisis also produced fresh wealth across the world. Brazil, Russia, China, India, Vietnam, Indonesia, and South Africa all became more prosperous than they were even just a decade ago. Capital, technology, and media brought the world together ever more closely. The movement of ideas and images across national

Occupy Wall Street. *Inspired by other stirrings around the world, this largely national movement was fueled by methods as novel as social media and as traditional as a sit-in. Here an Occupy Wall Street rally joins a labor union demonstration outside the New York County Courthouse in 2011.*

borders accelerated. Social media like Facebook provided new lines of communication and connections, particularly among the young. New aspirations for employment, prosperity, consumption, and political expression appeared. While these varied across the different regions of the world, as we shall see in the following sections, we can also identify certain emergent global patterns.

Juan Evo Morales came to power in Bolivia as the first president of Indian descent in 2005—and was reelected in 2009—on the basis of his activism as leader of peasants and working people. Thousands took to the streets in the Orange Revolution in Ukraine during 2004 and 2005, protesting electoral fraud and corruption. An upsurge against Vladimir Putin erupted in Russia in 2011, culminating in the dramatic protest staged in 2012 by Pussy Riot, a feminist punk rock band. The Arab Spring swept across the Middle East in 2011, offering new expressions of political transformation in sharp contrast to Islamic militancy. An anticorruption movement broke out in India in 2011, mobilizing people demanding transparency and accountability in politics. Barack Obama swept to power in 2008 as the first African American president. Even though his campaign of hope and change crashed at the shores of the economic crisis, he was reelected in 2012.

The global economic and political stirrings were full of paradoxes and contradictions. The growth of prosperity and wealth around the world was highly unequal and accompanied by an unprecedented rise in the power and influence of corporations and financial institutions. Even as a global middle class came into being, inequality deepened. This sparked protests, none more powerfully and dramatically than by Occupy Wall Street (OWS), a movement that started in September 2011 in New York and was organized by a Canadian anarchist group called Adbusters. It highlighted growing social and economic inequality and challenged the power of banks and corporations.

OWS was one among a wide range of emergent political upheavals around the world. Each one had a character specific to the region. Yet together they represent a new phenomenon. Almost all of them took shape outside conventional politics and ideological agendas. Expressing antiestablishment ideals and using social media to mobilize, the young took the lead in these new popular upsurges. We do not know if they will endure or what shapes they will take, but these global stirrings represent something new on the horizon.

Global Warming

Global warming is just one of numerous environmental issues that have gained prominence in the new millennium. As the world population continues to grow and as more areas industrialize, the pressure on vital natural resources (especially oil and water) has inspired calls for greater conservation and more environmentally sustainable economic development. But the U.S.

Hurricane Katrina. *As the hurricane dissipated in the tail end of August 2005, the U.S. Coast Guard surveyed the affected areas by aircraft and conducted damage assessment of what would be the costliest natural disaster in American history. This Coast Guard photograph captures New Orleans immediately after the passing of Katrina.*

government's resistance to global regulations, as well as a rising demand for resources (especially by China and India), has made the future of the earth's environment uncertain.

Despite difficulties in achieving a consensus on actions, there is growing recognition that the planet needs healing. Thus, when the Group of Eight (G8), a forum of leaders from Canada, France, Germany, Italy, Japan, Russia, the United Kingdom, and the United States, met in 2007, a key topic was global warming. It acknowledged that humankind is contributing to, if not causing, the increase in temperatures and that climate change will bring catastrophic storms, severe droughts, famine, and flooding. Hurricane Katrina in 2005, for example, left much of New Orleans and the Mississippi Gulf Coast in ruins. Hurricane Sandy had similar catastrophic effects on the shorelines of New Jersey and New York in 2013. As always, the impact of these changes may be uneven, but if the warnings are correct, global warming will reshape the lives of everyone on the planet. Indeed, global warming affirms just how integrated the world has become and how actions across national frontiers are required to nurse the planet.

THE UNITED STATES, THE EUROPEAN UNION, AND JAPAN

The global political and economic crisis had a deep impact on the United States. Americans moved from supporting Bush to electing Barack Obama, tiring of the wars in Iraq and Afghanistan. But the protection of citizens from terrorist attacks emerged as a continuing concern, posing a challenge to balance security against freedom. The recession following the economic crisis resulted in soaring foreclosures, dwindling tax revenues, and millions thrown out of work.

As the Obama administration sought to cope with the economic crisis while introducing health-care reform, it encountered a conservative backlash in the shape of the Tea Party movement. Consisting largely of older whites, the conservative activists espoused the ideals of small government and market freedom, helping to administer a stinging defeat to the Democrats in the 2010 congressional elections. From the opposite side of the ideological spectrum arose the Occupy Wall Street movement in 2011. Claiming to speak on behalf of the 99 percent against the 1 percent of people, the Occupy activists, consisting largely of young people, railed against the banks and financial institutions that the bailout had helped. Although the movement ran out of steam by the end of the year, it succeeded in inserting the growing inequality into political discussions. Partially helped by the focus on inequality brought about by the Occupy movement, Obama won reelection and his party fared better in the 2012 elections.

A Changing Western Europe

The American invasion of Iraq created fractures in the alliance between the United States and western Europe. During the 1990s, the collapse of the Soviet Union and the development of the European Union (EU) had caused some rumblings about the future of NATO, but disagreements remained muted prior to the American military's entrance into Iraq. In fact, in the immediate wake of September 11, European allies rallied behind the United States. But before and after the invasion of Iraq, leaders in France and Germany sharply criticized U.S. foreign policy.

Notwithstanding the internal divisions, what was striking from a historical standpoint was the region's continuing integration. By 2010, the European Union had widened its membership to twenty-seven countries, including ten nations that formerly had been part of the Soviet bloc. True, this unification faced some reversals, most notably when voters in France and the Netherlands rejected the EU constitution. Still, viewed against the backdrop of twentieth-century total wars and attempts at ethnic cleansing, it is remarkable that member states could bind themselves together in a union to which each relinquished significant degrees of sovereignty.

Demographic Issues

Looking forward, the greater threat to European integration—and to Europe's future peace and prosperity—remains the interlocking issues of aging and immigration. Roughly speaking, to maintain its population of 500 million people, each female in the European Union would have to bear a mean of 2 children, but women in the union now average only 1.5 offspring. Adding to the demographic and labor pressures is the aging of the population. With the percentage of elderly Europeans rising rapidly, sustaining the present workers-to-retirees ratio and paying for the region's burgeoning number of pensioners will require the European Union to attract around 15 million immigrants annually.

Although this number has not been reached, European populations have been boosted by millions of immigrants, many of them Muslims. As of 2010, Europe was home to 38 million Muslims, of whom 25 million (roughly 5 percent of the total population) resided within the European Union. Islam now represents the fastest-growing religion in Europe. In France, the figure has topped 10 percent. These immigrants often live in impoverished circumstances, and in many countries their status as guest workers (see Chapter 21) denies them the full benefits of citizenship. Their presence in Europe's larger cities threatens those who still equate Europe with Christendom and challenges those who believe that European integration requires complete assimilation of all inhabitants.

Europe is not alone in confronting the problems of an aging population and the integration of immigrants. As its baby boom generation ages, the United States faces a similar imbalance between retirees and workers that endangers its Social Security system. Likewise, the flood of immigrants, particularly from Asia and Latin America, continues to shift the nation's ethnic composition. According to U.S. Census Bureau projections, in 2010 people of Latin American descent in the United States will number nearly 48 million (about 15.5 percent of the population). The presence of so many Spanish-speakers troubles those who think the United States should remain an English-only country, and the degree to which immigrants should be required to assimilate remains a contentious issue. More heated still are debates about illegal immigration. (For a global look at population growth and life expectancies, see Maps E.1 and E.2.) It took an overwhelming turnout of Latino and Hispanic voters in the 2012 U.S. presidential election in support of incumbent Democratic Party candidate Barack Obama to bring Republicans and Democrats to the bargaining table to pass immigration reforms.

In many respects, the twin dilemmas of aging and immigration press hardest today on Japan. Like Europeans and North Americans, the Japanese are marrying later and having fewer children. Japan's female population now averages barely 1.37 children, compared with nearly 3.7 in 1950. At the same time, Japanese life expectancy has reached eighty-five, the highest in the world, which further tilts the nation's age pyramid. In 1970 the elderly (those over age sixty-five) represented around 7 percent of the population; in 2005 they reached 20 percent and are expected to hit 40 percent by 2050. Analysts surmise that Japan's population peaked at around 128 million and might decline to perhaps 90 million by 2050. Such a downturn bodes ill for Japan's dynamic economy, which is currently the world's second largest (although China's economy is poised to overtake it).

As in Europe and North America, Japan relies on immigrants to fill out its labor force. In the 1960s, the nation's booming economy experienced labor shortages, but neither the government nor major corporations chose to invite in foreign laborers. They preferred automation or recruitment of workers of Japanese descent from abroad. By the 1980s, however, deepening labor shortages and the yen's rising value led to an expanded dependence on immigrant workers. Recent estimates put the number of foreign nationals in Japan at nearly 2 million, or around 1.5 percent of the total population. Most of them hail from the Korean peninsula, the Philippines, Indochina, Brazil, and Iran.

Anti-Immigrant Sentiments

In Europe, where unemployment rates remain higher than in Japan or North America, the political reaction against immigration has been sharpest. Far right groups have demanded that immigration be halted or "foreigners" expelled. Support levels vary in each country, but across Europe the far right's electoral base appears to be around 15 percent; in some countries it is above 25 percent. The Freedom Party in Austria and the Northern League and National Alliance in Italy regularly place cabinet representatives in coalition governments. Ultra-right forces such as France's National Front, Denmark's People's Party, and the League of Polish Families sometimes pressure governing coalitions to slow EU integration and immigration, especially from Muslim countries.

In recent years, anti-immigrant sentiments in general and anti-Muslim ones in particular have risen in the wake of violent episodes. In Holland, the precipitant was the grisly murder of filmmaker Theo Van Gogh by Mohammed Bouyeri in 2004. Bouyeri claimed he was fulfilling his duty as a Muslim by killing Van Gogh, who had made a film about the abuse of Muslim women. Following the assassination, many in Holland questioned the nation's traditional tolerance of diversity and expressed concern that Muslims were too alien in their values to ever fit in Dutch society. Such questions about the assimilation (and assimilability) of Muslims arose again in 2006 after the publication of anti-Islamic cartoons in a Dutch newspaper generated violent demonstrations across Europe and throughout the Muslim world.

France confronted similar dilemmas after rioting rocked the mostly Muslim suburbs of Paris in 2005. This unrest highlighted the desperate plight of unemployed and alienated immigrants, but it also fed fears about Muslims' loyalties and led some politicians to take a harder line against foreigners. Nicolas Sarkozy, who was interior minister at the time, ordered the deportation of immigrants convicted of rioting, while Jean-Marie Le Pen, leader of the far right National Front, demanded that even naturalized rioters be stripped of their citizenship. In the 2007 race

French turban ban. *During French President Sarkozy's state visit to India in 2010, Indian Sikh students held a demonstration in New Delhi calling for the lifting of the French ban on the turban, a religious practice that dates back to the eighteenth century.*

GREENLAND
(Denmark)
ALASKA
(U.S.)
ICELAND
CANADA
GREAT BRITAIN
FR
SPAIN
UNITED STATES
MOROCCO
ATLANTIC OCEAN
WESTERN SAHARA
(Morocco)
MAURITANIA
HAWAII
(U.S.)
MEXICO
CUBA
DOMINICAN REP.
PUERTO RICO
(U.S.)
BELIZE
JAMAICA
HAITI
GUATEMALA
NICARAGUA
COSTA RICA
PANAMA
COLOMBIA
SENEGAL
SIERRA LEONE
LIBERIA
GALAPAGOS ISLANDS
(Ecuador)
PACIFIC OCEAN
PERU
BRAZIL
CHILE
ARGENTINA
Annual percentage population increase 2005–2010
Population loss
0.0%–0.9%
1.0%–1.9%
2.0%–2.9%
3.0% or more
No data
0
1000
2000 Miles
0
1000
2000 Kilometers

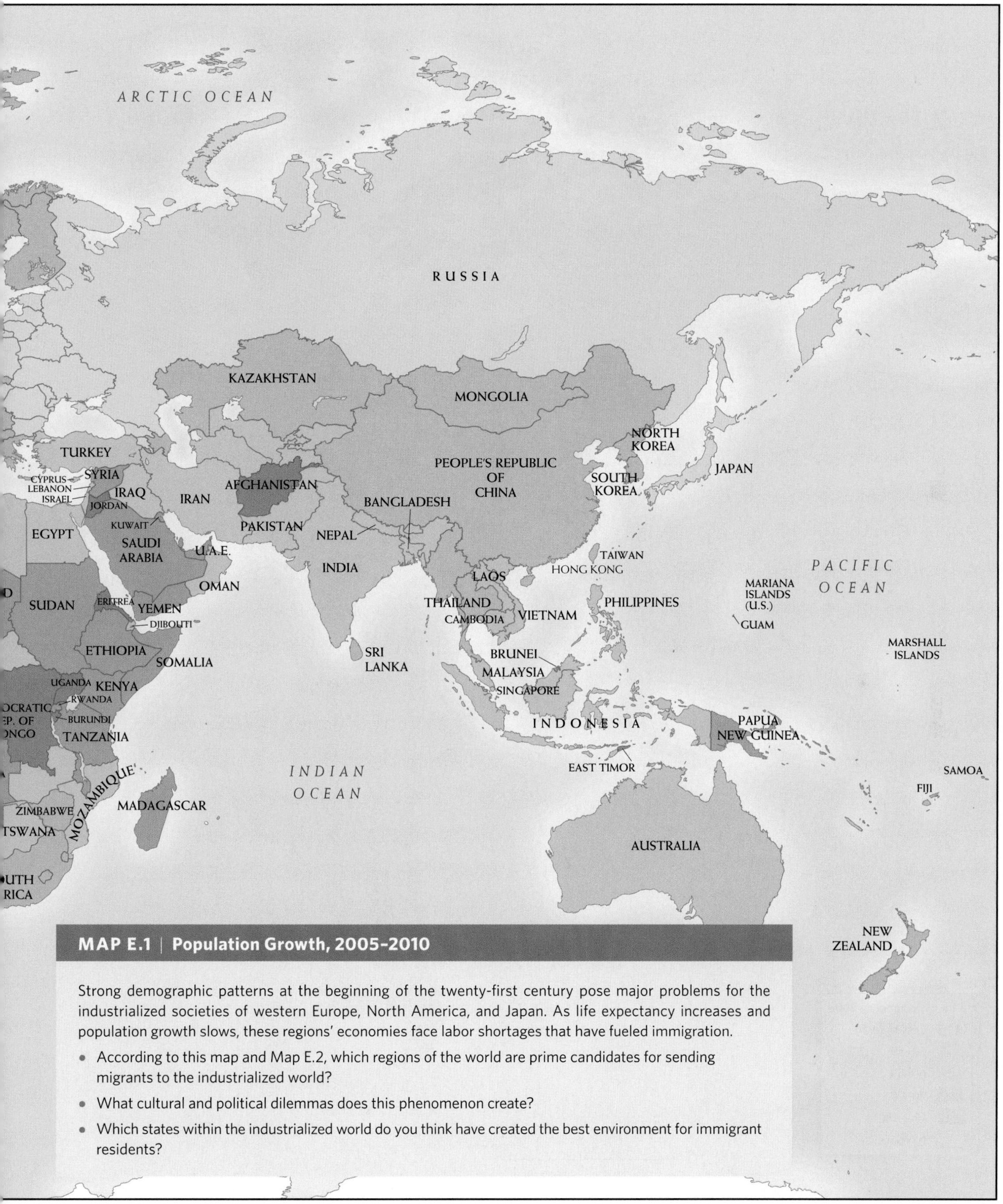

MAP E.1 | Population Growth, 2005–2010

Strong demographic patterns at the beginning of the twenty-first century pose major problems for the industrialized societies of western Europe, North America, and Japan. As life expectancy increases and population growth slows, these regions' economies face labor shortages that have fueled immigration.

- According to this map and Map E.2, which regions of the world are prime candidates for sending migrants to the industrialized world?
- What cultural and political dilemmas does this phenomenon create?
- Which states within the industrialized world do you think have created the best environment for immigrant residents?

GREENLAND
(Denmark)
ICELAND
ALASKA
(U.S.)
CANADA
UNITED
STATES
ATLANTIC
OCEAN
SPAIN
MOROCCO
WESTERN SAHARA
(Morocco)
MAURITANIA
SENEGAL
SIERRA LEONE
LIBERIA
HAWAII
(U.S.)
MEXICO
CUBA
DOMINICAN
REP.
PUERTO RICO
(U.S.)
BELIZE
JAMAICA
HAITI
GUATEMALA
NICARAGUA
COSTA RICA
PANAMA
COLOMBIA
GALAPAGOS
ISLANDS
(Ecuador)
PACIFIC
OCEAN
PERU
BRAZIL
CHILE
ARGENTINA
Life expectancies, 2008
Less than 50
50–59
60–69
70–79
Over 80
No data
0
1000
2000 Miles
0
1000
2000 Kilometers

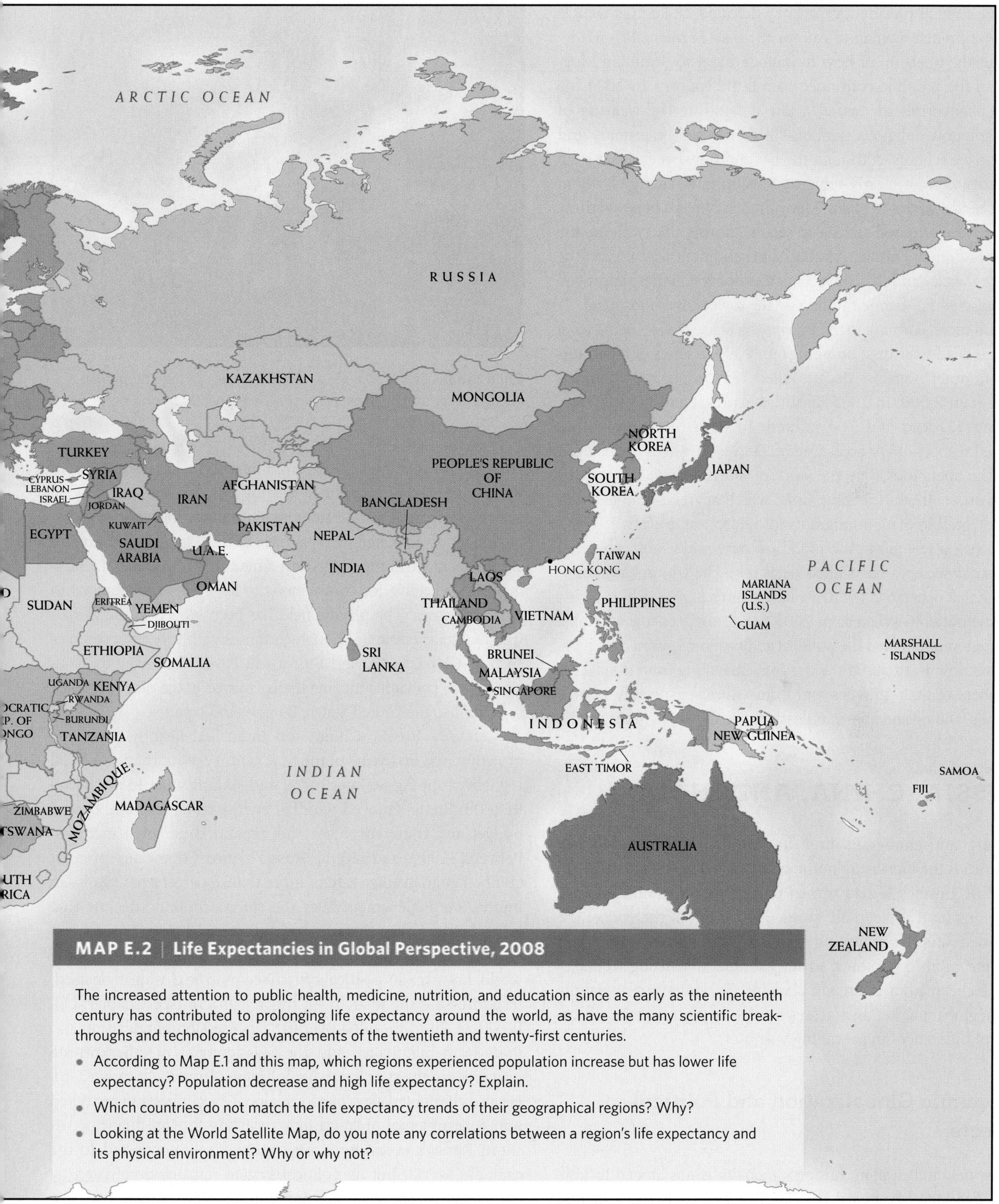

MAP E.2 | Life Expectancies in Global Perspective, 2008

The increased attention to public health, medicine, nutrition, and education since as early as the nineteenth century has contributed to prolonging life expectancy around the world, as have the many scientific breakthroughs and technological advancements of the twentieth and twenty-first centuries.

- According to Map E.1 and this map, which regions experienced population increase but has lower life expectancy? Population decrease and high life expectancy? Explain.
- Which countries do not match the life expectancy trends of their geographical regions? Why?
- Looking at the World Satellite Map, do you note any correlations between a region's life expectancy and its physical environment? Why or why not?

for the French presidency, Sarkozy defeated Le Pen (as well as the first French woman to run for the seat, Ségolène Royal).

But the question of how to include the 4 to 5 million Muslims in the republic continued to roil the country. In 2004 the French government passed a law forbidding the wearing of "conspicuous religious symbols" in French public primary and secondary schools. Although the law did not specify what such symbols were, it clearly targeted Muslim girls, many of whom wore head scarves, or *hijabs*. Many French officials believed these scarves undermined the basic secular norms that were at the heart of French culture. Anti-Muslim sentiment was also on the rise in Switzerland. In 2009, 57 percent of voters there approved a plebiscite that banned minarets (the towers over mosques).

Still more alarming to the Europeans' sense of well-being were several deadly terrorist bombings. In 2004, a series of bombings of commuter trains in Madrid killed 191 people and wounded more than 2,000; in 2005, terrorists struck London's subways, leaving 52 dead and 700 injured. In both cases, authorities pinned responsibility on al-Qaeda. But investigators also alleged that the operations were the work of Muslims who had resided in Spain or Britain for some time, which sparked doubts about the integration of all immigrants into European society.

In just a few years, the mood of the world's most advanced industrial societies has shifted decisively. The triumphant atmosphere that ushered in the new millennium has given way to a pessimistic outlook. Whereas in 2000 talk of the blessings of global integration dominated the political and economic scene, prognosticators now warn about the dangers emanating from disaffected members of their societies and from radicals, especially Islamic radicals, willing and able to unleash terror anywhere in the world.

RUSSIA, CHINA, AND INDIA

Fueling anti-immigrant fires in Europe, Japan, and North America is the increasing number of jobs being "outsourced." In the past, businesses had turned to immigrants to fill low-wage positions (and to keep all wages down). But at the end of the twentieth and the beginning of the twenty-first centuries, it has become more economical to relocate manufacturing to places where cheap labor is already available. To compete successfully in the global market, businesses need to be agile, to take advantage of differences in prevailing wages.

Economic Globalization and Political Effects

In the new millennium, business mobility is not limited to low-skilled and low-wage jobs. The *New York Times* columnist Thomas Friedman observed in a best-selling book that "the world" has become "flat." In other words, technological advances—particularly in computers and communication—have truly brought the world together by virtually erasing distances and enabling all sorts of enterprises to operate from almost any point on the globe. No longer do educated workers have to leave India and China for employment in Europe or North America, because it is increasingly cost-effective for corporations to shift certain operations to those countries. The playing field has been leveled in the globalized market economy, although countries with vast labor reserves such as China, India, and Russia still have a long way to go to achieve the per capita income levels enjoyed in the older capitalist societies like the United States, Europe, and Japan.

Child Labor. *Girls in a Javanese village work in a factory transferring bundles of cotton yarn to bobbins to be used in handlooms.*

Certainly, Russia, China, and India had healthy economic growth in the first years of the new century. With the price of oil regularly topping \$60 per barrel and spiking at \$140 per barrel in 2008, Russia enjoyed windfall energy revenues that boosted budget and trade surpluses and expanded personal incomes. Between 1999 and 2008, Russia's gross domestic product climbed at an average rate of more than 7 percent per year—an impressive achievement after the steep economic decline that followed the Soviet Union's dissolution in 1991.

At the same time that Russia's economy is opening to the world, however, its political system seems to be closing in on itself. In addressing the anarchy of the Yeltsin era (see Chapter 21), President Putin presided over the repossession of television stations from billionaires and the reassignment of other private properties to the state (or to his colleagues from the former KGB). He also eliminated elections for regional executives and restricted non-governmental organizations receiving foreign financing. In short, Russia's economy is now more firmly connected to the capitalist world, but its political system remains dominated by the executive branch. This situation has dashed hopes for the eventual consolidation of a real legislature and an independent judiciary that the Gorbachev-Yeltsin era seemed to promise.

The Chinese have followed a similar path, encouraging market economic reforms while quashing the possibilities for political liberalization. Their economic strategies seem to be successful. Over the last three decades, China's economy has grown at a breathtaking rate of over 9 percent annually, a spectacular ascent that shows no sign of abating. Consumer goods made in China dominate so many markets that it is virtually impossible, as several newspaper reporters have found, to supply an American family's needs on a "China-free" diet. As of 2010, China's economy was the third largest in the world, and projections—if current growth rates can be sustained—suggest that China will have the world's largest economy by midcentury (although its per capita income will still lag behind that of the United States).

In many ways, China's fortunes illustrate both the promises and the pitfalls of the economic reforms undertaken by many developing countries—what used to be called the Third World—in the era of globalization. On the one hand, despite the continued monopoly of political power by the Chinese communist party at home, China's entry into the World Trade Organization (WTO) in 2001 signified its full integration into the global capitalist economy. On the other hand, the reforms have caused political, social, and environmental problems that defy easy solutions. The disparity between the relatively prosperous coastal areas and the poor interior of the country—a problem that the communist government pledged to redress after it came to power in 1949—has once again become a glaring challenge.

At the same time, the gap between rich and poor in China's more economically developed urban areas has widened at an alarming rate. Government statistics indicate that the richest 10 percent of households own 45 percent of private urban wealth, while the poorest tenth command less than 1.4 percent of the wealth in the cities. Also, at home and abroad, there are concerns about the environmental impact of China's economic development. China's homes and factories, for instance, use 40 percent more coal than those in the United States, and Chinese city dwellers suffer from some of the world's worst smog and least healthy air quality.

As its energy consumption and economy have soared, so has China's global standing. In the period after 1949, China was the eager junior partner to the Soviet Union, slavishly imitating the Stalinist developmental model until the Sino-Soviet split of the 1960s (see Chapter 20). Subsequently, Richard Nixon and Henry Kissinger's courting of Mao in 1972 opened up a global option for China that Mao's successors have exploited. China's shift in foreign policy orientation from an alliance with the Soviet Union to a partnership with the United States has arguably been the most important geopolitical realignment in the contemporary world.

Moreover, China has become the number one trading partner with almost every country in Asia, displacing the United States. It has even become the top trading partner with Brazil as well as many countries in Africa. China has also replaced the United States as the number one customer for Saudi Arabian oil. China-India economic relations have strengthened, too. In parallel, the Chinese government has invested heavily in building an ocean-going navy. Although China faces numerous challenges, from environmental degradation to an aging population, it has regained the enormous global weight it held for centuries up to the eighteenth century. In fact, commentators have begun to speculate that China's authoritarian capitalism could be a model for other countries seeking rapid economic development without political liberalization.

Chinese Environmental Concerns. *Despite its prosperity, Hong Kong, like other major Chinese cities, suffers from severe air pollution, which threatens its future as a hub of international commerce. This picture shows part of the city's waterfront shrouded in smog.*

Internal Divisions, External Rivalries

Hindu-Muslim Tensions. *In 2002, Gujarat was consumed by sectarian riots, set off by a train fire in which fifty-nine Hindu pilgrims died. Although an Indian government investigation concluded that the fire was accidental, the incident sparked an orgy of violence by Hindu mobs against Muslims. Shown here is an angry right-wing Hindu party activist.*

Like China, India seems to be one of the success stories of economic globalization, yet internal divisions and external rivalries threaten to undo many benefits. After coming to power in 1998, a coalition led by the Bharatiya Janata Party (BJP), the Hindu nationalist party, embraced market liberalization. Over the next five years, the government opened India to the global market economy with spectacular economic results. Growth rates topped 7 percent annually, and India's stock market boomed. India is now a favorite destination for the flow of international capital, particularly in the information technology sector. Bangalore, Hyderabad, Mumbai, and Delhi have prospered as hot spots in the global economy.

At the same time that the BJP-led government promoted market reforms, it also championed *Hindutva* (Hinduness) as the bedrock of Indian identity. Nowhere were the effects of this twin strategy of economic liberalism and Hindu nationalism more visible than in the western state of Gujarat. Home to merchant communities for centuries, Gujarat has been in the forefront of capitalist manufactures and commerce. While aggressively participating in the global economy, the state has also been a fertile ground for Hindu nationalism.

The dark side of that nationalism erupted in February 2002 after sixty Hindus perished in a fire that consumed a train compartment. Although the circumstances of the fire remain disputed, a rumor immediately spread, authenticated by the BJP government in Gujarat, that Muslims and a "foreign hand" were responsible. For the next few months, Hindu mobs went on a rampage, burning Muslim homes and hacking the residents to death. Newspapers reported that government leaders and the police force assisted in this carnage or looked the other way as over 2,000 Muslims lost their lives. In the provincial elections of December 2002, the BJP aggressively projected itself as a Hindu nationalist and pro-business party. This strategy paid rich dividends, and the BJP was reelected to power with a commanding majority. It repeated its impressive electoral feat once again in the 2012 elections.

Yet another dark side is in fact related to market-led growth. In an effort to boost capitalist economy, the government has declared an open season on land acquisition for real estate development, industrial parks, and mining, leading to the eviction of farmers and forest dwellers. The displaced people have responded with Maoist insurgencies. The flood of corporate money has also corrupted politics, with scandal after scandal dominating the newspaper headlines. In 2011 an outburst of revulsion against politicians led to a movement against corruption.

The ongoing tension with neighboring Pakistan is yet another problem faced by India. Flexing its nationalist muscle, the Indian government exploded a nuclear device in 1998. Pakistan responded by exploding its own bombs, casting an ominous shadow over the two nations' unresolved conflict over Kashmir. In that contested province, terrorist violence repeatedly disturbed the peace and brought the nuclear-armed neighbors close to a potentially devastating war. The tension between the two countries escalated in 2008 when a small band of terrorists from Pakistan carried out raids in Mumbai, slaughtering many civilians and security personnel before being subdued.

Presently, India and Pakistan appear to have taken a step away from that brink, in part because national elections in 2004 returned a coalition headed by the Congress Party to power in India. Led by the Italian-born Sonia Gandhi (wife of the deceased Rajiv Gandhi, Nehru's grandson), the coalition included diverse caste, regional, and ideological interests. Its victory represented a setback to the Hindu nationalist effort to define India's identity in singular terms—at least for the time being. In 2009 the Congress Party again won national elections, and its leader, Manmohan Singh, became prime minister of a coalition government for the second time.

Projecting recent trends into the future, many observers forecast a rearrangement of the world's economic order, with China and India especially moving to the fore during the twenty-first century. Yet China, India, and Russia, like other parts of the world, have not escaped from the past. These societies, too, struggle with widening internal divisions and potentially devastating external rivalries. The impulse toward greater global integration conflicts with the desire to preserve local, regional, and national autonomy. (For a global look at hunger and disparities in income, see Maps E.3 and E.4.)

THE MIDDLE EAST, AFRICA, AND LATIN AMERICA

Although anxieties about terrorism and immigration add to the worries of the West, North American, European, and Japanese societies still boast the world's largest economies and longest life expectancies. Likewise, Russia, China, and India have benefited from bulging trade surpluses and rising per capita incomes. Elsewhere, however, it is harder to find signs of enduring peace or general prosperity.

The Arab Spring

In the 2011 report issued by the Eurasia Group, a multinational organization that assesses countries at risk for political instability, not a single Arab country appeared on their extensive lists. Their predictions were completely off target. The trigger for what became known as the Arab Spring occurred on December 17, 2010, with a seemingly futile act of an insignificant twenty-six-year-old Tunisian vegetable vendor and father of eight who set himself on fire outside a provincial office to protest constant police harassment. This singular act aroused the entire population of Tunisia against the ruling elite. Not only had the police confiscated Mohammed Bouazizi's vegetable stand, and not for the first time, but a policewoman had slapped him in the face. In explaining his decision to take his life, his sister exclaimed, "[I]n Sidi Bouzidi [where he resided] those with no connections and no money for bribes are humiliated and insulted and not allowed to live." As the story circulated through the country, large numbers poured out into the streets, demanding an end to the long-term dictatorship of Zine al-Abidine Ben Ali, who had taken over from Habib Bourguiba, Tunisia's president from independence in 1956 until 1978. Ben Ali was an easy target for reproach. Not only had he ruled with an iron fist, but his second wife, Leila Trabelsi, was a notoriously corrupt person, a former hairdresser who lived in splendor and spent lavishly on herself and her prominent European and Arab guests. Ben Ali's promises to change his behavior convinced no one. The catchword of the protesters was *degage*, "get out." With the army refusing to suppress the dissenters and the security police overwhelmed, Ben Ali took the only way open to him. He departed for Saudi Arabia on January 14, 2011.

Young Egyptian radicals watched events in Tunisia with growing interest. After all, if the Tunisians could get rid of their dictator, why not the Egyptians? On January 25, 2011, ironically a holiday to honor Egypt's police forces, by now an object of people's hatred, Egyptians of all backgrounds and ages—Copts and Muslims, workers and professionals—assembled in Cairo's major plaza, Midan al-Tahrir, or Liberation Square, to let Egypt's president, Hosni Mubarak, in office since 1981, know that he was no longer wanted. Their watchword, *irhal,* meaning "scram" in Arabic, expressed the protesters' utter contempt for him and his rule. His efforts to offer concessions by promising that he would not be a candidate for the presidency in the elections that were to take place at the end of the year had the same effect that Ben Ali's promised reforms had. On February 11, 2011, just three weeks after the first mass demonstration, Hosni Mubarak left office, turning the reins of power over to the Supreme Command of the Armed Forces, a small group of officers whom the president had chosen to lead Egypt's army.

The ouster of Ben Ali and Mubarak sent shock waves of excitement throughout the Arab world. Decades of pent-up rage could no longer be contained. An outpouring of protests occurred in all of the Arab world's major cities. The demands were consistent—the end of repression, the establishment of democratic institutions, and the ousting of rulers who had stayed in power too long and who did not represent the will of the people. The results were astonishing. Monarchs in Jordan and Morocco promised new constitutions; they said that going forward they would rule, not reign. Bahraini Shiites exacted a new constitution from their Sunni king, and Ali Saleh, ruler of Yemen since 1978, fled the country. Even Muammar Qaddafi, the Libyan strongman, in power since ousting King Idris in 1969, felt the sting of protest, though his ouster and eventual execution on October 20, 2011, in the city of Sirte, owed as much to NATO air power as it did to the rebel army that rose up to unseat him.

Although much of the world had misunderstood the causes of these uprisings, they were not hard to discern after the fact. In the first place, Arab populations, 60 percent of whom were under thirty years of age and had known no other rulers, resented the fact that the wave of democratic reforms that had swept through Russia, much of eastern and central Europe, and large parts of sub-Saharan Africa had passed them by. They saw no reason why they, too, should not have leaders who represented their wishes rather than rigged elections and fraudulent referendums that supported the wishes of the ruling elites. The young came to be known as the generation in waiting—waiting for jobs that never seemed to appear; waiting to have enough money to move out of their parents' homes; and waiting to get married and start families. The fact that Hafez al-Assad had passed power to his son, Bashar al-Assad, and Hosni Mubarak was grooming his son, Gamal, heightened the rage. Although the

GREENLAND
(Denmark)
ICELAND
ALASKA
(U.S.)
CANADA
UNITED
STATES
ATLANTIC
OCEAN
BERMUDA
(Br.)
HAWAII
(U.S.)
MEXICO
CUBA
DOMINICAN
REP.
PUERTO RICO
(U.S.)
BELIZE
JAMAICA
HAITI
GUATEMALA
NICARAGUA
COSTA RICA
PANAMA
COLOMBIA
GALAPAGOS
ISLANDS
(Ecuador)
PACIFIC
OCEAN
PERU
BRAZIL
CHILE
ARGENTINA
SPAIN
MOROCCO
WESTERN SAHARA
(Morocco)
MAURITANIA
SENEGAL
SIERRA LEONE
LIBERIA
Hunger
<2.5%, extremely low
2.5%–4.0%, very low
5.0%–19.0%, moderately low
20.0%–34.0%, moderately high
>35.0%, very high
No data
0 1000 2000 Miles
0 1000 2000 Kilometers

MAP E.3 | Hunger Is a Global Problem

Despite much optimism, globalization has not yet shown the ability to meet the basic human needs of the entire world population.

- According to this map, in which regions is hunger very high?
- Comparing this map with Map E.4, identify at least twelve countries where hunger is very high *and* per capita income is low ($825 or less). What other characteristics do these regions share?

GREENLAND
(Denmark)
ICELAND
ALASKA
(U.S.)
CANADA
UNITED
STATES
ATLANTIC
OCEAN
BERMUDA
(Br.)
BAHAMAS
CUBA
DOMINICAN
REP.
PUERTO RICO
(U.S.)
HAWAII
(U.S.)
MEXICO
BELIZE
JAMAICA
HAITI
GUATEMALA
NICARAGUA
COSTA RICA
PANAMA
COLOMBIA
GALAPAGOS
ISLANDS
(Ecuador)
PACIFIC
OCEAN
PERU
BRAZIL
CHILE
ARGENTINA
SPAIN
MOROCCO
WESTERN SAHARA
(Morocco)
MAURITANIA
SENEGAL
SIERRA LEONE
LIBERIA
CÔTE
D'IVOIRE
World income, 2007
$10,066 or more, high
$3,256–$10,065, upper middle
$826–$3,255, lower middle
$825 or less, low
No data
0
1000
2000 Miles
0
1000
2000 Kilometers

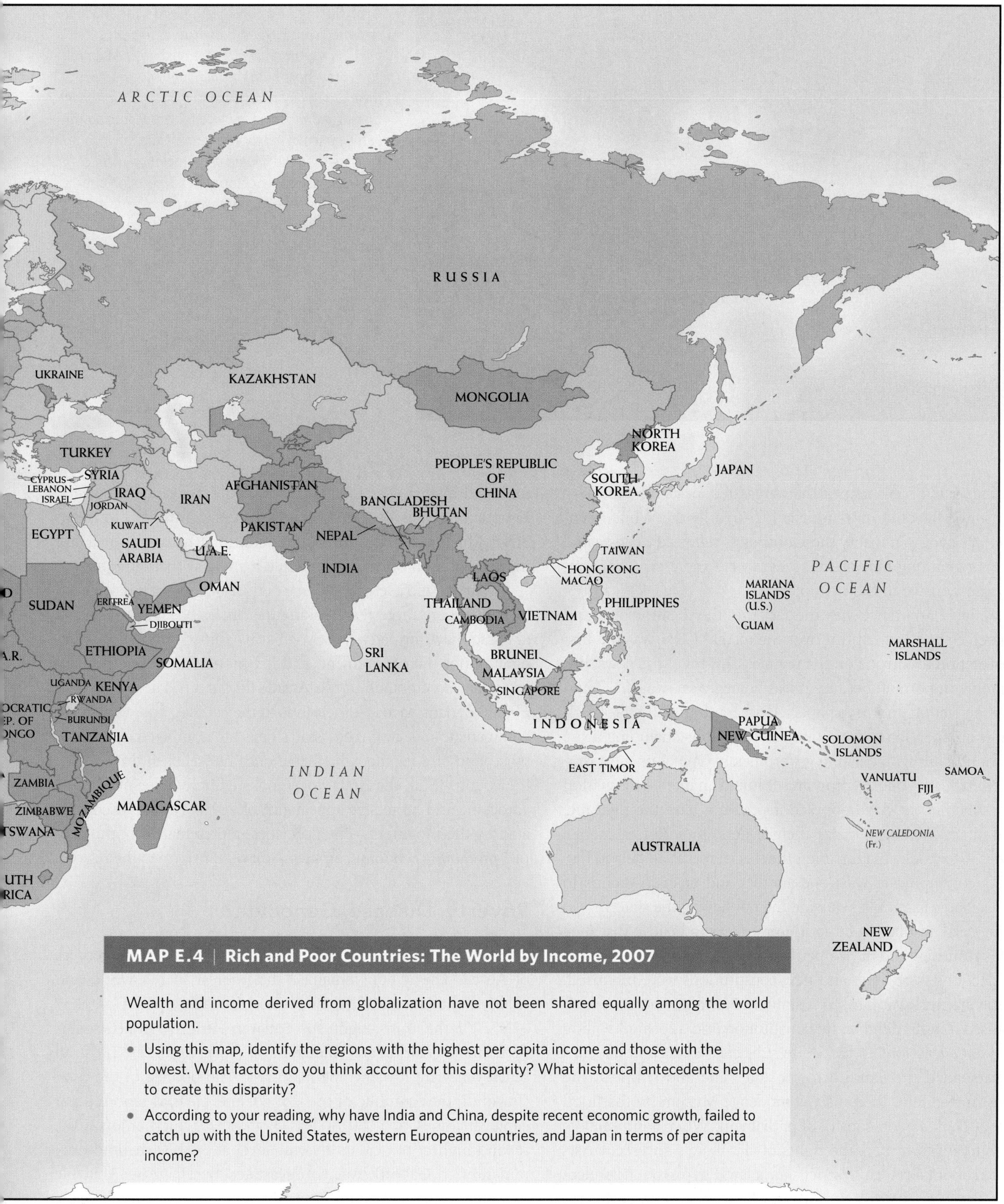

MAP E.4 | Rich and Poor Countries: The World by Income, 2007

Wealth and income derived from globalization have not been shared equally among the world population.

- Using this map, identify the regions with the highest per capita income and those with the lowest. What factors do you think account for this disparity? What historical antecedents helped to create this disparity?
- According to your reading, why have India and China, despite recent economic growth, failed to catch up with the United States, western European countries, and Japan in terms of per capita income?

Arab Spring. *Day and night, Cairo's Tahrir Square swarmed with Egyptians of all ages to protest the ongoing military rule after the ousting of Mubarak. Here protestors burn the midnight oil to decry the dissolution of Parliament by Egypt's Supreme Constitutional Court, a move to consolidate power in the hands of military generals. Note the man documenting the heated demonstration with his video camera* (bottom left), *whose footage would likely have found its way to the wide array of social media sites for discussion and further dissemination.*

uprisings often took names that suggested peaceful protest—the Jasmine Revolution in Tunisia followed by the White Revolution in Egypt—in reality these outbursts reflected deep-seated and long-standing fury at rulers who were repressive, corrupt, and unresponsive to their people.

Of high importance was the fact that the dictatorships and monarchies had lost control over the media. CNN was the first global station to intrude on the regimes' control of the news, but even more important, because it was homegrown, was the Qatari television station and newspaper, Aljazeera, founded in 1995. It became an open forum for all kinds of opinions, including those that found fault with existing governments. One of its most dramatic and widely quoted programs featured an intense discussion about whether the Arab populations did not have the right like those in the West to criticize their leaders. In addition, mobile phones, Facebook, Twitter, and other social media all helped dissenters communicate with one another and enabled groups to organize large assemblies outside the purview of the state.

The early results led euphoric protesters to believe that they could create new and more open societies. Dictators were ousted, free elections were held, and new constitutions were promised. But the progress was hard to sustain. In Bahrain, where the king promised a more democratic constitution and appeared willing to make concessions to his Shiite subjects, violence in the capital persuaded the Saudi army to intervene and suppress the protest movement. In Tunisia, a moderate Muslim Brotherhood party, al-Nahda, won control of parliament. While it affirmed its commitment to respect the rights of all, liberals and secularists worried about a return to strict *sharia* law. Egypt, too, held elections that were won by the Muslim Brotherhood party, Justice and Development, but nullified by the courts. It also elected a Muslim Brotherhood president, Muhammad Morsi, who was unseated after a year for his unchecked expansion of powers; Egyptian judge Adly Mansour now serves as interim president. Strict Muslims, in the meantime, continue to work for a full implementation of sharia law while many fear that outcome.

By far, the most lethal outcome of the Arab Spring has occurred in Syria where protesters, seeking the ouster of President Bashar al-Assad, have formed a free Syrian army, gained international recognition for their movement, and led protests that have resulted in violent confrontation with Assad's forces. To date, more than 60,000 Syrians have lost their lives in the conflict, and while most commentators believe that Assad's days are numbered, few know what kind of a regime will emerge once he has been driven from the country. Still, the Arab world looks entirely different from its autocratic and repressive appearance of 2010. The ideals enunciated by the protesters—open societies, representative of the people, promoting economic progress—have transformed the region.

Poverty, Disease, Genocide

The new millennium did not begin auspiciously for the peoples of Africa. The region remained the poorest in the world and suffered the uncontrolled and uncontrollable spread of HIV/AIDS. Of the thirty-eight sub-Saharan African countries surveyed in the World Bank *Annual Development Report* for 2009, all but seven were low-income countries. The poorest of the poor (Burundi, the Republic of the Congo, and Liberia) reported per capita incomes of $150 or less. Botswana, which enjoyed the second-highest per capita income level at $6,120 (behind only mineral-rich Gabon), was so devastated by HIV/AIDS that life expectancy, once the highest in Africa at close to seventy years, had tumbled to fifty-one years in 2007 and was one of the lowest in the world. (For a global look at HIV incidence, see Map E.5.)

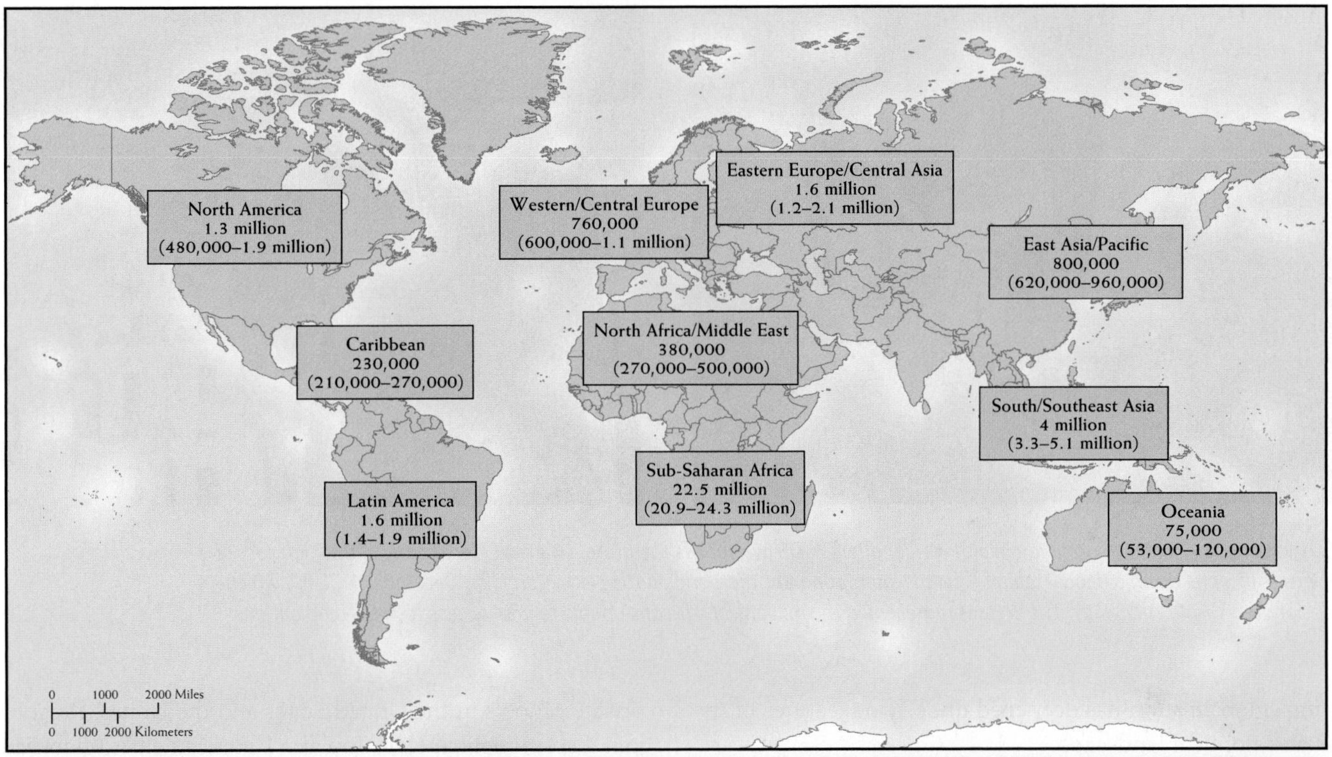

MAP E.5 | The Number of HIV-Positive People Worldwide, 2007

The spread of HIV threatens the development of human capital in the twenty-first century.

- According to this map, which region has the highest amount of HIV infection?
- Using Maps E.3 and E.4 as reference, what connections do you see between poverty and HIV prevalence?
- How does the spread of HIV compromise economic development in poorer regions of the world?

There are a few promising signs. Ghana embraced parliamentary and presidential elections. Civil strife ended in Mozambique and Angola. South Africa convened a Truth and Reconciliation Commission to put the trauma of apartheid behind it and to stay on the course of parliamentary democracy while addressing the gross disparities of income between whites and blacks that were legacies of the twentieth century.

But these have been exceptions to the rule in which political instability wrought misery and devastation. Three of West Africa's countries (Liberia, Sierra Leone, and the Ivory Coast) were torn asunder because of ethnic and personal rivalries and required foreign interventions. Nigeria finally rid itself of unwanted military dictatorial control and moved to a civil, parliamentary system. But Nigeria's democratically elected presidents have barely been able to hold the country together. The northern, mostly Muslim territories continue to fear and resent the southern, mainly Christian communities.

In 2003, just when Africa's longest-running civil war, pitting the animist and Christian southern Sudanese against the northern Muslim peoples, had been resolved and led to the creation of a new state carved out of Sudan and known as South Sudan, a new dispute broke out in western Sudan. In the region of Darfur the state allowed local horse-riding, nomadic tribesmen to carry out ethnic cleansing campaigns against settled agriculturalists. This has led to perhaps the worst case of displaced peoples in the early twenty-first century. Over 2 million refugees fled government terror and civil war to huddle in vast, miserable camps. As in Rwanda in the 1990s (see Chapter 21), genocide has once more visited Africa. But there is some hope. In the West African country of Liberia, after years of pitiless civil war, the belligerents agreed to put down their guns in 2004. In 2005, remarkable elections swept Ellen Johnson-Sirleaf into office to become Africa's first woman president.

Deepening Inequalities

Compared with sub-Saharan Africa, Latin America's situation is not so bleak. Globalization has had profound effects on Latin America, but it has not created an entirely new age. In some areas, globalization has changed the way Latin Americans see their worlds and their place in the wider world. In other

AIDS Awareness. (Left) *A Gambian health worker offers AIDS awareness literature.* (Right) *Due, in part, to the high cost of medicines, AIDS has taken a deadly toll on Africans, prompting this memorial in the Netherlands on December 1, 2009, which was designated World AIDS Day. The crosses represented the millions of Africans unable to gain access to AIDS medications.*

domains, globalization has deepened underlying features of the social and political landscape.

Across the region, the divide between haves and have-nots has widened what has historically been the world's most unequal region. The very rich in Buenos Aires live like the very rich in Boston; magnates of Mexico City drive the same cars, eat the same food, read the same books, and vacation in the same spots as their social cousins from Moscow. They send their children to private schools in the United States and the United Kingdom to join a cosmopolitan elite. To Latin American elites, globalization has been a boon to their wealth and has facilitated integration into the international circulation of goods, ideas, and people. Many, in fact, identify less and less with a particular place in the world.

Liberia's President. *Ellen Johnson-Sirleaf after her inauguration at the Capitol Building in Monrovia, on January 16, 2006. Johnson-Sirleaf is Africa's first elected woman president; she enjoys strong U.S. support and has vowed to fight graft and rebuild her country after years of war.*

Some of the same features hold for the social bottom. Being disadvantaged and poor in southern Mexico looks a lot like being on the losing end in southern Africa: people cling to tiny parcels of land, migrate long distances for seasonal jobs, and fight against insensitive authorities for their basic needs. Globalization has offered few opportunities to make it at home. Old factories have closed in Rosario, Argentina, when faced with competition from Japan; maize farmers in Mexico have to contend with imports from Iowa. In many cases, thanks to globalization, the main solution to the problem is to leave—to move to the city or across borders in search of opportunities elsewhere.

Latin Americans have responded to these challenges in many ways. One sweeping trend is for voters to elect left-wing governments. Most of these are not like the rebel firebrands of the 1960s. Instead, in Brazil, Chile, Argentina, and Uruguay, left-wing governments offer policies designed to soften the blows of globalization and meet basic needs for land, schools, and decent housing. Here the same pressures of globalization that contribute to leftist electoral triumphs limit what these fledgling governments can do. Elsewhere, a more nationalist and populist brand of politics has emerged, one that decries globalization altogether. Rather than softening its effects, leaders here promise to reverse them. In Venezuela, Ecuador, and Bolivia, presidents criticize imperialism and challenge American influence. Their message is that Latin America is better off being a world apart; being together, especially if it means cozying up to

São Paulo, Brazil. *An aerial view of one of São Paulo's biggest slums, Favela Morumbi; Favela Morumbi borders one of the city's richest neighborhoods, also called Morumbi.*

the United States, implies a future of subservience and impoverishment. But as many of these leaders also stifle criticism at home, being apart does not ensure empowerment and prosperity for all, either.

The appeal of anti-globalist politics is not limited to Latin America, or even to the underdeveloped world. In the most advanced industrial societies, as well as in rapidly rising nations like China and India, programs to check globalization or buffer people from its destabilizing effects have found receptive audiences. Still, opposition to deeper global integration continues to be greatest in the poorest parts of the world, where globalization's benefits are least apparent and its costs are often lethal.

Historians are better at interpreting the past than at forecasting the future, but what seems certain is that economic, cultural, political, and environmental developments will continue to encourage exchange and interaction, fostering the integration of peoples and cultures in the new millennium. But cultural and religious diversity, local political institutions and prerogatives, economic competition, and environmental particularities will also persist. And so will the dynamic tensions that both link our worlds together and keep our worlds apart.

Anti-Globalization. *Anti-globalization activists target annual summits of the leaders of the eight most industrialized countries. This one, in Germany in June 2007, saw riot police drive back protesters. Notice the New York Yankees baseball cap on one of the protesters.*

FURTHER READINGS

CHAPTER 1

Arsuaga, Juan Luis, *The Neanderthal's Necklace: In Search of the First Thinkers*, translated by Anthony Klatt (2002). A stimulating overview of prehistory that focuses on the Neanderthals and compares them with *Homo sapiens*.

Barham, Lawrence, and Peter Mitchell, *The First Africans: African Archaeology from the Earliest Toolmakers to Most Recent Foragers* (2008). New findings on the evolution of hominids in Africa.

Barker, Graeme, *Agricultural Revolution in Prehistory: Why Did Foragers Become Farmers* (2006). The most recent, truly global, and up-to-date study of this momentous event in world history.

Bellwood, Peter, *First Farmers: The Origins of Agricultural Societies* (2005). A state-of-the-art global history of the origins of agriculture including recent archaeological, linguistic, and microbiological data.

Bogucki, Peter, *The Origins of Human Society* (1999). An authoritative overview of prehistory.

Cauvin, Jacques, *The Birth of the Gods and the Origins of Agriculture*, translated by Trevor Watkins from the original 1994 French publication (2000). An important work on the agricultural revolution of Southwest Asia and the evolution of symbolic thinking at this time.

Cavalli-Sforza, Luigi Luca, *Genes, Peoples, and Languages*, translated by Mark Selestad from the original 1996 French publication (2000). An expert's introduction to the use of gene research for revealing new information about the evolution of human beings in the distant past.

Childe, V. Gordon, *What Happened in History* (1964). A classic work by one of the pioneers in studying the early history and evolution of human beings. Though superseded in many respects, it is still an important place to start one's reading and a work of great power and emotion.

Clark, J. Desmond, and Steven A. Brandt (eds.), *From Hunters to Farmers: The Causes and Consequences of Food Production in Africa* (1984). Excellent essays on the agricultural revolution.

Coon, Carleton Stevens, *The Story of Man; from the First Human to Primitive Culture and Beyond*, 2nd ed. (1962). An important early work on the evolution of humans, emphasizing the distinctiveness of "races" around the world.

Cunliffe, Barry (ed.), *The Oxford Illustrated Prehistory of Europe* (1994). The definitive work on early European history.

Ehrenberg, Margaret, *Women in Prehistory* (1989). What was the role of women in hunting and gathering societies, and how greatly were women affected by the agricultural revolution? The author offers a number of stimulating generalizations.

Ehret, Christopher, *The Civilizations of Africa: A History to 1800* (2002). Although this is a general history of Africa, the author, a linguist and an expert on early African history, offers new information and new overviews of African peoples in very ancient times.

Fagan, Brian, *People of the Earth: An Introduction to World Prehistory* (1989). An authoritative overview of early history, widely used in classrooms.

Fage, J. D., and Roland Oliver (eds.), *The Cambridge History of Africa*, 8 vols. (1975–1984). A pioneering work of synthesis by two of the first and foremost scholars of the history of Africa. Volume 1 deals with African prehistory.

Frison, George C., *Survival by Hunting: Prehistoric Human Predators and Animal Prey* (2004). An archaeologist applies his knowledge of animal habitats, behavior, and hunting strategies to an examination of prehistoric hunting practices in the North American Great Plains and Rocky Mountains.

Gebauer, Anne Birgitte, and T. Douglas Price (eds.), *Transition to Agriculture in Prehistory* (1992). Excellent essays on the agricultural revolution, especially those written by the two editors.

Johnson, Donald, Lenora Johnson, and Blake Edgar, *Ancestors: In Search of Human Origins* (1999). A good overview of human evolution, with insightful essays on *Homo erectus* and *Homo sapiens*.

Jones, Steve, Robert Martin, and David Pilbeam (eds.), *The Cambridge Encyclopedia of Human Evolution* (1992). A superb guide to a wide range of subjects, crammed with up-to-date information on the most controversial and obscure topics of human evolution and early history.

Ki-Zerbo, J. (ed.), *Methodology and African Prehistory*, vol. 1 of the UNESCO General History of Africa (1981). A general history of Africa, written for the most part by scholars of African descent.

Klein, Richard G., and Blake Edger, *The Dawn of Human Culture* (2002). A fine and reliable guide to the tangled history of human evolution.

Leakey, Richard, *The Origin of Humankind* (1994). A readable and exciting account of human evolution, written by the son of the pioneering archaeologists Louis and Mary Leakey, a scholar of equal stature to his parents.

Lewin, Roger, *The Origin of Modern Humans* (1993). Yet another good overview of human evolution, with useful chapters on early art and the use of symbols.

Loewe, Michael, and Edward Shaughnessy (eds.), *The Cambridge History of Ancient China: From the Origins of Civilization to 221 B.C.* (1999). A good review of the archaeology of ancient China.

Mellaart, James, *Çatal Höyük: A Neolithic Town in Anatolia* (1967). A detailed description of one of the first towns associated with the agricultural revolution in Southwest Asia.

Mithen, Steven, *The Prehistory of the Mind: The Cognitive Origins of Art and Science* (1996). A stimulating discussion of the impact of biological and cultural evolution on the cognitive structure of the human mind.

Olson, Steve, *Mapping Human History: Genes, Race, and Our Common Origins* (2003). Using the findings of genetics and attacking the racial thinking of an earlier generation of archaeologists, the author writes powerfully about the unity of all human beings.

Price, T. Douglas (ed.), *Europe's First Farmers* (2000). A discussion of the agricultural revolution in Europe.

Price, T. Douglas, and Anne Birgitte Gebauer (eds.), *Last Hunters– First Farmers: New*

Perspectives on the Prehistoric Transition to Agriculture (1996). An exciting collection of essays by some of the leading scholars in the field studying the transition from hunting and gathering to settled agriculture.

Scarre, Chris (ed.), *The Human Past: World Prehistory and the Development of Human Societies* (2005). An encyclopedia and an overview rolled up into one mammoth volume, written by leading figures in the field of early human history.

Shaw, Thurstan, Paul Sinclair, Bassey Andah, and Alex Okpoko (eds.), *The Archaeology of Africa: Food, Metals, and Towns* (1993). Up-to-date research on the earliest history of human beings in Africa.

Smith, Bruce D., *The Emergence of Agriculture* (1995). How early humans domesticated wild animals and plants.

Stringer, Christopher, and Robin McKie, *African Exodus: The Origins of Modern Humanity* (1996). Detailed data on why Africa was the source of human origins and why *Homo sapiens* is a recent wanderer out of Africa.

Tattersall, Ian, *The Fossil Trail: How We Know What We Think We Know about Human Evolution* (1995). A passionately written book about early archaeological discoveries and the centrality of Africa in human evolution.

Tattersall, Ian, *The World from Beginnings to 4000 BCE* (2008). A brief up-to-date overview of humanity's early history by a leading authority.

Tattersall, Ian, *Masters of the Planet: The Search for Our Human Origins* (2012). The most recent survey of human evolution.

Van Oosterzee, Penny, *Dragon Bones: The Story of Peking Man* (2000). Describes how the late-nineteenth-century unearthing of sites in China containing fossils of animals used for medicinal purposes led to the discovery of the fossils of the Peking Man.

Weiss, Mark L., and Alan E. Mann, *Human Biology and Behavior: An Anthropological Perspective* (1996). The authors stress the contribution that biological research has made and continues to make to unravel the mystery of human evolution.

Wrangham, Richard, *Catching Fire: How Cooking Made Us Human* (2009). The author shows how fire made it possible for humans to have a more varied and richer diet but also one that provided energy for the one organ—the brain—that consumes the most energy.

CHAPTER 2

Adams, Robert McCormick, *The Evolution of Urban Society* (1966). A classic study of the social, political, and economic processes that led to the development of the first urban civilizations.

Algaze, Guillermo, *The Uruk World System: The Dynamics of Expansion of Early Mesopotamian Civilization* (1993). A compelling argument for the colonization of the Tigris and Euphrates valley by the proto-Sumerians at the end of the fourth millennium BCE.

Andrews, Carol, *Egyptian Mummies* (1998). An illustrated summary of Egyptian mummification and burial practices.

Bagley, Robert, *Ancient Sichuan: Treasures from a Lost Civilization* (2001). Describes the remarkable findings in Southwest China, particularly at Sanxingdui, which have challenged earlier accounts of the Shang dynasty's central role in the rise of early Chinese civilization.

Bar-Yosef, Ofar, and Anatoly Khazanov (eds.), *Pastoralism in the Levant: Archaeological Materials in Anthropological Perspectives* (1992). Classic study of the role of nomads in the development of societies in the Levant during the Neolithic period.

Bruhns, Karen Olsen, *Ancient South America* (1994). The best basic text on pre-Columbian South American cultures.

Butzer, Karl W., *Early Hydraulic Civilization in Egypt: A Study of Cultural Ecology* (1976). The best work on how the Egyptians dealt with the Nile floods and the influence that these arrangements had on the overall organization of society.

Cunliffe, Barry, *Europe Between the Oceans, 9000 BC–AD 1000* (2008), a very up-to-date and spectacularly illustrated account of early Europe.

Habu, Junko, *Ancient Jomon of Japan* (2004). Study of prehistoric Jomon hunter-gatherers on the Japanese archipelago that incorporates several different aspects of anthropological studies, including hunter-gatherer archaeology, settlement archaeology, and pottery analysis.

Jacobsen, Thorkild, *The Treasures of Darkness: A History of Mesopotamian Religion* (1976). Best introduction to the religious and philosophical thought of ancient Mesopotamia.

Kemp, Barry J., *Ancient Egypt: Anatomy of a Civilization* (1989). A synthetic overview of the culture of the pharaohs.

Kramer, Samuel Noah, *The Sumerians: Their History, Culture and Character* (1963). Classic study of the Sumerians and their culture by a pioneer in Sumerian studies.

Pollock, Susan, *Ancient Mesopotamia: The Eden That Never Was* (1999). An analysis of the social and economic development of Mesopotamia from the beginnings of settlement until the reign of Hammurapi.

Possehl, Gregory L., *Indus Age: The Beginnings* (1999). The second of four volumes analyzing the history of the Indus Valley civilization.

Postgate, J. N., *Early Mesopotamia: Society and Economy at the Dawn of History* (1992). A study of the economic and political development of the Sumerian civilization.

Preziosi, Donald, and L. A. Hitchcock, *Aegean Art and Architecture* (1999). One of the best general guides to the figurative and decorative art produced both by the Minoans and Mycenaeans and by related early societies in the region of the Aegean.

Ratnagar, Shereen, *Trading Encounters: From the Euphrates to the Indus in the Bronze Age*, 2nd ed. (2004). A comprehensive presentation of the evidence for the relationship between the Indus Valley and its western neighbors.

———, *Understanding Harappa: Civilization in the Greater Indus Valley* (2001). Harappan site archaeological data of the last century organized into a historical narrative comprehensible to the general audience.

Rice, Michael, *Egypt's Legacy: The Archetypes of Western Civilization, 3000–300 BC* (1997). The author argues for the decisive influence of Egyptian culture on the whole of the Mediterranean and its later historical development.

Roaf, Michael, *Cultural Atlas of Mesopotamia and the Ancient Near East* (1990). A comprehensive compendium of the historical and cultural development of the Mesopotamian civilization from the Neolithic background through the Persian Empire.

Shaw, Ian (ed.), *The Oxford History of Ancient Egypt* (2000). The most up-to-date and comprehensive account of the history of Egypt down to the Greek invasion.

Thorp, Robert, *The Chinese Neolithic: Trajectories to Early States* (2005). Uses the latest archaeological evidence to describe the development of early Bronze Age cultures in North and Northwestern China from about 2000 BCE.

CHAPTER 3

Allan, Sarah, *The Shape of the Turtle: Myth, Art and Cosmos in Early China* (1991). Explains the roles of divination and sacrifice in artistic representations of the Shang cosmology.

Allen, James P., *Middle Egyptian: An Introduction to the Language and Culture of Hieroglyphs* (2000). An introduction to the system of writing and its use in Ancient Egypt.

Anthony, David W., *The Horse, the Wheel, and Language: How Bronze-Age Riders from the Eurasian Steppes Shaped the Modern World* (2007). A superb analysis of the origins and spread of the Indo-European peoples.

Arnold, Dieter, *Building in Ancient Egypt: Pharaonic Stone Masonry* (1996). Details the complex construction of monumental stone architecture in ancient Egypt.

Baines, John, and Jaromir Málek, *Atlas of Ancient Egypt* (1980). Useful compilation of information on ancient Egyptian society, religion, history, and geography.

Beal, Richard H., *The Organization of the Hittite Military* (1992). A detailed study based on textual sources of the world's first chariot-based army.

Bogucki, Peter, and Pam J. Crabtree (eds.), *Ancient Europe 8000 BC–AD 1000: Encyclopedia of the Barbarian World*, 2 vols. (2004). An indispensable handbook on the economic, social, artistic, and religious life in Europe during this period.

Bruhns, Karen Olsen, *Ancient South America* (1994). The best basic text on pre-Columbian South American cultures.

Bryant, Edwin, *The Quest for the Origins of Vedic Culture: The Indo-Aryan Migration Debate* (2001). Insight into the highly charged debate on who the Indo-European speakers were, where they originated, and where they migrated to.

Castleden, Rodney, *The Mycenaeans* (2005). One of the best current surveys of all aspects of the Mycenaean Greeks.

Chadwick, John, *The Decipherment of Linear B*, 2nd ed. (1968). Not only a retelling of the story of the decipherment of the Linear B script but also an introduction to the actual content and function of the tablets themselves.

Cline, E. H., *Sailing the Wine-Dark Sea: International Trade and the Late Bronze Age Aegean* (1994). An excellent account of the trade and contacts between the Aegean and other areas of the Mediterranean, Europe, and the Near East during the late Bronze Age.

Cunliffe, Barry, *Facing the Ocean: The Atlantic and Its Peoples, 8000 BC–AD 1500* (2001). An in-depth, highly useful treatment of western Europe during this period.

Cunliffe, Barry (ed.), *Prehistoric Europe: An Illustrated History* (1997). A state-of-the-art treatment of first farmers, agricultural developments, and material culture in prehistoric Europe.

Davis, W. V., and L. Schofield, *Egypt, the Aegean and the Levant: Interconnections in the Second Millennium BC* (1995). A discussion of the complex interactions in the eastern Mediterranean during the "international age."

Doumas, Christos, *Thera: Pompeii of the Ancient Aegean* (1983). A study of the tremendous volcanic eruption and explosion that destroyed the Minoan settlement on the island of Thera.

Drews, Robert, *Coming of the Greeks: Indo-European Conquests in the Aegean and the Near East* (1988). A good survey of the evidence for the "invasions" or "movements of peoples" that reconfigured the world of the eastern Mediterranean and Near East.

Finley, M. I., *The World of Odysseus*, 2nd rev. ed. (1977; reprint, 2002). The classic work that describes what might be recovered about the social values and behaviors of men and women in the period of the so-called Dark Ages of early Greek history.

Frankfort, Henri, *Ancient Egyptian Religion: An Interpretation* (1948; reprint, 2000). A classic study of Egyptian religion and culture during the pharaonic period.

Keightley, David N., *The Ancestral Landscape: Time, Space, and Community in Late Shang China, ca. 1200–1045 BC* (2000). Provides insights into the nature of royal kinship that undergirded the Shang court and its regional domains.

Kemp, Barry J., *Ancient Egypt: Anatomy of a Civilization* (2006). A definitive presentation of the history, culture, and religion of ancient Egypt.

Klein, Jacob, "The Marriage of Martu: The Urbanization of 'Barbaric' Nomads," in *Mutual Influences of Peoples and Cultures in the Ancient Near East*, ed. Meir Malul (1996).

Kristiansen, Kristian, *Europe before History* (1998). The finest recent survey of all the major developmental phases of European prehistory.

McIntosh, Jane, *Handbook to Life in Prehistoric Europe* (2006). Highlights the archaeological evidence that enables us to re-create the day-to-day life of different prehistoric communities in Europe.

Preziosi, Donald, and L. A. Hitchcock, *Aegean Art and Architecture* (1999). One of the best general guides to the figurative and decorative art produced both by the Minoans and Mycenaeans and by related early societies in the region of the Aegean.

Quirke, Stephen, *Ancient Egyptian Religion* (1992). A highly readable presentation of ancient Egyptian religion that summarizes the roles and attributions of the many Egyptian gods.

Robins, Gay, *The Art of Ancient Egypt* (1997). The most comprehensive survey to date of the art of pharaonic Egypt.

———, *Women in Ancient Egypt* (1993). An interesting survey of the place of women in Ancient Egyptian society.

Romer, John, *Ancient Lives: Daily Life in Egypt of the Pharaohs* (1990). A discussion of the economic and social lives of everyday ancient Egyptians.

Sandars, N. K., *The Sea Peoples: Warriors of the Ancient Mediterranean* (1985). A readable discussion of a very complex period of Levantine history.

Simpson, William Kelly (ed.), *The Literature of Ancient Egypt: An Anthology of Stories, Instructions, and Poetry* (1972). A compilation of the most important works of literature from Ancient Egypt.

Thorp, Robert L., *China in the Early Bronze Age: Shang Civilization* (2005). Reviews the archaeological discoveries near Anyang, site of two capitals of the Shang kings.

Warren, Peter, *The Aegean Civilizations: From Ancient Crete to Mycenae*, 2nd ed. (1989). An excellent textual and pictorial guide to all the basic aspects of the Minoan and Mycenaean societies.

Wilson, John A., *The Culture of Ancient Egypt* (1951). A classic study of the history and culture of pharaonic Egypt.

Yadin, Yigael, *The Art of Warfare in Biblical Lands in the Light of Archaeological Discovery* (1963). A well-illustrated presentation of the machinery of war in the second and first millennia BCE.

CHAPTER 4

Ahlström, Gosta W., *The History of Ancient Palestine from the Paleolithic Period to Alexander's Conquests* (1993). An excellent survey of the history of the region by a renowned expert, with good attention to the recent archaeological evidence.

Aubet, Maria Eugenia, *The Phoenicians and the West,* 2nd ed. (2001). The basic survey of the Phoenician colonization of the western Mediterranean and Atlantic, with special attention to recent archaeological discoveries.

Behringer, Wolfgang, *A Cultural History of Climate*, Translated by Patrick Camiller (2010). A summary view of the place of climate in historical change, written by an expert in historical climatology.

Briant, Pierre, *From Cyrus to Alexander: A History of the Persian Empire*, trans. Peter T. Daniels (2002). A complex and comprehensive history of the Persian Empire by its finest modern scholar.

Bright, John, *A History of Israel,* 4th ed. (2000). An updated version of a classic and still very useful overview of the whole history of the Israelite people down to the end of the period covered in this chapter.

Cook, J. M., *The Persian Empire* (1983). An older but still useful, and highly readable, standard history of the Persian Empire.

Fagan, Brian, *The Long Summer: How Climate Changed Civilization* (2004). An accessible overview of the role of climate in historical change, written by one of the leading historians of ancient history and an individual who has brought together considerable evidence about climatic change and historical development.

Falkenhausen, Lothar von, *Chinese Society in the Age of Confucius (1000–250 BC): The Archaeological Evidence* (2006). A timely reassessment of early Chinese history that compares the literary texts on which it has traditionally been based to the new archaeological evidence.

Frye, Richard N., *The Heritage of Persia* (1963). This classic study of ancient Iran gives the political and literary history of the Persians and their successors.

Grayson, A. K., "Assyrian Civilization," in *Cambridge Ancient History,* vol. 3, pt. 2, pp. 194–228. The Assyrian and Babylonian empires and other states of the Near East, from the eighth to the sixth century BCE.

Hornung, Erik, *Akhenaten and the Religion of Light*, translated from the German by David Lorton (1999). An important, brief biography of Egypt's most controversial pharaoh.

———, *History of Ancient Egypt: An Introduction*, translated from the German by David Lorton (1999). An accessible overview of the history of ancient Egypt by a leading Egyptologist.

Isserlin, Benedikt J., *The Israelites* (1998). A very well-written and heavily illustrated history of all aspects of life in the regions of the Levant inhabited by the Israelites, equally good on the latest scholarship and the archaeological data.

Keay, John, *India: A History* (2010). A useful, readable overview of the sweep of Indian history.

Lancel, Serge, *Carthage: A History*, trans. Antonia Nevill (1997). By far the best single-volume history of the most important Phoenician colony in the Mediterranean (the first three chapters are especially relevant to materials covered in this chapter).

Lemche, Niels Peter, *Ancient Israel: A New History of Israelite Society* (1988). A quick, readable, and still up-to-date summary of the main phases and themes.

Lewis, Mark Edward, *Writing and Authority in Early China* (1999). A work that traces the changing uses of writing to command assent and obedience in early China.

Markoe, Glenn E., *Phoenicians* (2000). A thorough survey of the Phoenicians and their society as it first developed in the Levant and then expanded over the Mediterranean, with excellent illustrations of the diverse archaeological sites.

Matthews, Victor H., and Don C. Benjamin, *Social World of Ancient Israel, 1350–587 BCE* (1993). A thematic overview of the main occupational groups and social roles that characterized ancient Israelite society.

Oates, Joan, and David Oates, *Nimrud: An Assyrian Imperial City Revealed* (2001). A fine and highly readable summary of the state of our knowledge of the Assyrian Empire from the perspective of the early capital of Assurnasirpal II.

Oded, Bustenay, *Mass Deportations and Deportees in the Neo-Assyrian Empire* (1979). A detailed textual examination of the deportation strategy of the Assyrian kings. Good for in-depth research of the question.

Potts, D. T., *The Archaeology of Elam: Formation and Transformation of an Ancient Iranian State* (1999). The definitive study of the archaeology of western Iran from the Neolithic period through the Persian Empire.

Shaughnessy, Edward L., *Sources of Western Zhou History: Inscribed Bronze Vessels* (1992). Detailed work on the historiography and interpretation of the thousands of ritual bronze vessels discovered by China's archaeologists.

Stein, Burton, *A History of India*, Second Edition, edited by David Arnold (2010). One of the standard general histories of India, brought up-to-date by a leading historian of the subcontinent.

Tanner, Harold M., *China: A History* (2009). A readable and up-to-date overview of the sweep of Chinese history.

Thapar, Romila, *From Lineage to State* (1984). The only book on early India that uses religious literature historically and analyzes major lineages to reveal the transition from tribal society to state institutions.

Tignor, Robert L., *Egypt: A Short History* (2010). A succinct treatment of the entire history of Egypt from the pharaohs to the present, with three chapters on the ancient period.

Tubb, Jonathan N., *Canaanites* (1998). The best recent survey, well illustrated, of one of the main ethnic groups dominating the culture of the Levant.

CHAPTER 5

Adams, William Y., *Nubia: Corridor to Africa* (1977). The authoritative historical overview of Nubia, the area of present-day Sudan just south of Egypt and a geographical connecting point between the Mediterranean and sub-Saharan Africa.

Buddha (2001). A readable and impressive account of the life of the Buddha.

Aubet, Maria Eugenia, *The Phoenicians and the West,* 2nd ed. (2001). The basic survey of the Phoenician colonization of the western Mediterranean and Atlantic, with special attention to recent archaeological discoveries.

Barker, Graeme, and Tom Rasmussen, *The Etruscans* (1998). The most up-to-date introduction to this important pre-Roman society in the Italian peninsula, with strong emphasis on broad social and material patterns of development as indicated by the archaeological evidence.

Burkert, Walter, *Greek Religion*, trans. John Raffan (1985). The best one-volume introduction to early Greek religion, placing the Greeks in their larger Mediterranean and Near Eastern contexts.

Burns, Karen Olsen, *Ancient South America* (1994). A very useful overview of recent debates and conclusions about pre-Columbian archaeology in South America, including both the Andes and the lowland and coastal regions.

Cartledge, Paul (ed.), *The Cambridge Illustrated History of Ancient Greece* (2002). An excellent history of the Greek city-states down to the time of Alexander the Great.

Chakravarti, Uma, *The Social Dimensions of Early Buddhism* (1987). A description of the life of Buddha drawn from early Buddhist texts.

Cho-yun, Hsu, *Ancient China in Transition* (1965). An account of the political, economic, social, and intellectual changes that occurred during the Warring States period.

Coarelli, Filippo (ed.), *Etruscan Cities* (1975). A brilliantly and lavishly illustrated guide to the material remains of the Etruscans: their cities, their magnificent tombs, and their architecture, painting, sculpture, and other art.

Coe, Michael, et al. (eds.), *The Olmec World: Ritual and Rulership* (1996). A collection of field-synthesizing articles with important illustrations, based on one of the most comprehensive exhibitions of Olmec art in the world.

Confucius, *The Analects (Lun Yü)*, trans. D. C. Lau (1979). An outstanding translation of the words of Confucius as recorded by his major disciples. Includes valuable historical material needed to provide the context for Confucius's teachings.

Finley, M. I., and H. W. Pleket, *The Olympic Games: The First Thousand Years* (2005). A fine description of the most famous of the Greek games; it explains how they exemplify the competitive spirit that marked many aspects of the Greek city-states.

Garlan, Yvon, *Slavery in Ancient Greece*, trans. Janet Lloyd (1988). A treatment of the emergence, development, and institutionalization of chattel slavery in the Greek city-states.

———, *War in the Ancient World: A Social History*, trans. Janet Lloyd (1976). A discussion of the emergence of the forms of warfare, including male citizens fighting in hoplite phalanxes and the development of siege warfare, that were typical of the Greek city-states.

Iliffe, John, *Africans: The History of a Continent*, 2nd ed. (2007). A first-rate scholarly survey of Africa from its beginnings, with a strong emphasis on demography.

Kagan, Donald, *The Peloponnesian War* (2004). A vivid description of the war that pitted the major Greek city-states, including Athens and Sparta, against each other over the latter half of the fifth century BCE.

Lancel, Serge, *Carthage: A History*, trans. Antonia Nevill (1997). By far the best single-volume history of the most important Phoenician colony in the Mediterranean.

Lewis, Mark Edward, *Sanctioned Violence in Early China* (1990). An analysis of the use of sanctioned violence as an element of statecraft from the Warring States period to the formation of the Qin and Han empires in the second half of the first millennium BCE.

———, *Writing and Authority in Early China* (1999). A revisionist account of the central role of writing and persuasion in models for the invention of a Chinese world empire.

Ling, Trevor, *The Buddha: Buddhist Civilization in India and Ceylon* (1972). An overview of Buddhism in India and Ceylon.

Lloyd, G. E. R., *Early Greek Science: Thales to Aristotle* (1970). An especially clear and concise introduction to the main developments and intellectuals that marked the emergence of critical secular thinking in the early Greek world.

Lloyd, G. E. R., and Nathan Sivin, *The Way and the Word: Science and Medicine in Early China and Greece* (2002). A comprehensive rethinking of the social and political settings in ancient China and city-state Greece that contributed to the different views of science and medicine that emerged in each place.

Mote, Frederick, *Intellectual Foundations of China* (1971). An early but still useful description of the seminal figures in China's early intellectual life.

Murray, Oswyn, *Early Greece*, 2nd ed. (1993). One of the best introductions to the emergence of the Greek city-states down to the end of the archaic age.

Osborne, Robin, *Archaic and Classical Greek Art* (1998). An outstanding book that clearly explains the main innovations in Greek art, setting them in their historical context.

———, *Greece in the Making, 1200–479 BC* (1999). The standard history of the whole early period of the Greek city-states characterized by an especially fine and judicious mix of archaeological data and literary sources.

Pallottino, Massimo, *The Etruscans*, rev. ed., trans. J. Cremona (1975). A fairly traditional but still classic survey of all aspects of Etruscan history, political and social institutions.

Redford, Donald B., *From Slave to Pharaoh: The Black Experience of Ancient Egypt* (2004). A description of Egypt's twenty-fifth dynasty, which was made up of Sudanese conquerors.

Schaberg, David, *A Patterned Past: Form and Thought in Early Chinese Historiography* (2002). A comprehensive study of the intellectual content of historical anecdotes by the followers of Confucius collected around the fourth century BCE.

Schaps, David, *The Invention of Coinage and the Monetization of Ancient Greece* (2004). A new analysis that offers a broad overview of the emergence of coined money in the Near East and the eastern Mediterranean and its effects on the spread of money-based markets.

Sharma, J. P., *Republics in Ancient India, c. 1500 B.C.–500 B.C.* (1968). Relying on information from early Buddhist texts, this book first revealed that South Asia had not only monarchies but also alternative polities.

Shaw, Thurston, *Nigeria: Its Archaeology and Early History* (1978). An important introduction to the early history of Nigeria by one of that country's leading archaeologists.

Shinnie, P. L., *Ancient Nubia* (1996). An excellent account of the history of the ancient Nubians, who, we are discovering, had great influence on Egypt and on the rest of tropical Africa.

Snodgrass, Anthony, *Archaic Greece: The Age of Experiment* (1981). A good introduction to the archaeological evidence of archaic Greece.

Taylor, Christopher, Richard Hare, and Jonathan Barnes, *Greek Philosophers* (1999). A fine, succinct, one-volume introduction to the major aspects of the three big thinkers who dominated the high period of classical Greek philosophy: Socrates, Plato, and Aristotle.

Torok, Laszlo, *Meroe: Six Studies on the Cultural Identity of an Ancient African State* (1995). A good collection of essays on the most recent work on Meroe.

Von Falkenhausen, Lothar, *Chinese Society in the Age of Confucius (100–250 BC)* (2006). The larger Chinese society under the influence of Confucian thought.

Welsby, Derek, *The Kingdom of Kush: The Napatan and Meroitic Empires* (1996). A fine book on these two important Nubian kingdoms.

CHAPTER 6

Bradley, Keith, *Slavery and Rebellion in the Roman World, 140 B.C.–70 B.C.* (1989). A description of the rise of large-scale plantation slavery in Sicily and Italy, and a detailed account of the three great slave wars.

Browning, Iain, *Palmyra* (1979). A narrative of the history of the important desert city that linked eastern and western trade routes.

Casson, Lionel, *The Periplus Maris Erythraei* (1989). An introduction to a typical ancient sailing manual, this one of the Red Sea and Indian Ocean.

———, *Ships and Seamanship in the Ancient World* (1995). The classic account of the ships and sailors that powered commerce and war on the high seas.

Colledge, Malcolm, *The Art of Palmyra* (1976). A well-illustrated introduction to the unusual art of Palmyra with its mixture of eastern and western elements.

Fowler, Barbara H., *The Hellenistic Aesthetic* (1989). How the artists in this new age saw and portrayed their world in new and different ways.

Green, Peter, *Alexander to Actium: The Historical Evolution of the Hellenistic Age* (1990). The best general guide to the whole period in all of its various aspects, and well illustrated.

Habicht, Christian, *Athens from Alexander to Antony*, trans. Deborah L. Schneider (1997). The authoritative account of what happened to the great city-state of Athens in this period.

Holt, Frank L., *Thundering Zeus: The Making of Hellenistic Bactria* (1999). A basic history of the most eastern of the kingdoms spawned by the conquests of Alexander the Great.

Hopkirk, Peter, *Foreign Devils on the Silk Road* (1984). A historiography of the explorations and researches on the central Asian Silk Road of the nineteenth and early twentieth centuries.

Juliano, Annette L., and Judith A. Lerner (eds.), *Nomads, Traders and Holy Men Along China's Silk Road* (2003). A description of the travelers along the Silk Road in human terms, focusing on warfare, markets, and religion.

Lane Fox, Robin, *Alexander the Great* (1973). Still the most readable and in many ways the sanest biography of the world conqueror.

Lewis, Naphtali, *Greeks in Ptolemaic Egypt* (1986). An account of the relationships between Greeks and Egyptians as seen through the lives of individual Greek settlers and colonists.

Liu, Xinru, *Ancient India and Ancient China* (1988). The first work to connect political and economic developments in India and China with the evolution and spread of Buddhism in the first half of the first millennium.

———, *The Silk Road in World History* (2010). A study of the history of the great trade and communications route that connected the different regions of Afro-Eurasia between the third century BCE and the thirteenth century CE.

Long, Antony A., *Hellenistic Philosophy: Stoics, Epicureans, Sceptics*, 2nd ed. (1986). One of the clearest guides to the main new trends in Greek philosophical thinking in the period.

Martin, Luther H., *Hellenistic Religions: An Introduction* (1987). An introduction to the principal new Hellenistic religions and cults that emerged in this period.

Mendels, Doron, *The Rise and Fall of Jewish Nationalism* (1992). A sophisticated account of the various phases of Jewish resistance in Judah to foreign domination.

Miller, James Innes, *The Spice Trade of the Roman Empire, 29 B.C. to A.D. 641* (1969). A first-rate study of the spice trade in the Roman Empire.

Pomeroy, Sarah B., *Women in Hellenistic Egypt: From Alexander to Cleopatra* (1990). A highly readable investigation of women and family in the best-documented region of the Hellenistic world.

Ray, Himanshu P., *The Wind of Change, Buddhism and the Maritime Links of Early South Asia* (1994). Ray's study of Buddhism and maritime trade stretches from the Arabian Sea to the navigations between South Asia and Southeast Asia.

Rosenfield, John, *The Dynastic Art of the Kushans* (1967). Instead of focusing on the Gandharan Buddhist art itself, Rosenfield selects sculptures of Kushan royals and those representing nomadic populations in religious shrines to display the central Asian aspect of artworks of the period.

Rostovtzeff, Michael Ivanovich, *Caravan Cities*, trans. D. and T. Talbot Rice (1932). Though published more than seven decades ago, this small volume contains accurate descriptions of the ruins of many caravan cities in modern Jordan and Syria.

———, *The Social and Economic History of the Hellenistic World* (1941). A monumental achievement. One of the great works of history written in the twentieth century. An unsurpassed overview of all aspects of the politics and social and economic movements of the period. Despite its age, there is still nothing like it.

Schoff, Wilfred H. (ed. and trans.), *The Periplus of the Erythraean Sea* (1912). An invaluable tool for mapping the names and places from the Red Sea to Indian coastal areas during this period.

Shipley, Graham, *The Greek World after Alexander, 323–30 BC* (2000). A more up-to-date survey than Peter Green's work (above), with more emphasis on the historical detail in each period.

Tarn, W. W., *Greeks in Bactria and India* (1984). The most comprehensive coverage of Greek sources on Hellenistic states in Afghanistan and northwest India.

Thapar, Romila, *Ashoka and the Decline of the Mauryas* (1973). Using all available primary sources, including the edicts of Asoka and Greek authors' accounts, Thapar gives the most authoritative analysis of the first and the most important empire in Indian history.

Vainker, Shelagh, *Chinese Silk: A Cultural History* (2004). A work that traces the cultural history of silk in China from its early origins to the twentieth century and considers its relationship to the other decorative arts. The author draws on the most recent archaeological evidence to emphasize the role of silk in Chinese history, trade, religion, and literature.

Wood, Francis, *The Silk Road: Two Thousand Years in the Heart of Asia* (2004). Illustrated with drawings, manuscripts, paintings, and artifacts to trace the Silk Road to its origins as far back as Alexander the Great, with an emphasis on its importance to cultural and religious movements.

Young, Gary K., *Rome's Eastern Trade: International Commerce and Imperial Policy, 31 BC–AD 305* (2001). This study examines the taxation and profits of eastern trade from the perspective of the Roman government.

CHAPTER 7

Bodde, Derk, *China's First Unifier: A Study of the Ch'in Dynasty as Seen in the Life of Li Ssu (280?–208 B.C.)* (1938). A classic account of the key Legalist adviser, Li Si, who formulated the Qin policy to enhance its autocratic power.

Bowman, Alan K., *Life and Letters on the Roman Frontier: Vindolanda and Its Peoples* (1994). An introduction to the exciting discovery of writing tablets at a Roman army base in northern Britain.

Bradley, Keith, *Slavery and Society at Rome* (1994). The best single overview of the major aspects of the slave system in the Roman Empire.

Chevallier, Raymond, *Roman Roads,* trans. N. H. Field (1976). A guide to the fundamentals of the construction, maintenance, administration, and mapping of Roman roads.

Coarelli, Fillipo (ed.), *Pompeii,* trans. Patricia Cockram (2006). A lavishly illustrated large volume that allows the reader to sense some of the wondrous wealth of the buried city of Pompeii.

Colledge, Malcolm A. R., *The Parthians* (1967). A bit dated but still a fundamental introduction to the Parthians, the major power on the eastern frontier of the Roman Empire.

Cornell, Tim, *The Beginnings of Rome: Italy and Rome from the Bronze Age to the Punic Wars, c. 2000 to 264 B.C.* (1995). The single best one-volume history of Rome through its early history to the first war with Carthage.

Cornell, Tim, and John Matthews, *Atlas of the Roman World* (1982). A history of the Roman world; much more than simply an atlas. It is provided not only with good maps and a gazetteer but also with marvelous color illustrations and a text that guides the reader through the basics of Roman history.

Csikszentmihalyi, Mark, *Readings in Han Chinese Thought* (2006). A volume presenting a representative selection of primary sources to illustrate the growth of ideas in early imperial times; a useful introduction to the key strains of thought during this crucial period.

Dixon, Suzanne, *The Roman Family* (1992). The best one-volume guide to the nature of the Roman family and family relations.

Garnsey, Peter, and Richard Saller, *The Roman Empire: Economy, Society, and Culture* (1987). A perceptive and critical introduction to three basic aspects of social life in the empire.

Giardina, Andrea (ed.), *The Romans,* trans. Lydia Cochrane (1993). Individual studies of important typical figures in Roman society, from the peasant and the bandit to the merchant and the soldier.

Goldsworthy, Adrian, *The Roman Army at War: 100 B.C.–A.D. 200* (1996). A summary history and analysis of the Roman army in action during the late Republic and early Empire.

Goodman, Martin, *The Roman World: 44 B.C.–A.D. 180* (1997). A newer basic history text covering the high Roman Empire.

Harris, William, *Ancient Literacy* (1989). A basic survey of what is known about communication in the form of writing and books in the Roman Empire.

Hopkins, Keith, *Death and Renewal: Sociological Studies in Roman History,* vol. 2 (1983). Innovative studies in Roman history, including one of the best on gladiators and another on death and funerals.

———, *A World Full of Gods: Pagans, Jews and Christians in the Roman Empire* (1999). A somewhat unusual but interesting and provocative look at the world of religions in the Roman Empire.

Juliano, Annette L., and Judith A. Lerner (eds.), *Nomads, Traders and Holy Men along China's Silk Road* (2003). A description of the travelers along the Silk Road in human terms, focusing on warfare, markets, and religion.

Kern, Martin, and Michael Hunter (eds.), *The Analects. A Western Han Text?* (2013): Challenges the assumption that the Confucian *Analects* was compiled before the Han Dynasty.

Kraus, Theodore, and Leonard von Matt, *Pompeii and Herculaneum: The Living Cities of the Dead,* trans. Robert E. Wolf (1975). A huge, lavishly illustrated compendium of all aspects of life in the buried cities of Pompeii and Herculaneum as preserved in the archaeological record.

Loewe, Michael, *The Government of the Qin and Han Empires: 221 BCE–220 CE* (2006). A useful overview of the government of the early empires of China. Topics include the structure of central government, provincial and local government, the armed forces, officials, government communications, the laws of the empire, and control of the people and the land.

Millar, Fergus, *The Crowd in the Late Republic* (1998). An innovative study of the democratic power of the citizens in the city of Rome itself.

———, *The Emperor in the Roman World, 31 B.C.–A.D. 337* (1992). Everything you might want to know about the Roman emperor, with special emphasis on his civil role as the administrator of an empire.

Potter, David, *Roman Empire at Bay: A.D. 180–395* (2004). A new basic text covering the later Roman Empire, including the critical transition to a Christian state.

Potter, David S., and David J. Mattingly (eds.), *Life, Death, and Entertainment in the Roman Empire* (1999). A good introduction to basic aspects of Roman life in the empire, including the family, feeding the cities, religion, and popular entertainment.

Qian, Sima, *Records of the Grand Historian: Qin Dynasty,* trans. Burton Watson, 3rd ed. (1995). The classic work of Chinese history in a readable translation. The Han dynasty's Grand Historian describes the slow rise and meteoric fall of the Qin dynasty from the point of view of the succeeding dynasty, which Sima Qian witnessed or heard of during his lifetime.

Southern, Pat, *The Roman Army: A Social and Institutional History* (2006). A fundamental guide to all aspects of the Roman army.

Todd, Malcolm, *The Early Germans,* rev. ed. (2004). A basic survey of the peoples in central and western Europe at the time of the Roman Empire.

Vainker, Shelagh, *Chinese Silk: A Cultural History* (2004). A work that traces the cultural history of silk in China from its early origins to the twentieth century and considers its relationship to the other decorative arts. The author draws on the most recent archaeological evidence to emphasize the role of silk in Chinese history, trade, religion, and literature.

Wells, Peter S., *The Barbarians Speak: How the Conquered Peoples Shaped Roman Europe* (1999). The cultures of the peoples of central and northern Europe at the time of the Roman Empire and their impact on Roman culture.

Wood, Francis, *The Silk Road: Two Thousand Years in the Heart of Asia* (2004). A work illustrated with drawings, manuscripts, paintings, and artifacts to trace the Silk Road to its origins as far back as Alexander the Great. The author stresses the importance of the Silk Road to cultural and religious movements.

Woolf, Greg (ed.), *The Cambridge Illustrated History of the Roman World* (2005). A good guide to various aspects of Roman history, culture, and provincial life.

——, *Rome: An Empire's Story* (2012). An up-to-date narrative of the Roman empire told according to major themes that are particularly relevant to world history.

CHAPTER 8

Brown, Peter, *The Rise of Western Christendom: Triumph and Diversity, A.D. 200–1000*, 2nd ed. (2003). The rise and spread of Christianity in Europe and Asia, with up-to-date bibliographies on all topics, maps, and time charts.

——, *The World of Late Antiquity: From Marcus Aurelius to Muhammad, AD 150–750* (1989). A social, religious, and cultural history of the late Roman and Sasanian empires, with illustrations and a time chart.

Bühler, G. (trans.), *The Laws of Manu* (1886). The classic translation of one of India's most important historical, legal, and religious texts.

Coe, Michael D., *The Maya*, 6th ed. (1999). A work by the world's most famous Mayanologist, with recent evidence, analyses, and illustrations.

Cowgill, George L., "The Central Mexican Highlands and the Rise of Teotihuacan to the Decline of Tula," in Richard Adams and Murdo Macleod (eds.), *The Cambridge History of the Native Peoples of the Americas*, vol. 2, *Mesoamerica, Part 1* (2000). A thorough review of findings about urban states in central Mexico.

Fash, William L., *Scribes, Warriors and Kings: The City of Copan and the Ancient Maya* (2001). A fascinating and comprehensive study of one of the most elaborate of the Mayan city-kingdoms.

Fowden, Elizabeth Key, *The Barbarian Plain: Saint Sergius between Rome and Iran* (1999). The study of a major Christian shrine and its relations to Romans, Persians, and Arabs.

Fowden, Garth, *Empire to Commonwealth: The Consequences of Monotheism in Late Antiquity* (1993). A study of the relation between empire and world religions in western Asia.

Gombrich, Richard F., and Sheldon Pollack (eds.), *Clay Sanskrit Library* (2005–2006). All major works from the Gupta and post-Gupta periods, in both Sanskrit and English versions. During the Gupta period, classical Sanskrit literature reached its apex, with abundant drama, poetry, and folk stories.

Gordon, Charles, *The Age of Attila* (1960). The last century of the Roman Empire in western Europe, vividly illustrated from contemporary sources.

Harper, Prudence, *The Royal Hunter: The Art of the Sasanian Empire* (1978). The ideology of the Sasanian Empire as shown through excavated hoards of precious silverware.

Heather, Peter, *The Fall of the Roman Empire: A New History of Rome and the Barbarians* (2006). A military and political narrative based on up-to-date archaeological material.

Herrmann, Georgina, *Iranian Revival* (1977). The structure and horizons of the Sasanian Empire as revealed in its monuments.

Hillgarth, Jocelyn (ed.), *Christianity and Paganism, 350–750: The Conversion of Western Europe*, rev. ed. (1986). A collection of contemporary sources.

Holcombe, Charles, *In the Shadow of the Han: Literati Thought and Society at the Beginning of the Southern Dynasties* (1994). A clear and concise account of the evolution of thought in China after the fall of the Han dynasty in 220 CE. The book presents the rise of Buddhism and Daoism as popular religions as well as elite interests in classical learning in a time of political division and barbarian conquest in North and South China.

La Vaissière, Étienne de, *Sogdian Traders: A History*, trans. James Ward (2005). A summary of historical facts about the most important trading community and its commercial networks on the Silk Road, from the early centuries CE to its demise in the ninth century CE.

Little, Lester (ed.), *Plague and the End of Antiquity: The Pandemic of 541–750* (2008). A series of debates over the nature and impact of the first great pandemic attested in global history.

Liu, Xinru, and Lynda Norene Shaffer, *Connections across Eurasia: Transportation, Communication, and Cultural Exchanges on the Silk Roads* (2007). A survey of trade and religious activities on the Silk Road.

Maas, Michael, *Readings in Late Antiquity: A Source Book* (1999). Well-chosen extracts that illustrate the interrelation of Romans and non-Romans, and of Christians, Jews, and pagans.

Maas, Michael (ed.), *The Cambridge Companion to the Age of Justinian* (2005). A survey of all aspects of the eastern Roman Empire in the sixth century CE.

Moffett, Samuel, *A History of Christianity in Asia*, vol. 1 (1993). Particularly valuable on Christians in China and India.

Munro-Hay, Stuart, *Aksum: An African Civilization of Late Antiquity* (1991). The origins of the Christian kingdom of Ethiopia.

Murdock, George P., *Africa: Its Peoples and Their History* (1959). A vital introduction to the peoples of Africa and their history.

Oliver, Roland, *The African Experience: From Olduvai Gorge to the Twenty-First Century* (1999). An important overview, written by one of the pioneering scholars of African history and one of the leading authorities on the Bantu migrations.

Postclassical World (1999). Essays and items for the entire period 150–750 CE. The volume covers the Roman, East Roman, Sasanian, and early Islamic worlds.

Pregadio, Fabrizio, *Great Clarity: Daoism and Alchemy in Early Medieval China* (2006). An examination of the religious aspects of Daoism. The book focuses on the relation of alchemy to the Daoist traditions of the third to sixth centuries CE and shows how alchemy was integrated into the elaborate body of doctrines and practices of Daoists at that time.

Tempels, Placide, *Bantu Philosophy* (1959). A highly influential effort to argue for the underlying cultural unity of all the Bantu peoples.

Vansina, Jan, *Paths in the Rainforests: Toward a History of Political Tradition in Equatorial Africa* (1990). The best work on Bantu history.

Walker, Joel, *The Legend of Mar Kardagh: Narrative and Christian Heroism in Late Antique Iraq* (2006). Christians and Zoroastrians in northern Iraq and in Iran.

Yarshater, Ehsan, *Encyclopedia Iranica* (1982–). A guide to all aspects of the Sasanian Empire and to religion and culture in the regions between Mesopotamia and central Asia.

Xuanzang, *Faxianzhuan Jiaoxhu*. Text excerpt translated by Xinru Liu.

Zürcher, E., *The Buddhist Conquest of China: The Spread and Adaptation of Buddhism in Early Medieval China*, 3rd ed. (2007). A reissue of the classic account of the assimilation of Buddhism in China during the medieval period, with particular focus on the religious and philosophical success of Buddhism among Chinese elites in South China.

CHAPTER 9

Ahmed, Leila, *Women and Gender in Islam* (1992). A superb overview of the relations between men and women throughout the history of Islam.

Aneirin, *Y Gododdin: Britain's Oldest Heroic Poem,* ed. and trans. A. O. H. Jarman (1988). A sixth-century Welsh text that describes the battle of the last Britons against the invading Anglo-Saxons.

Arberry, Arthur J., introduction to *The Koran Interpreted: A Translation,* trans. Arthur J. Arberry (1986). One of the most eloquent appreciations of this classical work of religion.

Augustine, *The City of God,* trans. H. Bettenson (1976). An excellent translation of Augustine's monumental work of history, philosophy, and religion.

Berkey, Jonathan P., *The Formation of Islam: Religion and Society in the Near East, 600–1800* (2005). A recent overview of the history of Islam before the modern era. It is particularly sensitive to the influence of external elements on the history of the Muslim peoples.

Bol, Peter, *This Culture of Ours: Intellectual Transitions in T'ang and Sung China* (1994). A study tracing the transformation of the shared culture of the Chinese learned elite from the seventh to the twelfth centuries.

Brown, Peter, *The Rise of Western Christendom: Triumph and Diversity, ad 200–1000,* 2nd ed. (2003). A description of the changes in Christianity in northern Europe and the emergence of the new cultures and political structures that coincided with this development.

Bulliet, Richard W., *Conversion to Islam in the Medieval Period: An Essay in Quantitative History* (1979). A study of the rate at which the populations overrun by Arab conquerors in the seventh century ce embraced the religion of their rulers.

Cook, Michael, *The Koran: A Very Short Introduction* (2000). A useful overview of Islam's holy book.

_____, *Muhammad* (1983). A brief but careful life of the Prophet that takes full account of the prolific and often controversial preexisting scholarship.

Creswell, K. A. C., *A Short Account of Early Muslim Architecture, Revised and supplemented by James W. Allan* (1992). The definitive treatment of the subject, brought up to date.

Cross, S. H., and O. P. Sherbowitz-Westor, trans., *The Russian Primary Chronicle* (1953). A vivid record of the Viking settlement of Kiev, of the conversion of Kiev, and of the princes of Kiev in the tenth and eleventh centuries.

Donner, Fred M., *The Early Islamic Conquests* (1981). The best account of the Arab conquests in the Persian and Byzantine empires in the seventh century.

Duncan, John, *The Origins of the Chosŏn Dynasty* (2000). A historical account of the early Korean dynasties from 900 to 1400.

Elman, Benjamin, *Precocious China: Civil Examinations, 1400–1900* (2013). Summary of civil exams in China from medieval times.

Fage, J. D., *Ghana: A Historical Introduction* (1966). A brief but authoritative history of Ghana from earliest times to the present.

Fisher, Humphrey J., *Slavery in the History of Muslim Black Africa* (2001). A general history of the relations between North Africa and black Africa, focusing on one of the most important aspects of contact—the slave trade.

Graham-Campbell, James, *Cultural Atlas of the Viking World* (1994). A positioning of the Vikings against their wider background in both western and eastern Europe.

Hawting, G. R., *The First Dynasty of Islam: The Umayyad Caliphate, A.D. 661–750* (2000). The essential scholarly treatment of Islam's first dynasty.

Herrmann, Georgina, *Iranian Revival* (1977). The structure and horizons of the Sasanian Empire as revealed in its monuments.

Hillgarth, J. N. (ed.), *Christianity and Paganism, 350–750: The Conversion of Western Europe,* rev. ed. (1986). A collection of contemporary sources.

Hodges, Richard, and David Whitehouse, *Mohammed, Charlemagne, and the Origins of Europe* (1983). A spirited comparison of Islam and the rise of Europe.

Hodgson, Marshall G. S., *The Venture of Islam: Conscience and History in a World Civilization* (1977), 3 vols. A magnificent history of the Islamic peoples. Its first volume, *The Classical Age of Islam,* is basic reading for anyone interested in the history of the Muslim world.

Holdsworth, May, *Women of the Tang Dynasty* (1999). An account of women's lives during the Tang dynasty.

Hourani, Albert, *History of the Arab Peoples* (2002). The best overview of Arab history.

Jones, Gwynn, *The Norse Atlantic Saga* (1986). The Viking discovery of America.

Kennedy, Hugh, *The Prophet and the Age of the Caliphate: The Islamic Near East from the Sixth to the Eleventh Century* (2004). A very good recent synthesis of the rise and spread of Islam.

Lee, Peter, et al. (eds.), *Sources of Korean Tradition,* vol. 1 (1996). A unique view of Korean history through the eyes and words of the participants or witnesses themselves, as provided in translations of official documents, letters, and policies.

Levtzion, Nehemia, *Ancient Ghana and Mali* (1980). The best introduction to the kingdoms of West Africa.

Levtzion, Nehemia, and Jay Spaulding, *Medieval West Africa: Views from Arab Scholars and Merchants* (2003). An indispensable source book on early West African history.

Lewis, Bernard, *The Middle East: Two Thousand Years of History from the Rise of Christianity to the Present Day* (1995). A stimulating introduction to an area that has seen the emergence of three of the great world religions.

_____ (trans.), *Islam from the Prophet Muhammad to the Capture of Constantinople* (1974). Vol. 2: Religion and Society. A fine collection of original sources that portray various aspects of classical Islamic society.

Lewis, David Levering, *God's Crucible: Islam and the Making of Europe, 570–1215* (2008). An exciting and well-written overview of the high period of Islamic power and cultural attainments.

Middleton, John, *The Swahili: The Social Landscape of a Mercantile Community* (2000). An exciting synthesis of the Swahili culture of East Africa.

Miyazaki, Ichisada, *China's Examination Hell* (1981). A study of China's examination system.

Nurse, Derek, and Thomas Spear, *The Swahili: Reconstructing the History and Language of an African Society, 800–1500* (1984). A work that explores the history of the Muslim peoples who lived along the coast of East Africa.

Peters, F. E., *Muhammad and the Origins of Islam* (1994). A work that explores the early history of Islam and highlights the critical role that Muhammad played in promoting a new religion and a powerful Arab identity.

Poursharíati, Parveneh, *Decline and Fall of the Sasanian Empire* (2008). Fundamental analysis of the end of the Sasanian empire and the reasons for the success of the Arab/Muslim invasions.

Robinson, Chase F., *The Formation of the Islamic World, Sixth to Eleventh Centuries*, vol. 1 in *The New Cambridge History of Islam* (2010). An authoritative and up-to-date six-volume overview of the history of Islam from the sixth century to the present.

Schirokauer, Conrad, et al., *A Brief History of Japanese Civilization*, 2nd ed. (2005). A balanced account; chapters focus on developments in art, religion, literature, and thought as well as on Japan's economic, political, and social history in medieval times.

Smith, Julia, *Europe after Rome: A New Cultural History, 500–1000* (2005). A vivid analysis of society and culture in so-called Dark Age Europe.

Totman, Conrad, *History of Japan* (2004). A recent and readable summary of Japanese history from ancient to modern times.

Twitchett, Denis, *The Birth of the Chinese Meritocracy: Bureaucrats and Examinations in T'ang China* (1976). A description of the role of the written civil examinations that began during the Tang dynasty.

———, *Financial Administration under the T'ang Dynasty* (1970). A pioneering account—based on rare Dunhuang documents that survived from medieval times in Buddhist grottoes in central Asia—of the political and economic system undergirding the Chinese imperial state.

Whittow, Mark, *The Making of Byzantium, 600–1025* (1996). A study on the survival and revival of the eastern Roman empire as a major power in eastern Europe and Southwest Asia.

Wood, Ian, *The Missionary Life: Saints and the Evangelization of Europe, 400–1050* (2001). The horizons of Christians on the frontiers of Europe.

CHAPTER 10

Allsen, Thomas, *Commodity and Exchange in the Mongol Empire: A Cultural History of Islamic Textiles* (1997). A study that uses golden brocade, the textile most treasured by Mongol rulers, as a lens through which to analyze the vast commercial networks facilitated by the Mongol conquests and control.

———, *Culture and Conquest in Mongol Eurasia* (2001). A work that emphasizes the cultural and scientific exchanges that took place across Afro-Eurasia as a result of the Mongol conquest.Bartlett, Robert, *The Making of Europe: Conquest, Colonization and Cultural Change, 950–1350* (1993). The modes of cultural, political, and demographic expansion of feudal Europe along its frontiers, especially in eastern Europe.

Bay, Edna G., *Wives of the Leopards: Gender, Politics, and Culture in the Kingdom of Dahomey* (1998). A work that stresses the role of women in an important West African society and dips into the early history of this area.

Beach, D. N., *Shona and Zimbabwe, 900–1850: An Outline of Shona History* (1980). A good place to start for exploring the history of Great Zimbabwe.

Brooks, George E., *Landlords and Strangers: Ecology, Society, and Trade in Western Africa, 1000–1630* (1993). A survey assembled from primary sources of early West African history that stresses transregional connections.

Buzurg ibn Shahriyar of Ramhormuz, *The Book of the Wonders of India: Mainland, Sea and Islands*, ed. and trans. G. S. P. Freeman-Greenville (1981). A collection of stories told by sailors, both true and fantastic; they help us imagine the lives of sailors of the era.

Chappell, Sally A. Kitt, *Cahokia: Mirror of the Cosmos* (2002). A thorough and vivid account of the "mound people"; it explores not just what we know of Cahokia but how we know it.

Christian, David, *A Short History of Russia, Central Asia, and Mongolia*, vol. 1, *Inner Eurasia from Prehistory to the Mongol Empire* (1998). Essential reading for students interested in interconnections across the Afro-Eurasian landmass.

Curtin, Philip, *Cross-Cultural Trade in World History* (1984). A groundbreaking book on intercultural trade with a primary focus on Africa, especially the cross-Saharan trade and Swahili coastal trade.

Dawson, Christopher, *Mission to Asia* (1980). Accounts of China and the Mongol Empire brought back by Catholic missionaries and diplomats after 1240 CE.

Foltz, Richard C., *Religions of the Silk Road: Overland Trade and Cultural Exchange from Antiquity to the Fifteenth Century* (1999). A study of the populations and the cities of the Silk Road as transmitters of culture across long distances.

Franklin, Simon, and Jonathan Shepherd, *The Emergence of Rus: 750–1200* (1996). The formation of medieval Russia between the Baltic and Black seas.

Gibb, Hamilton A. R., *Saladin: Studies in Islamic History*, ed. Yusuf Ibish (1974). A sympathetic portrait of one of Islam's leading political and military figures.

Goitein, S. D., *Letters of Medieval Jewish Traders* (1973). The classic study of medieval Jewish trading communities based on the commercial papers deposited in the Cairo Geniza (a synagogue storeroom) during the tenth and eleventh centuries; it explores not only commercial activities but also the personal lives of the traders around the Indian Ocean basin.

———, *A Mediterranean Society: An Abridgment in One Volume*, rev. and ed. Jacob Lassner (1999). A portrait of the Jewish merchant community with ties across the Afro-Eurasian landmass, based largely on the documents from the Cairo Geniza (of which Goitein was the primary researcher and interpreter).

———, "New Light on the Beginnings of the Karim Merchant," *Journal of Social and Economic History of the Orient* 1 (1958). Goitein's description of Egyptian trade.

Harris, Joseph E., *The African Presence in Asia: Consequences of the East African Slave Trade* (1971). One of the few books that looks broadly at the impact of Africans and African slavery on the societies of Asia.

Hartwell, Robert, "Demographic, Political, and Social Transformations of China, 750–1550," *Harvard Journal of Asiatic Studies* 42 (1982): 365–442. A pioneering study of the demographic changes that overtook China during the Tang and Song dynasties, which are described in light of political reform movements and social changes in this crucial era.

Historical Relations across the Indian Ocean: Report and Papers of the Meeting of Experts Organized by UNESCO at Port Louis, Mauritius, from 15 to 19 July, 1974 (1980). Excellent essays on the connections of Africa with Asia across the Indian Ocean.

Hitti, Philip, *An Arab-Syrian Gentleman and Warrior in the Period of the Crusades: Memoirs of* Usāmah *ibn-Munqidh* (1929). The Crusaders seen through Muslim eyes.

Hodgson, Natasha, *Women, Crusading, and the Holy Land in Historical Narrative* (2007). A book dealing with the Crusades and focusing on the place of women in them.

Holt, P. M., *The Age of the Crusades: The Near East from the Eleventh Century to 1517* (1984). The Crusades period as seen from the eastern Mediterranean and through the lens of a leading British scholar of the area.

Hymes, Robert, and Conrad Schirokauer (eds.), *Ordering the World: Approaches to State and Society in Sung Dynasty China* (1993). A collection of essays that traces the intellectual, social, and political movements that shaped the Song state and its elites.

Ibn Battuta, *The Travels of Ibn Battuta,* trans. H. A. R. Gibb (2002). A readable translation of the classic book, originally published in 1929.

Ibn Fadlan, Ahmad, *Ibn Fadlan's Journey to Russia: A Tenth Century Traveler from Baghdad to the Volga River,* trans. with commentary by Richard Frye (2005). A coherent summary of the observations of an envoy who traveled from Baghdad to Russia.

Irwin, Robert, *The Middle East in the Middle Ages: The Early Mamluk Sultanate, 1250–1582* (1986). Egypt under Mamluk rule.

Jeppie, Shamil, and Diagne, Souleymane Bachir, editors, *The Meanings of Timbuktu* (2008). New materials on the ancient Muslim city of Timbuktu by scholars who have been preserving its manuscripts and writing about its historical importance.

Lancaster, Lewis, Kikun Suh, and Chai-shin Yu (eds.), *Buddhism in Koryo: A Royal Religion* (1996). A description of Buddhism at its height in the Koryo period, when the religion made significant contributions to the development of Korean culture.

Levtzion, Nehemia, and Randall L. Pouwels (eds.), *The History of Islam in Africa* (2000). A useful general survey of the place of Islam in African history.

Lewis, Bernard (trans.), *Islam: From the Prophet Muhammad to the Capture of Constantinople* (1974). Vol. 2: *Religion and Society.* A fine collection of original sources that portray various aspects of classical Islamic society.

Lopez, Robert S., *The Commercial Revolution of the Middle Ages, 950–1350* (1976). An account focusing on the development around the Mediterranean of commercial practices such as the use of currency, accounting, and credit.

Lyons, Malcolm C. & D. E. P. Jackson, *Saladin: The Politics of the Holy War,* Cambridge (1984: reprint 2001). The fundamental revisionist work on one of the more important historical figures of the time.

Maalouf, Amin, *The Crusades through Muslim Eyes,* trans. Jon Rothschild (1984). The European Crusaders as seen by the Muslim world.

Marcus, Harold G., *A History of Ethiopia* (2002). An authoritative overview of the history of this great culture.

Mass, Jeffrey, *Yoritomo and the Founding of the First Bakufu: The Origins of Dual Government in Japan* (1999). A revisionist account of how the Kamakura military leader Minamoto Yoritomo established the "dual polity" of court and warrior government in Japan.

McDermott, Joseph, *A Social History of the Chinese Book: Books and Literati Culture in Late Imperial China* (2006). The history of the book in China since the Song dynasty, with comparisons to the book's role in other civilizations, particularly the European.

McIntosh, Roderik, *The Peoples of the Middle Niger: The Island of Gold* (1988). A historical survey of an area often omitted from other textbooks.

Moore, Jerry D., *Cultural Landscapes in the Ancient Andes: Archaeologies of Place* (2005). The most recent and up-to-date analysis of findings based on recent archaeological evidence, emphasizing the importance of local cultures and diversity in the Andes.

Niane, D. T. (ed.), *Africa from the Twelfth to the Sixteenth Century,* vol. 4 of *General History of Africa* (1984). The general UNESCO history of Africa's volume on four centuries of African history. This work features the scholarship of Africans.

Oliver, Roland (ed.), *From c. 1050 to c. 1600,* vol. 3 of *The Cambridge History of Africa,* ed. J. D. Fage and Roland Oliver (1977). Another general survey of African history. This volume draws heavily on the work of British scholars.

Peters, Edward, *The First Crusade* (1971). The Crusaders as seen through their own eyes.

Petry, Carl F. (ed.), *Islamic Egypt, 640–1517,* vol. 1 of *The Cambridge History of Egypt,* ed. M. W. Daly (1998). A solid overview of the history of Islamic Egypt up to the Ottoman conquest.

Polo, Marco, *The Travels of Marco Polo,* ed. Manuel Komroff (1926). A solid translation of Marco Polo's famous account.

Popovic, Alexandre, *The Revolt of African Slaves in Iraq in the 3rd/9th Century,* trans. Leon King (1999). The account of a massive revolt against their slave masters by African slaves taken to labor in Iraq's mines and fields.

Scott, Robert, *Gothic Enterprise: A Guide to Understanding the Medieval Cathedral* (2003). The meaning and social function of religious building in medieval cities in northern Europe.

Shaffer, Lynda Norene, *Maritime Southeast Asia to 1500* (1996). A history of the peoples of the southeast fringe of the Eastern Hemisphere, up to the time that they became connected to the global commercial networks of the world.

Shimada, Izumi, "Evolution of Andean Diversity: Regional Formations (500 BCE–CE 600)," in Frank Salomon and Stuart Schwartz (eds.), *South America,* vol. 3 of *The Cambridge History of the Native Peoples of the Americas* (1999), part 1, pp. 350–517. A splendid overview that contrasts the varieties of lowland and highland cultures.

Steinberg, David Joel, et al., *In Search of Southeast Asia: A Modern History* (1987). An account of the emergence of the modern Southeast Asian polities of Cambodia, Burma, Thailand, and Indonesia.

Tyerman, Christopher, *God's War: A New History of the Crusades* (2006). The balance of religious and nonreligious motivations in the Crusades.

Waley, Daniel, *The Italian City-Republics,* 3rd ed. (1988). The structures and culture of the new cities of medieval Italy.

Watson, Andrew, *Agricultural Innovation in the Early Islamic World: The Diffusion of Crops and Farming Techniques, 700–1100* (1983). An impressive study of the spread of new crops throughout the Muslim world.

CHAPTER 11

Bois, Guy, *The Crisis of Feudalism: Economy and Society in Eastern Normandy, c. 1300–1550* (1984). A good case study of a French region that illustrates the turmoil in fourteenth-century Europe.

Brook, Timothy, *Praying for Power: Buddhism and the Formation of Gentry Society in Late Ming China* (1994). An analysis of the role of a significant religious force in the political and social developments of the Ming.

Dardess, John, *A Ming Society: T'ai-ho County, Kiangsi, Fourteenth to Seventeenth Centuries* (1996). A work that covers the different changes and developments of a single locality in China through the centuries.

Dols, Michael W., *The Black Death in the Middle East* (1977). One of the few scholarly works to examine the Black Death outside Europe.

Dreyer, Edward, *Early Ming China: A Political History, 1355–1435* (1982). A useful account of the early years of the Ming dynasty.

Finkel, Caroline, *Osman's Dream: The Story of the Ottoman Empire, 1300–1923* (2005). The most authoritative overview of Ottoman history.

Hale, John, *The Civilization of Europe in the Renaissance* (1994). A beautifully crafted account of the politics, economics, and culture of the Renaissance period in western Europe.

Hodgson, Marshall, *The Venture of Islam: Conscience and History in a World Civilization*, vol. 3 (1974). A good volume on the workings of the Ottoman state.

Itzkowitz, Norman, *Ottoman Empire and Islamic Tradition* (1972). Another good book on the Ottoman state.

Jackson, Peter, *The Delhi Sultanate* (1999). A meticulous, highly specialized, political and military history.

Jackson, Peter, and Lawrence Lockhart (eds.), *The Cambridge History of Iran*, vol. 6 (1986). A volume that deals with the Timurid and Safavid periods in Iran.

Jones, E. L., *The European Miracle* (1981). A provocative work on the economic and social recovery from the Black Death.

Kafadar, Cemal, *Between Two Worlds: The Construction of the Ottoman State* (1995). A thorough reconsideration of the origins of one of the world's great land empires.

Karamustafa, Ahmed, *God's Unruly Friends: Dervish Groups in the Islamic Later Middle Period, 1200–1550* (1994). A book that describes the unorthodox Islamic activities that were occurring in the Islamic world prior to and alongside the establishment of the Ottoman and Safavid empires.

Levathes, Louise, *When China Ruled the Seas: The Treasure Fleet of the Dragon Throne, 1405–33* (1994). A book that provides a lively account of the Zheng He expeditions.

Lowry, Heath W., *The Nature of the Early Ottoman State* (2003). New perspectives on the rise of the Ottomans to prominence.

McNeill, William, *Plagues and Peoples* (1976). A pathbreaking work with a highly useful chapter on the spread of the Black Death throughout the Afro-Eurasian landmass.

Morgan, David, *Medieval Persia, 1040–1797* (1988). Contains an informative discussion of the Safavid state.

Peirce, Leslie, *The Imperial Harem: Women and Sovereignty in the Ottoman Empire* (1993). A work that describes the powerful place that imperial women had in political affairs.

Pirenne, Henri, *Economic and Social History of Medieval Europe* (1937). A classic study of the economic and social recovery from the Black Death.

Reid, James J., *Tribalism and Society in Islamic Iran, 1500–1629* (1983). A useful account of how the Mongols and other nomadic steppe peoples influenced Iran in the era when the Safavids were establishing their authority.

Singman, Jeffrey L. (ed.), *Daily Life in Medieval Europe* (1999). An introductory description of the social and material world experienced by Europeans of different walks of life.

Tuchman, Barbara W., *A Distant Mirror: The Calamitous Fourteenth Century* (1978). A book that shows, in a vigorous way, how war, famine, and pestilence devastated Europeans in the fourteenth century.

Wittek, Paul, *The Rise of the Ottoman Empire* (1958). A work that contains vital insights on the emergence of the Ottoman state amid the political chaos in Anatolia.

CHAPTER 12

Axtell, James, *Beyond 1492: Encounters in Colonial North America* (1992). A wonderfully informed speculation about Indian reactions to Europeans.

Brady, Thomas A., et al. (eds.), *Handbook of European History 1400–1600: Late Middle Ages, Renaissance, and Reformation, Structures and Assertions* (1996). A good synthetic survey of recent literature and historiographical debates.

Brook, Timothy, *Vermeer's Hat: The Seventeenth Century and the Dawn of the Global World* (2008). An interesting look at the connections forged across the globe through the works of a well-known European artist.

Cass, Victoria, *Dangerous Women: Warriors, Grannies, and Geishas of the Ming* (1999). An original study of Chinese female archetypes in memoirs, miscellanies, short stories, and novels.

Chaudhuri, K. N., *Trade and Civilisation in the Indian Ocean: An Economic History from the Rise of Islam to 1750* (1985). An excellent, comprehensive work that deals with the Indian Ocean economy and the appearance of European merchants there from the sixteenth century onward.

Clendinnen, Inga, *Aztecs: An Interpretation* (1991). Brilliantly reconstructs the culture of Tenochtitlán in the years before its conquest.

Crosby, Alfred W., *The Columbian Exchange: Biological and Cultural Consequences of 1492* (1972). A provocative discussion of the ecological consequences that followed the European "discovery" of the Americas.

———, *Ecological Imperialism: The Biological Expansion of Europe, 900–1900* (1986). Another important work on the ecological consequences of European expansion.

Curtin, Philip, *Cross-Cultural Trade in World History* (1984). A work stressing the role of trade and commerce in establishing cross-cultural contacts.

Febvre, Lucien, *The Problem of Unbelief in the Sixteenth Century: The Religion of Rabelais* (1982). A tour de force of intellectual history by the man who moved the study of the Reformation away from great men to the broader question of religious revival and mentalities.

Flynn, Dennis, and Arturo Giráldez (eds.), *Metals and Monies in an Emerging Global Economy* (1997). Contains several articles relating to silver and the Asian trade.

Frank, Andre Gunder, *ReOrient: Global Economy in the Asian Age* (1998). A reassessment of the role of Asia in the economic development of the world from around 1400 onward.

Gruzinski, Serge, *The Conquest of Mexico* (1993). An important work on the conquest of Mexico.

Habib, Irfan, *The Agrarian System of Mughal India* (1963). One of the best studies on the subject.

Hall, Richard Seymour, *Empires of the Monsoon: A History of the Indian Ocean and*

Its Invaders (1996). A very engaging journalistic account with fabulous details.

Hodgson, Marshall, *The Venture of Islam*, vols. 2 and 3 (1974). A magisterial work that includes the Indian subcontinent in its careful study of the political and cultural history of the whole Islamic world.

Hulme, Peter, *Colonial Encounters: Europe and the Native Caribbean, 1492–1797* (1986). Presents an interesting interpretation of the encounters of Europeans and Native Americans.

Lach, Donald F., *Asia in the Making of Europe*, 5 books in 3 vols. (1965–). Perhaps the single most comprehensive and innovative guide to the European voyages of discovery.

Lockhart, James, and Stuart Schwartz, *Early Latin America* (1983). One of the finest studies of European expansion in the late fifteenth century.

McCann, James, *Maize and Grace: Africa's Encounter with a New World Crop, 1500–2000* (Cambridge, MA, 2005).

Melville, Elinor G. K., *A Plague of Sheep: Environmental Consequences of the Conquest of Mexico* (1994). A history of the transformation of a valley in Mexico from the Aztec period to the era of Spanish rule.

Mignolo, Walter D., *The Darker Side of the Renaissance: Literacy, Territoriality, and Colonization* (1995). Uses literary theory and literary images to present provocative interpretations of the encounter of Europeans and Native Americans.

Pagden, Anthony, *European Encounters with the New World* (1993). A complex look at the deep and lasting imprint of the New World on its conquerors.

Parker, Geoffrey, *The Military Revolution: Military Innovation and the Rise of the West, 1500–1800* (1996). Traces the changes in technology and tactics in the early modern period and discusses the political significance of this "revolution."

Pelikan, Jaroslav, *Reformation of Church and Dogma (1300–1700)* (1988). An important overview of major religious controversies.

Phillips, William D., and Carla Rahn Phillips, *The World of Christopher Columbus* (1992). One of the finest studies of European expansion in the late fifteenth century.

Russell-Wood, A. J. R., *The Portuguese Empire, 1415–1808* (1992). An important survey of early Portuguese exploration.

Von Glahn, Richard, *Fountain of Fortune: Money and Monetary Policy in China, 1000–1700* (1996). Includes an excellent analysis of the history of silver in Ming China.

CHAPTER 13

Alam, Muzaffar, *The Crisis of Empire in Mughal North India* (1993). Represents the best of the new scholarly interpretations on the subject.

Bay, Edna, *Wives of the Leopard: Gender, Politics, and Culture in the Kingdom of Dahomey* (1998). A useful treatment of gender issues in Dahomey.

Blackburn, Robin, *The Making of New World Slavery: From the Baroque to the Modern, 1492–1800* (1997). A good place to begin when studying African slavery and the Atlantic slave trade, it compares the early expansion of the plantation systems across the Atlantic and throughout the Americas.

Calloway, Colin G., *One Vast Winter Count: The Native American West before Lewis and Clark* (2003). A sweeping survey of North American Indian histories prior to the nineteenth century.

Crossley, Pamela, *A Translucent Mirror: History and Identity in Qing Imperial Ideology* (1999). The author deals with the formation of identities such as "Manchu" and "Chinese" during the Qing period.

Eltis, David and Richardson, David, *Atlas of the Transatlantic Slave Trade* (New Haven, 2010). This work contains the most up-to-date data on the Atlantic slave trade, the numbers transported, where the captives came from, and where they landed.

Flynn, Dennis O., and Arturo Giraldez (eds.), *Metals and Money in an Emerging World Economy* (1997). A collection of articles about the place of silver in the world economy.

Forsyth, James, *A History of the Peoples of Siberia: Russia's North Asian Colony 1581–1990* (1992). A narrative overview of a violent history reminiscent of the western expansion of the United States.

Glahn, Richard von, *Fountains of Fortune: Money and Monetary Policy in China, 1000–1700* (1996). A discussion of the place of silver in the Chinese economy.

Halperin, Charles J., *Russia and the Golden Horde: The Mongol Impact on Medieval Russian History* (1985). A book on the rise of Muscovy, forebear of the Russian Empire, from within the Mongol realm.

Hämäläinen, Pekka, *The Comanche Empire* (2008). A book that inverts the conventional history of empires in North America by arguing that the Comanches were the most successful expansionist power in the middle of the continent during the eighteenth century.

Hattox, Ralph S., *Coffee and Coffeehouses: The Origins of a Social Beverage in the Medieval Near East* (1985). This work shows how widespread and popular coffee consumption and coffeehouses were around the world.

Huang, Ray, *1587, A Year of No Significance: The Ming Dynasty in Decline* (1981). An insightful analysis of the problems confronting the late Ming.

Lensen, George, *The Russian Push Toward Japan: Russo-Japanese Relations 1697–1875* (1959). A discussion of why and how Japan established its first border with another state and how Russia pursued its ambitions in the Pacific.

Lockhart, James, *The Nahuas After the Conquest* (1992). A landmark study of the social reorganization of Mesoamerican societies under Spanish rule.

Lovejoy, Paul, *Transformations in Slavery: A History of Slavery in Africa* (1983). An excellent discussion of African slavery.

Nakane, Chie, and Shinzaburo Oishi (eds.), *Tokugawa Japan: The Social and Economic Antecedents of Modern Japan* (1990). First-rate essays on Japanese village society, urban life, literacy, and culture.

Pamuk, Sevket, *A Monetary History of the Ottoman Empire* (2000). A discussion of the place of silver in the Ottoman Empire.

Parker, Geoffrey (ed.), *The Thirty Years' War* (1997). The standard account of the conflict and its outcomes.

Perdue, Peter C., *China Marches West: The Qing Conquest of Central Asia* (2005). This volume chronicles the expansion of the Qing Empire to its northwest, drawing comparisons to other colonial empires and their legacies.

Platonov, S. F., *Ivan the Terrible* (1986). Covers the controversies over Russia's infamous tsar.

Rawski, Evelyn, *The Last Emperors: A Social History of Qing Imperial Institutions* (1998). This volume explores the mechanisms and processes through which the Qing court negotiated its Manchu identity.

Reid, Anthony, *Charting the Shape of Early Modern Southeast Asia* (1999). A collection of articles by a leading historian of Southeast Asia.

Spence, Jonathan, and John Wills (eds.), *From Ming to Ch'ing: Conquest, Region, and Continuity in Seventeenth-Century*

China (1979). Covers the various aspects of a tumultuous period of dynastic transition.

Taylor, Alan, *American Colonies: The Settling of North America* (2001). Brings together British, French, and Spanish colonial histories and shows how the fortunes of each were entangled with one another and with those of diverse Native American peoples.

Thornton, John, *Africa and Africans in the Making of the Atlantic World, 1400–1800* (1998). A wonderful discussion of how African slaves played a large role in the formation of the Atlantic world.

Thornton, John K., *The Kongolese Saint Anthony: Dona Beatriz Kimpa Vita and the Antonian Movement, 1684–1706* (1998). An excellent monograph on religious movements in the Kongo.

Toby, Ronald P., *State and Diplomacy in Early Modern Japan: Asia in the Development of the Tokugawa Bakufu* (1984). The author shows that the Japanese, far from being isolated from the outside world, engaged in vigorous and successful diplomacy.

Vilar, Pierre, *A History of Gold and Money* (1991). An excellent study of the development of the early silver and gold economies.

CHAPTER 14

Axtell, James, *The Invasion of America: The Contest of Cultures in Colonial North America* (1985). Discusses the strategies of Christian missionaries in converting the Indians, as well as the success of Indians in converting Europeans.

Babaie, Sussan, *Isfahan and Its Palaces: Statecraft, Shi'ism and the Architecture of Conviviality in Early Modern Iran* (2008). An overview of the city of Isfahan, as the capital of the Safavid state.

Barmé, Geremie, R., *The Forbidden City* (2008). A concise introduction to the history of one of the most important physical emblems of Chinese imperial power.

Berlin, Ira, *Many Thousands Gone: The First Two Centuries of Slavery in North America* (1998). Surveys the development of African-American culture in colonial North America.

Brook, Timothy, *The Confusions of Pleasure: Commerce and Culture in Ming China* (1999). An insightful survey of Ming society.

Clunas, Craig, *Superfluous Things: Material Culture and Social Status in Early Modern China* (1991). A good account of the late Ming elite's growing passion for material things.

Collcutt, Martin, Marius Jansen, and Isao Kumakura, *A Cultural Atlas of Japan* (1988). A sweeping look at the many different forms of Japanese cultural expression over the centuries, including the flourishing urban culture of Edo.

Darnton, Robert, *The Business of the Enlightenment: A Publishing History of the Encyclopédie, 1775–1800* (1979). The classic study of Europe's first great compendium of knowledge.

Dash, Mike, *Tulipomania: The Story of the World's Most Coveted Flower and the Extraordinary Passions It Aroused* (1999). A global perspective on and lively account of the spread of the tulip around the world as a flower signifying both beauty and status.

Elman, Benjamin A., *On Their Own Terms: Science in China, 1550–1900* (2005). A study of the development of "native" Chinese science and how the process interacted with the introduction of western science to China over the course of three and a half centuries.

Eze, Emmanuel Chukwudi (ed.), *Race and the Enlightenment: A Reader* (1997). Readings examining the idea of race in the context of the Enlightenment.

Fleischer, Cornell, *Bureaucrat and Intellectual in the Ottoman Empire: The Historian Mustafa Ali (1540–1600)* (1986). Offers good insight into the world of culture and intellectual vitality in the Ottoman Empire.

Grafton, Anthony, April Shelford, and Nancy Siraisi, *New Worlds, Ancient Texts: The Power of Tradition and the Shock of Discovery* (1995). A concise discussion of the impact of the New World on European thought.

Gutierrez, Ramon, *When Jesus Came, the Corn Mothers Went Away: Marriage, Sexuality, and Power in New Mexico, 1500–1846* (1991). A provocative dissection of the spiritual dimensions of European colonialism in the Americas.

Harley, J. B., and David Woodward (eds.), *The History of Cartography*. Vol. 2, Book 2: *Cartography in the Traditional East and Southeast Asian Societies* (1994). An authoritative treatment of the subject.

Horton, Robin, *Patterns of Thought in Africa and the West: Essays on Magic, Religion, and Science* (1993). Reflections on African patterns of thought and attitudes toward nature, which can help us understand African-American religious beliefs and resistance movements.

Keene, Donald, *The Japanese Discovery of Europe: Honda Toshiaki and Other Discoverers, 1720–1798* (1952). A study of the ways Japan managed to incorporate knowledge from the outside world with the development of national traditions.

Ko, Dorothy, *Teachers of the Inner Chambers: Women and Culture in Seventeenth-Century China* (1994). Explores the lives of elite women in late Ming and early Qing China.

Lewis, Bernard, *Race and Color in Islam* (1979). Examines the Islamic attitude toward race and color.Morgan, Philip D., *Slave Counterpoint: Black Culture in the Eighteenth-Century Chesapeake and Lowcountry* (1998). Describes the development of African-American culture in colonial North America.

Munck, Thomas, *The Enlightenment: A Comparative Social History, 1721–1794* (2000). A wonderful survey, with unusual examples from the periphery, especially from Scandinavia and the Habsburg Empire.

Necipoglu, Gulru, *Architecture, Ceremonial, and Power: The Topkapi Palace in the Fifteenth and Sixteenth Centuries* (1991). A magnificently illustrated book that shows the enormous artistic talent that the Ottoman rulers poured into their imperial structure.

Publishing and the Print Culture in Late Imperial China (Special Issue). *Late Imperial China*, Vol. 17:1 (June 1996). Contains a collection of important articles with a foreword by the French cultural historian Roger Chartier.

Qaisar, Ahsan Jan, *The Indian Response to European Technology, AD 1498–1707* (1998). A meticulous, scholarly work on this little-studied subject.

Rizvi, Athar Abbas, *The Wonder That Was India*. Vol. 2: *A Survey of the History and Culture of the Indian Sub-continent from the Coming of the Muslims to the British Conquest, 1200–1700* (1987). A deeply learned work in intellectual history.

Smith, Bernard, *European Vision and the South Pacific* (1985). An excellent cultural history of Cook's voyages.

Smith, Richard J., *Chinese Maps: Images of "All under Heaven"* (1996). Provides a good introduction to the history of cartography in China.

Welch, Anthony, *Shah Abbas and the Arts of Isfahan* (1973). Describes the astonishing architectural and artistic renaissance of the city of Isfahan under the Safavid ruler Shah Abbas.

Whitfield, Peter, *The Image of the World: Twenty Centuries of World Maps* (1994). A good introduction to the history of cartography in different parts of the world.

Wilks, Ivor, *Forests of Gold: Essays on the Akan and the Kingdom of Asante* (Athens, OH, 1993). A study that focuses on the Asante's drive for wealth.

Zilfi, Madeline C., *The Politics of Piety: The Ottoman Ulema in the Post-Classical Age (1600–1800)* (1988). Explores the cultural flourishing that took place within the Islamic world in this period.

CHAPTER 15

Allen, Robert C., *The British Industrial Revolution in Global Perspective* (2009). The most recent and authoritative study of the industrial revolution in Britain and its implications around the world.

Anderson, Fred, *Crucible of War: The Seven Years' War and the Fate of Empire in British North America, 1754–1766* (2000). The best synthesis of the "great war for empire" that set the stage for the American Revolution.

Bayly, C. A., *Indian Society and the Making of the British Empire* (1998). A useful work on the early history of the British conquest of India.

Blackburn, Robin, *The Overthrow of Colonial Slavery*, 1776–1848 (1988). Places the abolition of the Atlantic slave trade and colonial slavery in a large historical context.

Cambridge History of Egypt: Modern Egypt from 1517 to the End of the Twentieth Century, Vol. 2 (1998). Volume 2 contains authoritative essays on all aspects of modern Egyptian history, including the impact of the French invasion and the rule of Muhammad Ali.

Chaudhuri, K. N., *The Trading World of Asia and the East India Company, 1660–1760* (1978). An authoritative economic history of the East India Company's operations.

Crafts, N. F. R., *British Economic Growth during the Industrial Revolution* (1985). A pioneering study that emphasizes a long-term, more gradual process of adaptation to new institutional and social circumstances.

de Vries, Jan, *Industrious Revolution: Consumer Behavior and the Household Economy, 1650 to the Present* (2008). A book on the lead-up to the industrial revolution, written by the leading economic historian who coined the term industrious revolution.

Diamond, Jared, and James A. Robinson (eds.), *Natural Experiments of History* (2010). This book consists of eight comparative studies drawn from history, archeology, economics, economic history, geography, and political science, covering a spectrum of approaches, ranging from a non-quantitative narrative style to quantitative statistical analyses.

Doyle, William, *The Oxford History of the French Revolution* (1990). A highly detailed discussion of the course of events.

Drescher, Seymour, *Abolition: A History of Slavery and Anti-Slavery* (2009). A recent and authoritative overview of slavery and its opponents.

Elvin, Mark, *The Retreat of the Elephants: An Environmental History of China* (2004). A study of the different ways in which China's natural environment was shaped.

Fick, Carolyn E., *The Making of Haiti: The Saint Domingue Revolution from Below* (1990). Provides a detailed account of the factors that led to the great slave rebellion on the island of Haiti at the end of the eighteenth century.

Findley, Carter, *Bureaucratic Reform in the Ottoman Empire: The Sublime Porte, 1789–1922* (1980). A useful guide to Ottoman reform efforts in the nineteenth century.

Geggus, David (ed.), *The Impact of the Haitian Revolution in the Atlantic World* (2001). A lively effort to disentangle the effects of the Haitian Revolution from those of the French Revolution.

Hevia, James, *Cherishing Men from Afar: Qing Guest Ritual and the Macartney Embassy of 1793* (1995). Offers a definitive interpretation of the nature of Sino-British conflict in the Qing period.

Hobsbawm, Eric, *Nations and Nationalism since 1780* (1990). An important overview of the rise of the nation-state and nationalism around the world.

Howe, Daniel Walker, *What Hath God Wrought: The Transformation of America, 1815–1848* (2007). A Pulitzer Prize–winning interpretation of how new technologies and new ideas reshaped the economy, society, culture, and politics of the United States in the first half of the nineteenth century.

Hunt, Lynn, *Politics, Culture and Class in the French Revolution* (1984). Examines the influence of sociocultural shifts as causes and consequences of the French Revolution, emphasizing the symbols and practice of politics invented during the revolution.

Inikori, Joseph, *Africans and the Industrial Revolution in England* (2002). Demonstrates the important role that Africa and Africans played in facilitating the industrial revolution.

Isset, Christopher Mills, *State, Peasant, and Merchant in Qing Manchuria, 1644–1862* (2007). A study of the relationships between the sociopolitical structures and peasant lives in a key region during the Qing.

James, C. L. R., *The Black Jacobins: Toussaint L'Ouverture and the San Domingo Revolution* (1938). A classic chronicle of the only successful slave revolt in history and provides a critical portrait of their leader, Toussaint L'Ouverture.

Jones, E. L., *Growth Recurring* (1988). Discusses the controversy over why the industrial revolution took place in Europe, stressing the unique ecological setting that encouraged long-term investment.

Kinsbruner, Jay, *Independence in Spanish America* (1994). A fine study of the Latin American revolutions that argues that the struggle was as much a civil war as a fight for national independence.

Landers, Jane, *Atlantic Creoles in the Age of Revolutions* (2011). A collection of fascinating and unique portraits of Atlantic World creoles who managed to move freely and purposefully through French, Spanish, and English colonies, and through Indian territory, in the unstable century between 1750 and 1850.

Mokyr, Joel, *Enlightened Economy: An Economic History of Britain, 1700–1850* (2009). Perspectives on the evolution of the British economy in the era that produced the industrial revolution.

———, *The Lever of Riches* (1990). An important study of the causes of the industrial revolution that emphasizes the role of small technological and organizational breakthroughs.

Naquin, Susan, and Evelyn Rawski, *Chinese Society in the Eighteenth Century* (1987). A survey of mid-Qing society.

Neal, Larry, *The Rise of Financial Capitalism* (1990). An important study of the making of financial markets.

Nikitenko, Aleksandr, *Up from Serfdom: My Childhood and Youth in Russia, 1804–1824*

(2001). One of the very few recorded life stories of a Russian serf.

Pomeranz, Kenneth, *The Great Divergence: Europe, China, and the Making of the Modern World Economy* (2000). Offers explanations of why Europe and not some other place in the world, like parts of China or India, forged ahead economically in the nineteenth century.

Rudé, George, *Europe in the Eighteenth Century* (1972). Emphasizes the rise of a new class, the bourgeoisie, against the old aristocracy, as a cause of the French Revolution.

Wakeman, Frederic, Jr., "The Canton Trade and the Opium War," in John K. Fairbank (ed.), *The Cambridge History of China*, Vol. 10 (1978), pp. 163–212. The standard account of the episode.

Wong, R. Bin, *China Transformed: Historical Change and the Limits of European Experience* (2000). Draws attention to the relative autonomy of merchant capitalists in relation to dynastic states in Europe compared to China.

Wood, Gordon S., *Empire of Liberty: A History of the Early Republic, 1789–1815* (2009). An excellent synthesis of the history of the United States in the tumultuous years between the ratification of the Constitution and the War of 1812.

Wortman, Richard, *Scenarios of Power: Myth and Ceremony in Russian Monarchy*, 2 vols. (1995–2000). Examines how dynastic Russia confronted the challenges of the revolutionary epoch.

CHAPTER 16

Anderson, David M., *Revealing Prophets: Prophets in Eastern African History* (1995). Good discussion of the prophets in eastern Africa.

Beecher, Jonathan, *The Utopian Vision of Charles Fourier* (1983). A fine biography of this important thinker.

Boyd, Jean, *The Caliph's Sister: Nana Asma'u, 1793–1865, Teacher, Poet, and Islamic Leader* (1988). A study of the most powerful female Muslim leader in the Fulani religious revolt.

Clancy-Smith, Julia, *Rebel and Saint: Muslim Notables, Populist Protest, Colonial Encounter (Algeria and Tunisia, 1800–1904)* (1994). Examines Islamic protest movements against western encroachments in North Africa.

Clogg, Richard, *A Concise History of Greece* (1997). A good introduction to the history of Greece in its European context.

Dalrymple, William, *The Last Mughal: The Fall of a Dynasty: Delhi, 1857* (2007). A deeply researched and riveting account of Delhi during the 1857 revolt.

Danziger, Raphael, *Abd al-Qadir: Resistance to the French and Internal Consolidation* (1977). Still the indispensable work on this important Algerian Muslim leader.

Dowd, Gregory E., *A Spirited Resistance: The North American Indian Struggle for Unity, 1745–1815* (1992). Emphasizes the importance of prophets like Tenskwatawa in the building of pan-Indian confederations in the era between the Seven Years' War and the War of 1812.

Guha, Ranajit, *Elementary Aspects of Peasant Insurgency in Colonial India* (1983). Not specifically on the Indian Rebellion of 1857 but includes it in its pioneering "subalternist" interpretation of South Asian history.

Hamilton, Carolyn (ed.), *The Mfecane Aftermath: Reconstructive Debates in Southern African History* (1995). Debates on Shaka's *Mfecane* movement and its impact on southern Africa.

Hiskett, Mervyn, *The Sword of Truth: The Life and Times of the Shehu Usman dan Fodio* (1994). An authoritative study of the Fulani revolt in northern Nigeria.

Johnson, Douglas H., *Nuer Prophets: A History of Prophecy from the Upper Nile in the Nineteenth and Twentieth Centuries* (1994). Deals with African prophetic and charismatic movements in eastern Africa.

Keddie, Nikki, *An Islamic Response to Imperialism: Political and Religious Writings of Sayyid Jamal ad-Din "al-Afghani" (1968)*. Definitive information on the Afghani's life and influence, coupled with a translation of one of his most important essays.

Michael, Franz, and Chung-li Chang, *The Taiping Rebellion: History and Documents*, 3 vols. (1966–1971). The basic source for the history of the Taiping.

Mukherjee, Rudrangshu, *Awadh in Revolt 1857–58* (1984). A careful case study of the Indian Rebellion.

Omer-Cooper, J. D., *The Zulu Aftermath: A Nineteenth-Century Revolution in Bantu Africa* (1966). A good place to start in studying Shaka's *Mfecane* movement, which greatly rearranged the political and ethnic makeup of southern Africa.

Ostler, Jeffrey, *The Plains Sioux and U.S. Colonialism from Lewis and Clark to Wounded Knee* (2004). Uses the lens of colonial theory to track relations between the Sioux and the United States, offering fresh insights about the Ghost Dance movement.

Peires, J. B. (ed.), *Before and After Shaka* (1981). Discusses elements in the debate over Shaka's *Mfecane* movement.

Pilbeam, Pamela, *French Socialists Before Marx: Workers, Women and the Social Question in France* (2001). Describes the development of a variety of socialist ideas in early nineteenth-century France.

Reed, Nelson, *The Caste War of Yucatan* (1964). A classic narrative of the Caste War of the Yucatan.

Restall, Matthew, *The Maya World* (1997). Describes in economic and social terms the origins of the Yucatan upheaval in southern Mexico.

Ruedy, John, *Modern Algeria: The Origins and Development of a Nation* (2005). Still the best overview of the modern political history of Algeria.

Rugeley, Terry, *Rebellion Now and Forever: Mayans, Hispanics, and Caste War Violence in Yucatán, 1800–1880* (2009). Explains the combination of economic and cultural pressures that drove the Mayans in the Yucatan to revolt in the Caste War.

Spence, Jonathan, *God's Chinese Son: The Taiping Heavenly Kingdom of Hong Xiuquan* (1996). A fascinating portrayal of the Taiping through the prism of its founder.

Wagner, Rudolf, *Reenacting the Heavenly Vision: The Role of Religion in the Taiping Rebellion* (1982). A brief but insightful analysis of the religious elements in the Taiping's doctrines.

White, Richard, *The Middle Ground: Indians, Empires, and Republics in the Great Lakes Region, 1650–1815* (1991). A pathbreaking exploration of intercultural relations in North America that offers a provocative interpretation of the visions of Tenskwatawa and the efforts of Tecumseh to resist the expansion of the United States.

CHAPTER 17

Berry, Sara, *Cocoa, Custom and Socio-Economic Change in Western Nigeria*, Clarendon Press, 1975), Innovative study based on interviews with local farmers that suggests that farmer enterprise and micro-economic theory better explain the spectacular growth in cocoa production than grand economic theory.

Cain, P. A., and A. G. Hopkins, *British Imperialism: Innovation and Expansion, 1688–1914* (1993). An excellent discussion of British imperialism, especially British expansion into Africa.

Cronon, William, *Nature's Metropolis: Chicago and the Great West* (1991). Makes connections among territorial expansion, industrialization, and urban development.

Davis, John, *Conflict and Control: Law and Order in Nineteenth-Century Italy* (1988). A superb study of the north-south and other rifts after Italian political unification.

Frankel, S. Herbert, *Capital Investment in Africa: Its Course and Effects*, Oxford University Press (1938). A careful study based on a mass of detailed figures and statistics on the general economic development of states in sub-Saharan Africa.

Friesen, Gerald, *The Canadian Prairies* (1984). The most comprehensive account of Canadian westward expansion.

Gluck, Carol, *Japan's Modern Myths: Ideology in the Late Meiji Period* (1985). A study of how states fashion useful historical traditions to consolidate and legitimize their rule.

Headrick, Daniel R., *The Tools of Empire: Technology and European Imperialism in the Nineteenth Century* (1981). A useful general study of the relationship between imperialism and technology.

Herbst, Jeffrey, *States and Power in Africa: Comparative Lessons in Authority and Control* (2000). An overview of the impact of colonial rule on contemporary African states.

Hill, Polly, *The Gold Coast Cocoa Farmer: A Preliminary Survey*, Oxford University Press (1965).

Hine, Robert V., and John Mack Faragher, *The American West: A New Interpretive History* (2000). Presents an excellent synthesis of the conquests by which the United States expanded from the Atlantic to the Pacific.

Hobsbawm, Eric J., *Nations and Nationalism since 1780: Programme, Myth, Reality* (1993). An insightful survey of the origins and development of nationalist thought throughout Europe.

Hochschild, Adam, *King Leopold's Ghost* (1998). A full-scale, eminently readable study of Europe's most egregiously destructive colonial regime in Africa.

Lee, Leo Ou-fan, and Andrew Nathan, "The Beginnings of Mass Culture: Journalism and Fiction in the Late Ch'ing and Beyond," in David Johnson, Andrew Nathan, and Evelyn Rawski (eds.), *Popular Culture in Late Imperial China* (1985), pp. 360–95. An important article on the emergence of a mass-media market in late-nineteenth- and early-twentieth-century China.

Lieven, Dominic, *Empire: The Russian Empire and Its Rivals* (2000). A comparison of the British, Ottoman, Habsburg, and Russian empires.

Mackenzie, John M., *Propaganda and Empire* (1984). Contains a series of useful chapters showing the importance of the empire to Britain.

Mamdani, Mahmood, *Citizen and State: Contemporary Africa and the Legacy of Late Colonialism* (1996). A survey of the impact of European colonial powers on African political systems.

McClintock, Anne, *Imperial Leather: Race, Gender and Sexuality in the Colonial Contest* (1995). A study of the imperial relationship between Victorian Britain and South Africa from the point of view of cultural studies.

McNeil, William, *Europe's Steppe Frontier: 1500–1800* (1964). An excellent study of the definitive victory of Russia's agricultural empire over grazing nomads and independent frontier people.

Mitchell, B. R., *International Historical Statistics: Africa, Asia, and Oceania, 1750–2005* Palgrave Macmillan. (2007). This comparative volume provides data from over two centuries for all principal areas of economic and social activity in both Eastern and Western Europe.

Montgomery, David, *The Fall of the House of Labor: The Workplace, the State, and American Labor Activism, 1865–1925* (1987). An excellent discussion of changes in work in the late nineteenth century.

Myers, Ramon, and Mark Peattie (eds.), *The Japanese Colonial Empire, 1895–1945* (1984). A collection of essays exploring different aspects of Japanese colonialism.

Needell, Jeffrey, *A Tropical Belle Epoque: Elite Culture and Society in Turn of the Century Rio de Janeiro* (1987). Shows the strength of the Brazilian elites at the turn of the century.

Pan, Lynn (ed.), *The Encyclopedia of Chinese Overseas* (1999). A comprehensive coverage of the history of the Chinese diaspora.

Porter, Bernard, *The Absent-Minded Imperialists: What the British Really Thought about Empire* (2004). A careful dissection of the ways in which empire changed the British—and did not.

Stengers, Jean, *Combien le Congo a-t-il coûté à la Belgique* (1957). A detailed financial accounting of how much Leopold put into the Congo and how much he took out, underscoring just how ruthlessly he exploited this possession.

Topik, Steven, *The Political Economy of the Brazilian State, 1889–1930* (1987). An excellent discussion of the Brazilian state, and especially of its elites.

Walker, Mack, *German Home Towns: Community, State, and the General State, 1648–1871* (1971, 1998). A brilliant, street-level analysis of the Holy Roman Empire (the First Reich) and the run-up to the German unification of 1871 (the Second Reich).

Wasserman, Mark, *Everyday Life and Politics in Nineteenth-Century Mexico* (2000). Wonderfully captures the way in which people coped with social and economic dislocation in late-nineteenth-century Mexico.

Weeks, Theodore R., *Nation and State in Late Imperial Russia: Nationalism and Russification on the Western Frontier, 1863–1914* (1996). A good discussion of the Russian Empire's responses to the concept of the nation-state.

White, Richard, *Railroaded: The Transcontinentals and the Making of Modern America* (2011). A seering exposé of the corruptions and a startling critique of the economic and environmental costs associated with the expansion of railroad lines across Canada, the United States, and Mexico.

Yung Wing, *My Life in China and America* (1909). The autobiography of the first Chinese graduate of an American university.

CHAPTER 18

Bayly, C. A., *The Birth of the Modern World, 1780–1914: Global Connections and Comparisons* (2004). A general study of the key political, economic, social, and cultural features of the modern era in world history.

Bergère, Marie-Claire, *Sun Yat-sen* (1998). Originally published in French in 1994, this is a judicious biography of the man generally known as the father of the modern Chinese nation.

Chatterjee, Partha, *The Nation and Its Fragments* (1993). One of the most important works on Indian nationalism by a leading scholar of "Subaltern Studies."

Conrad, Joseph, *Heart of Darkness* (1899). First published in a magazine in 1899, this novella contained a searing critique of King Leopold's oppressive and exploitative policies in the Congo and was part of a growing concern for the effects that European empires were having around the world, especially in Africa.

Esherick, Joseph, "How the Qing became China," in Joseph W. Esherick, Hasan Kayali, and Eric Van Young, eds., *Empire to Nation: Historical Perspectives on the Making of the Modern World* (2006). A study of the processes through which the Qing Empire became the nation-state of China.

———, *The Origins of the Boxer Uprising* (1987). The definitive account of the episode.

Everdell, William R., *The First Moderns: Profiles in the Origins of Twentieth-Century Thought* (1997). A rich account of the many faces of modernism, focusing particularly on science and art.

Finnane, Antonia, *Changing Clothes in China: Fashion, History, Nation* (2008). An exploration of changing Chinese identities from the perspective of clothing.

Gay, Peter, *The Cultivation of Hatred* (1994). A provocative discussion of the violent passions of the immediate pre–Great War era.

Gilmartin, Christina, Gail Hershatter, Lisa Rofel, and Tyrene White (eds.), *Engendering China: Women, Culture, and the State* (1994). Analyzes politics and society in modern China from the perspective of gender.

Hochschild, Adam, *King Leopold's Ghost: A Story of Greed, Terror, and Heroism in Colonial Africa* (1998). A well-written account of the violent colonial history of the Belgian Congo under King Leopold in the late nineteenth century.

Katz, Friedrich, *The Life and Times of Pancho Villa* (1998). An exploration of the Mexican Revolution that shows how Villa's armies destroyed the forces of Díaz and his followers.

Keddie, Nikki, *An Islamic Response to Imperialism: Political and Religious Writings of Sayyid Jamal ad-Din "al-Afghani" (1968).* Definitive information on the Afghani's life and influence, coupled with a translation of one of his most important essays.

Kern, Stephen, *The Culture of Time and Space 1880–1918* (1986). A useful study of the enormous changes in the experience of time and space in the age of late industrialism in Europe and America.

Kuhn, Philip, *Chinese among Others: Emigration in Modern Times* (2008). An overview of the history of Chinese migration.

McKeown, Adam, *Melancholy Order: Asian Migration and the Globalization of Borders* (2008). An examination of global migration patterns since the mid-nineteenth century and how regulations designed to restrict Asian migration to other parts of the world led to the modern regime of migration control.

Meade, Teresa, *"Civilizing" Rio: Reform and Resistance in a Brazilian City, 1889–1930* (1997). A wonderful study of cultural and class conflict in Brazil.

Pick, Daniel, *Faces of Degeneration: A European Disorder, c. 1848–c. 1918* (1993). A study of Europe's fear of social and biological decline, particularly focusing on France and Italy.

Pretorius, Fransjohn (ed.), *Scorched Earth* (2001). A study of the Anglo-Boer War in terms of its environmental impacts.

Sarkar, Sumit, *The Swadeshi Movement in Bengal* (1973). A comprehensive study of an early militant movement against British rule.

Schorske, Carl E. *Fin-de-Siècle Vienna: Politics and Culture* (1980). The classic treatment of the birth of modern ideas and political movements in turn-of-the-century Austria.

Trachtenberg, Alan, *The Incorporation of America: Culture and Society in the Gilded Age* (1982). A provocative synthesis of changes in the American economy, society, and culture in the last decades of the nineteenth century.

Wang, David Der-wei, *Fin-de-Siècle Splendor: Repressed Modernities of Late Qing Fiction, 1849–1911* (1997). A fine work that attempts to locate the "modern" within the writings of the late Qing period.

Warren, Louis, *Buffalo Bill's America: William Cody and the Wild West Show* (2005). A superb portrait of William F. Cody, the person; of Buffalo Bill, the persona Cody (and others) created; and of the popular culture his Wild West shows brought to audiences in Europe and North America.

Warwick, Peter, *Black People and the South African War, 1899–1902* (1983). An important study that reminds readers of the crucial involvement of black South Africans in this bloody conflict.

Womack, John, Jr., *Zapata and the Mexican Revolution* (1968). A major work on the Mexican Revolution that discusses peasant struggles in the state of Morelos in great detail.

CHAPTER 19

Bloxham, Donald, *The Great Game of Genocide: Imperialism, Nationalism, and the Destruction of the Ottoman Armenians* (2005). The definitive work on the Armenian genocide, set in a wide historical context.

Brown, Judith, *Gandhi: Prisoner of Hope* (1990). A biography of Gandhi as a political activist.

De Grazia, Victoria, and Ellen Furlough (eds.), *The Sex of Things: Gender and Consumption in Historical Perspective* (1996). Path-breaking essays on how gender affects consumption.

Dumenil, Lynn, *The Modern Temper: America in the 1920s* (1995). A general discussion of American culture in the decade after World War I.

Fainsod, Merle, *Smolensk under Soviet Rule* (1989). The most accessible and sophisticated interpretation of the Stalin revolution in the village.

Friedman, Edward, *Backward toward Revolution: The Chinese Revolutionary Party* (1974). An insightful look at the failure of liberalism in early republican China through the prism of the short-lived Chinese Revolutionary Party.

Gelvin, James, *Divided Loyalties: Nationalism and Mass Politics in Syria at the Close of Empire* (1998). Offers important insights into the development of nationalism in the Arab world.

Horne, John (ed.), *A Companion to World War I* (2010). A collection of articles written by leading scholars of World War I; the most comprehensive and up-to-date work on this war.

———, *State, Society, and Mobilization during the First World War* (1997). Essays on what it took to wage total war among all the belligerents.

Johnson, G. Wesley, *The Emergence of Black Politics in Senegal* (1971). A useful examination of the stirrings of African nationalism in Senegal.

Kennedy, David M., *Freedom from Fear: The American People in Depression and War, 1929–1945* (1999). A wonderful narrative of turbulent years.

Kershaw, Ian, *Hitler*, 2 vols. (1998–2000). A masterpiece combining biography and context.

Kimble, David, *A Political History of Ghana* (1963). An excellent discussion of the beginnings of African nationalism in Ghana.

Kotkin, Stephen, *Magnetic Mountain: Stalinism as a Civilization* (1995). Recaptures the atmosphere of a time when everything seemed possible, even creating a new world.

LeMahieu, D. L., *A Culture for Democracy: Mass Communication and the Cultivated Mind in Britain between the Wars* (1988). One of the great works on mass culture.

Lyttelton, Adrian, *The Seizure of Power: Fascism in Italy, 1919–1929* (1961). Still the classic account.

Marchand, Roland, *Advertising the American Dream: Making Way for Modernity, 1920–1945* (1985). An excellent discussion of the force of mass production and mass consumption.

Mazower, Mark, *Dark Continent: Europe's Twentieth Century* (1999). A wide-ranging overview of Europe's tempestuous twentieth century.

McKeown, Adam, *Melancholy Order: Asian Migration and the Globalization of Border* (2008). A major study of the vast movement of peoples around the globe between the middle of the nineteenth and twentieth centuries.

Morrow, John H., Jr., *The Great War: An Imperial History* (2004). Places World War I in the context of European imperialism.

Nottingham, John, and Carl Rosberg, *The Myth of "Mau Mau": Nationalism in Kenya* (1966). Dispels the myths in describing the roots of nationalism in Kenya.

Taylor, Jay, *The Generalissimo: Chiang Kai-shek and the Struggle for Modern China* (2009). The first serious biographical study of Chiang Kai-shek in English, although its reliance on Chiang's own diary as a source does raise some questions of historical interpretation.

Thorp, Rosemary (ed.), *Latin America in the 1930s* (1984). An important collection of essays on Latin America's response to the shakeup of the interwar years.

Tsin, Michael, *Nation, Governance, and Modernity in China: Canton, 1900–1927* (1999). An analysis of the vision and social dynamics behind the Guomindang-led revolution of the 1920s.

Vianna, Hermano, *The Mystery of Samba* (1999). Discusses the history of samba, emphasizing its African heritage as well as its persistent popular content.

Wakeman, Frederic, Jr., *Policing Shanghai, 1927–1937* (1995). An excellent account of Guomindang rule in China's largest city during the Nanjing decade.

Winter, J. M., *The Experience of World War* (1988). A comprehensive presentation of the many sides of the twentieth century.

Young, Louise, *Japan's Total Empire: Manchuria and the Culture of Wartime Imperialism* (1998). An innovative case study of Japanese imperialism and mass culture with broad implications.

CHAPTER 20

Aburish, Said K., *Nasser: The Last Arab* (2004). A recent and impressive look at Egypt's most powerful political leader in the 1950s and 1960s.

Anderson, Jon Lee, *Che Guevara: A Revolutionary Life* (1997). A sweeping study of the radicalization of Latin American nationalism.

Bayly, Christopher, and Tim Harper, *Forgotten Armies: Britain's Asian Empire and the War with Japan* (2004). A brilliant social and military history of the Second World War as fought and lived in South and Southeast Asia.

Chatterjee, Partha, *Nationalist Thought and the Colonial World: A Derivative Discourse?* (1986). An influential interpretation of the ideological and political nature of Indian nationalism and the struggle for a postcolonial nation-state.

Crampton, R. J., *Eastern Europe in the Twentieth Century and After* (2nd ed., 1997). Comprehensive overview covering all Soviet-bloc countries.

Dikötter, Frank, *Mao's Great Famine: The History of China's Most Devastating Catastrophe, 1958–1962* (2010). A recent detailed account of one of the greatest man-made disasters in twentieth-century history.

Dower, John W., *Embracing Defeat: Japan in the Wake of World War II* (1999). A prize-winning study of the transformation of one of the war's vanquished.

Elkins, Caroline, *Imperial Reckoning: The Untold Story of Britain's Gulag in Kenya* (2005). Pulitzer Prize–winning study of the brutal war to suppress the nationalist uprising in Kenya in the 1950s that ultimately led to independence for that country.

Feshbach Murray, and Alfred Friendly, Jr. (1992). *Ecocide in the USSR: Health and Nation under Siege*. A crucial study of ecological disasters in the Soviet Union.

Gao Yuan, *Born Red: A Chronicle of the Cultural Revolution* (1987). A gripping personal account of the Cultural Revolution by a former Red Guard.

Gordon, Andrew (ed.), *Postwar Japan as History* (1993). Essays covering a wide range of topics on postwar Japan.

Hargreaves, John D., *Decolonization in Africa* (1996). A good place to start when exploring the history of African decolonization.

Hasan, Mushirul (ed.), *India's Partition: Process, Strategy and Mobilization* (1993). A useful anthology of scholarly articles, short stories, and primary documents on the partition of India.

Iriye, Akira, *Power and Culture: The Japanese-American War, 1941–1945* (1981). A discussion that goes beyond the military confrontation in Asia.

Jackson, Kenneth T., *Crabgrass Frontier: The Suburbanization of the United States* (1985). An insightful and influential consideration of the movement of the American population from cities to suburbs.

Jalal, Ayesha, *The Sole Spokesman: Jinnah, the Muslim League and the Demand for Pakistan* (1985). A study of the high politics leading to the violent partition of British India.

Keep, John L. H., *Last of the Empires: A History of the Soviet Union 1945–1991* (1995). A detailed overview of the core of the "Second World."

Morris, Benny, *Righteous Victims: A History of the Zionist-Arab Conflict, 1881–1999* (2000). On the Arab-Israeli War of 1948.

Patterson, James T., *Grand Expectations: The United States, 1945–1974* (1996). Synthesizes the American experience in the postwar decades.

Patterson, Thomas, *Contesting Castro* (1994). The best study of the tension between the United States and Cuba. Culminating in the Cuban Revolution, it explores the deep American misunderstanding of Cuban national aspirations.

Roberts, Geoffrey, *Stalin's Wars: From World War to Cold War, 1939–1953* (2007). A reassessment of Stalin's wartime leadership that conveys the vast scale of what took place.

Ruedy, John, *Modern Algeria: The Origins and Development of a Nation* (1992). Gives the history of the Algerian nationalist movements and provides an overview of the Algerian war for independence.

Saich, Tony, and Hans van de Ven (eds.), *New Perspectives on the Chinese Communist Revolution* (1995). A collection of essays reexamining different aspects of the Chinese communist movement.

Schram, Stuart, *The Thought of Mao Tse-tung* (1989). Standard work on the subject.

Tignor, Robert L., *W. Arthur Lewis and the Birth of Development Economics* (2006). An intellectual biography of the Nobel Prize–winning, West Indian–born economist, who proposed formulas to promote the economic development of less developed societies and then sought to implement them in Africa and the West Indies.

Wiener, Douglas R. (2002). *A Little Corner of Freedom: Russian Nature Protection from Stalin to Gorbachev*. A groundbreaking book about Russian environmentalism.

Zubkova, Elena, *Russia after the War: Hopes, Illusions, and Disappointments, 1945–1957* (1998). Uses formerly secret archives to catalogue the devastation and difficult reconstruction of one of the war's victors.

CHAPTER 21

Collier, Paul, *The Bottom Billion: Why the Poorest Countries Fail and What Can Be Done About It* (2007). Shows that despite the world's advancing prosperity, more than a billion people have been left behind in abject poverty.

Davis, Deborah (ed.), *The Consumer Revolution in Urban China* (2000). A look at the different aspects of the recent, profound social transformation of urban China.

Davis, Mike, *City of Quartz: Excavating the Future in Los Angeles* (1990). Offers provocative reflections on the recent history, current condition, and possible future of Los Angeles.

Dutton, Michael, *Streetlife China* (1999). A fascinating portrayal of the survival tactics of those inhabiting the margins of society in modern China.

Eichengreen, Barry, *Globalizing Capital: A History of the International Monetary System* (1996). An insightful analysis of how international capital markets changed in the period from 1945 to 1980.

Gourevitch, Philip, *We Wish to Inform You That Tomorrow We Will Be Killed with Our Families: Stories from Rwanda* (1999). A volume that reveals the hatreds that culminated in the Rwanda genocide.

Guillermoprieto, Alma, *Looking for History: Dispatches from Latin America* (2001). A collection of articles by the most important journalist reporting on Latin American affairs.

Han Minzhu (ed.), *Cries for Democracy: Writings and Speeches from the 1989 Chinese Democracy Movement* (1990). A collection of documents from the events leading up to the incident in Tiananmen Square on June 4, 1989.

Herbst, Jeffrey, *States and Power in Africa: Comparative Lessons in Authority and Control* (2000). Explores the political dilemmas facing modern African polities.

Honig, Emily, and Gail Hershatter, *Personal Voices: Chinese Women in the 1980's* (1988). A record of Chinese women during a period of rapid social change.

Huang, Yasheng, *Capitalism with Chinese Characteristics: Entrepreneurship and the State* (2008). A sharp, unsentimental inside look at China's market economy and its future prospects.

Klitgaard, Robert, *Tropical Gangsters* (1990). On the intimate connections between corrupt native elites and international aid agencies.

Kotkin, Stephen, *Armageddon Averted: The Soviet Collapse, 1970–2000* (2001). Places the surprise fall of the Soviet Union in the context of the great shifts in the post–World War II order.

Mamdani, Mahmood, *When Victims Become Killers: Colonialism, Nativism, and the Genocide in Rwanda* (2001). Discusses the genocide in Rwanda in light of the legacy of colonialism.

Mehta, Suketu, *Maximum City: Bombay Lost and Found* (2005). Examines one of the great, and contradictory, cities in the era of globalization.

Mottahedeh, Roy, *The Mantle of the Prophet: Religion and Politics in Iran* (2nd ed., 2008). Perhaps the best book on the 1979 Iranian Revolution and its aftermath.

Nathan, Andrew, and Perry Link, *The Tiananmen Papers* (2002). An inside look at the divisions within the Chinese elite in connection with the 1989 crackdown.

Portes, Alejandro, and Rubén G. Rumbaut, *Immigrant America* (2nd ed., 1996). A good comparative study of how immigration has transformed the United States.

Prakash, Gyan, *Mumbai Fables* (2010). A spirited account of the rise of India's most modern city, a center of intellectual, commercial, and political vitality.

Prunier, Gerald, *Africa's World War: Congo, the Rwandan Genocide, and the Making of a Continental Catastrophe* (2009). A chilling discussion of the spillover effects of the Rwandan genocide on central, eastern, and southern Africa.

Reinhart, Carmen, and Kenneth Rogoff, *This Time Is Different: Eight Centuries of Financial Folly* (2009). Explains the latest financial crash using historical perspective.

Van Der Wee, Hermann, *Prosperity and Upheaval: The World Economy, 1945–1980* (1986). Describes very well the transformation and problems of the world economy, particularly from the 1960s onward.

Westad, Odd Arne, *The Global Cold War: Third World Interventions and the Making of our Times* (2007). A genuinely global perspective on the cold war and its consequences.

Winn, Peter, *Americas: The Changing Face of Latin America and the Caribbean* (1992). A useful portrayal of Latin America since the 1970s.

GLOSSARY

Abd al-Rahman III Islamic ruler in Spain who held a countercaliphate and reigned from 912 to 961 CE.

aborigines Original, native inhabitants of a region, as opposed to invaders, colonizers, or later peoples of mixed ancestry.

absolute monarchy Form of government where one body, usually the monarch, controls the right to tax, judge, make war, and coin money. The term *enlightened absolutists* was often used to refer to state monarchies in seventeenth- and eighteenth-century Europe.

acid rain Precipitation containing large amounts of sulfur, mainly from coal-fired plants.

adaptation Ability to alter behavior and to innovate, finding new ways of doing things.

African National Congress (ANC) Multiracial organization founded in 1912 in an effort to end racial discrimination in South Africa.

Afrikaners Descendants of the original Dutch settlers of South Africa; formerly referred to as Boers.

Agones Athletic contests in ancient Greece.

Ahmosis Egyptian ruler in the southern part of the country who ruled from 1550 to 1525 BCE; Ahmosis used Hyksos weaponry—horse chariots in particular—to defeat the Hyksos themselves.

Ahura Mazda Supreme God of the Persians believed to have created the world and all that is good and to have appointed earthly kings.

AIDS (Acquired Immuno Deficiency Syndrome) Virus that compromises the ability of the infected person's immune system to ward off disease. First detected in 1981, AIDS was initially stigmatized as a "gay cancer," but as it spread to heterosexuals, public awareness about it increased. In its first two decades, AIDS killed 12 million people.

Akbarnamah Mughal intellectual Abul-fazl's *Book of Akbar*, which attempted to reconcile the traditional Sufi interest in the inner life within the worldly context of a great empire.

Alaric II Visigothic king who issued a simplified code of innovative imperial law.

Alexander the Great (356–323 BCE) Leader who used novel tactics and new kinds of armed forces to conquer the Persian Empire, which extended from Egypt and the Mediterranean Sea to the interior of what is now Afghanistan and as far as the Indus River valley. Alexander's conquests broke down barriers between the Mediterranean world and Southwest Asia and transferred massive amounts of wealth and power to the Mediterranean, transforming it into a more unified world of economic and cultural exchange.

Alexandria Port city in Egypt named after Alexander the Great. Alexandria was a model city in the Hellenistic world. It was built up by a multiethnic population from around the Mediterranean world.

Al-Khwarizmi Scientist and mathematician who lived from 780 to 850 CE and is known for having modified Indian digits into Arabic numerals.

Allied powers Name given to the alliance between Britain, France, Russia, and Italy, who fought against Germany and Austria-Hungary (the Central powers) in World War I. In World War II the name was used for the alliance between Britain, France, and America, who fought against the Axis powers (Germany, Italy, and Japan).

allomothering System by which mothers relied on other women, including their own mothers, daughters, sisters, and friends, to help in the nurturing and protecting of children.

alluvium Area of land created by river deposits.

American Railway Union Workers' union that initiated the Pullman Strike of 1894, which led to violence and ended in the leaders' arrest.

Amnesty International Non-governmental organization formed to defend "prisoners of conscience"—those detained for their beliefs, race, sex, ethnic origin, language, or religion.

Amorites Name that Mesopotamian urbanites called the transhumant herders from the Arabian desert. Around 2300 BCE, the Amorites, along with the Elamites, were at the center of newly formed dynasties in southern Mesopotamia.

Amun Once insignificant Egyptian god elevated to higher status by Amenemhet (1991–1962 BCE). *Amun* means "hidden" in Ancient Egyptian; the name was meant to convey the god's omnipresence.

Analects Texts that included the teachings and cultural ideals of Confucius.

anarchism Belief that society should be a free association of its members, not subject to government, laws, or police.

Anatolia Now mainly the area known as modern Turkey; in the sixth millennium BCE, people from Anatolia, Greece, and the Levant took to boats and populated the Aegean. Their small villages endured almost unchanged for two millennia.

ancestral worship Religious practice in which the living honor their dead ancestors through performative rituals, under the belief that the dead intervene with their powers on behalf of the living.

Angkor Wat Magnificent Khmer Vaishnavite temple that crowned the royal palace in Angkor. It had statues representing the Hindu pantheon of gods.

Anglo-Boer War (1899–1902) Anticolonial struggle in South Africa between the British and the Afrikaners over the gold-rich Transvaal. In response to the Afrikaners' guerrilla tactics and in order to contain the local population, the British instituted the first concentration camps. Ultimately, Britain won the conflict.

animal domestication Gradual process that occurred simultaneously with or just before the domestication of plants, depending on the region.

annals Historical records. Notable annals are the cuneiform inscriptions that record successful Assyrian military campaigns.

Anti-Federalists Critics of the U.S. Constitution who sought to defend the people against the power of the federal government and insisted on a bill of rights to protect individual liberties from government intrusion.

apartheid Racial segregation policy of the Afrikaner-dominated South African government. Legislated in 1948 by the Afrikaner National Party, it had existed in South Africa for many years.

Arab-Israeli War of 1948–1949 Conflict between Israeli and Arab armies that arose in the wake of a U.N. vote to partition Palestine into Arab and Jewish territories. The war shattered the legitimacy of Arab ruling elites.

Aramaic Dialect of a Semitic language spoken in Southwest Asia; it became the lingua franca of the Persian Empire.

Aristotle (384–322 BCE) Philosopher who studied under Plato but came to different conclusions about nature and politics. Aristotle believed in collecting observations about nature and discerning patterns to ascertain how things worked.

Aryans Nomadic charioteers who spoke Indo-European languages and entered South Asia in 1500 BCE. The early Aryan settlers were herders.

Asante state State located in present-day Ghana, founded by the Asantes at the end of the seventeenth century. It grew in power in the next century because of its access to gold and its involvement in the slave trade.

ascetic One who rejects material possessions and physical pleasures.

Asiatic Society Cultural organization founded by British Orientalists who supported native culture but still believed in colonial rule.

A´soka Emperor of the Mauryan dynasty from 268 to 231 BCE; he was a great conqueror and unifier of India. He is said to have embraced Buddhism toward the end of his life.

Assur One of two cities on the upper reaches of the Tigris River that were the heart of Assyria proper (the other was Nineveh).

A´svaghosa First known Sanskrit writer. He may have lived from 80 to 150 CE and may have composed a biography of the Buddha.

Ataturk, Mustafa Kemal (1881–1938) Ottoman army officer and military hero who helped forge the modern Turkish nation-state. He and his followers deposed the sultan, declared Turkey a republic, and constructed a Europe-an-like secular state, eliminating Islam's hold over civil and political affairs.

Atlantic system New system of trade and expansion that linked Europe, Africa, and the Americas. It emerged in the wake of European voyages across the Atlantic Ocean.

Atma Vedic term signifying the eternal self, represented by the trinity of deities.

Atman In the Upanishads, an eternal being who exists everywhere. The atman never perishes but is reborn or transmigrates into another life.

Attila Sole ruler of all Hunnish tribes from 433 to 453 CE. Harsh and much feared, he formed the first empire to oppose Rome in northern Europe.

Augustus Title meaning "Revered One," assumed in 27 BCE by the Roman ruler Octavian (63–14 BCE). This was one of many titles he assumed; others included *imperator*, *princeps*, and *Caesar*.

australopithecines Hominid species that appeared 3 million years ago and, unlike other animals, walked on two legs. Their brain capacity was a little less than one-third of a modern human's or about the size of the brain capacity of today's African apes. Although not humans, they carried the genetic and biological material out of which modern humans would later emerge.

Austro-Hungarian Empire Dual monarchy established by the Habsburg family in 1867; it collapsed at the end of World War I.

authoritarianism Centralized and dictatorial form of government, proclaimed by its adherents to be superior to parliamentary democracy and especially effective at mobilizing the masses. This idea was widely accepted in parts of the world during the 1930s.

Avesta Compilation of holy works transmitted orally by priests for millennia and eventually recorded in the sixth century BCE.

Axis powers The three aggressor states in World War II: Germany, Japan, and Italy.

Aztec Empire Mesoamerican empire that originated with a league of three Mexica cities in 1430 and gradually expanded through the Central Valley of Mexico, uniting numerous small, independent states under a single monarch who ruled with the help of counselors, military leaders, and priests. By the late fifteenth century, the Aztec realm may have embraced 25 million people. In 1521, they were defeated by the conquistador Hernán Cortés.

baby boom Post–World War II upswing in U.S. birth rates; it reversed a century of decline.

bactrian camel Two-humped animal domesticated in central Asia around 2500 BCE. The bactrian camel was heartier than the one-humped dromedary and became the animal of choice for the harsh and varied climates typical of Silk Road trade.

Baghdad Capital of the Islamic Empire under the Abbasid dynasty, founded in 762 CE (in modern-day Iraq). In the medieval period, it was a center of administration, scholarship, and cultural growth for what came to be known as the Golden Age of Islamic science.

Baghdad Pact (1955) Middle Eastern military alliance between countries friendly with America who were also willing to align themselves with the western countries against the Soviet Union.

Balam Na Stone temple and place of pilgrimage for the Mayan people of Mexico's Yucatan peninsula.

Balfour Declaration Letter (November 2, 1917) by Lord Arthur J. Balfour, British foreign secretary, that promised a homeland for the Jews in Palestine.

Bamboo Annals Shang stories and foundation myths that were written on bamboo strips and later collected.

Bantu Language first spoken by people who lived in the southeastern area of modern Nigeria around 1000 CE.

Bantu migrations Waves of rapid population movement from West Africa into eastern and southern Africa during the first millennium ce that brought advanced agricultural practices to these regions and absorbed most of the preexisting hunting-and-gathering populations.

barbarian Derogatory term used to describe pastoral nomads, painting them as enemies of civilization; the term *barbarian* used to have a more neutral meaning than it does today.

barbarian invasions Violent migration of people in the late fourth and fifth centuries into Roman territory. These migrants had long been used as non-Roman soldiers.

basilicas Early church buildings, based on old royal audience halls.

Battle of Adwa (1896) Battle in which the Ethiopians defeated Italian colonial forces; it inspired many of Africa's later national leaders.

Battle of Wounded Knee (1890) Bloody massacre of Sioux Ghost Dancers by U.S. armed forces.

Bay of Pigs (1961) Unsuccessful invasion of Cuba by Cuban exiles supported by the U.S. government. The invaders intended to incite an insurrection in Cuba and overthrow the communist regime of Fidel Castro.

Bedouins Nomadic pastoralists in the deserts of the Middle East.

Beer Hall Putsch (1923) Nazi intrusion into a meeting of Bavarian leaders in a Munich beer hall; the Nazis were attempting to force support for their cause; Adolf Hitler was imprisoned for a year after the incident.

Beghards (1500s) Eccentric European group whose members claimed to be in a state of grace that allowed them to do as they pleased—from adultery, free love, and nudity to murder; also called Brethren of Free Speech.

bell beaker Ancient drinking vessel, an artifact from Europe, so named because its shape resembles an inverted bell.

Berenice of Egypt Egyptian "queen" who helped rule over the Kingdom of the Nile from 320 to 280 BCE.

Beringia Prehistoric thousand-mile-long land bridge that linked Siberia and North America (which had not been populated by hominids). About 18,000 years ago, *Homo sapiens* edged into this landmass.

Berlin Airlift (1948) Supply of vital necessities to West Berlin by air transport primarily under U.S. auspices. It was initiated in response to a land and water blockade of the city instituted by the Soviet Union in the hope that the Allies would be forced to abandon West Berlin.

Berlin Wall Wall built by the communists in Berlin in 1961 to prevent citizens of East Germany from fleeing to West Germany; torn down in 1989.

bhakti Religious practice that grew out of Hinduism and emphasizes personal devotion to gods.

Bhakti Hinduism Popular form of Hinduism that emerged in the seventh century. The religion stresses devotion (*bhakti*) to God and uses vernacular languages (not Sanskrit) spoken by the common people.

big men Leaders of the extended household communities that formed village settlements in African rain forests.

big whites French plantation owners in Saint Domingue (present-day Haiti) who created one of the wealthiest slave societies.

Bilad al-Sudan Arabic for "the land of the blacks"; it consisted of the land lying south of the Sahara.

bilharzia Debilitating water-borne illness. It was widespread in Egypt, where it infected peasants who worked in the irrigation canals.

Bill of Rights First ten amendments to the U.S. Constitution; ratified in 1791.

bipedalism Walking on two legs, thereby freeing hands and arms to carry objects such as weapons and tools; one of several traits that distinguished hominids.

Black Death Great epidemic of the bubonic plague that ravaged Europe, East Asia, and North Africa in the fourteenth century, killing large numbers, including perhaps as many as one-third of the European population.

Black Jacobins Nickname for the rebels in Saint Domingue, including Toussaint L'Ouverture, a former slave who led the slaves of this French colony in the world's largest and most successful slave insurrection.

Black Panthers Radical African American group in the 1960s and 1970s; they advocated black separatism and pan-Africanism.

black shirts Fascist troops of Mussolini's regime; the squads received money from Italian landowners to attack socialist leaders.

Black Tuesday (October 29, 1929) Historic day when the U.S. stock market crashed, plunging the United States and international trading systems into crisis and leading the world into the "Great Depression."

Blitzkrieg "Lightning war"; type of warfare in which the Germans, during World War II, used coordinated aerial bombing campaigns along with tanks and infantrymen in motorized vehicles.

Bodhisattvas In Mahayan Buddhism, enlightened demigods who were ready to reach *nirvana* but delayed so that they might help others attain it.

Bolívar, Simón (1783–1830) Venezuelan leader who urged his followers to become "American," to overcome their local identities. He wanted the liberated countries to form a Latin American confederation, urging Peru and Bolivia to join Venezuela, Ecuador, and Colombia in the "Gran Colombia."

Bolsheviks Former members of the Russian Social Democratic Party who advocated the destruction of capitalist political and economic institutions and started the Russian Revolution. In 1918 the Bolsheviks changed their name to the Russian Communist Party.

Bonaparte, Napoleon (1769–1821) General who rose to power in a post-Revolutionary coup d'état, eventually proclaiming himself emperor of France. He placed security and order ahead of social reform and created a civil legal code. Napoleon expanded his empire through military action, but after his disastrous Russian campaign, the united European powers defeated Napoleon and forced him into exile. He escaped and reassumed command of his army but was later defeated at the Battle of Waterloo.

Book of the Dead Ancient Egyptian funerary text that contains drawings and paintings as well as spells describing how to prepare the jewelry and amulets that were buried with a person in preparation for the afterlife.

bourgeoisie The middle class. In Europe, they sought to be recognized not by birth or title, but by capital and property.

Boxer Protocol Written agreement between the victors of the Boxer Uprising and the Qing Empire in 1901 that placed western troops in Beijing and required the regime to pay exorbitant damages for foreign life and property.

Boxer Uprising (1899–1900) Chinese peasant movement that opposed foreign influence, especially that of Christian missionaries; it was put down after the Boxers were defeated by an army composed mostly of Japanese, Russians, British, French, and Americans.

Brahma One of three major deities that form a trinity in Vedic religion. Brahma signifies birth. *See also* Vishnu *and* Siva.

Brahmans Vedic priests who performed rituals and communicated with the gods. Brahmans provided guidance on how to live in balance with the forces of nature as represented by the various deities. The codification of Vedic principles into codes of law took place at the hands of the Brahmans. They memorized Vedic works and compiled commentaries on them. They also developed their own set of rules and rituals, which developed into a full-scale theology. Originally memorized and passed on orally, these may have been written down sometime after the beginning of the Common Era. Brahmanism was reborn as Hinduism sometime during the first half of the first millennium CE.

British Commonwealth of Nations Union formed in 1926 that conferred "dominion status" on Britain's white settler colonies in Canada, Australia, and New Zealand.

British East India Company *See* East India Company.

bronze Alloy of copper and tin brought into Europe from Anatolia; used to make hard-edged weapons.

brown shirts Troops of German men who advanced the Nazi cause by holding street marches, mass rallies, and confrontations and by beating Jews and anyone who opposed the Nazis.

bubonic plague Acute infectious disease caused by a bacterium that is transmitted to humans by fleas from infected rats. It ravaged Europe and parts of Asia in the fourteenth century. Sometimes referred to as the "Black Death."

Buddha (Siddhartha Gautama; 563–483 BCE) Indian ascetic who founded Buddhism.

Buddhism Major South Asian religion that aims to end human suffering through the renunciation of desire. Buddhists believe that removing the illusion of a separate identity would lead to a state of contentment (nirvana). These beliefs challenged the traditional Brahmanic teachings of the time and provided the peoples of South Asia with an alternative to established traditions.

bullion Uncoined gold or silver.

Cahokia Commercial center for regional and long-distance trade in North America. Its hinterlands produced staples for urban consumers. In return, its crafts were exported inland by porters and to North American markets in canoes. *See also* Mound people.

Calaveras Allegorical skeleton drawings by the Mexican printmaker and artist José Guadalupe Posada. The works drew on popular themes of betrayal, death, and festivity.

caliphate Institution that arose as the successor to Muhammad's leadership and became both the political and religious head of the Islamic community. Although the caliphs exercised political authority over the Muslim community and were the head of the religious community, the *ummah,* they did not inherit Muhammad's prophetic powers and were not authorities in religious doctrine.

Candomblé Yoruba-based religion in northern Brazil; it interwove African practices and beliefs with Christianity.

Canton system System officially established by imperial decree in 1759 that required European traders to have Chinese guild merchants act as guarantors for their good behavior and payment of fees.

caravan cities Set of networks at long-distance trade locations where groups of merchants could assemble during their journeys. Several of these developed into full-fledged cities, especially in the deserts of Arabia.

caravans Companies of men who transported and traded goods along overland routes in North Africa and central Asia; large caravans consisted of 600–1,000 camels and as many as 400 men.

caravansarais Inns along major trade routes that accommodated large numbers of traders, their animals, and their wares.

caravel Sailing vessel suited for nosing in and out of estuaries and navigating in waters with unpredictable currents and winds.

carrack Ship used on open bodies of water, such as the Mediterranean.

Carthage City in what is modern-day Tunisia; emblematic of the trading aspirations and activities of merchants in the Mediterranean. Pottery and other archaeological remains demonstrate that trading contacts with Carthage were as far-flung as Italy, Greece, France, Iberia, and West Africa.

cartography Mapmaking.

caste system Hierarchical system of organizing people and distributing labor.

Caste War of Yucatan (1847–1901) Conflict between Mayan Indians and the Mexican state over Indian autonomy and legal equality, which resulted in the Mexican takeover of the Yucatan peninsula.

Castro, Fidel (1926–) Cuban communist leader whose forces overthrew Batista's corrupt regime in early January 1959. Castro became increasingly radical as he consolidated power, announcing a massive redistribution of land and the nationalization of foreign oil refineries; he declared himself a socialist and aligned himself with the Soviet Union in the wake of the 1961 CIA-backed Bay of Pigs invasion.

Çatal Hüyük Site in Anatolia discovered in 1958. It was a dense honeycomb of settlements filled with rooms whose walls were covered with paintings of wild bulls, hunters, and pregnant women. Çatal Hüyük symbolizes an early transition into urban dwelling and dates to the eighth millennium BCE.

Cathedra Bishop's seat, or throne, in a church.

Catholic Church Unifying institution for Christians in western Europe after the collapse of the Roman Empire. Rome became the spiritual capital of western Europe and the bishops of Rome emerged as popes, the supreme head of the church, who possessed great moral authority.

Cato the Elder (234–149 BCE) Roman statesman, often seen as emblematic of the transition from a Greek to a Roman world. Cato the Elder wrote a manual for the new economy of slave plantation agriculture, invested in shipping and trading, learned Greek rhetoric, and added the genre of history to Latin literature.

Caudillos South American local military chieftains.

cave drawings Images on cave walls. The subjects are most often large game, although a few are images of humans. Other elements are impressions made by hands dipped in paint and pressed on a wall or abstract symbols and shapes.

Celali revolts (1595–1610) Peasant and artisan uprisings against the Ottoman state.

Central powers Defined in World War I as Germany and Austria-Hungary.

Chan Chan City founded between 850 and 900 CE by the Moche people in what is now modern-day Peru. It had a core population of 30,000 inhabitants.

Chan Santa Cruz Separate Mayan community formed as part of a crusade for spiritual salvation and the complete cultural separation of the Mayan Indians; means "little holy cross."

Chandra Gupta II King who reigned in South Asia from 320 to 335 CE. He shared his name with Chandragupta, the founder of the Mauryan Empire.

Chandravamsha One of two main lineages (the lunar one) of Vedic society, each with its own creation myth, ancestors, language, and rituals. Each lineage included many clans. *See* Suryavamsha.

chapatis Flat, unleavened Indian bread.

chariots Horse-driven carriages brought by the pastoral nomadic warriors from the steppes that became the favored mode of transportation for an urban aristocratic warrior class and for other men of power in agriculture-based societies. Control of chariot forces was the foundation of the new balance of power across Afro-Eurasia during the second millennium BCE.

charismatic Person who uses personal strengths or virtues, often laced with a divine aura, to command followers.

Charlemagne Emperor of the West and heir to Rome from 764 to 814 CE.

chartered companies Firms that were awarded monopoly trading rights over vast areas by European monarchs (e.g., Virginia Company, Dutch East India Company).

Chartism (1834–1848) Mass democratic movement to pass the Peoples' Charter in Britain, granting male suffrage, secret ballot, equal electoral districts, and annual parliaments, and absolving the requirement of property ownership for members of the parliament.

chattel slavery Form of slavery that sold people as property, the rise of which coincided with the expansion of city-states. Chattel slavery was eschewed by the Spartans, who also rejected the innovation of coin money.

Chavín A people who lived in what is now northern Peru from 1400 to 200 BCE. They were united more by culture and faith than by a unified political system.

Chernobyl (1986) Site in the Soviet Union (in Ukraine) of the meltdown of a nuclear reactor.

Chiang Kai-shek (1887–1975) Leader of the Guomindang following Sun Yat-sen's death who mobilized the Chinese masses through the New Life movement. In 1949 he lost the Chinese Revolution to the communists and moved his regime to Taiwan.

Chimu Empire South America's first empire; it developed during the first century of the second millennium in the Moche Valley on the Pacific coast.

chinampas Floating gardens used by Aztecs in the 1300s and 1400s to grow crops.

China's Sorrow Name for the Yellow River, which, when it changed course or flooded, could cause mass death and waves of migration.

chinoiserie Chinese silks, teas, tableware, jewelry, and paper; popular among Europeans in the seventeenth and eighteenth centuries.

Christendom Entire portion of the world in which Christianity prevailed.

Christianity Religion that originated at the height of the Roman Empire and in a direct confrontation with Roman imperial authority: the trial of Yeshua ben Yosef (Joshua son of Joseph; we know him today by the Greek form of his name, Jesus). Jesus was condemned for sedition and crucified. His followers believed that he was resurrected and that his teachings were not that of a man, but a god who had walked among human beings. At first, the Roman Empire refused to recognize Christianity and persecuted its followers, but in the fourth century ce Christianity was officially recognized as the Roman state religion.

Church of England Established form of Christianity in England dating from the sixteenth century.

city Highly populated concentration of economic, religious, and political power. The first cities appeared in river basins, which could produce a surplus of agriculture. The abundance of food freed most city inhabitants from the need to produce their own food, which allowed them to work in specialized professions.

city-state Political organization based on the authority of a single, large city that controls outlying territories.

Civil Rights Act (1964) U.S. legislation that banned segregation in public facilities, outlawed racial discrimination in employment, and marked an important step in correcting legal inequality.

civil rights movement Powerful movement for equal rights and the end of racial segregation in the United States that began in the 1950s with court victories against school segregation and nonviolent boycotts.

civil service examinations The world's first written civil service examination system, instituted by the Tang dynasty to recruit officials and bureaucrats. Open to most males, the exams tested a candidate's literary skills and knowledge of the Confucian classics. They helped to unite the Chinese state by making knowledge of a specific language and Confucian classics the only route to power.

Civil War, American (1861–1865) Conflict between the northern and southern states of America; this struggle led to the abolition of slavery in the United States.

clan A social group comprising many households, claiming descent from a common ancestor.

clandestine presses Small printing operations that published banned texts in the early modern era, especially in Switzerland and the Netherlands.

Clovis people Early humans in America who used basic chipped blades and pointed spears in pursuing prey. They extended the hunting traditions they had learned in Afro-Eurasia, such as establishing campsites and moving with their herds. They were known as "Clovis people" because the arrowhead point that they used was first found by archaeologists at a site near Clovis, New Mexico.

codex Early form of book, with separate pages bound together; it replaced the scroll as the main medium for written texts. The codex emerged around 300 CE.

cognitive skills Skills such as thought, memory, problem-solving, and—ultimately—language. Hominids were able to use these skills and their hands to create new adaptations, like tools, which helped them obtain food and avoid predators.

Cohong Chinese merchant guild that traded with Europeans under the Qing dynasty.

coins Form of money that replaced goods, which previously had been bartered for services and other products. Originally used mainly to hire mercenary soldiers, coins became the commonplace method of payment linking buyers and producers throughout the Mediterranean.

cold war (1945–1990) Ideological conflict in which the Soviet Union and eastern Europe opposed the United States and western Europe.

colonies Regions under the political control of another country.

Colons French settler population in Algeria.

Colosseum Huge amphitheater completed by Titus and dedicated in 80 CE. Originally begun by Flavian, the structure is named after a colossal statue of Nero that formerly stood beside it.

Columbian exchange Movements between Afro-Eurasia and the Americas of previously unknown plants, animals, people, diseases, and products that followed in the wake of Columbus's voyages.

commanderies Provinces. Shi Huangdi (First August Emperor) divided China into commanderies (*jun*) to enable the Qin dynasty to rule the massive state effectively. The thirty-six commanderies were then subdivided into counties (*xian*).

Communist Manifesto Pamphlet published by Karl Marx and Friedrich Engels in 1848 at a time when political revolutions were sweeping Europe. It called on the workers of all nations to unite in overthrowing capitalism.

compass Navigation instrument invented by the Chinese and used to determine directions with a magnetized needle, which always points to the North cardinal direction on the compass rose.

Compromise of 1867 Agreement between the Habsburgs and the peoples living in Hungarian parts of the empire that the Habsburg state would be officially known as the Austro-Hungarian Empire.

concession areas Territories, usually ports, where Chinese emperors allowed European merchants to trade and European people to settle.

Confucian ideals The ideals of honoring tradition, emphasizing the responsibility of the emperor, and respect for the lessons of history, promoted by Confucius, which the Han dynasty made the official doctrine of the empire by 50 BCE.

Confucianism Ethics, beliefs, and practices stipulated by the Chinese philosopher Kong Qiu, or Confucius, which served as a guide for Chinese society up to modern times.

Confucius (551–479 BCE) Influential teacher, thinker, and leader in China who developed a set of principles for ethical living. He believed that coercive laws and punishment would not be needed to maintain order in society if men following his ethics ruled. He taught his philosophy to anyone who was intelligent and willing to work, which allowed men to gain entry into the ruling through education.

cong tube Ritual object crafted by the Liangzhu. A cong tube was made of jade and was used in divination practices.

Congo Independent State Large colonial state in Africa created by Leopold II, king of Belgium, during the 1880s, and ruled by him alone. After rumors of mass slaughter and enslavement, the Belgian parliament took the land and formed a Belgian colony.

Congress of Vienna (1814–1815) International conference to reorganize Europe after the downfall of Napoleon. European monarchies agreed to respect each other's borders and to cooperate in guarding against future revolutions and war.

conquistadors Spanish military leaders who led the conquest of the New World in the sixteenth century.

Constantine Roman emperor who converted to Christianity in 312 CE. In 313, he issued a proclamation that gave Christians new freedoms in the empire. He also founded Constantinople (at first called "New Rome").

Constantinople Capital city, formerly known as Byzantium, which was founded as the New Rome by Constantine the Great.

Constitutional Convention (1787) Meeting to formulate the Constitution of the United States of America.

Contra rebels Opponents of the Sandinistas in Nicaragua; they were armed and financed by the United States and other anticommunist countries (1980).

Conversion of Constantine A significant political and religious turning point in the Roman Empire. Before the decisive battle for Rome in 312 CE, Constantine supposedly had a dream in which he was told to place a sign with the opening letters of Christ's name on his soldiers' shields. Constantine won the ensuing battle; he soon issued a proclamation giving privileges to Christian bishops. The edict spread Christianity through the institutions and across the byways of the Roman Empire.

Conversos Jewish and Muslim converts to Christianity in the Iberian Peninsula and the New World.

Coptic Form of Christianity practiced in Egypt. It was doctrinally different from Christianity elsewhere, and Coptic Christians had their own views of Christology, or the nature of Christ.

Corn Laws Laws that imposed tariffs on grain imported to Great Britain, intended to protect British farming interests. The Corn Laws were abolished in 1846 as part of a British movement in favor of free trade.

cosmology Branch of metaphysics devoted to understanding the order of the universe.

Council of Nicaea Church council convened in 325 CE by Constantine and presided over by him as well. At this council, a Christian creed was articulated and made into a formula that expressed the philosophical and technical elements of Christian belief.

Counter-Reformation Movement to counter the spread of the Reformation; initiated by the Catholic Church at the Council of Trent in 1545. The Catholic Church enacted reforms to attack clerical corruption and it placed a greater emphasis on individual spirituality. During this time, the Jesuits were founded to help revive the Catholic Church.

coup d'état Overthrow of established state by a group of conspirators, usually from the military.

creed Formal statement of faith or expression of a belief system. A Christian creed or "credo" was formulated by the Council of Nicaea in 325 CE.

creoles Persons of full-blooded European descent who were born in the Spanish American colonies.

Crimean War (1853–1856) War waged by Russia against Great Britain and France. Spurred by Russia's encroachment on Ottoman territories, the conflict revealed Russia's military weakness when Russian forces fell to British and French troops.

crossbow Innovative weapon used at the end of the Warring States period that allowed archers to shoot their enemies with accuracy, even from a distance.

Crusades Wave of attacks launched in the late eleventh century by western Europeans. The First Crusade began in 1095, when Pope Urban II appealed to the warrior nobility of France to free Jerusalem from Muslim rule. Four subsequent Crusades were fought over the next two centuries.

Cuban Missile Crisis (1962) Diplomatic standoff between the United States and the Soviet Union that was provoked by the Soviet Union's attempt to base nuclear missiles in Cuba; it brought the world close to a nuclear war.

cult Religious movement, often based on the worship of a particular god or goddess.

cultigen Organism that has diverged from its ancestors through domestication or cultivation.

cuneiform Wedge-shaped form of writing. As people combined rebus symbols with other visual marks that contained meaning, they became able to record and transmit messages over long distances by using abstract symbols or signs to denote concepts; such signs later came to represent syllables, which could be joined into words. By impressing these signs into wet clay with the cut end of a reed, scribes engaged in cuneiform.

Cyrus the Great Founder of the Persian Empire. This sixth-century ruler (559–529 BCE) conquered the Medes and unified the Iranian kingdoms.

Daimyo Ruling lords who commanded private armies in pre-Meiji Japan.

dan Fodio, Usman (1754–1817) Fulani Muslim cleric whose visions led him to challenge the Hausa ruling classes, whom he believed were insufficiently faithful to Islamic beliefs and practices. His ideas gained support among those who had suffered under the Hausa landlords. In 1804, his supporters and allies overthrew the Hausa in what is today northern Nigeria.

Daoism School of thought developed at the end of the Warring States period that focused on the importance of following the Dao, or the natural way of the cosmos. Daoism emphasized the need to accept the world as it was rather than trying to change it through politics or the government. Unlike Confucianism, Daoism scorned rigid rituals and social hierarchies.

Dar al-Islam Arabic for "the House of Islam"; it describes a sense of common identity.

Darius I (521–486 BCE) Leader who put the emerging unified Persian Empire onto solid footing after Cyrus's death.

Darwin, Charles (1809–1882) British scientist who became convinced that the species of organic life had evolved under the uniform pressure of natural laws, not by means of a special, one-time creation as described in the Bible.

D-Day (June 6, 1944) Day of the Allied invasion of Normandy under General Dwight Eisenhower to liberate western Europe from German occupation.

Dear Boy Nickname of an early human remain discovered in 1931 by a team of archaeologists named the Leakeys. They discovered an almost totally intact skull. Other objects discovered with Dear Boy demonstrated that by the time of Dear Boy, early humans had begun to fashion tools and to use them for butchering animals and possibly for hunting and killing smaller animals.

Decembrists Russian army officers who were influenced by events in revolutionary France and formed secret societies that espoused liberal governance. They were put down by Nicholas I in December 1825.

Declaration of Independence U.S. document stating the theory of government on which America was founded.

Declaration of the Rights of Man and Citizen (1789) French charter of liberties formulated by the National Assembly that marked the end of dynastic and aristocratic rule. The seventeen articles later became the preamble to the new constitution, which the assembly finished in 1791.

decolonization End of empire and emergence of new independent nation-states in Asia and Africa as a result of the defeat of Japan in World War II and weakened European influence after the war.

Delhi Sultanate (1206–1526) Turkish regime of Northern India. The regime strengthened the cultural diversity and tolerance that were a hallmark of the Indian social order, which allowed it to bring about political integration without enforcing cultural homogeneity.

democracy The idea that people, through membership in a nation, should choose their own representatives and be governed by them.

Democritus Thinker in ancient Greece who lived from 470 to 360 BCE; he deduced the existence of the atom and postulated that there was such a thing as an indivisible particle.

demotic writing The second of two basic forms of ancient Egyptian writing. Demotic was a cursive script written with ink on papyrus, on pottery, or on other absorbent objects. It was the most common and practical form of writing in Egypt and was used for administrative record keeping and in private or pseudo-private forms like letters and works of literature. *See also* Hieroglyphs.

developing world Term applied to countries collectively called the Third World during the cold war and seeking to develop viable nation-states and prosperous economies.

Devshirme System of taking non-Muslim children in place of taxes in order to educate them in Ottoman Muslim ways and prepare them for service in the sultan's bureaucracy.

dhamma Moral code espoused by A´soka in the Kalinga edict, which was meant to apply to all—Buddhists, Brahmans, and Greeks alike.

***dhimma* system** Ottoman law that permitted followers of religions other than Islam, such as Armenian Christians, Greek Orthodox Christians, and Jews, to choose their own religious leaders and to settle internal disputes within their religious communities as long as they accepted Islam's political dominion.

dhows Ships used by Arab seafarers; the dhow's large sails were rigged to maximize the capture of wind.

Dien Bien Phu (1954) Defining battle in the war between French colonialists and the Viet Minh that secured North Vietnam for Ho Chi Minh and his army and left the south to form its own government to be supported by France and the United States.

Din-I-llahi "House of worship" in which the Mughal emperor Akbar engaged in religious debate with Hindu, Muslim, Jain, Parsi, and Christian theologians.

Diogenes Greek philosopher who lived from 412 to 323 BCE and who espoused a doctrine of self-sufficiency and freedom from social laws and customs. He rejected cultural norms as out of tune with nature and therefore false.

Directory Temporary military committee that took over the affairs of the state of France in 1795 from the radicals and held control until the coup of Napoleon Bonaparte.

divination The interpretation of rituals used to communicate the wishes of gods or royal ancestors to foretell future events. Divination was used to legitimize royal authority and demand tribute.

Djoser Ancient Egyptian king who reigned from 2630 to 2611 BCE. He was the second king of the Third Dynasty and celebrated the Sed festival in his tomb complex at Saqqara.

domestication Bringing a wild animal or plant under human control.

Dominion in the British Commonwealth Canadian promise to keep up the country's fealty to the British crown, even after its independence in 1867. Later applied to Australia and New Zealand.

Dong Zhongshu Emperor Wu's chief minister, who advocated a more powerful view of Confucius by promoting texts that focused on Confucius as a man who possessed aspects of divinity.

double-outrigger canoes Vessels used by early Austronesians to cross the Taiwan Straits and colonize islands in the Pacific. These sturdy canoes could cover over 120 miles per day.

Duma Russian parliament.

Dutch learning Broad term for European teachings that were strictly regulated by the shoguns inside Japan.

dynastic cycle Political narrative in which influential families vied for supremacy. Upon gaining power, they legitimated their authority by claiming to be the heirs of previous grand dynasts and by preserving or revitalizing the ancestors' virtuous governing ways. This continuity conferred divine support.

dynasty Hereditary ruling family that passed control from one generation to the next.

Earth Summit (1992) Meeting in Rio de Janeiro between many of the world's governments in an effort to address international environmental problems.

East India Company (1600–1858) British charter company created to outperform Portuguese and Spanish traders in the Far East; in the eighteenth century the company became, in effect, the ruler of a large part of India.

Eastern Front Battlefront between Berlin and Moscow during World War I and World War II.

Edict of Nantes (1598) Edict issued by Henry IV to end the French Wars of Religion. The edict declared France a Catholic country but tolerated some Protestant worship.

Egyptian Middle Kingdom Period of Egyptian history lasting from about 2040 to1640 BCE, characterized by a consolidation of power and building activity in Upper Egypt.

Eiffel Tower Steel monument completed in 1889 for the Paris Exposition. It was twice the height of any other building at the time.

eight-legged essay Highly structured essay form with eight parts, required on Chinese civil service examinations.

Ekklesia Church or early gathering committed to leaders chosen by God and fellow believers.

Ekpe Powerful slave trade institution that organized the supply and purchase of slaves inland from the Gulf of Guinea in West Africa.

Elamites A people with their capital in the upland valley of modern Fars who became a cohesive polity that incorporated transhumant people of the Zagros Mountains. A group of Elamites who migrated south and west into Mesopotamia helped conquer the Third Dynasty of Ur in 2400 BCE.

empire Group of states or different ethnic groups under a single sovereign power.

Enabling Act (1933) Emergency act passed by the Reichstag (German parliament) that helped transform Hitler from Germany's chancellor, or prime minister, into a dictator following the suspicious burning of the Reichstag building and a suspension of civil liberties.

enclosure A movement in which landowners took control of lands that traditionally had been common property serving local needs.

Encomenderos Commanders of the labor services of the colonized peoples in Spanish America.

Encomiendas Grants from European Spanish governors to control the labor services of colonized people.

Endeavor Ship of Captain James Cook, whose celebrated voyages to the South Pacific in the late eighteenth century supplied Europe with information about the plants, birds, landscapes, and people of this uncharted territory.

Engels, Friedrich (1820–1895) German social and political philosopher who collaborated with Karl Marx on many publications, including *The Communist Manifesto*.

English Navigation Act of 1651 Act stipulating that only English ships could carry goods between the mother country and its colonies.

English Peasants' Revolt (1381) Uprising of serfs and free farm workers that began as a protest against a tax levied to raise money for a war on France. The revolt was suppressed but led to the gradual emergence of a free peasantry as labor shortages made it impossible to keep peasants bound to the soil.

enlightened absolutists Seventeenth- and eighteenth-century monarchs who claimed to rule rationally and in the best interests of their subjects and who hired loyal bureaucrats to implement the knowledge of the new age.

Enlightenment Intellectual movement in eighteenth-century Europe stressing natural laws and reason as the basis of authority.

entrepôts Trading stations at the borders between communities, which made exchange possible among many different partners. Long-distance traders could also replenish their supplies at these stations.

Epicurus Greek philosopher who espoused emphasis on the self. He lived from 341 to 279 BCE and founded a school in Athens called The Garden. He stressed the importance of sensation, teaching that pleasurable sensations were good and painful sensations bad. Members of his school sought to find peace and relaxation by avoiding unpleasantness or suffering.

Estates-General French quasi-parliamentary body called in 1789 to deal with the financial problems that afflicted France. It had not met since 1614.

Etruscans A dominant people on the Italian peninsula until the fourth century BCE. The Etruscan states were part of the foundation of the Roman Empire.

eunuchs Loyal and well-paid men who were surgically castrated as youths and remained in service to the caliph or emperor. Both Abbasid and Tang rulers relied for protection on a cadre of eunuchs.

Eurasia The combined area of Europe and Asia.

European Union (EU) International body organized after World War II as an attempt at reconciliation between Germany and the rest of Europe. It initially aimed to forge closer industrial cooperation. Eventually, through various treaties, many European states relinquished some of their sovereignty, and the cooperation became a full-fledged union with a single currency, the euro, and with a somewhat less powerful common European parliament.

evolution Process by which the different species of the world—its plants and animals—made changes in response to their environment that enabled them to survive and increase in numbers.

Exclusion Act of 1882 U.S. congressional act prohibiting nearly all immigration from China to the United States; fueled by animosity toward Chinese workers in the American West.

Ezo Present-day Hokkaido, Japan's fourth main island.

fascism Mass political movement founded by Benito Mussolini that emphasized nationalism, militarism, and the omnipotence of the state.

Fascists Radical right-wing group of disaffected veterans that formed around Mussolini in 1919 and a few years later came to power in Rome.

Fatehpur Sikri Mughal emperor Akbar's temporary capital near Agra.

Fatimids Shiite dynasty that ruled parts of the Islamic Empire beginning in the tenth century CE. They were based in Egypt and founded the city of Cairo.

February Revolution (1917) The first of two uprisings of the Russian Revolution, which led to the end of the Romanov dynasty.

Federal Deposit Insurance Corporation (FDIC) Organization created in 1933 to guarantee all bank deposits up to $5,000 as part of the New Deal in the United States.

Federal Republic of Germany (1949–1990) Country formed of the areas occupied by the Allies after World War II. Also known as West Germany, this country experienced rapid demilitarization, democratization, and integration into the world economy.

Federal Reserve Act (1913) U.S. legislation that created a series of boards to monitor the supply and demand of the nation's money.

Federalists Supporters of the ratification of the U.S. Constitution, which was written to replace the Articles of Confederation.

feminist movements Movements that called for equal treatment for men and women—equal pay and equal opportunities for obtaining jobs and advancement. Feminism arose mainly in Europe and in North America in the 1960s and then became global in the 1970s.

Ferangi Arabic word meaning "Frank" that was used to describe Crusaders.

Fertile Crescent Site of the world's first agricultural revolution; an area in Southwest Asia, bounded by the Mediterranean Sea in the west and the Zagros Mountains in the east.

feudalism System instituted in medieval Europe after the collapse of the Carolingian Empire (814 CE) whereby each peasant was under the authority of a lord.

fiefdoms Medieval economic and political units.

First World Term invented during the cold war to refer to western Europe and North America (also known as the "free world" or the West); Japan later joined this group. Following the principles of liberal modernism, First World states sought to organize the world on the basis of capitalism and democracy.

Five Pillars of Islam The five tenets, or main aspects, of Islamic practice: testification or bearing witness that there is no God other than God (Allah, in Arabic) and that Muhammad is the messenger of God; praying five times a day; fasting from sunup to sundown every day during Ramadan (a month on the Islamic calendar); giving alms; and making a pilgrimage to Mecca.

Five-Year Plan Soviet effort launched under Stalin in 1928 to replace the market with a state-owned and state-managed economy, to promote rapid economic development over a five-year period of time and thereby "catch and overtake" the leading capitalist countries. The First Five-Year Plan was followed by the Second Five-Year Plan (1933–1937), and so on, until the collapse of the Soviet Union in 1991.

Flagellants European social group that came into existence during the bubonic plague in the fourteenth century; they believed that the plague was the wrath of God.

floating population Poor migrant workers in China who supplied labor under Emperor Wu.

Fluitschips Dutch shipping vessels that could carry heavy bulky cargo with relatively small crews.

flying cash Letters of exchange—early predecessors of paper cash instead of coins—first developed by guilds in the northwestern Shanxi. By the thirteenth century, paper money had eclipsed coins.

Fondûqs Complexes in caravan cities that included hostels, storage houses, offices, and temples.

Forbidden City of Beijing Palace city of the Ming and Qing dynasties.

Force Publique Colonial army used to maintain order in the Belgian Congo; during the early stages of King Leopold's rule, it was responsible for bullying local communities.

Fourierism Form of utopian socialism based on the ideas of Charles Fourier (1772–1837). Fourier envisioned communes where work was made enjoyable and systems of production and distribution were run without merchants. His ideas appealed to middle-class readers, especially women, as a higher form of Christian communalism.

free labor Wage-paying rather than slave labor.

free markets Unregulated markets.

Free Officers Movement Secret organization of Egyptian junior military officers who came to power in a coup d'état in 1952, forced King Faruq to abdicate, and consolidated their own control through dissolving the parliament, banning opposing parties, and rewriting the constitution.

free trade Domestic and international trade unencumbered by tariff barriers, quotas, and fees.

Front de Libération Nationale (FLN) Algerian anticolonial, nationalist party that waged an eight-year war against French troops, beginning in 1854, that forced nearly all of the 1,000,000 colonists to leave.

Fulani Muslim group in West Africa that carried out religious revolts at the end of the eighteenth and the beginning of the nineteenth centuries in an effort to return to the pure Islam of the past.

fur trade Trading of animal pelts (especially beaver skins) by Indians for European goods in North America.

Gandhi, Mohandhas Karamchand (Mahatma) (1869–1948) Indian leader who led a nonviolent struggle for India's independence from Britain.

garrison towns Stations for soldiers originally established in strategic locations to protect territorial acquisition. Eventually, they became towns. Alexander the Great's garrison towns evolved into cities that served as centers from which Hellenistic culture was spread to his easternmost territories.

garrisons Military bases inside cities; often used for political purposes, such as protecting rulers and putting down domestic revolts or enforcing colonial rule.

gauchos Argentine, Brazilian, and Uruguayan cowboys who wanted a decentralized federation, with autonomy for their provinces and respect for their way of life.

Gdansk shipyard Site of mass strikes in Poland that led in 1980 to the formation of the first independent trade union, Solidarity, in the communist bloc.

gendered relations A relatively recent development that implies roles emerged only with the appearance of modern humans and perhaps Neanderthals. When humans began to think imaginatively and in complex symbolic ways and give voice to their insights, perhaps around 150,000 years ago, gender categories began to crystallize.

genealogy History of the descent of a person or family from a distant ancestor.

Geneva Peace Conference (1954) International conference to restore peace in Korea and Indochina. The chief participants were the United States, the Soviet Union, Great Britain, France, the People's Republic of China, North Korea, South Korea, Vietnam, the Viet Minh party, Laos, and Cambodia. The conference resulted in the division of North and South Vietnam.

Genoa One of two Italian cities (the other was Venice) that linked Europe, Africa, and Asia as nodes of commerce in 1300 CE. Genoese ships linked the Mediterranean to the coast of Flanders through consistent routes along the Atlantic coasts of Spain, Portugal, and France.

German Democratic Republic Nation founded from the Soviet zone of occupation of Germany after World War II; also known as East Germany.

German Social Democratic Party Founded in 1875, the most powerful Socialist party in Europe before 1917.

Ghana The most celebrated medieval political kingdom in West Africa.

Ghost Dance American Indian ritual performed in the nineteenth century in the hope of restoring the world to precolonial conditions.

Gilgamesh Heroic narrative written in the Babylonian dialect of Semitic Akkadian. This story and others like it were meant to circulate and unify the kingdom.

Girondins Liberal revolutionary group that supported the creation of a constitutional monarchy during the early stages of the French Revolution.

global warming Release into the air of human-made carbons that contribute to rising temperatures worldwide.

globalization Development of integrated worldwide cultural and economic structures.

Gold Coast Name that European mariners and merchants gave to that part of West Africa from which gold was exported. This area was conquered by the British in the nineteenth century and became a British colony; upon independence, it became Ghana.

Goths One of the groups of "barbarian" migrants into Roman territory in the fourth century.

government schools Schools founded by the Han dynasty to provide an adequate number of officials to fill positions in the administrative bureaucracy. The Imperial University had 30,000 members by the second century BCE.

Gracchus brothers Two tribunes, the brothers Tiberius and Gaius Gracchus, who in 133 and 123–21 BCE attempted to institute land reforms that would guarantee all of Rome's poor citizens a basic amount of land that would qualify them for army service. Both men were assassinated.

Grand Canal Created in 486 BCE, a thousand-mile-long connector between the Yellow and Yangzi rivers, linking the north and south, respectively.

grand unity Guiding political idea embraced by Qin rulers and ministers, with an eye toward joining the states of the Central Plain into one empire and centralizing administration.

"Greased cartridge" controversy Controversy spawned by the rumor that cow and pig fat had been used to grease the shotguns of the sepoys in the British army in India. Believing that this was a British attempt to defile their religion and speed their conversion to Christianity, the sepoys mutinied against the British officers.

Great Depression Worldwide depression following the U.S. stock market crash on October 29, 1929.

great divide The division between economically developed nations and less developed nations.

Great East Asia Co-Prosperity Sphere Term used by the Japanese during the 1930s and 1940s to refer to Hong Kong, Singapore, Malaya, Burma, and other states that they seized during their run for expansion.

Great Flood One of many traditional Mesopotamian stories that were transmitted orally from one generation to another before being recorded. The Sumerian King List refers to this crucial event in Sumerian memory and identity. The Great Flood was assigned responsibility for Uruk's demise to the gods.

Great Game Competition over areas such as Turkistan, Persia (present-day Iran), and Afghanistan. The British (in India) and the Russians believed that controlling these areas was crucial to preventing their enemies' expansion.

Great League of Peace and Power Iroquois Indian alliance that united previously warring communities.

Great Leap Forward (1958–1961) Plan devised by Mao Zedong to achieve rapid agricultural and industrial growth in China. The plan failed miserably and more than 20 million people died.

great plaza at Isfahan The center of Safavid power in the seventeenth century created by Shah Abbas (r. 1587–1629) to represent the unification of trade, government, and religion under one supreme political authority.

Great Proletarian Cultural Revolution (1966–1976) Mass mobilization of urban Chinese youth inaugurated by Mao Zedong in an attempt to reinvigorate the Chinese revolution and to prevent the development of a bureaucratized Soviet style of communism; with this movement, Mao turned against his longtime associates in the communist party.

Great Trek Afrikaner migration to the interiors of Africa after the British abolished slavery in the empire in 1833.

Great War (August 1914–November 1918) A total war involving the armies of Britain, France, and Russia (the Allies) against those of Germany, Austria-Hungary, and the Ottoman Empire (the Central Powers). Italy joined the Allies in 1915, and the United States joined them in 1917, helping tip the balance in favor of the Allies, who also drew upon the populations and material of their colonial possessions. Also known as World War I.

Greek Orthodoxy Enduring form of Christianity that used the framework of the "Roman" state inherited from Constantine and Justinian to protect itself from Roman Catholicism and Muslim forces. The Greek Orthodox capital was Constantinople and its spiritual empire included the Russian peoples, Baltic Slavs, and peoples living in southwest Asia.

Greenbacks Members of the American political party of the late nineteenth century that worked to advance the interest of farmers by promoting cheap money.

griots Counselors and other officials to the royal family in African kingships. They were also responsible for the preservation and transmission of oral histories and repositories of knowledge.

Group Areas Act (1950) Act that divided South Africa into separate racial and tribal areas and required Africans to live in their own separate communities, including the "homelands."

guerrillas Portuguese and Spanish peasant bands who resisted the revolutionary and expansionist efforts of Napoleon; after the French word *guerre*.

guest workers Migrants looking for temporary employment abroad.

Gulag Administrative name for the vast system of forced labor camps under the Soviet regime; it originated in a small monastery near the Arctic Circle and spread throughout the Soviet Union and to other Soviet-style socialist countries. Penal labor was required of both ordinary criminals (rapists, murderers, thieves) and those accused of political crimes (counterrevolution, anti-Soviet agitation).

Gulf War (1991) Armed conflict between Iraq and a coalition of thirty-two nations, including the United States, Britain, Egypt, France, and Saudi Arabia. It was started by Iraq's invasion of Kuwait, which it had long claimed, on August 2, 1990.

gunpowder Explosive powder. By 1040, the first gunpowder recipes were being written down. Over the next 200 years, Song entrepreneurs invented several incendiary devices and techniques for controlling explosions.

gunpowder empires Muslim empires of the Ottomans, Safavids, and Mughals that used cannonry and gunpowder to advance their military causes.

Guomindang Nationalist party of China, founded just before World War I by Sun Yat-sen and later led by Chiang Kai-shek.

Habsburg Empire Ruling house of Austria, which once ruled both Spain and central Europe but came to settle in lands along the Danube River; it played a prominent role in European affairs for many centuries. In 1867, the Habsburg Empire was reorganized into the Austro-Hungarian Dual Monarchy, and in 1918 it collapsed.

Hadith Sayings attributed to the Prophet Muhammad and his early converts. Used to guide the behavior of Muslim peoples.

Hagia Sophia Enormous and impressive church sponsored by Justinian and built starting in 532 CE. At the time, it was the largest church in the world.

Hajj Pilgrimage to Mecca; an obligation for Muslims.

Hammurapi's Code Legal code created by Hammurapi, the most famous of the Mesopotamian rulers, who reigned from 1792 to 1750 BCE. Hammurapi sought to create social order by centralizing state authority and creating a grand legal structure that embodied paternal justice. The code was quite stratified, dividing society into three classes: free men, dependent men, and slaves, each with distinct rights and responsibilities.

Han agrarian ideal Guiding principle for the free peasantry that made up the base of Han society. In this system, peasants were honored for their labors, while merchants were subjected to a range of controls, including regulations on luxury consumption, and were belittled for not engaging in physical labor.

Han Chinese Inhabitants of China proper who considered others to be outsiders. They felt that they were the only authentic Chinese.

Han Fei Chinese state minister who lived from 280 to 223 BCE; he was a proponent and follower of Xunzi.

Han military Like its Roman counterpart, a ruthless military machine that expanded the empire and created stable conditions that permitted the safe transit of goods by caravans. Emperor Wu heavily influenced the transformation of the military forces and reinstituted a policy that made military service compulsory.

Hangzhou City and former provincial seaport that became the political center of the Chinese people in their ongoing struggles with northern steppe nomads. It was also one of China's gateways to the rest of the world by way of the South China Sea.

Hannibal Great Roman general from Carthage whose campaigns in the third century BCE swept from Spain toward the Italian peninsula. He crossed the Pyrenees and the Alps mountain ranges with war elephants. He was unable, however, to defeat the Romans in 217 BCE.

Harappa One of two cities that, by 2500 BCE, began to take the place of villages throughout the Indus River valley (the other was Mohenjo Daro). Each covered an area of about 250 acres and probably housed 35,000 residents.

harem Secluded women's quarters in Muslim households.

Harlem Renaissance Cultural movement in the 1920s that was based in Harlem, a part of New York City with a large African American population. The movement gave voice to black novelists, poets, painters, and musicians, many of whom used their art to protest racism; also referred to as the "New Negro movement."

harnesses Tools made from wood, bone, bronze, and iron for steering and controlling chariot horses. Harnesses discovered by archaeologists reveal the evolution of headgear from simple mouth bits to full bridles with headpiece, mouthpiece, and reins.

Hatshepsut Leader known as ancient Egypt's most powerful woman ruler. Hatshepsut served as regent for her young son, Thutmosis III, whose reign began in 1479 BCE. She remained co-regent until her death.

Haussmannization Redevelopment and beautification of urban centers; named after the city planner who "modernized" mid-nineteenth-century Paris.

Hegira "Emigration" of Muhammad and his followers out of a hostile Mecca to Yathrib, a city that was later called Medina. The year in which this journey took place, 622 CE, is also year 1 of the Islamic calendar.

Heian period Period from 794 to 1185, during which began the pattern of regents ruling Japan in the name of the sacred emperor.

Hellenism Process by which the individuality of the cultures of the earlier Greek city-states gave way to a uniform culture that stressed the common identity of all who embraced Greek ways. This culture emphasized the common denominators of language, style, and politics to which anyone, anywhere in the Afro-Eurasian world, could have access.

hieroglyphs One of two basic forms of Egyptian writing that were used in conjunction throughout antiquity. Hieroglyphs are pictorial symbols; the term derives from a Greek word meaning "sacred carving"—they were employed exclusively in temple, royal, and divine contexts. *See also* Demotic writing.

Hijra Tradition of Islam, whereby one withdraws from one's community to create another, more holy, one. The practice is based on the Prophet Muhammad's withdrawal from the city of Mecca to Medina in 622 CE.

Hinayana (Lesser Vehicle) Buddhism Form of Buddhism that accepted the divinity of Buddha himself but not of demigods, or bodhisattvas.

Hinduism A refashioning of the ancient Brahmanic Vedic religion, bringing it in accord with rural life and agrarian values. It emerged as the dominant faith in Indian society in the third century CE. Believers became vegetarians and adopted rituals of self-sacrifice. Three major deities—Brahma, Vishnu, and Siva—formed a trinity representing the three phases of the universe (birth, existence, and destruction, respectively) and the three expressions of the eternal self, or *atma*.

Hindu revivalism Movement to reconfigure traditional Hinduism to be less diverse and more amenable to producing a narrowed version of Indian tradition.

Hiroshima Japanese port devastated by an atomic bomb on August 6, 1945.

Hitler, Adolf (1889–1945) German dictator and leader of the Nazi Party who seized power in Germany after its economic collapse in the Great Depression. Hitler and his Nazi regime started World War II in Europe and systematically murdered Jews and other non-Aryan groups in the name of racial purity.

Hittites One of the five great territorial states. The Hittites campaigned throughout Anatolia, then went east to northern Syria, though they eventually faced weaknesses in their own homeland. Their heyday was marked by the reign of the king Supiliulimua (1380 to 1345 BCE), who preserved the Hittites' influence on the balance of power in the region between Mesopotamia and the Nile.

Holocaust Deliberate racial extermination of the Jews by the Nazis that claimed around 6 million European Jews.

Holy Roman Empire Enormous realm that encompassed much of Europe and aspired to be the Christian successor state to the Roman Empire. In the time of the Habsburg dynasts, the empire was a loose confederation of principalities that obeyed an emperor elected by elite lower-level sovereigns. Despite its size, the empire never effectively centralized power; it was split into Austrian and Spanish factions when Charles V abdicated to his sons in 1556.

Holy Russia Name applied to Muscovy and then to the Russian Empire by Slavic Eastern Orthodox clerics who were appalled by the Muslim conquest in 1453 of Constantinople (the capital of Byzantium and of Eastern Christianity) and who were hopeful that Russia would become the new protector of the faith.

home charges Fees India was forced to pay to Britain as its colonial master; these fees included interest on railroad loans, salaries to colonial officers, and the maintenance of imperial troops outside India.

hominids Humanlike beings who walked erect and preceded modern humans.

Homo A word used by scientists to differentiate between pre-human and "true human" species.

Homo caudatus "Tailed man," believed by some European Enlightenment thinkers to be an early species of humankind.

Homo erectus Species that emerged about 1.5 million years ago and had a large brain and walked truly upright. *Homo erectus* means "Standing man."

Homo habilis Scientific term for "Skillful man." Toolmaking ability truly made *Homo habilis* the forerunners, though very distant, of modern humans.

Homo sapiens The first humans; they emerged in a small region of Africa about 200,000 years ago and migrated out of Africa about 100,000 years ago. They had bigger brains and greater dexterity than previous hominid species, whom they eventually eclipsed.

homogeneity Uniformity of the languages, customs, and religion of a particular people or place. It can also be demonstrated by a consistent calendar, set of laws, administrative practices, and rituals.

horses Animals used by full-scale nomadic communities to dominate the steppe lands in western Afro-Eurasia by the second millennium BCE. Horse-riding nomads moved their large herds across immense tracts of land within zones defined by rivers, mountains, and other natural geographical features. In the arid zones of central Eurasia, the nomadic economies made horses a crucial component of survival.

Huguenots French Protestants who endured severe persecution in the sixteenth and seventeenth centuries.

humanism The Renaissance aspiration to know more about the human experience beyond what the Christian scriptures offered by reaching back into ancient Greek and Roman texts.

Hundred Days' Reform (1898) Abortive modernizing reform program of the Qing government of China.

hunting and gathering Lifestyle in which food is acquired through hunting animals, fishing, and foraging for wild berries, nuts, fruit, and grains, rather than planting crops, vines, or trees. As late as 1500, as much as 15 percent of the world's population still lived by this method.

Hyksos A western Semitic-speaking people whose name means "Rulers of Foreign Lands"; they overthrew the unstable Thirteenth Dynasty in Egypt around 1640 BCE. The Hyksos had mastered the art of horse chariots, and with those chariots and their superior bronze axes and composite bows (made of wood, horn, and sinew), they were able to defeat the pharaoh's foot soldiers.

Ibn Sina Philosopher and physician who lived from 980 to 1037 CE. He was also schooled in the Quran, geometry, literature, and Indian and Euclidian mathematics.

ideology Dominant set of ideas of a widespread culture or movement.

Il Duce Term designating the fascist Italian leader Benito Mussolini.

Iliad Epic Greek poem about the Trojan War, composed several centuries after the events it describes. It was based on oral tales passed down for generations.

Il-khanate Mongol-founded dynasty in thirteenth-century Persia.

Imam Muslim religious leader and politico-religious descendant of Ali; believed by some to have a special relationship with Allah.

imperialism Acquisition of new territories by a state and the incorporation of these territories into a political system as subordinate colonies.

Imperium Latin word used to express Romans' power and command over their subjects. It is the basis of the English words *empire* and *imperialism.*

Inca Empire Empire of Quecha-speaking rulers in the Andean valley of Cuzco that encompassed a population of 4 to 6 million. The Incas lacked a clear inheritance system, causing an internal split that Pizarro's forces exploited in 1533.

Indian Institutes of Technology (IIT) Institutions originally designed as engineering schools to expand knowledge and to modernize India, which produced a whole generation of pioneering computer engineers, many of whom moved to the United States.

Indian National Congress Formed in 1885, a political party deeply committed to constitutional methods, industrialization, and cultural nationalism.

Indian National Muslim League Founded in 1906, an organization dedicated to advancing the political interests of Muslims in India.

Indo-Greek Fusion of Indian and Greek culture in the area under the control of the Bactrians, in the northwestern region of India, around 200 BCE.

Indu What we would today call India. Called "Indu" by Xuanzang, a Chinese Buddhist pilgrim who visited the area in the 630s and 640s CE.

indulgences Church-sponsored fund-raising mechanism that gave certification that one's sins had been forgiven in return for money.

industrial revolution Gradual accumulation and diffusion of old and new technical knowledge that led to major economic changes in Britain, northwestern Europe, and North America, catapulting these countries ahead of the rest of the world in manufacturing and agricultural output and standards of living.

industrious revolution Dramatic economic change in which households that had traditionally produced for themselves decided to work harder and longer hours in order to produce more for the market, which enabled them to increase their income and standard of living. Areas that underwent the industrious revolution shifted from peasant farming to specialized production for the market.

innovation Creation of a new method that allowed humans to make better adaptations to their environment such as the making of new tools.

Inquisition Tribunal of the Roman Catholic Church that enforced religious orthodoxy during the Protestant Reformation.

internal and external alchemy In Daoist ritual, use of trance and meditation or chemicals and drugs, respectively, to cause transformations in the self.

International Monetary Fund (IMF) Agency founded in 1944 to help restore financial order in Europe and the rest of the world, to revive international trade, and to support the financial concerns of Third World governments.

invisible hand As described in Adam Smith's *The Wealth of Nations,* the idea that the operations of a free market produce economic efficiency and economic benefits for all.

iron Malleable metal found in combined forms almost everywhere in the world; it became the most important and widely used metal in world history after the Bronze Age.

Iron Curtain Term popularized by Winston Churchill after World War II to refer to a rift, or an iron curtain, that divided western Europe, under American influence, from eastern Europe, under the domination of the Soviet Union.

irrigation Technological advance whereby water delivery systems and water sluices in floodplains or riverine areas were channeled or redirected and used to nourish soil.

Islam A religion that dates to 610 CE, when Muhammad believed God came to him in a vision. Islam ("submission"—in this case, to the will of God) requires its followers to act righteously, to submit themselves to the one and only true God, and to care for the less fortunate. Muhammad's most insistent message was the oneness of God, a belief that has remained central to the Islamic faith ever since.

Jacobins Radical French political group that came into existence during the French Revolution and executed the French king and sought to remake French culture.

Jacquerie (1358) French peasant revolt in defiance of feudal restrictions.

jade The most important precious substance in East Asia. Jade was associated with goodness, purity, luck, and virtue, and was carved into such items as ceremonial knives, blade handles, religious objects, and elaborate jewelry.

Jagat Seths Enormous trading and banking empire in eastern India.

Jainism Along with Buddhism, one of the two systems of thought developed in the seventh century BCE that set themselves up against Brahmanism. Its founder, Vardhamana Mahavira, taught that the universe obeys its own everlasting rules that no god or other supernatural being could affect. The purpose of life was to purify one's soul in order to attain a state of permanent bliss, which could be accomplished through self-denial and the avoidance of harming other creatures.

Janissaries Corps of infantry soldiers recruited as children from the Christian provinces of the Ottoman Empire and brought up with intense loyalty to the Ottoman state and its sultan. The Ottoman sultan used these forces to clip local autonomy and to serve as his personal bodyguards.

Jati Social groups as defined by Hinduism's caste system.

Jesuits Religious order founded by Ignatius Loyola to counter the inroads of the Protestant Reformation; the Jesuits, or the Society of Jesus, were active in politics, education, and missionary work.

jihad Literally, "striving" or "struggle." This word also connotes military efforts or "striving in the way of God." It also came to mean spiritual struggles against temptation or inner demons, especially in Sufi, or mystical, usage.

Jih-pen Chinese for "Japan."

Jim Crow laws Laws that codified racial segregation and inequality in the southern part of the United States after the Civil War.

Jizya Special tax that non-Muslims were forced to pay to their Islamic rulers in return for which they were given security and property and granted cultural autonomy.

jong Large ocean-going vessels, built by Southeast Asians, which plied the regional trade routes from the fifteenth century to the early sixteenth century.

Judah The southern kingdom of David, which had been an Assyrian vassal until 612 BCE, when it became a vassal of Assyria's successor, Babylon, against whom the people of Judah rebelled, resulting in the destruction of Jerusalem in the sixth century BCE.

Julius Caesar Formidable Roman general who lived from 100 to 44 BCE. He was also a man of letters, a great orator, and a ruthless military man who boasted that his campaigns had led to the deaths of over a million people.

junks Trusty seafaring vessels used in the South China Seas after 1000 CE. These helped make shipping by sea less dangerous.

Justinian Roman or Byzantine emperor who ascended to the throne in 527 CE. In addition to his many building projects and military expeditions, he issued a new law code.

Kabuki Theater performance that combined song, dance, and skillful staging to dramatize conflicts between duty and passion in Tokogawa, Japan.

Kamikaze Japanese for "divine winds" or typhoons; such a storm saved Japan from a Mongol attack.

Kanun Highly detailed system of Ottoman administrative law that jurists developed to deal with matters not treated in the religious law of Islam.

Karim Loose confederation of shippers banding together to protect convoys.

karma Literally "fate" or "action," in Confucian thought; this is a universal principle of cause and effect.

Kassites Nomads who entered Mesopotamia from the eastern Zagros Mountains and the Iranian plateau as early as 2000 BCE. They gradually integrated into Babylonian society by officiating at temples. By 1745 BCE, they had asserted order over the region, and they controlled southern Mesopotamia for the next 350 years, creating one of the territorial states.

Keynesian Revolution Post-Depression economic ideas developed by the British economist John Maynard Keynes, wherein the state took a greater role in managing the economy, stimulating it by increasing the money supply and creating jobs.

KGB Soviet political police and spy agency, formed as the Cheka not long after the Bolshevik coup in October 1917. Grew to more than 750,000 operatives with military rank by the 1980s.

khan Ruler who was acclaimed at an assembly of elites and supposedly descended from Chinggis Khan on the male line; those not descended from Chinggis continually faced challenges to their legitimacy.

Khanate Major political unit of the vast Mongol empire. There were four Khanates, including the Yuan Empire in China, forged by Chinggis Khan's grandson Kubilai.

Kharijites Radical sect from the early days of Islam. The Kharijites seceded from the "party of Ali" (who themselves came to be known as the Shiites) because of disagreements over succession to the role of the caliph. They were known for their strict militant piety.

Khmers A people who created the most powerful empire in Southwest Asia between the tenth and thirteenth centuries in what is modern-day Cambodia.

Khomeini, Ayatollah Ruhollah (1902–1989) Iranian religious leader who used his traditional Islamic education and his training in Muslim ethics to accuse the shah's government of gross violations of Islamic norms. He also identified the shah's ally, America, as the great Satan. The shah fled the country in 1979; in his wake, Khomeini established a theocratic state ruled by a council of Islamic clerics.

Khufu A pyramid, among those put up in the Fourth Dynasty in ancient Egypt (2575–2465 BCE), which is the largest stone structure in the world. It is in an area called Giza, just outside modern-day Cairo.

Khusro I Anoshirwan Sasanian emperor who reigned from 530 to 579 CE.

He was a model ruler and was seen as the personification of justice.

Kiev City that became one of the greatest cities of Europe after the eleventh century. It was built to be a small-scale Constantinople on the Dnieper.

Kikuyu Kenya's largest ethnic group; organizers of a revolt against the British in the 1950s.

King, Martin Luther, Jr. (1929–1968) Civil rights leader who borrowed his most effective weapon—the commitment to nonviolent protest and the appeal to conscience—from Gandhi.

Kingdom of Awadh One of the most prized lands for annexation and the fertile, opulent, and traditional vestige of Mughal rule in India.

Kingdom of Jerusalem What Crusaders set out to liberate when they launched their attack.

Kizilbash Mystical, Turkish-speaking tribesmen who facilitated the Safavid rise to power.

Knossos Area in Crete where, during the second millennium BCE, a primary palace town existed.

Koine Greek Common form of Greek that became the international spoken and written language in the Hellenistic world. This was a simpler everyday form of the ancient Greek language.

Koprulu reforms Reforms named after two grand viziers who revitalized the Ottoman Empire in the seventeenth century through administrative and budget trimming as well as by rebuilding the military.

Korean War (1950–1953) Cold war conflict between Soviet-backed North Korea and U.S.- and UN-backed South Korea. The two sides seesawed back and forth over the same boundaries until 1953, when an armistice divided the country at roughly the same spot as at the start of the war. Nothing had been gained. Losses, however, included 33,000 Americans, at least 250,000 Chinese, and up to 3 million Koreans.

Koryo dynasty Leading dynasty of the northern-based Koryo kingdom in Korea. It is from this dynasty that the name "Korea" derives.

Kremlin Once synonymous with the Soviet government; refers to Moscow's walled city center.

Kshatriyas Originally the warrior caste in Vedic society, the dominant clan members and ruling caste who controlled the land.

Ku Klux Klan Racist organization that first emerged in the U.S. South after the Civil War and then gained national strength as a radically traditionalist movement during the 1920s.

Kubilai Khan (1215–1294) Mongol leader who seized southern China after 1260 and founded the Yuan dynasty.

kulak Originally a pejorative word used to designate better-off peasants, the term used in the late 1920s and early 1930s to refer to any peasant, rich or poor, perceived as an opponent of the Soviet regime. Russian for "fist."

Kumarajiva Renowned Buddhist scholar and missionary who lived from 344 to 413 CE. He was brought to China by Chinese regional forces from Kucha, modern-day Xinjiang.

Kushans Northern nomadic group that migrated into South Asia in 50 CE. They unified the tribes of the region and set up the Kushan dynasty. The Kushans' empire embraced a large and diverse territory and played a critical role in the formation of the Silk Road.

Labour Party Founded in Britain in 1900, the party that represented workers and was based on socialist principles.

laissez-faire The concept that the economy works best when it is left alone—that is, when the state does not regulate or interfere with the workings of the market.

"Land under the Yoke of Ashur" Lands not in Assyria proper, but under its authority; they had to pay the Assyrian Empire exorbitant amounts of tribute.

language System of communication reflecting cognitive abilities. Natural language is generally defined as words arranged in particular sequences to convey meaning and is unique to modern humans.

language families Related tongues with a common ancestral origin; language families contain languages that diverged from one another but share grammatical features and root vocabularies. More than a hundred language families exist.

Laozi Also known as Master Lao; perhaps a contemporary of Confucius and the person after whom Daoism is named. His thought was elaborated upon by generations of thinkers.

Latifundia Broad estates that produced goods for big urban markets, including wheat, grapes, olives, cattle, and sheep.

Laws of Manu Part of the handiwork of Brahman priests; a representative code of law that incorporated social sanctions and practices and provided guidance for living within the caste system.

League of Nations Organization founded after World War I to solve international disputes through arbitration; it was dissolved in 1946 and its assets were transferred to the United Nations.

Legalism Also called Statism, a system of thought about how to live an ordered life. It was developed by Master Xun, or Xunzi (310–237 BCE). It is based on the principle that people, being inherently inclined toward evil, require authoritarian control to regulate their behavior.

Lenin, Nikolai (1870–1924) Leader of the Bolshevik Revolution in Russia and the first leader of the Soviet Union.

Liangzhu Culture spanning centuries from the fourth to the third millennium BCE that represented the last new Stone Age culture in the Yangzi River delta. One of the Ten Thousand States, it was highly stratified and is known for its jade objects.

liberalism Political and social theory that advocates representative government, free trade, and freedom of speech and religion.

limited-liability joint-stock company Company that mobilized capital from a large number of investors, called shareholders, who were not to be held personally liable for financial losses incurred by the company.

Linear A and B Two linear scripts first discovered on Crete in 1900. On the island of Crete and on the mainland areas of Greece, documents of the palace-centered societies were written on clay tablets in these two scripts. Linear A script, apparently written in Minoan, has not yet been deciphered. Linear B was first deciphered in the early 1950s.

"Little Europes" Urban landscapes between 1100 and 1200 CE composed of castles, churches, and towns in what are today Poland, the Czech Republic, Hungary, and the Baltic States.

Liu Bang Chinese emperor from 206 to 195 BCE; after declaring himself the prince of his home area of Han, in 202 BCE, Liu declared himself the first Han emperor.

llamas Animals similar in utility and function to camels in Afro-Eurasia. Llamas could carry heavy loads for long distances.

Long March (1934–1935) Trek of over 10,000 kilometers by Mao Zedong and his communist followers to establish a new base of operations in northwestern China.

Longshan peoples Peoples who lived in small agricultural and riverine villages in East Asia at the end of the third millennium BCE. They set the stage for the Shang in terms of a centralized state, urban life, and a cohesive culture.

lord Privileged landowner who exercised authority over the people who lived on his land.

lost generation The 17 million former members of the Red Guard and other Chinese youth who were denied education from the late 1960s to the mid-1970s as part of the Chinese government's attempt to prevent political disruptions.

Louisiana Purchase (1803) American purchase of French territory from Napoleon, including much of the present-day United States between the Mississippi River and the Rocky Mountains.

Lucy Relatively intact skeleton of a young adult female australopithecine unearthed in the valley of the Awash River in 1974 by an archaeological team working at a site in present-day Hadar, Ethiopia. The researchers nicknamed the skeleton Lucy. She stood just over three feet tall and walked upright at least some of the time. Her skull contained a brain within the ape size range. Also, her jaw and teeth were humanlike. Lucy's skeleton was relatively complete and was the oldest hominid skeleton ever discovered.

Luftwaffe German air force.

Maastricht Treaty (1991) Treaty that formed the European Union, a fully integrated trading and financial bloc with its own bureaucracy and elected representatives.

Ma'at Term used in ancient Egypt to refer to stability or order, the achievement of which was the primary task of Egypt's ruling kings, the pharaohs.

Maccabees Leaders of a riot in Jerusalem in 166 BCE; the riot was a response to a Roman edict outlawing the practice of Judaism.

Madhyamika (Middle Way) Buddhism Chinese branch of Mahayana Buddhism established by Kumarajiva (344–413 CE) that used irony and paradox to show that reason was limited.

madrassas Higher schools of Muslim education that taught law, the Quran, religious sciences, and the regular sciences.

Mahayana (Greater Vehicle) Buddhism School of Buddhist theology that believed that the Buddha was a deity, unlike previous groups that had considered him a wise human being.

Mahdi The "chosen one" in Islam whose appearance was supposed to foretell the end of the world and the final day of reckoning for all people.

maize Grains, the crops that the settled agrarian communities across the Americas cultivated, along with legumes (beans) and tubers (potatoes).

Maji-Maji Revolt (early 1900s) Swahili insurrection against German colonialists; inspired by the belief that those who were anointed with specially blessed water (*maji*) would be immune to bullets. It resulted in 200,000–300,000 African deaths.

Mamluks (Arabic for "owned" or "possessed") Military men who ruled Egypt as an independent regime from 1250 until the Ottoman conquest in 1517.

Manaus Opera House Opera house built in the interior of Brazil in a lucrative rubber-growing area at the turn of the twentieth century.

Manchukuo Japanese puppet state in Manchuria in the 1930s.

Manchus Descendants of the Jurchens who helped the Ming army recapture Beijing in 1644 after its seizure by the outlaw Li Zicheng. The Manchus numbered around 1 million but controlled a domain that included perhaps 250 million people. Their rule lasted more than 250 years and became known as the Qing dynasty.

mandate of heaven Ideology established by Zhou dynasts to communicate the moral transfer of power. Originally a pact between the Zhou people and their supreme god, it evolved in the first century BCE into Chinese political doctrine.

Mande A people who lived in the area between the bend in the Senegal River and the bend in the Niger River east to west and from the Senegal River and Bandama River north to south. Also known as the Mandinka. Their civilization emerged around 1100.

Mandela, Nelson (1918–) Leader of the African National Congress (ANC) who was imprisoned for more than two decades by the apartheid regime in South Africa for his political beliefs; worldwide protests led to his release in 1990. In 1994 Mandela won the presidency in South Africa's first free mass elections.

Manifest Destiny Belief that it was God's will for the American people to expand their territory and political processes across the North American continent.

Mao Zedong (1893–1976) Chinese communist leader who rose to power during the Long March (1934). In 1949, he defeated the Nationalists and established a communist regime in China. Although many of Mao's efforts to transform China, such as the industrialization program of 1958 (known as the Great Leap Forward) and the Cultural Revolution of 1966, failed and brought great suffering to the people, he did instill a new spirit of independence in China and a sense of purpose after many decades of political and economic failure.

maroon community Sanctuary for runaway slaves in the Americas.

Marshall Plan Economic aid package given by the United States to Europe after World War II in hopes of a rapid period of reconstruction and economic gain, thereby securing the countries that received the aid from a communist takeover.

martyrs People executed by the Roman authorities for persisting in their Christian beliefs and refusing to submit to pagan ritual or belief.

Marx, Karl (1818–1883) German philosopher and economist who created Marxism and believed that a revolution of the working classes would overthrow the capitalist order and create a classless society.

Marxism Form of scientific socialism created by Karl Marx and Friedrich Engels that was rooted in a materialist theory of history: what mattered in history were the production of material goods and the ways in which society was organized into classes of producers and exploiters.

mass consumption Increased purchasing power in the early-twentieth-century prosperous and mainly middle-class societies, stemming from mass production.

mass culture Distinctive form of popular culture that arose in the wake of World War I. It reflected the tastes of the working and the middle classes, who now had more time and money to spend on entertainment, and relied on new technologies, especially film and radio, which could reach an entire nation's population and consolidate their sense of being a single state.

mass production System in which factories were set up to produce huge quantities of identical products, reflecting the early-twentieth-century world's demands for greater volume, faster speed, reduced cost, and standardized output.

Mastaba Word meaning "bench" in Arabic; it refers to a huge flat structure identical to earlier royal tombs of ancient Egypt.

Mau-Mau Revolt (1952–1957) Uprising orchestrated by a Kenyan guerrilla movement; this conflict forced the British to grant independence to the black majority in Kenya.

Mauryan Empire Dynasty extended by the Mauryans from 321 to 184 BCE, from the Indus Valley to the northwest areas of South Asia, in a region previously controlled by Persia. It was the first large-scale empire in South Asia and was to become the model for future Indian empires.

Mawali Non-Arab "clients" to Arab tribes in the early Islamic Empire. Because tribal patronage was so much a part of the Arabian cultural system, non-Arabs who converted to Islam affiliated themselves with a tribe and became clients of that tribe.

Maxim gun European weaponry that was capable of firing many bullets per second; it was used against Africans in the conquest of the continent.

Mayans Civilization that ruled over large stretches of Mesoamerica; it was composed of a series of kingdoms, each built around ritual centers rather than cities. The Mayans engaged neighboring peoples in warfare and trade and expanded borders through tributary relationships. They were not defined by a great ruler or one capital city, but by their shared religious beliefs.

McCarthyism Campaign by Republican senator Joseph McCarthy in the late 1940s and early 1950s to uncover closet communists, particularly in the State Department and in Hollywood.

Meat Inspection Act (1906) Legislation that provided for government supervision of meat-packing operations; it was part of a broader "Progressive" reform movement dedicated to correcting the negative consequences of urbanization and industrialization in the United States.

Mecca Arabian city in which Muhammad was born. Mecca was a trading center and pilgrimage destination in the pre-Islamic and Islamic periods. Exiled in 622 CE because of resistance to his message, Muhammad returned to Mecca in 630 CE and claimed the city for Islam.

Medes Rivals of the Assyrians and the Persians. The Medes inhabited the area from the Zagros Mountains to the modern city of Tehran; known as expert horsemen and archers, they were eventually defeated by the Persians.

megaliths Literally, "great stone"; the word *megalith* is used when describing structures such as Stonehenge. These massive structures are the result of cooperative planning and work.

Megarons Large buildings found in Troy (level II) that are the predecessors of the classic Greek temple.

Meiji Empire Empire created under the leadership of Mutsuhito, emperor of Japan from 1868 until 1912. During the Meiji period Japan became a world industrial and naval power.

Meiji Restoration Reign of the Meiji emperor, which was characterized by a new nationalist identity, economic advances, and political transformation.

Mencius Disciple of Confucius who lived from 372 to 289 BCE.

mercantilism Economic theory that drove European empire builders. In this economic system, the world had a fixed amount of wealth, which meant one country's wealth came at the expense of another's. Mercantilism assumed that colonies existed for the sole purpose of enriching the country that controlled the colony.

Mercosur Free-trade pact between the governments of Argentina, Brazil, Paraguay, and Uruguay.

meritocracy Rule by persons of talent.

Meroe Ancient kingdom in what is today Sudan. It flourished for nearly a thousand years, from the fifth century BCE to the fifth century CE.

mestizos Mixed-blood offspring of Spanish settlers and native Indians.

métis Mixed-blood offspring of French settlers and native Indians.

Mexican Revolution (1910) Conflict fueled by the unequal distribution of land and by disgruntled workers; it erupted when political elites split over the succession of General Porfirio Díaz after decades of his rule. The fight lasted over ten years and cost one million lives, but it resulted in a widespread reform and a new constitution.

***Mfecane* movement** African political revolts in the first half of the nineteenth century that were caused by the expansionist methods of King Shaka of the Zulu people.

microsocieties Small-scale communities that had little interaction with others. These communities were the norm for peoples living in the Americas and islanders in the Pacific and Aegean from 2000 to 1200 BCE.

migration Long-distance travel for the purpose of resettlement. In the case of early man, the need to move was usually a response to an environmental shift, such as climate change during the Ice Age.

millenarian Convinced of the imminent coming of a just and ideal society.

millenarian movement Broad, popular upheaval calling for the restoration of a bygone moral age, often led by charismatic spiritual prophets.

Millets Minority religious communities of the Ottoman Empire.

minaret Slender tower within a mosque from which Muslims are called to prayer.

Minbar Pulpit inside a mosque from which Muslim religious speakers broadcast their message to the faithful.

Minoans A people who built a large number of elaborate, independent palace centers on Crete, at Knossos, and elsewhere around 2000 BCE. Named after the legendary King Minos, said to have ruled Crete at the time, they sailed throughout the Mediterranean and by 1600 BCE had planted colonies on many Aegean islands, which in turn became trading and mining centers.

mission civilisatrice Term French colonizers used to refer to France's form of "rationalized" colonial rule, which attempted to bring "civilization" to the "uncivilized."

mitochondrial DNA Form of DNA found outside the nucleus of cells, where it serves as cells' microscopic power packs. Examining mitochondrial DNA enables researchers to measure the genetic variation among living objects, including human beings.

Moche A people who extended their power and increased their wealth at the height of the Chimu Empire over several valleys in what is now modern-day Peru.

Model T First automobile, manufactured by the Ford Motor Company of Henry Ford, to be priced reasonably enough to be sold to the masses.

modernists A generation of exuberant young artists, writers, and scientists in the late nineteenth century who broke with older conventions and sought new ways of seeing and describing the world.

Mohism School of thought in ancient China, named after Mo Di, or Mozi, who lived from 479 to 438 BCE. It emphasized one's obligation to society as a whole, not just to one's immediate family or social circle.

monarchy Political system in which one individual holds supreme power and passes that power on to his or her next of kin.

monasticism Christian way of life that originated in Egypt and was practiced as early as 300 CE in the Mediterranean. The word itself contains the meaning of a person "living alone" without marriage or family.

monetization An economic shift from a barter-based economy to one dependent on coin.

Mongols Combination of nomadic forest and prairie peoples who lived by hunting and livestock herding and were expert horsemen. Beginning in 1206, the Mongols launched a series of conquests that brought far-flung parts of the world together under their rule. By incorporating conquered peoples and adapting some of their customs, the Mongols created a unified empire that stretched from the Pacific Ocean to the shores of the eastern Mediterranean and the southern steppes of Eurasia.

Moors Term employed by Europeans in the medieval period to refer to Muslim occupants of North Africa, the western Sahara, and the Iberian Peninsula.

mosque Place of worship for the people of Islam.

"Mound people" Name for the people of Cahokia, since its landscape was dominated by earthen monuments in the shapes of mounds. The mounds were carefully maintained and were the loci from which Cahokians paid respect to spiritual forces. *See also* Cahokia.

Mu Chinese ruler (956–918 BCE) who put forth a formal bureaucratic system of governance, appointing officials, supervisors and military captains to whom he was not related. He also instituted a formal legal code.

muckrakers Journalists who aimed to expose political and commercial corruption in late-nineteenth- and early-twentieth-century America.

Muftis Experts on Muslim religious law.

Mughal Empire One of Islam's greatest regimes. Established in 1526, it was a vigorous, centralized state whose political authority encompassed most of modern-day India. During the sixteenth century, it had a population of between 100 and 150 million.

Muhammad (570–632 CE) Prophet and founder of the Islamic faith. Born in Mecca in Saudi Arabia and orphaned when young, Muhammad lived under the protection of his uncle. His career as a prophet began around 610 CE, with his first experience of spiritual revelation.

Muhammad Ali Ruler of Egypt between 1805 and 1848. He initiated a set of modernizing reforms that sought to make Egypt competitive with the great powers.

mullahs Religious leaders in Iran who in the 1970s led a movement opposing Shah Reza Pahlavi and denounced American materialism and secularism.

multinational corporations Corporations based in many different countries that have global investment, trading, and distribution goals.

Muscovy The principality of Moscow. Originally a mixture of Slavs, Finnish tribes, Turkic speakers, and many others, Muscovy used territorial expansion and commercial networks to consolidate a powerful state and expanded to become the Russian Empire, a huge realm that spanned parts of Europe, much of northern Asia, numerous North Pacific islands, and even—for a time—a corner of North America (Alaska).

Muslim Brotherhood Egyptian organization founded in 1938 by Hassan al-Banna. It attacked liberal democracy as a cover for middle-class, business, and landowning interests and fought for a return to a purified Islam.

Muslim League National Muslim party of India.

Mussolini, Benito (1883–1945) Italian dictator and founder of the fascist movement in Italy. During World War II, he allied Italy with Germany and Japan.

Muwahhidin Term meaning "unitarians"; these were followers of the Wahhabi movement that emerged in the Arabian Peninsula in the eighteenth century.

Mycenaeans Mainland competitors of the Minoans; they took over Crete around 1400 BCE. Migrating to Greece from central Europe, they brought their Indo-European language, horse chariots, and metalworking skills, which they used to dominate until 1200 BCE.

Nagasaki Second Japanese city to be hit by an atomic bomb near the end of World War II.

Napoleonic Code Legal code drafted by Napoleon in 1804; it distilled different legal traditions to create one uniform law. The code confirmed the abolition of feudal privileges of all kinds and set the conditions for exercising property rights.

National Assembly of France Governing body of France that succeeded the Estates-General in 1789 during the French Revolution. It was composed of, and defined by, the delegates of the Third Estate.

National Association for the Advancement of Colored People (NAACP) Founded in 1910, the U.S. civil rights organization dedicated to ending inequality and segregation for black Americans.

National Recovery Administration (NRA) New Deal agency created in 1933 to prepare codes of fair administration and to plan for public works. It was later declared unconstitutional.

nationalism The idea that members of a shared community called a "nation" should have sovereignty within the borders of their state.

nation-state Form of political organization that derived legitimacy from its inhabitants, often referred to as citizens, who in theory, if not always in practice, shared a common language, common culture, and common history.

native learning Japanese movement to promote nativist intellectual traditions and the celebration of Japanese texts.

native paramountcy British form of "rationalized" colonial rule, which attempted to bring "civilization" to the "uncivilized" by proclaiming that when the interests of European settlers in Africa clashed with those of the African population, the latter should take precedence.

natural rights Belief that emerged in eighteenth-century western Europe and North America that rights fundamental to human nature were discernible to reason and should be affirmed in human-made law.

natural selection Charles Darwin's theory that populations grew faster than the food supply, creating a "struggle for existence" among species. In later work he showed how the passing on of individual traits was also determined by what he called sexual selection—according to which the "best" mates are chosen for their strength, beauty, or talents. The outcome: the "fittest" survived to reproduce, while the less adaptable did not.

Nazis (National Socialist German Workers Party) German organization dedicated to winning workers over from socialism to nationalism; the first Nazi Party platform combined nationalism with anticapitalism and anti-Semitism.

Neanderthals Members of an early wave of hominids from Africa who settled in western Afro-Eurasia, in an area reaching from present-day Uzbekistan and Iraq to Spain, approximately 150,000 years ago.

needle compass Crucial instrument made available to navigators after 1000 CE that helped guide sailors on the high seas. It was a Chinese invention.

negritos Hunter-gatherer inhabitants of the East Asian coastal islands who migrated there around 28,000 BCE but by 2000 BCE had been replaced by new migrants.

Negritude Statement of the virtues of the black identity and the validation of African culture and the African past, even in a westernizing world. This idea was shaped by African and African American intellectuals like Senegal's first president, Léopold Sédar Senghor.

Nehemiah Jewish eunuch of the Persian court who was given permission to rebuild the fortification walls around the city of Jerusalem from 440 to 437 BCE.

Neo-Assyrian Empire Afro-Eurasian empire that dominated around 950 BCE. The Neo-Assyrians extended their control over resources and people beyond their own borders, and their empire lasted for three centuries.

neocolonialism Contemporary geopolitical policy or practice in which a politically, economically, and often militarily superior nation asserts control over a country that remains nominally sovereign.

Nestorian Christians Denomination of Christians whose beliefs about Christ differed from those of the official Byzantine church. Named after Nestorius, former bishop of Constantinople, they emphasized the human aspects of Jesus.

New Deal President Franklin Delano Roosevelt's package of government reforms that were enacted during the 1930s to provide jobs for the unemployed, social welfare programs for the poor, and security to the financial markets.

New Economic Policy Enacted decrees of the Bolsheviks between 1921 and 1927 that grudgingly sanctioned private trade and private property.

New Negro movement *See* Harlem Renaissance.

New World Term applied to the Americas that reflected the Europeans' view that anything previously unknown to them was "new," even if it had existed and supported societies long before European explorers arrived on its shores.

Nirvana Literally, nonexistence; nirvana is the state of complete liberation from the concerns of worldly life, as in Buddhist thought.

No–drama Masked theater favored by Japanese bureaucrats and regional lords during the Tokugawa period.

Noble Eightfold Path Buddhist concept of a way of life by which people may rid themselves of individual desire to achieve nirvana. The path consists of wisdom, ethical behavior, and mental discipline.

Nok culture Spectacular culture that arose in what is today Nigeria, in the sixth century BCE. Iron smelting occurred there around 600 BCE. Thus the Nok people made the transition from stone to iron materials.

nomads People who move across vast distances without settling permanently in a particular place. Often pastoralists, nomads and transhumant herders introduced new forms of chariot-based warfare that transformed the Afro-Eurasian world.

nongovernmental organizations (NGOs) Term used to refer to private organizations like the Red Cross that play a large role in international affairs.

nonviolent resistance *(Satyagraha)* Moral and political philosophy of resistance developed by Indian National Congress leader Mohandas Gandhi. Gandhi believed that if Indians pursued self-reliance and self-control in a nonviolent way, the British would eventually have to leave.

North American Free Trade Agreement (NAFTA) Treaty negotiated in the early 1990s to promote free trade between Canada, the United States, and Mexico.

North Atlantic Treaty Organization (NATO) International organization set up in1949 to provide for the defense of western European countries and the United States from the perceived Soviet threat.

Northern Wei dynasty Regime founded in 386 CE by the Tuoba, a people originally from Inner Mongolia, that lasted one and a half centuries. The rulers of this dynasty adopted many practices of the earlier Chinese Han regime. At the same time, they struggled to consolidate authority over their own nomadic people. Ultimately, several decades of intense internal conflict led to the dynasty's downfall.

northwest passage Long-sought marine passageway between the Atlantic and Pacific oceans.

Oceania Collective name for the lands of Australia and New Zealand and the islands of the southwest Pacific Ocean.

Odyssey Composed in the eighth century BCE, an epic tale of the journey of Odysseus, who traveled the Mediterranean back to his home in Ithaca after the siege of Troy.

Oikos The word for "small family unit" in ancient Greece, similar to the *familia* in Rome. Its structure, with men as heads of household over women and children, embodied the fundamental power structure in Greek city-states.

oligarchy Clique of privileged rulers.

Olmecs A people who emerged around 1500 BCE and lived in Mesoamerica. The name means those who "lived in the land of the rubber." Olmec society was composed of decentralized villages. Its members spoke the same language and worshipped the same gods.

Open Door Policy Policy proposed by American Secretary of State John Hay that would give all foreign nations equal access to trade with China. As European imperial powers carved out spheres of trade in late-nineteenth-century China, American leaders worried that the United States would be excluded from trade with China. To prevent this, Hay proposed the Open Door Policy.

Opium War (1839–1842) War fought between the British and Qing China over British trade in opium; resulted in the granting to the British the right to trade in five different ports and the ceding of Hong Kong to the British.

oracle bones Animal bones used by Shang diviners. Diviners applied intense heat to the shoulder bones of cattle or to turtle shells, which caused them to crack. The diviners would then interpret the cracks as signs from the ancestors regarding royal plans and actions.

Organization of Petroleum Exporting Countries (OPEC) International association established in 1960 to coordinate price and supply policies of oil-producing states.

Orientalism Genre of literature and painting that portrayed the nonwestern peoples of North Africa and Asia as exotic, sensuous, and economically backward with respect to Europeans.

orientalists Western scholars who specialized in the study of the East.

Orrorin tugenensis Predecessor to hominids that first appeared 6 million years ago.

Ottoman Empire Rulers of Anatolia, the Arab world, and much of southern and eastern Europe in the early sixteenth century. They transformed themselves from nomadic warrior bands who roamed the borderlands between Islamic and Christian worlds in Anatolia into sovereigns of a vast, bureaucratic empire. The Ottomans embraced a Sunni view of Islam. They adapted traditional Byzantine governmental practices but tried new ways of integrating the diverse peoples of their empire.

Pacific War (1879–1883) War between Chile and the alliance of Bolivia and Peru.

Pagani Pejorative word used by Christians to designate pagans.

palace Official residence of the ruler, his family, and his entourage. The palace was both a social institution and a set of buildings. It first appeared around 2500 BCE, about a millennium later than the Mesopotamian temple, and quickly joined the temple as a defining landmark of city life. Eventually, it became a source of power rivaling the temple, and palace and temple life often blurred, as did the boundary between the sacred and the secular.

Palace of Versailles The palace complex, eleven miles away from the French capital of Paris, built by Louis XIV in the 1670s and 1680s to house and entertain his leading clergymen and nobles, with the hopes of diverting them from plotting against him.

Palmyra Roman trading depot in modern-day Syria; part of a network of trading cities that connected various regions of Afro-Eurasia.

pan movements Groups that sought to link people across state boundaries in new communities based on ethnicity or, in some cases, religion (e.g., pan-Germanism, pan-Islamism, pan-Slavism).

Pansophia Ideal republic of inquisitive Christians united in the search for knowledge of nature as a means of loving God.

papacy The institution of the pope; the Catholic spiritual leader in Rome.

papal Of, relating to, or issued by a pope.

Parthians Horse-riding people who pushed southward around the middle of the second century BCE and wiped out the Greek kingdoms in Iran. They then extended their power all the way to the Mediterranean, where they ran up against the Roman Empire in Anatolia and Mesopotamia.

pastoral nomadic communities Groups of people that moved their domesticated animals from place to place to meet the animals' demanding grazing requirements. Around 3500 BCE, western Afro-Eurasia witnessed the growth and spread of pastoral nomadic communities.

pastoralism Herding and breeding of sheep and goats or other animals as a primary means of subsistence.

Paterfamilias Latin for "Father of the family," which itself was the foundation of the Roman social order.

Patria Latin, meaning "fatherland."

patrons In the Roman system of patronage, men and women of wealth and high social status who protected dependents or "clients" of a lower class.

Pax Mongolica Term that refers to the political and especially the commercial stability that the vast Mongol Empire provided for the travelers and merchants of Eurasia during the thirteenth and fourteenth centuries.

Pax Romana Latin for "Roman Peace"; refers to the period between 25 BCE and 235 CE during which conditions in the Roman Empire were settled and peaceful.

Pax Sinica Period of peace (149–87 BCE) during which agriculture, commerce, and industry flourished in East Asia under the rule of the Han.

Peace Preservation Act (1925) Act instituted in Japan that specified up to ten years' hard labor for any member of an organization advocating a basic change in the political system or the abolition of private property.

Pearl Harbor American naval base in Hawaii on which the Japanese launched a surprise attack on December 7, 1941, bringing the United States into World War II.

Peloponnesian War War fought between 431 and 404 BCE between two of Greece's most powerful city-states, Athens and Sparta.

Peninsular War (1808–1814) Conflict in which the Portuguese and Spanish populations, supported by the British, resisted the French invasion under Napoleon of the Iberian Peninsula.

peninsulars Spaniards who, although born in Spain, resided in the Spanish colonial territories. They regarded themselves as superior to Spaniards born in the colonies (Creoles).

Peoples' Charter Document calling for universal suffrage for adult males, the secret ballot, electoral districts, and annual parliamentary elections. It was signed by over 3 million British between 1839 and 1842.

periplus Book that reflected sailing knowledge; in such books captains would record landing spots and ports. The word *periplus* literally means "sailing around."

Persepolis Darius I's capital city in the highlands of Fars; a ceremonial center and expression of imperial identity as well as an important administrative hub.

Peterloo Massacre (1819) The killing of 11 and wounding of 460 following a peaceful demonstration for political reform by workers in Manchester, England.

Petra City in modern-day Jordan that was the Nabataean capital. It profited greatly by supplying provisions and water to travelers and traders. Many of its houses and shrines were cut into the rocky mountains. *Petra* means "rock."

phalanx Military formation used by Philip II of Macedonia, whereby heavily armored infantry were closely arrayed in battle formation.

Philip II of Macedonia Father of Alexander the Great, under whose rule Macedonia developed into a large ethnic and territorial state. After unifying Macedonia, Philip went on to conquer neighboring states.

philosophia Literally "love of wisdom"; this system of thought originally included speculation on the nature of the cosmos, the environment, and human existence. It eventually came to include thought about the nature of humans and life in society.

Phoenicians Known as the Canaanites in the Bible, an ethnic group in the Levant under Assyrian rule in the seventh century BCE; they provided ships and sailors for battles in the Mediterranean. The word *Phoenician* refers to the purple dye they manufactured and widely traded, along with other commercial goods and services, throughout the Mediterranean. While part of wider Mesopotamian culture, their major contribution was the alphabet, first introduced in the second millennium BCE, which made far-reaching communication possible.

phonemes Primary and distinctive sounds that are characteristic of human language.

piety Strong sense of religious duty and devoutness, often inspiring extraordinary actions.

plant domestication Process of growing plants, harvesting their seeds, and saving some of the seeds for planting in subsequent growing cycles, resulting in a steady food supply. This process occurred as far back as 5000 BCE, when plants began to naturally retain their seeds. Plant domestication was practiced first in the southern Levant and spread from there into the rest of Southwest Asia.

Plato (427–347 BCE) Disciple of the great philosopher Socrates; his works are the only record we have of Socrates' teaching. He was also the author of formative philosophical works on ethics and politics.

plebs In Rome, term that referred to the "common people." Their interests were protected by officials called tribunes.

Pochteca Archaic term for merchants of the Mexicos.

polities Politically organized communities or states.

polyglot communities Societies composed of diverse linguistic and ethnic groups.

popular culture Affordable and accessible forms of art and entertainment available to people at all levels of society.

popular sovereignty The idea that the power of the state resides in the people.

populists Members of a political movement that supported U.S. farmers in late-nineteenth-century America. The term is often used generically to refer to political groups who appeal to the majority of the population.

potassium-argon dating Major dating technique based on the changing chemical structure of objects over time, since over time potassium decays into argon. This method makes possible the dating of objects up to a million years old.

potato famine (1840s) Severe famine in Ireland that led to the rise of radical political movements and the migration of large numbers of Irish to the United States.

potter's wheel Fast wheel that enabled people to mass-produce vessels in many different shapes. This advance, invented at the city of Uruk, enabled potters to make significant technical breakthroughs.

pottery Vessels made of mud and later clay that were used for storing and transporting food. The development of pottery was a major breakthrough.

Prague Spring (1968) Program of liberalization under a new communist party in Czechoslovakia that strove to create a democratic and pluralist socialism.

predestination Belief of many sixteenth- and seventeenth-century Protestant groups that God had foreordained the lives of individuals, including their bad and good deeds.

primitivism Western art movement of the late-nineteenth and early-twentieth centuries that drew upon the so-called primitive art forms of Africa, Oceania, and pre-Columbian America.

progressive reformers Members of the U.S. reform movement in the early twentieth century that aimed to eliminate political corruption, improve working conditions, and regulate the power of large industrial and financial enterprises.

proletarians Industrial wage workers.

prophets Charismatic freelance religious men of power who found themselves in opposition to the formal power of the kings, bureaucrats, and priests.

Prophet's Town Indian village that was burned down by American forces in the early nineteenth century.

Protestant Reformation Religious movement initiated by sixteenth-century monk Martin Luther, who openly criticized the corruption in the Catholic Church and voiced his belief that Christians could speak directly to God. His doctrines gained wide support, and those who followed this new view of the Christianity rejected the authority of the papacy and the Catholic clergy, broke away from the Catholic Church, and called themselves "Protestants."

Protestantism Division of Christianity that emerged in western Europe from the Protestant Reformation.

Proto-Indo-European The parent of all the languages in the Indo-European family, which includes, among many others, English, German, Norwegian, Portuguese, French, Russian, Persian, Hindi, and Bengali.

Pullman Strike (1894) American Railway Union strike in response to wage cuts and firings.

puppet states Governments with little power in the international arena that follow the dictates of their more powerful neighbors or patrons.

Puritans Seventeenth-century reform group of the Church of England; also known as dissenters or nonconformists.

Qadiriyya Sufi order that facilitated the spread of Islam into West Africa.

Qadis Judges in the Ottoman Empire.

qanats Underground water channels, vital for irrigation, which were used in Persia. Little evaporation occurred when water was being moved through qanats.

Qing dynasty (1644–1911) Minority Manchu rule over China that incorporated new territories, experienced substantial population growth, and sustained significant economic growth.

Questions of King Milinda (Milindapunha) Name of a second-century BCE text espousing the teachings of Buddhism as set forth by Menander, a Yavana king. It featured a discussion between the king and a sophisticated Buddhist sage named Nagasena.

Quetzalcoatl Ancient deity and legendary ruler of Native American peoples living in Mexico.

Quran The scripture of the Islamic faith. Originally a verbal recitation, the Quran was eventually compiled into a book in the order in which we have it today. According to traditional Islamic interpretation, the Quran was revealed to Muhammad by the angel Gabriel over a period of twenty-three years.

radicals Widely used term in nineteenth-century Europe that referred to those individuals and political organizations that favored the total reconfiguration of Europe's old state system.

radiocarbon isotope C^{14} Isotope contained by all living things, which plants acquire directly from the atmosphere and animals acquire indirectly when they consume plants or other animals. When living things die, the C^{14} isotope they contain begins to decay into a stable nonradioactive element, C^{12}. The rate of decay is regular and measurable, making it possible to ascertain the date of fossils that leave organic remains for ages of up to 40,000 years.

Raj British crown's administration of India following the end of the East India Company's rule after the Rebellion of 1857.

raja "King" in the Kshatriya period in South Asia; could also refer to the head of a family, but indicated the person who had control of land and resources in South Asian city-states.

Ramadan Ninth month of the Muslim year, during which all Muslims must fast during daylight hours.

Rape of Nanjing Attack against the Chinese in which the Japanese slaughtered at least 100,000 civilians and raped thousands of women between December 1937 and February 1938.

Rashtriya Swayamsevak Sangh (RSS) (1925) Campaign to organize Hindus as a militant, modern community in India; translated in English as "National Volunteer Organization."

Rebellion of 1857 (Great Rebellion) Indian uprising against the East India Company to bring religious purification, an egalitarian society, and local and communal solidarity without the interference of British rule.

rebus Probably originating in Uruk, a representation that transfers meaning from the name of a thing to the sound of that name. For example, a picture of a bee can represent the sound "b." Such pictures opened the door to writing: a technology of symbols that uses marks to represent specific discrete sounds.

Reconquista Spanish reconquest of territories lost to the Islamic Empire, beginning with Toledo in 1061.

Red Guards Chinese students who were the shock troopers in the early phases of Mao's Cultural Revolution in 1966–1968.

Red Lanterns Female supporters of the Chinese Boxers who rebelled against foreign intrusions in China at the turn of the twentieth century. Most were teenage girls and unmarried women and dressed in red garments.

Red Turban Movement Diverse religious movement in China during the fourteenth century that spread the belief that the world was drawing to an end as Mongol rule was collapsing.

Reds Bolsheviks.

Reich German empire composed of Denmark, Austria, and parts of western France.

Reichstag The German parliament.

Reign of Terror Campaign at the height of the French Revolution in the early 1790s that used violence, including systematic execution of opponents of the revolution, to purge France of its enemies and to extend the revolution beyond its borders; radicals executed as many as 40,000 persons who were judged enemies of the state.

Renaissance Term meaning "rebirth" that historians use to characterize the expanded cultural production of European nations between 1430 and 1550. Emphasized a break from the church-centered medieval world and a new concept of humankind as the center of the world.

republican government Government in which power and rulership rest with representatives of the people—not a king.

Res publica Literally "public thing"; this referred to the Roman republic, in which policy and rules of behavior were determined by the Senate and by popular assemblies of the citizens.

Restoration period (1815–1848) European movement after the defeat of Napoleon to restore Europe to its pre-French revolutionary status and to quash radical movements.

Rift Valley Area of northeastern Africa where some of the most important early human archaeological discoveries of fossils were found, especially one of an intact skull that is 1.8 million years old.

river basin Area drained by a river, including all its tributaries. River basins were rich in fertile soil, water for irrigation, and plant and animal life, which made them attractive for human habitation. Cultivators were able to produce surplus agriculture to support the first cities.

riverine Term denoting an area whose inhabitants depended on irrigation for their well-being and whose populations are settled near great rivers. Egypt was, in a sense, the most riverine of all these cultures, in that it had no hinterland of plains as did Mesopotamia and the Indus valley. Away from the banks of the Nile, there is only largely uninhabitable desert.

Roman army Military force of the Roman Empire. The Romans devised a military draft that could draw from a huge population. In their encounter with Hannibal, they lost up to 80,000 men in three separate encounters and still won the war.

Roman Catholicism Branch of Christianity established by 1000 CE in western Europe and led by the Roman papacy. In contrast to ancient Greek Orthodoxy, Western Catholics believed that their church was destined to expand everywhere, and they set about converting the pagan tribes of northern Europe. Western Catholics contemptuously called the East Romans "Greeks" and condemned them for their "Byzantine" cunning.

Roman law Roman legal system, under which disputes were brought to the public courts and decisions were made by judges and sometimes by large juries. Rome's legal system featured written law and institutions for settling legal disputes.

roving bandits Large bands of dispossessed and marginalized peasants who vented their anger at tax collectors in the waning years of the Ming dynasty.

Royal Road A 1,600-mile road from Sardis in Anatolia to Susa in Iran; used by messengers, traders, the army, and those taking tribute to the king.

Russification Programs to assimilate people of over 146 dialects into the Russian Empire.

S.S. *(Schutzstaffel)* Hitler's security police force.

Sack of Constantinople Rampage in 1204 by the Frankish armies on the capital city of Constantinople.

sacred kingships Institutions that marked the centralized politics of West Africa. The inhabitants of these kingships believed that their kings were descendants of the gods.

Sahel region Area of sub-Saharan Africa with wetter and more temperate locations, especially in the upland massifs and their foothills, villages, and towns.

St. Bartholomew's Day Massacre (1572) Roman Catholic massacre of French Protestants in Paris.

St. Patrick Former slave brought to Ireland from Briton who later became a missionary, or the "Apostle of Ireland." He died in 470 CE.

Salt March (1930) A 240-mile trek to the sea in India, led by Mohandas Gandhi, to gather salt for free, thus breaking the British colonial monopoly on salt.

Samurai Japanese warriors who made up the private armies of Japanese daimyos.

Sandinista coalition Left-leaning Nicaraguan coalition of the 1970s and 1980s.

Santería African-based religion, blended with Christian influences, that was first practiced by slaves in Cuba.

Sargon the Great King of Akkad, a city-state near modern Baghdad. Reigning from 2334 to 2279 BCE, Sargon helped bring the competitive era of city-states to an end and sponsored monumental works of architecture, art, and literature.

Sasanian Empire Empire that succeeded the Parthians in the mid-220s ce in Inner Eurasia. The Sasanian Empire controlled the trade crossroads of Afro-Eurasia and possessed a strong armored cavalry, which made them a powerful rival to Rome. The Sasanians were also tolerant of Judaism and Christianity, which allowed Christians to flourish.

Sati Hindu practice whereby a woman was burned to death on the pyre of her dead husband.

satrap Governor of a province in the Persian Empire. Each satrap was a relative or intimate associate of the king.

Satyagraha *See* nonviolent resistance.

scientific method Method of inquiry based on experimentation in nature. Many of its principles were first laid out by the philosopher Sir Francis Bacon (1561–1626), who claimed that real science entailed the formulation of hypotheses that could be tested in carefully controlled experiments.

Scramble for Africa European rush to colonize parts of Africa at the end of the nineteenth century.

scribes Those who wield writing tools; from the very beginning they were at the top of the social ladder, under the major power brokers.

Scythian ethos Warrior ethos that embodied the extremes of aggressive mounted-horse culture, c. 1000 BCE. In part the Scythian ethos was the result of the constant struggle between settlers, hunter-gatherers, and nomads on the northern frontier of Europe.

Sea Peoples Migrants from north of the Mediterranean who invaded the cities of Egypt and the Levant in the second millennium BCE. Once settled along the coast of the Levant, they became known as the Philistines and considerably disrupted the settlements of the Canaanites.

SEATO (Southeast Asia Treaty Organization) Military alliance of pro-American, anticommunist states in Southeast Asia in 1954.

Second World Term invented during the cold war to refer to the communist countries, as opposed to the West (or First World) and the former colonies (or Third World).

second-generation societies Societies that expanded old ideas and methods by incorporating new aspects of culture and grafting them onto, or using them in combination with, established norms.

Seleucus Nikator Successor of Alexander the Great who lived from 358 to 281 BCE. He controlled Mesopotamia, Syria, Persia, and parts of the Punjab.

Self-Strengthening movement In the latter half of the nineteenth century, a movement of reformist Chinese bureaucrats that attempted to adopt western elements of learning and technological skill while retaining their core Chinese culture.

Semu Term meaning "outsiders" or non-Chinese people—Mongols, Tanguts, Khitan, Jurchen, Muslims, Tibetans, Persians, Turks, Nestorians, Jews, and Armenians—who became a new ruling elite over a Han majority population in the late thirteenth century.

sepoys Hindu and Muslim recruits of the East India Company's military force.

serfs Peasants who farmed the land and paid fees to be protected and governed by lords under a system of rule called feudalism.

settled agriculture Application of human labor and tools to a fixed plot of land for more than one growing cycle. It entails the changeover from a hunting and gathering lifestyle to one based on agriculture, which requires staying in one place until the soil has been exhausted.

Seven Years' War (1756–1763) World-wide war that ended when Prussia defeated Austria, establishing itself as a European power, and when Britain gained control of India and many of France's colonies through the Treaty of Paris.

sexual revolution Increased freedom in sexual behavior, resulting in part from the advances in contraception, notably the introduction of oral contraception in 1960, which allowed men and women to limit childbearing and to have sex with less fear of pregnancy.

shah Traditional title of Persian rulers.

shamans Certain humans whose powers supposedly enabled them to commune with the supernatural and to transform themselves wholly or partly into beasts.

Shamisen Three-stringed instrument, often played by Japanese geisha.

Shandingdong Man A *Homo sapiens* whose fossil remains and relics can be dated to about 18,000 years ago. His physical characteristics were closer to those of modern humans, and he had a similar brain size.

Shang state Dynasty in northeastern China that ruled from 1600 to 1045 BCE. Though not as well defined by borders as the territorial states in the southwest of Asia, it did have a ruling lineage. Four fundamental elements of the Shang state were a metal industry based on copper, pottery making, standardized architectural forms and walled towns, and divination using animal bones.

Shanghai School Late-nineteenth-century style of painting characterized by an emphasis on spontaneous brushwork, feeling, and the incorporation of western influences into classical Chinese pieces.

sharecropping System of farming in which tenant farmers rented land and gave over a share of their crops to the land's owners. Sometimes seen as a cheap way for the state to conduct agricultural affairs, sharecropping often resulted in the impoverishment and marginalization of the underclass.

sharia Literally, "the way"; now used to indicate the philosophy and rulings of Islamic law.

Sharpeville Massacre (1960) Massacre of sixty-nine black Africans when police fired upon a rally against the recently passed laws requiring nonwhite South Africans to carry identity papers.

Shawnees Native American tribe that inhabited the Ohio valley during the eighteenth century.

Shays's Rebellion (1786) Uprising of armed farmers that broke out when the Massachusetts state government refused to offer them economic relief.

Shiism One of the two main branches of Islam, practiced in the Safavid Empire. Although always a minority sect in the Islamic world, Shiism contains several subsects, each of which has slightly different interpretations of theology and politics.

Shiites Group of supporters of Ali, Muhammad's cousin and son-in-law, who wanted him to be the first caliph and believed that members of the Prophet's family deserved to rule. The leaders of the Shiite community are known as "Imam," which means "leaders."

Shinto Japan's official religion; it promoted the state and the emperor's divinity. The term means "the way of the gods."

shoguns Japanese military commanders. From 1192 to 1333, the Kamakura shoguns served as military "protectors" of the ruler in the city of Heian.

Shotoku Prince in the early Japanese Yamoto state (574–622 CE) who is credited with having introduced Buddhism to Japan.

shudras Literally "small ones"; workers and slaves from outside the Vedic lineage.

Siddhartha Gautama Another name for the Buddha; the most prominent opponent of the Brahman way of life; he lived from 563 to 483 BCE.

Sikhism Islamic-inspired religion that calls on its followers to renounce the caste system and to treat all believers as equal before God.

Silicon Valley Valley between the California cities of San Francisco and San Jose, known for its innovative computer and high-technology industries.

silk Luxury textile that became a vastly popular export from China (via the Silk Road) to the cities of the Roman world.

Silk Road Trade route linking China with central Asia and the Mediterranean; it extended over 5,000 miles, land and sea included, and was so named because of the quantities of silk that were traded along it. The Silk Road was a major factor in the development of civilizations in China, Egypt, Persia, India, and even Europe.

Silla One of three independent Korean states that may have emerged as early as the third century BCE. These states lasted until 668 CE, when Silla took control over the entire peninsula.

Silver Islands Term used by European merchants in the sixteenth century to refer to Japan, because of its substantial trade in silver with China.

Sino-Japanese War (1894–1895) Conflict over the control of Korea in which China was forced to cede the province of Taiwan to Japan.

Sipahi Urdu for "soldier."

Siva The third of three Vedic deities, signifying destruction. *See also* Brahma *and* Vishnu.

slave plantations System whereby labor was used for the cultivation of crops wholly for the sake of producing surplus that was then used for profit; slave plantations were a crucial part of the growth of the Mediterranean economy.

small seal script Unified script that was used to the exclusion of other scripts under the Qin, with the aim of centralizing administration; its use led to a less complicated style of clerical writing than had been in use under the Han.

social contract The idea, drawn from the writings of British philosopher John Locke, that the law should bind both ruler and people.

Social Darwinism Belief that Charles Darwin's theory of evolution was applicable to humans and justified the right of the ruling classes or countries to dominate the weak.

social hierarchies Distinctions between the privileged and the less privileged.

Social Security Act (1935) New Deal act that instituted old-age pensions and insurance for the unemployed.

socialism Political ideology that calls for a classless society with collective ownership of all property.

Socrates (469–399 BCE) Philosopher in Athens who encouraged people to reflect on ethics and morality. He stressed the importance of honor and integrity as opposed to wealth and power. Plato was his student.

Sogdians A people who lived in central Asia's commercial centers and maintained the stability and accessibility of the Silk Road. They were crucial to the interconnectedness of the Afro-Eurasian landmass.

Solidarity The communist bloc's first independent trade union, it was established in Poland at the Gdansk shipyard.

Song dynasty Chinese dynasty that took over the mandate of heaven for three centuries starting in 976 CE. It ruled an era of many economic and political successes, but it eventually lost northern China to nomadic tribes.

Song porcelain Type of porcelain perfected during the Song period that was light, durable, and quite beautiful.

South African War (1899–1902) Conflict between the British and Dutch colonists of South Africa which resulted in bringing two Afrikaner republics under the control of the British. Often called the Boer War.

Soviet bloc International alliance that included the east European countries of the Warsaw Pact as well as the Soviet Union but also came to include Cuba.

Spanish-American War (1898) War between the United States and Spain in Cuba, Puerto Rico, and the Philippines. It ended with a treaty in which the United States took over the Philippines, Guam, and Puerto Rico; Cuba won partial independence.

speciation The formation of different species.

specie Money in coin.

species Group of animals or plants possessing one or more distinctive characteristics.

spiritual ferment Process that occurred after 300 CE in which religion touched more areas of society and culture than before and touched them in different, more demanding ways.

Spring and Autumn period Period between the eighth and fifth centuries BCE, during which China was ruled by the feudal system. Considered an anarchic and turbulent time, there were 148 different tributary states in this period.

Stalin, Joseph (1879–1953) Leader of the communist party and the Soviet Union; sought to create "socialism in one country."

steel A metal more malleable and stronger than iron that became essential for industries like shipbuilding and railways.

stoicism Widespread philosophical movement initiated by Zeno (334–262 BCE). Zeno and his followers sought to understand the role of people in relation to the cosmos. For the Stoics, everything was grounded in nature. Being in love with nature and living a good life required being in control of one's passions and thus indifferent to pleasure or pain.

Strait of Malacca Seagoing gateway to Southeast and East Asia.

Strategic Defense Initiative ("Star Wars") Master plan, championed by U.S. president Ronald Reagan in the 1980s, that envisions the deployment of satellites and space missiles to protect the United States from incoming nuclear bombs.

stupa Dome monument marking the burial site of relics of the Buddha.

Suez Canal Channel built in 1869 across the Isthmus of Suez to connect the Mediterranean Sea with the Red Sea and to lower the costs of international trade.

Sufi brotherhoods Mystics within Islam who were responsible for the expansion of Islam into many regions of the world.

Sufism Emotional and mystical form of Islam that appealed to the common people.

sultan Islamic political leader. In the Ottoman Empire, the sultan combined a warrior ethos with an unwavering devotion to Islam.

Sumerian King List Text that recounts the making of political dynasties. Recorded around 2000 BCE, it organizes the reigns of kings by dynasty, one city at a time.

Sumerian pantheon The Sumerian gods, each of whom had a home in a particular floodplain city. In the Sumerian belief system, both gods and the natural forces they controlled had to be revered.

Sumerian temples Homes of the gods and symbols of Sumerian imperial identity. Sumerian temples also represented the gods' ability to hoard wealth at sites where people exchanged goods and services. In addition, temples distinguished the urban from the rural world.

Sun Yat-sen (1866–1925) Chinese revolutionary and founder of the Nationalist Party in China.

Sunnis Orthodox Muslims. The majority sect of Islam, Sunnis originally supported the succession of Abu Bakr over Ali and supported the rule of consensus rather than family lineage for the succession to the Islamic caliphate. *See also* Shiism.

superior man In the Confucian view, a person of perfected moral character, fit to be a leader.

superpowers Label applied to the United States and the Soviet Union after World War II because of their size, their possession of the atomic bomb, and the fact that each embodied a model of civilization (capitalism or communism) applicable to the whole world.

supranational organizations International organizations such as NGOs, the World Bank, and the IMF.

survival of the fittest Charles Darwin's belief that as animal populations grew and resources became scarce, a struggle for existence arose, the outcome of which was that only the "fittest" survived.

Suryavamsha The second lineage of two (the solar) in Vedic society. *See* Chandravamsha.

Swadeshi movement Voluntary organizations in India that championed the creation of indigenous manufacturing enterprises and schools of nationalist thought, in order to gain autonomy from Britain.

syndicalism Organization of workplace associations that included unskilled labor.

tabula rasa Term used by John Locke to describe the human mind before it begins to acquire ideas from experience; French for "clean slate."

Taiping Heavenly Kingdom (Heavenly Kingdom of Great Peace) Religious sect established by the Chinese prophet Hong Xiuquan in the mid-nineteenth century. Hong Xiuquan believed that he was Jesus's younger brother. The group struggled to rid the world of evil and "restore" the heavenly kingdom, imagined as a just and egalitarian order.

Taiping Rebellion Rebellion by followers of Hong Xiuquan and the Taiping Heavenly Kingdom against the Qing government over the economic and social turmoil caused by the Opium War. Despite raising an army of 100,000 rebels, the rebellion was crushed.

Taj Mahal Royal palace of the Mughal Empire, built by Shah Jahan in the seventeenth century in homage to his wife, Mumtaz.

Tale of Genji Japanese work written by Lady Murasaki that gives vivid accounts of Heian court life; Japan's first novel (early eleventh century).

talking cures Psychological practice developed by Sigmund Freud whereby the symptoms of neurotic and traumatized patients would decrease after regular periods of thoughtful discussion.

Talmud Huge volumes of oral commentary on Jewish law eventually compiled in two versions, the Palestinian and the Babylonian, in the fifth and sixth centuries BCE.

Talmud of Jerusalem Codified written volumes of the traditions of Judaism; produced by the rabbis of Galilee around 400 CE.

Tang dynasty (608–907 CE) Regime that promoted a cosmopolitan culture, turning China into the hub of East Asia cultural integration, while expanding the borders of their empire. In order to govern such a diverse empire, the Tang established a political culture and civil service based on Confucian teachings. Candidates for the civil service were required to take examinations, the first of their kind in the world.

Tanzimat Reorganization period of the Ottoman Empire in the mid-nineteenth century; modernizing reforms affected the military, trade, foreign relations, and civilian life.

tappers Rubber workers in Brazil, mostly either Indian or mixed-blood people.

Tarascans Mesoamerican society of the 1400s; rivals to and sometimes subjects of the Aztecs.

Tatish Ruler of Chan Santa Cruz during the Mexican Caste War. The term means "father."

Tecumseh (1768–1813) Shawnee who circulated Tenskwatawa's message of Indian renaissance among Indian villages from the Great Lakes to the Gulf Coast. He preached the need for Indian unity, insisting that Indians resist any American attempts to get them to sell more land. In response, thousands of followers renounced their ties to colonial ways and prepared to combat the expansion of the United States.

Tekkes Schools that taught devotional strategies and the religious knowledge for students to enter Sufi orders and become masters of the brotherhood.

temple Building where believers worshipped their gods and goddesses and where some peoples believed the deities had earthly residence.

Tenskwatawa (1768–1834) Shawnee prophet who urged disciples to abstain from alcohol and return to traditional customs, reducing dependence on European trade goods and severing connections to Christian missionaries. His message spread to other tribes, raising the specter of a pan-Indian confederacy.

Teotihuacán City-state in a large, mountainous valley in present-day Mexico; the first major community to emerge after the Olmecs.

territorial state Political form that emerged in the riverine cities of Mesopotamia, which was overwhelmed by the displacement of nomadic peoples. These states were kingdoms organized around charismatic rulers who headed large households; each had a defined physical border.

Third Estate The French people minus the clergy and the aristocracy; this term was popularized in the late eighteenth century and used to exalt the power of the bourgeoisie during the French Revolution.

Third Reich The German state from 1933 to 1945 under Adolf Hitler.

Third World Nations of the world, mostly in Asia, Latin America, and Africa, that were not highly industrialized like First World nations or tied to the Soviet Bloc (the Second World).

Thirty Years' War (1618–1648) Conflict begun between Protestants and Catholics in Germany that escalated into a general European war fought against the unity and power of the Holy Roman Empire.

Tiananmen Square Largest public square in the world and site of the pro-democracy movement in 1989 that resulted in the killing of as many as a thousand protesters by the Chinese army.

Tiers monde Term meaning "Third World," coined by French intellectuals to describe countries seeking a "third way" between Soviet communism and western capitalism.

Tiglath Pileser III Assyrian ruler from 745 to 728 BCE. This leader instituted reforms that changed the administrative and social structure of the empire to make it more efficient and introduced a standing army.

Tiwanaku Another name for Tihuanaco, the first great Andean polity, on the shores of Lake Titicaca.

Tlaxcalans Mesoamerican society of the 1400s; these people were enemies of the powerful Aztec Empire.

Tokugawa shogunate Hereditary military administration founded in 1603 that ruled Japan while keeping the emperor as a figurehead; it was toppled in 1868 by reformers who felt that Japan should adopt, not reject, Western influences.

Toltecs A Mesoamerican people who, by 1000 CE, had filled the political vacuum created by the decline of the city of Teotihuacán.

tomb culture Warlike group from northeast Asia who arrived by sea in the middle of the third century ce and imposed their military and social power on southern Japan. These conquerors are known today as the "Tomb culture" because of their elevated necropolises near present-day Osaka.

Topkapi Palace Political headquarters of the Ottoman Empire, located in Istanbul.

total war All-out war involving civilian populations as well as military forces, often used in reference to World War II.

transhumant migrants Nomads who entered settled territories in the second millennium BCE and moved their herds seasonally when resources became scarce.

Trans-Siberian Railroad Railroad built over very difficult terrain between 1891 and 1903 and subsequently expanded; it created an overland bridge for troops, peasant settlers, and commodities to move between Europe and the Pacific.

Treaty of Brest-Litovsk (1918) Separate peace between imperial Germany and the new Bolshevik regime in Russia. The treaty acknowledged the German victory on the Eastern Front and withdrew Russia from the war.

Treaty of Nanjing (1842) Treaty between China and Britain following the Opium War; it called for indemnities, the opening of new ports, and the cession of Hong Kong to the British.

Treaty of Tordesillas (1494) Treaty in which the pope decreed that the non-European world would be divided into spheres of trade and missionary responsibility between Spain and Portugal.

trickle trade Method by which a good is passed from one village to another, as in the case of obsidian among farming villages; the practice began around 7000 BCE. Also called "down the line trade."

Tripartite Pact (1940) Pact that stated that Germany, Italy, and Japan would act together in all future military ventures.

Triple Entente Alliance developed before World War I that eventually included Britain, France, and Russia.

Troy Important site founded around 3000 BCE in Anatolia, to the far west. Troy is legendary as the site of the war that was launched by the Greeks (the Achaeans) and that was recounted by Homer in the *Iliad*.

Truman Doctrine (1947) Declaration promising U.S. economic and military intervention, whenever and wherever needed, for the sake of preventing communist expansion.

Truth and Reconciliation Commission Quasi-judicial body established after the overthrow of the apartheid system in South Africa and the election of Nelson Mandela as the country's first black president in 1994. The commission was to gather evidence about crimes committed during the apartheid years. Those who showed remorse for their actions could appeal for clemency. The South African leaders believed that an airing of the grievances from this period would promote racial harmony and reconciliation.

truth commissions Elected officials' inquiries into human rights abuses by previous regimes. In Argentina, El Salvador, Guatemala, and South Africa, these commissions were vital for creating a new aura of legitimacy for democracies and for promising to uphold the rights of individuals.

tsar/czar Russian word derived from the Latin *Caesar* to refer to the Russian ruler of Kiev, and eventually to all rulers in Russia.

Tula Toltec capital city; a commercial hub and political and ceremonial center.

Uitlanders British populations living in Afrikaner republics; they were denied voting rights and subject to other forms of discrimination in the late nineteenth century. The term means "outsiders."

ulama Arabic word that means "learned ones" or "scholars"; used for those who devoted themselves to knowledge of Islamic sciences.

Umayyads Family who founded the first dynasty in Islam. They established family rule and dynastic succession to the role of caliph. The first Umayyad caliph established Damascus as his capital and was named Mu'awiya ibn Abi Sufyan.

Umma Arabic word for "community"; used to refer to the "Islamic politu" or "Islamic community."

Universal Declaration of Human Rights (1948) U.N. declaration that laid out the rights to which all human beings are entitled.

universitas Term used from the end of the twelfth century to denote scholars who came together, first in Paris. The term is borrowed from the merchant communities, where it denoted the equivalent of the modern "union."

Untouchables Caste in the Indian system whose jobs, usually in the more unsanitary aspects of urban life, rendered them "ritually and spiritually" impure.

Upanishads Vedic wisdom literature collected in the first half of the first millennium BCE. It took the form of dialogues between disciples and a sage.

urban-rural divide Division between those living in cities and those living in rural areas. One of history's most durable worldwide distinctions, the urban-rural divide eventually encompassed the globe. Where cities arose, communities adopted lifestyles based on the mass production of goods and on specialized labor. Those living in the countryside remained close to nature, cultivating the land or tending livestock. They diversified their labor and exchanged their grains and animal products for necessities available in urban centers.

utopian socialism The most visionary of all Restoration-era movements. Utopian socialists like Charles Fourier dreamed of transforming states, workplaces, and human relations and proposed plans to do so.

Vaishyas Householders or lesser clan members in Vedic society who worked the land and tended livestock.

Vardhamana Mahavira Advocate of Jainism who lived from 540 to 468 BCE; he emphasized interpretation of the Upanishads to govern and guide daily life.

Varna Caste system established by the Vedas in 600 BCE.

vassal states Subordinate states that had to pay tribute in luxury goods, raw materials, and manpower as part of a broad confederation of polities under the kings' protection.

Vedas Rhymes, hymns, and explanatory texts composed by Aryan priests; the Vedas became their most holy scripture and part of their religious rituals. They were initially passed down orally, in Sanskrit. Brahmans, priests of Vedic culture, incorporated the texts into ritual and society. The Vedas are considered the final authority of Hinduism.

Vedic people People who came from the steppes of Inner Asia around 1500 BCE and entered the fertile lowlands of the Indus River basin, gradually moving as far south as the Deccan plateau. They called themselves Aryan, which means "respected ones," and spoke Sanskrit, an Indo-European language.

veiling Practice of modest dress required of respectable women in the Assyrian Empire, introduced by Assyrian authorities in the thirteenth century BCE.

Venus figures Representations of the goddess of fertility drawn on the Chauvet

Cave in southeastern France. Discovered in 1994, they are probably about 35,000 years old.

Versailles Conference (1919) Peace conference between the victors of World War I; resulted in the Treaty of Versailles, which forced Germany to pay reparations and to give up its colonies to the victors.

Viet Cong Vietnamese communist group committed to overthrowing the government of South Vietnam and reunifying North and South Vietnam.

Viet Minh Group founded in 1941 by Ho Chi Minh to oppose the Japanese occupation of Indochina; it later fought the French colonial forces for independence. Also known as the Vietnamese Independent League.

Vietnam War (1965–1975) Conflict that resulted from concern over the spread of communism in Southeast Asia. The United States intervened on the side of South Vietnam in its struggle against peasant-supported Viet Cong guerrilla forces, who wanted to reunite Vietnam under a communist regime. Faced with antiwar opposition at home and ferocious resistance from the Vietnamese, American troops withdrew in 1973; the puppet South Vietnamese government collapsed two years later.

Vikings A people from Scandinavia who replaced the Franks as the dominant warrior class in northern Europe in the ninth century. They used their superior ships to loot other seagoing peoples and sailed up the rivers of central Russia to establish a trade route that connected Scandinavia and the Baltic with Constantinople and Baghdad. The Vikings established settlements in Iceland and Greenland and, briefly, North America.

Vishnu The second of three Vedic deities, signifying existence. *See also* Brahma *and* Siva.

viziers Bureaucrats of the Ottoman Empire.

Vodun Mixed religion of African and Christian customs practiced by slaves and free blacks in the colony of Saint Domingue.

Voting Rights Act (1965) Law that granted universal suffrage in the United States.

Wafd Nationalist party that came into existence during a rebellion in Egypt in 1919 and held power sporadically after Egypt was granted limited independence from Britain in 1922.

Wahhabism Early-eighteenth-century reform movement organized by Muhammad Ibn abd al-Wahhab, who preached the absolute oneness of Allah and a return to the pure Islam of Muhammad.

Wang Mang Han minister who usurped the throne in 9 CE because he believed that the Han had lost the mandate of heaven. He ruled until 23 CE.

war ethos Strong social commitment to a continuous state of war. The Roman army constantly drafted men and engaged in annual spring military campaigns. Soldiers were taught to embrace a sense of honor that did not allow them to accept defeat and commended those who repeatedly threw themselves into battle.

War of 1812 Conflict between Britain and the United States arising from U.S. grievances over oppressive British maritime practices in the Napoleonic Wars.

War on Poverty President Lyndon Johnson's push for an increased range of social programs and increased spending on social security, health, education, and assistance for the disabled.

Warring States period Period extending from the fifth century BCE to 221 BCE, when the regional warring states were unified by the Qin dynasty.

Warsaw Pact (1955–1991) Military alliance between the Soviet Union and other communist states that was established in response to the creation of the NATO alliance.

Weimar Republic (1919–1933) Constitutional Republic of Germany that was subverted by Hitler soon after he became chancellor.

Western Front Military front that stretched from the English Channel through Belgium and France to the Alps during World War I.

White and Blue Niles The two main branches of the Nile, rising out of central Africa and Ethiopia. They come together at the present-day capital city of Sudan, Khartoum.

White Lotus Rebellion Series of uprisings in northern China (1790–1800s) inspired by mystical beliefs in folk Buddhism and, at times, the idea of restoring the Ming dynasty.

White Wolf Mysterious militia leader, depicted in popular myth as a Chinese Robin Hood whose mission was to rid the country of the injustices of Yuan Shikai's government in the early years of the Chinese Republic (1910s).

Whites "Counterrevolutionaries" of the Bolshevik Revolution (1918–1921) who fought the Bolsheviks (the "Reds"); included former supporters of the tsar, Social Democrats, and large independent peasant armies.

witnessing Dying for one's faith, or becoming a martyr.

Wokou Supposedly Japanese pirates, many of whom were actually Chinese subjects of the Ming dynasty.

Works Progress Administration (WPA) New Deal program instituted in 1935 that put nearly 3 million people to work building roads, bridges, airports, and post offices.

World Bank International agency established in 1944 to provide economic assistance to war-torn and poor countries. Its formal title is the International Bank for Reconstruction and Development.

World War II (1939–1945) Worldwide war that began in September 1939 in Europe, and even earlier in Asia, and pitted Britain, the United States, and the Soviet Union (the Allies) against Nazi Germany, Japan, and Italy (the Axis).

Wu or Wudi Chinese leader known as the "Martial Emperor" because of his many military campaigns during the Han dynasty. He reigned from 141 to 87 BCE.

Wu Zhao Chinese empress who lived from 626 to 706 CE. She began as a concubine in the court of Li Shimin and became the mother of his son's child. She eventually gained power equal to that of the emperor, and named herself regent when she finagled a place for one of her own sons after their father's death.

Xiongnu The most powerful and intrusive of the nomadic peoples; originally pastoralists from the eastern part of the Asian steppe in what is modern-day Mongolia. They appeared along the frontier with China in the late Zhou dynasty and by the third century BCE had become the most powerful of all the pastoral communities in that area.

Xunzi Confucian moralist whose ideas were influential to Qin rulers. He lived from 310 to 237 BCE and believed that rational statecraft was more reliable than fickle human nature and that strict laws and severe punishments could create stability in society.

Yalta Accords Results of the meeting between President Roosevelt, Prime Minister Churchill, and Premier Stalin that occurred in the Crimea in 1945 to plan for the postwar order.

Yavana kings Sanskrit name for Greek rulers, derived from the Greek name for the area of western Asia Minor called Ionia, a term that then extended to anyone who spoke Greek or came from the Mediterranean.

yellow press Newspapers that sought a mass circulation by featuring sensationalist reporting.

Yellow Turbans One of several local Chinese religious movements that emerged across the empire, especially under Wang Mang's officials, who considered him a usurper. The Yellow Turbans, so called because of the yellow scarves they wore around their heads, were Daoist millenarians.

Yin City that became the capital of the Shang in 1350 BCE, ushering in a golden age.

Young Egypt Antiliberal, fascist group that gained a large following in Egypt during the 1930s.

Young Italy Nationalist organization made up of young students and intellectuals, devoted to the unification and renewal of the Italian state.

Yuan dynasty Dynasty established by the Mongols after the defeat of the Song. The Yuan dynasty was strong from 1280 to 1368; its capital was at Dadu, or modern-day Beijing.

Yuan Mongols Mongol rulers of China who were overthrown by the Ming dynasty in 1368.

Yuezhi A Turkic nomadic people who roamed on pastoral lands to the west of the Xiongnu territory of central Mongolia. They had friendly relationships with the farming societies in China, but the Yuezhi detested the Xiongnu and had frequent armed clashes with them.

Zaibatsu Large-scale, family-owned corporations in Japan consisting of factories, import-export businesses, and banks that dominated the Japanese economy until 1945.

Zamindars Archaic tax system of the Mughal Empire where decentralized lords collected tribute for the emperor.

Zapatistas Group of indigenous rebels that rose up against the Mexican government in 1994 and drew inspiration from an earlier Mexican rebel, Emiliano Zapata.

Zheng King during the Qin era who defeated what was left of the Warring States between 230 and 221 BCE. He assumed the mandate of heaven from the Zhou and declared himself First August Emperor, to distinguish himself from other kings.

Zheng He (1371–1433) Ming naval leader who established tributary relations with Southeast Asia, Indian Ocean ports, the Persian Gulf, and the east coast of Africa.

Zhong Shang Administrative central complex of the Shang.

Zhongguo Term originating in the ancient period and subsequently used to emphasize the central cultural and geographical location of China in the world; means "Middle Kingdom."

ziggurat By the end of the third millennium BCE, the elevated platform base of a Sumerian temple had transformed into a stepped platform called a *ziggurat*.

Zionism Political movement advocating the reestablishment of a Jewish homeland in Palestine.

Zoroaster Sometimes known as Zarathustra, thought to have been a teacher around 1000 BCE in eastern Iran and credited with having solidified the region's religious beliefs into a unified system that moved away from animistic nomadic beliefs. The main source for his teachings is a compilation called the Avesta.

Zoroastrianism Religion based on the teachings of Zoroaster that became the dominant religion of the Persian Empire.

Zulus African tribe that, under Shaka, created a ruthless warrior state in southern Africa in the early 1800s.

CREDITS

CHAPTER 1

Photo Credits Page 1: Erich Lessing/Art Resource; p. 7: Volker Steger/Photo Researchers; p. 8: Robert Preston/Alamy; p. 10: Kenneth Garrett/National Geographic Image Collection; p. 11 (top): John Reader/Photo Researchers; p. 11 (bottom): Staffan Widstrand/Corbis; p. 12: Pascal Goetgheluck/Photo Researchers; p. 15: Lionel Bret/Photo Researchers; p. 18: John Reader/Photo Researchers; p. 20: Images of Africa Photobank/Alamy; p. 21 (left & right): French Ministry of Culture and Communication, Regional Direction for Cultural Affairs–Rhone Alpes region–Regional department of archaeology; p. 22: Archivo Iconografico, S.A./Corbis; p. 26: Erich Lessing/Art Resource; p. 28: Copyright © Christie's Images Ltd. All rights reserved; p. 30: © Universal Images Group/DeAgostini/Alamy; p. 32: Bruce Smith: The Emergence of Agriculture (New York, 1998: Diane Pub Co.). p. 104; p. 32: Boltin Picture Library/Bridgeman Art Library; p. 37: © Images & Stories /Alamy.

Text Credits Page 5: Ainslee T. Embree, from *Sources of Indian Tradition, Vol. 1, From the Beginning to 1800*, edited and revised by Ainslie T. Embree, 2nd ed., pp. 18–19. Copyright © 1988 Columbia University Press. Reprinted with permission of the publisher; p. 19: Richard B. Lee & Irven DeVore, "Problems in the Study of Hunters and Gatherers," *Man The Hunter*, pp. 3 & 5. Copyright © 1968 by Aldine Publishers. Reprinted by Permission of AldineTransaction, a division of Transaction Publishers; p. 34: Adrian Recinos, Excerpt from *Popol Vuh: The Sacred Book of the Ancient Quiche Maya*, trans. Delia Goetz & Sylvanus G. Morley, pp. 165–168. Copyright © 1950 by the University of Oklahoma Press. Reprinted with permission of University of Oklahoma Press; p. 38: From *Mother Nature: Maternal Instincts and How They Shape the Human Species* by Sarah Blaffer Hrdy, copyright © 1999 by Sarah Blaffer Hrdy, published by Chatto and Windus. Used by permission of Pantheon Books, a division of Random House, Inc. and The Random House Group Ltd.

CHAPTER 2

Photo Credits Page 42: The Trustees of the British Museum/Bridgeman Art Library; p. 44: © Balage Balogh/Art Resource, NY; p. 50: Granger Collection; p. 52: Peter Bull Art Studio; p. 53: Dean Conger/Corbis; p. 54 (left): HIP/Art Resource; p. 54 (right): University of Pennsylvania Museum of Archaeology and Anthropology; p. 55: The Trustees of the British Museum; p. 56: University of Pennsylvania Museum of Archaeology and Anthropology; p. 58: Scala/Art Resource; p. 61: Diego Lezama Orezzoli/Corbis; p. 62 (left): Borromeo/Art Resource; p. 62 (right): Réunion des Musées Nationaux /Art Resource; p. 63: Roger Wood/Corbis; p. 66: © Kazuyoshi Nomachi/Corbis; p. 67 (left): Gianni Dagli Orti/Corbis; p. 67 (right): Christine Osborne/Corbis; p. 68 (left): Scala/Art Resource; p. 68 (right): Sandro Vannini/Corbis; p. 71: Asian Art & Archaeology, Inc./Corbis; p. 74 (left): HIP/Art Resource, NY; p. 74 (right): The Granger Collection, New York; p. 77: © Eric and David Hosking/CORBIS; p. 78 (top): Adam Woolfitt/Corbis; p. 78 (bottom): akg-images/De Agostini Picture Library; p. 80: Ashmolean Museum, University of Oxford; p. 81: Album/Art Resource, NY.

Text Credits Page 56: J. A. Black, G. Cunningham, E. Fluckiger-Hawker, E. Robson, and G. Zólyomi, from *The Electronic Text Corpus of Sumerian Literature* (University of Oxford, 1998–2006), www-etcsl.orient.ox.ac.uk; p. 60: Shereen Ratnagar, "The Mystery of Harrapan Writing" from *Understanding Harappa: Civilization in the Greater Indus Valley* (New Delhi: Tulika Publishers, 2001), pp. 60–62. We have made diligent efforts to contact the copyright holder to obtain permission to reprint this selection. If you have information that would help us, please write to Permissions Department, W. W. Norton & Company, Inc., 500 Fifth Avenue, New York, NY 10110; p. 70: James B. Pritchard (ed.), "The Admonitions of Ipuwer." From *Ancient Near Eastern Texts Relating to the Old Testament- Third Edition with Supplement.* Copyright © 1950, 1955, 1969, renewed 1978 by Princeton University Press. Reprinted by permission of Princeton University Press; p. 73: Kwang-chih Chang, from *The Archaeology of Ancient China*, 4th ed., pp. 287–88. Copyright © 1986 Yale University Press. Reprinted by permission of the publisher.

CHAPTER 3

Photo Credits Page 84: Scala/Art Resource; p. 87 (left): Art Resource; p. 87 (right): JTB Photo Communications/Alamy; p. 87 (bottom): Scala/Art Resource; p. 92: Roger Wood/Corbis; p. 93: Sandro Vannini/Corbis; p. 94: Sandro Vannini/Corbis; p. 96: bpk, Berlin/Art Resource, NY; p. 98: Eric Lessing/Art Resource; p. 100: Vanni/ Art Resource; p. 103: National Museum of India, New Delhi; p. 106: Yale University Art Gallery /Art Resource; p. 107: From Luo, Zhenyu ji, Yin xu shu qi jing hua. China: Shangyu; p. 110: Albrecht G. Schaefer/Corbis; p. 113 (left): Institute of Nautical Archaeology, Bodrum, Turkey; p. 113 (right): Gianni Dagli Orti/Corbis; p. 115 (top): Erich Lessing/Art Resource; p. 115 (bottom): The Art Archive/ National Archaeological Museum, Athens/Dagli Orti; p. 116 (top): Peter Clayton; p. 116 (bottom): University of Cincinnati; p. 117: Hermitage, St. Petersburg, Russia/The Bridgeman Art Library; p. 117: Giraudon/The Bridgeman Art Library.

Text Credits Page 97: "The Epic of Gilgamesh" from *Myths from Mesopotamia: Creation, the Flood, Gilgamesh, and Others*, pp. 100–101, trans. Stephanie Dalley.

© Stephanie Dalley 1989. Reprinted with permission of Oxford University Press; p. 105: Ssu-ma Ch'ien, "Sima Qian on the Ruler's Mandate" from *The Grand Scribe's Records*, ed. by William H. Nienhauser, Jr., Robert Reynolds, and Lu Zongli. Copyright © 2002 by William H. Nienhauser, Jr. Reprinted with permission of Indiana University Press.

CHAPTER 4

Photo Credits Page 122: Dagli Orti/Louvre/Bridgeman Art Library; p. 125 (left): A. Paul Jenkin/Animals Animals; p. 126 (right): S. Muller/Peter Arnold, Inc.; p. 129: ????? p. 131 (top): The Trustees of the British Museum; p. 131 (bottom): Erich Lessing/Art Resource; p. 133: British Museum/Bridgeman Art Library; p. 134: SEF/Art Resource; p. 136: Alinari/Art Resource; p. 137: Dagli Orti/Louvre/Bridgeman Art Library; p. 138: Erich Lessing/Art Resource, NY; p. 139: The Art Archive/Dagli Orti; p. 140: Lloyd Cluff/Corbis; p. 142 (top): Scala/Art Resource, NY; p. 142 (bottom): AKG images/Peter Connolly; p. 143 (left): Dagli Orti/Art Archive; p. 143 (right): The British Library/HIP/The Image Works; p. 150: Giraudon/Art Resource; p. 174: Asia Society, New York: Mr. and Mrs. John D. Rockefeller 3rd Collection 1979, 100a,b. Photograph by Lynton Gardiner; p. 155: Erich Lessing/Art Resource, NY.

Text Credits Page 136: Roland G. Kent, from *Old Persian: Grammar, Texts, Lexicon*, 2nd Revised Ed. Pp. 131–32. Copyright © 1953 American Oriental Society. Reprinted with permission; p. 141: "The Truce Erupts in War," from *The Iliad* by Homer, translated by Robert Fagles, copyright © 1990 by Robert Fagles. Used by permission of Viking Penguin, a division of Penguin Group (USA) Inc.; p. 152: Burton Watson (ed.), "Zhou Succession Story" from *Early Chinese Literature*, pp. 35–36. , Copyright © 1962 Columbia University Press. Reprinted with the permission of the publisher.

CHAPTER 5

Photo Credits Page 160 (left): National Library of China; p. 160 (right): Scala/Art Resource, NY; p. 161: Erich Lessing/Art Resource, NY; p. 165: © Asian Art & Archaeology, Inc./Corbis IH015825; p. 167: Viktor Korotayev/Reuters/Corbis; p. 169: Wikimedia Commons; p. 170 (top): Erich Lessing/Art Resource, NY; p. 170 (bottom): Smithsonian Freer Gallery of Art and Aurthur M. Sackler Gallery; p. 171: British Library; p. 173: Borromeo/Art Resource, NY; p. 174 (left): Paul Almasy/Corbis; p. 174 (right): Corbis; p. 178: Erich Lessing/Art Resource, NY; p. 179 (left): Gillett Griffin; p. 179 (right): Gillett Griffin; p. 183: Princeton University Art Museum; p. 184: JTB Photo Communications, Inc./Alamy; p. 185: The Art Archive/Xalapa Museum Veracruz Mexico/Gianni Dagli Orti; p. 189 (top): Erich Lessing/Art Resource, NY; p. 189 (bottom): Vanni/Art Resource, NY; p. 190: Michael Freeman/Corbis; p. 192: Erich Lessing/Art Resource, NY; p. 193 (top): Peter Willi/The Bridgeman Art Library; p. 193 (bottom): The Bridgeman Art Library; p. 194 (left): Erich Lessing/Art Resource, NY; p. 194 (right): HIP/Art Resource, NY; p. 195: Scala/Art Resource, NY.

Text Credits Page 168: "Confucianism vs. Daoism" from *Sources of Chinese Tradition, Volume 1*, 2nd Edition, pp. 55–56, 86. Eds. de Bary & Bloom, Copyright © 1999 Columbia University Press. Reprinted with the permission of the publisher.

CHAPTER 6

Photo Credits Page 200: © The Cleveland Museum of Art; p. 203: Erich Lessing/Art Resource, NY; p. 207: Lauros/Giraudon/The Bridgeman Art Library; p. 209: Vanni/Art Resource, NY; p. 210: AKG Images/Peter Connolly; p. 212: Illustration by Jean-Claude Golvin from *L'Afrique Antique*. Tallandier: Paris 2001; p. 213 (left): Bildarchiv Preussischer Kulturbesitz/Art Resource, NY; p. 213 (right): Landesmuseum, Mainz, Germany; p. 214: Stapleton Collection/Corbis; p. 215 (left): Brian A. Vikander/Corbis; p. 215 (right): The Bridgeman Art Library; p. 217: © vario images GmbH & Co.KG /Alamy; p. 219: Réunion des Musées Nationaux/Art Resource, NY; p. 220 (top, middle, bottom): Courtesy of Bill Welch, "What I Like About Ancient Coins" http://www.forumancientcoins.com/moonmoth/ancientcoins.html; p. 222: David Gurr/Eye Ubiquitous/Corbis; p. 226 (left): The Metropolitan Museum of Art. Gift of Muneichi Nitta, 2003 (2003.593.1) Image © The Metropolitan Museum of Art/ArtResource, NY; p. 226 (right): © The Metropolitan Museum of Art/Art Resource, NY; p. 231: Bruno Morandi/Robert Harding World Imagery/Corbis; p. 232: The Art Archive/Palmyra Museum Syria/Dagli Orti; p. 233: NASA/JPL.

Text Credits Page 218: Romila Thapar, from *Aśoka and the Decline of the Maurya*, 2nd Edition. Pp. 255–57. © 1973. Reprinted with permission of Oxford University Press.

CHAPTER 7

Photo Credits Page 236: Vanni/Art Resource, NY; p. 243 (top): Snark/Art Resource, NY; p. 243 (bottom): HIP/Art Resource, NY; p. 243 (right): National Library of China; p. 254 (top): The Bridgeman Art Library; p. 245 (bottom): Louis Mazzatenta/National Geographic Image Collection; p. 247: Lauros/Giraudon/The Bridgeman Art Library; p. 251 (top): British Museum/Art Resource, NY; p. 251 (bottom): Model of House, Chinese. 1st century C.E., Eastern Han Dynasty (25–220 C.E.) Earthenware with unfired coloring, 52 x 33 1/2 x 27 inches (132.1 x 85.1 x 68.6 cm); p. 252 (top): Royal Ontario Museum/Corbis; p. 252 (bottom): Asian Art & Archaeology, Inc./Corbis; p. 252 (right): Asian Art & Archaeology, Inc./Corbis; p. 254 (top): Erich Lessing/Art Resource, NY; p. 254 (bottom): AM Corporation/Alamy; p. 255: The Art Archive/Genius of China Exhibition; p. 257: Araldo de Luca/Corbis; p. 261: Image copyright © The Metropolitan Museum of Art/Art Resource; p. 262: Vanni/Art Resource, NY; p. 263: Robert Harding Picture Library Ltd/Alamy; p. 264 (top): The Art Archive/Museo Capitolino Rome/Gianni Dagli Orti; p. 264 (bottom): Atlantide Phototravel/Corbis; p. 265: Museo Arqueológico, Sevilla, Spain; p. 267 (left): Giraudon/Art Resource, NY; p. 267 (right): Roger Wood/Corbis; p. 268 (top): Scala/ Art Resource; p. 268 (bottom): Fridmar

Damm/zefa/Corbis; p. 272: HIP/ Art Resource, NY; p. 275: Erich Lessing/Art Resource, NY.

Text Credits Page 244: "A Qin Legal Document: Memorial on the Burning of the Books" from *Sources of Chinese Tradition, Volume 1*, eds. de Bary & Bloom, © 1999 Columbia University Press. Reprinted with the permission of the publisher; p. 246: Jia Yi, "Faults of the Qin" from *Sources of Chinese Tradition, Volume 1*, eds. de Bary & Bloom, © 1999 Columbia University Press. Reprinted with the permission of the publisher; p. 250: Dong Zhongshu, "Responsibilities of Han Rulership" from *Sources of Chinese Tradition, Volume 1*, eds. de Bary & Bloom, © 1999 Columbia University Press. Reprinted with the permission of the publisher; p. 266: J. Gonzalez, "The Lex Irnitanta: A New Copy of the Flavian Municipal Law", from *Journal of Roman Studies*, Vol. 76 (1986). Reprinted with permission of the Society for the Promotion of Roman Studies.

CHAPTER 8

Photo Credits Page 278: Charles & Josette Lenars/Corbis; p. 281: Réunion des Musées Nationaux/Art Resource, NY; p. 285 (left): Scala/Art Resource; p. 281 (right): Granger Collection; p. 286 (left): Jewish Museum/Art Resource; p. 286 (right): Scala/Art Resource, NY; p. 287 (top): Bettmann/ Corbis; p. 287 (bottom): Scala/Art Resource, NY; p. 291 (left & right): Cameraphoto Arte, Venice/Art Resource, NY; p. 292: Yann Arthus-Bertrand/Corbis; p. 294: © Julian Chichester/Bridgeman Art Library; p. 295: Scala/Art Resource, NY; p. 296: British Museum/Art Resource, NY; p. 298: British Library, London, Stein Collection; p. 299 (top): Dean Conger/Corbis; p. 299 (bottom): British Museum; p. 300: Werner Forman/akg-images; p. 301: bpk, Berlin/Art Resource, NY; p. 302: SEF/Art Resource, NY; p. 305 (left): Liu Xiaoyang/Alamy; p. 305 (right): Pierre Colombel/Corbis; p. 307: National Palace Museum, Taipei, China; p. 311: Gianni Dagli Orti/Corbis; p. 312: Charles & Josette Lenars/Corbis; p. 131: Angelo Hornak/Corbis; p. 314 (left): Werner Forman/Art Resource, NY; p. 314 (right): Giraudon/The Bridgeman Art Library.

CHAPTER 9

Photo Credits Page 318: Patrick Ward/ Corbis; p. 320: Suhaib Salem/Reuters/ Corbis; p. 323: Erich Lessing/Art Resource, NY; p. 326: Wikimedia Commons; p. 329 (left): Vanni Archive/Corbis; p. 329 (right): Patrick Ward/Corbis; p. 330: Bettmann/Corbis; p. 333 (left): Gavin Hellier/JAI/Corbis; p. 333 (right): Christine Osborne/Corbis; p. 338 (left): De Agostini Picture Library/The Bridgeman Art Library; p. 338 (right): akg-images; p. 339: The Art Archive/British Library; p. 340 (left): Werner Forman/Art Resource, NY; p. 339 (right): Kurt Scholz/ SuperStock; p. 341: Julia Waterlow/Eye Ubiquitous/Corbis; p. 346: Asian Art & Archaeology, Inc./Corbis; p. 347 (left): The Trustees of the British Museum; p. 347 (right): CulturalEyes-AusGS/Alamy; p. 349: Giraudon/Bridgeman Art Library; p. 351 (top): akg-images; p. 351 (bottom): The Art Archive; p. 352 (left): imagebroker/ Alamy; p. 352 (right): Robert Harding Picture Library Ltd /Alamy; p. 354 (top): Werner Forman/Art Resource; p. 354 (bottom): Interfoto/Alamy.

Text Credits Page 322: From *The Koran* translated with notes by N.J. Dawood (Penguin Classics 1956, Fifth revised edition 1990). Copyright © N.J. Dawood, 1956, 1959, 1966, 1968, 1974, 1990, 1993, 1997, 1999, 2003. Reproduced by permission of Penguin Books Ltd.

CHAPTER 10

Photo Credits Page 358: HIP/Art Resource, NY; p. 360: Nik Wheeler/ Corbis; p. 361: Granger Collection; p. 363: Wikimedia Commons; p. 367 (left): Werner Forman/Art Resource, NY; p. 367 (right): HIP/Art Resource, NY; p. 368 (left): Colin Hoskins/ Cordaiy Photo Library/Corbis; p. 368 (right): The Art Gallery Collection/ Alamy; p. 369: Peter Guttman/Corbis; p. 374: Macduff Everton/Corbis; p. 375: Keren Su/Corbis; p. 376: © The Metropolitan Museum of Art. Image source: Art Resource, NY; p. 379 (top): Wikimedia Commons; p. 379 (bottom): Granger Collection; p. 382 (top): akg-images/ Werner Forman; p. 382 (bottom): Christophe Loviny/Corbis; p. 385 (top): Erich Lessing/Art Resource, NY; p. 385 (bottom): Hubert Stadler/Corbis; p. 386: akg-images/Volker Kreidler; p. 388: The Art Archive; p. 389 (left): Charles & Josette Lenars/Corbis; p. 389 (right): Kevin Schafer/Corbis; p. 391: Snark/Art Resource, NY; p. 394 (left): Otto Lang/ Corbis; p. 394 (right): Michael S. Lewis/ Corbis; p. 395: akg-images; p. 399: Granger Collection; p. 401: Bettmann/ Corbis.

Text Credits Page 366: From *Sundiata: An Epic of Old Mali*, translated by D. T. Niane, pp. 40–41. Copyright © 1965 Longman Group. Reprinted with permission; p. 371: Goitein, S.D. (trans.); *Letters of Medieval Jewish Traders*. © 1973 Princeton University Press, 2001 renewed PUP Reprinted by permission of Princeton University Press; p. 381: From *Sources of Japanese Tradition*, Volume 1, pp. 177–79. Compiled by Ryu¯saku Tsunoda, Wm. Theodore de Bary, and Donald Keene Copyright © 1964 Columbia University Press. Reprinted with permission of the publisher.

CHAPTER 11

Photo Credits Page 404: Snark/Art Resource; p. 406: The Granger Collection, New York; p. 414: Album/Art Resource, NY; p. 415: Yann Arthus-Bertrand/ Corbis; p. 416: Stapleton Collection, UK/ Bridgeman Art Library International Ltd.; p. 417: Library of the Topkapi Palace Museum folio 31b, photograph courtesy of Talat Halman; p. 419: © 2007 The British Library; p. 423: Bibliotheque Nationale de France, Paris/Art Resource, NY; p. 427 (left): Scala/Ministero per i Beni e le Attività culturali/Art Resource; p. 427 (right): Scala/Ministero per i Beni e le Attività culturali/Art Resource; p. 429: Giraudon/ Art Resource, NY; p. 430: The Granger Collection, New York; p. 431: The Art Archive; p. 432: Réunion des Musées Nationaux/Art Resource, NY; p. 435: The Jan Adkins Studio.

Text Credits Page 412: Ahmet Karamustafa, "Dervish Groups I the Ottoman Empire 1450–1550" from *God's Unruly Friends: Dervish Groups in the Islamic Later Middle Period*, pp. 6–7, Oneworld Publications, Oxford, 2006. Reprinted with the permission of Oneworld Publications;

p. 420: "Nanak's Teachings in India" from *Sources of Indian Tradition*, ed. William T. de Bary, © 1958 Columbia University Press. Reprinted with the permission of the publisher; p. 422: Robertus de Avesbury, "The Flagellants in England" from *The Black Death*, Rosemary Horrox, trans./ed., pp. 153–154. Copyright © Rosemary Horrox 1994. Reprinted with permission of Manchester University Press; p. 433 Lily Hwa, "Proclamations of the Hong Wu Emperor." Reprinted with the permission of The Free Press, a Division of Simon & Schuster, Inc., from *Chinese Civilization: A Sourcebook, Second Edition*, revised & expanded by Patricia Buckley Ebrey. Copyright © 1993 by Patricia Buckley Ebrey. All rights reserved.

CHAPTER 12

Photo Credits Page 440: Courtesy Wychwood Editions; p. 442: Reunion des Musees Nationaux/ Art Resource, NY; p. 444 akg-images/Cameraphoto; p. 445 (top): Biblioteca Estense, Modena, Italy/ Scala/ Art Resource, NY; p. 445 (bottom): Science Museum, London/The Bridgeman Art Library; p. 450: Bildarchiv Preussischer Kulturbesitz/Art Resource, NY; p. 451: Granger Collection; p. 452 (left): Granger Collection; p. 452 (right): The Art Archive/Government Palace Tlaxcala Mexico/Mireille Vautier; p. 453 (left): Schalkwijk/Art Resource, NY © 2013 Banco de Mexico Diego Rivera Frida Kahlo Museums Trust, Mexico, D.F./ Artists Rights Society (ARS), New York; p. 453 (right): Granger Collection; p. 455: The Art Archive/Archaeological Museum. Lima/Dagli Orti; p. 457 (top): The Granger Collection, New York; p. 457 (bottom): Granger Collection; p. 459: © François Guenet/Art Resource; p. 462: Rare Books Division, New York Public Library, Astor; Lenox and Tilden Foundations; p. 464: akg-images; p. 467: Musee d'Archeologie et d'Histoire, Lausanne, Switzerland/Giraudon/The Bridgeman Art Library; p. 468: Reunion des Musees Nationaux/ Art Resource, NY; p. 473: The Art Archive/Maritime Museum Kronborg Castle Denmark/Gianni Dagli Orti.

Text Credits Page 461: Padden, R.C., editor, "Claudia the Witch," pp. 117–121, from *Tales of Potosi*. © 1975 by Brown University Press. Reprinted by permission of University Press of New England, Lebanon, NH and the author; p. 471: T'ien-Tsê Chang, *Sino-Portuguese Trade From 1514 to 1644: A Synthesis of Portuguese and Chinese Sources* (Leyden: E.J. Brill, 1934), pp. 51–52. Reprinted by permission of Koninklijke Brill NV.

CHAPTER 13

Photo Credits Page 476: Reunion de Musees Nationaux/ Art Resource; p. 478 (left): British Museum/Superstock; p. 478 (right): © The Trustees of the Chester Beatty Library, Dublin/The Bridgeman Art Library; p. 483: Granger Collection; p. 485: MPI/Getty Images; p. 486: MPI/Getty Images; p. 488: The Granger Collection, NY; p. 492 (left): © 1989 North Wind Picture Archives; p. 492 (right): Private Collection/ © Michael Graham-Stewart/The Bridgeman Art Library; p. 494: The Newberry Library, Chicago; p. 496: Mary Evans Picture Library/The Image Works; p. 497: The Art Archive/Museum der Stadt Wien/ Dagli Orti; p. 498 (left): British Library/ The Image Works; p. 498 (right): © The Trustees of the Chester Beatty Library, Dublin/The Bridgeman Art Library; p. 500: © The Metropolitan Museum of Art/Art Resource, NY; p. 503: Granger Collection; p. 504: Sotheby's/ akg-images; p. 505: The Art Archive; p. 507: Reunion de Musees Nationaux/ Art Resource; p. 509 (top): Granger Collection; p. 509 (bottom): Chris Hellier/ Corbis; p. 510: Wikimedia Commons; p. 511: bpk, Berlin/Art Resource; p. 512: Chateau de Versailles, France/ Bridgeman Art Library; p. 513: Private Collection/ The Bridgeman Art Library.

Text Credits Page 501: Huang Liu-Hung, "Elimination of Authorized Silversmiths" from *A Complete Book Concerning Happiness and Benevolence*, translated and edited by Djang Chu, pp. 190–191. © 1984 The Arizona Board of Regents. Reprinted by permission of the University of Arizona Press.

CHAPTER 14

Photo Credits Page 518: Scala/Art Resource, NY; p. 521: Topkapi Palace Museum, Istanbul; p. 522: Réunion des Musées Nationaux/Art Resource, NY; p. 523 (left): Topkapi Palace Museum, Istanbul; p. 523 (right): Victoria & Albert Museum, London/ Art Resource, NY; p. 524 (left): Giraudon/ Art Resource; p. 524 (right): Private Collection, courtesy of the owner and D.A. King; photo by Christie's of London; p. 525: Reproduced by the kind permission of the trustees of the Chester Beatty Library and Gallery of Oriental Art, Dublin; p. 526 (left): Scala/ Art Resource, NY; p. 526 (right): Granger Collection; p. 527: from World Civilizations (Addison Wesley Longman, 2001); p. 529: Werner Forman/Art Resource, NY; p. 530 (left): Underwood & Underwood/Corbis; p. 530 (right): Underwood & Underwood/Corbis; p. 531 (left): Underwood & Underwood/Corbis; p. 531 (right): The British Library, London; p. 532: The British Library, London/ The Bridgeman Art Library; p. 533: Reunion de Musees Nationaux/ Art Resource, NY; p. 534: The Fotomas Index; p. 536 (top): Wikimedia Commons; p. 536 (bottom): Euriskodata CDrom/Wikimedia Commons; p. 537: Bridgeman Art Library; p. 538: Bridgeman Art Library; p. 539: Musee des Beaux-Arts, Rouen/Superstock; p. 541 (top): Private Collection/ The Bridgeman Art Library; p. 541 (bottom): Private Collection/ The Bridgeman Art Library; p. 542: Image copyright © The Metropolitan Museum of Art/Art Resource, NY; p. 544: Bridgeman Art Library; p. 545 (left): Museo de America, Madrid; p. 545 (right): Museo de America, Madrid; p. 546: National Maritime Museum, London; p. 548 (left): HIP/Art Resource, NY; p. 548 (right): Granger Collection; p. 549: The Art Archive/Castle Howard/Eileen Tweedy; p. 550: Natural History Museum, London/ The Bridgeman Art Library.

CHAPTER 15

Photo Credits Page 554: Lauros-Giraudon/ The Bridgeman Art Library; p. 557: Library of Congress; p. 561: Granger Collection; p. 562: Hulton Archive/ Getty Images; p. 563: Musee de la Ville de Paris, Musee Carnavalet/ Giraudon/ Art Resource, NY; p. 565: Lauros-Giraudon/ The Bridgeman Art Library; p. 567: North Wind Picture Archives; p. 568: Granger Collection; p. 571 (left): The Art Archive /Museo Nacional de Historia, Castillo de Chapultepec, Mexico City/Dagli Orti; p. 571 (right):

Granger Collection; p. 573: Private Collection/ The Bridgeman Art Library; p. 574: Granger Collection; p. 576: Granger Collection; p. 578: Granger Collection; p. 581: Novotsi/ The Bridgeman Art Library; p. 583: Corbis; p. 584: Courtesy of the director, National Army Museum, London; p. 585: Wikimedia Commons; p. 586: Granger Collection; p. 588: The Art Archive; p. 589 (left): The British Library, London/ The Bridgeman Art Library; p. 589 (right): North Wind Picture Archives; p. 591: Roy Miles Fine Paintings/ The Bridgeman Art Library.

Text Credits Page 582: Abd al-Rahman al-Jabarti, From *Napoleon in Egypt: al-Jabarti's Chronicle of the French Occupation*, 1798, translated by Shmuel Moreh, pp. 24–29. (Princeton: Markus Wiener Publishing, 1993).

CHAPTER 16

Photo Credits Page 594: Harvard-Yenching Library, Harvard University; p. 599: Wikimedia Commons; p. 601 (left): The British Library, London; p. 601 (right): National Archives, Zimbabwe; p. 605: Granger Collection; p. 607: Corbis; p. 610: Granger Collection; p. 611: Alamy; p. 617 (left): Granger Collection; p. 617 (right): Granger Collection; p. 618: Wikimedia Commons; p. 619: Wikimedia Commons; p. 621: Getty Images; p. 623: Victoria & Albert Museum/Art Resource, NY.

Text Credits Page 602: "Gikku Bello" from *One Woman's Jihad* by Beverly Mack & Jean Boyd. Copyright © 2000 by Beverly B. Mack and Jean Boyd. Reprinted with permission of Indiana University Press; p. 606: From "The Principles of the Heavenly Nature," in *Sources of Chinese Tradition*, 2nd Edition, Volume 2, pp. 229–30. Compiled by Wm. Theodore de Bary and Richard Lufrano. Copyright © 2000 Columbia University Press. Reprinted with permission of the publisher; p. 612: Karl Marx and Friedrich Engels, from "The Communist Manifesto," in *The Marx-Engels Reader*, 2nd ed., pp. 473–83, 490–91, 500. Edited by Robert C. Tucker.

CHAPTER 17

Photo Credits Page 628: Granger Collection; p. 634 (left): Granger Collection; p. 634 (right): The Granger Collection, New York/The Granger Collection; p. 635: Granger Collection; p. 636: Time & Life Pictures/Getty Images; p. 637 (left): Hulton/Getty Images; p. 637 (right): Hulton/Getty Images; p. 642: Universal History Archive/UIG; p. 643 (top): Peter Newark American Pictures/The Bridgeman Art Library; p. 643 (bottom): Hulton/ Getty Images; p. 644: Bettmann/Corbis; p. 646 (top): Illustrated London News/ Mary Evans Picture Library; p. 646 (bottom): Private Collection (uncredited photo), from Judith Gutman's "Through Indian Eyes, Oxford University Press; p. 649 (left): Hulton /Getty Images; p. 649 (right): Private Collection/The Bridgeman Art Library; p. 650: Roger-Viollet, Paris/The Bridgeman Art Library; p. 651: Wikimedia Commons; p. 652: The Art Archive; p. 654 (top): Illustrated London News, 1872/ Mary Evans Picture Library; p. 654 (bottom): North Wind Picture Archives; p. 655: Erich Lessing/ Art Resource, NY; p. 656 (top): North Wind Picture Archives; p. 656 (bottom): The Art Archive; p. 657: Granger; p. 662: Sovfoto/ Eastfoto.

CHAPTER 18

Photo Credits Page 666: SuperStock; p. 673 (left): SuperStock; p. 673 (right): Hulton Archive/Getty Images; p. 675 (left): Corbis; p. 675 (right): ullstein bild/ The Granger Collection; p. 676: Empress Dowager Cixi and the imperial eunuchs, 1903–1905. Photographer: Hsun-ling Tz-u-hi, Empress Dowager of China, 1835–1908, Photographs, negative 261. Freer Gallery of Art and the Arthur M. Sackler Gallery Archives, Smithsonian Institution, Washington, D.C.; p. 678: SuperStock; p. 680 (left): akg-images; p. 680 (right): Hulton-Deutsch Collection/Corbis; p. 682: Bettmann/ Corbis; p. 685 (left): Culver Pictures/Art Archive; p. 685 (right): Sean Sprague/ Mexicolore/ The Bridgeman Art Library; p. 687: Wikimedia Commons; p. 688: © Estate of Pablo Picasso/Artists Rights Society (ARS), New York. Digital Image (c) The Museum of Modern Art/Licensed by Scala/Art Resource, NY; p. 689: Snark/ Art Resource, NY; p. 690 (left): © National Gallery, London/Art Resource, NY; p. 690 (right): Erich Lessing/Art Resource, NY; p. 690 (bottom): Album/Art Resource, NY; p. 691 (top): Sigmund Freud Copyrights/ Mary Evans Picture Library; p. 691 (bottom): The Palace Museum, Beijing; p. 693: Corbis; p. 694: Schalkwijk/ Art Resource, NY © 2013 Banco de Mexico Diego Rivera Frida Kahlo Museums Trust, Mexico, D.F./Artists Rights Society (ARS), New York; p. 696 (left): Wikimedia Commons; p. 696 (right): © SZ Photo/AV Photo/The Bridgeman Art Library; p. 697 (left): Wikimedia Commons; p. 697 (right): E.O. Hoppe/ Corbis; p. 698: Domenica del Corriere/Dagli Orti/ The Art Archive.

Text Credits Page 683: Qui Jin, "An Address to Two Hundred Million Fellow Countrywomen." Reprinted with the permission of The Free Press, a Division of Simon & Schuster, Inc., from *Chinese Civilization: A Sourcebook, Second Edition*, revised & expanded by Patricia Buckley Ebrey. Copyright © 1993 by Patricia Buckley Ebrey. All rights reserved; p. 684: Margot Badran & Miriam Cooke (eds.), "Industrialization and Women's Freedom in Egypt" from *Opening the Gates: An Anthology of Arab Feminist Writing*. Copyright © 1990. Reprinted with permission of Indiana University Press; p. 699: Sayid Jamal al-Din al Afghani and Abdul-Hadi Ha'iri, "Afghani on the Decline of Islam," in *Die Welt des Islams*, New Series, Vol. 13, No. 1/2 (1971): 121–125. Reprinted by permission of Koninklijke Brill NV; p. 700: Franziska von Reventlow, "Viragines oder Hetaere" in *Autobiographisches, Novellen, Schriften, Selbtzeugnisse*, edited by Else Reventlow, translated by Suzanne Marchand. Reprinted with the permission of Suzanne Marchand.

CHAPTER 19

Photo Credits Page 704: The Illustrated London News Picture Library, London, UK/The Bridgeman Art Library; p. 707: The Imperial War Museum; p. 709: Hulton-Deutsch Collection/Corbis; p. 712 (left): Sovfoto/Eastfoto; p. 712 (right): SuperStock; p. 716: Corbis; p. 717 (top): Ullstein bild/Granger Collection; p. 717 (bottom): Hulton/Getty Images; p. 719: SF Palm/Stageimage/The Image Works; p. 721: The Granger Collection, New York/The Granger Collection; p. 722: Library of Congress; p. 723 (left): Hulton Archive/Getty Images; p. 723 (right):

The Granger Collection, New York/The Granger Collection; p. 725: The Illustrated London News Picture Library; p. 726: Mary Evans Picture Library; p. 729 (left): Bettmann/Corbis; p. 729 (right): Getty Images; p. 730: Heinrich Hoffmann/Time & Life Pictures/Getty Images; p. 731 (left): The Art Archive; p. 731 (right): Genevieve Naylor/Corbis; p. 732: Granger Collection; p. 734 (left): The Illustrated London News Picture Library; p. 734 (right): Private Collection/ The Bridgeman Art Library; p. 736: Dinodia Picture Agency, Bombay; p. 737: Modern China Rare Photography Library, Sun Yat-Sen and the Guomindang Party (The Commercial Press, Ltd. 1994); p. 738: Getty Images.

Text Credits Page 727: Ernest R. Huber, "Fuhrergewalt," *Nazism 1919–1945: A Documentary Reader, Vol. 2: State, Economy and Society 1933–1939*, edited by J. Noakes and G. Pridham, pp. 198–199. Reprinted by permission of University of Exeter Press; p. 733: From *Facing Mt. Kenya* by Jomo Kenyatta, published by Vintage Books, a division of Random House, Inc. and Secker & Warburg. Used by permission of Alfred A. Knopf, a division of Random House, Inc. and The Random House Group Ltd.; p. 735: M. K. Gandhi, from *Hind Swaraj and Other Writings*, edited by Anthony J. Parel, pp. 26–91. Copyright © 1997 Cambridge University Press. Reprinted with permission.

CHAPTER 20

Photo Credits Page 742: F.D.R. Library; p. 746 (left): The Illustrated London News Picture Library; p. 746 (right): Sovfoto/ Eastfoto; p. 748: Hulton/Getty Images; p. 749 (left): Official U.S. Air Force Photo/ Cody Images; p. 749 (right): Yosuke Yamahata/ Cody Images; p. 749 (bottom): F.D.R. Library; p. 750: NATO Photo/ TRH Pictures/Cody Images; p. 752: Bettmann/Corbis; p. 754: Granger Collection; p. 756 (left): Henri Cartier-Bresson/ Magnum Photos; p. 756 (right): Xinhua News Agency; p. 756 (bottom): Bettmann/ Corbis; p. 760 (top): Bettmann/ Corbis; p. 760 (bottom): Bettmann/ Corbis; p. 762: Hulton-Deutsch Collection/Getty Images; p. 763 (top): Hulton-Deutsch Collection/ Corbis; p. 763 (bottom): Stroud/Express/ Getty Images; p. 764: FPG/Getty Images; p. 765: Hulton-Deutsch Collection/ Corbis; p. 766 (left): Bettmann/ Corbis; p. 766 (right): Bettmann/ Corbis; p. 767 (left): AP Photo; p. 767 (right): Fred Blackwell/State Historical Society of Wisconsin Visual Materials Archive; p. 768 (top): akg-images; p. 768 (bottom): Sovfoto; p. 769: Hulton-Deutsch Collection/ Corbis; p. 771: Wikimedia Commons; p. 772 (left): Roger-Viollet/The Image Works; p. 772 (right): Li Zhensheng/ Contact Press Images; p. 773: Itar-Tass/ Sovfoto; p. 774: AP Photo; p. 775: Bettmann/ Corbis; p. 776 (top): AP Photo; p. 776 (bottom): JP Laffont/Sygma/Corbis.

Text Credits Page 763: Léopold Sédar Senghor, excerpts from *African Socialism* (New York: American Society of African Culture, 1959), trans. Mercer Cook. Reprinted by permission of Moorland-Spingarn Research Center, Howard University, Washington, DC; p. 779: "The Problem That Has No Name" from *The Feminine Mystique* by Betty Friedan. Copyright © 1983, 1974, 1973, 1963 by Betty Friedan. Used by permission of W.W. Norton & Company, Inc. and Victor Gollancz, an imprint of The Orion Publishing Group Ltd.

CHAPTER 21

Photo Credits Page 784: AP Photo; p. 787: Hulton Archive/Getty Images; p. 789: Robert Maass/Corbis; p. 792: Peter Magubane/ Time Life Pictures/ Getty Images; p. 793: AP Photo; p. 795: George Esiri/Reuters/Corbis; p. 798: Uriel Sinai/Getty Images; p. 799 (top): Jeff Albertson/ Corbis; p. 799 (left): Getty Images; p. 799 (right): © Seth Wenig/ /AP; p. 801: Mary Evans/EROS INTERNATIONAL /Ronald Grant/Everett Collection; p. 804 (top): Serge Attal/ TimePix/Getty Images; p. 804 (left): Copyright © 2007 by Robert Frerck and Odyssey Productions, Inc.; p. 804 (right): Lee Jae-Won/Reuters/Corbis; p. 805 (left): Gisele Wulfsohn/ Panos Pictures; p. 805 (right): © Chris Johnson/ Panos Pictures; p. 808: Vanessa Vick/ Redux; p. 810: AP Photo; p. 811 (left): Susan I. Cunningham/ Panos Pictures; p. 811 (right): Douglas Engle/Corbis; p. 813: ASSOCIATED PRESS; p. 814: Sovfoto/ Eastfoto; p. 815: Tom Stoddart /Getty Images; p. 816: Peter Turnley /Corbis; p. 817 (top): © Jacques Haillot /Corbis; p. 817 (bottom): Bettmann/ Corbis; p. 818: AP Photo; p. 819 (left): Clive Shirley/ Panos Pictures; p. 819 (right): Schalkwijk/ Art Resource, NY, © 2013 Artists Rights Society (ARS), New York/ SOMAAP, Mexico City.

Text Credits Page 790: Ann Tusa, "A Fatal Error" in *Media Studies Journal*, Fall 1999, pp. 26–29. Copyright © 1999. Reprinted by permission of *Media Studies Journal*; p. 809: Reproduced with permission of the World Bank from "Using subsidies to close gender gaps in education," *World Development Report 2000–2001*, p. 122, Box 7.2. Copyright 2000 by World Bank. Permission conveyed through Copyright Clearance Center, Inc.

EPILOGUE

Photo Credits Page 824: ASSOCIATED PRESS; p. 826 (left): AP Photo; p. 826 (right): Matt McDermott; p. 827: Ali Haider/epa/Corbis; p. 828: AP Photo; p. 829 (top): ASSOCIATED PRESS; p. 829 (bottom): AP Photo/U.S. Coast Guard, Petty Officer 2nd Class Kyle Niemi; p. 831: AP Photo/ Mustafa Quraishi; p. 836: Dean Conger/ Corbis; p. 837: Timothy O'Rourke/ Bloomberg News/ Landov; p. 838: Sebastian D'Souza/AFP/ Getty Images; p. 844: ASSOCIATED PRESS; p. 846 (left): Liba Taylor/ Corbis; p. 846 (right): Herman Wouters/ Hollandse Hoogte/Redux; p. 846 (bottom): Jason Reed/Reuters/Landov; p. 847 (top): AP Photo; p. 847 (bottom): Alexander Hassenstein/Getty Images.

INDEX

Italic page references indicate maps, illustrations, or chronology entries.

NORTH POLAR REGION
ARCTIC OCEAN
NORTH AMERICA
ASIA
GREENLAND
North Pole
North Magnetic Pole
Hudson Bay
GREENLAND
QUEEN ELIZABETH ISLANDS
NORTH AMERICA
NORTH PACIFIC OCEAN
NORTH ATLANTIC OCEAN
Hawaii
TROPIC OF CANCER
EQUATOR
TROPIC OF CAPRICORN
GULF OF MEXICO
CENTRAL AMERICA
CARIBBEAN SEA
WEST INDIES
Amazon Basin
SOUTH AMERICA
ANDES
SOUTH PACIFIC OCEAN
POLYNESIA
MID-ATLANTIC RIDGE
SOUTH ATLANTIC OCEAN
Falkland Islands
Cape Horn
Drake Passage
ANTARCTIC CIRCLE
ANTARCTIC PENINSULA
WEDDELL SEA
Ellsworth Land
Marie Byrd Land
ANTA
180° 160° 140° 120° 100° 80° 60° 40°
GLOBAL SATELLITE MOSAIC
The beauty and complexity of Earth's landscapes above and below the oceans is revealed with the Global Satellite Mosaic. The mosaic was produced for the National Geographic Society by NASA's Jet Propulsion Laboratory using more than 500 satellite images from the National Oceanic and Atmospheric Administration. The cloud-free images show Earth in its natural colors as it would be seen from space. One can easily identify the world's major glaciers, deserts, mountain ranges, and rain forests. For example, follow the green ribbon of lush vegetation along the Nile into the stark, dry Sahara. The mountain ranges seem to rise off the map thanks to digital elevation databases from the Department of Defense. The deepest areas of the ocean realm are colored dark blue in contrast to the light blue areas highlighting continental shelves, submarine ridges, and underwater mountains.
BIOSPHERE
Thousands of satellite images
combined to show a picture of biospheric
productivity. In the oceans, red, yellow,
green indicate waters rich in phytoplankton. On
green areas show high-potential plant productivity; tan
suffer from productivity limitations due to aridity and temperature.
THE
SAT

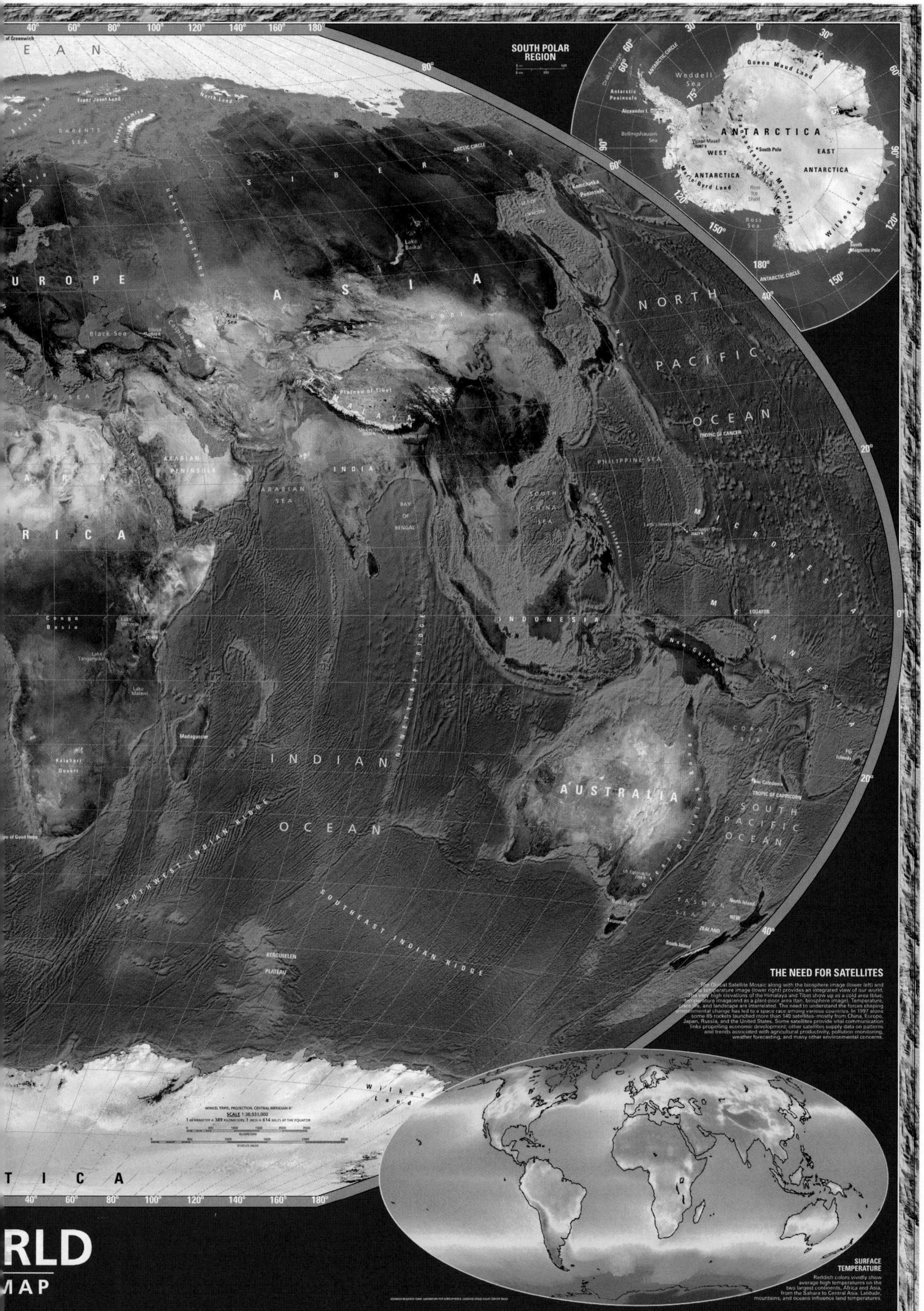

THE NEED FOR SATELLITES

The Global Satellite Mosaic along with the biosphere image (lower left) and the temperature image (lower right) provides an integrated view of our world. The very high elevations of the Himalaya and Tibet show up as a cold area (blue, temperature image)and as a plant-poor area (tan, biosphere image). Temperature, plant life, and landscape are interrelated. The need to understand the forces shaping environmental change has led to a space race among various countries. In 1997 alone some 85 rockets launched more than 140 satellites–mostly from China, Europe, Japan, Russia, and the United States. Some satellites provide vital communication links propelling economic development; other satellites supply data on patterns and trends associated with agricultural productivity, pollution monitoring, weather forecasting, and many other environmental concerns.

RLD

MAP

SURFACE TEMPERATURE

Reddish colors vividly show average high temperatures on the two largest continents, Africa and Asia, from the Sahara to Central Asia. Latitude, mountains, and oceans influence land temperatures.